A Book about the Film
Monty Python's Life of Brian

A Book about the Film
Monty Python's Life of Brian

All the References from Assyrians to Zeffirelli

Darl Larsen

Rowman & Littlefield

Lanham • Boulder • New York • London

Published by Rowman & Littlefield
An imprint of The Rowman & Littlefield Publishing Group, Inc.
4501 Forbes Boulevard, Suite 200, Lanham, Maryland 20706
www.rowman.com

6 Tinworth Street, London, SE11 5AL, United Kingdom

British Library Cataloguing in Publication Information Available

Library of Congress Cataloging-in-Publication Data
Names: Larsen, Darl, 1963– author.
Title: A book about the film Monty Python's Life of Brian : all of the references from Assyrians to
    Zeffirelli / Darl Larsen.
Description: Lanham : Rowman & Littlefield, [2018] | Includes bibliographical references and
    index.
Identifiers: LCCN 2017033575 (print) | LCCN 2017051435 (ebook) | ISBN 9781538103661
    (electronic) | ISBN 9781538103654 (hardback : alk. paper) | ISBN 9781538134443 (paperback
    : alk. paper)
Subjects: LCSH: Life of Brian (Motion picture)
Classification: LCC PN1997.L575 (ebook) | LCC PN1997.L575 L37 2018 (print) | DDC
    791.43/72—dc23
LC record available at https://lccn.loc.gov/2017033575

For Dad,
Norbert W. Larsen,
1935–2015

CONTENTS

CONTENTS

ACKNOWLEDGMENTS

This kind of book project doesn't happen without loads of help, so there are thanks to be given. A couple of years ago I was caught off guard by Doug Fabrizio of Radio West, who asked when a *Life of Brian* book might be expected. I'd just finished *A Book about the Film Monty Python and the Holy Grail*, so I was tired and maybe even cranky. I think I may have tactfully answered "Never." Just weeks later, that prompt turned into a niggling, then into the beginnings of this book, so a thanks to Doug is in order.

Stephen Ryan and Rowman & Littlefield were good enough to push the project through, and I'm grateful for their continuing enthusiasm. My BYU Theatre and Media Arts colleagues Wade Hollingshaus, Dean Duncan, Sharon Swenson, Tom Russell, Benjamin Thevenin, Brad Barber, Scott Christopherson, Tom Lefler, Kelly Loosli, Jeff Parkin, Megan Sanborn-Jones, and Amy Jensen helped make this book a reality; and Elizabeth Funk, Kyle Stapley, and the terrifically helpful front desk team all carried water—thanks. Profs. Roger Macfarlane and Rob McFarland assisted with Latin and German translations, respectively, and my research assistants Emily Bade, Jessica Cahill, and Helen Butcher provided wonderful, crucial material. Kimball Maw Jensen and Martha Rallison taught courses for me so I could have release time, while my dissertation advisor, mentor, and friend William Proctor Williams is ever in my corner, and I'm grateful. The Harold B. Lee Library and especially the resourceful people at Interlibrary Loan bent over backwards, again, to get me everything I needed for such an expansive subject.

Mom and Dad, Patricia and Norbert Larsen, continue to be as helpful and loving as can be imagined. My amazing wife, Nycole, my children and their spouses—Keir (Misti), Emrys (Cat), Brynmor (Chad), and Eamonn, Dathyl, Ransom, and Culainn—and granddaughter, Hayden, are constant fans who encourage me to work on what makes me happy. Thank you all.

INTRODUCTION

It is a tale of unrelieved horror—of brutalities committed . . . by provisional governors . . . by the leaders of the Jewish insurgents. . . . It is a tale of hopeless revolts, of suicidal strife between rival gangsters and warring factions, of incredible heroism achieving nothing but universal ruin and destruction.

—G. A. Williamson[1]

We're giving Pilate two days to dismantle the entire apparatus of the Roman Imperialist State.

—Reg

This country's a worse risk than Cuba. You're a banana republic. You're a mess.

—"Tony"

Tony is talking about Great Britain in the late 1970s; Williamson about Jerusalem in 70. In *Life of Brian*, Reg and the Pythons bring the two together, and we will, too.

In John Mackenzie's eschatological gangster picture *The Long Good Friday*, East London mob boss Harold Shand has run up against the new face of crime, the IRA, and the results are catastrophic. Shand (Bob Hoskins[2]) has been busy arranging his version of the future, a deal with the American mafia[3] for the legitimization of his corrupt empire, but after a series of bombings and assassinations, the Yanks are going home, their reasons mentioned above. The old way of doing things in the London crime world was coming to an end in 1979, the film tells us, as a more powerful, more vicious (and Rome-influenced) foreign element wrests control. The hints of epochal change were everywhere in the 1970s—across the Empire, in music and the arts, in the failing postwar "consensus" of Britain as a socialist utopia—and it's no surprise to find it in a Python film. Williamson's "insurgents" aren't the Peoples' Front of Judea but the Jewish Zealots, a fanatical sect that pricked the Romans (and Jewish theocrats) with a thousand pins before being crushed, their holy city and temple obliterated. But the PFJ *are* part of this tale. Promising brutalities against their hated governor, Pilate, the PFJ's revolt is a hopeless one, their strife suicidal. They will struggle with rivals; one among them will act heroically and in so doing invite *discrete* ruin and destruction. For the Pythons, the PFJ are the Zealots, yes, but also the PLO, the SLA, and the RAF, all terror groups active in the 1970s, and all fighting against their versions of the "bloody Romans." Kidnapping for ransom, to force regime change, or for leverage to free political prisoners had become so common as to pass nearly unnoticed in first-century Jerusalem and the world of 1977. This heady mélange of ancient and contemporary history isn't new for the Pythons.

In *Monty Python and the Holy Grail*, the Pythons presented a sub-Roman world populated by medieval filth and ignorance, but also characters mythological (King Arthur, the Legendary Beast), quasi-historical (tribe leader Arthur), and anachronistic (Dennis, policemen). The tensions between the fabular and the historical bits of Arthur, the early Middle Ages, and twentieth-century Britain threatened the integrity of the film at every turn, culminating in a police raid and an upended film projector. *Life of Brian* exhibits some of these tensions, but its connective tissue—a shadow version of the Christ story—keeps the narrative skeleton from collapsing, following Brian from his nativity to his stations of the cross in faithful, pilgrimatic steps. There are no direct-address moments in *Brian*, no helpful narrators, no acknowledgments of the artifice of filmmaking (it's almost never "only a model"). There are more made-up than historical characters in *Holy Grail* and *Brian*, with just Pilate and Jesus appearing from history in *Brian*, and Jesus making only a single, canonical appearance. Most others are just Bible types—lepers, sinners, tradesmen, disciples, Jews and Samaritans, Roman plutocrats, prefects, and soldiers; these figures appear in all biblical films, from *Ben-Hur* to *Jesus of Nazareth*. The period-appropriate dress, settings, and subject matter further situate the story in a believable biblical milieu. But this verisimilitude only creates a *more* classical Hollywood-type film than *Holy Grail*—purposely anachronistic language and references, irreverence for the spiritual, and a spaceship digression maintain the film's Pythonesque instability, its chimeric mode. And contrary to much clinkering fourth-estate scree, the film isn't really about Jesus, or things blasphemous—it's rather a Jesus-*type* story. In a millennial time of many claimant messiahs and healers and prophets, the Pythons present a baby mistaken for the "King of the Jews," and follow him as he grows, just off the way from where an actual Jesus is pursuing his ministry. *Life of Brian* is more about religious zealotry and terrorism in first-century Jerusalem and the twentieth-century world; it is about the British Empire as much as the Roman Empire; it is about institutional power and the efficacy of Davids versus Goliaths in the religious, colonial, and political regimes of ancient Rome and modern Britain. For two centuries the British Empire has been mentioned in the same breath as the Roman Empire, good and bad, by university doyens, Sir Clark-like presenters, and Fleet Street columnists.[4] James Morris[5] calls his first chapter in *Pax Britannica* "The Heirs of Rome," referring to the sprawling, muscular British Empire of 1897—the spirituous time of Victoria's diamond jubilee—the title a play on "*Pax Romana*," the controversial, celebrated "Roman peace" that embraced much of the known world for decades.

In March 1975 during a recording session for a forthcoming album, the troupe decided that their next film would be a "Monty Python and the Life of Christ" lark, with Chapman as Christ and featuring characters like "Ron the Baptist."[6] This was agreed about a week before the London premier of *Holy Grail*, the impetus for the decision being the creation of a continuing revenue stream for Python Productions.[7] The *Carry On*–like "Ron the Baptist" character never did materialize, nor would Chapman play Christ, but the film project eventually came to be. The troupe's individual television, book, and film projects would push this group effort off to 1976 and 1977; it would be late 1976 before they began writing, then drafting and rewriting in 1977, and finally September 1978 by the time they reached Tunisia for shooting.[8] *Monty Python's Life of Brian* premiered in August 1979, more than four years after it was conceived.

This book project, then, is a close look at the social, economic, and political zeitgeist of Britain, her vanishing Empire, and a version of the Holy Land, the lens being a film, in this case *Life of Brian*. The Pythons are creatures of their time, but they are also educated university wits who have access to historical and philosophical referents—their work can be unpacked for synchronic and diachronic influences, for its ontological and phenomenological motifs. There is much in the writing and references, but there is also much beyond, the episodes and films being truly heteroglossic. We will study this film in its time—as it responds to economic and political headlines of the day—as well as across time, in relation to the biblical epics it models and spoofs, the acts of terror occupying the news in the 70s and 1970s, and even films from the Pythons' youth that very clearly imprinted on them, including one starring the "Forces' Sweetheart" Vera Lynn. My earlier works on *Flying Circus* and *Holy Grail* focus as much on the worlds and words that inform the troupe's writing and performing as on the television series and feature film created.[9] These earlier efforts are referenced throughout this current book, necessary given that the Pythons, like Shakespeare, reflexively refer to themselves and their portfolio, trotting out favorite hobbyhorses for another go.[10] For *Life of Brian*, our time periods include first-century Jerusalem and late-1970s England, both caught on the horns of millenaric unrest involving collapses of leadership and economies, internal dissension, and crushing external forces. By the seventh decade, Roman rule had become intolerable to many, and those willing to fight, the Zealots, preached a messianic sermon with rabble-rousing, kidnappings, and murder. Just thirty-seven years after the death of Christ, Jerusalem fell to the Romans, its temple, homes, and palaces razed. Nineteen hundred years later, rule by Labour and the grasping British trade unions was not only becoming intolerable but unsustainable, with inflation undermining the economy's fortifications, and Thatcherism gathering to storm the breach in May 1979. The Jewish-but-philo-Roman historian Josephus paints a grim picture of the Jews advancing their own demise, not content to receive Rome's beneficence, not acknowledging what the Romans had "ever done for" them. Josephus points to the Zealots specifically, who brought deadly terror to the hearts of Romans and anyone supporting them across Judea; later, tabloid chronicles of the 1970s pitched bombings and kidnappings and hijackings committed by (or for) those who saw themselves as oppressed "have-nots," and generally targeting the "haves." The ultimate disaster for many as the 1970s waned—the fall of the Holy City, if you will—was the end of Labour's occupation of No. 10 for a good long time, and the myriad references to apocalypses and "Old Testament" prophets and a kind of "New Jerusalem" filled news shows and political diary pages. The Pythons brought Old and New Jerusalem together for *Life of Brian*, yes, but this terminology was everywhere, according to Peter Jenkins:

> Sir Keith Joseph had played the Baptist's role in Mrs Thatcher's coming. The analogy is apt because in conversations at that time he (like [Tony] Benn) had compared himself with a prophet come down from the mountains. Indeed, there was an Old Testament ring to his cries of woe from the wilderness as he urged repentance from the wicked ways of socialism and beat his breast in immolation for his own part in the betrayal of the ark of the Conservative covenant.[11]

All these players—Joseph, Benn, and Thatcher, Tory and Labour, Left and Right, wild-eyed and measured—we'll meet in the following pages.

Just months before Palin mentions the Pythons considering the life of Christ as their next project, Sir Lew Grade, his television network ATV, and director Franco Zeffirelli announced "with considerable fanfare" their *Jesus of Nazareth* six-part miniseries, slated for Easter 1976.[12] This certain "money-spinner" followed many recent revisitations from Jesus and the Gospels, including the play and film *Jesus Christ Superstar*, and the play *Godspell*. The controversial poem *The Love That Dares to Speak Its Name* brought these new examinations of the imagined life of Jesus into the Old Bailey, where "blasphemy" was eventually proven and punished. Jesus even became something of a Zealot and conjuror himself in the film *The Passover Plot*, also from 1976.[13] The 1970s were a time for the reevaluation of iconicity, with Jesus Christ treated as contestedly as any. A number of searching books were produced in the middle part of the decade—just when the Pythons were beginning their search for a new movie subject—treating belief, Jesus, and the Gospels. Just a few include Desmond Leslie's *The Jesus File*, Oscar Cullman's *Jesus and the Revolutionaries*, Malachi Martin's *Jesus Now*, Peter De Rosa's *Jesus Who Became Christ* and *Come Holy Spirit*, and G. A. Wells's *Did Jesus Exist?*.[14] When actor Paul Nicholas took on the lead role in *Jesus Christ Superstar* in 1972, he brought threads together, much as the Pythons would several years later. Nicholas hoped "that audiences . . . will feel at the end Jesus as a freedom fighter . . . [s]omeone along the Che Guevara lines, getting the only accolade he knows will last, martyrdom."[15] This wasn't a standalone conceit—in the postwar years there had appeared dozens of books and articles asking about Jesus as a Zealot, a terrorist, a revolutionary, a political figure, a Jewish national hero; these books and their reviews and then responses to those reviews became a cottage industry in academia. The Pythons could have hardly avoided being influenced. The ubiquitous, Jesus-like photo of Che gracing dorm rooms everywhere after 1968 serves as a neat pictograph for the age, at least for those who saw themselves as the young progressives shepherding a fairer future. The Pythons also may have decided on the subject just because so many institutional others were taking on the Christ story, with the *Jesus of Nazareth* producers (including screenwriter Anthony Burgess) promising a catholic, reverent look at Jesus, not the "modern, hippy travesties" and "sociological notions" of *Superstar* or *Godspell*, nor the *révolutionnaire du jour* revisionisms of *The Passover Plot*.[16] The historical "reality" of King Arthur and Camelot were front and center in the news of 1973, when the Pythons put pen to paper on *Holy Grail*;[17] a polymorphic Jesus occupied the same spaces in newspapers, magazines, on television and movie screens when *Life of Brian* came into being.

It shouldn't be a surprise to find a fixation on the Middle East during the Pythons' lifetimes. Palestine had been administered by Britain since the end of World War I, and, by 1948, joined other members of the former British Empire in the exodus from British domination. British territorial soldiers had toured, served, and died in the Holy Land, while British colonial administrators managed, erected, or reinforced cities and public works projects, all then left behind when the Mandate ended. Bernstein—acknowledging Britain's optimism after World War II—writes that the "Middle East, more than any other region, was an area where the British still saw themselves as a major player."[18] Those hopes were dashed in "the messiest of Britain's retreats from empire" just a few years later.[19] In 1956 the Suez Crisis exposed the frailty of the "sick man" Britain,[20] its influence in the region evaporating without the support of another former colony, the United States. In the 1967 and 1973 wars in these deserts, Britain had to watch from the bench as the new superpowers—the Americans and the Soviets—played the game. The Middle East was home base for a number of terror organizations of the day—Syria, Lebanon, Libya, and the teeming Palestinian refugee camps—becoming the last stop for many terrorists after high-profile hijackings or bombings. By 1973, an OPEC oil embargo would strangle Britain, helping bring down a Conservative government, and hobbling succeeding Labour administrations. This stagnation directly resulted in an anemic economy across the mid-1970s, its lifeblood drained by inflation, the powerful unions, and their unsustainable pay packet demands. By 1979, in the eyes of many, the death rattle of the "socialist commonwealth" wheezed out, and the "conviction politics" of Thatcherism frog-marched the country into an uncertain future. This is precisely where our film is situated—created 1976–1979, set in the heat of the Middle East, at the crux of radical change on a global scale, but also, ironically, shivering in the lowering cold of Britain's Winter of Discontent. In *Strange Rebels*, Caryl lays out the major world figures and events fulminating and culminating as the seventies came to a close:

> The forces unleashed in 1979 marked the beginning of the end of the great socialist utopias that had dominated so much of the twentieth century. These five stories—the Iranian Revolution, the start of the Afghan jihad, Thatcher's election victory, the pope's first Polish pilgrimage, and the launch of China's economic reforms—deflected the course of history in a radically new direction. It was in 1979 that the twin forces of markets and religion, discounted for so long, came back with a vengeance.[21]

These global changes, and those more local, will be revisited as we move forward.

The Pythons' Jerusalem is, like Britain, a "nation of shopkeepers,"[22] where (attempted) exchanges take place regularly, a favorite trope. In *Flying Circus* there were tobacconists and chemists, vendors of cheese, sexual favors, pornography, "fishy" toilet requisites, books, dung, lingerie, arguments, ants, and so on. Transactions in the Pythons' Jerusalem include the selling and buying of rocks for stonings, begging, the alleged exchange of sexual favors for sustenance, the vending of "imperialist titbits," haggling for a beard, and then a gourd, and on. Many of the film's scenes are shot in, or within earshot of, market sets, avoiding religious settings almost completely; government settings are reserved for Brian's arrest, "trial," and condemnation; and the few private spaces include Brian's home and the PFJ's hideout. The bulk of the film's action takes place in arenas of transactions—fighting for life in the arena, begging for alms at the city gate, haggling for bargains in rocks, beards, and gourds near the soukh. The "twin forces of markets and religion" mentioned by Caryl come together throughout, coming to a head in the epically silly—a valueless gourd that Brian struggles to give away becoming "the Holy Gourd of Jerusalem."

It's worth asking what's missing from this first-century story—meaning how near is *Brian* to being an orthodox, classical biblical tale, or a *Carry On*–like costume farce—and the answers are revealing. The reasons that the Romans treated the Jews differently from almost any other conquered peoples in their empire—the Jews' monotheism and demands for ritual purity—are obscured in *Life of Brian*. The Pythons' version of Jerusalem has no temple or cultus, the center of Jewish religious life. Foreign violations of these had provoked uprisings over and over again after Pompey's time, but there's not even the hint of a temple or synagogue. There is a single instance of slavery, even though slavery was common in cultures across Palestine, the Jews included; "Jew" and "Jewish" are mentioned only twice, this is more a "pre-Christian" tale told by white Church-of-England types; there is no obvious Sanhedrin—the "sacerdotal aristocracy" (the Jewish ruling class) are absent; the Sabbath is only mentioned once, and that in a *draft* of the script; we see just one Jewish official, at the stoning; there is no mention (beyond "Elders") of any high priest, even though Caiaphas worked closely with Pilate for much of his prefectship; and, finally, there is no temple tax collection. But maybe there's more evidence of accurate Roman life in first-century Judea? Marginally. There are centurions, a prefect, Romanized sculptures, and obvious Roman architectural hints, and there's also Roman justice on display. There is no obvious praetor beyond the Praetorian Guard; no aedile, even though we are shown games; no censor, pontiffs, or augurs, and no obvious polytheism (everyone in the film, Roman and Jew, uses singular "God" epithets); and no sign of significant Roman public officials beyond Pilate and those Romans lounging about at the Colosseum.[23] Roman emperors are mentioned, but not the current emperor, Tiberius. There are also no mentions of Roman contributions as important as concrete or arches (though public works will be listed, but not shown), and no tribute tax, no *publicani* (publicans), except in the script's draft form. Reasons for these conspicuous absences range from the practical (no looming Temple set needed to be built) to the cautious (why anger the Jewish world, too, with profaneness in relation to holy sites and sacred practices?), and will be discussed as we move along. The mise-en-scène looks as if it was mostly inspired by the various biblical epics the Pythons screened prior to making the film, with identifiable bits from *Ben-Hur*, *King of Kings*, and the recent *Jesus of Nazareth*, as opposed to scholarly work. In short, the Pythons haven't dug nearly as deep into the world they're populating—at least not as deep as they had for *Holy Grail*, where Palin and Jones's reading of scholarship on medieval Britain shone through. It could be that the topics of modern zealotry, rigidity of belief, and intolerance outweighed the demand for scholarly fastidiousness, the sets and characters merely useful backgrounds and vessels for the Pythons' talking points.[24]

The 1960s and 1970s was a fascinating time when much traditional social and religious thought and exercise came under scrutiny. The existence of a benevolent God had been under attack since the Bishop of Woolwich's *Honest to God* emerged in 1963; "Jesus freaks" appeared in Britain from America in 1971, and, to many Brits, there was one in the White House; Jesus and synoptic gospel stories were reimagined on Broadway and West End stages— Jesus as naif, as questioning, as political; and a spate of popular novelizations about Pontius Pilate (reassessing his role as a man between the Jews and Rome) problematized this already problematic figure. This was a self-flagellating period for Britain, when an emerging batch of "stand-by experts" set about to "decry common sense, defy public opinion and loathe hallowed tradition," ensuring a better, more progressive future by flaying the past.[25] It was also a period where serious films and poems looking at the physical, human life of Jesus raised blood pressures, hackles, and writs in London—"progress" wouldn't necessarily mean "anything goes." Comedy was a bit safer, yes. In a late 1972 *Flying Circus* episode, a Cleese character mentions following the Bergsonian theory of "laughter as a social sanction against inflexible behaviour"; for the Pythons, that generally meant poking fun at sociopolitical martinets, coxcombs, and middle England.[26] *Life of Brian* also embraces that conceit. We will laugh at the "inelasticity"[27] of uptight Romans and Jews, of single-minded individuals and singly driven mobs, and at "silly sods" who kill themselves because they can.

In the region, the Israelis were embracing archaeology (ambitious digs in Masada, Jerusalem) to underscore the preeminent importance of the Jewish (as opposed to Palestinian) presence in Palestine, historically, but also reexamining the life and significance of Jesus for the jaded 1970s. Israeli school texts were updated in 1973, conflating, collaterally, the British and Roman empires. Students new to Jesus were understandably confused: "In their identification of Jesus as a rebel, they frequently committed slips of the tongue calling the Romans 'British' and Pontius Pilate the 'High Commissioner,' the title of the British official who was the last foreign ruler in Jerusalem before Israel's independence."[28] This "confusion" sets us up perfectly for the Pythons to mean the PLO or JRA when they say PFJ, and to examine their prime minister alongside a Roman prefect, the failing British Empire in relation to the mature Roman Empire, etc.

The idea of a smaller, weaker body trying to influence or even overthrow a larger one can be appreciated on several levels in the film, and especially in the nuanced period of postwar Great Britain. Apart from myriad anticolonial activities going on in the remaining "pink bits" of Empire and around the world, in December 1973 a determined coal mining industry brought Britain to a near standstill, forcing a three-day work week and rationing—Christmas lights and electric hearths went dark across the country—just as the Pythons were creating their "impoverished plague-ridden" *Holy Grail* world.[29] This was precipitated by the small, distant, and decidedly foreign OPEC enacting an oil embargo, forcing Britain to rely on coal, putting miners in the catbird seat. The Heath government fell just two months later.[30] In the film, the PFJ is fighting to unseat the Roman Empire, just as Rhodesia and India and Malaya had recently shrugged off the cloak of Britain's empire; just as radicalized groups like the Japanese Red Army and the Red Army Faction struck against imperialist forces in their own countries; just as smaller, more radical sects of the Palestine Liberation Organization (viz., the Popular Front for the Liberation of Palestine) lashed against its own parent group, against Israel and the West; just like shadow governments tilted in vain opposition at sitting governments in Britain; just as the clumps of Liberals and ministers from Ulster and Edinburgh tried to influence policy during Callaghan's coalition government; and just like factions within the Labour and Conservative parties (the militant Left; the arch Right) attempted to force concessions from the center, etc. None of these actions came off without misery and bloodshed, metaphorical or very real. Peter Marin (1972) calls the twentieth century a time of "botched revolutions," so it would be very much surprising to see Brian or the PFJ succeed.[31]

A "Decent Controversy"

In 1977, when *Gay News* was in the dock for publishing an allegedly blasphemous poem, the prosecutor admitted that such publications had freedoms within the limits of "decent controversy," but that didn't keep publisher Denis Lemon from a fine and a suspended jail sentence. Though protested, weakly, and railed against to a limited extent, *Life of Brian* failed to reach a level exceeding "decent controversy"—it avoided litigation, and managed to be a popular film. Indecency aside, annotations responding to the characters and references in *Life of Brian* matter as they do for any work of art. Many of the images and references included in *Flying Circus* and *Holy Grail* have faded with time, especially the more topical bits. Important names and faces, key legislation, and political alliances mean a great deal, even everything, within earshot of an event or era; but the brilliance of lightning rods like Marcia Williams, Reginald Maudling, or even former PM Wilson have diminished with passing years. Political diarist Bernard Donoughue—special advisor during this period to two prime ministers—understood this only as he reread his diaries prior to publication: "It is chastening to my generation to realise how matters which seemed of great import and common knowledge at the time—the 'social contract,' the 1975 pay policy and the EEC renegotiations are but a few major examples—are today beyond the recollection of all but a few readers with a special interest or experience."[32] Annotating these cultural artifacts matter, Donoughue underscores: "Although the events described in this diary are only a generation ago, many current media commentators show little interest in and even less knowledge of them. This is sad because that decade of the 1970s contains matters of great significance for our nation's history."[33] *Monty Python's Life of Brian* is one such artifact, born in and responding to the detritus comprising 1976–1978 Britain and the world. Add to this the explosion of violence from dozens of terror groups—sloughing off colonialism or attempting to overthrow capitalism or just lashing out from lives of privileged boredom and *ennui*—many so agitated being just rudderless youth given a heading thanks to Marxist pamphlets, socialist professors, and the availability of small arms. Scores of books emerged describing current terrorism and its history; many somber TV specials, as well; all trying to account for the eruptions of unrest and violence. These same "matters" found their way into *Life of Brian*, and our task is to tease them out, revealing a "constellation of brilliant particulars."[34]

Sources for this study include the finished film itself, as well as a bound version of the printed script.[35] There are a number of versions of the script available online, offering diverse drafts, so many without provenance that including them is fruitless. "Missing" scenes involving classrooms and shepherds and Otto were either written and not filmed, or filmed and edited out, and will be mentioned only as appropriate. Another draft is the script as read aloud by most of the Pythons in July 1977, and now available as an audio track on the Blu-ray edition of the film. This oral performance does not follow the printed version of the script precisely, and will be referenced as needed. The film as finished and distributed is our primary source material. Our work is broken up by scenes, start to finish, with annotations given in order of screen/page appearance. This means that the animated title sequence annotations, for example, appear just after the nativity scene, and just before the Sermon on the Mount. An entry preceded by *(draft)* is one brought over from a draft version of the script. As for secondary sources, I've found that a mixture of the scholarly and the more popular is best. For *A Book about the Film* Monty Python and the Holy Grail, for instance, scholarly works on Britain of the tenth through fourteenth centuries were used alongside the most recent Arthurian scholarship, alongside Malory's *Le Morte D'Arthur* and even boys' comic books from the Pythons' youth. The goal in all this is an approximation of what the Pythons accessed in their writing, taking into account what they may have studied at university, for example. The latest academic scholarship available in 1976—on the Holy Land, the life of Jesus, Pontius Pilate, ancient and modern terrorism, etcetera—is key. But popular study is also crucial, since the Pythons often wrote based on what they'd read in newspapers, watched on TV, listened to on *The Goon Show*, and seen in *Private Eye*. This is why the critical works of scholars E. Mary Smallwood and Joachim Jeremias are important for "Jerusalem at the time of Jesus" information, as well as period journal articles from the likes of oft-published Solomon Zeitlin and S. G. F. Brandon. The work of Jewish scholar Josephus is crucial to understanding the period leading up to the fall of Jerusalem; his self-serving bias is acknowledged, but he's also one of the very few sources for this fascinating period in Jewish history. The celebrated Williamson editions of Josephus's work appeared in 1959 and 1964, and were well-received and much-discussed.[36] Josephus's work—part of assigned reading lists at both Oxford and Cambridge for centuries—will be cited throughout. British newspapers from the 1970s are a rich quarry for the latest, often overstated "discoveries" in relation to both the Dead Sea Scrolls and Holy Land and Roman archaeology, as well as salacious examinations of terror groups and their atrocities, and even the first "proof" of crucifixion. This last, for example, involved the discovery of bones in a Jerusalem neighborhood in 1968, bones that seemed to prove the practice of crucifixion in first-century Jerusalem. Surprisingly, despite the literary and filmic evidence depicting or discussing the use of crucifixion by Romans against Jews in first-century Judea—Josephus mentions it, as does the Bible, and many biblical epics revel in it—no archaeological evidence had been found to support the claims. This first-century victim had been buried, and then his bones reinterred into an ossuary, a metal spike still fixed through his ankle. This find was immediately written about in 1970, likely crucifixion "styles" presented, trumpeted in newspapers, then revisited with a bit more skepticism in scholarly journals across the 1970s and 1980s. As will be seen later, the Centurion's jibe about which way Brian wants to be crucified could well have come from the scholarly and public fascination with this single discovery. Historical fiction of the period is also useful. Books like Paul Maier's *Pontius Pilate* take existing scholarship and spin it into a readable tale that becomes sometimes indistinguishable, in the public mind, from the few hints left by history for such a significant figure. Newspapers of the mid-1970s offer an explanation for what seems to be a throwaway bit of background material, the glimpsed inscription "PILATVS IVDAEOS REGET OK" in Pilate's chambers. It seems innocuous, but it's actually referring to a current event covered in colorful tabloid detail. Finally, *Life of Brian* can fruitfully be described as *Jesus of Nazareth* meets *I'm All Right Jack*, the latter a 1959 Peter Sellers comedy satirizing unions and the working class in Harold Macmillan's Britain. The genesis of both Brian and the PFJ, at least, can be traced to this comedy. Long story short, to unpack a polyglot Python film, a mix of scholarship, popular media, tongue-in-cheek material, and popular (non-)fiction is just the starting point.

And Now for the Lacuna

Quite a bit has already been written about this film, much of it pretty good. Kim Johnson's *Monty Python's Tunisian Holiday* has plenty of day-to-day information about the film's production, while Julian Doyle's *The Life of ~~Brian~~ Jesus* spends less time on behind-the-scenes tidbits, rather deep thinking on the biblical world around Jesus and Pilate, the realities of crucifixion, and so on. The recent *Jesus and Brian* explores "the historical Jesus" in relation to the film, and scattered entries in autobiographical works from Chapman, Cleese, and Palin are also available, and worth reading. Robert Hewison's *Monty Python: The Case Against* and John O. Thompson's *Monty Python Complete and Utter Theory of the Grotesque* both look at the scandal surrounding the production and release of the film. I mention all these just to indicate where this book won't spend as much time or energy. As with my earlier forays into studies of *Monty Python and the Holy Grail* and *Monty Python's Flying Circus*, the dialogue and scenarios in the printed scripts and the eventual performance and production of those elements will guide and occupy us. Connecting this film to the Pythons' previous work is essential, illustrating what tropes have been carried over, and how this film fits into or chafes against other Python work. In *Life of Brian* the Pythons are drawing not only on their collective Sunday school memories of the life of Jesus, but the "Christmas and Easter" version of those same stories that populate holiday cards, television specials, and pews twice yearly. They are looking at religious fervor and the mob mentality, as well as terrorism of the first and twentieth centuries. *Holy Grail* was as much about 1970s Britain as the 930s; *Life of Brian* is occupied by the Roman and British Empires, the burdens and blessings of the Welfare State, and the dangers of radical thought in the Jerusalem of Pilate and pre-Thatcherite Britain.

Notes

1. From Williamson's introduction to the 1970 Penguin edition of Josephus's *The Jewish War*, 7.
2. Hoskins's name will be used for a character appearing later in *Life of Brian*.
3. This is where Tony (Stephen Davies) comes in, along with Charlie (Eddie Constantine), representing organized crime interests in America.
4. Brendon, *DFBE*, xvii–xx; Sir Kenneth Clark was a well-traveled academic and presenter (Larsen, *MPFC: UC*, 1.374; Larsen, *BAFHG*, 300–301).
5. Now Jan Morris.
6. Palin, *Diaries 1969–1979*, 224.
7. Most troupe meetings during this period seemed to involve financial issues or protecting their brand, or both. None of them seemed to want to do more television series; *Flying Circus* had ended its original broadcast run in November 1974.
8. Palin, *Diaries, 1969–1979*, 349 and 485.
9. *A Book about the Film* Monty Python and the Holy Grail (Rowman & Littlefield, 2015), and Monty Python's Flying Circus: *An Utterly Complete, Thoroughly Unillustrated, Absolutely Unauthorized . . .* (Scarecrow Press, 2013).
10. See Larsen, *MPSERD* (2003) for more.
11. Jenkins, *Mrs. Thatcher's Revolution*, 61.

12. "ATV in Alliance to Make £2.5m Series on Life of Jesus," *Financial Times*, 31 July 1974: 7.

13. Elements of all these projects and the time period will be discussed as we move forward.

14. See John Whale's *Sunday Times* article "In Search of the Saviour," 30 March 1975: 38.

15. See Jane Gaskell, "What It's Like to Play Jesus," *Daily Mail*, 29 September 1972: 7.

16. "ATV in Alliance," 7.

17. See *BAFHG*, 26–27, 39, and 54.

18. Bernstein, *Myth of Decline*, 88.

19. Bernstein, *Myth of Decline*, 107.

20. This is a phrase Thatcher would use in speeches.

21. Caryl, *Strange Rebels*, xiii.

22. Mentioned in "The Man Who Won the War," *The Goon Show*, by Frenchman Moriarty, but originally attributed to Napoleon. It first appears in print in the *Times* in October 1803.

23. See Richard, *WWAR*, 7.

24. More like Godard's garbage men in *Weekend* (1967) who complain about inadequate U.S. aid to the Congo, and Algerian oil company atrocities, while abusing their *bourgeoisie* guests.

25. Hitchens, *The Abolition of Britain*, 74. Hitchens is talking specifically about the move to comprehensive schools and the abandonment of grammar schools, but the fervor for change cut across society.

26. *ATW*, 2.35.166; *MPFC: UC*, 2.111–12.

27. Bergson's term (in translation). See "Laughter: An Essay on the Meaning of the Comic."

28. "Friendlier Israeli Image of Jesus," *Times*, 22 March 1973: 9.

29. *BAFHG*, 76–78.

30. See *BAFHG*, 86 and 104 for more.

31. "Meditations on the Jesus Movement," 60.

32. Donoughue, *DSD*, 1.xii.

33. *DSD*, 2.5–6.

34. *DFBE*, xx.

35. *Monty Python's The Life of Brian (of Nazareth)*, 1979.

36. New editions of Whiston's *Josephus*, from which we cite, were produced in 1960 and 1974.

ABBREVIATIONS

AJ	*Antiquities of the Jews*, Josephus
ASRI	*The Archaeology of Sanitation in Roman Italy*, Koloski-Ostrow
a.t.	Audio transcription
ATW	Monty Python's Flying Circus: *All the Words* (two vols.), Chapman
BAFHG	*A Book about the Film* Monty Python and the Holy Grail, Larsen
BBC	British Broadcasting Corporation
BCA	British Cartoon Archive
BRJ	*Blood and Rage: The Story of the Japanese Red Army*, Farrell
BRT	*Blood and Rage: A Cultural History of Terrorism*, Burleigh
DBI	*The Doré Bible Illustrations*
DDC	*The Doré Illustrations for Dante's Divine Comedy*
DFBE	*The Decline and Fall of the British Empire*, Brendon
DSD	*Downing Street Diary* (two vols.), Donoughue
EEC	European Economic Community (Common Market)
EJ	*Encyclopedia Judaica*
FCY	*Four Crowded Years*, Waugh
HLTJ	*The Holy Land in the Time of Jesus*, Kotker
HMB	*A History of Modern Britain*, Marr
IMDb	Internet Movie Database
JE	*Jewish Encyclopedia*
JTJ	*Jerusalem in the Time of Jesus*, Jeremias
JURR	*The Jews under Roman Rule*, Smallwood
JVL	Jewish Virtual Library
LBI	*Life in Biblical Israel*, King and Stager
MPFC: UC	Monty Python's Flying Circus: *An Utterly Complete, Thoroughly Unillustrated, Absolutely Unauthorized . . .* (two vols.), Larsen
MPSERD	*Monty Python, Shakespeare and English Renaissance Drama*, Larsen
NT	New Testament
OED	*Oxford English Dictionary*
OT	Old Testament
PSC	Printed Script Commentary

ABBREVIATIONS

TAD	*Those about to Die*, Mannix
WJ	*Wars of the Jews*, Josephus (Whiston translation)
WWAR	*Why We're All Romans*, Richard

(*Terror group and political party acronyms are included in the body of the book.*)

SCENE ONE
IN A BETHLEHEM MANGER

In a Bethlehem Manger—(PSC) Bethlehem continues to be a point of argument for Bible scholars, and even the Gospels disagree as to its exact significance in relation to Christ's birth. Luke's account notes that Jesus's parents traveled from Nazareth to Bethlehem, where the child was born (2:4); while Matthew avers that Joseph and Mary already resided in Bethlehem (2:1).[1] There is not complete agreement as to how old the child Jesus was when the magi finally arrived, either, with many arguing that the "infant" was two years old or more by the time of the visitation. What the Pythons are appropriating and then sending up is not scholarship, but the Christmas card, hymnal, and accreted *traditional* versions of the nativity,[2] often as depicted in films, and much *not* part of the Gospels accounts: Mary riding a donkey, the holy family being refused a place at an inn, the child born in a stable, angels singing to shepherds, the baby Jesus not crying, or even three kings on camels, and so on. The BBC's *Who Was Jesus?* summarizes the generally accepted scholarly view of the nativity in 1977, just as the Pythons were writing and planning *Brian*:

> Overall, the most likely conclusion must be that the nativity stories are not historical. They do not belong to the primitive tradition about Jesus, but were developed by the early Church out of the Old Testament. . . . There is no reference to ox or ass in the Gospels. Our modern version of the nativity story has borrowed them in just the same way from the Old Testament: "The ox knoweth his owner, and the ass his master's crib."[3]

In this same year, though, the BBC also produced a "schools programme" for children on the series *Watch*. Filmed in studio and on location in Bethlehem and environs, the show took children on a "gently religious" journey through the nativity.[4] Joseph and Mary's arduous journey, their rejection at every inn, and the birth in a stable are all depicted or sung about. What's more, this program echoed a believer's sentiment to a great degree, especially cohost James Adair's songs: "His name was Jesus, he came to save us / Open your hearts, and let him come in."[5] Many Christian believers likely disagreed with the "accreted nativity" interpretation, while "permissive society" types balked at the BBC indoctrinating children with religious claptrap.

The Pythons' argumentative approach to the subject of the nativity is then based on centuries of these disagreements that seemed to be reaching a critical mass in the mid-1970s, just when the Pythons were penning *Life of Brian*. In a special letter to the *Times*, professor of theology R. P. C. Hanson discusses the "state of deep confusion" around Jesus:

The articles and letters devoted to the origins of Christianity published in this paper during the past few months are sufficient to demonstrate this [confusion]. Drastic and diverse and often contradictory interpretations of the evidence are put forward by people whose competence cannot be doubted by even the most sceptical or the most imaginative critic. Further, it is perfectly clear that this community regarded itself as entrusted with authority from God as a result of the career (or what is believed to be the career) of Jesus, and that this authority included the power to forgive or not to forgive sins, and to include in or exclude from its number and to further the expansion of the community itself by disseminating the good news about Jesus of Nazareth (whatever it may have thought that good news to be).[6]

Professor Hanson goes on to assert that active, believing Christian communities across Britain would be the answer to this disconnect and disagreement.

Secondly, in late February 1976 the Church of England released *Christian Believing*, a report discussed in an article by Lord Hailsham. The conservative Hailsham saw three main problems with the tract. First, the absence of much discussion about the existence of God, or the spirit world in general; second, the use of "highly metaphorical, or almost unintelligible" language when making doctrinal statements ("What is, or can be meant by . . . 'conceived' by the Holy Ghost?"); and third, any thoughtful, scientific discussion of the "allegedly miraculous" events that pepper the Old and New Testaments, including the belief that the world is a mere six thousand years old.[7] The dangers of not drilling deeper into these areas include, for the first, an embrace of materialism rather than spirituality; second, confusion of terms leading to fractiousness; and, third, failure to even attempt to reach the "scientifically-minded modern man." Fittingly, the last such report had been issued in 1938, just as Hitler was busy annexing parts of Central Europe, a prelude to the horrors of World War II. In 1976 there followed a number of theologians who wrote in support of the new report, as well as a number (including the religion correspondent for the *Times*) who found the doctrine troubling. In short, after *Time* magazine had asked in 1966 "Is God Dead?" and after the race riots, political assassinations, kidnappings, acts of terror, predictions of environmental apocalypse, and years of economic malaise of the following decade, it's no surprise that letters to the editor tended to wax pessimistic, especially in regard to God, faith, and the more supernatural aspects of Christianity.

That being said, the Pythons' nativity account seems to have been mostly inspired by Luke, likely because it is better known than others in the Gospels. The Lucan isn't even the earliest gospel account, though the synoptic gospels share a good deal of material.

THREE WISE MEN on camels—The camels and magi are dressed very similarly to those seen just months earlier in Franco Zeffirelli's version of the Christ story, *Jesus of Nazareth*. The three kings wear flowing, draped robes that hang down well below their stirruped feet, and the camels they ride are similarly festooned. These "exterior" scenes were shot back at Shepperton Studio, west of London, while the manger scenes were filmed near Carthage.

A star leads them towards BETHLEHEM—This special effect star is actually moving across the night sky, and stops directly over what appears to be an image of *Jerusalem* (not Bethlehem)—from the viewers' point of view, meaning the Wise Men would have a different angle entirely. (Cinematically, a perspectival alignment would be confusing, so purposefully bad perspective actually looks better on film.) In this version of the Jerusalem silhouette, the Dome of the Rock can be glimpsed, which is the film's first, likely incidental anachronism. This Islamic structure wasn't completed until about six hundred and sixty years *after* Christ's crucifixion. This is the type of greeting-card Jerusalem image captured by dozens of Western artists in the seventeenth, eighteenth, and nineteenth centuries. If the Pythons (and most likely Gilliam) had chosen to use an image of Jerusalem, *circa* 33, audiences would likely not recognize the very different cityscape.[8]

Already missing from the film is a shepherd scene. They talk about the loveliness of sheep, except at shearing, and in their inattention, miss the star visiting other shepherds.[9]

Visual beanfeast with inspiring music—(PSC) In the 1977 recorded table read for the script (one of many script "drafts") Palin actually reads this as "*beau* feast," meaning he and writing partner Jones likely did not write this section. Aside from being mentioned by Veruca Salt[10] in her self-serving song from *Willy Wonka and the Chocolate Factory* (1971), a beanfeast is popularly a dinner given by an employer for employees. Appropriately, though, it also refers to the annual feast the night before Twelfth Day, also known as Three Kings Day. Politically, the term was often used in British newspapers when either party wanted to lambast the other over profligate spending proposals.[11]

(draft) **NARRATOR:** *(Audience thinks 'They're really doing it!' Uneasy tittering. Catholics gather their belongings)*—(PSC) From the moment the Pythons mentioned the possibility of doing a Christ or New Testament–based story they knew there would be many, even fans of the *Flying Circus* and *Holy Grail*, who would be offended by the irreverent treatment of sacred subject matter. At this point, however, the setting and treatment are quite on point, which, to Python-acculturated viewers, certainly meant that an undercutting was the other shoe waiting to drop. These asides have become common in Python scripts, though there are relatively few in this finished version of the *Brian* script. See the entry "*Or, could a shaft of light* . . ." below for more.

The Pythons only mention the Catholics as likely to be offended by this treatment. Perhaps they assumed that Anglican adherents wouldn't care enough to be offended, nor would Jews, and that American faiths would ignore the irreverence, as well. What they're presenting is a more catholic version of the sacred event, and it seems less likely to offend Christian viewers. As it turned out, it was often the more fundamentalist flocks within the larger, heterogeneous faiths that reacted most strongly. The Church of England, per se, wasn't against the film, but Mary Whitehouse and her more activist fellows reacted to any increase in the depictions or discussions of sex and amorality in schools, on television, and in films. There was nowhere near the eruption of public antagonism in regard to the forthcoming *Life of Brian* as there had been for the announced Danish film *The Sex Life of Jesus Christ* in 1975–1976.[12] There were minor protests against *Brian*, including one outside the Plaza in Lower Regent Street, though none terribly well-attended.[13] The real difference between *Life of Brian* and other projects decried as blasphemous (the film *The Sex Life of Jesus Christ*;[14] the poem *The Love That Dares to Speak Its Name*[15]) is the fact that the Pythons purposely avoided implicating Christ in any irreverent or sacrilegious setting. In *Brian*, both depictions of Jesus are straightforward and sober, with the Sermon on the Mount being almost reverent (before the camera pulls away from Christ, revealing a bickering flock at the back).

the town is very full—(PSC) This from the original printed script, as read. As the Wise Men enter the city in the finished film there is no indication of any other person, but the pathways are lined with stacks of goods and such, perhaps indicating a host of sleeping people. This sequence was shot long after location shooting, and back at Shepperton, to boot. British extras would have cost much more than the handful of dinars paid to extras in Tunisia, so a late-night setting and the cover of darkness cloaked the otherwise empty (studio) streets.[16]

plumb line from the star—(PSC) A plumb line and bob are used to determine the verticality of a structure; here, the indication is that the line and bob would reach from the star to the manger, meaning a fake star hanging above the manger set. This level of context-smashing— only suggested here in the scenic description—will be on display in the Pythons' final film,

Meaning of Life. In the closing sequence, "It's Christmas in Heaven," another nativity scene is depicted during a musical number, and a nimbed Mary eventually bursts through the stable roof, singing full-throat.

(Or, could a shaft of light shine, suddenly, directly on the roof of the stable?) (Think about it)—(PSC) Likely referring to the many illustrations of the nativity where such obvious, typographical elements are employed, including nimbs, spiritual radiances, and shafts of heavenly light.[17] In the painting of the nativity at the Church of the Shepherds in Bethlehem, for instance, the light does indeed shine *directly* from above, through cherubs on clouds and a star-like Chi Ro, onto the nimbed and glowing holy family.

This is one of only a handful of intertextual comments made by the scriptwriters to themselves, a carryover from both the *Flying Circus* and *Holy Grail* scriptings.[18] In the first television episode as written and recorded, the animated title sequence is described in the script as being "possibly connected with the stretching of owls" and "proceeding from a bizarre American's fevered brain."[19] Gilliam's animated contributions are often described this way, since the Pythons generally didn't see them until the day of the show's taping.[20]

A fairly typical manger scene—(PSC) The more "typical" the scene is, of course, the more effective the Pythons' undercutting of the moment will become. This is more like a St. Francis–type nativity scene, one staged before a cathedral or church during the Christmas season, or those appearing in paintings since about the fourth century.[21] The bright nimbs are disappearing from painted nativity images by the late fifteenth century, and may be used here since they are so iconic (and blindingly bright). This also resembles the very popular rehearsal of mystery plays at York (which Palin and others may have grown up seeing), though the mystery plays tended to use medieval costumes as opposed to first-century costumes. Gilliam will borrow a version of the baby Jesus from one such "typical" Doré work. See the entry for "*infant Brian on a cloud*" below for more.

Incidentally, there was also a very recent mystery play adaptation by Tony Harrison playing at National Theatre in 1977 and 1978. There, portions of the Wakefield, Coventry, York, and Chester cycles were performed in a new setting, with plenty of working-class tradesmen-actors and lots of broad northern accents and verbiage. The accent of Mrs. Big Nose (heard later) doesn't sound nearly as out of place after watching this remarkable play.

THREE MEN approach the manger (audience shift uneasily)—(PSC) The "shift uneasily" bit means the Pythons are also aware of what a Python audience might bring to the cinema—seeing just how far into reverent orthodoxy the boys will go before pulling the rug out from under the scene. There's almost a "Wait for it!" moment (heard much later) implied in this tension.

The First Wise Man is "blacked up" for the role, which the Pythons employed more than once during the run of *Flying Circus*.[22] The Goons also mention "blacking up," as well.[23] There had been a long tradition of blackface performances on British stages and screens, and the Pythons had called for blackface performances in Eps. 20 and 29. The popular *Black and White Minstrel Show* was, coincidentally, taken off the air just as the Pythons were producing *Life of Brian*. This depiction may also be simply another borrow from the recent *Jesus of Nazareth* film, where black American actor James Earl Jones plays one of the Wise Men (along with Donald Pleasance and Fernando Rey[24]), or one of hundreds of paintings, altarpieces, and frescoes that have depicted the nativity since about 500. A number of such images do depict a wise man of color (Balthazar, who generally represents Africa), though many also present three fair-skinned magi and the occasional black servant or slave carrying one of the gifts. By the time the Pythons are producing their final feature film *Meaning of Life*, the nativity is being broadcast on TV in heaven, Mary and Joseph are dancers, and the Three Wise Men are *all* black and pushing shopping carts loaded with their gifts.

(draft) (No ocelots. This bit is serious please.)—(PSC) Part of the Python humor has always been the appearance of normalcy and somber sobriety in both character and setting, followed by a transgressive intrusion that completely undercuts the situation. The more real the medieval world of *Holy Grail* looked and sounded, the funnier the moments of deflation. Well into the film, when frocked monks walk together through a small, filthy town, chanting, nothing seems amiss—it is a scene drawn from *The Seventh Seal*, and perfectly medieval. This is undercut when they whack themselves in the foreheads with large planks of wood—the Pythons' version of flagellant monkery.

The ocelot, as a New World animal, would qualify as an out-of-place manger inhabitant, thus spoiling the "serious" tone. The Pythons often telescope history and create anachronisms, of course, including coconuts in medieval England, "orangutans," "fruit bats," and "breakfast cereals" in the holy scriptures of the same period, and so on. In *Flying Circus* Ep. 25, a perfectly dramatic, realistic World War I scene—where a young private is trying to tell his sergeant of life back home—has to be cut short thanks to a sheikh, a mermaid, and a spaceman in the shot.[25] In the nativity scene as completed in *Life of Brian*, only a cow stands beside the manger (though a chicken can be heard at points).

The mother nods by the side of the child—This is Mandy, played by Terry Jones. She is never called Mandy in the film. In *Holy Grail* Jones played Dennis's mother, and she was draped similarly. There, her name was also never mentioned, nor was her relationship to Dennis. Most assumed they were husband and wife. "Mandy," incidentally, was the street name for Mandrax, a methaqualone and antihistamine recreational drug mix popular in the 1970s in Britain. In Ep. 41 of *Flying Circus*, Michael Ellis's mother (also Jones) mentions the drug as one to which her son's pet tiger is addicted.[26]

She wakes from a lightish doze, sees them, shrieks and falls backwards off her bale of straw—The Third Wise Man's response to this is an exaggerated eye roll, meaning the bloom of sacredness is already off this rose. This gestural acting is likely a nod to farce films, classic British TV, and even the music hall stage, where such gestures were necessary when playing to the back stalls. In *Holy Grail*, Arthur's first encounter in the film—with the battlement sentries who digress into swallow minutiae—ends with Arthur raising his eyes "*heavenwards*."[27]

She is a ratbag—(PSC) This description is a Python portmanteau reference for the slovenly Pepperpot-ish woman seen a number of times in *Flying Circus*, and then *Holy Grail*. "Ratbag" means frumpy and unattractive, a reader of the *Express* or *Telegraph*, and likely a racially insensitive Tory; the pejorative is used in Eps. 9, 16, and 21.[28] During the run of *Flying Circus* Jones specialized in playing this type of character, culminating in the outrageous mother character in Ep. 45's "*Most Awful Family in Britain*" sections. In *Holy Grail*, Jones plays yet another ratbag, this time mucking around in the filth as the mother of Dennis, the so-called "constitutional peasant."[29] Of the decision to cast Jones in *Life of Brian* as this recurring Python character, Palin wrote the following: "Casting completed this morning. Most of the main parts reaffirmed. Brian is Graham (unchallenged), Terry J Mandy (John being the only other one in the running, but it was felt that a motherly rat-bag was needed, and TJ's women are more motherly than JC's long, thin, strange ones), Eric Otto, me Pilate, and so on."[30] Palin would add a clarifying footnote to an entry from 1972, on the occasion of hearing Jones's mother had passed away: "I had got to know Terry's mum well in the days when I visited the family home in Claygate, Surrey. She was an endearing lady and we were very fond of each other. Some of Terry's drag roles on Python were uncannily like her, though absolutely not Mandy in *The Life of Brian*."[31]

FIRST WISE MAN—None of the visiting magi are given names in the printed script or in the finished film, they are just "Three Wise Men." Clearly, though, the Pythons are mimicking the most popular Christian tradition for these depictions, offering two "white" characters (Gaspar and Melchior) and one "black" (Balthazar). Many medieval manuscripts produced in Western Europe—such as the St. Albans Psalter and the St. Wulfram's Gospels—depict three very European-looking magi. Occasionally, the Gothic illustrators gave one Wise Man a darker beard, likely to indicate African ancestry.

THIRD WISE MAN: "We are astrologers. We have come from the East"—These visitors from the "East" only appear in Matthew's version of the Christ story: "Now when Jesus was born in Bethlehem of Judea in the days of Herod the king, behold, there came wise men from the east to Jerusalem."[32] There isn't a number provided there, and the astrologers aren't given names in the best-known versions of the story. It's also unclear where they came from, precisely, excepting somewhere east of Palestine. It's likely that since there are three gifts enumerated—gold, frankincense, and myrrh—it was assumed three men carried them.

MANDY: "Is this some kind of joke?"—In Ep. 41 of *Flying Circus*, the odd behavior of the clerks behind the ant counter prompt a complaint from Chris (Idle), and the Real Manager (Jones) tells him their "performances" are part of the store's "rag week": "A university tradition where students help raise money (via sideshow-type performances) for charities. Both Cambridge and Oxford participate in the long-standing 'raising and giving' tradition. The student fun and games during rag week could be rather over the top."[33] This explanation is actually able to elicit a donation from Chris for the store's charity; Brian's skeptical mother is able to (momentarily) collect charitable donations from the visiting magi.

FIRST WISE MAN: "We wish to praise the infant"—There are several versions of this scene in Matthew, chapter 2, that the Pythons could have used as their scriptural foundation. Both the Revised Standard Edition (1952) and the New International Version (1973) agree almost completely with the King James Version:

> 9 When they had heard the king, they departed; and, lo, the star, which they saw in the east, went before them, till it came and stood over where the young child was.
>
> 10 When they saw the star, they rejoiced with exceeding great joy.
>
> 11 And when they were come into the house, they saw the young child with Mary his mother, and fell down, and worshipped him: and when they had opened their treasures, they presented unto him gifts; gold, and frankincense and myrrh.
>
> 12 And being warned of God in a dream that they should not return to Herod, they departed into their own country another way.

See the next entry for the Pythons' word choice. Pilate's wife will also be warned in a dream that her husband should release Jesus; he does not follow her advice.

MANDY: "Homage!! You're all drunk . . ."—A Pythonesque misunderstanding, certainly. Perhaps Jones is riffing on the medieval, knightly definition of the term, meaning the acknowledgment of a vassal-lord relationship. Even though Jones is an avid and published medieval historian, it's more likely that Mandy simply hears "homage" and "balm" in her own way. In *Flying Circus* Ep. 5, a management training interviewer (Cleese) interprets an applicant's simple, seemingly obvious and normal gestures (sitting down, standing up, sitting down again, answering "Good morning") in aberrant, mystifying ways. The applicant (Chapman) has no way to interpret the odd goings-on during the interview, and eventually has a tantrum. In a later episode a character must learn to talk faster or slower, higher or lower (in register), louder or softer, just to facilitate a police report.[34] Communications in the Python world are very seldom straightforward, and often the characters involved have to work out, in scene, how to effectively communicate:[35]

> The importance . . . of communication in [*Flying* Circus] is a significant trope. In Ep. 14, the Minister delivers his answer in his "normal voice, and then in a kind of silly, high-pitched whine." Other characters only speak parts of words, so that only in a group can they utter complete sentences; one character speaks in anagrams; and one insults the listener with every other sentence, etc. In a nicely visual twist on the trope, in Ep. 30, gestures are offered to denote "pauses in televised talk."[36]

Mandy won't know what the magi mean by "Wise Men," "homage," "myrrh," "balm," "praising," and "Capricorn," and her interpretation of being "led by a star" is being "led by a bottle," a more human, earthy metaphor that's closer to her character's range of understanding and experience as a "ratbag" Pepperpot. She immediately comprehends when the Wise Men offer her gifts, however, specifically when they've mentioned "gold." She also understands "astrologers" and "star signs," like Mrs. O and Mrs. Trepidatious in Ep. 37 of *Flying Circus*. They—along with closet mice (Ep. 2), "Ideal Loons" (middle-Britain Conservatives; also Ep. 37) and awful British tourists abroad on package tours (Ep. 31)—read the *Daily Express* for its horoscope and sordid human interest stories.[37]

Most of the major versions of the Bible available to the Pythons as they wrote do not use the word "homage" in relation to the nativity. In one or two versions (e.g., the RSV for Catholics) "homage" appears in the Gospels, but only when Christ is being tortured and humiliated, and then only in Mark.[38] This might be one of the most identifiable influences, then, of the Zeffirelli version in *Jesus of Nazareth*. In the scene where the Wise Men are in the manger, and they've all agreed this is the king they were sent to find, they speak of their praising and gift-giving in this way:

> Balthazar: Accept these poor tokens of our homage. Incense, to perfume the holes in thy feet.
>
> *He places the vessel on the floor at Mary's feet.*
>
> Melchior: Gold, for kingly rule.
>
> *He places the box on the floor.*
>
> Gaspar: Myrrh, the most precious herb of the east, and the most bitter.
>
> *He places the vessel on the floor.*

The very seriousness of this moment, followed as it is by Melchior's warning to Mary that Herod is likely a threat to her son, means it's ripe for the Pythons. In most editions of the Bible, the Wise Men "worship" (also "worship," "worshipped," and "worshipping") the baby Jesus. The Pythons' version of the Three Wise Men will do this, as well, in unison, in a moment.

MANDY: ". . . some tale about Oriental fortune tellers . . ."—They are "from the East," and Mandy's decided that means the Orient, which was a generalization of the period. Babylon had been the center of Oriental trade, and the Jews had been exiled in Babylon, though this exile had ended some six hundred years prior to the film's stated time. Both frankincense and myrrh would have necessarily found their way to Jerusalem via the "Incense Route," as perhaps would tales of "Oriental fortune tellers." And since both frankincense and myrrh were burned as holy incense in the temple in Jerusalem, regular and dependable sources would have been crucial.[39] Mandy doesn't know what myrrh is, she'll admit in a moment, and that may mean she has no knowledge of the inner workings of the temple—a lack of knowledge likely shared by many everyday Jews (and perhaps especially female Jews) of her time.

MANDY: "Go and praise someone else's brat! Go on!"—This bossy, over-the-top characterization is typical of some of the Pythons' ratbags, but there is also a character in *Jesus of Nazareth* they likely drew from. In the manger scene, the woman taking care of Mary after the birth takes charge rather authoritatively, giving Joseph instructions and seeing to the new mother's needs. At this point shepherds appear at the manger door, and she immediately tries to give them the bum's rush: "Who's that? What do you want? This is no place for you! Get out! Get out, do you hear me?" At this point she aims to physically hustle them back out the door, like Mandy with her visitors: "Off! Off with you! Can't you see? The poor girl has just had a child!" After revealing by what means they were led there (a star, not a bottle), the shepherds are invited in by Joseph, *without* the promise of gifts.

MANDY: "Led by a bottle, more like"—The possibility of drinking spirits from a glass bottle was real during this period, though the more likely container for wine could have been amphora or oak barrels brought in by hated Romans. Later, the Peoples' Front of Judea will count imported Roman wine as one of the positive things about the Roman occupation.

FIRST WISE MAN: "Gold, frankincense, myrrh"—Wine mixed with myrrh will be offered to Christ as he is placed on the cross, in a passage found in Mark 15, "but he received it not." Myrrh was used in Roman times as a fairly effective painkiller, as well as for its fragrant properties.[40] The shepherds who visit the child in Harrison's *The Mysteries* miracle play bring gifts, as well: "a bob of cherries," a bird in a cage, and a tennis ball for the child to play with. And even though it sounds like a Pythonesque anachronism, the gift of the tennis ball comes from very old versions of the Wakefield cycle.[41]

THIRD WISE MAN: "It is a valuable balm"—This is an answer to Mandy's question "So what is myrrh, anyway?" a question many have likely asked over the years. The Johannine account tells of Nicodemus bringing a myrrh mixture to anoint Christ's body after his crucifixion, and with Pilate's approval.[42] Myrrh had both medicinal and sacerdotal applications, meaning it would have been both valuable and available in Jerusalem during this time.

MANDY: "What are you giving him a balm for? It might bite him"—It might seem that at first Mandy may have heard "bomb," and we could assume that in her world there are "Holy Hand Grenade"–type devices as there had been in *Holy Grail*.[43] She takes the reference sideways, of course, thinking a "balm" is some kind of wild animal. She's already assumed that "homage" is "disgusting," so her version of malapropery is betrayed. Misunderstandings and failures of communication are wrecking balls in the Python world, smashing contexts and diverting narratives onto seemingly unintended paths. In *Flying Circus*, the Pythons had merely carried on a long-standing English dramatic tradition of the "comic misunderstanding," leading to silly or (narratively) fatal results. In the first episode of the TV series, an Italian language class is underway, being taught to, of course, Italians:

> It's already clear that almost everyone in the classroom is Italian, and only the teacher seems to have missed this point. The irony of teaching introductory, conversational Italian to native Italians is the obvious joke, and it's compounded by Python's characteristic "comic misunderstanding" trope, thanks to the teacher's failure to recognize his students' nationalities. This comic misunderstanding occurs when peasants refuse to recognize kings, in the Python world, or when Thomas Dekker's lower-class characters consort with upper-class characters on the same social level, and without self-consciousness, in *The Shoemaker's Holiday* (1599). The tra-

dition is also carried on in myriad eighteenth-century plays (e.g., Sheridan's *The Rivals*) and novels (Fielding's *Tom Jones*).[44]

Cleese's Centurion and Palin's Nisus Wettus will struggle mightily as they try to communicate later with jailers, both fairly unhelpful, narratively speaking. Also in *Flying Circus*, a tobacconist's signs may or may not be sexual *double entendres* ("chest of drawers," "a bit of pram"),[45] and a man asking to be married at the Registry Office is mistaken for/as proposing *to* the Registrar. By the time that scene is complete, five men are happily married to each other.[46] Brian's mother's misunderstandings might simply be a comment on her ratbag rusticity, and her inability to differentiate between reality and what she might have dreamed.

MANDY: "Yes, it is. It's got great big . . ." *(she gestures)*—Tim the Enchanter (Cleese) describes the beast waiting for the knights should they approach the Cave of Caerbannog in a very similar way, including using his fingers to indicate the creature's "nasty, big pointy teeth."[47]

THIRD WISE MAN: "No, it isn't, it's an ointment"—In the printed script Mandy fingers the jar (offered by the helpful First Wise Man) to get a feel for the ointment, but in the finished film that "grubby finger" moment is elided. They obviously shot this moment, as well, then edited it out; all that's left in the finished film is Mandy enigmatically holding up her index finger, as if she's testing the breeze. Not being a woman of wealth, Mandy might be excused for not appreciating expensive unguents. If she had been wealthy and interested in perfumes, she would have "known that scents and 'ointments' were greatly in vogue, and often most expensive (Matt. 26:7). The latter were prepared of oil and of home or foreign perfumes, the dearest being kept in costly alabaster boxes."[48] As the film plays out, only Gregory and his wife, those Romans and preferred servants of Pilate's household, and the assembled Roman audience at the Colosseum would have ritually availed themselves of these luxuries.

MANDY: "Or did I dream it?"—The dream as portentous is common in the scriptures. In the New Testament, dreams related to the Savior include: the aged Zacharias being visited in a "vision" by an angel who told Zacharias that his son, John, would be "great in the sight of the Lord";[49] in Matthew, Joseph's concerns about putting away Mary "privily" are assuaged by the visitation of an angel;[50] and Joseph will be visited again with a supernatural prompting to take his wife and child out of Herod's reach.[51] Just prior to this last visitation, the Three Wise Men will also receive a message from God to "not return to Herod," but "[depart] into their own country in another way."[52] Later, Matthew 27:19 tells of Pilate's wife warning her husband to have "nothing to do with that just man," meaning Jesus—her dreams had made her "[suffer] many things."[53]

Mandy's dreams of a biting animal called a "balm" sound more like the visions given to John and recorded in Revelations, where there are myriad dragons and beasts. There is a "behemoth" mentioned in Job, but "he eateth grass as an ox," so isn't likely to bite anyone, as well as "leviathan" mentioned in Isaiah, Psalms, and Job.[54] With the vagaries of medieval translation noted, there are also unicorns, cockatrice, and even satyrs. These fanciful creatures can be seen in the margins of Gothic illuminated manuscripts, and on maps from the same period, when some of the major biblical translations were being accomplished.[55]

MANDY: "So you're astrologers are you?"—In the Zeffirelli film *Jesus of Nazareth*, just prior to finding the baby Jesus at the stable, the Wise Men gather with their astrologer's paraphernalia (maps, charts, etc.) and discuss the signs and meaning of the coming miracle.

MANDY: "What star sign is he?"—This "star sign" talk appears earlier in a Pete and Dud sketch from their 1968 BBC series *Goodbye Again*, when Dud visits the doctor (he fears he's been cursed by an angry palmist):

Dud: So I said "I am the Ram" . . .

Pete: Ares.

Dud: Ares. "Mercurial, quixotic . . ."

Pete: ". . . tempestuous—tempestuous. Given to sudden flights of fancy . . ."

Dud: (*laughing*) For Valerie Pearson at four in the morning . . .

Pete: Exactly.

Dud: Uh, "outgoing, ingoing, avoid brunettes, lucky number four." . . .

A number of tabloids, including the *Daily Express*, *The Sun*, and the *Daily Mirror*, boasted popular horoscope sections. In Ep. 37, "What the Stars Foretell" sketch in *Flying Circus*, two ratbags (Chapman and Idle) discuss star signs (". . . the zodiacal signs, the horoscopic fates, the astrological portents, the omens . . ."), reading especially from the *Daily Express*.[56]
FIRST WISE MAN: ". . . Capricorn"—Simply meaning that these Wise Men assume (and so do the writers of the film, and much of the world) that Christ was born sometime between 22 December and 20 January. This reference likely pricked the astute, younger audience members' memories, given that seven years earlier American singer and songwriter Kris Kristofferson had released the song and album "Jesus was a Capricorn":[57]

> Jesus was a Capricorn / He ate organic food
> He believed in love and peace / And never wore no shoes
> Long hair, beard and sandals / And a funky bunch of friends
> Reckon we'd just nail him up / If he came down again.

There are many opinions as to when Christ was actually born, differing for Jew, Christian, and pagan, though a winter birth seems unlikely given the cold weather. Arguments against a December nativity do include the cold—shepherds would not have been in their fields with flocks overnight, for example; also, the Augustan census was underway, which would have been scheduled in better travel weather to ensure a higher, more accurate count, etcetera. Calculating against Christ's cousin John's birth puts the blessed event sometime toward the end of September. If the date is set toward the end of September, then Brian (and Christ) would have been Libra, not Capricorn.

In December 1976, the Pythons were meeting fairly regularly to share story and scene ideas for the forthcoming film. On 10 December, a small story appeared in the *Times*, "Astronomy: The Star of Bethlehem," which was itself adapted from an article appearing the previous day in the scientific journal *Nature*. For the articles, D. W. Hughes of Sheffield University examined all the available information explaining the Star of Bethlehem, whether a comet, a nova, or even a particularly bright planet Venus. None of these match the astronomical situation of the period (about 7 BC), and he proposed instead a "triple conjunction," wherein Jupiter and Saturn moved very close together three times over a space of six months, appearing incredibly bright. He finds that the "triple conjunction (in the constellation Pisces) had been calculated and predicted" in Babylonian cuneiform tablets, and astrologers like these magi would have known (or even been responsible for) these predictions. And, "astrologically, the event could have been full of significance for Babylonians steeped in Jewish tradition. Not only is Pisces associated with the Jewish people, but in traditional Jewish astrology Saturn protected Israel. In addition, Jupiter was considered to be a lucky and royal star."[58] The "guided by a triple conjunction" explanation may have elicited the same response from Mandy ("You're drunk!"), but at the time the Pythons were actually writing the movie, it was the most recent and most defensible scientific explanation for the Star of Bethlehem.

FIRST WISE MAN: "He is the Son of God. Our Messiah"—Beginning in January 1976 George Lucas and the large film crew that would create *Star Wars* began work at Elstree Studios in Borehamwood. The *Star Wars* novelization[59] and first trailer appeared later in December 1976, when the *Brian* screenplay was still in its early stages. Parallels between the emerging Luke character and Brian, as eventually realized, can easily be drawn. The image of the young, infatuated naïf who aspires to greater things is common to both, for example. Palin's version of Brian and his trajectory read quite familiar:

> Today we decide on . . . the rough pattern of Brian's life—a bastard with a Roman father, toys with joining various Messiahs, is disillusioned, joins, or dabbles, with the resistance, is caught, escapes from the Romans, disguises himself as a prophet and gains a large and devoted following which he also tries to escape from.[60]

Luke follows the Joseph Campbell–inspired path of the mythic hero: He is introduced to the "problem" (the empire taking over the universe) but he demurs, for domestic responsibilities, until his family are killed and he is free to escape home and join the rebellion.[61] Brian must defy his mother to join the rebellion, he is thrust out of the (safety) of the community—he is hunted and eventually captured—and then he himself is the sacrifice. These aren't mirrored narrative journeys, but the Pythons were obviously very aware of the *Star Wars* world. (Both Luke and Brian eventually fly in spaceships, as well, a surprising but acknowledgeable coincidence for a scene intended to lampoon the special effects–laden space blockbusters of the day.) It's also hard to miss the *visual* similarities between Luke and Brian. Both are dressed in tunics that are light-colored, textured and woven, gathered at the waist, setting them apart from most of the characters around them.

It is noteworthy that the Pythons were thinking along the same lines as George Lucas at this point, though the historical, archetypal elements of these characterizations are probably clear anyway. Frank Herbert's 1965 *Dune* had also posited a bastard-type, insider-cum-outsider-cum-savior in young Paul Atreides.[62] There were plenty of messiahs in the news of the day, too, and of all stripes: from Charles Manson to Tony Benn to union activist Derek Robinson to Ted Heath—the epithet was used often and widely. Similarities to *Star Wars'* character and narrative construction become more possible after the Pythons begin principal writing in January 1978, when they were together in Barbados.[63] *Star Wars* had become a worldwide hit, released in the UK at Christmas 1977 to long lines and much hype. Palin specifically praises the film in his diaries, which he'd screened for the first time just days before heading to Barbados and the final group writing for *Life of Brian*.[64]

SECOND WISE MAN: "King of the Jews"—This is the title that Pilate applies to Jesus as he is sent to the cross. The priests who saw to Jesus's condemnation objected to the sign that Pilate had made, "The King of the Jews," and, in a Pythonesque bit of semantics, asked that the sign be changed: "Then said the chief priests of the Jews to Pilate, write not, The King of the Jews; but that he said, I am King of the Jews."[65] Pilate refused to change what he had ordered written. In Matthew, the Wise Men ask around to find "he that is born King of the Jews";[66] elsewhere in the NT, the phrase is *only* used in relation to Jesus's appearance before Pilate.

MANDY: ". . . Brian"—There's no sign of a Joseph figure here, and we'll soon learn that Mandy was raped ("at first") by a Roman soldier, who is Brian's alleged father. It's certain that Mandy, as the mother, will name Brian, which goes along with tradition, according to

Susan Ackerman: "In the Hebrew Bible, mothers are more often said to name their children than fathers."[67] But Ackerman also goes on to mention the significance of the name itself, discussing "Micah," which when fully extended means "Who is like God?": "Therefore, an Israelite audience would likely have understood that the mother had bestowed upon her son a name that celebrates Yahweh as the object of her religious devotion."[68] This last section is significant, at least for a Python audience, since it means Mandy has gone well away from a devotional naming, unless she is somehow devoted to Prince Charles (known as "Brian" in the pages of *Private Eye*), or the Brians mentioned below. Of Irish and Celtic origin, "Brian" is very familiar to Python fans:

> A Brian-named character appears in [*Flying Circus*] Eps. 2, 4, 9, 11, 13–14 (three characters), 19 (four characters), 20–23, 29, 36–37, 40–41, 43, and 45. There are many possibilities for the high status this name seems to occupy in Python, including [*Flying Circus*] staff member Brian Jones, and various BBC television commentators sharing the name. . . . The most likely, however, refers to Captain Brian Trubshaw, British test pilot and first pilot of the Concorde SST, whom the Queen referred to openly as "my Brian."[69]

One can also factor in popular cricketer Brian Close, sports commentator Brian Johnston, footballer Brian Clough, and boxer Brian London—each of these Brians is mentioned more than once during the run of *Flying Circus*. In the pages of *Private Eye*, Prince Charles was often referred to as "Brian," while his mother the Queen was known as "Brenda."

There are a number of seemingly out-of-place names in Jerusalem today like "Wilson's Arch" and "Robinson's Arch," ancient structures named for later imperialist adventurers who "discovered" them.

MANDY: "Oh! Well, if you're dropping by again do drop in"—According to the Gospels, the magi went home a different way to avoid having to report to Herod. From Matthew: "And being warned of God in a dream that they should not return to Herod, they departed into their own country another way."[70] These won't be "dropping by again," certainly.

MANDY: ". . .thanks a lot for the gold and frankincense . . . but don't worry too much about the myrrh next time . . ."—Given that the smoke of "frankincense and many other aromatics" were common "methods of controlling insects," Mrs. Cohen should have been quite happy to receive the resin—she is, after all, living in a stable. The "mosquitoes, flies and other insects" would have starved for oxygen in proximity to the smoke, and the rough room would have smelled much more pleasant.[71] Earlier, in Peter Cook and Dudley Moore's live stage show *Behind the Fridge*, newspaper correspondent Matthew (Moore) interviews a Shepherd (Cook) about the nativity events, and the shepherd mentions that the "atmosphere was very, very smelly" in the stable. The shepherd also points out that he thought the Wise Men were actually "bloody idiots" who gave the Christ child gold—"fair enough, a little nugget of gold always comes in handy"—but the gift of frankincense and myrrh was thoughtless: "What is a little kid gonna do with frankincense and myrrh? Myrrh is the stuff what poofs put behind their ears!"[72]

Lastly, Mandy clearly doesn't know the relative value of the gifts her child's being offered. In ancient Rome, myrrh was said to be valued much higher than frankincense. She's holding *three* treasures, at least for a few moments. In a draft version of the script Mandy "*gives them the presents back and receives a gift of cash.*" This is an example of a "flog back" where a prize (won on a game show) could be traded for cash. In the *Flying Circus* sketch "*It's a Living*," the Compère (Idle) recites the show's rules: "The winners will receive an additional fee, a prize which they can flog back and a special fee for a guest appearance on *Late Night Line Up*."[73]

The equating of a visitation to the blessed Son of God and a modern game show transaction should be noted, of course. This isn't a surprise, though, given that elsewhere in *Flying Circus* historical figures including Marx, Lenin, Mao, Che Guevara, John the Baptist's head, Genghis Khan, St. Stephen, Richard III, Julius Caesar, and King Edward VII all participated in TV game shows.[74] The Pythons regularly drag both respected and reviled persons of history out of their historical contexts and into the modern world of film and television.

MANDY: "Out of their bloody minds . . ."—The coarse accent is the first sign, but the use of "bloody"—a particularly English epithet—sets the tone for the rest of the film. These are various English men and women in the Holy Land setting, with no pretense of period language or accents. This practice had become *de rigueur* in Hollywood films, for example, with the mixing of American and British accents in films like *The Ten Commandments*, and the use of British accents in place of German accents in many Hollywood World War II films. *The Goon Show* had really led the Pythons here, no surprise, placing very British characters—including a "Nomad Arab" who'd gone to Cambridge to study Cockney—into Middle Eastern settings.[75] The various *Carry On* films, including *Carry on Cleo*, employed various British accents and mannered speech, from the high camp of Kenneth Williams (as Caesar) to the rough Cockney of Sidney James (as Marc Antony).

The use of "bloody" had also come of age in broadcasting and the movies as the Pythons came to be. A BBC internal document published in 1948 (and still in effect when the Pythons took to the air in 1969) laid out standards and practices on the use of expletives ("Bloody, Gorblimey, Ruddy"), with a "serious dramatic setting" being the general underpinning.[76] Though not beholden to the BBC, the British Board of Film Classification shared opinions with the Beeb as to expletives, and it wouldn't be until the advent of New Wave films and, specifically, Angry Young Men raging across screens in the late 1950s that words like "bloody" found their way into more common parlance at cinemas. In *I'm All Right Jack*, a comedy produced in 1959, Mr. Kite's wife rails at him for his stubbornness and politics: "Oh, yes, you're chairman of the Works Committee, don't we all know it. I'm sick to death of you and your Works Committee! Union this, union that. And your—blasted Soviet Union!" When saying "blasted," Mother Kite obviously curbs her own tongue, as she clearly (pausing, the "*b*" on her lips) wants to say "*bloody* Soviet Union." She doesn't, replacing it with her own "innocuous expression," but she could have just a few years later, even in a comedy.[77]

Later in *Life of Brian*, at the back of the crowd during the Sermon on the Mount, Mr. Big Nose hears "bloody" and tells Mr. Cheeky to not "swear" at his wife; the Ex-leper will also complain about "bloody donkey owners" and that Jesus, who healed him, is a "bloody do-gooder"; and Ben, hanging in Pilate's jail, is grateful that the Romans have brought discipline to the Jews, otherwise there'd be a "right bloody mess."[78]

(draft) They turn and we see an identical Manger Scene in the other corner of the barn— (PSC) Not so, precisely. This would perhaps have been even funnier, given that the actual infant Jesus and his nativity scene were just a head-turn away as the silliness with Mandy and Brian unfolded. In the finished film, Mary and Joseph are in a nearby manger, just across the way. Coincidentally, in a 1977 issue of *Private Eye*, the "November Books" column advertises a new book, *The Ted Heath Book of Bethlehem*: "The former Prime Minister tells the familiar Christmas story in his own inimitable style, with cut-out nativity figures, pop-up Xmas tree and free, giveaway record of well-loved Yuletide carols."[79]

MARY and JOSEPH and JESUS with haloes—There is a common mixing of depictions here, since Matthew mentions only Jesus's mother in attendance as the Magi visit. These nimbed versions of the nativity are plentiful, and Gilliam even used several (angels and perhaps a Mary figure) in the animated opening credits of *Holy Grail*.[80] Gilliam earlier included two versions of the Madonna and child imagery in *Flying Circus* animations, using Bellini's *Madonna of the Meadows* in Eps. 19 and 25, and di Credi's *Virgin and Child* in Ep. 26.[81]

Like the Sermon on the Mount scene earlier—at least that portion of it featuring Jesus—this is one of the few scenes in *Brian* played straight. This may have been why the Pythons chose to remove the proper nativity from the same manger where Mandy and infant Brian are found. Lifted right from popular versions of the Gospels, these scenes, if removed from the Pythonesque context, would fit into a completely orthodox production of the nativity. Here the holy family is in place, the proper animals are gathered, and the Wise Men approach and kneel just as they should, as if posing for a mystery play tableau. There is no other shoe waiting to drop, no undercutting. (That happens when we cut back to Mandy and Brian, and she slaps him for crying.) This was one of the earliest ideas for the entire film, where a "St. Brian" just misses the miracles, the events of the Passion, etc., always arriving too late.[82] It is perhaps the very reverent and traditional nature of these scenes as conveyed—both including the Savior—that inflamed public opinion against the film, given the language, nudity, and/ or irreverence in scenes before and after. It's equally possible, though, that a straight-ahead lampoon takes "the curse off it."[83] A sort of *Carry On Jesus* would have likely been clucked at but largely ignored. *Private Eye* had, in September 1977, offered a story from their "World of TV" section depicting presenter and host Bamber Gascoigne[84] as a Christ figure, complete with disciples, mentions of fishermen and famous Jews, and a sermon on the mount in rural Spain: "It was on a hillside very similar to this, on the outskirts of the little town of Granada, that Bamber first delivered his immortal challenge to his little group of young disciples. 'Here,' he told them, 'is your starter for ten.'"[85] A few months earlier the magazine had lampooned the BBC 2 documentary *Who Was Jesus?* in an article entitled "Will the Real Jesus Please Stand Up and Be Counted!"[86] The article tends to poke fun at the presenters and the show itself, and not Jesus. Peter Cook and Dudley Moore had treated stories from the Gospels several years earlier for their show *Behind the Fridge*, and sent them up.[87] In one scene, as an obviously iconic Jesus (Cook) walks on the water, his disciple (Moore) walks just behind him, chronicling the miracle, slowly sinking deeper and deeper (to audience giggles), until he splashes out of sight. Cook even finished with his arms outstretched, a gesture that could have offended, it seems, more sensitive viewers. Cook and Moore's approach to the Gospels was a lampoon, start to finish, and without nudity or cursing.

. . . pushing MANDY over—The obvious jerkiness of this movement results from the removal of a handful of frames from the action, causing a noticeable "jump" in the otherwise fluid motion. This effect has been used since film began, from Georges Méliès' "trick-film" *fin-de-siècle* shorts through Gilliam's *Time Bandits* and beyond.[88]

This unflattering, unattractive depiction of women is the Pythons' métier. By the final episode of *Flying Circus*, all stops are out. In Ep. 45 Jones plays a screeching, appalling mother figure (wearing a dress and wig but called "Dad") in the "Icelandic Honey Week" sketch. In that same episode, the mother (Idle) is equally appalling; she screams every bit of dialogue and worries about honey giving Dad "plop-plops"; the salesman is a man dressed in *female* Icelandic traditional costume, and hates his job but it gets him away from "gloomy" Iceland; and the son (Gilliam) is also cross-dressed and wearing garish makeup. Everyone here is cross-dressed at the actor level (four male actors dressed as females), while at the level of the fiction, the sketch, Jones's "Dad" character is a man dressed as a woman; Idle's "Mother" character is a woman dressed as a woman; the honey salesman (Chapman) is a man dressed as a woman; and the son (Gilliam) looks like he is a man dressed as a schoolgirl (school tie, cap, blazer, and skirt).[89]

MANDY and her brat—These characters have gone from being the holy mother of the Savior and the Messiah himself to a "ratbag" with "brat" rather quickly, as is customary in the

Python world. This setting is beginning to feel much more like the world of a Snoo Wilson play, perhaps especially *Vampire*, which premiered in 1973, and was then rewritten and re-staged in 1977.[90] One of Wilson's obituarists described him as "often overtly political, Snoo was a Marxist '*tendance* Groucho'; more subtly subversive and humorous" than other post-1968 British playwrights.[91] Wilson characters in his 1976 and 1977 plays included Afrikaners and ghosts, vampires and punks, and even "real" people like Eugène Marais, Lynda Marchal, and Enoch Powell as a bloodsucking vampire.[92]

(draft) (MANDY pokes it with a long pole)—(PSC) In the finished film, Mandy actually slaps the crying baby.[93] This off-camera slap was earlier used in Ep. 4 of *Flying Circus*. There, two art-loving mothers (Chapman and Cleese) visit an art gallery where their children (never seen) allegedly have "smeared tomato ketchup all over Raphael's *Baby Jesus*," manhandled a "Baroque masterpiece," smashed an entire contemporary sculpture exhibition, spray-painted Vermeer's *Lady at a Window*, and "eaten most of the early nineteenth-century British land-scape artists."[94] As the mothers tell each other of their children's bad behavior, each slaps her child several times, with sound effects provided by someone offscreen.

This seems to be a nearly direct reference to two recent and much-ballyhooed royal births—for Princess Anne and Mark Phillips,[95] and for the daughter-in-law of the Duke of Gloucester. The Phillips's child Peter was born 15 November 1977, and the papers carried information about his mother's normal pregnancy, the boy's weight and health, and even who his nanny would be. Quite interesting for us is an official statement made on 9 November, just days before the royal birth. The Palace announced that the royal child would *not* be awarded a title, and that he should be known as "Master Phillips." His un-royal father, Captain Phillips, would not receive a title, either, nor would his mother, Princess Anne, be created a duchess.[96] This was page-one news in most broadsheets and tabloids of the day. The *Sunday Times* went so far as to remind everyone that Master Phillips, grandchild of the Queen, was "technically a commoner"; just five days later, and in the same hospital, the daughter of the Duchess of Gloucester, Birgitte (van Deurs), was born *with* title, and officially known as Lady Davina Windsor.[97] The pregnancies had coincided with April announcements, July–August "retirements" from public engagements, then nearly-aligned November deliveries. *Private Eye*'s resident caustic Auberon Waugh[98] characterized the event in "lowly stable"–like terms:

> Rumours which continue to reach me that there is something terribly wrong with Master Peter Phillips can only be strengthened by the Queen's decision to have him improperly christened in a drawing room at Buckingham Palace instead of publicly in Church, as his religion demands. . . . First reports that the lad was born with five legs can surely be discounted. It is quite normal for the male organ to appear disproportionately large in new-born infants. The truth may be simpler, that the Princess Anne Dame Anne Phillips has given birth to a centaur. If so, it is hard to decide whether one should congratulate her on her good fortune or commiserate with her. It happens in the best families.[99]

So, baby Peter Phillips, grandson to the Queen, was slapped by the Palace, the peerage, and the press as he lay swaddled in hospital, the wise men of the day taking his gifts and moving off to a nearby birth of more significance. Fascinating.[100]

The music sweeps—desperately—The lyrics were principally written by Palin, well away from the rest of the troupe. Palin self-deprecatingly records that when the orchestrated version of the song was played for the group, it went over fairly well: "Played the Bassey *Brian*. Good reaction, especially from JC. All full of admiration for André's arrangement, though not for my lyric particularly. I agree."[101]

SCENE ONE

Notes

1. Unless otherwise indicated, Bible citations will be drawn from the King James Version.

2. In this book I will spell both "nativity" and "temple" without capital letters (except as part of a title or quote), with the understanding that they each refer to a singular event (Christ's birth) and structure (the temple in Jerusalem).

3. Cupitt and Armstrong, *Who Was Jesus?* 46; Isaiah 1:3.

4. Louise Hall-Taylor went on location; Adair made cutouts and sang songs in the studio. The show also presents canonical angels appearing to the shepherds, and the Three Kings' visitation with gold, frankincense, and myrrh, all guided by a star.

5. Audio transcription (a.t.) from the program.

6. "The Living Reality of the Christian Community," *Times*, 24 January 1976: 14.

7. "Urgent Questions Awaiting a New Doctor Angelicus," *Times*, 21 February 1976: 16.

8. A detailed model of first-century Jerusalem was built for the Holyland Hotel in 1966, and could have served as a photographic model, had the Pythons demanded period authenticity. Pictures of the large model were splashed across many British newspapers (i.e., *The Illustrated London News* 24 December 1966: 26–27). The 1976 film *The Passover Plot* used shots of this model as establishing shots.

9. Various DVD versions offer the missing scenes that were photographed, including "Shepherds," "Pilate's Wife," "Otto," "The Sign That Is the Sign," and "Souvenir Salesman."

10. Played by English actress Julie Dawn Cole.

11. "Labour Expected to Reject Secret List of MP's Interests," *Times*, 24 April 1973: 4.

12. Discussed in more detail later in the "Stoning" scene. Other period films, like the biblically themed and homosexual-oriented historical thriller *Sebastiane* (the life and death of St. Sebastian), directed by Derek Jarman, raised no fuss.

13. "Python Film Protest," *Daily Mail*, 9 November 1979: 19. Hewison's *Monty Python: The Case Against* covers these reactions thoroughly.

14. In the 1 October 1976 issue of *Private Eye* the film becomes "*The Sex Life of Her Majesty the Queen*," which "include[s] 'hard-core hand-waving scenes', and explicit, no-holds-barred close-ups of the royal hat" (12).

15. Also discussed in the "Stoning" scene.

16. Palin mentions the pay rate of extras for shooting in Tunisia (*Diaries 1969–1979*, 491–92).

17. This shaft of light is glimpsed behind the chatting shepherds in the elided "Shepherds" scene.

18. See Larsen, *MPFC: UC*, 1.21 for a discussion of this practice.

19. *ATW*, 1.2.15.

20. *MPFC: UC*, 1.5.

21. St. Francis began the practice of staging somewhat elaborate nativity scenes as early as the first quarter of the thirteenth century.

22. For the "blackface" and "blacked-up" moments in *Flying Circus*, see *MPFC: UC*, 1.104, 313, 315, 324, and 344; and 2.42, 46, and 209.

23. The "blacking up" moments (and references) are found in *Goon Show* episodes "Red Fort," "The Nasty Affair at the Burami Oasis," "The Raid of the International Christmas Pudding," "Ill Met by Goonlight," and "The Great Regent's Park Swim." *Private Eye* also occasionally employed blackface moments (18 March 1977: 13).

24. Jones had voiced Darth Vader in *Star Wars* this same year, and plays the traditional role of Balthazar here. Pleasance plays Melchior, and Rey plays Gaspar.

25. *ATW*, 2.25.20–21; *MPFC: UC*, 1.371–84.

26. *MPFC: UC*, 2.173.

27. Larsen, *BAFHG*, 64; also, 70n117.

28. *MPFC: UC*, 1.151, 260 and 335; 2.135.

29. See the entries for the "Dennis the Peasant" scene (*BAFHG*, 94–160).

30. Palin, *Diaries 1969–1979*, 434.

31. Palin, *Diaries 1969–1979*, 91.

32. Matthew 2:1.

33. *MPFC: UC*, 2.174.

34. *ATW*, 1.12.154–55.

35. *MPFC: UC*, 1.85.

36. *MPFC: UC*, 1.191.

37. See the index in *MPFC: UC* under "newspapers: *Daily Express*" for more. *Private Eye* would regularly run a snippet from the *Daily Express* horoscope section, poking sophomoric fun, like the following, for Gemini: "Uranus adds a touch of novelty to what you're doing this evening" (2 September 1977: 5). In *Private Eye*, the *Daily Express* was often the *Daily Getsworse*.

38. Mark 15:19.

39. See Cohen, "A Wise Man's Cure: Frankincense and Myrrh."

40. See Freese, "Medicinal Myrrh"; also Jeremias, *JTJ* 4, 8–9, 28, 95, and 121. In the 1976 film *The Passover Plot*, this offering is mixed with a sedative that Yeshua accepts, convincing attendants that he has died on the cross.

41. See Gillmeister's *Tennis: A Cultural History*, 27–28.

42. John 19:38–40.

43. "Bomb" is also a sixteenth-century term, so out of time here.

44. *MPFC: UC*, 1.12.

45. *MPFC: UC*, 1.165–66, 225–26.

46. *MPFC: UC*, 1.289, 299.

47. *BAFHG*, 437–40. Arthur and his knights simply mark the Enchanter's "eccentric performance," and go to the cave anyway.

48. From "Pharisees: Their Dress," *Bible History Online*.

49. Luke 1:5. Zacharias was very old, as was his wife, and he had to be struck dumb by God to convince him of the dream's accuracy. The Pythons *don't* include any John the Baptist, forerunner-type character. (The Baptist appears in both *The Passover Plot* and *Jesus of Nazareth*.) The hermit Simon is similar, but he has no connection to Brian, other than being stepped on by him.

50. Matthew 1:19–20. The Pythons also do without a Joseph-type character, rendering Brian's conception a few steps below "immaculate."

51. Matthew 2:19.

52. Matthew 2:9. There are no dreams, visitations, or visions depicted in the finished film. The nearest extranatural moment comes when Brian is accidentally swept into the *Star Wars*–type space dogfight.

53. Pilate's wife is included as an active character in the script, and there were even scenes shot featuring the actor, John Case, in the role. None of these scenes made the final cut.

54. Job 40:15 for the behemoth; Isaiah 27:1, Psalms 74:14 and 104:26, and Job 41:1 for the leviathan mentions. In one draft of the script, Pilate's wife is described as a "Leviathan" rising from her bed.

55. Discussed in relation to *Holy Grail* in *BAFHG*.

56. *ATW*, 2.37.197; *MPFC: UC*, 2.139.

57. Kristofferson had been in London in June 1972 appearing on Rolf Harris's very popular TV show, and he would return to British television in December of that same year.

58. *Times*, 10 December 1976: 19.

59. Ghost written by Alan Dean Foster.

60. Palin, *Diaries 1969–1979*, 355.

61. Lucas demands this of all his major characters in his early films—*THX 1138*, *American Graffiti*, and *Star Wars*.

62. A "Kwisatz Haderach," the universe's super being, is prophesied (and manipulated) by the Bene Gesserit order. Paul becomes this being earlier than predicted, and outside of the Bene Gesserit order's control. In *Star Wars*, Luke's assumed position as the second-most-powerful Jedi in the universe, to his father Darth Vader, is also hijacked by Luke's choices.

63. Palin, *Diaries 1969–1979*, 428–34. In the United States, *Star Wars* was still in first-run cinemas until almost November 1978. In late 1978, *Star Wars* was playing in London at the Dominion.

64. Palin, *Diaries 1969–1979*, 428. Palin would attend a party with Carrie Fisher, Mark Hamill, and Harrison Ford, among others, in June 1979 as the *Star Wars* cast worked in England on *The Empire Strikes Back* (559–60).

65. John 19:21.

66. Matthew 2:2.

67. Ackerman, "Women in Ancient Israel," unpaginated.

68. Ackerman, "Women in Ancient Israel."

69. *MPFC: UC*, 1.28–29.

70. Matthew 2:12. This is the KJV translation, which isn't remarkably different from the RSV, excepting in the KJV the warning is said to come "of God."

71. Neufeld, "Hygiene Conditions in Ancient Israel," 60.

72. *Behind the Fridge* was a live show shot in Australia in 1971, an offshoot of the popular *Not Only . . . But Also* television series (BBC 2, 1965–1970). This setup looks much like *Brian*'s elided "Shepherds" scene.

73. *Flying Circus* Ep. 19; see *MPFC: UC*, 1.294.

74. See the index for these names in *MPFC: UC*, as well as entries in Eps. 1 and 13 for more on where history and game shows intersect.

75. "The Gold Plate Robbery," February 1959.

76. *MPFC: UC*, 1.50.

77. Mr. Kite is allowed to say "bloody," however.

78. In Ep. 17 of *Flying Circus*, a BBC Man (Palin) lists the words not allowed on the BBC, including "bum," "botty," "pox," and "knickers" (*ATW*, 1.17.231; *MPFC: UC*, 1.264–77). The BBFC provided the Pythons with a list of words and images that could be removed from *Life of Brian* (and earlier, *Holy Grail*) if the Pythons wanted a lower rating. They eventually remove a swear from *Holy Grail*, but decided to keep the swearing in *Life of Brian*.

79. 11 November 1977: 10. Also, *Monty Python's Previous Record* features a "Teach Yourself Heath" demonstration.

80. This sequence is annotated in *BAFHG*, 265–69.

81. See *BAFHG*, 74, 290, 372, and 386. Haloes are a *pagan* addition to Christian iconography by Roman artists, part of the Romanization of the Church (Richard, *WWAR*, 275).

82. Palin, *Diaries 1969–1979*, 310–11.

83. On the Pythons' *Contractual Obligation Album*, an ad man (Cleese) is spit-balling ideas for a "string" sales pitch, proposing a nude woman in the bath with the string. "Too sexy," he concludes, and decides that putting an archbishop in the bath with her "will take the curse off it."

84. Gascoigne, host of the very popular quiz show *University Challenge*, has been mentioned earlier by the Pythons in *Flying Circus* Ep. 45 (*MPFC: UC*, 2.202).

85. "The Long Search for Things That Really Matter," *Private Eye*, 30 September 1977: 13.

86. 29 April 1977: 10.

87. The stage version of *Behind the Fridge* (directed by Joe McGrath) was playing at the Cambridge Theatre from November 1972 through fall 1973. The Pythons had lampooned McGrath as "McRettin" in Ep. 23's "Scott of the Antarctic" (*MPFC: UC*, 1.353–54).

88. In *Time Bandits* (directed by Gilliam; cowritten by Gilliam and Palin), one of Robin Hood's Merry Men sucker punches each of the poor as they receive gifts from the grinning Robin (Cleese). The punches are made all the more egregious with a crunchy sound effect.

89. *ATW*, 2.45.331–32; *MPFC: UC*, 2.202–10.

90. Contemporary reviews in the *Spectator* and the *Times* were enthusiastic for Wilson's mid-1970s work; "Marais Resurrected," *Times*, 4 February 1976: 9, and "Blue Rooms," *Spectator*, 25 March 1977: 26.

91. Dusty Hughes, *Guardian*, 5 July 2013.

92. Marais was a South African naturalist; Marchal (later Lynda La Plante) was an actress (*Coronation Street*) and author; and Enoch Powell was an MP during this period, and not leading the party. Coincidentally, Carol Cleveland was lifelong friends with La Plante ("The Monty Python Pin-Up Carol Cleveland," *Daily Express*, 13 January 2014).

93. Having now shown the actual Christ Child elsewhere, this is a point where the film demonstrates Brian is the Son of Mandy, not the Son of Man. The balance of the film follows the Brian-is-*not*-Jesus thread, which many critics missed or ignored.

94. *ATW*, 1.4.42–43.

95. In 1974, Princess Anne had also been the subject of an attempted kidnapping, which will be discussed in "The PFJ Plan Their Raid" scene. When asked to get out of the car at gunpoint, she reportedly retorted, "Bloody likely."

96. "No Title for Princess Anne's Baby," *Times*, 9 November 1977: 1; "No Title for Royal Baby," *Telegraph*, 9 November 1977: 1. Had Captain Phillips been offered and then accepted a peerage, he would have been titled, and his offspring could use courtesy titles. This was hashed through many times—beginning the day the pregnancy was announced—over the following months prior to the birth ("Princess Anne to Have a Baby," *Times*, 9 April 1977: 1).

97. "A Girl for the Gloucesters," *Sunday Times*, 20 November 1977: 1. Now married, she is Lady Davina Lewis; her father is Prince Richard, Duke of Gloucester.

98. Waugh's "diaries" discuss primarily news of the day along with politicians, novelists, and journalists. He also contributed to the *Spectator* for many years, and bashes the royals often.

99. Waugh, *FCY*, 31 December 1977.

100. Less than a year earlier the Pythons had cemented the *Brian* idea; just days before baby Peter's appearance they'd settled on Tunisia for location shooting (Palin, *Diaries 1969–1979*, 442).

101. Palin, *Diaries 1969–1979*, 443. The Shirley Bassey–like song was sung by Sonia Jones.

SCENE TWO

ANIMATED TITLE AND CREDIT SEQUENCE

Shot 1 *(clouds)*—

engraving-type clouds and shining sun—For the animations in *Flying Circus* and *Holy Grail*, Gilliam borrowed from photo reproductions in art, history, and technical books, and collections of works from Bosch, Bruegel, and Albrecht Dürer, among others. For *Life of Brian*, Gilliam focuses on biblical-looking characters and settings including, as will be seen, a number of Gustave Doré and Giambattista Piranesi images. Doré illustrated editions of the Bible and Dante, while artist and architect Piranesi sketched the ruins of Rome. The clouds across the bottom, left-center, and left of the frame, for example, are copied (and touched up) from Doré's "Dante, in a Dream, Carried Off by an Eagle" illustration in Canto IX of the *Purgatorio*.[1]

For *Holy Grail*, Gilliam would often cut and paste portions of one illuminated manuscript with another for a desired scene, like the "arse trumpeters" sequence, or the later "Springboard Novitiates" and "Passing Seasons" animations. In this last sequence, Gilliam uses up to six separate illustrations or portions of such to create his imagined world.[2] Here, Gilliam will piece together this cloud scene from several Doré prints.

Seen at the end of the credits, as well, this sun looks like it is also from the print "Dante . . . Carried Off by an Eagle," offering these same clouds, a brilliant sun, and a winged creature climbing skyward.[3]

"Brian" title song—Bond-like in its composition and presentation, this is meant to sound like the *Goldfinger* (1965) and *Diamonds Are Forever* (1971) title tracks written by John Barry and sung by Shirley Bassey. Bassey and friends had already lampooned themselves in 1967 with the recording of the *Goldfinger*-esque *The Liquidator* title track song. The actual "Brian Song" was sung by young Sonia Jones and written by Andre Jacquemin and Dave Howman. Jacquemin will work with Pythons again on *Ripping Yarns* (1979), *Live at the Hollywood Bowl* (1982), and Gilliam's *Zero Theorem* (2013); Howman will contribute the music to "Every Sperm is Sacred" for *The Meaning of Life*.

HandMade Films presents—HandMade Films belonged to former Beatle George Harrison and was run by Denis O'Brien. The company was set up specifically to distribute the seemingly undistributable *Life of Brian*. EMI Films had originally planned to finance and release the film, but backed out when public response to the film's allegedly blasphemous content began to heat up. HandMade would also distribute *The Long Good Friday* (1979), *Time Bandits* (1981), and *Withnail and I* (1986).

Monty Python's—This is in multicolored neon, likely to stand out from the biblical setting as much as possible. The title is plugged into another AC outlet on a cloud, though the receptacle appears to be the standard two-prong North American version, and not the three-prong version used in the UK. Gilliam would have been familiar with both, of course.

Shot 2 *(stone letters) including camera move*—

"Life of Brian" stone block letters—Also used in *Flying Circus*, the "New Cooker Sketch," where Gilliam was clearly trying to match the epic promotional titles of *Ben-Hur* (1959) for something as trivial as the arrival of a new gas cooker. The cover of the original soundtrack album for the William Wyler film features the title laid out just like Gilliam's version of *Life of Brian*—stacked, made to look like stone carvings, perspectively displayed—as does the cover of the promotional *The Story of the Making of Ben-Hur* picture book also released by MGM. Posters for the 1961 film *King of Kings* copied this layout quite accurately.[4] There are also a number of low-budget Hammer Studio films whose producers knew a good thing when they saw it, borrowing the majestic look for their titles. Midnight movie posters with identical lettering include *She* (1965), *The Brigand of Kandahar* (1965), *One Million Years B.C.* (1966), *When Dinosaurs Ruled the Earth* (1970), and *At the Earth's Core* (1976).

infant Brian on a cloud—This image is of course a version of the Christ-child, not Brian, this one borrowed from Doré, specifically "The Nativity" engraving from his illustrated Bible collection (c. 1866). Gilliam has colored the child's hair brown and given him some "flesh" tone, since the original is a black-and-white etching. The child is also nimbed in the Doré original, with a fiery glow as opposed to a halo-type nimb. In other illustrations from this same series, Joseph and Mary are both nimbed (conventionally), and baby Jesus bears the fiery glow.

It's likely that Gilliam pulled all of these biblical Doré illustration examples from the same book, *The Doré Bible Illustrations* reprinted by Dover in 1974. For *Flying Circus* and *Holy Grail,* he had also used Dover publications.[5]

falling "B"—This type of animated sequence is a Gilliam trope, where one portion of the animation can detach and affect following portions. In the opening credits for the first season of *Flying Circus*, for example, a corseted model's head pops off, upward and out of frame, hitting a cherub floating above, who then falls into another frame and onto a wheeled Cardinal Richelieu, who is crushed into a hole.[6] In the *Brian* credits, as the block title rises into the sky (and the camera "pulls back") the monolithic "B" in "BRIAN" somehow catches on the upper diegetic frame edge and is dislodged. This is Gilliam acknowledging the "edge" of the diegetic world, as well as his knowledge of cinematic history, but also a nod to the artist for much of his inspiration for these titles, Piranesi (discussed in a moment). In the "Pink Elephants on Parade" sequence in *Dumbo*, the elephants at one point march in line along all four edges of the film frame, drawing attention to the built-in (but almost never focused on) proscenium created around the mise-en-scène when the camera is static. The edge of the film world is rarely acknowledged in traditional, classical film and animation; it is in the context-smashing worlds of avant-garde film, and the animated films of Tex Avery, for example, that the *formal* elements of film itself are highlighted.[7] In Ep. 28 of *Flying Circus*, an animated medical drawing walks out of the frame and off the film stock itself:

This is not unlike the self-reflexive cartoon *Duck Amuck* (1953), where Daffy is confronted with the artificial and plastic nature of his ink and paint world, or many of Tex Avery's cartoons (at Warner Bros. and MGM). In one Avery cartoon (*Screwball Squirrel*, 1944), Screwy Squirrel lifts the edge of the frame he's in to see what's going to happen to him next, for example, and in *Duck Amuck*, Daffy ends up getting in a fight with an adjoining frame's version of himself. Most

21

precisely, in the Tex Avery cartoon *Dumb-Hounded* (1943) the wolf character runs off the frame right, past the racing sprocket holes, and into off-screen white space for a moment, before scampering back into the world framed by the film. These cartoons, with their hyperviolence, speed, and reflexivity, obviously had a profound influence on the Goons, first, for radio, and later on, the Pythons and the often-cartoony world they created for television [and film].[8]

The "B" will fall and disappear into oblivion, out of frame, and we will follow the falling Brian cut-outs, instead. (There is no indication why just the "B" manages to snag the frame edge, while the others slide past without a problem.) The "B" does not reappear in any of the lower portions of the "caverns" created by Gilliam.

The Piranesi connection is an interesting bit of context tampering, setting the stage for Gilliam's own "coloring outside the lines," as it were. In some of his elaborate Roman architectural drawings, Piranesi would allow a chunk of broken foundation or the foot of a tourist or, yes, even a loose clump of plinths to hang over the "front" of the frame, casting a shadow across the descriptive caption beneath. In his "Plan and View of the Tomb Supposedly of Alexander Severus," for example, parts of collapsed ornamented frieze project out of the drawing and into the world of the viewer, a remarkable acknowledgment of the edge of the picture frame and its tenuousness in relation to the viewer's position.[9] This bit of playfulness will be seen again in the "foundation view" rendering discussed below; another bit of fallen masonry lurching out beyond the flat page.

falling Brian baby—This image is different from the previous child image, but also borrowed from Doré. This "crouching" child is cropped from "The Deluge" flood scene from Doré's Bible series, and can be found directly in the middle of the picture, the child clambering at the top of the rock. Gilliam is likely counting on the viewer *not* making the connection between the original work (where the child will likely either drown or be eaten by the mother tiger and her cubs already on the rock) and the infant Brian falling, safely, onto the "Starring" credit block.[10] This same print will provide the next Brian figure, discussed below.

Shot 3—("Starring")

"Starring & Written By . . ."—Michael Palin, Terry Jones, Eric Idle, Terry Gilliam, John Cleese, and Graham Chapman, from bottom to top. The troupe often wrote in discrete units. Cambridge grads Chapman and Cleese wrote together (and had for years), while Oxford alums Jones and Palin also were a long-term team. Idle had often written on his own, then contributed to the group effort. Gilliam generally worked on the outside of the group, since he was primarily an animator and then bit actor; his contributions as an actor increased as the series matured. As their biblical film was being written, they tended to keep to these clusters, with Palin and Jones working together on their scenes and characters (including the Three Wise Men), and Cleese and Chapman meeting and writing together (Ex-leper; Stoning), as well. They'd all come together for semi-regular read-throughs, where all ideas were on the table.[11]

This layout—employing Renaissance perspective, for example—can be seen in many of Piranesi's drawings of Rome, but, as mentioned above, also copies the title sequences for both *Ben-Hur* and *King of Kings*.

earthquake and fissure—Though not associated with Christ's birth, an earthquake may have coincided with his death. Thanks to accounts in Matthew 27:51–54, Mark 15:38, and Luke 23:45,[12] an earthquake that tore the temple veil has been identified as accompanying Christ's death on the cross.[13] In Zeffirelli's *Jesus of Nazareth*, a storm is used at the time of Christ's death, but no earthquake; earlier, in George Stevens's *The Greatest Story Ever Told* (1965), a raging rainstorm accompanies his death, along with a hint (rumblings, birds spooked into flight) of earth tremors; and in *Barabbas* (1961), an actual eclipse during film-ing allowed for an eerie, stony silence and semidarkness, followed by wind as Christ's body is removed from the cross.[14]

In a semi-related event, the temple's foundation in Jerusalem had begun to settle and par-tially collapse the structure above almost as soon as it had been finished, and in the years lead-ing up to the revolt in 66, repairs were planned (to employ as many potential insurrectionists as possible) but never realized after the chaos of revolt set in.[15] Jewish historian Josephus (or Joseph ben Matthias[16]) mentions that the stones used for the temple were massive, measuring 25 cubits by 8 cubits by 12 cubits[17] (or 12.5 by 4 by 6 *yards*), reminiscent of the enormous blocks of letters Gilliam arranges for the title. These types of blocks are seen in DeMille's *The Ten Commandments*, as the Pharaoh's monumental works are being erected.

infant Brian is catapulted—It's the "AN" from "CHAPMAN" that bounces on "STAR-RING," sending the infant Brian into the Dantean abyss. The pile of monumental blocks left over from the collapsed names resemble the piles sketched again and again by Piranesi on his treks to Rome and Roman ruins. A number of these "fantastic" works are depicted in his *Prima Parte* series, the *Grotteschi* images, and images like "The Foundations of the Theatre of Marcellus," from *Antichità*.[18] The last image offers enormous cut blocks both in situ and lying about, and interested eighteenth-century men clambering and gesticulating.

Shot 4 *(downward camera move)*—

"falling" shot—The backgrounds as the infant (and then boy) Brian falls are borrowed from photos and illustrations of ancient architecture, including significant Roman ruins, as well as places not so Roman, as it turns out.

background one—The first visible background is a retouched interior shot of a lower hall-way arcade in the Flavian Amphitheater, Pozzuoli, Italy. Gilliam has removed some of the ceiling and openings at the top of the archways, inserting a blue-sky background. The lower section of this same shot is simply an upside-down image of the amphitheater hallway. The rocks inserted at the top right of the screen (perhaps to mask a caption found on the origi-nal) are borrowed from the same Doré print used for clouds elsewhere in this section, "The Tomb of Anastasius." The rocks have been turned upside down from their original position at the bottom left of the Doré print.[19] Gilliam has fused separate images into new buildings and vistas before, most notably in the animated sequences for *Holy Grail*. In the animated titles sequence for that film, Gilliam performs this same legerdemain, adding and obscuring as needed.[20] Earlier still, in Ep. 27 of *Flying Circus*, Gilliam creates a world inside a criminal's body from inverted, retouched images of Greek temples and the Panthéon (in Paris).[21] Kit-ted out with his own decorations—hand-drawn and airbrushed "entrails" and fluids—as well as sound effects (digestive noises), the scenes become quite authentic as animated policemen chase the bad guy, hoping to get out before he eats or, worse, has a bowel movement.

As for a source, there is a very nice, full-page photo of the tunnel section of the Flavian amphitheater in William MacDonald's *The Architecture of the Roman Empire*, published in 1965. The photo is the final plate in the book. Perhaps tellingly, some of the bright sunlight stripes on the original image can also be seen in Gilliam's version.

"With"—The baby falls past stones with cast member names inscribed on them, each somehow floating as Brian falls.

Terence Baylor—Actually a misspelling of "Bayler."[22] New Zealand-born Bayler was an early decision by the Pythons as a dependable extra.[23] Bayler had appeared on Idle's *Rutland Weekend Television* in 1975–1976, and *The Rutles: All You Need Is Cash* in 1978, also with Idle. He will also appear in Gilliam's *Time Bandits*.

Carol Cleveland—A longtime Python chum, Cleveland appears in the earliest publicity photos produced by the BBC for *Flying Circus*, though for a time she only contributed her female-ness to the show. She had likely only been included to broaden the new show's potential demographic, capturing young females as well as the requisite males, where possible. By the second season, though, Cleveland was often allowed to act with the boys and showcase her comedic gifts (along with her physical assets).

new falling Brian, youth—The block featuring Cleveland's credit hides the transition from the falling baby Brian to a falling youth Brian. Gilliam clearly wanted a Brian figure somewhere between child and adult. This new figure comes from Doré's Bible work "The Deluge," wherein drowning parents attempt to save their children by hoisting them onto exposed rocks. A tiger and her cubs are already waiting there, meaning the children might not last long. Gilliam has simply copied out the uppermost child, and turned him upside down.

Kenneth Colley—Veteran actor Colley would appear in *The Empire Strikes Back* and *Return of the Jedi* in 1980 and 1983, respectively. He also appeared in Gilliam's *Jabberwocky*. In *Life of Brian* he is tasked with playing Jesus Christ, which he does with restraint and feeling, especially in comparison with Jeffrey Hunter's somewhat affected performance in *King of Kings*, or the fiery rebelliousness of Zalman King in *The Passover Plot* (1976).

Neil Innes—Idle's friend and collaborator, the musician and actor Innes had appeared in the final season of *Flying Circus*, as well as *Holy Grail*, *The Rutles*, *RWT*, and earlier with his band and Palin, Idle, and Jones on *Do Not Adjust Your Set* (1969). Innes would also appear with the Pythons for their *Live at the Hollywood Bowl* shows.

projecting rock—Off to the right at this moment is a slab of rock (not original to the setting) that juts out into the cavern, serving no apparent purpose. It won't be until the end of the credits, when we are in this setting again (with different characters and titles), that it becomes apparent this background was designed for two uses. In the second iteration toward the end of the credit sequence a giant will be using the rock as a platform. See the "*stretched human*" entry below for more on this giant.

Charles McKeown—Just younger than the Pythons, McKeown had appeared on *Fawlty Towers* with Cleese, and would appear in *Ripping Yarns*, then *Time Bandits*, *The Missionary* (1982), and *Brazil* (1985).

John Young—Known to most Python fans as the "Famous Historian" who loses his life to a *Holy Grail* knight on horseback, as well as another memorable character: "In the 'Cast List' included as part of the printed script in [*Monty Python and the Holy Grail (Book)*], Young's characters are described as 'The Dead Body That Claims It Isn't,' and 'The Historian Who Isn't A.J.P. Taylor At All.'"[24]

Gwen Taylor—Taylor was originally being considered for the role of Judith, as were many others. According to Palin, they watched tape for actresses Gilda Radner, Kika Markham, and Penny Wilton, then "Judy Loe . . . Maureen Lipman, Diana Quick" and Taylor, and finally Sue Jones-Davies, who won the role. They'd met Radner on various *Saturday Night Live* forays; and while Markham was a serious actress, her politics, as a member of the radical Workers' Revolutionary Party, gave the Pythons concern about life on the set.[25] Judy Loe would get the call for *Meaning of Life*; Penelope Wilton missed out on *Brian* but made it comfortably into the popular *Doctor Who* and *Downton Abbey* series later; and Lipman later found fame in *Educating Rita* (1983), and had been part of the earlier *Doctor at Large* (cowritten by Chapman and Cleese; 1971). Finally, the leading contender for the role from the outset had been Diana Quick, who obviously read well and wowed all of the Pythons, according to Palin. Quick could be consoled by her casting into the popular *Brideshead Revisited* (1981), voice work on *Doctor Who* (2003), and a long career in British television. Gwen

Taylor eventually lost out on the Judith role because, in Palin's mind, they needed a "stroppy feminist" type, and Jones-Davies fit better after months of reading and consideration. Taylor had worked on *RWT* and later on *Ripping Yarns*.

Sue Jones-Davies—Her Welsh-tinged reading of Judith's "stroppy feminist" lines won the role for Jones-Davies. This casting took them more than half a year, according to Palin.[26]

Shot 5 *(downward camera move)*—

background two—This transition is a jump cut, essentially, with no real attempt to match the backgrounds, rather the vertical camera movement, which is continuous.

This second far background photo—a hodgepodge of small, rough doorways and wooden porches with laundry lines attached by Gilliam—is in fact the stacked, retouched image of an ancient Berber granary in Qasr al-Haj, Libya. The structure dates to much later than the Roman or Asian images seen in the rest of the title sequence.

new falling Brian, older—This version of Brian is provided by Doré, as well, but from an Old Testament source. This figure is one of the teasing children being set upon in *The Children Destroyed by Bears* (1866) illustration from 2 Kings (2:23–24). The prophet Elijah—whom the children had called "baldhead"—looms darkly in the background, his back half turned from the slaughter.[27]

Peter Brett—Veteran actor (and now writer) Brett had appeared in *Flying Circus* and *Fawlty Towers*, and earlier in *Dixon of Dock Green*, *Softly, Softly*, and *Doctor Who*, the last three common shows for casting calls with *Flying Circus*.[28] He was married to Carol Cleveland 1971–1983. Brett's name and roles do not appear on the *Dramatis Personae* list in the published version of the script.

figurative column—The "column" at the right is actually a photo of one of the Assyrian winged bull (*lamassu*) carvings at the Gate of All Nations, found at Persepolis, Iran. These gates date to the late fifth century, meaning well past the time of Christ, but old enough and exotic enough to pass muster for Gilliam background material. A little worse for the wear for time and the elements, these carvings are still in place. This historical site had been much in the news in the early 1970s when the Shah of Iran[29] decided to celebrate his family's achievements in association with the twenty-five-hundredth anniversary of the founding of the Persian Empire at Persepolis. The picturesque ruins became the backdrop for what Caryl calls "the jetset event of the century."[30] Many international figures, including the American vice president, the Duke of Edinburgh, Princess Anne, and Liberal Party leader Jeremy Thorpe, attended the lavish event.[31] Myriad stories and photos of Persepolis and the elaborate tent cities erected for the celebration (to which Iran Air promised smooth, comfortable flights) appeared in major British newspapers in 1971.

This background, coupled with the claustrophobic crowding of the bestatued columns at screen right and the laundry lines strung between buildings is more reminiscent of a "modern" British inner city than a Roman one of the first century.[32] The crowded and decrepit Victorian terraces had featured such images for decades, while areas like City Parish of Glasgow offered vistas just like Gilliam recreates. Frederick Engels would write that he "did not believe, until [he] visited the wynds [side alleys] of Glasgow, that so large an amount of filth, crime, misery and disease existed in one spot in any civilised country."[33] Some of Doré's London illustrations (c. 1872) were also clearly the basis for Gilliam's version of Brian's first-century Jerusalem home. The tower blocks that would replace many of these more awful Victorian slums held great promise but quickly decayed into sky-high versions of the same slums.[34] Gilliam seems to be creating a combination of these Victorian and Modernist living conditions, revealing their towering darkness as Brian falls and falls. The pages of Thomas Annan's *Photographs of the Old Closes and Streets of Glasgow* are replete with such images. Importantly,

25

a Dover reprint of this same book appeared in 1977, just as the Pythons were putting *Life of Brian* together.[35] Gilliam has, of course used Dover reprints before, as mentioned earlier.

SINGER: "He had arms. And legs. And hands. And feet . . ."—Gilliam had made a career manipulating, moving, and removing arms and legs and hands and feet for his animated characters. In this opening credit sequence alone we will see severed heads, moving arms, legs dismembered from torsos, disembodied lips and heads, and a human body stretched to banner size. Gilliam's work in *Flying Circus* set itself apart in this way[36]:

> Recognizable faces from the world of politics (Nabarro, Heath), sport or entertainment (W.G. Grace, Greer Garson) are given new, often grotesque bodies and/or abilities in Gilliam's world, and normal, unknown folk from traditional family photos also appear. The wholeness of the human body is the [audience's] expectation, and Gilliam takes every opportunity he can to dismember and make strange and monstrous that formerly sanctified figure. This "body horror" phenomenon isn't new to Gilliam or the Pythons, having crept into feature films (Hammer horror, bloody Peckinpah Westerns, George Romero's *Night of the Living Dead*, etc.) and on the nightly news as the color images from the day's fighting in Vietnam was reported.[37]

Parts of an entire episode of *Flying Circus* (Ep. 22) are devoted to identifying bits of the body. Later in *Brian*, pieces of combatants are strewn across the coliseum sand, the PFJ want to cut all Pilate's wife's "bits" off, and still later one of Brian's followers will parse the physical form in its potential godliness, calling for people to read Brian's sign as a providential direction to "think not of the things of the body but of the face and head." The Pythons and their characters tend to be corporeally-obsessed:

> They spend significant time referencing saliva, urine, vomit, mucous, fecal matter and bowel movements, as well as buckets and geysers of blood (*MPFC: UC*, 1.160). Characters in this carnivalesque and grotty world . . . can cough up blood (Ep. 29, "Salvation Fuzz"), spew aortal geysers of blood (Ep. 33, "Sam Peckinpah's Salad Days"), or die dramatically with blood arcing gracefully, even poetically from the chest (Ep. 23, "Scott of the Sahara"). In this world of corporeality, one can gob at great works of art (Ep. 4, "Art Gallery"), smell the pong at Victorian poetry readings (Ep. 41, "Es schmecken wie ein Scheisshauss!"), take delivery of dung and nearly dead Indians (Ep. 19, "Dead Indian"), and meet families like the Gits who don't exist except to revel in "warm pus" and "vomit and catarrh" (Ep. 21, "Mr. and Mrs. Git"). By Ep. 45 . . . wiping "the cat's doo" on the bread, toxic flatulence, diarrhea ("plop plops"), and monumental bowel movements define the Garibaldi and Jodrell families, both vying for the "Most Awful Family in Britain" award. Most of these situations had nothing to do with medieval times, either, meaning the Pythons were simply fascinated by excremental humor (or "fundamental" humor—humor of the lower parts of the body). In this they were neatly following in the footsteps of their literary predecessors Jonson, Voltaire, Rochester, Swift, Dryden, Smollett, Hogarth, et al., not to mention a number of New Wave filmmakers, including Pasolini, Polanski, Nagisa Oshima . . . and Walerian Borowczyk.[38]

This fascination likely comes from their heroes, the Goons, whose character Bluebottle (Sellers) ended many episodes by being "deaded"—blown to pieces, electrocuted or squashed, or simply having his knees fall off.[39] Like his cartoon antecessors, Bluebottle was always back hale and whole for the next episode.

John Case—Case was edited out of the film in the role of Pilate's enormous and dangerous wife, but remained as the looming Burt in the "Harry the Haggler" scene. His casting is a nod to the old Keystone tradition of hiring freaks and acrobats for their striking screen presence (tall and short, fat and thin, contortionists, etc.). Burt is also left off the semiofficial *Dramatis Personae* cast list in the printed version of the script.

Chris Langham—Langham is an actor and writer who wrote for *The Muppet Show* but also appeared, memorably, as the eager new MP Hugh Abbot in *The Thick of It* (2005). Langham was married to fellow *Brian* actor Sue Jones-Davies for a number of years.

Andrew McLachlan—The credits (in hanging laundry) spell this name incorrectly, as well, which means mistakes memorialized in stone, cloth, or film stock will remain forever. Scottish-born MacLachlan would reappear in *Time Bandits, Meaning of Life*, Cleese and Palin's *A Fish Called Wanda* (1988), and Jones's *Erik the Viking* (1989). MacLachlan had attended St. Edmund Hall, Oxford, Jones's alma mater.

Bernard McKenna—McKenna has a long list of writing credits, many with Chapman, including *Doctor in the House*, and *Yellowbeard* (1983). He also wrote for and with Ronnie Barker, Peter Cook, and Douglas Adams.

Spike Milligan—The Pythons' creative genie, *Goon Show* creator Milligan had already made a vocal appearance during Ep. 19 of *Flying Circus*, where he shouts from offscreen during *Election Night Special*.[40]

lamassu feet—The temple on which the *lamassu* stands is an inverted version of the Bacchus Temple at Baalbeck, Lebanon. This temple will appear later in the credit sequence, as well. There are a number of Doré prints in the Bible illustrations featuring these figures (*lamassu*) as gateway sentinels.[41]

etched cloud formation—This particular bit of cloud is copied out of Doré's work, specifically "The Tomb of Anastasius" found in his illustrations for Dante's *Divine Comedy*. Gilliam likely copied the image out of the 1976 Dover edition of *DDC*, page 31.

Roman columns—The columns to the right are inverted versions of the columns found at the Roman Theater of Merida, in Spain.

Shot 6 *(falling between columns)*—

statue head—This is an image of the head from the Roman "Colossal statue of Constantine" now found in a courtyard at the Musei Capotilini in Rome. The statue was originally created for the Basilica of Maxentius. This fourth-century head and the hand are the only complete parts of the large statue left. The falling Brian (see below) is pushed along now by the statue head.

new clinging Brian—This version of Brian—clinging to the statue's head—is a new version, also from Doré. This is a tiny version of David from "Saul Attempts the Life of David" found in Doré's Bible illustrations collection, page 76. In the print, young David clings to his harp as Saul prepares to skewer him "even to the wall" (1 Samuel 18:11). Gilliam has swapped the harp and wall for the statue's head.

Shot 7 *(lion statue and column)*—

cave ceiling rock—Gilliam lifted this section of "ceiling" from Doré's *Dante* work "The Gate of Hell," found on page eight of *DDC*. He's left a barely visible glimpse of the "All hope abandon, ye who enter here" sign at the top of the cave opening, and flipped the rock face image. Gilliam's cropped the cave mouth completely, except as the "ceiling" begins to fall the entrance to Hell can be seen, briefly. As it falls, the images of Dante and Virgil would be seen, had Gilliam not removed them, as well. Above this ceiling—as the columned surface above is revealed—the rocks from "The Tomb of Anastasius," used earlier, reappear.

lion statuary—This looks to be not a Roman lion (a Medici, for example), particularly, but perhaps a Greek-produced work (or copy); its pose—paws forward, together, and not on a sphere—and its facial features appear similar to earlier Greek statues from the fourth century BC. There is an example of such a statue at the Louvre, in the Roman section.

"horizon" rock—The surface upon which the lion stands isn't from the same source as the ceiling rock above, except that it is, oddly. Gilliam seems to have flipped the original image and is using a retouched version of the clouds as the new ground on which the lion stands. He has done this throughout *Flying Circus*, taking recognizable structures and settings and, with some simple manipulation, rendered them unfamiliar.

column and basis—The column on top of the lion appears to be a Roman Tuscan column, one perhaps pieced together by Gilliam. Similar columns will be seen later, in the "Julian Doyle" titled scene. The collapse of this scene brought on by the removal of the column support features characteristic cartoon physics. The support is removed, there is a pause, the lion glances upward, then back at us, and then there's a collapse. See the entries for the "stonemason" below for more on this cartoony effect.

Director of Photography—Peter Biziou—Biziou has lensed two dozen films, including *Time Bandits, Pink Floyd: The Wall* (1982), and *The Truman Show* (1998).

Shot 8 *(statues and columns)*—

The transition to this shot involves a wipe, where the new shot "falls" over the old one. In the shot, the cave ceiling above the lion collapses, revealing the surface above, where the columns are placed. This transition is accomplished in just a handful of film frames.

headless statue clutching severed head—Another Doré inclusion, this from his *Divine Comedy* illustrations published beginning in 1861.[42] The figure isn't a statue, as Gilliam has depicted, but the beheaded baron Bertran de Born, placed into the eighth circle of Hell by Dante for his schismatic influences. The trumpets his images bear are reminiscent of the ones Gilliam created for the title credits to *Holy Grail*. See the notes for the Title Sequence Animation (Scene 12) in *BAFHG*. This (live-action) trumpet theme will reappear in the "Colosseum" scene later in the film.

Shot 9 *(multiple statues and columned building)*—

columned building—The columned background building is a retouched photograph of the Bacchus Temple at Baalbek, Lebanon. Since this side of the building's columns (the southern side) have been partially collapsed for centuries, it's not as often photographed.

new etched cloud formation—This cloud is also sourced from the 1976 Dover edition of Doré's *Divine Comedy* prints, page 31. See the entry for *"etched cloud formation"* above.

man on horseback—At the bottom right of the frame are two tiny horses, one bearing a rider. The ridered horse is rearing up slightly, as well. These figures don't actually move and only the red coat attracts the eye to this far corner of the frame. This tiny bit of ephemera, almost marginalia, is not from a photograph but from one of Piranesi's prints originally drawn in Rome in the eighteenth century. "The Forum of Nerva" is part of Piranesi's celebrated *Views of Rome* series.[43] Piranesi almost always included human figures—tourists, gesticulating guides, and every day Romans—providing perspective for the massive remains he was capturing. It appears that Gilliam felt compelled to do the same, even though the images are separated by much time and geography.

Camera Operator—John Stanier—He would also work as a camera operator on *Midnight Express* (1978) and *Pink Floyd: The Wall*.

1st Asst. Director—Jonathan Benson—Assistant director and first assistant director on many films, working with the Pythons, Ken Russell, Paul Morrissey, and Franco Zeffirelli.

Continuity—Brenda Loader—Loader was a busy script supervisor for television commercials, TV movies, and feature films, from *Doctor Who* to Paul McCartney's *Give My Regards to Broad Street* (1984).

Dubbing Mixer—Hugh Strain—Having worked earlier on *Holy Grail*, Strain can claim dozens of sound projects, including *Britannia Hospital* (1982) and *Withnail & I*, as well as television work.

Dubbing Editor—John Foster—Along with Strain and Doyle (and Gilliam and Jones), Foster had worked on the *Holy Grail* postproduction sound team. Foster also worked sound on *Superman* (1978).

spinning statue—When the trumpeter spins, he has been replaced by a crude, Gilliam-drawn version of the headless figure, since Gilliam only had one angle to work from. As part of his work on *Flying Circus*, Gilliam would often redraw portions of a cut-out image for ease of movement.

Shot 10 *(pull back camera move)*—

Editor—Julian Doyle—On *Holy Grail* Doyle had helped seed the film, then, with the Pythons, carried it through production and postproduction. Doyle continued to work, with his wife and with Jones and Palin, after the film's budget ran out. He was clearly a sine qua non in regard to completion of *Holy Grail*.[44] By December 1978 the Pythons were summoned to the Sapphire Theatre to watch Doyle's first cut of *Brian*, and Palin reports very positive responses.[45] Doyle would later write a book based at least partly on the experience, *The Life of Brian Jesus*.

six columns—These are different from other columns used throughout. They appear to be made of Egyptian porphyry, a darker, shinier stone material. Roman columns were made from granite, marble, travertine, and even tuff. The entablature perched atop these columns is the very thing indignant Welsh coal miners in *Flying Circus* Ep. 26 argued about, eventually going out on strike. See the entries later in relation to Pilate's audience chamber for more on these architectural bits.

arch plinths—These appear to be plinths for a Roman arch, perhaps the cobbled-together Constantine arch seen later in the credit sequence. The columns above them have been installed by Gilliam, and aren't part of any Roman arch.

Sound Recordist—Garth Marshall—Marshall had also been sound recordist on *Holy Grail*, then continued his sound career on the documentary *The Song Remains the Same* (1976), *Meaning of Life*, *Prospero's Books* (1991), and *Outlanders* (2007).

SINGER: "And his face became spotty. . ."—A euphemism for acne, the Pythons are taking us through the part of Brian's life that is missing almost entirely from Jesus's life in any of the Gospels. We know of Jesus's birth, his encounter with the temple elders when he was about twelve (only found in Luke), and then when he begins his ministry as an adult. The many years between are a mystery. This song offers us at least some of the life experiences that Brian encountered before his short time in the sun commenced.

Shot 11 *(statue face close-up, then pull back)*—

Makeup and Hairdressing—Maggie Weston is Gilliam's wife, and a makeup artist who worked on *Flying Circus* and appeared in *Holy Grail* (it's her hand turning the pages of *The Book of the Film*). **Elaine Carew** has continued to work in makeup, most recently on Idle, Palin, and Jones's *Not the Messiah: He's a Very Naughty Boy* (2010).

carved face—The face this bubble emerges from is one of many found at a Roman ruin at Leptis Magna in Tripoli, Libya.

etched cloud—This cloud is a recolored but also slightly manipulated version of two separate cloud patterns found in *Doré's* "The Tomb of Anastasius," from which Gilliam has already sourced both clouds and rocks.[46]

multi-windowed background—This warren of openings is also from a Piranesi print, "View of the Upper Ruins of the Baths of Diocletian."[47] Gilliam has taken part of the large image, reversed it, and then copied and reduced portions for more background. To add height, Gilliam took bits of the structure further in the background—since it's perspectively smaller—and attached those to the top of the new structure. In his animations for *Holy Grail*, Gilliam would also piece together frames of illuminated manuscript pages to create new borders and new worlds.[48]

three ruined columns—The pillars in the left background appear to be from Persepolis, Iran. There is an image of these oft-photographed columns taken from the very same angle in Hammerton's 1952 book *Wonders of the Past*.[49]

Shot 12 *(archway monument; camera move downward)*—

archway monument—This monument is a retouched version of the Arch of Constantine in Rome, and it has been copied and stacked on top of itself to add height. A section of this monument will become separated and race through the animation, nearly to its end. All these names have been "etched" onto the monument. Gilliam has removed one of the Dacian statues from atop the columns and centered it, and added one or two more statues historically separate from the arch. (This arch is a bit of a jumble anyway, as will be discussed later.)

Costume Department—**Nick Ede** has had a long career as a costume designer, most recently working on the television series *Close to the Enemy* (2016); **Bill Pierce** also worked on *Jabberwocky* and *A Room with a View* (1985); **Sue Cable** had been with the crew on *Holy Grail*, and would also work on *Jabberwocky* and Ridley Scott's *Legend* (1985); **Zouleikha Ktari** is credited with two additional titles, both Spanish films; and **Leila Turki** also worked locations for *The English Patient* (1996).

SINGER: "And things started to grow"—This kind of lyric reflects Gilliam's animation *modus operandi*, frankly, where one thing can become another thing, and where plants, animals, humans, and even structures can grow and grow. The very first images offered to viewers as *Flying Circus* took to the air in October 1969 were sprouting flowers that blossomed into the title "*Monty Python's Flying Circus*."

For Brian, of course, this is connected to his physical and sexual maturation, referenced later as his mother chides him about always thinking of sex and the size of his manhood. The frankness of this display and discussion of emerging sexuality (and the freshness of the later "Are you a virgin?" question) is likely due to the influence of the sex education material made available to many youth in Britain in elementary and secondary schools. A 1970 sex education documentary depicting a sexual act between a husband and wife (and shown in schools), and a radio broadcast for children called *Growing Up* that described masturbation for boys and girls had many parents, clergy, and educators up in arms.[50] And like the pernicious foreign influence of the promised film *The Sex Life of Jesus Christ*, something equally disturbing was coming from the continent. *The Little Red Schoolbook* (1971) was a translation of a 1969 Danish book written for children, prompting youngsters to become more empowered, to see adults as "paper tigers," and to question every authoritarian institution. This was dangerous enough. The book also covered topics from classroom etiquette and homework to peer pressure, and from sex (with matter-of-fact, real-life descriptions of sexual acts) and drug use to drinking and smoking. There is even a long section on the significance of "marks," and a description of the British school system, with its inherent biases and discriminations—all incendiary stuff. The book was imported, then translated and rewritten for British schoolchildren, and was immediately blasted by Education Secretary Margaret Thatcher, the Pope, and campaigner Mary Whitehouse, who was able to bring a prosecution against the book under the Obscene Publications Act. In late 1976 the book was still in the news, with a British publisher claiming both human and civil rights were in play if the book was banned.[51] On the whole, however, sex education and the depiction of nudity and sexuality across European and British culture was much more liberal than during the same period in the United States. (Which is why the full-frontal nudity alone qualified *Brian* for an "R" rating—and opprobrium—in the United States.)

Props Department—Peter Grant was part of the art departments for *Time Bandits*, *The Abyss* (1989), and *The Adventures of Young Indiana Jones* (2000); **John Margetts** had worked on *Target of an Assassin* (1977); **Geoffrey Hartman** has only *Brian* to his credit; **Arthur Wicks** has worked steadily as a prop master, including *Jeeves and Wooster* (1991) and *Gangs of New York* (2002); **Gordon Phillips** later dressed props for *Memphis Belle* (1990); and **Darryl Patterson** has moved from the Pythons to blockbusters, working as assistant prop master on *Avengers: Age of Ultron* (2015) and *Guardians of the Galaxy* (2014).

Make Up and Hairdressing Departments—Susan Frear is now Susan Ignatius, recently doing makeup for *Jack the Giant Slayer* (2013); **Kenteas Brine** worked on *Chariots of Fire* (1981); **Diana Webber** worked on *Film (A Screen Play by Samuel Beckett)* in 1979; **Fatma Jaziri** continues to work in eastern film, most recently as a makeup artist on *Hedi* (2016); and **Faouzia Choura** has only *Brian* to her credit.[52]

Art Department: Asst. Art Directors—John Beard has moved into production design on larger films like *The History Boys* (2006) and *The Lady in the Van* (2015); and **Mohamed Abdennadher** previously worked locations in Tunisia on *Sergeant Klems*, in 1971.

Production Buyers—Peter Dunlop also worked on *The Winds of War* miniseries in 1983, and *Outland* (1987); and **Hassine Soufi** was also Tunisian production manager for *Raiders of the Lost Ark* (1981).

SINGER: "He was suddenly no/ No girl called Brian"—A comment on the maturation of Brian's male reproductive body parts, signaling his masculinity and emerging sexuality. Just after the stoning scene, Brian's mother will tell him to stop fixating on sex.

The sexually charged subjects of hermaphroditism and sex changes will be discussed later. The world's first well-known sex reassignment patient had been Christine Jorgensen; her story was somewhat badly told in the feature film *The Christine Jorgensen Story*, which appeared at the London Pavilion in September 1970.[53]

a newer clinging Brian—This version of Brian somehow clings backwards to the statue head. The head is moving quickly through these scenes, so a freeze frame is necessary to identify the source of the figure—yet another Doré. This figure is from the apocryphal work Maccabees, and the Doré print is known as "Mattathias and the Apostate."[54] The purloined figure is the Jew who attempted to sacrifice on the Modin altar, and he's just been mortally wounded by Mattathias. He clings to the altar and the upper step.

Construction Managers: John Patterson would work in the art department for *Casualties of War* (1989); and **Lotfi Layourni**'s only art credit is for *Brian*.

Set Dresser: Hassen Soufi—Another North African local who would work on *Raiders of the Lost Ark* two years after *Brian*.

working stonemason—There are many images of ladders up against ruins and monuments in Piranesi's myriad works of Rome, some featuring workmen, some inquisitive tourists with canes and tricorn hats. In the Piranesi etching "Tomb of the Household of Augustus," ten or so gentlemen wander around the catacombs, staring at the ancient wonders, and two ladders are visible leaning against a central arch support.[55] There are also ladders in the crucifixion scenes in Doré's work. Gilliam's stonemason appears to be a combination of figures from Doré, including the plates "Nailing Christ to the Cross," "Erection of the Cross," and "Descent from the Cross" in his *Bible* series.[56] Gilliam has combined upper and lower body portions, added a head covering and a hammer, etc.; Gilliam will put several bodies together for the final Brians seen in the next scenes.

There is also a pause here, just after the lower section of the arch is removed by the traveling lips/column/head/Brian, and before it falls, crushing the worker. This is clearly the influence of animation, especially Warner Bros.' Wile E. Coyote cartoons. In *Zoom and Bored* (1957), Wile E. has run off a cliff, but a cloud obscures the fact; he won't fall until he realizes there is nothing beneath his feet. Tex Avery's often context-smashing cartoons employed these "holds," as do those directed by fellow WB creator Robert Clampett. In *Falling Hare* (1943), the Gremlin holding Bugs's carrot disappears, but the carrot remains, suspended for a beat, then drops to the ground. Both the Goons and the Pythons employ this kind of cartoon physics. Apart from appearing with WB feature films in cinemas[57] for many years, characters like Bugs Bunny, the Roadrunner, and Wile E. Coyote had been seen on British television since at least 1959, when *The Bugs Bunny Show* began airing on ABC Midland and Northern TV.[58]

Shot 13 *(bridge and stone head; camera track up, pull back)*—What follows is a very busy shot, with several layers of animation that move, and with a camera movement, as well.

rope gang—The men raising the head are borrowed from the Doré engraving "The Erection of the Cross," also from his Bible illustration sequence.[59] Gilliam has removed the cross, all other bystanders and the backgrounds, and put the rope in place.

The hook and rope seen to the right appear to be drawn from Piranesi's "Methods of Raising Travertine Blocks . . . for the Tomb of Caecilia Meralla," found in his collection of Rome studies. There are also many such contraptions in Piranesi's *Carceri* drawings (where the later ring images will appear), though Piranesi generally depicts rope hanging from enormous block and tackle.[60]

statue head being raised—This may be Balbinus, a three-month Roman emperor (165–238). There were five other emperors in 238.

etched cloud pattern—Variations of the same cloud drawings, Gilliam had borrowed these for his *Animations of Mortality* book, which was published in 1978. The clouds can originally be found in Doré's *Dante* illustrations, "Marco the Lombard," page 98.

Hazel Pethig and Charles Knode—Pethig has been a Python associate from the earliest days, working on *Flying Circus*, *Holy Grail*, *A Fish Called Wanda*, and all the way up through *Not the Messiah*. Julian Doyle credits Pethig for making the vagabond and penniless *Holy Grail* work.[61] "Charlie" Knode has also worked over and over again with the Pythons, appearing in *Holy Grail* as a minstrel and castle guard, and as a leper in *Brian*, and as an award-winning costume designer for *Blade Runner* (1982) and *Braveheart* (1995).

inscribed arched bridge—The background behind the rising bust is a version of the Pons Fabricius, the oldest bridge in Rome. Gilliam has reversed the image so the readable inscription is backwards.[62] Gilliam has included the smaller center arch as well as a larger arch. It looks as if he used the Piranesi etching as his original, coloring and adding brick façade for the new lettering above the archways.

The inscription is technically graffiti (graffito), or "scratchings" in the stone, and is common throughout the Roman Empire. Brian will later create his own version, with paint, as he tries to insult the Roman occupiers in clumsy Latin. Painted signs and posters were common in this period, often as advertisements for political candidates, upcoming games, and businesses and services. Versions of these came to London in 1977 as part of the *Pompeii AD79* exhibit at the Royal Academy of Arts.[63] More on graffiti later, when Brian's "Romans Go Home" artwork is being discussed.

monolithic rock abutment—This looks to be a mountain, and it's not original to either Rome or the Piranesi sketches; Gilliam has likely sourced it from a "natural wonders" book of some sort. It may be a scene from the Petra, Jordan area (perhaps the Rum Wadi), where monumental structures were carved into the native sandstone. During post-production of

Holy Grail, Doyle needed a mountainous forest backdrop as an establishing shot for Sir Robin's scene, and, with no budget remaining, improvised with a still from a picture book.[64]

Roman emperor statue—This statue of Augustus (63 BC–AD 14) can be found as part of the Vatican Museums collection. The image has been reversed; the original holds out his right hand. This is one of the handful of figures included by Gilliam actually dating to the time of Christ.

portion of arch monument—This is again a portion of the Constantine arch, the same attic portion that was knocked free in the previous shot. The arch itself dates to the fourth century. The late date of this monument is part of the reason it's a bit hotchpotch, Richard mentions, and why it might be particularly appropriate for Gilliam's type of attentions: "By this point in Roman history, the emperor could no longer find enough skilled sculptors, so he was forced to loot panels from various Flavian and Antonine monuments with which to ornament his arch, his features replacing those of Hadrian, Marcus Aurelius, and others, while some subsidiary figures were expanded."[65] Gilliam does the same thing, frankly. The last falling Brian figure actually looks up after he's finally landed, looking at the camera, and that face appears to be a tiny version of an actual human (photographed) face. Gilliam's *modus operandi* pieces animated sequences together from often disparate images that span time, though most of these, and we've seen, are at least culled from the ancient Mediterranean world of monumental statues and buildings. Gilliam has pulled apart, xerographed, and put back together again the Arch of Constantine[66]—manipulating it, stacking it on itself, essentially—ironically creating a finished product that is remarkably similar to the magpie original.

bridge interior framework—Drawn from Piranesi's "A View of Part of the Intended Bridge at Blackfriars London" (1764), which was based on an architectural drawing Piranesi requested of a friend.[67]

Shot 14 *(tracking shot left)*—

This shot begins immediately tracking left, and quickly, past several structures, all drawn from Piranesi's versions of the remains of the Diocletian baths in Rome. Portions of these etchings appear earlier in the animated sequence. Here, the traveling monument-and-lips-and pillar-and-statue-and-clinging-Brian goes through a window seen at about the middle of the original print. Gilliam's copied the top of the window and added it to the bottom.

colonnaded wall—This is a classic Gilliam conceit. He has taken a xerographed copy of a portion of the Roman aqueduct,[68] copied it over and over, colored it, inverted the top half of the image, and connected all the portions, in diminishing perspective, as if the wall is disappearing into the distance.

etched cloud pattern—Yet another cloud from yet another Doré illustration, this lonely cloud is copied from "Marco the Lombard," a print made up almost entirely of clouds. This particular cloud is at the furthest left, and toward the top of the print.[69]

Shot 15 *(Brian falling; tracking downward, then pull back, then zoom in)*—

another new clinging Brian figure—A jump cut reveals a new figure, fully robed and with his hands stretched above his head. This figure comes from the page 198 print in the Doré Bible illustration source book, and is titled "Entry of Jesus into Jerusalem."[70] Gilliam has here chosen a bystander who is clearly praising Christ as he rides into town; if it is Brian, then he's supportive of this dangerous man/king.

The show so far: The illustrated Doré images chosen by Gilliam to represent the growing Brian have included (1) the baby Jesus himself; (2) an infant sure to drown in the Great Flood; (3) another, older child also sure to drown; (4) an image of the young David, about to be murdered; (5) an apostate Jew killed at the Lord's altar; and (6) and (7) (see below) two of Job's family mourning Job's losses. All of these come from *The Doré Bible Illustrations*.

SINGER: "And have one off the wrist"—Meaning to masturbate. In *Flying Circus*, a reference to masturbation as a hobby was censored, one of a handful of such outright elisions. In Ep. 31, in "The All-England Summarize Proust Competition," competitor Harry Bagot (Chapman) lists his hobbies as "strangling animals, golf, and masturbating."[71] The first two hobbies remained in the final version of the episode. This bit of censorship was also one of the few demanded from the BBC leadership, specifically Duncan Wood, head of Light Entertainment.[72] Masturbation had also been hinted at as early as Ep. 2, there as one of the perversions of mice-men.[73]

Art Director—Roger Christian—Christian would work on *Alien* (1979) as an art director, and then as a second unit director on several *Star Wars* films, and would direct the cult flop *Battlefield Earth* in 2000.

new falling Brian figure—This new Brian clutches his head, and is a bit of a hybrid. There are two figures in one Doré print, "Job Hearing of His Ruin," that Gilliam seems to have combined for this version of Brian. Both figures are at the left of the print, one lying on the ground, hands on her head, and the other just to her left, kneeling, one hand on her head. Neither figure is facing the viewer. Gilliam seems to have used the upper torso and arms and hair from the prostrate character, and the robe and lower limb(s) from the kneeling character. Both figures appear to be female, originally. Gilliam has combined these into one figure, hands on head, whose right foot is trailing and upraised, as if falling.[74]

The combination is made certain when the figure hits the ground. At that moment, Brian's position goes from both hands on head to one hand on head and one hand thrust to the side, just like the kneeling figure from the original. When the feet come to rest, it's clear that the lower half of the figure is from the prostrate character in the original; the upper half from the kneeling character. Gilliam has simply used two similarly dressed and helpfully posed figures to create two versions of one character, Brian—one in motion, and one at rest.

In the *Flying Circus* episode "Full Frontal Nudity" (Ep. 8), Gilliam employed Victorian nudes in various seated and standing positions, many sequential, to create the illusion that the cutout character was actually changing poses.[75]

Associate Producer—Tim Hampton—Hampton had production managed the very large *Superman* shoot in 1978 (also finished at Shepperton), after having performed postproduction chores on the Pythons' *And Now for Something Completely Different* (1971).

massive foundation wall—This is a version of yet another Giovanni Piranesi print, likely from a later printed version of his *Le Antichità Romane*, first published in 1756. This image is drawn from the "Foundations of the Mausoleum of Hadrian" etching, completed c. 1755.

Looking closely, Gilliam has left the tiny human figures Piranesi included—to evidence the massive scale of the foundations—beneath Hampton's name. These figures are so small and blending they're nearly impossible to see. Gilliam has also added another layer of the foundation, perspectively smaller, on top of the original etching. This is another Piranesi rendering featuring a bit of ruin masonry projecting out of the frame.

gateway arch—At the bottom of this foundation wall Gilliam has inserted a gateway arch; the original etching depicts only massive blocks and a ledge at that point. It's on this ledge that several tiny figures can be glimpsed in the original print, dwarfed by the enormous structure. The arch itself is actually the center portion of a Roman fountain façade as depicted by Piranesi in "View of the Fountainhead of the Aqua Felice."[76] The ring has been added by Gilliam (and will be pulled momentarily), and only one lion from the original four is included. Many of these rings appear in Piranesi's *Carceri* drawings. These same kinds of rings will appear later as part of the set decoration for the Colosseum, complete with ropes and chains draped from and between them. Gilliam and his team likely used the Piranesi prints as inspiration for the monumental set decorations throughout the film.

statues and obelisks—The congeries of artifacts at both the bottom right and left of this frame are also found in the pages of Piranesi's Roman etchings. Referred to as the "Idea of the Ancient Via Appia and Ardeatina," this 1756 work is stuffed with funerary objects. The lantern-shaped statue at the far left of Gilliam's frame occupies the same space in the original, while the half-statue, obelisks, and mausoleums are on the far right, but reversed, facing into the frame. The legs and torso of the half-statue on the pedestal off to the right appear to be from an Antinous statue, smashed apart in mid-torso, with remains at its feet.[77] The smaller obelisk has been moved into the frame, as well, by Gilliam; the far right side of the original etching, featuring Ardeatina road, has been cropped. As this was the frontispiece of this second volume of Piranesi's work, the title was included on the plinth, which Gilliam has cropped out.

Roman chariot—The Romans tended to use chariots for racing, not warfare. The chariot doesn't appear to actually run over the prostrate Brian, *Ben-Hur*-like. Gladiatorial games might have used these in staged battles (often against slaves, captured prisoners, etc.)

SINGER: "And go out and get pissed"—Slang, meaning to get drunk. In the Pythons' "Bruce's Song," it was Socrates who was both "permanently pissed" and "a lovely little thinker but a bugger when he's pissed."[78] *Private Eye* would use the phrase "tired and emotional" instead of "drunk" to avoid writs for defamation.

hand—Just prior to being squashed by the falling wall/gate, the prone figure looks up at the camera. Like in many cartoons and silent comedies, the first disaster is averted (a "phew" moment), only to be immediately followed by the cruncher. In the Buster Keaton short *One Week* (1921), a house that Buster and wife have been towing to a new lot is stuck on railroad tracks, as a train bears down. The couple give up and leap to safety, only to have the train roar by on a parallel track. Relieved, they hug, just as a second train, coming from the other direction, smashes the house to splinters.

Shot 16 *(rising flower, stone balloons)*—

Design and Animations: Terry Gilliam—Gilliam purposely stepped away from director's responsibilities on this film to concentrate on acting and the overall design of the film. He has worked as a writer and director ever since.

Shot 17 *(rising flower, gargoyle)*—

gargoyle face—This appears to be part of an ancient fountain. The beard may indicate this is a faun or satyr character.

Shot 18 *(rising flower, giant)*—

The background is the same background from the beginning of the credits, a reworked version of the Flavian amphitheater corridor in Pozzuoli.

headless "thinker"—From Doré's *Divine Comedy* work, this headless, contemplative character appears virtually unchanged (save coloring) from the original Doré print. Others in the original scene are limbless, or just suffering violently.[79]

Executive Producers George Harrison & Denis O'Brien—This film wouldn't have been distributed without the assistance of these two men, and likely never recouped its significant production cost. Film distributor EMI (*King Kong* [1976] and *Close Encounters of the Third Kind* [1977]) had agreed to back *Brian*, but eventually backed out. Harrison and O'Brien created HandMade Films to raise money for and then distribute *Life of Brian*.[80] O'Brien had been Harrison's attorney since about 1973. Harrison will make a brief appearance in the film as Mr. Papadopoulis, which will also be spelled "Papadopoulos" when he is introduced later. (Likely not a running gag; just a mistake.)

stretched human—The stretching figure is borrowed from another Doré illustration, "The Suicides."[81] The character in the original is "naked and scratched," and attempting to flee through a forest. His body position is similar to Gilliam's finished animated character, just not so stretched. This human sign is being stretched by yet another Doré creation, the Giant Antaeus from his *Divine Comedy* series. Gilliam has reversed the image for this scene, removing (almost completely) the tiny human characters (Dante and Virgil) from his large hand. This image is also found in *DDC*, there on page 66.

Shot 19 *(jumbled block letters)*—

Produced by John Goldstone—Goldstone's name is posted to a dingy billboard, even though he's not a typical Hollywood producer. Goldstone produced the Python films,[82] post-Python films and TV efforts, cult hits like *The Rocky Horror Picture Show* (1975), and most recently the documentary *The Ghost of Peter Sellers* (2017).

In this scene we are back to where we started, with the jumbled block letters that once spelled out the names of the Pythons. Our trajectory is worth mentioning. We have "fallen" with Brian through the earth, until he finally lands and is squashed. Then the flower and stem raises Brian back up, out into the sunshine, and when the flower opens an angel (Brian?) emerges. This area of jumbled ruins now looks like the Via Appia area where the landscape, as depicted by Piranesi, teems with funerary monuments, and consonant with a "resurrected" Brian.

Shot 20 *(blooming lotus, winged angel)*—

Directed by Terry Jones—Jones would go on to direct *Meaning of Life* and *Erik the Viking*. Both the winged figure and Jones's name emerge from the lotus flower. Hindu and Buddhist spiritual characters are often depicted seated or standing on a lotus flower; interesting that Gilliam has placed his Christ-like character on this non-Christian symbol, perhaps purposely, given Brian's cry for self-reliance and tolerance (in the face of organized Western religion) in his sermon.

cloudscape—These are the same clouds as seen in the first shot of the credits, from Doré's "Dante, in a Dream, Carried Off by an Eagle." We have returned to the precise point where we started. The *Holy Grail* credits progressed along a linear path, one that culminated in the film's title, and with no repeated images. Here the title has come first, and the rest will be a Dantean (and Messiah-like) journey from above to a Hell below and back. As will be seen, the image of Dante being lifted by the eagle will be hinted at in this final bit of animation.

a winged angel—This "angel" appears to be a recolored version of the John the Baptist figure from Van Eyck's *Ghent Altarpiece*. The wings are *not* part of the original altarpiece figure, and move smoothly enough to have been rotoscoped, not simply drawn by hand. The fact that the winged character can rise and rise, only to be scorched by the sun, Icarus-like, and fall to earth again, sets the tone for the rest of the film.

Notes

1. Found in the Dover edition of *The Doré Illustrations for Dante's Divine Comedy*, page 90. Gilliam had used Dover editions on *Holy Grail*.

2. See the entries for these sections in Larsen, *BAFHG* for a closer look at all these composite settings; pages 265–69, 322–26, and 424–34.

3. *DDC*, 90.

4. In a promotional film the Pythons made for the Birdseye company in 1971, Gilliam also created similar block letters for the title sequence: *The Great Birdseye Peas Relaunch 1971*.

5. Larsen, *MPFC: UC*, 1.5, 42, 235, and 245.

6. This credit sequence is discussed in the "*bizarre things happen*" entry in *MPFC: UC*, 1.5.

7. Avery enjoyed context-smashing in his cartoon work, always ready to draw attention to the medium's formal elements; his cartoony worlds greatly influenced the Goons and the Pythons.

8. *MPFC: UC*, 2.39.

9. Plate 143, page 123 in Scott's *Piranesi* (1975). In that same book, plates 151, 162, 164, 206, 212, 217, and 316 display this same subtle conceit.

10. Another Doré print—"The Massacre of the Innocents"—features two babies in this precise pose, both being skewered by Herod's soldiers. These are much darker images (thicker etching lines); Gilliam chose the lighter version for the "Deluge" print. See *DBI*, 165.

11. See Palin's *Diaries 1969–1979* for mentions of these scenes and writing teams.

12. Perhaps since the veil moment does not appear in any significant way in any of the major filmic influences, and the temple itself is missing entirely from *Life of Brian*, the Pythons stayed away from such events in their version. Also, adding the earthquake to Brian's crucifixion might have upset the film's critics even further.

13. Recent geologic research has pinpointed Friday, 3 April 33 as a likely date for that earthquake and, therefore, as the day of Christ's death. See the *International Geology Review* (May 2012). For a contemporary influence, the July 1976 Tangshan, China, earthquake had killed at least 250,000; the disaster remained in headlines for months.

14. In *King of Kings* it's also darkness and wind/thunder. These were all films that the Pythons screened, in part, as they prepared for the writing process (Palin, *Diaries 1969–1979*, 352).

15. Josephus, *AJ*, 15.11.3 (Whiston, 334); also Smallwood, *JURR*, 283. Josephus notes that these foundations were planned for repair "in the days of Nero," but circumstances intervened. Citations from the works of Josephus will be taken from the 1960 Kregel edition of *The Complete Works of Flavius Josephus*, the William Whiston translation. The page number *and* chapter/paragraph numbers will be provided.

16. For more on this fascinating figure riding the crest of a historical wave, see the foreword to Whiston's *Josephus*, Williamson's edition, and the entry for Josephus in the *Jewish Encyclopedia*. Since Josephus is one of the very few period sources writing about first-century Judea, his work has been cited for centuries.

17. *AJ*, 15.11.3 (Whiston 334).

18. See Scott's *Piranesi*, pages 62–63, plates 72–74; pages 71–73, plates 85–87; and page 129, plate 150, respectively.

19. Page 31 in the 1976 Dover edition.

20. *BAFHG*, 266–67.

21. *MPFC: UC*, 2.3.

22. During the run of *Flying Circus*, the Pythons misspelled quite a few title cards and captions (*MPFC: UC*, 1.159). Elsewhere in the series, they complain about the cost of captioning, so reshooting for a misspelling just wasn't in the budget. It's a little more surprising in a feature film, and with an actor they'd worked with before. (Bayler's name is spelled properly in the *Time Bandits* and *Brazil* credits, for instance.)

23. Palin, *Diaries 1969–1979*, 424.

24. Oxford historian and TV presenter Taylor is mentioned in *Flying Circus*, as well (*BAFHG*, 5); also the index under "Taylor, A. J. P." in *MPFC: UC*.

25. Palin, *Diaries 1969–1979*, 423–24.

26. Palin, *Diaries 1969–1979*, 472 and 475. In two July 1977 issues of *Private Eye* there coincidentally appear a stroppy Roman-era feminist in the "Hom. Sap." cartoons. In both cartoons a man is facing this fierce-looking feminist. In the first she brandishes a Roman standard topped by a Romanized version of the "female" symbol, and below a small banner reading "S. P. Q. R.—Rome Women's Movement" (8 July 1977: 8). In the 22 July issue, the very same setup instead ends with the woman telling the man what "S. P. Q. R." stands for: "Sexist Pigs Quit Rome!" (8).

27. *DBI*, 103.

28. In *MPFC: UC*, see the entries beginning with "Episode. . ." in every chapter for the listing of all extras and walk-ons scheduled for that episode; also the index under "*MPFC* extras and walk-ons (as scheduled)."

29. In the pages of *Private Eye* the Shah of Iran was known as the "Shit of Persia."

30. Caryl, *Strange Rebels*, 49.

31. Caryl, *Strange Rebels*, 49–50.

32. There existed Roman apartment buildings in the time the film is set, some reaching even six and seven stories, legally, and it's certainly possible that laundry could have been strung on lines between buildings (over narrow alleyways). Occupants would have been upper-middle class and below, meaning they might not have qualified as slums, except over time.

33. Quoted in Judith Flanders's article "Slums" at the British Library site.

34. The Pythons have already tackled the tower block and its checkered place in British life (*MPFC: UC*, 1.264–77). The clotheslined Victorian alleyway will also later appear in the *Oliver!*-inspired song and dance number "Every Sperm is Sacred" in *Meaning of Life*.

35. Similar images—dark, narrow, looming alleyways bedraped with clotheslines and drying laundry—can be found in Plates 2–3, 5–13, 15, 27, 30–33, 44, and 48 in Annan's *The Photographs of Old Closes and Streets of Glasgow 1876/77*.

36. See *Gilliam on Gilliam*, 38–40; also, index entries in *MPFC: UC* under "dismember (and remembering)."

37. *MPFC: UC*, 1.240.

38. *BAFHG*, 89–90.

39. *BAFHG*, 184n59.

40. *MPFC: UC*, 1.305–6.

41. See *DBI*, pages 119, 124, and 131, for example.

42. This image is on the cover and page 58 of *DDC*.

43. Ficacci's *Piranesi: The Complete Etchings* (2000), 712; Scott, *Piranesi*, plate 316, page 262. This is one of the drawings that featured jutting masonry at the bottom edge.

44. *BAFHG*, 16; also dozens of additional references to Doyle in the *BAFHG* index.

45. Palin, *Diaries 1969–1979*, 514–15.

46. *DDC*, 31.

47. Ficacci, *Piranesi*, 748.

48. In *BAFHG*, see pages 265–69 and 322–26, as well as all of appendix A (495–529).

49. Page 259, at the far right of the photo.

50. See *MPFC: UC*, 2.84.

51. Hansen and Jensen, *The Little Red Schoolbook*; "Court Rejects Appeal on 'Red Schoolbook,'" *Times*, 8 December 1976: 5.

52. Many of these credits are culled from IMDb and the BFI databases.

53. "The Naked and the Dead," *Times*, 18 September 1970: 6.

54. *DBI*, 149.

55. Scott's *Piranesi*, page 132, plate 157.

56. See plates 213, 214, and 217. In 213 the man is nailing with a hammer, for example.

57. In the days of classical Hollywood, the studios sent "blocks" of film product to cinemas. The blocks could contain at least one feature film, a newsreel, and a cartoon.

58. *MPFC: UC*, 1.20. See also the many entries in *MPFC: UC* discussing the influence of animation on both the Goons and then the Pythons.

59. *DBI*, 214.

60. Ficacci, *Piranesi*, 128–53.

61. *BAFHG*, 13–14.

62. It reads: *L FABRICIVS C F CVR VIAR / FACIVNDVM COERAVIT / EIDEMQVE / PRO-BAVEIT*, or "Lucius Fabricius, son of Gaius, Superintendent of Streets, undertook to have this built / and himself approved it." See Lansford's *The Latin Inscriptions of* Rome, 454–55.

63. See the commemorative catalog *Pompeii AD79*, Bristol: Imperial Tobacco (November 1977): 34–35, 39, 41, and 65.

64. *BAFHG*, 307.

65. Richard, *WWAR*, 80.

66. Gilliam chose the arch because it was iconically Roman, though the Arch of Titus—with images of the parade through Rome following the fall of Jerusalem, the victors carrying spoils of the temple—would have been more historically pertinent. See *JURR*, 324.

67. Ficacci, *Piranesi*, 492–93.

68. This portion looks like that found near Segovia, Spain.

69. *DDC*, 99; this cloud is in the background and quite dark, though well outlined against the sky, in the original print.

70. *DBI*, 1974.

71. *ATW*, 2.31.106. Just a few years later, an occasional letter writer to *Private Eye* would sign himself "BAGOT."

72. *MPFC: UC*, 2.70, 73.

73. *MPFC: UC*, 1.47.

74. *DBI*, 136.

75. *MPFC: UC*, 1.129. See entries in the *MPFC: UC* index for "Barker, Ronnie."

76. Ficacci, *Piranesi*, 715.

77. The inscription on the statue pedestal is dedicated to Antinous; Piranesi also executed a drawing of the complete Antinous statue, posed much like the large Pilate statue seen later.

78. Found on the *Matching Tie and Handkerchief* album (1973), and performed at live shows.

79. This plate, titled "Geri Del Bello," can be found on page 59 of *DDC*.

80. See Wilmut's *From Fringe to Flying Circus* and Hewison's *Monty Python: The Case Against* for more on the film's production and release history.

81. *DDC*, 37.

82. Excepting *And Now for Something Completely Different*, which was produced by Patricia Casey, Victor Lownes (of *Playboy* fame), and David Gil.

SCENE THREE
THE SERMON ON THE MOUNT

EXT. MOUNT—DAY—This sermon is only found in the book of Matthew, while a "Sermon on the Plain" in Luke includes four of the Beatitudes.

These kinds of often large gatherings did happen outside the city. In about the year 36, a Samaritan religious leader called for all faithful Samaritans to come out from the city to Mt. Gerizim, where he would "lead them to the summit and display to them the sacred vessels from the Tabernacle that were believed to have been buried there by Moses when the Israelites first settled in Canaan."[1] Pontius Pilate, fearing an insurrection (especially after the fairly recent crucifixion of Jesus), sent troops out to prevent the ascent, which led to bloodshed, including the execution, by order of Pilate, of the sect's leaders. With the exception of the fatal violence, the Pythons have set up a similar gathering in this opening scene. The Samaritans would officially complain to the Legate of Syria, and Pilate was recalled to Rome to answer before Tiberius.[2]

BIG CLOSE-UP OF JESUS—This is a shot composed with a telephoto lens, zoomed in to "crush" the perspective. The actor is Kenneth Colley, who would ironically appear as an Imperial commander in *The Empire Strikes Back* the following year.

pulling back and back (this is a helicopter shot)—No, this is not a helicopter shot; helicopters are expensive, and would likely have been a challenge to arrange in Tunisia. This is instead structured like the opening shot(s) of *Jesus Christ Superstar* (1973), where a telephoto lens is also used. The shots of people heading for the sermon are modeled on a similar scene in *Ben-Hur*, where townspeople gather around Jesus. Most of the "Jesus" films screened as the troupe prepared for *Brian* feature a version of this scene.

. . . the CAMERA has revealed the full extent of the crowd—The Mount scene is staged very much like Doré's "The Sermon on the Mount" illustration from his Bible collection, images from which Gilliam used throughout the animated title sequence.[3]

CAPTION: JUDEA A.D. 33—This is Judea under Roman occupation. The Roman version of this date would have been A.U.C. 786, meaning 786 years after the founding ("*ab urbe condita*") of the city of Rome. The Pythons had started their previous film *Monty Python and the Holy Grail*, with another date, AD 932, though that date had been less fixed.[4]

This is also one of the challenging and argued about "facts" related to Jesus—when he was born, how long his ministry was, and when he was crucified. There are many scholars who opt for around 30, meaning Jesus would have been born a few years earlier than generally accepted.[5] Again, the Pythons are employing a more popular conception of events, so 33 works without argument.

CAPTION: SATURDAY AFTERNOON—There is no indication as to why the Pythons chose to set this scene on Saturday, the Jews' Sabbath day. The chances of observant Jews making the long trek outside the city walls, often with pack animals and servants, seem slight: the Sabbath wouldn't have ended until the evening. Various rabbinical traditions also forbid any traveling, and virtually any activity (including the "work" of animals) that might detract from the remembrance of God. Some with camels even look as if they are carrying their wares to be sold. Observant Jews could assemble at synagogues on the Sabbath, of course, for scheduled instruction, but traveling to a mount outside the city is well beyond this allowance.[6] It's possible, though, that this upstart man preaching on the Sabbath is an early indication of his dangerous nature. Jesus will heal on the Sabbath, much to the consternation of the Pharisees, who went away to counsel "how they might destroy him."[7] For the Pythons, this pleasant Sabbath day excursion descends into a scrum, which shouldn't be a surprise.

CAPTION: ABOUT TEA-TIME—This caption didn't appear in the "original" script as read through in 1977. Captions and titles and even animated bits would have only been firmly decided well after principal photography was complete. In the postproduction phase of *Holy Grail*, Palin juxtaposed the sober opening credit sequence with silly, faux-Swedish subtitles as a last-minute and very cheap way to finish the film.[8]

JESUS (Ken Colley): "How blest are the sorrowful, for they shall find consolation"—Firstly, these versions are more like those found in Matthew than in Luke (second person as opposed to third person). Second, the text seems to be remotely drawn from at least two versions of the extant Bible, the New English Translation Bible (1971), and the New Life Version (1969). The latter is one of the very few versions that use the term "sorrowful" instead of "mourn," but the phrase "How blest" is used in *none* of the myriad English translations across the years, and "blest" appears in just one instance in The Living Bible (1971). The King James Version is more recognizable: "Blessed are they that mourn: for they shall be comforted."[9]

Perhaps not accidentally, Margaret Thatcher's reign as the Queen's First Minister, which began on 4 May 1979, started in a similar fashion as this introduction of Jesus by the Pythons. Standing on the steps of No. 10 for the first time as prime minister, she gave her own sermon:

> I'll strive unceasingly to try to fulfil the trust and confidence that the British people have placed in me and the things in which I believe. And I would just like to remember some words of St. Francis of Assisi which I think are really just particularly apt at the moment. "Where there is discord, may we bring harmony. Where there is error, may we bring truth. Where there is doubt, may we bring faith. And where there is despair, may we bring hope."[10]

JESUS: "How blest are those of gentle spirit; they shall have the earth as their possession . . ."—This is a version of Matthew 5:5, which most often reads "Blessed are the meek: for they shall inherit the earth." "Gentle spirit" is a translation that also appears in very few instances in most translations, and none in relation to the Beatitudes. This is in fact what the people at the back mishear—hearing "Greek" for "meek"—even though the beatitude as uttered is clearly "gentle spirit." This is some kind of disconnect between what Colley the actor utters (and the soundtrack provides) and what those at the far back actually hear and respond to. It's as if Colley is using one translation and the Pythons another—and there's no hint of any discord between the two. Jesus is saying one thing and his people, at least toward the back, are hearing something else. Just a few scenes later it will be the Centurion who mishears Pilate, responding with answers that don't fit the questions or statements as we've heard them.

JESUS: "How blest are those who hunger and thirst to see right prevail. They shall be satisfied . . ."—The New English Translation comes closest here: "Blessed are those who hunger and thirst for righteousness, for they will be satisfied." Other English translations use "justice" for "righteousness," and "filled" for "satisfied."

. . . revealing the enormous size of the crowd . . .—In terms of a film shoot this is a large crowd, and there are relatively few of these shots. According to Palin these extras were making about three dinars per day, plus meals.[11] Most other depictions of the Sermon on the Mount—in films like *The Greatest Story Ever Told* and *King of Kings*—either zoom in as opposed to zooming out, focusing on Jesus, or use static, discrete shots. In *Ben-Hur*, the camera is behind Jesus, the crowd at his feet, and Ben-Hur himself is alone in the distance, slowly moving closer. *King of Kings* employs a low angle close-up of Jesus, over-the-shoulder shots, and very little lens movement. *Jesus Christ Superstar* employs the "moving" lens more than any other; it also offers modern dress, obvious sets and props, and language of the everyday to ground the telling in the 1970s. The most recent version, however, Zeffirelli's *Jesus of Nazareth*, employs nearly the same zoom-out that the Pythons use, revealing the "size of the crowd" as Jesus speaks. The zoom lens had found new life in more "artistic" films of the 1970s, when the crushed perspective of the zoomed-in shot and the artificial movement created by the lens (used to great effect in films like *Butch Cassidy and the Sundance Kid*, *THX-1138*, and *Jaws*, for example) helped define the cinematic period.

JESUS: *(very faintly)* **"How blest are those whose hearts are pure. They shall see God"**—This last is very hard to actually hear on the soundtrack, and even as those at the back start to mutter and scuffle, Jesus continues speaking (he can just be heard, off-camera). In Matthew 5:8 this is recorded as "Blessed are the pure in heart: for they shall see God."

large contingent of Roman Soldiers on extra weekend duty—(PSC) There are actually only seven or eight Roman soldier types visible in the forepart of the scene, and another three or four at the back, where all the action happens. In the finished film, the Roman soldiers often watch ambivalently as their charges argue and fight among themselves, including later at the stoning, where the wrong man is stoned. In the later printed version of the script, the description reads: "*Standing nearby, isolated but alert, is a large contingent of Roman soldiers drawn up in serried ranks, armed, impassive, foreign soldiers on extra-weekend duty. . . .*"[12] The "serried ranks" language appears in the final battle descriptions for *Holy Grail*, as well.[13]

In 1947, ironically, it was British troops acting this part in Haifa as unapproved ships crammed with Jewish refugees attempted landings in the Holy Land. Foreign Secretary Bevin's ill-advised attempt to "teach the Jews a lesson" led to three former death camp survivors being killed. Union Jacks painted over with swastikas greeted newsreel cameras in this propaganda disaster.[14]

These images of bolstered police and military presences at mass events would have been common by the late 1970s, in postcolonial hotspots and in London. There had been dozens of police officers assigned to the long-running Grunwick strike[15]—holding back picketers from assaulting busloads of "scabs," keeping the entrance to the factory clear, and protecting the many female Asian strikers in the otherwise burly, male crowd. As Mark Garnett mentions in *From Anger to Apathy*, all sorts of public gatherings, permitted and wildcat, drew a police presence in the mid-to-late-1970s as the Wilson and Callaghan administrations attempted to keep anti-government (or even just anti-malaise) sentiment from exploding into street violence.[16]

. . . the large and potentially anti-Roman crowd . . .—(PSC) There is nothing "potentially anti-Roman" about this crowd as presented. Like most filmic versions of the Sermon on the Mount, crowds of people gather quietly on a low hillside (though in Stevens's *The Greatest Story Ever Told*, Christ stands, arms perpetually raised, atop monolithic sandstones of the Canyonlands in southern Utah—quite striking). In George Stevens's version Herod Antipas

(José Ferrer) sends Roman soldiers to arrest Jesus, and the beginnings of the Sermon are heard over the image of soldiers leaving Herod's fortress; this may account for the Pythons' inclusion of vigilant soldiers. There are no visible Romans in this scene, though the camera is pulled back to such a respectful distance—likely to capture the majesty of the setting, too—it's difficult to be certain. In the Sermon scene in *Ben-Hur*, there are no soldiers visible, and the crowd is quiet, and seated; in *King of Kings*, no soldiers, but a more restive crowd (they ask for signs); and in *Jesus of Nazareth*, a very respectful crowd (many crowd shots of intent faces), and no visible Romans. In the unusual (and low-budget) *The Passover Plot*, the Beatitudes are delivered in a jumbled rush to a gathering in town.

In the end, only the non-Romans cause trouble with other non-Romans (Jews grappling with Jews), and Reg and the PFJ wander away complaining that it's Jesus who doesn't understand contemporary politics.

. . . MANDY, older now by thirty-three years, but still a ratbag—(PSC) Mandy doesn't seem to have changed much at all, excepting the color of her costume.

MANDY: "Speak up!"—In the final Python film *Meaning of Life*, as the Catholic father tells his enormous family of their destitution, and the fact that he has to sell them all for scientific experimentation, one child in the back yells "Speak up!" Father (Palin) helpfully repeats: "I can't keep you all here any longer!"

MANDY: "Well I can't hear a thing. Let's go to the stoning"—In a printed draft of the script, it's Brian who wants to go to the stoning, and Judith who wants to stay and listen; in that earlier version Brian's mother Mandy isn't in this scene, appearing just after, as part of the stoning crowd.

MRS. BIG NOSE (Gwen Taylor): "Don't pick your nose"—In the printed script, this character is known both as "Wife" and "Mrs. Big Nose." Taylor was in the running for the Judith role, which eventually went to Sue Jones-Davies.

Flying Circus was stocked with hectoring wives and angry husband types. In Ep. 5, Mr. A (Palin) tries to explain the family cat's problem to a visiting vet (Chapman) only to have his wife, Mrs. B (Jones), "shush" him at every turn; in Ep. 9, though, Mrs. Equator (Jones) is both rude and incontinent, while her husband (Cleese) is abusive and groping; in Ep. 13, the husband (Cleese) is constantly apologizing for (and thereby insulting) his dim, rambling wife (Idle). Prior to his Monty Python experience, Cleese was part of a similar husband and wife sketch act, in *I'm Sorry I'll Read That Again*, with Jo Kendall.[17]

There had also been a very visible couple the Pythons could draw from, who had been front-page news for years in the *Times*, on the cover of *Private Eye*, and in the gossip-page quagmire of the *Express* and *Mail*: Marcia Williams and Harold Wilson.[18] These two weren't married, but their relationship read (in *Private Eye* and in various biographies and autobiographies from those around No. 10) as corrosive, painful, and retributive as any convenient but doomed marriage. Wilson's senior policy adviser, Bernard Donoughue (disliked by the *Private Eye* staff and hated by Williams), writes of Wilson's and Williams's relationship as he saw it, later, from 1974, at the threshold of Wilson's last premiership. It's clear that even as late as 2005, when now-Lord Donoughue's diaries were being edited for publication, he felt the need to tread lightly when referring to the writ-happy[19] Lady Falkender, but the lingering enmity seeps through:

[Wilson] listened to and accepted her views more readily than those from any other source. He often indulged her wildest whims almost like a daughter (for example treating honours like chocolates given to her to keep her quiet and happy) and equally feared her like a fierce mother (as when he is seen hiding from her menacing phone calls). She, as I observed in the diary early in

1974, had the magical power both to switch on and switch off his lights. She was also very adept at mobilising his demons, stimulating his nightmares and evoking his alleged enemies. Theirs was a relationship of great intensity and complexity which no one coming late to the scene as I did could presume to fully analyse and understand. But its existence mattered greatly to everyone who worked in Number Ten[20] trying to serve Harold Wilson as Prime Minister.[21]

Williams knew Wilson's habits—she would have known if he was picking his nose—and wasn't afraid to use the threat of revealing whatever secrets she thought she had in managing her boss. Wilson's press secretary Joe Haines announced in his *The Politics of Power* that Wilson and his administration could not be fully understood without understanding his relationship with and dependence upon Marcia Williams—their stories were and would ever be interwoven. In the Sermon scene in *Brian*, it's Mrs. Big Nose's reaction to a "do you mind" that forces her husband to get involved, leading to a wild punch and then a dusty scrum. In the end, neither Mr. nor Mrs. Big Nose is being dragged from the scuffle; others around them have been drawn in, instead.

MR. CHEEKY (Idle)—(PSC) This is a character never named in the film, only in the printed script. "Cheeky" means fresh or even rude, and Mr. Cheeky's willingness to say what's on his mind fits those descriptors.

BIG NOSE: "Don't you swear at my wife"—"Bloody," as defined in the *OED*, "constituted the strongest expletive available. This is reflected in the regularity with which dashes, asterisks, etc., were formerly used to represent the word in print, and in the large number of euphemistic forms to which it has given rise [bee, bleeding, blerry, plurry, etc.]." The term is only used once in *Holy Grail*, when Arthur, clearly frustrated past the breaking point by the obstreperous Dennis, calls him a "Bloody peasant."[22] There it's also an anachronism, since the word as an intensifier doesn't appear until the sixteenth century. Here, it's out of place simply because it's an English invective heard in first-century Jerusalem. Controversial *Till Death Us Do Part* character Alf Garnett (Warren Mitchell) would use the term often as he decries, for example, the "bloody coons" ruining his beloved Britain.[23] Mary Whitehouse particularly disliked the show due to its use of the words "Jesus" and "bloody."[24]

In 1970, critic Maurice Wiggin wrote an article decrying television's language, "Poverty by the Mouthful."[25] Wiggin admits that he dislikes Mary Whitehouse and her attempts at censorship and that he himself can swear up a storm when it's called for, but "not in front of the children," he chides, "there's a time and place." Film and TV language and depictions of things sacred or private were decried often in the newspapers, and Wiggin is essentially echoing Mr. Big Nose in a not-in-front-of-my-wife way: "Everyone's free to speak as he pleases, in his privacy or in congenial company. And of course colourful obscenity can be amusing, for a short time. But we simply must preserve an area of public communication wherein we all speak the same language—preferably at its best."[26] Part of the reason the Pythons included coarse language and nudity in *Life of Brian* was clearly to tweak those who would let themselves be tweaked.

MR. CHEEKY: "Well he has got a big nose"—Clearly, this "isn't meant to be taken literally," at least as these characters appear here—both Idle and Chapman have more prominent noses than Palin. This is likely an easy, obvious moment of racial identification, with Mr. Big Nose, as a (Samaritan) Jew, described by a stereotypically larger nose (even though the actor, Palin, has no such nose, and is not fitted with a prosthesis for the scene). Such depictions would have been recognizable to English viewers, at least, given the broadside caricatures and jargon of infamous London-born Jewish fence Ikey Solomon, and the recent performances of the character Fagin in *Oliver Twist* adaptations.[27]

. . . another rather well-heeled Jew in a Toga turns around—This is New Zealand-born actor Terence Bayler. According to Palin, Bayler was one of the company that the Pythons quickly and universally agreed upon.[28] In the film as shot, he and his wife (Cleveland) are standing between Mr. Big Nose and Mr. Cheeky.

The class struggles as criticized by Dennis in *Holy Grail* are all but invisible in *Life of Brian*. The historical social division among Jews isn't a leg in this stool (the rich and the poor, the priestly class and the commoners, etc.); instead, the Romans occupy the evil, oppressive role for the film, with Jewish internecine problems only hinted at. Gregory may be "well-heeled," but he and his wife are never treated as posh types, though they act the part. Later, Gregory will attempt to have Brian heal his wife of a headache, and he is concerned that he be crucified in "a purely Jewish section" of Calvary.[29] They act like upper crust, but they aren't judged as such—no narrative retribution that's any more venal than anyone else, since myriad non-Roman types are hanging on crosses as the film ends. The more Marx-lite sentiments are reserved for Reg and the PFJ as they lay out their case for revolution, but the arguments describe the Romans as invaders and occupiers, not powerful *haute bourgeoisie*.

A similar argument was made by some Marxist scholars, interestingly, about Jesus. Not a Christian himself, Karl Kautsky tried to situate Jesus within the history of Jewish anti-Roman activities—akin to the role and work of the Zealots (who will be discussed later)—representing "Jesus as a rebel engaged in a first-century Marxian class-struggle."[30] He saw Jesus as a man with a socialist mission, and not the Son about his "Father's business."[31] In the 1960s–1970s some offered Jesus as "a kind of nationalist freedom-fighter," the Christ-like Korda image of Che Guevara, for example, drawing the two revolutionaries together, or even the opposite, positing "Judas [as] the man who wanted a liberation-struggle, and he betrayed Jesus because Jesus wouldn't join him."[32] The zeitgeist of the liberating, revolutionary 1960s clearly influenced many in their views of Jesus, moving him from lamb to lion; it's evident the Pythons are also affected by the world around them as they approach their first-century Jerusalem story and characters. Given this, the idea of a militant group determined to shrug off the shackles of the colonizer isn't narratively radical at all—it was happening in first-century Jerusalem, in the remnants of the twentieth-century British Empire, and across the Third World.

(draft) He constantly has trouble with his toga and has to keep pushing it back in place—Not part of the finished film, this is a sight gag borrowed from *Holy Grail*, though it even had life before that. In *Holy Grail*, Sir Bedevere (Jones) expends a great deal of energy holding open his faulty visor. This is in turn a mannerism borrowed from the Pellinore character found in T. H. White's *Once and Future King* (1958).[33] The irritations of everyday life, distractions, digressions, and something as simple as a bit of misbehaving clothing is comedic grist for the Pythons' mill. The tantalizing repetition of the sagging taffy or the squeaky door hinge in Jacques Tati's *M. Hulot's Holiday* (1953) can also be mentioned. But Gregory's specific tic—the slouching toga—is reminiscent of Mickey's too-long sleeve in *Mickey's Band Concert* (1935), as well as dozens of similar tiny gags from the likes of Chaplin, Keaton, the Marx Brothers, and Tati. The Pythons' (and The Goons') collective debt to physical comedy, cartoons, and the "cartoony" is explored elsewhere.[34] Palin writes about the *Three Wise Men* scene potentiality, in his *Diaries*, describing why something like a slipping sleeve could be funny: "In the classic Python mould of the humour of frustration; irritation at constantly being diverted by trivia."[35] Other diversions: Pilate's guards allow Brian to escape thanks to their narrative sidetracking, Harry the Haggler's gourd deal with Brian falls apart for lack of focus, and the wrong man gets stoned to death thanks to the word "Jehovah."

His voice is very cultured—Gregory speaks with a posh English accent, of course, not a posh Jewish or Greek or even Samaritan accent. G. B. Shaw's quip about one Englishman despising another Englishman the moment he opens his mouth is a bit far, but throughout *Flying Circus* and *Holy Grail* the Pythons have used language and especially accent to identify class and social position. In Ep. 16, one character points out the "poshness" of another character, via pronunciation of a single word:

> Mr. Chigger (Jones): Look, I came here to learn to fly an aeroplane.
>
> Mr. Anemone (Chapman): A what?
>
> Mr. Chigger: I came here to learn to fly an aeroplane.
>
> Mr. Anemone: (*sarcastically; affected*) Oh, "an aer-o-plane." Oh, I say, we are grand, aren't we? (*imitating a posh accent*) "Oh, oh, no more buttered scones for me, mater. I'm off to play the grand piano." "Pardon me while I fly my aer-o-plane." Now get on the table![36]

Mr. Anemone says "grahnd" and "piahno," and then slips back out of the accent so that the "a" in "table" sounds more like the "i" in "Bible," decidedly less posh. By the end of *Brian*, when Mrs. Gregory is on the cross, her posh accent turns "rather" into the very affected "raw-thur," and we understand why the Gregorys don't want to be crucified among the great unwashed.

A small boy holds a large parasol . . .—The boy is clearly meant to represent an African slave, perhaps of Nubian descent. Jeremias notes that the presence of both Jewish and Gentile slaves in Jerusalem was a given for centuries, and he spends a good deal of time describing the types of and laws regarding slavery among the children of Israel.[37] As it turns out, both types of slaves were defined and even protected by law.

If there is anything here worth noting beyond the presence of the slave owned by a wealthy Jew, it is the fact that there is *only* one.[38] A medieval king like Arthur would have been followed by an impressive retinue, and not just Patsy.[39] Koloski-Ostrow writes that the wealthy in the empire defined and displayed that wealth often by sheer numbers: "We do have a passage by Ammianus Marcellinus . . . in which he describes retinues of up to fifty servants accompanying imperial aristocrats to the baths at Rome."[40] The patrician Jew Gregory is being quite conservative, then, as he leans on just one slave to listen to the sermon. The budget for the film would have precluded such displays of (even cinematic) wealth, with the masses being used only occasionally as background extras. This boy will also be at Calvary, shading the crucified Gregory.

MAN FURTHER FORWARD (Charles McKeown): "I think it was 'Blessed are the Cheesemakers'"—Another misunderstanding, a miscommunication, the kind that can send narratives sideways in the Python world. In the post-Python film *Brazil*, written by Gilliam and Tom Stoppard, a single typo—"Buttle" for "Tuttle"—dooms an innocent man to torture and death, and propels Sam (Jonathan Pryce) on a mission to save the woman of his dreams. In Ep. 29 of *Flying Circus*, a Victorian explorer mentions that it's been "a great expedition," prompting an immediate cut to jaunty music and *an engraving of Crystal Palace*, where the 1851 Great *Exhibition* took place. The explorer has to say "Great expedition" again, more precisely, to refocus the story.[41]

This rehearsal is a slight rewording, as well, as this Christ figure here would have said "*How blest* are the peacemakers . . . ," and not "Blessed are the peacemakers," to be bibliographically precise.

WIFE OF GREGORY: "What's so special about the cheesemakers?"—Nothing, probably. This is only the Wife of Gregory's ill-stated *Sitz im Leben*—she's wondering how this blessing came to be attached to cheesemakers, or what it's "setting in life" can mean.[42] Jeremias describes the food trades active in first-century Jerusalem, and the making of cheese, by inference, can be assumed, if not in the city then nearby. In a paragraph describing the production of oil, bread, and processed meats in Jerusalem, he mentions that "an Athenian is said to have had cheese and eggs bought from a Jerusalem market," meaning cheese was at least available for purchase.[43] In *Life in Biblical Israel*, King and Stager identify milk products (primarily from goats) as part of the Israelites' staple diet, including milk, curdled milk, yoghurt, curds, and cheese.[44] And though there were dozens of occupations described as impure or unholy in Jewish everyday life, cheesemaking wasn't one of those professions.[45] Josephus mentions the Tyropoeon Valley, also known as Valley of the Cheesemongers (or Cheesemakers), which was likely named for the tradesmen who occupied it at some point. This valley had actually been an unofficial dump and landfill site for the city for decades.

The Pythons exhibited a fun fixation on cheese in *Flying Circus* Ep. 33, "The Cheese Shop" sketch, where Mr. Mousebender (Cleese) asked Mr. Wensleydale (Palin), the proprietor, about the availability of forty-three types of "cheesy comestibles," none of which were actually available for sale.[46]

GREGORY (Terence Bayler): "It's not meant to be taken literally. Obviously it refers to any manufacturers of dairy products"—In the July 1977 issue of *Private Eye*, in the article "Jesus Was 'Ordinary Bloke,'" the reverends Stupitt and Flannel[47] sound very much like Gregory: "In a new book entitled *A God for the Seventies*, a group of radical theologians . . . have put forward what they call 'a radical re-orientation of the Christ-myth to provide an ongoing belief-structure for Christians and non-Christians alike.'" Then the nail is driven: "The Rev. Stupitt and his colleagues argue that Christ, despite his claims to be God, did not mean to be taken literally."[48] Christ did teach in parables, often, where deeper meanings could be hidden from or lost on scribes and Pharisees, or those who had hardened hearts and didn't have "ears to hear."[49] In *Jesus of Nazareth*, when Jesus is dragged before Caiaphas, one of the men admits this pointedly: "Rabbi, we fail to understand the meanings of many of your sayings." Mrs. Gregory is also missing the point. The Beatitudes are sectional, a condition followed by a result. Mrs. Gregory is just remembering the condition, or at least a version of the condition, and one that skews the condition-result relationship badly. Blessing one group of tradesmen seems unfair, of course, since not everyone could or should aspire to cheesemaking; blessing a peacemaker likely makes the world a better place, and assures membership in God's household. In a moment, the blessed will be a single man (or even woman) of Greek extraction, at least as heard.

The satire in the *Private Eye* article seems to be pointed at recent fashionable writings from men like Bishop John Robinson in *Honest to God* (1963), who posited no God "up there," no mythological or supernatural being, since man has "come of age" and merits a different, less preternatural reality. Many would respond in print over the following years, and the arguments about God or no God would carry on through the bleak 1970s. Brian will later tell his "followers" that they don't need an organized belief system, that they don't need to follow anyone but themselves. The followers and Judith will intensely agree with him, and then promptly try and follow him.[50]

Later in the life of the Roman Empire the increasing employment of "replacement theology" and the use of allegory to interpret scripture became commonplace, according to Richard, as the Christian church became more Romanized:

Though the replacement theology of the late empire was largely the product of a new anti-Semitism that accompanied the increasing Romanization of a once Judaic religion, it was also partly the result of the destruction of the nation of Israel and the dispersion of the Jews by Vespasian and Hadrian. Fourth- and fifth-century Christians could not imagine that Israel would ever be restored as a nation; therefore, they naturally inclined to the view that the Bible's end-time prophecies must refer to "spiritual Israel," the Christian Church, God's new (and exclusive) chosen people. Since such an interpretation of Scripture was extraordinarily non-literal, it also serves as an illustration of another development of the late empire—the increasing tendency to interpret Scripture allegorically. In the hands of theologians like Augustine, the Millennium of Christ's rule became a figurative reference to the Church Age, another interpretation that involved an extraordinary departure from the literal biblical text.[51]

Once again, Gregory's reminder to not take (the misheard versions of) Christ's parables too "literally," thus a "cheesemaker" can and should be a producer of any dairy product. Interestingly though, when it's heard that a "Greek" is set to inherit the earth, Gregory becomes much more literal, wanting to know the lucky man's name, likely to secure an introduction.

MR. CHEEKY—(PSC) Many of these names aren't spoken during the film, so names like "Mandy," "Mr. Cheeky," and "Gregory" have been missed by viewers for years. Idle plays this type of fresh character often. In *Flying Circus* he is the quintessential cheeky character in the form of Norman in the "Wink, wink, nudge, nudge" sketch from Ep. 3, as well as the irritating interloper Arthur Name in Ep. 9.[52] In Ep. 35 he appears as Mr. Badger, a Scottish hijacker who will tell the flight crew where he hid a bomb for, first, a thousand pounds, then just a pound, and finally *offering* the crew a pound to retrieve it. He will also later promise to not interrupt sketches for a pound.[53]

MR. BIG NOSE: ". . . I'll take you to the fucking cleaners"—This is the kind of language removed from *Holy Grail* so that an AA rating could be achieved. As an intensifier, the word has only been part of the English lexicon since the later nineteenth century.[54] Earlier drafts and readings of the film featured many more uses and variations of the term. Also, the phrase "take you to the cleaners" is much younger than ancient Judea, and, as an American colloquialism, generally means to separate someone from his money, to fleece him, not assault him physically.[55]

MR. CHEEKY: ". . . not so bad yourself, Conkface . . ."—Kind of a double meaning here, since "conk" can mean the nose, but also "nosey," which fits the situation quite well. This may also be a racial joke, relying on the age-old stereotype of a Jew having a large nose. The Goons had poked fun at mate Max Geldray's larger (yes, Jewish) nose across the seasons of *The Goon Show*, sometimes even hinting at the *double entendre* of a large nose and a large male member, as Mandy will reference later, talking to Brian about sex. It's worth pointing out the perhaps obvious—Idle's nose isn't appreciably smaller than either Chapman or Palin's. In Palin's estimation, part of the reason Chapman was cast as Brian was that he was "Roman-looking, which helps," meaning he possessed an aquiline profile.[56]

ANOTHER PERSON FURTHER FORWARD (Gilliam): "I think it was 'Blessed are the Greek'"—Miscommunication here again, and this time taking a blessing meant for all mankind (who humble themselves) and reserving it instead for a Greek man whose name isn't known. Again, the condition has been misheard, and it's as if there is no result even considered. Gregory will want to know the man's name, but he's not asking why the Greek is fit to be "blest" in the first place. He's jumping from the condition, over the result, and to what likely he hopes could be a profitable introduction to this blessed man. Famous Greeks in the news in the 1970s included Stavros Niarchos, Archbishop Makarios, and Aristotle Onassis and family. Magnate Onassis is referenced in *Flying Circus* and many times in the pages of *Private Eye* (there as O'Nassis), known for his mega-yacht, his buying of islands, and for marrying Jackie Kennedy in 1968. Niarchos was an oft-married and often-in-the-news shipping multibillionaire.[57] The Church of Cyprus archbishop (and President of the Republic of

Cyprus) Makarios is mentioned in *Private Eye*, and even in the Python sketch "String," found on *The Contractual Obligation Album*.[58] The Greek with the highest visibility in Britain's tabloids during this period, however, would have Gregory asking about "her name." Arianna Stassinopoulus is now Arianna Huffington of liberal *Huffington Post* fame, but in the 1970s

> she was everywhere: on the radio, on television, in the opinion columns of the *Times*, addressing right-wing think tanks, literary lunches and Conservative Women's conferences. The name, the hair, the voice, the strident opinions—everything was instantly recognisable. . . . For a dozen heady years [c. 1966–1978], everything she wished for was in Britain. She had fame; she was controversial; she was admired by distinguished old men and escorted by ambitious young ones. There were books, lectures and after-dinner speeches; there were appearances on *Any Questions* and *Face the Music*. There was a [successful] libel action against *Private Eye*. There was even her own chat show.[59]

Of the three, a man like the wealthy Gregory would have identified with the (then) right-leaning Stassinopoulus and the multi-millionaires Onassis and Niarchos; less so the church-man Makarios who had been deposed by junta in 1974. All four of these Greeks could be regularly found in the news of the day in Britain.

MRS. BIG NOSE: "Oh it's the Meek . . . Blessed are the meek!"—Actually, unless this Christ is offering several versions of his own Beatitudes, or repeating himself, he's already well past "Blessed are the meek." Moments earlier, as the camera zooms out from the close-up, he said, "How blest are those of gentle spirit. They shall have the earth as their possession," a version chosen for a reason, according to Palin. The verbiage Ken Colley employs is "a modern translation of the Beatitudes . . . in preference to the St James version," Palin writes in his *Diaries*, "because it felt less like a set up for a joke, and more of an attempt to portray Jesus as honestly as possible."[60] This fidelity was seen earlier, in the (actual) manger scene, as well.

MR. CHEEKY: "Who hit yours then? Goliath's big brother?"—Some rabbinical literature does posit Goliath as a sibling, one of four sons to Orpah, the sister of Ruth. Additional giants are also mentioned in Samuel 21. Mr. Cheeky is mentioning Goliath's *big* brother purposely, likely meaning Mr. Big Nose's nose is so big it has to have been smashed by a giant among giants. In the end, this simply sounds like a schoolyard insult, like "Big Nose" and "Conkface," the kind of talk heard on playgrounds across the years.

WIFE OF GREGORY (Carol Cleveland): "Oh do pipe down . . ."—Another more recent term, this one from the nineteenth century. Novelist Evelyn Waugh would use the phrase as an indicator of the speaker's class. In *Brideshead Revisited*, for example, prisoners—"various tramps and pickpockets"—employed the shouted phrase to help them get some kip.[61] Perhaps this is a sort of "Move yer bloomin' arse" moment, where Mrs. Gregory reveals a more ill-refined upbringing? She does manage to say this coarser phrase in a posh accent, though.

. . . a group of three intense young men whose dress sets them apart from the rest—In the finished film Judith is a part of this group (she was standing with Brian in earlier versions.) This little cabal does seem to be intense, and their dress, though perhaps darker in color, seems quite similar to the others, excepting Brian. Brian's tunic is a bit more threadbare, looser, and woven more coarsely than the robes of the PFJ. These *jeunesse dorée* sport tightly woven and fashionably black robes, and they are clean-shaven, something that really sets them apart from the adult males around them.

These better-dressed individuals seem to be the disaffected, upper-middle-class youth who will talk about fighting the imperialists, the capitalists, the "system." None of them seem to be employed, nor are they at school, serving in religious capacities, etc. It may be that these young men are simply more Hellenized than others in their city. But these are also characters seen on the streets of larger British cities at the time when the film was being written. In the transition in Britain from glam rock to punk rock in the mid-1970s, it was often the "look" that youngsters embraced first as they tried to be different. One man who adopted the new fashions looked back in an interview for *Eyewitness 1970–1979*, fully appreciating the irony of his bold antiestablishment choices: "Oh, yeah, I mean we were individuals because we were wearing a uniform, no doubt about that, we really were. How seriously you were into punk rock was measured by how completely and strictly you adhered to wearing this uniform. And that's when I got my Mohican haircut."[62] We meet this black-clad[63] and fashionable confederacy as they attend Jesus's Sermon on the Mount, where it's clear they have ideological misgivings about Jesus and the Beatitudes; we'll see them again as they attend the gladiator fights in the amphitheater, where they don't want, initially, the "imperialist" food of the oppressors; and then again as they've gathered to discuss their assault on Pilate's palace, where we see their reasonably argued and nearly unanimous commitment to violence against the state.

Voice of the New Left Herbert Marcuse had talked about "outsiders" emerging in the 1960s and 1970s to reinvigorate socialist revolutions, according to Dobson and Payne:

> [Marcuse's] examination of the new industrial societies had led him to the belief that scientific and technological revolution had changed the structure of the working class and thereby altered a number of Marxist assumptions. In the new technologically-based society of the West a labour aristocracy had developed, and a new alliance had grown up between big business and the working class which was no longer revolutionary or intent on overthrowing the established order.
>
> This development created a situation in which only what he called the "outsiders" were now the true revolutionaries. *The outsiders were those forced from the system because they were unemployable by it; those persecuted for their colour; the exploited masses of the Third World, and the students and intellectuals disgusted by comfortable consumerism in the West.*[64]

The PFJ won't seem part of any system, they don't seem to be employed, they are persecuted because they are not Roman, and they are ironically comfortable thanks to what the Romans have done for them, but still petulant in that comfort.

And here is how they see themselves, these high-minded revolutionaries, in Bakunin and Nechaev's *Revolutionary Catechism*[65] terms, according to Demaris:

> The revolutionary is a dedicated man. . . . Everything in his life is subordinated towards a single exclusive attachment, a single thought, and a single passion—the revolution. . . . He has torn himself away from the bonds which tie him to the social order and to the cultivated world, with all its laws, moralities, and customs. . . . Night and day he must have but one thought, one aim— merciless destruction. . . . He must be ready to destroy himself and destroy with his own hands everyone who stands in his way.[66]

It will become evident that this is how Reg and the PFJ see themselves, but their commitment to paying the ultimate price will waver in the face of both Roman retribution and the comfortable, infrastructural benefits of the Roman occupation.

(draft) BIG NOSE lets fly an almighty punch and hits GREGORY in the face—In the earlier drafts it is Gregory who asks Mr. Big Nose to "pipe down," and Gregory who takes the punch to the face. A fight still breaks out at the back of the group, near Brian and Mandy, and Roman soldiers move in to break it up.

This punch is also one of those moments where, during the editing process, a handful of frames were removed to make the motion seem faster than the actual movement. This is a cartoony process used often by the Pythons—and in slapstick comedy films in general. For example, when Robin Hood's men are distributing treasure to "the poor" in Gilliam's *Time Bandits*, each recipient is also gifted with a vicious, sped-up sucker punch. Robin (Cleese) asks if the punches are "absolutely necessary," and the Merry Man replies that he's "afraid it is."

(draft) **JUDITH: "Roman bastards!!"[67] We don't want you here!"**—In these earlier drafts Judith is much more fired with revolutionary zeal than in the final version, with Brian trying to explain away the presence and influence of the Romans. At this stage of the screenplay process it is Brian who is keen to go to the stoning, not his mother, and Brian and Judith are already acquainted.

(draft) **JUDITH: "Imperialist pigs!"** . . . **"They're an army of <u>occupation</u>"**—In the earlier drafts of the script the Roman guards were more menacing and inflammatory, with Judith responding here to catcalls. These barbs have disappeared by the finished film, replaced by the Jews fighting each other, and the Romans intervening only to unpack the scrum.

"Imperialist pig" and "army of occupation" is the language of the leftish, postcolonial world, heard in relation to British troops in Northern Ireland; American forces in Japan, Germany, and especially Vietnam; Israeli interests in contested Palestine and Jerusalem; and even earlier in regard to the French in North Africa and the British in Levant. The British had employed self-styled British Armies of Occupation in parts of defeated Germany after both world wars, when the term was likely more reassuring to natives afraid of postwar reprisals from the nearby Soviet forces. By the period of postcolonialism, however, the phrase had been co-opted by student movements, rebel groups, and Communist governments like Mao's PRC.[68] Judith is using the phrase here as an epithet, an invective meant to urge others to action. (She is mostly ignored, and shushed by Brian, who in this draft doesn't want trouble.)

The use of this modern phraseology makes it clear that in addition to a first-century Judea setting and focus, the Pythons are addressing the contemporary world of colonial oppression, postcolonial power vacuums, and the budding terrorism brought on by Western hegemony across the Third World. The frictions between these foci actually push the film forward, past the potential shuntpoints of cul-de-sac arguments ("What have the Romans ever done for us?") and alien space rides, and toward a final song-and-dance number on the crosses.

This "pig" reference also might have been a particularly insulting insult, given the orthodox Jews' views on pig flesh. Why pigs? Various traditions identify pigs as defiled because they have "fully split hooves," they are filthy and disease-carrying, and, simply, forbidden by God's commandment. One ancient text even helpfully equates pigs and the hated Romans: "*It is a symbol of hypocrisy*: It pretends to be a kosher animal. The Midrash draws a comparison between the Roman empire and the pig. . . . Just as the pig sticks out its hooves when it is resting, as if to say 'I am kosher,' so did the Romans put on a show of justice to mask their avarice and corruption."[69] "Imperialist pig" is a more modern framing, but the insult works across time and cultures.

FRANCIS (Palin): "Well, Blessed is just about everyone with a vested interest in the status quo . . ."—Again, the hearers of the Word are hearing "Blessed"—and even saying "bless-ed" when they speak it—when Jesus has clearly been saying "blest," an odd disconnect between parts within a single scene, separated by some space but not time. This may be due to the fact that the actual portion of this scene where Jesus is talking was filmed well apart from the furor toward the back, according to Kim Johnson.[70] The "blessed" mentions would have been shot and recorded first, and then days later the "blest" sayings from Colley as Jesus.

This "status quo" charge was one of the main complaints against PM Wilson. Emerging as a leftish member of the Labour Party after the war, Wilson followed Aneurin Bevan but was never considered Left enough by those on the Left. It seems that early on Wilson realized how pragmatic the center space could be, understanding that "extreme" prime ministers were few, far between, and short-lived, and that holding the party together (Reg-like?) trumped all else. Once he became PM, Wilson tried to balance the fringes of the Party, but thanks to an up and down economy, a struggling pound, and stroppy unions, the great plans for change often failed to materialize, and discord was inevitable:

> The old Tory style of government by clique and clubmen gave way to government by faction and feud, a weakness in Labour politics throughout the party's history. Wilson had emerged by hopping from group to group, with no settled philosophical view or strong body of personal support in the party. Instead of a "Wilson party," represented in the Commons and country, he relied on a small gang of personal supporters—Marcia Williams most famously, but also the Number Ten insiders Peter Shore, Gerald Kaufman, George Wigg and, for a while in these early years, Tony Benn too. . . . Suspicious of the Whitehall establishment, with some justification, and cut off from both the right-wing group of former Gaitskellites, and the old Bevanites, Wilson felt forced to create his own gang . . . [turning] to an eclectic group on one-offs and oddballs, producing a peculiarly neurotic little court, riven by jealousy and misunderstanding.[71]

Some of these names will be mentioned again as we go, along, with others not named, including Bernard Donoughue[72] and Joe Haines. The PFJ are caught between the Jews and the Romans, and tinctured by both the first and the twentieth centuries; Wilson's "one-offs and oddballs" managed to run the country from the isolated center from 1964 to 1970, and then again for a last dash from 1974 through Wilson's sudden retirement in 1976.[73] As the film comes to an end, Francis could have complained that Reg's version of the PFJ was as guilty as any—the status quo had been maintained by purposeful inaction, the essential core of the PFJ were still in place, the Romans were still in place, and only the agitator Brian was set to suffer as a result of the momentary disequilibrium.

Francis's complaint is fundamentally accurate, though, in relation to what Jesus is suggesting. If Jesus is promising in the Beatitudes that those who are oppressed and downtrodden will eventually inherit riches and kingdoms, then keeping the Romans in power and the Jews in bondage does satisfy the status quo, keeping things the way they are and have been. "Real change" revolutionaries would have gone away from the Sermon a bit deflated, having hopes that this whispered-about messiah might have been the one to lead a military uprising against the Romans. Turning the other cheek meant more oppression, more subjugation, with rewards promised but delayed.

These beardless thinkers are clearly part of the New Left, an early version of PM Wilson's "tightly knit group of politically motivated men" who had never had the luxury of failing at the ballot box.[74] This minority of voices at the left of the Labour Party, in Wilson's view, combined their Marxist sentiments with political intrigue, meddling in the unions to agitate for dock and transportation strikes, hoping to benefit from every downturn of the pound and rise in prices. Wilson saw them lurking everywhere. The PFJ aren't so devious, of course, hewing closer to what groups like Britain's own Angry Brigade got up to, which wasn't all that much:

> Though in many ways the Angry Brigade were a non-event they represent the only direct confrontation between revolutionary protest, supposed to be one of the key ingredients of the sixties, and the evolving economy of pleasure which was the sixties' real story. Other left-wing groups,

mainly Trotskyists would argue with each other and march, protest and publish about employment and foreign affairs.[75]

For the PFJ, "revolutionary protest" is mollified by the admitted "pleasure" of subjugation by the Roman Empire. The long list of reasons to not hate the Romans will be enumerated later. "The English revolution," Marr would write of the Angry Brigade's failures, "was again postponed for lack of interest."[76] One journalist would neuter them completely, calling them "a quaint Pythonesque version of their more murderous continental counterparts."[77] Reg, Francis, and Stan aren't the Jews inspired by revolutionaries and teachers including "Judas, Zadok, and other Pharisees" of the first century; they're not demanding an end to Roman rule because it is an offense to God, rather, an offense to the individual liberty of the twentieth-century, postcolonial Man.[78]

In the space between the camera and the PFJ is the result of the disagreement. Gregory, his wife, Mr. and Mrs. Big Nose, and two of the others gathered (Gilliam and McKeown) are rolling around in the dirt, while Mr. Cheeky—who really started it all—is helpfully pointing into the melee so the Centurions can make proper arrests. This is also a kind of status quo, when the Jews fight among themselves and seem to forget their Roman oppressors. Historically it was often the more violent gladiatorial games that brought *crowd* members into confrontation, not quiet sermons outside the city walls. Nero had to cancel games for a decade when Pompeii fans couldn't keep from fighting with rival fans.[79] More recently, even after myriad concessions offered to both sides in the decades-long struggle in Northern Ireland, including the short-lived "power-sharing executive" in the form of the Sunningdale Agreement in 1973–1974, nothing seemed to alter the status quo—killings and reprisals went on.[80] Lecturer Vernon Bogdanor notes sardonically that almost twenty-five years (and many deaths) later the Good Friday Agreement of 1998 essentially aped Sunningdale, which Irish politician Seamus Mallon ruefully called "Sunningdale for slow learners."[81]

REG (Cleese): "Yeah, well what Jesus blatantly fails to appreciate . . ."—The pre-revolutionary nihilism amongst the intelligentsia in Russia exhibited itself in similarly contrarian ways. The PFJ dress and groom themselves differently, and denounce Jesus's radicalism as just the "status quo." In nineteenth-century Russia, "nihilism meant an inordinate credulity towards any numbers of 'isms'. . . [including] terrorism," with the young radical adopting "a contrived boorishness" and "conforming nonconformity"—the very picture of the PFJ.[82] The revolutionary verbiage is nearly identical to that heard in the more sober *Jesus of Nazareth*. After Jesus has been performing healing miracles his disciples are worried about appearances:

Disciple 1: He doesn't seem to realize the scandal it would cause. Peter, you tell him!

Peter: I've told him.

Disciple 2: Well tell him again. The whole place is talking about it!

Disciple 3: Meaning some Pharisees I suppose . . .

Disciple 2: Well they know the law!

Like the PFJ in *Brian*, these four are apart from their "leader" when they discuss him.

Reg and the PFJ clearly didn't see the messiah they wanted, one who was going to "appreciate" their situation and overthrow the Romans, freeing all Israel. There were likely quite a few Jews who listened at the Sermon on the Mount for a sign that this man was their avenging, sword-wielding shepherd, and who went away disappointed. In 1969 the PLO-supporting Al Fatah[83] posed similar questions about Jesus and his image to the modern world, asking Christians, essentially, what they really believed: "In an anonymous letter addressed to both Catholic and Protestant Churches in West Berlin at Christmas 1969,[84] the supporters of the Palestine Liberation Front, Al Fatah, challenged the pastors of these churches to speak out openly in favour of this Front, presenting Christ as an example 'who fought against the Roman occupation power.'"[85] As mentioned earlier, a number of scholars in the 1960s were rereading Jesus's life and finding revolutionary planks, supports that could justify twentieth-century anti-establishment thought and action. The PLO and Al Fatah will be discussed in more detail later, in the PFJ scenes.

REG: ". . . it is the Meek who are the problem"—Reg is speaking for many followers of Jesus who didn't want the Romans "blessed," but sent packing: "Many of Jesus's followers found it difficult to accept his message," Kotker writes. "What they wanted most was a political Messiah, a divinely sent king who would drive the Romans out of the country. The crowds who came to hear him, and even the Disciples who followed him closely, pleaded for a sign from Jesus indicating that he was sent by God to end Roman power and usher in the rule of God.[86] Many were tired of the "go along/get along" attitudes that leaders in the Jewish communities of Judea had adopted: as long as the Romans left the Jews' religious lives alone, some taxes, tributes, and occupation were tolerable. But the PFJ is different from other Zealot-type terrorists of the first-century. If they are Jews, then something is missing. Brandon describes the overall breakdown of the relationship between Jews and their masters, the Romans, and that a Jew didn't have to be a member of a terror group to feel "the natural resentment of any subject people towards the unjust government of their foreign masters." He went on, noting, for us, what is missing from the PFJ: "there must be added the profound devotion of the Jews to their peculiar religion which logically envisaged Israel as a theocracy."[87] The PFJ show no Jewishness, to be fair, nor are they Samaritans or Idumaeans. (Their "leaders" are all clean-shaven, if that's a noteworthy commonality.) Even if they are Jews, they don't seem to be waiting for a Messiah to free them; they're not arguing for a theocratic government; they don't participate in the temple cultus; and they don't mingle with other Jews or priests or almost anyone outside their clique.

This is part of the script more closely connected first to postwar Britain, and thence the world of 1970s political and terror movements, and further away from first-century Jerusalem. The wretched "meek" beatified by Christ but mistrusted by Reg could be found in the immediate postwar period, when millions of war refugees descended on Western and Central Europe, and then Britain. Former POW camps in England changed roles but not populations as prisoners became refugees. Though happy and privileged in Stinchcombe, novelist Evelyn Waugh[88] worried about the postwar changes, fearing he could smell "the reek of the Displaced Persons Camp," and, ultimately, that Britain had changed forever.[89] This same rabble will be waiting for Brian in his living room later—lepers, those possessed with devils, adulteresses, wailing babies, *bourgeoisie* with headaches, foreign promoters like Mr. Papadopoulos—all wanting his attention, most wanting to touch him or be touched by him.

That being said, Reg and the PFJ also don't seem to be following the *modus operandi* of emerging 1960s and 1970s radical groups like those in the Shah's Iran, for instance. There, the all-powerful Shah had "closed off every possible avenue for political expression," according to Caryl, pushing many radicals—of the intelligentsia and working class—right into the arms of a radicalizing Islam.[90] The PFJ aren't turning to their inchoate Jewishness or even to the new and radical tenets of Christianity—they seem to think that direct revolutionary action (at least as discussed) is the only way to achieve the "world supremacy" they're seeking.

In a 1978 interview with the New Left thinker Herbert Marcuse, interviewer Bryan Magee's last question seems to well describe the PFJ as presented in *Brian*. Magee is asking about the admitted failings of the New Left:

> For example, it's commonly said of the New Left movement that has developed to such a large degree out of your work that it is elitist, that you have these little groups of, for the most part, middle-class—some would say self-admiring—intellectuals divorced from the working class as you have yourself acknowledged earlier, regarding themselves as the instruments of revolution . . . and that the whole thing has become trendy and has become fashionable, and above all has become dissociated with the real working class that it was all supposed to originally be about.[91]

There is no indication that Reg and the PFJ have any real connection to the working class of Jerusalem—we never see them at jobs, in queues, at worship, and almost never mingling with the unwashed general public. Their cleanliness, smart dress, and well-fed appearance means they are actually middle-class, and can be "tarred with the epithet" of "dissolute middle-class revolutionaries"—the same attached to Britain's own Angry Brigade.[92] When they do find themselves surrounded by the rabble—in Brian's living room—they are curt and dismissive toward lepers and children, the sick and possessed. They are clearly intellectuals and have had some schooling; they have a command of revolutionary jargon and parliamentary procedure. Italian New Wave director Pier Pasolini would likely have called them "anthropologically middle-class," meaning they are incapable of bringing about real change because they are too interested in the things of the world.[93] They are in the end fashionable—when push comes to shove and they have an opportunity to act in a revolutionary way (by saving Brian from the cross), they demur, saving themselves and the movement. This New Left, *attentisme*-like, will wait for the day that oppression overthrows itself, perhaps.

JUDITH *(the girl BRIAN has been admiring)*: **"Yes . . . yes . . . I see . . ."**—In the film as shot, Judith is styled as an acolyte, a kind of outsider (perhaps not unlike Brian, in a following scene). She is clearly looking up to Reg here, and not just because of his height (a joke that would be different if they'd cast Jones or Palin in the role; see the "short one's" entry below). Perhaps Judith is the first and only female sibling in the movement, hence her sycophancy, but it also could be just standard acolytic behavior in small groups. Judith sees positives in Reg—he doesn't seem afraid or constrained and is (almost) endlessly self-confident—and she won't be proven wrong until later, when Reg stays behind from the raid, hides from the Romans, and finally he and the rest of the PFJ leave Brian on the cross to suffer for all of them.[94] But Judith, too, will ultimately understand the "wonderful" side of Brian's sacrifice as explained to her by her leader, Reg, and abandon Brian to his fate.

These kinds of sycophantic, worshipful relationships existed in the terror organizations of the day. Even in prison, Andreas Baader led via cult of personality in the Red Army Faction, "[infatuating] all those who ventured close to him with a Promethean mission of fire and immolation."[95] His lawyers regularly delivered mission instructions to his followers, and to a degree the revolutionary work of the RAF carried on even as its leaders languished in maximum security cells.[96] Charles Manson and Carlos the Jackal[97] held sway over followers and the public differently, but to similarly manipulative ends. The ultimate example might be the case of heiress Patty Hearst, who was abducted by the Symbionese Liberation Army and eventually came to ally herself with the group, and willingly participate in their criminal activities.[98]

(draft) **JUDITH: "The short one's Reg"**—Remembering that Cleese stood about six-foot-five, this might have been a joke, a purposeful mistake, a reference to someone else

scheduled to play Reg or, most likely, that this Reg was at least originally based on the "pint-sized" trade union firebrand Reg Birch.[99] A lifelong and ardent Communist (or better, Maoist), Birch had been expelled from the Communist Party in 1966 for being too radical, and had formed the Communist Party of Britain (Marxist-Leninist) in February 1968.[100] Like Reg, Birch would talk loudly and determinedly about holding to principles. In an April 1968 strike action, the "right-wing moderates" of the Amalgamated Union of Engineering and Foundry Workers had overridden the more militant left-wing and settled for "a token strike." Coverage of the negotiations saw the split in the AUEW:

> Mr. Reg Birch, a left-wing member of the executive council said: "Now we are either to be in unity or at the parting of the ways." Not to give the mandate to the executive to take action would make nonsense of any decision to call a one-day token stoppage. "Either you say we are in a battle or you use, as an excuse, this hypocritical display of militancy of a one-day stoppage because you do not know how to retreat", he said.[101]

Birch was often front-page news until his retirement in 1979, just as *Life of Brian* was being completed. He was particularly on point during the ongoing Ford strikes in the late 1960s and into the early 1970s, his name and union being mentioned in article after article, his thoughtful, carefully crafted declarations making good copy.

(draft) **JUDITH: "He may not be personally attractive, but he's the sort of man we need if we are to liberate ourselves"**—On the way to the stoning in an earlier draft, Judith is talking to Brian about the "short one," Reg, and perhaps even figures like Carlos (Ilich Ramirez Sanchez), who was chubby and "normal" in appearance; and Charles Manson, who was just over five feet and wiry. They are perhaps even referring to Jesus, whose physical appearance in recent biblical epics had been generally Waspish—tall and fair and beautiful, and likely inaccurate.[102] A number of contemporary reviewers took Zeffirelli's *Jesus of Nazareth* to task for its worshipful dullness, and for its love affair with star Robert Powell's face. Critic and playwright Dennis Potter wrote: "Indeed, a score of minor miracles may yet follow the screenings, though none, I fear, will be quite so astounding as the grace which apparently enabled Jean Rook of the *Daily Express* to hold her breath for three hours last Sunday and yet still survive to rhapsodise in her bilious tabloid about Powell's still, lake-blue, green eyes."[103] Potter posits what a "real" Jesus might have looked like, and how even eager youngsters (like Potter once was) learning songs about Jesus might receive him:

> We may have had scrubbed faces, polished shoes, and clean hankies, but most of us warbling that childhood hymn would have been only too prepared to hurl a stone or a jibe at the strange young Jew barely recognisable as the "real" Jesus. Of all the many faces of Christ, indeed, the one we would surely never acknowledge is that one, the wandering rabbi down from the sour hills with the Torah in his head and wild figs in his stomach.[104]

The BBC documentary *Who Was Jesus?* made its debut in April 1977 on BBC 2, less than two weeks after Zeffirelli's *Jesus of Nazareth* appeared for the first time on BBC 1. In the documentary and accompanying book,[105] authors Cupitt and Armstrong lay out the "facts" of Jesus as known or accepted in 1977. In the section on archaeology, they include a note in regard to Jesus's physical appearance, pointing out "early traditions" that posited a glorious and beautiful Jesus "in his risen or transfigured state," as well as "a frail and ugly" Jesus in his "human appearance."[106] Christian art took up the glorious version, but the "older writers" remembered "the frailty of Jesus' human appearance":

Clement of Alexandria . . . says his face was ugly. The pagan writer Celsus . . . asked "How can the Son of God have been such an ugly little man?"; and the Christian writer Origen . . . usually so quick to rebut slanders, on this occasion accepts the description and quotes Isaiah 52ff.[107] The great Latin Father, Tertullian . . . opposing heretics who regarded Jesus as some kind of angelic visitant, repeatedly emphasized Jesus' frail human form. He was like a "puerulus," a wretched little boy.

Where did the idea come from? The most ingenious answer was given by Robert Eisler,[108] who put together a description of Jesus from Byzantine citations of a now-lost version of Josephus. It is a string of adjectives: three cubits tall, crooked or stooping, long-faced, long-nosed, with connate or continuous eyebrows, with scanty hair, looking older than his years, dark-skinned.[109] Eisler argued that this is the language of a police description, that an official record of the trial of Jesus must have existed and that Josephus (and perhaps Tacitus too) would had access to it. . . . As Tertullian remarked, Jesus' physical appearance may have partly prompted the barrage of mockery and insults which the Gospels so surprisingly preserve.[110]

Cupitt wonders about the historical accuracy of these descriptions, but sees the descriptions as "the most religiously beautiful ever produced." The above quote is lengthy but important, given that within a span of a fortnight two separate BBC shows offer such remarkably different depictions of Jesus, and just when the Pythons are creating their own version. The Pythons' initial thoughts of casting of a "short" or unattractive actor for Reg (or Brian, even) might well have been a forward-thrusting move past most biblical epic depictions of Jesus. As it played out, Cleese took the role of Reg and anything beyond humor evaporated.

(draft) **BRIAN: "I wish you'd liberate yourself"**—Brian is talking about sex—and with Judith, clearly—and not about the nascent women's liberation movement that had been gaining momentum in many countries, including Britain. Women's Liberation Conferences convened starting in 1970, and the feminist magazine *Spare Rib* premiered in 1972.[111] Germaine Greer's 1970 book *The Female Eunuch* would have disappointed Brian—her version of liberation is more than sexual: "Now as before, women must refuse to be meek and guileful, for truth cannot be served by dissimulation," she writes. "Women who fancy that they manipulate the world by pussy power and gentle cajolery are fools. It is slavery to have to adopt such tactics."[112] Brian will have to impress if Judith is to "liberate" herself in the way he means; her goals seem well beyond a physical relationship. Greer just might be the "stroppy feminist" the Pythons were thinking of when they created Judith's role. Judith may see a relationship at this point in her political life as another form of enslavement, no different from the hated Roman occupancy, but one that offers (as we'll see) a modicum of security, as well: "Abandonment of slavery is also the banishment of the chimera of security. The world will not change overnight, and liberation will not happen unless individual women agree to be outcasts, eccentrics, perverts, and whatever the powers-that-be choose to call them."[113] Judith will be a bit of an outcast from the men of the PFJ; she will agree to a relationship with Brian, but she will ultimately abandon the relationship for, ironically, the security of PFJ membership *and* the continuing Roman occupation.

In 1978 Herbert Marcuse would say that "far more attention needs to be paid to the women's liberation movement," and that he saw in that contemporary "movement . . . a very strong, radical potential."[114] Here Judith wants to change society; Brian is amenable to that, but post-coitally, if he has his druthers. Brian's forwardness (especially about sex) will disappear from the final drafts of the script, as will most of Judith's protestations about the "bloody Romans."

(draft) **JUDITH: "It's positively Chaldean"**—Meant to indicate ancient, backwards, or even "stone age," but perhaps also violent and repressive, the Chaldean empire was active six

and more centuries earlier than the time of Christ. The Old Testament prophet Habakkuk, whose name will be mentioned later in relation to the failed raid on Pilate's palace, perhaps set the example for Judith in the prophet's description of these marauders. Habakkuk cries to the Lord about the "terrible and dreadful" Chaldeans; he knows they are coming, and he knows that his people haven't behaved in such a way as to merit God's protection. *Spectator* religion writer Martin Sullivan discusses Habakkuk's "dilemma" in a 1974 Easter article: "He admits that the social evils of Judah deserve Divine chastisement. What is God up to, using as His instrument a nation which by its rapacity and its arrogant impiety was an infinitely worse offender? How could these Chaldeans, conquerors of Babylon, marching over the face of the earth with an unbridled savagery, be agents of God's purposes?"[115] What's also interesting here is that the early version of Judith was one who wanted to participate in men's activities even if those activities were painful and punitive. She's arguing for the right to stone someone to death, the stone-thrower's gender notwithstanding.

As the film concludes it seems as if the PFJ have also come to acknowledge the Roman's significant part in bringing God's (political) will to fruition. They will allow Rome to crucify Brian, perhaps seeing the act as a necessary step toward their eventual freedom.

Notes

1. Smallwood, *JURR*, 170. The discussion of prophets in and around Jerusalem will be broached again in the "Street Preachers and Haggling" scene.

2. *JURR*, 170. Tiberius would die just before Pilate reached Rome, but Pilate's governorship of Judea was finished. He was replaced by a temporary governor in 37.

3. See page 175 of *DBI*.

4. The Pythons had discussed and even tried other time settings, including 787, 1167, and 1282 for the events of *Holy Grail*. See Larsen, *BAFHG*, 28–32.

5. See, for example, *JURR*, 167–68, and especially note 82 on page 168; also, see the most contemporary summary of popular Jesus scholarship in Cupitt and Armstrong's *Who Was Jesus?* published in 1977.

6. *JURR*, 133. Also see the index entries in *JURR* for descriptions of Sabbath in first-century Judea.

7. Mark 3:1–6.

8. *BAFHG*, 14.

9. Matthew 5:4.

10. Margaret Thatcher Foundation, http://www.margaretthatcher.org/document/104078. It has been pointed out that the words are only *attributed* to St. Francis, and are actually of the Victorian era—this may fit Thatcher even better (Marr, *HMB*, 385).

11. Palin, *Diaries 1969–1979*, 492–93.

12. From *Monty Python's The Life of Brian (of Nazareth)*, 8.

13. *BAFHG*, 485.

14. Burleigh, *BRT*, 106.

15. The loud and long strike at Grunwick will be discussed in more detail later, in relation to women at the stoning and the missing "Popular Front."

16. Garnett, *From Anger to Apathy*, 78–83; also Sandbrook's *Seasons in the Sun*, 599–618.

17. Larsen, *MPFC: UC*, 1.205.

18. Wilson was prime minister 1964–1970, and 1974–1976, and leader of the Opposition in between; Williams (later Lady Falkender) was part of Wilson's "kitchen cabinet" as his private and then political secretary. Williams had been with Wilson since 1956. For his part, Donoughue referred to the *Private Eye* reporters as "lice" (*DSD*, 1.512).

19. As recently as 2007 Lady Falkender was awarded £75,000 in damages from the BBC for libelous depictions in the 2006 drama *The Lavender List*. As part of the settlement the BBC agreed to never air the show again.

20. The first (and much feared, in No. 10) version of this relationship and these events at the top of Britain's government emerged in 1977, when Wilson's former press secretary, Joe Haines, published *The Politics of Power*. Haines dedicated thirty pages to the relationship between Wilson and Williams, and to the temblors that their collusions and collisions propagated.

21. Donoughue, *DSD*, 1.14.

22. *BAFHG*, 149–51.

23. *BAFHG*, 279–80. *Till Death Us Do Part* aired 1965–1975 on the BBC.

24. "'Need for Good Sense on TV," *Times*, 23 June 1965: 8. By 1970, Mrs. Whitehouse had achieved almost mythic status, according to David Wade: "Certain public figures acquire reputations so powerful that it becomes almost impossible to hear what they actually say. One [is] Mary Whitehouse, heard last week in *What Happened to Authority?* (4). We all know Mrs. Whitehouse, scourge of the B.B.C., defender of the national morality, the St. Joan of clean living and thinking: Angel or demon according to your point of view" (*Times*, 19 September 1970: 18).

25. Wiggin has been mentioned in *Flying Circus* Ep. 38 as being a "looney." *Private Eye* also lampooned him more than once. See *MPFC: UC*, 2.144–45.

26. *Sunday Times*, 29 March 1970: 53.

27. Solomon was a popular rogue, escaping from or accidentally being released from prison more than once, and giving the authorities a run during his long criminal career; for Fagin see David Lean's 1948 film, and the West End musical (1960) and film *Oliver!* (1968).

28. Along with Neil Innes, Roger McGough, and Ken Colley (Palin, *Diaries: 1969–1979*, 423–24).

29. He's protesting the presence of a Samaritan, who is also Jewish, ironically.

30. Brandon, *Jesus and the Zealots*, 23n1.

31. Luke 2:49.

32. Cupitt and Armstrong, *Who Was Jesus?* 9. See Pathrapankl's "Jesus: Freedom-Fighter or Prince of Peace?," as well as the 21 June 1971 *Time* magazine, including "The New Rebel Cry: Jesus Is Coming!" There was also an entire series of articles on Jesus appearing in *Der Spiegel* in 1966. In the (1965 book and) 1976 film *The Passover Plot*, Jesus allied himself with active Zealots to ensure his martyr status. Alberto Korda's famous picture of Che, taken in 1960, adorned the flats of students from Berlin to Tokyo (*BRT*, 223–24).

33. White, *The Once and Future King*, 16, quoted in *BAFHG*, 192–93.

34. From *BAFHG*: "The surrealistic and context-smashing world of these cartoons was clearly influential for both the Goons and the Pythons. See *MPFC: UC*, 1.19–20, as well as the index in those volumes under 'cartoony' for more" (321n29)." Oversized props, exaggerated sounds, and unreal violence can be found throughout *Flying Circus* and *Holy Grail*.

35. Palin, *Diaries 1969–1979*, 348.

36. *ATW*, 1.16.206–8.

37. Jeremias, *JTJ*, 312–51, passim.

38. The "weedy Samaritan" seen later in the colosseum might be a slave, but he also might be a captured combatant whose only role is to die in the arena. (A Samaritan so captured might have been shipped off to Rome for more elaborate games demonstrating the strength and scope of the Empire.) The use of Christians as games fodder is a later development.

39. *BAFHG*, 32–33. The film's meager budget played a large part in this economy, as well.

40. Koloski-Ostrow, *The Archaeology of Sanitation in Roman Italy*, 31.

41. *ATW*, 2.29.84; *MPFC: UC*, 2.42.

42. Guelich, "The Matthean Beatitudes," 418.

43. *JTJ*, 8.

44. King and Stager, *LBI*, 102–3.

45. The herdsman, though, *was* on the list of despised trades, as he was considered to be "dishonest and thieving" (*JTJ*, 304). It's not clear how cheesemakers could get their hands on milk to make cheese, except that law and practice often diverged. Shepherds were also on these lists, proving that such trades could be prone to prejudice in one place or time, and celebrated in another (305–7).

46. *ATW*, 2.33.142–45; *MPFC: UC*, 2.91–100.

47. Generally meaning soft-headed or nonsensical. "Stupitt and Flannel" is a play on the contemporary Jesus scholars Cupitt and Armstrong mentioned earlier.

48. 8 July 1977: 14.

49. Mark 4:9.

50. This moment is an echo of the two guards in Swamp Castle in *Holy Grail*. They listen carefully to orders from their king: (1) guard the prince, and (2) keep the prince from leaving the tower. They agree, and when the king turns to leave, they immediately follow him. This movement to a more approachable God is discussed in *MPFC: UC*, 1.28, 33.

51. Richard, *WWAR*, 273.

52. *ATW*, 1.3.40–41 and 1.9.118–19, respectively.

53. *ATW*, 2.35.165–79.

54. The *Oxford English Dictionary* (*OED*) is consulted for definitions and etymologies.

55. See *MPFC: UC*, 1.33, 48, 74, 99, 103, and 106; 2.44 and 46. These terms crept into British and English culture thanks to the flood of Hollywood films and television, as well as the presence of American troops and personnel on English soil during and since World War II. Fittingly but unevenly, the BBC tried to suppress these linguistic infiltrations into domestic programming as early as 1948 (1.50, 59, 89, and 276).

56. Palin, *Diaries 1969–1979*, 395–96.

57. Lifelong competitors in the oil tanker business (and sharing at least one wife), Onassis and Niarchos were often mentioned in the same newspaper columns and profiles. See "The Two Millionaires Relish Their Rivalry and Enjoy Their Fortunes," *Times*, 3 June 1972: II.

58. In the 1970s, *Private Eye*'s offices were located on Greek Street, as well.

59. Brian Cathcart, "Rear Window," *Independent*, 15 October 1994.

60. Palin, *Diaries 1969–1979*, 505.

61. See the *OED* entries under, first, "pipe," then "to pipe down" beneath.

62. "The Emergence of Punk 1," in *Eyewitness 1970–1979: A History of the Twentieth Century in Sound* (London: BBC, 2005), CD, a.t.

63. They appear to be wearing linen robes, likely meaning they are more expensive as the weaving is finer.

64. Dobson and Payne, *The Carlos Complex*, 222; italics added.

65. Available at the marxists.org website. Mikhail Bakunin was a Russian revolutionary and anarchist; Sergei Nechaev is also credited with working on this tract. See *BRT*, 37–38.

66. Demaris, *Brothers in Blood*, 382; see also *BRT*, chapter 2.

67. "Bastards" will be discussed later in relation to Brian's status as one of uncertain parentage.

68. *MPFC: UC*, 2.23.

69. See Mendy Kaminker, "Pigs and Judaism," at http://www.chabad.org/library/article_cdo/aid/2376474/jewish/Pigs-Judaism.htm.

70. Johnson, *Monty Python's Tunisian Holiday*, 20–21.

71. Marr, *HMB*, 307–8.

72. Donoughue was Callaghan's adviser and head of the government's Policy Unit, and had worked previously at No. 10 under Wilson.

73. These events and figures are covered extensively in myriad books, including those from Donoughue, Marr, and Sandbrook, and in the pages of daily newspapers and *Private Eye*.

74. *HMB*, 297.

75. *HMB*, 333–34.

76. *HMB*, 333. The Angry Brigade will be discussed in more detail later, in the "PFJ Plan their Raid" scene.

77. See Martin Bright, "Look Back in Anger," *Observer* 2 February 2002.

78. Horsley, "The Sicarii," 443.

79. *WWAR*, 69; also Grant, *Gladiators*, 79.

80. Demaris, *Brothers in Blood*, 298.

81. "Collapse of the Postwar Settlement, 1964–1979," a.t.

82. *BRT*, 33.

83. Also "al-Fatah," "Al-Fatah," and later just Fatah, depending on which newspaper or communique is mentioning the group.

84. For timeline perspective, the Pythons had just broadcast Ep. 10 of *Flying Circus* on 21 December, and recorded Ep. 12 on that same day.

85. Pathrapankal, "Jesus: Freedom-Fighter or Prince of Peace?," 79.

86. Kotker, *HLTJ*, 62.

87. Brandon, *Jesus and the Zealots*, 107.

88. Waugh and his writings on Englishness are discussed in *MPFC: UC*, in notes to Eps. 2, 10, and 31. His oldest son, Auberon, wrote for *Private Eye* and *Spectator* for many years.

89. *HMB*, 47. The nearest large camps were more than fifty miles away from Waugh's village, so he was speaking more poetically. Homeless British families began squatting on deserted military bases and in empty government buildings across the country as early as summer 1946, changing ancient regional populations overnight (*HMB*, 71). By fall, it was estimated that there were more than forty-five thousand of these "meek" squatting on government land, and many more followed, even into Kensington, through the winter (72–73).

90. Caryl, *Strange Rebels*, 46.

91. Marcuse, "Interview with Herbert Marcuse," a.t.

92. Cleese's Mr. Praline character utters the first phrase in *Flying Circus* Ep. 23 (*MPFC: UC* 1.349–59); the second is from Martin Bright's article on the Angry Brigade (*Observer* on 2 February 2002). Members of the Angry Brigade had, for the most part, come from middle-class homes and were at one time enrolled in university programs.

93. Discussed in Ricciardi's *After La Dolce Vita*, 55–56. For Pasolini, "consumerist 'ideologies' and modernist 'tolerance'" have replaced revolutionary fervor (55). The truth of this becomes evident at the end of the film; the PFJ want to stay alive and keep fighting the fashionable fight.

94. Not unlike the Irish situation, when, in 1919, Republicans in vain sought American influence from President Woodrow Wilson, "patron of the rights of small nations": "He refused, as a Chicago priest said, 'to take poor Ireland down from the Cross on which she has been hanging for seven long centuries'" (Brendon, *DFBE*, 312).

95. Lasky, "Ulrike Meinhof and the Baader-Meinhof Gang," 10.

96. Lasky, "Ulrike Meinhof and the Baader-Meinhof Gang," 10–11.

97. Carlos was nicknamed "The Jackal" by a journalist *after* the release of both the novel and film *The Day of the Jackal*. The 1971 novel was written by Frederick Forsyth—mentioned later in relation to its influence on coup actions. Manson had been incarcerated since late 1969.

98. Carlos, Hearst, and Baader will be discussed in much more detail later.

99. "Pint-sized" comes from Terry Pattinson's obituary (*Independent*, 16 June 1994).

100. Birch's version of Communism favored more rigorous Chinese and Albanian practices. See "Maoist Party Is Planned," *Times*, 3 February 1968: 2. A series of interesting articles looking at the various arms of the New Left—including Birch's Maoism—began appearing in the *Times* in 1971 ("The Revolutionaries," *Times*, 15 February 1971: 12). Birch would lead a small delegation to Communist China in January 1971 ("The Times Diary," *Times*, 14 January 1971: 14).

101. "Moderates Win as Engineers Settle for Token Strike," *Times*, 30 April 1968: 1.

102. The 1964 Pasolini film, *The Gospel According to St. Matthew*, offered a darker, swarthy Jesus (played by a Spanish-Italian student). Pasolini was well-known for casting non-professionals who could bring an honesty to the role.

103. Dennis Potter, "The Celluloid Messiahs," *Sunday Times*, 10 April 1977: 33.

104. Potter, "Celluloid Messiahs," 33.

105. The BBC often produced books to accompany special productions (*MPFC: UC*, 1.361; 2.22).

106. Cupitt and Armstrong, *Who Was Jesus?* 27.

107. Isaiah 52:14: "As many were astonied at thee; his visage was so marred more than any man, and his form more than the sons of men."

108. Robert Eisler was an Austrian historian (who was also Jewish). His controversial rereading of Josephus, *The Messiah Jesus and John the Baptist* was published in English in 1931. Chapter 15 discusses Eisler's reading of Josephus's remarks on the physical appearance of Jesus.

109. This is much like Pasolini's choice for his Jesus, including the unibrow.

110. Cupitt and Armstrong, *Who Was Jesus?* 27–28.

111. Cleese had appeared on the cover of *Spare Rib* on 6 December 1972.

112. Greer, *The Female Eunuch*, 328.

113. Greer, *The Female Eunuch*, 328.

114. Marcuse, "Interview with Herbert Marcuse."

115. "One Who Embraces," *Spectator*, 6 April 1974: 10. The Pythons have mentioned the Chaldeans, in Ep. 43, in relation to authentic "police" helmets or headwear (*MPFC: UC* 2.188).

SCENE FOUR
THE STONING

Cut to MANDY and BRIAN walking along towards the city...—Ahead of Mandy can be seen the city of Jerusalem set on a faraway hill. This is a forced perspective technique as old as film itself and where, if this were *Holy Grail*, Patsy would have chirped: "It's only a model."[1] The Pythons are obviously not as interested in drawing attention to this film's artifice as in their previous film. Since there are no full-size trees or other buildings to give an actual perspective to this hill shot, building a scale model and shooting it from a low angle would have been rather simple. Tiny trees were added nearby to complete the illusion of a larger city set on a hill further away than it appears. A matte shot *could* have been employed, as will be seen at the beginning of the Colosseum scene and after Brian's graffiti endeavor, and had been used to create an entire castle where ruins stood in Polanski's *Macbeth*.[2] Cost-wise, it may have been cheaper to build the model on location than create a matte painting during the postproduction process.

MANDY is fiddling away putting on a very obvious false beard—(PSC) Later we'll see that there is a designated hook in their home where she can hang her beard as she comes in, indicating, in the world of the film, that beards for Jewish women were an everyday item. In Ep. 43 of *Flying Circus*, there is a special hanging place on a bedroom wall for a rather nasty-looking, gold-plated knobkerrie, used to bang on the wall to silence the neighbors.[3]

The wife of the pharaoh Thutmose II, Hatshepsut, may have donned a beard after the death of her husband, and ruled Egypt as co-regent, king, and then pharaoh for a total of more than twenty years (according to Josephus). The sculptured images of Hatshepsut depict her as wearing a beard, as pharaohs did for ceremonial occasions, even when she is attired in identifiably female clothing. (She may have shaved her head, as well, which was also the custom of the elite.) It's also clear Hatshepsut was *not* trying to hide behind the beard; it may just have been that false facial hair was an important part of the ruler's expected attire of state.

MANDY: "Oh, I hate wearing these beards"—Mandy is wearing the beard so she can participate in a ritual set apart for men only—like priestly activities, and some access to the temple (often forbidden due to a woman's ritual uncleanliness or impurity). This separation of sexes wasn't confined to first-century Jerusalem, though. Public discussion of equality for women in the mid-to-late-1970s became even more heated after the passage of the Sex Discrimination Act in November 1975. *Times* Columnist Bernard Levin wrote a blistering article directed at those "sniggering" at the prospect of more women in shipyards and foundries, comparing the sniggerers to those who laughed at NHS recipients in the late

1940s wearing their state-provided "false teeth and spectacles": "Today, the similar reaction to the new law is based on what might be called attitudes of sexual class; a particular kind of man thinks that women have no business being equal, and similarly ought to bear their lesser status without complaint."[4] Levin goes on to point a finger at women who refused to support the recent election of Margaret Thatcher to the Tory leadership, calling it "an enormous achievement" that brought only "sneers" from the "sisterhood." Bad form, that, and a missed opportunity:

> But if [women] do succeed in using the Act to press on towards genuine equality of opportunity they will indeed pose a threat to the male domination of our society, and in particular to the way in which that domination has enabled men to retain a wildly disproportionate share both of power and of the loot that goes with it. . . . [The Act] *can* have explosive effects; but only if women, and their allies among men, can use it creatively and usefully.[5]

The bearded women in the scene have used their ally among the men, the beard salesman, to secure participation in a man's event, the effects being at least concussive, if not explosive. Levin's call for civility prompted some sniggering from Auberon Waugh just nine days later:

> I fear I'm beginning to lose my admiration for the Thoughts of Bernard Levin. . . . Why has he joined the chorus of randy London bachelors saying we must not snigger at sexual equality? . . . Perhaps you have to be a married man living in the country to understand the cruel and unnatural thing which is being done to our women. But the Labour government's action in 1948 was not nearly as cruel as *these new proposals to equip our women with free beards and moustaches, make them work as navvies[6] and beat them from a tender age.*[7]

Only women will be casting stones, we'll see in a moment, all because they've taken advantage of the tacitly approved offer of beards—a kind of odd equality—allowing them to participate in what had been a man's world.

In relation to the temple, women were expected to pray at the northern gate, and men nearer the temple, in the inner court.[8] Ackerman points out that even though the bulk of written work pertaining to ancient Israel and the Hebrew Bible was recorded by, for, and about (often elite) men's lives, female duties and roles can be "painstakingly teased out."[9] Not surprisingly, the female's area of influence tended to be in the household, and with(in) the family.[10] In an earlier draft of the script, Judith is at Brian's home, inviting Brian to dinner with her parents. In the finished film, Judith has no domestic responsibilities or role, excepting as a bedmate for Brian. Even that chore ends with her defending Brian as a "great leader," and not a great lover or provider or even boyfriend. Mandy's domestic presence is limited, as well; she tells Brian to clean his room, and provides sexual favors to Roman soldiers for an income.

The beard as forming a disguise, however, also has precedent in this period, and for men, specifically. During his tumultuous reign in Judea, Herod would sometimes don a disguise and go out into Jerusalem (where he lived most of the year) to converse with and listen to his people, gauging their mood and opinions of him.[11] Later, at the time of the unrest following the opening of Pilate's aqueduct (built at the temple treasury's expense), Pilate sent out dozens of his men, armed and disguised, to infiltrate the gathered mob and deal with the most vocal of the rabble.[12]

Lastly, the Goons had mentioned beards as part of a disguise in the "I Was Monty's Treble" episode. There, a song is determined to be fake because it's wearing a beard, and clean-shaven beneath.[13]

BRIAN: "Why aren't women allowed to go to stonings, Mum?"—A version of this exchange can be found in the earlier drafts, but there it's Judith and Brian discussing the laws, with Judith decrying the backwardness.

The oral traditions gathered into the third-century Mishnah do allow for stoning, after a proper trial and conviction. The book also explains how the stoning should be carried out, with instructions varying slightly for a male as opposed to a female stonee (generally, how they are to be dressed and situated). There does not seem to be a *specific* mention in the Mishnah that women are forbidden from participating in the stoning.[14] Leviticus 24:14 actually mentions that "all the congregation" is to participate in the stoning of the blasphemer, though there has been much disagreement as to how to decipher "all." (All men? All men, women, and children? All adults?) The sentencing would have come from men of the Sanhedrin, the witnesses would likely have been male, and at this time the Roman authorities would have had to approve the execution—again, all men. The fact that this was a religious proceeding in a patriarchal society—and the woman's place tended to be in the home—indicates little chance of women being invited or allowed to participate in such a potentially unsettling event. Those things being said, it makes perfect sense for women in the Python world to cross-dress (put on beards) so they can participate in the man's world.

(draft) JUDITH is wearing a beard—Judith isn't in this scene in the finished film. In earlier drafts, she may be a revolutionary, but she's clearly still participating in the repressive activities of this world, though the stonings would have been part of the Sanhedrin's punishments, therefore Jewish and religious, not Roman and secular. The Sanhedrin did have the power to punish capital crimes, as well, to "conduct trials and execute sentences for capital crimes perpetrated by Jews in Judea,"[15] but, as Smallwood points out in *Jews Under Roman Rule*, "the question of the composition, powers and presidency of the Sanhedrin in Jerusalem [during Hyrcanus's time] is intensely complicated."[16] That power was eventually taken from the Sanhedrin by Pilate (perhaps even before) to become part of the *jus gladii*, or "law of the sword" held by Roman prefects in Judea. The challenging factors include the nature of Brian's crime, as well as his race: Is he a Jew or Roman? Or neither?

MANDY: "It's written, that's why"—It is Josephus who offers this Sadducean,[17] letter-of-the-law conceit, essentially, in *Antiquities of the Jews*, telling us who *cannot* stand as an official witness in ancient Israel: "But let not the testimony of women be admitted, on account of the levity and boldness of their sex."[18] Deuteronomy 21:21 affirms that "all the *men* of his city shall stone him with stones, that he die," and verse twenty-two says essentially the same. This would seem to preclude women from participating in these stonings as stone-throwers, too. (Women are fair game to be stoned, incidentally.) Translator Whiston can't account for this proscription: "The Pentateuch says not a word about the exclusion of women as witnesses in courts of justice," Whiston admits, before dropping the other shoe: "It is very probable, however, that this was the practice of Jews in the days of Josephus."[19] So Whiston himself is saying he doesn't know, "It's written, that's why."[20]

It would often have been wise to at least know *what* was written during this period, even if one didn't know *why* it had been written. Josephus mentions an inscription in the temple in Jerusalem, likely carved in Greek and Latin so foreigners could read it, a warning to trespassers.[21] A large engraved tablet from the temple itself was discovered in 1871, and was translated: "*No stranger is to enter within the balustrade round the temple and enclosure. Whoever is caught will be responsible to himself for his death, which will ensue.*"[22] This is a sort of "All hope abandon, ye who enter here" mentioned earlier in the opening titles discussion.[23] No one other than the Jews and, perhaps, even then only the highest-ranking priests would *really* know why the temple was such a forbidden place—for all else, it's off-limits simply because "it's written, that's why." Those that did manage to make it into the Holy of Holies, including invaders Pompey and later Titus, were quite surprised to find an austere, barren room.[24] It's clear many polytheists didn't believe the Jews meant it when they said no likeness of Yahweh could be managed, so none should be made.

There were plenty of "it's written" texts (and oral litanies) that laid out rules for behavior and belief for the Jews. The ascetic Qumran Essenes had their Manual of Discipline, there were Pharisee rules and Sadducee rules (many of which conflicted), and dozens of books of scripture and apocrypha. There were laws regarding what to eat and what not to eat, what to do in the temple, with what (and by whom), there were "laws of property and laws that dealt with criminals . . . [and] laws of conduct," including the Ten Commandments.[25] Mandy and Brian would most likely have only heard these texts as read aloud by Pharisees and scribes.[26] There were also varying degrees of ritual adherence in first century Jerusalem, ranging from spirit of the law to an almost fanatical letter of the law precision,[27] and this just among the Jews. Add in the Roman laws and the presence of many foreigners and their religions in the city, and the comprehension of all things "written" becomes virtually impossible.

Another version of "because it's written" during this period comes from an unusual source: a novel. Frederick Forsyth's *Dogs of War* was published in 1974, and, like Marighella's *Minimanual*, became required reading for would-be revolutionaries. The book is essentially the recipe for a successful coup, Wheen notes. The first maxim posits that "a mere handful of mercenaries can overthrow a regime."[28] This is just the heady stuff that the PFJ (and the RAF and JRA, etc.) wanted to hear, and where some likely stopped reading before embarking on their piratical adventures. The rest of the recipe is crucial, though. A "mere handful" like the PFJ can suffice *if*, the formula continues, "the republic is weak enough and power concentrated in the hands of a tyrant." The PFJ would have done well to think on the last two requirements.[29] Demaris underscores this point effectively: "Terrorism has failed as a tactic because it is ineffective against a ruthless tyranny or strong democracy. Unlike organized revolution, it has never overthrown or even seriously threatened a totalitarian state."[30]

Pilate may have been tyrannical, but he did have to answer to the Syrian Legate and then Rome, the latter being as powerful an empire as could have been imagined. These are the reasons that coups seldom succeed in democratic or even benignly fascistic countries—the symbols of power aren't just symbols, they represent actual weapons, active militaries, and acceptable levels of economic and social stability. The banana republic is a different story, and one that Forsyth was telling. Forsyth's methods were tried and tested in the field, when mercenaries were planning an Equatorial Guinea coup d'état in 1973, but were arrested before the plot could unfold, or others successfully overthrew the Comoros, on several occasions.[31] Forsyth's plot and methods were uncannily similar to the planning and execution of a number of such attempts across Africa, the Seychelles, and on. Soldier of fortune Robert Denard led four coups against the Comoros, and Mike Hoare led one in the Seychelles, sorties that Forsyth commented on later: "It was remarkable. In Denard's attack, I learned, every mercenary had a copy of *Les Chiens de Guerre* stuck in his back pocket and in Hoare's attack they all had a copy of the English version."[32]

Lastly, the facts of life in Britain, economically speaking, would remain set in stone as long as the popular "postwar consensus" remained in effect. The wide-ranging social programs, the safety nets of social security and single-payer health, the nationalized (subsidized) industries, and the promises of full employment kept the free market wolves away from the door from 1945 through most of the 1970s. The changing global economy (thanks in part to Middle East oil), Britain's moribund manufacturing (thanks to entrenched trade unions and practices), and Britain's waning influence beyond her borders reduced the size and vitality of the domestic economy to a point where there weren't enough taxes to subsidize blossoming public responsibilities. A sort of "because it's written" mentality persisted as long as the pound was strong enough and jobs were available for all who wanted to work. This postwar consensus—that the welfare state was a comfortable and dependable fact of life—had been "the bedrock of British politics," according to Caryl, but would have to change utterly from 1979, under Thatcherism.[33]

Packets of gravel are piled in cone twists—These look like traditional chip servers (as in fish and chips), and they'll be seen again when Brian is selling otters' noses at the Colosseum.

(draft) BRIAN: "No. Not in the beard"—In a draft version of the script, Judith is walking with Brian to the stoning, she's already donned her beard, and she's just snapped at him, comparing him unfavorably to Reg:

BRIAN is hurt. Pause. JUDITH looks at him. Takes his hand.

Judith: Sorry.

Brian: Don't.

Judith: Come on.

Brian: No . . . not in the beard.

Here she's wanting Brian to cuddle with her in front of Harry and the woman carrying the donkey, but Brian is clearly uncomfortable with the potentially homoerotic image this would convey. The OT mentions "sodomites" practicing their "abominations" in 1 Kings 14:24, while the Torah calls the act abhorrent; the Lord's displeasure with that act would certainly keep public displays of homosocial affection to a minimum. Leviticus 20:13 even calls for a death sentence for both participants in a homosexual union. Ancient Roman and Greek views of same-sex relationships would have been much more relaxed, as discussed by Jason von Ehrenkrook in "Effeminacy in the Shadow of Empire":

> "Normal" sexual behavior for a *vir* [a fully masculine male] encompassed three orifices: the *vir* who penetrates the vagina (*fututor*), the *vir* who penetrates the mouth (*irrumator*), and the *vir* who penetrates the anus (*pedicator/pedico*). That a *pedicator* might penetrate a male anus, or an *irrumator* a male mouth, was of no consequence to the penetrator's status as a *vir*. Conversely, the corresponding receptive behavior that did in fact compromise one's status as a *vir*, placing him into the category of gender deviant, included performing oral sex on a female (*cunnilinctor*) or male (*fellator*) and receiving anal intercourse (*pathicus* or *cinaedus*).[34]

Jewish religious authorities of Jerusalem would have been much less receptive to these more permissive categories; if Brian is going to be public about his affections, then it will be with the unbearded Judith. It's during this very period in Britain that the great struggle between religious fundamentalists and the more permissive society was being waged, featuring campaigners like Mary Whitehouse and Malcolm Muggeridge on one side, and Germaine Greer and Roy Jenkins on the other.

Beyond the local employment of beards to mask female faces at religious events open only to men, the image of the "bearded revolutionary"—facial hair somehow signifying the anti-authoritarian credentials of the wearer (Lenin and Trotsky, Guevara and Castro, for example)—comes forward through the 1920s and into the 1970s. In a 1966 story covering the south Wales elections, the winning Liberal candidate is described, probably tongue-in-cheek, as wearing colors that are "dangerously revolutionary," and "his beard adds to the impression."[35] In this same election cycle, the headline "All Beards are Suspect to Labour" graced a *Telegraph* column in January 1966; the story beneath reads as silly as the leader, and comes from Hull:

> Growing a beard is a time-honoured form of disguise, but Mr. Gott, the Radical Alliance[36] candidate, who has a luxuriant nut-brown one, will have to reverse the process if he wants to gatecrash another Labour meeting here. Stewards at the two Labour meetings last night were told to watch for anybody with a beard seeking admission. Mr. John Gittings, Mr. Gott's agent, who is also bearded, was asked if he was Mr. Gott. Mr. Peter Jackson, Labour's prospective candidate for High Peak, Derbyshire, was also challenged. Mr. Gott, who was escorted from a Labour meeting on Sunday, told me he is now thinking of sending a few "doubles" to attend meetings.[37]

Mr. Gott was able to claim 253 votes in this by-election, but the seat remained safely Labour.

In 1970s Britain, the image of the bearded person had taken on very definite political connotations, and as early as 1971 the suggested image must have been rather widely accepted, too. In an article about the contentious Industrial Relations Bill,[38] the influence on/from the Left by the Communist Party was presented as a given: "It is not a revolutionary party in the bearded, grenade-draped sense of the word but a formidable political organization with a single-minded devotion."[39] Moderates and those on the right of the Conservative and even Labour (and Liberal) parties and their sympathetic newspapers now identified the dangerous Far Left by appearance, including the "progressive" and bearded teachers discussed later.[40] Bernard Donoughue met with a reporter friend, Brian MacArthur, of the *Evening Standard*, who passed on that "working on the *Standard* is now terrible. They are instructed to get pictures of pickets with beards, but that is all. No analysis."[41] Donoughue also notes that when he was first part of the 1974 Wilson administration he and his staff were vetted for security purposes, one older official asking "about one of my staff. 'Is he vulnerable to subversion? He has a beard.'"[42] Two years later times hadn't changed, as Donoughue noted the "positive vetting" of a newer member of his staff by British intelligence even though the intelligence man has "worried that [his] housing man had a beard."[43] By the mid-1970s in Britain beards were still considered by many to be something to hide behind. But bearded women? On a later trip to Ruskin College, Oxford in October 1976, Donoughue records that at the tea after Callaghan's education speech,[44] "the PM went to discuss the [education] issues with some student representatives, all—including the girls, I'm sure—with beards."[45]

And even though it's considered fairly certain that Israelite males during Jesus's time all wore beards[46]—including Jesus, his disciples, and his detractors—the nuclei of the PFJ do not. The social stigma attached to beardlessness in the later Talmudic period seems to argue against being clean shaven—a beard was "the adornment of a man's face," and in the Talmud "a man without a beard was compared to a eunuch."[47] The PFJ's clean-shaven appearance sets them apart from most everyone else at the Sermon—these beardless rebels—and will be discussed later as they plan their raid on Pilate's palace. It's not likely that the Pythons de-bearded the PFJ for any other reason beyond presenting them as very young and rebellious, but it also did give the troupe a break from hair and makeup sessions as the shoot wore on.

HARRY, the stone salesman—This quick moment is unusual and worth mentioning. The rock and gravel sale is a commercial transaction[48] that actually goes to plan—a rarity in the Python world. In *Flying Circus*, there are a handful of such transactions, including a City Gent buying a copy of the *Times* before embarking on the famous "Silly Walk" sketch (Ep. 14), a native guide leads intrepid explorers right to a "smashing little restaurant" and is paid for his efforts, and a man buys and then receives an argument (both in Ep. 29). Most transactions, whether financial or informational, go awry in *Flying Circus* and *Holy Grail*—for example, Arthur's attempts to gather adherents or even guidance ("What knight lives in that castle?") on his quest prove incredibly frustrating. In *Flying Circus* we are presented with the Pythons' version of Britain as the "nation of shopkeepers" mentioned earlier by Spike Milligan (and earlier still by Napoleon and Adam Smith, et al.).[49] These vendors sell encyclopedias (Ep. 5), pet parrots (Ep. 8), lingerie (Ep. 10), albatross (Ep. 13), jokes and novelties (Ep. 15), fishy aftershave (Ep. 17), meat and insults (Ep. 18), tobacco and newspapers (Eps. 6 and 25), arguments, abuse, and "being hit on the head lessons" (Ep. 29), cheese (Ep. 33), pornography (Ep. 36), and Icelandic honey (Ep. 45). Most of the transactions in these establishments come to naught, while the customer is often frustrated as the narrative is hijacked in some other direction. The British and Roman empires had been sustained and expanded thanks to goods and human trade—"trade and empire went hand in hand"[50]—creating more nations of shopkeepers in far-flung provinces: "The spearhead, one could say, of Roman expansion . . . was as much economically based as it was militarily based," Hendrix points out. "We have a lot of evidence that tells us about Roman venture capitalists out there on the fringes of Roman economic spheres, beginning to build their small economic empires, and in some cases rather larger economic empires, that brought with [them] Roman rule."[51] The "venture capitalists" in *Life of Brian* don't seem to be molested by the Romans, carrying on their trade ("How much for the gourd?") around the city walls and as a backdrop to the actions of Brian, the PFJ, and the Roman soldiers. The more contemporary British Commonwealth also relied on favored exchange between member states, agreements that had been (and continue to be) one of the main points of contention in the EEC.

MERCHANT (Idle): "Stone, madam?"—This woman is wearing no beard, so she's clearly a woman; it's then interesting that Harry is offering to sell her stones, since "it's written" that she, being a woman, cannot actually attend stonings, and he would know that. He's not flouting a Roman, civil law, but a religious one important to the Jews of Judea, meaning, if he's an observant Jew, he would have to answer to religious authorities, the same men who would have condemned Matthias to death for blasphemy.

Selling stones for a stoning is just the Pythonesque version of the active commercial life Jerusalem enjoyed, especially around Passover, one of the three pilgrimage festivals that gathered thousands into the city.[52] Sellers of animals (doves, goats, sheep, cattle) for temple sacrifices were needed, as were moneychangers to convert foreign money into that which was acceptable for the required half-shekel temple tribute, as well as the sellers of pilgrimage souvenirs and trinkets. The pilgrim coming to the temple for Passover would need a sacrificial animal, and could buy one in the streets outside the temple; the Pythons' pilgrims coming to the stoning will need a stone to participate fully in this other "religious" activity, and can buy one from Harry on his (or her) way.

This also likely tells us that this works along the lines of the black market during World War II—illegal but always a wink and a deal made if there's money available. The Pythons grew up in wartime and postwar England, where black market goods were on offer if you knew who to ask, an underground economy cautioned against in newspapers and government radio broadcasts of the period.[53] During and after the war, when rationing was in effect, sought-after items ranged from any meat not from a horse to budgie seed to affordable liquor (even legitimate pubs were having to depend on black market vendors).[54] Alcohol and cigarettes weren't rationed, but thanks to the German naval activity around the United Kingdom, both became harder and harder to find as the war dragged on. In Dunstable, A. W. Morgan remembers that a kind of charcoal-gray black market developed as rationing bit harder: "Our neighbour managed to get meat from a butcher in exchange for surplus eggs and my mother exchanged some of my 'sweet' coupons for 'sugar' coupons from another neighbour and thereby was able to build up a stock for jam making when fruit was plentiful."[55] So, not stolen goods flogged from the back of a lorry or out of a trench coat, but daily necessities acquired through clever bargaining and trades of rationed items—this is the England the Pythons knew as youngsters.

An elderly woman, almost bent double by the weight of a huge donkey on her shoulders, staggers past—See the "donkey rides" sight gags from *Flying Circus*, Eps. 3 and 35.[56] Also, this "elderly woman" isn't so elderly, and is played by the same woman who played the wife to Mr. Big Nose in the previous scene, Gwen Taylor.

The stone salesman whips open his coat, revealing rows of artificial beards . . .—This is the sure sign of the street peddler, and more than likely one who is selling black market goods. The legal products, rocks and gravel, are on display, while the illegal goods, the beards, are hidden in the coat. This "open-coat" trope has been seen in cartoons, on television, and in films for many years. Idle often played this type of fast-talking "spiv" character in *Flying Circus*, as a burglar selling encyclopedias, a door-to-door jokes and novelties salesman, and as a vicar hawking water heaters, Cup Final tickets, biros, the lot.[57] In the popular *Dad's Army* (1968–1977), Private Walker (James Beck) played this role, always ready for a quick sale of whisky, cricket balls, or King George VI "coronation beer mugs."

WOMAN: "I haven't got time to go to no stonings. 'E's not well again"—Ailing animal aside for a moment, in *Holy Grail* it was Dennis and his mother who were too busy gathering "lovely filth" to be bothered by their king's (re)quest. These are early medieval characters whose feet are planted firmly in their lives and work, and whose connections and allegiances to any representation of the state is ephemeral at best.[58] The clannish nature of a Jewish existence likely prevented this kind of dislocation, since even the Diaspora gathered together wherever found themselves in the postexilic period. In Jerusalem of the first century, Jews would have been necessarily attached to the religious activities and expectations of the temple cult and festivals; the quotidian nature of sacerdotal life likely kept *most* from wasting much time at stonings or sermons or meeting with terrorist cells.[59] Bogdanor notes that in Britain such individual-State interactions are a recent development, and that up until about the end of the nineteenth century, the "role of the State" was a limited one:

> If you look at 1900, the average British person, provided he or she kept out of the hands of the police and did not commit a crime, would have nothing whatever to do with the State—the State would not impinge: there was no health insurance, no unemployment insurance, nothing to connect you with the public authorities. But, gradually, all that changed: from the First World War, the Liberal reforms and so on.[60]

This change has much to do with the increase in the British people's "confidence in the State," something the PFJ and Brian don't seem to share. Auberon Waugh described this type of person who would avoid a stoning—or perhaps the modern equivalent in Britain, the picket line's attack on scabs—as someone whose everyday life mattered more:

> On such days as this one realises that England still survives. Beneath the notice of television or colour supplements there exists a whole world of quiet, intelligent people going about their daily lives pretty well as they have always done, untroubled by trade unionists or transistor radios or comprehensive schools. The secret is to take no interest in what people say is happening, and disbelieve everything you read in the newspapers.[61]

The health of the family's donkey might have meant the difference between life and death, between sustenance and starvation, or even between being lower-middle class and poor. In this the Elderly Lady perhaps represents what later came to be called the "Essex Woman" (and "Essex Man"), the quasi-real C2[62] working-class voters who elected Margaret Thatcher in 1979. This is a rare figure in the Python oeuvre, the seemingly normal person who, even when given the opportunity, refuses to become or remain a part of the narrative folderol. Dennis's mother in *Holy Grail* is another such character.

The donkey is also an indication that the woman isn't a slave, and that she owns at least one animal, setting her above the beggars seen later, and perhaps even above Brian and his mother. As a method of transportation, the ass was oft-used in first-century Jerusalem, according to Jeremias, and an important beast of burden for tradesmen.[63] The class arguments that were heard in *Holy Grail* are not really part of this world, though class and privilege meant a great deal in ancient Judea.[64] Magness writes: "Social categories among Jews were religiously based (for example, priest versus Israelites or being a member of a sect or movement), not economically defined."[65] (Example: The "wealthy Jew" Gregory and his wife end up on crosses just behind Brian, underscoring this classlessness.) There's also no indication as to how the woman actually uses the ass, whether for milk or for personal transportation or hauling, or, worse, whether she is somehow associated with one of the so-called "despised" trades, an ass-driver. Despised trades included most anyone who drove animals or transported goods, the lot being seen as conniving and dishonest.[66] Incidentally, the peddler selling the stones is also considered a despised trade participant, as would anyone selling "rich Imperialist titbits," or haggling for beards or gourds. Jeremias notes that "there can be few reputable trades left," so most of what we see in the streets of *Life of Brian*'s Jerusalem is ritually impure.[67]

Finally, carrying a sick donkey isn't an odd act, considering the way animals might be treated in the ancient world. It didn't pay to be a sacrifice-worthy animal, of course, since most of the major religions, pagan and otherwise, spilled blood as part of elaborate, crucial rituals to please various gods. The temple in Jerusalem was said to "resemble a busy slaughterhouse" at times.[68] A number of the film versions of the nativity featured shepherds carrying a lamb, and there are scores of devotional paintings, old and new, depicting Christ carrying a lamb. Roman beliefs put animals in odd situations, too. Inside the Senate chamber, and next to the altar to Apollo, a "coop of sacred chickens" served as auguries when important decisions were considered. The chickens were fed "hallowed grain" and then watched closely for their signal of the omens, good or ill.[69]

HARRY *(to Mandy)*: **"Stone, sir?"**—The salesman has switched adroitly from addressing the donkey-bearing woman as "madam" to calling Mandy "sir," likely since she's sporting the called-for beard. It's not clear whether he knows he's addressing a woman dressed like a man, there's no wink-wink moment between them. In fact, he deals with Mandy as a straight-ahead customer, pointing out the craftsmanship of the stones he sells.

In *Flying Circus*, the cross-dressed man isn't often identified, at least textually. In Ep. 9 the lumberjack (Palin) admits to dressing like a woman, and in Ep. 14 two characters admit to cross-dressing. One, played by Chapman, is an MP appearing on a news show to discuss housing (and dressed completely as a woman), and the other, played by Cleese, admits to being a female impersonator who has dated Dinsdale Piranha.[70] Other than that, the characters dressed as female are treated as female, and sometimes rat-bag females, but as women, even if there is a sexual setting, as in Ep. 17, when a Poet Inspector (Palin) is being cooed over by a lusty, lonely housewife (Jones).

Lastly, American novelist Herman Melville visited Jerusalem in 1857, and was greatly disappointed at the gray, barren tattiness of the entire region. In *Clarel*, he soliloquized on the wretched stones he found at every turn:

> Stones of Judea. We read a good deal about stones in Scriptures. Monuments & stumps of the memorials are set up of stones; men are stoned to death; the figurative seed falls in stony places; and no wonder that stones should so largely figure in the Bible. Judea is one accumulation of stones—stony mountains & stony plains; stony torrents & stony roads; stony walls & stony fields, stony houses & stony tombs; stony eyes & stony hearts. Before you and behind you are stones. Stones to the right & stones to the left.[71]

Melville—whose Jerusalem was a Pythonesque "half melancholy, half farcical"—is clearly not appreciating the stones as either Harry or Mandy will, and leaves the Holy Land uninspired.[72]

MANDY: "Nah, they've got them up there lying around on the ground"—In Zeffirelli's version, there *are* stones just "lying around" ready to be used for a stoning. The *Brian* script does call it "The Stoning Place," after all, but it's not quite the same as described in the Mishnah. In the Zeffirelli version, which the Pythons clearly emulate, Christ refuses to convict the woman, and after asking those who are without sin to cast their stones first, the crowd (of men) drop their stones, rather cinematically, and wander off. The woman is then forgiven. The final shot of the scene depicts Christ standing where the woman had cowered, discarded stones scattered around his feet.

HARRY: ". . . feel the quality of this—that's craftsmanship"—Craftsmanship seems to have been very important in Jerusalem during this period, perhaps thanks to the well-known work on Herod's palace: "Both in exterior decoration and interior appointment, in the selection of materials as in their treatment, in wealth of variety as in costly detail, the various crafts competed: the sculptor, the tapestry maker, the planner of fountains and ornamental gardens, the goldsmith and the silversmith, were all engaged in the work."[73] This is the palace that Pilate would have likely been occupying, and which we will see later in a state of remodeling. There, we will also see an example of an elaborate mosaic in tile on the palace floor, representing another of the surviving hints of Jerusalem's place in architectural history. Harry is probably thinking of himself as a stonemason, a rather high-ranking position among Jerusalem's craftsmen, according to Jeremias.[74] His off-the-books job is more in the gray market area of beard manufacture and selling.

Gilliam and his crew actually handcrafted the stones for this and the following stoning scene, according to Palin.[75]

MANDY stops and appraises the stone. Weighs one up professionally—She's obviously done this before, and knows the kind of stone she likes for such forbidden events. In the Zeffirelli version, there are women glimpsed in the shots, but they are at the back, watching—none are clasping stones.

BRIAN: "Can I have a flat one, Mum?"—Brian makes the mistake of betraying Mandy's gender, but a simple "shush" is enough to keep the illusion in place, at least for Harry, who wants to make a sale. In *Holy Grail*, Patsy's "reveal"—a remark that "It's only a model"—is also shushed, and the diegetic fiction is maintained.

MANDY (adopts a lower register)—(PSC) In Ep. 10 of *Flying Circus*, the police are only able to communicate with one another (and the general public) once they've learned each other's speaking idiosyncrasies, including higher and lower registers, loudness, etc.[76] In the film as shot Mandy does *not* attempt to change her voice, and the rock salesman doesn't seem to notice (or just doesn't care, given he's making a sale) that she might be a woman.

HARRY: "Should be a good one this afternoon . . . local boy"—Given that this is a religious punishment, it's likely that most of the condemned would be "local." The local versus foreign argument might be more applicable to those figures appearing in the games, especially the gladiatorial combats. The Emperor Commodus, born near Rome, fought in hundreds of gladiatorial combats, and appears to have been a popular "local boy" to the bloodthirsty masses, though not necessarily to the military or city fathers.[77] He would eventually be assassinated. In contemporary terms, "local" boys like boxer Alan Tottoh of Manchester were touted this way, drawing larger home crowds than visiting stars on the fight circuit, even though they may have been no more accomplished.[78] The term appears in relation almost exclusively to boxing and politics across the years.[79]

The STONING PLACE—(PSC) This is set up almost precisely as the scene from *Jesus of Nazareth* where the "woman taken in sin"[80] was set to be stoned—featuring ancient stone walls[81] and a crowd of assembled priests and stone-clutching Jews. The Pythons had worried prior to shooting that using some of the same sets and backdrops might be too familiar to viewers, since *Jesus of Nazareth* had broadcast to enormous viewership in April 1977, but they chose this setting anyway.

By the way, even though Brian and Mandy are pictured hustling toward the stoning so as to not miss it, once the scene begins they aren't pictured at all. They aren't part of the crowd of "men" ready to throw stones, nor do we see either of them throw a stone or even watch as others throw. There are surviving frame captures[82] that show both of them at the back of the crowd, but the Pythons obviously decided to cut them out of the finished film.

An OFFICIAL stands here, with some helpers—This official must represent the high priests of the city, members of the Sanhedrin, of which there may have been two separate bodies, according to Zeitlin,[83] the *Jewish Encyclopedia*, and others:

> For neither Josephus nor the Gospels in speaking of the Sanhedrin report any of its decisions or discussions referring to the priests or to the Temple service, or touching in any way upon the religious law, but they refer to the Sanhedrin exclusively in matters connected with legal procedure, verdicts, and decrees of a political nature; whereas the Sanhedrin in the hall of hewn stone dealt, according to the Talmudic sources, with questions relating to the Temple, the priesthood, the sacrifices, and matters of a kindred nature. Adolf Büchler assumes indeed that there were in Jerusalem two magistracies which were entirely different in character and functions and which officiated side by side at the same time. That to which the Gospels and Josephus refer was the highest political authority, and at the same time the supreme court; this alone was empowered to deal with criminal cases and to impose the sentence of capital punishment. The other, sitting in the hall of hewn stone, was the highest court dealing with the religious law, being in charge also of the religious instruction of the people (Sanh. xi. 2–4).[84]

As described above, it's still not clear which body would have dealt with a Jew who blasphemed and deserved capital punishment, especially at a time when such punishments may have been enforceable only with Roman permission.

The Official's costuming, and especially his headdress, is actually less like those seen in *King of Kings* or *Jesus of Nazareth*, and more like the exaggerated hats created for the priests to wear in *Jesus Christ Superstar*. The costume designers have done their homework here, though. The Official's tunic is not held together with buttons, which wouldn't be used in this way until about the thirteenth century, but brooch-like ornamentation at the chest and a thong that runs up the side of the body and inside of the arms. These can be untied and loosened to put on or remove the tight-fitting garment. He appears to wear the ritual fringes required of all observant adult males (Deut. 22:12), though it's not clear whether he's wearing only woolen clothing, another requirement, and not a mix of linen and woolen clothing (Deut. 22:11). His clothing is also white—more expensive, harder to make (bleaching is required), and harder to keep clean.

The timeline here isn't completely clear, but it should be pointed out that if this is the Passover eve—and the presence of Biggus Dickus might support that—then the Sanhedrin seems to be running afoul of its own laws. The Mishnah was very clear in these matters, Rosenblatt reminds us:

> One of the characteristics of the Pharisees that made them particularly objectionable in the eyes of the authors of the [NT] was that they were sticklers for the letter of the law. If this characterization is correct, then they could never have had anything to do with either the trial of Jesus or his death by crucifixion. Under the rules of Pharisaic law as summarized in the tractate of Sanhedrin of the Mishna no hearings in a case involving capital punishment could be initiated on the eve of a major holiday like Passover. No conviction was permitted to be brought in at night. No sentence might be executed on the day of a festival.[85]

So Matthias could not have been tried and convicted if the Passover were the following day, nor could he be executed, if the letters of laws were followed. Rosenblatt notes that since even note taking was forbidden on this day, as well, no court proceeding could have been accomplished.[86] The Roman prefect would have to have given his permission, as well, meaning an earlier meeting with Pilate (which could have happened, off-screen). All these are letter of the law rules, certainly, which the Pythons have never slavishly followed in their citing of history and historical characters.

Ultimately, in the stoning scene from *Jesus of Nazareth*, the visual influence for this scene in *Brian*, all of these same juridical considerations are also ignored or, less likely, perhaps accomplished off-screen. The woman taken in adultery is simply dragged into the scene/shot, like Matthias, she is accused by her captors, and the priests(?) tell them to take her to Jesus for his condemnation.

. . . the potential stonee, MATTHIAS—Matthias is wearing a simple loincloth, a clear indication of his role as a convicted man ready for punishment. He is essentially "naked" wearing only this undergarment. The "weedy Samaritan" will be dressed similarly when he's pushed onto the Colosseum sand, and Brian will be stripped to a loincloth as he's affixed to the cross.

OFFICIAL (Cleese): "Matthias son of Deuteronomy of Gath"—There are at least two "Matthias" possibilities to note here. The first is a Matthias who, like our Matthias, got himself into trouble with Jerusalem's leadership. This Matthias was the High Priest Matthias who, in about 5 BC, was sacked by Herod for "allowing" several overzealous rabbis and their pupils to tear down an eagle Herod had installed on a wall of the temple.[87] Another Matthias only appears in the New Testament, and is known for being the disciple who replaced Judas. Matthias was later (perhaps) martyred in Ethiopia. Our Matthias is in trouble here with the religious authorities and threatened with stoning; later he is in dutch with the Roman authorities and threatened with crucifixion. He seems to be what Pilate might have termed a "notowious cwiminal," even more so than the later mentioned "wapist," "wobber," and "pickpocket"—and yet Matthias escapes unharmed, as far as we can tell.

Deuteronomy is the fifth book of the Hebrew Bible, and rarely used as a name. It is, however, one of the OT books cited often in regard to Mishnah laws, and, along with Leviticus, would have been the books the Pythons scanned as they prepared for the film, as well as the Synoptic Gospels and John. Gath is one of the Philistine cities mentioned in the OT, and a place name found throughout the OT. The name "Gath" appeared in British newspapers often, in relation to many new Israeli settlements being created as thousands of Jews returned to their homeland. "Gath" also appeared as a clue for a number of crossword puzzles appearing in the *Times* after 1963.

OFFICIAL: ". . . found guilty by the elders of the town of uttering the name of our Lord . . ."—Richard describes this phenomenon in the first century: "By contrast [to the polytheistic Roman religion], the Hebrew religion involved the worship of Yahweh, an omniscient, omnipotent, and inscrutable but loving and creative God who appeared in various forms (e.g., as a burning bush) and whose name could not be uttered."[88] It's not clear where "could not be uttered" comes from, except as an accretion over time, or as the influence of one rabbinical school over another. There don't seem to be such prohibitions in either the Torah or the Mishnah, according to the very popular *Judaism 101*[89]:

> Nothing in the Torah prohibits a person from pronouncing the Name of God. Indeed, it is evident from scripture that God's Name was pronounced routinely. Many common Hebrew names contain "Yah" or "Yahu." Part of God's four-letter Name [YHVH]. The Name was pronounced as a part of daily services in the Temple. The Mishnah confirms that there was no prohibition against pronouncing The Name in ancient times. In fact, the Mishnah recommends using God's Name as a routine greeting to a fellow Jew.[90]

The site goes on the mention that later, "some rabbis" began to treat the utterance of God's name more proscriptively, condemning to death or damnation (in principle, not practice) those who pronounce the four-letter name rather than using a substitute.

This is one of the very few Jewish religious references in the film, which is fascinating given the setting, first-century Jerusalem, and the subject matter, the crucifixion of a misunderstood messianic figure. The "elders" would have been high priests who were members of the Sanhedrin bodies, those authorized to hear complaints, conduct trials, and pass sentences of corporal and capital punishment. Most of the biblical movies the Pythons screened as they prepared for *Brian* feature at least one scene—often the trial of Jesus—where these bearded and somber men are gathered. With the exception of one of their officials seen here (who may be a lower level priest), there are no obvious priests or high priests depicted in the film, and no religious gathering. Brian will be condemned by Romans and Roman law, for an attempt on the life or safety of the prefect's wife; he will face no religious charges or authorities. No such scenes seem to have been part of any draft of the script.

This sentence is the result of an actual trial, it seems (he reads from an official transcript or recommendation from that trial), which was one of the avenues through which such executions were made possible. In those cases, the accused would have been brought before the priests to answer to charges brought by witnesses. Spontaneous stonings could also be found, though those throwing the stones would likely have to have personally witnessed the crime. "Stoning to death could occur as the spontaneous action of a mob enraged against an individual . . . since it was a form of killing for which weapons could usually be found immediately at hand," Bauckham writes. "Formal trial is evidently not required, since those who undertake to stone [Jesus for the crime of blasphemy] have themselves witnessed the crime."[91]

In *Jesus of Nazareth*, the stoning of the sinful woman seems to be fairly spontaneous, though the scriptures say that it was the "scribes and Pharisees" who brought her before Jesus, meaning she could have been at a trial already (John 8:3). The Johannine account makes it clear that Jesus is being tested by those who would trick him into a blasphemous trap, and the scene as depicted in *Jesus of Nazareth* may be just as spontaneous as it appears. As played out, the scene in *Brian* very much resembles the "She's a Witch" scene in *Holy Grail*, discussed below.

OFFICIAL: ". . . as a blasphemer . . ."—There is an interesting angle from which this scene and the eventual conviction of Brian by Pilate can be examined. Death by stoning (or burning or hanging, etc.) *did* happen in first-century Jerusalem, and the Romans *did* crucify thousands as they built and then protected the empire. These scenes of sanctioned violence may be included for reasons similar to those for a plague cart heaped with bodies or a witch brought for burning in *Holy Grail*—both of which can be historically verified and have come to define an image of the Middle Ages for modern viewers. The specter of violence is also always at the Python feast, a nod to hyper-violent postwar cartoons, New Wave films, and the more "grown-up" postwar generations of film viewers. It seems clear that the Pythons weren't out to damage the name and legacy of Jesus, to hold him up to ridicule, or cast him into a narrative that degraded, sexualized, or even "normalized" him, as other recent depictions had been accused of or attempted.[92] Those sensational books, poems, plays, and films will be discussed as we move forward.[93] The mobs who follow the messiah du jour in *Brian* and who are willing to physically put down any opposing voice are the obvious targets, though belief and believers also take body blows as the Pythons promote a more laissez faire version of the spiritual man.[94] The Pythons have gone out of their way to depict Jesus in what can only be called conservative, traditional settings, and to handle those settings and Jesus himself with kid gloves. The silliness and undercutting goes on in a manger well away from the baby Jesus, and it's only at the back of the Sermon on the Mount that mishearings become fighting words. It could be argued that the conviction of Jesus by the Sanhedrin, for blasphemy, and thence by the Romans, for sedition, are offered by proxy in *Life of Brian* by Matthias and later Brian himself.[95] The film parses the trials and convictions Jesus faced onto two characters, one of whom, Matthias, even manages to escape his execution when the stoning descends into a melee.[96] Brian does not escape, except by the diegetic "out" of the film ending before he dies, and when we last see him, he looks as happy on the cross as we've seen him in the film.

One of the reasons Mary Whitehouse and a handful of British faith-based organizations were so ready to pounce on even the whiff of a film like *Life of Brian* was the announced Danish film *The Sex Life of Jesus Christ*. In May 1975 the Danish government admitted that it had granted artist Jens Jørgen Thorsen funding to produce the incendiary film.[97] Thorsen then stoked the flames in preproduction interviews by promising depictions of Christ participating in both heterosexual and homosexual acts, and even orgiastic set-pieces.[98] The controversy saw members of the Danish Film Institute resign, the Vatican speak out against the project, the Queen call the idea "obnoxious," and France withdraw permissions for location filming. Mrs. Whitehouse went to the trouble of having the script translated from Danish into English so that vicars, MPs, Home Secretary Merlyn Rees, and anyone interested could read it.[99] By September 1976 hundreds of letters had been sent and received, from parishioners to prelates, and from prelates to politicians, asking that the Danish filmmaker be banned from Britain, and—if made—the film banned, as well.[100] Britain's home secretary eventually denied the filmmakers entry into the UK in February 1977.[101] No other accessible locations were granted before the film's funding guarantee expired (Denmark, Sweden, France, West Germany, Britain, and Israel all said no), and the project was dead.[102]

Closer to home, editors of the underground magazine *OZ* had been put on trial in 1971 for obscenity (for an issue put together by and directed at teens), and were eventually given prison sentences.[103] In 1977 the *Gay News* and publisher Denis Lemon had been found guilty of blasphemy at the Old Bailey in July, thanks to Mrs. Whitehouse's private prosecution charges against a poem the magazine was to publish. The poem—*The Love That Dares to Speak Its Name*, by James Kirkup—depicted a centurion's physical love for and to the crucified Christ. Prosecutor J. J. Smith was interviewed by the *Times'* Stewart Tendler:

He said that the Crown had to prove two ingredients of the offence. One was an attack on Christianity that undermined the doctrines of Christianity or the Bible. The other was an attack made in such a manner as to pass the limits of decent controversy or discussion and outrage the feelings of any sympathizer of Christianity. "The nub lies in the second ingredient, the tone of this publication, the language used, such as to outrage a sympathizer," he said.[104]

Here is where the Pythons likely situated themselves, to be safe from similar attentions:

[Smith] asked the jury to note that "we have freedom of speech, which means that you can say anything about religion . . . within limits of decent controversy. You can say Christ was a fraud or a deceiver or Christ may have been a homosexual, provided you say it in a reasonable, measured, reflective, decent way."[105]

And since Lemon was eventually only fined and given a suspended sentence, this may have given the Pythons all the impetus needed to push forward with their story that did not feature Christ himself in any controversial way.[106]

By April 1979, however, as *Life of Brian* was being prepped for distribution, nervousness still wracked the film's backers and the BBFC, who would have to give the film a rating. Palin writes on 12 April:

[Producer] John Goldstone says the censor has been along to see *Brian* and reckons it would be an AA,[107] and he liked it, but he is concerned about licensing a movie against which there could be legal proceedings. He is sure that the Festival of Light will try and use the blasphemy law (upheld in the *Gay News* case) to try and stop the film. Lord Justice Scarman's judgement in the *Gay News* case gives them a ridiculously wide area to play with. JG wants to be sure of the church's attitude and so does the censor.[108]

EMI did flee, leaving a scramble for backing met by George Harrison's HandMade Films, and the film was completed. Ultimately Matthias is condemned for something that happened offscreen and for which there seem to be no witnesses present (these witnesses could/should cast the first stones). Matthias manages to escape this religious punishment, and he also evades punishment by the Romans. Brian is never condemned by the Jews, interestingly—separating him further from Jesus—just the Romans, which turns out to be condemnation enough.

OFFICIAL: ". . . you are to be stoned to death"—The actual practice of stoning, as carried out when the Sanhedrin enacted a death penalty, may have been quite different than the one depicted by the Pythons:

At the place of stoning, his clothes would have been stripped off. Then one of the Sanhedrists, as witness to his "blasphemy," would have shoved him off a precipice onto the rocks below. If he were still alive, a second member of the Sanhedrin would have dropped a boulder onto his heart. If he still survived, the entire Sanhedrin and any others present would have been obliged to hurl stones down on him until he died.[109]

Not long after the crucifixion of Christ, a fellow Nazarene, Stephen, whose Christ-centered preachings and acts angered many Jews, was stoned to death for blasphemy.[110] Rather than being turned in by his wife or neighbor, like Matthias, or trapped by false charges, as Jesus was, Stephen blasted the Sanhedrin for their evils—essentially asking for a public execution.

Punishment for sins against God was very real for Jews, but could also be applied to Romans, as it turned out, especially when political expediency was involved. During the procuratorship of Cumanus (AD 48–52), an imperial slave was robbed somewhere between Jerusalem and Joppa; Roman reprisals included raids on nearby villages ostensibly looking for terrorists, but more to set a reminder of imperial power. One Roman soldier went the extra mile and destroyed, in front of horrified villagers, a "Laws of Moses" scroll, tearing it, burning it, and using "reproachful language" as he did so.[111] This "act of unspeakable desecration" led to a mob march on Caesarea, where Cumanus lived, who acted quickly in the name of peace: "Cumanus had the soldier, who was probably guilty of military insubordination as well as of a breach of the Roman law declaring the sacred rolls in the synagogue sacrosanct, beheaded in front of his accusers, a firm and uncompromising action that restored calm by satisfying Jewish indignation."[112] The Roman soldier's actions weren't blasphemous, to put a fine point on it,[113] but certainly sacrilegious and ill-advised, given the volatile political situation of Judea. The Pythons' stoning is also clearly a use of punishment as a means of maintaining public order, not by or thanks to the Roman occupiers, but by the Jews themselves,[114] perhaps understandably so:

> Because blasphemy is an intolerable profanation of the sacred, it affronts the priestly class, the deep-seated beliefs of worshippers, and the basic values that a community shares. Punishing the blasphemer may serve any one of several social purposes in addition to setting an example to warn others. Punishment propitiates the offended deities by avenging their honor, thereby averting divine wrath: earthquakes, infertility, lost battles, floods, plagues, or crop failures. Public retribution for blasphemy also vindicates the witness of the believers and especially of the priests; it reaffirms communal norms; and it avoids the snares of toleration.[115]

Zeitlin reads Jewish history similarly, and sees the Sadducees as the likely force be behind a stoning such as this one. Holding to the *written* laws and nothing else, the Sadducees

> maintained that a man should be rewarded for his good deeds in this world, and held that a person who transgressed a precept of the Bible involving a death penalty should be punished accordingly. They were of the opinion that the [Jewish] State was the foundation of the existence of the Jewish people. Therefore, they held that the State was responsible[116] for the deeds or acts of the individual and that the court should punish those who transgressed the laws of the Pentateuch.[117]

According to the Sanhedrin Tractate (43a) in the Babylonian Talmud, a herald announced that Jesus himself was slated for stoning after news of the miracle of Lazarus circulated, standing accused of sorcery. Forty days later, he was crucified.

And the Roman non-interference in this religious event was typical, not odd or absurd. Rome had been dealing with the dispersed Jews since at least the second century BC, and since the year 6 with Jews in Judea and their Holy City, Jerusalem. E. Mary Smallwood describes Rome's treatment of these "peculiar people":

> Two alternatives faced Rome in dealing with a religion of this sort—suppression, or toleration and protection. Rome chose toleration and protection. There is nothing surprising in this. It was in line with her general policy towards provincial cults. Unless they were politically dangerous or morally objectionable—and Judaism was not suspected of being either—no attempt was made to suppress them. . . . It was therefore only natural that the Jews should be allowed to go on worshipping their own God. . . . But Rome went further than mere toleration, and safeguarded Jewish religious liberty.[118]

Smallwood is seconding Zeitlin, who writes twenty-five years earlier:

> It seems to me that there is no doubt that the Jews had full religious freedom under the Romans. The Romans never interfered in their internal affairs. As Josephus records, Fadus and Tiberius

Alexander abstained from all interference with the customs of the country and kept the nation at peace, since it was not the policy of the Romans to intervene in the religious and cultural life of the peoples whom they conquered.[119]

So the Pythons are right here: Roman soldiers are going to shake their heads at the silly religious claptrap about "blasphemy," but they won't step in and stop a religious exercise, even if it's a capital punishment. If the punishment had been for a crime against the Romans, then the Jews would have had no authority to carry it out, and Rome's interference would have been expected.[120]

MATTHIAS: ". . . all I said to my wife was 'That piece of halibut was good enough for Jehovah'"—These are all English versions of first-century languages spoken in Jerusalem, but "Jehovah" itself is a much later term. In Tyndale's Bible of the earlier sixteenth century, it's printed "Iehouah," while in the earlier Wycliffe Bible it's "Adonay," one of the replacement versions of God's name.[121] The version as uttered by Matthias, "Jehovah," can't be found in popular print until Milton's *Paradise Lost* (1667).

According to long-standing tradition, more than one witness is required to confirm the offense before an execution can be carried out: "At the mouth of two witnesses, or three witnesses, shall he that is worthy of death be put to death; *but* at the mouth of one witness he shall not be put to death."[122] It's not clear in the scene (from the charge read out by the official) whether the wife is a witness, beyond hearing the utterance in the first place, and if Matthias were turned in by his wife. Deuteronomy 17:7 also demands that the witnesses be the first to cast stones, meaning some of the gathered should be witness to the crime. This latter isn't likely, though, since the stoners are all bearded women, and Josephus tells us that women and slaves are disqualified.[123]

It's also not likely that Matthias would have been able to get his hands on halibut, since these are deep-water fish found in the northern Atlantic and Pacific oceans. Trade across the vast Roman Empire might have brought the fish all the way to Jerusalem, but almost certainly not to Matthias's plate. The halibut gets top billing here likely for reasons closer to home. In Ep. 23 of *Flying Circus*, for instance, Mr. Praline mentions that his pet fish, Eric, "is an halibut."[124] Earlier, in Ep. 17, one of the sought-after "fishy" requisites (aftershaves) was something "a little bit more halibutish."[125] The reference even goes back to the Goons, where "Halibut" is a silly name for a wealthy family.[126] Fish from the nearby Red Sea included St. Peter's fish, carp, and catfish.

This is a slightly different version than the more elaborate "outing" in the original version of the script. In this earlier version Matthias finishes his explanation by saying "and she turned me in," meaning his wife had turned him over to the religious authorities for blasphemy.[127] These few additional words are themselves leftovers from an entire scene that appeared in an earlier draft of *Brian*. There, a wife (dragging two children) works very hard to convince the centurions that her husband is the Brian they are looking for. It's not clear why she wants to turn him in, except that he's described in the script as "*wretched*," but she is quite persistent that he's Brian, not "Errol," as he's claiming. Other scenes mentioned and now missing include an early shepherd scene (which Palin was rehearsing on set[128]), the fight with Pilate's enormous wife, the Pythons' version of the Last Supper featuring Brian and two "easy" disciples, and additional Otto and Sermon on the Mount–type scenes. These either disappeared before being filmed—like the "King Brian the Wild" scene for *Holy Grail*—or were filmed and later edited out.[129]

OFFICIAL: "Blasphemy! He's said it again"—Saying it more than once makes it worse? Perhaps, if there were a warning from the elders about some violation of religious law, and then the violation was repeated. If one sign of devotion to the Lord were good, then many or repeated indications should be much better, some thought: "It was said that Moses had received the law of their observance from God on Mount Sinai; that the 'tephillin' were more sacred than the golden plate on the forehead of the high-priest, since its inscription embodied only once the sacred name of Jehovah, while the writing inside the 'tephillin' contained it not less than twenty-three times."[130] So at least in one rabbinical tradition, repetition did matter, but in this case making someone more holy, as opposed to more condemned.

This may be a reference to Peter's infamous denial, which appears in all four of the Gospels.[131] Jesus has told Peter that before the morning the follower would deny or disown his Lord three separate times; Peter was certain he would rather die. Sure enough, Peter was given three chances to admit that he knew and followed Jesus, and three separate times he denied such. In this case one would not have been enough, the second and third utterances did in fact make "it worse"—the repetition was necessary to fulfill Jesus's prophecy. Incidentally, the (Sanhedrin) Official does not tear his mantle here after hearing this repeated blasphemy, an act we've seen in various iterations of Jesus's trial in recent popular film, where Caiaphas is depicted.[132]

OFFICIAL: "Are there any women here today?"—The cross-dressing gets confusing here, as the Pythons are men dressed as women who are then pretending to be men. On the Elizabethan stage this kind of confusion was quite normal: a young male actor always played the younger female roles, and sometimes those roles required the female character to pretend to be male. Boys pretending to be girls pretending to be men upset many anti-theatricalists in Elizabethan and Stuart times, where both "aesthetic and erotic pleasure" was feared and realized.[133] That's not the case here, nor with most Python cross-dressings. In the stoning scene the women are dressing as men to participate in the man's religious world, a world off-limits to them because of their gender. They are trying to deceive the Official, otherwise they couldn't participate, meaning a sin is being committed here, too. There are no uneasy sexual moments in this scene, though; that will happen in the following scene, when Mandy seems ready to offer a sexual favor to a Roman soldier. That specter was also raised moments earlier, in the draft version, when Brian resists Judith's amorous advances because she's wearing a beard.

But it wasn't just the strict Sadducees or Pharisees who kept women at bay. The Pythons had been taking the female roles since before they were Pythons. The revues at Cambridge and Oxford were, if not forbidden to women, certainly not welcoming. The Pythons had written and performed all their own work, only giving away the female roles that called for actual femininity or, more honestly, actual breasts. The troupe ran a fairly closed shop.

In the world outside the film and the Pythons, other areas historically seen as a bastion of men began to change during the 1970s: the unions and the picket line. The workers at Grunwick who initially went on strike in 1976 were primarily Asian females, and were soon joined by sister members of the Communist Party Women's Group, assorted "stroppy feminists," and even Labour minister Shirley Williams showed up to have her picture taken with the strikers.[134] Pictures of the strike featured more female faces than previous strike actions—not women as spouses but women as workers—and especially women of color. One of those interviewed during the strike had this to say: "If you look 'round at this strike or if, you know, as the build-up to this big mass—mass day of support, I think you'd find that the number of women who have participated in it have been fantastically high."[135] The singing of songs of solidarity had been a mainstay of strikes for many years in Britain, and the Grunwick strike was no different, except that here female voices rang through.[136] One of the songs pointed up the female presence:

Hey Susie are you comin'? / With us in the van?
Bring the kids 'round our place, / They'll stay with my old man.
We're going to join our sisters / On the march to victory,
With union might and women's rights / In solidarity.[137]

The role husbands played might have been exaggerated, yes, but the Grunwick action will be discussed in more detail later.

MATTHIAS: "Ow. Lay off . . ."—A twentieth-century term, and leaning more American than British, according to the *OED*. The Official won't cancel the stoning because of one stoner who false starts, but, as in middle school, the troublemaker gets sent to the back.

During this they keep their voices as low as they can, in pitch but not in volume—These ladies are trying to keep from betraying their femaleness, though the chance that one will be outed seems unlikely. In the wider shots there are *only* females wearing beards in the stoning, no men (men will be seen in the close-ups). The child behind the Official might be male, but it's not certain. Brian is not part of the crowd, either.

OFFICIAL: "Who threw that stone? Come on!"—This is suddenly a school classroom setting, one that appears often in *Flying Circus*. In the very first episode an Italian class is being taught to Italian speakers, in Ep. 2 a Cambridge Don is beaten up, a handful of students put on a bad version of *Seven Brides for Seven Brothers* (Ep. 18), and the newer "plate-glass" universities (East Anglia, e.g.) are home to idiots and idioting degrees (Ep. 19). Here Cleese is the headmaster, as will be seen in full flower later in *Meaning of Life*.

Sensation!!!!! The WOMEN gasp—(PSC) At the mention of the name "Jehovah" again, the assembled crowd gasps as one. The printed script reflects this outrage by resorting to comic book expressions, multiple exclamation points, and a music hall (or even silent film) kind of printed verbiage. In the 1963 film *Tom Jones*, the opening sequence is structured like a silent film, complete with title cards. When the foundling is discovered in the Squire's bed, a card reads: *"Abandoned!!!"*[138] This is also one of those moments in a Python script written for the reader, and for the other Pythons. This has been a staple since *Flying Circus*, where the printed script spoke to other members of the troupe, as well as to the director and production designers at the BBC. In Ep. 12, a character bangs on his desk, then falls through a hole and into the earth. In the script as presented for production, it reads: *"He thumps on the desk and he falls through the floor. (Yes Mr Director you did read that right: he fell through the floor and added a fortune to the budget)."*[139] Here *Sensation!!!!!* is intended as a scene direction for a particular reaction, but one that might only be known to the other cast members, and only because they'd worked together and agreed on a language in their scripting. This is a tabloid headline; in fact the word "Sensation" followed by one or more exclamation points, has been used a number of times in the banner headline of the *Daily Mirror* over the years. The *Mirror* was competing with the *Sun* and *Daily Mail* for best-circulated tabloid in the later 1970s. Moments later, when Matthias begins dancing and singing "Jehovah, Jehovah" the script direction reads *Greater Sensation!!!!!*

OFFICIAL: "You're only making it worse for yourself"—Probably the only way an execution could be made worse is if it is designed to be prolonged. A stoning as laid out in the Jewish laws is quite specific, with steps that need to be followed to ensure a fairly swift death. As described above, the victim is pushed awkwardly from a fairly high and rocky point, landing on rocks; if still alive, a large rock is immediately used to finish the task. There are also OT versions where the entire populace pick up stones and conduct the execution for the good of the community, all under God's direction. As the Centurion will point out to Matthias later, crucifixion could take hours or longer, depending on the method of affixion.[140] Being burned alive sounds quite horrible, though it can't last terribly long, and wasn't attached to very many crimes, while strangulation and the sword were also possible.[141] If God is listening at this religious event, then Matthias might also suffer from reoffending God with his repetition, according to the apocryphal *Wisdom of Solomon* 1:6: "For wisdom is a kindly spirit and will not free a blasphemer from the guilt of his words; because God is witness of his inmost feelings, and a true observer of his heart, and a hearer of his tongue." He's "making it worse" as he dances and sings "Jehovah," then.

But the Official may also be referring to what the stonee can expect once he's ushered from this world, though this would betray the Pythons' Christian upbringing. "Jewish teachings on the subject of afterlife are sparse," the *Encyclopedia Judaica* notes. "The Torah, the most important Jewish text, has no clear reference to afterlife at all."[142] The noncanonical scriptures also offer hints along these lines, including the Wisdom of Solomon 3:9: "The godless will meet with the punishment their evil thoughts deserve, because they took no heed of justice and rebelled against the Lord." Perhaps the Official is certain that Matthias is one of these "godless." The rock ends up on the Official, anyway, postponing Matthias's adventure into the afterlife.

MATTHIAS: "How could it get any worse?"—For international terrorists serving life sentences for their crimes, there weren't many "get any worse" possibilities. In March 2017, however, the infamous Carlos—already serving two life sentences for bombings and kidnappings—was found guilty of murder and sentenced to yet another life sentence for his bombing of the Publicis pharmacy in Paris, September 1974.[143] Carlos was working on behalf of the Popular Front for the Liberation of Palestine (PFLP) at the time.

OFFICIAL: "If you say 'Jehovah' one more time" *(A stone hits him on the side of the head. He reacts.)*—This is a classic Python moment, where the tables are turned on the accuser or antagonist. In *Holy Grail*, it's the Bridgekeeper being flustered on the Bridge of Death—uncertain whether his question to Arthur hinges on the swallow's particular geographical heritage, "African or European"—and he is thrown in the chasm after the others.[144] Here the Official is also hoisted with his own petard, and the literality of the crowd, as he is stoned for the same utterance as Matthias.[145]

More up to date, on 23 June 1977 the aggressive strike action against Grunwick in Willesden was going well until someone in the crowd threw a bottle, hitting a policeman on the head. The stark, graphic image of PC Trevor Wilson lying in a pool of his own blood made the front page of newspapers across Britain; the image changed almost immediately the tenor of the strike, especially in the minds of the general public, who had either been sympathetic to the strikers, or had been ignoring the fracas entirely.[146] In Brian's world, though, not even the Roman guards can muster any real feeling or effort as the religious Official is pelted, then squashed entirely. The Romans won't interfere if Jews kill Jews; and likely the effects of the bottle incident would have been quite different if it were simply one of the strikers who'd taken the hit.

Matthias also cackles noticeably as the first stone comes to a rest, happy that the Official is in for the same punishment.

Five WOMEN carry a huge rock, run up and drop it on the OFFICIAL—(PSC) This looks silly and cartoony, and was likely meant to be seen as such, but it's actually not far from the prescribed ritual as found in the Tractate Sanhedrin. According to the Mishnah, the condemned was to be pushed by his thighs from a low cliff so that he would land face first on rocks below, but not so high that his body becomes "mangled."[147] If he survived the fall, he would be turned over, and one of the witnesses was to drop or place a large rock on his chest. In some versions the stone had to be so large that it required a minimum of two men to carry it. The stoning as carried out in the film is likely a more modern, less ritualized, more spontaneous version—as seen, for example, in *Jesus of Nazareth*—but the coup de grace rock is spot-on.[148] That, or the Pythons are referring to the Lord's OT description of how a stoning should be administered when the Children of Israel were in the wilderness, and who should administer it. In Leviticus 24:10–16, the son of an Egyptian and an Israelite blasphemed during a scuffle, he was brought before Moses, and Moses prayed for guidance. Soon, his prayer was answered:

13 And the LORD spake unto Moses, saying,

14 Bring forth him that hath cursed without the camp; and let all that heard *him* lay their hands upon his head, and let all the congregation stone him.

15 And thou shalt speak unto the children of Israel, saying, Whosoever curseth his God shall bear his sin.

16 And he that blasphemeth the name of the LORD, he shall surely be put to death, *and* all the congregation shall certainly stone him: as well the stranger, as he that is born in the land, when he blasphemeth the name *of the LORD*, shall be put to death.

Moses continues his lecture, reciting the "breach for breach, eye for eye, tooth for tooth" dictum, and then: "And Moses spake to the children of Israel, that they should bring forth him that had cursed out of the camp, and stone him with stones. And the children of Israel did as the LORD commanded Moses."[149] It's not clear just how the Egyptian-Israelitish man used the Lord's name in a blasphemous way, but it's also clear that it was more than just an utterance of the Lord's name—it was likely uttered as part of an oath or condemnation.

During the run of *Flying Circus*, these oversized, cartoony props appeared often. A sixteen-ton weight fell from nowhere to end a character and/or a scene, a helpfully labeled "anarchist's bomb" is handed to a character, a giant hand of God points out the guilty man who is then arrested[150]—visual absurdities that point up the cartooniness of the violence—as well as an oversized hammer that banged people on the head.[151] The rock brings this stoning scene to a close with another "thud," a scene that wouldn't have been nearly as funny if only smaller, more obviously realistic rocks had been used. In this age of acts of terror playing out on the nightly news, a comical hijacking can't end with dead hostages or a burning plane; it has to end with the hijackers absurdly commandeering a city bus to Cuba (*Flying Circus* Ep. 16), or a forgetful bomber asking for help in finding his bomb somewhere on the plane (Ep. 35), or a Chinese army trying to take over an English school prize-giving ceremony (Ep. 19). The ridiculousness takes the curse off the tender subject, much in the same way the Allies created derisive, ridiculing propaganda during the war, even as Hitler and the Nazis seemed poised to overrun most of Europe, and even Britain.[152]

This is also a classic "escalation" sketch structure, which the Pythons used often in *Flying Circus*. In this sketch type something starts small and then gets bigger, in this case rocks, from one rock hitting the intended target, to one hitting an unintended target, to many hitting another target, and then to the giant payoff rock squashing a man completely. The stoning begins properly, with Matthias being hit, then goes off the rails in quick order as the Official is stoned, then squashed. In the "Accidents Sketch" in Ep. 18 of *Flying Circus*, a man waiting to see someone starts a chain of accidents that get larger and larger, culminating in the house exploding into rubble.[153] The very serious and lethal act of stoning, which was still in practice when the film was being produced, is made less threatening by this ridiculous treatment, and the same approach will be used in treating both the Romans and Jews of this period.

Lastly—harking back to the discussion of empowered women thanks to the 1975 Sex Discrimination Act—the women here not only took advantage of a leveling element (the beards) to participate in what had been a males-only state-religious activity, they managed to save one of their fellow-sufferers, Matthias, and destroy the embodiment of their oppression, a Sanhedrin official. Two birds killed with that cartoony stone.

Everyone claps. The GUARDS sadly shake their heads—(PSC) Note that these guards— who don't seem sad but bored—don't attempt to intervene or break up the melee, as they eventually did earlier, at the Sermon dust-up. There are at least two reasons for this. First, as Elisabeth Vikman, quoting William V. Harris, points out, the Roman soldier had by this point become inured to violence, such that "Roman warfare was malignant":

> "Almost every year the legions went out and did massive violence to someone—and this regularity gives the phenomenon a pathological character. . . ." The otherwise abnormal behaviour adopted by soldiers surrounding battle must have been normalised, as war turns into everyday experience. Killed, violated and mutilated people must eventually become a regular feature for the soldiers. Harris claims that the Roman army had a particular taste for savage behaviour: "the regular harshness of Roman war-methods sprang from an unusually pronounced willingness to use violence against alien peoples." He believes Romans were worse in this respect than other, contemporary societies.[154]

Secondly, these Romans seem content to allow the Jews to kill each other, likely because this began as a sanctioned Sanhedrin execution. Roman soldiers as police forces had a fairly straightforward function, according to Aristides, writing of Flaccus's governorship in Alexandria, Egypt: "He instructed . . . the soldiers individually not to interfere in matters outside their military duties, but to remember that they had also been ordered to maintain the peace."[155] The large public gathering at the Sermon had the potential to devolve into a scrum—there were Jews and Samaritans in attendance—so the soldiers stepped in to separate combatants. They leave this Jewish-only religious melee alone completely. It might even be said that since a Jew was stoned to death, then this was a successful ritual, at least in the eyes of the Roman sentinels. George Bernard Shaw had voiced a similar conceit in regard to British military activity in Northern Ireland: "After all, what business is it of the British if we Irish want to slaughter each other?"[156] This would be revoiced many times and from both sides of the longstanding conflict in Northern Ireland in the 1960s and 1970s.

Josephus also relates an event toward the end of procurator Felix's rule in Jerusalem, where the high priests and the "principal men" of Jerusalem began some kind of disagreement. Gangs were formed on either side and the hurling of epithets and rocks followed. What surprised Josephus was the lack of institutional control displayed: "And there was nobody to reprove them; but these disorders were after a licentious manner in the city, as if it had no government over it."[157] Felix and his Roman garrison obviously did not step in and separate these rival factions,[158] allowing the high priests to cut off tithes and offerings from those lower priests who opposed them, leaving "the poorer sort of the priests" to die "for want."[159] Confident in their position and power, our Roman guards watch as the potential stonee, Matthias, escapes his punishment, and the Sanhedrin Official takes on the chest a cartoony rock like the dozens that fell on Wile E. Coyote. These soldiers seem completely confident that they themselves are untouchable, that the Roman system is in full control, and that any intervention on their part is unnecessary. Emperors including and since Caesar Augustus had set the parameters in place for the tolerance of things particularly Jewish in Judea, and even in Rome itself and throughout the empire. These soldiers are like the sentries at the gates of Swamp Castle in *Holy Grail* (*sans* nosegay garlands) as they watch guests filter into the wedding, unchallenged. Here, though, there does not seem to be even the slightest concern that these Roman soldiers are in any danger from any kind of Launcelot figure—phlegmatic, they watch their charges killing each other in a sanctioned (by Rome and the Sanhedrin) religious activity.

In one of the earlier drafts Mandy thanks a remaining Official for a lovely stoning before moving off after Brian and the others. In the finished film, neither she nor Brian are seen in any of the shots.

Notes

1. Larsen, *BAFHG*, 238–39.
2. *BAFHG*, 239.
3. Larsen, *MPFC: UC*, 2.188.
4. "Sniggering Does Nothing for the Cause of Equality," *Times*, 13 January 1976: 14.
5. "Sniggering," *Times*, 13 January 1976: 14.
6. Slang for heavy construction worker.
7. Waugh, *FCY*, 22 January 1976; italics added.
8. Ezekiel 8:14, 16; see the entirety of Ackerman's article, "Women in Ancient Israel and the Hebrew Bible," in the *Oxford Research Encyclopedia of Religion*.
9. Ackerman, "Women in Ancient Israel." Ackerman reminds us of a rather telling fact: "Indeed, over 90 percent of the 1400 or so individuals who are given names in the Hebrew Bible are men." Given the actual ratio of named men to women in the scriptures, the Pythons can be credited with making more robust the female presence in their version of first-century Jerusalem.
10. Ackerman, "Women in Ancient Israel," passim; also, King and Stager, *LBI*, 21–60.
11. Kotker, *HLTJ*, 40–41.
12. Discussed in more detail later, in "The PFJ Plan their Raid" scene.
13. 10 November 1958.
14. A searchable version of the Mishnah is available at the Jewish Virtual Library site, http://www.jewishvirtuallibrary.org/tractate-sanhedrin.
15. Maier, *Pontius Pilate*, 129.
16. Smallwood, *JURR*, 32n36. Smallwood summarizes the complicated, contentious issue, concluding that there were essentially two Sanhedrins, one more political, one more religious. It's no wonder the Pythons avoided the Sanhedrin entirely. See also *JURR*, 149–50.
17. See Zeitlin's very helpful delineations of the major sects of this period, the Sadducees, Pharisees, and Essenes, in "The Crucifixion of Jesus Re-Examined," 328–32. He characterizes the Pharisees as beholden to "the unwritten law," to tradition.
18. Josephus, *AJ*, 4.8.15 (Whiston, 97). The twelfth-century rabbi Maimonides also disqualifies nine others, those who "are not competent to affirm or testify," including "slaves, minors, lunatics, the deaf, the blind, the wicked, the contemptible, relatives, and the interested parties." ("Witness," *EJ*). Women cross-dressed as men might also make this list. See Zeitlin's "The Crucifixion of Jesus Re-Examined" for more on these divisions.
19. *AJ*, 4.8.15n (Whiston, 97).
20. See also the lengthy, cross-referenced entry for "witness" in *EJ* found at www.jewishvirtual library.org.
21. Josephus, *WJ*, 5.5.2 (Whiston, 554).
22. Only the Greek version was found. Smallwood discusses this warning in *JURR*, 92–94.
23. See the entry for "*cave ceiling rock*" in the notes on the opening titles.
24. Smallwood notes (following Josephus and Cicero) that Pompey did not loot the temple, which would have been replete with gold, expensive furniture, and tithes, and he allowed it to be re-sanctified the following day, so that regular Jewish rituals could continue (*JURR*, 23–27). Pompey understood that allowing the Jews their practices simply made his job easier. Later, Titus would allow his men to sack the temple and the city (*HLTJ*, 128–29).

25. *HLTJ*, 50.

26. See Kotker, *HLTJ*, chapters two and three.

27. This potential leeway may have been where some congregations or cities forbade female participation in events like stonings, and others might have tolerated their presence.

28. Wheen, *Strange Days*, 148.

29. The final requirement is one the PFJ don't mention at all: having a ready substitute leader for the overthrown country (Wheen, *Strange Days*, 145). Reg never promises any version of post-coup leadership.

30. Demaris, *Brothers in Blood*, 383.

31. *SD*, 147–50. Donoughue mentions the reading/viewing of Forsyth's very influential *The Day of the Jackal* and *The Odessa File* in *DSD*. International terrorism and espionage were clearly both fascinating subjects and much in the public view in the 1970s.

32. *Strange Days*, 148.

33. Caryl, *Strange Rebels*, 5.

34. Quoted in *BAFHG*, 341.

35. "Strange Political Landscape," *Times*, 31 March 1966: 8.

36. The RA was a short-lived offshoot of the Campaign for Nuclear Disarmament (CND) movement, and the Independent Nuclear Disarmament Election Committee (INDEC). All these parties/movements/splinters were tagged with real and imagined Communist influences, diminishing their candidates' electability. Mr. Gott was just twenty-seven at this time, confirming his dangerous status. See "Added Hazard for Labour," *Telegraph*, 5 January 1966: 34.

37. 19 January 1966: 24.

38. Trade union reaction to the restrictive bill would eventually lead Heath to call an early election, a loss to Wilson and Labour in 1974.

39. "The Revolutionaries," *Times*, 16 February 1971: 12.

40. In *Holy Grail* Arthur "must be a king" because of his appearance, and the witch was certainly a witch because "she looks like one"; in the Python world, appearance matters.

41. *DSD*, 2.438.

42. *DSD*, 1.121.

43. *DSD*, 1.634.

44. This was the celebrated "back to basics" education speech intended by Callaghan to claw back control of the schools and curricula from "progressive," "trendy," Far Left elitists. See *DSD*, 2.82–84, and Sandbrook's *Seasons in the Sun*, 684–88.

45. *DSD*, 2.84. This may also be a sideways, sanctimonious slap at the students attending Ruskin, a school affiliated with Oxford but not actually part of it. Ruskin was set up to educate mature students who couldn't achieve the necessary qualifications for Oxford or Cambridge.

46. This facial hair admonition is traced to Leviticus 19:27 and 21:1–5.

47. "Beards and Shaving," *EJ*, 235.

48. Harry the "spiv" will be discussed again, when he haggles with Brian for a beard and a gourd.

49. Uttered by the wily Frenchman Moriarty (Milligan) in *Goon Show* episode "The Man Who Won the War" (18 September 1955).

50. Kenneth Morgan, "Symbiosis: Trade and the British Empire"; see also Brendon's *DFBE*, passim.

51. Holland L. Hendrix, from the *Frontline* PBS program *Jews and the Roman Empire* (1998), a.t.

52. One of Pilate's soldiers and Pilate himself will later mention Passover; no one else in the world of the film, even the observant Jews, mention it at all. This must have been a late addition, as well—none of the earlier drafts include references to the holiday.

53. Stiff fines and prison sentences were handed out to those who would buy truckloads of eggs directly from farmers for resale, or to families who received extra ration books by mistake and used them anyway, or kept using a ration book after the death of its owner, and on.

54. Garfield, *Private Battles*, 247, 333.

55. See *WW2 People's War*, "Dunstable Town Centre," a BBC website.

56. *MPFC: UC*, 1.52.

57. Found in Eps. 5, 14, and 28, respectively.

58. *BAFHG*, 94–160. Dennis's mother didn't even know they "had a king" (*BAFHG*, 116).

59. Also, for most Jews the Roman occupiers might have been more supernumerary, meaning their direct rulers were the priestly Jews (Sanhedrin).

60. "Character of the Postwar Period," a.t.

61. *FCY*, 18 December 1976.

62. A demographic classification created by the National Readership Survey (NRS) identifying the "skilled working class" in Britain, the voters Thatcher identified as wanting to move into the middle class, and whom she said she represented. See Bogdanor, "Thatcherism," a.t.

63. Jeremias, *JTJ*, 31, 59.

64. Aside from Gregory and his wife, and perhaps the religious officiator at the stoning, the Pythons don't present us with characters who can be called members of the "priesthood and secular aristocracy," those who would most benefit from "the taxes and tithes flowing into the expanding temple city of Jerusalem," quoting Silberman and Meyers ("The Politics of First-Century Judea," 39). For the most part, we keep on a level with the working classes. Privilege won't keep Gregory and his wife from the cross, or the religious official from death by incidental stoning (this is a Python world, after all).

65. Magness, *Stone and Dung*, 11.

66. *JTJ*, 303–4.

67. *JTJ*, 303.

68. *HLTJ*, 31.

69. Maier, *Pontius Pilate*, 159. Livy mentions the sacred chickens, as well, used earlier in preparations for battles against the Samnites (Book X).

70. *MPFC: UC*, 1.151, 228.

71. Sugarman, "Melville in Jerusalem" (from *Clarel*, 1876).

72. Sugarman, "Melville in Jerusalem."

73. *JTJ*, 15; also, from *WJ*, 5.4 (Whiston, 553–54).

74. *JTJ*, 15–16.

75. Gilliam was pushing for the stoning scene to be filmed on Saturday, 16 September, the first day of filming, knowing the stones would have to be prepared by Thursday at the latest. Cleese had been unwilling to shoot such an important scene on day one (*Diaries*, 486–88).

76. *MPFC: UC*, 1.191–92; *ATW*, 1.154–55.

77. He enjoyed games more than administration, his appearances at the combats cost the city a great deal of money, and his opponents were often said to be more weedy than the Samaritan we'll see later. See chapter 2 in Toner's *The Day Commodus Killed a Rhino* (2014).

78. "McAlinden Stopped by the Quiet American," *Times*, 14 March 1972: 11.

79. The *Telegraph* ran a story in 1961 that pointed out how effectively the Liberal Party contested local council seats, winning a much higher percentage in relation to their national positions than larger parties. The story was headlined "Local Boy Makes Good" (7 January 1961: 6).

80. John 8:1–11.

81. Plus one constructed for the *Jesus of Nazareth* film, and then left in place.

82. *Monty Python's Life of Brian (of Nazareth)*, 11.

83. "The Crucifixion of Jesus Re-Examined," *JQR*, pages 327–69.

84. *JE*, "Sanhedrin."

85. "Crucifixion of Jesus Re-Examined," 317–18.

86. Rosenblatt, "The Crucifixion of Jesus from the Standpoint of Pharisaic Law," 318.

87. *JURR*, 99.

88. Richard, *WWAR*, 252.

89. Found at http://www.jewfaq.org.

90. "Pronouncing the Name of God"; these are (translated) versions of "God be with you" and "God bless you" (jewfaq.org).

91. Bauckham, "For What Offence was James Put to Death?," 219.

92. If they'd stayed with the original title and concept, *Jesus Christ: Lust for Glory*—a nod to the movie title *Patton: Lust for Glory*, the title of *Patton* (1970) when it was distributed in the UK (the film aired on ITV on 31 December 1976)—there might have been a different reception.

93. Including the novel *The Last Temptation of Christ*, the plays/films *Godspell* and *Jesus Christ Superstar*, the announced Danish film *The Sex Life of Jesus Christ*, and the poem *The Love That Dares to Speak Its Name*.

94. This will become even more pronounced in the later *Spamalot* musical, where the euphemism for such unquestioned freedoms is "Find Your Grail."

95. From Zeitlin (1941): "According to the Gospels, Jesus was arrested and brought before the Sanhedrin and the High Priest, charged with blasphemy, while the Sanhedrin, in presenting the case to Pilate, maintained that Jesus was a rebel against the State" ("Crucifixion of Jesus Re-Examined," 359).

96. Jesus was a target for stoning, as well, but he evaded angry mobs just weeks before his eventual arrest and crucifixion (John 8:56–59; 10:27–36).

97. "Danish Grant for Film on Christ," *Times*, 29 May 1975: 5. In January 1976 the Danish attorney general announced that he would not seek a blasphemy charge against Thorsen ("Script on Sex Life of Christ 'Not Blasphemy,'" *Times*, 3 January 1976: 3).

98. These wouldn't have been terribly unusual, given recent New Wave films from Ken Russell, Pier Paolo Pasolini, and Jean-Luc Godard, among others. The presence of Christ would have been the cruncher (see *BAFHG*, xi–xxx). Pasolini's final film, *Salo*, appeared in London in July 1977 and was confiscated by police at the Compton Cinema Club; obscenity charges brought against the private Soho club were later dropped.

99. "Mrs Whitehouse Delivers 'Obscene' Danish Script of Jesus Film to Mr Rees," *Times*, 5 October 1976: 1. Note that this was front-page news.

100. See "Proposed Film about the Sex Life of Jesus Christ," *Times*, 4 September 1976: 13. The Pythons seem to have, in creating *Brian*, responded to what contemporary critic (and no fan of Thorsen) Bernard Levin called the "thuggish intolerance of some of the Christians involved in the argument, together with the pre-judging element in their attitude" toward a film they'd not seen ("Fight the Good Fight by all Means," *Times*, 7 September 1976: 12).

101. See Nash's *Blasphemy in the Christian World*, 182. The Pythons were writing together in both December 1976 and March 1977 on *Brian* ideas. Palin doesn't mention the Thorsen film or accompanying controversy anywhere in his diaries.

102. Waugh wrote that he had been considering *The Sexual Life of Jesus Christ* [sic] in a planned series, but decided against it when he'd concluded "such a film would require a cast of only one and might get us into trouble with Equity." He continued: "Instead, we are working on the sexual lives of Karl Marx, Mahatma Gandhi, Queen Victoria, Sir Harold Wilson, Lord Goodman, Arianna Stassinopolous, and many hundreds of others" (*Private Eye*, 29 October 1976: 15). The film that never was truly had legs in the British media.

103. The sentences were eventually overturned, but not until those imprisoned had their hair cut and spent time in Her Majesty's prison system. See *MPFC: UC* 2.124–25, 126.

104. "Blasphemy Charge over Poem about Christ," 5 July 1977: 2.

105. "Blasphemy Charge," 2.

106. Palin reports that the Pythons donated £500 to *Gay News* in April 1976 to help fight the case (*Diaries 1969–1979*, 376n). For a contemporary account of Whitehouse and her movement in the wake of the *Gay News* ruling, see Caroline Moorehead's article "Mrs. Mary Whitehouse: A Certainty That Everything Is Either Black or White," *Times*, 31 October 1977: 8.

107. *Holy Grail* had gone out with an "A" rating, meaning all audiences five and older could attend; an "AA" stipulated that audiences had to be fourteen and older. Palin makes it clear that as they shot and edited *Brian* the Pythons agreed they shouldn't bend to censorial demands: "We discuss our attitude to censorship, on which there is total agreement within the group that we do not and will not change anything because we're told to, unless we happen to agree that it isn't funny anyway. We're all happy to go to court in defence of the movie" (Palin, *Diaries 1969–1979*, 556).

108. Palin's note: "Scarman upheld the ruling under the Blasphemy Act of 1697 that the *Gay News* had offended by claiming that Christ was homosexual" (547). Justice King-Hamilton had made the initial ruling against *Gay News* in 1977, discussed later in the "In Pilate's Jail" scene.

109. Maier, *Pontius Pilate*, 213; this is a work of historical fiction, though quite well-researched. It is useful here in that, like Mannix's gladiator fiction *Those about to Die*, it was a popular and oft-cited text focusing on portions and practices of the Roman Empire at the time the Pythons were creating their own work of "historical fiction," *Life of Brian*.

110. See Acts 7. The scriptures tell us that Saul (he would become Paul) was a willing witness to this stoning.

111. *AJ*, 20.5.4 (Whiston, 419). See also *Jesus and the Zealots* (106–7) for events tied to Cumanus's volatile procuratorship.

112. Smallwood, *JURR*, 265.

113. Many passionate voices responding to *Life of Brian* invoked the term, though it was also often pointed out that this was a religious charge, and not a crime punishable in civic courts. (See Hewison's *The Case Against*.) The Jews of first-century Judea weren't interested in the hair-splitting, and demanded the Roman soldier's life for his crimes.

114. The Roman authorities wouldn't have involved themselves unless someone had "blasphemed" the official cult, perhaps defacing Roman iconic badges or displays. These distinctions came into play when the Sanhedrin demanded Christ's death, and Roman authorities (Pilate and even Herod Antipas) argued against capital punishment—favoring corporal punishment—for a religious offense.

115. Levy, *Blasphemy*, 3.

116. Again, this would be separate and distinct from crimes against the Roman occupiers, which Brian will be charged with; Matthias is charged with crimes against God and the Jewish State.

117. "Crucifixion of Jesus Re-Examined," 330.

118. Smallwood, "Jews and Romans in the Early Empire," 233.

119. Zeitlin, "Crucifixion of Jesus Re-Examined," 344.

120. See Zeitlin, "Crucifixion of Jesus Re-Examined," 344–46 for more.

121. Mentioned in the "God's Name" section of *Judaism 101*, and there spelled "Adonai." See the *OED* entry under "Jehovah" for more.

122. Deuteronomy 17:6.

123. *AJ*, 4.8.15 (Whiston, 97).

124. *ATW*, 1.23.316.

125. *ATW*, 1.17.232.

126. *MPFC: UC*, 1.188; *The Goon Show*, "Silent Bugler," 23 February 1958.

127. See the printed/read aloud version of the original script available as a special feature on DVD and Blu-ray editions of the film.

128. Palin, *Diaries 1969–1979*, 488. By the point of a February 1979 screening of the film, the Shepherds scene and most of the raid on Pilate's palace had been removed, Palin mentions, and the film plays better for the absence (531).

129. See *BAFHG*, 421–23 and additional index entries under "King Brian the Wild."

130. Edersheim, *Sketches of Jewish Social Life*, 222.

131. Matthew 26:33–35; Mark 14:29–31; Luke 22:33–34; and John 13:36–38.

132. Anthony Quinn performs the service in the recent *Jesus of Nazareth*.

133. Larsen, *MPSERD*, 180–81.

134. Sandbrook, *Seasons in the Sun*, 607–8; also Benn's *Conflicts of Interest*, 172–74. Palin's *Diaries* ignores the strike entirely, while Donoughue's *DSD* mentions it only in passing.

135. *Look Back at Grunwick* (1980), a.t.

136. This strike was also unusual in that it was covered so closely by news outlets. With hundreds of hours of footage shot and thousands of still images captured over many months, it is likely the most fully documented strike action in British labor history.

137. *Look Back at Grunwick*, a.t.

138. Directed by Tony Richardson and starring Albert Finney.

139. *MPFC: UC*, 1.186; *ATW*, 1.12.160.

140. Yeshua in *The Passover Plot* counted on this delay, planning for his rescue from the cross.

141. "Capital Punishment," in the *EJ* at the Jewish Virtual Library http://www.jewishvirtuallibrary .org/capital-punishment In Roman prisons, strangulation tended to be the favored method.

142. See "Jewish Concepts: Afterlife," Jewish Virtual Library, http://www.jewishvirtuallibrary.org/ afterlife-in-judaism.

143. Indiscriminate bombings of public, "bourgeoisie" places was a hallmark of nineteenth-century anarchist movements across Europe (see Burleigh, *BRT*).

144. See *BAFHG*, 472.

145. Though it's not shown or mentioned in the finished film, Matthias escapes his death sentence in the confusion of the Official's stoning, just like Brian will later escape Pilate's court; Matthias will reappear later, with the PFJ.

146. Sandbrook, *Seasons in the Sun*, 611–12. Donoughue mentions in passing that the PM's "irritated" and "grumpy" mood at Question Time on 30 June 1977 was due to the ongoing, ugly strike at Grunwick (*DSD*, 2.208).

147. *Sanhedrin* chapter 6, Mishnah 4; see the searchable JVL site. These ritual executions would have been a real challenge since the body had to be preserved in its sanctity, even in death.

148. Stonings for adultery in Saudi Arabia and for heresy in Afghanistan were still regularly occurring in the 1960s–1970s, and often made international news. British forces were also regularly pelted with stones in Northern Ireland postings.

149. Leviticus 24:23.

150. For the sixteen-ton weight, see Eps. 4, 12, 23, and 38; for the anarchist bomb see Ep. 8; for the hand of God see Ep. 29 and *Meaning of Life*; and for the giant hammer see Eps. 17, 30, and 35.

151. *MPFC: UC*, 1.270–71.

152. Hollywood produced many cartoons lampooning Hitler—comparing his face to a horse's hindquarters, chasing him into hell—while the British MOI created a "Doing the Lambeth Walk" spoof that caricatured the goose-stepping Nazis. See *BAFHG*, 517; also, the *MPFC: UC* index for the entries under "scorn/ridicule/derision" and "cartoons" for more.

153. *MPFC: UC*, 1.279.

154. "Ancient Origins: Sexual Violence," 29.

155. Davies, "Police Work in Roman Times," 700.

156. Demaris, *Brothers in Blood*, 299.

157. *AJ*, 20.8.8 (Whiston, 422); see also *JURR*, 280–81.

158. "The Roman authorities, for some unexplained reason, did not intervene" (Brandon, *Jesus and the Zealots*, 113–14).

159. *AJ*, 20.8.8 (Whiston, 422).

SCENE FIVE
ALMS FOR AN EX-LEPER

JERUSALEM, outside the city gate—(PSC) This setting—outer walls of Ribat, Monastir—might have been recognizable to those who had watched the recent *Jesus of Nazareth*. That film version staged the crucifixion at this precise location, and with the same iconic city wall backdrop.

. . . enormous statue of PILATE is being dragged . . .—(PSC) This work seems to be modeled after a combination of two statues, Michelangelo's *David* and a bronze statue of Julius Caesar in Rimini, Italy. The head and face are fashioned to look like Palin as Pilate. Auberon Waugh presaged this move in his "Diary" entry for 17 February 1978: "Perhaps it would be a good idea for public statues to be made with disposable heads that can be changed with every change of popular fashion. The same bodies could be used for Churchill, Wislon, Grocer, or whoever was the hero of the moment."[1] In a way this is also the approach used when the Arch of Constantine (seen during the title sequence) was created between 312 and 315. Portions of the new arch came from previous structures built during the Trajan, Hadrian, and Marcus Aurelius administrations, making it much more like a Gilliamesque bit of animation.[2]

Gilliam has already used an image of the David statue in *Flying Circus*, there as part of a title card for *It's the Arts* in Ep. 6.[3] Gilliam has also included an image of an Augustus statue in the title sequence for *Brian*.

Later in the printed script there is a suggestion from Reg that a priapic version of a Julius Caesar should be commissioned; this was a Peoples' Front of Judea (PFJ) demand that could be sacrificed in negotiations with Pilate.

Pilate learned through hard experience that the Roman penchant for displayed cult statues, emblems, and images wouldn't be tolerated in Jerusalem, the city of the temple. Commissioning statues of one's self did occur across the empire, and at many levels, as Wiedemann points out: "A *duumvir* from Cirta in Numidia thought of a cheap way of immortalizing his *munus* [public works, games]: he raised a statue to himself out of the revenue from entrance fees."[4] The new Pilate statue is likely associated with the ongoing modifications to Pilate's palace seen later. Being a prefect, Pilate would have been living in quarters built by Herod and occupied by other prefects before him, so some remodeling is understandable.[5] Notoriously, Caligula would later demand that a statue of himself as Jupiter be erected *within* the Holy of Holies in the temple in Jerusalem, according to Philo.[6] Cooler heads prevailed, putting off Caligula's rash move, and the emperor would die before seeing this sacrilegious renovation to completion.[7]

This is likely a reference to an incident related by Josephus in his *Antiquities of the Jews*, when the newly appointed Pilate "introduced Caesar's effigies" into Jerusalem from Caesarea. Josephus notes that previous procurators (or prefects) had entered the city with such effigies removed from ensigns and the like, in deference to the Jews' law forbidding "the very making of [such] images."[8] The images were part of the standards carried before the troops newly stationed in Judea, at Pilate's command, and what likely inflamed the situation was that the standards could be glimpsed from the temple.[9] There was a great tumult that followed Pilate's thoughtlessness (or guile), with Jews coming "in multitudes" to Caesarea to ask Pilate to remove the images; Pilate refused, claiming it would be an "injury" to Caesar. The multitude of voices against the images continued to crescendo, and Pilate quietly directed his armies to equip themselves and lie in wait. Surrounded by these heavily armed men Pilate sat in his judgment-seat and threatened to kill every protestor who would not leave Caesarea. Their collective response surprised him:

> But they threw themselves upon the ground, and laid their necks bare, and said they would take their death very willingly, rather than the wisdom of their laws should be transgressed; upon which Pilate was deeply affected with their firm resolution to keep their laws inviolable, and presently commanded the images to be carried back from Jerusalem to Caesarea.[10]

In the Pythons' version of this scenario, the statue is only noticed by Brian, and his mother is certain that's only because the statue is naked and Brian is consumed by thoughts of sex. No one else seems to really notice at all, nor will they notice the corpses nailed to crosses in this same area. As for the Pythons' Jews' willingness to die for a cause (or for God), Matthias seems ambivalent about a painful death, and Otto's crack suicide squad kill themselves for nothing in particular. Everyone else in the film possesses (and enacts) a sense of self-preservation, as will be seen.

A comical version of this historical scene will be enacted toward the end of the film, when Pilate attempts to gain favor with the "people of Jewusalem" and "welease" prisoners from Roman jails as a Passover gift. There, the crowd will also be on the ground, but laughing at the speech impediments of both Pilate and his "gweat fwiend fwom Wome," Biggus Dickus.

Near us are some old crosses with one or two twisted skeletons hanging on them—As recently as 71 BC, after the escaped slave Spartacus had been killed in battle, the Romans crucified six thousand rebel slaves along the Appian Way, Rome's major highway, as a warning to the rest of the enslaved masses that insurrection was a fatal mistake. The British Empire had committed similar atrocities and for similar reasons in India, where Col. James O'Neill executed six thousand Indians during the "Great Mutiny," and another Englishman wrote of his desire to see India transformed into "groves of gibbets" as a lesson to mutineers.[11]

Jewish historian Josephus writes at some length of the Romans' proclivity toward public punishments: "Now it happened at this fight that a certain Jew was taken alive, who, by Titus's order, was crucified before the wall, to see whether the rest of them would be affrighted, and abate of their obstinacy."[12] The detail Josephus relates betrays his clear fascination (and, Ben-like, even admiration) for Roman order, justice, and even mercy and fair-handedness:

> Some of these were indeed fighting men, who were not contented with what they got by rapine; but the greater part of them were poor people, who were deterred from deserting by the concern they were under for their own relations; for they could not hope to escape away, together with their wives and children . . . nor could they think of leaving these relations to be slain by the robbers on their account; nay, the severity of the famine made them bold in thus going out. . . . This

miserable procedure made Titus greatly to pity them, while they caught every day five hundred Jews; nay, some days they caught more: yet it did not appear to be safe for him to let those that were taken by force go their way, and to set a guard over so many he saw would be to make such as guarded them useless to him. The main reason why he did not forbid that cruelty was this, that he hoped the Jews might perhaps yield at that sight, out of fear lest they might themselves afterwards be liable to the same cruel treatment. So the soldiers, out of the wrath and hatred they bore the Jews, nailed those they caught, one after one way, and another after another, to the crosses, by way of jest, when their multitude was so great, that room was wanting for the crosses, and crosses wanting for the bodies.[13]

Public executions happened, and often, but the leaving of the corpses on their crosses to rot and feed scavengers might have been more challenging in such close proximity to the Holy City and the temple. Those Jews subject to capital punishment could be publicly burned, stoned, beheaded, strangled, or crucified, but then their corpses would have to be dealt with immediately: "Even [after public execution] their lifeless bodies were not permitted to remain exposed overnight, because, as it is stated in the Pentateuch, '(the sight of) a hanged man is an insult to God.'"[14] It may be that *outside* the walls of the city there was more leeway, though when the self-proclaimed messiah Theudas was captured and beheaded by the Romans some twenty years after the time of Christ, according to Rosenblatt, "his cut-off head was displayed in Jerusalem as an example to other would-be rebels."[15] It may have been that the high priests picked their fights with the Romans carefully, protecting the sanctity of the temple while looking away from lesser offenses. Given the Roman emperors' historical acknowledgment of the special case of Jews and their beliefs, even after subjugation by the Romans, the chances that a procurator or prefect would agitate his Jewish population unnecessarily are slim (though Pilate seems the exception here).

From film to film, the Pythons are interested in quite similar set pieces—social and/or communal violence, governmental oppression, and small-group dynamics, as well as piercing, slicing, and segmenting the human body, and earnest journeys brought to dispiriting conclusion. These crucified remains (even though they are being ignored) are window dressing, not unlike the Catherine Wheel and draped skeleton deployed in *Holy Grail* to help set the tone of a violent, barbaric medieval world.[16] Later, as Brian is about to be nailed up, one of these bodies will be in the process of removal, perhaps "thrown into a nearby charnel pit," as well. And as "normal" as this might seem to be—skeletal remains had been part of Disneyland's Pirates of the Caribbean ride since it opened in 1967, and have been found on film sets, in carnival "haunted" rides and freak shows for decades—it was only in 1968 that archaeological *proof* of crucifixion was discovered. There had of course been talk of crucifixion in the classical writers' works, in canonical scriptures and apocryphal texts, and in modern literature and eventually movies. Most of the major feature films about the events of the Passion at least hint at the crucifixion, and later films, like *Ben-Hur*, *King of Kings*, and the particularly gruesome *The Passover Plot* and *Jesus of Nazareth*, all feature extended crucifixion scenes.[17] But these were all inspired by literature, and not hard evidence:

> The accidental discovery in 1968 of a burial cave at Giv'at ha-Mivtar, in which the remains of a male crucified during the Roman period were found, has over the years generated considerable scholarly interest. Despite ample literary evidence attesting to the frequency of crucifixion in the Mediterranean region, this was the first direct anthropological evidence of the practice. The original report on the skeletal remains therefore aroused wide public interest and prompted a number of articles by scholars in Israel and abroad.[18]

Three years later, when the scholarly papers began to emerge, British newspapers carried stories about this significant find, as did many newspapers around the world.[19]

This is a common sight—no one pays any attention . . .—(PSC) This could simply be a Pythonesque trope, of course. Theirs is a world where a de-limbed knight can deny his deficit, where characters can live and function with impalements and dismemberments, and where the most obvious atrocities and absurd outrages can pass with just a glance. In Ep. 19 of *Flying Circus*, for example, a school awards ceremony is interrupted by a common thief and Chinese Communists, before descending into a pitched gun battle; all the while, the members of the governing board smile vacantly.[20]

In Roman times, heavily traveled roads were often used as sites of crucifixion, avowedly "for deterrent purposes," according to Cook: "The Spartacus revolt is a famous example. . . . [Six thousand] of the vanquished slaves were crucified on the road from Capua to Rome by Crassus."[21] Almost 136 years later the Judean procurator Florus tried to put down a budding rebellion in Jerusalem by rounding up rebels and others, executing three thousand six hundred, "many by crucifixion."[22] (This rebellion led to the fall of Jerusalem to rebel forces, and initiated Rome's destruction of the city four years later.) The Pythons included this kind of "punishment on display" in *Holy Grail*, as the *visibility* of the fruits of justice were key: "The high visibility afforded these public sorts of punishments served a social purpose in the Middle Ages, according to [Barbara] Tuchman. . . . 'In everyday life passersby saw corpses hanging on the gibbet and decapitated heads and quartered bodies impaled on stakes on the city walls.'"[23]

There are many instances in the Python oeuvre where "no one pays any attention," no matter how odd or violent the visible act might be.

BRIAN: "Have I got a big nose, Mum?"—Mandy will interpret this as Brian wondering about girls and sex, but it also goes right back to the "big nose" jibes being thrown around in the previous scene. Perhaps it's easier for her to answer questions about her son's budding sexuality than his parentage, which will be discovered in the following scene. For some reason, Mandy is still wearing her beard, even though she's no longer participating in a male-only public act, and there are other females out in public who do not have their faces covered. This reddish fake beard also looks very much like the disguise that Woody Allen's character dons in the 1967 farce *Bananas*, as they attempt to liberate lunch from a local café.

BRIAN: "I'm only just starting to get interested in it, Mum"—If there were those who could only see side-by-side comparisons between Brian and Jesus, this is a moment of divergence. It's likely not an accident that at the point the Christ is about his Father's work, Brian is just getting interested in the birds and bees. Later, he won't "really want to" leave the beguiling Judith alone, sexually, just before he is arrested and taken before Pilate.

(draft) **MANDY: "It's time you got interested in a job, my lad!"**—In the film, *none* of the PFJ seems to have a job—*except* initiate Brian—none seems to be suffering overly, and none seems particularly worried about the plight of their fellow working men. Perhaps they've managed to achieve a level of "wantlessness," citing Magness. Are these few we meet the typical "lower-class Jews who populate the Gospel accounts"? Are they "villagers who own houses and have a few possessions but are not destitute like the leper who begs Jesus to heal him"?[24] No, not really. These are city dwellers with political agendas and leisure time, situating them closer to the 1970s than 33.

They *could* be a version of Nechaev and Bakunin's "doomed man" revolutionary, the man who "has no personal interests, no business affairs, no emotions, no attachments, no property, and no name."[25] Not likely. The members of the PFJ are situated somewhere between the working class and the city's leadership. Perhaps the most apt comparison of this little clique is to the Works Committee in the seminal *I'm All Right Jack*, a film the Pythons homage throughout *Brian*. The stewards march from meeting to meeting, from stoppage to stoppage, from pronouncement to pronouncement, doing little actual labor. And the "brothers" they represent spend much more time on the picket line than the assembly line; there's no such thing as redundancy in this labor-friendly world. This isn't one of the Pythons' anachronisms, though. Jeremias talks at some length about just this type of "idler" in first-century Jerusalem, describing them in very familiar terms:

> However there are others besides beggars that we must mention as support for the impression that Jerusalem had already in Jesus' time become a city of idlers, and that the considerable proletariat living on the religious importance of the city was one of its most outstanding peculiarities. It was said that it was of the essence of a city that it was a place where "ten idle men" were to be found . . . i.e. people who had renounced ordinary employment to devote themselves to worship. There were men like this in Jerusalem too.[26]

Chief Steward Kite and friends are living on the "organized labour importance" of their city, and they've given up "ordinary employment" for union leadership; the PFJ are somehow living off the "political importance" of their occupied city, having given up employment for insurrectionary organizing, the latter without obvious means of support. Jeremias goes on, telling us what these idle men of Jerusalem got up to in the second half of the first century:

> It is amazing how many people of this kind emerged in the last decade before the destruction of Jerusalem; they formed themselves into gangs and terrorized the whole city . . . and later carried on the civil war within its walls. These revolutionaries of course included ardent patriots and men full of religious feeling, but others were simply men whom Josephus rightly describes as a rabble of slaves and the dregs of the population.[27]

Like the shop stewards of *I'm All Right Jack*, the PFJ are more homogenous than those who would become Zealots, but no less idle.

Employment and family benefits were front and center in the British mind across the postwar period. Into the mid-1970s the policy of "family allowances" (eventually called the "child benefit") had only been paid to families *after* the first child, meaning a Mandy-and-Brian-like family wouldn't have qualified; by 1977, all children qualified for child benefits. Unemployment insurance was improved and expanded during this same period, "earnings-related supplements" were implemented and increased, and old-age pensioners (like Mandy?) were, by 1975, included in these improvements. A single-parent benefit was also added during this expansion of benefits, with support from both Labour and Conservative parties.[28]

Employment was another matter, given the recent worrying uptick in the ranks of the unemployed. There were almost 1.5 million unemployed in 1977, having sailed passed the greatly feared one million mark in 1975–1976. By the first third of the next decade (when *Meaning of Life* was produced) employment would be three times as high, as Thatcherism allowed the economy to adjust itself, full employment no longer being a high-water mark. (And unemployment obviously not the poison pill party leaders had feared it would be—Thatcher and the Tories would remain in power until 1997.)[29]

And if Brian doesn't have a job at his age, the question might be, why not? The answer is that the world had changed dramatically in just the Pythons' lifetimes, and jobs in the mills, the mines, in heavy industry, or in the trades weren't as available or as attractive as they had once been. More young people went to university, fewer went to work on the factory floors, and a newer, more diverse society was partly to blame. As part of Harold Wilson's first administration, Home Secretary Roy Jenkins set out to "modernise" Britain, nearly top to bottom.[30] Since the late 1950s Jenkins had been arguing that Britain needed to come into the "progressive" age in regard to its views on abortion, homosexuality, divorce, crime, capital punishment, and censorship.[31] In *Holy Grail*, the mythical, Middle Ages Arthur is consistently flummoxed by the world he's encountering—it's not the world of the divine right of kingship, courtesy, or myth, or even knowing your place:

> The Britain Arthur might represent here (across the ages), the "older Britain with its military traditions, its thousands of slow industrial and village backwaters, its racism, its clear divisions of class and geography," was being nosed out ([Marr], 265). And far from being the "anarcho-socialist paradise" many in the 1960s hoped for, the new Britain was one that might seem alien to both Left and Right, to the old order or the new. [. . .] Jenkins's Britain was a place where the "State's powers over individual freedoms" were dramatically reduced, and termed "social reform" (251–52). The laundry list of reforms is especially compelling when it's remembered how quickly the changes were implemented, and how far-reaching their effects would be. State executions (by hanging), judicial flogging, the persecution and prosecution of homosexuals, the censoring of plays, the forbidding of abortions, and repressive divorce and immigration laws were all tinkered with or thrown out entirely, and all between 1965 and 1968 (Marr, 251–56).[32]

The generation coming of age during or born just after this period would have necessarily been affected by this abrupt sea change. The Pythons, for example, became entertainers as opposed to entering the traditional workforce, distinctly separating themselves from their parents' generation.[33] By the mid-1970s the punk culture screeched into life in decaying urban areas where there were few job prospects, if jobs were wanted at all. Hardest hit were the "Third World" areas of the UK: Northern Ireland, Scotland, and northern England.[34] In January 1976, the government announced it had spent a staggering £340 million in unemployment benefits in 1975, not counting December.[35] The poverty rate in Great Britain rose from about 11 percent in 1977 to more than 13 percent in 1979, meaning the numbers of those on the dole—"scrounging," like the lepers and even the birds in *Brian*—increased dramatically.

The following scene features another job-related character and incident.[36] The Ex-leper who, by virtue of being healed by Jesus, loses his ability to pursue his occupation as an effective beggar, manages to only wrangle "half a denary" from Brian. In the scene following "Ex-leper," Brian actually does have a job, selling snacks at the Colosseum. There's no indication how long he's been employed. This setup scene (where Mandy encourages Brian to find a job) may have been cut simply because it didn't jibe with the following "full employment" scene, where Brian is clearly working. The Angry Young Men tended to have jobs they didn't like, too—Joe Lampton works in a low-level municipal office, Arthur Seaton is a factory machinist, and Frank Machin is down at the coal face—their sights were always set higher, though none were able to reach what they thought was the goal without sacrifice and crippling regret.[37] None of the other members of the PFJ seem to have jobs. This may be a nod to the fact that many 1960s and 1970s revolutionaries tended to come from privileged backgrounds, meaning two-parent homes, an education, and prospects.[38] It's likely no accident that the SLA terrorist/victim, Patty Hearst, listed her occupation as "unemployed urban guerrilla" when she was being processed into jail before trial in 1975.[39] As a dope-smoking, disaffected heiress lost in the decadent 1970s, she was the ideal candidate for membership in these groups, coerced or not. Brian's difference from the PFJ's unemployed urban guerrillas may also signal the eventual ease with which Reg and siblings distance themselves from Brian in his new role/job as martyr.

It's also significant that an *absence* of work was one of the hallmarks of this period. In 1978, as the film script was being polished during the Pythons' Barbados working vacation, 9.3 million working days were lost in Britain to strike actions. The following year, as the film was being edited and finished, a whopping 29.5 million days were lost.[40] It seemed to many that more people in Britain were striking than working, with the Labour government under Callaghan first losing control of the unions, then the Party, the Commons, and finally No. 10. The specter of joblessness was everywhere. A *World in Action* program, "Starting on the Dole," looked at the incredibly high unemployment rate for school leavers in summer 1977, while another episode from the following spring, "Working on a Pittance," examined the low-paying work available to the physically and mentally disabled of Britain. Youth like the Ex-leper would have had a struggle being employed in the Britain of 1977–1978 as a union member out on strike; he's an Ex-leper without a marketable trade.

As they pass through the city gate . . .—The printed script offers no physical description of either the setting or the other beggars sitting around Palin's Ex-leper. There are actors and actual lepers (a local extra sans fingers can be glimpsed) lined up against the wall just inside the city's gate. There is a faux-leper sitting to Palin's right played by Charlie Knode, a costume designer on the film, who also worked on and appeared as a Swamp Castle guard and one of Robin's minstrels in *Holy Grail*.[41]

Beggars would have been a daily sight at the gates of Jerusalem, though Jeremias writes that there are almost no "Palestinian papyri which give information about Jerusalem," meaning "literary sources" have to suffice.[42] This Ex-leper beggar, then, is most likely a nod to a filmic source like *Ben-Hur*, which features an ungrateful leper (discussed later). Jeremias can say that Jerusalem had become a "centre for mendicancy," likely due to its role as home to the temple and religious festivals, and to the "meritorious" giving to the poor that often accompanied these holy events.[43] And since there were more people willing to give to the poor in the Holy City, advantages were bound to be taken, according to Jeremias:

> It is not surprising that even in those days there were complaints of people who pretended to be blind, dumb, dropsical, deformed and lame. . . . The situation had changed so little that even lepers, whose established begging-place only a few decades ago was on the road to the Garden of Gethsemane, were also to be found in Old Jerusalem.[44] Since they were not allowed to enter the Holy City, they sat sheltering from the weather under the gates, which did not count as part of the city.[45]

The Ex-leper isn't pretending, but he is hanging on to at least the name of his former affliction as he tries to ply his trade in relation to his new affliction, that of a whole, healthy man.[46] "Begging in Jerusalem was concentrated around the holy places," Jeremias continues, meaning around the temple, but the Pythons have clearly made no effort to build or even reference the bulk of Jewish spiritual life in the film.[47] Thus, the lepers and beggars in *Brian* are merely at the city gates, as they'd been in other biblical films, before they disappear entirely from the story. Similarly, in *Holy Grail* the images of a plague-ridden countryside disappear after the initial plague village scene.

The lives of the poor would have been less frequently documented, anyway, and wouldn't even become of interest in Britain, for example, until the Victorian era, when surveys of those living at or beneath the poverty line were first conducted.[48] Jeremias also notes that there were clearly two types of poor in Jerusalem of the first century: those who worked and supported themselves, and those who lived on "relief." Our lepers here at the gate seem to fall into the latter category, though Palin's Ex-leper admits that begging had been his vocation, and now that he's healed he's unfit for such employment, placing him in an odd position between the working and nonworking poor.[49] Bernstein notes that even during the years when Britain's economy was officially "booming" (between 1945 and 1973)—meaning improving and expanding, though other countries (Germany, France, Japan) improved and expanded much more, in comparison—poverty doggedly thrived in Britain. People living below the poverty line at the time of the film's production accounted for about 3–5 percent of the British population, though "if one includes those *at* as well as below the level at which income support kicked in," Bernstein writes, "the percentage jumped up to 14 per cent in 1979."[50] It was this group of people that suffered most during the Winter of Discontent of 1978–1979, and whose plight filled the pages of newspapers as the Pythons completed *Brian*.

Finally, Gilliam and his team worked hard on these sets, though as filming proceeded he would complain about how the sets, props, and costumes were being underexploited, according to Palin:

> Today [26 September] has shown signs of strain in the unit. Terry G is worried that TJ is driving everyone along at such a frenetic pace that he isn't leaving enough time to get the best shots. Gilliam is especially irked that the elaborately splendid detail of his market place is not being seen. He keeps muttering that this might as well have been done at Shepperton[51] for two million less.[52]

Palin earlier called this option the "Jesus of Shepperton" movie, which they'd considered.[53] Money had been secured for the more expensive location work, Gilliam was overruled, and they eventually found themselves in Tunisia.

EX-LEPER: (Palin): "Bloody donkey owners—they're all the same, innay?"—The ass-driver was one of the "despised trades" in Jerusalem of this period. Most of the trades involving transport of any kind were suspect, and therefore "despised," given the historical potential for rooking of customers by drivers, herders, carters, haulers, etc.[54] Additionally, many of these jobs were occupied by slaves, so ass/donkey "owners" would be rated higher, socially, than their slaves who operate them. (The woman seen earlier who was *not* going to the stoning because of her donkey, is an example.) The donkey owner the Ex-leper is complaining about is actually riding the donkey, not leading it, but it's only clear that the Ex-leper thinks he is an owner, and not a slave.

Jeremias reports that the donkey was used often for "local transport" in Judea, so this would have been a regular sight.[55] Remember that Mary was said to have ridden on a donkey traveling to Bethlehem, and Jesus entered Jerusalem on Palm Sunday riding an ass. Donkeys were also apparently appropriate conveyance for merchants and teachers, as Jeremias reports that Rabbi Simeon b. Shatach, who was also either a comber or merchant of flax (or both) was "offered [by his pupils] a donkey so that his work would not tire him so much."[56] King and Stager mention that, since horses and horsemen tended to be poorly regarded by "prophets and psalmists,"[57] the donkey was naturally elevated:

> The kings of Israel rode on donkeys or mules instead of horses when performing official functions. A letter of admonition to King Zimri-Lim from the prefect of the Mari palace conveys the impression it was a long-standing custom: "Since you [Zimri-Lim] are the king of the Khana tribesmen . . . my lord ought not to ride horses; rather, it is upon a palanquin or on mules that my lord ought to ride."[58]

This "bloody donkey owner" could have been a rabbi or royalty, then, for all the lepers knew.

This is also one of the few places in the film where *class* politics trump the us-versus-them (Jews v. Romans) language. Class had been a big part of the conversation between

Arthur, Dennis, and Dennis's mother in *Holy Grail*,[59] and it raised its head often during the run of *Flying Circus* (i.e., "Upperclass Twits"; City Gents) but, since the Pythons chose to not depict or deal with the religious hierarchy of Jerusalem in the film, class isn't much of a narrative thrust in *Brian*. Gregory is clearly a wealthy Jew, and he and his wife speak with posh accents, but their social and economic advantages don't get them special access to Brian for a healing, or keep them from the cross. The Ex-leper is implying that the owner of a donkey is at a certain level of success in society, and that he's probably not a slave (since he "owns" something of value). The fact that such owners are "all the same," and that his afflicted mate nods along in agreement, means that at least the poorest in first-century Jerusalem understand these societal strata.

EX-LEPER: "**Oh, here's a touch**"—Meaning a mark, someone to put the "touch" on for a handout of money, generally. The lepers here are obviously sizing up the crowds that pass through the gate, looking for who might be more willing to part with their money—more willing than donkey owners, clearly.

LEPER: "**Alms for a leper?**"—Most of these actors and extras are not afflicted in any way, though one, to Palin's left, is missing the fingers on his right hand. (He's also on crutches, likely meaning his legs and feet are affected, as well.) Recent medical archaeology has found *no* evidence of actual leprosy (Hansen's disease) in first-century Jerusalem, the presence of which would be indicated by skeletal necrosis in the fingers, toes, and on the face. The references in the scriptures to afflicted individuals tend to be broader than just leprosy:

> The term *zara'at* is traditionally rendered "leprosy" because of its translation by Greek *lepra*. . . . The Greek covers a wide range of diseases that produced scales. Greek *lepra* may have included true leprosy, i.e., Hansen's disease, but is definitely not limited to it. In fact, biblical descriptions of *zara'at* do not include the necrosis associated with Hansen's disease. Thus far no skeletons of the biblical period show any signs of Hansen's disease. The term *zara'at* is a generic name, embracing a variety of skin ailments, including many non-contagious types.[60]

The Pythons have included lepers and leprosy not based on actual historical evidence, but on Bible stories and cinematic biblical depictions like those in *Ben-Hur* and *The Greatest Story Ever Told*. This means that a leper scene likely seemed as important for the Pythons in this biblical film as a plague scene was for a Middle Ages film like *Holy Grail*.

These types might also be here due to their presence across the British Empire. In the first decade of the twentieth century, the recently "freed" Egypt welcomed flocks of tourists eager to see the pyramids. They were as often "horrified by the squalor and confusion that reigned in Egypt . . . assailed by touts, pimps and deformed beggars whining for baksheesh" (alms).[61] In *The Decline and Fall of the British Empire*, Brendon concludes: "Egypt provided [for the British traveler] a memento mori of imperial greatness as sublime as the wreckage of classical Rome."[62] The Pythons' version of Jerusalem is likely jaundiced by the Englishman abroad Evelyn Waugh's colorful, acrid accounts of the sights and smells encountered as he traveled around the Mediterranean in the 1920s, earlier enacted by the ranting tourist in *Flying Circus*.[63] Novelist Herman Melville happened to tour the classical sites in 1857 when he was ill, and reportedly detested almost everything: "He hated the Holy Land—'Must have suggested to the Jewish prophets their ghastly theology . . . whitish mildew pervading whole tracts of landscape— bleached—leprosy—encrustation of curses—old cheese, bones or rock— crunched, gnarled, mumbled.'"[64] Melville had called his own unappreciated work "the Gospels," incidentally.[65]

EX-LEPER (Palin): "**Spare a talent for an old ex-leper . . .**"—An enormous amount of money, as Mandy indicates in her reaction. During the First Punic War, for instance, the

Roman fleets were able to destroy and seize dozens of Carthaginian ships, force the surrender of Sicily, and demand 3,200 talents in payments. Just a few years later the Romans "seized Sardinia and Corsica and demanded another 1,200 talents."[66] Just a little later (about 35 BC), Cleopatra was demanding and receiving 200 talents annually from Herod as she leased back to him bits of Jericho over which she'd assumed control.[67] Jeremias estimates that Herod Antipas could claim more than 1,000 talents in taxes from his entire kingdom, throwing into relief the Ex-leper's rather outrageous request.[68] Much closer to the film's proposed time, a talent was still quite valuable. It's estimated that the aqueduct Pilate built leading from springs near Bethlehem to Jerusalem's city walls was bid out at about 750 talents.[69] By 66, the intemperate procurator Florus was demanding a 17-talent tax payment from the temple treasury, inciting a Jewish riot, Roman reprisals, and even executions.[70] The Ex-leper's demands, then, are just as ransomous, but will only merit a "piss off" from Mandy.[71]

The amount is likely relative, and plucked from the Bible's pages without much historical research on the Pythons' part. In *Holy Grail*, they'd done the same thing. The wedding guards killed by Launcelot "cost fifty pounds each," and the Cart Driver demands "ninepence" to pick up a nearly dead man in the plague village. In the times depicted in *Holy Grail*, a yearly income for a master carpenter, for instance only came to about fifteen pounds, and if you had income of twenty-five pounds or more you were considered wealthy and thence owed service to the king.[72] As for the "ninepence" quote, during the high times of plague in England a skilled wage-earner could only make about four and a half pence a day, an unskilled laborer even less. At those rates burying a family member could mean three days' salary for the working poor, which was likely unmanageable.[73]

MANDY: "That's more than he earns in a month!"—It would actually have been more than many earned in a month. In ancient Greece, the value of just one talent (perhaps 10,000 Attic silver drachmas[74]) was incredible: "One *talent* was the equivalent of around nine years' worth of wages for a single skilled laborer working five days a week, 52 weeks a year, according to the wage rates we know from 377 B.C."[75] A more contemporary valuing for the talent can be found in the worth of a rich tunic that one priest was provided by his mother, "worth 100 minas, that is, one talent"; while another priest's mother gave her son a finely sewn tunic worth 20,000 denarii, or two talents.[76] Given that Brian is wearing coarse, crudely woven clothing, one or two talents must represent a fortune. Earlier, Mandy had hinted that Brian didn't have employment, and that he should be more interested in getting a job than sex. It may be that she meant he needed a *better* job than the one we see him plying later—selling snacks at the Colosseum performances in the very next scene.

This situation—where a beggar of sorts demands money from someone of lesser means—is also found in first-century Jerusalem. Since scribes weren't allowed to charge for their services and it was considered "meritorious" for those with some means to give to the poor religious educators, many scribes adopted the lucrative "habit of sponging on the hospitality of people of limited means," which often included "widows" like Brian's mother.[77]

MANDY: *(to Ex-leper)* **"Buzz off!"**—A rather more recent colloquialism, the *OED* sets the Cockney phrase to the early twentieth century.

EX-LEPER: "Say you open at one shekel, I start at two thousand . . ."—This isn't simply a first-century Jerusalem financial lesson. In *Life of Brian* the Pythons grapple with all four contested areas of the postwar economy—"full employment, an expanding economy, stable prices and a strong pound"—balls that had been juggled by No. 10 since at least Macmillan's premiership.[78] Mandy will bemoan Brian's job status, the Ex-leper's chances of "full employment" end when he's healed, and financial transactions and references to currency value occur throughout, including the buying of stones, donating to ex-lepers, and haggling for beards and gourds. Brian's later inability to afford an attorney keeps him on the crucifixion queue, and the PFJ's rapine charges against the "bloody Romans" ("they've bled us white") is simply a tax and tribute lament. There was even a "paying of taxes to Rome" question—followed by a PM-like, platitudinal answer—in an earlier draft of the script.[79]

This kind of upward haggling was very contemporary for later 1970s Britain. The unions targeted PM Callaghan's ministers and economic functionaries as they clutched after fatter pay packets and higher bumps in new pay adjustments, even as the government kept to a flat 5 percent increase (or lower) in the public sector. Inflation—which "transforms an ordered society into an undisciplined mob"[80]—had climbed to historic highs, forcing Callaghan to hold down pay with a voluntary incomes policy across 1976 and 1977, and which the unions assumed would end in 1978,[81] when inflation had dropped appreciably. The Callaghan administration pushed on, hoping to beat inflation *and* the unions, and the rank and file members then demanded a return to free collective bargaining.[82] The major shift points came when an assumed election was *not* called in the fall of 1978, and then in October 1978 Ford crumbled to union demands and, instead of offering the agreed-upon 5 percent bump (against the 25 percent increase the union asked for), the car company agreed to give 17 percent. The dominoes began to fall after that, and union after union, big and small, scrambled to force employers into similar pay increases, many of which were approved just to avoid prolonged and expensive strike actions.[83] With a whisper-thin margin in the Commons, Labour had no wiggle room. The government's pay policy was now officially in tatters, and the Winter of Discontent howling under the door.

All this haggling worked on employers and the government, and here works on Brian, too. Instead of giving nothing—as was the original intention—he gives half a denarii, and the Ex-leper is just a little better off.

MANDY: ". . . so piss off!"—The *OED* sites this mild epithet to the Pythons' youth, coming into use by about 1935. This was one of the phrases recorded for eventual looping work on *Holy Grail*, when Galahad tells Tim the Enchanter to "Get stuffed" at the Killer Rabbit's lair. The goal was to have a handful of possible insertions for sound editors to choose from as they edited the film's soundtrack, keeping in mind the potential ratings implications of various words.[84]

giant statue feet—Two of the many set decorations included by Gilliam and his crew in this market set are feet, *giant* feet from an obviously giant statue. They can be seen behind Brian, Mandy, and the Ex-leper as they round a corner, as the Ex-leper changes his tactics and drops his asking price. These feet are likely meant to remind the viewer of Gilliam's animated, crushing foot from the *Flying Circus* credits, but they are also part of Gilliam's classical source material for this film. In Piranesi's frontispiece ("Statue of Minerva") to the *Vedute di Roma* collection there is a jumbled arrangement of broken statues and crumbled monuments. Part of this mess is an enormous, carved foot, which had obviously been part of a statue larger than anything else visible in the frame.[85] Bits and pieces of unused Roman buildings and stone works of all kinds had been plundered over the centuries, so it's not a surprise to see these feet, perhaps even on sale, in a first-century Jerusalem marketplace.

BRIAN: "Did you say 'Ex-leper'?"—This is where the scene goes sideways, in true Python fashion. Brian could have offered the coin at the outset, and then there's no haggling. Instead, he is curious about the odd situation—the man is a *former* leper—and that curiosity propels them both through the soukh and the scene. In *Holy Grail*, the sentries could have answered directly about their master, and not sidetracked into coconuts and swallows; later peasants could have simply said that "no one lives" in the nearby castle and they have no lord, rather than espousing a political doctrine not yet hatched. In the latter instance Arthur in his frustration ends up exposing "the violence inherent in the system," and in the first Arthur and Patsy have to simply move on without the information or acolytes they'd sought.

In an earlier *Flying Circus* iteration of "ex-," found in "The Dead Parrot" sketch of Ep. 8, the prefix means the bird is dead—"This is an ex-parrot"—the way Praline uses the phrase.[86] The term here means *former* leper, not dead leper or even dead man, a significant difference.

Behind Brian, Mandy, and the Ex-leper can be seen the great wall used in both *Jesus of Nazareth* and *Life of Brian*. In *Jesus of Nazareth*, the wall—with its diagonal staircase—can be glimpsed in the distance behind the crowd as Pilate (Rod Steiger) addresses the braying crowd who want Jesus crucified. In *Brian*, the wall is dressed as the side of Pilate's palace, where he addresses jeering citizens from his porch. Here, Gilliam and friends have added pole-and-fabric stalls running up the ramp way.

EX-LEPER: ". . . sixteen years behind the bell . . ."—Likely a play on the "behind the badge" phrase heard in regard to police officers.

This scene, featuring a "donkey owner," professional lepers, and Brian (who, we'll see, has a concessions job at the Colosseum), is key in that everyone seems to be gainfully employed or at least able to sustain themselves separate from the state's teat. It actually flies in the face of where Britain found itself in 1974–1979, when millions of "gawdelpus" types were unemployed and the strain on the welfare system was spreading misery all around.[87] Here, a passerby owns a donkey, a valuable animal in the period, meaning he might be a businessman involved in the (despised, but paying) trade of haulage, or it might be a family animal for work and milk products around the house. Brian is on his way home, to a small house he shares with his mother. She seems to make some kind of living offering sexual services to at least the one Roman we see in their home—tawdry, but an income nonetheless—and Brian will go off to his own job soon. The lepers and ex-lepers are begging, but they're obviously treating begging as a legitimate source of regular income—it's their job, they're not unemployed, by their own definition. In this world of first-century Jerusalem there doesn't appear to be mass unemployment or even the suffering brought on by a lack of jobs or underemployment, unlike what was happening in the world outside the film, or even in the unsettled, starving Jerusalem leading up to the 66 revolt. In 1977, when the bulk of the film's writing took place, the yearly average for unemployment exceeded 1.48 million, more than doubling from 1970. Unemployment would exceed 2 million by 1981, and then 3 million in 1981–1982.[88]

This is one of the few moments where the Pythons don't directly take an obvious, real-world situation plaguing Britain and lampoon it in their creative work. In *Holy Grail* the anti-Anglo French position regarding the Common Market, as well as union leaders like Jack Scargill shouting down management and government took center positions in key scenes.[89] In *Life of Brian*, teeming humanity and even squalor might be hinted at, but with the noted exceptions of the masses of people willing to follow messiahs whenever they appear, and those who can find time in their day to attend stonings, the working class appear to be working. But these mobs disappear as quickly as they form—they're nowhere in sight, for instance, by the time Brian really needs them to save him from the cross. In *Holy Grail* there was an assembled crowd of villagers set on burning a witch, behaving very much like the mob who eventually carry off Simon in *Brian*. The difference for the villagers in *Holy Grail* was that many of them were carrying instruments of their trade—scythes, bread-baking paddles, axes, blacksmithing instruments, rakes, threshing tools, barber instruments, brooms, and so on. These are working people caught out during their working day. In *Life of Brian* the crowds do not march around with their tools or dressed for any particular tradecraft. In this they seem more like ready-made religious mobs simply waiting for a messiah to follow, which is the comment the Pythons are trying to make.

EX-LEPER: ". . . a bloody miracle, sir . . ."—Typically Pythonesque phrasing here, combining a reference to a sacred act with a course intensifier.

BRIAN: "Who cured you?"—Not "how," but "who," meaning these healings must have happened or at least been broadcast about in Brian's lifetime. Brian isn't surprised that the man's been healed, he just wants to know who did the actual healing, which is of course the script's setup to introduce Jesus again, this time as a worker of miracles. In *Antiquities of the Jews* Josephus wrote of one Eleazar who "healed" men of spiritual ills, like the great King Solomon, who had

> left behind him the manner of using exorcisms, by which they drive away demons, so that they never return; and this method of cure is of great force unto this day; for I have seen a certain man of my own country, whose name was Eleazar, releasing people that were demoniacal in the presence of Vespasian, and his sons, and his captains, and the whole multitude of his soldiers. The manner of the cure was this: He put a ring that had a Foot of one of those sorts mentioned by Solomon to the nostrils of the demoniac, after which he drew out the demon through his nostrils; and when the man fell down immediately, he abjured him to return into him no more, making still mention of Solomon, and reciting the incantations which he composed. And when Eleazar would persuade and demonstrate to the spectators that he had such a power, he set a little way off a cup or basin full of water, and commanded the demon, as he went out of the man, to overturn it, and thereby to let the spectators know that he had left the man; and when this was done, the skill and wisdom of Solomon was shown very manifestly.[90]

Those possessed by demons will be seen later, when Brian is thronged by followers, just before he is arrested for the final time. A contemporary of Jesus, Rabbi Hanina ben Dosa, was known for miracles brought about by his prayers—healings, stopping and bringing rain, and even surviving a serpent (or poisonous lizard) bite where the serpent died, instead.[91] There were others during this period striving to heal, as well, according to Hankoff, with similar ingratitude displayed in the process: "When Jews in the first century attempted healing in the name of Jesus, the Talmud condemned the practice."[92]

EX-LEPER: "Jesus did. . . . One minute I'm a leper with a trade, next moment me livelihood's gone. Not so much as a by your leave"—This is the second mention of Jesus, by name, in the film. A fairly common name, there was a Jesus known to be a leader of a band of brigands-for-hire who were paid to help protect the "pro-Roman city Sepphoris in the summer of 66," as well as one of the high priests (along with Ananus) "hunted down" by the Idumaeans, according to Josephus.[93] The Pythons could have easily used the common name Jesus for their hero, resulting in a confusion of Jesuses.[94] Very early story ideas for the film, according to Palin, centered on this trope of misidentification and unmet expectations involving a Jesus-like character, with more actions and set pieces involving the actual Jesus throughout.[95]

Given this Ex-leper's reaction to being cured on spec, it's not likely that he followed the prescribed routine for cleansed lepers. He would have had to show himself to a "director of the weekly course" whose job it was to "perform rites of purification" for women after childbirth, adulterous women, and lepers.[96] If satisfactorily cleansed, the Ex-leper would then be pronounced clean at the Nicanor Gate, which would have likely been an inner gate nearer the temple, not one leading into the city proper (as used in the film). In Matthew 8:4 Jesus tells the leper to show himself to the priest after he's been cleansed, meaning the official pronouncement at the gate would have followed that step.

(gestures in the manner of a conjuror)—(PSC) Here he touches his forehead, more like a faith healer might do. "Healing by touch" is well-documented in scriptural sources, as Hankoff explains:

Healing by touch figured dramatically in the career of Jesus. It is also mentioned in the Talmud although no unequivocally first-century episode is to be found. An interesting sequence involves a late second-century rabbi, Johanan ben Nappaha. Johanan was able to cure colleagues of illness by simply taking the sufferer's hand and raising it. When he became ill, another sage visited him and cured him by raising Johanan's hand. It was, of course, asked why Johanan could not cure himself, to which the reply was, "The prisoner cannot free himself from jail." The description of the healing by Jesus of Simon Peter's mother-in-law of a fever uses almost exactly same formula in one Gospel as that of Johanan's healing. Jesus "took her by the hand and lifted her up." This same language appears in the healing by Peter of a lifelong cripple seen at the Temple gate. Peter told the cripple to rise, took him by the right hand and raised him up. The cripple's bones were strengthened, and he leaped up. Jesus cured a leper by touching him, and demonstrated in addition his willingness to make physical contact with this sufferer. Jesus restored sight to two blind men by simple touch.[97]

These stories could be found in the Pythons' modern Britain, as well. The *Times* carried one such note in January 1969, titled "Faith 'Cure'": "After suffering from misplaced vertebrae for more than 10 years, Mr. Richard Pratt, Chief Constable of Bedfordshire, claims to have been completely cured in five minutes by Mr. Kenneth Hebbelthwaite, who practises faith healing."[98] Also in the headlines during this period was US president Jimmy Carter's sister Ruth Carter Stapleton, who was a well-known faith healer. In January 1977 Mrs. Stapleton admitted to being so overworked after her brother's election that blessings sometimes went sideways: "I was giving the blessing in a meeting a while back," she said at a book signing, "and instead of saying 'In the name of Jesus Christ' I said 'In the name of Jimmy' by mistake."[99] The article didn't say whether, given the slight error, the blessing was efficacious. *Private Eye* and even the usually respectful British press treated Carter like a fervent Jesus freak.

The term "conjuror" has historically often had a negative, shady context in British English. In John Wycliffe's c. 1382 version of the Bible, Jews who claimed exorcist powers were known as "*coniureris*," or conjurors. Hankoff notes that many of the maladies cured in the pages of the Bible were those connected to possession, and not just bodily illness: "Eight of the 24 healing episodes of Jesus in the Gospels and four of the 12 in Acts refer to an unclean or evil possessing spirit. The New Testament descriptions of demonic possession cover a wide variety of illnesses."[100] Illness was often attributed to possession in the NT as opposed to the Talmud, where "an internal pathological state needed correcting, most usually by removal of a physical bane."[101] The Markan version[102] of this incident is a bit different, certainly. There, the leper comes to Jesus and asks to be made clean, and Jesus, "moved with compassion," touches the man and heals him immediately. (The lepers in Luke 17 also cry unto Jesus, asking for his blessing.) Jesus also tells the man to tell no one excepting his priest, and to give offerings in thanks for the healing. The man was obviously too excited about his new health to remember the charge: "But he went out, and began to publish *it* much, and to blaze abroad the matter, insomuch that Jesus could no more openly enter into the city, but was without in desert places: and they came to him from every quarter."[103] This healing (and subsequent advertisement) meant Jesus wouldn't be left alone.[104] Brian will gain this kind of following after *not* finishing a portion of his mostly nonsensical preaching, his disciples glomming on to the promise of a "secret" something meant just for them, as opposed to a demonstrated blessing or anything he's actually said. Our Ex-leper is only telling of his Jesus encounter to Brian, though perhaps he's been rehearsing the unfortunate turn of events to any "touch" encountered at the gate.

There was a very interesting but related sideshow going on in June and July 1972, when *Daily Mail* cartoonists Gary Keane and Neville Randall produced a "Secrets of the Scrolls" series (about eighteen in all) looking at current Dead Sea scroll "discoveries" and controversies. Several are based on the pronouncements of Manchester University's John Allegro, who'd published a book claiming the Essenes had created the Christ figure and stories, and that Jesus was more factually a "magician" than a savior.[105] Allegro's translations and conclusions were roundly criticized.[106] The Dead Sea Scrolls and various interpretations and claims remained in the news from 1948 through 1978, and beyond.

This particular shot appears to be one that they picked up much later, back at Shepperton Studio in late June 1979, to try and patch holes in the film's narrative flow. The background used is a re-dressed version of a set used first for the 1968 film *Oliver!*, according to Palin: "We shoot at the main gate of the old *Oliver* set—in itself a sad and crumbling place, with memories, for me, of *Jabberwocky*.[107] The shooting, between showers and aeroplanes, goes along well and we even do some hand-held dialogue shots."[108] Palin's hair is quite a bit shorter here, and the bright North African sunshine of October 1978 has given way to the English damp of June 1979.

EX-LEPER: "You're cured mate. Bloody do-gooder"—In an earlier draft of the printed script, he says "You're cured mate, sod you," which is a more profane version and likely one they worked out of the finished film. As *Holy Grail* moved from rough draft script to "shooting" script, the character of God, for example, changed considerably:

> In the first draft of the printed script, it turns out there are multiple grails found or cobbled together, and eventually they're all presented to God in the coffee shop at Harrods. . . . God isn't pleased, and tells Arthur and mates to go and find the true Grail "somewhere in Italy." . . . Just one page later, the questers steal a chalice from a church in Italy, race outside to where God waits in a VW "getaway van," and they speed off, militarized clergy on their tail. Their van plunges into the sea as God promises to "part this lot" (the sea)—the van sinks, and the credits roll. . . . The ending of the original draft would have likely brought the reproach [*Brian*] invited, but this shirty God who dies with his holy accomplices never made it off the typed page. God, the ultimate authority figure, can expect the same treatment as an Upperclass Twit or a "King of the Britons" in the Pythons' carnivalesque, topsy-turvy world.[109]

The original draft of *Holy Grail* was a handful of unrelated sketches (a boxing match, a department store, a car chase) stitched together by bits of Arthur and his peripatetic knights searching for the Holy Grail at the command of a rather nasty God. Eventually, Palin and Jones ditched the more modern scenes (several found their way in the fourth season of *Flying Circus*) to focus on the Arthurian tale, and God's appearances (and ill-temper) diminished. The *Brian* structure also became much more focused as the script matured.

(draft) **EX-LEPER: "But it was a living . . ."**—This Ex-leper could have pursued other period jobs *not* directly attached to a salary, or to his ability to beg. Scribes (teachers) of first-century Jerusalem weren't allowed, by religious law, to charge for their services. They either had to hold trade jobs (carpenter, shopkeeper, tanner, etc.) as well, or rely on, essentially, the kindness of strangers. Jeremias writes that "in the main the scribes lived on subsidies": "The learned, or teachers of the wise . . . were dependent on the gratitude of their pupils . . . on some consideration at the distribution of tithes for the poor, and in certain cases also on support from the Temple treasury."[110] Not being a slave, the Ex-leper could have pursued education and then teaching, by his own choice, and still made his "living" by begging.

(draft) **EX-LEPER: ". . . my family has been in begging six generations"**—Temple slaves working for the Jewish high priests were generational, it seems. Jeremias mentions that Joshua appears to have "given" Gibeonites—"hewers of wood and drawers of water"—to the temple, and that descendants of those slaves continued in that capacity from generation to

generation. Jeremias is quick to point out that by the time of Jesus, "in no case do we ever find the slightest indication . . . either in Jerusalem or other Jewish territory, there were still slaves of the Temple."[111] There could have been sixth- and seventh-generation slaves working at the temple in the earlier post-exilic period.

The Ex-leper's laments are of a kind heard since the beginning of the Industrial Revolution in Britain, when massive mills and factories opened, replacing the decades-old cottage industries in weaving and textiles. The early nineteenth century in Britain saw the Luddite movement lash out against the new technologies, trying in vain to slow the progress toward machine-made goods, or at least to keep individual jobs from becoming redundant.[112] The trade unions plied these waters across the twentieth century, struggling to keep up the "full employment" promise even as new machinery, new technologies, and new industries replaced an outmoded past. Britain watched as postwar Europe (especially Germany and France), the United States, and even Japan raced ahead by *not* kowtowing to big labor but embracing production streamlining and industrial efficiency. Britain's entrenched trade unions—clinging to the Social Contract with Labour—kept such updating from having any real effect, and Britain's economy suffered as a result. Men whose families had been coal miners or shipyard or mill workers found themselves unemployed and unemployable in the mid-to-late 1970s. Bogdanor calls the 1970s and beyond a time when there was, euphemistically, "a more flexible labour market," encouraged by the economy's natural travails as the world changed in the postwar period, as the labor force adapted or did not, and as Thatcher's policies (including relegation of the trade unions) took effect in the early 1980s.[113]

(draft) **EX-LEPER: "I'm not about to become a goat-herd, just because some long-haired conjuror starts mucking about"**—The phraseology should ring familiar, and it may indicate that Palin (and Jones) wrote this Ex-leper sequence as well as the rantings of Dennis the "Constitutional Peasant" from *Holy Grail*:

> Arthur: Be quiet!
>
> Dennis: You can't expect to wield supreme executive power just because some watery tart threw a sword at you . . .
>
> Arthur: Shut up!
>
> Dennis: I mean, if I went round saying I was an Emperor because some moistened bint had lobbed a scimitar at me . . .

EX-LEPER: ". . . a goat-herd . . ."—The Ex-leper clearly sees a shepherd—someone entrusted with angelic visits to announce the birth of Christ a little more than thirty years earlier—as a member of the lower class. And rather than seeing this type as a herder of goats, the Ex-leper may simply see the type as a rustic, someone not fit for life in the city, and therefore beneath him, even if he is a low-born leper (with a trade). Jeremias writes "that there were circumstances—quite independent of ancestry—which carried a whole series of trades which were despised, and those who practised them were, to a greater or less degree, exposed to social degradation."[114] The people of Jerusalem at Jesus's time understood which trades were "crafts of robbers," which were "repugnant" (those often creating noxious smells), and which were "despised," including those connected with women, or those based on trickery, Jeremias continues.[115] As mentioned earlier, the herdsman appears on the same list as the ass-driver, camel-driver, and butcher, as each was considered likely to rook his customer at any turn. Jeremias reminds us that herdsman . . . did not enjoy a very good reputation. As proved by experience, most of the time they were dishonest and thieving; they led their herds on to other people's land . . . and pilfered the produce of the herd. For this reason it was forbidden to buy wool, milk or kids from them.[116] . . . The favourable picture of the shepherd which we are given in Jesus's teaching is quite isolated; in rabbinic literature in general there are unfavourable references to herdsmen, if we abstract those passages which have developed from Old Testament texts, and present Yahweh, the Messiah, Moses and David as shepherds.[117]

During Passover, however, the herdsmen would by necessity and demand descend on Jerusalem to provide animals for the daily sacrificial rites, meaning they were an *essential* part of Jewish religious life.

EX-LEPER: "Which is a pain in the arse, excuse my French, sir"—The phrase "Excuse my French" or "Pardon my French" has been part of the English lexicon since at least the mid-nineteenth century, and is clearly out of place in first-century Jerusalem.

EX-LEPER: ". . . half a denary for my bloody life story!"—Obviously taken as a mean offering, this amount was occasionally phrased into an insult during this period. An Alexandrian nationalist who had been arrested and brought before Claudius used the phrase "twopenny-halfpenny Jew" to insult the emperor and his well-known tolerance of the Jews.[118] On the other hand, the money-tax to support the temple cult in Jerusalem, a tax applied to all adult male Jews between the ages of twenty and fifty, no matter where they lived, came to two denarii (half a shekel) per year.[119] The Ex-leper has been gifted with a quarter of what Brian would have been expected annually to give to the temple—fairly generous.

It's hard to measure the value of the denarii in today's terms, but a daily wage in first-century Palestine wouldn't have exceeded a handful of denarii, certainly. Jeremias writes that a common day laborer in Jerusalem earned about "one denarius a day . . . with keep."[120] The great Jewish scholar Hillel worked as a day laborer for just *half* a denarius a day, and after the fees to attend school he was left with only half of that for "the maintenance of himself and his family."[121] Smallwood mentions, when discussing large temple gifts (of money, in about 60 BC), that "800 talents = 4,800,000 drachmae or denarii," meaning one talent was equal to 6,000 denarii.[122] (The Ex-leper asks for the equivalent of 6,000 denarii, but settles for just half a denarii; if this is accurate at all, the Ex-leper was masterfully haggled down by Mandy's obstinacy and Brian's inquisitiveness.) If a typical sewer worker (in high-rent Rome) was paid about twenty-five denarii per day, though, as Koloski-Ostrow estimates, then "half a denary" isn't really much, and the Ex-leper's complaint understandable.[123] By way of comparison, the *tributum capitis* was, by the year 30, set at about "one Roman denarius per head, the 'tribute money' of the Gospels."[124] This money paid to Rome is addressed in an earlier draft of the script, but does not survive into the finished film. Another comparison: The Emperor Augustus "broke the legs of his secretary Thallus for having betrayed the contents of a letter for 500 *denarii*"[125] So Thallus lost use of his legs for a long while in exchange for twenty days' wage of a working man.

Incidentally, the Tunisian extras who roll about as Pilate and Biggus try and speak were paid three (modern) dinars each, and Palin reports a near-riot when the payments were being handed out.[126] Palin would also pay the boy who regularly turned down his bed at the hotel one dinar daily.[127]

In the Pythons' everyday life, the value of British sterling and the pound had been in flux, trending downward for some time by 1976–1977, when this film was being written. Living standards fell "two years out of four" after Labour reentered No. 10 in 1974, and "real disposable income (which is what the pay packet will buy after all deductions) fell by about 1.5 per cent from mid-1975 to mid-1977."[128] Between November 1974 and June 1975, the value of sterling against major foreign currencies dropped a precipitous 9 percent, an uneven tide that Thatcher would eventually ride into No. 10.[129] Thanks to inflation, the British version of "half a denary" simply didn't buy what it used to. It should be remembered that much of this "crisis" had been, in the opinion of many, kickstarted thanks to the Arab oil cartel's stranglehold on oil production and exports, and so could be directly connected to Middle Eastern political terrorists and Middle Eastern oil terrorists—not far from the Holy Land of *Brian*.

BRIAN: "There's no pleasing some people"—This is likely influenced by a famous scene from *Ben-Hur*. Ben-Hur returns to the city after finding his leprous mother and sister. As they approach, we can hear a man with a bell calling out, "Alms for the blind." The blind man takes Ben-Hur's coin, at first grateful, but then realizes there are lepers before him. He drops the coin, fearing defilement, providing a neat "there's no pleasing some people" moment.

In January 1976 the *Telegraph* carried a story about Albert Thorogood, a man who had been unable to find (or had been unwilling to accept) "suitable employment" since 1950. In the intervening twenty-six years he had worked a total of thirty-six weeks, while accepting more than £12,000 in unemployment benefits. He lost his "livelihood" (he was a carpenter) in 1950, and had lived on state benefits ever since. He had been offered a reported one hundred jobs in the past seven years alone, and had rejected all of them because they didn't "suit" him: "The labour people keep on sending me to the wrong sort of jobs," Thorogood told the paper. Mr. Thorogood was sentenced to a month in jail in February 1976 for benefits malfeasance. His wife blamed the newspapers for her husband's predicament, and was certain he would never get a job after his release.[130] In this period of rising dole participation there were dozens of stories about "dole fiddlers," or those who did everything they could—legal and otherwise—to stay on the dole, increase their benefits, complain about the meagerness of the stipend, and avoid a real job at all costs.[131]

EX-LEPER: "That's just what Jesus said, sir!"—The other well-known leper story involves Christ healing ten lepers (Luke 17:11–19), and ends with only one who has been healed returning to Jesus to thank him. Christ asks after the other nine, and the man can only answer that he doesn't know, prompting Christ's response: "And he said unto him, Arise, go thy way: thy faith hath made thee whole." In that case, the one who gives thanks sets himself apart from others, as opposed to the one here who expresses ingratitude at his loss of trade. Jesus doesn't actually say "there's no pleasing some people."

(draft) **EX-LEPER: "Thank you sir, you're a real Jew"**—Far from an insult, which it likely has become over the intervening centuries, according to the scholar Hillel one sign of a "real Jew" was his almsgiving largesse.[132] But perhaps the Ex-leper is using Brian's Jewishness as evidence that he's "a touch" for money? A Roman woman, Fulvia, made a large donation to the temple, given as an offering in good faith. The Jews who collected the money then misappropriated it. Fulvia's husband complained, and the Emperor Tiberius responded by having all Jews expelled from Rome.[133] The unscrupulous Jews saw the kind-hearted Fulvia as "a touch." Here it's likely that the Ex-leper is a Jew trying to wheedle money from another Jew, Brian, meaning the Roman authorities wouldn't be terribly concerned.

Notes

1. "Wislon" is *Private Eye*'s name for Harold Wilson; Ted Heath was "Grocer."
2. Gilliam also added to and manipulated the Arch of Constantine.
3. Larsen, *MPFC: UC*, 1.100.

4. Wiedemann, *Emperors and Gladiators*, 17–18.

5. The prefect immediately preceding Pilate was Valerius Gratus, who held the office 15–26. In *Ben-Hur*, Gratus is the man nearly killed when the tile falls from Judah Ben-Hur's home.

6. Brandon, "Pontius Pilate in History and Legend," 524; also, Maier, *Pontius Pilate*, 319–20.

7. This will be further discussed later in response to Reg's demand that a grotesquely phallic statue of Caesar be erected in the city. See "The PFJ Plan Their Raid."

8. Josephus, *AJ*, 18.3.1 (Whiston, 379).

9. Maier provides an entertaining version of these events in his work of historical fiction, *Pontius Pilate*, published (and very popular) in 1968. See chapter 6, pages 63–80.

10. *AJ*, 18.3.1 (Whiston, 379); also Smallwood, *JURR*, 161–62

11. Brendon, *DFBE*, 135–36.

12. Josephus, *WJ*, 5.6.5 (Whiston, 558).

13. *AJ*, 5.11.1 (Whiston, 565).

14. Rosenblatt, "The Crucifixion of Jesus from the Standpoint of Pharisaic Law," 315–21.

15. Rosenblatt, "The Crucifixion of Jesus," 319.

16. See Larsen, *BAFHG*, 27, 64n7, 80, 209, 210, 517, and 519.

17. The Pythons screened bits of these "heavy and turgid" biblical epics as they prepped for the film, meaning there were plenty of crucifixion images they could have referenced (Palin, *Diaries 1969–1979*, 351–52).

18. Zias and Sekeles, "The Crucified Man," 22.

19. "Israelis Unearth Crucifixion Clue," *Times*, 4 January 1971: 1. The authors of "The Crucified Man" article set out in 1985 to address the inaccuracies generated by the earliest forensic analysis, namely N. Haas's seminal work. Newspapers published Haas's grisly versions of the crucifixion pose (knees bent and to the side, feet together, iron nail driven through both heels). See Haas, "Anthropological Observations on the Skeletal Remains from Giv'at ha-Mivtar." The 1977 BBC documentary/book *Who Was Jesus?* also reported this crucifixion information as the latest archaeological *fact* regarding the time of Jesus (*Who Was Jesus?*, 24). When this crucifixion report was reassessed in the mid-1980s, there wasn't similar front-page coverage.

20. *MPFC: UC*, 1.319, "School Prize-Giving" sketch.

21. "Envisioning Crucifixion," 281 and 281n. This scene is memorably reimagined in Stanley Kubrick's 1960 film.

22. Kotker, *HLTJ*, 114. Josephus notes that Florus's soldiers killed rather indiscriminately, rounding up "quiet people" as well as alleged rebels. If they weren't killed where they fell in the streets, they were brought to Florus, "chastised with stripes, and then crucified" (*WJ*, 2.14.9 [Whiston, 485]).

23. *BAFHG*, 248–49.

24. Magness, *Stone and Dung*, 14.

25. Burleigh, *BRT*, 37.

26. Jeremias, *JTJ*, 118.

27. *JTJ*, 118–19.

28. Bernstein, *Myth of Decline*, 309.

29. See Dennan and Macdonald for more. *Meaning of Life* will have two distinct corporate-themed sections, *The Crimson Permanent Assurance* featurette, and the "Very Big Corporation of America," while "Every Sperm is Sacred" deals with unemployment in Yorkshire mill towns.

30. Jenkins will be discussed later in relation to the Pythons' Pilate, with whom he shares an affectation of speech.

31. Capital punishment in Great Britain, for instance, ceased in 1965. In 1974–1975, when IRA attacks reached a particularly bloody pitch, the reintroduction of capital punishment as a weapon against terrorism was discussed. The call for capital punishment appeared again just after the Tory victory in 1979, but also failed to gain widespread acceptance. *Flying Circus* episodes dealt with all of these social aspects, from birth control and divorce (Ep. 13) through homosexuality (Ep. 28), censorship (Eps. 17, 25), and capital punishment (Eps. 3, 35).

32. *BAFHG*, 142; the citations in the indented block quote are from Marr's *HMB*.

33. Cleese had qualified as a barrister, and Chapman as a doctor, but neither pursued those careers once their writing and performing talents became evident.

34. Speaking for the Pythons, the *Meaning of Life* narrator calls Yorkshire "the Third World."

35. "£340m Dole Paid," *Telegraph*, 21 January 1976: 30. On this same day the Labour government's Employment Secretary, Michael Foot, told the Commons that unemployment wasn't Labour's fault. Given Foot's record of splashing Tory governments with blood-red unemployment statistics in the past, this moment of supreme irony—a Labour government in power while unemployment climbs—allowed the article's author to savor twisting the knife: "So yesterday it was as if Mrs Mary Whitehouse had been caught presiding over a saturnalia" ("Foot Proclaims His Virtue at a Dole Queue Saturnalia," *Telegraph*, 21 January 1976: 30).

36. And later Brian will mangle another Jesus saying (Matthew 10:29–31) when he asks whether the birds have jobs, confusing his potential disciples.

37. Lampton is played by Laurence Harvey, *Room at the Top* (1959); Seaton is Albert Finney, *Saturday Night and Sunday Morning* (1960); Machin is Richard Harris, *This Sporting Life* (1963).

38. The fact that none of the PFJ have beards, either—which would have been de rigueur for a male Jew of this time—indicates they are meant to be young and impressionable, therefore more likely to harbor revolutionary feelings alien to their fathers, and their father's fathers, and so on.

39. On advice of counsel Hearst would rather quickly try and get that bit of revolutionary nose-thumbing changed to "none," as it became prime fodder during her trial ("Miss Hearst No Longer 'Urban Guerrilla,'" *Times*, 26 September 1975: 8).

40. Jenkins, *Anatomy of Decline*, 103.

41. *BAFHG* 9, 23n41 and 42.

42. *JTJ*, 109.

43. Some of Freud's examined jokes in *The Joke and Its Relation to the Unconscious* involve beggars and the sacred *expectation* for charity in Jewish law (45, 107–8).

44. This is likely figured from the time of the book's first publication (in German) in 1967.

45. *JTJ*, 116–17.

46. He will also complain (in an earlier draft) that "waving muscular suntanned limbs in people's faces demanding compassion" is "a bloody disaster," as far as begging goes, which is the visual part of the joke here—a leper without leprosy.

47. *JTJ*, 117.

48. Including, for example, the work of Charles Booth in the 1880s and 1890s, *The Life and Labour of the People of London*. The nineteenth century also saw the formation of many charities in Britain, designed to assist the poor, children, unwed mothers, and so on.

49. *JTJ*, 110.

50. Bernstein, *Myth of Decline*, 321.

51. Shepperton is the film studio where as late as 25 June 1979 they were shooting pickup shots (trying to salvage the Ex-leper scene), and where Palin had been a member of the governing board since late 1976 (Palin, *Diaries 1969–1979*, 494).

52. Palin, *Diaries, 1969–1979*, 493–94.

53. Palin, *Diaries 1969–1979*, 445.

54. *JTJ*, 304.

55. See also King and Stager, *LBI*, 115–16, and 186–87.

56. *JTJ*, 310n36.

57. The "negative attitude" toward horses seems to arise from their use in warfare and for the ostentatious displays of men. See the biblical citations listed by King and Stager (115).

58. *LBI*, 115.

59. The "Dennis" scene is discussed at length in *BAFHG*, 94–160.

60. "Leprosy," *EJ*, Jewish Virtual Library, http://www.jewishvirtuallibrary.org/leprosy.

61. Brendon, *DFBE*, 182.

62. *DFBE*, 182.

63. *MPFC: UC*, 2.71; *Flying Circus* Ep. 31.

64. Bruce Chatwin, *Spectator*, 4 Dec. 1976: 30.

65. Sugarman, "Melville in Jerusalem," *Tablet*, 16 August 2012.

66. Richard, *WWAR*, 7.

67. In *Meaning of Life*, the Hospital Administrator (Palin), proudly points out a machine that goes "ping": "This is my favorite. You see, we lease this back from the company we sold it to, and that way, it comes under the monthly current budget and not the capital account." All clap.

68. *JTJ*, 91.

69. Maier, *Pontius Pilate*, 105.

70. *JURR*, 289.

71. In 201 BC, when Hannibal's troops were defeated by Scipio and the Romans, part of the payment penalty was 10,000 talents (*WWAR*, 9).

72. *BAFHG*, 387–88.

73. *BAFHG*, 83.

74. *JTJ*, 91n13.

75. Engen, "The Economy of Ancient Greece," *Economic History* (unpaginated).

76. *JTJ*, 97.

77. *JTJ*, 114.

78. Jenkins, *Mrs. Thatcher's Revolution*, 5.

79. See the entry "Is it right that we should pay taxes . . ." in scene 19.

80. Raymond Fletcher, quoted in Tomlinson, "The Politics of Decline," 44.

81. Former TUC leader David Lea mentioned this hope, speaking at a conference commemorating the Winter of Discontent in 2009 ("1978–1979: Winter of Discontent," 553–54).

82. Much public opinion ran against the unions. Pundit Waugh was certain that his union (National Union of Journalists) was run by "pigs, stoats, [and] child-murderers," and that other unions were little better: "In Blackpool the Trade Union Congress deliberates its next programme of theft, chaos and destruction in the name of Workers' Power" (Waugh, *FCY*, 10 March and 6 September 1977).

83. "1978–1979: Winter of Discontent"; also Black and Pemberton's "The Winter of Discontent in Britain" (2009). This period is covered in great detail by Sandbrook, Marr, Morgan, and Donoughue.

84. *BAFHG*, 446.

85. Scott, *Piranesi*, 32.

86. *ATW*, 1.8.105.

87. Dennan and McDonald, "Unemployment Statistics from 1881 to the Present Day."

88. Dennan and McDonald, "Unemployment Statistics," 10–11.

89. See the index in *BAFHG* under "Common Market" and "Charles de Gaulle" for more, as well as entries for "Arthur Scargill." The comments for the scenes "Dennis the Peasant" (94–160) and "Taunting by Frenchmen" (270–90) are also helpful for understanding these topicalities.

90. *AJ*, 8.2.5 (Whiston, 173).

91. Hankoff, "Religious Healing in First-Century Christianity, 388; "Hanina B. Dosa," *JE*.

92. Hankoff, "Religious Healing," 393.

93. Horsley, "The Zealots," 167 and 171, respectively. The high priest Jesus flourished 62–65, while Jesus Barabbas was alive during Jesus Christ's lifetime.

94. Julian Doyle—editor on *Brian* and jack-of-all-trades on *Holy Grail*—mentions several more Jesus namesakes in his very interesting book *The Life of Brian Jesus*, pages 246–47.

95. See the various entries for the writing of *Life of Brian* in Palin's *Diaries 1969–1979*.

96. *JTJ*, 163–64.

97. Hankoff, "Religious Healing," 391.

98. "In Brief," *Times*, 30 January 1969: 2. The short notice is delivered without tongue in cheek or a wink from the paper—it's just reported.

99. "Overwhelmed," *Telegraph*, 24 January 1977: 14.

100. Hankoff, "Religious Healing," 392–93.

101. Hankoff, "Religious Healing," 393.

102. Mark 1:40-45. This leper encounter is also mentioned in lesser detail in Matthew 8.

103. Mark 1:45.

104. This is rather eerily handled in *The Passover Plot*, where Yeshua is besieged at night by moaning sufferers.

105. *Daily Mail*, 5 July 1972: 27.

106. See "Apostles May Be Myths," *Sunday Times*, 16 January 1966: 6; and Geza Vermes, "Neglected Facts in the Dead Sea Scrolls," *Daily Telegraph*, 9 April 1966: 8, among many.

107. Palin and Gilliam had completed *Jabberwocky* at Shepperton, shooting July–August 1976.

108. Palin, *Diaries 1969–1979*, 561.

109. *BAFHG*, xvii.

110. *JTJ*, 112–13. The longer quotation is from Franz Delitzsch, *JTJ*, 113.

111. *JTJ*, 342–43.

112. See Bruce Watson's "For a While, the Luddites Had a Smashing Success."

113. "Collapse of the Postwar Settlement," a.t.

114. *JTJ*, 303.

115. See *JTJ*, chapter 14, "Despised Trades and Jewish Slaves," 303–12.

116. This prohibition meant that herdsman would sell to approved city vendors before the public could buy the products, perhaps diminishing the number and frequency of dishonest transactions.

117. *JTJ*, 305–6.

118. Smallwood, "Jews and Romans in the Early Empire," 238.

119. *JURR*, 124–25.

120. *JTJ*, 111.

121. *JTJ*, 116.

122. *JURR*, 126n20.

123. See the entry for ". . . we are sewage workers" in scene 11, "In the Palace Sewers," for more on the typical sewer worker during this period.

124. *JURR*, 151; also, Matthew 17, where the tribute is listed as half a shekel.

125. Wiedemann, *Emperors and Gladiators*, 76.

126. Palin, *Diaries 1969–1979*, 492–93.

127. Palin, *Diaries 1969–1979*, 492.

128. Jenkins, *Anatomy of Decline*, 92.

129. "Fresh Slump by Sterling Puts Shares in Retreat," *Times*, 27 June 1975: 15.

130. "Man Jobless for 25 Years Is Jailed for a Month," *Times*, 21 February 1976: 3.

131. In the Goons' "World War One" episode, a man is celebrating fifty years' unemployment, always dodging the "fear of work" bell (24 February 1958).

132. *JTJ*, 126–27.

133. *JURR*, 203–7.

I'M NOT A ROMAN, MUM!

MANDY: "Oh hello, Officer . . ."—"Officer"? A late fourteenth-century term borrowed from French, according to the *OED*, though Mandy here is addressing the Centurion as a man of the law, not unlike those in the *Flying Circus* world confronted with a constable or detective.[1]

BRIAN: ". . . we don't owe the Romans anything"—Brian is likely speaking about him and his mother, though he could also be taking the grander view, opining about what the PFJ will be on about soon—"bloody Romans" in Judea. Mandy's response brings the reference back home, and makes it quite personal for Brian.

MANDY: ". . . you were asking about your . . . er . . ."—Simply a comment about the more Roman, aquiline nose of Brian, meaning he has a Roman father. The "hook nose" caricature of a Jew—not common until much later—can be very similar to a Roman nose, meaning Brian can't tell where his particular nose might come from, his father or his mother. In a moment Brian will even embrace his "hook nose" Jewish stereotype, along with several others. (To be fair, when arrested he will claim to be a Roman.)

MANDY: ". . . your father isn't Mr. Cohen"—We never do meet this bearded father figure, nor will we see the alleged "Nortius Maximus." As far as the film presents the situation, Brian's conception is, if not immaculate, certainly immethodical. The name Cohen is a version of *kohen*, the Hebrew word for priest (or augur, soothsayer). If Mr. Cohen *were* Brian's actual father, Brian might be priestly by birth and tradition (not a Levite, but a Kohen), and therefore higher in the social, religious, and political strata of Jerusalem. As a son of uncertain parentage, however, Brian can be no more than a bastard, which is generally described as "depraved" and worse.[2] See "The bastard!" entry below for much more on this term.

In the final Monty Python film, *Meaning of Life*, one of the piratical chartered accountants is named Mr. Cohen.

MANDY: "None of your cheek!"—A common English colloquialism, "cheek" can be impertinence, rudeness, or just freshness. The in-your-face Mr. Cheeky—seen at the Sermon on the Mount and later as part of the crucifixion queue—fits this term well.

MANDY: "He was a Roman, Brian!" *(dramatic chord)*—The "dramatic chord" moment is a borrow from not only *Holy Grail* and the run of *Flying Circus*, but also years of radio dramas the Pythons grew up hearing, as well as *The Goon Show*. In Ep. 7 of *Flying Circus*, for example, a similar chord is struck, and a slightly dim-witted female character thinks it's a doorbell. The scientist (Chapman) has to tell her "It's just the incidental music for this scene."[3] Similarly, in the "Ralph Mellish" sketch included on the *Matching Tie and Handker-chief* album (1973), a number of these flourishes can be heard, even as the narrator continues to tell us that nothing out of the ordinary is happening.

MANDY: "He was a centurion in the Roman army"—A centurion was a commander in the Roman army, meaning he ranked with the other centurion depicted in the film (played by Cleese). Given his swift disappearance, however, he easily may have exaggerated his rank to impress young Mandy.

As will be discussed later, Brian should actually be happy about this new fact, since the likelihood of a Roman citizen—more specifically the *honestiores*—being crucified was extremely rare.[4] Other methods of capital punishment, however, were still at the prefect's disposal, especially for *humiliores*, the lower classes of Roman culture. The fact that Brian is also part Jewish problematizes his situation.

BRIAN: "You mean . . . you were raped?"—This would have been a tricky legal definition at the time. Rape was illegal under Roman law, and women could bring charges against an accused rapist, but the woman had to be a Roman citizen. If the woman were a slave, then the rape charge could be downgraded to a violation or even theft of chattel—property owned by another Roman citizen. In a time of war and conquest, especially, the chances of any prosecution being brought for a rape among the enemy seem unlikely.

Elisabeth Vikman writes of the use of sexual violence in antiquity, noting that the ancient Greeks, Romans, and even the Israelites practiced (and often defended) rape against their conquered. The easiest and perhaps most understandable reason is the use of violence as justified against the "other," especially "during these early holy wars" among the Israelites.[5] In fighting the Midianites, for example, "the victorious may do as they wish with defeated peoples," and prophetic, scriptural backing underscored it all.[6] And since the Israelites practiced it, Mandy shouldn't be surprised when the Roman invaders did the same. If, as Paul Bentley Kern mentions, "the raping that frequently followed the fall of a city starkly symbolized total victory in a total war," then the subjugation of Judea qualifies as total war for the Roman forces. As depicted by the Pythons here, though, Mandy admits to the initial violence of the act, then backpedals as she admits the promised benefits—exotic travel, food, and riches—changed her view of the rape. This walking back will be revisited later, when Reg's charges against Rome are questioned by the rest of the PFJ, who remind Reg of how good life is in Jerusalem after the initial violent, penetrative act.

Problematically, it's mentioned (by Ziolowski) that the "sexual attractiveness" of the potential victims meant that "fair women" had a much better chance of survival, even including the rape scenario: "It is important to remember the subsequent enslavement of enemy women common in ancient warfare. Attractive women would then hold a higher economical value and this may be an additional motive to spare their lives."[7] This being said, was Mandy "sexually attractive" thirty years earlier? She was raped, she admits, and she did survive. But the script calls her a "rat-bag" when we first see her, with the infant Brian, and she's now just an older rat-bag. This is the Pythonesque trope of using men-as-ugly-women who somehow manage to still be attractive, in the narrative world. Remember that Nortius also promises Mandy gifts and *la dolce vita* back in Rome, essentially honey-talking her into a premarital romp—it sounds less like a marauding conqueror raping at will, and more like a hormone-besotted twenty-something willing to say anything to get *everything*.

MANDY: "Well at first . . . yes . . ."—Nineteen-year-old Patty Hearst was, at first, a kidnap victim, taken by the Symbionese Liberation Army because she was the coddled scion of a powerful, moneyed clan representing everything rotten in modern America.[8] Kidnapped from her Berkeley apartment in February 1974, authorities assumed that her participation in the group's insurrectionary efforts became voluntary very quickly (she was participating in an armed robbery by April 1974), which is why she was eventually convicted of bank robbery and sentenced to prison. During the course of the sensational trial the sexual activity between Hearst and members of the SLA became prime fodder. Hearst and her lawyers claimed that she was raped by leader "Cinque" and that sex with Willy Wolfe happened because she was "afraid," but prosecutors were convinced she had entered into a willing physical relationship with at least Wolfe, a.k.a. "Cujo." The more tawdry portions of the trial were covered in depth in local (Bay Area) newspapers, and especially graphically in countercultural underground papers like the *Berkeley Barb*, university papers including UC Berkeley's *Daily Californian*, and even *Playboy*.[9]

MANDY: "Nortius Maximus . . ."—The two names indicate this man at least could claim to be a free Roman citizen before entering the military.[10] There are many Maximus-named men in history, including a handful of Roman generals and governors. One Magnus Maximus (335–388) had usurped the empire's throne as a commander in Britain, and would lose the seat in battle five years later. Maximus was technically *from* Britain when he usurped Gratian's authority, bringing him closer to these English-speaking Romans depicted in *Brian*. As will be discussed below, "Nortius Maximus" is most likely a *Carry On*–type name, meant to wink at the character's extreme level of naughtiness.

MANDY: ". . . promised me the known world . . . taken to Rome . . . house by the Forum . . . slaves . . . asses' milk . . . as much gold as I could eat . . ."—Reminiscent of the excesses enjoyed by the ex-slave character Trimalchio in Petronius's *Satyricon*, who "has scores of slaves around him to pick up fallen objects, carry him, offer their hair as towels, massage him, and make music."[11] Mandy's version of this "absurd feast" includes milk from an ass and "as much gold" as she can eat. But given that *Satyricon* dates to approximately Nero's reign (54–68), Nortius Maximus couldn't have read it (or heard it read) and simply be aping the portions he remembers. (The Pythons could be allowing him this anachronism, of course, something they've enjoyed in *Flying Circus* and *Holy Grail*.) Brian himself will later try to emulate Jesus's teachings to escape the Roman soldiers, mangling Beatitudes and parables almost beyond recognition. This actually just seems to be Nortius's line to convince young Mandy he's a real catch.

Mandy doesn't say if she was promised marriage, but if she had then that should have been the first clue that something was amiss: Roman soldiers were actually *forbidden* to marry until 193, during the reign of Septimus Severus. More recent archaeology indicates that a number of Roman outposts offer clear evidence of women and children in domestic situations, so practice may have kept its distance from principle.[12] Perhaps she was to be a mistress, and not a wife, but Mandy isn't forthcoming.

The fringe benefits that allowed Nortius Maximus into Mandy's garden of earthly delights include:

". . . taken to Rome"—Interesting that Mandy's idea of bliss is to leave Jerusalem and head for Rome, the heart of the empire that has enslaved her people. For many, though, Rome was the center of the universe, hence the medieval adage, "All roads lead to Rome."

These philo-Romans would include the historian Josephus, who was born a Jew but ended his life as a celebrated and favored Roman citizen. As the Jewish military leader Joseph, he had surrendered in Jotapata (discussed in detail later) and been taken to Rome, likely for execution. Instead, the clever man offered Vespasian an aggrandizing version of a known prophesy, and Vespasian allowed Joseph to live. Once Nero and his short-lived successors Galba and Otho died, Vespasian was, with some military intrigue, in line for the throne, and

Joseph's future was also assured. Josephus would enjoy many of the niceties on Mandy's list as he later wrote his histories, safely nestled in Rome.

This also may be a contemporary reflection of the very split opinion in Northern Ireland (and Ireland in general) over the significance of *Catholic* Irish "popery"—a "Home Rule as Rome rule"[13] that the *Protestant* Irish wanted to avoid at all costs—the Irish themselves split down the middle. For many in Ireland, then, the specter of being ruled by Rome, with a host of staunch Catholic citizen foot soldiers ready to do the pope's bidding—so it was feared—was a frightening reality throughout most of the Pythons' lifetimes.[14] Men like the Rev. Ian Paisley, "a fire-breathing standard bearer of Protestantism"[15]—likely asked the rhetorical "And what have they ever given us in return?" among themselves, as their Catholic neighbors welcomed their faith's allegedly foreign influence.

"House by the Forum . . ."—Essentially the center of the public life in Ancient Rome, the Forum was actually a handful of buildings around a rectangular courtyard. The contemporary equivalent might be the promise of a house in London's Kensington, or a Park Avenue apartment in Manhattan.

". . . slaves . . ."—In *Life of Brian* there is only one identifiable slave, a "small boy" holding a parasol over Gregory at the Sermon on the Mount and on the cross. The script doesn't identify the boy's color or race, though in the film he's black, and likely a local North African extra. Jeremias mentions that slaves seem to have comprised an insignificant portion of Jerusalem's population, and were generally domestic servants. In other more Roman cities, including Rome itself, slaves would have been more plentiful (all able-bodied peoples conquered by Roman forces were fair game for enslavement), and slaves were needed for public works projects and the popular, deadly games staged regularly across the empire.[16] Many countries and ancient peoples took slaves as spoils of war, including the Israelites and Greeks. Homer would write, according to Vikman, of a "gendered ideal; men are slaughtered whereas women and children are enslaved."[17] This seemed to be true across many peoples in Greece; while among the Israelites there were both Hebrew and Canaanite slaves, and laws for treatment of each group. Like the temple and most of Jewish religious life, slavery is another practice prevalent in first-century Judea that the Pythons avoid in *Life of Brian*.

". . . asses' milk . . ."—Mentioned earlier by the Ex-leper, the donkey had been a crucial part of Ancient Israel's life for several thousand years. Pliny the Elder wrote of the benefits of donkey's milk, as Jill Bough records in her book titled, appropriately, *Donkey*:

> It is generally believed that asses' milk effaces wrinkles in the face, renders the skin more delicate, and preserves its whiteness; and it is a well-known fact, that some women are in the habit of washing their face with it seven hundred times daily, strictly observing that number. Poppaea, the wife of Emperor Nero, was the first to practice this; indeed, she had sitting-baths, prepared solely with asses' milk, for which purpose whole troops of she-asses used to attend her on her journeys.[18]

Pliny's *Historia naturalis* also includes other benefits of this milk, noting the liquid could "combat poisonings, fever, fatigue, eye strains, weakened teeth, face wrinkles, ulcerations, asthma and certain gynaecological troubles."[19] Milk from the donkey doesn't seem to have been high on the lists of fresh milk sources for ancient Israelites, but many Romans clearly enjoyed its benefits. Nortius may have mentioned the milk's cosmetic and health properties, perhaps another one of the reasons Mandy is willing to travel to Rome. Given this list of uses, it's no wonder the woman seen earlier carrying her donkey home would want to nurse the valuable creature back to profitable health.

In *Carry on Cleo*, the voluptuous Cleopatra (Amanda Barrie) is bathing in asses' milk when she first meets Mark Antony, an image the Pythons likely encourage viewers to conjure in relation to our Mandy and Nortius.

". . . as much gold as I could eat . . ."—In the Goons' "The Fear of Wages" episode, two corrupt Army Pay Corps' representatives are trying to abscond with all the wages in their charge. At one point they are hiding as much as they can on Moriarty's person—£10,000 in the linings of his socks, £100 under his wig, and "£50,000 in loose silver" that he needs to swallow.

Gold wasn't meant to be eaten, nor was expensive and much-coveted marble meant to be trod under foot, but that's where Jerusalem found itself a few years before the city fell to the Romans. In the year 64, the temple was finally completed and celebrated. Unfortunately, the thousands of workmen who had been gainfully employed for years as the temple slowly progressed were now without work. The city's fathers decided to create more public works to help offset the unemployment—hopefully staving off idlers' violence and even revolt—and with the leftover marble from the building of the temple, began to repave the streets of Jerusalem.[20]

Just six years later, the plight of Jerusalem had gone well beyond a lack of employment for ex-lepers or public workers. With Titus's forces surrounding the city, then breaching first one wall and then another, many Jerusalemites tried to sneak out of the city to escape both the Romans and starvation. Many "ate" their gold and silver and jewelry, and then fled in the dark of night. These furtive decampments dwindled when word spread that those who were captured by the Romans were immediately slit open, and their guts searched.[21]

MANDY: ". . . then—he, having his way with me, had, voom! Like a rat out of an aqueduct"—In the well-known "Dead Parrot" sketch in Ep. 8 of *Flying Circus*, the Shopkeeper (Palin) assures Praline (Cleese) that the parrot would fly away—"voom"—if it hadn't been nailed to the perch. Praline is certain that even "four thousand volts" wouldn't make this exparrot "voom."[22]

Rats could move around from area to area on grain carts, on ships, in deliveries of all sorts across the ancient world. Rats would have used these waterways as sources of fresh water, of course, but also safer pathways under, above, and simply away from the city's human inhabitants. During times of flooding, parts of Rome could experience significant rising water levels, forcing populations of rats out of sewers and waterways and into homes.[23] (It may be that Nortius Maximus had been stationed in Rome initially, and was simply serving in the Jerusalem garrison when his honeyed words seduced Mandy, and then "voomed" back to Rome.) Koloski-Ostrow even tells of an octopus said to have used the Puteoli sewer to clamber up into a home, regularly pilfering pickled fish from a wealthy merchant's larder.[24] Of more concern than rats in aqueducts, especially in Jerusalem, were rats and other vermin living and dying in the city's cisterns, where fresh water was stored.[25] These complex subterranean waterways were necessary to keep the city's meager water supplies from rapidly evaporating in surface storage. Aqueducts will be discussed again in more detail in relation to PFJ member Xerxes asking about one of the benefits of the Roman occupation.

Auberon Waugh fortuitously points out an equally "advantageous" relationship in the real world that is echoed in Mandy's experience with Nortius Maximus. In a 1977 issue of *Private Eye*, he mentions Mary Whitehouse's attempt to prosecute *Gay News* for blasphemy:[26]

Mrs Mary Whitehouse is an old friend and very remarkable woman. I also happen to find her very attractive physically. But I can't help feeling she has let zeal outrun her discretion in prosecuting *Gay News* for allegedly blasphemous libel. Normally, of course, some kind High Court judge would restrain her from making a fool of herself in this way. On this occasion, she had the misfortune to draw a fanatical enemy of the Press in Judge Bristow *and is left holding the baby, as the saying goes.*[27]

The obviously "physically attractive" Mandy was confronted not by an authority figure who puts her in her place as one conquered by Rome; it's her "misfortune" to be taken advantage of by a "fanatical" enemy of Jewry, a centurion named Nortius Maximus who has his own agenda, and Mandy is eventually left holding the baby, Brian.

(draft) **MANDY: "I went down to the barracks . . . you've been had, Missus"**—In this draft version Judith is part of this conversation, and has invited Brian over to her house for dinner. Her parents are the "Iscariots," meaning she's actually "Judith Iscariot," a very *Carry On*–sounding name. There were more of these easy gags in the early days of the idea and then script, including a Fourth Wise Man who always gets shushed, a "Ron the Baptist," an Otto who was much more clearly a "Nazi-rene" looking to annex neighboring countries and cleanse the homeland, etc.[28] This Nortius Maximus moment won't reemerge until later, when Pilate asks the Centurion if such a man is part of the local garrison.

These barracks would have likely been found within the impressive Antonia Fortress, one of Herod's many military and civic structures built during his reign. The high priest's vestments were also kept in this fortress.

BRIAN: "The bastard!"—In first-century Jerusalem this wouldn't have been just a mild insult. There was disagreement over just what constituted a bastard in the eyes of Jewish law, including whether betrothals or promises had been made when there was conception, whether the woman was already married, etc., but these were minor arguments that paled in relation to the larger question:

> Who were regarded as bastard in Jerusalem before the destruction of the Temple? Traditional teaching allows only the following conclusion to be drawn. M. Yeh. iv.13 relates: "R. Simeon b. Azzai (c. AD 120) said: 'I found a family register in Jerusalem and in it was written: Such-a-one is a bastard through [a transgression of the law of] thy neighbour's wife.'" We see then that in Jerusalem children conceived in adultery were declared bastards.[29]

We don't know if there actually was a "Mr. Cohen" to whom Mandy was married when she had relations with Nortius, or whether the centurion was already married. Likely Mandy was young and single, and so was Nortius, and therefore the act was not adulterous. The subsequent birth was still problematic, even if Brian wouldn't have been considered a bastard by the mores of the time.[30] He could have been called "fatherless," if his true father were indeed not known, which clearly could have been the case when rape was alleged. Both fatherless and "foundling" children were blemished, and were nearly forbidden to marry at all. The reason? Since their parentage was unknown, there was no certainty that a forbidden, incestuous marriage might not be accidentally entered into with a close relative.[31]

According to Jeremias, Jewish law treated "tainted" births and peoples quite punitively, at least in principle. For example, a bastard like Brian could only intermarry within the group including "the proselyte, freedman, bastard . . . [temple slaves] . . . [fatherless] and . . . [foundlings]."[32] He could not intermarry with "priestly, levitic and (full-)Israelitish stocks," nor even in the second category, which added "impaired priestly stocks."[33] Brian's family would have been described as having "grave blemishes of ancestry," so his chances of finding a suitable wife or be accepted as a son-in-law were slim. Other lists of appropriate marriage partners forbade bastards from marrying other bastards, given their uncertain parentage.[34] Brian was also a bastard of a Gentile father, which pushed him further down the list,[35] and as a bastard he could also never be part of the Sanhedrin or hold public office.[36]

This is another of those moments in the film where the Pythons will make direct connections to the time they are portraying, if only by accident, and even to Jesus. Given the Jews' strictures regarding birth and parentage, Brian, as the illegitimate son of a Roman soldier, and Jesus, the alleged (to many) son of God, both carry "grave blemishes of ancestry" (or at least charcoal gray areas), and it's no surprise that Brian ends up suffering the same fate as Jesus—crucified, in part, for being on the outside of acceptable Jewish culture in first-century Jerusalem. Finally, from Jeremias: "When we consider that the stigma of bastardy marked every male descendant . . . for ever and indelibly, and that a bastard family's share in Israel's final redemption was most vigorously disputed . . . we shall understand that the word 'bastard' constituted one of the worst insults to a man; and anyone using it was sentenced to thirty-nine lashes with the whip."[37] No one is punished for saying "bastard" in the world of the film, just "Jehovah."[38] It's clear the Pythons *didn't* truly appreciate the volatile concept of bastardy in relation to Brian specifically and ancient Jerusalem in general.

BRIAN: "I'm a Kike! A Yid! A Hebe! A Hook-nose! I'm Kosher, Mum. I'm a Red Sea Pedestrian and proud of it!"—More of a childish temper tantrum than anything else, this is a shortened version of a Python staple, the "thesaurus sketch" trope, in this case a "vituperative verbal list" that Cleese and Chapman pioneered in *Flying Circus*.[39] This Python favorite will be discussed again, when Reg has to be reminded of the Roman contributions to Jerusalem, and where Reg finally puts a stop to the unhelpful flow of information with a characteristic "Shut up!"

Also, it's interesting that Brian is here claiming his provincial, even *humiliores* status in front of not only his mother, but a Roman centurion. If only he'd appreciated that later, in front of Pilate, he would need to change his tune and claim Roman kinship and status.[40] There he could have enlisted this man—a Roman citizen and soldier, with all attendant rights and privileges—as a witness to his Roman heritage, and therefore his rights, one of which was the chance to avoid execution, as will be discussed later.

"Kike" is a derogatory Jewish epithet, more American than British, and likely emerging from the nineteenth or twentieth century, perhaps in relation to the increased immigration of Jews into the United States. The British TV character Alf Garnett spewed these terms regularly on the edgy and incredibly popular sitcom *Till Death Us Do Part*.[41]

A "Yid" is another nineteenth and twentieth century insult, which, according to the *OED*, was often used by Jewish persons to refer to other Jews. Oswald Mosley's Blackshirts (the British Union of Fascists) were known to shout "anti-Yid slogans" as they marched through the East End in the 1930s, and later Hitler was known to call Churchill "this Yid-ridden, half-American souse."[42] "Bloody Yid" and "filthy Yid" seemed to have been fairly popular epithets in Britain during the 1970s, spoken just before a fight got out of hand.[43] When novelist Evelyn Waugh's *Diaries* were released in September 1976, the *Sunday Times'* Frederic Raphael reviewed the work in the article "Portrait of the Artist as a Bad Man." The language Waugh often used (and that Brian uses here) is the language of the public schoolboy, and Waugh is acknowledged by the reviewer as being both "odious" and "terribly funny":

> Surely there was more to him that that? Yes: he was also mad, and quite possibly bad, and undoubtedly dangerous to know. "Mad" is a term which recurs *un peu partout* in his Diaries. It is applied to the unremarkable schoolboys whom he was forced to teach, because he needed the money after coming down from Oxford in a haze of expensive alcohol (there were not better hazes in his long experience) and it is applied, thirty and more years later, to assorted wor-

thies and unworthies, including his dearish dearest friends, Cyril Connolly and also Randolph Churchill.[44] (Well, he didn't call them niggers or hook-nosed Jews or oiks or wops, did he, the eternal Public Schoolboy?) Was he mad? Hilaire Belloc[45] was asked, after a first muted meeting with the unusually deferential enfant terrible, what he made of him. "He is possessed," replied the sage-old Yid-hating, Papist semi-Frog. Well, touché certainly. For if the Comic Muse was his enviable familiar, there were always more sinister demons leering at his shoulder. Such are the cradle gifts of the Gods: you cannot, and Waugh certainly could not, be blessed with the one without being cursed with the others.[46]

The Pythons are also clearly "eternal public schoolboys," ready for a poop joke or racial slur should the need arise, *un peu partout*.

"Hebe"—short for Hebrew—is a more recent, Depression-era epithet, and seemingly more popular in the United States than in Britain. In July 1972 critic Alan Brien was watching DeMille's *Ten Commandments* with his son at the Casino cinema, and began to wonder why the Jews were never called "Jews," rather "Hebrews" or "Israelites." Even the Pharaoh dances around the name, leading Brien to conclude:

> This reluctance to give your enemy the name he calls himself is usually the mark of the discreet racialist. He prefers to say "the Chosen People," or "those of the Hebrew persuasion," or "coloured folk," or "those of African descent"—thus giving the impression, even to some Jews and blacks, that "Jew" and "Black" are the equivalent of "Yid" and "nigger."[47]

"Hebe" was also the approved and oft-used shortening for "Hebrew" in the pages of *Variety* for many years.[48] Much of the Hollywood film industry had been run by Jewish families and individuals, *Variety* included.

These kinds of racial slurs (and insensitive racial depictions) seemed to be everywhere as the Pythons grew up, in cinema cartoons, advertisements, political cartoons, on the radio and TV, and in letters to the editor. A "Golliwogg" character (based on a Negro minstrel doll) became very popular during the Pythons' youth, appearing on dozens of consumer items, from greeting cards to jam.[49] The Goons regularly made racial jokes at the expense of their only colleague of color, bandleader Ray Ellington—who was often the initiator (at the performance level) of the joke. The Goons also presented Scotsmen as penny-pinching, the Welsh as dim but pleasant, the French as "frog-eaters," and Arabs as "wogs." The Goons' harmonica player, Max Geldray, a Dutch-born Jew (Ellington was also Jewish), also got to hear about the size of his "conk" on a regular basis. Principal writer and Irishman Spike Milligan wrote as many self-deprecating Irish jokes as others; his "racialist" references seemed to be on par with the more racially insensitive spirit of the times.

"Hook-nose" is the only insult here not specifically connected to the Jewish people. There are many instances historically where "hook-nose" has been used to simply describe the facial features of a criminal, for example, or a character introduced in literature, distinct from any racial or religious attachment. (The nose prosthesis worn by Alec Guinness—playing Fagin—in David Lean's *Oliver Twist* is a noted exception to this race-free description.) A 1975 archaeological find in Sakkara, Egypt, for example, was a bas-relief image of King Tut's general, Horemheb (later pharaoh himself), which, according to contemporary news reports, depicted "a fat man with a hooked nose and a double chin."[50]

"Kosher" simply means Brian is claiming to live according to Jewish custom and law, including eating meat that has been properly killed and prepared. Both the Pythons and the Goons made "kosher" jokes. In *Flying Circus* Ep. 3, a barrister (Cleese) is running late after having trouble finding a "kosher car park," while:

in *The Goon Show* episode "King Solomon's Mines," Bluebottle (Sellers) is thrown into the river, and shouts out: "Help! I've fallen into non-kosher water!" Other instances include "kosher margarine" in "The Tales of Old Dartmoor," "yellow kosher boots" in "The International Christmas Pudding," and "kosher wine gum" in "The Pevensey Bay Disaster."[51]

In *Flying Circus* Ep. 26, the lost-at-sea sailors are worried not about having to eat one of their fellows, but that he be killed and prepared in accordance with kosher laws if he is to be eaten.[52]

Finally, a "Red Sea Pedestrian" is fairly self-evident, though its origins are clouded. Slang dictionaries cite it as both an Australian and British reference, and it simply means one who crossed the Red Sea on foot (Exodus 14:21).[53] Unlike some of the other slurs, this one is generally considered to be more jocular. The slanted references to Jews in *Flying Circus* are few, and are missing entirely from their look at Britain of the early Middle Ages, where such references might seem most appropriate:

> The Pythons make no direct or even glancing references to Jews or Jewishness in [*Holy Grail*], even though the place and plight of Jews in the medieval period was significant—they were allowed to lend money with interest (their souls were damned anyway, was the prevailing thought), and they suffered horrifically during the many pogroms, especially following the worst of the plagues.[54]

In *Meaning of Life*, a Jew-baiting reference from a charwoman results in a bucket of vomit being dumped on her head.

Alf Garnett himself erupts with a splenetic along this same vein, though it's only after his son-on-law has goaded him, the *Telegraph*'s Alan Yentob remembers in an article looking at Jews in the British entertainment business:

> Over the years, the British approach has been more subtle—on occasion, even subversive. One of the funniest moments in any sitcom that I can remember is when Alf Garnett, the irredeemable but likeable "bigot" from *Till Death Us Do Part* is confronted by his socialist son-in-law and accused of being a Jew. "How would you like it if I called you a Yid? You're Jewish, aren't you," he taunts him, only to be greeted by an expression of utter horror and humiliation, and Alf's repeatedly hysterical response, "What are you talking about! I am not a Yid!! I am not Jewish!! It's lies. It's all lies."[55]

She moves towards the CENTURION—Nothing in the printed scripts say anything about why the Centurion waits, or what actual relationship he might have with Mandy. As filmed, Mandy moves toward the Centurion and just begins to kneel in front of him. The implication is that she performs sexual favors for him, he pays her or rewards her somehow, and she and Brian live on in this way without a husband or master. (This after chiding and tsk-ing Brian for only thinking about "Sex, sex, sex!") As will be discussed later, the scriptures offer very few similarly *unattached* women who are capable of supporting themselves, so Mandy and Brian have managed to buck the odds; that, or she is more of a 1970s construct, a "liberated" female who chooses her lifestyle.

Notes

1. See the many entries for "constable" in the index for Larsen, *MPFC: UC*.
2. See Prawer's *The History of Jerusalem*, 272.
3. *ATW*, 1.87–88.
4. Cook, "Envisioning Crucifixion," 263–64.

5. The Pythons have previously "othered" homosexuals, women, toffs, and so on, often culminating in a violent act. See the index entry in *MPFC: UC*, "othering/others," for more.

6. Vikman, "Ancient Origins: Sexual Violence," 23; see Deuteronomy 21: 10–14; Numbers 31.

7. Quoted in Vikman, "Ancient Origins: Sexual Violence," 28.

8. She was the granddaughter of newspaper magnate (and ur-Charles Foster Kane) William Randolph Hearst. She and the SLA will be discussed later.

9. For more see "The Parts Left Out of the Patty Hearst Trial, Parts 1 and 2" (2002), at disinfo .com, by Paul Krassner, who also wrote *Patty Hearst and the Twinkie Murders* (2014).

10. Adoption was possible. Jewish historian Josephus (born Joseph ben Matityahu) added "Titus" and "Flavius" to his name as a token of respect (or obsequy) to the Flavian dynasty, and specifically to Vespasian and Titus. He became known as Titus Flavius Josephus.

11. Rodriguez, *The Historical Encyclopedia of World Slavery*, 549. Both Trimalchio and Petronius's *Satyricon* and Horace's *Satires* will be discussed later in the scene at the Colosseum, where Brian is flogging "Roman rubbish" to the audience.

12. Archaeologist Elizabeth Greene discussed her new interpretations of female figures found on Trajan's Column at a conference; her own article on the subject has yet to be published. For coverage, see "Women Present, No 'Second Fiddle' in Roman Military," in *Western News*, 5 February 2015.

13. Brendon, *DFBE*, 304.

14. Remember the earlier-mentioned invasion of the IRA, in its conception at least a Roman church-following body armed to the teeth and bent on domination?

15. "Paisley's £180,000 Church," *Times*, 4 October 1969: 6.

16. See the entries later in the "Colosseum" scene for more on slaves, gladiators, and the games.

17. Vikman, "Ancient Origins: Sexual Violence," 26.

18. Bough, *Donkey*, 39–40.

19. Bough, *Donkey*, 40.

20. Kotker, *HLTJ*, 114.

21. *HLTJ*, 123. This search for plunder was payment to the Roman soldiers for their sufferings as the siege went on, depredations that also included rape and murder of the city's inhabitants.

22. *ATW*, 1.8.105.

23. See Aldrete's *Floods of the Tiber in Ancient Rome*, 127.

24. Koloski-Ostrow, *ASRI*, 83.

25. See Ernest L. Martin's notes (esp. footnote 15) related to reviews of his book, *New Evidence of the Site of the Temple in Jerusalem* (2000), Associates for Scriptural Knowledge website.

26. See entries in the "The Stoning" scene for more on this case, and its influence on the Pythons and the in-progress *Life of Brian*.

27. *Private Eye*, 7 January 1977: 16; italics added.

28. Palin, *Diaries 1969–1979*, 352 and 224, respectively.

29. Jeremias, *JTJ*, 340.

30. Palin summed up Brian's story as they worked out the film treatment (a pre-script) in December 1976, referring to Brian as a "bastard," simply meaning born out of wedlock.

31. *JTJ*, 343.

32. *JTJ*, 271.

33. *JTJ*, 271.

34. *JTJ*, 271–72.

35. *JTJ*, 273.

36. *JTJ*, 298n102.

37. *JTJ*, 342.

38. The word is used at least fourteen times in the film, and *always* as just a simple insult.

39. *MPFC: UC*, 1.43.

40. As the Apostle Paul (of the free city Tarsus) did to avoid corporal punishment and ensure a fair trial; see Acts 22. Brian, born in Bethlehem and living in Jerusalem, doesn't appear to be a Hellenistic Jew. This will be discussed later when Brian claims to be a Roman, in the "Court of Pontius Pilate" scene.

41. Viewership reached upwards of half the homes in Britain in the late 1960s, and Garnett "went on to supercede fictional status and became a cultural phenomenon, attracting seismic media coverage" (Malik, *Representing Black Britain*, 93). See also Larsen, *BAFHG*, 279–80.

42. "Mosley's Blackshirts," *Times*, 25 October 1968: 11; and "Plays That Remain," *Times*, 22 May 1976: 10.

43. ". . . And Tranquilisers Can Make People Violent," *Sunday Times*, 2 February 1975: 2; "The 'New Left,'" *Telegraph*, 26 March 1971: 18. In February 1978, just after the Pythons returned from Barbados, an Islington-area comprehensive school created a list of words that would be banned on campus, including "coon," "wog," and "yid." This was following the discovery of a National Front recruiting leaflet at the school ("Head Bans Race Words in National Front Drive," *Telegraph*, 3 February 1978: 6).

44. Cyril Connolly was a writer and literary critic. Evelyn's son Auberon blasted Connolly often in the pages of *Private Eye* and *Spectator*, and for years promised he was writing a book about him. The Pythons mention him in their song "Eric the Half-a-Bee." Randolph Churchill was both a journalist and a Tory MP.

45. The Pythons have also mentioned Belloc—an "ardent Catholic"—in Ep. 2 as perhaps "a closet sexual deviant" (*MPFC: UC*, 1.28).

46. Frederic Raphael, "Portrait of the Artist as a Bad Man," *Sunday Times*, 5 September 1976: 27.

47. "Alan Brien's Diary," *Sunday Times*, 30 July 1972: 24.

48. Rawson, *Wicked Words*, 189.

49. See *MPFC: UC*, 2.31, the "Nigger-Baiter" entry.

50. "Pharaoh Was Probably Fat," *Telegraph*, 21 February 1975: 17.

51. *MPFC: UC*, 1.55.

52. *MPFC: UC*, 1.390.

53. See *The New Partridge Dictionary of Slang*, as well as Rawson, *Wicked Words*.

54. *BAFHG*, 289n57.

55. "Now That's What I Call Chutzpah," *Telegraph*, 22 May 2011.

SCENE SEVEN
THE COLOSSEUM, JERUSALEM

A huge Roman amphitheatre sparsely attended—Found in Carthage, Tunisia, this location is actually an ancient Roman amphitheatre, though quite dilapidated, and had to be dressed considerably by Gilliam and crew. The low wall with arches and rings, the gated entry, and the podia had to be built and decorated onsite, while a (postproduction) painted glass matte provided the upper background.

The matinee could be "sparsely attended" simply because the Pythons have a habit of creating mock epic moments in their film and television worlds. In Ep. 12 of *Flying Circus* a handful of cheering debutantes watch the Upperclass Twits compete themselves to death, while in Ep. 28 one small flag-waving child stands ready to send off the intrepid Mr. and Mrs. Brian Norris (Palin and Chapman) as they set off to trace the historic migration from Surbiton to Hounslow.[1] It's also true that by the year 33 the Roman emperor Tiberius would have been in power for almost nineteen years, and he was known to be "notoriously hostile to public shows."[2] By the year 57, the emperor Nero would announce the "banning [of] provincial governors and imperial procurators from giving gladiatorial *munera*, *venationes*, or theatrical shows of any kind in the provinces."[3] This means a provincial ruler like Pilate (or the local *aedile*) would have been unable to stage the pitiful gladiatorial display in Jerusalem or anywhere else in Judea after 57.[4] Gladiators and their games would remain viable, however, through the fourth century at least, in smaller contests (perhaps tatty ones like this), and further away from seats of power.[5]

Considering the film's budget, the Pythons had likely shot their wad (in regard to extras) for the "Sermon on the Mount" and the "Pilate's Address" scenes, where dozens of costumed extras wend their way toward the mount and roll in the dust, respectively. There are handfuls seen in the bazaar scenes, as well, but other scenes feature fewer and fewer people. It's also possible that they could have added any number of games audience members on the matte painting portion of the shot, if they'd wanted to go that way. As presented, the painted upper portion of the Colosseum is as sparsely populated as the live portion below.

SUPER TITLE: The Colosseum, Jerusalem—Herod the Great is known for his massive building program that included almost all of Caesarea, and the temple, fortresses, theaters, and games arenas near Jerusalem, the last bringing Hellenized Rome and Roman games to Judea.[6] There was no Colosseum-type building in Jerusalem, but Herod's quinquennial games to honor the emperor (Augustus) meant gladiators were likely fighting in or near Jerusalem, and Josephus found that disturbing:

On this account it was that Herod revolted from the laws of his country, and corrupted their ancient constitution, by the introduction of foreign practices, which constitution yet ought to have been preserved inviolable; by which means we became guilty of great wickedness afterward, while those religious observances which used to lead the multitude to piety were now neglected; for, in the first place, he appointed solemn games to be celebrated every fifth year, in honor of Caesar, and built a theater at Jerusalem, as also a very great amphitheater in the plain. Both of them were indeed costly works, but opposite to the Jewish customs; for we have had no such shows delivered down to us as fit to be used or exhibited by us; yet did he celebrate these games every five years, in the most solemn and splendid manner.[7]

Games were held regularly in Caesarea, where Pilate would live, though Jewish residents refused to participate: "[The Jews] could not forgive [Herod] for insulting their religious feelings by forcing upon them heathen games and combats with wild animals."[8] It was also in Caesarea in 70 that many Jewish captives rounded up in the fall of Jerusalem were slaughtered in gladiatorial games. The Herodian theater, amphitheater, and a hippodrome described by Josephus do not survive, except by description, and in archaeological remains.[9] The "sparsely attended" events the Pythons have presented reflect the Jewish resistance to these pagan celebrations: "The Pharisees scorned the Greek civilization that Herod encouraged in the country," Kotker writes, "and they were shocked when he built a hippodrome for chariot racing in Jerusalem and an amphitheatre outside the city walls where men fought with wild beasts and with one another in gladiatorial combats."[10] Smallwood suggests that rather than being *religiously* offended (as they might be by graven images), the Jerusalem Jews "were disgusted by the barbarity of the bloodshed of the amphitheatre . . . not any actual contravention of the Law."[11]

In the closing pages of his fascinating and oft-reprinted book *Those about to Die*, Daniel Mannix gives a handy list of regions beyond Rome but still part of the empire where large, games-related amphitheaters had been constructed, and where the spectacles were well attended: "So all over the Roman world great amphitheaters appeared, hardly less magnificent than the one in Rome itself: at Capus, Pompeii, Pozzuoli[12] and Verona in Italy; at Arles and Nimes in France; at Seville in Spain; at Antioch in Palestine; at Alexandria in Egypt; at Silchester in Britain; at El Djem in Tunisia."[13] Judea and Jerusalem are not part of this list.[14] Wiedemann's comments indicate this absence shouldn't be surprising: "References to gladiators in Hebrew texts are virtually non-existent."[15] The possibility of confusion as to which Roman-occupied cities might have had amphitheaters built to feature gladiatorial events is understandable. In the popular picture book *Wonders of the Past*, for example, the two-page spread of an image of Jerusalem during Herod's time clearly depicts a large (circular) Roman colosseum in the far distance, inside the city walls.[16] As a city occupied by the Romans, it makes sense that artists would have assumed the Romans had eventually built *all* their usual entertainment structures.

Under the "The Colosseum, Jerusalem" title is a medium, zoom lens shot of heralds blowing trumpets,[17] each trumpet draped with red and gold banners. These types of banners have been seen earlier, in the opening credit sequence, there with the names and job titles of production personnel.[18] These banners clearly pay tribute to the revered Caesar Augustus (SPQR DIVO AUGUSTO CAESARI[19]), who had died in the year 14, about nineteen years before the depicted events. Tiberius had been the Roman emperor since 14, and would be until 37. It is certainly possible that these paltry games are being staged in tribute to the deceased emperor.[20] In the third century Tertullian will write of the games as honoring the dead, at least initially, and that "what was offered to appease the dead was counted as a funeral rite. . . . It is called *munus* (a service) from being a service due—a rendered . . . service to the dead."[21] If this is the case, then the memory of Augustus is being served in a paltry way, with a "weedy" victim and a weak-hearted gladiator—very Pythonesque. This historical infidelity could be a simple mistake, or a purposeful inclusion for convenience sake. In *Jesus of Nazareth*, Pilate's Great Hall is decorated with what appears to be a statue of the emperor Trajan, who wouldn't be born until twenty years *after* the events depicted in the film. His may have been the most convenient large statue to acquire for the film's needs, the producers knowing most filmgoers would never notice. Could the banners have been leftovers from some previous games? There's no textual support for this, but, as Richard reminds, "the typical provincial hardly noticed any change from one emperor to the next," so remaking expensive decorations from past celebrations might be a moot point.[22]

Perhaps the Romans assume the crowd was illiterate, and wouldn't know the difference between a living and dead emperor's printed name? The survival of many coarse, clever bits of graffito and myriad advertisements across the empire would belie this: "Election posters, shop signs, and public notices were intended primarily for common people."[23] The lowly born Brian can only write grammatically inelegant Latin, yes, but he can still read and write.[24] Whatever, Pilate and his household would have known at which emperor's convenience he served, even if he was only in charge in Judea for about a decade. The Pythons had spent the run of *Flying Circus* (and, separately, on shows like *I'm Sorry I'll Read That Again*, *At Last the 1948 Show*, *Do Not Adjust Your Set*, and *The Complete and Utter History of Britain*[25]) showing off their collective university educations, citing and even being conversant with ancient and modern philosophy, history, and high culture through the mouths of Pepperpots, Pewteys, and Pralines.[26] They even, for particularly on-point historical mentions in Ep. 26, referenced and cited the author they were relying on, G. M. Trevelyan, and included the page number of the citation.[27] So, to flesh out an argument between coal miners about the Treaty of Utrecht (Ep. 26), and later to make precise a description of Charles XII's troubles in the Northern War (Ep. 37), the Pythons resorted to an old-fashioned, academic practice—they looked it up.

This is all brought in to suggest that the Pythons' inclusion of Caesar Augustus in the time of Tiberius *might* have been an accident. It may also have been purposeful, given the fact that most viewers who had any grounding in Bible stories would have heard and could recognize the famous passage from Luke: "And it came to pass in those days, that there went out a decree from Cæsar Augustus, that all the world should be taxed."[28] Moreover, just one chapter later, in 3:1, Tiberius is much less memorably mentioned as being in the "fifteenth year" of his reign, and Pontius Pilate is his governor in Judea. Emperors Augustus and Tiberius are mentioned within pages of one another in the early section of the Christ story, and the Pythons chose the historically inaccurate but better known one anyway. To illustrate this process from another angle: In September 1978 at the Trades Union Congress in Brighton, PM Callaghan teased journalists (who were desperate to hear a proposed election date) by singing a bit from a music hall ditty made famous by Vesta Victoria.[29] The PM remarked, however, that the tune came from Marie Lloyd, and sang away. Adviser Donoughue recorded in his diary that the PM *knew* when he wrote the speech that the performer was Victoria and not Lloyd, but Callaghan and his civil servants who read the drafts were certain that the more well-known Lloyd was the better, more identifiable name for the anecdote.[30] (Interestingly, just nineteen days later, a columnist in the *Sunday Times* took up the unreality, referencing the PM's "Marie Lloyd song and shuffle," perpetuating this new myth.[31]) "Marie Lloyd" it was, and the anecdote went over well; "Caesar Augustus" is acknowledged for the games, and he's also given nominal credit for the sewer the PFJ will later crawl through.

In the background can also be seen a marble archway, labeled PILATVS IVDAEOS RE-GET OK. This bit of the set will be seen later, in Pilate's main room, and will be discussed at that point.

Shot 1—As the camera pans along the trumpets the set decoration comes into view. A bas-relief border of miniature Elgin-type marble figures adorn the podium where the nobles are meant to sit. On closer inspection these do appear to be plaster cast versions (or simply reproductions) of several Parthenon frieze sections now housed in the British Museum, specifically the "hydria-bearers" (north frieze) and a version of the procession of horsemen (west frieze). Gilliam and the Pythons have used images from the collections of British museums and art galleries since the first season of *Flying Circus*.[32] In the title sequence for the first series, for example, local gallery visits become apparent as four separate works from the National Gallery are featured.[33] The bas-relief frieze section is here much more accessible and viewable than when it was originally part of the frieze section above the shaft, capital, and architrave of the Parthenon, more than twenty-five feet above most visitors' craning vantage points.

As the camera movement ceases, the back end of an animal statue and portions of an inscribed obelisk are also revealed. Both are made to look as if they have been cast in bronze. The statue actually appears to be a version of Dürer's very popular 1515 woodcut "The Rhinoceros." The Pythons have already used a version of the print in their first episode created for German television, known as *Monty Python's Fliegender Zirkus*, in 1971. The Dürer sections of that episode were created to "celebrate" the five-hundredth anniversary of the artist's birth.[34]

The obelisk looks to be a type of conical pillar, inscribed, not unlike those found at the turns of the Circus Maximus track. The carvings on this pillar also make it look like a version of Trajan's Column—which sports a spiral *bas relief* depicting Trajan's victory in the Dacian Wars—or the Column of Marcus Aurelius. The conical shape, however, more resembles the three obelisk-like *metae* at the ends of the *spina* in Rome's Circus Maximus.

This is also perhaps a version of Jean Goujon's rhinoceros and obelisk statue, created in 1549. This same statue, set on a tall plinth, can be seen behind the Centurion in the "Latin Lesson" scene, as well. The statues and set decorations are used more than once in the film, due to budget constraints, but this economy had also become standard for the Pythons. As they shot *Holy Grail*, the original plan to use multiple castles in Scotland and Wales was scaled back dramatically, thanks to time and money concerns. Doune Castle served for almost all of the interior shots, and many of the exterior ones, as well, while Castle Stalker served as the Grail Castle at the end of the film, necessity being the mother of invention:

> Three other castles are depicted in the film. One is the "model" castle built from plywood as noticed by Patsy; the second is a filmed image of Kidwelly Castle, doubling as the exterior of the "Swallows" castle; and the third is a filmed image of Bodiam, meant to be Swamp Castle. Doyle captured the Kidwelly and Bodiam footage separate from the Pythons, after principal photography was completed.[35]

On the *Life of Brian* shoot, the same handful of walls and alcoves will be dressed and used as a setting, then redressed and reused for a new scene setting. The wall Brian graffitis becomes the backdrop for the soukh, which becomes Pilate's outside porch area, and so on.[36]

SUPER TITLE: Children's Matinee—While there weren't special children's shows at these life-and-death events, the day's events were divided up, according to Wiedemann. The *venatio* (killing of wild animals) was scheduled for the morning, followed by the *munus* (gladiator games) in the afternoon. In between, lunch was taken. During lunch, "public executions of prisoners of low status" were displayed, though "the audience was not required to stay."[37] Wiedemann continues: "The educated classes were free to leave after the *venatio* . . . to take their lunch and their siestas before the gladiators appeared in the afternoon."[38] These were clearly games conducted by some of the more humane emperors. Suetonius[39] notes that the "macabre" Caligula would go out of his way to offend and disgust. He would "have the canopies removed at the hottest time of the day and forbid anyone to leave; or cancel the regular programme, and pit feeble old fighters against decrepit criminals; or stage comic duels between respectable householders, who happened to be physically disabled in some way or other."[40]

Emperors Claudius and Commodus would also delight in the blood-spatter and debauched killings, truly enjoying the pleasures of others' sufferings.[41]

The scene we're being presented in *Life of Brian* seems to be one following on the heels of a particularly gruesome *munus*, where several gladiators lost lives and limbs.

Shot 2—This is a lower angle shot aimed up at the podium, composed so that the majesty of the games and the Colosseum can be seen in the background, and the decapitated gladiator being dragged off as a visual gag in the foreground. In the middle ground can be glimpsed a version of the famous Romulus and Remus statue, just to the left of the Roman archway. There are a number of these statues in Rome, including the Lupa Capitolina in Pallazo dei Conservatori.[42]

Suspended above the draped viewing stand is an *aquila* (eagle), an insignia carried before most legions across the Roman Empire. This version looks much more like the Nazi version of that same symbol, however, the *Reichsadler*, perhaps purposefully. Incidentally, this was the same Roman Eagle image that had so incited the sophists Matthias and Judas during Herod's reign, though there adorned in brilliant gold. These men and their students conspired to pull the symbol down from the temple, where Herod had placed it, and were executed by Herod for their efforts.[43] See the entry for "What's this then?" in scene nine, "The Latin Lesson," for more on the significance of such idolatrous images to the Jewish people.

This shot is clearly modeled on the famous Jean-Léon Gérôme painting, *Pollice Verso* (1872). In both the painting and the scene as filmed by the Pythons, the point of view (or camera setup) is nearly on the sandy floor of the arena, looking identically up toward the inner wall, spectators, royal podium, and, in the far background, even the upper, statue-graced ring of the Colosseum. The Pythons have also dressed their gladiator very much like the one depicted by Gérôme. In the painting he is a Secutor with his foot on the throat of a Retiarus, the defeated Retiarus's trident and net on the sand next to him. See the notes for "*A huge GLADIATOR*" later for more on these arena characters.

The upper third of this shot is clearly a matte painting created and inserted in the postproduction process, and is meant to resemble the original splendor of Rome's Colosseum (including liminal statues). The source is likely a borrow from a pen-and-ink-type work from an artist like Hector D'espouy, and looks to be an image of the third floor of the structure. Several of the most distant audience members are standing, and their heads are cut off by the lower line of this process shot. During the shot, one spectator even sits, coming fully back into view. This same technology is used on dozens of biblical epics, including *Quo Vadis* and *Ben-Hur*, so that only the lower portions of the large, city-size sets had to be built; the upper portions could be added later, less expensively, as part of a glass painting.

The Pythons dress their Colosseum appropriately, with regularly spaced spears jutting into the arena from the lowest wall, and netting strung between them. The Colosseum in Rome was similarly decorated, with large elephant tusks thrusting into the gaming space, and thick nets draped between them. The nets and sharp objects were meant to prevent the wild animals from leaping into the crowd, and especially onto the platform where the nobility would have gathered to watch.[44] These nets would only have been in place, however, when the wild animals were part of the show; as soon as the venator (hunter) segment of the performance was complete, the nets were removed to allow a better view.[45] In the Python version there are also a number of large metal rings hanging from the walls between the half-arches. These are likely inspired by Piranesi's *Carceri* drawings mentioned earlier, which Gilliam used as source material. The rings don't seem to serve any practical purpose, but they look forbidding. This scene, in its entirety, looks like a tatty version of the big budget *Quo Vadis*.

. . . a large group of Romans . . .—The editor of the games (or perhaps the *aedile*) would have been among this group, the wealthy man who paid for the staging, and who—if this were Rome—may have been running for public office and looking for votes.[46] He may be the man who complains that what he sees is "dreadful." These patricians are not seen again in the film.

. . . OLD LADIES are busy cleaning up . . . putting limbs into their baskets—Mannix mentions that these bodies and parts of bodies were cleaned up between events, and quickly, with the carcasses often chopped into food for the animals.[47] Slaves would have performed this grisly function, and then quickly spread clean sand to cover the bloodstains.

This level of grotesquery isn't overstated, given the Roman penchant for public spectacle, especially during hard times. To try and quell two weeks of riots in the streets of Rome, Nero announced the staging of two full weeks of games, the likes of which had never been seen:

> Special announcement was made by heralds that the finest chariot races on record would be held at the Circus Maximus. Three hundred pairs of gladiators would fight to the death and twelve hundred condemned criminals would be eaten by lions. Fights between elephants and rhinos, buffalo and tigers, and leopards and wild boars would be staged. As a special feature, twenty young women would be raped by jackasses. Admission to the rear seats, free. Small charge for the first thirty-six tiers of seats.
>
> Everything else would be promptly forgotten. The gigantic stadium, seating 385,000 people, was jammed to capacity. For two weeks the games went on while the crowd cheered, made bets and got drunk. Once again the government had a breathing space to try to find some way out of its difficulties.[48]

It's not likely that the slaves cleaning up after the battles would be allowed to keep anything of value. For one thing, those that were fighting were slaves of a sort to begin with, so their adornment would have been provided by owners. Secondly, those in the ring as prey would also have been prisoners or slaves of the lowest sort—no worldly goods there. In any event, the organizer of the games would have kept any valuables as spoil.

COLOSSEUM ANNOUNCER (OS) (Palin): "Frank Goliath, the Macedonian Baby-Crusher . . . and Boris Meinberg"—This is an example of the sweetening and finishing work that goes on during postproduction on any feature film. As happened during the finishing work on *Holy Grail*, Jones and Palin spent the most time on the editing and sound process, often dubbing and adding voiceovers to assist continuity.[49]

In *Flying Circus* there are several fighting-ring sketches. In Ep. 2, a monsignor and a Cambridge don wrestle to prove the existence of God; in Ep. 5 there is a surreal boxing match where the opponents change as the fight moves on; and in Ep. 18, Ken Clean-Aire Systems (Cleese) boxes his tiny female opponent (Connie Booth), beating her badly.[50] A ring announcer accompanies most of these. In a film insert for the second *Fliegender Zirkus* episode, as well as *Live at the Hollywood Bowl*, Colin "Bomber" Harris (Chapman) wrestles himself into submission.

"Frank Goliath, the Macedonian Baby-Crusher"—Names meant to inspire fear and awe could be found in the Pythons' world, with "Carlos the Jackal" occupying headlines around the world in the 1970s. "Frank Goliath"[51] is likely meant to mimic the over-the-top announcers and names from professional wrestling like Andre the Giant or Killer Kowalski. There were a number of gladiators who enjoyed this kind of fame (or infamy), including Flamma and even the emperor Commodus, but they didn't sport similar names. Caligula's name meant "little boots," which isn't nearly so fear-inducing (his acts of madness were terrifying, though). As he battled the Seleucids, Jewish guerrilla leader Judas came to be known as Judas "Maccabee," which many interpreted as meaning "The Hammer (of God)." Contemporary figures would have been Martin McGuiness, the IRA leader whose reputation had led to him being called the "Butcher of Bogside," as well as the fanatical Shankill Butchers and Lenny Murphy who regularly kidnapped, tortured, and murdered Catholics in Belfast.[52] More "affectionately," according to journalist Hugo Young, Labour MP Dennis Skinner was known as "Beast of Bolsover."[53] This is also the second time that "Goliath" has been mentioned. Mr. Cheeky asked about "Goliath's big brother" at the Sermon on the Mount dust-up.

Macedonia was a Roman province from 146 BC, and one of the regions in the area was Thrace, home of the vaunted Thracian gladiators, including the rebel Spartacus. Caligula's favorite gladiators were also Thracian, and he "chose Thracian gladiators to officer his German bodyguard."[54] The "baby-crusher" sobriquet was, unfortunately, based in actual events across this period. Marauding soldiers, often acting on an emperor's orders, killed rivals as well as their families, all ages. One of Dore's illustrations for the Bible, "The Massacre of the Innocents," depicts the killing of children.[55] There they are being stabbed or crushed against stone walls.

There was also the unfortunate contemporary case of Nigel Briffett, who killed his young stepson Wayne Brewer and earned the nickname "baby crusher" from those around him. The death followed the boy's release into his stepfather's custody, even after the local social services recommended against it. Briffett was found guilty of manslaughter, and served five years.[56]

"Maurice Feinberg"—Or, since the recording isn't clear, it could be "Boris Weinberg." Likely chosen to represent a recognizably Jewish name, like Brian's last name, Cohen, and a particularly spindly opponent for an accomplished gladiator. (The ancient men of the Crimson Permanent Assurance—hard of hearing, wearing pacemakers, dentures, and glasses—will manage to best the Very Big Corporation of America in *Meaning of Life*.)

He has a tray round his neck and is selling tit-bits—Chapman had gone door-to-door with a tray in *Flying Circus* Ep. 45, trying to flog Icelandic honey; Idle had done the same but with novelties items in Ep. 15; and Cleese carries a tray of albatross (and "gannet on a stick") for sale, without "bloody wafers," in Ep. 13.[57]

BRIAN: "Larks' tongues . . . Wrens' livers . . . Chaffinch brains . . . *(with spirit)* Jaguars' earlobes!"—Mannix notes that the "wealthy class of Rome" actually ate very similarly, noshing on "thrushes' tongues in wild honey and sow's udders stuffed with fried baby mice."[58]

As the camera follows Brian, the upper edge of the existing amphitheater can be glimpsed, consisting of rubble, fencing, and light posts. This delimitation was covered by a matte painting in the previous shot, but the film crew clearly hoped the composition of this shot could hide the horizon, and they were nearly right. This theater is still in use today. This shot also clearly reveals the dais where the emperor would have sat with his guests. His expensive chair is there, under the canopy and *aquila*, along with four *curule*-type seats, but there is no sign of an emperor, his prefect, Pilate, or even an editor or *aedile* for these games.

REVOLUTIONARIES—REG, FRANCIS, STAN and JUDITH—At this point the camera begins a zoom in on the huddled revolutionaries seated across the arena. The sparse crowd watches with little interest whatever is going on down on the bloody sand, perhaps because the most popular part of most games, chariot racing, isn't part of this event. The film also acknowledges the significance of the audience as opposed to the games—"The great spectacle at the circus is not the games but the spectators"—and we focus on the members of the PFJ rather than the combat below.[59]

JUDITH: ". . . Any Anti-Imperialist group . . ."—The Pythons have cast their first-century rebels in a favorable light, which wasn't always the case in academia. Brandon notes that, following Josephus, much Western scholarship depicted these Zealot types as "brigands and fanatics, who by political murder and sabotage pushed their nation into its fatal revolt against Rome."[60] And the reasons? "Josephus' [negative] evaluation . . . evoked a ready acceptance from people proudly conscious of their imperial mission of bringing well-ordered government and civilisation to non-European nations," Brandon writes. "Accordingly, to those troubled by revolutionaries, whether Russian, Irish or Indian, who threatened the stability of Western capitalist society or British rule, the character and activities of the Zealots in first-century Palestine seemed only too familiar."[61] So, the British Empire. Brendon notes again and again how voices across the years of the British Empire favorably compared it to the Roman Empire, bringing order and democracy to a violent, backwards world.[62] And even though, as Bernstein notes, "from the 1890s on, generations of British children were educated to identify national pride and power with the empire," the Pythons have lampooned the British version and especially its waning influence (in their lifetimes) since the first days of *Flying Circus*.[63] By the end of the second season, they were, like Gray, tolling "the knell of parting day," chronicling the empire's diminution. In Ep. 25, a caption crawl announced: "In 1970, the British Empire lay in ruins":

> By 1970, the British empire had changed drastically since Queen Victoria's day, and perhaps especially since the end of WWII. Australia, Canada, and New Zealand were granted "Dominion" status in 1926 (translating to autonomy in the Empire), followed in 1947 by Pakistan and India being granted a peaceful independence. Many others, including Cyprus, Zambia, the Seychelles, Zimbabwe (Rhodesia [Ep. 45]), and Malaysia also were separated (forcibly, often) from the British Empire in the twentieth century. So in the short lifetimes of the Pythons, the British Empire had indeed diminished in size and international significance.[64]

Brandon sees the partisan experiences of the Second World War as key to changing this perception of the irritating revolutionary. During the war, significant anti-Nazi resistance activity helped carry the war in the Allies' favor, concomitantly stirring "a new and sympathetic interest in the Zealots."[65] The Pythons grew up in the immediate postwar era, and went to school under the academics writing these new appraisals of first-century Judean revolutionary activity.

This "anti-imperialist" rhetoric had been part of the political lexicon since at least 1949, when Mao's guerillas came down from the mountains and took control of China. The term was thrown around in pronouncements from the Soviets, East Germans, and forces in Northern Ireland, as well as most African countries seeking independence from colonizers. In 1965 the president of Indonesia called for an "Anti-Imperialist Axis" across Asia to counter the American influence in Vietnam and beyond.[66] Students in France in 1968 were staging regular anti-imperialist days, while those in London tried and failed to motivate the working class into joining their anti-Vietnam War, anti-American demonstrations.[67] Many of these student organizations were as woefully ineffective as the PFJ will prove, their failures likely influencing the Pythons as they wrote the film. Entertainments weren't left out, either. Critic Alan Brien writes of a performance of a new play in London in 1972, one clearly meant to point the finger at the British establishment, but which ended up just looking silly:

> At the Aldwych,[68] *The Island of the Mighty*, by John Arden "with Margaretta D'Arcy." (Why not "and"?). He claims it is anti-imperialist, but the director, David Jones, has made it pro-imperialist. If anyone gets the wrong end of the stick, it is the audience. Three acts, each one hour and twelve minutes, with two twelve (more like twenty) minute intervals. Who does he think we are—the delegates at a Congress of the Communist Party of the Soviet Union?[69]

The PFJ is clearly performing theater, as well, and the inner core—Reg, Francis, Stan/Loretta, and Judith—will know just when to leave the stage.

JUDITH: ". . . group like ours must <u>reflect</u> such a divergence of interests within its power base"—Not so, often. By the 1960s, the solidly anti-West Soviets and Chinese couldn't see eye to eye on anything, with China smelling a Soviet-American conspiracy to encircle East Asia for destruction and the disputed lands between the countries trembling beneath an awful two-edged axe.[70] That slow-motion wrestling match would rumble on through the 1970s. As for terror groups, both the German Red Army Faction and the Japanese United Red Army, to name just two, dealt harshly with members who backslid, moved from Marxist to Maoist or the opposite way, or displayed "ideological weakness" or "counterrevolutionary thought" of any kind. The infamous purging of less-motivated URA members in the frozen mountains of Japan in winter 1972, followed by the murder of former RAF member Ulrich Schmücker in June 1974 meant that ideological fidelity couldn't flag—there couldn't be an acknowledged "Uh, well one" among them who didn't believe what everyone else believed.

As for student groups, the attempted October 1968 uprising in London started off well. The National Liberation Front had put out the call for all students and trade unions to mass together and confront the United States (and Britain, in her support for the United States) over Vietnam. The "divergence of interests" within this movement meant that some of the marchers were against the war, clearly, while some were plotting the downfall of the capitalist British government. So some wanted a war to end, while others actually wanted a revolution. In this row, the Vietnam Solidarity Campaign (VSC) and the Maoist Britain-Vietnam Solidarity Front (MBVSF) could never agree on coordinated goals. What happened to these "splitters" should read very familiar:

> The Maoists insisted on a march on the American Embassy in Grosvenor Square as the main objective and the adoption of the slogans "Victory to the N.L.F." and "Long Live Ho Chi-minh." The V.S.C.'s October 27 ad hoc committee could not accept that the "imperialist lair" should be the main target, and so the front decided to act on its own. With it went some nine smaller groups.[71]

The PFJ's ad hoc committee will experience similar dissension. And in a prescient moment for the coming PFJ-Campaign for Free Galilee tussle, the VSC also decided that it would be appropriate to use their own march to block off the MBVSF march on Grosvenor Square. So, one activist group fights another activist group somewhere near the seat of power, and both fail to shift the oppressor—their "divergence of interests" clearly too divergent.

This call for a respect for differing interests wouldn't hold water within and between other terror groups, either, as will be discussed later, when Brian nearly brings the "Fifth Legion" to the PFJ's headquarters.

FRANCIS: ". . . provided the Movement never forgets that it is the inalienable right of every man . . ."—"Inalienable" is a charged political term, a manifesto word, heard and read often in the volatile postwar years, emanating from the Sino-Soviet blocs and the emerging Third World colonial and postcolonial countries. The "First Conference of Solidarity of the Peoples of Africa, Asia and Latin America" convened in Havana in January 1966, hosted by Cuba and the Communist Party, and the conference resolution is telling: "The Conference proclaims the *inalienable right* of the peoples to total political independence and to resort to all forms of struggle that are necessary, including armed struggle, in order to conquer that right."[72] The January 1973 peace accords to end the war in Vietnam declared that "the South Vietnamese people's right to self-determination is sacred, inalienable, and shall be respected by all countries."[73] A 1974 UN resolution for the recognition of the PLO announced "the inalienable right of the Palestinians to return to their homes and property from which they have been displaced and uprooted," and acknowledged the right to "self-determination without external interference" and "national independence and sovereignty."[74]

This same Jeffersonian language is employed during this period by Biafrans demanding their own country, by unions reminding the world of their rights to strike, by OPEC asserting its rights as a cartel, by Britain clearing all blocks to North Sea oil flow, by journalists demanding access to "secrets" held by the Civil Service, by the National Trust demanding their right to "inalienable" declarations, by Jews in confirming their rights to a peaceful Passover, and by Young Liberals demanding squatter's rights for the homeless of England.[75] This was an "I know my rights" time—as *Holy Grail's* Dennis confirms—and with the help of a voracious media, everyone else could know them, too.[76]

FRANCIS: "Where was I?" REG: "I thought you'd finished"—Likely a very telling moment, where the endgame to the PFJ's hoped-for revolution was to have been presented, discussed, and perhaps even agreed upon, parliamentarily. Thanks to Stan/Loretta, however, they are sidetracked and the goal remains undefined. But this isn't just the Pythons as the PFJ engaging in expected Pythonesque silliness, it's a reflection of the late 1970s and the decade-old student-cum-revolutionary movement, according to Dobson and Payne:

> They became intellectuals "with a pistol in the drawer." Revolution and terror became the first priority and eventually ends in themselves for people who no longer had clear ideas about what sort of world they would try to build once they had torn down the old system. The very act of destruction was sufficient, they argued. Something better was certain to emerge from the ruins.[77]

The PFJ wants to overthrow the Roman Empire, but they're not claiming their own place as leaders in the vacuum that follows. Reg later calls for "world supremacy," but without a transition plan. Most of the terror organizations of the 1960s and 1970s had short-term goals that were reachable—acts of terror drawing attention to a minority cause—but no plan for what to do if they succeeded, or even what "success" might look like.

In an early draft of the script, it is Otto who talks about the future. He sees a Jewish Reich, essentially. Otto is styled somewhat after the German terrorist Gabriele Kröcher-Tiedemann, who led the attack on Air France Flight 139 in June 1976.[78] With her German accent she barked orders at passengers, separated Jews from others, reminding many on board of a Nazi death camp worker.[79] Kröcher-Tiedemann had already been arrested for terror activity and freed as part of a ransom demand in the Peter Lorenz kidnapping, discussed later.

REG: "Furthermore, it is the birthright of every man . . ."—In 1977, this was not only a Third World political issue but a First World body issue. Dr. Helena Wright, of International Planned Parenthood, interviewed in the *Sunday Times* as she contemplated turning ninety, announced that "the voluntary control of fertility is the birthright of everyone." Stan/ Loretta would have likely agreed.

Francis's gendered language was also under attack in Britain at this time. In 1975 the World Council of Churches had agreed to remove "all 'sexist' language from its constitution and its deliberations."[80] New and trendy books like *Words and Women* published in 1977 laid out the "thesis that sexist language contributes to downgrading women," and were popular reading and made for good newspaper copy.[81] Elsewhere, a move that Stan/Loretta would have applauded occurred in California two years before work on *Brian* began. In 1974 the voters of California agreed that "reverence for the status quo was obsolete," so language in the state's documents could change: "They voted to remove words like *congressmen*, *assemblymen*, and the pronoun *he*, *his*, and *him* from their Constitution entirely."[82] And since Stan/Loretta will be seen to be in charge of the group's recorded minutes, he/she could facilitate that change, too.

REG: "Why don't you shut up about women, Stan. You're putting us off"—The then-editor of *Punch*, William Davis, wrote a column about this very topic in March 1973.[83] He had recently returned from a visit to the United States where he appeared on *The Dick Cavett Show*, and was followed around New York thereafter by boisterous feminists unhappy with his allegedly backward views on women. In the editorial "Let's Get Laughter into Lib," Davis bemoans the "solemn, dogmatic" and "intolerant" feminists who "don't have a sense of humour." He sounds like Reg as he patronizingly tells women everywhere to lighten up:

> In their eagerness for publicity they invite ridicule by concentrating on trivial issues—and get angry when one takes up the invitation. One of the sillier causes is the argument about "sexist language." There is no reason why we should not have chairpersons, and I dare say we could bring ourselves to name hurricanes "George" instead of "Agnes." But these are unimportant subjects, detracting from the very real arguments which gave birth to women's lib.[84]

Davis is being put off by the women like Reg is being put off by Stan, thinking he's just overly "on about" women. Reg is certain that Stan's idée fixe is going to put them all onto a side-track, which it actually does. They've digressed from defining their movement and its goals, now twice, and won't get back on track until Brian accepts his "little job."

STAN: "Women have a perfect right to play a part in our movement, Reg"—Again, yes and no. In Tsarist Russia, "terrorism was one of the few areas where women could play an active role," Burleigh writes, "with their views being accorded equal respect to those of men."[85] Closer to home, many Tories were certain that Margaret Thatcher wouldn't survive more than a few months as leader of the party, with some almost immediately planning for the next leadership fight when "normalcy"—white male leadership—would be restored.[86] To many, Thatcher was always "that bloody woman," her gender front and center in their opprobrium.[87] Marcia Williams must be mentioned here, as she and Thatcher were the two highest-profile women in British government (well beyond MPs Barbara Castle and Shirley Williams, or even the Queen) during the 1970s, but for different reasons. Williams had been Wilson's kitchen cabinet leader—and her temperament, penchant for nepotism, and venality jaundiced Wilson's final years at No. 10. The tendentious Williams was an easy target for pundits and a blessing to *Private Eye*—responding to criticism with insults, expensive writs, and political threats.[88] In 1975, when Williams's book *Inside Number 10* about her Downing Street years appeared, her publisher, George Weidenfeld, put "her face on the front of every No. 11 bus," so she was very much in the public eye.[89]

As for guerrilla terror cells, those revolutionary groups in Britain, Germany, Japan, and the United States were made up of men and women (mostly men), but as will be discussed, women *did* "play a part" in many terror operations, building on the Russian example. Herbert Marcuse saw this as a potential positive, since "all domination up to today has been patriarchal," and the New Left had the opportunity to change that imbalance.[90] This wasn't so in first-century Judea, where women would have had their place in above-board life, and likely had *no* place elsewhere, Jeremias writes: "We have therefore the impression that Judaism in Jesus's time also had a very low opinion of women, which is usual in the Orient where she is chiefly valued for her fecundity, kept as far as possible shut away from the outer world, submissive to the power of her father or her husband, and where she is inferior to men from a religious point of view."[91] This understanding of contemporary culture would have precluded Judith from participating with the PFJ in any meaningful way, meaning this inclusiveness is a modern affectation, something borrowed from the Red Armies and SLAs of the 1970s.

Given this conflict between a woman's place in the years 33 and 1973, we should have expected the pope to chime in here for the official viewpoint of the Church. Paul VI's 1974 Apostolic Exhortation *Marialis Cultis* positions Mary as a model for the "modern woman." The pope writes that the "Modern Woman" who wants to participate in the community of decision makers already knows that Mary gave "active and responsible consent"—in "dialogue with God"—to be the mother of Jesus; that Mary chose virginity to "consecrate herself," and moreover:

> The modern woman will note with pleasant surprise that Mary of Nazareth, while completely devoted to the will of God, was far from being a timidly submissive woman or one whose piety was repellent to others; on the contrary, she was a woman who did not hesitate to proclaim that God vindicates the humble and the oppressed, and removes the powerful people of this world from their privileged positions (cf. Lk. 1:51–53).

She does sound Judith-like in her support of the oppressed (people of Jerusalem) and the appeal against the powerful (Romans). The pope goes on to remind that Mary was actively strengthening the apostolic community and was a maternal exemplar—"clearly . . . the figure of the Blessed Virgin does not disillusion any of the profound expectations of the men and women of our time but offers them the perfect model of the disciple of the Lord."[92] Skeptic Auberon Waugh can only say this of the pope's missive to the modern woman: "His latest claim that the Mother of Christ was a thoroughly Modern Mary and early apostle of women's lib will put a heavy strain on the credulity of the faithful."[93] Judith doesn't seem ready to accept this kind of role, either. (Nor does Loretta, for that matter.)

"Women played key roles in the Baader-Meinhof gang," is the flat statement from Ovid Demaris, and not just in the Red Army Faction.[94] In contemporary terror groups, the place and employment of women varied, depending on the group. The JRA could claim a number of highly-placed, intelligent, and dangerous women in their organization; six of the twelve founding members of the SLA were women (while abductee Patty Hearst became an infamous de facto member); Leila Khaled led PFLP hijackings in 1969 and 1970; women (including the Price sisters of the Provisional IRA) fired guns, planted bombs, and waged hunger strikes; and the RAF of West Germany boasted dozens of committed women, including Gudrun Ensslin and Ulrike Meinhof. The German and Japanese terror groups were particularly open to women, it seems. According to Dobson and Payne, speaking of the RAF:

> Even greater distress was caused to traditionally-minded Germans when they realised how great a part in the terrorist campaigns was played by women. In the original Baader-Meinhof band there were no fewer than twelve women among the force of twenty-two. The girls carried and used guns as willingly as their menfolk. As Dr. Stumper[95] put it: "There is a very high female

content in the terrorist organisations . . . We often find that they are the ones who ginger up the men and push them on to greater deeds of violence."[96]

In *Private Eye*, Claud Cockburn discussed an article written by an Irish woman, Christina Murphy, for a German newspaper focusing on the place of women in the Baader-Meinhof gang. Murphy pointed out that most of the faces on the "hundreds of thousands of posters advertising wanted terrorists" in Germany are female, and that a German police source told her "the majority of terrorists we are looking for are women."[97] Cockburn's take on the situation was guided by an Irishman, Andrew Fowler, writing in response to Murphy's article, alleging that the women were being "used to do the dirty work" by the men, who led the group from a safe distance. In *Life of Brian*, Reg remains behind while the novitiate Brian makes the dangerous attack on Pilate's home, where he is caught. Judith has no part in the planning or execution of this raid. Judith was also not part of Brian's assault on the walls of Pilate's palace. Rather than the men being "gingered up" by the women, however, as Dobson and Payne allege, Fowler is certain that bombing is "a particularly vicious type of crime which appeals more than any other to the temperament of the female terrorist," no male prodding needed.[98] So female party members like Judith are clearly leading the way toward the more violent acts, for Fowler. Cockburn has now found the thread he's looking for, and turns his "eyes homeward" to see Margaret Thatcher:

> Indeed . . . turn them backward along the grim vista of history. Think of Heath. Confrontation. Three-day week. Ruin. Defeat. At that moment in time, was there any sane man, repeat man, who wanted to be a Tory leader? There were a couple of obvious zanies, but no one that counted. The Tories—the sane male Tories—caucused. They realised that leading the Tories was, in Fowler's words, "a particularly vicious type of crime which appeals more than any other to the temperament of the female terrorist." That Tory male caucus realised, too, that even in this day and age the power of men is such that it can draw women into hideously undesirable activities. "If," they reasoned, "it can be done in Germany, it can be done here. Women," they said in their essentially male way, "are women." And the next thing you knew, they had handed the dirty work to poor little Margaret Thatcher. . . . Of the faces which "peer dourly from the posters," hers is among the most prominent. The whole affair will go down in history as a monstrous example of male cunning and malevolence.[99]

So the female leader of the opposition party as an active but mind-controlled terrorist? In one of the most fitting last-laugh moments in history, sixteen months later Margaret Thatcher would become prime minister.

As for levels of commitment, the JRA and especially the United Red Army, its more violent splinter, could boast particularly nefarious female activity, according to Demaris:

> Of the sixteen jailed for the [internecine] killings,[100] six were women. About a third of the URA members who followed Fusako Shigenobu to the Middle East were women. Some Japanese argue that the URA and other radical factions provide an extreme outlet for women's frustrations in a society where they are still very much second-class citizens.[101]

But what about the women who weren't part of the admittedly patriarchal Japanese society? Less internationally known but no less violent, there was a women's section of the Ulster Defense Association (UDA) in the Sandy Row area of Belfast. In February 1975 "The Faces of Terrorism" frowned from the pages of the *Daily Mail*—ten unsmiling mugshots, all female. They had just been found guilty of stomping another woman and leaving her to die by a roadside. None of the defendants expressed remorse, no matter how young. Perhaps influential for the Pythons, for most of September 1970 the PFLP's Leila Khaled had been under arrest and held in the Ealing area, Greater London. The Pythons were shooting the first and second series of *Flying Circus* in Ealing area at this time—their BBC home was then in nearby Shepherd's Bush—and they had a high-profile female terrorist living just around the corner.

The media did notice the inclusion of the fairer sex in these violent men's clubs, and, citing Kipling and his *The Female of the Species*, some columnists and terror experts were certain that the future promised more women terrorists and much more appalling female-wreaked violence. Perhaps the title of an October 1975 editorial comment in the *Daily Mail*—"The Day of the Female Jackal"—says it all. Short mentions therein of Marion Coyle, Patty Hearst, Leila Khaled, Lynette Fromme, Ulrike Meinhof, and the Price sisters—"callous harpies" all—opine that they have abandoned "all mercy and tenderness for the sake of a political abstraction."[102] It's likely the author was male.

Lastly, in a February 1978 issue of *Private Eye*, the "Wayside Pulpit" column addresses the recent elevation of Anna Ford to lead presenter at ITN news, following Angela Rippon's earlier ascendancy to a similar post at the BBC. There were voices against these front-and-center females on the previously male-dominated news desks, which *Private Eye*'s pseudonymous "Rev. J. C. Flannel" sends up, kindly connecting us to first-century Jerusalem, as well:

> We hear a lot these days about whether women should be allowed to administer the news on television. Already the BBC has permitted a woman, Miss Angela Rippon, to preside over its traditional 9 O'clock News spot. Is nothing sacred, some people ask? Others ask, under what authority are we contemplating this great break with the time-honoured way of doing things? What would our Lord himself have done? Certainly there is nothing in the scriptures to indicate guidelines one way or the other, on this supremely important question. It is true that when Our Lord himself sent out his team to preach the "Good News," he did not name a woman as one of the Squad. There was no "Angela" among the "Evangelists"! But times have changed.[103]

The PFJ won't have much use for their token woman, Judith, as she is simply put up with, and isn't in on the actual combat missions or much of the decision making. In this same issue of *Private Eye*, another short blurb allegedly from BBC Radio mentions a typical BBC panel seated for a typical roundtable discussion, including three men of note—"Lord Longford, Malcolm Muggeridge, Lord Robens"—as well as "Ms Statutory Woman," the token stroppy feminist who doesn't even get a name.[104]

FRANCIS: "Why are you always on about women, Stan?"—In the 1959 film *I'm All Right Jack*, young Cynthia Kite (Liz Fraser) listens as the company directory (Dennis Price) lectures in the canteen at lunchtime on the benefits of working hard and selling their product abroad ("'Export or Die' is no empty phrase!").[105] Cynthia leans over to her beau (Ian Carmichael[106]) and whispers: "What's he on about, Stan?" The design of the working PFJ has come directly from this film, with the officious Mr. Kite leading the way as chief shop steward. Our Stan will want to be called "Loretta," of course.

Terrorist Evelyne Barges[107] may have felt that the male-dominated French press damned her with faint praise, or perhaps just indulged in a ham-handed compliment when the *Journal du Dimanche* called her alternately "a true revolutionary, a professional of clandestinity and of terror attacks," and also, "Carlos in a skirt."[108] Judith, at least, seems to want to rise above this kind of sexism. But Carlos could have also been understandably "on about women," because so many had helped him do his work. He had lived an unassuming life in London with his mother, quiet and seeming the comfortable, apolitical son, simply enjoying the sweets of Western culture. By July 1975 three women were being charged with aiding the terrorist:

a Columbian student, a Paris bank worker, and a quiet British secretary. Guns, explosives, forged passports, and detailed maps, journals, and plans for future actions were found in relation to these arrests, exposing a good deal of the complex terror network.[109] (When the Romans search Matthias's flat later, they will find a spoon.)

The most recognizable female in a position of power during this period wasn't any terrorist, of course (unless the Far Left was being polled), it was Margaret Thatcher, Tory leader from 1975, and prime minister from May 1979. Thatcher was most often treated with the same smirking toleration seen in Reg's attitude toward Judith, and of course Loretta/Stan.[110] Over the course of many Prime Minister's Questions in 1975 and 1976, Labour special adviser Donoughue gloats every time he records a win for his "relaxed and amusing" bosses, Wilson, then Callaghan, stinging their opposite shadow number, Thatcher, and "putting [her] down gently but with patronising contempt." Donoughue concludes: "Even the Tories were roaring with laughter."[111] Thatcher had no support or respect from Labour, little support and little respect from her own party, but she would grab the ring just two years and nine months later when she entered No. 10 as the new prime minister. Labour would then be in opposition for eighteen years.

STAN: "I want to be a woman. . . . I want you all to call me Loretta"—So in the midst of the PFJ's struggle against the Roman Empire's oppression, one of its few members is sidetracked by a gender reassignment fixation, and another Pythonesque digression emerges. We know that the movement cannot be taken seriously after this, what with the constant niggling of appropriate gender identifications threatening to sidetrack any PFJ decision. Loretta isn't alone in being politically committed and distracted. The members of West Berlin's Commune 1 wanted the world to change, yes, but there were priorities: "The Vietnam War is not what interests me," one member said in 1967, "but difficulties with my orgasms do."[112]

Patty Hearst had become "Tania X" in April 1974, completing her transition from heiress to revolutionary. Other SLA members also "became" as their revolutionary personalities emerged, including Patricia Soltysik, who wanted to be known as "Mizmoon," Willy Wolfe, who answered to "Cujo," and leader Donald "Cinque" DeFreeze. *Salon* writer Andrew O'Hehir grew up in the Bay Area in the same neighborhoods as Hearst, and remembers that it didn't take long for the shock of her kidnapping, crime spree, arrest, trial, and conviction to become a neighborhood joke, so much so that his school-age friends could get in on the fun:

> In other words, by the time my friend Jennifer performed her Tania shtick on the stage of the Berkeley Community Theater [in 1979] . . . the story of Patty Hearst really had receded into the background clutter of California insanity and become kind of a joke. The earnest but deranged Berkeley radicals of the SLA . . . were a joke. So was their ludicrous vision of revolution—along with the simultaneously hysterical and incompetent reaction from officialdom. The bewildered finishing-school princess with a submachine gun was a joke, and so were her anguished old-money parents.[113]

Baiting the Roman Empire, the PFJ share this same "ludicrous vision of revolution." From the distance of London, the joke must've been all the funnier—the Pythons poke fun at revolutionaries Cujo, Mizmoon, Cinque, Tania X, "Brian, who is called Brian," and "Loretta."

STAN: "Don't you oppress me!"—Women in biblical Israel would have been regularly, or *ritually* "oppressed" as part of the patriarchal culture:

> The Bible was written and compiled by males who had no special interest in women's roles. They focused principally on the male aspects of life, such as warfare, governing, economy, and worship, in which women were not directly involved or to which they contributed only minimally. In

addition, Israel's laws were addressed only to men. The domain of a woman's activities was the household, where she exercised authority in her role as mother.[114]

Reading back over this, the Pythons' written world across *Flying Circus*, *Holy Grail*, and *Life of Brian* follows most of these same rules. They had little interest in women's roles, except in *playing* those roles themselves. *Brian* focuses on warfare (the terror "waid"; Roman reprisals), governing (Pilate; the Chief Shop Steward Reg), and economy (buying rocks and beards; begging and haggling) and ignores worship completely; and the woman in the households the Pythons offered were generally cross-dressed and exaggerated.

REG: "I'm not oppressing you, Stan—you haven't got a womb. Where's the foetus going to gestate? You going to keep it in a box?"—This might sound like a scene from David Lynch's experimental film *Eraserhead* (1977), but the years 1976–1978 were exciting times for "alternative" pregnancies. As early as 1968 headlines like "Embryos Outside the Body" were becoming commonplace, and the term "test-tube baby" had entered the cultural lexicon.[115] Principal work in the area was being conducted in Britain, as well, and British newspapers would bid for the rights to the exclusive story.[116] The world's first test-tube baby was born 25 July 1978, and the pregnancy had been front page news since before October 1977—when she was "conceived"—which of course coincides with the writing, reading out, and rewriting of *Brian*.

This subject would have definitely had Catholics "tittering" nervously and gathering their belongings; one letter from a concerned Englishwoman speaks for many, placing the blame for such adventures on the dark, changing world:

> Sir.—The recent news of the possibility of a "test tube" baby fills me with despair for the future. I cannot refrain from trying to express my horror and to register some measure of protest. . . . Over the last 10 years the "permissive" society with its emphasis on licence, on abortion and sterilization, its insistence that Christianity is utterly outdated has turned our country into a travesty of the England which is so dear to many people. I cannot believe that it is only those of my generation who feel this. For the sake of the thousands of young men and women who I am convinced still believe in and know the meaning of love, I beg the leaders of Christian thought and morals to call a halt before we reach the nadir of the slippery slope. Yours faithfully, Mary Middleton Murry.[117]

Reg isn't tut-tutting Loretta's personal, moral choice to become a mother who can "have babies" (remember, that was a choice ascribed to Mary by the pope, so it is an ennobling act), just the scientific, biological impossibility of such a thing. And Reg is right, actually, since even the eventual celebrated "test-tube baby" was only *conceived* in vitro; the nine-months gestation took place after the fertilized egg was returned to the mother's uterus.

JUDITH: ". . . which is nobody's fault, not even the Romans', but that he can have the *right* to have babies"—In October 1975 a failed Liberal candidate Mr. John Campbell embarked on a "symbolic fast" to draw attention to the lack of Liberal MPs in the current parliament. There is a wonderful picture of him in the *Times* stolidly refusing a glass of milk proffered by "Mr. Cyril Smith, MP," and "Mr. Jeremy Thorpe, the Liberal Party leader."[118] Campbell drank only water for thirteen days, one for every sitting Liberal MP. Campbell certainly had the "right" to perform this protest, but it was as ineffective as Stan's wish to be "Loretta" and have babies—David Steel's Liberals *lost* two seats in the following election.

REG: "What's the point of fighting for his right to have babies when he can't have babies?"—Fighting for a symbolic thing is an age-old concept, and this silly version—fighting for a right to something that is impossible or at least unlikely—is another borrow from the shop stewards group in *I'm All Right Jack*. Mr. Kite and the other stewards find out that a non-union man is on a forklift, then march in to management to demand action. They want him fired, and management is keen to agree. This quick agreement unnerves the stewards, certain that something must be up. They withdraw and confer (as the PFJ will do at the end of the film), and upon reentering:

> Kite: My colleagues here have instructed me to put to you one question, Major.
>
> Major: Certainly! Go ahead my dear fellow.
>
> Kite: Is it or is it not your intention to sack this man?
>
> Major: Sack him, of course.
>
> *Kite withdraws again for a brief whisper with the gathered stewards outside the door, then returns.*
>
> Kite: I'm obliged to point out, Major, that if you sack this man the company is in breach of its agreement with the union.
>
> Major: Surely he's not a union member?
>
> Kite: Correct, but that is merely technical.
>
> Major: But didn't you say that he was incompetent and couldn't do his job properly?
>
> Kite: We do not and cannot accept the principle that incompetence justifies dismissal. That is victimisation.
>
> *The other stewards all nod in agreement.*

The shop stewards will now fight for the man's right to work even though it is a symbolic fight—he isn't a union member and he isn't qualified for nor able to do the job. This shambolic silliness will reach a head when both union and management begin to look ridiculous in the media, and then agree to work together to get rid of the man, and all will be well again.

FRANCIS: "It is symbolic of our struggle against oppression"—Verbiage from terror group manifestoes across the middle of the century, really. Chilling contemporaneous references for these symbolic struggles can be found in the aftermath of two kidnappings and a mass killing, all three in South America.

The US ambassador to Brazil, Charles Elbrick, was kidnapped in Rio de Janeiro by the Revolutionary Movement 8th October and held for ransom in 1969. The demands involved freeing fifteen political prisoners, and the threat was the life of the ambassador, whom the group labeled "a symbol of exploitation" in its manifesto released to newspapers.[119] Elbrick was released after the Brazilian government met kidnappers' demands. In Uruguay in January 1971, British Ambassador Geoffrey Jackson was kidnapped by the Tupamaros guerrilla group. Jackson was targeted, according to the Tupamaros, as "a national symbol of institutional neocolonialism," and was held for eight months.[120] He was released unharmed in August 1971 after more than one hundred Tupamaros guerrillas escaped from prison. Uglier were the mass murder and mass suicides in Jonestown, Guyana, in November 1978. The leader of the People's Temple, Jim Jones, and more than nine hundred of his followers died in an eschatological frenzy. The paranoid and drug-addicted Jones was reportedly concerned that "CIA infiltrators" were planning a raid, and would keep the faithful from being "translated" to another planet.[121] Cyanide- and sedative-laced fruit drink was mixed and given to everyone.[122] Thomas Szasz reported on 24 March 1979 that these "struggles" were happening often, and for myriad reasons: "During the weeks and days immediately preceding the

[Jonestown] massacre [it] is evident . . . that a dinner benefit, called 'A Struggle Against Oppression,' was planned for the People's Temple in San Francisco for 2 December 1978. . . . It was cancelled after the massacre."[123] Jones had lectured about his version of Marxist Christianity for many years prior to taking his followers into the jungle.

Many of the kidnappings, bombings, and acts of insurrection in general were communicated as being "symbolic" of neo- and postcolonial oppression. References were made in Africa and Argentina, where shanty towns had become symbols of "colonialist oppression," and in the postcolonial West Indies, it was the "British Crown" acting "as a symbol of past oppression."[124] Francis and Judith are simply quoting from the headlines of the 1960s and 1970s.

REG: "It's symbolic of his struggle against reality"—Most of the terror groups' actions—lashing out against monolithic institutions, even in discrete, symbolic acts—were themselves symbolic of the guerrilla groups' struggle against reality, of course. Western democracies were not brought down by the Angry Brigade or the Baader-Meinhof gangs, nor was political or economic equality achieved by the efforts of Carlos or the PLO. Virtually all of the terror cadres were eventually run to ground, ending their active, reactionary lives in prison, in exile, or in death.

A SAMARITAN is pushed out into the arena—There is no visual indication of this man's race or background, but in the credits he is called a "Weedy Samaritan." "Weedy" means he's a bit of a weakling, kind of wet, and not much of a physical specimen. According to Cupitt, observant Jews viewed the Samaritans as "schismatic and half-pagan," so seeing one committed to the brutality of the games is understandable.[125] *Cheering* for that unrepentant outsider is a bit more surprising, except that this means the PFJ are now really cheering against the Romans, which indicates their revolutionary bona fides. In *Flying Circus* Palin and Jones play characters also described as "weedy."[126]

There is a small spattering of applause from the sparse CROWD—This description belies the historical record, at least for the bulk of larger cities in the Roman Empire. By this period, according to Mannix, the popularity of the games had reached new heights, with the number of gladiatorial combats rising significantly during Julius Caesar's reign, and even higher in the new millennium under emperors Claudius and Marcus Aurelius.[127] Given Jerusalem's Jewish population and theocratic leadership, it's unlikely that Roman, pagan blood sports would have been tolerated within Jerusalem's walls. The combats held further away in Caesarea, where Pilate lived, were as bloody as any.

The atmosphere resembles the second day of a mid-week cricket match between Northamptonshire and the minor counties at Kettering—(PSC) Northants Cricket had a secondary field at Kettering, where the matches were likely smaller, more intimate. Those matches seem to have stopped as of 1971, though the Pythons are likely thinking of the years they were growing up and watching cricket as impressionable youngsters. In newspaper coverage of the matches it was regularly reported that even though a "full day's cricket" was planned for Kettering or Derby, for example, attendance was often "sparse," while there were also plenty of "sleepy" matches where not much happened. Northamptonshire is west of Cambridge and north of Oxford, and just south of Leicester, where Chapman grew up, and east of Wolverhampton, where Idle went to school. Both Northants and Kettering are mentioned in *Flying Circus*.[128] In the Ep. 20 mention, a handful of old gentlemen watch a cricket match, and one dies as the match moves on. The announcer (Cleese) tells us it's the "second day of the first test," and nothing has happened ("already they are nought for nought"). The film clip then shows a bowler bowling to the batman, and nothing happens. The batman is eventually carried off, stiff, and replaced by a piece of furniture. The ball is "extremely well not-played."[129] This likely would have qualified as "dreadful" play to many fans of county cricket.

The sparsely attended or even tatty games reproduced here aren't ahistorical, either. The further from Rome, the more likely the games could be second tier, or worse, in Martial's[130] eyes, especially if elected officials or even "city-priests" weren't in charge:

> Outside Rome, there were many other givers of games, too, and Martial is extremely caustic and snobbish about the low status of some of the men who succeeded in achieving this ambition. He complains that a shoe-maker sponsored contests at the cultured city of Bononia, and a fuller at Mutina (Modena), wondering sarcastically which will be the first town to have a show organized by a publican.[131]

SAMARITAN: "It's dangerous out there!"—This is voiced as the unwilling fighter is pushed back out onto the bloodied sand. The actor is Neil Innes, but the voice has been added later by Idle. This alcove was built for the film.

A huge GLADIATOR advances on him . . .—This man would have been one of only three types: a captured warrior from another kingdom, a man condemned and "of servile status," or a nobleman who has broken ranks with his class to join the combats.[132] The last would be the least likely and fewest in number; there were criminals aplenty for *naumachia* or to reenact famous land battles; while the most elaborate, entertaining games featured colorful, exotic enslaved combatants from the far reaches of the empire. If he did happen to be a free man who chose to associate himself with this low level of society, he would have taken "the gladiator's oath":

> The words of this most noble oath are the same as those of that most dishonourable one: to be burnt (i.e., branded), to be chained up, and to be killed by an iron weapon. A binding condition is imposed on those who hire their hands out to the arena and consume food and drink which they are to pay back in blood, and that they should suffer such things even if do not wish to.[133]

As for the gladiator the Pythons have placed into the arena, there are no indications as to what brought him into service—his crime, servile status, or personal choice as a free man.

. . . the SAMARITAN sets off at full speed . . .—Many of the more staged acts in these arenas did require the victims to flee in terror, and as the victims tended to be criminals, slaves, or prisoners of war (often women, children, and the elderly), running for their lives was likely a natural response, though ultimately a futile one.[134] Just as often, however, the victim was chained or tied to an animal, a post in the arena, or to another victim, and fleeing wasn't an option.

Juvenal, writing of the effeminate Gracchus[135] in the arena, illustrates a period version of this fleeing Samaritan:

> The games! Go there for the ultimate scandal,
> Looking at Gracchus who fights, but not with the arms of a swordsman,
> Not with a dagger or shield (he hates and despises such weapons),
> Nor does a helmet hide his face. What he holds is a trident,
> What he hurls is a net, and he misses, of course, and we see him
> Look up at the seats, then run for his life, all around the arena
> Easy for all to know and identify.[136]

In the notes to this section, the "running" is explained, and also explains the props our gladiator and prey are carrying, beginning with the trident the Samaritan drops immediately:

Fuscina, a sort of three-pronged fork or trident, used by a particular kind of fencer or gladiator, who was armed with this, and with a net; hence called Retiarus. His adversary was Mirmillo . . . and was armed with a shield, scythe, and headpiece, with a figure of a fish on the crest. The Retiarius tried to throw his net over the Mirmillo's head, and so entangle him. . . . The Mirmillo is sometimes called the secutor or pursuer, *because if the Retiarius missed him, by throwing his net too far, or too short, he instantly took to his heels, running about the arena for his life, that he might gather up his net for a second cast; the Mirmillo, in the mean time, as swiftly pursuing him,* to prevent him of his design.[137]

So the fleeing looks silly and Pythonesque, but is based in actual events as played out numerous times on the arena sand. It's not likely, though, that many pursuers had to give up the chase due to heart attack. Also, if the pursuer did fail, his life might be forfeit, and his prey might be granted a reprieve; that, or the editor or emperor could rematch the pursued with another gladiator, and the fight would continue.

. . . the CROWD is disgruntled . . .—At the height of the games, a baying, bloodthirsty crowd could decide which gladiators or victims lived or died, which acts were successes and which were not, and the canny editor and emperor allowed the public its head:

If a convict fought bravely enough, the community might be sufficiently impressed to be prepared to give him back his life. A brave fighter might rise from the dead, and re-join the society of the living. That was not in the gift of the president of the games, magistrate or even emperor, but in the gift of society as a whole: of the Roman people, present in the amphitheatre.[138]

The scattered crowd in this arena don't seem to be any real threat to Roman power, and as the assembled rabble cheer for the nimble Samaritan, the reclining Romans simply mutter their disgust. Also, the crowd won't be giving this gladiator "back his life," but clearly the Samaritan has won their admiration.

Gladiator crowds did tend to be excitable, especially if the fighters didn't perform as expected, according to Lactantius: "They are angry with the fighters, if one of the two is not quickly killed, and as though they thirst for human blood, *they hate delays.* They want similar and fresher fighters to be given to them, so that as soon as possible they can satisfy their eyes."[139] The emperor could also disapprove of the events as they unfolded. Suetonius reports one such fight in front of Caligula, Grant quotes:

A group of net-and-trident *retiarii*, dressed in tunics, put up a very poor show against the five *secutores* with whom they were matched. But when the emperor sentenced them to death for cowardice, one of them seized a trident and killed each of his opponents in turn. Caligula then publicly expressed his horror at what he called "this most bloody murder," and his disgust with those who had been able to stomach the sight.[140]

The "dreadful" display of blood seemed to have upset Caligula infrequently (if ever, truly).

The Pythons' gladiator is costumed as a "Secutor," complete with armor on one arm and one leg, and wearing a helmet.[141] The victim is given a two-pronged spear[142] and a net, and is clearly meant to be seen as a "Retiarus." The Secutor was the "chaser," while the Retiarus was the "netman," and as the frightened potential victim runs away, he's performing just the way his "role" demands, and would have been expected by knowledgeable spectators.

In the "final" version of the printed script—that which appears in book form—this is essentially the end of the scene, at least as far as the contestants in the arena are concerned. We are left with the image of the lumbering Gladiator chasing the Weedy Samaritan, and "the Samaritan is going to take a lot of catching."[143] The balance of the scene focuses on Brian and the PFJ, and transitions to Brian's nocturnal graffiti mission. Another version of the script (as read aloud) offers a quick cutaway to the staggering Gladiator as he has a heart attack. In that version, the quick-thinking Samaritan grabs the Gladiator's sword and stabs him, to muted applause from the Jews, and disgust from the Romans.

Notes

1. *ATW*, 1.12.155–58 and 2.28.60–62, respectively; also, see the entries for "Upperclass Twit" (1.12.184–200) and "Emigration from Surbiton to Hounslow" (2.20–39) in Larsen, *MPFC: UC*.

2. Wiedemann, *Emperors and Gladiators*, 133. This reluctance to host games was overcome about twenty years later as the Colosseum was under construction in Rome, eventually setting the high-water mark of theatrical presentations for eager crowds.

3. Wiedemann, 134.

4. Pilate had been, of course, deposed and recalled to Rome by 36. Part-Jewish Agrippa II (27– c. 100) was in charge of Judea at this time.

5. Grant, *Gladiators*, 122–24.

6. See Ames, "Herodian Judea"; also, Smallwood, *JURR*, 83–85. Unlike Pilate, who lived in Caesarea, Herod had spent most of his rule living in Jerusalem, and it's likely Herod's palace that Pilate calls his own in the film.

7. Josephus, *AJ*, 15.8.1 (Whiston, 328); Josephus doesn't specifically mention gladiators fighting in these Jerusalem arenas, but he does describe in some detail full-fledged gladiatorial games in "the Roman colony of Berytus," where "seven hundred pairs were made to fight, including any condemned criminals Agrippa had available" (Wiedemann, *Emperors and Gladiators*, 146). Wiedemann concludes that "there was a substantial feeling amongst those versed in Jewish law . . . that Agrippa's behaviour was improper" (146). Perhaps the scattered crowd offered by the film wasn't far from the reality of *Jewish* attendance at these games.

8. "Herod the Great," *JE*. Remember that Herod was an Edomite, raised as a Jew (his father had converted), and clearly pleased the Romans enough (he kept order, which should have impressed the PFJ) to secure his throne for many years.

9. Jerusalem has been built up, torn down and scattered, and built up again over many generations (see the introduction section of Smallwood's *JURR*). The image the film begins with is a much later version of Jerusalem than Christ's time, one that features structures not present in the first century. It's only as recently as 1999–2000 that archaeologists announced the potential discovery of more parts of Herod's palace, the substructures of which have been intermittently uncovered since the 1960s. See Schürer, 45–46.

10. Kotker, *HLTJ*, 40.

11. *JURR*, 84.

12. Gilliam uses a photograph of a portion of this structure in the opening credits animation.

13. Mannix, *TAD*, 141.

14. Wiedemann, citing Golvin, sets the number of cities "certain" to have these structures across the empire at 186, "with another 86 probable, purpose-built amphitheatres" (22).

15. Wiedemann, *Emperors and Gladiators*, 146.

16. *Wonders of the Past* was first published in 1923, and reprinted often thereafter. The view is from the Mount of Olives. The Hippodrome structure is a part of many later Jerusalem cityscapes, though it moves around a bit. The editors of the book attribute the image as a version "after the painting by H. C. Selous," who created *Jerusalem in Her Grandeur* (c. 1860).

17. Gilliam had created these kinds of images for the animated sequences of the titles in *Holy Grail*, and had, as Patsy, blown a herald note at the French-held castle.

18. The first to unfurl is for "1st Asst. Director Jonathan Benson."

19. Translated as "The Senate and People of Rome [make this donation to] the Divine Augustus Caesar." Thanks to Dr. Roger Macfarlane, who also points out that the Latin on the banner is "utterly conventional and grammatically correct," so kudos to the Pythons there.

20. An example of a tribute like this would be Julius Caesar (100–44 BC) holding games in the memory of his daughter Julia (c. 76–54 BC), who died as a young wife during childbirth (Richard, *WWAR*, 34; also *Gladiators*, 27). In the draft version, Reg will later mention Julius Caesar in relation to demands the PFJ are making for the safe release of Pilate's wife, and it's not clear there, either, why the sitting emperor Tiberius isn't the emperor mentioned.

21. Grant, *Gladiators*, 11.

22. The possibility that the Pythons and their production team gathered the banners and other props from previous Holy Land film and TV productions is a real one, too—they'd utilized the BBC's vast wardrobe and prop department throughout the run of *Flying Circus*. They are reusing some of the same buildings, walls, and Sousse/Ribat settings the Zeffirelli production had used in 1977.

23. *WWAR*, 90. These are common *Roman* people, of course; those made subjects to the empire were likely tasked with learning the language of the oppressor on their own.

24. Reg also reads from prepared scrolls twice, Francis is able to create a workable map, and Stan/Loretta takes notes on a wax tablet more than once.

25. *I'm Sorry, I'll Read That Again* (BBC Radio, 1964–1973) starred Cleese and was cowritten by Idle; the *1948 Show* (ITV, 1967) featured Chapman and Cleese; *Do Not Adjust Your Set* starred Idle, Jones, and Palin (1967–1969); and *Complete and Utter History of Britain* was created by Jones and Palin in early 1969 for London Weekend TV. These shows are discussed in more detail in *MPFC: UC*.

26. The Pepperpots are the doughty but indefatigable women (played by the Pythons) who can be both "ratbag" and "revisionist"; Arthur Pewtey is a myopic nebbish; and Mr. Praline is the slick-haired, Mac-wearing know-it-all. See the *MPFC: UC* index for much more on these characters.

27. See *MPFC: UC* 1.394 and 2.133. They transposed the page number slightly, by the way—the reference is on page 486, not 468.

28. Luke 2:1.

29. This portion of the speech appeared in major British newspapers, including the *Times*, *Telegraph*, and *Daily Mail* the following day (6 September 1978).

30. See Donoughue's *DSD*, 2.356, and Shepherd's *Crisis? What Crisis?*, 28.

31. See Kenneth Fleet, "The Baskets Get at Jim," *Sunday Times*, 24 September 1978: 53.

32. The young Pythons would have made the trek to these galleries on occasion as school outings. To this day, clusters of uniform-clad schoolchildren roam the halls of these spaces, listening (allegedly) to a docent and taking notes.

33. *MPFC: UC*, 1.5.

34. *MPFC: UC*, 1.350, 372; 2.111, 128.

35. *BAFHG*, 227n2.

36. During *Flying Circus* the Pythons drew from the same BBC prop department as shows like *Doctor Who* and *Benny Hill*—shared props can be glimpsed from time to time (*MPFC: UC*, 1.154, 248).

37. Wiedemann, *Emperors and Gladiators*, 63.

38. Wiedemann, *Emperors and Gladiators*, 63.

39. Suetonius (c. 69–122) was a Roman poet.

40. Grant, *Gladiators*, 104.

41. Grant, *Gladiators*, 113.

42. There is a two-page spread of these statues in the Timmers and Van Der Heyden picture book *The Glory of Rome*, pages 10–11.

43. The two rabbis refused to recant or give any obeisance to Herod, and were burned to death (Brandon, "The Zealots," 633); also Smallwood, *JURR*, 99.

44. *TAD*, 43–44.

45. *TAD*, 69–70.

46. Grant, *Gladiators*, 51.

47. *TAD*, 69.

48. *TAD*, 5.

49. This voiceover line doesn't appear in various printed versions of the scripts, and was likely created by Jones and Palin as they stitched the film together. Idle was obviously also in on the postproduction

work; it's his voice that says "It's dangerous out there!" when the Samaritan (Neil Innes) is pushed into the arena. At the end of the "fight," when the gladiator is dying, it's Jones's voice we hear.

50. See *MPFC: UC*, 1.26–49, 79–92, and 278–88.

51. There is also a "Mr. A. T. Hun" in *Flying Circus* who turns out to be Alexander the Great, or "Mr. A. T. Great" (*ATW*, 1.13.173–74).

52. See Burleigh's *BRT*, 304–9.

53. Skinner was a miner, union official, and Leftist Labour MP.

54. Grant, *Gladiators*, 62.

55. *DBI*, 165.

56. "Inquiry Accuses JPs in 'Baby Crusher' Case," *Telegraph*, 3 March 1977: 3.

57. See the entries in *MPFC: UC* for these.

58. *TAD*, 6.

59. *TAD*, 18.

60. Brandon, *Jesus and the Zealots*, 24.

61. Brandon, *Jesus and the Zealots*, 24.

62. See Brendon, *DFBE*, index under "Rome."

63. Bernstein, *The Myth of Decline*, 8; see "British Empire" in the *MPFC: UC* and *BAFHG* indexes.

64. *MPFC: UC*, 1.373.

65. Brandon, *Jesus and the Zealots*, 24.

66. "President Sukarno Proposes Anti-Imperialist 'Axis,'" *Times*, 18 August 1965: 6.

67. "French Confusion Over Students' Revolt," *Times*, 17 May 1968: 12; and, "Why Revolutionary Firebrands Failed to Spark the Workers," *Times*, 28 October 1968: 8.

68. The Pythons had shot a portion of Ep. 36 at the back door of the Aldwych Theatre, the home of the Royal Shakespeare Company of Stratford-upon-Avon at this time, and the debut stage for many more frankly political and sexual plays of the day (*MPFC: UC*, 2.121).

69. "Alan Brien's Diary," *Sunday Times*, 10 December 1972: 32.

70. "Peking Forces Final Rift," *Daily Mail*, 24 March 1966: 2.

71. "Why Revolutionary Firebrands Failed to Spark the Workers," *Times*, 28 October 1968: 8.

72. Dobson and Payne, *Carlos Complex*, 13; italics added.

73. "23 Steps to End the Killing," *Daily Mail*, 25 January 1973: 18–19. Less than two years later North Vietnam forces overran South Vietnam.

74. Peter Strafford, "Pro-Palestinian Votes by General Assembly," *Times*, 23 November 1974: 6.

75. Respectively: *Times*, 8 November 1967: 7; "CBI Mood Hardens," *Times*, 15 October 1969: 22; "Solemn Declaration," *Times*, 18 March 1975: 9; "Full Speed Ahead for Britain's Oil," *Daily Mail*, 1 February 1974: 1; "Scandal of the Street of Secrets," *Daily Mail*, 11 September 1975: 6; "National Trust Fears Threat by the State," *Telegraph*, 3 June 1974: 9; "Passover and Its Message of Freedom," *Times*, 22 March 1975: 16; "Young Liberal Group Urges Support for Squatters," *Times*, 9 September 1975: 14.

76. *BAFHG*, 122–23.

77. Dobson and Payne, *Carlos Complex*, 11.

78. Kröcher-Tiedemann had also been Carlos's number two earlier in the storming of the OPEC offices in Vienna in 1975, where she had killed two people. This will be discussed later in relation to Brian's graffiti attack, and the PFJ's failed raid for Pilate's wife.

79. Demaris, *Brothers in Blood*, 203–6.

80. "Grievance Cultivation," *Telegraph*, 27 May 1975: 12.

81. "Sexist Language," *Times*, 14 December 1977: 15.

82. Miller and Swift, *Words and Women*, 128.

83. Auberon Waugh calls Davis "Kaiser Bill Davis," a poke at Davis's birth in Germany. Waugh's editors seem certain that Davis (born "Gunter Kase") was also a member of the Junior League of Hitler Youth (Waugh, *FCY*, 21 April 1975).

84. *Punch*, 27 March 1973: 13.

85. *BRT*, 30.

86. Sandbrook, *Seasons in the Sun*, 666–67.

87. Bogdanor, "Thatcherism, 1979–1990," a.t.

88. The *Evening Standard*, for example, paid libel damages to Williams (known as "Lady Fork-bender" in *Private Eye*) in 1975 rather than face trial (*FCY*, 19 July 1975).

89. Donoughue, *DSD*, 1.520.

90. From a 1978 interview with Bryan Magee, which will be discussed later in more detail.

91. Jeremias, *JTJ*, 375.

92. Section 37 of the 1974 *Marialis Cultus* found at http://www.papalencyclicals.net/Paul06/p6marial.htm.

93. *FCY*, 9 April 1974.

94. Demaris, *Brothers in Blood*, 224. The RAF made its first violent attack in May 1972, setting off bombs at military, civil, and political installations. The RAF blamed the bombings on US military activity in Vietnam.

95. Dr. Alfred Stumper was the chief of police, Interior Ministry of Baden-Wurtemberg.

96. Dobson and Payne, *Carlos Complex*, 151.

97. *Private Eye*, 9 December 1977: 12.

98. Nineteenth-century Russian terrorist Vera Figner is discussed in this vein in *BRT* (29–32).

99. *Private Eye*, 9 December 1977: 12.

100. The winter 1972 killings. See entries in scene 10, "The PFJ Plan Their Raid," for more on this grisly series of events.

101. *Brothers in Blood*, 29.

102. *Daily Mail*, 30 October 1975: 6. Coyle was a Provisional IRA member who spent a decade in prison for political kidnapping; Lynette "Squeaky" Fromme was a Manson family member who tried to assassinate President Ford in 1975; Hearst, Khaled, Meinhof, and the Prices are discussed elsewhere in this book.

103. 17 February 1978: 12.

104. "Any Questions," *Private Eye*, 17 February 1978: 13. Muggeridge along with the Bishop of Southwark will later upbraid Cleese and Palin for *Life of Brian*. See Hewison's *Monty Python: The Case Against*. The first pages of Miller and Swift's *Words and Women* looks at this same absent name, absent identity issue.

105. This film was based on Alan Hackney's novel *Private Life*, published in 1958. Like the Pythons' work, Hackney's novel reflected the social and economic unrest of the time, as his obituary acknowledged: "In the film's main character . . . Hackney created one of those comic figures . . . who seem to embody a particular moment in British social history" (*Telegraph*, 19 May 2009). Hackney lampooned contemporary labor and class in everyday dress; the Pythons do the same, draping their contemporary satire across a biblical setting.

106. Liz Fraser would also appear in a number of *Carry On* films in the following two decades.

107. Barges had helped in September 1970 hijackings, and the bombing of Rotterdam oil refineries.

108. Dobson and Payne, *Carlos Complex*, 29.

109. "British Woman Charged in Paris with Aiding 'Carlos the Jackal,'" *Times*, 7 July 1975: 3; also "The Cocktail Party Revolutionary," *Daily Mail*, 7 July 1975: 14–15.

110. See the "feminists" entry later, in scene 21, "The PFJ Discusses," for more.

111. *DSD*, 2.59. To be fair, Donoughue acknowledged Thatcher's triumphs, as well. In January 1979, during the Winter of Discontent, Thatcher used a Commons debate to blast Labour's truckling to the trade unions. Donoughue called the shadow leader's arguments "extremely effective, passionate" and "[t]ypical of her at her best, articulating popular resentment and prejudices" (*DSD*, 2.424). See also Sandbrook's *Seasons in the Sun*, pages 738–39, where he notes that even the Labour-leaning *Guardian* offered Thatcher deserved kudos for this "blazing attack."

112. *BRT*, 228.

113. O'Hehir, "Insane Time and Place."

114. King and Stager, *LBI*, 49.

115. "Embryos Outside the Body," *Times*, 4 May 1968: 6.

116. Associated News, owners of the *Daily Mail*, won the bidding.

117. "'Test Tube' Life," *Times*, 27 February 1970: 9.

118. "Fast Is Unbroken," *Times*, 24 October 1975: 4. Jeremy Thorpe lost his seat in the following election, as well as the leadership of the party (earlier, in 1976).

119. See Richard Wigg, "Brazilian Urban Guerrillas," *Times*, 9 September 1969: 8; also, Elbrick's entry in Newton's *The Encyclopedia of Kidnappings*, 96.

120. "Sir Geoffrey Jackson," in *Eyewitness 1970–1979*. See also the entry for Jackson in Newton's *Encyclopedia of Kidnappings*, 147. More on these kidnappings later, as the PFJ are discussed.

121. "The Cyanide Messiah," *Sunday Times*, 26 November 1978: 17. See also Ligasor, "The Art of Attrition: The Erosion of Peoples Temple and Jim Jones." The Rev. Jones even called his armed guards "Red Brigade."

122. This is where the macabre phrase "Drinking the Kool-Aid" comes from.

123. "Was Jim Jones Mad or Bad?" *Spectator*, 24 March 1979: 15.

124. See "Argentina's Revolt is Part of a Social War," *Sunday Times*, 7 April 1963: 4; and "Royal Tour Shows West Indies Are Still Loyal," *Sunday Times*, 6 March 1966: 6, respectively. The flip side of this last coin: For many years, the working thesis of the British Empire as a power that could project itself around the globe and thrive as an economic superpower had to be attenuated—"after 1850," Bernstein writes, "This empire was more a symbol of power than a source of power" (Bernstein, *Myth of Decline*, 22). See also Brendon's *DFBE*, passim.

125. Cupitt and Armstrong, *Who Was Jesus?*, 62.

126. *ATW*, 1.1.11 and 1.21.280.

127. *TAD*, 34–35.

128. *MPFC: UC*, 1.320, 2.68.

129. *ATW*, 1.20.274–76.

130. Martial (c. 38–102) was a Roman poet born in what is now Spain.

131. Grant, *Gladiators*, 52.

132. Wiedemann, *Emperors and Gladiators*, 102.

133. Quoted in Wiedemann, *Emperors and Gladiators*, 107.

134. See Grant's *Gladiators*, passim.

135. According to Madan, "Gracchus had been one of these Salii [priests of Mars] but had left them and had sunk into . . . effeminacies and debaucheries" (*Juvenal and Persius*, 56).

136. Quoted in Grant, *Gladiators*, 61.

137. Madan, *Juvenal and Persius*, 58–59; italics added.

138. Wiedemann, *Emperors and Gladiators*, 105.

139. Cook, "Crucifixion as Spectacle," 75; italics added.

140. Grant, *Gladiators*, 62.

141. *TAD*, 21–22; *Gladiators*, 58–59.

142. This should be a trident for a proper Retiarus, and the armor-clad Secutor would have sported a "fish insignia on his helmet as did the Gauls" (Mannix, 21). It's not clear what designs are on this character's helmet. See also *Gladiators*, 57–63.

143. *Monty Python's The Life of Brian (of Nazareth)*, 17.

SCENE EIGHT
THE PEOPLES' FRONT OF JUDEA

This scene is very nearly continuation of action of the previous scene, and the actions will overlap as Brian and the PFJ meet and converse.

BRIAN: "Larks' tongues . . . otters' noses . . . Ocelot spleens"—In one of Auberon Waugh's diary entries for 1973, he describes Mrs. Walter Annenberg's "very dainty *fricassee* of nasturtium leaves, served in a sauce of brandy, cram, Grand Marnier, *foie gras truffe*, caviar and crushed nightingales' tongues."[1]

In the world of the film, this list implies that there is ample food available in the Pythons' Jerusalem, at least for purchase. Juvenal wrote that satisfying the Roman people (of the empire, not the republic) eventually came down to two items: bread and circuses (*panem et circenses*). Once they had abdicated their duties, as Juvenal saw them, the Roman people and subjects could be well controlled by simply being fed and entertained.[2] The PFJ complain about Roman rule, but they also attend Roman entertainments and eat Roman food after just a token fuss. (To be fair, they also second-guess Jesus's message earlier, and will eventually abandon Brian to his fate, but also plan an insurrection while watching the Roman *munera*.) Later they'll tick off a long list of the benefits of Roman rule, too. In life, these terror types often came from privileged First World backgrounds, not Third World poverty—Burleigh mentions that there was no consideration of the *lumpenproletariat* in the literature of West Germany's RAF-type groups—so contradictions are plentiful.[3]

As it is, no one in *Brian* is seen to be starving. Lepers and ex-lepers beg, but as a job; in a draft of the film script Brian has been invited to dinner with Judith's family, and there is also a "Last Supper" scene; and a mob (and a single hermit) can be fed on wild berries. Food and eating are not a major part of the world of the finished film. As in *Holy Grail*, the Pythons don't spend much time on feeding their characters, nor on plot points that hinge on either food abundance or scarcity. Food is a major part of the settings and props throughout *Meaning of Life*: A lack of work meaning lack of food forces the Catholic father to sell his children for medical experiments, and there are dinner/meal settings in the "fiercely proud" Protestant scene, the World War I, medieval Hawaiian restaurant, Live Organ Donor, and dinner party scenes, as well as in the penultimate "Christmas in Heaven" scene. This film is, admittedly, often more domestically sited—like *Flying Circus* was, as well—meaning kitchens and dining rooms (and the routines therein) are more likely to appear.

REG: "You got any nuts?" . . . "I don't want any of that Roman rubbish"—Perhaps a sign that these are truly rebels, since Magness notes that many Jews had come to enjoy

149

Roman foods, that they were "open to Roman culinary influences and prepared to try and taste new food."[4] Simple foods would have been the fare for most Romans, though, and for most citizens of the Roman Empire. Nuts would have been available, including almonds, pistachios, pine nuts, and peanuts.[5] "Roman rubbish" includes any food that was exotic, difficult to prepare, or just rare and expensive. Spices from across the empire—cinnamon, nutmeg, or pepper—and unique dishes like roasted thrush or stuffed dormice could be found at Roman banquet tables. Horace's *Satires*, written about sixty years before the events depicted in the film, list a similar array of exotic and perhaps grotesque delicacies served by "Nasidienus, the rich man," whose slaves

> carried to the table, followed by a giant board, a crane served into parts and coated well with salt and crumbs, the liver of a fig-fed, albino gander, and rabbit legs torn from the trunk: that way they're daintier etc. than if still connected to the rabbit. Next course was boiled blackbird breasts served with de-assed doves, quite a treat without the lecture his lordship gave about their cause and essential natures.[6]

The guests then "fled" before tasting any of these latter delicacies, dismissing this haute cuisine like Reg and the PFJ. Other tidbits served earlier at this feast included "Lucanian boar," all sorts of expensive wines, skirret root, fish-pickle, cakes, birds, oysters and fish, various livers, sugar apples, and Lamprey eel on a bed of prawns.[7] This same disdain for unacceptable items is heard in *Flying Circus* Ep. 37, when peasants reject the latest items of "bloody silver" from the redistributor of wealth, Dennis Moore, demanding "Venetian silver," instead.[8]

Trimalchio's feast as described in Petronius's *The Satyricon* is equally rich and exaggerated—the Pythons' "ocelot spleens" and "otters' noses" fit right in:

> On arches built up in the form of miniature bridges were dormice seasoned with honey and poppy-seed. There were sausages, too, smoking hot on a silver grill, and underneath (to imitate coals) Syrian plums and pomegranate seeds . . . [and] a lot of peafowl's eggs. . . . Trimalchio turns his head at this, saying, "My friends, it was by my orders the hen set on the peafowl's eggs yonder; but by God! I am very much afraid they are half-hatched. Nevertheless we can try whether they are eatable." For our part, we take our spoons, which weighed at least half a pound each, and break the eggs, which were made of paste. I was on the point of throwing mine away, for I thought I discerned a chick inside. But when I overheard a veteran guest saying, "There should be something good here!" I further investigated the shell, and found a very fine fat beccafico swimming in yolk of egg flavored with pepper. . . .
>
> An immense circular tray bore the twelve signs of the zodiac displayed round the circumference, on each of which . . . a dish of suitable and appropriate viands: on the Ram ram's-head peas, on the Bull a piece of beef, on the Twins fried testicles and kidneys, on the Crab simply a crown, on the Lion African figs, on a Virgin a sow's haslet, on Libra a balance with a tart in one scale and a cheesecake in the other, on Scorpio a small sea-fish, on Sagittarius an eye-seeker, on Capricornus a lobster, on Aquarius a wild goose, on Pisces two mullets. In the middle was a sod of green turf, cut to shape and supporting a honey-comb. Meanwhile an Egyptian slave was carrying bread around in a miniature oven of silver, crooning to himself in a horrible voice a song on wine and laserpitium.[9]

Also, imagine and add as much liquor and wine as the guests could drink.

JUDITH: "Why don't you sell proper food?"—For Jews, meat would have been boiled, generally, though occasionally roasted, as a paschal lamb on a spit. Other foods included bread, made daily, "flour cakes sweetened with honey or figs," griddle and barley cakes, myriad vegetables, figs, olives, wine and parched grain, beans, fruit, cheese, stews made with lentils and herbs, and meat sparingly.[10] This is quite a variety of food, but we see almost no eating or producing of food in the finished film. Jeremias notes that there was plenty of food and wine for the buying during festivals, but that Jerusalem was also prone to food shortages exacerbated by drought or times of siege.[11]

The idea of what's "proper" changes over time, of course, and by culture. Much in the news during this period was the Iran situation, where the long-reigning Shah had begun to institute the White Revolution, an attempt to curtail Islamic sectarian activism while borrowing the more progressive ideas for modernization.[12] Influence from the West, and specifically America and Israel, were the targets of these Islamic religious backlashes, with the notion of "proper" food, dress, and behavior changing as their influence grew. Under the influence of the Westernized Shah, Iran had been dining on American food, "Zionist" food, if you will, and the Shiite clerics wanted an end to this gluttony.

During the Pythons' youth there had been significant and mandatory rationing of food in the UK, both during the war and for several years after. In *Flying Circus* Ep. 29, Klaus (Idle) is being offered "rabbit fish" by his irritated wife (Jones), in place of "proper food":

> Rationing (from January 1940) was a part of life in the UK for many years, with coffee, meats, sugar, butter, bacon, etc., all diminished as the war pushed on—remaining scarce in the frugal postwar years, until at least 1954. (A Milligan character in "The Fireball of Milton Street"—Sir Jim Nasium—asks several times if anyone knows what happened to "that crisp bacon" they had "before the war," and is shot for his troubles.) Beginning in 1940 each family registered with the local government and were given coupons for precisely what they deserved, by age and number of family members, and no more.
>
> In the larger cities especially, where there was less chance of growing a useful garden, Brits had to scrounge and resort to illicit sources for all sorts of items, from cigarettes to tea and, eventually, even bread. Londoners reported many days when bread and milk were the only meals, when housewives had to travel outside the city to buy black market vegetables and dairy products from small farms, and when virtually any kind of animal—including horse—could be justified as a meal.[13]

Marr mentions that beyond even the horsemeat ("regarded as disgusting") made available to a hungry population, Ministry officials imported whale meat from Commonwealth partner South Africa, which was meant to be eaten like tuna, as well as the tropical fish "snoek," also tinned and also from South Africa, but also ignored by British consumers except for the making of "a great joke in the newspapers and in Parliament."[14] On the whole, the young Pythons and their countrymen turned up their noses at food they considered to not be "proper."[15]

Moving away from food, one of the genesis points for Irish nationalism was the decline of the speaking and teaching of Gaelic in Ireland across the mid-nineteenth century. Activists sought to increase the presence of Gaelic speech and literature, the "proper" language of a free Ireland.[16]

BRIAN: *(reluctant to move away)*: "Are you the . . . Judean Peoples' Front?"—This would have been an easy mistake to make in the 1970s. There were diverse political action groups at most British universities, for example, including the Campaign for Nuclear Disarmament (CND) and its splinters, as well as the Radical Student Alliance (RSA), the Revolutionary Socialist Students' Federation (RSSF), the National Front (NF), the British-Vietnam Solidarity Front (BVSF), and the Vietnam Solidarity Campaign (VSC). There were many more of these groups, large and small, as well as versions of many that were more and less Trotskyist, Marxist, Maoist, or Revisionist.[17]

In 1975 the *Times* profiled Japan's young terror groups, finding a dizzying array of names and leftish ideologies. "Besides the Red Army and the three major rival movements of student radicals," Hazelhurst[18] writes, "the Chukakua (6,500 supporters), the Kakumarha (the Revolutionary Marxists, with 4,500 supporters), and the Hanteigakuhyo (the Anti-Imperialist Student Council with a force of 2,000)—it is estimated that another 25 militant and fanatical groups, supporting different shades of left-wing ideology, exist in Japan today."[19] The JRA would become inextricably connected to the PFLP after leader Fusako Shigenobu went to work with the PLO, and spent more than thirty years in the Middle East.

REG: "Fuck off!"—An equivalent of this phrase that has been traced to this period—and even found scrawled on the wall of the Stabian baths in Pompeii—is "*in cruce figarus*," or "get nailed to a cross."[20] Graffiti in the Roman Empire will be further discussed later, in relation to Brian's anti-Roman slogans painted on the palace walls.

This language was one of the reasons that the film offended so many upon its initial release, but the specter of larger-than-life (and in this case "biblical") characters using such language shouldn't have been a surprise. The recent revelations from the Watergate affair, for example, displayed an American president's penchant for cursing and racial slurs,[21] and *Private Eye* reported the following in March 1976:

> The recent vote against the Government on the public spending cuts seems to have gone to Chancellor Healey's head. On the evening of the vote he was seen to be in the House of Commons, standing over a mild-mannered Scottish Tribunite MP, Denis Canavan, and shouting over and over again, very loudly indeed: "You—you're a *fucker*. You, you're a *fucker*. A *fucker*, do you hear?" (And so on for about ten minutes.)[22]

Other filmmakers had already slipped things holy into bed, often literally, with things profane. Buñuel's ascetic saint Simon (in *Simon of the Desert* [1965]) is tempted by worldly things, including sex and popular culture; Pasolini's celebrated *Canterbury Tales* (1972) and *The Decameron* (1971) offered everything Mary Whitehouse and the NVLA could have found offensive: "This Italian New Wave retelling of the Boccaccio work . . . features mud, filth, excrement, sex, Church-bashing, death, plague, etc.—quite Pythonesque, actually."[23] The fact that such films weren't greeted with the same righteous indignation as James Kirkup's poem in *Gay News*[24] or Pythons' *Life of Brian* might be the fact that this "filth" was both foreign (Pasolini an Italian; Buñuel an itinerant Spaniard), and that both attacked, at some levels, popery and the Catholic Church, no sin for many English "Christians." Pasolini's nuns were breaking their vows, but Jesus himself wasn't implicated.[25]

Incidentally, this was where Palin, at least, thought the film was heading most fruitfully in the early days of writing. As the troupe tried to write funny sketches based on actual Gospels events, moments like the Immaculate Conception and the miracle of Lazarus were subjected to sketch treatment, to fitful results, Palin records:

> The sketches, or fragments, which work least well at the moment are those which deal *directly* with the events or characters described in the Gospels. I wrote a sketch about Lazarus going to the doctors with "post-death depression," which, as I read it, sounded as pat and neat and predictable as a bad university revue sketch. The same fate befell John and G's sketch about Joseph trying to tell his mates how his son Jesus was conceived. The way the material is developing it looks as though the peripheral world is the most rewarding, with Jesus unseen and largely unheard, though occasionally in the background.[26]

The fact that these types of sketches—where Christ could have played a significant role—were not working early in the script process likely saved the Pythons from even more backlash as the film was being completed.

REG: *(incredulously)* **Judean Peoples' Front!??? We're the Peoples' Front of Judea"**— This is a misunderstanding that would have been common in the postwar period, as anti-imperialist groups proliferated in various colonial countries. The Goons had made this joke already as early as October 1954. In that year the French military control of Vietnam was ended, Vice President Nixon admitted the possibility of American troops going to Vietnam, the Algerian struggle for independence from France began in earnest—in the guise of the Algerian National Liberation Front—and the unsettled Labour Party swirled helplessly in the eddy of a thirteen-year absence from No. 10. *Goon Show* writer Milligan adroitly tosses all political groups—new and old, traditional and revolutionary—into the mix. In "The Lone Banana" episode a single banana tree, characterized as "the last symbol of waning British prestige in South America,"[27] is the focus of an armed incursion:

> Moriarty: It is the revolution señor—everywhere there is an armed rising.
>
> Seagoon: Are you in it?
>
> Moriarty: Right in it—you see, señor, the United Anti-Socialist Neo-Democratic Pro-Fascist Communist Party is fighting to overthrow the Unilateral Democratic United Partisan Bellicose Pacifist Co-belligerent Tory Labour Liberal Party!
>
> Seagoon: Whose side are you on?
>
> Moriarty: There are no sides—we are all in this together.[28]

Among the expected antis, pros, fronts, and -isms Milligan has lumped in all three British political parties, picking no favorites. This jab at domestic politics is apropos, given the contentious and divisive nature of the ongoing "Gaitskellite" coup endeavors in the Labour Party of the 1950s and 1960s. The Gaitskellites[29] of the right side of the Labour Party, named for Hugh Gaitskell, had been working to pull the party away from the extreme Left, led by Aneurin Bevan. The application of the principles of socialism—whether forced upon, suggested for, or chosen by the electorate—were the sites of contention in this fight. There were many who believed—perhaps Milligan, too—that this political chasm helped keep Labour out of power between 1951 and 1964, when Harold Wilson's more moderate views and colleagues finally brought Labour out of opposition status. In other words, internecine squabbling *can* prevent anything significant being accomplished in a political group, as the PFJ will discover before the film is done.

Later, during the 1970s, the anti-imperialist revolutionary groups proliferated, split from each other, and renamed themselves with confusing regularity. Even earlier, though, in the violent postwar years across the Middle East and spawned from the sprawling Palestinian refugee camps in Gaza and Jordan, for example, came many new terror groups:

> This period saw a proliferation of Palestinian "resistance" groups. The Arab Front of the Liberation of Palestine was formed when three other organizations combined: the National Front of the Liberation of Palestine, the Palestinian Revolutionary Movement, and the General Command of Palestinian Self-Organization. Societies calling themselves the Red Hand and the Black Hand came into being and were followed by the Palestinian Military Organization and the Arab Palestinian Fedayeen. . . . The Palestinian Rebels Front of Mohammed Abu Sakhila; the Palestinian Liberation Front; and, most notable, the Arab Nationalist Movement (ANM), which merged with the Palestinian Liberation Front to form the PFLP, still exist today [in 1977].[30]

In 1969, Burleigh identifies at least fifty-two separate, active "armed Palestinian groups" in Jordan alone.[31] By the period closer to the film's creation there were terror groups whose names weren't as easily shortened, including Shining Path (Peru), the Red Army Faction (West Germany), the Japanese Red Army, the 2 June Movement (West Germany), the First of May Group (Spain/England), and the Tupamaros (Uruguay), among many. A short list of terror groups active in the 1970s offers a confusing array of acronyms, including the DFLP, PLF, PLO, PFLP, PFLP-EO, PFLP-GC, PNLM, PPSF, PRFLP, SLA, and SOT, to mention just a handful.[32] A number of these groups are offshoots of the PLO and Fatah (based in the Middle East and North Africa), splinter groups either more or less dedicated to the use of violence in attaining, for example, the liberation of Palestine, or, in the case of the American-born SLA, the overthrow of capitalism, patriarchalism, racism, sexism, and on.

Dobson and Payne note that specifically Arab groups in the 1970s could be fairly cavalier in regard to names, aims, and revolutionary goals, though all tended to have an anti-Zionist plank, at least, and then an axe to grind with the Western (read: imperialist) powers supporting Israel. When in 1975 Carlos's motley group stormed the OPEC headquarters in Vienna, they demanded all sorts of comforts and supplies, and that a missive be read out on Austrian radio:

> This was easily agreed to. It was a verbose and banal document couched in all the clichés of Arab extremism. The gang announced that they were "The Arm of the Arab Revolution." The name means nothing except that it places them in the left-wing of the Arab spectrum. Every operation is undertaken by *groups which seem to choose their own names, either for glorification of some martyr or to confuse their origins.* Black September[33] was itself chosen as a name to hide its Fatah parenthood.[34]

The Pythons have already mined this ore, in *Holy Grail*, where the "Knights Who Say Ni" announce their name change ("We are now no longer the Knights who say Ni!").[35]

Clearly the closer-to-home "Troubles" in and from Northern Ireland also produced a hodgepodge of acronymed, terror-bent groups, with British newspapers taking great pains to separate the IRA from the Provisional IRA (and then from the Official IRA) from the Royal Ulster Constabulary (RUC) from the Ulster Volunteer Force (UVF) from the Ulster Defence Association (UDA), and on. It didn't help when one group, for example, the IRA, blamed another group, the USC (Ulster Special Constabulary, the B-Specials), for explosions in April 1969, explosions that had been blamed on the IRA by the government just days earlier.[36] In an Ireland Cabinet Committee meeting in December 1974, Bernard Donoughue admits to passing a note to a new private secretary "comparing the IRA to the PLO."[37] The Pythons would simply take the next step and create their own acronymed group, the PFJ, reflecting the actual terror organizations so prevalent in newspapers and on the evening news.[38]

The most active group directly involved with Holy Land terror in the 1970s was the Popular Front for the Liberation of Palestine (PFLP), a more radical PLO "splinter." In September 1970, for instance, the PFLP were responsible for multiple hijackings and attempted hijackings, holding hostages to secure the release of comrades, and generally showing up the Israelis and the world with their "daring piece of 'theatre.'"[39]

FRANCIS: "Wankers ... "—This can mean masturbaters, but it also has a more general, desexualized connotation that means the person is merely "objectionable or contemptible."[40] In his diaries for 27 September 1977, Bernard Donoughue mentions a very PFJ-type group he came across: "Then went to North St Pancras Labour management committee. What a bunch of wankers!—not a serious working person there. All part-time polytechnic lecturers. Terrible. Did not finish till 11."[41] Similar epithets, like "sod," have also accrued both sexual and simply pejorative meanings, depending on the situation and usage. In the lyrics for the "*Brian*" song under the opening credits, Brian is mentioned as having "one off at the wrist," meaning he masturbates. His mother will later tell him to "leave it alone; give it a rest."

JUDITH: "Splitters!"—"Party splitter" was a common term in parliamentary politics of the day. In July 1974, Roy Jenkins was being called a "splitter" by the Left of the Labour Party, including Ian Mikardo, just after he "called for more moderate policies" to address the country's "grave economic conditions."[42] The Left wanted to move closer to state control of industry, following up on their 1973 manifesto, and moderates like Jenkins, Shirley Williams, and especially Harold Wilson knew such a move would cost many votes in the middle. This squabbling didn't derail Labour, though, as it narrowly won the next election.

BRIAN: " . . . Which are you again?"—It's a fun irony likely not missed by the Pythons and thoughtful others that government acronyms can sound very much like these terror group initials. In Ep. 15 of *Flying Circus*, a civil servant-type policy briefing begins with a barrage of acronyms, some legitimate, some silly: "Gentlemen, our MP saw the PM this AM and the PM wants more LSD from the PIB by tomorrow AM or PM at the latest. I told the PM's PPS that AM was NBG so tomorrow PM it is for the PM it is nem. con. Give us a fag or I'll go spare."[43] Through Bernard Donoughue's *Downing Street Diary* volumes, acronyms come hard and fast, including PM James Callaghan being referred to fittingly as "JC," and more than once Donoughue complains about the underhanded terror tactics of the dreaded "PLP," or Parliamentary Labour Party—his own political party.[44]

BRIAN: "May I join you?"—This may be Brian's Pauline moment, his conversion to the righteous cause. He was clearly struck earlier, as he saw Judith out at the sermon, and now he's wanting to be part of anything she's doing. His road to Damascus conversion is as much sexual attraction as political commitment. In recent films like *Bonnie and Clyde*, *Butch Cassidy and the Sundance Kid*, and *Badlands*, it had been the interested woman who, attaching herself to an attractive man, was drawn into a journey of violence and destruction.

REG: "No. Piss off"—A milder version of the phrase Reg uttered moments before, and already heard from Mandy when she's seeing off the pesky Ex-leper. This may have been just one of several tried as they shot the scene, given their experience with ratings and on-set work on *Holy Grail*, where multiple versions of "swears" would be recorded.[45] This is the kind of language that the BBC was uncomfortable with during the first season of *Flying Circus*.

BRIAN *(referring to tray)*: **"I don't want to sell this stuff you know . . . it's only a job"**—In Ep. 45 of *Flying Circus*, the man at the door (also Chapman, dressed in Icelandic costume) doesn't want to be selling Icelandic honey, either:

Mother (Idle): Well why do you come in here trying to flog the stuff?

Man (Chapman): Listen Cowboy. I got a job to do. It's a stupid, pointless job but at least it keeps me away from Iceland, all right? The leg of a worker bee has . . .[46]

This "I'm only doing my job" line had been in the collective consciousness (and conscience) of Europe since the Nuremberg Trials. There, a long line of Nazi functionaries tried to defend themselves by saying they were merely following orders, saving their own lives, participating in the new "empire" without knowing the atrocities, etc.

BRIAN: "I hate the Romans as much as anybody"—In yet another distinction from Brian being simply a Python stand-in for Jesus, it's clear that Brian does have opinions about the Roman occupiers, that he is not "insulated" from the current political situation, as some representations of Jesus seemed to posit: "The Johannine presentation of Jesus sharply defines a problem that is implicit in the accounts of the Synoptic Gospels," Brandon writes. "It is constituted by the fact that these documents agree in representing Jesus as insulated from the political unrest which was so profoundly agitating contemporary Jewish society."[47] Brandon also points out that it simply defies belief that a potential Messiah and Son of God could or would allow or support (Ben-like) "an abiding challenge to Yahweh's sovereignty" like Roman taxation and "obligation."[48] The Yeshua of *The Passover Plot* (book and film) was more aware of the Zealots of his day, and even quietly aligned himself with them and their goals.

The REVOLUTIONARIES all look around anxiously to make sure no one has heard— (PSC) The revolutionaries in any oppressive society have to operate this way, always expecting the KGB, NKVD, Stasi, (Hoover's) FBI, or Praetorian Guard loyal to the government at any turn. Herod was reported to have a network of spies in place in Jerusalem, ready to ferret out disloyalty among cabals like the PFJ, while Pilate is said to have forbidden gatherings of men, six or more.[49] In Poland in the 1970s, the secret police were the SB (Służba Bezpieczeństwa), and as the new pope's homecoming visit approached in 1979, eager Poles had to remember to be of two minds:

> Poles of this era had grown up in a society where life was split into two parallel realms, the public and the private, each with its own versions of language and history. As in so many other authoritative states, citizens . . . of Poland learned from early on to parrot their allegiance to official ideology in public while keeping their real opinions to themselves and their families. Communist rule depended on ensuring that people persisted in paying public tribute to the official version of truth, thus preventing them from seeing how many of them actually rejected it.[50]

Reg, Francis, Judith, and the PFJ also have their public and their private lives; they never talk about revolution in any mixed company, they meet furtively, and generally keep to themselves. There were characters in earlier drafts who were not members of the PFJ who were given interactions with the PFJ (two groupie girls, for example, and even Otto), but those characters were eventually written or edited out of the film, or those intersections were removed. (Otto is still part of the film, but he doesn't ever talk with Reg, as he did in earlier drafts.) Like many of the terror groups of the 1970s, the PFJ keep their own company.

REG: "Listen, if you wanted to join the P.F.J., you'd have to really hate the Romans"— This is the first mention of their little group as an acronym, an indication that contemporary audiences would have recognized the "acronymizing" phenomenon for terrorist groups immediately, as it had occupied headlines for at least a decade. Writing in 1977, Ovid Demaris discusses the relative importance of terrorism as a foundational concept for world change (to Guevara and Marighella, specifically, who disagree with one another), and easily resorts to the lexicon of the day:

> The idea is to show that the capitalist state depends for its continued existence upon the use of violence and its own terror. This is the conventional wisdom of a wide spectrum of terrorist groups—IRA, FLQ, ERP, RAF, ETA, URA, ALN, MIR, FAR, PLO, PFLP, PDFLP, ALF, ELF, TPLA—a veritable alphabet soup of terror, not to mention the separatist movements active all over the globe.[51]

A Rand Corporation report outlined what it saw as the future, given the fractiousness of the postcolonial world, "a world in which the acronyms of various self-proclaimed revolutionary fronts may take their place in international forums alongside the names of countries."[52]

The IRA had recently brought the specter of terrorism right into the English streets, which might account for its significance in the film. The year 1974 witnessed attacks on a military coach (killing twenty-six), and bombs detonated at the Tower of London, and in pubs in Guildford and Birmingham.[53] One of the less deadly but more spectacular attacks had been directed at the very heart of British power, the Houses of Parliament, on 17 June 1974. An IRA bomb exploded that day, injuring eleven. The Pythons had brought this up earlier, when Launcelot reminds Arthur that they have the Holy Hand Grenade, and then they use it effectively.[54] By the time the Pythons are contemplating *Life of Brian*, the hatred of the IRA for everyone who disagreed with a united Ireland, free from Westminster and free for Roman Catholicism, had become despairingly evident. Everything violent that happens or is even talked about in *Life of Brian*—kidnappings, ransoming, torture, body mutilation, intimidation, and even an overwhelming military presence and response—had also been front-page news (and regularly erupting) in Northern Ireland and Britain.

REG: "Right, you're in"—Since Brian hates the Romans "a lot," he's welcomed into the secret society. Admission to the Essene society at Qumran was more difficult. Only "full members" could take part in communal meals, and then only after taking "tremendous oaths," and even then, the novitiate could only have the solid food for a year, and after two years the liquid.[55]

FRANCIS: "And the Judean Popular Peoples' Front"—Homegrown revolutionaries and terrorists, meaning those of Jewish origins, were as old as the oppression the Jews lived under. Jesus Bar Abbas (also "Barabbas") was one such figure, active during Christ's lifetime, who will be discussed later, when Pilate is considering his Passover gift to his people. In the Pythons' lifetime it was the Irgun Zvai Leumi,[56] an extreme right-wing "Revisionist National Military Organization" set on the creation of a Jewish state, by force. "Jewish paramilitary organizations were not new," Demaris writes. "There had been Jewish self-defense forces in Europe for years. In Russia the Hashomer . . . and in Poland the Betar had attempted to defend the people against the savage pogroms instituted there. . . . They were the forerunners of the Hagana[57] and the Irgun Zvai Leumi in Palestine."[58] Also according to Demaris, just a few years earlier, in the 1920s, revisionist Jews were reacting negatively to any suggestion of Arabs allowed anywhere near Palestine:

> Vladimir Jabotinsky[59] [rejected Chaim] Weizmann's gradualism and his acceptance of an Arab presence on the east bank of the Jordan[;] the revisionists were maximalists who wanted not only all of Palestine but all territory that had been part of King David's kingdom at its height. And they were ready to use violence to gain their ends.[60]

During and after WWII the Stern Gang (also "Lehi"[61]) were actually Jewish terrorists trying to drive the British out of Palestine.[62] Even earlier, there were Special Night Squads formed by the Brits with Jewish (Hagana) help in 1938, put together to protect oil pipelines, power stations, and villages from Arab attacks. Their actions tended to be quite vicious, according to Demaris.

STAN: "And the Peoples' Front of Judea"—Everyone initially agrees here, caught up in the moment. Even in straight-ahead, registered political parties, *not* revolutionary groups, name confusion abounded in the tumultuous postwar period. By the mid-1970s there was a small Democratic People's Party in Hungary vying for votes, while in the Sudan, Pakistan, Sri Lanka, and Afghanistan, versions of a People's Democratic Party attempted to gain electoral traction. In Portugal in 1974 the situation approaching elections was recognizably confused. In a lengthy interview with Portuguese Minister of Foreign Affairs Mario Soares, a typical question and answer betrayed the Left's predicament:

> *Times*: Will the grouping of the parties of the left be forming a popular front to counter the danger of a right-wing reaction?

> Soares: No, for the time being strategy for the elections has not yet been made clear, but there is every reason to believe that parties will be standing as single units. So there will be a Socialist

Party list [of candidates], a Communist list, a PPD (People's Democratic Party) list—the three parties in the government—and who knows what other groups?[63]

Soares concludes that when the election results are in, alliances will then be explored. (This could have benefited the PFJ and members of the CFG whom they struggle with beneath Pilate's palace.) A similar series of discussions took place after the 1974 General Election put Wilson back into No. 10, but with a slim majority. By 1977 that majority was failing, and both the Lib-Lab pact and agreements with the Unionist parties were collapsing, as well. The Liberal Party had agreed to "struggle together" with Labour and the smaller parties, but never felt sufficiently empowered. This ever-loosening concatenation of like-minded votes couldn't overcome the Tories' no-confidence vote in March 1979, forcing an election, which the Conservatives won.

The Pythons weren't the first pundits to lampoon the party name confusion, either. In May 1973, *Times* contributor Richard Harris reports on Asian elections (in Cambodia, Ceylon, India, etc.), noting that Western journalists need to better understand the fundamental differences between those contests and ones held in France and Britain. The differences tended to include historic tribal structures, racial and religious divides, and the difficult transition in these Third World countries from colonialism, monarchism, or despotism to perhaps just a more democratic version of those three regime types, and not necessarily to democracy. Harris's summation of the fate of fringe parties in these "consensus" countries sounds like the PFJ's discussion: "No hope then for those dedicated hopefuls on the left in the People's Socialist Party or the Democratic Revolutionary Party, or the Revolutionary Socialists or the Democratic People's Party?"[64] Harris then directly connects the Western world, and specifically Britain, to these Third World parties, and he even seems to be talking about the (im)possibility of success for a group like the PFJ:

The obvious reason why these opposition parties have little chance of power is not just that they were all born in the 1930s in the London School of Economics (or whatever centres of left-wing thought have succeeded that institution), but that they have never been reshaped by the reality of their own society. Their revolutionary passions are Western-made, their jargon comes off the assembly line, they are urban, theoretical, far too world conscious ever to win support from the slowly changing minds of their own peasants. Moreover, as parties that seek the overthrow of the exciting society they seem more like enemies of the consensus than advocates of a new one.[65]

Clearly, the PFJ has not "been reshaped by the reality of their own society." Trapped in the peak of the Roman Empire's power, their jargon is borrowed from other groups of the 1960s and 1970s, and they never do try and enlist the support of the enslaved Jews around them. This is why their version of "consensus" can justify surrendering Brian to the cross, labeling him a useful martyr, then going home to continue the quiet talk of action-free revolution.

Just three years after Harris's article in the *Times*, the paper produced an eight-page special section in its 12 August 1976 issue dedicated to Portugal. Two years earlier, Portugal had endured the "Carnation Coup," so-called for its lack of bloodshed and violence, in April 1974, where a democratic government replaced the fascist, authoritarian government. The news stories on the political page of this special section look closely at Portugal's hopes for a secure NATO link, and the fact that the fractured radical left in Portugal couldn't agree on enough basic principles to form any kind of lasting coalition. To illustrate this second story, the *Times* editors provided a semi-serious illustration laying out the political parties vying for ascendancy in Portugal, labeling it "The Party Game." The fourteen parties appearing on the

1976 Portuguese ballot were listed in the bit of artwork, each with its accompanying logo, and a brief (and sometimes funny) descriptor. These included (name, descriptor, and acronym):

Centre Social Democrats (Conservative): CDS
Left Socialist Movement (Marxist-Catholic intellectuals): MES
Communist Party of Portugal (Marxist-Leninist) (officially recognized Maoists): PCP M-L
People's Socialist Front (ultra-left split from main Socialist party: FSP
Revolutionary Party of the Workers (Trotskyist schism): PRT
Movement for the Reorganization of the Proletariat Party (unofficial Maoist): MRPP
People's Monarchist Party (regal with bizarre anarchist shades): PPM
Popular Democrat Party (liberal: number two in national strength): PPD
Christian Democrat Party (failed Christian Democrats—do not count): PDC
Portuguese Communist Party (Stalinist inclined): PCP
Workers' and Peasants' Alliance (alleged ultra-left: suspected Socialist Party front): AOC
International Communist League (orthodox Trotskyists): LCI
People's Democratic Union (ultra-left Stalinist): UDP
Socialist Party (officially Marxist and government: moving rightwards): PS[66]

The last, PS, became the leading power in the Socialist-pluralist government, headed by Mario Soares. In this same eight-page spread, Christopher Reed writes that "the confusing glut of party initials" (as many as fifty emerged in the weeks after the coup) might have only "encouraged many commentators to dismiss the ultra-left as the fanatical fringe." Even the major, centrist parties "provided enough initials to make a molecular biologist feel he had an easily explicable discipline compared with Portuguese politics."[67]

So it seems the joke about political (and revolutionary) party acronyms was making the rounds in 1976. The first real meeting with all the Pythons to discuss ideas for their biblical film took place just two weeks after these stories and illustration appeared.[68]

STAN: " . . . I thought we were the Popular Front"—Generally a catch-all term for an agglomeration of leftist groups who have banded together to increase their chances of electoral success.[69] This is a term even used in Benn's voluminous diaries.[70] When laying out just a short list of those far-left groups participating in the loud and lengthy Grunwick Strike in June–July 1977, Sandbrook makes the obvious connection for us. "Active groups included the Communist Party of Great Britain, the Socialist Workers' Party, the Workers' Revolutionary Party, the Revolutionary Workers' Party (Trotskyist), the Communist Party of Britain (Marxist-Leninist), the International Marxist Group, the International Communist Current, the Indian Workers' Movement/Caribbean Workers' Organization, and so on. No doubt the People's Front of Judaea [*sic*] were there too, if only in spirit."[71]

This naming challenge isn't limited to newspapers and terror groups of the 1970s. Even though Josephus spends a great deal of time and energy describing the agitating activities of group(s) outside the Sadducees, Pharisees, and Essenes, identifying and vilifying a fourth group, it's their name he withholds: "Even if he thus later admitted this connection with Pharisaism, Josephus still omits to give a name to the followers of Judas and Saddok in the *Antiquities*, as he had omitted to name those of Judas only in the *Jewish War*. The omission is very curious."[72]

It's possible the group was so scattered and shadowy that no name was settled on, and descriptors like "brigands" had to do. But if the group was large and influential enough to be called a fourth philosophical sect by Josephus, an actual name should have emerged over time, especially given the widespread spoliations attributed to them. It's fun to think of Jewish patriots like Judas, Saddok, and others (like initiate Brian-types) struggling with unrecognizability, splitters, and perhaps having to eat "rich imperialist titbits" as they fought their good fight.

REG: "Peoples' Front. Twit"—Peoples' Front parties (traditional political and reactionary) had been active in Java, Singapore, Yugoslavia, Japan, Italy, Finland, Chile, Hungary, and a score of other countries. The largest and most well known in the immediate postwar period were those in Hungary and Yugoslavia. There were of course many versions of this name, as well, including Peoples' Popular Front, People's Democratic Front, the *New* People's Democratic Front, and the People's Progressive Front.

FRANCIS: "Whatever happened to the Popular Front, Reg?"—Reg answers that "He's over there," and we are shown a lone man sitting below them. They shout "Splitter!" at him, and he turns to see what the fuss is about. At the 1975 Labour Party Conference in Blackpool, Bernard Donoughue noticed another splitting of ideological factions, this within the ranks of the more liberal (and usually lock-armed) side of the party: "At lunch it was noticeable that the Left is split up. In the old days they all sat at one table. Now they are split up around the room. Michael Foot is very separate—the Tribune Group have dropped him from their recommended slate (in favour of Dennis Skinner!)."[73] The Labour Party and Wilson's government worried a great deal about this fractiousness, especially as the strength of coalition votes (Irish and Scottish MPs) vacillated with every whiff of cordite in Belfast or devolution referenda in Edinburgh. Donoughue, Haines, and Wilson are talking about these splits as early as 1975, divides that lead to Callaghan's tottering administration from 1976. By December 1976, the Left's Tribune Group was hotly divided, many wanting to detonate the Chancellor of the Exchequer's dismayingly moderate economic proposals. Foot tried in vain to keep them from fighting each other, while the Shadow Cabinet "decided to abstain on the procedural vote to adjourn the House, leaving the field open for Labour MPs to quarrel amongst themselves," which they then did.[74] By 1979, the inability of the Labour Party to agree on enough points to fight a concerted general election battle saw the ascension of Thatcherism.

The answer to the obvious question, "Whatever happened to the Popular Front (for the Liberation of the Occupied Arabian Gulf)?" is: "It's over there" (in Oman and Bahrain). The Popular Front for the Liberation of the Occupied Arabian Gulf (PFLOAG, formerly the Dhofar Liberation Front) were a small Maoist group fighting against the sultan in Oman. The sultan's forces were trained and commanded by British officers.[75] In 1974 the group divided, becoming the Popular Front for the Liberation of Oman and the Popular Front for the Liberation of Bahrain. In early 1975, two British officers were even killed in battle in Oman. Even after Palestine, Aden, and Suez, the British military presence in the Middle East and Gulf continued.

REG: "He's over there"—The man representing the Popular Front sits alone, watching the gladiator contest, and certainly not plotting the downfall of the empire. Newton notes that the IRA went through a fracturing, and with a similar result:

> In January 1970, political dissension in the IRA produced a rift in the organization, with "official" and "provisional" wings adopting different philosophies and tactics. Since that time, the Provisional Irish Republican Army (PIRA) has carried out the bulk of armed resistance to British rule in Northern Ireland, while the "official" wing has withered to a tiny, passive remnant.[76]

The "official" Popular Front doesn't look "withered," but he certainly looks disinterested.

GLADIATOR: "I think I'm going to have a cardiac arrest"—Some criminals or slaves not only accepted their gladiatorial sentence, but attempted to magnify their situation. Success in the arena offered a few combatants the chance to eventually buy their lives and even freedom, but there was even more, according to Wiedemann: "The criminal condemned *ad ludos* was a socially 'dead man' who had a chance of coming alive again." Surviving could mean not only *surviving*, as in the body, but a social recuperation of sorts, where this lowest of the low could reenter Roman society and retire into mythdom. The Pythons' version of this potential recuperation is typical—the gladiator dies ignominiously, and his prey celebrates.[77]

Structurally, the rampaging Legendary Beast in *Holy Grail* had only been stopped by fortune of the animator's fatal heart attack, a simple, obvious narrative tie-off. In *Flying Circus*, the Pythons had followed the Goons' example of such narrative trickery, as described by Peter Sellers:

> We wanted to express ourselves in a sort of surrealistic form. We thought in cartoons, we thought in blackouts, we thought in sketches. We thought of mad characters. *We thought of—take a situation and instead of letting it end normally, let it end the other way—twisted around.*[78]

These narrative side doors are used throughout *Flying Circus*, though nowhere more blatant than in Ep. 34, "The Bicycle Tour." In that episode—unusual for the Pythons in that it is a self-contained, singular-narrative story of Mr. Pither's (Palin) bicycle adventures—Jeremy Pither and Gulliver (Jones) find themselves in a predicament. They are about to be bayoneted by Soviet soldiers when a "SCENE MISSING" caption appears over a black screen. When that ends, our heroes are safe on a "*Cornish country lane.*"[79] In *Holy Grail*, the expense of additional postproduction animation work or additional pickup shots precluded the sweetening most films enjoy, so the "cartoon peril" can end self-consciously, aligning *Holy Grail* with both the art films of the period *and* the cartoons the Pythons had grown up watching:

> The intrusions of the modern world have already been blessed with believability in the Python's Dark Ages, so a cartoony death (farcical, fast-motion) fits well. It's also likely that the Pythons were drawing on their medieval sources yet again, since Chrétien de Troye's masterful work Perceval also ends abruptly—in midsentence, even: "When the queen saw her she asked her what was the matter—", and scholars assume the author died before finishing,[80] perhaps even as the sentence was being composed.[81]

The characters, settings, and situations are very often cartoony in *Life of Brian* (including a spaceship interval and the condemned singing and dancing on crosses), there are several blackout transitions (including one in a few moments that finds Brian approaching the palace wall), and the film is almost entirely composed of stitched-together sketches (The Sermon on the Mount, The Stoning, Harry the Haggler), just as *Holy Grail* had been. During the run of *Flying Circus*, characters could agree to stand up and leave an overly silly situation (Ep. 35), an authority figure could stop the film and transition the show into another scene (Ep. 15), or the camera and narrator could just meander away from uninteresting characters to something else entirely (Ep. 7). Ultimately, *Holy Grail* itself is brought to a close by a constable's hand covering the camera lens, causing, miraculously, the film to slip out of the gate and the projector to fall.

An animal version of the "heart attack" ending can be found in the actual history of the games. Mannix cites a report from one Christian martyr, Polycarp, of just such a spectacle in a *provincia* amphitheater.[82] In the period when Christians were regularly tortured and executed as part of the games, editors did allow for public recanting, and a prisoner could agree to acknowledge the Roman gods right there at the arena—where an altar was kept ready—thus saving his life:

> One man . . . held out until actually in the arena. Then he collapsed and begged to be allowed to sacrifice. The editor refused and demanded that the animals be released. The only animal was a lion who had been starved to make him savage. But the *bestiarius* had overdone it and when the lion was released, the poor brute just lay down and died. The martyr had to be burned at the stake.[83]

Severed limbs in the background—Behind the dying Gladiator a lower leg dangles from one of the nets strung between spears. For most arena spectacles, especially those closer to Rome, such messiness wouldn't have been tolerated. Between performances slaves would clean the bodies and body parts, human and animal, change scenery (desert rockscape, forest, even flooding the arena for a sea setting) and would then lay out fresh, clean sand to cover all the bloodstains.[84]

(draft) The ROMANS in the audience look at each other in disgust—This is modeled after the audience response to Ben-Hur's win in *Ben-Hur*, where many had clearly been betting against Sheik Iderim's horses (which Ben-Hur drives), and instead on the favored Roman, Messala.

Muttered comments in versions of the script include "pathetic," "terrible," and "appalling"; these Romans are clearly appalled not by the bloodshed and carnage, but the fact that their man lost, and lost in such a disappointing, nonviolent way.[85] Marcus Aurelius's inurement to the depravity and gore—swollen by an unslakable "morbid taste" shared, evidently, by his people—is evident as he comments on these public spectacles: "I wouldn't mind the games being brutal and degrading if only they weren't so damned monotonous."[86] The games were an ongoing attempt to distract both the lower class Romans from their difficult lives, and men of ambition from their ambitions—games often staged, successfully, simply to quell food riots or mutinous movements.[87] In 1970s Britain, this clear separation is identified by columnist Peter Jenkins as the "Two Nations" concept, where those ten millions living at or even near the "supplementary benefit level" (essentially the poverty level) found life a daily, unremitting challenge. Britain's continuing decline simply deepened these people's sufferings.[88]

But the violent, fantastical Roman Empire games also served as an escape from the boredom of a privileged life, just as sexual debauchery of every kind helped distract outside the arena. Also from Mannix: "As the mob gradually lost all interest in finding work, serving in the legions or taking any responsibility, the games became increasingly brutal and lewd. Finally they were simply excuses for sadistic debauches."[89] This specter of damaging, caustic boredom has been broached by the Pythons in *Flying Circus*, there "expressing a Kierkegaardian complaint voiced in *Either/Or*—namely, that for the aesthete—whose life is devoted to the pursuit of pleasure and amusement—boredom is the single greatest corrosive."[90] These games-goers fit this bill. Mandy is ready to leave the Sermon on the Mount so she can get to something a bit more exciting, a stoning. Later it's Pilate who seems to be spending his time on interior decorating rather than running Judea, perhaps building another useless Babel, in Kierkegaard's terms, and the prospect of a little violence is a pleasant distraction—it's his version of Kierkegaard's "crop rotation." The members of the PFJ aren't depicted doing anything apart from bloviating and circular planning, meaning they're not unlike the other upper-middle-class revolutionaries of the 1970s, or even the disaffected have-not generations often depicted in postwar New Wave cinemas. In Bunuel's *Los Olvidados* it's Jaibo and the kid gang; in Pasolini's *Accattone* it's the layabout gang of pimps and scroungers with nothing to do but scavenge, eat, and swim; and in Godard's *Breathless*, our "hero" drifts from larceny to murder before dying in the street.[91]

This Samaritan gives an "up yours" (or *bras d'honneur*) sign to the assembled Romans, who already think the day's events have become "dreadful." *An Encyclopedia of Swearing* gives credit for this gesture to the Italians, suggesting American and British servicemen brought it back with them after World War II.[92] The fact that our Samaritan is giving it right back to these Romans is quite fitting, though anachronistic. This is one of the few *épater la bourgeoisie* moments that goes unpunished in the world of the film, incidentally. The Roman spectators are appalled by the success of the Samaritan prey/victim, as opposed to the blood and gore scattered across the arena floor, but the crowd made up of the people of Judea clearly appreciate the fact that the slave managed to best the gladiator.

A fight like this is described in some detail in *Those about to Die*. Flamma, Mannix imagines, might have been a trained soldier whose unknown crime "sentenced him to the arena."[93] Once there, Flamma was cast in the role of Secutor, giving him bulky armor and helmet, and pitting him against an unarmored gladiator, a more nimble Retiarus. Flamma was likely supposed to fight well but lose to the better-trained, faster, and more seasoned gladiator. As it turned out, Flamma found he had a knack for this gladiatorial fighting, tricking the better fighter into mistakes that allowed him to win. Mannix notes that the standard response to this unforeseen victory (actually a loss for the promoter or editor of the games) was the emperor's signal to another Retiarus "to come out and finish him off." The crowd—who had started out cheering against the mutinous ex-soldier—turned immediately and cheered for him, and, according to Mannix: "Very few emperors dared to ignore the will of the people in the circus."[94] In the Pythons' Colosseum, the non-Roman sections of the crowd cheer lustily for the surviving Samaritan, while the lounging Romans simply grumble and accept the will of the people. It's possible (though not likely) that the wily Samaritan will be promoted to a gladiator school and spend the rest of his days performing for appreciative audiences, as Flamma did.

The non-Roman audience claps and cheers the triumphant Samaritan—This happiness and celebration will likely be short-lived. Depending on the *editor* of these paltry games, a second gladiator can be sent out to finish the kill, or the victim will be recaptured and held over for the next games. It's unlikely that a slave or criminal or just captured foreigner (any of which this victim might be) would have benefited from the crowd's appreciations, except to live one more day. Refusing to fight in the arena was also a mistake, as Cicero relates "in a letter of 43 BC about L. Cornelius Balbus, Caesar's quartermaster, who was said to have tried to force a Pompeian officer called Fadius to fight twice as a gladiator in Balbus's home town of Gades, and when he refused to have had him burnt alive in a gladiatorial school."[95] There are also many instances where Jews and, later, Christians thrown into the arena with wild animals refused to defend themselves, with grisly and predictable results.[96]

REG: ". . . bruvver!"—Reg seems to say "brother" as he cheers along with most of the crowd for the successful Samaritan, identifying another sibling, at least in spirit. Anyone who manages to best the Romans is family, it seems. Seneca spent energies attacking the crowds who attended these games, those cheering on the "ludicrous cruelties at midday"[97] with unattractive gusto: "Nothing is so morally degrading as the spectators at the games. As if armed combats are not bad enough, the midday intermission, when criminals have to fight without helmet or armour, are sheer murder," Seneca wrote. "Many spectators prefer this to the regular programme. In the morning they throw men to the lions, at midday they throw them to the spectators."[98]

"Bruvver" is a much-caricatured Cockney version of "brother," heard earlier on *Flying Circus* when Palin and Jones played the Vercotti brothers, shaking down the military.[99] This may also be a nod to the contemporary punk/skinhead trend in Britain, where "cropped hair, levis and braces, and Cherry Red boots" brought disaffected "siblings" together in the poorest white areas of Britain.[100] These "aggro" punks were lashing out at any semblance of authority in the 1970s, at immigrants and unemployment and—given the moribund economy of the later 1970s—perhaps just at the awful prospects of their lives.[101] The Pythons have provided versions of shorter-haired young "punks" (the PFJ) in the stands cheering against "the Man," and a long-haired hippie type (he's even "weedy") giving the up-yours to the Roman establishment—successive antiauthoritarian cultures from 1960s and 1970s Britain.

BRIAN: "Brian . . . er . . . Brian Cohen"—He knows by this time that he's not actually the son of "Mr. Cohen," whom we never meet, but the very Jewish name is likely a better calling card for introduction to an anti-Roman terror group than "Brian Maximus."

REG: "We may have a little job for you, Brian"—The "weedy Samaritan" has "defeated" the gladiator, upsetting the status quo in the Roman world, where the stratigraphic divisions in society were essential. Is it simply coincidental that at this moment Reg announces to Brian and the rest of the PFJ that there is a further antisocial activity in the offing? Or is this decision directly connected to the performance they just witnessed? Many found fault with these violent and passionate games; moralists feared a deleterious effect on the audience-cum-mob. Plato, the Stoics and Epicureans, and many Roman writers agreed that these spectacles did not bring out the masses' most noble natures: "Nothing is so damaging to good character than the habit of wasting time at the Games; for then it is that vice steals secretly upon you through the avenue of pleasure. . . . I come home more greedy, more ambitious, more voluptuous, even more cruel and more inhumane, because I have been among human beings."[102] If the Samaritan had lost, would Reg have had "a job" for Brian, or would the reinforced social order have been settled comfortably, and the PFJ just gone home? We can't know. The gladiator dies, the crowd cheers the victorious Samaritan, and the PFJ sends off their pledge to make his bones.

And who was the Labour Party's go-to man for unattractive little jobs? During this period there was at least one man who was always ready to be the David taking on Goliath, or the Samaritan besting the Macedonian Baby-Crusher—Tony Benn.[103] This very-Left Labour minister and Cabinet member was ever the wild card, the most "out there" (meaning active and willing) member of the Cabinet during this decade; both a "left-wing prophet" and "bogeyman," Benn could be called upon to do the painful, unthanked, unpopular, and politically dangerous heavy-lifting of Labour's extreme Left.[104] Donoughue complained about him often because Benn seemed to push and pull and threaten from and toward the left, and when blocked he'd promise to resign and bring down the house. Wilson and Callaghan both could have taken him up on this promise, but then he'd back off, keep his Cabinet job, and quietly manipulate centrist Labour positions leftward, from within.[105] And even though Benn irritated those at No. 10 with his prickly, assumed, man-of-the-worker shtick, Donoughue at least, saw the potential usefulness of such a strong-willed (and *expendable*) foot soldier:

> I am deciding, slowly I realise, that Benn and Bennery could be useful in getting this country's manufacturing industry out of its mess. Not his ad hoc subsidies to any bunch of shop stewards. Not his marginal co-operatives. But the NEB[106] at the van[guard] of a proper policy of industrial regeneration. He would not be my chosen instrument—he is too fanatical. *But he is all we have, and if controlled might just pull it off.*[107]

Benn did spend much of his time trying to drag British industry into reorganization, into the hands of the workers, a Dennisean task of "anarchosyndicalism" that could never have achieved but seemed noble and worth fighting for. Along with Ian Mikardo he was generally the conscience of the Left (and, like Jiminy Cricket, often ignored).

This is Brian's *rite de passage* for his potential membership in this secret society, the PFJ.[108] And while many of the nineteenth-century revolutionary syndicalists[109] believed in the *reprise individuelle*, an "individual expropriation" of wealth or goods from the bourgeoisie, Brian and the PFJ don't "liberate" ill-gotten deposits from banks, nor do they rob the temple or moneychangers or rich men like Gregory, even though in first-century Jerusalem these latter targets would have been ripe for plucking.[110] What Brian is asked to enact instead is a sort of *proclamation individuelle*—he will adorn the palace walls with an anti-imperialist slogan. Russian scientist and activist Peter Kropotkin would have characterized this act as essential and epoch-changing:

> By actions which compel general attention, the new idea seeps into people's minds and wins converts. One such act may, in a few days, make more propaganda than thousands of pamphlets. Above all, it awakens the spirit of revolt; it breeds daring. . . . One courageous act has sufficed to upset in a few days the entire governmental machinery, to make the colossus tremble.[111]

An anarchist, essentially, Kropotkin would have had much in common with the more anarchic individualism[112] Brian espouses later, as he naively counsels people to not follow authority blindly and to think for themselves, and even later telling the crucifying centurion that he doesn't "have to follow orders." (The crowd parrots Brian's words back to him and the Centurion says he likes following orders, so the individualist argument is consistently mooted.)

This "individual terror" is more at home, likely, in the modern world, where students and disaffected minorities declaim by voice, banner, and graffiti, using media of all kinds to rail against the oppressive system, institution, or state.[113] Brian and the PFJ haven't these means, so a man and a paint brush must suffice. When Brian succeeds—and Reg and Francis seem surprised that he does—he will be welcomed into their group, given the secret salute, and added to the commando raid on Pilate's palace, with predictable results.

Notes

1. Waugh, *FCY*, 5 March 1973. Walter Annenberg was an American publisher and philanthropist; Mrs. Annenberg was the former Leonore Cohn.
2. Juvenal's *Satire X* (Loeb Classical Library), 373.
3. See Farrell, *BRJ*, chapter 6.
4. Magness, *Stone and Dung*, 56.
5. *JVL*, "Jewish Food"; also, King and Stager, *LBI*, 105.
6. Horace, *Satires*, 2.8.85–93; from Fuchs, *Horace's Satires and Epistles*, 1977.
7. Fuchs, *Horace's Satires*, 45–46.
8. *ATW*, 2.37.207.
9. Petronius, *The Satyricon*, chaps. 5 and 6.
10. *LBI*, 64–69; also, Jeremias, *JTJ*, passim.
11. *JTJ*, 121, 131.
12. Caryl, *Strange Rebels*, 7–9.
13. Larsen, *MPFC: UC*, 2.47.
14. Marr, *HMB*, 82–83.
15. Marr does mention that the snoek purchases—"millions of tins"—ended up satisfying cat food producers, who bought most of it at a greatly reduced price (83).
16. Burleigh, *BRT*, 1.
17. Like Mrs. Conclusion (Chapman) in Ep. 27 of *Flying Circus* (*MPFC: UC* 2.15–16).

18. Peter Hazelhurst provided additional stories on Japan's terror groups for the 7 and 14 October editions of the *Times*.

19. "Japan's Terror Groups," *Times*, 22 October 1975: 16.

20. See Cook's "Envisioning Crucifixion," 276–78 for more on this insult.

21. The 1977 *Monty Python and the Holy Grail (Book)* had included on the back cover many names from the Nixon administration, and specifically those recently convicted in relation to the Watergate affair (*BAFHG*, 13).

22. 19 March 1976: 4. In an example of the cross-fertilization within the entertainment industry of Britain, Blake Edwards was also shooting at Shepperton during this period, finishing *The Pink Panther Strikes Again*, and was also obviously reading *Private Eye*. To this same issue he contributes a short letter, responding to an earlier "Grovel" column: "*Sir, About Grovel; BOLLOCKS . . . BLAKE EDWARDS.*" On 1 May 1974, Bernard Donoughue diaried that Marcia Williams had attacked Harold Wilson for "mentioning *Private Eye* in the Commons"—an indication of the magazine's scope and influence in British culture (Donoughue, *DSD*, 1.111).

23. Larsen, *BAFHG*, 74–75. Buñuel's *The Milky Way* (1969), had actually attacked what the film-maker saw as "Catholic heresies," perhaps rendering him less threatening to Christians like Whitehouse and NVLA. Again, Buñuel isn't attacking or even depicting the figure of Christ, which is likely why these films avoided attention.

24. See the " . . . as a blasphemer . . . " entry earlier in "The Stoning" scene for more on the poem, its publication, and the subsequent trial for blasphemy.

25. Likely one of the reasons a filmed version of *The Last Temptation of Christ*, originally published in 1955, had to wait for a later generation.

26. Palin, *Diaries 1969–1979*, 349–50.

27. Britain's shrinking empire is a consistent locus of comedy and self-deprecation for both the Goons and the Pythons. See the index of *MPFC: UC* and *BAFHG* under "British Empire."

28. 26 October 1954. As the country tried to rebuild after the war while still supporting the principles and fiscal realities of the Welfare State, Britain's international influence declined while domestic commitments rose.

29. Important Labour figures like Callaghan and Donoughue were identified as Gaitskellite (belief in personal liberty, etc.), while Bevan, Tony Benn, and Michael Foot were the "Bevanites," much further to the Left (where the public would own the means of production, etc.). PM and Party leader Wilson was seen as a moderate. See Sandbrook, Haines, and Donoughue for more.

30. Demaris, *Brothers in Blood*, 134.

31. *BRT*, 152–53.

32. The acronyms stand for, in order (including establishment dates): the Democratic Front for the Liberation of Palestine (1969), the Palestinian Liberation Front (1961), the Palestine Liberation Organization (1964), the Popular Front for the Liberation of Palestine (1967), the Popular Front for the Liberation of Palestine—General Command (1968), the Palestinian Popular Struggle Front (1967), the Popular Revolutionary Front for the Liberation of Palestine (1972), the Symbionese Liberation Army, and the Sons of the Occupied Territory (both c. 1973) (Demaris, *Brothers in Blood*, 35, 150–58). This last group (SOT) hijacked a Japanese airliner out of Amsterdam in July 1973, landed in Benghazi, then blew up the plane after everyone (excluding one hijacker, already dead) had left the plane. This was the group's one and only operation. See entries in scene 16, "Hiding with the PFJ," later for more.

33. Black September is the terrorist group that stormed the Israeli athlete rooms at the 1972 Munich Olympic Games, killing eleven.

34. Dobson and Payne, *Carlos Complex*, 112; italics added.

35. *BAFHG*, 416.

36. "IRA Blame Police for Explosions," *Times*, 22 Apr. 1969: 10.

37. *DSD*, 1.265.

38. See Demaris, *Brothers in Blood*, passim.

39. Dobson and Payne, *Carlos Complex*, 21. This explosion of activity was followed by an all-out assault by King Hussein of Jordan, in whose territory the Palestinians resided, and hundreds of terrorists

and refugees were killed (21–22). This was the first "Black September." In this case Hussein acted more like the Romans depicted in *Brian*—hunting down and destroying the enemies of Rome.

40. Later, when Biggus Dickus is being laughed at, "wank" will be mentioned again.

41. *DSD*, 2.240.

42. "Labour's Left Raps 'Splitter Jenkins,'" *Sunday Times*, 28 July 1974: 1; also "Jenkins Sparks Fury on the Left," *Sunday Times*, 11 March 1973: 1. Jenkins was attempting during this period to bring Labour back from the furthest left, in the hope of fighting a more winnable election without resorting to austerity (lurching to the right) or out-and-out socialism (keeping left).

43. *ATW*, 1.196; *MPFC: UC*, 1.246–47.

44. *DSD*, 2.82.

45. *BAFHG*, 446.

46. *ATW*, 2.45.332.

47. Brandon, *Jesus and the Zealots*, 17.

48. Brandon, *Jesus and the Zealots*, 17.

49. Levine, *Jerusalem*, 173; the latter figure is whispered to a Centurion in *The Passover Plot*, and may be a Herodian leftover. In seething post-WWI India—where Home Rule was the native goal—the British Empire's representative, General Reginald Dyer, forbade assemblies of any kind, hoping to quash rebellion (Brendon, *DFBE*, 266). The April 1919 Amritsar Massacre followed, anyway.

50. Caryl, *Strange Rebels*, 200.

51. Demaris, *Brothers in Blood*, 383–84.

52. Demaris, *Brothers in Blood*, 385.

53. The presence of the Holy Hand Grenade in *Holy Grail* can be directly connected to the explosive events of 1974.

54. *BAFHG*, 452.

55. Magness, *Stone and Dung*, 80. The Essenes will be discussed later in relation to the ascetic hermit Simon.

56. Israeli PM David Ben-Gurion would call these types of men "Jewish Nazis," suggesting a genesis for the Pythons' Otto (*DFBE*, 477).

57. Military wing of the Zionist Congress. After the war and when it became clear that the British weren't ready to support a sovereign Jewish homeland, Hagana and the Stern Gang worked more closely together in acts of sabotage and civil disobedience against the British (Demaris, *Brothers in Blood*, 81).

58. Demaris, *Brothers in Blood*, 74.

59. Vladimir Ze'ev Jabotinsky was a Russian Jew who founded the Jewish Self-Defense Organization; Chaim Wiezmann was also a Russian Jew who would become Israel's first president in 1949. For a survey see Demaris's *Brothers in Blood*, 73–75; and *BRT*, chapter four.

60. Demaris, *Brothers in Blood*, 74.

61. *Lohamei Herut Israel*—"Fighters for the Freedom of Israel." See Brendon, 474–76, as well.

62. Demaris, *Brothers in Blood*, 78–80.

63. "A Country Eager to Make Up for Lost Time," *Times*, 3 December 1974: I, VI.

64. "Ne'er the Twain Shall Meet, Particularly in Politics," *Times*, 4 May 1973: 18.

65. "Ne'er the Twain Shall Meet," 18.

66. *Times*, 12 August 1976: iii.

67. "Ultra-Left May Yet Swamp Nation," *Times*, 12 August 1976: III.

68. Palin, *Diaries*, 310–11. In the general elections of 1974 and 1979 in the UK, the three "major" parties were Conservative, Labour, and Liberal, but there were also the following parties to choose from: Scottish National, Ulster Unionist, Plaid Cymru, Social Democratic and Labour, Independent, Communist, Socialist Unity, Vanguard, Socialist Party of Great Britain, Democratic Unionist, Independent Labour, Marxist-Leninist, Independent Conservative, Workers' Revolutionary, Independent Republican, and on.

69. As discussed earlier, the Labour Party in 1974 had to make agreements with the Liberals, and then the Unionist (Irish and Scottish) parties to ensure a working majority, creating a British version of a popular front. This popular front held together for almost four years.

70. Sandbrook, *Seasons in the Sun*, 36.

71. Sandbrook, *Seasons in the Sun*, 610.

72. Brandon, *Jesus and the Zealots*, 38–39.

73. Left-leaning Labour politician and writer/editor Foot worked in the Wilson and Callaghan administrations. Donoughue mentions him often and warmly, especially in comparison to Tony Benn, whose conduct tended to alienate even fellow travelers. The Tribune Group was so-named because they circled around the democratic socialist magazine *Tribune*. Foot was editor of the magazine 1955–1960. Skinner was mentioned earlier as the "Beast of Bolsover." *DSD*, 1.513.

74. "Foot Divides Tribune Group," *Financial Times*, 21 December 1978: 1.

75. "Gulf Guerrillas 'In Peking,'" *Financial Times*, 5 March 1970: 9; "British Officers 'Killed in Oman Battle.'" *Times*, 13 January 1975: 5.

76. Newton, *Encyclopedia of Kidnappings*, 233.

77. Shakespeare killed off his enormously popular character Falstaff in the most uncharitable way possible, for a stage favorite—*off*-stage (Larsen, *MPSERD*, 164). The Pythons kill both Gawain and Robin's minstrels this way in *Holy Grail*, as well. Gawain isn't mentioned until he's been killed, and the minstrels are happily eaten during voiceover narration (*BAFHG*, 226 and 309, respectively). Our gladiator dies well away from his milieu, the fight, a "dreadful" death indeed.

78. *MPFC: UC*, 1.20.

79. *ATW*, 2.34.163–64; *MPFC: UC* 2.101–9.

80. Similarly, Thucydides's *History of the Peloponnesian War* ends mid-sentence, in 411 B.C. (Richard, *WWAR*, 169).

81. *BAFHG*, 466.

82. Polycarp (69–155) was one of the Apostolic Fathers and bishop of Smyrna. Generally, the best circus performances could be had in the major cities of the Empire, with Rome and the Colosseum or Circus Maximus claiming to be elite, while further flung settings could feature less accomplished fighters and fewer, perhaps ill-trained animals.

83. *TAD*, 137.

84. See Mannix, *TAD*, passim.

85. There's no sign of the most popular games-related activity, gambling. A loss by the gladiator would have cost these men thousands of *sesterces*, perhaps prompting their muted outrage.

86. *TAD*, 117; also Grant, *Gladiators*, 75–76.

87. See *TAD*, passim. One magistrate complained about the escalating price of this onerous necessity: "It's cost me three inheritances to stop the mouth of the people" (131).

88. Jenkins, *Anatomy of Decline*, 101.

89. *TAD*, 133.

90. *MPFC: UC*, 2.177–78, 1.97.

91. *BAFHG*, xxi–xxv *passim*, xxxn56, xxxn62, and 3; and the entries for New Wave in the *BAFHG* index.

92. Hughes, *Encyclopedia of Swearing*, 259–60.

93. *TAD*, 21.

94. *TAD*, 21–22.

95. Quoted in Wiedemann, *Emperors and Gladiators*, 140; see also Grant, *Gladiators*, 32.

96. See Mannix's creative story about Carpophorus and his encounters with the old rabbi and captured Jews (*TAD*, 80–89).

97. See Cook, "Crucifixion as Spectacle," 76n26.

98. Quoted in Bauman, *Human Rights in Ancient Rome*, 124.

99. "Army Protection Racket," Ep. 8. There it's "fings" for "things," "bruvver" for "brother," and "dunnay" for "don't they."

100. From Meriel McCooey's article "Skinhead," *Sunday Times*, 28 September 1969: 53.

101. "Aggro" was a shortened version of "aggressive" seen often in newspapers of the day. The term doesn't appear until 1969, with the rising concern about youth "antisocial behavior."

102. Seneca, *Letters* 7.3; quoted in Wiedemann, 142–43.

103. Lightning rod Enoch Powell was his opposite number on the Tory side of the Commons divide, always willing to take the hard line when it came to the damaging potential of mass immigration, for instance.

104. "Act Like a Prime Minister," *Economist* 17 May 1975: 9–11.

105. See *DSD*, 1.575, but also the index there for the many, many references to Benn and his relationship with Wilson and Callaghan.

106. The National Enterprise Board, established in 1975.

107. *DSD*, 1.247; italics added.

108. Laqueur, *Terrorism*, 23.

109. See the discussions of syndicalism in *BAFHG*. There, Dennis lectures Arthur on the value of the anarchosyndicalist worldview; Arthur eventually throttles him.

110. See *JTJ* for more on the financial systems of the city during Christ's lifetime.

111. Quoted in Iviansky, "Individual Terror," 45.

112. For a very contemporary take on the types and tints of both "Individualism" and "individualism" in Britain, see Shirley Letwin's "Can Individualists Be Compassionate?" in *Spectator*, 2 June 1978: 14. Brian may be speaking here for Chapman and the other Pythons as they see the approach of Thatcher's Britain at the expense of Labour, the Liberals, and England in general. More on this later, when Brian addresses the multitudes beneath his window.

113. See Iviansky's "Individual Terror" for more.

THE LATIN LESSON

Darkened streets. Night time. Figures flit from shadow to shadow—Painting at night isn't at all unusual, as it turns out, even if the text and message weren't illegal, even treasonous. Cook notes that "in a graffito discussed by Jacobelli, the *scriptor* describes himself (*Scr(ipsit) / Aemilius / Celer sing(ulus) / ad luna(m)*; Aemilius Celer painted this by himself, by moonlight)."[1]

Most graffiti would need to be done under the cover of darkness, anyway, just to be safe. Mannix reports that under a painted advertisement (done in red paint, coincidentally) for an upcoming games edited by "the generous Flaccus, who is running for duumvirate," is a signature by the artist: "Marcus wrote this sign by the light of the moon. If you hire Marcus, he'll work day and night to do a good job."[2]

The first shot here is a low angle shot, set at the foot of the newly placed Pilate statue seen earlier. Behind is an elaborate portico on a staircase, and a handful of plinthed statues scattered around as set decoration. None of these plinths, statues or the portico were actually part of the extant city wall. They had built a covering for the lower wall so that they could add the plinths and portico, but also paint on the set without damaging the underlying monastery wall. They had also constructed these kinds of temporary additions at the Colosseum set, giving the illusion of a Roman-influenced setting.

Statues—Some of these are identifiable. The second statue from the right is Sophocles, from Rome's Lateran Museum collection; the statue at the far left, just glimpsed, appears to be a version of the Caesar Augustus statue used in the opening credits; while the statue on the larger plinth at the left appears to be a beardless version of the Sophocles statue.

Pilate's Palace—Creating a monumental graffito on the walls housing a ruling power isn't recommended at any time. Brian's act is akin to a Russian painting "Communists Go Home" on the Kremlin in 1919, or a Chinese peasant scrawling "Mao Go Back to the Mountains" in Peking in 1949. The disposition of this particular Judean governor, Pontius Pilate, would likely have given even the most zealous of the Zealot bandits, or *sicarii*,[3] pause before the first brush stroke. Contemporary historian Philo had little good to say about this appointed prefect, the Hellenized Jew philosopher describing Pilate as mean, at best, for he was "a man of a very inflexible disposition, and very merciless as well as very obstinate . . . in respect of his corruption, and his acts of insolence, and his rapine, and his habit of insulting people, and his cruelty, and his continual murders of people untried and uncondemned, and his never ending, and gratuitous, and most grievous inhumanity. Therefore, being exceedingly angry, and being at all times a man of most ferocious passions."[4]

According to Smallwood, "[Pilate demonstrated] a disregard for his subjects' religious sensibilities, which could be described charitably as tactless or uncharitably as deliberately provocative."[5] A number of these descriptors will be underscored later—and some dismissed—as we are introduced to the Pythons' version of Pilate.[6]

It's fair to ask just how much of the hated Richard Nixon is part of the Pythons' version of Pilate's imperious, vengeful leader. The recently released transcripts of the Nixon White House tapes revealed a vain, profane, and conspiratorial man who punished his detractors and those who disagreed with his policies using the power of the state. Haynes Johnson of the *Washington Post* called the papers "candid beyond any papers ever made public by a President."[7] More WH tape revelations were to come as the Pythons wrote *Life of Brian*:

> The Watergate affair had returned to world headlines in May 1977 with the release of previously secret and then much-talked-about White House tapes, some featuring recordings of special counsel Colson and the president discussing the need to "stonewall" investigations into the Watergate burglary. For the Pythons and many political pundits of the day, Nixon and his administration represented everything that could be wrong with the conservative right, a barbed comedic gift that kept on giving.[8]

Add to this the fact that Nixon had agreed to an essentially no-holds-barred televised interview series with David Frost that aired in the first week of May 1977 (in both the United States and Britain), and it would actually be a surprise if the Pythons *weren't* influenced by Nixon and his paranoid regime. The interview opened "old wounds" and reignited the harsh criticism of the former president.[9] Palin also mentions that in August 1976 he was reading Woodward and Bernstein's book *The Final Days*, their account of Nixon's demise.[10] Pilate, however, isn't immediately worried about secrecy, cautious candor, or old wounds in relation to his adversarial relationship with the Jews—for now he's working with impunity as the Roman prefect.

Graffiti is another plot point where the influential *I'm All Right Jack* also pipped the Pythons to the post. Major Hitchcock is certain that if he hadn't installed a suggestion box in the workers' canteen (loaded with scribbled responses he calls "sheer porno") "they'd be writing all over the walls." Just a few minutes later in the film, outside Fred Kite's house, a brick wall bit of graffiti advertises a union rally for 3pm the coming Sunday.

The 1970s were a time of graffiti and decay in England's larger cities. The noxious combination of economic torpor and political malaise (at home; marches and rioting abroad) led to all sorts of sloganeering. Graffiti decried this or promoted that: "Squatters Rights" images (a scrawled house that peaks in a clenched fist), or "Every Where Offices—No Where Homes," and "Peoples Power," as well as the more general "Anarchy," "Fight Back," and finally the very specific "Stoke Newington Eight" graced walls and fences and hoardings everywhere.[11] During the trial of the homegrown terrorists the Angry Brigade (a.k.a. Stoke Newington Eight) in 1972, someone spray-painted "Whose Conspiracy?" along a wall of the Old Bailey, where the trial was being conducted.[12] (Compare these impactful examples to the 1978 Tory poster created by Saatchi & Saatchi, "Labour Isn't Working," and featuring an endless dole queue.[13] Many saw this as the most strikingly effective anti-incumbent arrow in Thatcher's quiver.) Most of these scribblers had no fear of severe punishment, and likely most weren't even apprehended. A letter to *Private Eye* detailed one man's encounter with graffiti in northern Britain:

> Sir, [a] few (3½) months ago I was apprehended for daubing (the misspelt) slogan "Khymer Rouge Assassins!"[14] in firm letters on the wall of Elvet Bridge, Durham City. This venture cost

me £130.50p, of which £100 was for "costs of removal." The slogan remains, continuing, in the words of the magistrate officiating at my trial, to stand as a "vicious insult to the citizens of Durham, which they will not tolerate."[15]

The graffiti craze could be found in most developed (meaning nominally democratic) societies of the period. (Again, such demonstrations of political outrage were too dangerous in totalitarian states.) Nanterre offered spray-painted images of "REVOLUTION!"[16] In Frankfurt in January 1969 the budding Baader-Meinhof movement garnered support via graffiti. A possible strike by students at the Free University of Berlin led to leaflets and discussion about the predicted use of violence *by* students, and concerns about when and how the police might respond with force prompted this painted sign, chillingly reminding the older generation of their Nazi guilt: "Heute Relegation, Morgen Liquidation? Besser: Revolution."[17]

But graffiti *could* happen in more repressive societies, like a first-century Roman Jerusalem. In September 1978, in a well-traveled area of downtown Beijing, a group of youngish radicals created and posted a row of *dazibao*, or "big-character posters," on a long wall where thousands could read their "revolutionary" claims.[18] This became known as the "Xidan Democracy Wall," and it would even boast "Romans Go Home"-type anti-Mao posters,[19] something unheard of just weeks earlier: "The importance of Democracy Wall was not limited to its role as a proving ground for new ideas. It also had eminently practical effects . . . criticism focused on those who had engineered the Cultural Revolution and still clung to the doctrine of Mao's infallibility."[20] Similarly, in late 1976 *Private Eye* offered a silly article looking at the British political waters in the wake of Wilson's surprise retirement several months earlier. The article is posted by *Private Eye*'s "Chinese Correspondent," and tells of the throngs of Chinese people who took to the streets of "Lon Don" to read "the latest wall posters denouncing the late Chairman Wis Lon." The long-suffering Wis Lon had allegedly been "'nagged to death by the so-called red-hot running bitch of Threadneedle Street capitalists,' Mao Cha." Wis Lon is of course former PM Wilson, and Mao Cha is his longtime secretary Marcia Williams, called a shrieking, abusive, "sharp-clawed tigress" in the article. Order should be restored, the correspondent hopefully concludes, now that "the moderate Kal Ah Han" (new PM Callaghan) is in charge.[21] On the actual streets of China, freedom of expression would last only about a year, and by 1980 the right to post these kinds of opinions was rescinded.

When he reaches the foot of the high wall he starts painting on it in pathetically small letters— **"Romanes Eunt Domus"** . . . —Graffiti was actually quite a common sight during this period, with advertisements (products and services), announcements (upcoming gladiatorial events and games, prostitutes), and political messages ("Vote for Bruttius: he'll keep the tax rates down"[22]) found on walls and arches and tombs throughout the Roman Empire.[23] There were also scrawled political attacks on famous people, including, obliquely, the emperor. Domitian was known to erect triumphal arches "to commemorate his slightest achievements"—one of them was finally defaced with an emphatic "That's enough!" Richard notes.[24] Most of the (surviving) examples aren't painted, of course, but scratched or etched into the limestone or tufa walls. There are also dozens of lavatorial and profane humor scrawls, many discovered in the excavation of Pompeii, the indelicate subjects of which wouldn't have surprised Mandy.

A very recent and headline-grabbing graffiti incident in Leeds can be connected to Brian's attempt here, as well the earlier-glimpsed PILATVS IVDAEOS REGET OK. Supporters of an imprisoned minicab driver, George Davis, had busied themselves in 1975 painting versions of "George Davis Is Innocent" on many buildings and hoardings in London. There was so much paint going up that Davis's wife asked publicly for supporters to "stop daubing walls" so that the public wouldn't turn against her family.[25] Vandals then upped the ante when they not only painted these same scrawls on the walls outside Headingley Cricket ground, but went inside and tore up the pitch, forcing the cancellation of a Test Match. Arrests followed, the official response (including no bail for those arrested) prompted yet another outcry.[26] Davis's case and especially the texts of various graffiti will be discussed later, in scene 20, "Brian Is Arrested, Again."

Monumental inscriptions like these were actually part of the Israelites' history and law: "The Bible attests that the Israelites were directed," King and Stager note, "after crossing over the Jordan into the land of Canaan, to set up large stones and cover them with plaster, and 'You shall write on them all the words of this law' (Deut. 27:3)."[27] The antagonism toward the Romans might not fit into the earlier directive, but perhaps Brian is simply and unconsciously enacting a cultural tradition. Though already being scrubbed away by the evening, the painted letters telling the Romans to go home are also semi-permanent, at least as testimony against Brian and the PFJ (and just as God has promised): "The sin of Judah is written with an iron stylus; with an adamant point it is engraved on the tablet of their hearts."[28]

CENTURION (Cleese): "What's this then?"—Cleese has assumed the authoritarian role of policeman here, as seen many times in *Flying Circus*, including the "Naughty Chemist" sketch of Ep. 17:

> This ["What's all this then?"] is a reflexive moment, wherein the fiction of the show refers to itself, another fiction. The Chemist character (Palin) here notes that this catchphrase has become synonymous in [*Flying Circus*] with police officials (including constables, detectives, inspectors) as they enter a room. See Eps. 5, 7, and 11 for earlier PC entrances. Python often quotes itself, accessing its own history.[29]

So the possibility of an avuncular *Dixon of Dock Green*–type character is posited here, one that Python audiences would have recognized immediately. They also immediately *undercut* expectations, as this version of the helpful authority figure will promise to emasculate Brian if he doesn't finish his community service by dawn. The only "human" Roman character offered by the Pythons will be Nisus Wettus, a Centurion genuinely troubled by the violence of his people.

CENTURION: "'*Romanes Eunt Domus*'? People called Romanes, they go the house?"— The Centurion has learned his Latin fairly well, it appears. Most specifically, the "hysterically wrong"[30] phrase could be rendered as, "People called Romanes, they go, the house"—perhaps understandable to the embittered people of Jerusalem, but certainly without the emphatic tone Brian intended. As will be discussed in a moment, the Centurion will also slip up in his proper Latin, meriting his own "write it a hundred times" lesson. A more contemporary but similarly challenged bit of graffiti collected in the 1960s is reported by Reisner: "U.S. is the more ignorant nation on earth."[31]

Additionally, it becomes clear that this is one of the Python sketches that relies on the verbal and not the visual, like the "Tall Tower" scene in *Holy Grail*, or the "Dead Parrot" scene in *Flying Circus*. These sketches are directly related to *The Goon Show* and the music hall stage traditions. The Pythons wrote sketches for the hearer only, often, producing a number of very popular record albums.[32]

BRIAN: "It says "Romans Go Home""—There are myriad examples of such scrawled anti-imperialist slogans across history, with an increase in the colonial and postcolonial era, when students were taking to the streets armed with aerosol spray paint, not bucket and brush. Versions of "Yankee Go Home" were seen on walls in Tehran in the 1950s, in Greece and Turkey in 1964,[33] in Indonesia in 1965,[34] also Japan, Thailand, and South Korea in the

1970s. As the British slowly pulled out of Palestine in 1948, versions of "Tommy Go Home" could be seen on Jerusalem walls.[35] In an article carried in the *Daily Mail* in May 1967, someone even beat the Pythons to the punch on this specific bit of silliness. Writing about graffiti and Norman Mailer, of all subjects, Jeffrey Blyth notes: "Whether Caesar's legions, when they invaded Britain, were greeted with signs that read 'Romans go Home,' hasn't been recorded."[36] A decade later the Pythons have Brian paint this very same slogan, but in clumsy Latin. Blyth goes on to mention the recently discovered scribbles in Pompeii, as well as the Reisner booklet *Graffiti—Selected Scrawls from Bathroom Walls*, first published in 1967. This useful book mentions a "Yankee Go Home" sign near the Buenos Aires airport where, underneath, some clever dick added "Via Pan American"; a similar sign in this same area reads "Yankee go home—and take me with you."[37] This last sentiment sounds very PFJ-ish, if you will, since the revolutionaries will be certain that the Romans have to go, but the stuff they've brought and built is pretty wonderful ("the sanitation, the medicine, education, wine").

The British and empire were also on the receiving end of this anti-imperialist slogan-eering. In Cyprus in 1950, the anti-British scrawl "Greeks, liberty is won with blood" was "typical";[38] in Edinburgh in 1959 there was a reported "English Go Home!!" painted across walls;[39] and in 1964 it was reported that a large hospital in Aden had its "corridor walls . . . smeared with slogans demanding 'Go Home British.'"[40] The more frightening, violent strain of this graffiti culture could be found across Northern Ireland, where versions of "Go Home British" covered hoardings and walls, and "No Pope Here" and "Up the IRA" slogans in contested Belfast neighborhoods.[41] These demands were backed up by bullets and bombs, altogether more destructive than the PFJ. And, in a less deadly vein, the respected French magazine *New Economist* in 1976 published "a four-page attack accusing Britain of blocking progress in European affairs," an attack the *Mail* characterized as a "British go home" (from the Common Market).[42] As a failing, falling imperial power, the British were confronted with this graffiti often.[43]

Finally, it could simply be that the Pythons are acknowledging the fluctuation of Latin across the centuries, as, for example, Petrarch's "classical Latin, as exemplified by Cicero," would eventually win out "over the less elegant, scholastic Latin that had developed during the Middle Ages."[44]

CENTURION: "No it doesn't"—The intense study of *unverständliche Kritzeleien*, or "indecipherable scrawl," has become a sub-emphasis in Roman studies over the centuries, perhaps first enacted here by the Centurion.[45] There are hundreds of surviving paintings and etchings in Roman cities large and small, and many have sparked disagreements as to what the author intended to say, precisely. The vagaries of not only Latin, but the command of proper Latin by ancient scribblers come into play as these texts are approached.[46] When Apollinaris, one of Titus's own doctors, visited Herculaneum he left the following note, allegedly: "APOLLINARIS. MEDICUS. TITI IMP. HIC. CACAVIT. BENE." Koloski-Ostrow translates this as "Apollinaris, doctor of the emperor Titus, crapped well here." Some scholars have accepted "the text at face value," a simple statement of fact, while others, like Koloski-Ostrow, believe it was meant as a joke.[47] In the latter interpretation, a respected, highly placed man of Rome is brought down to the level of every man, rich and poor, base or noble—we all excrete.[48] These juxtapositions are common in the marginalia of Gothic manuscripts, where learned, respected, or even feared figures—of the Church, of the nobility—are ridiculed by their associations with bodily functions, perverse sexuality, animal metaphors, and myriad *obscaena*.[49] Koloski-Ostrow also notes that Roman citizens and slaves weren't above this kind of excremental humor, describing an Ostian latrine that featured paintings of dignified, robed Greek philosophers lecturing on the best ways to achieve a satisfactory bowel movement.

Each is also holding a cleaning stick (a sponge on a stick) used to wipe oneself, as a kind of lecture baton. Smaller images at the bottom of the panel offer similar discussions from everyday Romans, but "in a more coarse manner."[50]

Misinterpretation of a bit of perhaps *unverständliche* graffiti, then, is clearly possible, even when the scholars of the ages are involved. Wiedemann demonstrates the fluidity of Latin "intentions," when discussing the Roman belief in man's domination over animals as moral justification for games-related slaughters of especially the "cruel" lion and bear:

> Such animals are as "cruel" as the death they inflict on humans, and their killing is hardly a moral problem: the inscription commemorating games given at Minturnae in AD 249 does not celebrate sadism by boasting that ten bears were killed "cruelly" (reading *crudel[iter]* with Hopkins, "Murderous Games" p. 26), but rather that the world was rid of ten cruel bears (*ursos crudel[es]*): savage bears deserve to be killed.[51]

Whether the beasts were cruel or not, or whether the games could be morally justified isn't the point for our purposes; rather, we look at the various translations of the author's use of "cruel," interpretations that can change the meaning of the assertion significantly (and keep classics scholars employed). Brian finds himself in this same dilemma, and his Latin tutor has a sword and the power of the Roman Empire behind him.

One scrawl in a Vesuvian city leaves a message that can be translated in more than one way, with significantly different results. The graffito *cacator cave malu(m)* can be rendered, according to Koloski-Ostrow: "'Crapper, beware of the danger (the evil eye?) [from not crapping well? Or from crapping in this spot?].'"[52] The first is concerned with the gastrointestinal health of the occupant, while the latter is a warning about the location itself. Many tombs have been found to have such threats scrawled on them, warning potential pissers, crappers, and even fornicators to find another tomb for their cursed activity.

And among the *Jewish* population of the empire, the availability of education would likely have affected any attempted graffiti:

> In the ancient world the Jew was generally not envied for his wealth but despised for his poverty, and the Jewish beggar is a familiar figure in Roman literature. The poor material, crude workmanship and eccentric spelling and syntax of many of the epitaphs in the Jewish catacombs point to a lack of both education and money in those who set them up. About three-quarters of them are in Greek and only about a quarter in Latin, with a negligible number in Hebrew or Aramaic.[53]

So, there are reasons that Brian's command of Latin might differ from the Centurion's.

CENTURION: "What's Latin for Romans?"—The genesis for this set piece can be tracked along two routes. We can go directly back to the young Pythons' school days, and their often rigid, authoritarian prefects and headmasters. There are many such figures in *Flying Circus*, mumbling through restaurants (Ep. 3), marshaling a stilted production of *Seven Brides for Seven Brothers* (Ep. 18), giving school prizes while under Chinese Communist assault (Ep. 19), and haranguing boys for a rogue unit-trust scheme in Ep. 28. By *Meaning of Life*, the headmaster figure is teaching sex education (with his good wife) to a very bored roomful of pupils. The headmaster-type in *Holy Grail*, styled "The Famous Historian," is cut down in mid-lecture for his headmasterly temerity.[54]

The second route takes us back, as well, but not nearly as far. In April 1976 the Pythons brought their live show to Broadway. There they performed a medley of favorites from *Flying Circus* ("Llamas," "World Forum," "The Lumberjack Song") and were generally well received.[55] Audiences dressed up as favorite characters, and critics including the venerable

Clive Barnes of the *New York Times* found the Pythons "vulgar, sophomoric, self-satisfied, literate, illiterate, charmless, crass, subtle and absolutely terrific."[56] But not everyone was thrilled. The *New York Daily News* critic responded negatively, and was characterized recognizably, for our purposes, by Iain Johnstone,[57] *Sunday Times* arts critic for New York, seeing that amid the raucous Americans "there were some who forbore to cheer." Johnstone continued: "The critic of the *New York Daily News*, under the headline 'Anglos with Dirty Minds' ticked them off in a finger-wagging review, somewhat in the manner of a headmaster who has discovered some graffiti in the lavatories."[58] The Centurion's demonstrative voice can be heard here. The Pythons did regularly see and read their reviews, so this dressing down from a major New York critic wouldn't have escaped their notice. Johnstone was certain that the Pythons would have actually relished the bad review from a stuffy establishment critic, pushing the Roman-Emperor-and-gladiator theme even further: "I suspect this might have given more pleasure to the cast (who, like a pop group, have undergone the change from quasi-rebels to cult figures) than the life-giving thumbs-up from Emperor Barnes in the *New York Times*. As with the Beatles, most of the tickets had been sold anyway."[59] The PFJ are still quasi-rebels as the film ends, with Brian alone making the unhappy transition to cult(us) figure as a sacrifice on the cross.

During the run of the New York show, the Pythons had also discussed and agreed upon a Holy Land-themed feature film as their next project.[60] Just five months after this series of performances the Pythons are regularly gathering to write what will become *Life of Brian*.

CENTURION *(drawing his sword and holding it to Brian's throat)*: **"Dative!"**—The sword the Centurion is using to help improve Brian's Latin looks to be a typical Roman double-edged short sword known as a *gladius*, a pedagogical tool many frustrated teachers wished for.

BRIAN: "Er . . . accusative . . . er . . . domum . . . ad domum . . . the locative . . . "—It's "domus" and the locative where the Centurion actually falters, according to a helpful colleague, Dr. Roger Macfarlane:

> The noun DOMUS, it is true, is in a particular class of nouns that manifest the locative for expressing "place where"—proper names of cities, towns, small islands, plus *domus*, *humus*, and *rus*. To express "place to which" with these nouns, Classical Latin uses only the noun in the accusative case omitting the preposition—i.e., "home(ward)" is not '*ad domum*' but rather '*domum*.' Thus the Centurion coaxes Brian to the grammatically correct *Romani, ite domum*. But DOMUM is not in the locative.[61]

Macfarlane calls the error "quite minor," but still "technically wrong." It's the kind of wrong that sparks disasters in the Python world, causing knights to be flung into the depths, for example.

CENTURION: "So we have . . . *Romani, ite domum* . . . now write it out a hundred times"—A well-worn school assignment, often as a punishment, or as a rote memorization tool, or both, this solidifies the public school nature of this lesson for Brian. The Goons had gotten here first, in the episode "The Fireball of Milton Street." There, Neddie tasks the audience to write "I must not try and guess the end of *Goon Show* gags" one hundred times.[62]

CENTURION: "I'll cut your balls off"—The emperor Domitian (51–96) was known to "scorch" the genitals of suspected traitors as he tried to gather names of accomplices.[63] Castration would render Brian a eunuch, yet another figure meriting judgment in Jewish culture during this period. Eunuchs were in the same "gravely blemished" class as bastards, so a double mark against Brian: "To sum up, it must be said that bastards and eunuchs were included among those Israelites with grave racial blemish," Jeremias writes. "Rabbinic legislation, appealing to Deuteronomy 23: 2–3,[64] was ever watchful to keep the community, and the clergy in particular, apart from these elements by marking them as a caste outside the law."[65] One of the lists of approved marriage categories places eunuchs, those of "deformed sex," and hermaphrodites below even bastards, slaves, and proselytes.[66] Brian is of uncertain parentage and he is later threatened with castration; and Stan wants to become Loretta, even though he doesn't have a womb. The PFJ have as members some of the potential outcasts from acceptable Jewish life. On the other hand, the eunuch in Roman culture could be held in much higher esteem, with many serving in governments and households at the highest levels, and being trusted with the secrets of bedchambers across the empire.[67]

This turnabout, where the friendly policeman has become aggressive and threatening, has been heard on *The Goon Show*, not surprisingly. In "Dishonoured Again," Neddie is out in the cold on Christmas Eve, sleeping rough, when a constable approaches:

> Constable (Sellers): Er, you two men, what you doing 'ere? Move along now. That bench is for royalty of no fixed abode.
>
> Seagoon (Secombe): Constable, have pity, 'tis Christmas, the time of goodwill.
>
> Constable: 'Strewth, so it is. Well, a Merry Christmas on ya, mate.
>
> Seagoon: And the same to you!
>
> Constable: Now move along there before I belt you![68]

BRIAN: "Hail Caesar, sir . . . "—Historically, as a Jew living in an area controlled by Rome, men like Brian would have, according to Smallwood, "enjoyed the privileges of religious liberty guaranteed for the Diaspora by Julius Caesar and Augustus." Smallwood continues: "The right to practise Judaism carried with it automatically the privilege of exemption from participation in the imperial cult."[69] This would seem to extend to hailing Caesar. The more restive Judea grew in the latter half of the first century, the more elusive these freedoms became, certainly, so Brian may have felt compelled to return the salute, just to get home safely.

If, however, Brian were truly a Zealot, meaning he was fighting in the first place because there was only one God to whom he could give obeisance, then he never would have said "Hail Caesar," nor anything like it, according to Josephus, no matter the consequences:

> And indeed six hundred of them were caught immediately . . . and brought back, whose courage, or whether we ought to call it madness, or hardiness in their opinions, everybody was amazed at. For when all sorts of torments and vexations of their bodies that could be devised were made use of to them, they could not get any one of them to comply so far as to confess, or seem to confess, that Caesar was their lord; but they preserved their own opinion, in spite of all the distress they were brought to, as if they received these torments and the fire itself with bodies insensible of pain, and with a soul that in a manner rejoiced under them. But what was most of all astonishing to the beholders was the courage of the children; for not one of these children was so far overcome by these torments, as to name Caesar for their lord. So far does the strength of the courage [of the soul] prevail over the weakness of the body.[70]

Brian is threatened with castration, and he confesses Caesar as his lord, essentially, and escapes with his life. Castration for Brian, of course, would have rendered his reason for being in the PFJ in the first place (the lovely Judith) perhaps moot, so his choice is more understandable.

Since Brian feels he has to do this, it also might be the equivalent of Herod's semi-regular "declaration of loyalty" demanded of his subjects. Levine notes that in about the seventeenth year of his reign, Herod "imposed an oath of allegiance to himself and to the emperor" as a way to ensure stability.[71] The text of the oath does not survive.

ROMAN SOLDIER STIG (McKeown): "Right. Now don't do it again"—This is one of the many character names only appearing in the printed script and credits, and not voiced anywhere in the film. Characters named Stig have already appeared in *Flying Circus*, including episodes 5, 14, and 23, and those characters also are not named except in the printed script.[72]

It's likely this is a reference to impresario Robert Stigwood. He had produced *Hair* and *Jesus Christ Superstar*, and managed both Cream and the Bee Gees. Idle was connected to the music industry during this period, and may have contributed the nickname. The real connection to the Pythons likely came from Stigwood's on-again, off-again relationship with EMI, who'd helped distribute *Holy Grail* (after passing on funding the film), and then were on board early in the pursuit of *Life of Brian* participation, before being scared off by the "blasphemous" content, allowing George Harrison and HandMade Films into the picture. Palin never mentions EMI in his *Diaries* without a bit of a shudder.[73]

The walls are covered with graffiti; Brian climbs down from the ladder—This shot and the following chase sequence are not part of the printed version of the script. The chase transition is more effective dramatically, likely why it was added during production. In this shot the Pythons have created a palace wall for painting purposes, one which will be used later for Pilate's Passover address. There are six statues visible, five along a diagonal wall portion and one in the square, as well as a large Corinthian portico leading into Pilate's palace. When the camera pulls back completely, we are presented with another process shot, where the upper portion of the extant walls have been covered with Brian's painting after-the-fact, during postproduction.

Notes

1. Cook, "Crucifixion as Spectacle," 74.
2. Mannix, *TAD*, 26.
3. Actual terror groups nearly contemporary with Reg and the PFJ, including the Zealots (c. 67–68) and sicarii (c. 50–59)—active in the "Jewish freedom movement"—will be discussed later. The differences between the groups have been the focus of much critical writing over the decades. See the pertinent works of Richard Horsley, Morton Smith, Mary Smallwood, and S. G. F. Brandon, for example. Writing in an article published the same year as *Life of Brian* appeared, Horsley says the sicarii can be best understood as "terrorists," which will be discussed in a later entry. The term "zealot" appeared often in 1970s British political commentary, referring, for instance, to men surrounding new party leader Thatcher's "throne," including Keith Joseph and Ian Gilmour (Jenkins, *Anatomy of Decline*, 71).
4. Philo, *Embassy to Gaius*, 38.301–3.
5. Originally from Philo's *Embassy to Gaius*, this version edited by E. M. Smallwood in 1961 and 1970. See also Smallwood, *JURR*, 160–61.
6. Pilate is both laughable and vicious here. Alternately, by about the beginning of the third century the Carthaginian Christian writer Tertullian was claiming "that Pilate was already a Christian in his conscience" (quoted in Maier's "The Fate of Pontius Pilate," 362). This may be as much an anti-Jewish sentiment as a rehabilitation of Pilate, of course.
7. *Washington Post*, 1 May 1974.
8. Larsen, *BAFHG*, 13.
9. "Mr Nixon's Television Interview Opens Old Wounds . . . ," *Times*, 6 May 1977: 10.
10. Palin, *Diaries 1969–1979*, 336.
11. See the documentary film *The Angry Brigade*, directed by Gordon Carr, 1973.
12. Carr, *The Angry Brigade* (book, 1975): photo opposite page 32.

13. See Sandbrook's discussion of the poster and its immediate, immense impact on the electorate in *Seasons in the Sun*, 665–66.

14. Between 1975 and 1979, Pol Pot and the Khmer Rouge are responsible for the deaths of as many as two million Cambodian citizens. Mr. Walker's crime was only mild, indirect political vandalism in the safety of northeast England, and the punishment, unlike Brian's, was not lethal. Like Brian at Pilate's wall, imagine if a Cambodian had attempted such a daring act in Phnom Penh? The Pythons are clearly not using the Khmer Rouge as their revolutionary model—the PFJ are much more like the "reasonably violent" men of the Crimson Permanent Assurance.

15. *Private Eye*, 3 September 1976: 7.

16. Image from Carr's documentary *The Angry Brigade*, 1973.

17. "Today Relegation, Tomorrow Liquidation? Better: Revolution."

18. Caryl, *Strange Rebels*, 126–27.

19. Mao had died two years earlier, in September 1976. Rather than telling Mao to leave China, the posters tended to point up the failings of the Great Leap Forward, the Cultural Revolution, and the current, backwards-looking administration led by Hua Guofeng (see Caryl, *Strange Rebels*).

20. Caryl, *Strange Rebels*, 126–27.

21. "Wis Lon 'Nagged to Death' by Secretary," *Private Eye*, 29 October 1976: 10.

22. Richard, *WWAR*, 28.

23. See Cook's "Crucifixion as Spectacle" for more; also, a more contemporary batch of graffiti collected by Robert Reisner in *Graffiti*, 1967.

24. *WWAR*, 24. An image of an arch like this is used in the opening credits, the Arch of Constantine, finished in 315 to celebrate the emperor's military victories.

25. She was worried that the canceled cricket matches would turn the tide against her husband. (Rain would have "stopped play" anyway, officials said.) See "Calm It Down Plea by Davis's Wife," *Telegraph*, 28 August 1975: 1. George Davis would be rearrested in September 1977 for another robbery. See the entries "*columned doorway/window*" and "*wun for our money*" later for the ironic ending(s) to this story, one that parallels Brian's.

26. "Yard Inquiry into Conviction of Minicab Driver," *Times*, 20 August 1975: 1; also, "G. Davis, a New Name in Wisden," *Telegraph*, 20 August 1975: 1.

27. King and Stager, *LBI*, 304.

28. *LBI*, 305; Jeremiah 17:1.

29. Larsen, *MPFC: UC*, 1.277.

30. Dr. Roger Macfarlane, e-mail communication to the author (26 April 2017).

31. Reisner, *Graffiti*, 27.

32. *BAFHG*, 377.

33. See respectively "American Fleet Puts Off Visit to Greece," *Times*, 5 March 1964: 11, and "Ankara Attack on Greek Embassy," *Times*, 29 August 1964: 6.

34. "Indonesians Stone U.S. Consulate," *Times*, 31 July 1965: 6.

35. Brendon, *DFBE*, 485. This slogan appeared on West German walls, as well, in 1950.

36. "The Writing on the Wall Turns into a Best Seller," *Daily Mail*, 29 May 1967: 6.

37. Reisner, *Graffiti*, 28.

38. *DFBE*, 621. This was the same year "the Greek" Makarios III, discussed earlier, was elected archbishop of Cyprus.

39. From Ramsay Lane, photographed by Al Lorentzen.

40. "Resignation Threats by Aden Ministers," *Times*, 27 June 1967: 4. The Radfan's National Liberation Front (NLF) had been very active in anticolonial strikes since the early 1960s (*DFBE*, 511). Also, "NLF Promises a Safe Aden," *Daily Mail*, 11 November 1967: 2.

41. "The Storming of Stormont," *Sunday Times*, 1 December 1968: 7.

42. "'British Go Home' Attack by French," *Daily Mail*, 4 December 1976: 4.

43. On a much happier note, there was also a travel agency in central London, Jetback, whose vacation advertisements took advantage of the oft-heard phrase and advertised "Yankee, Go Home!" in summer 1976, offering flights to New York from £108.

44. *WWAR*, 121.

45. Cook, "Crucifixion as Spectacle," 70n8.

46. It's also possible that Brian's grasp of Latin simply isn't up to snuff. The Pharisees were very concerned that Jewish children be taught to read, but that likely meant their own language, and not Latin or even Greek (Kotker, *HLTJ*, 39). Jews of the Diaspora, like those slaves and manumitted slaves in Rome, may have had lower literacy rates. And, as Smallwood reminds us, Dispersed Jews often spoke Greek as opposed to Hebrew or Aramaic: "This is not necessarily evidence that the Jews in Rome remained a predominantly Greek-speaking community for centuries. They may have retained Greek solely for epitaphs, as the language of their former home, and traditionally appropriate for the purpose. The authors of the countless Latin epitaphs in our churches did not talk Latin in everyday life" (*JURR*, 133).

47. Koloski-Ostrow, *ASRI*, 112.

48. It's not clear whether Apollinaris would have been so bold as to create this himself, as proud of his bowel movement as he may have been. More likely one of the doctor's put-upon retinue or a cheeky local created the graffito, after the fact.

49. See *BAFHG* entries in the index under "arse trumpeters" for more on this monkish merriment.

50. *ASRI*, 115–16.

51. Wiedemann, *Emperors and Gladiators*, 63.

52. *ASRI*, 112.

53. *JURR*, 133.

54. For a discussion of the significance of the "Famous Historian," see *BAFHG*, 299–306.

55. The show ran from 14 April through 2 May 1976. A live recording was made for an album release, *Monty Python Live!*

56. Barnes called the show "pure, unadulterated madness" (*New York Times*, 16 April 1976: 11).

57. Johnstone would later cowrite the film *Fierce Creatures* with Cleese.

58. "Python in New York," *Times*, 23 April 1976: 23; italics added.

59. *Times*, 23 April 1976: 23.

60. Palin, *Diaries 1969–1979*, 310–11.

61. E-mail correspondence, 6 May 2017.

62. *Goon Show*, 22 February 1955.

63. *WWAR*, 24. Earlier, the brash Roman satirist Persius (34–62) condemned his own generation of uninteresting poets as having "been born without balls" (208); later, Apuleius's character Lucius, after being turned into a jackass, is threatened with, among other things, emasculation, and is himself owned by "a band of Syrian eunuchs" (220).

64. 1 A man with crushed or severed genitals may not enter the assembly of the LORD.

2 A person of illegitimate birth may not enter the assembly of the LORD; TO THE TENTH GENERATION NO ONE RELATED TO HIM MAY DO SO.

3 An Ammonite or Moabite may not enter the assembly of the LORD; TO THE TENTH GENERATION NONE OF THEIR DESCENDANTS SHALL EVER DO SO. (Deuteronomy 23:1–3)

65. Jeremias, *JTJ*, 344.

66. *JTJ*, 272; also 272n4–5.

67. There were types of "genitally different" men, including those born without testicles, those whose testicles had been tied off or crushed, boys who were castrated to become catamites, or those whose sex was indeterminate due to a congenital defect. In many instances, being a eunuch actually improved job and life prospects in the empire. See Stevenson, "The Rise of the Eunuchs in Greco-Roman Antiquity."

68. *Goon Show*, 26 January 1959.

69. *JURR*, 147.

70. Josephus, *WJ*, 7.10.1 (Whiston, 407).

71. Levine, *Jerusalem*, 173–74.

72. *MPFC: UC*, 1.89, and 357–58.

73. See the index in Palin's *Diaries 1969–1979* for those entries.

SCENE TEN
THE PFJ PLAN THEIR RAID

... a group of six other eager revolutionaries—This conflation of terror forces and Rome isn't out of the blue, or even from Zealot accounts, but off the front pages of 1970s newspapers. In one of the silly-but-true sections of *Private Eye* the often absurd but equally often deadly political scenes around the world were highlighted, including "Letter from Jerusalem" (cited later), "Letter from Malta," etc. In the July 1977 issue, "Letter from Rome" rehearsed an almost unbelievable list of violent events plaguing Italy:

> Since 1972, there have been 7,500 explosions, 70 successful and 500 unsuccessful assassination attempts . . . [and b]ombs and murders in trains and banks. . . . This year [1977] alone there has been at least one kidnapping a week not to mention bank robberies and innumerable explosions. Extra-parliamentary groups with "red" connections[1] spring up like mushrooms. They have access to a great deal of money . . . some of the money comes from so-called "political" kidnappings.[2]

Depicting one failed kidnapping and one successful graffiti protest, the Pythons are severely understating the contemporary threat to the Italian people and government, where "knee-cappings," assassination attempts, and explosions were daily events. The article goes on to lay out reasons for the crisis and warns that Italy is slipping toward a Middle East-level of ungovernability:

> Open chaos, fear, a new and worrying regime where the Communists become accomplices of the old institutions: terrorism—often financed from abroad; a deep economic crisis—over 20% inflation despite the fact that shops are full and all expensive, luxury goods find a buyer; the government, threatened by crisis, dismantling industry in the south. Italy could soon become Lebanon.[3]

The violence and ungovernability in Lebanon had found its way to Italy; the violence and ungovernability in the Pythons' first-century Jerusalem is a mirror of conditions in Britain, West Germany, and Japan.

The interior of MATTHIAS'S HOUSE—This is described as a "conspiratorial," "cellar-like room," though, later, Brian will go to the window to hide, and the window is revealed to be on at least the second story of the dwelling. The fact that this is a house at all, and not a cave or outbuilding, means the Pythons are thinking of more contemporary terror groups as well as their first-century predecessors. The Zealots had found that living in a city like Jerusalem was inadvisable, given the proximity to the Roman garrisons and the Jewish authorities, forcing them out of doors:

The strongholds of such resistance groups were undoubtedly in the desert areas of Palestine: indeed the caves discovered recently [1960–1961] in Nahal Hever, near En Gedi, which had been occupied by the forces of Bar Kochba during the revolt of A.D. 132–5, attest the type of refuge and mode of life of those who fought for Israel's freedom a generation or two before. The records of Josephus contain abundant evidence of this Zealot connection to the desert.[4]

The PFJ seem to have one connection to the desert—their trip to hear Jesus speak at the Sermon on the Mount. Earlier drafts of the script placed them back out at the mount (owned by Mr. Papadopoulis) for Brian's paid sermons, as well. Otherwise, the PFJ is an urban terror group, like the Baader-Meinhof Gang, the SLA, and the Japanese Red Army of the 1970s.

In a May 1968 speech,[5] rightist Tory MP Enoch Powell describes this kind of backroom cabal, though he places them in the past (right where we encounter the PFJ, coincidentally):

We live in an age of conspiracies. They are far more successful and well-managed conspiracies than the conspiracies of history. Perhaps the improvement in efficiency is one of the benefits which we owe to the technological revolution. At any rate, the age of the old-fashioned conspirator is no more. He no longer gathers with his fellows in tiny groups, admitted by password to huddle round a dark lantern in a dingy garret. Today the conspirators sit in the seats of the mighty.[6]

Powell is describing the Pythons' version of the classic conspirators' bolthole, though both the group's privacy (security) and effectiveness are placed in question as the film moves on. Theirs is the conspiracy born of conviction.[7]

FRANCIS, dressed in commando gear . . . is standing by a plan on the wall—"They had delusions of grandeur," said Helmut Schmidt, former West German Chancellor. "They thought they were the messiahs of the revolution."[8] He was describing the revolutionary Baader-Meinhof or 2 June Movement groups, and members of the radical cadre wouldn't have disagreed: "Our idea was to destroy the system, to strike at its heart," remembers Margrit Schiller, a Baader-Meinhof member.[9]

Francis lays out the plan, starting the presentation with a map hanging on the wall. The map appears to be based on typical plans produced of Roman villas in Rome and Pompeii.[10] The map does feature readable labels. The lower labels are "FORUM" and "HYPOCAUST," and the upper one appears to be "BASILICA." This is clearly not meant to be a map of Pilate's (Herod's) palace in Jerusalem, as there was no forum or basilica. This map is likely an amalgam of an existing plot plan for a Roman or Pompeian villa, as well as perhaps the layout of the Cloaca Maxima, Rome's Grand Sewer, which passed by (or under) at least two basilicae and five fora. According to Burleigh, the Algerian authorities would employ diagrams known as "organograms"—based on informant information—to help map out their FLN opponents' organizational structures and bases of operation.[11]

This scene is important because it is the first indication of the PFJ's real talent: planning. In this scene they will plan the downfall of Pilate and the Romans in Judea; they will later plan the Roman Empire's fall and the PFJ's attainment of "world supremacy"; finally, they will plan for a life of perpetual, noble resistance after Brian's "glorious martyrdom." They can plan, discuss, and observe parliamentary procedure to an admirable degree. For the Britain of the Pythons' youth, "planning" was one of the two so-called "magic words" according to Vernon Bogdanor. After the devastations of the interwar strikes, the Great Depression, and World War II, it was planning that would be "putting things right," for it was planning that had rebuilt the powerful French economy, for example, and pushed the industrial output of France, Germany, and Italy (and Japan) well ahead of Britain in the 1950s–1960s.[12] Comprehensive planning was supported by "all sensible-minded people" in Britain in the 1960s—it sparked the creation of the National Economic Development Council (NEDC), where "representatives of government, management and the unions" got together to "plan the economy," as well as the National Incomes Commission (NIC), where, yes, all incomes and wages could be planned and controlled.[13] Harold Wilson would come to No. 10 in 1964 to apply the "white heat of technology" to these well-intended plans, and even Ted Heath's Conservative government couldn't claw back what seemed to be working for and popular to most voting Britons. The wheels wouldn't really begin to come off until 1972–1974, when coal miners had had enough of wage restraint and the Arab oil embargo sent shudders through Britain's fragile economy. Planning then gave way to simple survival, which the PFJ will come to understand, as well.[14]

. . . *eight MASKED COMMANDOS*—These commandos are likely garbed to remind viewers of the haunting images seen during the hostage crisis of the 1972 Munich Olympics, where Black September terrorists killed Israeli hostages. The grainy, telephoto images of a balaclava-wearing terrorist leaning over a balcony, as well as a negotiator in a white hat pulled low, were likely still fresh in 1979. There were also images of IRA marches in Northern Ireland where men and women all wore dark hoods or masks, and ETA (Basque separatists) members often wore white masks. These "commandos" are something like the briefly popular "Situationists"—an artistic-cum-political movement interested in fomenting change (in art, then in life) via demonstration and spectacle—whose movement peaked with the May 1968 riots in France. The PFJ is clearly trying to make a spectacular showing as they attempt to kidnap the wife of their oppressor and hold her to ransom, but there's a fork in the path of revolutionary sentiment and action. The artistic genesis of the movement feels like the PFJ in that Situationists didn't generally recruit for new membership (Brian had to be willing to audition), they only wanted like-minded "geniuses for the avant-garde task" they'd set (like them, Brian "really hates the Romans"), they rejected "compromise" or "conformism" ("No blackmail!"), and "they immediately exclude those of their number who fail in practice to maintain any of the strict positions of the group."[15] Brian actually *does* something, he's a "doer," which impresses Reg but is obviously a strike against him, as it leap-frogs the PFJ's strict practice of "immediate discussion." Brian is rejected in the sense that he is left on the cross to die for the cause; he has become the spectacle that the PFJ think they need in their continuing struggle against the oppressor. And also like the PFJ, exclusivity and rigor kept the Situationist movement small and easily fractured. The Situationists officially disbanded in 1972. By summer 1989, all that was left of the movement was an art showing at the Institute of Contemporary Arts on The Mall;[16] the Situationists, like Brian, were left hanging for all to see.

As mentioned earlier, these "commandos" are also clean-shaven, those we can see, which sets them apart. It's likely they are shaven to indicate their youth and vigor (in the world of the film), traits of those who would consider revolt against the ways of their fathers:[17]

> In the ancient world, older men equated beards with sagacity, but as the fashion for shaving grew more widespread, younger men began to ridicule the sight of a man with a full beard. In the first century AD, Lucian of Samosata, a Greek satirist and writer, famously commented, "If you think that to grow a beard is to acquire wisdom, a goat with a fine beard is at once a complete Plato."[18]

Most Jewish men wore beards, anciently, and the only regulations had to do with how to trim (or not trim) the beard. Thus, clean-shaven men stood out: "Of the other nations coming in contact with Israel, the Hittites and the Elamitic nations shaved the Beard completely, as the earliest Babylonians had done."[19] Josephus, describing the beginnings of the revolt that would end Jerusalem, blames Judas, Saddok, and their followers, who "filled the lands with troubles and planted the roots of the evils that flourished there later." Josephus concludes very specifically that the "youth" had "caused the ruin of our land."[20]

REG: "Tell us about the raid on Pilate's palace . . ."—A royal palace had been raided before, but with slightly different motives. Josephus reports that the brigand Judas, son of Ezekias, targeted a Herodian palace:

> This Judas, having gotten together a multitude of men of a profligate character about Sepphoris in Galilee, made an assault upon the palace [there,] and seized upon all the weapons that were laid up in it, and with them armed every one of those that were with him, and carried away what money was left there; and he became terrible to all men, by tearing and rending those that came near him; and all this in order to raise himself, and out of an ambitious desire of the royal dignity; and he hoped to obtain that as the reward not of his virtuous skill in war, but of his extravagance in doing injuries.[21]

This assault seems similar to the one depicted by the Pythons, especially in the eruption of violence, the "tearing and rending" that eventually left Brian standing alone. Judas and friends were looking for weapons and money, both likely to be used to fight the Roman occupancy, while the PFJ (and CFG) looked for leverage, essentially. The end results were the same, however. This and other insurrection activities led to significant Roman reprisals, and, as in *Life of Brian*, the crucifixion of the rebels (about two thousand in all).[22]

FRANCIS: "We get in through the underground heating system here . . . "—An example of the Pythons doing their homework. During the 1960s and 1970s there were many Roman finds (villas, baths) in Britain, with excavations revealing and describing in detail the hypocausts at Woodchester, Bath, Fishbourne, Guernsey, York, Cirencester, and St. Alban's, among others. A number of these hypocaust sections were up to three feet high, meaning an army could crawl through them, if needed. In Jerusalem, Herod had built what Roller calls "a Roman town house," not as large or elaborate as his palace at Herodeion, though the fortifications around the Jerusalem house were formidable.[23] Archaeological finds were regular news coming out of Jerusalem, as well, as the Israelis had set about nation building by demonstrating the significance of the past, and especially the place of Jews and Jerusalem in the life of the Holy Land.

FRANCIS: ". . . Pilate's Wife . . . "—There isn't much known about Pilate either well before or long after his decade as Judean prefect. One mythology attaches the partly royal girl Procula[24] (or Procla) to young Pilate as the wife he leaves (on their wedding night) to take up the Judean post offered by Tiberius. These personal details about Pilate and his life—his marriage, if he had children, his service or death after being recalled to Rome—are actually unknown to historians.[25] Whatever she was in history, Pilate's wife isn't a pretty young girl here. The Pythons cast the towering John Case to play her, and then cut all his/her scenes out of the finished film. (In the scenes in her bedroom and adjoining hallway, she physically overwhelms the PFJ, throwing each out, before hitting Brian on the head,[26] ending the raid.) In a real world parallel, Burleigh reports that one Red Brigades kidnappee, Pietro Costa, was not only very large (he joked that they should have tried for one of his smaller siblings), he also had a very big appetite—they had trouble hiding and feeding him. He was soon able to talk his kidnappers' demands down to an affordable level, and he was freed unharmed.[27]

And why would Pilate's wife be fair game to these revolutionaries? She likely had little or no direct influence on Pilate's decision-making process, his administration, or on the continuing subjugation of Jews in Judea,[28] and thus wouldn't likely be a target for political assassination or violence, at least anciently. This is one of the moments in the film where the influence of the modern world can be glimpsed. Nineteenth-century Russian revolutionaries, for example, would have targeted the likes of Pilate's wife and household as a justifiable "blow at the centre."[29] For these revolutionaries the tsar and his family existed as practicable, obvious targets, the so-called "weakest link in the existing order, its Achilles heel" at the heart of the government.[30] "Those to be judged and destroyed are not public figures or rulers," Iviansky writes in 1977, "but the social order in its entirety, the economic establishment, the absolute or foreign rule." Iviansky continues:

> Therefore, "individual terror" maybe defined as a system of modern revolutionary violence aimed at leading personalities in the government or the Establishment (or any other human targets). . . . The motivation is not necessarily personal but rather ideological or strategic. . . against the foreign conqueror, the social order, or the Establishment embodied in the individuals.[31]

For the more contemporary Red Brigades, she could simply be seen as a "demiurge of bourgeois power," as she clearly supported and benefited from her position as an oppressor.[32] The PFJ see Pilate's wife as this weak link, the bargaining chip they need to leverage the government. This is the modern terrorism of "national liberation," using Iviansky's terms.[33]

If this were the ancient Jewish *sicarii* choosing a target, it would have been a precisely "discriminate" target, "chosen . . . with a maximum of political or religious symbolic value . . . symbols of 'the normative structures and relationships that constitute the supporting framework of society.'"[34] Horsley reminds us that the sicarii were not only "highly discriminate," but, unlike the PFJ, they made their attacks against "fellow Jews, not against Roman soldiers or citizens."[35] The sicarii will attack Jews assisting the occupying force, like their first target, the High Priest Jonathan, assassinated for "collaboration with the alien Roman rulers and its exploitation of the people."[36] The "innocent" wife of the most powerful man in the colonizing, imperialist force, then, would likely have *not* been a sicarii target—such an attack would have demanded a full retaliation by Pilate and the Roman garrison, something sicarii wished to avoid.

Most revolutionaries from the eighteenth-century and onward, however, would have argued that any means of support—military, political, economic, or even familial—for the colonizer, anything that fueled the imperialist machine, existed and could be justified as a potential target for violence. One of the Anarchist movement's most strident voices, German-born Johann Most, identified the need to focus on *individuals* even as it was the system ultimately being targeted, according to Laqueur:

> There were no social systems which were not represented and, indeed, made to work, by persons. The system was defended by the forces of "law and order"; to kill them was not murder, for policemen and spies were not human. The enemies were pigs, dogs, bestial monsters, devils in human shape, reptiles, parasites, scum, the dregs of society, *canaille*, hellhounds.[37]

As they prepared for this raid, Reg had given his list of grievances against the empire, reminding the PFJ that, vampire- or parasite-like, Rome had "bled . . . white" the Jews. He calls them "bastards," a damning, dislocative charge in these times, as discussed earlier, and they are "Bloody Romans" to Judith, the PFJ, and the Jewish populace. Lastly, Reg charges the Romans with thievery, Rome having "taken everything from" not only the current generation, but from their ancestors. Dehumanizing Pilate, his wife, and the Romans renders them easy and even obvious targets for these revolutionaries. And as far as the specter of potential collateral damage, most modern terrorists believed "it was not [the innocent's] business to be in places where a bomb was likely to explode."[38] The PFJ seems ready to cut her up, violating the body of the government as they do so, because retributive violence was the only recourse left to them. By the 1970s, terror groups were justifying their attacks on so-called innocent victims similarly. The IRA began planting bombs in England for these very reasons; and the URA and PFLP considered any passenger on an El-Al jet, traveling through an Israeli airport, or flying to or from Israel for *any* reason a potential, justifiable target in their pursuit of the destruction of Israel and Zionism.

FRANCIS: ". . . having grabbed his wife . . . "—This plan will read like a chapter from the very popular 1969 underground terror treatise, *Minimanual of the Urban Guerrilla*, by Carlos Marighella:[39]

> Kidnapping is capturing and holding in a secret place a spy, political personality or a notorious and dangerous enemy of the revolutionary movement. Kidnapping is used to exchange or liberate imprisoned revolutionaries or to force the suspension of torture in jail by the military dictatorship. The kidnapping of personalities who are well-known artists, sports figures or who are outstanding in some other field, but who have evidenced no political interest, can be a useful form of propaganda for the guerrillas, provided it occurs under special circumstances, and is handled so the public understands and sympathizes with it. The kidnappings of foreigners or visitors constitutes a form of protest against the penetration and domination of imperialism in our country.[40]

The manual became internationally known very quickly, and by October 1970 it was already being mentioned in slightly mirthful ways, as when a member of the Quebec government based in London asked publisher *Agitprop* for two copies of the manual, even including payment. The requester, counsellor André Laurion, was simply keen to understand the motives of the revolutionary and violence-prone Quebec Liberation Front, to "find out what sort of people my government is up against," he said. (The FLQ had very recently kidnapped two highly placed government economic and trade officials, one a Brit and the other from Quebec.) *The Times Diary* saw the kind of Pythonesque absurdity of the situation, especially as it unfolded per the attempted purchase—a classic "unsuccessful transaction":[41]

> Laurion will not, however, receive his manuals although he sent nine shillings to pay for them. Agitprop has replied that as "the Canadian Government, of whom you are an agency, is at present in confrontation with the FLQ, a group organised to struggle for the control of Quebec to be placed in the hands of the people of Quebec . . . we have decided that it would be in the best interests of the people of your state to send two copies of the manual to the FLQ." Nor will Laurion get his money back. Agitprop say they are instructing the FLQ to deduct the nine shillings from their ransom demand if they find the manuals to be of use.[42]

This bit of humor, admittedly dark, took on a much darker tone just three days later, when the Canadian hostage, Pierre Laporte, was found dead, perhaps "accidentally" murdered by his nervous kidnappers. Two days after that, on 19 October, the *Times* printed a somber, stern condemnation of the kidnapping and murder.[43] The next time the *Minimanual* was mentioned in the often silly *The Times Diary* section, then in relation to Argentinian revolutionaries, there was *no* remnant of lightheartedness.[44]

The IRA even considered kidnapping royal scion Prince Charles in 1976, following a deadly season of bombings and shootings that seemed to be turning public opinion against the organization, rather than toward its political goals.[45]

FRANCIS: ". . . she is in our custody and forthwith issue our demands"—This is an example of what came to be called "organized violence in the form of highly politicized terrorism" by the late 1960s.[46] Tiny, unknown fringe groups with any political axe to grind—generally waving the flags of anticapitalism, anticolonialism, or antifascism—could take hostages, issue demands, and count on sensational media coverage. The infamous Patty Hearst kidnapping is a prime example, one played out in the years leading up to *Life of Brian*.[47] The PFJ could have been reading from the SLA's guerrilla handbook, the way the FBI describes the kidnapping: "Why'd they snatch Hearst? To get the country's attention, primarily. Hearst was from a wealthy, powerful family; her grandfather was the newspaper magnate William Randolph Hearst. The SLA's plan worked and worked well: the kidnapping stunned the country and made front-page national news."[48] The PFJ would have liked to "stun" Judea and make "front-page news" with their situational action, even if just to show that those who had been bled white were "not to be trifled with." The Hearst affair will be discussed in more detail later.

Much earlier, sicarii had set the table for the SLA, JRA, RAF, and PDFLP as they resorted to kidnapping as a "typical terrorist tactic," according to Horsley, generally to get attention and bargain for the release of "some of their own number who had been taken prisoner by the authorities."[49] From Josephus: "This was the beginning of greater troubles; for the brigands contrived by one means or another to kidnap some of Ananias' staff and would hold them in continuous confinement and refuse to release them until they had received in exchange some of the sicarii."[50] As mentioned above, Brazilian terrorists kidnapped an American ambassador in 1969, and followed this same scheme. One of the first discussed acts of revolution from the Japanese Red Army was the planned kidnapping of PM Sato Eisaku in late 1969. The PM was set to travel to America to meet with President Nixon in regard to Okinawa's return to Japanese sovereignty; the hostage-taking would have forced the ongoing and unpopular security agreements between the United States and Japan into more public discussion, the JRA hoped. A police raid at the inn where they were training for this kidnapping ended the operation, and twenty-seven members spent time in prison.[51]

There were dozens of politically motivated kidnappings in the 1970s, meaning the Pythons had plenty of real-world events on which to model the exploits of their PFJ. The *modus operandi* was very similar, event to event (they'd all read the same source material, as mentioned earlier), and typically as laid out by Francis above: take a significant political prisoner, threaten harm, make demands, collect ransom. An incomplete but representative survey of the decade's notable hostage-and-ransom events and news follows.

In March 1970, a left-wing guerrilla was released by the Guatemalan government in exchange for the release of US diplomat Sean Holly; more kidnappings were promised if police continued their battles against Guatemalan guerrilla groups.[52] Also in March, *Punch* provided a wanly comedic take on the recent spate of violence, printing a "Can you keep alive till the end of this Quiz?" story, which tested readers' readiness for political kidnappings and bombings.[53] This playfulness would disappear in a few years, after scores of deaths abroad and in Northern Ireland. In October 1970, Quebec separatist kidnappings ("FLQ Oui!") led to what became known as the "October Crisis" and to the employment of the War Measures Act, culminating in many arrests, troops in streets, etc. The year 1970 was a busy one for terror, with dozens of kidnapping events (most involving demands for and eventual release of political prisoners) occurring in Northern Ireland, and up and down Central and South America. Westerners and Israelis tended to be the prime targets in many of these international kidnappings.

The year 1972 signaled the end of the imploding United Red Army (most died in the mountainous massacre, winter 1972), and the beginning of the Japanese Red Army's international terror activities, both discussed later. The year also witnessed the start of "The Disappeared," a spate of kidnappings by (primarily) the IRA. Some bodies have been found over the years, and some have not. There are at least seventeen names on the list. The following year saw the Provisional IRA abduct Grundig factory manager Thomas Niedermayer in December in Belfast. A "Provos" splinter planned to trade him for the Price sisters, who were being held on bombing charges by the British.[54] Niedermayer tried to escape, was hit with the butt of a gun, and died. He was dumped in a rubbish tip, his remains only discovered in 1980.[55]

In 1973 a Getty heir was kidnapped; this will be discussed later, in relation to the PFJ's bona fides. In March 1974 there was an odd, isolated attempt to kidnap Princess Anne by a slightly deranged man, Ian Ball. His goal was to ransom her for a £2 million payment in £5 notes from the Queen. The police tried to find an IRA connection, but the man assured them he'd worked it out all on his own. The Eritrean Liberation Front (ELF) was also quite active in 1974, kidnapping several foreigners to draw attention to their struggle for freedom from Ethiopia.[56]

The most famous political kidnapping, perhaps of the decade, had happened just the month before in California. Newspaper heiress Patricia "Patty" Hearst was kidnapped by the SLA in February, and the group's first demands fit right into the weird mood of the day. Rather than funds for their own use, the kidnappers demanded that Hearst's father, Randolph Hearst, donate millions of dollars to feed needy people in California. They had actually asked for a donation of $70 of food "be given to every needy Californian," and those handouts began almost immediately, funded by the Hearst family.[57] The SLA also demanded that two of their imprisoned colleagues be allowed to hold a broadcast press conference. After the food donations had run their course, as demanded, the SLA ceased communicating with authorities, and the next event was the spectacular Hibernia Bank robbery. From that point on, the ill-gotten funds were used to finance their own activities.

In 1975, the RAF-affiliated 2nd of June Movement kidnapped CDU[58] chairman Peter Lorenz in February, then successfully demanded the release of six RAF colleagues. Lorenz was released unharmed.[59] Ulrike Meinhof and the RAF had also plotted to kidnap German Chancellor Willy Brandt, and issue demands, but the plan didn't pan out.[60] The RAF continued to be active even as its leadership languished in specially built German prison cells—with their courtroom attached—and even after several had taken their own lives.[61] A domestic British flight (Manchester to London) was hijacked on 7 February 1975, with the Iranian hijacker demanding first a flight to Paris, then just £100,000 and a parachute. He would later settle for a flight to Stansted, where he was arrested.[62] (He seems to have bargained like our Ex-leper.)

In September 1977 German industrialist Hans-Martin Schleyer was kidnapped by the RAF (also made possible by "the praxis of the Tupamaros in Uruguay"[63]), with demands including another prisoner release; those prisoners died, so Schleyer was killed by his kidnappers in October 1977. Schleyer had been targeted only after another kidnap attempt went wrong, and the victim was killed.[64] The ripple effects of these kidnappings and attempted kidnappings were very real—British PM Callaghan decided to put off a scheduled September 1977 trip to Bonn because of the Schleyer kidnapping.[65]

And finally in 1978, Italian Christian Democrat Aldo Moro was kidnapped and killed by the Red Brigades. The kidnappers wanted prisoners released for Moro's life. The Red Brigades' manifesto called for a "concentrated strike against the heart of the State, because the state is an imperialist collection of multinational corporations."[66] The Red Brigades kidnapped for political reasons (right-wing figures) and for ransoms (industrialists), but also set fires, explosions, employed sabotage, and shot journalists, lawyers, judges, and politicians.

The spirit of the times obviously encouraged other profiteers to try their hand at the kidnap-and-ransom game. A Vermeer painting (*The Guitar Player*) was "kidnapped" in February 1974 and held for ransom; thieves threatened to burn it if the ransom was not paid.[67] One ransom call demanded £500,000 of food be flown to Grenada.[68] The caller also said that more paintings would be stolen and destroyed if the food demands were not met. Other ransom callers also demanded that the Price sisters be immediately released from prison and returned to Ireland.[69] The proposed reasons for such a theft should read familiar:

> There are two possible explanations for the theft of priceless and unsalable paintings like the Vermeer. The first is that they have been taken by a crank for political reasons. In September 1971, "The Love Letter" by Vermeer was stolen from an exhibition in Brussels in that way. It was later returned damaged. Goya's portrait of the Duke of Wellington was similarly stolen and returned to the National Gallery five years ago. After the incident the Treasury provided more money to tighten security there. The second possibility is that the picture was taken with the hope of negotiating a ransom for its return with the insurance company.[70]

The ransom possibility seemed to have been the real motivating factor. The painting was recovered in May 1974.

COMMANDO XERXES—(PSC) Xerxes was a Persian emperor, ruling in the fifth century BC. The name was likely just pulled from history, but Xerxes is mentioned in *The Goon Show* episode "The History of Communication." In this setting, it's not any more odd than a "Stan," "Loretta," or "Reg."

REG: "We're giving Pilate two days . . . "—Here, Reg is allowing Pilate just forty-eight hours to "dismantle" an enormous (and functioning) bureaucracy in Judea, one that's been building some ninety years by this time. Later, as Brian is carrying his cross to the crucifixion hill, and the PFJ are meeting, yet again, Francis points out that their five-year plan to "attain world supremacy" is likely "optimistic," unless they manage to overthrow the entire Roman Empire in just one year. This level of optimism and confidence isn't unique to the PFJ, but has a home in revolutionary groups, political parties, and committed special interest groups.

With much of the heavy lifting done across preceding decades, in early June 1947 the British tasked themselves with ending the Raj, slated just seventy-three days later—this after a build-up encompassing two hundred years.[71] Andrew Marr notes that just a few years later the committed, directed pressure of relatively few people, applied at opportune moments, brought about enormous social changes at home in Britain of the 1950s and 1960s. When Home Secretary Jenkins[72] set out to modernize Britain, he counted on grassroots organizations already marching against capital punishment, against the continuing criminalization of homosexuality, against arts censorship and age-old divorce laws. He found celebrities and politicians and everyday people—"apparently marginal people"—ready to take up the cause for change.[73] The general public and the major political parties weren't banging the drum for such sweeping changes, so the "eggheads and experts" and the always-the-bridesmaid Liberal Party stoked the fires.[74] If social change was made possible by those outside the established system, then why not economic or political change? Why couldn't a PFJ-type group shift the mountain of the Roman Empire? Because, as Francis admits later, "as far as empires go, this is the big one."

In his lecture "The Character of the Postwar Period," Vernon Bogdanor notes that such overestimations could be found across the challenging postwar decades. In a speech at Mansion

House in 1942, then-PM Winston Churchill saw in the dark days of the war a bright future for Britain and her international interests: "We mean to hold our own. I have not become the King's First Minister in order to preside over liquidation of the British Empire."[75] Bogdanor drops the other shoe, acknowledging the history that followed: "Of course, the British Empire was liquidated fairly soon after he made that speech."[76] Bogdanor also quotes the 1945 Labour Party manifesto and then the Labour Party leader, Clement Attlee, both brimming with righteous optimism that the future held no hope for capitalism, and that the emerging "Social Commonwealth of Great Britain" would destroy the "outworks" of the oppressive capitalist system.[77] Aside from sounding positively Dennisean,[78] Labour expected far too much. History would again blunt the point of this idealism, as by the time *Brian* is being filmed, Britain's ability to support its socialist commitments had atrophied thanks to a constricting economy. Attlee's phraseology sounds like Francis and Reg, revolutionary terminology meant for revolutionary victories: "The outstanding thing is not so much the growth in the strength of the forces which attack the citadel of capitalism, as in the loss of the outworks, the crumbling of the foundations, and the loss of morale of the garrison."[79] Reg and friends seek to attack the citadel of Roman occupation, beginning in its outworks of Judea; the foundations don't crumble, of course, nor do the garrisons lose any morale ("I like taking orders!" says one eager Centurion, in fact, as his underlings fix Brian to the cross). Here the PFJ echoes the handwringing sentiments of Labour and Conservative mandarins in the 1960s and 1970s. The optimistic but impatient parties struggled with the country's moribund economic growth—especially when compared to Western European or Japanese improvements.[80] Positive change couldn't come fast enough, nor could the economy grow large enough to suit either party. Twelve months or five years can be political lifetimes. Time is a commodity the seated government simply didn't have, leading to impatience, frustration, and short-term, politically expedient solutions, according to Bogdanor:

> The rate of growth in the 1960s was lower than the 1950s, and economists did not know how to secure it. . . . All they can say . . is that the *policies that are likely to improve growth are very long-term*. For example, one way to improve growth at the time might have been better management education and better technical education, but the effects of that would not be seen in the lifetime of one Government—they would be *seen over a long period*. Another example—of which we are perhaps seeing the benefits today [2012]—would be to achieve a more flexible labour market through reform of the trade unions. That was done by Margaret Thatcher in the 1980s, and it took time for its benefits to be seen. I think it is reasonable to say that we can see them now, that the recession has not led to such a high level of unemployment because of a more flexible labour market. However, it is also fair to say that productivity has not increased as much as it might have done, but the benefits of a flexible labour market *took some years to have their effect*. So, all that we do know about economic growth is that *it is a long-term matter, but of course politicians did not and do not want to hear that*. They are considering the next few years of the election, so that is a serious problem.[81]

Neither Wilson's nor Heath's governments had the time for such long-term percolation, and Callaghan in 1976 was really stuck with the stultifying effects of every stop-go measure both parties had laid on over the previous decade. The PFJ aims to end the Roman Empire in either as little as two days (by Roman submission) or as many as twelve months (by the PFJ's attacks) now appear equally ludicrous, given the lessons of history and time.

REG: ". . . dismantle the entire apparatus of the Roman imperial state . . . "—This would have included not only the small, local garrison that remained in Jerusalem, but the garrisons nearby that protected roads and waterways, the courts and municipal administration that kept the cities running smoothly and relatively crime-free, the transportation infrastructure for food and goods from across the empire that Jerusalem had come to depend on, and perhaps most importantly the protection of the Jews to perform their unique temple cult rites and live their lives as a conscientious, religious people. Many of these had been guaranteed as part of the Roman occupancy. An immediate dismantling would have thrown all that into chaos, a chaos that would appear leading up to and after the fall of Jerusalem in 70.

As crazy as this sounds, it should be remembered that, as Josephus points out, certain of the sicarii believed firmly that, given Rome's corruptness (and even *after* the Roman sacking of Jerusalem), a Jewish "victory over the Romans was possible."[82] It did not happen, but the point is there were those who were certain that it *could* happen. This "cleared field" policy—where a new future can be built from nothing but sheer will—is an echo from the Pythons' youth, when the so-called Beveridge Report emerged in 1942, and was embraced after the conclusion of the war, at the birth of the Welfare State: "Now, when the war is abolishing landmarks of every kind," William Beveridge wrote, "is the opportunity for using experience in a clear field. A revolutionary moment in the world's history is a time for revolutions, not patching."[83] This plan and its implementation were often credited with leading Britain to a possible "New Jerusalem," incidentally, that panaceatic phrase appearing in dozens of newspaper stories from September 1942 and beyond. The PFJ aren't looking for representation by the Romans, coexistence with their oppressors, or crumbs from the colonialist's table—they want everything, and fast. There is even a topical wartime cartoon that appeared in the *Daily Mirror* showing two men—Churchill and Beveridge—laying dynamite deep underground, ready to blow up the "Anti-Social Interests" overlay.[84] At that point both men seemed ready to totally redo the economy and social security after the war. The PFJ will attempt their overthrow in a similar manner, from beneath.

In contemporary jargon, this is a "rejectionist" argument, one employed by the more radical splinter group of the PLO, the Arab Rejection Front—created in 1974 in the wake of the epic failure of the 1973 Yom Kippur War—when PLO leader Yassir Arafat had adopted a more moderate stance toward the continuing existence of an Israeli state.[85] The rejectionists' "goal," according to Demaris in *Brothers in Blood*, "is nothing less than the total dismantling of Israel."[86] Reg and friends don't want to live with the Romans, they want their rule ended, though they may settle for just the freeing of Judea, and not the entire empire.

Even earlier than the 1970s, though, the Jewish terror group Irgun had made similar demands, including impossible-to-meet, even ridiculous deadlines. As the Allies fought the Axis at the outbreak of the war, this group (as well as Lehi) fought the Allies—specifically the British—trying to force them out of the Mandate. In January 1944, the group issued a statement ending their self-imposed truce (enacted earlier in the war), demanding the "immediate transfer of power" over the Mandate from Great Britain to "a Provisional Hebrew Government."[87] This "immediate transfer" did not happen, of course, and the struggle for control of Palestine continued after the war.

The 1970s were a coup-rich period, across Asia, Africa, and Central and South America, the sentiment and appeal of throwing off the yoke of imperialism were everywhere. A mad dictator led to slaughter in Equatorial Guinea in the late 1960s, following independence from Spain, and a smallish, PFJ-type coup was attempted. The plotters never made it past the Canary Islands, where they were arrested. The Forsyth novel *The Dogs of War* is a nearly identical depiction of this failed coup undertaking, except in the book the mercenaries are successful. "Thus art imitated life," Wheen writes of this mirroring, "and, as so often in the Seventies, life returned the compliment by devising narratives that even a thriller writer might have thought too extravagantly fanciful."[88] The Pythons present a heady band of revolutionaries trying to overthrow an empire; those very boasts and actions are happening in the world outside the film.

The Pythons had explored the phenomenon of international terrorism earlier in *Flying Circus*. In the first instance, the hijacker demands that the plane be diverted to not Cuba but Luton;[89] in Ep. 35, a passenger on an international flight asks for ransom or he'll blow up the plane. Both the JRA and the PFLP had made similar threats, and even followed through:

> Skyjackings began in earnest in about 1961, with a number of domestic American flights being rerouted to Cuba. Skyjacking was seen as a significant political tool for smaller, leftist terrorist cells such as the . . . PFLP, which began skyjacking planes in 1968, the first an international El Al flight from Rome to Tel Aviv. The phenomena had become so prevalent during the late 1960s that *Time* magazine devoted its 21 September 1970 cover to these "Pirates in the Sky."[90]

The Pythons' bomber in Ep. 16, of course, isn't so canny, asking to be tossed out over Basingstoke; he boards an equally convenient waiting bus, which is then immediately hijacked to Cuba.[91]

REG: ". . . we execute her"—If the PFJ managed to not only kidnap Pilate's wife but also kill her—no one here ever says "kill" or "murder," the jargon is more clinical—then as murderers they would be liable by Roman law for not only crucifixion but death by fire or wild beast: "Martial talks of the penalty *ad bestias* as applying to a slave who has cut his master's throat with a sword, has been mad enough to rob a temple of the gold deposited there, or has set Rome on fire with destructive torches," Wiedemann writes. "Public law therefore prescribed particular punishments for those whose crimes had set them outside the pale of civilized society: murderers and arsonists."[92] And given the fact that the PFJ's target was Pilate's wife, a different kind of gold in a different kind of sanctuary, and that they intended to torture and murder her, their punishments likely could have included all of these grisly tortures, and more.

MATTHIAS: "Cut her head off?"—Given that the PFJ's first bit of anti-imperialist action was essentially "guerrilla theater"—a harmless act meant to embarrass or annoy the oppressor—the chances that they would then torture or kill are slim, especially via something as gruesome as a beheading. From graffiti to murder in one go would have been a stretch for most terror groups. The Angry Brigade targeted *symbolically*, injuring only one bystander in two dozen bombings, while the Red Army Faction in West Germany initially just robbed banks and blew up US military targets, police stations, and newspapers not sympathetic to student causes. The Pythons had even set up a likely mode of action in Ep. 15, "The Spanish Inquisition." When the three snarling Inquisitors have their victim securely tied to a comfy chair, they begin to torture her with demands for a confession, followed by the threat of more shouting, soft cushions, and "only a cup of tea at eleven" before lunch.[93] She never does confess.

In the time of the Roman occupancy, death by beheading was generally reserved for political crimes and foes, while stoning was the punishment for a "capital charge against the religious law."[94] Politically dangerous enemies like John the Baptist were killed by the sword, while religious enemies like Stephen, and James, the brother of Jesus, suffered death by stoning.[95] Pilate's wife is obviously seen here as a political target, and therefore subject to death by sword. Earlier, the blasphemer Matthias was set to be stoned for his religious transgression.

In more modern times, execution was an approved method of attacking the imperialist state for many terror groups, though not all. For many, murder was a last resort. Often, the kidnapped victim was quite valuable—a large ransom could be demanded, or political leverage against the terror group's enemies gained. Britain's own Angry Brigade engaged in bombings to damage property, not necessarily people, hoping that the spectacle created by the explosions would energize the populace into a higher consciousness and, eventually, revolution.[96] In their first communique to the press and people of Britain in 1970, the Angry Brigade admitted their role in the "machine-gunning" of the Spanish embassy in London in August of that year, and also admitted to precision aiming: "We were careful not to hit the pigs guarding the building."[97] In their fifth communique, they reminded the public that after a handful of bombings no one had been hurt: "We are no mercenaries. We attack property not people. Carr, Rawlinson, Waldron, would all be dead if we had wished."[98] Body mutilation, including decapitation, carries such a stigmatic horror that it is often an ultimate threat. The PFJ realize that a penultimate threat might be needed, however, so they also discuss cutting "all her bits off" and sending them back to Pilate to prove their grit. The Getty kidnappers followed this plan, beginning with a piece of their captive's ear.[99] During the Hanafi Siege in Washington, D.C., in 1977, kidnappers threatened to behead hostages if demands were not met.[100]

The Pythons themselves depicted beheadings and mutilations by the score in *Flying Circus* and *Holy Grail*, many animated, some live-action. In *Flying Circus*, someone is beheaded in a bit of violent French film footage[101] (Ep. 23), a woman is decapitated by a piano keyboard (Ep. 33), and a boxer loses his head entirely in a bout (Ep. 43).[102] Gilliam's animations take apart and sometimes monstrously refashion the human body throughout the series. In Ep. 15, Reg's head is sawn off by BBC workers (he's promised "expenses"[103]) and dropped into an animated setting where

> his right iris is eventually "borrowed". . . for use as a cannonball. Gilliam's animations are often built on borrowing—on the dismembering and re-membering of the human figure, specifically. Recognizable faces from the world of politics (Nabarro, Heath), sport or entertainment (W. G. Grace,[104] Greer Garson) are given new, often grotesque bodies and/or abilities in Gilliam's world, and normal, unknown folk from traditional family photos also appear. The wholeness of the human body is the expectation, and Gilliam takes every opportunity he can to dismember and make strange and monstrous that formerly sanctified figure. This "body horror" phenomenon isn't new to Gilliam or the Pythons, having crept into feature films (Hammer horror, bloody Peckinpah Westerns, George Romero's *Night of the Living Dead*, etc.) and on the nightly news as the color images from the day's fighting in Vietnam was reported.[105]

The body "bits" removed from their normal context and then displayed in the Python world include the foot, shoulder, "naughty bits," navel, elbow, kneecap, ear, and big toe (Ep. 22), as well as myriad arms and legs, breasts, faces, eyes, hands, and heads. The violence continues in *Holy Grail*, where the Three-Headed Knight threatens to cut off Sir Robin's head, and Bors loses his head to the Killer Rabbit. The Black Knight loses all his limbs, the alleged witch is set to be immolated, a servant is squashed flat by a Wooden Rabbit, knights are mauled to death by a Killer Rabbit, Brother Maynard is eaten by the Legendary Beast, and men are thrown to their deaths from the Bridge of Death. The threats of the PFJ aren't beyond what the Pythons have already committed on and to their characters earlier, which may explain why Matthias would discount crucifixion as a "doddle," unnerving the Centurion, and with good reason.

Most revolutionary groups were aware that the public could be swayed to empathy with carefully staged kidnappings, ransom demands, and even bombings that targeted government, military, or industrial sites. The "Pilate's wife"–types of the world could be justified as targets, the ransom demands targeted the obscenely wealthy, and bombing sites tended to be faceless, featureless government or military installations. The outright murder of public servants, industrialists, and eventually police forces and ordinary citizens hardened public feelings, leading to calls for crackdowns and the reestablishment of law and order.[106] Marighella lays out which suggested targets for lethal attacks were acceptable, including foreign spies, agents of the sitting dictatorship, any "dictatorial personality in the government involved in crimes and persecutions against patriots," and *anyone* who works with the authorities against the guerrilla movement.[107] Though we don't know her in the finished film, Pilate's wife can likely be finessed into one or more of these categories, making her a natural target. These same justifications were applied by the Provisional IRA when they targeted Prince Philip's uncle Lord Mountbatten in August 1979: "The IRA claim responsibility for the execution of Lord Louis Mountbatten. This operation is one of the discriminate ways we can bring to the attention of the English people the continuing occupation of our country."[108] Two teens—one Mountbatten's grandson—were also killed, while four other family members were critically injured in this "discriminate" explosion. Just hours later, the IRA also killed eighteen soldiers near Warrenpoint with two more explosions. The *Guardian* would call Mountbatten "the IRA's most illustrious victim," a Pilate's wife-like appellation.[109]

FRANCIS: "Cut all her bits off . . . "—Cutting up the Roman prefect's wife (or cutting off whatever "all her bits" might mean) was one thing, and dangerous enough. If this had been a holy man, instead, the ramifications were more shaded. Under Jewish law[110] a mutilated body rendered the holy man unfit for the priesthood, and Josephus tells us that Hyrcanus's nephew Antigonus purposely cut "bits off" his uncle: "Being afraid that Hyrcanus, who was under the guard of the Parthians, might have his kingdom restored to him by the multitude, he cut off his ears, and thereby took care that the high priesthood should never come to him any more, because he was maimed, while the law required that this dignity should belong to none but such as had all their members entire."[111] Other versions translate into the grisly "bit his ears off," but the end result is the same. This edict would mean the lepers, seen earlier, were also blemished and not physically worthy of the priesthood. During Titus's lengthy siege of Jerusalem in 70, rather than killing Jerusalemite soldiers who escaped the city, the Roman forces would cut one hand off the deserter, then send the man back into the city. Titus's reasoning was sound: the maimed man could no longer wield a sword, but he still had to be fed, meaning the city's stores would disappear all the faster, hastening a surrender.[112]

But this gruesome threat wasn't reserved for ancient times. John Paul Getty III—grandson of oil billionaire J. Paul Getty—was kidnapped in Rome in July 1973. The ransom demand was received along with a portion of the boy's right ear, and a lock of his hair. The ransom note promised more violence against the boy if demands were not met:

> In their message, the kidnappers gave a warning that unless the newspaper published the photographs [of the boy's severed ear], the family would receive "another piece of Paul's flesh." The letter added: "It does not bother us—we like cutting up your son bit by bit and sending him to you. It is not we who are the sadists."[113]

Initially, J. Paul refused his son's request to help pay the ransom for his grandson, not wanting to encourage others to target his family. A ransom was eventually paid ($2.9 million), the boy was released, and most of the kidnappers were arrested. This sounds familiar, as well, as the kidnappers put the blame for any harm on the shoulders of those who refuse to cooperate— Reg will remind the PFJ in a moment that the Romans "bear full responsibility" for anything that happens to Pilate's wife. (In February 1974, just a few months after the Getty scion was kidnapped, the Vermeer painting *The Guitar Player*, mentioned earlier, was treated similarly, when a small piece of the painting was sent to the *Times*.[114])

Certainly the committed PFJ can be compared to the followers of one Judas from Galilee, as detailed by Smallwood:

> Josephus describes Judas' followers as forming a religious sect, the Jewish "fourth philosophy," parallel to the sects of the Pharisees, Sadducees and Essenes, and their doctrines as an extreme form of Pharisaism, mainly characterized by an overpowering passion for freedom and a refusal to call any man master. To them the only lawful ruler of the Jews was God, and they were prepared to kill or be killed and to suffer any hardship for the sake of their principles and would countenance no compromise with Rome such as the main body of the Pharisees was ready to make provided that they were allowed to practice their religion in peace.[115]

The above description sounds very much as if Francis dictated it. And the sicarii also have something in common with the Peoples' Front of Judea:

> They were not a rural phenomenon, but urban. They operated in the heart of the holy city of Jerusalem, even in the Temple. They did not commit armed robbery at all, but murder, assassination. In contrast to bandits, who made attacks and then fled to their hideaways because their identity was already known only too well, the Sicarii, although operating in broad daylight and in public places, assassinated their victims surreptitiously. Because of this clandestine manner of operation, no one knew who the assassins were, and they could continue to lead normal public lives in the city.[116]

The actual willingness or ability of the PFJ to make good on their threats of violence and murder is only certain until they and the CFG fight each other to the death beneath Pilate's bedroom.

The Japanese Red Army was the most cutthroat of these 1970s terror groups, ready to kill or die virtually anywhere, as long their aims of "fomenting worldwide revolution" were in play. In the Lod Airport massacre in 1972,[117] the three gunmen simply opened fire with submachine guns on queuing travelers. One gunman survived, and was quoted in his trial confession: "War involves killing and destruction. We cannot limit warfare to the destruction of buildings. We believe that the killing of humans is inevitable."[118] IRA apologist Gerry Adams would echo this, describing the killing of Mountbatten in August 1979 as "unfortunate" but necessary, that the career of Mountbatten symbolized the continuing oppression of the Irish people, and that the IRA "achieved its objective," which was to draw attention to the Irish situation.[119]

FRANCIS: ". . . we're not to be trifled with"—An odd terror story from the period can be related here. In 1974 director Otto Preminger was in France filming the Peter O'Toole film *Rosebud*. Even though the film told the story of a *successful* Palestinian raid on a yacht, Palestinian groups felt the film was pro-Zionist (perhaps because the director and screenwriter were Jewish), and the filming site in southern France was subjected to a bombing attempt, according to *Private Eye*. The messy script included media-driven terrorists and an over-the-top English bad guy (played by Richard Attenborough[120]). When the shoot relocated to Paris, another bomb threat was received, this time targeting star (and Irishman) O'Toole for "betraying revolutionaries throughout the world."[121] This second threat was determined to be a hoax, likely perpetrated by critic Kenneth Tynan, whom O'Toole would later rough up as payback.[122]

(draft) **REG: ". . . a ten-foot mahogany statue of the Emperor Julius Caesar with his cock hanging out . . ."**—This is one of the demands that Reg and the PFJ suggest in an early draft of the script. There were an abundance of priapic statues, friezes, and paintings across

the Roman Empire. Images of fertility could be found in homes and public spaces. Several surviving examples of these works—terracotta wall plaques and a large wall painting, all from Pompeii—were part of the *Pompeii AD79* exhibition mentioned earlier.[123] Why Reg has chosen Julius Caesar for his statue of ridicule, and not the current emperor, Tiberius, is puzzling. Julius Caesar had died some 77 years prior to the events of the film. In the earlier Colosseum scene, the banners on display had been dedicated to Caesar Augustus, even though he had also been dead for a number of years prior to the events depicted in *Brian*. Absolute historical accuracy has not been a hallmark of the Pythons, though they clearly pride themselves on their university educations and access to knowledge both empyrean and arcane.

Mahogany is a tropical hardwood not generally associated with the Middle East, since it is indigenous to the Americas. It would be the seventeenth century before mahogany found its way out of the Americas and into the homes of the wealthy in the Old World.[124]

A statue designed to enrage the Romans is an echo of a similar statue that had inflamed the Jews in the latter part of Gaius's reign. In about 40 the increasingly unstable emperor Gaius (Caligula) ordered an enormous statue of himself as Jupiter to be created and subsequently installed *inside* the walls of the temple in Jerusalem.[125] Given the Jews' abhorrence of effigies intended for worship—and especially Roman effigies and Roman cultus worship in any proximity to the temple—the emperor's order could not have been more inflammatory. Realizing that such a move would lead to a bloodbath, the Syrian leader Petronius stalled and even attempted to dissuade Gaius from his course. Only Gaius's untimely death put a halt to the potential desecration.[126]

(draft) **REG: "That's just a bargaining counter"**—Terrorists like members of the JRA, the RAF, and even Carlos often made demands that couldn't be met by responding governments, with an initial list being winnowed down to accomplishable goals, often including cash ransoms, transportation to a friendly country, and release of some or all of the group's imprisoned compatriots. Since most terror groups were asking for wholesale changes in nominally democratic countries, the first level of demands tended to be pie-in-the-sky, essentially unachievable, and were likely more of a means of identifying the groups' political stance. Demands made by Carlos and his group as they held hostages in Vienna included the cessation of American involvement in Arab oil production and distribution, and the withdrawal of Western influence from the Middle East.[127] The SLA had also demanded that the Hearst family feed *every* poor person in the Bay Area. None of these demands were met, nor were they even logistically possible except over many years. Many demands were accomplishable, however, given a certain political will, including the oft-heard demand for the release of terror colleagues, to which the Japanese government, for example, regularly agreed. This is a tactic the PFJ never attempts, one that could have benefited Brian.

This resort to force and violence to accomplish a political goal is understandable, especially considering not only the intransigent occupation by the Romans in first-century Judea, but the mindset of twentieth-century terrorists fighting entrenched colonialism and Western power in general. In life, however, Cleese, for example, participated in a number of nonviolent demonstrations, conveniently rubbing elbows with political figures, entertainers, and policy makers. Donoughue notes that Cleese was in attendance at a gathering of the Fabian Society—a Labour-friendly organization promoting the peaceful implementation of Communism in democratic countries—in November 1976, and earlier, in October 1970, Cleese had been a signatory on a call for the Heath government to support antiapartheid efforts in South Africa.[128] It's not clear whether these incidents define Cleese's liberal Left credentials, or show that he simply ran in a number of politically varied circles. It's not likely that signing broadsheet pledges or attending dinners would "shift one Roman soldier," though, as Reg acknowledges, and perhaps Cleese's actual liberal bent is less bendy than assumed, given his opinion of Left icon Tony Benn: "In a later conversation recorded by Michael Palin in his *Diaries*, Terry Jones is said to have opined for a Benn-led Labour government, after which Cleese was seen to 'twitch uncontrollably.'"[129] Reg will, after all, leave Brian on the cross and vow to fight on, likely in a less physically committed way.

REG: "And of course, let me point out . . . "—Reg is the gifted public speaker here, the leader of the Peoples' Front declaring the movement's grievances, principles, and intent. In this he is like his namesake, Reg Birch. Speaking during a round of negotiations with the Heath government in 1973, AEUW leader Birch laid out his union's position: "We regard any formula which places restraint on wages as a freeze," Birch said. "The Phase 2 formula of a £1 plus 4 per cent norm is a freeze, and any other formula that holds down wages will be a freeze since there will be no power to negotiate."[130] And here Reg and Reg sound very similar in their soaring rhetoric, confident in their abilities to both inspire their members to action and influence the governments they oppose:

> We say that there must be total opposition to what is a direct interference in the functions of the unions. This movement must have no truck with this Government. We should not join with them in this artificial debate. Under no circumstances should we confuse the minds of our members. There must be no conference about a wage freeze or any more attempts to restrict our freedom.[131]

In early February 1974—just weeks before Heath's unseating and during some of the most historically disruptive trade union activities—*Times* columnist PHS, writing in "The *Times* Diary" space, set about to list just what kinds of (and how many) "Reds" there might be under the bed. He cobbled together a list of the most visible and active Communist- and Socialist-influenced parties, and how they were responding to the crises of the go-slows, the three-day work week, and the yawning energy crisis. The third party listed is Reg Birch's Communist Party of Britain (Marxist-Leninist), and PHS's slightly mocking description of the group and its goals should sound very familiar, as if the *modus operandi* for the PFJ were born right here:

Communist Party of Britain (Marxist-Leninist)
Leading member: Reg Birch of the AUEW is chairman.
Run by: A central committee elected by a congress of members, and a secretariat chosen from the central committee. No paid officials.
Aim: The overthrow of capitalism by revolution and the recognition that the force to accomplish this is the working class with Marxist-Leninist ideological developments.
Paid-up members: Secret.
View of the crisis: No general strike: "This is a protracted struggle, requiring guerrilla tactics at all levels, with some taking strike action, others overtime bans, and others other form of industrial action."[132]

Two weeks later, PHS followed up on this strain, apologizing that in his earlier list of Reds under the bed he'd forgotten to include "the Communist Party of England (Marxist-Leninist) . . . on no account to be confused with the Communist Party of Britain (Marxist-Leninist), Reg Birch's outfit."[133] The Peoples' Front and the Popular Front, of Judea, again.

To put a topper on Birch's time in the public eye, in March 1978 it was announced that he had been included in the latest edition of *Who's Who*, while in April of that same year, Birch was instrumental in leading a work stoppage at the *Times* itself, which was covered in detail in the *Spectator* and other Fleet Street publications.[134]

REG: ". . . they bear full responsibility. . . we shall <u>not</u> submit to blackmail"—First, the demands that will follow are quite different from the "original" Judean terror group, the Zealots. Reg's opposite in the Zealots, Judas, was likely an educated, religiously trained man capable of teaching others from the Torah that paying tribute to Rome was an affront "to the absolute sovereignty of Yahweh."[135] Reg and the PFJ never do argue from a religious point of view—they're not even labeled as Jews, textually—they are a political group seeking the "absolute sovereignty" of, first, the PFJ, and then maybe Jerusalem and Judea.

This revolutionary jargon is very much from the manifestoes and terrorist ransom demands of the 1970s. Specifically, the continuing actions of the imperialist aggressors are given as the direct cause of the bombings and kidnappings—if imperialism would stop its march, violence would stop, as well, went the argument. As hostage negotiations took place, for example, in September 1977 with JRA hijackers on JLA flight 470, as the night dragged on the hijackers communicated that if their demands[136] weren't met, hostages would begin to be killed, the Japanese government being "directly responsible" for those deaths.[137] Four years earlier, the unknown "Sons of the Occupied Territory" group had hijacked a Japan Air Lines jet, then blown it up in Benghazi as a punishment to Japan for payment of victim compensation after the Lod airport massacre (carried out by Japanese terrorists) in 1972.[138] This new group promised more attacks if the Japanese continued to reimburse those affected by its own terrorists.

Baader-Meinhof member Horst Mahler would give an interview (from prison) for Alexander Kluge's *Germany in Autumn*, a docudrama released in 1978. Mahler had been the group's cofounder, and in the interview he tries to explain the Left's move from peaceful action to violence and how such thinking—justifying violence against potentially innocent targets—comes into being. Seven years into his prison sentence, he clearly sees it as a failed movement—his words describing well both the PFJ's conundrum and the zeitgeist of the late 1960s and early 1970s, where left-wing radicals itched to act on their principles:

Of course, it was all more or less abstract, removed from the existing social context, and in particular, removed from the mentality of the people, who were not in any way ready to wage war against the state or to support a war against that state. At the time, we weren't aware of this; otherwise we would never have put this policy . . . into effect on a practical level. The development that came about leading up to the Schleyer kidnapping, and this is really the crux of the problem, leading up to Mogadishu. . . .[139] That created the conditions to bring the crisis . . . I see it as a crisis of the Left, of our left-wing thinking . . . it finally came to attention as a crisis, as a weakness of ours, an object of our critique. I think you can't imagine it as a more radical culmination than this opposition that we initiated with our protest that we began with our uprising against imperialism. . . . The fact that we took to the streets because of My Lai, for example, a massacre against the Vietnamese people. And now we have to watch as one group of this movement, in order to free prisoners, with which the general population does not in any way identify, takes innocent and defenseless civilians—women, children, old people—takes them hostage, and threatens their lives, threatens to massacre them apparently without ever having asked the question: "Does this in any way have anything to do with left-wing politics?" The question is how can a person like Ulrike Meinhof kill another person, or find his death acceptable? A criminal murderer removes himself from the system of moral values; a revolutionary carries himself too far. This means that the moral rigor of the revolutionary which can spiral into a subjectively presumptuous arrogance is at the same time the prerequisite for overcoming the scruples that one has as a left-winger, when it comes to killing a person. You see the moral corruption of the capitalist system, you see the people in the system acting in a corrupt way, and you judge them morally, you condemn them. And based on that moral judgment, you consider them the embodiment of evil. Thus you have the idea that personal guilt plays a role, and that it is necessary and just, for the sake of liberation, to eradicate this evil, including where it is personified. This means eradicating people. This is why there's so much talk about sympathy for terrorists. There exists a common starting point, and that is the moral indignation about the current state of society.[140]

Mahler identifies the problems facing a group like the PFJ and later the Red Army Faction: the masses (especially in a democratic state) aren't ready to be liberated or assist in an over-throw, the revolutionary "goes too far" and simply becomes a murderer of the same people he or she has sworn to free, and the moral quandary can impair both revolutionary and public sentiment toward the rebels. With the dozens of hijackings (jumbo jets, ships, trains) over the previous decade, the hundreds of bombs at military sites and in crowded markets, and the scores of kidnappings for principle and then just for money and terror, it's no wonder that Mahler and many others saw the end of any potential sympathy for such political causes, and just when the Pythons are creating their spectacularly unsuccessful PFJ.

REG: "They've bled us white . . . "—In Britain's own empire, these same cries had been heard, and most often ignored. In late nineteenth-century India, nationalist voices decried the "'constant drain of wealth' from the subcontinent to the United Kingdom, plausibly as-serting that 'India is bleeding to death.'"[141] In Australia, the most strident voices began to be heard after the Anzac troop fiasco at Gallipoli—the "British Vampire" was sucking the life from the Antipodes.[142] In Ireland, the "centuries of ruthless tyranny" of Britain charged in the Irish Declaration of Independence in 1919 were followed by incredible "progress" in educa-tion, railway building, "health and welfare services," housing, and an improved economy.[143] And in Africa, attorney-cum-freedom-fighter Nelson Mandela would be "radicalized by the thousand quotidian systemic slights that . . . White mastery entailed."[144] But across the British Empire, being "bled white" was always an argument that could be countered by what colonialism ostensibly provided, at least in practical terms.

In December 1976 representatives of Britain's wine industry sent three half-empty bottles to Chancellor Healey, one cleverly labeled "Bled Dry White." The Wine and Spirits Asso-ciation attached labels to all three bottles: "Produce of Hard Work, Taxed and Taxed Again by HM Treasury." According to the Association, the British tax man was positively Roman, with taxes on wine inflating "table wine prices by 100 [percent], and sherry by more than 70 [percent]."[145] Many industries during this period of higher taxation (to cover the expand-ing costs of the Welfare State) claimed to be "bled white." For example, the bread industry blamed price controls and governmental "interference"; in the financial world, unit trust groups reported a depressing decade (including the Slater[146] fiasco); and regional organiza-tions for many villages were concerned that thanks to a floundering economy, "depression, unemployment and poverty" were bleeding whole rural areas white.[147] And on a *60 Minutes* broadcast in November 1976, economist Milton Friedman seriously asked if England was going the way of Chile—from communist dictatorship to military coup, its middle class "bled white by high taxes and 20 and 30 per cent inflation."[148] When the National Enterprise Board (Tony Benn's baby) was created in February 1975, the fear from the right was that Benn and his "Soviet" friends would intervene in British industry to a point that collapse was inevitable: "They are like the medieval apothecary who bled his patient white," said Opposition spokes-man Eldon Griffiths, "and then wondered why he was anemic."[149] Taxation seemed to bring the "bled white" phrase out of the woodwork during the 1970s.

Historically, the phrase also appears in the first pages of the popular book on the life of a gladiator, *Those about to Die*. There, Nero's appalling leadership and administration had led to continuous rioting, the peoples of Rome starving and strained to the breaking point thanks to a staggering economy. The mammoth expense of maintaining Rome's military machine of empire had led to fighting in the streets, according to Mannix, "bleeding the nation white."[150]

In the UK, supporters of Scottish nationalism in 1974 voiced the refrain "Scotland has been bled white by the English."[151] The labyrinthine process of Scottish "devolution" was well underway by 1977, with the Labour party very set on pushing it through the House. Callaghan adviser Donoughue even saw the political future of the party at stake, since Labour had come to depend on votes from Scottish members and many promises had been made to support devolution.[152] Perhaps this image—a smaller, "invaded" country trying to shrug off a colonial master—influenced the Pythons as they thought of secondary situations for their "Life of Christ" story. In this sense the situations in Scotland, Wales, and Northern Ireland, to varying degrees, mirrored what the PFJ (and the CFG) experienced in first-century Jerusalem.

What Reg is getting to is the idea that state violence must lead understandably, inevitably, to a peoples' revolutionary violence, and this is the oppressed, bled-white peoples' justification for action. Frantz Fanon, an Algerian doctor-cum-revolutionary, nurtured, according to Dobson and Payne, "a blazing hatred for colonialism and racial oppression," and in his fiery writings "elevated violence into mystique."[153] Fanon was a fundamental influence on terror groups of the 1960s: "Violence alone," Fanon wrote in *The Wretched of the Earth* (1961), "violence committed by the people, violence organised and educated by its leaders, makes it possible for the masses to understand social truths and gives them the key."[154] In the introduction to *Wretched of the Earth*, Jean-Paul Sartre echoes and supports Fanon (and the big-talking PFJ), that "no gentleness can efface the marks of violence; only violence itself can destroy" those colonizers and their violent ways.[155] The PFJ must, then, resort to kidnap at least, and perhaps even torture and murder to throw off the bonds of their oppressor, their colonial masters, the Romans. Dobson and Payne continue, outlining the importance of violence for the oppressed, and underscoring why groups like the PFJ, the CFG, and the real-life PFLP and Red Army could have embraced such views when faced with a seemingly unbeatable foe:

> Fanon preached that violence was not simply a means of ending colonial rule, but also an improving element in itself. "Violence is a cleansing force," he wrote (a sentiment to be echoed by Gaddafi, among others). "It frees the native from his inferiority complex and from his despair and inaction; it makes him fearless and restores his self-respect."[156]

Writing of the fragmented and volatile student movements in the late 1960s Japan, Farrell describes their obvious shortcomings, their likely Achilles' Heel of the near future:

> The birth of numerous factions within the radical movement indicated that. . . objectives were many and diverse. This fragmentation was further compounded by different methods available for achieving any stated goal. *Many called for the removal of "evil," while having no plan for implementing the "good."*[157] *There was little vision of the positive, only dissatisfaction with the status quo.* The only answer seemed to be rebellion, not reconstruction.[158]

Dobson and Payne concur, describing the odd mélange of multiple successful "robberies and kidnappings" by the Red Army and the members' fractiousness prior to the formation of the United Red Army: "There was, however, no consistency in the membership or loyalties of the group in Japan. It formed and reformed in a number of minute factions, all dedicated to the destruction of rival groups."[159] Reg and the PFJ will decry the rapacity of the Romans, but it doesn't take long for them to remind themselves of some of the very positive, even life-giving benefits of the status quo—roads, medicine, wine, infrastructure, and so on—eventually rendering their revolution patently absurd, and, like most revolutions, doomed to fail.

REG: "They've taken everything we had, not just from us, but from our fathers . . ."—Here also is the PFJ's *ultima ratio rebellium*, their excuse for action and violence, as they are "free men facing intolerable persecution," at least by their own measure.[160] They don't seem to be what Dr. Johnson would have called scoundrel types taking their "last refuge" in patriotism, though they do cite their heritage and they are fighting for a free Judea.[161] In his book *Terrorism*, Walter Laqueur points out that over the centuries both noble and ignoble causes have raised this same banner, from horse thieves in South America to the Red Army Faction in postwar West Germany.[162] Frantz Fanon saw it similarly, "everything" taken, including the necessities for life: "When we revolt it's not for a particular culture. We revolt simply because, for many reasons, we can no longer breathe."[163] The colonizer bleeds white the colonized, as Reg has already said. Laqueur goes on to discuss the "frustration-aggression concept" as it related to terrorism from the 1960s and beyond, the idea that to some "aggression is *always* a consequence of frustration," a clear case of haves and have-nots:

> [This] concept was widely accepted for a while by students of conflict who regarded protest and violence as the result of discontent caused by frustration. And they saw social discontent as the discrepancy between demand and fulfillment. Or, in more scientific language, the higher the social-want formation and the lower the social-want satisfaction, the greater the systematic frustration. Violence . . . is the result of socialization patterns which either encourage or discourage aggression and of cultural traditions sanctioning collective responses to various kinds of deprivation.[164]

Short answer: The Romans have "taken everything," and the victims have turned to violence,[165] not unlike German radical democrat Karl Heinzen, who was ready to justify the blowing up of "half a continent" and the pouring out of "a sea of blood" for his cause; 1960s radicals were prepared to kidnap, torture, and kill in the name of their versions of freedom. The PFJ's justifications might be a tad less noble, their commitment a mite less complete.[166]

This particular cri de coeur is generally read in the manifestoes and graffiti of oppressed minorities[167]—political speech designed to justify insurrectionary behavior, for example, and even persuade the unaffiliated to join the cause. It begins this way here, too, but is undercut by the helpful reminders given to Reg in regard to the Roman Empire's contributions to the quality of life in Judea—*Tristram Shandy*–like (and Pythonesque) digressions that put a human face on the dictatorial colonizer and render Reg's anti-Roman splenetic almost moot. If it helps, the Romans did this to their own, as well. A version of this cry is heard from Sallust (c. 86–35 BC), a Roman historian and politician. In *The Jugurthine War* Sallust decries the rapacious nature of the luxury-seeking, post-Carthage Roman aristocrats who had succeeded their more frugal, more noble ancestors: "When they conquered a foe, they took nothing from him save his power to harm. But their base successors stuck at no crime to rob subject people of all that those brave conquerors had left them, as though oppression were the only possible method of ruling an empire."[168] This is a lower-born Roman castigating wealthy Romans for "taking everything," to paraphrase Reg, yes, but Carl Richard points out an irony: Sallust had himself been a provincial governor (not unlike Pilate) in North Africa, and had enriched himself and his family greatly, and at the expense of the people of his province.[169] Richard goes on to mention that this narrative—earlier Romans were "province looters" who needed to be tarred as such—"had apparently grown so popular as to be employed by all factions," no matter its degree of accuracy. Reg calls his occupying Romans province-looters, having "taken everything" from Judea. Another Roman historian, Tacitus (56–120), will use similarly larcenous language, cursing the "savage and hostile" emperor Domitian (b. 51): "Rome of old explored the utmost limits of freedom; we have plumbed the depths of slavery, robbed as we are by the informers even of the right to exchange ideas in conversation. . . . Fifteen whole years . . . taken from us . . . so many of our best years have been taken from us."[170] The unpopular Domitian would be assassinated in the year 96. But Reg gets second-guessed by his own colleagues, and immediately; Sallust and others read back across history for their useful if not always completely accurate narrative, and second-guessing waits well into the future.

This cry was also heard loud and long in two specific political arenas of postwar Britain, *viz.*, the rising cost of maintaining the Welfare State, and potential British membership in the European Economic Community. In the first, Anthony Crosland's[171] rosy visions of just what Britain could be—given the proper application of socialist principles—began to collapse as Britain's economy sputtered in the late 1960s and into the 1970s. The increasing influence of organized labor after about 1957[172] meant that every government—Labour, Conservative, or coalition—had to bow to the Trades Union Congress, encouraging reduced competition, protectionism, restrictive practices,[173] and the fever dream of "full employment." British industry fell behind the often more austere but forward-thrusting economies of France, Germany, and Japan. Funding universal health care and social security could be accomplished in times of a robust and *continually* growing economy;[174] an overheated or stagnant economy meant existing commitments to funding still had to be serviced even as the economy slowed and contracted. The money had to come from somewhere, and this somewhere was the undiscovered country of the income tax:

> This in itself represented a change scarcely less profound than that brought about by the Welfare State which had ensured universal access to medical care and social security. The working classes were not used to paying income tax. Now the great mass had for the first time become taxpayers. In the lowest income bracket the rate they paid was the highest in the world, according to Denis Healey in his 1976 Budget speech. The Welfare State had made us into a nation of taxpayers.[175]

The Pythons had been born into an England recovering from the effects of the Great Depression and then World War II, and in their formative years endured the privations of postwar scarcity as the rest of Western Europe rebuilt across the Channel. The economy's contractions bashing headlong into expanding obligations of this later period was the proverbial turnip trying to give blood it didn't have. Secondly, in the lead-up to Britain's applications and then entry into the Common Market in the 1960s and 1970s, those *against* this foray into the EEC saw the continental agreements as nothing short of a surrender of British sovereignty to anti-Anglo *fauves* in France and market-savvy *Technokrats* in West Germany, and a transfer of sovereign power from Westminster to Brussels.[176] Journalist Peter Jenkins, though not an alarmist, put it bluntly: "There is no denying that a consequence of Britain's accession to the European Community is the loss of some national power."[177] Parliamentary power was being undermined as Britain agreed to "accept the existing rules and regulations of the Community but also agreed to be bound by its future rules and regulations."[178] Existing laws in conflict with EEC laws would have to change, and no future law could be enacted that flouted the EEC. So future British generations of Euroskeptics could echo Stan about everything being taken from "our fathers," but could also add, "and from our children." Jenkins continued, trying to remind voters in the month leading up to the referendum in 1975 that power once given wasn't easily reclaimed: "Power lost in this way cannot simply be said to have been transferred or delegated, or, as some like to argue, pooled."[179] The Romans exercised this kind of "negative power" from far-off Rome, able to make decisions for Judea that could not be counteracted by any legal means, upsetting "Romaskeptics" like the PFJ. Jenkins continues:

> The power of veto within the Council of Ministers [of the EEC, in Brussels], for example, is a negative power, which can be used to prevent decisions against our national interest, but there is no equivalent power for obtaining decisions in favour of our national interest within areas which are the subject of Community decisions and hence no longer within the power of national decision.[180]

It's easy to see how the anti-Europe or even the pro-British voter in Britain might feel completely powerless and dismayed when faced with this apparent arrogation of sovereign power. Even Parliament's powers of taxation took a hit in this agreement, as EEC tax policies rose to the top, by law. (Meaning the tax draw could still bleed Britons white, but those decisions were being made in Brussels, not Westminster.) Many Britons felt afterward they were being ruled by a foreign cabal, and that Britain's best interests were no longer at the forefront of either foreign or domestic policy: "Ever since, many of those among the 8.5 million who voted against, and younger people who share their view, have suggested that Heath and Jenkins and the rest lied to the country, at least by omission," Marr writes. "Had it been properly explained that Europe's law and institutions would sit above the ancient Westminster Parliament, it is said, they would never have agreed."[181] The following forty years has seen an on-again-off-again struggle to claw back some of these powers, culminating in the success of the Brexit Referendum in 2016.[182] Rome never had to worry about soft-peddling or sugar-coating—Roman occupancy was what it was.

A loud voice from the Left against EEC membership was Tony Benn, who, in an open letter to his constituency in January 1975, characterized "continuing membership" as "the end of Britain as a completely self-governing nation and the end of our democratically elected parliament as the supreme law-making body in the United Kingdom." Benn lays out five basic rights the British voter enjoys in their relationship with Parliament, and sees EEC membership as compromising all five, concluding, gloomily:

> In short, the power of the electors of Britain, through their direct representatives in Parliament to make laws, levy taxes, change laws which the courts must uphold, and control the conduct of public affairs has been substantially ceded to the European Community whose Council of Ministers and Commission are neither collectively elected, nor collectively dismissed by the British people nor even by the peoples of all the Community countries put together.[183]

Benn's views on EEC membership were expected, given his position at the extreme left of the Labour Party, where state ownership and/or syndicalism in industry were the highwater marks.[184] Jenkins notes that voices like Benn, Mikardo, Foot, and others *couldn't* have been happy, simply because "the [EEC] is inimical to their brand of socialism," though, Jenkins continues, "their brand of socialism would find itself in conflict not only with the European Economic Community but also with the international trading order of the non-Communist world."[185] The PFJ's brand of freedom is also inimical to both the Roman Empire's and Jewish religious authority's allowances for behavior and unproscribed activity in first-century Jerusalem.[186]

Closer to the hearts of the Pythons (especially Welshman Jones), Welsh rugby football captain Phil Bennett was able to make such a "they've taken everything" declarative as he addressed his team in the run-up to their 1977 match against England, and both the now-fabled text and subtext referenced much more than just sport:

> Look what these bastards have done to Wales. They've taken our coal, our water, our steel. They buy our homes and live in them for a fortnight every year. What have they given us? Absolutely nothing. We've been exploited, raped, controlled and punished by the English—and that's who you are playing this afternoon. The English.[187]

Reg will very nearly quote this speech in the film not many months later. It's fun to imagine what Bennett's response might have been if some player *had* raised his hand and piped in, like Xerxes does to Reg, perhaps asking what England's rugby team had to do with Britain's coal, steel, or housing policy, or to remind Bennett of any one of the benefits Wales enjoyed as a member of the United Kingdom. History and folklore give us nothing beyond Bennett's memorable exhortation, sadly. The following year, however, provides an eerily familiar example of one such awkward moment, also in rugby, and also involving Bennett and teammates, as related in the *Independent*:

> The story dates from [February] 1978, and is counted among the classics. Bill Beaumont, up there alongside Martin Johnson as the most venerated of England captains, was delivering his final dressing-room exhortation before a Five Nations Championship game with Wales at Twickenham. "Right," he fumed, steam billowing from his nostrils. "This Welsh team has had it. The Pontypool front row? Past it. Allan Martin and Geoff Wheel? No good. Terry Cobner? Too slow."
>
> At which point a nervous voice emerged from some dark corner of the inner sanctum. "Yeah, but what about Gareth Edwards, Phil Bennett, Gerald Davies and JPR Williams?" Profoundly flummoxed, Beaumont wracked his second-rower's brain for a suitable response. "For Christ's sake," he said eventually. "Even we're good enough to beat four men."[188]

Beaumont may as well have just barked "Shut up!" as Reg does. In a perfectly Pythonesque ending, Wales wins the match, defeating England (three penalty goals to two), perhaps giving groups like the PFJ false hope in their quest for victory over the oppressor.

STAN: "And our fathers' fathers' fathers' fathers. . . ."—Stan/Loretta is laboring the point, yes, but he's in good company. Taking us back to the football pitch, in one pregame speech Welsh rugby coach Clive Rowlands urged his players to play for more than just their "fathers' fathers' fathers"—he demanded his team "perform 'not just for yourself but for your father, your mother, your long-lost aunt, the miners, the steelworkers, the teachers, the schoolchildren."[189] The list begins to read more like a Python thesaurus sketch than a pep talk, reminding us of the Tourist's rant in *Flying Circus* Ep. 31, or more precisely the Narrator in *Holy Grail* as he introduces Scene 24, and gets sidetracked by bird references. The "list" generally found in a thesaurus sketch in the Python world follows immediately here, as the PFJ remind Reg just how much the Romans *have* actually contributed.

This listing of fathers and grandfathers was also part of Heath's immigration agenda upon taking No. 10 in 1970. "Anti-immigration" had been a key point of contention throughout the recent election, having come to a frothy head after Powell's infamous "Rivers of Blood" speech in 1968.[190] Asian and African immigration had been swelling since the 1950s, with many neighborhoods in cities from Brixton to Bradford to Birmingham experiencing rapid demographical changes. Heath's proposed legislation became known as the Immigration Act, and "removed any right to immigrate to Britain from anyone who did not have a parent or grandparent born in the country."[191] So if potential immigrants could identify British-born fathers or father's fathers, and so on, the new Act welcomed them into Britain. This left thousands of the so-called "detritus of empire"—like thousands of African Asians—in immigration limbo. Opponents made much hay of this restrictive, even racialist language.[192]

Not much later, Sir Keith Joseph's book *Monetarism Is Not Enough* (1976) castigated the postwar consensus governments' (Labour *and* Conservative) attachments to full employment no matter the cost. In the introductory pages Joseph—Margaret Thatcher's mentor, essentially—reels off his own list of Britain's ills under socialist economic policies: "We are over-governed, over-spent, over-taxed, over-borrowed, and over-manned."[193] But Joseph is simply reacting to a list proffered by the Beveridge Report more than thirty years earlier, wherein the hoped-for postwar Welfare State could tick off and then administer the cradle-to-grave needs for all Britons. Beveridge and Bevin were set to guarantee a list of three "pre-suppositions" that would undergird the government's ability to manage the country's needs, including full employment, family allowances[194] (not means-tested), and a vibrant NHS, all funded by taxation. With these pre-suppositions in place, according to Bogdanor, all the remaining social security problems could be dealt with by national insurance, and in return for a single weekly contribution, you would receive a pension, sickness benefit, and unemployment benefit when you were unemployed, and that would apply to everyone—all wage earners, all the self-employed, and their families. So, it was a new unified system, which would cover everyone in the country, in place of the piecemeal patchwork. That this was to be financed not out of taxation but out of contributions was fundamental for Beveridge because he said that was a mark of citizenship.[195]

What the "Great Socialist Commonwealth" was prepared to give to the people of Britain—*while* bleeding them white through, first, taxation and then what Beveridge benignly called "contributions"—was absolute peace of mind: near-guarantees of a job, household allowances, and "free" medical care, as well as lifelong insurance, a pension, and "disaster" benefits in case of illness or unemployment. No aqueducts, but unprecedented largesse, to be sure, and all administered by the so-called "nanny state." Taxes and forcible tribute to Rome helped pay for the administration of the empire, which in turn offered services and protection to her subjects, willing and not.[196] Bogdanor notes that Beveridge's offer to the British people of the former empire wasn't at all voluntary, either. If Britain was to combat "want, disease, ignorance, squalor and idleness," then everyone would have to participate: "[Beveridge] said that anyone who was not prepared to work should be sent to a compulsory re-training camp, and he said that young people who were not working should be given no benefit at all; that they should get trained and get a job."[197] The Britain where the young Pythons came of age (through at least the 1950s) very nearly achieved the dream of a more equal, more safe, and more healthy society, a place where the ingratitude represented in the "And what have they ever given us in return?" phraseology could actually be defensibly argued down. When this socialist Utopia ran up against changing economies brought on by postwar rebuilding, industrial and demographic upheaval, empire-reduction, and the age of technology, however, a collapse was inevitable.

REG: "All right Stan don't labour the point"—Specifically, Rome had only been *directly* involved in Judea for about ninety-six years, given the beginning of Roman rule in Syria in 63 BC. If a "generation" is about twenty to twenty-five years, then Stan's phrasing isn't "labouring" the point, it's actually underscoring how many generations these Jews have endured Roman rule.

REG: "And what have they ever given us in return?"—Meant as an unanswered bit of impassioned rhetoric, what begins here instead is a recitation of the significant contributions of the Roman occupiers to the infrastructure, especially, but also the quality of daily life for the people of Jerusalem. These are the "apparatus" of the "Roman imperial state" mentioned earlier by Francis. The answer to Reg could simply have been *Pax Romana*—the monumental, perhaps ironic, perhaps surprising peace brought by Rome's empire-building acumen.

"Roman rule," Brandon writes, "despite its ruthless enforcement and its often vicious officials, was not intolerable; and, after the sufferings of the initial period of conquest, most peoples settled down and prospered under the *Pax Romana*."[198] "Most peoples," but not the Jews, who would never accept a non-Jewish ruler or worship more than one god. But that's not as funny as a laundry list of the demonstrable benefits of Roman oversight in Jerusalem, followed by Reg's defensive, dismissive "shut up."[199]

In more contemporary terms, the continuing and, to many, humiliating[200] "little brother" relationship—Andrew Marr calling Britain a "junior partner"[201]—with the former colony United States can be discussed here. It wasn't bad enough that there had been for some time popular beliefs that the United States had "saved" Britain during World War II, and that the Marshall Plan after the war *seemed* to favor the defeated as opposed to the allies.[202] (Germany, Japan, and Italy rebuilt and improved while Britain continued wartime rationing, e.g.) In September 1976—when the Pythons were preparing for a November *Life of Brian* writing session and just two months after the official bicentennial celebrations in the United States—the Sterling Crisis came to a head. Inflation and unemployment were rising and seemingly beyond normal controls. Callaghan's Labour government and Chancellor Healy agreed to approach the International Monetary Fund (IMF), based in and greatly influenced by the United States, for a loan. "The purpose of this request," Healey would write in December 1976, "is to support the policies that have been adopted by the government to strengthen the balance of payments and create the conditions in which it will be possible to get both unemployment and domestic inflation down from their present unacceptable levels and keep them down."[203] Healey was asking for an unprecedented £2.3 billion, and only received it by agreeing to £2.5 billion in forced expenditure cuts and the selling of British Petroleum shares. The IMF demanded cuts and accepted no compromises, according to Donoughue, who saw the Americans as willfully, gleefully gouging Labour, forcing them to adopt essentially Tory monetary policies to save the country's economic bacon.[204] Callaghan had been adamant that British lives would not be run by "foreign bankers," an echo of Reg's tirade.[205] By the end of 1976 and on into 1977, there was no room for such high-minded quibbling, and the Callaghan government danced to the tune called by the IMF.[206]

These narrative digressions had become hallmarks of the Python writing style, appearing throughout *Flying Circus* and *Holy Grail*. In Ep. 7 the camera moves away from Mr. and Mrs. Brainsample simply because they don't seem as interesting as Mr. Potter, and the science fiction story can continue.[207] In Ep. 27 the narrative trajectory of *Njorl's Saga* is sidetracked again and again, and in Ep. 37 Dennis Moore's attempted robbery becomes a "botany lesson."[208] In *Holy Grail*, bird-fixated castle guards, Dennis, and The Knights Who Say Ni manage to sidetrack Arthur and his companions throughout the film.

Granted, the Romans as an occupying force would have endeavored to fix things up a bit given their residency status—meaning some/many of these changes would have been necessarily self-serving—but the public works programs alone demonstrate the improving quality brought about by membership (even unwillingly) in the Roman Empire.[209] Reg is trying to make a point about a foreign, authoritarian influence making life miserable for a formerly free and happy people, but the facts of life are going to get in the way. Herod's ambitious building program improved many aspects of life in Judea, improvements the members of the PFJ can't truly appreciate—they're too young. Roman garrisons kept familiar wolves from Jewish doors, something Reg, Francis, and Stan seem to have forgotten.[210] The Augustan Age poet Ovid[211] (43 BC–AD 17) suffered from similar selective memory, according to Richard: "Because he was too young to remember the civil wars, he was also too young to be grateful for the Augustan peace."[212] This is the same time of peace the PFJ's would-be revolutionaries enjoyed.

In postwar Uruguay, a fascinatingly similar "revolution" took place, with entirely unintended consequences. The Tupamaros group went from a political organization to a terror group in the 1960s, fighting against political, economic, and social inequities in a strict but *democratic* government atmosphere. The point here is that they were fighting against an *elected* government, unlike most typical insurrections, especially in Latin America. These young "idealists" remembered their misgivings about their government, but forgot about their rather special place: living in a country that could boast "an unbroken democratic tradition of many decades."[213] The effects of their move to assassinations and kidnappings (including the kidnapping of British ambassador Geoffrey Jackson in 1971) forced the sitting government's hand, according to Laqueur:

> The Tupamaros' campaign resulted in the emergence of a right-wing military dictatorship; in destroying the democratic system, they also destroyed their own movement. By the 1970s they and their sympathizers were reduced to bitter protests in exile against the crimes of a repressive regime which, but for their own action, would not have come into existence. The gravediggers of liberal Uruguay, as Regis Debray later wrote, also dug their own grave.[214]

Reg and the PFJ aren't living in a democratic paradise, of course, but they can't even remember "what the city used to be like" before their oppressors, the Romans, arrived and cleaned it all up. Their disturbing of the hornet's nest simply provided what many such terror groups discovered across the ages, concludes Laqueur: "Terrorism from below produced massive and infinitely more effective terror from above."[215] What the PFJ will get for their anti-establishment and anti-colonial efforts, eventually, is a much smaller (thanks to "martyr" deaths) and likely less politically agitated group that can live a quiet, domestic exile protected by the unshifting "bloody Romans" and their own parliamentary procedure.

This same "What have they ever given us in return?" complaint could be heard from disappointed supporters of both Conservative and Labour governments, and Northern Ireland when Westminster ruled; from Scots dead set on devolution, frustrated Liberal voters, and union members angry at their Party or their representation. The excitement and promises of the 1960s faded in the 1970s as two superpowers moved forward—neither of them Britain. Even the great postwar recovery in West Germany couldn't elicit party feeling from imprisoned revolutionary Ulrike Meinhof, who wrote a letter to fellow RAF member Hanna Krabbe from prison. Meinhof ticks off her version of what's wrong with the rebuilt Germany: "Given the environment in which we are struggling—the postfascist state, consumer culture, metropolitan chauvinism, media manipulation of the masses, psychological warfare, and social democracy—and faced with the repression that confronts us here, indignation is not a weapon. It is pointless and empty."[216] This is the great question likely asked in every British colony as it began to lean toward home rule, and by every revolutionary group remaking words into action.

XERXES: "The aqueduct?"—First, this is a typically Pythonesque moment where something certain or axiomatic is challenged. In *Holy Grail* it was Arthur's identity, kingship, and mission that were second-guessed, and often; later in this film it will be Brian's certainty that what he's painted says "Romans go home"; here it's the assertion that the Roman occupation has provided nothing of value to the Jews. There is an interesting historical version of this, with roles a bit reversed. Suetonius records that the men condemned to fight to the death on

Fucine Lake for Claudius's amusement called out "Hail, emperor, greetings from men about to die!" The emperor, Suetonius relates, "spoilt the effect by calling back 'Or not!'":

> This example of fatuous humour caused a momentary hitch, since the men thereupon refused to fight, insisting that his words had excused them and amounted to an imperial pardon. "Claudius grew so angry that he was on the point of sending troops to massacre them all, or burning them in their ships. However, he changed his mind, jumped from his throne and, hobbling ridiculously down to the lakeside, threatened and coaxed the gladiators into battle."[217]

Xerxes's riposte isn't fatuous but factual, the "hitch" being a narrative hiccup, cured when Reg has listed all the benefits of Roman occupation while still maintaining that such an occupation is intolerable. And Xerxes is right, since water is the lifeblood of these desert regions, and no human settlement would be possible without engineering or simply accessing a consistent water supply.[218] Josephus recalls Pilate's designs for the bringing of "a current of water to Jerusalem," which seems both necessary and practical, but that he accessed "sacred money" for the expensive undertaking, which outraged many in Jerusalem. Jeremias, discussing the industries of Jerusalem, describes the situation: "Next, as a building in the grand manner, the aqueduct built by Pontius Pilate deserves mention," says Jeremias. "Because he financed the project from the Temple treasury, his action provoked a public uproar, and the furious crowd had to be quietened by soldiers with cudgels."[219] The opening of this engineering marvel was one of the special occasions that brought Pilate (and likely his household) to Jerusalem.[220] Josephus is more colorful in his description of this cudgeling, his version arming Roman soldiers (dressed down as local people) with "daggers"; Pilate then signals his men to attack those "boldly casting reproaches upon him," resulting in "a great number of them slain. . . and thus an end was put to this sedition."[221] Jeremias elsewhere points out that this bloody to-do may not have been the Romans' fault, completely. The temple treasury was actually *supposed* to be paying out for maintenance of works like any "water-channel":

> The passage can also refer to the aqueduct mentioned above, p. 14 [in *JTJ*]. If this is true, Pilate, when drawing upon the Temple treasury to finance the project, did no more than punish a neglect on the part of Jerusalem's municipality, the Sanhedrin, by assuming, however illegitimately, the latter's duty. His action would have meant that the Temple money was spent for the purpose for which it was intended.[222]

These water projects brought water for drinking and cooking, for bathing and the cleaning of streets and latrines, and for storage during times of drought or even siege, into cisterns beneath the city.

This ancient construction had been rediscovered and even refurbished during the 1860s, thanks to the ongoing efforts of the Palestine Exploration Fund, whose work continued through the 1870s. These types of finds—long-lost aqueducts, feeder tunnels, cisterns, and even Roman bath houses—were in the news again in the mid-1950s as Masada was explored. By the mid-1960s these kinds of archaeological finds were being used to sell package tours to the Holy Land.[223] (A piece of Pilate's aqueduct itself was brought back to England in 1938 by a Rev. Gentle-Cackett of the Bible Lands Mission Aid Society.[224]) And as recently as 1971, finds like the aqueduct leading from the royal gardens to the Pool of Shiloam were being touted in international newspapers.[225]

Xerxes's question is a reminder that many in the Roman Empire were well aware of the benefits that Roman occupation had forced on subdued peoples, the aqueduct being one that Romans like Frontinus (c. 35–103) held up as the peak of Man's *useful* achievements: "With such an array of indispensable structures carrying so many waters, compare, if you will, the idle Pyramids or the useless, though famous, works of the Greeks."[226] Frontinus, who wrote an entire treatise on Rome's aqueduct system, gives his version of Reg's plaintive phrase: "What have the Egyptians (or Greeks) ever given us?" The answer? Not an aqueduct.

Finally, there is an intriguingly familiar tone to a news article coming from Jerusalem in August 1918. In the course of fighting World War I the British Expeditionary Force had captured Jerusalem from Turkish control in late 1917, and also controlled the Levant by October of 1918. Public works improvements began before the surrounding region was even fully in hand, with an adequate water system the first order of business. In August of 1918 the British press is already trumpeting the overhaul of Jerusalem's water supply and storage capabilities as "a triumph for the Royal Engineers." But what's fascinating is the language used by correspondent W. T. Massey, sounding as if he's a Roman news correspondent covering Pilate's public works programs in faraway Jerusalem: "It is doubtful whether the population of any city within the zones of war has profited so much at the hands of the conqueror as that of Jerusalem. In a little more than half a year a wondrous change has been effected in the condition of the people."[227] He's probably right about the benefits of a clean water supply, though the oft-conquered people of Jerusalem and Palestine may have asked almost immediately, in regard to losing their freedom yet again: "What have the British ever given us in return?" The British would administer Palestine for the next thirty years.

MASKED COMMANDO: "And the sanitation"—In a scene from the very popular 1976 BBC 2 series *I, Claudius*, Derek Jacobi addresses the audience while seated on a toilet, placing Romans and sanitation into the same scene just as the Pythons were writing *Life of Brian*. This first broadcast of the award-winning series appears when the Pythons are deciding, finally, to settle on a Cleese-suggested "Monty Python and the Life of Christ" story, Palin writes, and they are in the midst of a two-month long writing binge as a group.[228] The series would be rebroadcast in June 1978—when the Pythons were going through the entire script for the first time.[229]

Even after the Roman occupation, the disposal of waste in a city like Jerusalem would have been a challenge. There wasn't enough consistent running water to carry away waste, if that had been desired; what little water was available was reserved for agriculture and livestock, human ingestion, and ritual purification. Chamber pots were in use in homes, and then emptied into the streets, often.[230] There were no "Roman luxury latrines" available in Jerusalem, where constant running water would have carried away waste.[231] Toilet seats have been discovered in Jerusalem excavations, according to Koloski-Ostrow, one even found still atop its cesspit at the back of a home.[232] These cesspits would have to have been emptied manually, and the contents taken into the street, then carted outside the city walls and dumped. It's also likely that public urination and defecation in "filthy alleyways" would have been rampant given the lack of public latrines.[233] There would have been a smell, certainly, to a city like Jerusalem.

Recent work has uncovered Jerusalem's first-century sanitation system, information that at least partially belies the PFJ's complaint. An impressive landfill on the slopes of the Kidron Valley, just outside the city walls of Roman-occupied Jerusalem, was the subject of an archaeological dig in 2013–2014:

> It isn't that the people of ancient Jerusalem organized to collectively and obediently throw their dross over the city walls. "It looks like there was a mechanism in place that cleared the streets, cleared the houses, using donkeys to collect and throw away the garbage," [Yuval] Gadot speculates. The system may have developed out of a combination of Roman administrative knowhow and a growing observance among Jews of religious purity norms, researchers theorize. Jews in early

Roman Jerusalem were obsessed with purity and impurity, as shown by the proliferation of *mikvehs* (ritual baths), the frequent use of stone vessels (which were believed to be impervious to impurity) and the near absence of imported pottery. "It could be that it became a norm in Jerusalem that you have to take out the garbage, because it's impure and has to be brought outside the city," Gadot suggests. "It's not the municipality saying so: God says so, and that makes it easier."[234]

The landfill is noteworthy for its carefully layered design, with regular coverings of soil to keep odor under control. Garbage day pickup would have been a smelly affair, of course, with piles of garbage and human waste left in the streets, waiting for collection and transportation.[235] What this suggests is that the city streets may have been even cleaner than Rome's.

But an efficient waste removal system and the presence and even use of public baths wouldn't have helped in other areas of "public health," a term Reg will mention in his summation. In recent studies of Roman-era fecal matter (coprolites), the indication is that Roman practices actually magnified health problems. The incidence and travel of parasitic worms (roundworms, whipworms) and dysentery across the empire is blamed on the Roman penchant for warm baths and the exportation of often uncooked epicurean delicacies, like fish sauce.[236] Higher standards of cleanliness in other areas (like the idea of regular bathing) didn't keep these infection rates from climbing. If the Jews kept to their own foods and their own systems of preparation and purification,[237] they would likely have avoided many of the gastrointestinal issues that many others in the empire had to endure.

STAN: "Remember what the city used to be like"—Likely inaccurate for *all* of ancient civilization, but it's funnier than the facts. It's been noted in many studies that since the ancient Hebrews were religiously concerned about cleanliness, they were likely more clean and healthy than "most":

> The ancient Hebrews were among the earliest peoples to incorporate cleanliness and hygiene into their religious observance and everyday life. Some attribute Moses' upbringing in an Egyptian royal household for his emphasis on the purifying aspects of water. Washing, bathing and cleanliness played a prominent role in the religious rotes of the Jews, and indirectly afforded the people a greater measure of health than enjoyed by most ancient societies.[238]

Sanitary laws, likely Mosaic in origin, had accompanied the Israelites for centuries, and Hasmonean-ruled Jerusalem (the long period before Roman occupancy began) could boast engineered water sources, latrines, and sewer works. The appropriately named "Dung Gate" was the understood exit for the waste of the city, for example, and had been for many years. But Magness reminds us that "the Roman world was a filthy, malodorous, and unhealthy place," and "human waste fouled the streets and sidewalks of even the most advanced Roman cities."[239]

Putting a finer point on it, however, Stan isn't actually old enough to remember "what the city used to be like." Pompey had besieged Jerusalem sixty years or so before Stan or any of the PFJ were born,[240] and Herod is named "King of the Jews" some twenty years after that, signaling the start of his ambitious building and rebuilding of the war-torn city. So many of the Roman improvements to Jerusalem would have been in place or at least underway before Stan was born. Additionally, Ben-Sasson comments that things might have been unusually quiet in the Jerusalem of the PFJ's youth: "But after the first agitation (which occurred in the wake of the first Roman census) had faded out, we no longer hear of bloodshed in Judea until the days of Pilate."[241] The PFJ's collective memories seem to ironically picture a filthy, disorderly, unsafe Jerusalem,[242] but also an understanding that the Romans actually made things better.

This collective, selective memory could be found in the British general public after the war, as well. The privations of the war and the need for united, unselfish action to accomplish victory, at the fronts of battle and home, primed the pump for Attlee's great socialist advancement, the Welfare State. "At that time," Bogdanor says, "socialism was thought to be the wave of the future, and in particular people thought that it was given a great push by the war."[243] From the ashes of the war, and through the careful but complete nationalization of "production, distribution, and exchange," and via the promises of universal health care and social security, capitalist principles would naturally give way to a kind of Socialist Utopia, many thought, and all Britons could live in peace and relative prosperity.[244] A society erected on the "highest instincts of mankind" and "the principles of fellowship" (as opposed to "profit and incentives") falters when the populace feels "bled white," when the restrictions of that society—whether economic or simply anti-individualist—cast the remarkable benefits in a bad light.[245] Again, it would be the realities of the world and specifically Britain's changing status from "empire" to what Bogdanor calls a "second-ranking power" (behind, at least, the United States, USSR, France, and Germany, and soon Japan and China) that would call the tune. Having everything they might need or want couldn't keep need and want—of varying types—at bay, according to Bogdanor:

> The Labour Party has also clearly abandoned its commitment to socialism, at least in the form in which Attlee put it forward. It faced a great problem, which . . . derived from the success of the Attlee Government. A measure of this success is that if you had said to people in the 1920s and 30s that Britain would soon become a society in which there was full employment, as there was in the 1950s, that it would have a National Health Service which was free and open to everyone and universal, that it would have the Welfare State, guaranteeing to everyone a social security minimum . . . they would not have believed you. . . . When it did come about in the 1950s and '60s, people did not think it was utopia, and they wanted different sorts of things, and so the socialist ideal gradually came under criticism.[246]

The success of the Roman occupation meant more comfortable lives for most everyone in Jerusalem; even the perhaps chronically disaffected youth (of the PFJ) found silver linings on every horizon. The sort of utopian society the Romans have offered makes for better living, certainly, but the "different sort of things" the PFJ want—including freedom from oppression—means the Roman rule must also "gradually [come] under criticism." The world wherein the Pythons came of age had bitten the (socialist) hand that fed it, and it's no surprise to see characters in their films doing the same.

REG: ". . . are two things the Romans have given us. . . "—In the mid-1970s the actions of trade unions raised hackles across political lines. With the pound under such pressure, the country having to go to the IMF for a shoring-up, and inflation ticking upward, the major and minor unions continued to press their case for larger increases, wanting to get theirs before a clampdown could be implemented. Voices on the left and right bombarded the newspapers and news shows with opinions about the unions' actions and culpability, so much so that *Private Eye*'s Claud Cockburn dedicated a column to the cacophony. Essentially, Cockburn gives a how-to for criticizing the unions without truly ruffling feathers—organized labor was too powerful to be totally denounced, and politicians and pundits knew it.[247] Cockburn could be describing the stop-go PFJ, as well, their trade union–like revolutionary intentions breaking against the seawall of the Roman occupation:

> Always work both sides of the street. E.g. describe [Trade Union] leaders as Dictators (or Barons) driving their massed dupes into vile actions. But do not hesitate to accuse them also of palsied incompetence: accuse them of being powerless to control the actions of their mass membership. Again, this helps keep the consensus in good fighting order.

> In the same way, make it clear that the [Trade Union] leadership is run by sinisterly cunning doctrinaires Marx-drunk and ruthless in pursuit of evil long-term objectives, and also under the control of bumbling old fogies, ignorant of the simplest facts of modern economic life.[248]

The PFJ leadership is offered to us as both motivated and mealy-mouthed, their minions duped into going on a suicide mission while Reg, for example, stays home nursing a bad back. Reg and Francis do seem to be somewhat Marx-drunk and want to overthrow the empire in months; they are also clearly "ignorant" of the Roman way of life around them, from the benefits of the aqueduct to improved public health. Their rank-and-file remind them, helpfully, of these "simplest facts," and Reg can only answer with a "Shut up!"

The semantic elements of this argument could also very easily be adjusted, and it becomes an attempted diatribe against the postwar and contemporary New Jerusalem in Britain—the Welfare State. By the time the Pythons were in their early adolescence, 1951, "about twenty percent of the British economy was under public ownership," according to Caryl, touching on most of what Reg is allowing the Romans to have contributed.[249] Public health, in the form of a single-payer system (the NHS), access to education for all was increased dramatically, and public works of all kinds were taken fully into government management and control in the late 1940s and into the 1950s. And, Caryl mentions: "It all proved enormously popular."[250] This meant that free market Conservative types like Margaret Thatcher, or middle-of-the-road party men like Labour's Harold Wilson and Jim Callaghan, and even Tory Ted Heath couldn't stop the "consensus" express. When Reg admits to a list of the benefits of Roman occupation—"the sanitation, the medicine, education, wine, public order, irrigation, roads, the freshwater system, and public health,"—he's actually very close to ticking off the existing and hoped-for "freedom-from-want" Attlee-world of the welfare state in Britain.[251] And if the government didn't directly control all of these areas, it was the Labour government's influence (and dependence) on the trade unions to pick up the slack that kept Britain's New Jerusalem chugging forward—frankly right up to 1978–1979, when changes in the world's economy shunted Britain onto a side track, and the great postwar consensus came to a halt.[252]

MATTHIAS: "And the roads"—The Pythons might have had a more firsthand understanding of this example of Roman beneficence. Roman roads in Britain were critical to the invader and, eventually, the invaded: "London first became an important city not only because it was the first convenient crossing place of the Thames, but also because it was the chief modal point of the Roman road system in England."[253] That being said, the Pythons made no attempt to show any Roman-era structure or remains as they made *Holy Grail*. Arthur and Patsy's walk/ride would have been smoother on a paved Roman road, which are still visible in parts of Britain.[254]

In Judea, the King's Highway and Via Maris (or The Great Trunk Road) were major Roman roads during this period, and there were many minor roads, including at least two (one east-west, one north-south) running right through Jerusalem. Travel to and from Rome was made much easier thanks to these roads, as were troop movements between cities in the empire.

REG: ". . . obviously the roads, the roads go without saying"—Now we've heard the three things that, for many, indicate a thriving civilization: running water, controlled sewers, and maintained roads.[255] An admirer of Cloaca Maxima, "Dionysius of Halicarnassus, writing at the time of Augustus in the late first century B.C., mentions Rome's sewers as one of the most magnificent constructions of Tarquinius Priscus," writes Koloski-Ostrow. "In fact, he measures the greatness of the Roman Empire of his day by the sewers, along with Rome's aqueducts and paved roads."[256] The Greek geographer Strabo shared these views, celebrating the Romans (in favor of the Greeks) for "paving roads, laying out aqueducts, and constructing sewers to wash away filth."[257] James Joyce would see not only the benefits of Roman civilization, but bring in the Jews and the British to boot:

> What was their civilisation? Vast, I allow: but vile. Cloacæ: sewers. The Jews in the wilderness and on the mountaintop said: *It is meet to be here. Let us build an altar to Jehovah.* The Roman, like the Englishman who follows in his footsteps, brought to every new shore on which he set his foot (on our shore he never set it) only his cloacal obsession. He gazed about him in his toga and he said: *It is meet to be here. Let us construct a watercloset.*[258]

Modernist Joyce, like the Pythons, manages to reduce the sum total of the Roman Empire to a WC. The helpful members of the PFJ are simply restating what they've likely heard for many years—that Rome has made Jerusalem more livable.

ANOTHER MASKED COMMANDO: "Irrigation . . . "—We don't actually see any irrigation undertaken in the finished film. There is only talk of aqueducts, and we won't see an actual Roman road, either.[259] These are all mentions from a list shared by those who may have studied the Roman Empire in school.[260] More recently, the influx of Jews into Palestine after World War I, while displacing in situ Arabs, was easily rationalized—"everyone would benefit from improved irrigation, medicine and sanitation."[261]

The conclusions drawn about why Britain so convincingly voted to remain part of the EEC in 1975 are germane here. Jerusalem has been under the thumb of Rome for about ninety-six years by AD 33, and it would seem that those so oppressed would have had ample time to be convinced that the situation was intolerable. The following list, a list agreed upon and even added to by everyone in attendance, gives the reasons why the Roman occupation had, for many common Jews, been far better than tolerable. Life was admittedly better in a safe, clean, and well-administered city.[262] For the people of Great Britain in 1975, foreign "domination" at home could be easily explained away: "The truth revealed by opinion polls is that sovereignty as an issue," Marr writes, "did not concern the public nearly as much as jobs and food prices."[263] Marr continues, describing the PFJ's (and the nationalist left of the Labour Party like Benn and Foot, and the right of the Tories, Powell) cabal mentality perfectly: "It may be that sovereignty is always of absorbing interest to a minority—the more history-minded, politically aware—and of less interest to the rest, except when a loss of sovereignty directly affects daily life and produces resented laws."[264] Everyday Britons of the 1970s wouldn't complain about Common Market membership until food prices jumped, but by then it was too late. They had been warned of this outcome, too. Two months before the day of the referendum, the British government had set up an EEC Referendum Information Office, and on that first day (3 April 1975)- hundreds of phone calls came in, most asking about food prices.[265] The vote for remaining in the EEC reached a majority, anyway. Members of the PFJ have clearly had sovereignty on the mind, but they, too, are nearly overwhelmed by all the benefits of being subject to Rome. When the Brexit Referendum emerged in 2016, the issue of sovereignty regained was much discussed, and likely helped carry the day for the narrow "Leave the European Union" victory.

OTHER MASKED VOICE: "Medicine . . . "—There are no examples of Roman medicine offered in the finished film. Spiritual healing is the only healing we see.

Roman medicine was a bit dodgier than a passable road or a watertight aqueduct, but still better than some of the local remedies. The Romans (often from Greek influences) used many medical devices (rectal and vaginal specula, trephination tools, levers for setting bones or removing teeth, probes and catheters), many made of brass and finely crafted. Roman physicians were also better trained in anatomy, thanks to many Greek texts and practice on criminals and dead gladiators. They also regularly employed herbal medicines.

The Jews of first-century Judea, on the other hand, had been taught that illness tended to be a result of God's wrath, punishment for misdeeds or inadequate faith, or as a refiner's fire to make men more holy (think Job). As a consequence, "in ancient Israel, unlike Egypt, medicine as a profession was held in low esteem."[266] God was both the deliverer of pestilence and the true healer: "The fact that Yahweh was regarded by the earlier biblical writers as sole healer . . . accounted in part for the negative attitude toward human physicians."[267] There was probably a better chance that in a Romanized city like Jerusalem at this time, a Jew could seek out medical treatment not generally suggested by the priests, who had God's will in mind.

Caring for the health of the temple priests was the temple doctor, whose practice didn't seem to stretch beyond the vested few:

> He was called upon, not only when the priests hurt themselves in the course of their duties . . . but beyond that had an extensive practice since the priests had to go around barefoot on the flagstones of the Temple floor even in winter time, and so easily fell ill. Even more injurious to their health was their diet, which had a high meat content with only water to drink, as wine was forbidden them.[268]

Jeremias also records that there were doctors in virtually every town in the region, they worked on a fee-paying basis, and were lumped in with the manual laborers of the day.[269]

One noble goal of the British Empire had been for many years "the promotion of public health and morality."[270] This was easier said than done. Conditions in Uganda, Nigeria, and Kenya in the 1930s were poor by Britain's standards, with meager budgets stretched thin paying for local health and education, but more money was being spent than if these countries weren't under Britain's colonial wing. In Africa and the West Indies in the early part of the twentieth century "overall government expenditure on [blacks] was never more than a few shillings per head":

> For the West Indies a Royal Commission set up in 1938 painted an almost identical picture of past neglect: the social services still "all far from adequate for the needs of the population," schools ill-staffed, hospitals impoverished, housing "deplorable," sanitation "primitive in the extreme." In twenty years almost nothing had been done to fulfil what Britain always claimed was her "positive trust" to her colonial subjects: little to justify the claim.[271]

These empire subjects could ask the "What have they ever done for us" question, as well, but the answer might fairly be "Something, at least."

OTHER MASKED VOICE: "Education . . . "—This is one of the "benefits" of Roman occupation for which there is no textual reference in the film, excepting this statement. The only real instruction we see is the Centurion correcting Brian's Latin.

Education for observant Jews during this period would have been reserved primarily for priestly types, and for the wealthy, according to Jeremias. There were scribes and teachers and "academics" in first-century Jerusalem, though few or none dependent on the Romans for their education.[272] Women from wealthier families *could* be secularly educated, being taught Greek, for example, but in all cases "daughters came behind the sons," meaning "their education was limited to learning domestic arts, especially needlework and weaving."[273] "Better to burn the Torah than to teach it to women" was the saying of one ancient scholar.[274] "In every case," Jeremias concludes, "schools were solely for boys, and not for girls."[275] The likes of a Judith would have been few and far between in first-century Jerusalem.

This is one of those comments that seems better suited for the British Empire than the Roman one. Education is seen by many as one of the main successes of the British Raj in India, for example. In a lecture delivered in 1893 in Auckland, the Right Rev. W. G. Cowie laid out the benchmarks of the last forty years of British-run education in India, including the distribution of grants-in-aid, the founding of universities and teaching colleges, and educational opportunities for men and women (in an overtly patriarchal native culture). He quotes the former governor of Bombay, Sir Richard Temple, who pointed out the value of this education, especially in controlling the native population: "Among the educated natives, the first fruit of the new education was an improved standard of rectitude and integrity." Temple concluded: "The men themselves saw that this was the case, and attributed it unhesitatingly to educational influences."[276] These men were educated to be more British than Indian, he seems to be saying, and were thereafter more trustworthy. The Romans admittedly provided the people of Jerusalem with many life-improving projects and services, perhaps even knowing that a healthy, well-fed, and educated subject might actually begin to chafe at the subjection. As presented in the film, the power and will of Pilate and his garrison easily deal with any such eruption. Not so in the actual world of the British Empire. As Cowie concludes his speech, he admits that the British educational program in India is sowing dragon's teeth,[277] but nobly admits there is no other conscionable way:

> It is said that there is a growing spirit of discontent amongst the educated classes from the very course which the Government during the last 40 years have followed for the general elevation of the people. The extending and improving of the system of public education has been described as a suicidal policy on the part of the State. How, it has been asked, can the people of India be expected to remain in contented subjection to a European State, when their rulers, through their colleges, make them acquainted with the writings of Milton and Mill, and other prophets of freedom? How can men be satisfied with an autocracy of foreigners, however paternal, when those who exercise it themselves glory in the representative institutions and the constitutional Government of their own native land? These arguments are not to be gainsaid; and it is to be expected that the discontent of the class to whom I have referred will continue to increase. But the Government must not on that account desist from the course that it believes is to be for the best interests of the people.[278]

The British Empire sowed the seeds of its own destruction as it educated its colonial subjects, and at least some in the empire seemed to understand that from the beginning. The Roman Empire as depicted by the Pythons doesn't seem to be nearly as progressive or inward-looking; Pilate can deal with an educated and enlightened Brian on the cross.

Elsewhere in the postwar, inter-colonial period, education has been seen by scholars as one of the crucial catalysts for unrest in Japan. There the postwar experiment to teach democratic principles and move Japan away from feudalism and fealty to the emperor had a similar effect already seen in the later stages of Britain's empire in India—freer thinking that compounds itself. In Farrell's *Blood and Rage*, he traces the wholesale changes made by General MacArthur to Japan's educational system as part of the occupation after the war. Hundreds of thousands of students who (with their parents) had never considered college and then university were suddenly thrust into the competition for this new path to success. These educational experiences varied from public universities to private, promising more than could be delivered in the rubble of postwar Japan, and disaffected students (those who might feel they were in a diploma mill with no real prospects) formed and joined student groups, which proliferated in the late 1940s and beyond. Farrell points out that these easy pickings were taken advantage of by Japanese Communists[279] (thousands of whom had recently been released from prisons), leading to hundreds of thousands of students and recent graduates who saw a world they wanted to change utterly.[280] The largest and most influential Japanese student association, the *Zengakuren*, was controlled almost completely by the Japanese Communist Party, and its goals and practices aligned with the JCP's as they moved through the 1950s and toward the portentous 1960s.[281] MacArthur had a noble goal: Japanese youth could best recover from their parents' folly and Japan's feudalism by not only becoming educated, but by being allowed to "evaluate critically and intelligently the content of instruction," as well as "engage in free and unrestricted discussion of issues involving political, civil, and religious liberties."[282] This largesse led to the youth of Japan growing into cadres that wanted to not only throw off their parents' oppressions (including imperial fascism), but also the paternalistic Americans who invaded as a spoil of war, and who were, ironically, making this education available.

This is the very kind of outcome that the Romans hoped to avoid by not seeing to the education of the Jews. The insularity and refusal-to-be-governed mentality of the Jewish culture of this time, however, as well as their willingness to self-educate, kept the embers of perpetual revolution fanned anyway.

OTHER MASKED VOICE: "Health . . . "—Where there is a higher degree of cleanliness there tends to be better health, certainly. The fact that there may have been regular waste removal from the streets and an elevated sense of the need for ritual purity—washing with water—means good health might have been more possible in Jerusalem.[283] Hand washing, both before and after meals, a regular practice, may have gone farther than any other routine in keeping people healthy.[284] Also, staying away from undercooked and parasite-laden Roman foods likely helped in overall healthiness.[285] Significantly, Jeremias spends very little time discussing the health of first-century Jerusalemites, likely because there isn't much evidence to draw conclusions. As depicted in the film, the only real threat to a non-Roman's health is Pilate's willingness to decorate crosses.

COMMANDO NEARER THE FRONT: "And the wine . . . "—King and Stager note that the Jews didn't have to thank the Romans for wine, necessarily, since they'd made and consumed it regularly for generations: "Mentioned 185 times in the Hebrew Bible, wine served as the commonly consumed beverage in ancient Israel, since water was often contaminated."[286] Priests, though, "were . . . forbidden wine during their days of duty," and had to drink water only.[287] It could be that the PFJ simply liked Roman wine better, or it's mentioned because the Pythons know Italy as a home to significant wine production, and that wine making and consumption were important to Roman culture and cultus across the empire. Magness notes that the "gentile" Roman wine should have been off-limits for more sectarian Jews, though many Italian amphorae have been discovered in the homes of the Jewish elite. She cites Nahman Avigad, who concludes: "It would seem there have always been more and less observant Jews."[288]

A sort of sideways suggestion that the Romans *did* provide wine (and other necessities) to the Jewish population in first-century Jerusalem can be found in Jeremias, in the section "Local Trade":

> Rabbinic literature provides a further piece of evidence on the chief requirements of foodstuffs in Jerusalem. . . . At the time of the outbreak of rebellion against Rome [three councilors] declared that they would supply the city with food for twenty-one years. The first intended to furnish wheat and barley, the second wine, salt and oil, the third wood. The only omission here is cattle.[289]

Clearly this indicates that the city leaders were concerned about loss of certain foodstuffs should the Romans be driven out, and then lay siege to the city. These were items that may have been produced in and around Jerusalem, but not in sufficient amounts without Roman-protected importations. Francis will conclude this section of the list by saying, in relation to Roman wine: "Yeah, yeah. That's something we'd really miss, Reg, if the Romans left." It looks like they might also "miss" wheat, barley, salt, oil, wood, and perhaps cattle, if the Romans left.[290]

MASKED COMMANDO AT BACK: "Public baths"—Given the Jews' views on modesty it's unlikely that even the Romans were able to build and promote the public bath concept in Jerusalem proper, at least during the first century. There were baths in relation to the temple, Jeremias notes, given that ritual purification was required, and laborers were employed specifically to maintain these baths.[291] As Koloski-Ostrow demonstrates, most Roman cities were expected to have public baths and public latrines; Jerusalem, being a Jewish city occupied by the Romans, seems to be an exception.[292] There have been private baths (and foot baths), and ritual baths (*mikveh*) found in various places in the city, but the clearly "public bath" has remained elusive, according to Levine: "While a number of baths (i.e., tubs) and bathrooms were found in the Upper City—some that even functioned as steam rooms with heating units (hypocausts) beneath the floors—no public bathhouses have been discovered to date [2002] in Second Temple Jerusalem, and none is ever mentioned in any literary source."[293] Levine goes on to say that it's possible the baths have simply yet to be discovered, archaeologically, and/or these bathhouses were so common that they weren't mentioned in writing; but also, such baths might not exist because the Jews of Jerusalem did not embrace the more public version of bathing that Romans (and others) did.[294]

After the destruction of Jerusalem in the early 70s, the rebuilding around the new Hadrianic "Aelia Capitolina" (c. 135) *did* see the erection of Roman public baths, likely by and for Rome's Tenth Legion. This would have occurred about one hundred years after the events depicted in the film. Aelia Capitolina was a Roman-built city sited squarely on the remains of Jerusalem, and would be known as such for almost five hundred years.

This is also one of the ironies that is turned back on itself upon closer inspection. In the scene, Reg is being politely gainsaid by his siblings, who are helpfully pointing out the *positive* aspects of the Roman presence in Jerusalem (and by extension, in any occupied city where public works would/could be erected). This ironic but factual stream of thought can't be denied or second-guessed—it can only be shunted by a very Cleese-like, "Shut up!"[295]

The other penny waiting to drop is the implication that thanks to the advent of public baths, the "sanitation" and "public health" of the city and its inhabitants have concomitantly improved—this is clearly accepted as a given by the assembled PFJ. As Mitchell points out much later, however, the typical Roman public bath (had there been one in Jerusalem to enjoy) would likely have been an initially refreshing but ultimately foul place, with perhaps predictable health consequences. Mitchell sounds positively Reg-like, at least for a moment:

> Despite their large multi-seat public latrines with washing facilities, sewer systems, sanitation legislation, fountains and piped drinking water from aqueducts, we see the widespread presence of whipworm (*Trichuris trichiura*), roundworm (*Ascaris lumbricoides*) and *Entamoeba histolytica* that causes dysentery. This would suggest that the public sanitation measures were insufficient to protect the population from parasites spread by fecal contamination. Ectoparasites such as fleas, head lice, body lice, pubic lice and bed bugs were also present, and delousing combs have been found. The evidence fails to demonstrate that the Roman culture of regular bathing in the public baths reduced the prevalence of these parasites.[296]

Again, there's no indication that the PFJ are a "Jewish" political or religious group (in fact, they style themselves as a terrorist cell who hate the Romans "a lot"—that's all), though they may be, and perhaps are a more sectarian "splitter" like the Essenes, or Jewish political group like the Zealots. (Brian does make sure he mentions that his last name is "Cohen," meaning he at least thinks they are cousinly Jewish rebels.) In either case, the PFJ's use of the very Roman (pagan) public baths isn't a given, and they'll fight this religious or political intermeddling as they would anything else offered by their occupiers. Perhaps what Reg (or Cleese and the Pythons?) is really saying is that what once appeared as a positive aspect of the Roman occupation—the improvement of public works and public health—has instead further afflicted the people of Jerusalem.[297] Any colonized peoples could and have voiced similar concerns. The British tended to build schools and roads, bridges and railways, hospitals and sewers wherever they planted the Union Jack, but those improvements didn't keep the people of India, Malaya, or Palestine from feeling subjugated and disenfranchised.[298] The PFJ have fallen prey to what Koloski-Ostrow calls the "old view" of Roman life:

> While some work has begun to explore the nature of hygiene and the quality of living conditions in ancient Rome, an old view persists, established over the last hundred years and propagated by a number of scholars, even those writing on Roman medicine. The argument states that the very presence of sewers, public latrines, baths, and aqueducts in the city must reflect a serious Roman concern for health and hygiene. Because the notion seems so logical to our modern, Western, sewer-lined outlook, it has been perpetuated.[299]

The Pythons grew up during this "hundred-years" time of propagation, so their view that the Roman way of life must have been a cleaner, more orderly life is understandable. Except for Reg as leader of the PFJ. Reg is the standard-bearer for the movement, and he can't let the realities of a better daily life de-yellow his jaundiced views of the Roman Empire. He is the production team of *The British Empire* (1972) documentary that can cast into a harsh light the failings, inadequacies, and "petty atrocities"[300] perpetrated by the well-intentioned empire, demanding an answer to an Anglo version of "What have the Romans ever done for us?" (The insulted viewers and letter writers are Xerxes and friends who raise timorous hand to rebut.)[301] What have the Romans done for the people of Jerusalem? The answer, as Mitchell points out, could have been that the Romans provided whipworm, roundworm, and dysentery. Characteristically, the Pythons are talking as much about themselves as they are about the Jews and Romans. The arguments made during the Pythons' lifetimes to support and defend British imperialism were quite similar—after all, India has benefited immensely from its British-built railway system, bridges, and manufacturing industries, hasn't it?[302]

STAN: "And it's safe to walk in the streets at night"—The level of safety provided by the Romans is estimable and even supportable: "The condition of things was the same for the Romans of the second century of the Christian era. To the period of war had succeeded the period of organization. After having conquered the world, Rome 'pacified' it."[303] This wouldn't be true between about 68 and 70, when the Holy City was under constant siege by the Romans from without. Inside the city, sicarii assassins crept through the streets at night, ready to knife anyone suspected of being a Roman sympathizer or who might be willing to surrender the city or even "make peace."[304]

FRANCIS: "They certainly know how to keep order. . . they're the only ones who could in a place like this"—This is one of those many moments in the film where the Pythons are commenting on both Jewish history and contemporary British events. First the Jewish reference. Smallwood would have agreed with Francis—"in fairness to the procurators it must be admitted that governing Judaea was a tough proposition"—but it wouldn't be until *after* the year 50 that the series of procurators and their understaffed Roman garrisons began to have regular trouble keeping order."[305] Eleven years after the events depicted in the film, the façade of order begins to crack: "The story of the period 44–66 is largely the story of the progressive breakdown of law and order throughout the province."[306] This disorder would lead to Jerusalem's destruction by Roman troops in 70.

Quite a bit earlier than the film's setting, in 133 BC, King Attalus III of Pergamum died, leaving no heir. A longtime ally of Rome, Attalus III "left his kingdom to Rome," Richard writes. "Fearing a popular revolt when he died, he knew that the Romans would maintain order. . . ."[307] This was likely a good part of the reason that many regions later also welcomed Roman control, according to Kotker:

> But wherever Roman legionaries went, they established order and the rule of Roman law. Where before there had been squabbling city-states, constantly at war with one another, princes murdering their brothers to gain thrones, petty monarchs vying for a few square miles of land, pirates terrorizing the sea lanes, and highwaymen robbing travelers, there was now peace and safety. . . . Most of the conquered nations accepted Roman rule.[308]

But order could be illusory, or at best short-lived, especially in Jerusalem: "It is no wonder that the constant threat of messianic risings and brigandage made the procurators so nervous that they were perhaps over-severe when they had to face trouble," Smallwood writes. "Then a vicious circle was created: Roman severity inflamed Jewish nationalist antagonism to Rome, and this in turn led to fresh disturbances for the Romans to suppress.[309] These same prefects and procurators also had to deal with Jews fighting with Samaritans and Gentiles and Greeks, and with other Jews—a tall order, the PFJ know too well. Smallwood continues:

> The Jews' peculiar combination of what the ancient world regarded as fanaticism on both the political and the religious planes made them extremely difficult to handle, and even from Josephus' pro-Jewish narrative it is clear that they were often in the wrong and were responsible for disturbances, and that when trouble occurred the fault did not always lie with the Roman administration.[310]

At the heart of Britain's colonial influence in the Middle East, the Balfour Declaration in 1917 had acknowledged the rights of Jews in Palestine, just after the McMahon-Hussein agreements had already quid pro quo given the nod to *Arab* control of Palestine if the Arabs rose against the Ottoman Empire during World War I.[311] Schneer writes of the contested Declaration: "Because it was unpredictable and characterized by contradictions, deceptions, misinterpretations, and wishful thinking, the lead-up to the Balfour Declaration . . . produced a murderous harvest, and we go on harvesting even today."[312] It seems that neither Turks nor Brits, Arabs nor Jews could control "a place like this." By 1948, the British-administered Mandatory Palestine was moving into history, and the British Empire was growing smaller and smaller.

The specter of "ungovernability" was everywhere in 1970s Britain. Jenkins notes, for example, that crime had been on the rise since the Pythons' youth:

> The increases in crime which was the cause of such anxiety was real enough, even when allowances are made for increases and changes in the reporting of crimes. Violent crimes had turned sharply upwards from the mid-1950s and rose steeply through the 1960s. Reported crimes against the person increased from 38,000 in 1969 to 95,000 in 1979.[313] The rise was especially alarming among young persons.[314]

Starting with the coal miners' wresting control of the country's narrative in 1972 and leading inexorably through the eruption of punk music and violence and the events of the Winter of Discontent—to many, Britain seemed untethered and ungovernable.[315] After about 1968 the latter term appears hundreds of times in British newspapers, often referring to various banana republics,[316] but increasingly—as the 1970s move on—to Britain herself. There was even talk of a kind of palace coup in May 1968, when several leading figures—a newspaper baron, his editor-in-chief, a former chief of the Defence Staff, and the government's "chief scientific adviser"[317]—gathered to discuss the state of the Wilson administration, the country, and what could be done to effect immediate change. From Marr:

> There is no evidence that the talk of a coup was truly serious, or that the security services were involved, as has been publicly asserted since. Yet the Cecil King story counts in two ways. First, it gives some indication of the fevered and at times almost hysterical mood about Wilson and the condition of the country that had built up by the late sixties—a time now more generally remembered as golden, chic and successful. A heady cocktail of rising crime, student rioting, inflation, civil rights protests in Northern Ireland and embarrassments abroad had convinced some that the country was ungovernable.[318]

Francis sounds as if he could have been the fifth at this May 1968[319] tryst, perhaps ready to offer the Romans as effective rulers. Just a few years later it was Sir Walter Walker, former Commander-in-Chief of Allied Forces Northern Europe, who busied himself in 1974 starting an anti-Communist league, and then—since the country was sliding down the slippery slope—he planned for a kind of civilian standing army to fight long-haired Communism in the form of industrial anarchists in the streets, if and when that became necessary.[320] So many Britons seemed to find this new call for order and security appealing that by September 1974, MP Airey Neaves was speaking out in Parliament about the dangers of such private armies. Neaves, Margaret Thatcher's man,[321] so to speak, worried that the organizations might attract "political extremists" rather than patriots.[322] Sadly and ironically, Neaves would be killed by a car bomb, set by the IRA, on 30 March 1979, while Lord Mountbatten, who *supported* Walker wholeheartedly, was himself killed by an IRA bomb in August 1979. With these types of deaths—targeted and indiscriminate—and continually dreary headlines during the Winter of Discontent 1978–1979, it's easy to see why many in Britain felt discouraged about the future.

Heath and the Tories would famously ask in 1974 "Who governs Britain?" and the answer was not Heath, nor the Tories, and not even Labour (thanks to a hung parliament), but the trade unions. Even that could only last so long. Going hat in hand[323] to the IMF in 1976 meant that the Americans and other international interests were setting the agenda for Britain, fiscally, since she couldn't get her own house in order. Days lost to strike actions ballooned, into the tens of millions by the end of the decade, and even successful strikes (where the union received its increase) didn't improve production; Britain was falling further and further behind:

> It was this level of industrial inertia and the compounded results that would lead to Heath's ousting, a lackluster Labour win in 1974, a torpid mid-1970s that included supplication to the IMF, and the staggering Tory victory in 1979, led by Margaret Thatcher as an organized labor-crusher. As early as October 1970 (just after Labour somehow lost the [General Election]) one former Labour minister opined about the stop-and-go (-and-stop) policies of the party tied inextricably to the labour unions; these policies were "the perfect prescription for keeping Labour out of power through all eternity."[324]

By the time James Callaghan stepped in for Harold Wilson in 1976 the unions were lining up for enormous pay increases, raises that Wilson and Heath before him had tried to stem, and that the overheated economy couldn't possibly afford. This malaise also gave rise, according to Bogdanor, to an increase in "nationalism and protest parties," further diminishing the possibility of single-party rule, and leading directly to Callaghan's inability to re-form a coalition in 1979.[325] Bogdanor continues:

> People were worried about political decline as well as economic decline. Some people felt in the '70s, particularly at the time of the Winter of Discontent in '78/'79, but also in '74, that they were looking into an abyss, that there was something very wrong with the country. Thatcherism was born out of that. It is a British equivalent of Gaullism in France, born out of economic and political decline.[326]

The very real question being asked by many was whether the country could be run without the trade unions' say-so, and had ungovernability by an elected body given way to governance by a self-imposed authority—not unlike a dominating Roman presence in the lives of the Jewish rebels of the PFJ. In an article leading up to the October 1974 election, David Wood asks the question: "Who can govern the ungovernable?":

> Mr. Wilson and Labour ministers have spent most of the week trying to establish their claim that Labour alone can carry Britain through the gathering crisis in conditions of industrial peace. One by one they have come forward to boast that they have yielded all the TUC's demands. One by one they have offered policy prospectuses that anticipate, they hope, the TUC's next demands. In return, the TUC has subscribed to the so-called social contract, although even Labour ministers know, from painful past experience and with the Ford strike before their eyes, that the TUC has neither the constitutional power nor the moral authority to sign a contract of any kind.[327]

It seemed to many that even though Labour had been in opposition since 1970, it was Labour and the trade unions—and more directly the trade unions themselves—calling the shots, since the unions had the power to make things stop or make things go across Britain.

FRANCIS: ". . . only ones who could in a place like this"—This comment elicits a knowing laugh from everyone excepting Reg, whose incendiary moment is being stepped on. They are all agreeing that they can't police themselves. This seems like a particularly English, not Jewish, reference, with the Pythons referring to themselves, and may be most directly connected to the perception of Britain spiraling out of control in the 1970s. In May 1975 American newsman Eric Sevareid famously said that Britain was "drifting slowly toward ungovernability," setting off a firestorm in Britain of denials (from Wilson and friends) and affirmations (from many on the Right). A banner headline in the *Wall Street Journal* had just days earlier proclaimed "Goodbye, Great Britain."[328] For those in the know across the pond, the writing seemed to be clearly on the wall, and on newspaper and monograph pages. Books like Christopher Booker's *The Seventies* (1980), written just as the decade ended, and *From Anger to Apathy* (2007) by Mark Garnett, tend to underscore this bleak assessment. George Bernstein's *The Myth of the Decline* (2004), Andy Beckett's *When the Lights Went Out* (2009), and Black, Pemberton, and Thane's *Reassessing 1970s Britain* (2013), however, push back at these "declinist" versions of history, providing more nuanced explanations of the days' events, drawing conclusions for which banner headlines are ill-suited.

For the Pythons, the evidence of an ungovernable Jerusalem could be found, of course, with a religious body telling the State how to do its business in relation to Jesus, for example, followed by the scourge of the Zealots and the chaos leading up to the sack of the city in

70. Those are historical and defensible examples. Outside their windows in Britain, "order" seemed to be a thing hoped for, without much evidence, to paraphrase Hebrews. The labor-related stoppages put everyone in a bind; inflation cut into spending on all fronts; school-leavers could find few jobs; policemen were caught up in organized crime; the military and Britain's international influence were shrinking; some youth opted for loud music, anarchy, and the dole; the Callaghan government had no leverage and struggled to lead; and, in 1976, Britain's international financial prestige took a gut-punch. And this was all before the infamous Winter of Discontent. These were all historical and defensible examples available as the Pythons wrote and produced *Life of Brian*.

So who are the "only ones who could [keep order] in a place like this"? In reality for the film's setting, Pilate and the Romans effectively and brutally enforced Roman rule in Judea, which is why he is remembered (by Philo and Josephus, for example), and the PFJ grudgingly acknowledge there is no other way. Prior to the Romans coming to stay, the Jewish authorities had for generations[329] managed to maintain order in this overtly religious group, a laudable feat. Many in Britain in the seventies saw the erosion of such authority and accountability in their day as a worrying sign of the times, so it's no surprise to hear about a bleak future, and that some kind of revolution was coming, even inevitable.

REG: "... and public health"—Reg and the PFJ seem to agree here that the coming of the Romans brought all sorts of improvements in their daily lives, and in the life and health of the city. On the surface, it does seem to make sense that improved "sanitation" conditions would improve "public health," but both Mitchell and Koloski-Ostrow (and many others) have since observed the situation conditions as more nuanced. Paleoparasitologist Piers Mitchell discusses the actual *increase* in infection across the empire, thanks to the increased trade (of infested foods) from city to city, and the warm, shared bath waters (which went unchanged for long periods) in the public baths, among other vectors. Sanitary improvements in the city might have, ironically, made life less hygienic. One example cited by Mitchell seems a win-win, but there's a third, darker side. The human waste that was so carefully washed out of the public latrines or scooped from private toilets and cesspits, for example, often was sold and carried straight into nearby agricultural fields as fertilizer. The latrine was then clean, which seems like a win, and the crops were given some much-needed biological nourishment in the otherwise sandy soils, another win. The sandal waiting to drop is an ominous one, according to Mitchell:

> The Romans were known to have used the human feces collected from towns to fertilize crops growing in the fields. . . . This has been shown in modern research to increase crop yields. . . . However, unless the feces are composted for many months before being added to the fields, this can result in the spread of viable parasite eggs to the plants grown. . . . Hence, it may be the use of human feces as crop fertilizer under the Romans that led to an increase in roundworm and whipworm despite their use of sanitation technologies.[330]

So the good intention of keeping a cleaner latrine led to a higher rate of disease, which sounds quite Pythonesque. Reg is perhaps justified in his "Shut up!" then. In this way, the Roman Empire couldn't claim any higher level of hygiene than that found in non-Romanized countries, or even in the supposedly darker early Middle Ages, where *Holy Grail* hung its hat.[331]

REG: "All right. But apart from the sanitation, the medicine, education, wine, public order, irrigation, roads, the freshwater system, and public health—what have the Romans ever done for us?"—A couple of reads here. First, this revision of Reg's diatribe of decline sounds very much like what came to be known as "declinism." The same chord struck by many in and just after the 1970s was that decline had set in, and that everything just got worse and worse. The media had taken up the talking points of the parties, and then the parties recycled the media predictions, and then candidates quote the media, and decline became a reality. Lawrence Black suggests a cultural move from actual decline to just perceived decline, even though this declinism flavored readings of the decade's tea leaves for long after.[332] The helpful terrorists in front of Reg may just be the revisionists who saw the 1970s as more nuanced than the decliners.

Second, this list leaps right off the pages of more contemporary sources, but in relation to the British Empire. The effects of the empire on its colonies and protectorates had been cataloged for decades, positive and negative. The struggles to get and then hold Egypt, for example, were well-rewarded as Cairo's stock exchange flourished under British control, and fortunes were made. Under Lord Cromer at the turn of the century, Egyptian prosperity increased; taxes were reduced; the "administrative and judicial systems" were improved, as were education, tourism, and the telephone system; and "vast irrigation works which nearly doubled the crop area" could be claimed as a result of the British presence.[333] Still, these were only possible with the dominating presence of British troops and administration; strangers in a strange land weren't always welcomed. In Burma, British works—railroads, "public health work, agricultural improvements and so on" completely failed to win widespread public approval; the Burmese remained "a nation of rebels."[334] Further, in India there was a similar story, though to a greater degree given India's place as the "jewel in the crown." Brendon notes that "good government was the raison d'être of the Raj," with Viceroy Lord Mayo listing "Sanitation, Education, Hospitals, Roads, Bridges, [and] Navigation" as the colonizers' accomplishments in just "half a century."[335] British colonial efforts often improved lives, but inevitably destroyed centuries-old ways of life. Reg and the PFJ are citing from the Romans, yes, but also their shared history of the British Empire as taught in grammar schools.

In 1972 a new and fashionably revisionist thirteen-part series, *The British Empire*, aired on the BBC, and the public response was immediate. In April the *Daily Telegraph* printed a series of reactions from outraged viewers.[336] Letters from veterans and socialites came in, as well as historians, journalists, television figures, and even the head of the BBC.[337] Most viewers were certain that producers had decided to focus on only the darkest, least flattering events in the empire's history, undermining entirely the British attempts to make the world a better place. One respondent, Kathleen Wayland, complained about what was "omitted" from the series, particularly those things that *ennobled* the empire and its role, and she provided a helpful list: "Peace, order, justice, schools, communications, public health, growing trade and prosperity."[338] This line was picked up and quoted by the *Telegraph* editorial staff, and was reprinted several times—a laundry list of what was *right* with the empire. It's as if Lady Wayland is quoting the frustrated Reg before he can cinematically say anything.

Reg's acknowledgments and Lady Wayland's aplomb are versions of what British PM Harold Macmillan had famously said in July 1957 in the midst of a long Conservative term of leadership. Speaking at a Tory fete in Bedford, Macmillan reminded the faithful that "most of our people have never had it so good."[339] He cited a robust economy, plenty of jobs, and Britain's high place on the world scene, and predicted a bright and prosperous future.[340] Two years later, voters would seemingly agree with him, giving the Tories an increased majority in the 1959 General Election. The Goons used the phrase—ironically, of course—a number of times during the latter part of *The Goon Show*, especially when the penurious Grytpype-Thynne and Moriarty could be found dining on boiled newspapers, cutlery, laundry soup, or fish bones.[341] Macmillan's point was that with life going so very well after the war and the ending of postwar scarcities, no one—not even the Labour opposition—had the right to complain.[342]

This is certainly an impressive list, but it's not complete. One of the most important allowances the Romans made for the Jews involved religious liberty. If Reg and his PFJ activists are practicing Jews, then they are only such because the Romans decided it was the best way to keep order in Judea. Very little of the film involves Jewish life or rituals, but we have seen a likely representative of the Sanhedrin officiating at a religiously sanctioned stoning that Roman guards allowed. Elsewhere in the empire, Rome reserved that privilege for herself as part of *jus gladii*—the right to take or spare a life. In Judea, the Jewish religious authorities held that power for noncapital crimes (until well into Pilate's prefecture). So Rome went out of its way over the years to not only avoid "religious persecution," but to protect those liberties: "When dealing with the Jews of the Dispersion, it was not enough for Rome just to say that they should have religious liberty," Smallwood notes. "Definite steps had to be taken to ensure that their Gentile neighbours respected that liberty and did not molest them when they exercised it."[343] Julius Caesar and Augustus managed "the details of Rome's methods of protecting the Jews," and later emperors and provincial governors wrote many letters "informing or reminding [cities in the eastern empire] that the Jews had certain rights and were not to be molested in the exercise of them."[344] Ultimately, they could worship as they saw fit, they did not have to participate in the Imperial cult or house soldiers, and were also encouraged, even cautioned (by Claudius) to practice religious toleration themselves. So we can add an eleventh gift (not forgetting "Brought peace") from the Romans to the Jews—religious liberty[345]—and Reg's list becomes more accurate (and more frustrating, to Reg).

Proof that the Python influence continues to be felt, a subheading in the first chapter of Andrew Marr's *A History of Modern Britain* is titled "What the Romans Did for Us."[346] Versions of the phrase have been used in scholarly settings dozens of times since 1979. Without putting too fine a point on it, Marr is aligning the postwar Attlee government with the Roman Empire, suggesting that the influence, oversight, and overreach of both states are comparable. The Britain that the Pythons grew up in may have seemed as controlled and managed by the Labour government as Reg and the PFJ view their Roman occupancy—bled white by taxation and restricted by few choices, but with a list of begrudged benefits that can be ticked off at a moment's notice. All this order and restriction and, yes, safety is seen to dissipate after the advent of the Progressive Society and the long march into the uncertain 1970s. Before all that, the Attlee Labour government

> created the National Health Service. It brought in welfare payments and state insurance from "cradle to grave." It nationalized the Bank of England, the coal industry, which was then responsible for 90 percent of Britain's energy needs, and eventually the iron and steel industry, too. It withdrew from India. It demobilized much of the vast army, air force and navy.[347]

The list goes on, and includes the retrofitting of armament factories to consumer goods production, thousands of new homes, a reworked school system, food acquisition and distribution, fighting Communism overseas, developing the atomic bomb, and it even organized a positive and forward-looking Festival of Britain to cheer weary citizens.[348] This remarkable set of accomplishments was perceived in varied ways, of course. For those who had *never* had access to dental or vision care, the new NHS was a life-changer; for those who feared the influence of government in every financial institution, industry, and mode of transportation, it was far more Orwellian. It's easy to see how the Pythons (and others more conservative) could make the connections to the securely oppressive mantle Rome had draped over Jerusalem.

XERXES: "Brought peace!"—As hard as it might be to imagine, Xerxes's halting suggestion might be as accurate (and even prescient) as anything that's been said, according to Carl Richard, and specifically in regard to our first-century time period:

> For all of its horrible abuses, the system of imperial government established by Augustus [fl. 27 BC–AD 14] created unprecedented security, stability, and prosperity throughout the Western world for over two centuries. In the process it saved the political, cultural, and social heritage of Greece and Rome, which had been threatened by the instability, chaos, and violence of the late Roman republic.[349]

Ironically, the order imposed by the Romans led to peace, making possible the sharing of all the goods (medicine, infrastructure, education) saved from Roman chaos, to the current benefit of Judea and Jerusalem. To this neat syllogism the practical but incendiary (and frustrated) Reg can only say "Shut up!"

This list of Roman contributions to the well-being of the Jewish people having been presented, Reg still isn't ready to acknowledge the Romans' right to occupy Judea. (That won't happen until later, when Reg and the PFJ climb down from their active revolutionary platform, and leave Brian on the cross.) This same buildup and then letdown was happening as the Pythons were writing the film, and it was colloquially known in Great Britain as "devolution." After years of stillborn attempts to get various governments to push through devolution legislation—so that Scotland and Wales could shake off the "occupying" English—the concerned players in Wales and Scotland finally had their referendum on 1 March 1979. But faced with the inevitably challenging changes such a separation would bring, and perhaps because many Welsh and Scottish citizens could tick off their own lists of the benefits of a united United Kingdom—voters acted in a familiar, cautious, way. Wales defeated the proposal by a four-to-one margin, while Scottish voters, slightly more than half, voted in favor. Even so, the minimum 40 percent threshold for voter participation was not reached, and both devolution efforts failed.[350] Similarly, given the opportunity to finally and with prejudice denounce the Roman Empire and its right to occupation, most of the PFJ demur, grateful for the sanitation, education, roads, medicine. . . .

REG *(scornfully)*: **"Peace, yes . . . shut up!"**—Cool-and-officious-but-easily-frustrated Cleese characters often erupt this way, including in Ep. 11 of *Flying Circus*, where Dove (Cleese) shouts off-camera at his wife to "Shut up!"[351]

> Cleese's characters often try and control their environments by resorting to this (shutting off or shouting down opposition), including the nervy interviewer (Ep. 1), the ex-RSM (Ep. 4), the psychiatrist (Ep. 13), Praline (Ep. 18), Jim the TV commentator (Ep. 20), and so on. On *The Goon Show*,[352] "Shut up, Eccles!" had become a catchphrase, while Minnie Bannister and Henry Crun often shouted "shut up" to each other.[353]

In the penultimate sequence of *I'm All Right Jack*, when Stanley is on trial for inciting to riot, Mr. Kite's daughter begins to cry. Mr. Kite tells her to "Shut up!", and then tells his wife the same, and the proceeding moves on, both women back in their place.

The Reg of the outside world, Reg Birch, Maoist union executive, also found that his colleagues, even those on the far left with him, didn't always (or even often) see eye to eye. Birch regularly locked horns with Hugh Scanlon and John Boyd,[354] men on the left and right of the AUEW leadership, respectively, and would even vote against what might be considered leftist orthodoxy, precipitating the PFJ's version of parliamentary trade unionism:

> [This] may also explain why, on occasion, Mr Birch has voted in solidarity with Mr Boyd, rather than his natural, if more orthodox, left-wing colleagues. Indeed the voting record of the AUEW's executive would show some very strange alignments. *All of which points to the danger of attempting to import the standards of conventional parliamentary politics into analysis of the trade*

union movement. It can only be misleading and, in the case of the AUEW, destructive of serious analysis. Consider, on any single trade union question there are at least three answers. Because most leading trade unionists are first and foremost trade union patriots, they will divide in all sorts of ways depending on their own experience and estimation of the interests of the union. Even the allegedly disciplined battalions of the [Communist Party] have found themselves on different sides on a number of occasions.[355]

The PFJ is attempting to function as a terroristic parliamentary trade union—Carlos meets Mr. Kite, essentially—and the results will be as jumbled and unsatisfactory as might be expected.

Instantly everyone leaps into various ill-concealed hiding places—It's clear immediately that in this room and in the small city itself there would be very few places to hide. Josephus and his coconspirators were able to hide in the tunnels and caverns beneath Jotapata, though the Romans likely could have waited them out, eventually forcing them to appear, as evidenced by Josephus's own description of the vain hopes of other "tyrants" and "robbers":

> So now the last hope which supported the tyrants, and that crew of robbers who were with them, was in the caves and caverns underground; whither, if they could once fly, they did not expect to be searched for; but endeavored, that after the whole city should be destroyed, and the Romans gone away, they might come out again, and escape from them. This was no better than a dream of theirs; for they were not able to lie hid either from God or from the Romans.[356]

The anti-Roman prophets and Zealots had wisely made their homes in the caves and wastes of the deserts. What the PFJ won't be able to appreciate is the challenge of urban terrorism, since for contemporary terror operations, "the main scene of the action was in the countryside."[357] The South and Central American (and even Asian) guerrilla groups of the 1950s and 1960s realized very quickly that the countryside offered myriad hiding places and friendly enclaves, while the city offered something else entirely: "Castro and Guevara were firmly convinced that the city was the 'graveyard' of the revolutionary freedom fighter."[358] Brian will later be clapped on the shoulder and taken into custody near his home, in a populated section of the city.

REG: "What went wrong?"—This pessimistic tone *should* have been what the wet PFJ and most revolutionary groups kept on hand for their inevitable failures, but even collateral, accidental success breeds optimism. The terror forces who managed to assassinate their way into power in 66 and 67 in Jerusalem built on that accomplishment by sending forces to attack the Herodian fortresses at Jericho and Machaeros.[359] Those smallish garrisons were routed, and victories claimed for the Jewish rebels. The sideways victory for Reg, and thanks only to Brian's graffiti skills, is used as the springboard for the next and more ambitious assault, the attempt on Pilate's wife. The Jewish rebels of 66–67 were able to claim victories and justify more actions and more bloodshed. In other cities, Greeks and Jews began killing one another, the Greeks "settling old scores" against the Jewish minority, according to Smallwood, and anarchy reigned.[360] The temporary "breakdown of Roman authority" in the region—after procurators fled but before Roman troop reinforcements could arrive—led rebels to the fatally optimistic conclusion that Rome's days in the region were numbered.

The "What went wrong?" paranoia is also endemic to the period of the film's production, and is found on both sides of the Atlantic. Reg and the PFJ hide their anti-Roman sentiments—they meet in small numbers, keep to themselves, shout in darkened garrets and whisper in the streets—because they do indeed "know the penalty" for sedition.[361] But this paranoia is also without, in the world beyond the film; and as is so often the case, the outside world informs the world of a Python film.[362] The immediate period leading up to the writing and filming of *Life of Brian* coincided with one of the most infamous revelations in modern political history, the Watergate affair. Palin records and comments on many of the names and events from Nixon's administration, right through to his jubilation at the Watergate investigation results, Nixon's resignation, and the prison sentences for those involved in break-ins and cover-ups.[363] The Nixonian paranoia crept everywhere during these years, finding its way into many Hollywood films—*The Conversation, The Parallax View, Three Days of the Condor, All the President's Men*, and others—and the depths of secrecy and paranoia of Nixon's administration, and especially Nixon the man, had only become more apparent as the subpoenaed White House tapes emerged.[364] It's no surprise, then, that the PFJ want to whisper their anti-Roman epithets when in public, hide as they plot and plan, and eventually distance themselves from their man for crimes originally committed in "solidarity."

Jenkins discusses a recent book on American political paranoia by Richard Hofstader,[365] and the definitions ring quite familiar, especially remembering Reg's very recent laundry list of complaints the Roman occupiers:

> The conspiracy is always "gigantic" or "vast"; the message is always apocalyptic; it is always a turning point; time is always running out. The enemy is firmly ensconced in high places; usually he controls the press. The paranoid is often a pedant. "The enemy, for example, may be the cosmopolitan intellectual, but the paranoid will out-do him in the apparatus of scholarship, even of pedantry." Paranoid literature tends to begin with defensible assumptions but proceeds, through amassing facts or what appear to be facts, towards an overwhelming proof of the conspiracy and a total, or final, solution of the crisis brought about by conspirators.[366]

Reg has facts and proofs of the Romans' ill intentions, and to a certain extent he also has history on his side—we know that the Roman Empire imposed and dominated where it would—but his seemingly iron-clad argument is undercut by his own admissions of the upside to occupation by Rome. It's conspiratorial without being a conspiracy. The occupation is assisted by many conspirers—Pilate and his demands for obedience, willing Roman soldiers, turncoat Jews like Ben who take the Roman side, everyday Jews and Samaritans who simply want to get on with their lives, and ineffective radical groups like the Judean Peoples' Front (suicide on demand), the Campaign for Free Galilee, and the Peoples' Front of Judea.

JUDITH: "The first blow has been struck . . . "—Most radical groups began their terror activities modestly, like the Angry Brigade, who fired discriminately at an embassy, and then followed up with a printed communique explaining why. The previously unknown Sons of the Occupied Territories started bigger, taking a plane and then blowing it up. "Terrorism is the strategy of the weak," Dobson and Payne write, "and historically the only successes of this form of war are recorded when the aim is precise and the conditions right":

> That is the point about terrorism. The planning of an act of violence involves so many different interests that there is no telling where it will lead, or what the final result will be. The process starts with a man, or group, fired by a political objective and by the belief that it is a good and necessary one. It cannot be achieved through argument and the conventional means of persuasion. The opposition is too powerful and too entrenched. So a short cut has to be taken. The zealot, often neurotic and self-obsessed, never pauses to reflect that perhaps his aim is unreasonable, and unacceptable to a majority of other citizens. So he and his group take the fast road marked terrorism. When other people become involved in organisation the consequences cannot be contained, even if the original objective is gained.[367]

The use of this kind of dangerous, threatening message—as near a manifesto as the Romans are to get from the PFJ—is critical to the revolutionary *modus operandi*, according to Demaris.

Describing the significance of Carlos's propagandistic missive read out over Vienna radio during the OPEC conference ordeal, "in an age of instant communication [1975], propaganda is now a *sine qua non* of terrorism."[368] Similarly, the PFJ have announced their presence and intentions with "letters ten-foot high"; their "spectacle" will be the raid on Pilate's palace.

JUDITH: ". . . in letters ten-foot high!"—Size and height actually did matter, according to Cook, in Roman-era signage as today:

> The height of the letters in the first line indicates in part the function of the text as an advertisement to those who could read about the promised spectacle. The words of the greeting from Cuniculus to Lucceius are .08, .05, and .04 meters high respectively. The letters in the second line of the inscription are .09 meters high and those in the third line are .075 meters high.[369]

Clearly spectacle is the key, the spectacle of the advertisement, as well.

This idea of watching and spectacle could have been influenced by the media coverage given to seminal events of 1972—the Munich Olympics massacre and the siege of Asama Sams in Japan. In the latter episode—where a handful of Red Army terrorists held off hundreds of police for more than ten days—it's been estimated that television coverage of the tragic event reached 90 percent in Japan, a record that still stands.[370]

He flashes a brief look of alarm at FRANCIS, then returns to his revolutionary authority—This is Reg's first exhibition of his "stop-go" nature. In Britain the twin specters of pressure on the pound and inflation kept the economy unsettled through the 1950s. With so many overseas defense commitments costing so much money—as Britain attempted to keep its irons in the fire alongside superpowers America and Russia—the domestic situation was bound to be volatile. The answer tended to be a sporadic, fitful one, hence "stop-go": "Defend the pound and Britain's global self-image or let it fall and help Britain's exporters?" Marr writes. "'Stop-go' saw sudden tightenings of fiscal policy, then a stab on the accelerator, as government tried to break into a new era of growth, before slamming on the brakes to deal with the resulting surge in inflation."[371] Reg will flash hot, whipping up his siblings with revolutionary fervor, only to draw up short when action is imminent or actually accomplished. He has given Brian a "job" to perform, then regrets the too-bold assignment; he will send Brian and the rest of the PFJ to assault Pilate's palace, but will keep himself behind the lines (he has a bad back); and he will later boldly lead the surviving PFJ through the busy streets of Jerusalem to mark Brian's crucifixion. There, he will put the brake on again, reading out a proclamation rather than saving Brian from his fate.

As will be discussed later, there was often concern in these revolutionary groups that successful actions against strong imperialist aggressors could lead to devastating reprisals. There were also members of these groups who were only interested in civil disobedience and change through accepted channels, drawing the line at violence. Here, the PFJ and especially Reg (who hides the longest, and seems most surprised at any achievement) have no idea that their "little job" given to the acolyte Brian would have a positive effect—it was absolutely a shot in the dark. In his last term as PM, Harold Wilson knew the feeling. In 1974 the Wilson Cabinet had endured a particularly subfusc meeting at Chequers[372] discussing the faltering economy. Chancellor Healey had joked about Britain becoming a Third World country, perhaps only as a member of OPEC (North Sea oil being the impetus for this "joke"), but Foreign Secretary Crosland wasn't laughing, maybe better understanding the "relative decline" in Great Britain that could allow for such a thought. As industrial productivity fell quarter after quarter, union demands rose, and real buying power dropped, Crosland admitted that the government truly had no answers: "All we can do is to press every button we've got. We do not know which, if any of them, will have the desired result."[373] The PFJ are in a similar boat, struggling against the unshiftable Roman Empire, willing to try almost anything but with no certainty anything tried could work, no matter how much will was involved.

REG: "Oh great, great. We need do-ers in our movement, Brian"—Britain's own Angry Brigade performed acts of more theatrical violence, including gunfire aimed at buildings, bombs planted to damage property, and bold manifestoes. There seems to have been quite a bit of talk, though, according to Gerald Priestland, reviewing a new book:

> And according to Gordon Carr's new book *The Angry Brigade*, the so-called Stoke-Newington Eight . . . would sit round debating "the violence of the production line, of the high-rise flat, state violence perpetrated on people in their everyday lives." All of which is dangerous nonsense.[374]

At some level Brian's message on the wall is propaganda. It is a message directed at the Romans, but meant to influence and encourage the Jewish people to join the PFJ's cause. Revolutionary groups engaged in this kind of innocuous propaganda often, in graffiti, leaflets, booklets, manifestoes, and eventually (and most effectively) for the television cameras. A short propaganda film made by/for the Japanese Red Army (and the PFLP) describes the war in Vietnam as the ultimate example of imperialist aggression against a smaller, more worthy foe.[375] This is the kind of message that Reg would have liked. The fact that the "propaganda machine" of the United States can't sell the war as one that is justifiable, and that many Americans are taking to the streets in protest, is just what groups like the Red Army need:

> This is propaganda, our propaganda. Propaganda is action and struggle. That is the only supreme form of propaganda. However, that action has to be supported by firm solidarity with various leftist parties, factions, and by the revolutionary propaganda system. Regardless, the basic is armed struggle by the masses.[376]

Another example: In early 1972, just months after the arrests of the Angry Brigade members at a flat in Hackney, a handmade pamphlet was published by the Stoke Newington 8 Defence Group. The pamphlet laid out what had happened during and after the arrest of the "brothers and sisters" of the Brigade, denied many charges brought by prosecutors, and then offered a list of the oppressed peoples' charges against the State, not unlike Reg's list earlier.

REG: ". . . there is not one of us here who would not gladly suffer death to rid this country of the Romans once and for all . . . "—The Python world is full of these mock epic moments, where a deflation or deflection undercuts the solemnity. In *Holy Grail*, Prince Herbert's father is talking up the kingdom:

> This deflation is a borrow from the mock epics of history—the whole of *Don Quixote* . . . or Pope's *Rape of the Lock*, where a bit of snipped hair is the cause of great turmoil, Swift's "Big-endian" civil war of *Gulliver's Travels*, and Dryden, Gay, and Fielding, et al.—and from their own sketches, including "*Njorl's Saga*," "Restaurant Sketch." . . . Herbert's father is talking grandly about lands and inheritances and the future, like any medieval lord; Herbert can only see the draperies.[377]

Reg here sounds like many of the Irish patriots on the eve of the Easter Uprising in 1916, especially the sanguine Patrick Pearse, who spoke rhapsodically about the glories of dying for the cause.[378] More recently, factions of the Japanese Red Army purged its ranks with the capture, torture, and execution of its own members and sympathizers whose "ideological fervour" was found to be "insufficient." Contemporary news reports pegged this fratricidal death toll at twelve in 1972, leading to a police hunt and epic standoff over ten days in February 1972.[379] This is also the first moment where we know of the PFJ's intent—to throw off the colonial yoke of the oppressor. This aligns the PFJ more with nationalist, liberation groups like the IRA, ETA, and Eritrean People's Liberation Front, and less with the Red Army Faction or Japanese Red Army, or even Britain's Angry Brigade.

COMMANDO: "Uhh, well one"—In the West German RAF and 2 June Movement circles there were those who did not share the full commitment to shedding blood, and especially the killing of innocent bystanders; they were known as *Aussteiger*, or "drop-outs."[380]

REG: "Oh yeah. There is one. . . but otherwise we're solid. Are you with us?"—So there's one member of the PFJ not ready to give his life to the cause, and Reg will miss the slog through the hypocaust due to a bad back. The various unions represented in *I'm All Right Jack* were also "solid," according to Mr. Kite, as they held out against management's unreasonable production demands. The only "one" on the outs ends up being Stanley himself, even though he's willing to work, and even work "not very hard" if that's more suitable.

Perhaps surprisingly, after all the atrocities and declarations and fanatical determination demonstrated by Japanese United Red Army members, commitments could wane. A married member of the URA, Yamamoto Junichi, had actually brought his wife and child to the communal hideout in December 1971, and, since he "acted just as an ordinary husband to his wife . . . and not as a revolutionary," he was soon suspect. Under interrogation he was revealed as having only a "third party interest" in the revolution, and was tortured and killed.[381] In August 1975 other members of the faction were able to take fifty-two diplomatic hostages in Malaysia, then force the Japanese government to release imprisoned URA brethren from Tokyo-area prisons. The terrorists had demanded, by name, seven of their incarcered URA colleagues, and the Japanese government quickly capitulated, fearing another Lod Airport-type massacre.[382] Five of the imprisoned terrorists were released and readied for transport to Malaysia (thence to Kuwait or Lebanon, e.g.), but two others balked. One claimed to be too ill to leave Tokyo, and the other, Hiroshi Sakaguchi,[383] "indicated he preferred solitary confinement in Japan to the uncertainty of finding asylum with his comrades."[384] It's possible that the horrific events of February 1972, when the more militant members of the Red Army (including Sakaguchi) tortured and killed a dozen less enthusiastic (or just ideologically divergent) members—leaving many bound to trees to freeze to death in the harsh Japanese winter—had soured the revolutionary wine for these two former zealots.[385] Even the seemingly indomitable Fusako Shigenobu, who masterminded the JRA's activities for much of the 1970s from the Middle East, realized there were limits to terrorist activity successes. After the arduous bargaining that had to be done to successfully complete a hostage-taking operation at the French embassy at The Hague in September 1974—the ransom demand had to be reduced, and international terror figure Carlos also had to weigh in to keep negotiations with the French and Dutch moving forward—Farrell describes the operation "as a bit of a comedown," and a lesson: "Shigenobu had come to realize that as a terrorist group the JRA had to depend on others for some kind of support. While there were many Japanese leftist sympathizers in Europe, *not everyone was willing to fight or die for the cause*."[386] In the silly world of Python, a third-party interest from a revolutionary doesn't mean expulsion or death, and even a bad back can trump anti-imperialist fervor.

REG: ". . . you shall be called Brian who is called Brian"—This Brian is clearly meant to be a new man, at least in relation to the revolutionary *Geist der Zeiten* of the early 1960s. Postcolonial revolutionary and writer Frantz Fanon argued that the dominant national bourgeoisie could be overcome by a strong, decentralized peoples' political party that effectively educates: "The purpose of political education is to invent souls."[387] The peasant stock must be educated and formed into new men and women,[388] Burke notes, and Fanon's version of this new political party sounds a lot like Reg's PFJ:

> The party now becomes nothing less than the mechanism that will create the new man; his appearance will mark a new beginning in the history of mankind. This new man—political man—is the creation of the intellectuals. Is it totally an accident that just where Fanon is being the most straightforwardly descriptive, we suddenly find ourselves plunged into his utopian dream of the revolution?[389]

Brian the *political man* is invented here, and he is ready to embark on his admittedly utopian challenge to the dominant power structure, the Roman Empire. Like Fanon, as well, Brian, Reg, and the PFJ have "seriously underestimated the staying power of the national bourgeoisie."[390] According to Burke, Fanon didn't take into serious account the connection between the ruling class and the military, something Reg and friends should have been able to see clearly given the constant presence of Roman soldiers at every event we see, on the streets, and in the market place. Fanon was primarily focused on the plight of the underrepresented peasant classes of North Africa (and then Africa) where, coincidentally, the Pythons shot *Life of Brian*.

But the Pythons immediately undercut the idea of the "new revolutionary man," which should be expected, given their *modus operandi*. Instead of assuring Brian of his anonymity—crucial to his task of enacting revolution, according to anarchists and nineteenth-century Russian terrorists—Reg and friends double down on his Brian-ness, naming him "Brian Who Is Called Brian." Certainly not understanding that "the use of a pseudonym was an expression of liberation from all private and individual attachments," the PFJ instead underscore Brian's identity as the Brian the Romans will be looking for, essentially guaranteeing his arrest and execution, and even martyrdom.[391] And in a perfectly Pythonesque twist by the end of the film, Brian's notoriety is the reason he will be sent to the cross (he *is* recognized as the Brian who raided the palace), and his anonymity the reason he won't be saved from the cross (he *isn't* recognized as the Brian who was sentenced to death). Even the centurion who arrested him, twice, won't recognize the Brian we know to be Brian. He will be a martyr, still, at least to Judith and the PFJ, since they seem to be certain he is Brian, "the whole purpose of [whose] life and death is nothing but a last will and testament for generations to come."[392]

Finally, when *Dogs of War* mercenary Bob Denard completed the successful coup in the Comoros Islands in 1978, he took citizenship there, converted to Islam, married a local, and became known as Moustapha M'Ahdjou.[393] Sounds like a Brian dream.

REG: "Tell us about the raid on Pilate's palace, Francis"—The Pythons have aligned the PFJ with the revolutionary spirit of the times (the postwar and postcolonial years), but just a few years earlier and in Palestine, no less, similar work was afoot. Mentioned earlier, the Lehi freedom fighter group had formed in 1940 to push the Zionist cause, publishing their nationalist intentions to use terror "as proof of our war against the occupier. . . . It is not aimed at persons, but at representatives, and is therefore effective. And if it also shakes the population out of its complacency, so much the better. Thus and for no other reason, the battle for liberation shall commence."[394] The PFJ's war is against "the occupier"—theirs is a nationalist fight—and they've chosen Pilate's wife as a de facto representative of that occupying power. In scenes edited from the final film Pilate's wife is a grotesquely large woman, and quite capable of defending herself. Had this scene remained, the audience's sympathy for her would likely have been diminished, and the topical commentary regarding ideologically similar terror groups being their own worst enemies would have been lost. Either way, though, violence would have accompanied the attempted kidnapping scene, embracing what Burke characterizes as the best known and perhaps least understood conceit of Fanon's *The Wretched of the Earth*: the efficacy of violence. Burke notes the collective adoption of the book's myths by radical groups, including "the liberating force of violence in the anti-colonial struggle," this adoption occurring without the understanding of Fanon's larger, later argument, that "violence, while it may be an understandable response to colonial domination, is far from being an adequate one."[395] It's as if the budding terror cells stopped reading after Fanon's first chapter, missing the necessary "howevers" across the balance of the book. The PFJ will "raid" Pilate's palace and then "kidnap" and even "cut" Pilate's wife; the palace and the prefect's wife are manifest representations of the oppressors—Pilate and the Roman Empire—and allow for, according to Burke, "an escape from the colonial stalemate. The way out is through violence. Because the system was established and perpetuated through violence, it must be destroyed through violence."[396] This act of violence will lead to reprisals, of course, to an increased level of vigilance and violence on the part of the colonizer, which will in turn make the oppressed more agitated, which will escalate to an ultimate act of violence in the form of a crucifixion.

Notes

1. Offshoots from or just sycophantic cadres loyal to Italy's notorious Red Brigades terror group, mentioned earlier. There were also internecine struggles within these, between those who sought world-wide revolution, and those who had come to enjoy the killing (Burleigh, *BRT*, 217).
2. *Private Eye*, 22 July 1977: 8; see also Burleigh's chapter 6.
3. *Private Eye*, 22 July 1977: 8.
4. Brandon, *Jesus and the Zealots*, 55.
5. Delivered at Chippenham on 11 May 1968. The now infamous "Rivers of Blood" speech would be delivered at Birmingham just over a month later. See www.enochpowell.net.
6. Jenkins, *Anatomy of Decline*, 32.
7. The "conviction politics" of Thatcher, Michael Foot, and the modern two-party system will be discussed in some detail later, after the fiasco at Pilate's palace.
8. From the television documentary *Baader-Meinhof: In Love with Terror* (BBC, 2002).
9. From the BBC film *Baader-Meinhof: In Love with Terror*. Some of the Pythons will continue this study of so-called freedom fighters waging a war against an oppressive regime. In Gilliam's *Brazil*, a terror group has been setting off bombs for thirteen years as they fight the all-seeing Ministry of Information. Margrit Schiller would spend much of the later 1970s in prison.
10. Reproductions of these original maps and plans were part of the large museum exhibition installed in 1976–1977 at the Royal Academy of Arts, Piccadilly. See the *Pompeii AD79* book published in 1977 by Imperial Tobacco. *Private Eye* lampooned this exhibition in their 26 November and 10 December 1976 issues.
11. *BRT*, 123.
12. Bogdanor, "Collapse of the Postwar Settlement," a.t.
13. Bogdanor, "Collapse of the Postwar Settlement," a.t.
14. See Donoughue, Sandbrook, and Marr.
15. "The Situationist International," *Times Literary Supplement*, 3 September 1964: 781. During the mid-1970s the term "situation" popped up in coded, progressive speech relating to education, literature, white collar crime, the arts, and politics—so maybe the Situationists had more influence than imagined—and *Private Eye* even dedicated a section to lampooning these "situational" moments of high pseudery in 1976–1977.
16. "The Situationist International 1957–1972," *Sunday Times*, 9 July 1989: 1.
17. Facial hair is discussed earlier in relation to the stone and beard salesman.
18. "Facial Hair's Formative Years," *Telegraph*, 11 November 2014.

19. *JE*, "Beard"; see also the entry for "Shaving."

20. Quoted in Brandon, *Jesus and the Zealots*, 33–34.

21. Josephus, *AJ*, 17.10.5 (Whiston, 271).

22. Brandon, *Jesus and the Zealots*, 29.

23. Roller, *The Building Program of Herod the Great*, 97.

24. Most of Rome's provincial governors (or prefects, procurators) have been lost to history, so knowing just a little about Pilate is a boon. Historian Jona Lendering and the information at Livius.org are very useful for summaries of the characters and main events of this period.

25. See the entry for "Other Evidence" under "Pilate" at Livius.org for the most up-to-date information. Years of scholarship about Pilate have come to these same open-ended conclusions.

26. Another borrow from *I'm All Right Jack*. During the melee on the TV show, a large woman is counting her ill-gotten money when someone tries to grab them. She socks him on top of the head.

27. *BRT*, 206.

28. In the only mention of Pilate's wife in the Gospels, sans name, Pilate ignores his wife's warning and gives in to the chief priests. See Matthew 27:19.

29. Quoted in Iviansky, "Individual Terror," 49. This "centre," according to Iviansky, went beyond the targeting of a leader, whether a tsar or king or general, to that leader's most vulnerable points—family, friends, supporters, and on. This transition in thinking about the efficacy and employment of violence helped many anarchists and syndicalists (of the nineteenth century) rationalize the throwing of bombs into "soft targets" that included cafes (Carlos would do this), storefronts, and popular hotels. See Iviansky and Laqueur, *Terrorism*, for more.

30. Iviansky, "Individual Terror," 49.

31. Iviansky, "Individual Terror," 50.

32. *BRT*, 207. Aldo Moro will be branded with this epithet as justification for his kidnapping and killing in 1978.

33. Iviansky, "Individual Terror," 50–51.

34. Horsley, quoting Thomas Thornton, in "The Sicarii," 440.

35. Horsley, "The Sicarii," 439.

36. Horsley, "The Sicarii," 440.

37. Laqueur, *Terrorism*, 79.

38. Laqueur, *Terrorism*, 60.

39. Marighella was a Brazilian, a Marxist revolutionary who, after a series of robberies and kidnappings, was killed by police in São Paolo in 1969. His *Minimanual* has been photocopied and reprinted thousands of times, and used by virtually every revolutionary group mentioned in these pages, from the SLA in the United States to the Red Brigades, JRA, RAF, and the Provisional IRA.

40. Marighella, *Minimanual*, 62.

41. See the index in Larsen, *MPFC: UC*, "transactions," for many more unsuccessful transactions ("Dead Parrot," "Cheese Shop," "Argument Clinic," e.g.) in the Python world.

42. PHS, *The Times Diary*, 14 October 1970: 10.

43. "Murder as a Political Act," *Times*, 19 October 1970: 11.

44. "Argentina's Unlikely Guerrillas, *Times*, 25 May 1971: 12; see also "Death of a Guerrilla, *Economist*, 25 September 1971: 45, and "The Cult of Political Violence," *Illustrated London News*, 31 October 1970: 9. These terrorists and their activities occupied many column inches across this period.

45. Demaris, *Brothers in Blood*, 348.

46. *Eyewitness 1970–1979*, "Sir Geoffrey Jackson," a.t.

47. Hearst was arrested in September 1975, convicted in March 1976, and began her sentence in May 1978; the story was front page news for almost three years as the Pythons discussed, wrote, and then shot *Brian*.

48. See https://www.fbi.gov/history/famous-cases/patty-hearst.

49. Horsely, "The Sicarii," 441.

50. Quoted in Horsely, "The Sicarii," 441. Ananias was a high priest.

51. Farrell, *BRJ*, 93–94.

52. "Guatemalan Abductions Warning," *Times*, 10 March 1970: 8.

53. *Punch*, 11 March 1970: 381.

54. "The Man Who Fell Off the Earth,'" *Daily Mail*, 16 December 1974: 14.

55. "Kidnap Envoy Died after Bid to Escape," *Daily Mail*, 17 February 1981: 10–11.

56. See the entry for the ELF in Newton, *Encyclopedia of Kidnappings*, 98. The group would also kidnap three Brits in 1976, holding them five months ("Rebels Treated Us Well," *Daily Mail*, 6 October 1976: 18).

57. "Hearst Food Plan Altered to Meet Kidnapper's Demands," *Times*, 12 March 1974: 6.

58. The Christian Democratic Union of Germany, a conservative political party.

59. "Lorenz, Peter," in Newton, *Encyclopedia of Kidnappings*, 174; "The Angry Young Terrorists Who Shocked a Nation of Violence," *Daily Mail*, 3 March 1975: 4.

60. "The Fatal Flaw of Ulrike Meinhof," *Times*, 10 May 1976: 4.

61. "Red Army Faction," in Newton, *Encyclopedia of Kidnappings*, 244.

62. Four British-owned planes had been hijacked, all overseas, prior to this incident. See "First UK Hijacking: Questions Raised," *Flight International*, 16 January 1975: 57. Bernard Donoughue reports that PM Wilson stayed up all night following the negotiations with the hijacker, "directing the hijack affair till midnight." Donoughue concludes: "It ended successfully and he apparently enjoyed himself enormously—just like a schoolboy" (Donoughue, *DSD*, 1.275).

63. Demaris, *Brothers in Blood*, 229.

64. "Now Free Our Friends," *Daily Mail*, 7 September 1977: 4; "Schleyer, Hans," in Newton, 265.

65. *DSD*, 2.235.

66. See Orsini and Node's *Anatomy of the Red Brigades* (2011) and Catanzaro's *The Red Brigades and Left-Wing Terrorism in Italy* (1991) for more.

67. A Vermeer had been stolen three years earlier in Brussels, with the ransom demand asking for relief monies to Catholic charities serving East Pakistani refugees ("Waiter Charged with Theft of £1M Vermeer," *Times*, 8 October 1971: 6).

68. See also "Fear for £1M Painting Grows," *Times*, 26 February 1974: 3.

69. The Provos-affiliated Price sisters were being held in Brixton prison for their roles in a car bombing at the Old Bailey in 1973. See Demaris, *Brothers in Blood*, 364–65.

70. "Review of Security at Kenwood Promised," *Times*, 25 February 1974: 2.

71. *DFBE*, 414.

72. Discussed later in relation to Palin's characterization of Pilate.

73. Marr, *HMB*, 257–60.

74. *HMB*, 259.

75. "Britain in the 20th Century," a.t. This speech (part of the famous "End of the Beginning" speech) can be found in its entirety at the Churchill Society website. The war and postwar period saw the complete dismantling of the great British Empire—the "pink bits" on most period maps, Hitchens calls them—from India and Palestine through the Suez Crisis and Rhodesia. See Hitchens's chapter "The Pink Bits" in *The Abolition of Britain*.

76. Bogdanor, "Character of the Postwar Period," a.t.

77. Cited in Bogdanor's lecture. There is also a very interesting article from the Marxist journal *The Militant*, titled "Labour's Programme—1964–70 Disaster was a Warning," by Ted Grant, which also identifies the postwar Labour Party's overly optimistic reliance on weakness and vulnerability in the capitalist system.

78. As in the person of Dennis the Peasant, as seen in *Holy Grail*.

79. Quoted in Bogdanor's "Character of the Postwar Period," a.t.

80. See Bernstein, *Myth of Decline*, 61–62.

81. "Collapse of the Postwar Settlement," a.t.; italics added.

82. Laqueur, *Terrorism*, 8.

83. Beveridge, *Beveridge Report*, 6.6.

84. Philip Zec, *Daily Mirror*, 4 November 1942.

85. The Arab Rejection Front was comprised of or supported by "the PFLP, the PDFLP, the PFLP-GC, the Arab Liberation Front (Iraq), and the Popular Struggle Front. . . All were against the plan [for peace with Israel]" (Demaris, *Brothers in Blood*, 188).

86. Demaris, *Brothers in Blood*, 8.

87. Demaris, *Brothers in Blood*, 80.

88. Wheen, *Strange Days*, 147. See all of chapter 6 in Wheen's book for more.

89. *MPFC: UC*, 1.255–56.

90. *MPFC: UC*, 2.117.

91. *ATW*, 1.16.212.

92. Wiedemann, *Emperors and Gladiators*, 77.

93. *ATW*, 1.15.198.

94. Brandon, *Jesus and the Zealots*, 97.

95. Brandon, *Jesus and the Zealots*, 97n2.

96. See Carr, *The Angry Brigade*.

97. Carr, *The Angry Brigade*, 71–72; also a more complete collection at The Anarchist Library. At the end of this first communique, the Brigade couldn't promise to be as careful if Britain continued to "assist" France in the fight against Basque separatists—the threat of physical harm was there.

98. Secretary of State for Employment Robert Carr, Attorney-General Peter Rawlinson, and Metropolitan Police Commissioner John Waldron—all targets of Angry Brigade attacks in 1970–1971. Also found as part of "Communique 5," The Anarchist Library; "Bombing at the Home of Attorney General," *Times*, 28 January 1971: 1.

99. See the entry for "cut all her bits off" for more on this gruesome ordeal.

100. Bernard Donoughue was in the US capital during this time, and he comments about the events (*DSD*, 2.158–59). Demands included the release of men who had allegedly killed family members of the leader of the assault, Hamaas Khaalis, and the destruction of the movie *Mohammad, Messenger of God*, which they saw as sacrilegious. See "Terrorists Threaten to Behead Hostages in Washington Siege," *Times*, 11 Mar 1977: 1.

101. Part of what is allegedly a French New Wave film, *Le Fromage Grand*, à la Godard, where the imperialist "violence inherent in the system" is juxtaposed with the violence of everyday life (*MPFC: UC*, 2.349–59).

102. See the entries for those episodes in *MPFC: UC*, volumes 1 and 2, for much more.

103. *ATW*, 1.15.195.

104. Cricketer Grace appears as the face of God in *Holy Grail*, for example.

105. *MPFC: UC*, 1.240.

106. This is the time-honored resolution to most terrorist outbreaks. "There is no known case in modern history of a small terrorist group seizing political power; society usually tolerates terrorism only so long as it is no more than a nuisance," Laqueur writes (266). The flare-up is doused by authorities with a level of force that exceeds anything the terrorists could manage, often followed by increased oppression. Following the Quebec attacks Trudeau's government cracked down brutally on leftist groups, while in California the FBI ran SLA members to ground, killing most of them. Israel's reputation for revenge after the Munich massacre became legend.

107. Marighella, *Minimanual*, 61–62.

108. IRA communique, 28 August 1979; Wharton, *Wasted Years*, 235.

109. "The Carnage: Despair or a New Resolve?" *Guardian*, 28 August 1979: 14.

110. Leviticus 21:17–24.

111. *AJ*, 14.13.10 (Whiston, 307).

112. Kotker, *HLTJ*, 123.

113. *Times*, 23 November 1973: 6.

114. "Yard Testing 'Vermeer' Piece," *Times*, 7 March 1974: 1.

115. Smallwood, *JURR*, 154.

116. Horsley, "The Sicarii," 438.

117. See scene 16, the "Hiding with the PFJ," later for more on the Lod attack.

118. Fisk, Robert. "Spectacular, Ruthless Terrorists," *Times*, 5 August 1974: 5.

119. Wharton, *Wasted Years*, 235.

120. Lampooned in *Flying Circus*, Ep. 39.

121. "World of Theatre," *Private Eye*, 24 June 1977: 6.

122. The film's torturous existence is discussed in the book *Soon to Be a Major Motion Picture* by Theodore Gershuny (1982). Tynan is referenced in *Flying Circus* Ep. 21.

123. *Pompeii AD79*, 56.

124. The hardwood is in good company—there are coconuts and orangutans in *Holy Grail*.

125. This was in response to the Jews in Jamnia destroying an altar built by "heathens" to honor Gaius. See the entry for "Caligula" in the *JE*.

126. Brandon, *Jesus and the Zealots*, 85–86.

127. "Terrorists Raid OPEC Oil Parley in Vienna, Kill 3," *New York Times*, 22 December 1975: 59. For details of the raid and demands, see Dobson and Payne, *The Carlos Complex*, 89–123.

128. *DSD*, 2.94; "No Arms for South Africa," *Times*, 29 October 1970: 8.

129. Larsen, *BAFHG*, 19; Palin, *Diaries 1969–1979*, 602. Also further left than Cleese, Palin is upset when Nixon beats McGovern so easily in the 1972 presidential election (*Diaries 1969–1979*, 96).

130. "Unions and Downing Street Talks," *Times*, 28 June 1973: 1.

131. *Times*, 28 June 1973: 1.

132. "A Tight Squeeze under the Bed," *Times*, 4 February 1974: 12.

133. PHS, "The *Times* Diary: Britain's Black Revolutionaries," *Times*, 20 February 1974: 14.

134. At this time the Pythons were working on varied individual projects, and trying to get financial backing for *Life of Brian*. See Palin's *Diaries* for spring 1978.

135. Brandon, *Jesus and the Zealots*, 32.

136. Not unusually, these demands included the release of jailed JRA members, a significant cash ransom, and safe passage to a friendly country. See *BRJ*, 186–91.

137. *BRJ*, 190.

138. "New Guerrilla Group Says Hijack Was Revenge," *Times*, 27 July 1973: 6.

139. In October 1977 Lufthansa Flight 181 was commandeered by the PFLP, the goal being the release of RAF members in German prisons. All hostages were to be killed if demands were not met. A raid by a West German counterterrorist unit rescued the hostages and ended the standoff.

140. *Germany in Autumn*, a.t.

141. *DFBE*, 243.

142. *DFBE*, 269.

143. *DFBE*, 295.

144. *BRT*, 137.

145. "'Grapes of Wrath' Hint for Healey," *Telegraph*, 14 December 1976: 1.

146. *MPFC: UC*, 2.59.

147. See "A B Foods' Attack on Price Controls," *Times*, 15 July 1978: 19; "Bled White as Sellers Take Over," *Sunday Times*, 10 January 1971: 54; "Stop Drift from 'Grey' Areas," *Telegraph*, 11 October 1969: 19, respectively.

148. "Friedman Warning on 'UK Road to Disaster,'" *Times*, 30 November 1976: 1.

149. "Majority of 14 for Labour's Bill to Intervene in Industry," *Telegraph*, 19 February 1975: 7.

150. Mannix, *TAD*, 5. This is simply an old (Dickensian) phrase referring to the pallor of flesh when an animal (or human) had lost a great deal of blood; it is not a racial-tinged phrase. It simply means the giver has given so much he can no longer give. There are racial phrases in the film—"You're a real Jew"—which do carry flip or negative connotations.

151. Geoffrey Smith. "Scottish Nationalism Now Commands More Than Courteous Boredom," *Times*, 22 October 1974: 14.

152. *DSD*, 2.257.

153. Dobson and Payne, *Carlos Complex*, 209.

154. Dobson and Payne, *Carlos Complex*, 209–10.

155. Sartre in Fanon, *The Wretched of the Earth*, lv.

156. Dobson and Payne, *Carlos Complex*, 210.

157. Remember that novelist Forsyth listed the absolutes for a successful coup, the last one being a workable substitute for the dictator being deposed.

158. *BRJ*, 72–73; italics added.

159. Dobson and Payne, *Carlos Complex*, 168.

160. Laqueur, *Terrorism*, 13–14.

161. In *Holy Grail*, King Arthur also cites his lineage and justification for claiming kingship. His battle is equally hopeless, as his claims are never recognized outside of his small band of followers (*BAFHG*, 169).

162. Laqueur, *Terrorism*, 13–14.

163. From Fanon's *Black Skin, White Masks*, 201.

164. Laqueur, *Terrorism*, 137.

165. Laqueur also points out that these assumptions were actually "highly arbitrary" (169), since the social and economic situations, to name just two potential areas of frustration, varied from culture to culture and across time. In a moment, Reg's entire foundation for the use of such violence will be undermined by his comrade's reminders of the benefits of Roman occupation—another frustration that Reg and the PFJ must deal with.

166. Laqueur, *Terrorism*, 39–40; also *BRT*, chapter 3. Heinzen was more like the gingered-up Reg—he retired to domestic life in 1860 New York, and died quietly in 1879.

167. And, in the case of Carlos's takeover of the OPEC meetings in Vienna, dramatically read out over the state's public radio waves.

168. Quoted in Richard, *WWAR*, 176.

169. *WWAR*, 176.

170. *WWAR*, 181.

171. Crosland was a Labour minister, the author of the influential *The Future of Socialism* (1956), a former Treasury Secretary. He was Foreign Secretary at the time *Brian* was being written. Crosland will be discussed later, in the "'He's Not the Messiah' (Panto)" scene.

172. Following a wave of redundancies in 1956, national strikes involving shipbuilding and engineering unions in March 1957 led to significant increases in trade union membership among younger, formerly disinterested workers, and also to more energized, even "radicalized" unions, including the Amalgamated Engineering Union (AEU) and the Transport and General Workers' Union (TGWU). Governments began to deal with these large unions as partners, not constituents, the bad fruits of which wouldn't fully ripen until Callaghan's administration, 1976–1979.

173. Bogdanor discusses this period in his lecture "The Collapse of the Postwar Settlement, 1964–1979," looking at events that set the table for Thatcherism.

174. Tories had envisioned a minimum annual growth of 4 percent, while Labour (specifically under Wilson) expected more. The fly in the ointment was the sobering reality of recent history:

> There was one very small problem with the four percent growth rate: we had not achieved it since mid-Victorian times. . . . Wilson said four percent was far too unambitious and the Labour Party would have a much higher rate of growth. As I said, the rate of growth in the 1960s was lower than the 1950s, and economists did not know how to secure it. ("The Collapse of the Postwar Settlement," a.t.)

175. Jenkins, *Mrs. Thatcher's Revolution*, 9.

176. See, for example, Jenkins's discussion in "At the Head of the Queue for Collapse" in *Anatomy of Decline*, 73–77. Britain was also being told that EEC membership would require a step away from the embrace of the Americans, which sent a Cold War shudder through many.

177. Jenkins, *Anatomy of Decline*, 74. Jenkins wrote this article in May 1975, less than one month prior to the referendum where 67 percent of the British electorate voted to remain part of the EEC. Conservatives tended to vote for membership as almost a bloc, while Labour was fractured badly, many voting against. See Williamson's "The Case for Brexit."

178. Jenkins, *Anatomy of Decline*, 74.

179. Jenkins, *Anatomy of Decline*, 75.

180. Jenkins, "At the Head of the Queue for Collapse," *Anatomy of Decline*, 75.

181. *HMB*, 349–50.

182. During the time this book was being written, the Brexit referendum was organized, voted, and reacted for and against; then put into limbo by a High Court ruling confirming Parliament's role in its implementation; finally Royal Assent was given to the bill on 16 March 2017. Article 50 was signed by PM Theresa May on 29 March 2017.

183. "Anthony Benn on the Common Market," *Spectator*, 18 January 1975.

184. *BAFHG*, 94–160; also *BAFHG* index under "Tony Benn" and "syndicalism/syndicalist."

185. Jenkins, *Anatomy of Decline*, 77.

186. Palin devotes a handful of paragraphs to his thoughts on the referendum, seeing it as one of the few national subjects that crossed party and class lines in positive ways; he votes "Yes" (*Diaries 1969–1979*, 238–39).

187. Reprinted in the *Telegraph*, 9 March 2006.

188. "Rugby Union: Welsh Caught in Time Warp," *Independent*, 4 February 2005.

189. Quoted in *Seasons in the Sun*, 512.

190. See *MPFC: UC*, 1.88, 90, 290, and 375 for Powell references; also *BAFHG*, 277–81, for more on contemporary immigration issues in Britain.

191. *HMB*, 321.

192. See Pitchford, *The Conservative Party and the Extreme Right, 1945–1975*, 193–94. *Private Eye* also covered this rather shameful course of events, bringing the episode back into public view as Callaghan was preparing to take office following Wilson's surprise resignation in March 1976 ("Julian's Caesar," 2 April 1976: 16). Asian immigrants would be at the forefront of the Grunwick strike later.

193. Joseph, *Monetarism*, 19. This was delivered as the Stockton Lecture in 1976, and available at the Margaret Thatcher Foundation website, http://www.margaretthatcher.org/document/110796.

194. Money paid directly to families for each school-age child (excepting the eldest child), and which was initially set at five shillings per week.

195. "Character of the Postwar Period," a.t.

196. Roman taxes are mentioned in a *draft* version of the *Brian* script, in relation to the questions to Jesus about appropriate tribute to Caesar (Matthew 22.17, Mark 12:14, and Luke 20:22).

197. "Character of the Postwar Period," a.t.

198. Brandon, "The Zealots," 632.

199. *WWAR*, 43–44, 101–2.

200. Donoughue calls it both a "national humiliation" and "a prime example of a Cabinet government operating at its best" (*DSD* 2.5). The latter comment reads understandably like he's putting a good face on an otherwise bad situation.

201. *HMB*, 9.

202. American Secretary of State Dean Acheson credits PM Attlee with admitting that the United States had indeed "come to our rescue in the war," so this opinion may have been quasi-official (*HMB*, 25–26). As for the distribution of Marshall Plan funds, Great Britain had actually been given almost $3.2 billion in European Recovery Program aid after the war, *more than any other single country*. Britain's Welfare State demands during the same period and the "total war" had exhausted the country's strategic reserves in every way.

203. "1976 Sterling Crisis Details Made Public," *Financial Times*, 9 December 2005.

204. *DSD*, 2.108.

205. *DSD*, 2.39.

206. Bernstein sees Callaghan's handling of these negotiations, as "masterful," given the initial IMF demands (*Myth of Decline*, 264–66).

207. *ATW*, 1.7.84

208. See the index entry for "narrative disruption/transgression" in *MPFC: UC*.

209. This is also a sideways glance at Britain's Empire efforts in places like India and Ceylon, where improvements to transportation, industry, agriculture, and education were fundamental parts of the occupying presence.

210. The prisoner Ben (Palin)—much older than these revolutionaries—is more likely to remember difficult times in the city, so he can praise the Romans. The celebrated Augustan reign began sixty years prior to the film's setting; if Ben is seventy he has a very different conception of what might merit complaint. See the entries later in the "In Pilate's Jail" scene for more.

211. Ovid's magnum opus, like the Pythons' work, is reflexive: "*The Metamorphoses* is an egocentric work, constantly drawing the reader's attention back to the author through personal asides, puns, alliteration, and the author's sheer virtuosity in re-telling well-known tales" (*WWAR*, 107). For Python reflexiveness, see *BAFHG*, 310–11.

212. *WWAR*, 102.

213. Laqueur, *Terrorism*, 146.

214. Laqueur, *Terrorism*, 146.

215. Laqueur, *Terrorism*, 146.

216. *The Red Army Faction*, 1.401.

217. Grant, *Gladiators*, 73.

218. The site of Jerusalem (or the City of David) was particularly ill-suited for large-scale habitation, given its distance from sufficient, consistent potable water (and arable land). For generations, the Gihon Spring was the city's only water supply, with waterways carved into the rock beneath the city helping capture the water. A second, dependable (and defensible) water source would seem necessary, which might have been Pilate's goal.

219. Jeremias, *JTJ*, 14.

220. Maier, *Pontius Pilate*, 112–13.

221. *AJ*, 18.3.2 (Whiston, 379); see also *JURR* 162–63.

222. *JTJ*, 16n30.

223. See "The Palestine Exploration Fund," *Times*, 21 May 1866: 11; "A Palace of Herod the Great," *Times*, 22 April 1955: 14; a picture of the aqueduct at Caesarea is included in "An Introduction to Israel," *Illustrated London News*, 30 March 1968: 34; and "Israel on a Package Tour," *Times*, 22 April 1967: 21.

224. "Pilate's Aqueduct: Stone Pipe Brought from Bethlehem," *Times*, 2 February 1938: 9.

225. "Jerusalem Yields Its Ancient Secrets," *Times*, 1 January 1971: 6; also, "The Temple Mount of Jerusalem," *Illustrated London News*, 24 February 1973: 54.

226. *WWAR*, 59.

227. "Jerusalem's New Water Supply," *Times*, 10 August 1918: 5.

228. *I, Claudius* aired November 1976; *Diaries 1969–1979*, 348–49.

229. On 16 June 1978, Palin diaries that they had all agreed to invite The Who drummer Keith Moon into the small "repertory company" of players for the film, which would also include John Young, Sue Jones-Davies, and Terence Bayler, among others (*Diaries 1969–1979*, 472–73). Moon may have been eyed for a "Psychopath" role, which was not included in the final film. Moon died of a drug overdose in September 1978, just before he was scheduled to fly to Tunisia and join the film shoot.

230. Magness, *Stone and Dung*, 131–32.

231. Magness, "What's the Poop," 81.

232. Koloski-Ostrow, *ASRI*, 42–43.

233. Magness, "What's the Poop," 82.

234. David, "Ancient Romans, Jews."

235. These workers would have qualified for the "despised trades" descriptor, dealing in haulage and, even worse, haulage of impure waste. See *JTJ*, for more.

236. See Mitchell, "Human Parasites in the Roman World," 1–3.

237. Jewish sectarians prohibited the consumption of "fish blood," even from approved fish handled properly, but evidence indicates that after 70 Roman fish sauce became quite popular among Jews (Magness, *Stone and Dung*, 39).

238. "The History of Plumbing in Jerusalem," *P&M* (unpaginated).

239. Magness, "What's the Poop," 80.

240. Pompey conquered most of the Seleucid Empire by about 62 BC (*WWAR*, 14–15).

241. Ben-Sasson, *A History of the Jewish People*, 251. Ben-Sasson is commenting on the absence of unrest detailed in Josephus's descriptions of the period.

242. The images of medieval life in *Holy Grail* were also filthy. There is an "*impoverished, plague-ridden village*," and a scene of peasants digging for "lovely filth." Arthur is identified as a king simply because "he hasn't got shit all over him," though by the end of the film he has a load of ordure dumped on his head. Robin will also soil his armor when confronted by the Killer Rabbit. With the exception of the Castle Anthrax, this is a filthy world.

243. From Bogdanor, "The Character of the Postwar Period," audio transcription.

244. Bogdanor, "Character of the Postwar Period," a.t.

245. Bogdanor, "Character of the Postwar Period," a.t.

246. Bogdanor, "Character of the Postwar Period," a.t.

247. As much as twenty percent of the population were dues-paying union members in 1977; add their dependents, and this is a significant voting bloc.

248. *Private Eye*, 22 July 1977: 15.

249. Caryl, *Strange Rebels*, 55–56. The NHS, to cite just one state-owned entity, is lampooned often by the Goons and Pythons, poking at the one-size-fits-all standardization, rationing, and inefficiency of such a bureaucracy. The Goons mention "the dreaded National Health hospital at Hampton Court" ("The Last Smoking Seagoon"), and that peace and quiet at an NHS hospital is much louder than at a private hospital ("The End").

250. Caryl, *Strange Rebels*, 55.

251. Caryl, *Strange Rebels*, 56. Attlee had routed Churchill in the 1945 General Election; pundits concluded that British voters believed Labour and Attlee were much more likely to enact the Beveridge Report policies than Churchill and the Conservatives. The PFJ might be enjoying what Jenkins terms the "gentle decadence" Britain found itself in by the mid-1970s, when virtually every measuring point of prosperity showed long-term decline, but a "perpetual lagging behind" had yet to produce absolute decline from which there was no escape (Jenkins, *Anatomy of Decline*, 95–96). In this, the PFJ more resemble the educated, affluent, upper-middle-class members of the overtly political RAF or JRA groups, et al.

252. See Bogdanor's "Thatcherism, 1979–1990," for much more on consensus and its demise.

253. *WWAR*, 57.

254. *BAFHG*, 94.

255. By the end of the second century, the Romans had "constructed over fifty-three thousand miles of major highways and two hundred thousand miles of secondary roads" across the Empire (*WWAR*, 57). These roads fell into disrepair across much of Britain after the Romans left, and before the Victorian Age.

256. The fifth king of Rome, living ca. 616–579 BC. He is also credited with erecting the original Circus Maximus; *ASRI*, 63.

257. Quoted in *ASRI*, 63–64.

258. Joyce, "The Grandeur That Was Rome," in *Ulysses*, 131; Koloski-Ostrow mentions this alliance in *ASRI*, 103.

259. This is likely a holdover from *Holy Grail*, where the world of the Middle Ages is posited, but there are few visual indicators of that time. See *BAFHG*, xiv–xv for all that's "missing" from the Python's medieval film setting. In *Life of Brian*, the archaeological evidences of Roman occupation in their corner of Tunisia were all the Pythons had, so evidence would have to do.

260. See the entries later in the list for more on the benefits of Roman occupation, as well as the *absence* of those benefits as the film unfolds.

261. *BRT*, 89.

262. There were of course factions, like the Zealots, who could never stomach a foreign power ruling the Holy City, especially an idolatrous power praying to both men and multiple gods.

263. *HMB*, 351.

264. *HMB*, 351.

265. "EEC Referendum," *Times*, 4 April 1975: 6.

266. King and Stager, *LBI*, 76–77.

267. *LBI*, 77.

268. *JTJ*, 26.

269. *JTJ*, 17. Chapman acted as physician on the film set, incidentally.

270. "Our British Empire," *Sunderland Daily Echo and Shipping Gazette*, 19 March 1902: 3.

271. Porter, *The Lion's Share*, 281.

272. See the entries in *JTJ* under "education" for more.

273. *JTJ*, 363.

274. *JTJ*, 373n70.

275. *JTJ*, 373.

276. "The British Empire in India," *New Zealand Herald* (reprinted), 21 October 1893: II.

277. This is how many Englishmen saw the Raj: a nursery in which India "matures" and from which it is eventually weaned. See Brendon, *DFBE*, passim.

278. "The British Empire in India," *New Zealand Herald* (reprinted), 21 October 1893: IV.

279. These had been active in prewar days, prior to the army and the Right assuming control in 1937. The proletarian and "tendency" films popular in the 1920s and 1930s, for example, had disappeared along with their producers as the country moved toward ultranationalism.

280. *BRJ*, 39–46.

281. *BRJ*, 46.

282. *BRJ*, 45.

283. *LBI*, 69–70.

284. *LBI*, 71.

285. *LBI*, 73–75; also, Mitchell's "Human Parasites in the Roman World," passim.

286. *LBI*, 101.

287. *JTJ*, 170–71, also 26. Wine was such a part of daily and even ritual life that Jeremias is able to mention grapes, wine, and wine production over and over again in *JTJ*.

288. Magness, *Stone and Dung*, 57.

289. *JTJ*, 38.

290. Jeremias notes one item the PFJ leave off their list of gratitudes, wheat, was usually the first to fail in times of famine; much of it had to be imported to begin with (*JTJ*, 39).

291. *JTJ*, 174.

292. See the index entries for "baths" in *ASRI*.

293. Levine, *Jerusalem*, 329–30.

294. Levine, *Jerusalem*, 330.

295. Cleese plays this slow-burn-but-eventually-hyperbolic, frustrated, upper-middle-class type throughout the run of *Flying Circus*, as will be discussed later.

296. "Human Parasites in the Roman World," 1.

297. See also Borowski, *Daily Life in Biblical Times*, 78–80.

298. In India, "between 1850 and 1947, more than 40,000 miles [of rail track] were laid, involving heroic feats of embanking, tunneling, and bridging," leading a Scottish engineer in 1890 to rate Britain's building program in "dependent" lands higher than even Rome's (*DFBE*, 148).

299. *ASRI*, 49.

300. A defendant's phrasing as he apologizes for multiple murders in Ep. 27 of *Flying Circus*, congratulating the counsel, jury, and judge for successfully condemning him. See *MPFC: UC*, 2.3–19; *ATW*, 2.27.46.

301. This obvious genesis moment is discussed in detail below, just as a slightly crabbed Reg sums up the benefits of the Roman occupation.

302. See Adrian Lee's "The Remarkable Raj: Why Britain Should Be Proud of Its Rule in India," *Express*, 22 June 2013; and Lalvani's *The Making of India*.

303. Pellison, *Roman Life in Pliny's Time*, 228.

304. *HLTJ*, 116–17.

305. "Jews and Romans in the Early Empire," 316; also, Smallwood's *JURR*, chapter 11.

306. *JURR*, 257.

307. *WWAR*, 10.

308. *HLTJ*, 11.

309. Smallwood, "Jews and Romans in the Early Empire," 318.

310. Smallwood, "Jews and Romans in the Early Empire," 319.

311. See Bernstein, *Myth of Decline*, 101–2. The announcement coincided to the day with another uprising, the Bolshevik coup in Russia (*DFBE*, 319).

312. From Schneer, *The Balfour Declaration: The Origins of the Arab-Israeli Conflict*, 376.

313. The entirety of the Pythons' combined working lives stretched across this volatile period.

314. *Mrs. Thatcher's Revolution*, 74.

315. See the introduction to Black, Pemberton, and Thane's *Reassessing 1970s Britain*.

316. One of the more clever versions—from the Sex Pistols' manager Malcolm McLaren—referred to Britain as a "banana republic without the bananas" ("Proud Pirate of Punk," *Times*, 27 May 1983: 10). To be fair, an *Irish Times* columnist had made the same reference in regard to Ireland seven months earlier.

317. In order: Cecil King, of IPC and the *Daily Mirror*; Hugh Cudlipp; Prince Philip's uncle Lord Louis Mountbatten; and Solly Zuckerman. Of these, it seems that only King truly wanted to foment rebellion.

318. *HMB*, 307.

319. Not coincidentally, the student-led sit-ins and riots in France had begun in earnest just six days before this odd congress.

320. Profiled in the film *The Lost World of the Seventies*, presented by former BBC journalist Michael Cockerell. The film also looks at 1970s-era interviews with Lord Longford ("Lord Porn"), Metro Police Commissioner Robert Mark, and the writ-happy James Goldsmith. See also "Gen. Walker May Recruit 'Three Million,'" *Telegraph*, 28 August 1974: 2.

321. Neaves was her adviser and campaign manager, and she called him a "dedicated warrior for freedom." See the text of her speech at his memorial service, 16 May 1979, at the Margaret Thatcher Foundation (http://www.margaretthatcher.org/document/104085).

322. "MP Warns on Private Armies," *Financial Times*, 5 September 1974: 11.

323. Black et al. remind us that "cap in hand," "ungovernable" and "decline" are used over and over again by the more pessimistic assessors of the decade (*Reassessing 1970s Britain*, 4–5). I will try to be mindful of that.

324. *BAFHG*, 156n98; the quote within the block quote comes from David Wood, "Mr. Wilson Fails to Smother Vote," *Times*, 1 October 1970: 1. He was slightly exaggerating, of course, but Labour would be out of power for eighteen long years.

325. Bogdanor, "Thatcherism, 1979–1990," a.t.

326. Bogdanor, "Thatcherism, 1979–1990," a.t.

327. "Who Can Govern the Ungovernable?" *Times*, 30 September 1974: 15.

328. See Peter Stafford's "An American Wonders Who Is Controlling a Once-Reliable Ally," *Times*, 8 May 1975: 1; Garnett's *From Anger to Apathy*, 18–19, 21; "In Answer to Our Ungovernable Friends," *Financial Times*, 9 May 1975: 19.

329. Think of the First Temple Period, for example. See Levine, *Jerusalem*, xiii.

330. Mitchell, "Human Parasites," 7.

331. See Mitchell, "Human Parasites," passim. See also the entries in the index in *BAFHG* under "filth," "grotesque," and "sewage" for more.

332. Black et al., *Reassessing 1970s Britain*, 6.

333. *DFBE*, 178–81.

334. *DFBE*, 432.

335. *DFBE*, 235.

336. Produced in association with the American *Time-Life* book series, which the Pythons would lampoon in *Flying Circus* Ep. 31 (*MPFC: UC*, 2.75). Episode 31 was recorded in April 1972, and written in the months before, just when this documentary uproar hit the pages of newspapers.

337. The kerfuffle was such that the BBC's director-general, Charles Curran, was forced to apologize and admit the program was "not entirely up to standard" ("BBC Chief Rocks British Empire," *Daily Mail*, 6 April 1972: 3). Journalist Peregrine Worsthorne even called for the BBC to lose its privileged public charter in the wake of this scandal ("Disestablish the B.B.C.," *Sunday Telegraph*, 9 April 1972: 20). (Waugh makes fun of the earnest Worsthorne a number of times in his diaries.) The program ran in both February and March 1972 on BBC 1.

338. Lady Wayland's letter to the editor: "Benefits from British Rule," *Telegraph*, 6 April 1972: 16; an unsigned *Telegraph* editorial: "BBC's British Empire," *Telegraph*, 7 April 1972: 16; the documentary series' producers' reply (Max Morgan-Witts [b. 1931]): "British Empire on Television," *Telegraph*, 14 April 1972: 18, and "BBC Empire Series," *Times*, 11 July 1972: 15. There are dozens of other letters both decrying and supporting the controversial documentary series. There was even a follow-up series of articles in *The Listener* looking at reactions to the series, featuring comments of scholars who worked on the documentary.

339. The phrase was already in newspaper editorial-page parlance (appearing within quotation marks, and perhaps as an adaptation of a similar American phrase from the war) as early as 1954, and used regularly by 1956, always in relation to what the Tories saw as the results of successful Conservative policies since 1951.

340. Presciently, inflation was the only hiccup that seemed to worry Macmillan during this rosy stretch; rising inflation would maul the Wilson, Heath, and Callaghan administrations over the next two decades.

341. Listen to *Goon Show* episodes "Pam's Paper Insurance Policy" (24 November 1958); "King Solomon's Mines" (2 December 1957); "The Spanish Doubloons" (21 January 1960); and "The Spon Plague" (3 March 1958). *Never Had It So Good* is the title of Sandbrook's 2006 book about the post-Suez period in Britain.

342. The one complaint that could be made, justifiably, was that even though Britain's economy was strong and growing, it was consistently growing at a slower rate than most other developed countries in the West. See Marr and Bernstein.

343. Smallwood, "Jews and Romans in the Early Empire," 234.

344. Smallwood, "Jews and Romans," 234. The fact that these writs and letters continued to appear across the years indicates that the actual practice of such tolerations (i.e., intolerant prefects) was less effective than the ideal of toleration (i.e., Rome's good intentions) ("Jews and Romans," 313–14).

345. For a deeper discussion of this subject, see Smallwood's *JURR*, chapter 6, "The Diaspora and Jewish Religious Liberty."

346. *HMB*, 61.

347. *HMB*, 61.

348. *HMB*, 61.

349. *WWAR*, 35.

350. Bernstein, *Myth of Decline*, 266–67. In 2014 Scottish voters were offered another bite at the apple. The "No" votes accounted for more than 55 percent of the final tally, defeating the measure yet again.

351. *ATW*, 1.11.142.

352. In *So, Anyway*, Cleese calls *The Goon Show* "the Greatest Radio Comedy Show of All Time. . . . I love this show with an intensity that almost defies analysis" (71–72).

353. *MPFC: UC*, 1.180.

354. Hugh Scanlon, a proponent of workers' control (along with Tony Benn), is discussed in *BAFHG* (119–20). John Boyd was the general secretary of the AEU during this period.

355. "Trade Unions," *Spectator*, 29 November 1975: 10.

356. Josephus, *WJ*, 6.7.3 (Whiston, 585).

357. Laqueur, *Terrorism*, 33.

358. Laqueur, *Terrorism*, 33.

359. Machaeros was the fortress where John the Baptist was held, and eventually killed.

360. *JURR*, 295.

361. For the safety of his kingship, Herod earlier had "prohibited all unauthorized gatherings, even if only a few people were involved," with the punishment for violation "harsh, including death" (Levine, *Jerusalem*, 173).

362. *Holy Grail* is as much about Britain in the 1970s as it is about Arthur and the Middle Ages. See *BAFHG*.

363. Palin, *Diaries, 1969–1979*, 142, 186–87. Nixon is referenced a number of times in *Flying Circus*. As a noted antagonist of the Left, Nixon was an easy target. He also appears (via his signature) in *Holy Grail*, meaning he holds a pivotal position in the upper echelons of world leadership and in the Pythons' pantheon of evildoers. Some of the troupe had also just recently (1977) finished assisting with the production of the *Monty Python and the Holy Grail (Book)*, which featured a number of Nixon references on the back cover (*BAFHG*, 13, 24n58, 24n59, and 24n61).

364. The times tainted biblical films, as well. *The Passover Plot* depicts a Jesus-led conspiracy to survive the cross and "prove" his messiah-ship via subterfuge.

365. Hofstader, *The Paranoid Style in American Politics* (Jonathan Cape, 1966).

366. Jenkins, *Anatomy of Decline*, 33.

367. Dobson and Payne, *Carlos Complex*, 206–7.

368. Demaris, *Brothers in Blood*, 14.

369. Cook, "Crucifixion as Spectacle," 71.

370. See *BRJ*, 19–28.

371. *HMB*, 134.

372. The PM's official retreat, in Buckinghamshire, since about 1921.

373. This comment was recorded by Barbara Castle, Secretary of State for Health and Social Services, and quoted in Jenkins's *Mrs. Thatcher's Revolution*, 45. Jenkins is citing *The Castle Diaries*, 223.

374. *Spectator*, 18 July 1975: 18.

375. *The Red Army/PFLP: Declaration of World War* is a 1971 agit-prop film by Masao Adachi and Kôji Wakamatsu made in Lebanon.

376. *The Red Army/PFLP: Declaration of World War*, a.t.

377. *BAFHG*, 367.

378. *DFBE*, 305–6; *BRT*, 19. Pearse was executed on 3 May 1916.

379. "Toll of Japanese Terror Murders Rise to 12," *Times*, 14 March 1972: 6; also, "Tale of Guerrilla Torture Killings Shock Japan," *Times*, 9 May 1972: 7. The final death toll would rise to fourteen, not including law enforcement deaths.

380. *BRT*, 259.

381. *BRJ*, 15.

382. Tel Aviv, 30 May 1972; see "Cut all her bits off" earlier for more on that tragic event.

383. Sakaguchi, the third-ranking URA member at the time, had been sentenced to hang as early as 1993, and remained on death row through 2013, when his death sentence was again upheld.

384. "Nine Hostages Freed in Malaysia," *Times*, 6 August 1975: 1. It was reported that Malaysia was having trouble finding a country willing to allow the Japanese plane to land with its load of terrorists, even though they were seeking asylum, and even though many of the countries—including Lebanon, Syria, and North Korea—had histories of accepting such "freedom fighters." See also "Japan Releases Terrorists," *Times*, 5 August 1975: 1; *BRJ*, 164–68; and Dobson and Payne, *The Carlos Complex*, 182–84. Some members of terror groups, once incarcerated, refused to be released when other hostages had been taken—they wanted to finish their sentences and be done.

385. At this writing, Sakaguchi is still on death row.

386. *BRJ*, 163; italics added. Incidentally, a German police team tasked with attacking 1972 Olympic Black September kidnappers at the airfield took a vote and opted out of the deadly encounter (*BRT*, 166).

387. Quoted in Burke, "Frantz Fanon's *The Wretched of the Earth*," 134.

388. In prison awaiting trial, members of the Red Army Faction had plenty of time to consider these kinds of existential questions. They would communicate with one another and the outside (through their attorneys, often) using aliases; Ulrike Meinhof became "Therèse," while Baader wanted to be called, revealingly, "Ahab" (Lasky, "Ulrike Meinhof and the Baader-Meinhof Gang," 12).

389. Burke, "Frantz Fanon's *The Wretched of the Earth*," 134.

390. Burke, "Frantz Fanon's *The Wretched of the Earth*," 133.

391. See Iviansky, "Individual Terror," 56.

392. Iviansky, "Individual Terror," 56.

393. "Ex-Mercenary Is Police Chief," *Telegraph*, 6 June 1978: 4.

394. Quoted in Iviansky, "Individual Terror," 46.

395. Burke, "Frantz Fanon's *The Wretched of the Earth*," 131–32.

396. Burke, "Frantz Fanon's *The Wretched of the Earth*," 132.

SCENE ELEVEN
IN THE PALACE SEWERS

(draft) . . . eight MASKED COMMANDOS. Their faces are partially hidden—Even though this film is carefully crafted to reflect the look and atmosphere of first-century Judea (just like *Holy Grail* displayed a tenth-to-fourteenth-century mien), the connections between the "then" and the "now" are detectable, perhaps most initially and most identifiably in visual forms. The commando attire in this scene reflects not only the *sicarii* religious/terrorist sect, but the very recent and harrowing images of balaclava-wearing terrorists leaning out of hijacked airliners in the Jordanian desert[1] or peering over balconies of the athletes' village at the Munich Olympics. Our "masked commandos" are at least partially based on the notorious sicarii terror group, whom Laqueur describes as "a highly organized religious sect consisting of men of lower orders active in the Zealot struggle in Palestine."[2] What differentiates these men from the Zealots of the first century is that the Zealots were "primarily a coalition of peasants turned brigands [who] first challenged and then successfully opposed the high priestly regime in Jerusalem."[3] The PFJ are fighting the Romans, period.

Incidentally, the term "commando" is relatively young, harking back to the activities of the Boers across South Africa, where "commandos" were armed, civilian-led raids into native territories to recover stolen cattle, goods, and kidnapped women and children.[4] By the mid-1970s, commando missions were more military in nature—heavily armed military units inserted into inimical and (often) postcolonial territory to "rescue the innocent from the consequences of terrorism."[5] The West German military snuck into Mogadishu in October 1977 to save hostages taken by the PFLP from Lufthansa Flight 181; this less than a year after the Israeli commando raid at Entebbe—which set the example for action for many governments' future responses to terrorism—had saved more than one hundred hostages from Air France Flight 139.[6] The Entebbe raid had spawned not only worldwide news coverage but three separate films from which the Pythons could draw influence: *Victory at Entebbe* and *Raid on Entebbe*, both 1976, and *Operation Thunderbolt*, 1977. *Victory* began life as an ABC television movie; *Raid* was a Hollywood feature film for cinemas; and *Thunderbolt* was an Israeli-influenced production helmed by Menahem Golan, with appearances from some of the actual participants in the raid. *Times* critic David Robinson reviewed both *Raid* and *Victory* in the same column in late December 1976, with *Raid on Entebbe* coming out as the better viewing choice.[7] *Operation Thunderbolt* didn't appear in London cinemas until October 1977, though Robinson judged it "certainly the best" of the three Entebbe films.[8] *Private Eye* offers a mock advertisement for a selection of "New Year Films"—*The Entebbe Memorandum, Carry On, Entebbe! Confessions of an Entebbe Pilot*.[9]

Lastly, another well-publicized and contemporary image of the balaclava is attributed to the so-called "Black Panther," Bradford-born Donald Neilson. Neilson perpetrated a crime spree across West Yorkshire 1971–1974, kidnapping and killing Lesley Whittle, killing three in various Post Office robberies and trying to kill others, and all stemming from myriad house burglaries that grew progressively more violent. Neilson's crimes were enumerated in 1976 during his trials, and he was eventually sentenced to several life sentences. During testimony, Neilson claimed that "he always remained hooded in the kidnapped Lesley Whittle's company."[10]

Wide shot exterior of PILATE'S palace. Night time—So far this undertaking is a "raid and penetration," helpfully described in some detail in Marighella's 1969 *Minimanual*. These operations are "rapid attacks on establishments located in neighborhoods, or even in the center of the city, such as small military units, commissaries, hospitals, to cause trouble, seize weapons, punish and terrorize the enemy, take reprisals, or to rescue wounded prisoners or those hospitalized under police guard."[11] The cover of darkness is important, too. "Raids and penetrations are most effective," Marighella writes, "if they are carried out at night."[12] The PFJ is certainly out to "cause trouble," to "punish and terrorize," and to certainly undertake "reprisals" against the hated Roman Empire in the form of Pilate (and his wife). The kidnapping element—a separate section in Marighella's book—has been appended here by the PFJ, though they are more considerate than Marighella and his Brazilian counterparts: he promotes the ancillary aim of the raid and penetration as a means to "destroy vehicles and damage installations."[13] Ever thoughtful, Francis will want his brothers to be careful to *not* damage the newly tiled sewers.

FRANCIS (VO): "This is the palace at Caesar Square . . . "—This was likely Herod's palace, initially, taken over by Pilate when he became prefect, and it is in the process of being redone, as we will see. This palace wouldn't be discovered by archaeologists until 1999.

Francis's voiceover is not part of early editions of the scripts as printed, nor the version read aloud in July 1977. It may be that for the purposes of narrative continuity this voiceover was added in the postproduction phase, likely by Palin and Jones. After principal photography had been completed on *Holy Grail*, a cheap credit sequence was needed (animation was ruled out and the production budget was gone), so Palin produced the "silly Swedish subtitles" idea for the film's opening credits.[14]

Many ROMANS are attempting to scrub off BRIAN'S slogans by torchlight—These would likely have been slaves, historically, as opposed to Roman citizens. During some of the worst of The Troubles in Northern Ireland, it was reported that "Catholics paint the sides of houses and other buildings white so patrolling troops will be clearly outlined for IRA snipers. The [British] army resprays the walls with black or purple paint. 'The loser may be the side that runs out of paint first,' joked a British officer."[15] The remnants of the antisocial actions perpetrated by those defending George Davis weren't so easily cleared away. Those that broke into the Headingley Cricket Ground and ruined the turf were able to boast a lasting effect—the pending cricket match had to be canceled. This case will be discussed in detail later in relation to an inscription seen in Pilate's quarters.

FRANCIS (VO): "Our commando unit will approach from Fish Street . . ."—One of Jerusalem's gates was known as Fish Gate; it was located near where "Tyrian fish merchants" kept shop.[16] There was a Fish Street in Oxford, where Jones and Palin attended university. This is likely a more period reference, referencing the "fishes and loaves" story in the Bible (or even "Jesus fish" the "Ichthys").

. . . black-robed figures—The revolutionaries are dressed in black flowing robes, with yellow ties around their heads. This isn't unlike the "uniform" some Dark Ages Muslim rulers

demanded their Jewish citizens wear, including "distinctive clothing, a black habit with a sash and a yellow piece of cloth as a form of identification."[17] The PFJ are dressed this way in the film for a less sinister reason, likely. Later, when they come across the terrorists from the Campaign for Free Galilee, who will be wearing black robes and red sashes, it will be easier to distinguish them.

FRANCIS (VO): ". . . we are sewage workers on the way to a conference"—It's no stretch for the PFJ to employ this mode of entry into Pilate's sanctuary, especially given recent, highly visible events. There had been much talk between 1974 and 1978 in both the British and American press of the "plumbers" used by Nixon's White House to initially plug information and security leaks, and later burgle enemies' offices for sensitive or damaging information. The infamous Watergate break-in was just one such attempt. Palin writes of these sordid details a number of times, and for obvious reasons: "The whole Watergate case has taken up more press and broadcasting time than any other cause célèbre I can remember."[18]

There may well have been such men "employed" in Jerusalem's waterways; there were elsewhere in the Roman Empire. Carl Richard mentions that slaves were often assigned to keep the sewers clean, and not the trade union or guild members Francis seems to be describing.[19] Koloski-Ostrow notes that Augustus's *aedile* (the man responsible for maintaining public buildings), Marcus Agrippa (c. 64–12 BC), "apparently employed a team of about 240 specially trained enslaved workmen, who were later inherited by the state in accordance with Agrippa's will."[20] The emperor Trajan (53–117) would later write to Pliny (c. 23–79) in regard to the building of a water-controlling sewer in Amastris, Turkey, advising him that "the work of maintaining the sewer on a more regular basis might be effected by workers 'not far removed from punishment' (that is, convicted criminals) and by communal slaves."[21] Francis and the PFJ clearly see their disguised persons not as slaves, but as working freedmen, even guild members on their way to a trade union meeting where management (like the Romans) would get a verbal hiding from the righteously indignant rank and file. (In short, the meeting we've just seen with Reg and the PFJ, and those depicted in *I'm All Right Jack*.) There are estimates as to what a "trained sewer worker," a *clocarius*, might have earned around this time: "Based partly on the Price Edict of Diocletian, we can speculate that the salary . . . could not have provided more than a meager daily subsistence, perhaps twenty-five denarii per day," writes Koloski-Ostrow. "Such men were subjected to nightmarish pathogens in the wastewaters of the sewers, such as leptospirosis, sometimes causing a type of jaundice that is potentially fatal."[22] A network of sewers for water run-off and waste has been found in Jerusalem; the only question might be how many latrines or cesspits, public or private, were actually attached to this system. The most likely time for this upgrade would have been *after* the fall of the city, however, when Rome (and later occupants) could build and rebuild without the worry of desecration. Francis and the PFJ terrorists might be fairly safe with their cover story, then, given the filthy, disease-ridden, poorly remunerated nature of their work.

Across the British Empire, though, there were similar workers who wouldn't have been given a pass with this claim. In India, during the height of the colonial "sinecurist" afflictions, the Public Works Department acronym, PWD, was popularly known as "Plunder Without Danger," this "byword for villainy" pilfering wherever and whatever it could.[23]

FRANCIS: "Reg, our glorious leader and founder of the PFJ. Will be coordinating consultant at the drain head . . ."—The terrorist Carlos often led his acolytes into their attacks, and carried out his own. He attempted to assassinate the "Zionist" businessman Joseph Sieff in 1973, engineered several explosive-type attacks in London and Paris, and even attempted rocket-propelled grenade attacks at Orly Airport in 1975. He also led the Vienna OPEC raid that killed three. This increased notoriety forced Carlos's backers and protectors to withdraw, fearing international reprisals.[24] If Reg had gone on this glorious mission, he would either have been killed or taken hostage, like Brian. Either way, his terrorist days would have been over.

The JRA's Fusako Shigenobu, on the other hand, went to the Middle East in 1971, and was able to plan and set into motion terror actions both in Japan and abroad from a place of relative safety. Shigenobu was the "coordinating consultant" for the JRA, and with good reason. She didn't have a bad back, but she did realize that increasing police anti-terror action in Japan, as well as the bad taste left in the public's mouth after the internecine torture and murders of URA members had rendered the homeland inhospitable for the JRA. She would remain abroad for nearly thirty years.[25] Upon returning to Japan in 2000, she was arrested, tried, and sentenced to two decades in prison, where she remains at the time of this publication.

REG *(making revolutionary gesture)*: **"Solidarity, Brother"**—Ironic, of course, that Reg's devotion to the cause is only as solid as his bad back allows, and Brian picks up on that, clearly, as he wanly returns the salute. This variation in revolutionary fervor and usefulness has been categorized, helpfully. Nechaev and Bakunin's famous *Catechism* divides society into six categories: (1) the "intelligent and energetic" (a threat—they are to be killed first); (2) those whose "monstrous crimes" could be used to "[foment] revolution" (they'd still be killed, but later); (3) next came the "high ranking, the rich and the powerful" (useful as dupes and for blackmail); and (4) politicians are of value as long as they are manipulable (meaning weak and blackmail-prone).[26] Reg and perhaps Francis and Stan fall into Bakunin's fifth category, the "loudmouths," whose description should sound familiar: "those platonic advocates of revolution, should be engineered into making dangerous declarations, most would perish in the struggle but a few might become authentic revolutionaries."[27] The PFJ advocate revolution without being fully committed to the violent acts necessary for its conduct, they talk a good game (as long as Romans aren't within earshot), but on their first raid they all perish, but one, another somehow slipping away. They are "loudmouths," at best. The one, however, Brian, manages to become something of an authentic revolutionary as he successfully delivers an anti-imperialist message, escapes from the oppressors' clutches, and *perhaps* sows the seeds for future insurrection with his glorious death. Perhaps just the fact that at the end of the film, there are 140 non-Romans who agree "crucifixion's a doddle" as they sing and dance on the crosses is the glimmer the revolution needs? The sixth segment of society Bakunin mentions is women; that category will be discussed later, when Judith tries to spur the PFJ into action following Brian's second arrest.

FRANCIS (VO): "Once in the sewer . . . there is a Roman feast later in the evening so . . . don't wear your best sandals"—Pilate's house would have certainly had a private toilet, for he and his family, and likely more than one, separate spaces designated for men and women. Latrines connected to the palace for soldiers and staff should be assumed, as well as the possibility that a larger, public latrine would have been attached to the palace for use by visitors and guests. It might be assumed that all of these would have likely been plumbed to empty into a larger sewer beneath the palace or under the streets adjacent, but that's not necessarily the case. Koloski-Ostrow mentions that in Pompeii and Herculaneum, for example, "virtually every house . . . had its own private toilet," meaning the ruling and wealthy classes would have almost certainly enjoyed this amenity in Jerusalem.[28] And if Seneca is to be taken at his word as he castigates the Romans—"they vomit that they may eat, and they eat that they may vomit, and they do not deign even to digest the feast for which they ransack the world"[29]— then what's on its way to the scuttling PFJ will include ejecta from every human orifice. But Koloski-Ostrow goes on to say that even though in Rome, where *private* toilets could legally be connected to the city's massive sewers, most were not—"sewers were really a last resort to problems of waste removal in the Roman city"—meaning these toilets had to be emptied in some other way.[30] The Cloaca Maxima network, Koloski-Ostrow believes, was designed to channel not sewage but the city's river and storm water. Sewage overflow into the drains was inevitable, but not their primary function. If the same held true for Jerusalem, the PFJ wouldn't need to be worried about offal or vomit, but floodwaters.[31]

FRANCIS (VO): ". . . the Caesar Augustus Memorial Sewer . . ."—The Goons would use a water pipe said to be buried beneath the Via Appia (the famous Appian Way road) to escape from the Romans in their "Pliny the Elder" episode, and in "Ten Snowballs That Shook the World," Bluebottle sings "Sideways, through the Sewers of the Strand on a Sunday Afternoon" ("Ankle-deep in sludge, dear/ We'll walk hand in hand").[32]

The Romans did name their monumental structures, several of which we've already seen in the images Gilliam gathered for the opening credits. In that credit sequence, the Pons Fabricius (bridge), portions of the Baths of Diocletian, and the Arch of Constantine are used as backgrounds for the falling Brian image. Rome's main sewer was known as the "Cloaca Maxima." One of its main aqueducts, the "Aqua Claudia," was named for Claudius, who finished the project. Claudius was also responsible for an ambitious tunnel project meant to control flooding on Fucine Lake.[33] Perhaps the largest and quite complex water system built by the Romans was also named for Caesar Augustus, the Aqua Augusta, near the Bay of Naples. (This wouldn't have been a "memorial," since Augustus lived until fourteen.)

There were also many buildings in the empire connected to sewage, both literally and figuratively. Structures like the Forum of Julius Caesar, the Baths of Titus, and the Domus Tiberiana all bear the names of Roman emperors and all have been identified as housing latrines connected to sewers that channeled waste away from the city.[34] Koloski-Ostrow notes that to this building-mad race, all structures had similar significance, including those associated with waste:

> In almost every case we have considered in some detail, the public toilets were connected to the piping system of the urban infrastructure in a permanent way that required an impressive amount of technological know-how and advance planning. Latrines were not to be a passing experiment in Roman urban architecture. When latrines were built inside Roman cities, they were built to last.[35]

And, as Koloski-Ostrow concluded earlier: "As with so many other features of Roman architecture, the Romans dealt with sewage problems in a practical, levelheaded manner, in some instances with the sophisticated engineering skills they employed in other fields of architecture."[36] It's perhaps no wonder that Francis wants his fellow terrorists to be careful of the new tilework—any public latrines and sewers of Jerusalem would have served everyone, rich and poor, Roman, Jew, and Samaritan.

This same kind of subterranean entry—in Jerusalem, against an oppressive government, and with violent intent—had been tried to grisly success when the Pythons were young, and even well before. First, the ancient example: Zealots helped sicarii slip into Jerusalem via secret passages, according to historians, "where they committed atrocious acts."[37] These activities would eventually lead to Titus bringing the full force of the Roman military to bear against Jerusalem. More recently, on 22 July 1946 the Irgun conducted what was the most egregious and bloody attack on the British government in the Middle East to that point: the bombing of the King David Hotel in Jerusalem. The hotel was in part a government facility, housing British military police and investigations personnel, likely the bombers' primary targets. On 22 July "a dozen men in flowing Arab robes carried milk cans" into the basement of the hotel, which had been left unprotected. At about half past noon that same day the cans exploded, leveling parts of the hotel, and killing more than ninety.[38]

The REVOLUTIONARIES . . . enter the main hypocaust or central heating duct . . . — (PSC) As ever, the Pythons have done a bit of homework here, accurately describing the Roman structures for providing heat to villas and baths; they also know that this kind of system was expensive, so only a place like a former Herodian palace or Roman fortress could claim such amenities. Study aside, these structures were actually much in the news during the run-up to *Life of Brian*. A number of separate archaeological digs in England—including Bishophill, Chichester, Woodchester, Southwark, and Wetherby—featured significant hypocaust finds and descriptions; the term was certainly much in the public lexicon between 1973 and 1977.[39]

Also, on 17 June 1974 the IRA detonated a bomb *beneath* Parliament, injuring eleven and doing significant damage.[40] *Private Eye*'s Waugh attributed the blast not to the IRA but to a particularly gassy Commons' Serjeant at Arms who happened to have a long-standing grudge against *Private Eye*.[41]

FRANCIS (VO): "This has just been retiled, so terrorists: careful with those weapons!"—This sounds particularly Pythonesque, but there is a precedent in the world of terror organizations for such consideration. In 1970 as the Japanese Red Army was conducting robberies to finance its political activities, they would stay at rented "hideouts"—apartments, really—far away from their targets. When they moved from one hideout to another, they cleaned the apartment "thoroughly": "Not only was this done to remove possible evidence and fingerprints," Farrell writes, "but it also insured return of the rent deposit and a happy landlord who knew that these nice clean tenants could not have been radicals."[42]

Secondly, even though the script direction calls them "*REVOLUTIONARIES,*" Francis actually uses the term "terrorists" here, and in a positive way, which hasn't usually been the case, historically. Laqueur notes that the terms "terrorism" and "terrorist" are relatively new, dating to the end of the eighteenth century, to the Jacobins, and "the period in the French Revolution broadly speaking between March 1793 and July 1794," where it was "a synonym for 'reign of terror.'"[43] (In newspaper coverage of the 1970s terror world, the terms "terrorist" and "revolutionary" tend to be used interchangeably, often one in the headline and another in the body of the story.)

Also, the fact that these terrorists are armed with seemingly pointed, sharpened weapons—those that could scratch the ceramic sewer tiles—identifies them, generally, as sicarii, or brigand types who bear at least short swords. In Latin, "sicarius" is a common term for "assassin," and "has the same general meaning" in the Mishnah, and "sicæ" is a small dagger—they were known as "dagger-men"—according to the *Jewish Encyclopedia*.[44] Josephus mentions the sicarii conducting a raid very much like this one:

> But now the *Sicarii* went into the city by night, just before the festival, which was now at hand, and took the scribe belonging to the governor of the temple, whose name was Eleazar, who was the son of Ananus [Ananias] the high priest, and bound him, and carried him away with them; after which they sent to Ananias, and said that they would send the scribe to him, if he would persuade Albinus to release ten of those prisoners which he had caught of their party; so Ananias was plainly forced to persuade Albinus, and gained his request of him. This was the beginning of greater calamities; for the robbers perpetually contrived to catch some of Ananias's servants; and when they had taken them alive, they would not let them go, till they thereby recovered some of their own *Sicarii*. And as they were again become no small number, they grew bold, and were a great affliction to the whole country.[45]

The sicarii in the first century set the tone, clearly, for the tactics of the JRA, the Baader-Meinhof group, and the PFLP nineteen-hundred years later.

FRANCIS (VO): ". . . directly beneath Pilate's audience chamber. . . "—Part of the reason that revolutionary groups transitioned from targeting high-profile figures to more collateral or indiscriminate groups and places was simply availability—nineteenth-century tsars and first-century Roman prefects alike tended to be "well-guarded and almost inaccessible."[46] The PFJ's enemy is Rome, as they've said, not necessarily Pontius Pilate or the Roman soldiers in Judea (most of whom weren't Roman, by birth), but Rome qualifies as "inaccessible," and there are likely far too many soldiers in even the Jerusalem garrison to consider a head-on assault. Even Pilate himself—the local representative of Roman authority and oppression—has likely been considered and dismissed as a potential target. Pilate's family, then—like the scions of wealthy bourgeoisie from the Romanovs to the Gettys to the Hearsts,[47] or the representatives of foreign, colonizing governments (part of the "invisible enemy who afflicts and distorts . . . lives")—become the "accessible targets," and Third World terrorism is born.[48] In our case the PFJ manage to make their way into the sewers and heating space beneath Pilate's household, and, at least in the earlier drafts of the script, even accost Pilate's wife in her own bed—surely the *sanctum sanctorum* of the Pilate family. This accessibility doesn't help the PFJ, of course, since in the draft version Pilate's wife is an enormous woman who can easily defend herself, and in the finished version, the PFJ get into a scrap with the CFG terrorists, never even reaching the bedroom.

FRANCIS (VO): ". . . the moment for Habakkuk to get out his probe"—Habakkuk will be mentioned later as one who does not survive this raid. He was one of the so-called "minor prophets" gathered into the Hebrew Bible. His might be a name drawn from the newspapers of the day. Beginning in the early 1950s there was much scholarly and public discussion of new finds among the Dead Sea Scrolls relating to Habakkuk.[49]

This assault might also be modeled on the popular biblical version(s) of David's successful penetration of Jerusalem, as mentioned in 2 Samuel 5: "And David said on that day, Whosoever getteth up to the gutter, and smiteth the Jebusites, and the lame and the blind, *that are* hated of David's soul, *he shall be chief and captain.*"[50] Other translations use the word "shaft" instead of "gutter" as a translation for "zinnor," including the English Standard Version. Joab's troops climbed the fourteen-meter shaft, entered the city unmolested, and led the successful assault. Some also see this assault referred to in a passage in 1 Chronicles 11, where Joab "climbed" ("went up") into the city and, arriving first, became the "chief" or leader based on David's prophecy.[51] For many, this interpretation rang true, certainly even through the 1960s as archaeological work continued under Kathleen Kenyon in the area of the eastern slope of the City of David.[52] Not all scholars agreed with these interpretations, Reich notes, but they certainly could have impressed the Pythons as the PFJ's assault on Pilate's palace was being blocked. The actual genesis, construction, and use of this vertical shaft was the subject of much discussion during this period. By the late 1990s, additional digs and reinterpretations of the strata determined that Warren's Shaft was actually a *natural* formation, and was an unlikely water source or siege avenue.

. . . a large, rather erotic mosaic, in which a naked couple are embracing. The man wears a fig leaf—(PSC) On the title card for the "*It's the Arts*" animation in *Flying Circus*, there is a Statue of David wearing a fig leaf, and at some point that fig leaf gets yanked away, revealing a face. This same statue is seen later, in Ep. 32, also covering its modesty, and there is a story behind that leaf:

There has been a David cast replica of the original statue housed at the Victoria & Albert museum since 1857. . . . The V&A website reports that upon receiving the unannounced gift, Victoria was so shocked by the nudity she commissioned a fig leaf to be made, and ordered that it be installed before any royal visit. It seems the Pepperpots and Mary Whitehouse may have had something of a patron saint in their Queen Victoria.[53]

This is a Python inclusion of the fig leaf, since the models for these erotic works, drawn from the frescoes in the brothels and bathhouses of Pompeii, left *nothing* to the imagination. This mocked-up version appears to be based on an image found in the Lupanare brothel in Pompeii. These would have been paintings and mosaics kept hidden from public view, adorning the walls of the back rooms of the small brothel/tavern, so it's odd seeing them here. Perhaps, since this setting is supposed to be the more private rooms of Pilate's house (even though it is an "audience chamber"), such adornment can be depicted. A very popular museum installation featuring Pompeian artifacts occupied the Royal Academy for many months in 1976, just as the Pythons were formulating the world of *Life of Brian*.

FRANCIS emerges from the tunnel . . . —If this moment *were* modeled on Joab's alleged assault on the city and the Jebusites, then Francis would now be leader—thanks to David's own words that the first to emerge becomes "chief and captain"—an outcome Reg, the "glorious leader and founder of the PFJ," might not have anticipated or appreciated.

Tunneling would also be used later as Titus's forces surrounded and attempted to lay siege to Jerusalem in 69. As the Roman troops built "earthworks" to support siege engines, the Jews tunneled beneath, eventually undermining the earthworks and forcing Titus to opt for waiting and starvation, rather than frontal assault.[54] Titus was eventually successful, and Jerusalem fell.

. . . an IDENTICAL GROUP appears . . . —This "identical" group scenario would have been quite recognizable to the astute viewer in 1979. The 1960s–1970s had seen the eruption of dozens of militant groups around the globe, in developed and developing countries, in those countries recently decolonized, still colonized, or in the painful process of decolonization. These terror groups, large and small, could be found in Britain, Northern Ireland, France, Germany, Italy, Palestine, Israel, Syria, Bolivia, the United States, and on and on. There were multiple "Red" groups (Red Army, Red Brigades), various "Popular Front" and "Peoples' Front" and "Revolutionary Front" cadres, and eventually subgroups—"splitters"— from many of these, as well. With so many contenders, it was inevitable that a potential target for one group had already been chosen by another.

From another angle, as the Angry Brigade went to trial for their crimes, prosecutors managed to lump together several terror groups into one conspiracy, and successfully convict many. Also, the US-based carrier Eastern Airlines was identified as receiving more hijacking attempts than other airlines, meaning more terrorists competing for targetable Eastern flights (those within fuel range of Cuba), and in 1969 Eastern confirmed they were introducing security measures to try and deal with this unwanted attention.[55]

The LEADER of the OTHER REVOLUTIONARIES is called DEADLY DIRK—(PSC) "Deadly Dirk" is never named in the finished film, just in the script. A "dirk" is also a ceremonial dagger ("skean dhu") worn in the stocking as part of Highland dress, and was occasionally in the news when a particularly nationalist Scottish MP decided to wear full costume into the Commons. The dirk had become ceremonial over time, and so was allowed by the Serjeant at Arms. In this, the dagger version of the dirk and the terrorist version end up equally ceremonial—both are just for show.

More seriously, in 1977, Northern Ireland could offer a very similar situation, where two seemingly aligned but rival terror groups cancel out each other's efforts. Militants (calling themselves "loyalists") at the Ballylumford power station had called for a general strike, even though the majority of workers in the region and the population were against such an action. "Loyalist paramilitants" were using the critical power plant as a tool to leverage the British government, demanding a return to "majority rule at Stormont," and threatening terror against any who opposed.[56] The bellicose preacher Ian Paisley was one of the loudest voices behind the strike action. *Private Eye* read the situation with a cocked eye, as usual, seeing less-than-pure motives everywhere:

> The newspaper reporting of the ultra-Loyalist "strike" in Ulster has been at its usual abysmal level. Thus, the heroic workers of the vital Ballylumford power station have been portrayed as nobly resisting the calls of Paisley and his ilk because of a deep-seated loyalty to non-sectarianism. In fact, many of the workers are members of the rival para-military organisations, the UDA and the UVF,[57] and it is the split between the two organisations that has frustrated the strike-call in the area. The UVF, who have condemned the strike, are still reeling from the effects of a recent trial in the area two months ago, when 27 of their members received a total of 700 years of imprisonment on a variety of charges including the murder of two members of the UDA. In the circumstances, members of the rival armies are far too concerned in carrying out their private vendettas to be able effectively to organise a strike at the plant.[58]

So while the UDA and UVF struggle together, Northern Ireland continued to be ruled from Westminster, and another "common enemy," the IRA (not the Judean Peoples' Front) was free to attack all sides.

DEADLY DIRK *(saluting)*: **"Campaign for Free Galilee"**—First, the silliness. The "salute" Dirk gives is a Three Stooges borrow, a hand between the eyes to prevent an expected, two-fingered eye gouge.

There are contemporary and historical influences for the coming dustup, not surprisingly. First, an *au courant* to-do. *Private Eye*'s semi-regular column "Letter from . . . "[59] included one dispatch from the Holy Land that reads quite familiar. In November 1976 two Jewish groups—the Asian-descended Sephardi Jews and the European-descended Ashkenazi Jews—disagreeing over a Sephardi synagogue on Mount Zion, led to fighting between two rabbis and their followers: "[Ashkenazi Jew] Rabbi Goldstein was to be seen in the front rank, hitching up his skirts and blowing a whistle. In the battle several holy books were desecrated and fighting was only stopped by the Jerusalem police after several days had passed and Rabbi Goldstein had been arrested."[60]

Much earlier, as the battle for Jerusalem would heat up significantly in late summer 66 (after temple sacrifices for the well-being of the emperor were halted), there were at first just rivalries between those factions more devoted to Rome (and peace) and those fighting for freedom from Rome. As passions became more inflamed and war was certain, battles between "rival factions of insurgents" increased (led by Menahem and Eleazar, e.g.), making fatally certain that when Titus's troops finally surrounded the city, the city wasn't nearly ready.[61]

Even before the penultimate battle for Jerusalem, Galilee had "a history of guerilla warfare," according to Smallwood, with the "Galilean rising in 4 B.C. amounting to a revolt."[62] Josephus tells of "a certain Judas from Galilee" who called the Roman census "nothing but downright slavery."[63] This Judas saw it as "a confession of weakness for people who regarded God as their only master . . . to accept a human overlord and pay tribute to Rome."[64] Smallwood goes on to say that even though only "a certain amount of active opposition" arose directly from the census, the writing on the wall, to bring Brian and the PFJ back into this, *should* have been clear to the Romans. The seed planted was a "nationalist party," an ur-PFJ, growing out of anger over the tax imposition, and flowering eventually into extremist thought and action.[65] But it wasn't just Judas, and anti-Roman feelings weren't confined to just Galilee. Yadin notes that there were multiple parties seeking independence from Rome: "The discovery of [the *Songs of the Sabbath Sacrifice*] scroll at Masada allows us to conclude that the Great Revolt was not restricted to the 'Zealot' sect alone: rather, as Josephus also states, many sects of Jewry took part in it, including the sect of the Essenes, either as a whole or in part, or at a certain stage of its development."[66] The Campaign for Free Galilee could be the Pythons' nod to the Zealots, who, under their leader, another Judas of Galilee, were known to operate from the Galilee area.[67]

More recently, Caryl notes the postwar fracturing of seemingly similar political movements after the war, and especially through the 1960s: "To be sure, the appeal of Marxism-Leninism was waning in the developed world, where leftist ideology was splintering into a kaleidoscope of options: Social Democracy, Trotskyism, Eurocommunism, Maoism, the New Left, the Extra-Parliamentary Opposition."[68] Every oppressed people during this period could declare a "Campaign for a Free Something, Somewhere," from Aden to Zimbabwe. This was a popular phrase in the 1960s and 1970s. There were "campaigns for free trade unions," Tony Benn's left-leaning "Campaign for Press Freedom," and a right-wing "Campaign for Free Speech" on campuses.[69] Despite its popularity, this will be the last we hear of the Campaign for Free Galilee, or any other terror group other than the PFJ.

During the 1971–1972 trial of the Angry Brigade, the prosecution laid at the Brigade's feet additional charges for bombings that had been initially claimed by other groups. The prosecution was certain that bombs allegedly set by the "First of May Group, Revolutionary Solidarity Movement," "Butch Cassidy and the Sundance Kid," the "Wild Bunch," and "Lotta Continua," were actually placed by this Stoke Newington gang.[70] The "Stoke Newington 8 Defence Group" pamphlet denied these additional charges. There were so many disaffecteds looking for a measure of revenge on the "Man" and his world that it's no surprise that they might have trod on each other's toes and then been blamed for each other's actions by authorities.

DEADLY DIRK: "We're going to kidnap Pilate's wife . . . take her back . . . issue demands"—This is a classic example of political hostage-taking, a tactic employed over and over again in the world of international terrorism of the 1970s, but which also occurred in the first-century Roman Empire, with the Romans even acting the part. First the Jewish machinations.

The High Priest Ananias's son, Eleazar, was captain of the temple in Jerusalem. As mentioned earlier, when sicarii kidnapped Eleazar's secretary, he was held for a ransom involving the release of ten other sicarii already imprisoned. The procurator, Albinus, released prisoners more than once, succumbing to the extortionate acts at the insistence of Ananias and Eleazar. Not much later, Albinus cleverly put an end to the problem by executing the remaining sicarii in his prisons, and releasing criminals with "trivial charges" against them.[71] The PFJ never do consider rescuing or ransoming for Brian, even though many terror groups like the sicarii and more recently, the Japanese Red Army and the Baader-Meinhof Gang, successfully forced such transactions.[72]

As for the Romans, procurator of Jerusalem Agrippa II had a new dining room built as part of his palace, one that allowed him to see down into the Temple's inner courts while he ate. The Sanhedrin and the high priest Ishmael objected to this intrusion, and erected a higher inner courtyard wall, blocking Agrippa's view. The disagreement led to a delegation journeying to Rome from Jerusalem—including the high priest, the Temple treasurer, and others—to argue before the emperor. The case was actually heard by Poppaea, the wife of Nero, who decided in the Jews' favor. Poppaea, after ruling favorably, then detained the delegation, "ostensibly as hostages against the misuse of the privilege of privacy," a reminder that all the Jews' privileges came at Rome's pleasure.[73]

More contemporarily, after Black September carried out its successful, deadly raid on the Israeli athletes during the 1972 Olympics, details of the familiar plan emerged following the interrogation of Abu Dawud, Black September "chieftain":

> Mohammed Masailah had taken with him the instructions for the operation from Abu Iyad and a list of the names of the prisoners held by the Israelis who were to be bargained in exchange for the Israeli hostages. He had a statement prepared in English setting out the aims of the operation and Black September's conditions for releasing the hostages.[74]

The Japanese Red Army seemed particularly adept at hostage taking, according to Farrell:

> Political hostage taking attempts to flavor the incident with an air of legitimacy. The hostage takers are perceived as having some reason or motivation worth considering. Since the government has *allowed* this heinous act to occur in the first place it now *owes* it to the victims to listen to the demands and perhaps give in so that the incident might be resolved.[75]

As Farrell continues, we can fit the PFJ alongside the JRA's place in the equation:

> Since the JRA's [PFJ's] objective was not negotiation but rather capitulation, the political flavor to the demands worked to the group's advantage. Communiques issued by the group during the hijackings of the 1970s [attempted kidnapping of 33] made it perfectly clear that the onus was on the Japanese [Roman] government and not the JRA [PFJ]. The government [Pilate] had a choice: give in or accept responsibility for the deaths of its citizens [his wife, a Roman citizen].[76]

The JRA have more success in the 1970s than the PFJ enjoy in 33. The PFJ's hostage taking fails miserably (they scrap with the CFG instead), and leads quite directly to Brian's execution, *not* his ransoming by the PFJ so that he can fight another day. The situation in first-century Jerusalem is different, since Pilate is in a position to win by the use of overwhelming force—he has at his command the "shock and awe" of the empire, if necessary. Unlike modern democracies, where public opinion matters, Pilate does not worry much about local, national, or even international approval, short of pleasing Rome. His position as Judean prefect won't be untenable until Rome loses faith in his ability to keep order; after that, Pilate's days are numbered.

This was also the failed Roman consul candidate Catiline's (and his associates') plan as they readied their overthrow of Pompey's Rome in 63 BC. Cicero uncovered the plot, and Catiline fled to Etruria. One of the Catiline coconspirators "still in Rome plotted to kill all of the senators and to take Pompey's children hostage," a familiar-sounding plan.[77] And even though the usually tempestuous Julius Caesar argued for calm and a fair trial, Cicero and Cato—Pilate-like—insisted on immediate execution of the conspirators.

The oddest version of this hostage-taking-accompanied-by-demands scenario has to be what happened to English ex-pat Charlie Chaplin. The entertainer died in Switzerland on Christmas Day 1977, and was buried soon thereafter. On 2 March 1978—just when the Pythons were reeling from the shock of losing EMI's backing for *Life of Brian*—grave robbers stole Chaplin's body and immediately demanded a $600,000 ransom. His widow balked, and the robbers threatened the Chaplins' children next. A little more than a month later the hapless villains were arrested and the body recovered and securely reinterred.[78]

DEADLY DIRK: "We're not telling you"—Disagreements between seemingly similar revolutionary movements weren't unusual in the 1960s and 1970s, in life or in film. In 1967 Japan, "leaders of the three main *Zengakuren*[79] factions" were invited by a liberal professor to come to university and discuss their platforms for change, but all three refused to appear if they had to share the stage, and each denounced the other in his response to the professor.[80] One student spokesman concluded that "the qualitative difference [between] the movement[s] is so great that we do not think of seeking their aid, even if our power is weak."[81] A foreign visitor made the following observation, comparing the German and Japanese student movements: "There is a difference: in Germany the students fight the police; in Japan the bitterest battles are fought among the students."[82] Similarly, the Galilee and Judean factions, even though they seem to have the same goals and even methods, can't agree to work together for the betterment of Jerusalem.

FRANCIS: "Tough titty for you, fish face"—In an early *Goon Show* episode "fish face" is used as an insult, with Peter Sellers delivering the line in a Jewish accent, while "tough titty" is a very recent American colloquialism.[83] Auberon Waugh's father, Evelyn, used the term "Fuddy-Duddy Fish-Face" as a slighting nickname for Peter Quennell.[84]

DEADLY DIRK poke FRANCIS in the eye—Another Three Stooges (and by extension, cartoony) moment, akin to the "salute" Dirk displayed earlier. In the 1934 Tex Avery cartoon *Porky in Wackyland*, a three-headed creature performs these same Stooges' slaps and pokes.[85]

BRIAN: "Brothers, we should be struggling together . . . "—There are versions of a penultimate scene like this one found in several films, and even in life. First, in the influential *I'm All Right Jack*, a panel discussion show ("*Argument*") involving all sides of the industrial strike erupts into wrestling and fisticuffs. The shop steward, Mr. Kite, stands amid the punch-up and tries to call for order from all sides: "Brothers, please brothers! Use your self-control!" He is immediately socked, and the donnybrook continues. Also, in the Woody Allen film *Bananas* (1971), Fielding (Allen) is telling his psychiatrist about his childhood. In a Bergmanesque dream sequence we see two groups of flagellating monks carrying two crosses, with Fielding strapped to one of them. When both processions vie for the same parking space, a fight erupts, and the monks slaughter each other.

In the world outside the film, the Grunwick Strike[86] in the summer of 1977 pitted the Association of Professional, Executive, Clerical and Computer Staff (APEX) union against the Grunwick film processing laboratories. APEX represented many female, immigrant employees (most East African Asian). In this strike action, vocal and active support from the famed Arthur Scargill and his miners came to picket and chant, and to happily be arrested for their union sisters. *Private Eye* pointed out the irony of this very loud and photogenic support, citing recent history:

> Why was Miners leader Arthur Scargill arrested (with maximum publicity) outside Grunwicks? Scargill and his pack have never been noted for their concern for the union APEX (which is on strike at Grunwicks). In fact, six years ago, during the big national miners' strike,[87] extremely bad publicity was attracted by the miners picketing the Coal Board Doncaster HQ—Coal House. Miners and their wives were shown on television and in the papers kicking APEX members trying to get into Coal House. Teenage girls were kicked, punched and spat upon. Publicity was so bad[88] that during the next miners' strike Scargill had to tell the pickets to moderate their violence because the general public was thought to be in support of those APEX members trying to keep the Coal Board working.[89]

Art can imitate life as the PFJ and CFG struggle together in common cause, party feeling being wrestled into submission as Roman sentries watch.

"Struggling together" has been the warning heard from the earliest days of modern socialism. Socialists fighting each other, factionally, ideologically, means they are not fighting their "common enemy," just fatiguing themselves. In Petr Lavrov's *The State Element in the Future Society* (1876), the proper focus of "the struggle" and "solidarity" (precious terms for the revolutionary) is laid out:

> The working out of a socialist morality therefore requires one thing only: struggling against the Old World and unavoidably making use of the monopolies that exist, we must never even temporarily give ourselves the aim of creating new monopolies as instruments in the struggle for the socialist principle; never and in no case must we resort to monopoly, to exclusive control of any instruments in the social struggle, for the purposes of group rivalry among the socialists themselves, who, whatever their differences [. . .] are obliged, in the name of the solidarity which they have established as their aim (workers' socialism), and of their one and only hatred, towards their common foes (the present-day state and capitalism), [and not to] to fight amongst themselves . . . which . . . undermines the solidarity among all the builders of a world of solidarity, the world of workers' socialism.[90]

The right cause could unite even bitter ideological foes. In the years leading up to World War II, Chiang Kai-Shek's Kuomintang and Mao's Chinese Communist Party laid aside their political enmity in the face of the invading Japanese troops, fighting for a free China together.[91] After the war, they started up again, right where they'd left off.[92] John Sinclair, writing in the *Militant Irish Monthly* in June 1976, says the same of James Connolly's fractured Irish Socialist Republican Party in the first decade of the twentieth century, where ideological hairsplitting would lead to "years of further splits and fusions among tiny groups." Bringing the argument forward, Sinclair concluded: "As today [1976] these groups spend more time fighting amongst themselves than fighting for workers' interests."[93] During this very same period (1975–1976), and in the region our film is focused on, the Lebanese Civil War raged into life—Christian, Palestinian, and Muslim forces fought with and against one another, killing and displacing thousands.[94] The charter distributed by the PLO at its inception in July 1968 echoes Brian's plaintive cry:

> Article 8: The phase in their history, through which the Palestinian people are now living, is that of national (*watani*) struggle for the liberation of Palestine. Thus the conflicts among the Palestinian national forces are secondary, and should be ended for the sake of the basic conflict that exists between the forces of Zionism and of imperialism on the one hand, and the Palestinian Arab people on the other. On this basis the Palestinian masses, regardless of whether they are residing in the national homeland or in diaspora (*mahajir*) constitute—both their organizations and the individuals—one national front working for the retrieval of Palestine and its liberation through armed struggle.

The PFJ and CFG could have benefited from creating, then reading such a "work and play well together" declaration.[95]

But not just social progressives and terror groups, of course, suffer these internecine challenges. In the late 1960s, the French Fourth Republic was attempting to climb back from the depths (having fallen after the Algiers fiasco[96]), but scrapping among themselves threatened their ascension; in Israel the contentious premier race also featured infighting; and in the supposedly united new version of the Common Market, infighting among European members helped Britain forge better deals for the home country.[97] The 1970s in Britain were also a decade of turbulence for the middle class, especially as the home economy sputtered;[98] higher education failed to provide promised success; and the manufacturing base in Britain struggled, restructured, nationalized, and ultimately became perpetually uncompetitive.[99] The former bedrock of British life, both economic and social, the middle class, responded to this uncertainty with perhaps understandable worry and agitation, according to Will Ellsworth-Jones in September 1975: "The middle classes are on the warpath, fighting with all their considerable armoury a very bitter little battle. Their enemy, though, is not Harold Wilson, or Tony Benn, nor even Arthur Scargill;[100] their fight is with each other."[101] Ellsworth-Jones goes on to outline the vicious but sad and even silly infighting between two groups with seemingly similar goals—saving the endangered British middle class—styled the "Middle Class Association" and the "National Federation of the Self-Employed," the "MCA" and "NFSE," if you will. These so-called "fanatical moderates" had tried to put aside their differences when confronted with the breakdown of the world around them, but the leadership couldn't agree on tactics, vision, or useful actions. The MCA would become VOICE, or the Voice of the Independent Centre, and a "palace revolution" brought down MCA's original leader in favor of another, more strident and colorful leader (derisively called "the middle-class answer to Gary Glitter").[102] Like Reg and Francis, each group promised "dynamic action," even an "autumn full of action." Each group and factions within each group, though, ended up spending donated funds on fraternal squabbling rather than concerted external political activity, with the result, one insider admitted, that they were "looked upon as a bit of a joke."[103]

Circling back to our film's depicted world, in the city of Jerusalem in 70 there were at least three separate factions of "Zealots who were all determined to win the war," Kotker writes, but who disagreed on how to do it. One group—with their cry "No king but God"—seized the Temple and used it as a fortress. They continued to perform the Temple sacrifices, even while under attack from a rival band, which was itself being assaulted by soldiers of the third Zealot group. The Zealots were so full of hatred for one another that they seemed to have lost their senses. Members of the three groups even burned one another's food supplies.[104]

These three bands managed to agree they had a common purpose once Titus's forces had completely surrounded the city—a case of too little, too late. In the depicted 33, Pilate's best scenario for survival couldn't have imagined two like-minded fanatical groups bent on undermining his government actually killing each other almost completely before they reached their target—*and* leaving Pilate with one survivor to punish as a public demonstration of the power of the empire. In Britain of 1975, the status quo of the Labour party had nothing to fear from the "moderate militants" of the MCA, the NFSE, or even VOICE; they'd all killed each other long before coming within earshot of No. 10.

BRIAN: "We mustn't fight each other"—The circumstances of historical infighting among specifically revolutionary and terror groups would be risible—if the results weren't so deadly for so many. In the Pythons' lifetime and earlier, such bloody internecine scuffles occurred regularly, including rival Irish groups in the early 1920s, Bulgarian terrorist factional "feuds" between 1924 and 1934, and later "the killing of IRA regulars by Provisionals and vice versa."[105] In 1966 the emerging Palestinian leader Yassir Arafat and his newly formed al-Fatah "resistance" group faced a hostile takeover attempt from one of its backers, the Syrian government, leading to both assassination orders and attempts from either side.[106] The consolidated PFLP under Dr. Habash were, by 1968, the scourge of the more "patriotic" Palestinians—often killing those who opposed them ideologically—they were a "gang . . . of rascals and ruffians . . . trying to tear the revolutionary movement into pieces," according to the organs of competing resistance groups.[107] A pamphlet from another, competing terror organization charges al-Fatah with, essentially, "ruining it for the rest of us": "Habash is trying to tear the resistance movement into pieces from the inside," Demaris records. "This fascist gang is sabotaging the security of the resistance movement and is opening the way for counterrevolutionary forces to intervene in order to destroy the resistance movement."[108] The line "sabotaging the security of the resistance movement" meant that al-Fatah was rocking the boat, not only killing alleged friendly forces but possibly inviting, thanks to the chaos, a larger, more violent response from the Israelis, who had become known for both pinpoint assassinations and attack jet retaliations by this time.[109] Earlier, when Judith announced to the PFJ that Brian as a "do-er" had "struck a blow" against the Romans and for their movement, Reg and Francis were momentarily concerned, knowing that *actual* action might draw unpleasant reprisals from the Romans.

In early June 1948, a large shipment of arms and ammunition was sent from a French port to what had become the State of Israel less than one month earlier. The Irgun faction saw an opportunity to improve its position in (or situate itself in place of) the new government, and wanted the weaponry. The nascent, democratic government under David Ben-Gurion needed the "arms . . . [to] go to the army, whatever happens," and devised a plan to head off Irgun and seize the shipment aboard the *Altalena*.[110] Ben-Gurion's Hagana troops swarmed the beach where the landing was to take place, while Menachem Begin led the Irgun fighters. Ben-Gurion's concern that he voiced to his lieutenants was that they were fighting each other, and not the Arabs. He told his commander, Yigal Allon: "We are faced with open revolt. . . . The very future of the state is at stake. You are to take personal command of the Tel Aviv area. Your new assignment may be the toughest one you've had so far. This time you may have to kill Jews. But I'm depending on you to do what is necessary for the state of Israel."[111] A pitched battle did erupt between Begin's Irgun fighters and the legitimate members of Israel's army, all Jewish combatants, but Begin, who had boarded the *Altalena*, tried to call (Brian-like) for a cease-fire: "Stop shooting! Do not kill your own brothers!"[112] The ship was partly unloaded, then set afire in an artillery barrage from the shore. Begin allegedly refused to surrender, and wanted to die as a witness to the democratic government's "evil" nature, but he was ordered to be tossed overboard, and, like Brian, survived the failed mission.[113]

BRIAN: ". . . surely we should be united against the common enemy"—The immediate answer here is the mysteriously feared Judean Peoples' Front, but they realize it should actually be the Romans. In February 1974 the JRA and the PFLP had worked together to take over the Japanese embassy in Kuwait, their demands being the release of comrades being held in Singapore. By August 1974, there was real concern that the rumored "joint autumn operations of the Japanese Red Army Group and the PFLP" might mean bloody attacks on the Asian Games in Tokyo.[114] By 1976, police were finding evidence of cooperation between the IRA, PFLP, RAF, and Red Youth, a Dutch group.[115] The PFJ and CFG could have benefited from such cooperation, and perhaps survived the palace raid. The "odd bedfellows" idea of these groups linking up, "struggling together," was at this time being discussed in relation to the Japanese Red Army's seemingly suicidal bent, in juxtaposition to the various Al-Fatah groups who espoused more political (and survivable) motives and activities. Of the groups depicted in the film, only the briefly seen Judean Peoples' Front seem as set on self-destruction as the JRA.[116]

In terms of governance, the mid-to-late 1970s was a period of forced coalition, of unusual bedfellows "united against the common enemy," in this case the Tories. Heath's government had enjoyed a sizable majority in June 1970; Wilson's 1974 victory was by a much smaller margin (301–297 seats), and Labour *lost* the popular vote in that same election. The Conservatives were unable to convince the smaller parties to join them in a coalition to break the hung parliament, and Labour was then asked to form a government. Writing in August 1974, Peter Jenkins pointed up Labour's real challenge, and it had to do with "struggling together":

> To discuss coalition within the Labour Party is as perilous as to lecture on genetics at the London School of Economics. The taboo makes it difficult to be realistic about the possibilities of our politics which at the moment, with first holidays and then the election to come, have the appearance of being stuck. The biggest log in the jam is the wooden inability of the Labour Party to develop the potential which exists for a winning alliance on the Left of the centre of British politics.[117]

"Coalition is not some form of conspiracy against Labour," Jenkins would conclude, nor against the Peoples' Front of Judea or the Campaign for Free Galilee, we can conclude, the latter two seeming to have identical plans and goals.[118] Even though Labour had a visible, tilt-worthy opponent in Heath's Tories, they could not put aside ideological differences—the far Labour Left yawing further left, the center doubling down on moderation, and the Right skewing conservative—so coalition became the party's only lifeline. And rather than embrace the like-minded others in the metaphorical tunnel beneath Pilate's palace, Wilson will push on "alone," trusting the fact that he'd managed to win three of four national elections.[119]

The hastily called October 1974 "snap" election gave Wilson the small majority he needed to govern *sans* coalition, but just (319–277). Callaghan's Labour government (from April 1976) officially lost its majority on the day he took office, forcing a series of coalition balancing acts over the next several years. A Lab-Lib pact[120] helped for a while, offering a sort of power-sharing agreement with the smaller, third-party Liberals in return for their bloc votes or abstentions, whichever was necessary, followed by a turn to aggregate support from the fringe nationalist parties—the SNP, the Ulster Unionists, et al. The simple goal was to maintain a majority in the House so that Labour's policies could continue to move forward thanks to control of No. 10, especially as the country's economy seemed on the verge of positive change,[121] with inflation easing and North Sea oil ready to flow.[122] Donoughue notes over and over again that such associations and even concessions represented the greater good—Labour remaining in power, and Labour's agenda remaining in gear.

The PFJ will find that power-sharing to fight the common enemy isn't an option—the PFJ and CFG immediately kill each other in Pilate's house—and the PFJ especially will discover that revolutionary *in*action is a much safer path to remaining in power (and remaining alive).

A ROMAN GUARD walks by at the end of the hallway—This guard is clearly in ear shot of the arguing and whispers, meaning this is yet another cartoony moment; after he passes, they can continue.

DEADLY DIRK *(to Francis)*: **"Right. Where were we?"**—Francis reminds Dirk that he was about to punch him, the CFG leader does so, and the melee can continue. This kind of acknowledgment of the artifice of the action is seen in Tex Avery cartoons. In *Screwball Squirrel* (1944; MGM), Meathead the Dog is chasing Screwy to a frenzied version of the "William Tell Overture," when the action begins to cycle, as if they're stuck. Screwy steps out of frame (the camera pans with him) to an old Victrola, which is stuck in a groove and repeating itself; he jogs the needle, steps back into the frame with the dog, who is waiting patiently, and then the chase continues. Ten years later, in the fight scene (for Laurie's affections) in *The Searchers*, even after biting, eye-gouging, and a kick to the chin, both fighters stop when a fiddle is about to be crushed. They find out who it belongs to, hand it back, and the fight immediately resumes.

Around him lie the remains of the two REVOLUTIONARY GROUPS—A substantially longer fight scene between the PFJ and CFG, an attempted tryst between effeminate centurions, and the "Leviathan"-like appearance of Pilate's enormous wife were gone by the time the film was completed. In that version, Pilate's wife inflicts most of the damage seen here.

By the 1970s the formerly cohesive Students' Socialist League of Japan had splintered badly, leaving dozens of smaller groups with individual axes to grind against Japan, the United States, the war in Vietnam, the emperor, and on. By late 1975 the bomb attacks and assaults of all kinds were coming from myriad tiny groups, their lack of coordination making it much harder for the police to infiltrate and track them. Peter Hazelhurst covered the events in a series of columns for the *Times*, and he may as well have been describing the ridiculous PFJ-CFG clash:

> With each faction accusing the other of betraying Marxist ideals, hardly a day passes without reports of violent clashes. In most cases groups of radicals, wearing crash helmets and masks and wielding steel pipes, surround a small group of rivals and beat them senseless, and in many cases to death, before escaping in broad daylight. Again in most cases, the public do not intervene. Sixteen victims [have] died in political infighting this year so far. A total of 39 radicals have been killed and another 283 have been injured since 1969.[123]

(draft) Her vast fist descends on BRIAN'S head . . . —Right out of a score of Warner Bros. cartoons, including *Baseball Bugs* (1946), and a throwback to the Pythons' use of both the rubber chicken and the giant hammer in *Flying Circus*. In the finished film, this thump on the head happens offscreen, after the screen's gone black. There, it's not clear who actually hits him, but it's hinted that it's one of the guards, and not Pilate's Wife.

Notes

1. See Burleigh, *BRT*, 155.
2. Laqueur, *Terrorism*, 18. The murderous sicarii may or may not have been actively involved with the actual Zealot movement, which appeared a full decade after the rise of sicarii bandits. The Zealots appear to have been a confederation of "brigand bands" forced together by the Roman armies as they pursued a "scorched earth" policy across Judea in 67–68 (Horsley, "The Zealots," 159-71). The PFJ are clearly meant to be more of a political, nationalist group.
3. Horsley, "The Zealots," 189.
4. See the *OED*.
5. "Beating Terrorism," *Spectator*, 21 October 1977: 3.
6. The Air France hijacking was led by individuals from the PFLP-External Operations and (German) Revolutionary Cells terror groups. All four of the hijackers were killed in the Israeli rescue operation, as were three hostages.
7. David Robinson, "The Year the Cinema Looked Back," *Times*, 31 December 1976: 24.
8. "A Swiss Film That Stands Apart," *Times*, 21 October 1977: 17.
9. *Private Eye*, 7 January 1977: 13.
10. "Whittle Kidnapper Always Hooded," *Times*, 23 June 1976: 2.
11. Marighella, *Minimanual*, 53–54.
12. Marighella, *Minimanual*, 54.
13. Marighella, *Minimanual*, 54.
14. Larsen, *BAFHG*, 14 and 20.
15. Demaris, *Brothers in Blood*, 313.
16. Jeremias, *JTJ*, 20; also 2 Chronicles 33:14.
17. Demaris, *Brothers in Blood*, 115.
18. Palin, *Diaries 1969–1979*, 120. Palin was also reading John Dean's *Blind Ambition* in early 1978. Dean was White House Counsel for Nixon. See *BAFHG*, 24 for more.
19. Richard, *WWAR*, 29.
20. Koloski-Ostrow, *ASRI*, 80; also *WWAR*, 59–60.

21. *ASRI*, 81.

22. *ASRI*, 81.

23. Brendon, *DFBE*, 236.

24. Dobson and Payne, *Carlos Complex*, 235, 239–41; also Follain, *Jackal*, 192–93.

25. See Dobson and Payne, *The Terrorists*, 53–55.

26. Laqueur, *Terrorism*, 43–44.

27. Laqueur, *Terrorism*, 44.

28. *ASRI*, 32–33.

29. Quoted in Sandnes, *Belly and Body in the Pauline Epistles*, 85.

30. *ASRI*, 68, 83.

31. *ASRI*, 63–70.

32. First broadcast 28 March 1957 and 10 February 1958, respectively.

33. Claudius had chosen this larger lake many miles east of Rome to present an enormous *naumachia*, or staged naval battle, as part of his grand plan for the finest games ever. To keep the lake from flooding, a three-and-a-half-mile tunnel was cut as a water channel, taking eleven years to complete. The result was a lake large enough to stage the fifty-strong armada of full-size attack boats (Mannix, *TAD*, 36–37). The tunnel collapsed not long after it was completed (and rebuilt more than once), which may be why it does *not* bear Claudius's name.

34. *ASRI*, 13.

35. *ASRI*, 32.

36. *ASRI*, 30.

37. See the entry for "sicarii" in *JE*.

38. Demaris, *Brothers in Blood*, 83. In the months that followed, dozens of hoax bomb threats were reported ("Lessons of Jew Bomb Outrage," *Aberdeen Journal*, 25 July 1946: 1); see also *DFBE*, 481.

39. See the "Archaeology Report" sections in the *Times*, including 26 September 1973: 5, 15 November 1973: 21, 28 February 1974: 15, 12 April 1975: 3, and 13 August 1977: 14.

40. There were at least six other bombings attributed to the IRA in 1974.

41. Waugh, *FCY*, 13 June 1974.

42. Farrell, *BRJ*, 97.

43. Laqueur, *Terrorism*, 16–17. *Private Eye* also pokes fun using the current terrorist climate. In a February 1977 issue, a gala awards ceremony is interrupted by the appearance of "a number of highly trained Marxist guerrillas" who "broke into the hall and clubbed Mr. [Ivor] Richard to death with Soviet-made *knobkerries*" (7 January 1977: 10). Richard had been very recently (and, to some, ineffectively) helping to broker the Rhodesian negotiations at the 1976 Geneva Conference.

44. See the "sicarii" entry, penned by Richard Gottheil and Samuel Kraus, in *JE*.

45. Josephus, *AJ*, 20.9.3 (Whiston, 424).

46. Iviansky, "Individual Terror," 53.

47. J. P. Getty III and Patty Hearst are discussed elsewhere in this section. Frank Sinatra Jr. had been kidnapped and ransomed in California in 1963; the former child actress Shirley Temple Black had also been a target, it was discovered much later, for possible kidnapping by the JRA (*Daily Mail*, 18 March 2016). Black had become US ambassador to Ghana in 1974.

48. See Iviansky's "Individual Terror" and Laqueur's *Terrorism* for more.

49. "New Light on Habakkuk," *Times*, 30 May 1950: 3.

50. 2 Samuel 5:8.

51. See Reich's interview/presentation, "The Question of the Biblical 'Zinnor' and Warren's Shaft." Reich translates the words used in both the ESV and the KJV, "went up," as "climbed," meaning Joab and his men may have climbed upward through a shaft.

52. See Reich and Shukron's "Light at the End of the Tunnel," 22–33, 72.

53. Larsen, *MPFC: UC*, 1.100; 2.81.

54. Smallwood, *JURR*, 321.

55. "Airlines Want Inter-government Action to Combat Hijacking," *Financial Times*, 21 October 1969: 19.

56. "Troops Called in to Block Ulster Strike Measures," *Times*, 30 April 1977: 1.

57. The Ulster Defence Association and the Ulster Volunteer Force, respectively, both Protestant loyalist paramilitary groups.

58. *Private Eye*, 13 May 1977: 4.

59. This column featured real news from troubled areas of the world, usually detailing sad political and military absurdities that made life miserable for many.

60. *Private Eye*, 24 December 1976: 7.

61. *JURR*, 292–93.

62. *JURR*, 153n40.

63. *JURR*, 153.

64. *JURR*, 153.

65. *JURR*, 153–54. In 1969 Peter Lewis wrote a lengthy *Daily Mail* article on Judas Iscariot and his motivations in betraying Christ. Lewis spent a number of column inches discussing Barabbas, the Zealots, and first-century Judea anti-Roman movements ("Can We Really Believe Judas Did It Just for Money?" *Daily Mail*, 3 April 1969: 8).

66. Yadin, *Excavation of Masada*, 108; quoted in Brandon, *Jesus and the Zealots*, 62n4.

67. Maier's historical fiction, *Pontius Pilate*, also places the Zealots in Galilee (195).

68. Caryl, *Strange Rebels*, 38–39.

69. For the last reference, see "Rival Union Fights," *Daily Mail*, 6 October 1976: 11.

70. "How the Angry Brigade Cracked," *Daily Mail*, 7 December 1972: 16–17. The "Revolutionary Solidarity Movement, First May Group" claimed credit for shooting up the US Embassy in London in 1967 ("Sequel to Shots at US Embassy," *Times*, 25 August 1967: 3); at least two bombs were claimed by "Butch Cassidy and the Sundance Kid" and "Wild Bunch" ("Explosions Case Court Told of Letters," *Times*, 28 April 1971: 4); and Lotta Continua was an Italian terror group with reported links to the IRA. Jesus and his disciples' "raid" on the temple in *The Passover Plot* is structured just like one of these demonstrative Angry Brigade actions.

71. *JURR*, 281–82; *AJ*, 20.9.2–3 (Whiston, 424).

72. The Japanese government was especially prone to making deals with terrorists, hoping to avoid additional collateral damage.

73. *JURR*, 279; for Josephus's version, see *AJ*, 20.8.11 (Whiston, 422–23).

74. "How Black September Threatens Europe," *Telegraph*, 15 July 1973: 6.

75. *BRJ*, 231.

76. *BRJ*, 231.

77. *WWAR*, 114–15. For more on this incident, see "The PFJ's Plan" scene.

78. The bizarre Chaplin story stayed in the news through most of 1978, with a well-attended retrospective of his films and memorabilia running at the National Film Theatre starting in May and the trial for the grave robbers being conducted in December 1978.

79. An acronym for *Zen Nihon Gakusei Jichikai Sorengo*, or the "All-Japan Federation of Student Self-Governing Associations," a student offshoot of the Japan Communist Party.

80. *BRJ*, 61.

81. *BRJ*, 61.

82. *BRJ*, 62. Farrell goes on to note that between just 1968 and 1975, there were more than 1,770 "internal factional disputes" among these student groups—and those were just the fights "violent enough to require police involvement" (62). The PFJ and CFG are in good company.

83. *The Goon Show*, 22 January 1952.

84. "Peter Quennell," *New York Times*, 31 October 1993.

85. *BAFHG*, 315.

86. Discussed in more detail in the "Stoning" scene section.

87. This is the strike that hobbled Heath and the sitting Tory government, forcing power rationing and the three-day work week, and eventually a losing election for the Conservatives in 1974. *Holy Grail* was being written during this cold, dark period. See *BAFHG*, 86, as well as the entries in that index under "strikes" for more.

88. This "bad publicity" was worse than anyone assumed at the time—it helped sour the electorate to big labor causes, preparing the way for a Thatcher victory in 1979.

89. "Blackleg," *Private Eye*, 8 July 1977: 4.

90. Sapir, *"Vpered!" 1873–1877*, 326.

91. Caryl, *Strange Rebels*, 29.

92. There are even incidents of the authorities in charge of fighting insurrection "struggling together." *Private Eye* reports the following: "General Minguel Arracha, head of the anti-urban guerrilla section, Buenos Aires north, was blown to pieces by a bomb that his friend General Carlos Mendoza had forgotten to take away with him after their weekly game of dominoes" ("True Stories," 26 November 1976: 8).

93. Reprinted at http://redlug.com/LabHist/LabOrigins.htm. James Connolly was an Irish Republican activist who also spent time in the United States. He would be executed by the British in 1916. The *Militant Irish Monthly* began publishing in June 1972 to "put forward a clear and consistent Marxist view of the bloody events in Ireland," according to the broadsheet for its third issue.

94. Laqueur, *Terrorism*, 235–36.

95. "Rejectionist" groups—PFLP and PFLP-GC—targeted the more moderate PLO after 1974, so both Mossad and "friendly" agents were killing Palestinian "brothers" (*BRT*, 178).

96. "The Fourth Republic Creeps out of the Shadows," *Daily Mail*, 9 May 1969: 2.

97. "Who Steps In?" *Daily Mail*, 27 February 1969: 2. In the first case, François Mitterrand was a contender, but Georges Pompidou won the race; in the latter, Golda Meier. See also, "Hard Pounding on the Bargaining Table," *Daily Mail*, 19 October 1972: 6.

98. Wage inflation, for example, had just scaled to a new record of 30 percent, and "the irresistible surge of prices and wages" was bringing "the tide of inflation" to "monstrous proportions" (Sandbrook, *Seasons in the Sun*, 332 and 344).

99. See Sandbrook, *Seasons in the Sun*.

100. Labour leader Wilson was still at this point the sitting PM, having narrowly won reelection in February 1974, and strengthened his position (slightly) in the October 1974 election. His government's policies seemed to be having no positive effect on the moribund economy. The far left of the Labour party featured Benn, secretary of state for energy, who was busy trying to reshape entirely British industry and economy and life into a more state-controlled workers' paradise. Scargill was the NUM leader whose earlier strike activities had essentially brought down the Heath government (*BAFHG* 119, 120, and 238).

101. "The Middle-Class Warriors Split Down the Middle," *Sunday Times*, 14 September 1975: 2.

102. See Will Ellsworth-Jones, "The Middle-Class Warriors Split Down the Middle," *Sunday Times*, 14 September 1975: 2. Gary Glitter was a glam rocker of the period.

103. Ellsworth-Jones, "The Middle-Class Warriors," 2.

104. Kotker, *HLTJ*, 118.

105. Laqueur, *Terrorism*, 129.

106. Demaris, *Brothers in Blood*, 144.

107. Demaris, *Brothers in Blood*, 152–53.

108. Demaris, *Brothers in Blood*, 152.

109. "Jets Take Revenge for Cinema Raid," *Daily Mail*, 13 December 1974: 4.

110. Demaris, *Brothers in Blood*, 109–10.

111. Demaris, *Brothers in Blood*, 111.

112. Demaris, *Brothers in Blood*, 111.

113. Begin, a Jew devoted to the idea of a historically large Israel, would go on to form a right-wing political party, Herut, and after a coalition with other opposition parties, would become prime minister in 1977. Reflecting on his time in Palestine leading up to and including the British withdrawal in 1947 and the declaration of statehood the next year, Patrick O'Donovan would write of these men of leadership:

> Ben-Gurion was in Britain quickly accorded the rank of elder statesman and the many British journalists who stayed behind were treated courteously and helpfully. The only exception to all this was Menachem Begin. We

hated him. Ben-Gurion hated him. The Israeli Foreign Minister of the time, Moshe Shertok, told me that he was a "pathological phenomenon." ("Memories of Begin," *The Spectator*, 19 November 1977: 9)

114. "Games May Face Guerrilla Attack," *Daily Mail*, 31 August 1974: 4.

115. "Swoop on Terrorists with an IRA Link," *Daily Mail*, 30 September 1976: 4.

116. "Death Wish of a Red Army," *Times*, 7 February 1974: 5.

117. Jenkins, *Anatomy of Decline*, 60.

118. Jenkins, *Anatomy of Decline*, 63.

119. In a post-election column (12 October 1974), Jenkins would remind readers that Heath was neatly juxtaposed to Wilson, having "played four, lost three"; Jenkins was certain that Heath's political prospects, especially as leader of his party, were snuffed out (*Anatomy of Decline*, 66). Jenkins was prophetic. The next leadership tilt for the Tories went to Thatcher, and Heath faded into surly, same-party opposition status. (Jenkins, like most everyone else, gave Thatcher little chance to overcome the "Carlton Club" misogyny and carry the day [67].)

120. Made with Liberal leader David Steel, these were colloquially known as "understandings," where it was agreed that "Labour would take full account of the Liberal point of view" in selected areas of policy (*DSD*, 2.214). The fact that the agreements didn't last terribly long gives an idea of just how much "account" Labour gave to Liberal policies.

121. This optimism was short-lived, as was Callaghan's premiership. By the winter of 1978–1979, the trade unions began to flex their muscles again (*viz.*, the ramping-up of exorbitant pay claims), helping crush not only Britain's fragile economic recovery, but its labor-friendly Labour government, as well. Labour would be relegated to opposition until 1997.

122. Donoughue, *DSD*, 2.167. Interestingly, this was also the period that the leash held by Big Labour—the trade unions—went slack. The PM and his Labour Party minions had to concentrate on staying in power, meaning the bulk of the behind-the-scenes machinations were directed not at trade union representatives like Jack Jones or Hugh Scanlon, but toward the Ulster Unionists like Paisley and Powell, the SNP, and other outliers whose votes were not owned by the Tories. The daily newspapers were filled with rumors and realizations of such deals. See Donoughue and Sandbrook.

123. "Japan's Terror Groups Raise Fears of a Police State," *Times*, 22 October 1975: 16.

SCENE TWELVE
IN PILATE'S JAIL

He wakes up with a smile on his face to find himself being dragged along . . .—This is likely meant to indicate that Brian's been dreaming pleasantly, and even that everything he just went through was actually a dream. The camera is fixed on him in such a way that he seems to be asleep in his bed, his hand under his cheek, a pleasant look (not really a smile) on his face. A quick zoom out reveals his actual condition—he's being dragged down stairs and into Pilate's dungeon.

This may be one of the less obvious connections to the more "human" Christ figure depicted in *The Last Temptation*, the 1955 novel by Nikos Kazantzakis. There, Christ falls into a dream state while on the cross, lives a long and happy life, only to wake up still on the cross in time to make his ultimate sacrifice. In this controversial novel Christ possesses all the human weaknesses and strengths, including physical lust, and still manages to remain sinless and accomplish his role as savior.

. . . flings him into the dark damp cell, slamming the iron gate . . .—In "The Spanish Inquisition" sketch from *Flying Circus* Ep. 15, the Inquisitors drag the Dear Old Lady down into a "torchlit dungeon" where they will torture her with a comfy chair and soft cushions.

The contemporary version of Pilate's jail would have been the infamous Lubyanka, the headquarters of the KGB as well as a much-feared prison. Waugh mentions Lubyanka often in his diaries, sometimes in relation to its well-known former guest Aleksander Solzhenitsyn, and sometimes in relation to the *Daily Mirror*'s looming, brutalist-style headquarters in Holborn Circus.[1] The Roman version would have been the *Carcer Tullianum*, where inmates included Simeon bar Giora, former leader of the Jerusalem resistance as the Romans besieged the city; Vercingetorix, the Gaulish chieftain captured by Julius Caesar; and the apostles Peter and Paul. Ben is actually in good company when the notoriety of other Roman prisoners is considered.

. . . an emaciated figure, suspended from the wall . . .—Borrowed from the clapping figure seen outside Camelot in *Holy Grail*, an odd juxtaposition to this "silly place" of singing and dancing. The Goons had offered an almost identical setup in their second "Robin Hood" episode. When Robin (Secombe) is thrown into jail, Friar Balsam (Sellers) is hanging in chains on the wall behind him.[2] There is also a very similar set piece in the 1976 film *The Passover Plot*. There, John the Baptist (Harry Andrews) is being interrogated in a Herodian prison; he hangs against a stone wall, his arms chained above him.

We aren't ever told why Ben is here, whether he's Jewish or Samaritan or a Roman; we don't know if he's a slave or a free man convicted of a crime. If Ben was ever a Roman citizen, then he must have been "condemned as a result of a fair trial to corporal capital punishment, [the] consequence of which was a slave-like exclusion from the civic community, technically known as a *servitus poenae* [slavery of the punishment]."[3] He is also hanging from the wall, his feet off the ground—considered a sacrilege—exacerbating the victim's suffering and confirming his status as a *noxius* (criminal).[4] His verbiage later, when he credits the Romans with being "fair" and a "terrific race," means he's likely not from Rome, but he still may be a citizen, based on his residence in the empire, past Roman military service, or the like.

BEN: "I sometimes hang awake at nights dreaming of being spat at in the face"— One of the rituals found in ancient Israel surrounding a marriage refusal (involving a man and his brother's widow) included the woman loosening his shoe, then spitting in his face "in the presence of elders."[5] In other mentions, Jesus spits to make clay for healing, while Job was spat at due to his lowliness. Perhaps Ben is simply longing for the physical acknowledgment of his existence that being spat upon implies.

In Roman prisons like the Carcer Tullianum, according to Whiston, prisoners weren't held long, generally just until trial and/or execution. Ben's longer sentence is then more a reflection of the contemporary prison situation in Britain—life sentences had become the upper limit of state punishment after the abolition of hanging in 1965. Most Roman-era prisoners were simply strangled to death in the prison.[6] Jewish rebel leader Simeon bar Giora was taken to Rome, paraded through the streets, scourged, and executed as soon as he reached the prison.[7]

And speaking of "fair" treatment, during the Patty Hearst trial, the court heard of Hearst's "jailer" (members of the SLA) taking sexual liberties with her, which Hearst described in a Stockholm Syndrome kind of way. The prosecution argued the relationships were consensual.

BEN: "Manacles! Oooh" *(his eyes go quite dreamy)*—Firstly, these impedimenta would have been standard for prisoners in Roman jails, according to Plautus. If Ben were a slave, for example, and still able to work, he would have been "chained up by night in a prison and [taken] to work in the quarries during the day."[8] Plautus writes of a "slave . . . ordered to be taken to a smith, Hippolytus, who makes thick shackles forged of iron and attached them to the slave."[9] (Perhaps Ben is an old slave, then?)

Secondly, there exists an almost sexual gratification here, with Ben being dominated by a powerful "partner" (in this case, the Centurion, and even Rome) in a sadomasochistic relationship. He may be a Stockholm Syndrome sufferer. Popular in the news media of the day, captor and captive formed unexpected bonds. This relationship was noticed during the 1970 hijackings orchestrated by the PFLP, with passengers/hostages reporting they were "treated pretty well," and a number of hostages even felt significant sympathy not only for the young hijackers, but for their stated cause. A *Time* magazine correspondent interviewed a young American girl who had been held, and when it was all over she was certain that the Palestinians had been "kicked out of their homes," and that even though the pamphlets she was given to read were certainly "propaganda," she "believed that some of it was true."[10] Our Ben has been hung upside down for a number of years, and his captors have only recently righted him—for this he's clearly grateful. The Romans have not taken the next possible step—execution—so Ben is relieved and grateful. This almost groveling response to a kidnapper's supposed largesse isn't odd (or even Pythonesque) at all; an aberrant behavior psychiatrist of the period called it "common as dirt":

Dr. [David G.] Hubbard[11] says that the phenomenon is caused by the fact that the hijacker does not use all the force that is available to him. This makes the victims feel grateful. "The fact that he has no right to use the force doesn't come through because the people are so damned scared they are not thinking."[12]

Ben exhibits these same characteristics as a five-year hostage to Rome's imperial ambitions; he's grateful because they could have left him upside down, increased his pain and suffering, or even killed him. Rome isn't using all its force against Ben, though Brian won't be so lucky, or so grateful.

BEN: "They must think you're Lord God Almighty!"—This is a Hebrew classification—the one ruling God—and we're already far away from the hypersensitivity of the stoning scene, where the simple utterance of "Jehovah" (not as part of an oath) is sufficient to condemn Matthias.

BEN: "Oh, you'll probably get away with crucifixion"—Perhaps Ben has read his Livy (59 BC–AD 17), who had recently written of Rome's "gentle" punishments, at a time when those punishments included both immolation and crucifixion.[13] Strangulation inside a prison was also practiced, and often, generally after the victim had been paraded through the streets.

Josephus mentions quite a number of Roman executions by crucifixion, primarily for sedition, but not entirely: "But Varus sent a part of his army into the country, against those that had been the authors of this commotion, and as they caught great numbers of them, those that appeared to have been the least concerned in these tumults he put into custody, but such as were the most guilty he crucified; these were in number about two thousand."[14] Josephus also describes Ummidius Quadratus going to Caesarea and crucifying "all those whom Cumanus had taken alive,"[15] and:

> Felix took Eleazar the arch-robber, and many that were with him, alive, when they had ravaged the country for twenty years together, and sent them to Rome; but as to the number of the robbers whom he caused to be crucified, and of those who were caught among them, and whom he brought to punishment, they were a multitude not to be enumerated.[16]

And:

> they also caught many of the quiet people, and brought them before Florus, whom he first chastised with stripes, and then crucified. Accordingly, the whole number of those that were destroyed that day . . . was about three thousand and six hundred. And what made this calamity the heavier was this new method of Roman barbarity; for Florus ventured then to do what no one had done before, that is, to have men of the equestrian order whipped and nailed to the cross before his tribunal; who, although they were by birth Jews, yet were they of Roman dignity notwithstanding.[17]

As a member of the lower class *humiliores* (even though his father may have been a Roman), Brian might also have been eligible for two other approved methods of execution. While the nobleman could expect a quick beheading, or even be allowed an honorable suicide,

> the rest of the population (the *humiliores*) found themselves subject in late antiquity to the forms of the death penalty to which only non-citizens had been liable in earlier centuries. These were: crucifixion, being torn to death by animals (*ad bestias*), and being burnt to death (*ad flammas* or *crematio*)—the first two perhaps borrowed from the Carthaginian military practice at the time of the first Punic war.[18]

As Nisus Wettus will say later: "Crucifixion? Good." Perhaps, then, Ben isn't diminishing Brian's punishment—he might actually see crucifixion, like Matthias later, as preferable to death by wild animals or fire.

More contemporary with the Pythons themselves, but still in Judea, after World War II the Jewish nationalist terror groups put aside their internecine disagreements and began to cooperate against the "occupying" British in the Mandate of Palestine. This united front engaged in dozens of acts of sabotage (against rail lines, power stations, oil installations, police and government offices), as well as bombings, shootings, and even murders of British police and government officials across the region. The British reaction in January 1946 was to announce "new Emergency Regulations that called for the death penalty for acts of terror and in some cases even for membership in a terrorist group."[19] Pilate's immediate resort to the death penalty for anti-Roman activities was well within his purview as prefect of the region (maintaining order being paramount). To try and curb the violence as well as appease the Arabs clamoring for British control in Palestine, the British high commission took the same tack.

An uprising in colonial Jamaica in 1865 led the governor, Edward Eyre, to "declare martial law," and he "then hanged and flogged many hundreds of black people, and burned over a thousand dwellings."[20] Acting in a Pilate-like manner, the governor also executed a Baptist preacher, G. W. Gordon. Eyre was recalled to London (like Pilate to Rome), but never punished, and Jamaica then "came under direct rule as a crown colony."[21] Coincidentally, Gordon was the mixed-race son of a Scotsman and a Jamaican slave.

BEN: "Yeah, first offense"—The fact that Ben not only leads with such a gruesome punishment, but he also sees it as an *expected* and *fair* penalty for a first-time offender says that such Roman punishments were common, at least in the Pythons' version of first-century Jerusalem. We've already seen the grisly evidence of past executions on display as Mandy and Brian walk home, and the script directions have alerted us that they've become commonplace—they aren't noticed. This is interesting because it might indicate lacunae in some period biblical scholarship, specifically the originality of some of Jesus's words as recorded in the Gospels. In the 1977 BBC production (and accompanying book) *Who Was Jesus?*, Don Cupitt look at Mark 9:34: "If any man would come after me, let him deny himself and take up his cross and follow me," noting that there are similar sections in both Matthew and Luke. He concludes:

> Now if one thinks oneself back into the situation during Jesus' lifetime, before it was known that he was going to be crucified, and certainly before any idea that being a follower of Jesus meant sharing in his crucifixion, then it seems clear that the saying would not have been intelligible before Jesus' death. So it cannot be a saying of the historical Jesus.[22]

In the Python version of Judea, the specter of death on the cross was visible and talked about, long before Brian or any of the other 139 condemned find themselves on crosses at the end of the film.[23] And since the Romans had been employing crucifixion as a method of punishment for at least a century by this point, and Jesus was being accused of defying Rome (charged with sedition) by at least some of his Jewish antagonists, Rome's wrath would seem a possibility for a rouser of rabble like Jesus (or Barabbas or Judas, et al.).[24] Therefore, Jesus might actually have meaningfully and sincerely told his disciples to "take up his cross," assuming or even knowing where he would end his life.

BEN: "Best thing the Romans ever did for us . . ."—Ben isn't a voice in the wilderness, either. Jewish historian Josephus had no patience or praise for the violent action of the Zealots, whose activities he saw as undermining the Jews' beneficial relationship with Rome.[25] He would blame the Zealots "for the ruin of Israel and found no term too damning with which to condemn them."[26] And the "peace" that Xerxes earlier credits the Romans with bringing to the region (at which Reg snorts) is also key here. The idea of a *pax Romana* would be celebrated by Romans and Greeks, conquerors and conquered, blossoming from the acts and personality of Augustus (it's even known as *pax Augusta* by some). "Herod wholeheartedly advocated identification with the *pax Romana*," Levine writes, "and many followed suit":

> Indeed, most people probably reconciled themselves, to one degree or another, with Roman rule. Nicholas of Damascus, Herod's trusted adviser and a prominent historian in his own right, regarded Roman patronage as a blessing for all peoples. A generation later, R. Hananiah, a high-ranking Temple official, succinctly worded the merits of Roman rule: "One must pray for the welfare of the empire . . . for were it not for the fear of it, each person would swallow the next alive."[27]

Carl Richard supports Levine and Ben, underlining, like the PFJ, the benefits of Rome's rule:

> The Romans were not merely the modifiers and transmitters of Greek culture and of Christianity. They also made original contributions to the Western world. They not only provided the conditions of peace and prosperity necessary for the transmission of Greco-Roman culture and Christianity but also proved themselves the most capable administrators and lawgivers in human history. They effectively administered an empire of unprecedented size with minimal bureaucracy and technology and bequeathed to the West a system of law whose principles of equity and justice endured long after the fall of the empire.[28]

The PFJ have also already agreed that the Romans are the "only ones" who can keep order in Jerusalem. The Greek Aelius Aristides (c. 117–181) waxed positively Ben-like in his praise and admiration for what the Romans offered. Aelius saw the world outside the empire's influence as pitiable; those not under Rome's protection were "denied" the "blessings" of being subjects. Aelius cites the security of even the remote, formerly treacherous parts of the empire, "for safety it is enough to be a Roman, or one of your subjects."[29] Aelius isn't done (and in his exuberance sounds appreciably like the helpful PFJ in response to Reg's rhetorical question):

> In very deed you have made real Homer's dictum that the earth is the property of all; you have measured the whole world, spanned rivers with bridges of divers kinds, cut through mountains to make levels roads for traffic, filled desolate places for farmsteads, and made life easier by supplying its necessities amid law and order. Everywhere are gymnasia, fountains, gateways, temples, factories, schools, and it could be said in technical phrase that the world which from the beginning has been laboring in illness has now been put in the way of health.[30]

Reg has complained of his people being bled white, the Romans taking "everything" for several generations. But history also seems to be on Ben's side, and not the PFJ's:

> As the year 68 unfolded, the city of Rome was approaching a century of unbroken peace. Prosperity reigned and dangerous times seemed buried in history as people pursued lives of comfortable routine. They rose at dawn and prepared to make, or receive, morning visits. . . . "We are now in such a happy time of peace," the elder Pliny wrote.[31]

Pliny was writing during the time the film's events are unfolding, as well. He was writing about Rome specifically, but the bulk of the empire in Augustus's and Tiberius's lifetimes could claim unprecedented peace. Lastly, the Greek Plutarch (46–120) also had mixed feelings about being a Roman subject, but managed to balance those feelings:

> Plutarch was no imperial lackey; he characterized Augustus' early career as ruthless and bloodthirsty and his republican opponents as heroes. Yet Plutarch clearly valued the peace Augustus

had restored to the devastated Roman world after a century of civil war and appreciated his skill-ful administration of the empire. Nor did Plutarch bewail the Greeks' loss of freedom to Rome, despite his nostalgia for the eras of Greek greatness. Like Polybius and Josephus . . . Plutarch considered the Roman Empire the product of a divine will that was irresistible.[32]

BEN: ". . .if we didn't have crucifixion this country would be in a right bloody mess . . ."—This sounds like those who favored keeping capital punishment in the face of sweep-ing changes that ushered in the so-called "permissive society" in the mid-1960s, as well as a contemporary judge in a high-profile legal action important to *Life of Brian*.

In the first, one of Home Secretary Jenkins's "updates" in law and society was the aboli-tion of the death penalty in Great Britain in 1965,[33] ending generations of capital punish-ment for myriad offenses.[34] Between 1965 and 1977 there had been plenty of criminal atrocities (including the Moors Murders, the Yorkshire Ripper, the Black Panther, and IRA bombings in England) that reignited the calls for a death penalty,[35] but the will for such a change couldn't be sustained in either the Commons or No. 10. This didn't stop backbenchers from often stridently calling for capital punishment's return, including Colo-nel Carol Mathers, MP for Esher:

> His concern is to reassure the public, particularly the old people and the widows, who are fright-ened to go out alone at night. He says the nation must show that it is determined to stamp out serious crimes. There is no proper deterrent to the serious criminal. . . . His main argument for a Government initiative and a parliamentary *volte-face* is that the dimension of crime has changed completely since the death penalty was abolished in 1965. He said: "We have terrorism spilled over into this country from Northern Ireland."[36]

Finally, Mather was asked about his move to the right of the Tory party, and he offered this fa-miliar litany of unpleasant changes seen in Britain over the previous decade: "It was the general situation, violence, mugging and the very real effect which permissive legislation introduced during the Labour Government had on the deterioration of standards. Abortion, relaxation of censorship, the homosexual bill, all that lot. The system seemed to be collapsing."[37]

In *Flying Circus*, the Pythons had already offered a judge who's had it "up to here" with a whinging society that feels sorry for criminals and excuses such behavior. He is "emigrat-ing to South Africa" where he can dish out corporal and capital punishment, and for his last "fling" he sentences the man in front of him to be burnt at the stake.[38] The actual legal case that had many watching and wondering how the more permissive society would fare in court involved the *Gay News* prosecution in 1977. Judge Alan King-Hamilton presided over what was known as *Whitehouse v. Lemon*, and the editors of *Private Eye* (friends of those accused) published a helpful list of the judge's pro–corporal punishment views that read like Ben's own pronouncements. The article notes that in 1965 King-Hamilton told an offender that he regretted he was unable to "order capital punishment," and to a car thief in 1975 he said: "A great many people would not appear in the dock if they had corporal punishment when they were younger. It's a great pity the courts no longer have the power to order capital punish-ment," the judge complained. "The best form of psychiatric treatment is administered not to the head but to the backside."[39] It was believed at the time that King-Hamilton was also in favor of flogging, but that may have been just a law clerk rumor running around the Inns of Court.[40] During the weeklong trial, King-Hamilton had said that blasphemy included "any attack on Christ which has in it some irreverence," an incredibly broad definition that should have sobered the Pythons as they moved their film forward. He didn't call for corporal pun-ishment for the *Gay News* editors, but he did sentence them to prison time and fines.

And since running an empire took time and energy, the Romans didn't handle all these executions, as a matter of course. Many condemned *noxii* became a product of trade and entertainment: "The Roman imperial treasury could sell the *noxii* to a sponsor who in turn was responsible for the executions."[41] It might be that in the provinces the executions were handled closer to the institution, meaning Pilate's soldiers would have carried out these sentences.[42] The Pythons don't exploit this historical tidbit.

BEN: "Nail 'em up I say!"—The curmudgeonly journalist Claud Cockburn responded to a report on "attitudes of the youth" in eleven countries that was published in 1977. The report concluded, according to Cockburn's summary of the *Sunday Telegraph*'s coverage, that the youth seemed to be more conservative than not, and "the so-called generation gap is much narrower than we are often led to suppose." They even seem to be in favor of the return of capital punishment by hanging, so Cockburn argues for a return of hanging, and that such hangings should be "easily accessible to huge streams of family cars," and continues:

> An imaginative Government, in tune with youthful thinking, should have no difficulty in erecting scaffolds and gibbets at convenient sites on the country's principal motorways. . . . It will. . . be desirable that hangings be timed and sited so that the young families can eat their sandwiches, drink from their thermos etc., watch a man or woman being killed, and still have time to get on to beauty spot or beach. . . . It is surely obvious that to be effective, hanging must be no sort of hole-and-corner namby-pamby business, but conducted in full view of the maximum public.[43]

Ben would have agreed completely. Eckstein notes that if the masses aren't really willing to be "liberated," revolution gets trickier.[44] Citizens like Ben are obviously attached to the Roman way of life, and even with a dedicated revolutionary like Brian before him, he won't be swayed. Eckstein accounts for this "inertia": "More likely than not [the masses'] opposition to the terrorists will cause them to cling more closely to the already existing state structures."[45]

BEN: "It's taught me to respect the Romans"—The PFJ and Brian haven't learned this lesson. We don't ever know what crime Ben has been accused of or charged with, but he is certain that the Romans have done right by him and even his nation, and he's grateful. This is an echo of the obsequious response offered by Stig O'Tracey (Idle) when quizzed about his treatment by the Piranha brothers:[46]

> Interviewer (Jones): But the police have film of Dinsdale actually nailing your head to the floor.
>
> Stig: Oh yeah, well, he did do that, yeah.
>
> Interviewer: Why?
>
> Stig: Well he had to, didn't he? I mean, be fair, there was nothing else he could do. I mean, I had transgressed the unwritten law.
>
> Interviewer: What had you done?
>
> Stig: Er, well he never told me that. But he gave me his word that it was the case, and that's good enough for me with old Dinsy. I mean, he didn't want to nail me to the floor, I had to insist. He wanted to let me off. There's nothing Dinsdale wouldn't do for you.[47]

Another man (Chapman) *isn't* unhappy that Dinsdale nailed his head to a floor and screwed his pelvis to a cake stand, while Stig's wife (Chapman) is able to *deny* having her head nailed to a coffee table (which we see nailed to her head). These grateful victims are clear precursors to Ben, the ideal Roman prisoner, as Wiedemann points out, speaking specifically of captured opponents:

The marginal position of such captives in Roman eyes is clear. Defeated military opponents were enemies of the Romans who had refused to accept the benefits of subjection to Roman order. The Romans notoriously convinced themselves that no one might legitimately oppose their rule: to fight Rome was to rebel. Such rebels had forfeited any right to a place in Roman society.[48]

In this Ben also sounds like the ideal British subject, at least according to Labour MP Douglas Jay. In his somewhat infamous book *The Socialist Case*,[49] Jay would describe the proper relationship between the common man and his (Labour) government: "In the case of nutrition and health, just as in the case of education, the gentleman in Whitehall really does know better what is good for people than the people know themselves." This would become, to Conservative pundits, "The man in Whitehall knows best," and a rallying cry for the opposition.[50] And where would this *nem. con.* consideration for a government have come from, for the Pythons? Likely, their own childhoods. The ubiquitous voice and presence of the government during the war had become something of a comfort for most of the British public, and the necessary rationing of finite resources had placed the British man and woman in an abject position in relation to the various ministries of the government— depending on ration cards and travel permissions—a "meekness" that was likely difficult to shake in the postwar years.[51] Those in government keen on the socialist version of Britain's future saw a continuation of this masochistic relationship as necessary, and no one should or could legitimately oppose this march into a new world. Ultimately, redistribution of wealth and the dismantling of the class system was going to be a long and painful process, so pliable, long-suffering citizens were a must.

Ben has now accepted the Romans and their notorious legitimacy, and seems fairly happy in his chains.[52] Wiedemann goes on to describe these rebels and the PFJ fairly well, as both "had excluded themselves from the community of civilized peoples."[53] The PFJ hide in Matthias's and then Mandy's house and plan furtively, jumping at every door knock, subject to arrest upon discovery. Wiedemann goes on to mention that the only possible way these types survived was if the Romans offered them slavery—"whole peoples as well as individual soldiers"—as the "only escape from the death" they all deserved.[54] In the end, Reg and what remains of the PFJ choose their own version of this clemency—they put their revolutionary plans on the back burner, leave Brian safely on the cross, and remain subjects of the Roman Empire.

But Josephus points out rather curtly that the one thing Judas and his Zealot followers would not accept was a continuation of their current condition. These rebels' unwillingness to acknowledge the status quo, Roman rule, seems to have perplexed philo-Romans like Josephus and even most of the Jewish ruling class. Like Xerxes, sympathizers found value in the peace that Roman order delivered. Ben has embraced suffering—his version of peace—and now enjoys his masochistic relationship with his jailers and the empire. There seems to be pleasure in these hardships. Ben is willing to suffer in his imprisonment; the Zealots were willing to suffer to *throw off* their bondage, which seemed to frighten many, including Josephus, who wrote:

They have an inviolable attachment to liberty, and say that God is to be their only Ruler and Lord. They also do not value dying any kinds of death,[55] nor indeed do they heed the deaths of their relations and friends, nor can any such fear make them call any man lord. And since this immovable resolution of theirs is well known to a great many, I shall speak no further about that matter; nor am I afraid that any thing I have said of them should be disbelieved, but rather fear, that what I have said is beneath the resolution they show when they undergo pain. And it was in Gessius Florus's time that the nation began to grow mad with this distemper, who was our procurator, and who occasioned the Jews to go wild with it by the abuse of his authority, and to make them revolt from the Romans.[56]

Josephus saw these unbending characters (Judas, Saddok, their followers) and their "pernicious influence" as the reason Jerusalem would be destroyed in 70.[57]

BEN: ". . .you'll never get anywhere in this life unless you're prepared to do a fair day's work, for a fair day's . . ."—Ben sounds like a reproving parent or headmaster here, but there are also two quite specific sources for this phraseology. In yet another influence from *I'm All Right Jack*, company director Tracepurcel (Dennis Price) delivers a purposely inflammatory talk to his malingering, strike-prone workers, calling on them to eliminate their "slackness," aspire to "greater efficiency," and finally, "do an honest day's work for a fair day's pay—for a change." He tells his workers that what they lack is "honesty, hard work, and a sense of duty." They don't want to hear it any more than Brian wants to listen to similar reprovings from Ben. But it's also not unlike King Agrippa's speech to the leading Jerusalemites on the eve of open revolt. Agrippa had listened to the various complaints of "his" people, and, according to Josephus, tried to walk a line between condemning the procurator's actions and chiding the Jews for their actions of rebellion:

> Your first occasion is, the accusations you have to make against your procurators: *now here you ought to be submissive to those in authority, and not give them any provocation*: but when you reproach men greatly for small offences, you excite those whom you reproach to be your adversaries; for this will only make them leave off hurting you privately, and with some degree of modesty, and to lay what you have waste openly. *Now nothing so much damps the force of strokes as bearing them with patience*; and the quietness of those who are injured diverts the injurious persons from afflicting. But let us take it for granted that the Roman ministers are injurious to you, and are incurably severe; yet are they not all the Romans who thus injure you; nor hath Caesar, against whom you are going to make war, injured you: it is not by their command that any wicked governor is sent to you; for they who are in the west cannot see those that are in the east; nor indeed is it easy for them there even to hear what is done in these parts. Now it is absurd to make war with a great many for the sake of one; to do so with such mighty people for a small cause; and this when these people are not able to know of what you complain: nay, such crimes as we complain of may soon be corrected, for the same procurator will not continue for ever; and probable it is that the successors will come with more moderate inclinations.[58]

Agrippa (again, via Josephus) then goes on to remind the Jews of the invincibility of the Roman Empire, of the benefits to be had under the protection of its wing, and that it's very nearly ungrateful to not embrace their Roman rulers: "Moreover, ten thousand other nations there are, who had greater reason than we to claim their entire liberty, and yet do submit. You are the only people who think it a disgrace to be servants to those to whom all the world hath submitted. . . . Will you not carefully reflect upon the Roman empire?"[59] Agrippa is even careful to remind, like Ben, that he himself also shares in the empire, its benefits and challenges. He uses "we" four times in (this translation of) the speech, and "our" and "us" twice (though "you" and "your" he uses dozens of times, yes). Agrippa concludes:

> I call to witness your sanctuary, and the holy angels of God, and this country common to us all, that I have not kept back anything that is for your preservation; and if you will follow that advice which you ought to do, you will have that peace which will be common to you and to me; but if you indulge your passions, you will run those hazards which I shall be free from.[60]

Again, it's not certain how much of this is Agrippa, and how much is Josephus, but the sentiment from either would be similar. Ben isn't, certainly, "free from" the consequences of some indulgence; he will be hanging in his cell, jeering at the crucifixion party (he wants to taste this version of Roman justice, too), as the film ends.

The character "Spike" will later attempt to deliver this type of stirring speech as the various followers of Brian race after him into the hills. He raises his hands in a prophetic kind of way, but only gets as far as "Stop! Stop I say! Let us pray. Yea, he cometh to us like the seeds of the grave . . ." before the multitude run or just wander off after Brian. Agrippa's speech goes on, uninterrupted, for more than three thousand five hundred words.[61]

CENTURION: "I think he wants to know which way up you want to be crucified"—This actually sounds very much like the Pilate described by most historians, with the exception of Josephus, who painted a more complicated and complimentary picture of the prefect. This was no surprise, since by this time Josephus was Flavius Josephus, a Roman "convert" living and working in Rome.

As we've seen already, the preferred Jewish method of capital punishment tended to be stoning.[62] Roman death sentences for the common man could be by crucifixion, wild animals, strangulation, or immolation. Roman crucifixions were reportedly carried out on at least three types of "crosses." One type looked like a capital "T," another like a lowercase "t," and the third simply any cross-shaped tree.[63] For the first two, the central post often remained in the ground,[64] the victim carried the *patibulum* (crossbar) to the place of execution, and then both the crossbar and the victim were hauled up into place. The Pythons have chosen to emulate the crosses used in most of the big-screen biblical epics, most especially *King of Kings*. Brian and his "crucifixion party" carry their full crosses to the place of execution where, interestingly, there are many empty crosses already in place—this looks more cinematic than a barren hill. Upside-down crucifixions have actually been reported, as well. The Apostle Peter has traditionally been credited with requesting an upside-down crucifixion, seeing himself as unworthy to be compared with his Lord in this way. According to Eusebius (c. 260–340), the Christian martyr Blandina (c. 162–177) was crucified head-down "as bait for wild beasts," bringing together both threats Pilate will later make in relation to Brian and the sniggering Praetorian guard.[65]

Additionally, Josephus reports that the "which way" question in relation to crucifixion took on new meaning when Titus allowed his armies to vent their rage on rebellious Jews. The troops "nailed those they caught, one after one way, and another after another, to the crosses, by way of jest"—meaning every manner of contortion was possible (whatever likely elicited a laugh) on these hundreds of crosses.[66]

BEN: "Terrific race the Romans . . . terrific"—Ben isn't an isolated voice, actually, according to Levine: "As a result of the Roman conquest, a new constellation of leadership appeared in Judea that viewed the *pax Romana* as a positive force and pursued a policy of full cooperation with the conqueror."[67] These were not the Hasmoneans but "a marginal group" from Idumaea, headed by "Antipater, his son Herod, and their descendants."[68] Ben is in good company, allying himself with the leading family of Judea.

Perhaps, though, Ben is experiencing what psychologist Erich Fromm called "flight from freedom," wherein "an insecure nation frightened by war and crime and hallucinatory abandon[69] feels more secure under the firm hand of a mean man," trading freedom for security.[70] Fromm was trying to explain the appeal of a leader like Hitler to the average German in the Weimar period, but it works for a Ben character, too, who is part of a population recovering from Hasmonean infighting and looking to the steadying hand that the Roman Empire proffered in 63 BC.[71] Judea had asked Rome for a change to provincial status—they asked for the

Romans (in the figure of Pompey) to protect them from Hasmonean internecine wars. Ben is clearly "pro-Roman" and therefore an enemy to those chafing against Roman rule, but he's not "notable," he's probably not the wealthy, landed type that later sicarii would have targeted for assassination, plundering, etc.[72] The Herodians and others bent over backwards to try and help the Romans successfully put down the Zealots and banditry in general in 67–68, and there were many villagers (especially those of means) in Judea who either fled the villages and cities or actively assisted the Romans as they moved from place to place, cleaning up insurrection around the region before encircling Jerusalem.[73]

But Ben might be operating at a more realistic level than Brian, admitting that revolution is a costly and painful endeavor, and echoing many first-century Jews in Jerusalem. Even safely incarcerated, Ben just might possess "a shrewd appreciation of what revolt would cost in bloodshed and material loss . . . [and] counsel[s] a passive acceptance of injustice, and consequent national and religious degradation," Brandon writes. "Such a policy was adopted by some Jews, of whom Josephus was a well-known example; but Josephus has generally been despised by Jew and Christian alike as unpatriotic and mean."[74] Ben seems ambivalent about being despised or loved, and only marks his behavior by the standards of his Roman jailers.

In this near-lachrymosity Ben himself sounds like Josephus, of course, who found many laudable aspects of the Roman way of life, and who "pretends not to have flattered the Romans, though he is distinctly partial to them."[75] Historians since have approached Josephus's works with care, never certain which stories are self-serving, which are more factual, and which are factually self-serving. As an example, the Josephus work *Wars of the Jews* bears Titus's imprimatur, so it might easily be called "official propaganda."[76] The fact that Josephus at first fights but then joins the Romans, even adopting Vespasian's family name, perhaps renders him more obsequious than his voluminous writings are wont to betray.

Following are a handful of passages from Josephus, giving the reader an idea of how Ben-like this Jewish fighter-cum-historian-cum-Roman-citizen really was. (Reading these and hearing Ben's voice is an interesting experience):

- *Josephus describes the manner in which Roman soldiers bivouac together:* When they have thus secured themselves, they live together by companies, with quietness and decency, as are all their other affairs managed with good order and security.[77]

- *Josephus describes the Roman legions' planning and foresight:* But when they are to fight, they leave nothing without forecast, nor to be done off-hand, but counsel is ever first taken before any work is begun, and what hath been there resolved upon is put in execution presently; for which reason they seldom commit any errors; and if they have been mistaken at any time, they easily correct those mistakes. They also esteem any errors they commit upon taking counsel beforehand to be better than such rash success as is owing to fortune only; because such a fortuitous advantage tempts them to be inconsiderate, while consultation, though it may sometimes fail of success, hath this good in it, that it makes men more careful hereafter; but for the advantages that arise from chance, they are not owing to him that gains them; and as to what melancholy accidents happen unexpectedly, there is this comfort in them, that they had however taken the best consultations they could to prevent them. Now they so manage their preparatory exercises of their weapons, that not the bodies of the soldiers only, but their souls may also become stronger.[78]

- *Josephus concludes his laudatory "digression" on the Roman army's acumen:* Nor can we find any examples where they have been conquered in battle, when they came to a close fight, either by the multitude of the enemies, or by their stratagems, or by the difficulties in the places they were in; no, nor by fortune neither, for their victories have been surer to them than fortune could have granted them. In a case, therefore, where counsel still goes before action, and where, after taking the best advice, that advice is followed by so active an army, what wonder is it that Euphrates on the east, the ocean on the west, the most fertile regions of Libya on the south, and the Danube and the Rhine on the north, are the limits of this empire? One might well say that the Roman possessions are not inferior to the Romans themselves.

This account I have given the reader, *not so much with the intention of commending the Romans, as of comforting those that have been conquered by them, and for the deterring others from attempting innovations under their government.* This discourse of the Roman military conduct may also perhaps be of use to such of the curious as are ignorant of it, and yet have a mind to know it. I return now from this digression.[79]

Much earlier than these events, during the second century BC, the Jews signed and re-signed treaties with Rome, sought and concluded by Judas Maccabaeus (*fl.* 167–160 BC). Over the following several decades, Smallwood notes, the Romans failed to deliver much beyond lip service to the Jews, Rome's actions always ending with an issued "remonstrance" to Jewish antagonists. Ben-like, the Jews were for some reason satisfied: "Nevertheless [the Jews] clearly felt that even this was valuable (or else they were incurable optimists), for they renewed the treaty several times."[80] Ben can be an incurable optimist, and he can also be seeing what Brian and others couldn't, certainly that his relationship with the Romans—like Josephus's just a few years later—can be characterized as "very fair." Josephus's admittedly self-serving prayer is eloquent but does him no favors, in the eyes of history: "I willingly surrender to the Romans and consent to live; but I take thee to witness that I go, not as a traitor . . . but as thy minister."[81] Brandon concludes: "The reaction of his fellow Jews was very natural: they tried to kill him on this and other occasions."[82] Brian treats Ben as a bit mad, and not as a threat; as a Roman sympathizer, however, it's likely safer for Ben to be in manacles than on the streets with the other "lucky bastards" headed for crucifixion.

And finally, several decades later than the events depicted, in the years leading up to the revolt in 66, there were clearly two active but distinct Jewish groups: those "loyal to Rome in general and hostile only to Florus" (the rather venal procurator, *fl.* 64–66), and those set on ridding Judea of Roman invaders entirely, the sicarii and its sympathizers. The first and likely more numerous (or at least more visible) party were allied with "the moderate, philo-Roman party," according to Smallwood, with the nationalist cause being aggressively pushed by the more violent sicarii.[83] Ben is clearly much more philo-Roman than sicarii (though we never are told what he's done to merit incarceration), while the PFJ see themselves as extremist dagger-men, with no love lost for the "bloody Romans." Neither Ben nor the PFJ seem terribly effective in promoting their views, being Pythonesque characters, certainly.

Notes

1. Waugh, *FCY*, 8 February 1974.
2. A Christmas special recorded 2 December 1956.
3. Pölönen, "Plebeians and Repression of Crime in the Roman Empire," 219.
4. Cook, "Crucifixion as Spectacle," 76.
5. See Deuteronomy 25:9, and Gaskill, "The 'Ceremony of the Shoe.'"
6. Smith, *A Dictionary of Greek and Roman Antiquities*, 240–41.

7. "Simon bar Giora," JVL.

8. Cook, "Envisioning Crucifixion," 268.

9. Cook, "Envisioning Crucifixion," 268

10. Demaris, *Brothers in Blood*, 171.

11. Quoted by Demaris, Dr. Hubbard is the author of *The Skyjacker—His Flights of Fantasy* (Macmillan, 1971); he became a minor celebrity during the 1970s for his behavioral studies of the skyjacker, as well as interviews with skyjackers.

12. Demaris, *Brothers in Blood*, 171–72.

13. Richard, *WWAR*, 177. Perhaps Livy was referring to deaths the nobility could perhaps expect—a quick beheading or the "honor" of suicide.

14. Josephus, *WJ*, 2.5.2 (Whiston, 474).

15. *WJ*, 2.12.6 (Whiston, 482).

16. *WJ*, 2.13.2 (Whiston, 482–83).

17. *WJ*, 2.14.9 (Whiston, 485).

18. Wiedemann, *Emperors and Gladiators*, 69; also 75–77.

19. Demaris, *Brothers in Blood*, 81–82.

20. Brendon, *DFBE*, 152–53.

21. *DFBE*, 153.

22. The "historical" Jesus as opposed to, say, Jesus, the Son of God. In the doubting Thomas 1970s, it was easier to defend a conspiratorial Jesus (*The Passover Plot*) than a divine Jesus. Cupitt and Armstrong, *Who Was Jesus?* 56–57.

23. The dead on the crosses are seen early, Ben mentions death by crucifixion, Pilate mentions it, the Centurion threatens it, Matthias dismisses it, Nisus Wettus and the jailers seem to *only* know crucifixion as a Roman punishment, and Judith announces that the Romans are going to "crucify" Brian, not just execute him. It's all very specific.

24. Rosenblatt reminds us that the Roman Tacitus and the philo-Roman/Jewish scholar Josephus mention the frequency of Roman execution by crucifixion (Rosenblatt, "The Crucifixion of Jesus," 316).

25. Brandon, "Josephus: Renegade or Patriot?," 835.

26. Brandon, "Josephus: Renegade or Patriot?," 835. See the entry "Zealots" in *JE* for more on these "freedom fighters" or "brigands."

27. Levine, *Jerusalem*, 157.

28. Richard, *WWAR*, 43.

29. Quoted in *WWAR*, 44. See the entries earlier in the scene "The PFJ Plan Their Raid" for more on just what the Romans had done by the time of Christ.

30. Quoted in *WWAR*, 44.

31. *The Roman Empire in the First Century*, a.t.

32. *WWAR*, 237–38.

33. The Murder (Abolition of Death Penalty) Act was made permanent in 1969.

34. Jenkins's manner of working these changes involved support for Private Member's Bills as they came through Parliament. This bill came from Labour MP Sydney Silverman.

35. "Tory MPs Back Fresh Death Penalty Call," *Times*, 20 March 1973: 3.

36. "Colonel in Search of an Ultimate Deterrent," *Times*, 31 March 1973: 14.

37. "Colonel in Search," *Times*, 31 March 1973: 14.

38. *ATW*, 1.15.203; *MPFC: UC* 1.240–51.

39. *Private Eye*, 22 July 1977: 17.

40. "Hamilton Diabolical," *Private Eye*, 22 July 1977: 17–18.

41. Cook, "Crucifixion as Spectacle," 79.

42. Incidentally, the men tasked with actually nailing victims to the crosses in *Brian* are dressed like the jailers seen earlier, not soldiers, meaning they're likely just local employees.

43. *Private Eye*, 14 October 1977: 13.

44. After the fall of the Soviet Union in 1991, for example, it wouldn't take long living with the uncertainties of the quasi-capitalist new world before (especially older) Russians were pining for the

certainties of the Soviet era ("Why Do So Many People Miss the Soviet Union?" *Washington Post* 21 December 2016).

45. Eckstein, "Terror as a Weapon," 74.

46. Ep. 14, *Flying Circus*, "The Piranha Brothers." Based on the real-life Kray brothers, East End criminals committed to long prison sentences for underworld murders. *MPFC: UC*, 1.221–39.

47. *ATW*, 1.14.187.

48. Wiedemann, *Emperors and Gladiators*, 103.

49. Reprinted in 1946, the book was first published in 1937. This quote is found on page 317. See also Toye's "'The Gentleman in Whitehall' Reconsidered."

50. Bogdanor, "The Character of the Postwar Period," a.t. This unflattering quotation would be denied emphatically by Jay himself in 1950.

51. See the entry for "rabbit fish" in *MPFC: UC*, 2.47 for more on the wartime relationship between the British citizen and his/her government. Also, peruse the many entries for "World War II" in the index of that same book set.

52. The recent American film *Rolling Thunder* dealt with a returning Vietnam prisoner of war (William Devane) who can't adjust to life outside of his POW existence, finding comfort only when he is reenacting the dependable, torturous conditions of his Hanoi prison time.

53. Wiedemann, *Emperors and Gladiators*, 103.

54. Wiedemann, *Emperors and Gladiators*, 103.

55. Remember Matthias's dictum: "Crucifixion's a doddle."

56. Josephus, *AJ*, 18.1.6 (Whiston, 377).

57. Brandon, *Jesus and the Zealots*, 34.

58. *WJ*, 2.16.4 (Whiston, 487–88).

59. *WJ*, 2.16.4 (Whiston, 488).

60. *WJ*, 2.16.4 (Whiston, 490).

61. *WJ*, 2.16.4 (Whiston, 486–90).

62. This would be for religious reasons, generally. Josephus reports that the Hasmonean king Alexander Jannaeus crucified eight hundred rebellious Pharisaical Jews in about 87 BC, also slaughtering the rebels' wives and children (*WJ* 1.4.6 [Whiston, 433]).

63. There is also evidence that in some instances the victim could have been tied or nailed to an upright post alone, and likely a tall, thin tree could serve the same purpose. See Tzaferis, "Crucifixion—The Archaeological Evidence."

64. Many scholars believe that given the scarcity of wood in the area of Jerusalem, the building of dozens and then hundreds of crosses seems unlikely. (When the Romans encircled Jerusalem in the siege of 68–70, the building of siege engines was slowed by the lack of nearby trees.) The upright post (stipe) that remained in place appears to be the most likely answer to this scarcity, as well as tying a victim's hands and arms to the *patibulum*, rather than driving nails into the wood over and over again. See Zias and Sekeles, "The Crucified Man from Giv'at ha-Mivtar."

65. Wiedemann, *Emperors and Gladiators*, 82. Blandina lived through the crucifixion, and was further tortured before death.

66. *WJ*, 5.11.1 (Whiston, 563).

67. Levine, *Jerusalem*, 154.

68. Levine, *Jerusalem*, 154.

69. Fromm, *The Fear of Freedom*. Ben's "hallucinatory abandon" seems firmly in place as he "pines for" Roman corporal punishment, and Brian asks to be removed from the shared cell.

70. Jenkins, *Anatomy of Decline*, 50.

71. That firm hand will soon be glimpsed in Pilate's throne room, where the fair hand of Rome sits atop a Roman standard. Alleged revolutionary Francis has already argued (and others in the PFJ agreed) that the Romans were likely the "only ones who could" maintain order considering the rabble of Judea. At some level, then, the PFJ themselves have tickets on the "flight from freedom," and, by the end of the film, they leave Brian on the cross and board that flight happily.

72. Horsley, "The Sicarii," 441.

73. See Horsley's "The Zealots," passim.
74. Brandon, *Jesus and the Zealots*, 25.
75. *JE*, "Josephus, Flavius."
76. Brandon, "Josephus: Renegade or Patriot," 834.
77. *WJ*, 3.5.3 (Whiston, 505).
78. *WJ*, 3.5.7 (Whiston, 506).
79. *WJ*, 3.5.8 (Whiston, 506); italics added.
80. Smallwood, *JURR*, 7.
81. *WJ*, 3.8.3 (Whiston, 515). Quoted in Brandon, *Jesus and the Zealots*, 25n2.
82. Brandon, *Jesus and the Zealots*, 25n2.
83. *JURR*, 290–91.

SCENE THIRTEEN
IN THE COURT OF PONTIUS PILATE

PILATE'S AUDIENCE CHAMBER . . . big and impressive, although a certain amount of redecorating is underway—The portion of Pilate's palace where Pilate acted "in the capacity of judge, was called the Prætorium."[1] The guards in here are then, by definition, Praetorian guards, mentioned later as Pilate berates his men for snickering. This set is at least partly modeled after the larger, more elaborately lit and decorated throne room of Pilate as seen in *Ben-Hur*—the throne, the dais, even the columns are in place, though here they're all about one-half scale or so.

This construction work in progress (on the walls and floors) is likely an indication that Pilate is just visiting, and the palace (which was Herod's originally) is being brought up to his standards of decoration and comfort. Richard points out that it was these regional governors who actually oversaw nearly directly the large-scale improvements to their prefects, including "the construction of major highways, bridges, tunnels, forts, walls, canals, and even markets and baths."[2] Pilate's central administrative palace would have been in Caesarea, a larger port city, at this time, where the Sanhedrin representatives trekked to complain about the Roman insignia breach, and where Pilate would undertake the building of the Tiberium. The Passover celebration, mentioned by the Centurion later, is the likely reason Pilate's household and an important Roman like Biggus are in Jerusalem all together, as Smallwood writes, "The presence of both Pilate and a number of Herodian princes in Jerusalem suggests that this episode [Pilate's initial balking at the removal of aniconic shields from his Jerusalem residence], like those of the standards and the aqueduct, occurred at a festival."[3] Pontius Pilate was hand selected by Sejanus and ultimately the emperor Tiberius as prefect administering Judea, including Jerusalem, replacing Valerius Gratus, who had served in the position for eleven years. Pilate ruled from 26 to 36. (Herod Antipas was another Rome-appointed procurator from this same time, but over Galilee.)[4]

This same setup—an interview with a ruler while construction work is underway—is another historical borrow for the Pythons. Gaius (Caligula) had already let it be known to horrified Jewish leaders that he was thinking of adding an enormous statue of himself, as Zeus/Jupiter, *inside* the Temple at Jerusalem, so his penchant for renovation was certain.[5] Just weeks before his death, and when his madness seemed to be in full bloom, the emperor Gaius gave audience to a Jewish embassy from Alexandria. The Alexandrian prefect, Flaccus, had allowed the Greek population free reign in their treatment of Jews, which first involved ghettoization and then advanced to harassment, torture, and finally murder. This flew in the face of Rome's demands that the Dispersed Jews be granted protected status across the empire. (Flaccus would eventually be arrested and executed for maladministration, according to Philo.) The Jewish entourage waited and waited, and were finally admitted for an audience in late September, 40. They laid out their complaint, described the horrors, and reminded the emperor of their status granted in perpetuity by Rome, then waited for his answer. Philo records that Gaius—"a ruthless tyrant with a menacing frown on his despotic brow"—*rambled about proposed renovations to the mansions and gardens* rather than the matter at hand. The emperor later seemed fascinated by the Jews' unwillingness to eat pork, and couldn't understand why these "god-haters" did not treat him as a god, as well.[6] Gaius would be dead just a few months later, and Claudius would reset the *status ante quo* sometime in early 41.[7]

The camera pans across the large room here, revealing the usual attention to historical detail and design the Pythons earlier employed to create the believable Middle Ages world of *Holy Grail*. The visible painted frescoes (likely researched and then produced by Gilliam and his crew) are borrowed from known sources, and will be described in the order each appears as the camera moves. The heart of the scene "begins" when the camera rests on Pilate standing before his throne, and Brian is being "thwown" to the floor; prior to that moment, the camera pans across the set:

throne dais backdrop—A painted triptych is visible behind Pilate and the throne, with versions of three recognizable "Second Style" frescoes, all from Pompeii. The first is borrowed from the Villa of the Mysteries series,[8] and features men sharing a drink from an urn. It's not a surprise to see these large murals around Pilate's room, even though the juxtaposition is a historical anachronism.[9] On 23 November 1976, the Royal Academy in London hosted the exhibition *Pompeii AD79*. The exhibition featured "huge colour photographs, of the great mural from the Villa of the Mysteries, the finest of all surviving Pompeian paintings," according to contemporary news coverage of the show.[10] This same week, the Pythons would meet together in London to discuss scenes for their upcoming Holy Land movie, as well as take in a handful of biblical epic films for inspiration.[11] Rather than photo versions of the murals, it looks as if Gilliam and his team painted their own versions[12] of the large images, carefully replicating the famous Pompeian red backgrounds, a color further employed in some of Pilate's furnishings. And even though this well-publicized museum display would have raised Pompeii's visibility in the eyes of the general public, it isn't likely that the frescoes' inclusion in *Life of Brian*—a film ostensibly set in 33—would have struck many as anachronistic. As they had in *Holy Grail*—announcing a tenth-century setting but using thirteenth-century costumes and fourteenth-century castles, for example—the Pythons (like Shakespeare) telescope time(s) to serve the purpose of setting and historical mood; for them, historical fidelity might actually detract from their version of the medieval or ancient world.[13] The employment of such anachronisms have become hallmarks, tropes of the Python world. Gilliam and his crew would have found elements that "looked" Roman and could be at home in a Roman-held city like Jerusalem, even though, as we'll see, these props, costumes, and sets and set decorations could be taken out of their context (like the Pompeian frescoes), or out of another time (the Dürer-like rhinoceros-and-obelisk statue). Together, they resemble as much as anything Piranesi's *Appian Way*,[14] so a cluttered bricolage of historical objects and fantasy, a fetishized detritus of the Roman *cultus* world, biblical epics, and the Pythons' imagination.

Serious excavations at Pompeii wouldn't begin until the mid-eighteenth century, and archaeologists wouldn't begin work on this villa until the early twentieth century. And since the Villa of Mysteries, for example, was built in about 65–50 BC, admirers of the style and images like Pilate (or Herod) *could* have seen them on a visit to Pompeii and copied them, meaning they are not necessarily anachronistic, just out of place in Jerusalem. All the Roman-type villa amenities expected—a bath-house, hypocaust, even an altar—were found in a dig at Horvat 'Eleq south of Haifa, Israel, along with "Pompeian Red Ware cooking vessels," meaning the trade across the empire spread both wares and influences far and wide.[15]

The middle panel—directly behind the throne—is a reverse image from *The Dalliance of Mars and Venus* (Ares and Aphrodite) series, from the House of Punished Love in Pompeii.

The third panel is a version of Maenad in orgiastic dance and fear of the bride/initiate, another Pompeii fresco. This fresco is part of the Villa of the Mysteries, hall of the megalograph ("life-size paintings").[16]

Two standards—There is a brace of standards (or *signum*) on either side of this dais. These standards would have indicated which century, cohort, or legion was which, in battle and wherever the unit was garrisoned. The standards could bear the images of animals, the hand of Rome (*manus*),[17] the eagle, a flag, *philarae* (disks), and even likenesses of the emperor. The first one we see is topped with the manus and *SPQR*, meaning "The Senate and People of Rome" have promulgated and awarded this unit. The standards here *might* bear images of the emperor (the largish gold disks at the middle of either staff), which would have been in silver or gold, but it's difficult to see clearly. These last were the types of military and religious items that Pilate brought into Jerusalem in about 26 under the cover of darkness. As the images were part of the worshipped Roman *cultus*, and there were likenesses on the images, the high priests of Jerusalem demanded they be removed. Pilate initially refused, setting off a near-riot among his Jewish subjects.[18] It's likely that an orthodox Jew would have thought himself (or been ruled) unclean by simply being in this same room with the iconic images, especially so close to the temple. Trajan's Column in Rome depicts soldiers carrying standards that look very much like these.

column—There are both Doric and Ionic columns in this setting. The first columns behind Pilate's throne are fluted Ionic columns, each with a frieze and architrave on top, and above each of those can be glimpsed busts.[19] The bust at the far right appears to be an image of Augustus, in robes, and the one to its left may be Augustus in the dress of a Centurion. This attention to architectural detail is significant in the Python world given their penchant not only for arcane knowledge but for the showing off of that knowledge. In *Flying Circus*, Welsh coal miners can argue about classical architecture just after a disagreement over the Treaty of Utrecht has almost led to a punch-up:

A fourth miner runs up.

Fourth Miner (Ian Davidson): Hey gaffer can you settle something? Morgan here says you find the abacus between triglyphs in the frieze section of the entablature of classical Greek Doric temples.

Foreman (Idle): You bloody fool, Morgan, that's the metope. The abacus is between the architrave and aechinus in the capital.

Morgan (Gilliam): You stinking liar![20]

The production team for *Life of Brian* would have gone to great lengths to project historical verisimilitude, knowing that the anachronistic and undercutting humor works all the better against such an authentic backdrop. A very "real" version of the early Middle Ages set the table for the silliness and anachronisms in *Holy Grail*; a similarly serious version of first-century Jerusalem prepares the viewer for another such juxtaposition. Though describing *Holy Grail*, both films fit neatly into this mode: "The film is polymorphic and heteroglossic: it is an example of its subgenre as well as a genre-transgressing work that threatens the integrity of the [biblical] film. It can operate as an authentic-looking [biblical] film . . . and by virtue of its authenticity (its authentic 'look' thanks to careful production design) it effectively parodies that same genre."[21] *Life of Brian* will almost always look like a biblical epic—especially like the very recent *Jesus of Nazareth*—allowing for more complex parody and reflexivity.

columned doorway/window—The inscription above the doorway (on the frieze)—"PILATVS IVDAEOS REGET OK"—reads more like graffito than a monumental inscription, and a bowdlerized English-Latin version, at that. It could be interpreted as "Pilate Rules Judea—Got It?"[22] ("OK" not being a Latin term or abbreviation.) It wouldn't be a surprise to find fractured English in a Python world, remembering the French sentries in *Holy Grail*, and the "Dirty Hungarian Phrasebook" and the man suffering from Thripshaw's Disease in *Flying Circus*. But there's subtly more to this mangled inscription.

This is more precisely a reference to a much more contemporary story: The 1975 graffiti image—"George Davis Is Innocent OK"—found scrawled on a brick wall in Salmon Lane, London, and which appeared in newspapers and on news broadcasts of the time.[23] Even with a fairly solid alibi, Davis had been arrested for allegedly participating in a robbery that resulted in the wounding of a police officer. In March 1975 he was sentenced to twenty years in prison, and the slogans bearing his name began appearing across England—Tower Bridge Road, on the walls of the Headingley Cricket ground, on bridge spans, and even on a banner hung from atop St. Paul's Cathedral. The Who lead singer Roger Daltrey sported a "George Davis Is Innocent" T-shirt in a December 1975 concert performance, and Davis's brothers-in-law protested nude at the Victoria Park boating lake. Davis would be freed in 1976 (after support from Home Secretary Jenkins, as well), when it was determined that evidence against him wasn't truly sufficient.[24] He wouldn't be officially found innocent until 2011.[25]

Private Eye is in on the reference, too—meaning the slogan has officially entered the public lexicon—and mentions a wall near the "Ellen Wilkinson Estate" with "MUGGERS RULE—OK?" scrawled across it.[26] A few months later, it's "Jim Rules—OK?" when *Private Eye* responds to the Lib-Lab pact reached in March 1977. This minor power-sharing agreement kept "Jim" Callaghan and Labour in No. 10 for a further eighteen months, until the pact officially collapsed, and a new election was called.[27] By April of this same year *Private Eye* cartoonist Ed McHenry offers the graffitied meta-slogan "OK RULES, OK!"[28]

This combination of period Latin and more colloquial English is Pythonesque, to be sure, but this kind of conflation was also at the heart of a long-running and well-publicized disagreement between scholars in relation to the Dead Sea Scrolls. In the heady rush to examine and create scholarly articles (and make judgments) about these scrolls in the 1950s and 1960s, archaeologists and their anxious publicists made claims about the scrolls' ages, authorship, readership, and connections between them and both the Jewish faith and emerging Christianity of the latter part of the Second Temple period. Initial examinations of the scrolls were conducted in absolute secrecy, with announcements about discoveries seeping out slowly over a period of years, irritating many in the academic community. When select images of the scrolls and scholarly articles (primarily from archaeologists and theologians) began to circulate, the consensus seemed to confirm that the scrolls dated to between the years 1 and 68 or so, and represented invaluable additions to extant written material from first-century Palestine. This initial enthusiasm was tempered by some, including Solomon Zeitlin, a Jewish historian who argued for years that the Dead Sea scrolls were *not* created in the first century. He describes the fracas as he saw it:

> Shortly after the finding of the Scrolls was made known it was heralded that they would revo-lutionize our knowledge of Judaism and the beginnings of Christianity. To propagate these

views all media of publicity were employed,—press reviews, radio and television, media not characterized by the dignity of true scholarship. The Hebrew Scrolls became a sensation. The matter was no longer one for scholars. Persons with no scholarly equipment jumped on the band wagon, published their opinions in the popular press and over night became authorities on the Dead Sea Scrolls.[29]

(This is very similar to the carnivalesque atmosphere surrounding the Cadbury-Camelot dig in the late 1960s in England.[30]) Zeitlin's claims were based on word/symbol usage and phraseology of the original Hebrew text, and he identified many examples of words and edits in the scrolls that, he asserted, did not come into vogue among Hebrew scribes until hundreds of years later, even into the Middle Ages.[31] The clashes between academic points of view appeared on the BBC, in newspapers, and dozens of journal articles. The Pythons may well have been commenting on this dustup and one closer to home—the Silbury Dig—in their *Flying Circus* Ep. 21, "Archaeology Today," where rival archaeologists (one jealous of the other based on his height) fight to the death over their findings and archaeological credentials.[32] Zeitlin would write in 1964:

> In numerous essays I have maintained that the expressions and terms employed in the Scrolls militate against their antiquity . . . [and t]he physical signs used in the Scrolls, parentheses, connecting lines between two words and ellipses indicating that a word or words had been omitted, which also militate against the antiquity of the Scrolls, have never been referred to by the professors.[33]

In the Pythons' inscription, the "expressions and terms employed in the [inscription *do*] militate against [its] antiquity," and quite purposefully. Zeitlin would conclude his 1964 essay by bemoaning the "paradox" of such "medieval minds" existing and running the world in his more enlightened "atomic age"—a fun mixed metaphor itself.[34]

It was 1961 before any *monumental* inscribed evidence of Pilate's rule in Judea could be proven. The building constructed by Pilate in Caesarea, known as the Tiberieum (dedicated to Tiberius), featured the inscription "CAESARIENS. TIBERIEVM PONTIVS PILATVS PRAEFECTVS IVDAEAE DEDIT" ("Pontius Pilate, Praefectus of Iudaea bestowed a Tiberieum upon the People of Caesarea").[35] This was also the first indication that Pilate was known as a prefect, not a procurator.

half-finished fresco—In the background just behind Pilate is yet another Pompeian fresco, this one featuring a pre- (or post-) coital couple, the woman astride the man. Only the upper portion of the fresco is visible in the movie scene. This one looks to be a slightly altered version of a coupling scene from the Great Lupanar, and now part of the National Archaeological Museum in Naples collection.

The door opens, the CENTURION and some SOLDIERS carry BRIAN in—Certainly Brian is a prisoner, so being either shackled or manhandled in this way is to be expected, especially en route to an audience with the representative of Rome. Being brought before a judge of reportedly vicious temperament should have Brian in fear of corporal punishment. If he is a conscientious Jew, however, Brian might feel he is in *spiritual* peril here, as well. Emmerich notes that Jewish priests would have to have been dragged into this place, just like Brian. Stone seats placed at the edge of the forum in Pilate's palace were more than just for decoration or relaxation:

> It was at these seats that the Jewish priests stopped, in order not to defile themselves by entering the tribunal of Pilate, a line traced on the pavement of the court indicating the precise bound-

ary beyond which they could not pass without incurring defilement. . . . The marble staircase ascended by persons going to the governor's palace led likewise to an uncovered terrace, and it was from this terrace that Pilate gave audience to the priests and Pharisees, when they brought forward their accusations against Jesus. They all stood before him in the forum, and refused to advance further than the stone seats before mentioned.[36]

Wherever this understood line might have been in the film's version of Pilate's palace, Brian has clearly been carried across it, and he is now defiled. As this is the latter portion of the Second Temple period,[37] it's very likely that this defilement—which means an impurity has been acquired, and demands a purification action—would have been in full force, and Brian answerable to the priests. The fact that the Pythons have clearly, purposely avoided many (or any) direct references to the more rigorous, religious aspects of the Jews in Jerusalem in the first century—the temple, the Sanhedrin, Passover, the cultus, even "the Sabbath"—means they're not considering Brian's spiritual but physical well-being as he faces Pilate.[38]

frescoes on either side of doorway—Behind the entering Centurion (Cleese) is a decorated doorway bordered by two large, red-backed frescoes. The fresco to our left is another from the Villa of the Mysteries, featuring the character playing a lyre. Gilliam has reproduced these figures out of context (which he's done often creating animations for *Flying Circus* and *Holy Grail*), since the winged figure just glimpseable left of the lyre-player is from another portion of the long fresco. In the original work, the reaching figure (whose arm is glimpsed) is actually reaching for the winged figure, not the lyre player.

On the right side of the doorway appears to be a fairly traditional satyr and nymph scene. It is not part of the Villa of Mysteries fresco collection, as the column behind the action is fluted, a type not found in the Villa of the Mysteries. It may be inspired by the William-Adolphe Bouguereau *Study for Nymphs and Satyr* series from the later nineteenth century, and/or another erotic mosaic featuring a satyr and nymph found in the House of the Faun in Pompeii.

The doorway itself is framed by a patterned border borrowed directly from the labyrinth fret border found around the top edge of the frescoes in the Villa of the Mysteries. These were likely created from a book owned or borrowed by Gilliam. A very similar pattern was found as part of an elaborate mosaic floor from the Herodian period, uncovered during a 1969–1971 archaeological dig in the Jewish Quarter of Jerusalem.[39]

tile man—There is a worker carefully placing and tamping down tiny tiles for the floor mosaic, which appears to be a version of an erotic scene from the House of the Centenary in Pompeii. Surviving versions of these elaborate floors (and walls and even ceilings) have been uncovered in many villas the Romans erected, including those in Britain.[40] Roman mosaic remains were found near Fishbourne, then Lincoln (dug in 1976), Dewlish (1975 and 1976), and Wetherby (1977), while package trips to Cyprus and Sicily promised tours of Roman villas complete with mosaic tile floors during this same period.[41]

CENTURION: "Only one survivor, sir"—Francis obviously survived, as well, but managed to escape, perhaps without notice, while the CFG were obliterated. This "one survivor" is actually quite important, especially when considering the latitude allowed for Roman Empire regional governors in meting out punishments. Over and over in the historical records (as well as the plays and fictional accounts of the period) Roman leaders are restricted by Roman law, especially before an official condemnation has been issued. Imprisonment and torture of alleged criminals was often justified as the means necessary to search for criminal accomplices, torture eliciting the names of conspirators, it was hoped, so that the emperor and empire could be protected from further attack. According to Pölönen, "in the case of Roman citizens the torture of convicted criminals to make them reveal accomplices was traditionally the only legal form of torture known to the Romans."[42] In Brian's case, the Centurion has already admitted that all Brian's associates—at least those in the hypocaust—are already dead, meaning Brian could or even should be spared torture. The search for shadowy outside conspirators, of course, is likely motive enough for a regional governor to apply physical torture to even a non-condemned man. (And Pilate's reputation was for violence and suffering, not work-to-rule lawfulness.) Pölönen notes that even in the face of strict Roman law, there are many recorded instances of Roman authorities inflicting severe torture and eventual death in the pursuit of conspirators, turning "dictatorship into tyranny."[43]

As for more recent survivors of terror attacks, JRA terrorist Kozo Okamoto—trained by the PFLP—survived the deadly Lod bombing attack in Tel Aviv in 1972 and was arrested and interrogated. He was imprisoned in Israel, and his supporters even tried to bargain him out in 1973 with further kidnappings, but the Israelis refused. Okamoto wasn't released until 1985.[44]

In what might be the clearest case of outside influences affecting the film, the "only survivor" of the Symbionese Liberation Army—as constituted on the day Patty Hearst was kidnapped—was Hearst herself. Most of the SLA died in a shootout with police in May 1974, but Hearst and two companions remained on the loose. After her arrest in September 1975, it was Hearst alone who was put on trial in January 1976 for bank robbery, the surveillance images of which had become internationally famed. Hearst and her lawyers always maintained that she was a drugged and coerced hostage, not a willing participant in any of the SLA's activities. Hearst was also summarily convicted, and sentenced to seven years in prison.[45]

PILATE: "Thwow him to the floor"—This is more complicated than just a silly speech pattern, though there's plenty of that. First, the script has been written to take into account the speech impediment of Pilate. This is unusual for the Pythons. In *Flying Circus* wild Chinese and Hungarian accents and over-the-top regional British accents were performed, and often, but rarely part of the script as typed out. This means that this part of the script was likely completed with an after-market in mind—the printed script as it would appear in a *Life of Brian* book.[46] This idea—a fearsome ruler with a risible accent—was an early goer with all the Pythons as they put the script together. Palin mentions this "r"-challenged character as early as December 1977, with all troupe members high on the idea.[47]

This characterization is at least partly modeled on two very visible leaders of the day—both of whom enjoyed long political careers; both of whom endured jibes and barbs about the way they talked: Roy Jenkins and Margaret Thatcher.

The most obvious candidate for the Pythons' mocking was Labour mandarin Jenkins, home secretary, then president of the European Commission as *Life of Brian* was being written. Born and raised in Wales in a coal-mining family, Jenkins's accent changed as he mingled at Balliol College, Oxford, and in the upper echelons of British life; a reviewer of a Jenkins biography described him as "essentially a Whig who enjoyed life too much for the Left-wing puritans."[48] As an adult public figure, his speech sounded very much like Pilate's: he'd say "wationally" for "rationally," "countwy" for "country" and "awound" for "around."[49] *Private Eye* was obviously in on the joke, calling him "Woy Jenkins" (and "Smoothiechops"), mentioning him in a November 1976 "Grovel" titbit:

> Piers Paul Read, the talented young Yorkshire novelist, recently bearded Smoothiechops at a party to tell him the glad tidings that he was a convert to Socialism. "I've joined the Labour Party!" cried the man of letters. "How vewy surpwising!" Smoothie replied. "If I were you, young man, I would have done the pwecise opposite."[50]

In his own column, Auberon Waugh would describe Jenkins as having "various speech deformities."[51] There is even a terrific surviving bit of footage from a 1968 appearance on *University Forum,* where a studio audience of "wowdy webels" shout mercilessly at Jenkins about his Labour government's lack of socialist commitment, presaging Pilate on the balcony in *Brian* ten years later. Jenkins's friend and colleague Shirley Williams describes his speech and mannerisms in a familiar way, when thinking of Palin's performance of Pilate: "Roy is in some ways a shy man, and he's partly overcome the shyness by building up this façade, and style of, a very characteristic style of speaking, of mannerisms, of the way he uses his hands, like the turning bird cage." Williams concludes: "That becomes a barrier between him and other people.[52] Proving their fascination with pronunciation, the Pythons also offered the "Teach Yourself Heath" tutorial on *Monty Python's Previous Record* in 1972, offering accurate Heath-like word and letter pronunciations. Our Pilate struggles to communicate with his guards and with the Centurion. Jenkins's good friend and fellow Welsh MP Leo Abse would say that when returning to Pontypool and interacting with Welsh constituents, he felt like he was "acting as an interpreter between Jenkins and his own people."[53]

The second influence is more complicated, but no less significant. Minister and then Prime Minister Margaret Thatcher, raised in middle-class Grantham, also changed her accent. Her voice was characterized as "shrill," "hectoring"—her accent "cut glass"—throughout most of her pre-No. 10 career. PM Wilson would tell his adviser Donoughue that her voice was simply "terrible."[54] In the years leading up to the 1979 General Election, she took extensive voice coaching lessons to "lower her pitch and develop a calm, authoritative tone."[55] Over and over again in newspaper stories, news broadcasts, and political diaries from both sides of the aisle, Thatcher's "ghastly accent" had been used as evidence demonstrating her weakness, her unattractiveness (as a female and a politician), and even her falseness.[56] A parliamentary correspondent—allegedly an unbiased source of reportage—waxed poetic as front bench Opposition member Thatcher attacked sitting PM Callaghan over a capital gains tax question: "By this time she was in full stride, her impeccable accent beginning to hammer on Labour ears like some devilish Roedean hammer."[57] Even the articles that treated her more fairly couldn't avoid the de rigueur subjects—her appearance, her manner, and, of course, the way she talked:

> She has changed since she took over the leadership. The Cartland perm has gone, her hair is soft and wings over her ears in a traditional Tory, Macmillanish way. The voice has changed too, deeper, richer and deliberate, flowing on without an ah or um like Carnation milk pouring out of a tin. Not a trace of the Lincolnshire accent of her childhood remains.[58]

Roy Jenkins's accent was mentioned, but rarely; very few mentions of Margaret Thatcher could avoid the topic. The Pythons had spent the better part of the previous decade listening to both Jenkins (as home secretary) and Thatcher (as a rare frontbench female Tory), time enough for a character like Pilate and his affectation to be created.

Pilate's impediment is not just a display of silliness, but also the Python trope of miscommunication. He can't speak directly or effectively to his own (allegedly) Roman guard,[59] nor to the "wapscallion" Brian, nor later to the jeering Jewish "wabble." In the 1960s–1970s—the decades of political assassinations, race riots, anticolonialism, student marches in Europe and the United States, and a deepening of the Vietnam conflict—no buttoned-down politician, male or female, was likely to get any better treatment.

But Pilate's character, according to most sources remotely historical, was quite different from the Pythons' version: "According to Philo . . . [Pilate's] administration was characterized by corruption, violence, robberies, ill treatment of the people, and *continuous executions without even the form of a trial*. His very first act nearly caused a general insurrection."[60] Josephus, an apologist for the Jews but clearly not in the business of offending Romans, paints a less bloodthirsty picture of this prefect, though by no means creating a hagiography. Pilate's several offers to the mob condemning Jesus weren't accepted, and Pilate punished Jesus and released him to be crucified. This act of attempted leniency led to Pilate's sanctification by several faiths, complicating the portrait of Pilate for generations. Still, later historians agree that Pilate's disposition was by most measures nasty, mercurial, and retributive, his oppressions leading to an explosion of anti-Roman sentiment and activity: "The capture of a brigand who had ravaged the country for twenty years in or soon after 54 . . . is further evidence that it was as a reaction to Pilate's rule that brigandage became endemic."[61] Beyond the small and ineffective PFJ, however, there is little evidence of revolt against Pilate or the Romans in *Life of Brian*.

CENTURION: "What sir?"—There is no indication that the historical Pilate suffered from any speech defect or tic. The historical record for Pilate is so slim, however, that nothing can be ruled out. The future emperor Claudius (10 BC–AD 54) suffered from lasting effects of a childhood illness, to the point that when the purge was instituted before and after the death of Tiberius he, Claudius, was spared, likely being seen as no real threat. A noticeable speech impediment might have been just the thing that saved him.

PILATE: "Now . . . what is your name, Jew?"—Here, Pilate is using "Jew" as a catch-all epithet, likely because he assumes only a non-Roman would be capable of such a crime, and that no Roman would be brought before him in chains. His usage of the term is accurate, though, when it's understood how "Jews" was used in the Gospels. Zeitlin points out that the term appears in the Bible primarily when the audience was thought to be Christian-Gentile, not Jewish-Christian. He notes that Matthew, Mark, and Luke appear to have been aimed at Jewish-Christians based on terminology, for example, while Mark (writing from Rome) may have also had "not only the Jews of the Diaspora but the Gentiles as well" in mind.[62] He sees the Gospel of John directed at Gentile-Christians, those outside of the Jewish community and perhaps unfamiliar with the Jewish lexicon and eschatology:

> That the Gospel according to John was written not for the Jewish-Christians but for the Gentile-Christians may be proved by his usage of the word . . . Jews. The name Jews is used in John over sixty times, while in the Synoptic Gospels the expression Jews is mentioned only in connection with the trial of Jesus, or when the Jewish people were referred to by Gentiles.[63]

Zeitlin goes on to say that in Matthew,

> the term Jews is used by the wise men, who came from the East to Jerusalem, saying, "Where is He that was born King of the Jews?" Here the word Jews is used because it came from the lips of Gentiles. In the same manner is to be explained the use of the word Jews in the Gospel according to Luke: "And a certain centurion's servant, who was dear unto him, was sick, and ready to die. And when he heard of Jesus, he sent unto him the elders of the Jews, beseeching him that he would come and heal his servant." The name "Jews" is quite appropriate here, since it was used by a Gentile, while in the Gospel according to John the term "Jews" is constantly used. When the Feast of Passover or the Feast of Tabernacles are mentioned there, they are linked with the word Jews, as "Jews' Passover" or "the Jews' Feast of Tabernacles." The term "Jews' Passover" is never used in the Synoptic Gospels, simply Passover, or the Feast of the Unleavened Bread.[64]

So Pilate's usage of the term, even though it's uttered as if it were an invective, is actually wholly appropriate for this encounter between a Jew and a Gentile.

The Ayatollah Khomeini had railed against the Shah of Iran in 1963, asking publicly whether the Shah might actually be a "Jew" or an "infidel," certainly using Jew in a racially pejorative sense. Like many oppressed in the postwar period, it was the specter of the Shah's toadying relationship with the over-reaching United States that angered clerics like Khomeini. The "Jew" slur meant that, like the hated Israelis (more precisely, Zionists), the Shah was in the pocket of a postcolonial power, a puppet for Western policy and culture.[65]

Also, Pilate's immediate identification (by name) of Brian as a "Jew" might be a bit odd, given the fact that most of Pilate's subjects would have been Jews, unless he's using it as a kind of slur, a display of the prefect's built-in suspicion of and prejudice against all Jews. This will be glimpsed in prerevolutionary Russia, where Jews accounted for a disproportionately high percentage of those involved in "political crimes" against the tsar, according to Burleigh.[66] It also may be that Pilate is simply reminding the cowering man before him that he is *not* a Roman, and therefore an Other, with few rights in the Roman Empire. The conception of Pilate in the media of the 1960s and 1970s is also important. In 1961, at about the same time that news of the "Pilate stone" inscription was being discussed, the former Nazi who had fled to South America, Adolph Eichmann, was captured in Argentina by Mossad agents and returned to Israel for trial. During his trial, Eichmann attempted to explain away his culpability, saying he had only been following orders, and that he was "harnessed" into service and unable to turn left or right. In June 1961 Eichmann even compared himself to our prefect, in that he disagreed with Hitler's plans and even argued against them, but in the end was unable to avoid participation: "I sought a final solution of the Jewish problem which would be decent, feasible, and workable . . . but when the elite, the veritable popes of the regime, cast the die, there was nothing for me to do but to conform. . . . I had a satisfaction like Pilate and then I felt free of any guilt."[67] The Pilate reference in relation to the massacre of millions of Jews played well in the newspapers of the day, and was reprinted often. It didn't help Eichmann, though. He was hanged for his crimes in 1962.

Interest in Pilate was renewed in 1963 when a letter purportedly written by Pilate to Tiberius was uncovered in Liverpool, of all places. The letter caused a sensation in that it tells of Pilate's wholehearted attempts to save Jesus from crucifixion, even asking for reinforcements to his garrison to suppress the revolt that would occur when he pardoned or simply whipped Jesus. The Vatican would eventually call the letter a "fake," though it was assumed to have been written sometime in the fourth or fifth century.[68] Authorities did admit that the information contained in the letter, though not corroborable, wasn't necessarily fake or inaccurate.

Lastly, the metaphorical (and often hyperbolical) use of "Pontius Pilate," especially the "washing hands" trope to avoid responsibility, is language heard in the political sphere hundreds of times over the years, and from all major political players. It was said *by* Enoch Powell, it was said *about* Harold Wilson, it was used to describe government action *and* inaction. In January 1971 the general secretary of the Transport and General Worker's Union (TGWU), Jack Jones,[69] rather famously invoked the name of the maligned prefect: "It is no good the Chancellor of the Exchequer [Anthony Barber] standing aside like Pontius Pilate washing his hands while 750,000 working people are crucified by unemployment."[70] This kind of inflamed rhetoric played well in pubs, trade union halls, and to television cameras.

PILATE: "No, no, spiwit . . . bwavado . . . a touch of dewwing-do"—The script is careful to include words that feature "r" sounds for Pilate to mispronounce. "Derring-do" is actually not only a fourteenth-century creation, but a phrase mistaken from the first after Chaucer offered it, and then Lydgate and Spenser picked it up and used it inaccurately.[71]

In the very recent *The Mysteries* (1977) play cycle created by Tony Harrison, Herod's son is depicted as having a pronounced stutter, making communications with his father particularly challenging.[72]

CENTURION *(still not really understanding)*: **"Ah. About eleven, sir"**—In *Flying Circus* all manner of miscommunication is presented, a Python hobbyhorse borrowed from the Goons and the Modernists. There are characters who can't pronounce the letter "c," who can only speak the beginnings, middles, or ends of words, who insert the wrong word at the wrong time, who are insulting with every other sentence, who misread adverts as sexual come-ons, who speak in a roundabout way, who shout everything, who speak in anagrams or spoonerisms or Shakespearean jabber, and even a character who speaks so boringly that the studio camera can't stay focused on him. Miscommunication plays a crucial role in the Pythons' oeuvre.

PILATE: "So you dare to waid us?"—This is the only hint as to why Brian is being held, even though the PFJ's *attentat* had failed so miserably as to be almost absurd, and would have been even more silly had the scenes featuring the gargantuan wife of Pilate remained. There is also no interrogation that we see, or any indication that Brian has given details of their plan.

An overthrow challenge to an emperor or regional governor was less likely in these kinds of events than an attempted attack on the *person*, as Pölönen points out: "All the evidence indicates that the Emperors were more concerned about threats to their lives than potential challenges to their constitutional position."[73] This is likely due to the Roman bureaucratic apparatus being so intricate and vast—it was too large to fail, and a single death, even of an emperor, couldn't foul the smooth-running mechanism. Pilate directs Brian and the PFJ's "raid" at himself, and not his authority or position. Brian has dared to assume the right to attack the palace, the right to steal Pilate's property, his wife, actions that Roman leaders dealt with summarily:

> Caligula paraded a criminal whose hands had been amputated through the city with a placard stating what his crime had been. The physical pain inflicted on the criminal was also intended to degrade him. An evildoer may be perceived as someone who arrogates to himself certain rights which he does not have (rights to appropriate property belonging to another, for example, or the right to inflict harm on another person). In a society based on status differentiation, such an arrogation of rights is perceived as claiming a status to which the accused has no claim. His action thus overturns the proper hierarchy of statuses public recognition of which is essential if society is to function smoothly. The public humiliation of the criminal re-establishes social order by cancelling the criminal's exercise of rights which he did not have.[74]

Brian has dared to arrogate rights to himself that aren't available to him, and Pilate will reset the order of Roman society in Jerusalem via a very public humiliation.

This "dare" was also present in the language William Beveridge would use when describing the structure and effectiveness of what he wanted to call the "social service state," but others (especially opponents) termed the "Welfare State," a pejorative appellation that has stuck. Beveridge's ally in these socialist designs was Nye Bevan, who would use terms that, taken out of context, disturbed many. According to Bogdanor, Bevan told a gathering of the Fabian Society that he "wanted to create a new kind of authoritarian society—and that shocked people."[75] Stopping there, as many Conservatives did, it sounds as if a new fascistic menace lay on Labour's horizon. Not so, at least in Beveridge and Bevan's vision, which instead relied on "some very optimistic assumptions about human beings."[76] Bevan was drawing on "fellowship" and the Dunkirk spirit that had seen Britain through the war, his authoritarian society one wherein "the authority of moral purpose is freely undertaken" by all classes and for the common good, a move away from capitalism, away from "fear and acquisition."[77] (These last terms, of course, describe the Roman Empire at its apex, especially in the eyes of Reg and the PFJ.) But what of the outliers? Those who would "dare" separate themselves from the social service system could be dealt with:

> Beveridge did admit that there would be some people who just could not work under the system, so you would have public assistance for those people, and that would be means-tested out of taxation. There would be a small number of people—what he called "inadequates"—who would not be able to work or help society, and that would be funded out of taxation, and therefore means-tested, but this was a residual element. He said to a delegation of trade unionists, "There are not many people who will not behave properly." Again, you may think that was optimistic. *"There are not many people who will not behave properly, but those who do not behave properly have got to be made to do so."* So, there would be a stigma attached, in those days, to getting what he called "public assistance," and Beveridge thought that no irreducible class of the feckless and lazy people who didn't want to work, independent of the "inadequates"—everyone, he thought, wanted to work.[78]

In the case of shirkers who refused to contribute to and share in the benefits of the new system, Bevan and Beveridge weren't talking about prison or crucifixion, but *metaphora*. Improper behavior would be shamed and stigmatized by the balance of the population who admitted to and agreed on the benefits of the system. Reg, the PFJ, and Brian are treated as "inadequates" by Pilate and his forces—they "dare" to buck the functioning system—and so Brian is given literal stigmata on a cross, separated from the society he won't embrace. Along with other inadequates (Jews, Samaritans, Mr. Frisbee III), he is an effective negative example of Rome's systemic power to the rest of the population.

CENTURION: "And throw him to the floor, sir?"—The proper chain of events is now in place, and the Centurion wants to make sure he acknowledges the structure Pilate demands. He's also restating to ensure he understands Pilate's language, a wise move given Pilate's reported (and later displayed) temper. Many characters in the Python world have to discover the rules of the exchange before a successful transaction/communication can even begin, as in the "Buying a Bed" sketch from *Flying Circus* Ep. 8.[79]

PILATE: ". . . Jewish wapscallion"—"Rapscallion" is a seventeenth-century term, but it's really here because it begins with an "r." It's used in *The Goon Show* episode "House of Teeth," as well.

BRIAN: "I'm not Jewish . . . I'm a Roman!"—This *civis romanus sum* moment is an understandable turnabout. Very recently Brian was claiming angrily to be as Jewish as anyone, a "Red Sea pedestrian" and the like. Now, faced with a Roman judge, Brian wants his Roman blood taken into consideration. There were some Roman communities outside of Rome granted the "right of *conubium*, where the child of a Roman father and provincial mother was considered a Roman."[80] This might have some validity with the centurion who assaulted Mandy, though a province like Judea wouldn't likely be included in the citizenship deal. And even if it did, and Brian could be considered for citizenship, the fact that he's committed a crime could mean its immediate revocation.

But this is likely a purposeful allusion to the Apostle Paul's call to his Roman captors recorded in Acts 22: "And as they bound him with thongs, Paul said unto the centurion that stood by, Is it lawful for you to scourge a man that is a Roman, and uncondemned?"[81] The chief captain interviewing Paul had bought his own freedom, but Paul argues he himself is a free born Roman. The soldiers and the chief leave Paul, afraid that they've broken the law by binding a Roman citizen. So there's a reason that Pilate pulls up and seriously inquires about Brian's parentage—an actual Roman citizen's rights could have already been violated with his arrest and incarceration.

This plea/ploy actually *could* have been more effective, at least in delaying corporal punishment, than the Pythons allow. Roman law was quite precise, as Janne Pölönen points out: "Modern scholarly tradition has established that two fundamental rules regulated the use of torture in ancient Rome: torture must not be applied to Roman citizens or to slaves against their owners."[82] Pölönen goes on to admit that it's perhaps not so simple:

> It is commonly thought that during the Republic these principles were breached but exceptionally, whereas under the Empire their violation became ever more frequent as the extraordinary *cognitiones* invaded the criminal procedure. Expansion of torture has been associated with the political interests of imperial regime inaugurated by Augustus that took increasingly inquisitive and harsh measures against those convicted, or even suspected, of threatening the well-being of the Emperors and the Empire. The torture spread slowly but gradually to investigation of wider range of crimes, until the generalization of its use at the latest under the Severan emperors.
>
> The progress of torture during the first two centuries of the Empire is not, however, without contradiction, as scholars note the legal doctrine prohibiting the torture of freemen was duly maintained. Yet it is often taken for granted that at least the underprivileged inhabitants of the Roman Empire, the so-called *humiliores* in the legal jargon, in practice, if not in theory, lost protection against torture.[83]

And since the Pythons have decided to set their tale in Jerusalem, and in about the year 33, this qualifies as a time of the Roman Empire and not the Republic, meaning miscarriages of even Roman justice were quite possible. It wouldn't be until well later, in 212, that the Constitution of Caracalla declared *all* free men in the empire could be considered Roman citizens, so Brian has to hope that his claim to be Nortius's son carries some weight with Pilate.[84]

Cook mentions that a known Roman citizen, one Gavius, was wrongly flogged and then crucified by the ex-governor of Sicily, Verres, according to Cicero's stern reprimand:

> Gavius of Consa, a citizen and merchant, had been imprisoned in Verres' stone quarries. On escaping he reviled Verres in Messina, not realizing the danger he was in. "Suddenly he [Verres] ordered him to be snatched (from custody) into the middle of the forum, to be stripped and bound, and that rods be prepared." "He ordered him to be flogged vehemently all over his body. A Roman citizen was beaten with rods in the middle of the forum of Messina, members of the jury." In the midst of the cracking of the blows the only sound heard was "I am a Roman citizen." The *lex Julia de vi publica* (the Julian law on public violence) protected Roman citizens from torture (before conviction and appeal). Verres had falsely condemned Gavius as a spy.[85]

But the power of a provincial Roman governor could trump any of this. In 177 Christians were being thrown to the beasts in arenas in Lyons and Vienne, and at least one victim, Attalus, claimed to be a Roman citizen to save himself. He was immediately "returned to prison" to await the emperor's ruling. After Marcus Aurelius's response, the non-citizens were thrown to the wild beasts, and Attalus was legally beheaded.[86] And as Wiedemann reminds us: "Outside Italy, the authority of a Roman governor within his province was so absolute that no one could effectively challenge his decision to punish anyone in any way he decided, whatever the formal legal rights of the accused."[87] The Roman governor in Spain, Galba (3 BC–AD 69), is said to have responded to a prisoner set for crucifixion claiming Roman citizenship, like Brian, that he should be "hung on a higher cross than other criminals."[88] It seems that the Centurion's macabre joke about which way Brian wanted to be crucified wasn't strange for the period at all.

Akin to Brian's hope for exception are the so-called "Manchester Martyrs." These were Irish Fenians charged in 1867 with the murder of a police officer during a rescue of one of their own. They were fighting against an occupying force, the British, and were summarily indicted, found guilty, and executed. One member, Edward O'Meagher Condon, was given a reprieve because he could claim American citizenship, and the British wanted to "avoid diplomatic complications with the U.S."[89] There was no other empire the Romans likely feared in the year 33, so Brian can only hope his Roman rights can be enacted.

PILATE: "So your father was a <u>Woman</u>. Who was he?"—Pilate has assumed, rightly, just what Brian is—a bastard son of a Roman soldier and a Jewish mother—why he would conclude this, except for narrative convenience, isn't made clear. Perhaps Brian's appearance—his nose?—led Pilate to assume his parentage, meaning appearances mattered:

> In ancient Rome, as elsewhere, not only did the body help to define essential identities such as those based on gender and age, but the presentation of the body through aspects such as dress, adornment and gesture could further codify the individual. . . . Appearance could evoke respect, sympathy or revulsion. Public presentation and self-image were crucial aspects of how the identity of the living was both constructed and perceived.[90]

Ultimately, given what Brian is accused of, and the fact that he's not high-born, even if he were part-Roman, means there's little chance he'll escape a summary execution.

BRIAN: "He was a centurion in the Jerusalem Garrison"—As it turns out, this was no guarantee that Nortius was actually of Roman stock. His name is Roman, but could have been adopted, like "Josephus Flavius." Pilate's men housed in the Antonia Fortress would have most likely been a mixture of Syrian and Samaritan, "recruited locally for imperial service," according to Maier.[91] Only a handful of Pilate's household would have accompanied him all the way from Rome.

BRIAN: "Nortius Maximus"—For some reason this is spelled "Nortius" in the printed script and not "Naughtius" (and just *pronounced* "Nortius"), which fits the silliness. This is a *Carry On*–type name, a silly music hall borrow. The *Carry On* franchise began in 1958. The Goons paved the way, here, however, beginning in 1951. Announcer Wallace Greenslade's Roman name in an episode set in Roman Britain history—"Pliny the Elder"—is "Stomachus Grossus" (Greenslade was quite fat), Neddie is a "Charlius Britannicus" known as "Caractacus Seagoon," while Moriarty is "Brutus Moriartus." Caesar and the Roman army have come to Britain in 49 BC, and eventually take several characters back to Rome as Colosseum slave combatants. Later in the episode, a "Sparatacus of Protugal" is mentioned, as well.[92] In *Carry on Cleo* (1964) there is a "Senna Pod";[93] in Frankie Howerd's *Up Pompeii* (1971) there was "Ludicrus Sextus," "Ammonia," "Pussus Gloria," "Mucus," "Castor Oilus," "Bilius," "Erotica," "Biggius," "Boobia," "Odius," "Prodigious," "Plumpa," and "Noxious."

PILATE: "I have a vewwy gweat fwend in Wome . . ."—It's likely that both Pilate and Biggus are visiting in Jerusalem for the Passover celebration, as Pilate normally would have been in Caesarea, where he kept his household and headquarters.[94]

As hinted at earlier, Pontius Pilate is something of an enigma, historically. Maier points out that there are only seven separate texts that discuss the Judean prefect, with four of those being the New Testament Gospels, along with mentions in Josephus and Philo. "Of these seven writings," Maier notes, "one is hostile to Pilate [Philo], while the other six range from slightly critical to favorable."[95] The Pythons lean closer to Philo's description of a man capable of much cruelty; Philo writes of the "briberies, the insults, the robberies, the outrages and wanton injuries, the executions without trial constantly repeated, the ceaseless and supremely grievous cruelty."[96] Everything beyond Philo is less condemnatory.

PILATE: "Biggus Dickus"—An expected schoolyard Roman name, akin to those mentioned above in the *Carry On* and *Up, Pompeii* predecessors. The existence of so many

Roman priapic statues, frescoes, and graffiti likely made such a name less odd during this period. It's also clear that since Biggus has a lisp, his name (and dialogue) had to have plenty of "ess" sounds.

PILATE: "You will find yourself in gladiator school vewwy quickly . . ."—There were actually very active gladiator schools—*Ludi gladiatora*—in Rome and in a number of larger cities in the empire. These schools were both privately and publicly owned, and provided bodyguards for their masters as well as entertainment for the paying customers of the amphitheaters and colossea. The Thracian gladiator Spartacus was trained in a *ludus* in the Capua, Italy, area, for example. This was also perhaps a crushing insult, since Juvenal in his *Satires* tells us that such depravities outstripped even the despised job of an actor: "There is only one lower depth, the gladiator's school."[97]

They both try to stop giggling—This is "corpsing," and it's something the Pythons often tried to do to each other during live stage shows. In *Holy Grail*, during the "She's a Witch" scene, Cleese purposely held off delivering the line "Because she's made of wood?" just to force the others into laughter. It worked. Idle tries to cover his corpsing with the blade of a scythe in front of his mouth.[98]

PILATE: "Take him away! I want him fighting wabid, wild animals within a week!"— The alliteration is designed to undercut Pilate's threatening nature, creating a sing-song effect to his pronouncements. As this soldier sniggers, it seems that Pilate immediately designates him as *servitus poenae*, or "slavery of the punishment," meaning the soldier is now no better than a slave and can be treated as such.[99] This likely Roman citizen (he is a Roman soldier, and part of the Praetorian Guard) did have certain significant rights, which even Pilate should have to acknowledge:

> In principle, a Roman citizen had a right to halt torture and capital punishment after his condemnation by means of an appeal to the Emperor under the *lex Iulia de vi*. This recourse to the Emperor was, however, soon restricted as the number of citizens in the provinces increased and the official repression of crime called for concessions. The right of appeal was altogether denied to stage performers, persons with earlier criminal record, those who confessed, those who resisted summons, *and those who committed something against the public order*. The denial of appeals authorized the derogation of plebeians' citizen rights.[100]

It seems that both Brian and this giggling soldier have flouted the public order, at the very least, and deserve punishment by the letter of the law. And perhaps by a slight exaggeration, both have committed the crime *maiestas*, meaning their acts have contributed to "the diminution of the majesty of the Roman people." The *maiestas* charge became popular in regard to many forms of treason and revolt.[101]

Sentencing to the arena was a common punishment for soldiers who misbehaved, though. Mannix notes that Flamma was likely an insubordinate Roman soldier who was condemned to fight in the gladiator arena, where he became a cult hero.[102] But non-soldiers and non-slaves could also find themselves facing the toothy or tusked end of a wild animal; judges could sentence men convicted of "robbery, murder, sacrilege or mutiny" to fight in the arena. High arena turnover (meaning the deaths of combatants) increased vacancies steadily: "The demand for gladiators far exceeded the supply. In the law courts, 'sentenced to the arena' was the commonest of all verdicts."[103] It's not unusual at all, then, to see a soldier condemned to death by animal for giggling. Fighting wild animals was a newer twist on the gladiatorial pitch, and became very popular: "By the time the Colosseum was built . . . dangerous animals such as lions, leopards, wild boars and tigers were introduced and gladiators sent out to kill them," Mannix writes. "Augustus had a bandit named Selurus dropped into a cage of wild beasts and this sight made such a hit that the execution of condemned prisoners by wild animals became a regular part of the shows."[104] The games provided in the film offer no hint of wild beast entertainments.

PILATE: ". . . wabid, wild animals . . ."—As for the condition of these arena animals, great care was actually taken to make sure they were housed, trained, and fed well until they were needed in a fight. This was just good business. The Emperor Claudius was known for micromanaging his games, and would even throw the workers of games machinery to the beasts if their equipment broke down.[105] The trainers of unwilling or ineffective animals could likely share that fate. The area below the sand of the Colosseum that housed animals was far more comfortable than where slaves and other combatants were held, including running fresh water.[106] *Bestiarii* like Carpophorus were known to meticulously train their carnivores (leopards, tigers, lions) to favor human flesh, and have them ready to attack as soon as the Emperor signaled the beginning of the event. A rabid animal would have been dangerous to everyone—intended victim and animal handler alike—so healthy animals were prized. In the regional circuses, the smaller venue likely meant reduced attention to such details, and tatty men and "scrofulous" animals could be found.[107]

PILATE: ". . . the common soldiewy"—As mentioned earlier, Pilate would have surrounded himself with carefully picked bodyguards and perhaps a "cwack legion" from Gaul or Thrace, or the like. The common Roman soldier could come from across the empire, and by this period were expected to serve twenty-year terms. The somewhat unusual term "soldiery" is used several times in the Whiston translation of *Josephus* (1960), though it's likely used for Pilate because it has a useful "r" that can be rendered a "w."

revealed fresco—A new portion of the background fresco series is revealed as Pilate moves toward his sniggering guards. Also from the lengthy Bacchanalian fresco sequence found at the Villa of the Mysteries, Pompeii, this panel features a reversed version of a young woman grasping her shawl, which billows behind her. Gilliam would often reverse original images as needed for the new layouts he planned—in the *Holy Grail* sequence featuring the monk/scribe disturbed by the "Bloody weather," and throughout *Flying Circus*, including a Flemish baroque painting in the first series' title sequence, a Battle of Trafalgar print (Ep. 11), a Civil War–era military leader (Ep. 14), a seventeenth-century Jan Vredeman de Vries print (Eps. 15 and 19), Union Civil War encampment, artillery battery, and Union personnel photos (also Ep. 15), and a Civil War train (Ep. 22).[108]

PILATE: "Incontinentia Buttocks"—Yet another joke name meant to appeal to the seventh-grader in all of us. No guard snickers, interestingly, when hearing "Incontinentia," which seems to indicate the so-named cannot control her bowels; it's only when "Buttocks" is appended that giggling breaks out.

PILATE: "Call yourselves Pwaetowian guards. Silence!"—Specially trained "Praetorian" guards had been used for many years by Roman emperors. These tended to be hand-picked guards, meaning Pilate would likely have had a hand in selecting those working so close to him. Just two years before this scene is (allegedly) set, the Praetorian guards serving Tiberius in Rome had nearly been sicced on their own emperor by Sejanus, prefect of the imperial bodyguard, who was arrested and executed in 31.[109] Our Pilate may have had reason, then, to distrust his seemingly most loyal soldiers.

PILATE: "You cwowd of cwacking up cweeps"—Pilate is purposely sounding more and more like Elmer Fudd all the time, a Warner Bros. character voiced by Arthur Q. Bryant. His alliteration and speech impediment mean he won't be taken seriously again in the film, except when he sends "Bwian" off for crucifixion, and then tries to spare him. He's never taken seriously by the Jews.

PILATE: "Blow your noses and seize him! Oh my bum"—"Bum" is one of the terms that the Interviewer (Cleese) doesn't want to say as he interviews a man with three buttocks in Ep. 2 of *Flying Circus*.[110] It was also one of the words that, by Ep. 17, was allegedly forbidden for utterance by the BBC.[111]

Brian performs a cartoony escape here, and is able to rejoin Judith and their Peoples' Front of Judea comrades, ostensibly to carry on the work of ridding Judea of the Romans. In this he is very much like a number of later terrorists, including Osamu Maruoka. Maruoka became the de facto leader of his JRA cadre during the hijacking of Japan Air Lines flight 404 in July 1973 after the accidental death (by grenade) of their female leader. The plane was successfully commandeered to Libya, then blown up on the tarmac. Maruoka was arrested by Libyan authorities, a trial was promised, but he was later quietly "released without trial" by the sympathetic Qaddafi government, escaping, essentially, from his imperialist enemies' justice. Free to keep fighting the revolutionary cause, Maruoka in 1977 would assist in the hijacking of JAL flight 472, forcing the plane to eventually fly to Algeria.[112] Demands included a ransom and the release of JRA prisoners, both of which the Japanese government met.[113] Maruoka would be free for another ten years, when he was arrested trying to enter Japan in 1987. He would die in prison in 2011.

As serious as all these hijackings were, the sheer number of them across the 1960s reached absurd proportions, meaning the subject could understandably become sardonic and then satirized. Airlines flying routes toward the southeastern United States even provided their pilots landing instructions for Havana's airport.[114] A Ronald Giles political cartoon from September 1969 tweaks the hijackers' penchant of targeting valuable hostages for their prisoner release demands. The panel depicts an "X Channel Air 'Ops" plane being unloaded of its passengers, who look to be frumpy working-class types from well outside of civilized London somewhere. One dismayed terrorist says to another: "This lot won't fetch much on the hijack exchange, Gonzalez."[115]

Notes

1. Emmerich, *The Dolorous Passion of Our Lord Jesus Christ*.

2. Richard, *WWAR*, 57. This is also precisely what Palin (as Herbert's father), was doing to Swamp Castle when Launcelot came slashing through—he was renovating. See the entry for ". . . have all this knocked through" in Larsen, *BAFHG*, 392–95.

3. Smallwood, *JURR*, 166.

4. Brandon provides a very readable overview of these events in "Pontius Pilate in History and Legend," *History Today* 18.8 (1968): 523–30.

5. In the face of violent Jewish opposition relayed to him by his very brave Syrian legate Petronius, Gaius would eventually rescind this order. See Philo and companions' response to this proposed outrage in Colson's translation of *Embassy to Gaius*, 97–99.

6. Philo, *The Embassy to Gaius*, 175–77; italics added. See also *JURR*, 244–45.

7. Smallwood, "Jews and Romans in the Early Empire, Part I" 239.

8. The large, peristyle court in the Pompeii villa is known as "The Initiation Chamber," as it is thought to depict an initiation rite sequence, specifically for a young maiden, in well-preserved frescoes adorning its walls. (*Sala di Grande Dipinto*, Scene VI in the *Villa de Misteri*.)

9. The frescoes were likely painted sometime in the mid- to late first century BC, according to Seaford, "The Mysteries of Dionysos at Pompeii," then buried for centuries in 79, perhaps forty years after Pilate's death. Photographic versions of some of these frescoes were available in the book accompanying the exhibition.

10. Paul Overy, "A Stroll Round Pompeii," *Times*, 23 November 1976: 11.

11. Palin, *Diaries 1969–1979*, 352.

12. In Ep. 25 of *Flying Circus*, Gilliam and the production team for the BBC created a "large Titian canvas" for the beginning of the "Art Gallery Strike" sketch. The mocked-up version of the Titian is the first remade picture seen, followed by a Landseer called *Nothing at Bay* by the auctioneer (Larsen, *MPFC: UC*, 1.382–83 and 378, respectively).

13. Shakespeare created ahistorical characters like Falstaff around which his historical figures and events could revolve. See Larsen, *MPSERD*, especially chapter 3. Brian serves this function to a certain extent in this film, while the mythical Arthur tries to navigate the overlapping worlds (historical England, mythological England, and 1970s England) in *Holy Grail*.

14. Gilliam is well aware of these influences. He uses Piranesi's work throughout the title and credit sequence at the beginning of the film, as well as images from across the ancient world.

15. Magness, *Stone and Dung*, 12.

16. See Dal Masio, *Pompeii: The Art of Loving*, 63, 67.

17. Incidentally, this open hand symbol was a prominent part of both the UDA and UVF ultra-Loyalist paramilitary groups' insignia in Northern Ireland.

18. Both Philo and Josephus report this sacrilege.

19. This mixing of columnar types isn't unusual—the Theater of Marcellus boasts Doric, Ionic, and Corinthian columns, respectively, on its three tiers (*WWAR*, 65).

20. *ATW*, 2.26.30.

21. *BAFHG*, xix.

22. Perhaps better: "Pilate shall govern the Jews," according to Dr. Roger Macfarlane who, like, the Centurion, mentions the significance of tense ("Translate it with a future tense and you're nearly right") in a proper translation.

23. As of 2011, that graffiti was still visible. The *Daily Mail* ran a clever headline in 1978—when Davis had been put back in jail for *another* armed robbery—reading "George Davis Is Guilty OK" (25 July 1978: 16–17).

24. Davis had maintained all along that he had been miles away driving his minicab. He even passed a lie detector test supporting that alibi. Davis would be re-arrested for another robbery months later.

25. "George Davis IS Innocent," *Daily Mail*, 24 May 2011.

26. *Private Eye*, 30 April 1976: 13, in the "Gnome Bicentennial Exhibition" advertisement.

27. *Private Eye*, 1 April 1977: 14.

28. *Private Eye*, 15 April 1977: 7; *PE* cartoonist John Kent would run a series during the Thatcher administration called "Maggie Rules OK."

29. Zeitlin, "History, Historians," 99.

30. Mentioned later as Brian's followers argue over the holiness of a shoe, a sandal, or a gourd.

31. See Zeitlin's "The Idolatry of the Dead Sea Scrolls" and "History, Historians and the Dead Sea Scrolls." Zeitlin writes of being a "voice in the wilderness" across this span of years, seeing himself as one of the few cautious voices in the otherwise circuslike world of the Dead Sea scrolls.

32. See *MPFC: UC*, 1.327–38 for notes to Ep. 21, as well as *ATW*, 1.279–82 for the script pages. The Silbury Dig had been completed, rather on a down note, in 1969, just before the Pythons began writing the second series of the show (*MPFC: UC*, 1.336).

33. Zeitlin, "History, Historians," 100.

34. Zeitlin, "History, Historians," 116. Prof. Zeitlin would die in 1976. In the 1990s, the Dead Sea scrolls themselves were finally scientifically tested (via carbon dating), and the findings would have perplexed the emphatic Zeitlin. The "newest" scroll ("4Q258") seems to have been created no later than about 300, and almost all of the others were at least 100 and as many as 700 years *older* than this newest scroll. To be fair, during Zeitlin's lifetime, only the woolen wrappings around some of the scrolls had been age-dated, meaning the jury *should have* still been out as to the antiquity of the scrolls.

35. Special thanks to my helpful colleague Dr. Roger Macfarlane for accurate Latin translations throughout, and for noting that "there is only one attestation of the term 'Tiberieum' in all extant Latin . . . in the inscription from the Tiberieum at Caesarea" (e-mail correspondence with the author, 19

October 2016). For the first scholarly report on these findings, see Lifshitz's "Inscriptions latines de Césarée (Caesarea Palaestinae)."

36. Emmerich, *The Dolorous Passion*, 180.

37. The Second Temple Period is considered to end with the sacking of Jerusalem and the destruction of the temple by Roman forces in 70.

38. None of the surviving drafts of the script feature significant "Jewish" religiosity.

39. Yadin, *Jerusalem Revealed*, 40.

40. In fall 1975, it was reported that forty Roman villas had been identified in the Cotswolds alone. See "Cotswolds: Iron Age and Roman Remains," *Times*, 13 October 1975: 14.

41. "Lincoln: Signs of a Pre-Conquest Revival," *Times*, 22 January 1976: 16; "[Dewlish] Roman Pavement," *Times*, 17 July 1976: 2; "[Yorkshire] Villa Site: Remains from Three Epochs," *Times*, 13 August 1977: 14; "There Are Tigers in Cyprus," *Times*, 29 January 1977: 11; "The Sicilian Sun IS Waiting for You," *Times*, 21 November 1975: III.

42. Pölönen, "Plebeians and Repression of Crime," 219.

43. Pölönen, "Plebeians and Repression of Crime," 224.

44. Burleigh, *BRT*, 162.

45. Hearst's sentence was eventually commuted by President Jimmy Carter.

46. This same is true for portions of the *Holy Grail* script, which are word-for-word typed from the film as finished, not a draft version of the script. See *BAFHG* for more.

47. Palin, *Diaries 1969–1979*, 356. Originally, this had been a centurion, but quickly became Pilate.

48. "Roy Jenkins: Politics, Parties, and Guilt-Free Adultery," *Telegraph*, 13 March 2014.

49. This being said, it should be noted that Jenkins's accent isn't unlike Terry Jones's northern Welsh accent, where an "r" can slip into a "w" quite easily, and often. Perhaps, then, Palin's performance was also an unacknowledged tribute to his writing partner of many years.

50. *Private Eye*, 12 November 1976: 5. In a July *Private Eye* comic panel (by John Kent) Jenkins is also featured, there saying "sewies" for "series," "pewils" for "perils," "democwacy" for "democracy," and "countwy" for "country" (23 July 1976: 15). Jenkins's speech pattern appears in comic panels in myriad newspapers across the years, from many artists. See the University of Kent's British Cartoon Archive.

51. Waugh, *FCY*, 24 March 1976.

52. Cockerell, *Roy Jenkins: A Very Social Democrat*, 1996; a.t.

53. These quotes are from the Michael Cockerell film *Roy Jenkins: A Very Social Democrat*.

54. Donoughue, *DSD*, 2.356.

55. "From 'Shrill' Housewife to Downing Street: the Changing Voice of Margaret Thatcher," *Telegraph*, 25 November 2014.

56. "The Lessons Mrs T Will Have to Learn," *Sunday Times*, 28 June 1970: 9; see also Alan Watkins, "The Tory Style," *Sunday Times*, 25 October 1970: 61. As part of Heath's government from June 1970, Thatcher was much more in the public eye, as well as its crosshairs.

57. "A Woman Scorns Jobs Levy," *Times*, 6 May 1966: 14. The speech was called "a minor triumph" for Thatcher, though her gender and appearance and voice continued to be necessary identifiers. Enoch Powell had allegedly once described her simply as the woman "with those hats and that accent" ("The Times Diary," *Times*, 11 September 1974: 14). (The following day Powell would write to PHS denying this statement ["The Times Diary," *Times*, 12 September 1974: 18].) PHS apologized.

58. "Jilly Cooper Talks to . . . Margaret Thatcher," *Sunday Times*, 12 December 1976: 4.

59. Only a small number of guards closest to the prefect or procurator would necessarily be Roman, the balance from trusted neighboring provinces or countries, making the possibility of miscommunication even more likely. Herod, for example, was gifted (by Augustus) "a bodyguard of four-hundred Gauls," and there also may have been Thracians and Germans serving him. Plenty of languages, plenty of accents, and plenty of opportunity for miscommunication (Levine, *Jerusalem*, 172).

60. "Pontius Pilate," *JE*; italics added.

61. *JURR*, 164–65n71.

62. Zeitlin, "Crucifixion of Jesus Re-Examined," 348.

63. Zeitlin, "Crucifixion of Jesus Re-Examined," 349.

64. Zeitlin, "Crucifixion of Jesus Re-Examined," 349–50; see the original Zeitlin article (1941) for several in-text citations not included here.

65. Caryl, *Strange Rebels*, 48. Khomeini saw Zionist plots everywhere, it seems, attaching the term to myriad actions of the Shah's government over the years (88). During his exile, Khomeini would use donated "religious taxes" to help support the PLO in its fight against Israel (91).

66. *BRT*, 58.

67. "Eichmann 'Felt Like Pilate Free of Any Guilt,'" *Times*, 27 June 1961: 10.

68. "Faked Letter May Be Correct," *Times*, 5 October 1963: 7.

69. Jack Jones is discussed in *BAFHG*, as one of the types referenced by the Pythons as they created the pleasantly pugnacious Dennis the Peasant character. See *BAFHG*, 119–20.

70. "'Cut Bank Rate to Save Jobs' Appeal," *Times*, 20 January 1971: 2.

71. See the *OED* under "derring do."

72. The play premiered on Easter Sunday in 1977 at the National Theatre.

73. Pölönen, "Plebeians and Repression of Crime," 225n12.

74. Wiedemann, *Emperors and Gladiators*, 70–71.

75. Bogdanor, "The Character of the Postwar Period," a.t.

76. Bogdanor, "The Character of the Postwar Period," a.t.

77. Bogdanor, "The Character of the Postwar Period," a.t.

78. Bogdanor, "Character of the Postwar Period," a.t.; italics added.

79. *MPFC: UC*, 1.127–42.

80. Wasson, "Roman Citizenship" (http://www.ancient.eu/article/859/). Later, after the collapse of the Easter Uprising, combatant Eamon de Valera—later president of Ireland—escaped execution "perhaps because of his . . . American citizenship" (Brendon, *DFBE*, 309).

81. Acts 22:25.

82. Pölönen, "Plebeians and Repression of Crime," 217.

83. Pölönen, "Plebeians and Repression of Crime," 217–18.

84. Radin, *The Jews Among the Greeks and Romans*, 361–62.

85. Cook, "Envisioning Crucifixion, 268.

86. Bauman, *Human Rights in Ancient Rome*, 125.

87. Wiedemann, *Emperors and Gladiators*, 68.

88. Wiedemann, *Emperors and Gladiators*, 68. Galba would be emperor for about seven months, in 68–69.

89. *BRT*, 6.

90. Hope, "Contempt and Respect," 104.

91. Maier, *Pontius Pilate*, 63–64.

92. "The Histories of Pliny the Elder" was first broadcast 28 March 1957.

93. A plant used to make laxatives, the Goons have an entire episode dedicated to this gag, "The End, or Confessions of a Secret Senna Pod Drinker" (22 March 1955).

94. See *JURR*, 163.

95. Maier, *Pontius Pilate*, 353.

96. Quoted in Maier, *Pontius Pilate*, 353.

97. Juvenal, *Satire 8*.

98. Mentioned in the audio track recorded by the surviving Pythons, as included on the *Monty Python and the Holy Grail* DVD.

99. See Lawrence, "Servi Poenae," in Rodriguez's *The Historical Encyclopedia of World Slavery*, 1.7, 577–78.

100. Pölönen, "Plebeians and Repression of Crime," 256; italics added.

101. See *JURR*, 169; and "maiestas" in the *Oxford Dictionary of the Classical World*.

102. Mannix, *TAD*, 21–32.

103. *TAD*, 91.

104. *TAD*, 47.

105. Bauman, *Human Rights in Ancient Rome*, 124.

106. *TAD*, 84.

107. Toner, *The Day Commodus Killed a Rhino*, 48–50.

108. *BAFHG* 363; also 500, 509, and 516. For additional mentions of manipulated images in *Flying Circus*, see *MPFC: UC*, 1.5, 173, 222, 240–41, 290, and 344.

109. *JURR*, 166–67.

110. *ATW*, 1.2.17–18.

111. *ATW*, 1.17.231; also, *MPFC: UC*, 1.264–77.

112. "Skyjack Led by Lod 'Killer'," *Telegraph*, 5 October 1977: 19.

113. See Farrell's "Legacy of Violence" chapter in *BRJ*.

114. *BRT*, 153.

115. Found in the 7 September 1969 *Sunday Express*. See the BCA.

SCENE FOURTEEN
THE SPACE MOVIE INTERRUPTION

Suddenly BRIAN emerges at the top of the tower . . .—An illusion already employed in *Holy Grail*. When the obstreperous French sentry (Cleese) shouts down insults at Arthur and his knights, he appears to be standing on the high parapet of the castle. In fact, the film crew have built a mock-parapet that was then mounted a few feet above the ground, and placed the camera, angled up, at its base. The top of the tower Brian leaps from is likely built in a similar fashion.

. . . a passing space ship careers underneath him . . . animated Star Wars type space fight— The ship is yellow, perhaps a nod to either George Lucas's favored deuce coupe seen in *American Graffiti* or a bulbous New York Checker cab—both bright yellow. None of the models in *Star Wars* were this color. This sequence is the most "out there" section of the film, a complete rupture in the depicted time period, one that can't be papered over like those in *Holy Grail* where bits of the tenth, thirteenth, and fourteenth centuries often shared the screen. Gilliam will do this again on the following film, *Meaning of Life*, there creating a section initially intended to mesh with the rest of the narrative—*The Crimson Permanent Assurance*—but eventually dubbed a "supporting feature" that has to be quashed.

As discussed earlier, *Star Wars* and the Luke character exerted a profound influence on the life journey created for Brian, and perhaps Gilliam is saying that even a period film set at the time of Christ isn't safe from the intrusion of the blockbuster space saga.

Private Eye had lampooned the epic television event *Jesus of Nazareth*, quoting the movie's screenwriter, "famous British novelist Anthony Bargess," who defends his choice in "rewriting the story in modern terms," including the inclusion of the "surprise ending where Jesus goes off to Sirius in a UFO."[1] The *Sunday Times* Business News editor Kenneth Fleet inadvertently also put *Star Wars* and the Middle East together for a New Year's Day editorial in 1978. His first wish for the new year: "The star newly risen in the east may not explode[2] but herald a settled peace between Israel and Egypt, better still between Jew and Arab. Israel's energy and intelligence, allied with the human and mineral resources of the Arab world, would transform the Middle East into one of the great growth areas of the world."[3] Josephus describes his own miraculous, familiar escape from the Romans during the siege of Jotapata, in 67:

> And now the Romans searched for Josephus, both out of the hatred they bore him, and because their general was very desirous to have him taken; for he reckoned that if he were once taken, the greatest part of the war would be over. They then searched among the dead, and looked into the most concealed recesses of the city; but as the city was first taken, *he was assisted by a certain*

supernatural providence; for he withdrew himself from the enemy when he was in the midst of them, and leaped into a certain deep pit.[4]

This siege was led by Vespasian, whom the Pythons mention earlier in *Flying Circus* Ep. 24.[5]

The proximity of a messianic figure to an alien one isn't reserved for the satirical pages of *Private Eye*. Bishop Robinson's *Honest to God* facetiously refers to the Incarnation of God not only as "God dressed up—like Father Christmas," but that a "traditional" Christian view of God "leaves the impression that God took a space-trip and arrived on this planet in the form of a man."[6] A "jammy bastard" moment, indeed.

. . . and by pure chance BRIAN lands in the cockpit . . .—This narrative intrusion by another narrative has happened before in the Python world, and will happen again, in *The Meaning of Life*. During the run of *Flying Circus*, the epic Viking saga of Ep. 27 can never get a head of steam—other narrative elements continue to break in, including appearances by the saga's narrator, two Pepperpots looking for Jean-Paul Sartre, and the business people of North Malden.[7] In *Meaning of Life*, when a boardroom of American corporate executives are discussing the meaning of life and the wearing of more hats, the earlier-seen "supporting feature" makes an unwelcome appearance, only to be waylaid by the film itself:

> Voice Over: We interrupt this film to apologise for this unwarranted attack by the supporting feature. Luckily, we have been prepared for this eventuality, and are now taking steps to remedy it.
>
> *Outside in the street, an enormous glass skyscraper falls and crushes the pirate ship building flat.*
>
> Voice Over: Thank you.

A crash ends this *Star Wars*–type intrusion into the Holy Land film, and the first-century chase can continue. Remember also, in *Holy Grail*, the voice-over narrator for Scene 24 is eventually bashed on the head, ending his intrusion, the sudden death of the animator allowed Arthur and his knights to escape the cartoon beast, and the arrival of uniformed policemen ended the film entirely.

In similar contemporary news, in late December 1977 the Soviet satellite Kosmos 954 was struggling to maintain its programmed orbital trajectory, and by the new year it was quietly announced that the nuclear-powered satellite would fall back to Earth. In late January 1978 the satellite reentered the atmosphere and broke apart, scattering itself (including a chunk of uranium-235) across northern Canada. A small percentage of the satellite was recovered over the next year.[8] The Canadian government would eventually present a bill to the USSR for the recovery efforts, comprising £2.5 million of the total £6 million allegedly spent trying to find the satellite's radioactive core.[9] *Private Eye* carried a newswire story clipped from the *Evening Standard* referring to the falling Russian object, while the American TV show *Saturday Night Live* offered a sketch in January 1978[10] about the falling satellite's radiation creating mutant, marauding lobster creatures. In this same episode Bill Murray sings what will become his famous, "Nick Winters'" lounge version of the theme song to *Star Wars*, both events—the crashing Soviet satellite and the *Star Wars* reference—setting the tone nicely for Gilliam's falling (and Lucasian-yellow) alien ship.

. . . plunging back to earth at the foot of the tower . . .—The backdrop here is a mocked-up version of Jerusalem, not unlike the backdrop used in *Flying Circus* Ep. 7 during the "Science Fiction Sketch."[11] This is a composite image of bits of spires, mosque domes, and city walls from both Monastir, where the Pythons were shooting, and Jerusalem. The tower Brian jumps from is supposed to be the Ribat, looking over the rest of the city.

BRIAN staggers out from the wreckage—The prop ship resembles the ships designed for the 1936 *Flash Gordon* and 1939 *Buck Rogers* serials starring Buster Crabbe. The model created by Gilliam also looks similar to the mid-1930s toy ship created to promote the *Buck Rogers* radio show, and a poster for the 1936 Flash Gordon film *Rocket Ship* displays a bulbous, bright yellow rocket very similar to this one. Gilliam also adds race car sounds to the scene—screeching tires and brakes, a revving engine—furthering the silliness of the sequence. (The car sounds nudge the ship closer to the *American Graffiti* deuce coupe, as well.)

The script calls for the attacking ship to be destroyed by Brian's ship, but this does not happen; only Brian's ship is shot down.

PASSER-BY (Charles Knode): "You jammy bastard"—A recent colloquialism meaning someone who is very lucky or fortunate. Knode has already appeared in the film as one of the begging lepers.

Notes

1. One of the film's screenwriters had been Anthony *Burgess*, author of *A Clockwork Orange*. The "Sirius" reference is to the recently released book *The Sirius Mystery* by Robert Temple, which looks at amphibian alien visitation to Earth.

2. Likely referring to both the Star of David and the Death Star.

3. "*Star Wars* & Polish Jokes," *Sunday Times*, 1 January 1978: 13.

4. Josephus, *WJ*, 3.8.1 (Whiston, 514); italics added.

5. Larsen, *MPFC: UC*, 1.369.

6. "Mixed Thoughts on Religion from Under a Mitre," *Times*, 4 April 1963: 17. Robinson has been mentioned earlier in regard to Gregory's "not to be taken literally" comment during the Sermon on the Mount.

7. See the entries for Ep. 27, specifically those for "Njorl's Saga" and "Mrs Premise and Mrs Conclusion," in *MPFC: UC* 2.3–19.

8. "Soviet Nuclear Satellite Crashes in Canada," *Times*, 25 January 1978: 1.

9. "Cosmos Debris Bill," *Telegraph*, 24 January 1979: 5.

10. Listed as season three, episode 10, and hosted by comedian Robert Klein. Michael Palin will host *SNL* in April 1978; followed by *Star Wars* alum Carrie Fisher in November 1978, Eric Idle in December 1978, and Palin again in January and May 1979, all before *Life of Brian* was completed. Idle had already appeared as host of *SNL* in 1976 and 1977.

11. *MPFC: UC*, 1.121.

SCENE FIFTEEN
STREET PREACHERS AND HAGGLING

BRIAN runs off towards the crowded market square . . . inside the soukh . . .—This market set was Gilliam's pride and joy according to Palin. Palin mentions that the Ex-leper scenes were, for example, being shot so fast that Gilliam was concerned none of his crew's hard work was going to be seen. Gilliam laments this a bit, as well, calling himself the film's "resigner" as opposed to "designer," he felt like he had to give up so much.[1]

. . . many strangely bearded and oddly dressed PROPHETS . . .—These are only named in the printed script, and are known in order as the "Blood & Thunder Prophet" (Gilliam), the "False Prophet" (Charles McKeown), and the "Boring Prophet" (Palin).

Once again the Pythons have homaged *I'm All Right Jack*. In the scene where a crowd has gathered outside Stan's aunt's home, protesting the strike and praising Stan, a self-styled prophet wearing a placard marches through the shot, declaring: ". . .and the children of Babylon are destroyed, and become an abomination in the eyes of lasciviousness." His placard reads: "The day of wrath is at hand." There were many in Britain across this era of inflamed union activity who believed that doomsday would inevitably follow in the wake of such societal disruption. (Things would get much worse by the mid-to-late-1970s, when work stoppages and strike days missed often brought Britain to a halt.) The words and phrases appearing over and over again in newspaper columns included "anarchy," "ungovernable," and a bewailing of the "bloody-minded" moments of "mounting chaos" as labor and the economy soured.[2]

The first century seems to teem with this kind of prophetic figure and especially in the region of Jerusalem, the Holy City. The Romans might have been in charge, but they looked away from religious fervor when it didn't impinge on civic order. John the Baptist was perhaps the prototype for these strange prophets and was described quite favorably (in stark contrast to other period "messiahs") by Josephus,[3] as Goldberg describes:

> One wonders what the difference is between John and the men whom Josephus disparages as "deceivers" . . . and "enchanters" . . . such as Theudas and the Egyptian. It isn't simply that John did not represent a direct threat to Rome—Josephus always stresses the folly of those who do oppose Rome—as many of the others also seemed apolitical. All of these, including John, seemed to be killed solely because they had a large following, which in itself was seen as a threat to those in power: there was room for only one crowd and only one leader. We are left to conclude that Josephus himself was touched favorably by the philosophy of John, just as many of his countrymen were. While he was probably working from a source that was itself positive toward John, his choice of that source would have reflected his own attitude.[4]

306

In 1974, on a Belfast campaign platform for Tory outlier Enoch Powell, the Rev. Paisley even mentioned that he saw himself as a modern-day John the Baptist. (In this same speech, he also compared the current government of the Republic of Ireland to the communist, guerrilla government of North Vietnam.[5])

There were a number of such figures in the first century, according to Kotker. Paul criss-crossed Asia Minor, Greece, and the Holy Land preaching eternal life with belief in Christ, preaching in synagogues and on the streets, and founding Christian churches. The promise of a salvation into eternal bliss had many guises, though. There were Persians preaching of the god Mithras, Egyptian priests presenting Isis cults, and "missionaries of the Greek goddess Demeter" offering "mysteries" in a cave near Eleusis.[6] Around 44, according to Smallwood, there emerged "a series of impostors who added to the general unrest by posing as messiahs and attracting large followings with their promises of signs and wonders and deliverance from oppression."[7] One of these, appearing in and around Jerusalem, was Theudas, mentioned by Goldberg above, who promised Jesus-like miracles, according to Josephus:

> Now it came to pass, that while Fadus was procurator of Judea,[8] that a certain magician whose name was Theudas, persuaded a great part of the people to take their effects with them, and follow him to the river Jordan; for he told them he was a prophet, and that he would, by his own command, divide the river, and afford them an easy passage over it; and many were deluded by his words. However, Fadus did not permit them to make any advantage of his wild attempt, but sent a troop of horsemen out against them; who falling upon them unexpectedly, slew many of them, and took many of them alive. They also took Theudas alive, and cut off his head, and carried it to Jerusalem.[9]

Like Pilate, Marcellus, Marullus, and Agrippa before him, Fadus walked the tightrope between controlling and antagonizing his Jewish subjects. The "Egyptian prophet," also mentioned by Goldberg earlier, allegedly led a *sicarii* revolt according to Josephus, and was clearly seen as a threat to Rome, which John the Baptist never was.[10]

This locus of speechifying could also be found in the London of the Pythons' time, at Parliament Square. This tacitly approved area for peaceful protest and demonstration was in the news in May 1974 when an IRA bomb exploded there, injuring eleven.

A STRANGE FIGURE . . . two severed hands on a pole . . . —This is who the printed script calls the "Blood & Thunder Prophet," a mud-caked man of the wilderness, played by Gilliam; Palin calls him "gargoylical."[11] The "severed hands on a pole" could simply be a grisly version of the carved hand, the *manus*, placed atop many Roman standards, and seen earlier in Pilate's chambers.

There were plenty of modern prophets the Pythons could have chosen as inspiration for these biblical-era figures, many quite close to home. Northern Ireland provides two such figures. Seen by many in the press as a cross between a seventeenth-century "religious fanatic" and an American televangelist, the Reverend Ian Paisley raged *against* the pope and popery and *for* a Protestant Ireland from the mid-1950s onward.[12] He was called a "blood-and-thunder Evangelical" and an "Old Testament figure" many times, his public speaking was so renowned, and unfiltered.[13] On the death of Pope John XXIII, for example, Paisley said: "This Romish man of sin is now in hell!"[14] He called John Paul the "scarlet woman of Rome," was certain that alcohol was "the devil's buttermilk," and he regularly called "down the curse of God" on anyone who wanted to stretch "hands across the border."[15] It was Paisley who was instrumental in undermining the Sunningdale Agreement in 1974, which led to many more deaths before accepting a very similar agreement in 1998. He alternately sounded like the Blood & Thunder and the False prophet as he denounced the evil practices of men: "How base and despicable God's people become! Did you ever notice that? How base and despicable the people of God can become when they're covered with the sin of unbelief!"[16]

In February 1969 Paisley was campaigning in Belfast, covered by Philip Howard for the *Times* and a photographer from *Paris Match*, "who [had] been following 'the circus Paislee.'" Howard describes a "blood and thunder" moment, one with all the theatricality and noise of our snarling prophet:

> The small grinning boy clashes his cymbals as vehemently as if he is banging together the heads of the Pope, Captain Terence O'Neill, the B.B.C. and the conspiratorial, Romanist-infiltrated press. . . . Here . . . a considerable crowd of voters huddle together, to have their hearts warmed by the Demon King of the election, the Rev. Ian Paisley . . . [who] thunders for 50 minutes, from the back of a Land Rover, roaring out great guts of rhetoric. O'Neill is a traitor, a tyrant, a viper who wants to bring back the darkness of priestcraft, to make everyone kiss the big toe of Old Red-Socks (the Pope). "The press is against me. The TV is against me. The Old Devil is against me. But we believe that the God who was with us at the Battle of the Boyne will intervene. No surrender."[17]

Politician Leo Abse[18] writes of both Paisley and Powell, two of the loudest voices of the day, bringing "Jerusalem" and modern-day Britain together:

> We can no more annihilate our aggression than we can rid ourselves of the toxic waste of a fast-breeder reactor. The buried aggression seeps through: and so we have the Church Militant. The pacifism of Christianity unhappily leads not to the New Jerusalem but to Belfast. And in the environment of Ulster the Reverend Ian Paisley and Enoch Powell can in their pulpits preach doctrines which guarantee the continuation of the admixture of race and religion which is destroying the province.
>
> The danger of their doctrines is, of course, their terrible exclusiveness. They are envious of the claims of the chosen people whose Book they read, and overcome their jealousy by usurping the Jews and either explicitly or gnomically present themselves as the new elect, undeterred by the catastrophe that the Jews, by hubris, brought down upon themselves. Their creeds . . . have a long and sometimes ugly tradition: the ideal of the superior Holy People, the true Israel, separate, scrupulously protecting its identity through adherence to the Law, always brought with it the corollary of intolerance to foreigners and prohibitions against marrying out of the community. The Nehemiahs and Ezras of Judaic literature are the source books of our contemporary chauvinistic Christian preachers and politicians.[19]

In February 1969 a Gerald Scarfe exhibition at the Grosvenor Gallery featured scathing likenesses, coincidentally, of both Paisley and the Pope.[20]

In the other pews of this argument was Bernadette Devlin, equally vocal and equally certain that her point of view—a united Catholic Ireland as the true Ireland—would win the day. She was a witness to both the Battle of Bogside and Bloody Sunday, and was elected to Parliament in 1969. For her maiden speech, Devlin spoke directly about the situation in Ireland, a breach of protocol, it seems, but one she admitted and embraced. In this portion of her speech, she is taking to task Lord Chichester-Clark—MP for Londonderry since 1960, and Prime Minister of Ireland from May 1969—asking how well he understood Ireland:

> The hon. Member for Londonderry said that he stood in Bogside. I wonder whether he could name the streets through which he walked in the Bogside so that we might establish just how well acquainted he became with the area. I had never hoped to see the day when I might agree with someone who represents the bigoted and sectarian Unionist Party, which uses a deliberate policy

of dividing the people in order to keep the ruling minority in power and to keep the oppressed people of Ulster oppressed. I never thought that I should see the day when I should agree with any phrase uttered by the representative of such a party, but the hon. Gentleman summed up the situation "to a t." He referred to stark, human misery. That is what I saw in Bogside. It has not been there just for one night. It has been there for 50 years—and that same stark human misery is to be found in the Protestant Fountain area, which the hon. Gentleman would claim to represent. . . . The people of Northern Ireland have been forced into this situation. I was in the Bogside on the same evening as the hon. Member for Londonderry. I assure you, Mr. Speaker—and I make no apology for the fact—that I was not strutting around with my hands behind my back examining the area and saying "tut-tut" every time a policeman had his head scratched. I was going around building barricades because I knew that it was not safe.[21]

These kinds of exchanges continue to this day. Demaris concludes of Devlin: "She shares with Paisley, however, a major portion of the blame for the polarization of opinion on both sides that has led to so much bloodshed in Ireland."[22]

Blood & Thunder Prophet—The phrase itself is drawn from Colley Cibber's play *Love's Last Shift* (1696), and has been heard in over-the-top football punditry and from opera critics describing particularly effusive productions. In 1965 Granada television was producing two Thomas Middleton plays, *The Changeling* (1622) and *Women Beware Women* (c. 1624), "under the general heading BLOOD AND THUNDER," according to the *Spectator* (appearing in the "Not by Shakespeare" column).[23] These are primarily prophets of the eschatological harbingers, those who "see" the last days and the torments of death and hell. (Josephus railed against these types.) When Brian takes his place alongside them, he attempts a more Christ-like, beatific tone, and that, coupled with the open-endedness of his preaching, gains him followers almost immediately.

B & T Prophet: ". . . ride forth on a serpent's back . . ."—These are cobbled together from across the Old Testament, generally, but also Revelations. For example, Isaiah 27:1: "In that day the LORD with his sore and great and strong sword shall punish leviathan the piercing serpent, even leviathan that crooked serpent; and he shall slay the dragon that *is* in the sea."

B & T Prophet: ". . . eyes shall be red with the blood of living creatures . . ."—There are more than three times as many mentions of "blood" in the Old Testament as in the New Testament. Blood can be a part of purification, as in the Blood of the Lamb, or more punitive, as in those with spotted garments. In Revelations, the "woman . . .[is] drunk with the blood of the saints, the blood of the martyrs of Jesus." (17:6). In Ezekiel, Jerusalem has become the harlot, and is "polluted" in her own blood (16:6), which may be what this prophet's on about. The "whore of Babylon" character appears in dozens of woodcuts, and is often associated with the Roman Catholic Church and the pope, as in a vivid illustration from the 1545 edition of the Luther Bible.[24] The Pythons are pulling from the more hyperbolic portions of the scriptures for both the Blood & Thunder and the False prophets.

***(draft)* B & T Prophet: ". . . the hill of excitement . . . a great rubbing of parts . . ."**—This sexualized language is from condemnatory sections of the Bible, too, with connections to later English literature, and thence to the Pythons. The "earthy" poetry of Sidney and Spenser come to mind, first as the Pythons sexualized the hymn *Jerusalem* in *Flying Circus* Ep. 4:

> The glossing of "England's Mountains Green" as overtly sexual becomes much easier here, especially if "a man's life" is meant to include copulation . . . . "Mountains" can be either (or both) the female's breasts or pubic area. See Sidney's *Astrophil and Stella* and his object of lustful affection's "Cupid's hill." Also, cf. the Gardens of Adonis in Spenser's *Faerie Queene*, where the "stately Mount" is just one erotic section of this highly sexualized landscape.[25]

The "sweet gum" and "precious dew" in the "pleasant arbour" is Sidney at his most salacious, most Ovidian. The potential for "rubbing of parts" on this "hill of excitement" seems highly denunciable by this pelvis-thrusting prophet. These "secret parts" of the daughters of Zion are to be discovered by the Lord because they are "haughty," "wanton," and "mincing" (Isaiah 3:17).

FALSE PROPHET—Played here by Charles McKeown, but there's no reason or indication to believe he's any more or less truthful than any of the other street preachers here. This may have been a reflection of the Pythons' study as they prepared the film, perhaps accessing Josephus and his denunciations of false prophets like the Egyptian, discussed earlier.

FALSE PROPHET: ". . . a nine-bladed sword . . ."—There are sharp, two-edged swords in the scriptures, swords becoming ploughshares, and many references to death, justice, and suffering by sword, but none with multiple blades. In Revelations are beasts with seven heads and ten horns, which is likely where this mixed reference began. In Ep. 23 of *Flying Circus*, *Albrecht Dürer's Apocalypse of St. John, The Dragon with the Seven Heads* is used by Gilliam as part of a mail delivery animation.[26]

FALSE PROPHET: ". . . which he will wield on all wretched sinners . . ."—This prophet is properly fixated on numbers, as Arthur was in *Holy Grail*, but he's also nearly quoting from Isaiah 3, where Judah and Jerusalem are castigated by the Lord:

> 9 . . .they declare their sin as Sodom, they hide it not. Woe unto their soul! for they have rewarded evil unto themselves.
>
> 10 Say ye to the righteous, that it shall be well with him: for they shall eat the fruit of their doings.
>
> 11 Woe unto the wicked! it shall be ill with him: for the reward of his hands shall be given him.
> . . .
>
> 24 And it shall come to pass, that instead of sweet smell there shall be stink; and instead of a girdle a rent; and instead of well set hair baldness; and instead of a stomacher a girding of sackcloth; and burning instead of beauty.
>
> 25 Thy men shall fall by the sword, and thy mighty in the war.
>
> 26 And her gates shall lament and mourn; and she being desolate shall sit upon the ground.

(One of Brian's followers later will want to be healed of his "bald patch," perhaps believing it's a curse from on high.) This prophet perhaps most resembles John the Baptist. John had retreated away from cities and into the wilderness, preaching in the desert about the wretchedness of sin and the fact that when the Messiah did finally come, judgment came with him. He is mentioned by Josephus and in the Bible, and for good reason:

> John was a stirring preacher. With his unkempt beard and his rough clothes, his face weathered and tanned by years of exposure to the desert sun, he must also have been a striking figure. And his uncompromising and stern command "Repent, for the kingdom of heaven is at hand" helped him gather a devoted following in the years around A.D. 25. *To the Jews he was another of that line of fiery prophets who had long preached in Jerusalem and in the countryside of Palestine.* As others before had done, he called on the people to follow the ethical teachings of the Torah as well as its ritual prescriptions.[27]

We have our own line of prophets here, calling to repentance, or just condemning.

FALSE PROPHET: ". . . and that includes you sir"—This specificity, this personal touch, is mentioned as a key component for the particularly effective public speaker, according to Murray Sayle, covering Rev. Paisley for the *Sunday Times*:

Whatever one thinks of his doctrine, Paisley is a master orator. He is the only speaker I have heard who comes close to Fidel Castro. Their techniques are oddly similar, probably as old as the art of mob oratory itself: an almost schoolmasterly exposition broken by asides, savage humour, endless repetition of key phrases, picturesque abuse, and above all a total absorption in the changing moods of the audience.[28]

Brian will borrow the touch in a moment, when he effectively addresses one man in his audience, and the man happily thanks him.

FALSE PROPHET: ". . . the horns shall be on the head . . ."—The beast in Revelations has ten horns on its head, but a cuckold is also horned. In Daniel, he describes the dream beasts he's seen, including a fourth, ten-horned beast with "great iron teeth."[29] By verse twenty, he's explaining that the fourth beast is actually a fourth kingdom on Earth, and the ten horns are ten kings. In Revelations, creatures are multiple-headed, multiple-horned, and multiple-crowned—the bewildering array of creatures and sights in the apocalyptic works isn't really exaggerated by our prophets here. The cuckolded husband has typically been depicted wearing horns, but he is most often laughed at, not feared or even pitied.[30] The leader of the Knights Who Say Ni in *Holy Grail* is also wearing horns on his helm, as did Tim, but they're both also more ridiculous than feared.

BORING PROPHET: ". . . rumours of things going astray . . ."—The Children of Israel regularly went astray, as do the Lord's "sheep," with Jesus being the Good Shepherd who will find them. The "great confusion" this prophet mentions may simply be the dense works he's referencing, including Daniel, Revelations, and especially Isaiah, who offered: "But the cormorant and the bittern shall possess it; the owl also and the raven shall dwell in it: and he shall stretch out upon it the line of confusion, and the stones of emptiness."[31] Jeremiah was also certain that his enemies would be smitten with "everlasting confusion" and they "will not prosper."[32] The Second Coming may have been imminent for many during this period, or it may have been well in the future, but eschatological writings often mention the confusing, tumultuous days leading up to Christ's triumphal return. Following this line of prophets we have encountered prurience, fear and shame, and now spiritual bewilderment—all things Brian will encounter on his short journey to the cross.

". . . little things with the sort of raffia work base . . ."—He's waxing Goonish here. The Goons often list things absolutely necessary to carry out a particular task—retrofitting the Albert Memorial into a rocket ship, for example, or the crucial gear needed to reach Shangri-La or scale Everest—including two of the "one thin thing with lumps on," and one of the "one long thin object with no fixed abode."[33] Palin notes that he simply talked and talked here, spinning pseudo-scriptural nonsense so that they could choose from minutes of footage as they edited.[34]

Palin's quiet, rambling preacher version might be based on Peter Cook's popular E. L. Wisty character, who was himself based on a high butler Cook had known while at Radley.[35] One of the odd, droning stories this man delivered to Cook involved—coincidentally, for our purposes—a "Bee of Ephesus" that flew around the crucified Christ.[36] See also the Pythons' ramblings of pseud-talk in *Meaning of Life* church sermon ("And spotteth twice they the camels before the third hour . . ."), in *Holy Grail* with the reading monk (". . . and sloths, and carp, and anchovies . . ."), and in *Flying Circus* where Idle is in the dock, spouting faux-Shakespeare (". . . or wakes the drowsy apricot betides . . .").[37] This kind of obscurant, reference-laden, and frowsy speech comes from the Modernists (Eliot, Joyce), from the Goons, and has been a hallmark of the Pythonesque from the beginning.

311

BORING PROPHET: "... shall lose his friend's hammer and the young shall not know where lieth the things possessed by their fathers ..."—There was a "prophet" during this period who spoke of sacred, secret things buried by Moses on Mount Gerizim. This Samaritan prophet convinced thousands to follow him to the sacred mountain in 36, but Pilate sent troops to head off the crowd, leading to an all-out battle (many of the Samaritans were armed) and the eventual execution of the Samaritan leadership.[38] This was the incident that led to Pilate's recall to Rome, and perhaps to the termination of his prefecture that same year.[39] The Boring Prophet isn't calling anyone to anything, so he's likely no threat to Rome or the Sanhedrin.

BORING PROPHET (OS): "It is written in the Book of Cyril ..."—There are a number of apocryphal texts, those not included in the Bible, for example, but still considered scriptural to many. Cyril was a bishop of Jerusalem, in the fourth century, but there was also critic Cyril Connolly, already mentioned in the Python song "Eric the Half-a-Bee," and even Cyril Smith, the largish Liberal MP for Rochdale mentioned in *Flying Circus* Ep. 45.[40]

HARRY: "Oh. Twenty shekels"—Even if a talent was worth 3,000 shekels, 20 shekels seems like a rather high price for a false beard. Remember, though, the Ex-leper asked for a talent earlier, before settling for half a denarii.

HARRY: "We're supposed to haggle"—Here Idle seems to be playing Harry like a "spiv," a shonky character who appears in his element during but especially after the war in Britain, when rationing was firmly in place. Harry is selling a beard to a man, which is likely not illegal to Rome or in violation of Sanhedrin laws, except that Brian clearly tells Harry that it's for "the wife." With it, the wife will likely participate, against Jewish law and custom, in a religio-judicial ceremony not meant for women. Harry is abetting the flouting of the law, at the least. In postwar Britain, the spiv flourished when sub-legal trade became available and even oddly fashionable, when rationed (or exotic) food items might only be had through black market means. In Parliament there were groans about the "spiv economy," one that flowed almost without notice beneath the actual, heavily taxed economy, siphoning money from the state's coffers and lining the pockets of bookmakers and black marketeers.[41] The government even tried to have these spivs and "drones" (an idler, a non-worker) registered with the (Labour government) authorities so that their time and energies could be better managed by the state—sent to the mines alongside Polish former POWS, for example. It came to be known as "The Spivs and Drones Order."[42] The Socialist Party of Great Britain looked askance at both the Labour government's windy attacks on these "parasites" and the ill-defined spivs themselves:

> It has been said that the Spiv is at least a rebel. Some people have even sentimentalised him as a kind of revolt against the conditions imposed by the nature of capitalist exploitation. The Spiv's own anti-Government and anti-authoritarian outlook might seem to lend colour to this view. The Spiv, however, generally lacks the class loyalty and class sentiment that goes to the making of the class-conscious social revolutionary. The zeal and selfless devotion of the socialist, with his illimitable vista of a world based on production for use and the Brotherhood of Man, lights no fires in the mind and imagination of the Spiv. A good time and plenty of fun at the expense of others gravely limits his social horizon. Pleasure and "the easy way" becomes basic to his existence. His mode of life constitutes a form of social parasitism which conflicts with the healthy social instincts of the vast majority of workers.[43]

After much talk in the press and in Parliament, not much changed until the economy stabilized, desirable food became more available, and the spiv fascination petered out naturally. In his memoirs published in 1971, Lord Butler opined that with the cessation of state controls over food and the sales of goods and importation by the mid-1950s, characters like Harry disappeared, practically overnight.[44] Harry isn't an idler, certainly, since he sells both rocks for stonings and beards for disguises, and he doesn't seem to be gouging (another complaint from the Socialist Party assessment), but he does seem to be making his living on the Jewish authority system's teat, benefiting from what observant Jews *need* to participate in an approved, even sacred act like a stoning. Perhaps Harry has just positioned himself perfectly, in a business sense, with goods that he knows practicing Jews need and want. This has a first-century Jerusalem iteration, as well. The moneychangers and sellers of temple cult material (like those who sold animals for sacrifice, who baked shewbread, made incense, weaved and knitted for the temple curtain, and so on) made cultic participation—mandatory on some levels—more possible for many Jews.[45] If the Pythons had decided to include the religious aspects of Jewish life in the film, then people like Harry would have sold doves to the poorest Jews, who couldn't afford "more expensive animals such as sheep."[46] However proper his capitalist intentions and practices, Harry and these purveyors were the types, among others, that Jesus forcibly cleared from the temple as recorded in the Synoptic Gospels. In *Life of Brian*, the merchants tend to be more backdrop and set dressing than characters, not unlike the vaguely defined villagers digging for filth, attending a deadly wedding, or carrying a witch for execution in *Holy Grail*.

But is this capitalist go-getter and his milieu simply a distraction from the Jews' awful lives of servitude to Rome? Later, supporters of the Baader-Meinhof group and the student unrest in Europe after 1968 thought as much in relation to postwar Germany: "The so-called economic miracle was invented as a distraction to stop us thinking about our Fascist past. Consumerism put the lid back on history. We were no longer meant to know what our past meant."[47] In our case, is it to distract the people of Jerusalem from dwelling on the fact that they are ruled by Romans? The PFJ might think so.

BURT appears, he is very big—This is John Case again, his only surviving appearance in the film. He was cast to play Pilate's wife who, in earlier drafts, physically fought off the PFJ during their "waid."

On the night that a vote of confidence was called for in the House, 28 March 1979, it was reported by Donoughue that one of the hoped-for votes the government did not get was from the Irishman Frank Maguire, who seemed to respond to a similar, Burt-like looming influence: "I saw Stan Orme, who told me that he had done everything to get [Gerry] Fitt[48] and Maguire into the lobbies [to cast a vote], but nothing would move them." Donoughue continued: "Maguire's wife had come with him—along with two sinister Republican 'heavies'—and they forbade him to vote."[49] Fitt and his family had already been intimidated by the IRA, when

> sympathisers broke in, one night in 1976, as the Fitts were getting ready for bed. They were fended off by Gerry, in his underwear and waving a Browning automatic, issued officially to him during the period of the power sharing executive. But no amount of protection could stop the Fitt home being a target to Loyalists and the IRA.[50]

The possible threat from the IRA against, ostensibly, one of its own was one of those threads woven daily through British newspapers and evening news stories.[51]

Burt is also clearly Harry's employee, meaning Harry is one of Keith Joseph's anointed ones. Harry is an entrepreneur who sells rocks for stonings, enriches the economy with gourds, and offers beards for women who want to participate in the Jewish male religious world. With the Tories in opposition from 1974, Joseph found himself in the wilderness, but using particularly interesting language, this prophet[52] preached a consistently conservative message to local constituencies and Party conferences and in the House of Lords:

> Through constant repetition of his favourite themes, he hoped that he could still exert some influence over "the climate of opinion." The entrepreneur was praised on numerous occasions, and the scarcity of these *market place gladiators* was bemoaned in speech after speech. . . . He made several attempts to encapsulate the work of the entrepreneur—"the character who works the magic, the Aladdin who creates the jobs."[53]

Harry would have been an ideal figure for Joseph.

HARRY: "Haggle properly"—This is a long-standing stereotype also affixed to the Scots, being thrifty and always ready to bargain. The Goons mention Bluebottle's Scottish uncle who hides him in a "brown paper parcel" under the seat of a bus so that he doesn't have to pay the boy's fare; Neddie's Scottish uncle "Laird McGool" invites Neddie in to warm himself by a "roaring candle"; and in "Robin Hood," a Jewish character (Sellers) tells Robin Seagoon—who's been told a thousand "splonders" is needed to save him from the Sheriff—to "offer him nine-fifty and take a chance."[54] Karl Marx called haggling "the language of the Jews," according to Gilman:

> The Jew as money-changer is the prototypical Jew, who speaks a language of commerce which is deceptive but which remains immutable. The mask of the Jew may shift. He may articulate his deeds in English, German, or French, but these national languages are mere camouflage for the language by which he dupes his prey, the language and rhetoric of the Jews, "haggling." And this remains constant.[55]

There were several very public hagglings going on in this period. As already discussed, the Callaghan administration attempted to keep the trade unions on board through 1976–1978, hoping for a stable economy more favorable for a successful election. The unions refused to "haggle properly," pay increases were demanded and then granted, destroying the government's attempted curbs on inflationary activity. During the IMF loan crisis in 1976, the Americans and the IMF refused to "haggle properly," as well, holding the British government to onerous reductions on spending before the loan was granted. The haggling would change dramatically once the Thatcher years kicked in, when the unions were no longer as welcome at the policy-making table.

BRIAN: "Tell me what to say Please!"—This is a marvelous portmanteau Pythonism: miscommunication as part of a financial transaction. Brian is desperate to buy a beard as a disguise, and he even has sufficient money for the purchase, but he doesn't understand the "Jewish" language necessary to complete the transaction. This is because, textually, the transaction itself is the comedy bit, not a setup for a following scene or pay-off. (Think of the back-and-forth between the king of Swamp Castle and the guards watching Herbert in *Holy Grail* as an earlier example.) This two-minute bit has its own internal language and pace that must be learned by Brian for the scene to end, which means it's also slightly disconnected from the rest of the film, a kind of pause in the narrative flow.[56] But it's also about as Pythonesque as a scene can be. In Ep. 23 of *Flying Circus*, a French film is being reviewed, and the reviewer notes that the film is about the "breakdown in communication in our modern society":

> In a nutshell, this defines *Flying Circus*. There are very few examples in the series of a successful communication or transaction. In most cases, the message is misunderstood, delivered improperly, or perceived incorrectly. . . . The communication issue is key for the Pythons, and is based

on the recent interest in semantics and semiotics, the growing awareness that meaning isn't just "there," it is imbued by and for society/culture, and that meaning can and does fluctuate depending on context. The separation of a word from its "meaning" allows for new meanings and even multiple meanings to be temporarily affixed to a word—there now exists the possibility of "wiggle room" in the world of language. Modernist authors like Joyce, Stein, Pound, Woolf, and Eliot pushed this separation, this slippage, this interchangeability, and the Pythons came along at just the right time to explore that new ambiguity in the television format.[57]

The Pythons are exploring communication in transactions here, as well, and Brian will eventually have to run away, just short of completing the deal for the free gourd (though he keeps the gourd).

Again, the headlines offered plenty of painful haggling for the Pythons to cull through, including a sticking point when the government held firm at a 4.5 percent offer but the unions demanded a flat 5 percent in 1976. Chancellor Healey and the unions went back and forth, with PM Callaghan refusing to back down.[58] After more than a month of this, the government capitulated, and the unions got their 5 percent. At this moment, many in the government likely saw "TUC" as just another terror group acronym. And just two years later, the explosion of pay demands that eventually crippled the economy and sank the Labour government started at 5 percent, then rapidly became 10, 13, and eventually 22 percent for road haulage drivers, the government having no clue what the unions would ask for next.[59] That was "the red flag to the inflationary bull," Jenkins concludes.[60]

HARRY gives BRIAN a gourd—These gourds were plentiful in the region, and quite prominent, as it turns out. The colocynth is an architectural inspiration in both the Solomonic temple and the Tel Dan gate.[61] Gourds figure into a story involving Elisha in 2 Kings. There, a stew containing poisonous wild gourds was prepared for Elisha's "company of minor prophets," and Elisha added flour to dilute the poisonous effect, rendering it harmless.[62]

HARRY: "Yes but it's *worth* ten"—What's economic peace worth? This was being asked by Labour insiders during the latter days of the Callaghan administration. As mentioned, the government had agreed that inflation could be dealt with if pay rises stayed at or lower than 5 percent. Reg Birch and the like were having none of it. The government ended up surrendering more than 20 percent pay rises to the trades, and the "Labour Go Home" writing was on the wall. Opposition leader Thatcher tolled the bell in her 1978 Party Conference speech, damning the self-interested bargaining:

> Now, you, the trade union leaders, have great power. . . . But look at the position of your members today and compare it with the position of workers in other free countries. Can you really say, can anyone say, you have used your powers well? . . . You want higher wages, better pensions, shorter hours, more government spending, more investment, more-more-more. But where is this "more" to come from? There is no more. There can be, but there will not be, unless we produce it. . . . And here, let me say to trade union leaders, you are often your own worst enemies. Why isn't there more? Because too often restrictive practices rob you of the one thing you have to sell—your productivity.[63]

Thatcher would ride this horse to a General Election victory in May 1979.

HARRY: "Seventeen. My last word. I won't take a penny less . . ."—Harry of course ends up sealing the deal seconds later at sixteen shekels, down from his original asking price of twenty. He has already told Brian that "it's worth" ten shekels, but that he paid twelve shekels (or it cost him twelve shekels to manufacture it). The point is the haggling unfixes the value from the commodity, and in the flurry a rather arbitrary (and in this case lower) price is agreed upon. This kind of exchange is found throughout the run of *The Goon Show*. In "The Mystery of the Marie Celeste," for example, a reward for information starts at £5,000 and ends up, when it trickles down to Bluebottle, at "seventeen and ninepence."[64]

HARRY: "Ah, well there's one born every minute"—Famous quote *attributed* to nineteenth-century circus impresario P. T. Barnum.

Notes

1. Gilliam, *Gilliamesque*, 182.
2. "Why Are We All So Bloody-Minded?" *Times*, 25 August 1970: 9.
3. Josephus, *AJ*, 18.5.1 (Whiston, 382).
4. See Goldberg, "The Popularity of John the Baptist."
5. "Mr Powell Shows His Unity with Ulster," *Times*, 30 September 1974: 4.
6. Kotker, *HLTJ*, 98. These cave mysteries remain mysterious; adherents were "sworn to secrecy," and kept that oath (99).
7. Smallwood, *JURR*, 257.
8. Circa 45 or 46, according to Whiston. Cuspius Fadus followed Agrippa I as procurator of Judea, ruling 44–46 (*JURR*, 257–62).
9. *AJ* 20.5.1 (Whiston, 418).
10. See Acts 21:37–38, where Paul is mistaken for the dangerous Egyptian; also, *AJ*, 20.8.6 (Whiston, 422), and *WJ* 2.13.5 (Whiston, 483).
11. Palin, *Diaries 1979–1979*, 494.
12. Donoughue calls him "the awful Paisley" (*DSD* 2.165). Fascinating, too, that following the hung parliament outcome in the June 2017 general election, the Conservatives under Theresa May reached out to and brought into bed Paisley's party, the Democratic Unionist Party, securing a coalition government.
13. "O'Neill Carries Fight to His Enemies," *Sunday Telegraph*, 16 February 1969: 1.
14. "The Sayings of Ian Paisley," *Belfast Telegraph*, 12 September 2014.
15. Demaris, *Brothers in Blood*, 293.
16. From a sermon delivered 1 March 1968.
17. "Third Force Emerges as Paisley Thunders," *Times*, 21 February 1969: 3.
18. Waugh called Abse a "socialist MP" with an interest in "pretty serving boys" (*FCY*, 15 December 1974).
19. "Spong and British Politics," *Spectator*, 21 October 1977: 12.
20. Paul Grinke, "Stuffed Dummies," *Spectator*, 13 February 1969: 21.
21. The entire Commons exchange is available via Hansard at http://hansard.millbanksystems.com/commons/1969/apr/22/northern-ireland#S5CV0782P0_19690422_HOC_271.
22. Demaris, *Brothers in Blood*, 294.
23. "Not by Shakespeare," *Spectator*, 1 January 1965: 12.
24. Probably based on an original Lucas Cranach the Elder illustration.
25. Larsen, *MPFC: UC*, 1.71.
26. *MPFC: UC*, 1.350.
27. Kotker, *HLTJ*, 50; italics added. John's is an example of transcending the "it's written that's why" school of belief (mentioned by Mandy); he reminds his followers of the importance of the spirit *and* the letter of the law.
28. "Inside the Mind of Ian Paisley," *Sunday Times*, 9 February 1969: 13.
29. Daniel 7:7–8.
30. Larsen, *BAFHG*, 450.
31. Isaiah 34:11.
32. Jeremiah 20:11.
33. "The Albert Memorial," 23 March 1958; "Shangri-La Again," 8 November 1955.
34. Palin, *Diaries 1969–1979*, 494.

35. Thompson, *Peter Cook*, 24–25, 175–77.

36. See Wendy Cook's *So Farewell Then* (2006), and Thompson's *Peter Cook* (1997).

37. Cleese delivers this sermon in *Meaning of Life*, Palin is reading from the *Book of Armaments* before they blow up the rabbit in *Holy Grail*, and a prisoner, Mr. Larch (Idle), has lapsed into an "Olivier impression" in Ep. 3 of *Flying Circus* (*ATW*, 1.3.29; *MPFC: UC*, 1.50–62).

38. Brandon, "Pontius Pilate in History and Legend," 528.

39. The Syrian legate, Vitellius, essentially sacked Pilate before his trip to Rome, and Tiberius passed away just before Pilate arrived in Rome for his audience. The demonstrable record for Pilate disappears at this rather crucial juncture.

40. Auberon Waugh called Connolly "our Greatest Living Englishman," tongue in cheek; "Eric the Half-a-Bee" appeared on *Monty Python's Previous Record* album.

41. "Tax Structure Monstrous," *Times*, 19 July 1947: 4.

42. This became the Regulation of Employment Order 1947, and was enacted in December 1947, though to middling success. See also Thomas, *Villain's Paradise*.

43. *Socialist Standard*, October 1947.

44. "The Choice between Genteel Bankruptcy and Floating the Pound," *Times*, 20 May 1971: 12. Rab Butler had been Chancellor of the Exchequer 1951–1955.

45. Jeremias, *JTJ*, 25–27.

46. Safrai, *The Economy of Roman Palestine*, 100.

47. Dieter Kunzelmann, student leader, Kommune Eins, from *Baader-Meinhof: In Love with Terror* (BBC, 2002).

48. Fitt would be targeted by the IRA later, as well, when his family home in Antrim was burned to the ground in 1983.

49. *DSD*, 472.

50. Anne McHardy, *Guardian*, 26 August 2005.

51. This is discussed in more detail in Arnold Kemp's *Confusion to Our Enemies* (2012).

52. Marr actually calls Joseph an "Old Testament prophet denouncing his tribe" (*HMB*, 355). Wilson would call Tony Benn "an Old Testament prophet without a beard" (*Financial Times*, 12 May 1975: 30). Many of these raging, fire-and-brimstone types seemed to be on the Left, and often predicting doom under Tory policies.

53. Denham and Garnett, *Keith Joseph*, 420; italics added. See also Bogdanor's version of this quote found in "Thatcherism, 1979–1990."

54. "Emperor of the Universe," 3 January 1957; "The Treasure in the Lake," 28 February 1956; "Robin Hood," 2 December 1956.

55. "Karl Marx and the Secret Language of the Jews," 35. Found in Jessop and Wheatley, *Karl Marx's Social and Political Thought, Vol. Veo*. Marx is depicted several times in earlier Python work (*MPFC: UC*, 1.378–79).

56. This is one of those sketches that could play as well on an album as on film. Visuals aren't necessary for the humor to come through, a tribute to the *Goon Show*'s influence.

57. *MPFC: UC*, 1.350.

58. Sandbrook, *Seasons in the Sun*, 468–69.

59. Jenkins, *Mrs. Thatcher's Revolution*, 21–22.

60. Jenkins, *Mrs. Thatcher's Revolution*, 22.

61. King and Stager, *LBI*, 81.

62. *LBI*, 82; 2 Kings 4:40–41.

63. Conservative Party Conference speech, 13 October 1978 (margaretthatcher.org).

64. 16 November 1954.

SCENE SIXTEEN
HIDING WITH THE PFJ

STAN is striking the names of the dead REVOLUTIONARIES from his list—Stan appears to be using a wooden writing board, likely coated with beeswax. These types of "books" had been in use for hundreds of years by this point, from as early as 1300 BC.[1] The fact that Stan, at least, can read and write sets these men apart from many in this period.

FRANCIS: "Habbakuk"—Actually "Habakkuk," it is one of the smaller books nearer the end of the Old Testament. It was Habakkuk who broke through the tile floor earlier. This starts a list of "probationary martyrs" to the PFJ's cause—Daniel, Job, Joshua, Judges, and Brian—and is just like the listing of dead knights after the first assault on the Killer Rabbit in *Holy Grail*, where it's announced that Uther, Gorlois, Urien, Ector, and Bors were killed by the rabbit. (None of these characters had appeared before, some having fallen prey to script revisions as the project moved forward.[2])

Midway between Job and Habakkuk, the Book of Daniel's language and apocalyptic imagery fueled some of the wild prophets earlier. Daniel was a captive in Babylon. In the KJV, the Book of Job appears eleven books after Judges (the older, wealthy Job seeming an odd choice here). Joshua was the leader of the children of Israel after Moses's time, actually leading them into the Promised Land. Being a spy for Moses, as well, means he fits here. Joshua and Judges are listed in the correct order for the traditional Christian version of the Old Testament, though Judges isn't a personal name like Joshua. Judges is the name of the book that records the activities of people like Othniel, Deborah, and Jephthah, as well as Samson. In the draft version, a "Daryl called Andy" was also killed in the raid.

REG: ". . . probationary martyrs to the cause"—Perhaps this is the inevitable result of the restive relationship between most actual terror groups' "philosophy of the bomb" and those more like the Pythons' PFJ, where the "philosophy of the permissive society" precludes any of the well-known tit-for-tat brinksmanship enacted whenever, for example, the Japanese Red Army took hostages and made demands, and the Japanese government bowed to those demands.[3] Like the Labour Party after Attlee's administration, the gradual abandonment of the quest for a socialist Utopia or even the "good society" for all Britain changed Labour from fiery revolutionary zealot to a milder, less threatening seeker (and then provider) of consensus.[4] In the film, saving Brian from the cross would be an act of escalation, which would draw out the Romans against the PFJ, which would demand a new act of terror, and so on. Antagonizing a sitting government is challenge enough: "It was far more difficult," Laqueur concludes, "to survive the backlash of a military dictatorship."[5] The Roman Empire represented the pinnacle of such dictatorships. Reg, Francis, and Stan-Loretta seem ready to abandon *propagande par le fait*, and fall comfortably back into the safer *propagande par mot*, their version of "consensus" (the version where they survive). In this they've also clearly agreed to change their conception of Brian's acts and purpose, from revolutionary leader to martyr. This "readjustment" of expectations is an echo of those disciples around Jesus after his crucifixion, according to Brandon:

> Now, since current Messianic belief did not envisage the death and resurrection of the Messiah, the disciples had to readjust their ideas concerning Jesus to the new situation that confronted them. Before his crucifixion they had recognised him as the Messiah who would redeem Israel. . . . His death at the hands of the Romans . . . was a shocking contradiction of their hopes. If Jesus were the Messiah, he had died without accomplishing his mission. The conviction, stemming from their Resurrection experiences, that he was alive again, still left them with the problem of the unfulfilment of their expectations of him. The evidence of the New Testament documents shows that the readjustment of their faith took the form of a revised version of Jesus' Messianic role.[6]

Jesus would henceforth be adjusted into a "martyr for Israel" as well as a "Messiah for Israel" who would later "return, with supernatural power and glory, to redeem Israel from oppression."[7] Brian's role as "Chosen One" now means chosen for glorious, functional martyrdom, not messianic leadership to overthrow the Roman oppressors. Versions of "martyr to the cause" were printed quite often in period newspapers and heard on news broadcasts in the 1960s and 1970s, especially as myriad revolutionary causes heated up around the globe. In China, it was Li Ta-ch'ao, a "nationalist who believed in self-reliance," an early figure in Mao's assault on ancient China;[8] in Northern Ireland it was Frank Stagg, a Provisional IRA member who died in 1976 as a result of a hunger strike;[9] and the question was being asked by journalist Eric Marsden at Easter 1972 whether Jesus Christ was martyr, messiah, or both.[10]

REG: "Thank you, Loretta. On the nod"—Meaning there is general agreement that doesn't merit discussion; this is a bit of parliamentary procedure. Later, when Brian is on the cross, the PFJ actually hand-vote when agreeing to sing to him. There was also a Kenneth Rose column in the *Telegraph* called "On the Nod," which, yes, looked at *affaires du parlement*.

REG: "Let's not be down-hearted!"—Reg continues to keep the upper lip stiff in the face of this admitted hecatomb, but not all revolutionary leaders were so upbeat. After being sentenced to life imprisonment for murder and attempted murder, Red Army Faction leader Andreas Baader was told by followers outside of prison to cease his hunger strike, that a new and devastating terrorist strike was being planned—those on the outside were going to continue the fight, essentially. Increased police monitoring and the sobering sentences that had been given to the group's leadership must have dampened the revolutionary enthusiasm, though, as a September 1977 letter from Baader indicates:

> To the rabble who call themselves the RAF: our patience with you has run out! What's up with you lot? We only want to read one thing from you: a statement that you have carried out the operation. If you don't take the initiative, we will take away your right to call yourself RAF![11]

Following this missive, the outside members gathered, discussed their situation, and green-lighted the kidnapping of Hans Martin Schleyer, a business executive. Schleyer was to be held as hostage until the German authorities released RAF members in prison. Schleyer was killed by the RAF in October 1977, just after his captors learned of the suicide deaths of Baader, Ensslin, and Jan-Carl Raspe, all at Stammheim Prison.

Elsewhere, the spirit of revolution was also clearly felt, and even being acted upon. In the simmering pot that was 1970s Afghanistan, "Islamic radicals" decided to attempt an overthrow of the country's first president, Daoud Khan, a reform-minded man. The results should read familiar:

> In 1975, [religious scholars and university students] tried to overthrow Daoud in a dilettantish coup attempt. His security forces made short work of the rebels. They styled themselves as a new kind of political movement that they called the "Islamic Society". . . organized according to the same cell structure used by underground communist groups. (Like the Iranians [and, seemingly, the PFJ]), they had learned much from the Marxists.) For the moment, though, that was little help to the militants. Most of them disappeared in Daoud's jails or execution cellars; the rest fled to Pakistan.[12]

A military-led coup (supported enthusiastically by the Soviets) would successfully unseat Daoud in April 1978; he died in the fighting.

REG: "One total catastrophe like this is just the beginning!"—If this incident isn't just terror-related, for the historically minded Pythons the best "catastrophe" involving English-accented troops would have likely been the Suez Crisis. For many, the Suez failure was the swan song for Britain's empire, the unsightly denouement to decades of flag-waving colonialism. In October 1956, just after Egypt's President Nasser nationalized the Suez Canal, Israel invaded Egypt, supported in principle by both France and Britain. In November, British and French paratroopers joined the fray, resulting in Nasser blocking the canal with scuttled ships. The United States did not support the British in this affair, and it would eventually be revealed that the three aggressors had carefully planned the invasion to both re-seize control of the canal (built by the French and partly owned by the British) *and* end Nasser's rule.[13] Pressure from the United States and the international community (especially financial pressure from the United States) forced the invaders to withdraw; the canal had to be closed for four months to be cleared. At home, British protesters marched against the government, and the press were generally outraged by this sordid return to gunboat colonialism. Bernstein calls the raid a "catastrophe" and the resulting world tumult (including Britain's "allies'" attacks on the British financial system as punishment) a "fiasco," showing "how much Britain's world had been transformed."[14]

But then there were the terrorists, as well. Jenkins points out that the hoped-for socialist revolution in the 1960s Western world and Britain specifically, whispered and shouted about during the period of the Pythons' flourishing, never actually came to be:

> The events of 1968 in Britain were peaceful by the standards of those which took place in Paris, Berlin and Berkeley. There were big anti-Vietnam demonstrations in Grosvenor Square, one of them violent, and campus disturbances notably at the LSE and the newer plate-glass universities of Essex and Sussex, which the architects seemed to have designed for purposes of confrontation. The revolutionary project was well summed-up in the metaphor of masturbation with which Trevor Griffiths began his play *The Party*. *There was never the slightest prospect of socialist revolution in Britain between 1968 and 1979.*[15]

The beginnings of Fatah were also humble, for example. The hope in 1964 was that "apparently futile" attacks against Israel "would provoke a massive reaction" and bring international sympathy to the Palestinian cause.[16] *Life of Brian* may also simply be a historically cloaked version of what the young Pythons were witnessing in their Britain—cries of revolutionary sound and fury, ultimately signifying nothing.

And perhaps this failure is the PFJ's Entebbe moment? What starts as a glorious and promising revolutionary mission implodes in the face of overwhelming force—for the PFLP-EO at the Entebbe Airport it was grimly determined Israeli forces; for Brian and the PFJ, it's the Romans (and the bungling CFG). Terror expert Bowyer Bell had researched and written of the Irgun guerrilla campaign in British Palestine,[17] and in 1970 he published a book on the history of the IRA, *The Secret Army*. In the latter he waxes quite Reg-like: "But Ireland desperately needed a glorious failure to awake the latent revolutionary tradition."[18] Describing the IRA bombing campaign of 1939–1940, Bell writes in very familiar terms, for us:

> For terror the IRA lacked, perhaps commendably, the instinct for the jugular. That the IRA did not want to murder in the streets and could not cut the sinews of order meant that the campaign was doomed to futility—spluttering on until hope and haven had been lost and the men interned, imprisoned or expelled. Prudent men, even with 10 times the personnel and equipment, would have thought the prospects dim, but with the scanty resources available even the optimistic should have drawn back.[19]

In the age of "[t]errorist groups . . . springing up like mushrooms" but then fizzling into the heat waves of the Middle Eastern deserts, inept combat missions were bound to happen. The first raid into Israel by the newly minted "Heroes of the Return" group "was a total failure," according to Demaris, and, as with Brian's mission with the PFJ, there was only one survivor.[20] The combined Arab armed forces that participated in the Six-Day War in 1967 limped home after a catastrophic incursion that eventually saw Israel not only protect herself but push back her enemies on all sides across the "administrated" territories.[21]

Dobson and Payne described Libyan strongman Qaddafi as similarly ineffective in 1977, even though he sponsored terrorism with great enthusiasm, seeming perhaps—like Reg—to appreciate at least the theatrical element of the endeavor:

> To understand Qaddafi . . . it is necessary to appreciate his romantic and fanatical ideas about Arab unity. He sees himself as a kind of Napoleon of the Arab world. . . . Yet he does not have the capacity to sustain his efforts and by trying to do so many things at once he fails to achieve his aims. Only sporadically are his aims translated into action, so that on the spur of the moment and in a fit of enthusiasm he decides on a course of action. The Libyan enthusiast has neither the time nor the intellectual capacity to follow through the consequences of his decisions.[22]

Through Brian the PFJ had achieved their first (and likely only) noteworthy success—the painting of the slogans on the palace wall, but even then, Reg is of two minds, flashing "*a brief look of alarm at FRANCIS.*" Insurrectionary success brings the scrutiny of the mightiest empire on Earth, while simple ineffectiveness or base cowardice can be relatively safe.

REG: "Their glorious deaths shall unite us all—"—The pie-eyed self-deception practiced by many revolutionary groups—namely that their actions were not only justified but would trigger wide-ranging, permanent change in the world—was manifest in press releases and news reports across the 1960s and beyond. More somber accounts detailed the costs of such activities, settling this revolutionary fervor into the more torpid, miasmic strata of real life. Writing about the "brief fame" of such terrorists, Robert Fisk notes that by late summer 1975 elements of the JRA, the PFLP, and the ELF had been hunted to ground to a single building in Tripoli, while a few notable others had been accepted into Beirut, where they were all relatively safe but unable to act out their anti-imperialist agenda. Many of their comrades weren't so lucky:

Israel, on the other hand, is holding an estimated 67 Arab guerrillas in prison. Japan still has 14 Red Army men behind bars. Israel still holds Kozo Okamoto, the lone terrorist survivor of the Lod airport massacre. Two of the Red Army extremists died at Lod. Five of the Arabs who held the Israeli hostages at Munich in September, 1972, died with the 11 Israelis. One of the five Baader-Meinhof terrorists died from wounds sustained during the West German embassy siege in Stockholm in April this year; his four colleagues were captured by the police. According to United State's State Department figures, 520 people have been killed in incidents of international terrorism between 1968 and April this year. At least 50 of these are believed to have been terrorists.[23]

Reg hasn't learned a lesson that, frankly, many political figures have also failed to learn over the generations. In 1979 and 1980 the Conservative government under Thatcher battled mightily with the leftovers of the Winter of Discontent, while attempting to reign in the powers of the trade unions and remake Britain's economy. In opposition, the Labour Party, led by Michael Foot, gainsaid virtually every Tory move, especially those involving the economy—inflation, employment, manufacturing, and the usefulness of monetarist policies. Peter Jenkins marked the official end of postwar consensus politics in Britain, pointing out that Thatcher was trying to run the country from the far Right, and Labour was simply sniping back from further Left. Consensus had given way to "conviction":

> Mrs Thatcher and Mr Foot both speak with the rhetoric of conviction. That will make them exciting opponents across the floor of the House of Commons and it will be fun to see who first gets the better of the other. But we should not be misled by this entertainment into thinking that "conviction politics" are a substitute for a firm basis of governmental authority[24] or that passion in advocacy is the same thing as strong or effective leadership.[25]

Reg has a passion, a conviction in his politics that clearly exceeds his mechanisms for achieving those political ends. He wants to get rid of Roman rule but proffers no alternative, and no real way to accomplish the change. There can be no consensus because Rome and especially Pilate (in the film) won't consider it, nor do they need to.

They hide extremely badly—This scene is more cartoony than other parts of the film. Playing like a Warner Bros.' cartoon or a Marx Brothers' routine, the silly bit is reminiscent of the Pythons' *How Not to Be Seen (Public Service Film No. 42)*, a filmed sketch from *Flying Circus* Ep. 24.[26]

A heavy imperious knocking on the door—This knocking is underscored by a foreboding musical flourish, just how *The Goon Show* created the illusion of a fully realized world using only sound.

CENTURION: "... you may be hiding one Brian of Nazareth ..."—When hearing that the foretold son of Joseph had been found in Nazareth, the "Israelite" Nathanael resorts to what must have been a longstanding joke in the region: "Can there any good thing come out of Nazareth?"[27] There doesn't seem to be a pejorative slant to the town's name as mentioned here by the Centurion, though, so the joke may have missed the Pythons.[28] They don't find Brian this time; that will come later. The Centurion then had to return to the volatile Pilate *non est inventus*, which couldn't have been a pleasant experience.

This tableaux—furtive men hiding from the Roman authorities—is an echo of events depicted in Zeffirelli's *Jesus of Nazareth*. After Christ's death, and just before they learn of his resurrection, the remaining disciples are hiding in their garret, afraid of every knock at the door. This same scene will be an inspiration for a later *Life of Brian* scene, where Judith barges into the PFJ headquarters to announce Brian's execution.

A Brian-like figure in life comes to mind here. The former Black Power leader Michael X (born Michael de Freitas) was executed by hanging for murder in 1975 in Trinidad. Celebrities including John Lennon had campaigned for Michael X's release, including donating money and writing op-eds. A Privy Council plea was even attempted to stay his execution. No appeal was successful, and for good reason: he was clearly guilty of at least two murders, both former "disciples." In 1977 the book *False Messiah* emerged, offering a more complete picture of this revolutionary, who also happened to be a hustler, a pimp, a drug dealer, and a con man, before he was ever a murderer.[29] Brian is guilty of vandalism and attempting to kidnap Pilate's wife, and he's being punished for those crimes in an understandable way, for the time.

MATTHIAS: "My eyes are dim, I cannot see. . . . I'm just a poor old man . . ."—Matthias may be the most wily of all the PFJ, as he has already escaped Jewish religious justice by fleeing the stoning when it descended into chaos, he didn't have to go on the failed "waid," and here he will talk his way out of a Roman raid, partly because the Centurion ends up thinking he's just "weird." The last we see of him will be when he is puttering around what is alleged to be Mandy's kitchen as the PFJ plot their "rescue" of Brian.

The "poor old man" image was one much in the news and discussed in the Commons in the postwar period, and especially later, as the trade union activities in the late 1970s made life quite miserable for many who depended on the state for their care and sustenance. The wildcat strike actions of the Winter of Discontent period were especially challenging to the elderly, since "local authorities"—who had assumed the responsibility for care of the older generation after the war—were hardest hit by localized strikes.[30] The newspapers and evening newscasts were filled with images of this chaos, thanks to the unions' "massive public sector strikes against incomes policy," according to Bogdanor. "Uncollected rubbish was left piled in the streets," Bogdanor continues, "cancer patients were sent home because the hospital porters were on strike, the dead were left unburied in Liverpool and had to be buried at sea."[31] Essential services at hospitals where, understandably, more elderly patients than younger would have been found, reduced food and orderly services to a miserly degree thanks to porter strikes.[32] Like Matthias, the elderly in Britain of the twentieth century "tended to live alone," they depended more on subsidized housing, public transportation, subsidized health care, home welfare visits, and just the daily availability of a meager means of existence—like "the shops" not only being open, but offering a few tins of affordable this and that—so these scattered but countrywide strikes and slowdowns were very nearly catastrophic.[33] The actions in and against hospitals was the last straw for many: "The Winter of Discontent really frightened people—a sort of breakdown of consent—and it even frightened people in the Labour Party," says Bogdanor, acknowledging Labour's historical reliance on the older vote.[34] "The elderly," Bernstein concludes, "were the largest single block of people below the poverty level" in Britain, even as late as the 1990s, and may have been most likely to vote for change, given the opportunity.[35] Bogdanor concludes:

> Labour Party people were deeply shocked that these anti-social actions could be carried out by people within the Labour movement, and the country was even more deeply shocked. It did not just affect the election of 1979 but elections right through to 1992. The Winter of Discontent became a deep folk memory, as important as the memory of the Jarrow Marches[36] and unemployment in the interwar years.[37] If you had to choose one factor to explain why the Conservatives and Margaret Thatcher were in power for eighteen years, I think that the fear of similar strikes was a key factor—a fear that, if you voted Labour, you would have the same all over again.[38]

As it turns out, this "poor old man" is surprisingly resilient, plucky, and self-sufficient. Matthias will *almost* disappear from the narrative after these scenes. He can be seen in the background of the later "Discussion" scene with the PFJ—when Judith interrupts to say Brian is being crucified—though this was likely filmed when they filmed this searching scene. At any rate, there's no indication he is arrested or condemned, like Brian.

CENTURION: "Quiet! Silly person"—Again, Cleese's characters can often be flustered by prattling types, and his response tends to be to try and shut them up. During the run of *Flying Circus*, Chapman's "Colonel" character performed this same function, stopping scenes and calling for transitions when things became too "silly."

CENTURION: "Guards! Search the house"—The soldiers are likely only looking for Brian, and not other types of evidence, though they will find a spoon. In contemporary Britain, the Angry Brigade were able to evade police for more than a year, even as their twenty-five bombs targeted Scotland Yard, a British territorial army recruitment center, the BBC, a Biba boutique, and the homes of politicians and leaders of industry.[39] A police raid on a home where suspected sympathizers lived in August 1971 yielded not a spoon but an address book, and four of the gang were rounded up, signaling the beginning of the end of the Angry Brigade.[40] In summer 1972, when West German police raided a suspected Baader-Meinhof hideout in Stuttgart, their suspicions were confirmed when they found "[Andreas] Baader's favorite reading materials . . . Mickey Mouse comics."[41]

CENTURION: "You know what the punishment laid down by Roman law is for harbouring a known criminal"—"The Roman governor naturally had the power of life and death over the Jews in the case of political offences, a power which he exercised in many episodes recorded by Josephus."[42] The Jewish ruling body, the Sanhedrin, also had some influence over capital punishment, as the case of Christ indicates, but there is no trace of the Sanhedrin in the world of the film.

Ulpian wrote of the Romans' effective policing in the empire, touching on the "harbouring" element, as well:

> It is the mark of an efficient and conscientious governor to see to it that the province under his control is peaceful and quiet. This will not be difficult, if he acts diligently to search for wicked men and removes them from the province; he must search for the temple-robbers, brigands, kidnappers, thieves, *and punish anyone committing these offences, and suppress the people who harbour them, without whose aid a brigand cannot lie low for long.*[43]

Davies also writes:

> Bandits tended to flourish in Judaea; and there are many references to the use of Roman soldiers to hunt and capture them, and to search villages lest the villagers should be harbouring them, or their loot had been hidden there. The two criminals executed with Christ were brigands, captured in a security operation by the Roman forces. Barabbas, too, was a terrorist who had been arrested after leading an insurrection and committing murder in Jerusalem; he was in military custody and awaiting execution.[44]

It's likely that all Jerusalemites of age knew the penalties for defying the Romans.

MATTHIAS: ". . . at least it gets you out in the open air"—This could be a sentiment from the prisoner Ben, who sees the positives in his situation. A switch from hanging upside down to hanging right-side up makes all the difference, and he's grateful for it. Ben and Matthias are much older than most others we meet; the older generation remembering the Jerusalem of pre-Roman improvement, perhaps? As the crucifixion party makes its way to their destination, Ben will be seen again, upside-down, but at a window, which he is likely grateful for.

CENTURION: "You're weird"—What's really at stake here is the fear and respect the occupying, ruling Roman force has counted on for decades to support their minority rule of Judea, and perhaps especially Jerusalem. Brian has poked a finger in the eye of Rome by defacing the prefect's palace walls, attempting the kidnap of a "royal" person, and escaping from Pilate's custody—all serious offenses, two at least carrying a death sentence. Anyone harboring such a felon is subject to public torture and death, as well. The gravity of the situation seems to have escaped Matthias completely, much to the Centurion's surprise. This supposed-to-be-cowering Jew isn't, and he's not even daunted by threats of public torture and execution. The Centurion responds by singling out Matthias as an anomic "weirdo," likely since he's afraid to admit the possibility that the Roman grip on the throats of the people of Judea might be slipping.

This concept would have been one ingrained in the Pythons, who grew up learning lessons about the British Empire—the vast swathes of pinkish-red (the "Queen's Dominions") on world maps and globes—and then watched as it ebbed and faded in their lifetimes. In the 1960s, the white minorities in African countries, including British colonial South Africa, Rhodesia, and Kenya trod this same tightrope—a handful of white settlers holding on to power over millions of oppressed natives. In *Life of Brian* it's a small band of (British-sounding) Jews trying to rid themselves of Roman colonizers; in India in 1857 it's the Great Revolt, where Indians take up arms against British colonialists, killing many and being killed in the thousands.[45] A century later, in Kenya of the Pythons' youth, it was the white English settlers defending themselves against Mau Mau insurgents who wanted the colonizers out and their country back.[46] These turnabouts result in clashes between settlers (colonizers) and activists (the colonized) that can read quite Pythonesque, almost as odd as successfully hiding in a basket or behind an arras. The "domestic order" the English had so treasured in these colonized lands is the order the Romans expect, and which is being upset, to a small degree, by Brian and the PFJ. In 1953 Kenya, a white family was attacked in their front room by local "boys" wielding machetes; the white women calmly shot and killed three of the invaders, relating the story in low-key, matter of fact tones.[47] The Pythons had to craft their David v. Goliath narrative carefully and ironically, since as British citizens they had been by association affiliated with the colonizers and not the colonized. This is further complicated when they cast themselves into the roles of the oppressed (and the oppressors)—postmodern turnabouts that undercut themselves, and then turnabout again. India had finally been surrendered in 1947; in the 1950s and 1960s the British were slowly forced out of these African regions by "weirdos" who didn't want to be colonized anymore.

Horsley notes the real threat behind the *sicarii*'s program of targeted assassinations was just this "Matthias effect":

> The attack on the symbolic religiopolitical figures, such as the high priest, is particularly important with respect to the masses in a nascent revolutionary situation, for the Sicarii thus attacked the religiopolitical symbols which held the social structure together. The effect . . . was bound to be a lessening of the "habit of obedience" on which any government depends for its monopoly of power. With the breakdown of this habit of respect and obedience to symbols of power and authority, the government loses its monopoly of power.[48]

So the Centurion is concerned here that an indifferent subject is a dangerous one, something the British had been dealing with, in colonial terms, for many years.

MATTHIAS: "Big nose"—Matthias seems to be trailing his coat here, tweaking the Centurion for a fight, but getting a half-hearted response. This same Centurion will later warn Judith about smacking his helmet and threaten an obnoxious bystander with crucifixion. By the end of the film, this same Centurion will have helped in the interrogation of Brian, rearrested him, reminded Pilate that there is a "Bwian" who can be released, and then attempts to make good that release. He's actually a fairly well-intentioned, Whitehall-type civil servant, and responds pretty well to being insulted.

During the well-publicized trial of the Baader-Meinhof Gang across the spring and summer of 1975, those on trial not only refused to cooperate, they also regularly insulted the judges, the system, and the proceedings. On the twenty-sixth day of the trial the accused simply refused to take their seats:

Chairman: "Defendants are standing. What is that supposed to mean?"

Raspe: "That we want to be excluded by you."

Chairman: ". . . I would like to speak with the defendants for a moment. Do you have the wish to be excluded, or . . ."

Baader: "Exactly, yes . . . we shall not continue to take part in these proceedings."

(Then a few similar exchanges between the Chairman and both Baader and Raspe.)

Meinhof and Ensslin: "Exclude us, also."[49]

Baader would tell the chairman to "go ahead" and exclude all of them, calling him an "old monkey." The following day, this same scenario was rehearsed, with the chairman deciding to not exclude the defendants if they chose to stand, so the defendants took their antagonism a step further. Baader spoke out of turn often, and when challenged he called the chairman "the archetype of a fascist," and a "fascist pig," leading to the following closing remarks:

Chairman: "Do you wish to behave in the same manner that you are behaving at this moment?"

Baader: "We do not wish to change our behavior. We want to be excluded, damn it."

Chairman: "Do the other defendants go along with this declaration?"

Raspe: "Yes, of course."

Meinhof: "Yes, you fascist pig."

Chairman: "The defendants will be, according to a decree by the Senate, excluded from these proceedings for the rest of the week."[50]

These defendants knew they were safe from at least immediate physical reprisals, given the challenges the German legal system faced in the wake of the Nazi era—the system had erred on the side of restraint and progressiveness to avoid charges of totalitarianism. "Even thirty years after the end of the Third Reich the new West German democracy is extremely sensitive to the shadows of the Nazi past," writes Melvin Lasky in a 1975 profile of Ulrike Meinhof. "The rule of law must be protected for fear of charges of "*Gestapo*" methods and attitudes."[51] Matthias, Judith, and the other suspect Jews did not have such assurances, though the Romans do knock on their hideout door. Matthias seems to understand that the Centurion does not have the authority to act unilaterally, so he taunts. Back in their cells, of course, the German defendants were out of the public eye and therefore vulnerable. After months of soundproof solitary confinement, constant bright lighting, and the rigors of hunger strikes and the trial itself, Meinhof, Baader, and Ensslin would all take their own lives.

During the period of emerging student protest across Europe there were multiple demonstrations, sit-ins, and occupations, most nonviolent. When those achieved no significant results, violence was often contemplated, especially as the protests against the war in Vietnam increased, and group leaders (like Ensslin) began to see violence as the only act imperialists might notice.[52] During the attempted occupation of the Free University of Berlin in January 1969, students were keen to know just when the police *might* resort to the use of force:

> Rumors were passed up and down the stairs: "The police will only intervene when the glass doors to the government offices have been shattered." That was almost enough to kick them in. "The police will still not intervene if the glass doors are shattered." That gave rise to a peaceful alternative: the majority decided to give up occupying the place.[53]

In the Pythons' version of this world, spoken insults like "Big nose" from an old man, as well as annoying slaps on the helmet from a small woman don't merit corporal reactions, but that avenue is available. Toward the end of the film, as the Centurion is racing to save Brian from crucifixion, he pushes a vendor, who then snaps "Bloody Roman!" "Watch it!" the Centurion snaps back, "We've got a few crosses left." This is a bit of an empty threat, however, given the Romans' actual ability to effectively police not only Rome and Italy, but the vast expanses of the empire. In regard to ferreting out Christians, for example, who refused to sacrifice to Roman gods, Toner reminds us:

> that Rome was a relatively unsophisticated preindustrial society. It had no police force. Enforcing imperial decrees demanding universal sacrifice was an impossible task. It was probably quite easy to avoid persecution by leaving your home town and staying with friends or Christians elsewhere. Or you could go into hiding. Or get a pagan friend to sacrifice on your behalf . . . or buy a fake certificate.[54]

In all likelihood Brian could have managed to evade capture, especially if he left the city for the safety of the desert, but that wouldn't have served the narrative's purpose.

REG: ". . . he's sorry he led the Fifth Legion straight to our official headquarters"—Reg gets to be sarcastic here, and will have to do with Brian's apology, but in the real world of terror, organization turncoats—or "nightingales," as they were known in Germany—were treated quite harshly for betrayals of the cause. The United Red Army's disturbing treatment of its unfaithful has been mentioned earlier, but the Germans proved they could be as merciless as their Japanese counterparts. In Brandenburg in June 1973, twenty-two-year-old Ulrich Schmücker was found dying, a single gunshot wound in his forehead. Schmücker had been a member of the RAF-influenced 2 June Movement, and he had been trying to become known as a dependable maker of bombs.[55] The 2 June Movement had also proven its interconnectivity with other terror groups and causes, planting a bomb at the British Yacht Club in Berlin in 1972 in direct response to deaths in Londonderry.[56] An elaborate plan to blow up the Turkish Embassy in Bonn was hatched, and Schmücker was in charge of gathering the needed explosives. Police were able to easily track the group in relation to the purchase of the explosive gear: "A routine check in Bad Neuenahr, Schmücker's home town, trapped the entire gang sleeping in a parked Fiat—packed with bombs, detonators, walkie-talkies, false number plates, and house-breaking tools" (much more than a spoon, yes).[57] The willing nightingale then sang to interrogating authorities, laying out in great detail the identities, targets, and locations of his siblings. Police were able to make raids and many arrests, and prosecutors rewarded Schmücker with a sentence of time served. It is assumed that the several members of 2 June who had not been arrested in the police dragnet caught up with and executed Schmücker for his betrayal. A letter claiming responsibility for Schmücker's death was signed by Black June Commando, whose *Volkstribunal* had found Schmücker a "traitor and counter-revolutionary."[58] Brian is found to be simply a "klutz."

REG: ". . . the Fifth Legion . . ."—One of Rome's Fifth ("*V*") legions would be participating in the suppression of the Great Jewish Revolt, the *V Macedonia* sent by Nero to Vespasian. This was more than thirty years *after* the time period depicted in *Life of Brian*. There was another Roman fifth legion, but they were stationed along the Rhine during this period. Since Jerusalem was a smaller and, at least between the years 6 and 33, quieter than other parts of the empire, the Romans kept the garrisons understaffed, with larger cohorts further away in Caesarea and Syria.

REG: ". . . that's all right. Sit down. Have a scone . . . You KLUTZ!! You stupid, bird-brained flat-headed . . ."—Reg clearly calls Brian a "cunt" here as part of his cashiering, but the word is dubbed over later for "klutz." The Pythons performed this same kind of self-censorship as they prepared *Holy Grail* for distribution. To secure a milder, more audience-friendly rating, they dubbed over some of the harsher language. It's likely that as they shot *Life of Brian* they also shot multiple versions of these scenes to be sifted through later.

"scone"—Flat breads, griddle cakes, and fried bread (scones, essentially), were a regular part of Jewish diets during this period.[59] In Britain, scones eaten as part of a cream tea has been common for many years.

(draft) **"cunt"**—A very old (early thirteenth-century, at least) word used in Britain, and was a carryover from an Old English version. The fact that a number of streets in a number of English towns were named with versions of "Gropecunt"—indicating the thoroughfares may have been known for the business of prostitution—meant that "cunt" was part of the English spoken lexicon through the later Middle Ages. The use of the term as a way to insult a man is much newer, appearing sometime in the mid-nineteenth century, according to the *OED*.

As for the time period depicted by the film, a surviving mosaic in the Hadrianic Terme della Trincria baths announces very matter-of-factly "STATIO CVNNVLINGIORVM," meaning the local prostitutes might have offered *cunnilingus* services for clients seeking such attentions; that, or this is an insult to men using the bathhouse.[60] Koloski-Ostrow translates the phrase into common vernacular: "The station of those who lick cunts."[61] In other words, the Latin version of this term would have been part of the lexicon in first-century Jerusalem, and likely across the Roman Empire.

"bird-brained"—A twentieth-century phrase, according to the *OED*, while "flat-headed" is a nineteenth-century phrase found in both America and Britain.

CENTURION: "Have you ever seen anyone crucified?"—Of course he has, especially given his age. We've already seen crosses with desiccated victims attached, and we will again. Crucifixions were purposely public spectacles designed to discourage others from choosing acts of *laesa maiestas*, or acts that tend to "injure majesty," meaning the king or ruler, which would have warranted the death penalty.

MATTHIAS: "Crucifixion's a doddle!"—There was one Englishman who might have agreed with Matthias's assessment, as he lived through such an event. In July 1968 a Hampstead Heath park caretaker heard an unusual pounding and went to investigate. He found an odd tableau: Several men attempting to nail another man to a cross. They had already nailed his hands to the crossbar and were on to his feet when they were interrupted. The "attackers" were all arrested and the man, Joseph Richard de Havilland, was "saved" from the cross. It turns out, however, that de Havilland had arranged the crucifixion himself, after hearing voices and seeing visions for several years telling him to perform the crucifixion, and after he had talked friends into helping. When asked why he did it, he answered rather directly: "I had been told to by things not of this world. I am very religious."[62] He had also been told by the voice to confront the Archbishop of Canterbury just before the crucifixion, which he apparently did. The nonchalant way de Havilland describes the event (to a judge) would have likely disturbed the Centurion, as well:

> "I stretched out my left hand and I told Mr. Leach I was ready," he said. "He looked at me and I looked at him and he placed the nail in the centre of my palm and drove it through. He did the same thing with my right hand. Conklin and Pollydore were just watching."[63]

A bit later, in a May 1976 *Private Eye* story, it was reported that a mystic, Edward Shingler, wanted to have himself crucified "to prove the power of God to a world where people have lost faith." Mr. Shingler was planning to charge £3 for the privilege of watching the nails driven through his palms, but only 50p to view him on the cross near the Dunkirk Social Club.[64] Mr. Shingler did not explain how the "power of God" was to be made manifest via his public crucifixion. Auberon Waugh also had a hand in trivializing this most Christian of symbols. In July 1976 he reports that while attending a fundraiser (to help *Private Eye* pay its legal bills), he was so bored, "deafened and sweating like a horse" that all he could do was sit there and "try to think of Jesus at his crucifixion. . . . It is all in a good cause," he concluded.[65]

But what this riposte also represents is the continuing and increasing loss of *deference* seen as Britain emerged from the war and into the more permissive, modern world. Deference to authority figures in Britain had been at least assumed by society, even if that assumption was more myth than reality,[66] and the Pythons made a career of flicking authority's nose at every turn. Bogdanor calls it the "collapse of deference," and notes that the trade union rank and file membership, for example, seemed to change by the 1970s.[67] Essentially walking in lockstep for the first half of the twentieth century, unions had negotiated reasonable pay packages and benefits while often putting the needs of the country (during the war, for example) before their members' individual needs, securing for the trade unions a great deal of rapprochement with(in) the Labour Party.

When the uniting crises ended, however, so did much of the camaraderie among British workers. The transition from coal power to oil, for example, signaled the end of the miners' ability to set government policy—the Heath government had been brought down by angry, organized miners—and other unionized workers saw the potential for their own demise as cheaper imported goods flowed in from Asia while improving industrial technologies were kept at bay by insular, restrictive practices. The threat of progress and rigid incomes policies put the fear into all wage earners. By the time of the Callaghan administration in 1976, most of the older union leadership had retired—the ones who commanded respect from the government and deference from their members—and union workers (led by proactive shop stewards[68]) were ready to strike and strike and strike just to make sure their pay packets kept pace with inflation, no matter the effect on the rest of their neighbors, or even neighbor unions. Couple this with the decline in deference in schools, in the media, and even at home, and it's no surprise to hear a Python commoner like Matthias shrugging off something as "nasty" as crucifixion. The British state power to threaten or punish antisocial behavior in the 1960s and 1970s had diminished as caning and slippering in schools disappeared, capital punishment was done away with, and the "permissive society" reduced the number of punishable offenses.

The SOLDIERS come rushing out—This shot is sped up, like a farce comedy moment, and is one of the places in the film most like the *Carry On* series, the kind of film Palin, at least, had earlier hoped *Holy Grail* wouldn't become.[69] The faster-than-life movement is a filmic conceit that draws attention to itself, to the film stock even, distracting from the unambiguous reality most classical films try to project. These kinds of effects—fast and slow motion, jump cuts, unnatural juxtapositions, etc.—are part and parcel of both avant-garde and (especially physical) comedy films, both of which came of age in the 1920s, sharing many cinematic tropes. Both flew in the face of traditional narrative films, one for shock or *ars gratia artis*, and the other for laughs. *Flying Circus* employed many of these, often the more outrageous and "cartoony" the better, and *Holy Grail* offers a handful, as well (over-the-top violence, killer rabbits, cartoon monsters).[70] The Pythons have moved closer to classical Hollywood film as they've moved from *Flying Circus* to *Holy Grail*, adhering to their own version of the pastiche (though not mosaic) narrative structures found in both Shakespeare and Modernism:[71]

> The Pythons then, are purposely moving beyond the seemingly *wirrwarr* but still self-aware structures of the [*Flying Circus*] episodes (which typified the first draft of *Holy Grail*) and closer to a visually and thematically consistent narrative set in the medieval world, but peppered by persistent (and increasingly multipotent) irruptions of modernity. The ultimate intrusion will be modern, uniformed policemen bringing the two strands of parallel narrative timelines together, and the film to an abrupt end.[72]

There are fewer such narrative fractures and intrusions in *Life of Brian*, and as a result it is the most complete narrative film the Pythons produced.[73]

MATTHIAS: "My sight is weak, my eyes are poor and my nose is knackered"—Matthias is repeating himself already (talking about his poor "sight" and "eyes"), though the Centurion doesn't seem to notice. To have one's nose "knackered" is interesting, given that it often means to be very tired (even "shagged out"), but can also mean "severely damaged." As it turns out, the nose being tweaked is the Centurion's, and he will seem to appreciate that.

SERGEANT: "We found this spoon, sir"—If nothing else, the spoon might be important only because it was used by Francis earlier as his pointer, thus a tool in the continuing struggle against Roman oppression? This sounds silly, and it is, but the spoon (likely accidentally) figures into Pilate's relationship with the Jews in Jerusalem in a significant way. As mentioned, Pilate had earlier brought troops with him into the Holy City whose standards had "bosses adorned with portrait-busts of the Emperor," meaning they were "objects of cult in the Roman army," and therefore a sacrilege to the Jews.[74] The threat of mob hysteria and bloodshed forced Pilate to remove the standards. Later, Pilate commissioned the creation of almost featureless votive shields to honor Tiberius and brought those into Jerusalem; the Jews demanded those be removed, as well. Thwarted twice by the peace with the Jews his superiors demanded, Pilate may have purposely then struck coins that "show a similar disregard for Jewish feelings," according to Smallwood.[75] The coins didn't feature the profile of an emperor or any god, as was usual for coins struck in predominately Jewish regions, but Pilate seemed to be trying to slip one past his subjects:

> The coins of all the other procurators bear designs of objects such as an ear of corn, a vine-branch, a flower, or a palm-tree, which were inoffensive to the Jews. They appear on coins struck by the Jews both before the Roman annexation and during their revolt of 66–70. Some of Pilate's coins, however, show implements of pagan worship, the augur's staff *and the ladle with which the wine was poured in sacrifices*. These designs on coins handled every day cannot have failed to annoy the Jews.[76]

So the innocuous (ladle-like) spoon, in the crucible of Roman-Jewish relations, is much more important than even the bemused Centurion seems to think.

The Pythons may just like the sound and non-threatening appearance of the spoon, as well, since it crops up in their oeuvre a number of times. In *Holy Grail*, one of the villagers hustling the accused witch to her judgment is a young boy who wears a large wooden spoon as part of his hat.[77] One of the names floated for the original series in spring 1969 was *A Horse, a Spoon and a Basin*,[78] and spoon is one of the words an Italian student in an Italian class, has already mastered ("Il cucchiaio").[79] In Ep. 19 of *Flying Circus*, the "School Prize-Giving" sketch, a spoon is awarded as an academic plaudit, even though

> at Cambridge it was the student who performed worst in math who was awarded a wooden spoon, and later any academic or sport contestant/team could be eligible for such an honor. The sometimes very large spoons were last officially awarded in the early twentieth century, but live on unofficially at the Oxbridge schools and in public life (and are especially favored by UK consumer affairs gadflies).[80]

In sporting events, for example, no one wanted to be left "holding the wooden spoon," or be forced to "take the wooden spoon," because it often meant being shut out (victories, runs, tries, etc.), or winding up in last place like, for example, Ireland's rugby team in the mid-1950s.[81] For British viewers, then, this image—the Centurion holding the results of careful military search, a wooden spoon—is a recognizable jibe at headmasters, sergeant majors, and sporting sad sacks across the Commonwealth.

. . . there is yet another knock at the door—This is the fulfillment of the tried and true "rule of threes" in comedy, wherein the third iteration is where the gag is set to pay off. Attached to this setup and payoff is the balcony on which Brian has been hiding—at his third go, the balcony collapses, and he neatly replaces the Boring Prophet below.

MATTHIAS: "You haven't given us time to hide!"—Here the entire façade that's been constructed—soldiers earnestly searching for (and not finding) terrorists who hide in plain sight—is admitted to be false. In a more "real" world this would lead to recriminations against Matthias and the PFJ, but here it's simply a tossed-off line as we cinematically escape the room with Brian. The following scene, where Brian is preaching but the soldiers looking for him for some reason don't recognize him (he hasn't even put a beard on), is equally silly. (Earlier in the film the Roman guards beneath Pilate's rooms have somehow walked right past the rather noticeable tussle between the CFG and PFJ, so the die has been cast.) These moments abound in the Pythons' work—coconuts can be used instead of horses and a castle on the hill is "only a model." The Goons pulled back the curtain on the nuts and bolts of dramatic radio production—acknowledging the artifice—calling attention to sound effects and actors switching voices to create the next character. In the episode "World War One," the scheming Grytpype-Thynne, thinking on the fly for the best means of fleecing the credulous Neddie, nakedly reveals his plan: "Do you know, I have certain information that I've just thought of."[82] Neddie somehow hears the "information" part but misses that it's fake, which Grytpype-Thynne baldly admits. In their "Robin Hood and His Merry Men" episode, the Goons comment on the fact that they've been using sound effects rather than actual fighting throughout.[83]

This is also the last we'll clearly see of old Matthias. In the later scene where Judith bursts into Mandy's home to tell the PFJ of Brian's imminent crucifixion, Matthias is puttering around in the background. It could be that Rome no longer sees Matthias as a threat, given his advanced age and knackered-ness. Convicts in the empire (who had entered gladiatorial ranks) could, if they survived their term, retire after active games service. In a series of letters from Emperor Trajan to Pliny, the emperor mentioned that those who have been convicted within these ten years, and whose sentence has not been reversed by proper authority, must be sent back again to their respective punishments. But where more than ten years have elapsed since their conviction, and they are grown old and infirm, let them be distributed in such employments as approach penal servitude: that is, either to attend upon the public baths, cleanse the common sewers, or repair the streets and highways, the usual offices to which such persons are assigned.[84]

There is no hint as to what will happen to Matthias as the PFJ's beard; perhaps his was an ideological separation?

Notes

1. King and Stager, *LBI*, 309.
2. Larsen, *BAFHG*, 450–51.
3. See Laqueur's *Terrorism*; Farrell's *BRJ*; also Dobson and Payne's *The Carlos Complex*.
4. See Bogdanor on this transition to postwar consensus in "The Character of the Postwar Period."
5. Laqueur, *Terrorism*, 177.
6. Brandon, *Jesus and the Zealots*, 19–20.
7. Brandon, *Jesus and the Zealots*, 20.
8. "The Unfinished Revolution in China," *Times*, 2 July 1971: 16.
9. "Republicans Battle with Police at Stagg Memorial Service," *Times*, 23 February 1976: 1.
10. "Did Jesus See Himself as the Messiah?" *Times*, 1 April 1972: 14.
11. *Baader-Meinhof: In Love with Terror*, 2002.
12. Caryl, *Strange Rebels*, 12.
13. See Bernstein, *Myth of Decline*, 91–93; Carlton's *Britain and the Suez Crisis*; and Brendon, *DFBE*.
14. Bernstein, *Myth of Decline*, 92–93. The Goons mentioned both the canal and the crisis a number of times during the later years of *The Goon Show*.
15. Jenkins, *Mrs. Thatcher's Revolution*, 72; italics added.
16. Burleigh, *BRT*, 134. The African National Congress endured similarly failed but "symbolic" attacks in the early days of the fight against apartheid South Africa (144).
17. See Bell, *Terror Out of Zion* (1977).
18. Bell, *The Secret Army*, 6.
19. Bell, *The Secret Army*, 149; also "The IRA Bomb Campaign That Fizzled Out in Despair," *Times*, 14 September 1973: 16.
20. Demaris, *Brothers in Blood*, 144.
21. Demaris, *Brothers in Blood*, 149.
22. Dobson and Payne, *Carlos Complex*, 130.
23. "Brief Fame of a Terrorist," *Times*, 14 August 1975: 14.
24. This phraseology should sound familiar. When Dennis is arguing with Arthur about the benefits of syndicalism versus a monarchy, he talks a similar line: "Listen—strange women lying in ponds distributing swords is no basis for a system of government. Supreme executive power derives from a mandate from the masses, not from some farcical aquatic ceremony" (*BAFHG*, 143–44). Six years later, a noted political columnist echoes this "conviction politics" peasant.
25. Jenkins, *Anatomy of Decline*, 122.
26. Part of the Pythons' first film, *And Now for Something Completely Different*.
27. John 1:46.
28. There is typecasting in the film: The Ex-leper is certain that all donkey owners "are the same," and the Gregorys won't want to be crucified in anything but a Jewish section.
29. "Life without Michael X," *Sunday Times*, 26 June 1977: 32.
30. Bernstein, *Myth of Decline*, 279.
31. Bogdanor, "Collapse of the Postwar Settlement," a.t. Much of this has been overstated over the years, certainly, as Bernstein discusses in *Myth of Decline*.

32. Bogdanor, "Collapse of the Postwar Settlement," a.t.

33. Bernstein, *Myth of Decline*, 279.

34. Bogdanor, "Collapse of the Postwar Settlement," a.t.

35. Bernstein, *Myth of Decline*, 279.

36. Massive hunger marches of October 1936. Mentioned in Eps. 15 and 32 of *Flying Circus*, and discussed in *MPFC: UC*, 1.246 and 2.83.

37. In the interwar period (and coincident to the effects of the Great Depression), upwards of 20 percent of employable British workers were often out of jobs. These are the times and figures that would haunt both Labour and Conservative governments for many years to come, and the real reason that the election plank of "full employment" was clutched so tightly by both parties, until Thatcherism. See Bernstein, Marr, Turner, or Sandbrook for more.

38. Bogdanor, "Collapse of the Postwar Settlement," a.t.

39. Martin Bright, "Look Back in Anger," *Observer*, 2 February 2002.

40. "The Angry Brigade 1," *Eyewitness 1970–1979*, a.t.

41. *BRT*, 243.

42. Smallwood, *JURR*, 149.

43. Davies, "Police Work in Roman Times," 700; italics added.

44. Davies, "Police Work in Roman Times," 702.

45. See *DFBE*, chapter 5.

46. Similar struggles were underway in Northern Rhodesia and Nyasaland, as well.

47. *MPFC: UC* 2.62.

48. Horsely, "The Sicarii," 451.

49. Quoted in Demaris, *Brothers in Blood*, 258–59.

50. Demaris, *Brothers in Blood*, 259–60; also "Terror Trial Accused Ordered Out," *Times*, 11 July 1975: 6.

51. "Ulrike Meinhof and the Baader-Meinhof Gang," *Encounter* (July 1975): 11.

52. She and her accomplices firebombed a department store, Schneider's, wondering if the sellers and consumers of capitalist goods would appreciate a small taste of the fires that were raining down on the flesh of Vietnamese civilians. All were quickly arrested.

53. Hilke Schlaeger, "Vernunft gegen Gewalt"; translation provided by Prof. Robert McFarland.

54. Toner, *The Day Commodus Killed a Rhino*, 111.

55. Kemna, "Death of a Nightingale."

56. Kemna, "Death of a Nightingale," 61.

57. Kemna, "Death of a Nightingale," 61.

58. Kemna, "Death of a Nightingale," 62.

59. *LBI*, 18, 65–67.

60. See http://www.ostia-antica.org/regio3/16/16-7.htm for several versions of what this advertisement might have meant; also, Koloski-Ostrow, *ASRI*, 19.

61. *ASRI*, 19.

62. "Crucified Man Tells Visions," *Times*, 15 January 1969: 7. Terry Gilliam lived on Hampstead Heath, as did Julian Doyle. Many of the postproduction pickups and special effects backgrounds for *Holy Grail* were shot on the Heath.

63. *Times*, 15 January 1969: 7.

64. 14 May 1976: 8.

65. Waugh, *FCY*, 13 July 1976.

66. See Erickson's "Youth and Political Deference in England," where she discusses the differences between social and political deference.

67. Bogdanor, "Collapse of the Postwar Settlement," a.t.

68. Again, Fred Kite in *I'm All Right Jack*.

69. Palin, *Diaries 1969–1979*, 146. These films and their influence on the Pythons are discussed in *BAFHG*. Perhaps it was inevitable that some critics couldn't see the hoped-for distinction, seeing *Life of*

Brian as, at least partly, just another *Carry On* product. See, for example, Ackroyd's review in *Spectator*, 17 December 1979: 28.

70. See index entries for "cartoony" and "reflexivity" in both *MPFC: UC* and *BAFHG* for more.

71. See Larsen, *MPSERD*, 73–74 for more.

72. *BAFHG*, 46.

73. With the noted exceptions of interruptive and purposely intrusive *Star Wars* moments, yes. One of the Pythons' complaints about their next and final film, *Meaning of Life*, is that they felt as if they'd regressed, simply linking sketches together with a loose narrative arc.

74. Smallwood, "Jews and Romans in the Early Empire," 316.

75. Smallwood, "Jews and Romans in the Early Empire," 316. See also *JURR*, 167–68.

76. Smallwood, "Jews and Romans in the Early Empire," 316.

77. *BAFHG*, 187–225 discusses the "She's a Witch!" scene.

78. *MPFC: UC*, 1.45.

79. *ATW*, 1.1.2; *MPFC: UC*, 1.11.

80. *MPFC: UC*, 1.306.

81. "Significance of To-Morrow's Rugby Match in Dublin," *Times*, 24 February 1956: 4.

82. "World War One" was first broadcast 24 February 1958.

83. 2 December 1956.

84. Grant, *Gladiators*, 30.

SCENE SEVENTEEN
BRIAN GIVES A SERMON

*. . . knocking the **BORING PROPHET** cleanly off his perch*—Another cartoony moment of physical gaggery, wherein the audience's response should have been shock and horror, but in the Python world they are merely entertained by the "trick." These bits of dark humor can be found in New Wave films of this same period, many of which greatly influenced *Holy Grail*, including Herzog's *Aguirre: The Wrath of God*, which

> features the murderous, traitorous Aguirre (Klaus Kinski) who, after seizing control of the expedition by force, casually notes that one of his less motivated minions is a head too tall. His second-in-command takes the hint, drawing his sword. The doomed, clueless man is counting through their meager food stores aloud—"acht, neun"—as the fatal stroke is delivered—his head flies off and lands on the ground, and says: "Zehn."[1]

The assembled crowd is simply happy that they are being entertained, and that another diverting speaker has taken the Boring Prophet's place. Remember that Brian's earlier space ride and spectacular crash only elicited a "jammy bastard" from a passerby. (In fact, the only physical double-take in the movie comes from the alarmed aliens in the spacecraft, wondering where this odd creature, Brian, has come from.)

There is a smattering of applause from the crowd. They clearly like tricks—(PSC) This is one of the film's direct references back to *Flying Circus*. There, as early as the second episode, stock footage of the Women's Institute applauding some sketch punchline is inserted as the payoff for one scene and the transition to the next. In the first case, "A Man with Two Noses" has just blown his second nose, to polite applause.[2] A similar response will later be had from a leering group of "shabby men in filthy macs" as a doctor examines a well-endowed patient, to stripper music.[3]

Off to Brian's side we get a quick glimpse of an angle we've not seen yet. There are two other prophets haranguing the crowd, one dressed in flowing white robes and carrying a crook, and the other a rougher, wilder prophet all in black, and played by Jones.

BRIAN: "Don't pass judgment on other people, or else you might get judged yourself"—Here we're back to the conclusion of the Sermon on the Mount, the part that, we thought, Brian and Mandy couldn't hear.[4] Apparently he'd heard Jesus preach before, since this is a fairly unbowdlerized version of the teaching.

COLIN (Jones): "Me?"—There were many instances where Christ's disciples (and his detractors, as well) asked for or demanded clarification of his parables, stories crafted to confuse nonbelievers.[5] Sometimes the disciples were left puzzled, given Jesus's move away from the strictures of the Mosaic Law. (Colin seems quite happy with the answer he receives, though.) When Jesus announced that he would be betrayed, the disciples immediately asked "Lord, is it I?" while at another point argued among themselves as to which of them was the greatest disciple.[6] There is very little "discipleship" in the finished film, however. The haggling for endorsements, the additional sermons, the discussion of the future of the movement, etc.—these all remain in the various unfilmed drafts of the script.

DENNIS (Terence Bayler): "That's a nice gourd"—This is "Dennis," who is otherwise unnamed in the film. Most of the characters after this remain unnamed, even those like Simon the Hermit, who have larger speaking parts (ironically). The balance of the film often involves mobs and chasing (like a silent comedy or a Fleischer brothers cartoon), so characters referring to one another by name would be unusual. Like *Bonnie and Clyde* and *Butch Cassidy and the Sundance Kid*,[7] this film has become a chase film, and will only pause for Brian and Judith's night together. Also as depicted in those earlier films, the sexual encounter (or the significant appearance of a female character in an otherwise man's world) signals the beginning of the end for the male leads.

WOMAN: "Consider the lilies?"—This is adapted from Luke 12, where Jesus is asking his hearers to consider "the ravens" and the "fowls," as well as the "lilies" and the "grass."[8] In the "final" printed script, this question is given to a character named Geoffrey (to have been played by Gilliam). Here, it's delivered by an unnamed character (later called "Elsie"[9]) played by Gwen Taylor. Gilliam will appear in a moment, as a man named "Frank." The other characters named in this scene—named in the bound version of the script—include "Dennis," who wants to haggle for the gourd, Geoffrey, "Eddie," asking about the birds, "Arthur," and "Frank." None of their names are uttered, so these are just crowds.

ARTHUR (Cleese): "He say the birds are scrounging"—The listeners are responding with all the skepticism that isn't often seen in the scriptures, especially coming from the rank and file follower. Priests and scribes do nitpick Jesus's words, looking for ways to turn them into incriminatory weapons, but there are generally no persons asking about "cheesemakers" or the names of servants from a parable—that's the skeptical modern world talking. In Cook and Moore's Jesus sketch, words like "abiding" get worked over in ways that don't happen in more sacred settings. The Shepherd is "abiding" in fields that he can't "abide" because they're not very "abideable," and on.

BRIAN: "No, look, the point is they're doing do all right, aren't they?"—Brian has identified the parable problem—so many listeners misunderstood or just missed the significance of the message. When he keeps having to say "it doesn't matter" he's pointing to the portions of the stories that tend to distract modern men like the Pythons, where details can mean everything.[10] He actually explains it rather well, reminding his listeners that they are more important than the birds or flowers, and that the Lord will look after them. But in the 1970s world of second-guessing and reading between the lines, the dismissal of deference means that no statement will go unchallenged. The sentries in *Holy Grail* can't get past Arthur's mention of coconuts, then swallows; quests and Lords and masters get lost in the skeptical shuffle. This is the kind of language Bogdanor was referring to when he talked about the place Britain found itself in the 1970s. When Heath tried to overcome the miners in the earlier 1970s, he was almost speaking a lost tongue:

> He called an election under the slogan "Who Governs?" and appealed to the country in language which would have had a lot of effect in the 1940s but which, by the 1970s, was greeted with a belly laugh. He said: "Think nationally. Think of the nation as a whole. Think of these [statu-

tory incomes] proposals as members of a society that can only beat rising prices if it acts together as one nation." Now, in the time of Attlee and the Churchill peacetime Government, I think people would have responded to that language. There was a great deal of deference, a sense of social obligation, resulting from the War. By the 1970s, that sense of social obligation had worn out and different groups, including the miners, started asking, if they could use the market to get more, why shouldn't they?[11]

This is also the mythological Arthur waxing Maloric before the credulous Dennis—mystic swords and strange women are simply "no basis for a system of government" in the fallen world of the now. Those listening to Brian are closer to the 1970s than 33, as is their cynicism. Interestingly, once Brian trails off, leaving an unsaid potential blessing, the mob become followers.

ARTHUR: "He's having a go at the flowers now"—In the Python world, there is no possibility that a feel-good saying like this could go unchallenged. Arthur discovered this uncooperative, context-destroying behavior in the medieval-meets-mythology-meets-the-modern-world confusion of *Holy Grail*, where peasants, sentries, knights, and enchanters—all "Britons," he assumed—meet Arthur at their level, not his.

Brian is clearly trying to deliver a sermon or parable as he heard Christ do on the mount, but his memorialized version is spotty, at best. Add to this that his hearers aren't hearing at all; Jesus had to explain and re-explain to his disciples, as well: "Unto you it is given to know the mystery of the kingdom of God: but unto them that are without, all these things are done in parables: That seeing they may see, and not perceive; and hearing they may hear, and not understand."[12] It's clear Brian couldn't explain this explanation, either.

ARTHUR: "What were they called?"—Likely the beginning of the parable of the talents, but he can't remember the details. In Matthew 24 and 25 Jesus is teaching his disciples at the Mount of Olives, but no one else is mentioned (as being in attendance), meaning Brian must have heard the parables second hand, at best. The parables of the fig tree, the ten virgins, the talents, and the sheep and the goats follow in close succession in these verses.

This heckling might simply be related to the questions that his disciples had of his other teachings; there's no indication, especially in chapters like Matthew 25, of any response from his listeners. Start to finish, Jesus simply delivers three parables without pause or comment between. Arthur here is more like a less-polite Xerxes, raising a hand to ask for clarification or specifics, and not unlike those attending a speech at a party conference, where such shouted questions from the assembled delegates weren't welcome. This last possibility is made more realistic when a deleted scene is considered. In an earlier draft, Reg and the PFJ have become more involved in Brian's messiahship, organizing a for-pay sermon on the mount marshalled by fences and a gate, and set up much more like a concert or conference than a Jesus sermon. As the sermon ends Brian is hustled off to a waiting donkey and another paying engagement.

BRIAN: "Oh, they were called 'Simon' and 'Adrian.' Now . . ."—A Simon will appear later as the hermit in the wilderness, and an Adrian has already appeared in *Flying Circus*, Ep. 19, in the speeding credits appended to the "Timmy Williams Interview."[13]

SAM (Cleese): "He's making it up as he goes along"—Brian might not be "making it up," either. In 1909 the scholar Walter Bauer gathered "vast apocryphal material about Jesus's life, miracles, relatives" and so on, with the page count exceeding five hundred and, according to Koester, another five hundred pages could have been compiled by the time he wrote his own article, "One Jesus and Four Gospels," in 1968.[14] That apocrypha could have included a Simon and an Adrian, and likely did include mangled versions of the Beatitudes and parables, especially as they were adapted over time for more contemporary needs.

BRIAN: "Three. Well stewards really . . ."—The mystical number three, again, which so bedeviled Arthur in *Holy Grail*.[15] Brian is ad-libbing here, put on the spot by his precarious position as a wanted, fleeing man stuck on the preachers' rostrum. He's now "saying things in a very roundabout way," a character he's already played on Flying Circus.[16] In Luke 16:1–9 there is the parable of the "unjust steward," so the confusion between steward and servant is understandable.[17] "Steward" is only used in the KJV translation seventeen times, while "servant" appears almost nine-hundred times.

BRIAN: "Blessed are they . . . who convert their neighbour's ox . . . for they shall inhibit their girth . . ."—Brian is going from memory here, trying to mimic Christ's Beatitudes. The real world danger of this mimicry was mentioned earlier, when the preacher Theudas promised miracles *like* those Jesus and his followers claimed, including a parting of the river Jordan. The Judean procurator Fadus didn't wait for the miraculous events, and had the man arrested and summarily executed.[18]

This also may be a sideways nod to the teaching (or rantings) of the pseudonymic *Might Is Right* author "Ragnar Redbeard," whose Social Darwinist worldview offers a mangled, hateful (not just confused) version of the Beatitudes. His version blesses the strong, the "battle-blooded," the "iron-handed," and "the destroyers of false hope," and curses the "God-adorers," the "vanquished," and the "feeble-brained." This splenetic reads like a Python sketch, actually. "Ragnar Redbeard" was a pseudonym for, perhaps, Arthur Desmond but, for obvious reasons, the author kept his actual identity a secret, even though the work may have been an elaborate satire.[19] A new edition of this inflammatory book had appeared in 1972.

BRIAN: ". . . and to them only shall be given . . ."—Brandon points out that some earliest Christ-focused scholarship did actually see Jesus and his teachings as potentially combustive, as political rather than religious speech:

> It is significant that in what may be regarded as the first critical study of the life of Jesus the political aspect of his Messiahship was boldly asserted. In his *Von dem Zwecke Jesu und seiner Jünger*, Hermann Samuel Reimarus interpreted Jesus's preaching of the coming of the Kingdom of God as incitement to revolt against the government of Rome.[20]

This and following works along a similar vein have been "repudiated by orthodox Christian scholars," of course, but it's clear that a number of thinkers in the field of Jesus studies saw a political aspect to his ministry, one that would make him a target of the Romans as well as the Sanhedrin.[21] The Pythons seem to have chosen to bypass any Jewish judgment of their central figure, Brian, posing him as a threat to Roman rule alone.

***BRIAN** climbs down from the ledge to leave*—Josephus records that the high priest Jesus addressed "Idumaeans from the city wall" during the Zealots' siege of Jerusalem.[22]

BLIND MAN: "What was't he said?"—This garbled line was to have been spoken by a "Youth" who'd just arrived (perhaps even the "Intensely Dull Youth" of the "Dramatic Personae," set as Eric Idle). It was given instead to McKeown, playing a blind man. Gilliam's character Frank will grab the blind man's staff and push him out of the way in a moment. The blind man will later fall into Simon the Hermit's hole, just as he assures everyone he's been healed.

GIRL: "Is it the secret of Eternal Life?"—According to Hegesippus's account, these are the kinds of questions asked of James by "Sadducean leaders" eager to catch him out as a revolutionary, like Jesus, and then condemn him.[23] He would answer boldly, affirming Christ's divinity, and be stoned to death. The oddness of some of the questions and conclusions that follow—including the worship of a shoe as opposed to a sandal as opposed to a gourd—

mirrors one of the Sadducean questions that was posed to James, according to Hegesippus: "Tell us, what is the gate of Jesus?" "This expression has never been satisfactorily explained," according to Brandon, and he concludes "that it is likely a corruption of some Aramaic expression."[24] (Meaning, Jesus as the gate to heaven, essentially.) Later Brian's mother Mandy will be asked, quite seriously, if she is "a virgin," meaning that the crowd either accepts the Immaculate Conception cult or has *no* conception of how biological impregnation actually occurs (or both?). These head-scratching bits of logic appeared earlier in *Holy Grail*, when, from the back of the crowd, the wise King Arthur calls out "A duck," helping Bedevere complete his chain of (il)logic, successfully identifying a witch.[25]

GIRL: "Tell us, Master"—He has gone from "Brian" to "Master" in one go. In the elided, paid-admittance Sermon on the Mount scene, the "regional organiser" Reg and the rest of the PFJ call him "Lord," and fawn over even his garbled Beatitudes as they count gate receipts.

GIRL: "Is that . . . his gourd?"—Objects associated with Christ or his disciples can evoke warm feelings from devotees. From the alleged gathering of his blood as he hung on the cross (into the "Holy Grail") to his death shroud (of Turin), and including the myriad parts of the true cross and bits of the nails, religious relics of all kinds were said to be imbued with healing or saving power, and became significant parts of pilgrimages and devotion.[26] In *Holy Grail*, the French sentries tease Arthur and his devoted knights, saying they already have a grail, and don't need to search for another.[27] The woman here is correct, though, she does have a gourd that Brian actually held, and they will find and carry "his" sandal, as well.

In the years leading up to the film, the Shroud of Turin was in the news often, including a round of age-dating testing making front-page news in 1977. The fact that the fabric was eventually found to be likely of thirteenth-to-fourteenth-century origination hasn't dimmed the hopes of believers. In fall 1978 (when the Pythons were polishing the *Brian* script, casting, and doing costume fittings[28]) the shroud went on display to the public for the first time in many years in the Turin Cathedral.[29]

DENNIS: "It's under offer. . . . Ten then"—Dennis immediately raises the price (or the value) of the gourd when it's been attached to the new "master." He first offered to buy it from Brian for one shekel, than two, and now he's bumped it to ten. Once Brian becomes a "savior," a value can be attached to what he does, says, and even touches. This leads to his disciples—in the earlier drafts of the script—setting up promotional agreements for products and concert events where an admission can be charged. He is both messiah and rock star, at least in those drafts. Much of that cynicism disappeared by the finished cut of the film.

GIRL: "It is His gourd! We will carry it for you, Master . . ."—(PSC) In a moment made for the readers of the script only, the possessive pronoun "his" has been capitalized to indicate a reference to deity. This had been common in print for a long while, since by the nineteenth century editors were recommending the "old practice" of an initial capital letter when referring to deity for "Him" or "His." This was certainly reverential, but also practical—the same pronoun ("his") could show up in the same scriptural sentence and be referring to both man and God, leading to confusion.

YOUTH (Idle): "He's gone! He's been taken up!"—Christ would be "taken up" after forty days of ministration following the resurrection. This is recorded in Acts 1, which postdates this moment. Perhaps this crowd of ready-made believers (one admits to following a few saviors) had read or heard Psalms 68:18, and acknowledged it as a prophecy for their day.

ARTHUR: "No there he is, over there"—This moment of deflation is a Python trope, but also found in the classical Roman works. Herodotus (c. 484–425 BC) writes of Darius I's accession to the Persian throne, as discussed by Richard:

The seven Persian aristocrats decided to ride their favorite horses to a certain spot before dawn the next day. The owner of the first horse to neigh after sunrise would become the new emperor. Darius' lowly groomsman found a way to fix the contest. Before dawn, he rubbed the genitalia of the favorite mare of his master's horse and stuffed his hands in his cloak to preserve the smell. Then, as the sun rose at the designated location, the groomsman pretended to fasten the horse's bit. The horse smelled his hands and neighed. That is how Darius became emperor of Persia, the most powerful man in the world. This story is typical of Herodotus *because it demystifies an important event*, attributing its outcome to a clever human, rather than to the gods. (In reality, it was not quite as easy as that; Darius had to win a brief but bloody civil war to secure his throne.)[30]

Richard concludes that Herodotus, "like a favorite uncle," takes the fun path through history, his "hilarious digressions" endearing the reader to him.[31]

Indicates BRIAN disappearing round a corner. At once the crowd gives chase—Brian is running away from those who would follow him as a spiritual leader (calling him "Master," "Messiah," and "Lord"), but who also see him as a potential political tool (Reg and the PFJ acting as his "handlers").[32] The Romans would find the latter much more troubling, given the number of Jews in Judea compared to the number of Roman troops. Jesus found it necessary to elude large crowds, as well, which is likely the Gospel incident that spawned the scene:

> The Gospel of John, though not adhering to the Markan chronological framework and being much later in date, appears to know a tradition concerning Jesus that must be primitive and authentic. According to this tradition, during his Galilean ministry, the miracles of Jesus caused so great an impression on the people that there was a concerted movement to proclaim him king: "Jesus therefore perceiving that they were about to come and take him by force, to make him king . . . withdrew again into the mountain alone." The account suggests that Jesus was the unwilling subject of the popular excitement which his display of supernatural power had occasioned, and that he eluded the intent of the crowd. It is, however, significant that this popular enthusiasm was so strong that it took a political form.[33]

The Jewish and Roman authorities took these circumstances as "politically serious" in the Gospel of John, and Jesus was eventually a target for both. In *Life of Brian*, remember, the Jewish authorities are nowhere to be found in relation to either Jesus or Brian, continuing the Pythons' avoidance of delving into the Jewish world of first-century Jerusalem.[34] The Romans *are* concerned, and it's just after Brian's last mob moment—in his mother's home when he's surrounded by the PFJ, the diseased, and kindly promoters like Mr. Papadopolous—that the Romans catch up with him, and he is arrested and sent for execution.

Notes

1. Larsen, *BAFHG*, 174.
2. Larsen, *MPFC: UC*, 1.26.
3. *MPFC: UC*, 1.319; *ATW*, 1.20.265.
4. Recorded in Matthew 7:1–2 and Luke 6:37.
5. Vermes, *The Authentic Gospels of Jesus*, 140. See Mark 10:10, for example.
6. Matthew 26:22 and Luke 9:46, respectively.
7. And obvious comedies like the *Carry On* films and *It's a Mad Mad Mad Mad World* (1963), which is just an extended chase narrative.
8. Luke 12:24–28.
9. In the "Dramatis Personae" for the printed version, Carol Cleveland was to have played Elsie; she does not appear anywhere in the street preaching scene as filmed. This kind of change happened often during the run of *Flying Circus* (*MPFC: UC*, 2.32).

10. In Ep. 30, a simple anagrammatic problem—a sign says "Mary Recruitment Center"—can easily be switched to "Army Recruitment Center," and a line of nuns queuing up for a job are dispersed. Also, in Gilliam's *Brazil*, a typo—"Buttle" for "Tuttle"—ends a man's life, destroys a family, and sets the film on its narrative course. The broad strokes of a parable just won't do in the postmodernist age. Finally, in *Meaning of Life*, a serious discovery about the meaning of life is sidetracked by the mention of hats.

11. Bogdanor, "Collapse of the Postwar Settlement," a.t.

12. Mark 4:11–12.

13. *MPFC: UC*, 1.291.

14. Page 204. That book was *Das Leben Jesu im Zeitalter der neutestamentlichen Apokryphen* (Tübingen, 1909).

15. See the *BAFHG* index entries under "threes" for more.

16. Ep. 26, "The Queen Will Be Watching."

17. Vermes, *The Authentic Gospels of Jesus*, 161–62.

18. There is some disagreement as to Theudas's actual place in the timeline of known events; see Thiessen and Merz, *The Historical Jesus* 71, 143, and 154.

19. Laqueur, *Terrorism*, 77–78. Otto would have enjoyed this book.

20. Brandon, *Jesus and the Zealots*, 22.

21. Brandon, *Jesus and the Zealots*, 23. Reimarus's work was first published after his death, c. 1774. See also Thiessen and Merz's *The Historical Jesus*, chapter 14, for more.

22. Horsley, "The Zealots," 173.

23. Brandon, *Jesus and the Zealots*, 123–24.

24. Brandon, *Jesus and the Zealots*, 124n2.

25. See *BAFHG*, 190–91, for more on this moment.

26. See Chaucer's *Canterbury Tales*, for example.

27. For a discussion of some of the relics and shrines pertinent to Christianity, see *BAFHG*, 273.

28. Palin, *Diaries 1969–1979*, 475–80.

29. "Turin Shroud to Be Shown in Bullet-Proof Case," *Times*, 28 August 1978: 10.

30. Richard, *WWAR*, 167; italics added.

31. *WWAR*, 166.

32. Importantly, Brian is only called "King of the Jews" and "Son of God" once, in the nativity scene, being a mistake immediately admitted and corrected in the world of the film.

33. John 6:15; Brandon, *Jesus and the Zealots*, 16.

34. Perhaps due to the potentially sticky consequences from Israeli and/or Jewish backlash in the wake of an already controversial film. The Pythons also spent the run of *Flying Circus* avoiding significant references to the "Irish situation," perhaps to avoid an IRA-placed car or letter bomb. Scotland and Wales took the brunt of the Pythons' spoofing instead.

SIMON THE HERMIT

BRIAN appears at the gates of the city . . . along the lower slopes of the hill toward Calvary— Clearly meant to indicate they're in Jerusalem, this is precisely the same location (and almost, even the same camera angle) seen in *Jesus of Nazareth.*

ARTHUR: "He has given us a sign!"—Christ would tell the scribes and Pharisees that only a "wicked and adulterous generation seeketh after a sign."[1] These followers didn't ask for a sign, but they'll take one (or two, or three) when it's gifted to them.

EDDIE: "He has given us . . . his shoe!"—In Ruth 4, the lowly shoe is shown as importantly symbolic in an example involving Boaz, marriage, and inheritance, and the "ceremony of the shoe":

> 7 Now this was the manner in former time in Israel concerning redeeming and concerning changing, for to confirm all things; a man plucked off his shoe, and gave it to his neighbour: and this was a testimony in Israel.

> 8 Therefore the kinsman said unto Boaz, Buy it for thee. So he drew off his shoe.

According to Josephus, the shoe ritual was part of a levirate marriage ritual (which some scholars have since disputed), but articles of clothing were often invested with meaning in relation to holy places (i.e., where shoes were removed, heads covered or uncovered), and here, in this ritualized transaction: "So [Boaz] called the senate to witness, and bid the woman to loose his shoe and spit in his face, according to the law; and when this was done [Boaz] married Ruth, and they had a son within a year's time."[2] Perhaps now the spittle that Ben was so longing for earlier makes more sense in this public, ritualized setting?

GIRL: "Cast off the shoe!"—"Putting off the shoe" was the phrase for the published refusal made so that a woman whose husband had died (and left her without a son) could remarry.[3] The mob here don't seem to be appreciating the symbolic element of the shoe, except that it represents their "master."

GIRL: "Follow the Gourd! The Holy Gourd of Jerusalem"—Again, this sounds silly and over the top, but sacred vessels were a significant part of life in ancient Israel. "Pure goods" were kept in special "ovoid and cylindrical jars" at Qumran, for instance, some labeled as "fit for the purity of hallowed things," and the jars were often destroyed when the sacred use was complete.[4] This gourd only seems to be holy by association with Brian.

The search for allegedly sacred vessels was part of the reason that hundreds (or even thousands) of Samaritans followed a self-proclaimed prophet into the wilderness of Mount Gerizim.[5] This messiah figure—whom Josephus labeled as a man "who thought lying a thing of little consequence"—promised that these sacred vessels had been buried on the mountain by Moses, and invited followers to make their way to the holy site. For some reason many were armed, Josephus reports, and Pilate, fearing sedition, attacked the energetic "multitude." Many were killed in the battle, and more were executed afterward.[6] So, following the "Holy Vessel of Gerizim" wasn't a particularly wise decision. This was the cruelty that would eventually unseat Pilate, according to Josephus. The film does not offer any consequences or punishment for those who follow Brian, the shoe, a sandal, or the gourd, and only the hermit Simon might later suffer the multitude's wrath as an "unbeliever" and "heretic."[7]

Later, and closer to the Pythons' own time, there was waged a vigorous debate in regard to the authenticity of clay pots. These pots would have been as insignificant and unimpressive as the gourd in this scene had they not purportedly held portions of the Dead Sea scrolls found in a cave at Qumran. Scholars including Yigael Yadin promoted the authenticity of the ancient jars (he had bought them at a dear price, after all), while other scholars, like contemporary gadfly Solomon Zeitlin, pooh-poohed the claims in often withering terms:

> Muhammad ed-Deeb who supposedly discovered the scrolls in the cave said in his interview that he broke all the jars; none were left intact. How could Dr. Yadin possess two intact jars which he claims had come from the cave and which contained the scrolls? Why did Dr. Yadin never mention that the potteries had fresh breaks in them? Is there not a likelihood that the Bethlehem merchants perpetrated a hoax on the archaeologists and sold them jars which never contained the seven scrolls? These jars became a popular feature in the press, on the jackets of books published on the Dead Sea Scrolls, and on television.[8]

This very public set-to is similar to the one surrounding the popular and publicized archaeological dig for "Arthur's Camelot" at Cadbury Castle; there, the claims of discovery outpaced actual discoveries, and the whole endeavor became a made-for-television event.[9]

HARRY: "It's a sandal"—Eddie (Palin) has called for the group to "Follow the Shoe," and the nitpicking can begin when Harry reminds him it's a sandal. In the KJV, the translation to "sandal" only happens twice, while there are more than thirty references to "shoe." These are the kinds of details that derail many scenes and sketches in *Flying Circus* and *Holy Grail* (like riding on a horse or using coconuts, or how or what type of a swallow could carry a coconut, or yellow or blue as a favorite color). Specifics matter in the Python world.[10]

ARTHUR: "Follow the shoe-ites!"—Various "factions" in Jerusalem of the first century include those who aligned themselves with either the Pharisees or Sadducees, while the "splitters" might be the more ascetic Essenes (perhaps like Simon, who we'll meet in a moment), who saw themselves as practicing a purer form of devotion. (They even believed the Jews had defiled the temple and its righteous purposes.) These parties disagreed on interpretations and definitions of scripture, on priestly authority, on Hellenization, on the concepts of freewill and the afterlife, and on the temple services, at the least. The outsider, terrorist types were the Zealots, who actively agitated and even murdered in their quest for freedom from Rome.

ARTHUR: "Let us, like him, <u>carry</u> one shoe . . ."—Brian isn't actually carrying one shoe. He's lost one, and he's now running from them with just one shoe. This is likely a nod to the mutability of devotional practice following Christ's crucifixion. Various groups added to, modified, or rejected teachings they'd heard or read, leading to multiple Christian faiths, often varying by city. See Paul's letter to the Galatians in relation to circumcision, for example.

EDDIE: "No! Gather shoes!"—So one follower has called for carrying one shoe, another wants shoes to be gathered, and then a girl calls for shoes to be "cast off" and the gourd followed instead. There were myriad disagreements between and within sects, and for myriad reasons. The differing interpretations of life and scripture from the Hillel and Shammai schools, for instance, colored Jewish everyday life for centuries. Magness notes that the disagreements involving the letter or spirit of the law were constant between Pharisee and Sadducee, also observing only what was written or acknowledging oral traditions, and between practices of purity in the desert, in the city, and near the temple. There were more and less strict rabbinical traditions, and schools that taught scripture and schools that taught custom. The Qumran sect was so outraged by practices in Jerusalem and even smaller cities that they separated themselves to the desert, choosing a more ascetic, and to them, a more faithful life.[11] Simon, whom we'll meet in the following scene, is one such man.

Terror groups of the 1970s had similar disagreements, leading the Palestine-based groups to fracture into nonviolent and violent splinters, and sometimes targeting each other, similar to the divisions within groups on *both* sides of the issue in Northern Ireland.

In the political realm, it had been disagreements of conviction that fatally split Labour. Some on the far left wanted a more socialist state where the government set prices and incomes and oversaw all manner of production, others a more syndicalist worker-controlled industrial model that got rid of management and the upper crust. There was also a populated middle ground between these two poles simply trying to keep Labour in competition with the Tories for votes. The more moderate Labour figures like Wilson spent endless energy trying to keep the Left from keeping too far left, alienating the more conservative Labour supporters. The disagreements in the PLP, Whitehall, and No. 10 often sound like shoes versus sandals—to defeat inflation, for example, some argued for artificial stimulants to the economy, others said that higher unemployment was the answer, others that conservative pay policies needed to be nurtured, dividends needed to be restrained, and on.[12] As they dithered and jockeyed in Wilson's last administration, Thatcher and friends managed to win their Party leadership, then the confidence of a frightened country, and then a general election. Brian's followers don't let their disagreements break up their mob, happily.

YOUTH: ". . . we must like him think not of the things of the body but of the face and head"—It's not clear where this deviation comes from, except that hair-splitting rabbinical traditions make every action parsable. Brian gave up a gourd and lost a shoe—from that, the Youth has divined a focus on parts of the body. If it's a simple matter of hygiene, then this is accurate. Given the scarcity of fresh water, most people of this period would have washed only parts of their bodies—hands, face, and (the ritual washing of) feet.[13] Actual bathing in Jerusalem proper was likely a rarer thing, for observant Jews. (The Romans likely bathed, but in their quarters, apart from the Jews.) There is a great deal of rabbinical disagreement focusing on the body, its potential for defilement and purity, even down to specific parts of the body. Magness notes one tradition arguing that the hands can be defiled when touching an impurity but not the rest of the body, while another tradition argues that the entire body is defiled; there were disagreements about bathing before mentioning "the divine name" in the morning, or bathing afterward; whether the inside of a vessel or only the outside of a vessel can be impure; and whether scrolls—and even parts of scrolls (even depending on what is written on the scrolls)—can "impart uncleanness" to the hands that touch them.[14] It's also possible this is a more Augustinian admission, acknowledging the profaneness of the "naughty bits" of the body, especially, and its proclivity for sensuality and sin.[15]

GIRL: "All ye who call yourself Gourdenes!"—Perhaps a nod to the Pythons' study as they prepped for the film. This seems related to the Essene sect, since they could have said "Gourdites," but did not. The Essenes had been in the news often over the previous decade as Dead Sea scrolls researcher John Allegro published his controversial (and often refuted) findings.

SPIKE: "He cometh to us, like the seeds of the grave . . ."—Spike has raised his hands appropriately here, praying as in ancient Israel, arms reaching heavenward, as mentioned a number of times in the OT.[16] He is still ignored. Perhaps the time has passed for discrete followers to listen to preachers like this, having now aggregated into a "crowd" of disciples who will chase Brian back to his home. Also, the Prophet Spike isn't preaching on the prophet's wall, meaning he's indistinguishable from the rest of the mob.[17]

But SPIKE is left alone as the crowd sets off . . .—This is one of the Pythons' comedy heroes, Spike Milligan, who wrote most of *The Goon Show* episodes they grew up with. Milligan had also made a (vocal) appearance during the run of *Flying Circus*, yelling from off-camera during the "Election Night Special" in Ep. 19.[18] This is actually sadly prophetic. In the 1991 documentary *At Last the Go On Show*, Milligan is interviewed, and notes ruefully that his brand of comedy had been rejected by contemporary producers, leaving him "totally unemployed." Even in 1979, most Python fans wouldn't have recognized the Python hero in this scene.

The abandoned, crackpot-type character might just be a nod to the infamous John Stonehouse, a former Labour Party politician (and Wilson junior minister) who had tried to fake his own disappearance and death in November 1974 while on holiday in Florida. Most didn't actually think he'd died—Tony Benn doubts it in his diaries, echoing many others[19]—rather that Stonehouse had concocted an escape from financial and legal problems. He would be arrested in Australia just five weeks later, and even though he had run away and clearly wanted people to think he was dead, he was still eligible for his seat in the House (much to the chagrin of Wilson and the PLP), and was still trying to participate in parliamentary functions. On 20 October 1975 Stonehouse stood in the benches on the *Tory* side of the House and tried to explain his disappearance to the Commons, speaking of himself in the third person, like an odd prophet:

> A new parallel personality took over—separate and apart from the original man, who was resented and despised by the parallel personality for the ugly humbug and sham of the recent years of his public life. . . . The collapse and destruction of the original man came about because his idealism in his political life had been utterly frustrated and finally destroyed by the pattern of events beyond his control, which had finally overwhelmed him.[20]

Bernard Donoughue characterized it as "bizarre, but not mad, and crudely calculated. . . . The House looked embarrassed."[21] Spike's character looks quite embarrassed, too. Stonehouse was eventually sentenced to three years in prison for insurance fraud. His resignation diminished Labour's already slim majority, and would factor into PM Callaghan's struggles to maintain a functioning Lib-Lab pact necessary for a minority government.

. . . a hole . . . in which crouches a bearded mystic, in a meditative position—This bearded, unkempt[22] holy man with a cup and a bowl is likely inspired by an Essene hermit whom Josephus followed:

> Banus[23] . . . lived in the desert, and used no other clothing than grew upon trees, and had no other food than what grew of its own accord, and bathed himself in cold water frequently, both by night and by day, in order to preserve his chastity, I imitated him in those things, and continued with him three years.[24]

The Essenes were much more ascetic than either the Pharisees or Sadducees, and kept themselves apart (on the cliffs at Qumran, for instance), from the general Jewish population. There were deep disagreements between and even within these sects; the arguments we've just seen regarding sandals, shoes, and gourds are not outré in the least. Simon isn't mentioned specifically as an Essene, though he is in the wilderness, and has clearly renounced the things of the world. Simon doesn't seem to be waiting for the arrival of the promised Messiah, though, as the Essenes vowed.[25] He's likely related to the ascetic in Buñuel's *Simon of the Desert*, though that Simon is in the wilderness atop a pillar.[26]

His hirsuteness is reminiscent of St. Mary of Egypt, a hermitess who lived in the fourth century, and whom Gilliam sketched as he prepared for the animations on *Holy Grail*.[27] These eremites or anchorites seemed to have become more common later, from the third and fourth centuries, after St. Anthony of Egypt (c. 251–356). Gilliam had also sketched from Boschean versions of this hermitic saint as he prepared for the *Holy Grail* animations.[28]

SIMON: "Eighteen years of total silence . . ."—Ascetics could take all sorts of vows distancing themselves from the world, including a refrain from speaking, or bathing, or clothing, or relationships, or a refrain from taking in or putting on *anything* of Man's making (think of John the Baptist's diet of locusts and wild honey).[29] It's probably telling that his first words are oaths—"damn" and "blast it."

Now that his "fast" from speaking is over, he admits that he has wanted to "shout and sing and scream" his name out. The goal of the ascetic was often to put off the things of the world as well as the things of the self, so that a concentration on the godly could be achieved. Simon's is an odd situation, though. He isn't speaking to men, and his isn't praying (speaking) to God, so the point of his devotion (or accidie?) is a mystery, unless he is rejecting both the world and God. And since language and communication are key elements to being human, the refusal to speak (even to God) and, by removal to the wilderness, the refusal to be spoken to have denied his human identity. It's no surprise then that the first thing Simon wants to do is reaffirm his identity by screaming his own name. He also admits that he hasn't enjoyed this fast (he wants to "enjoy" himself now). The consequences of his vow-breaking become evident quickly: his sanctuary is violated, his berries are eaten, and he is carried off for execution as if he were a medieval witch.

The hermits that the Pythons offered in Ep. 8 of *Flying Circus* were far more chatty and convivial than Simon. Those hermits had left modern life to get away from it all, and ended up in a sort of hermit suburb where they could mingle with each other, gather berries and water, and chastise themselves. This silliness would be stopped by Chapman's "Colonel" character.[30]

SIMON: "'Hava Nagila'!"—This is a very modern song, composed when Britain administrated the Mandate of Palestine after World War I. Russian dancer Valery Panov and wife, who had petitioned to emigrate to Israel and subsequently suffered at the hands of Soviet authorities, were finally granted their freedom in 1974. Panov remembers passengers on their plane heading for Tel Aviv singing "Hava Nagila," a song he'd "heard on a thousand Radio Israel broadcasts."[31]

CROWD: "A blessing! A blessing!!"—The crowd have taken Brian's "Go away!" as the first words of his ministry to them. These would have attended Jesus's Sermon on the Mount, maybe followed some of the other minor prophets, listened to the various prophets preaching in the city, and even attended Brian's for-profit sermon, so they assume there's more preaching to follow. This same "A blessing!" moment happened in *Holy Grail*, as well, just after God appeared to the knights and called them to their quest.[32]

ARTHUR: "How shall we go away Master?"—A fair question, given that the Pharisees, Sadducees, Essenes and perhaps even the "Fourth Philosophy" sects might have differing answers. Moving away from the proscription of the Mosaic Law was a challenge for many.

Following Jesus's teachings, the easily observed (for most) Ten Commandments were in the process of giving way to just two charges: Love God and love your neighbor. Having to be taught how to "go away" fits right in with the more proscribed rabbinical Judaism of the post- and Second Temple period.

ELSIE: "Give us a sign"—Signs have been mentioned earlier, where Brian allegedly gave a sign without being asked (or meaning to). Jesus and his apostles warned about seeking signs,[33] but there's neither a warning nor punishment for the asking in *Brian*. Vermes notes that Jesus answers (in the Gospels) several different ways to those who ask him for signs, several negative (like Arthur's response in a moment), but some more positive, as well.[34]

ARTHUR: "There is no food on this high mountain"—What follows is a loaves-and-fishes moment, where Brian is said to have made the juniper bushes fruitful "by his word." In Cook and Moore's *Not Only . . . But Also* "Jesus" sketch, the loaves-and-fishes miracle is mentioned, when Jesus tells his landlady he has five-thousand lunch guests on the way, and she says she only has a little fish and bread. When Jesus returned with twelve baskets full, his landlady puts it down to his ability to carve delicately. Brian hasn't, of course, made anything fruitful, but the crowd sees all this as "a good sign, by any standard." This scene will simply follow the Pythons putting Brian through the "accidental messiah" wringer, with versions of Jesus's miracles and words peppered throughout.

Remembering John the Baptist's locusts and wild honey, these berries indicate that Simon, like John, has "a concern with purity," and eats "only wild, not processed food."[35] Earlier, the Jewish revolutionary Judas Maccabeus had also escaped into the wilderness, eating only "what grew wild."[36]

ELSIE: "The bushes have been made fruitful by his word"—More often than barren trees made fruitful, unfruitful trees were cursed, as in the fig tree mentioned in Mark and Matthew.[37] "Fruitful" only appears twice on the KJV New Testament, and only a handful of times in the Old Testament relative to actual vines and trees.

ARTHUR: "Do not tempt him, shallow ones. Is not the miracle of the juniper bushes enough?"—In Luke 4:12 Jesus tells Satan "Thou shalt not tempt the Lord thy God," while sign-seekers were treated similarly. Arthur is echoing Jesus from Matthew 12. When Jesus chastised the scribes and Pharisees for demanding a sign, Jesus not only said that no new sign would be provided, but that the sign given anciently to Jonas should be enough.[38]

ARTHUR: "They are a gift from God"—The wandering Children of Israel were granted manna, quail, water from a rock, bitter water made sweet, healing by a gaze at the brazen serpent—all gifts of God as they spent forty years in the wilderness. In the New Testament, the gifts from God include the more abstract (spiritual) grace and eternal life, for example, building on the newer teachings of Jesus and his apostles. These wouldn't be as interesting to this lot.

SIMON: "They're all I've bloody got to eat!"—John the Baptist survived (and even thrived) on the fruit of the desert, including that of the carob tree, as well as wild honey and locusts.[39] Early "desert prophets" like Elias drank from natural sources and were often fed by local people.[40] Banus ate only what the desert offered him, and was clothed from the things of nature, Josephus mentions. Later eremites like Mary of Egypt also ate what the desert provided, though many hermits relied on local people offering food as alms.

HARRY: "Lord! I am affected by a bald patch!"—Most of the healings ascribed to Jesus involved chronic afflictions, including leprosy-type diseases, withered limbs, hemorrhaging, deafness, blindness, and paralysis. Brian will be asked for more pedestrian miracles—curing a rich woman's headache so she can make it to a dinner party, and baldness. The blind man will claim to be cured, but he falls face first into the hole, anyway.

BLIND MAN: "I was blind and now I can see!"—The man immediately falls into the hermit's hole, since he cannot see. This scene is staged very much like the moment in *Jesus of Nazareth* where Christ heals the palsied man. Healed and called by Jesus to stand and walk home, the man gets up, healed arms outstretched, and walks around in front of the assembled crowd, rejoicing. The Pythons are careful not to even hint that Brian might actually be a healer, a Christ-like figure, or anything beyond a harried man keen for time alone with his beloved. It is the baying crowd following another savior for signs and self-serving miracles that seems to take the brunt of the film's ridicule.[41]

ALL: "A miracle! He is the Messiah!"—Brian is not called the Son of God here, of course, but he is confused with a messiah, or one who might deliver the Jews from their current oppressed state. The only mention of Brian as the potential savior is in the manger at the beginning, before the Wise Men realize their mistake. As Brandon points out, in the Markan Gospel Christ is very clearly recognized "as the Messiah of Israel, [and] is also accorded a far higher status, namely, that of the Son of God."[42] The Pythons likely skirted this potential land mine by pushing the fervor of the misguided crowd as opposed to any claims by Brian. In a moment he will tell them very clearly that he is not the messiah.

ALL: "Hurt my foot Lord!!"—Simon's complaints—that he speaks, that he only eats juniper berries, and that his foot has been trod upon by Brian—are interpreted as Brian's miracles and signs by the enthusiastic crowd. They seem to want whatever their Messiah sees fit to provide, including pain. In Gilliam's (and Palin's) film *Time Bandits*, Evil's minions will thank him profusely when he promises to turn them "inside-out over a very long period of time."

BRIAN: "I'm not the Messiah"—The proof may be in Brian's answer, actually. Jesus offered many "I am" utterances ("I am the way, the truth, and the life"), but spent less time saying what he was *not*. Brian's mother will also tell Judith that her son is "not the Messiah," rather a "very naughty boy." Brian is also smart in saying this aloud, since the Romans would deal harshly with messianic contenders both prior to and after Christ, seeing the possibility of sedition at every turn.[43]

ARTHUR: "I say you are Lord, and I should know. I've followed a few"—There was an eschatological outburst following the death of the oppressive Herod in 4 BC, and "the whole countryside erupted in spontaneous rebellion led by messianic pretenders in each of the principal districts, Galilee, Peraea, and Judea:[44] "Judas of Galilee, the founder of the Zealot movement, probably advanced Messianic claims, and it seems certain that Menahem, his son, did," Brandon writes. "It seems likely that the Theudas of Acts v. 36 . . . was a Messianic pretender . . . as was also the Egyptian (Jew) mentioned by Josephus . . . who, however, disappeared after the failure of his coup."[45] These pretenders would have included the later agitators like Menahem and Simon bar Giora, whose feats ended with the mass suicide at Masada.[46] Given these potentials, Reg would have had plenty of Messiahs to follow.

This "I say you are" argument is addressed in the author's earlier work in relation to the Pythons' and Shakespeare's willingness to use language as a tool for the making or remaking of characters, situations, and even alternate histories. Richard III was able to cast those he wanted to destroy (Clarence, Margaret, Hastings, the young princes, et al.) into "Others," remaking them either before or after their deaths, to suit his needs.[47] If "Richard *says* someone is a traitor, that person *becomes* a traitor, and can be dealt with accordingly. A married woman can become an available woman; a cousin can become a foe; rightful heirs can become seditious, and so on. Richard is perhaps the ultimate 'maker' in English literary history."[48] Naming and totemic words also carry a significant power in the Python world. Arthur Jackson becomes "Two Sheds," and that moniker becomes inescapable; "Ni" is somehow magical, and must be obeyed after its utterance; a police inspector becomes Sir Philip Sidney after being named as such, even though we know (or we think we know) he is Inspector Gaskell.[49] Here Brian can become a messiah to these people, he will play out that role for one night and morning, and then be arrested.

GIRL: "Only the true Messiah denies his divinity"—Jesus doesn't deny who he is, but he also doesn't go about trumpeting the fact, preferring to allow those around him to come to their understanding of him as they will. When Simon Peter answers Christ's own question about who his disciples think he is, his disciple say "You are the Christ, the Son of the living God." Rather than simply agree with him, Jesus tells him he is blessed because he learned it from "my Father in heaven."[50] It is an admission that is not a damning admission, since everyone within earshot could also say they had a father in heaven.

Brian denies he is the Messiah, but then will say that he is the Messiah, just to be left alone. This is the answer the crowd has been waiting for, however, and he *is* now their Messiah.

BRIAN: "Now fuck off!!!"—This of course doesn't insult the crowd, they simply seek a way to follow their new leader's perhaps rabbinical command. This juxtaposition of spirituality and harsh language isn't just the Pythons' conceit, of course. When it was announced that the Rev. Ian Paisley would be leading a march through Catholic sections of Derry, a *Sunday Times* correspondent recorded this reaction, likely from a Roman Catholic: "D'you think I'm goin' to let that f—n' Paisley walk through the f—n' streets of f—n' Derry to curse the f—n' Pope?"[51]

ARTHUR: "An unbeliever . . . Persecute! Kill the heretic!"—This bell, book, and candle condemnation is weakly protested by Brian, those protestations overcome by the appearance of comely Judith. And rather than Jewishness, the mob here is responding to the new messiah-type—"Christian" if they had decided to follow Christ (who is still somewhere just offscreen in the world of the film)—or "Brianian" as they try and follow Brian. The continuing disaster that was Northern Ireland prompted this assessment from a period journalist: "Despite all its protestations to the contrary, Christianity has always been a bloody religion, whether crusading against infidels, or persecuting Jews, or suppressing heresy with the rack and stake, or turning nation against nation or brother against brother. It has preached peace and made wars."[52] The mob of followers seems to bear this out as they bear Simon away to certain death.

This kind of public manifestation of condemnation had been witnessed very recently. Heartbreaking images and stories from China emerged as the Cultural Revolution went through its most violent period (1966–1968). "Unbelievers" ("counter-revolutionaries," using Mao's term) perhaps "harbouring bourgeois tendencies"[53] were arrested by the youth of the Red Guard, paraded through the streets wearing signs and dunce caps, tortured, and even killed. Fixing counter-revolutionary "revisionism" was the mob's main goal (like anyone who might not recognize Brian as Messiah, once the crowd has so anointed him). These "shock troops" in China's Cultural Revolution were

> the Red Guards, young people and students whose task, as they saw it, was to weed out all manifestations of creeping revisionism in Chinese society. This included bureaucracy, privilege, political cliques, excessive reliance on material incentives, failure to use local resources to deal with local problems, and many other phenomena which have a tendency to creep into sociality systems. . . . Elements among the Red Guards also committed severe excesses in the treatment of people they regarded as class enemies.[54]

Of course the Pythons didn't have to rely on current Chinese politics and society for examples of mob justice. These same kinds of summary judgments (and executions) were being made among contemporary revolutionary groups like the URA and the 2 June Movement, in Belfast and Derry, across the Middle East and Asia, stretching all the way back to Zealots and the *sicarii* of first century Judea. As this scene closes, the mob leader's language escalates. He first calls Simon an "unbeliever," then says he is guilty of heresy (likely an actionable charge) and must be persecuted, and from there it's an easy step to "kill"—his language has made Simon into a target:

> But this is an important part of revolutionary technique. Language must be redefined to support the revolutionary thesis, make real understanding impossible and thus leave no other form of communication but violence. Violence gives the illusion of doing something, not just talking. It forces the authorities to pay attention to people they have hitherto despised and rejected. Above all, violence baptises the revolutionary into the faith.[55]

Simon is then carried off "to his doom," the script says, just like the "It's a fair cop" witch in *Holy Grail*.

Notes

1. Matthew 12:39, 16:4.
2. Josephus, *AJ*, 5.9.4 (Whiston, 121).
3. Jeremias, *JTJ*, 372n65; cf. Deuteronomy 25:9–10.
4. Magness, *Stone and Dung*, 27 and 19.
5. *AJ*, 18.4.1 (Whiston, 380).
6. See also Brandon's *Jesus and the Zealots*, 80.
7. The ending of the Simon scene is very similar to the ending of the "She's a Witch" scene in *Holy Grail*, as will be discussed later.
8. "The Idolatry of the Dead Sea Scrolls," 265.
9. Larsen, *BAFHG*, 26, 54, 252–53, 304–5.
10. An influence from the Goons. In "The Secret Escritoire," the characters go to great lengths to differentiate between an escritoire and a writing desk: "And does it mean, all in all, a writing table with tiroirs? And pigeonholes? As distinct from a writing desk which has a sloping front?" (27 September 1955).
11. Magness, *Stone and Dung*, chapter 1.
12. Donoughue's many entries on these subjects are fascinating reading; see *DSD*.
13. Borowski, *Daily Life in Biblical Israel*, 78–79.
14. Magness, *Stone and Dung*, 22–25.
15. Richard, *WWAR*, 276–78.
16. See Calabro, "Gestures of Praise."
17. In *Brazil*, Sam won't get anywhere wearing the suit he's wearing, for some reason, and has to be given another, very similar suit. He then is recognized and effective.
18. Larsen, *MPFC: UC*, 1.305–6.
19. Palin, *Diaries 1973–1976*, 272–73.
20. Quoted in Sandbrook, *Seasons in the Sun*, 175–76.
21. *DSD*, 1.534–35. See "Speaker Halts Mr. Stonehouse Five Times in His Commons Statement," *Times*, 21 October 1975: 1.
22. In 1 Samuel 21:14, an unkempt beard is a sign of madness.
23. Some scholars have said Banus may have been a follower of John the Baptist.
24. *The Life of Flavius Josephus*, 2 (Whiston, 1).
25. Kotker, *HLTJ*, 46. See Norman Bentwich's discussion of Josephus and Banus in *Josephus*, 40–41, as well as the entry for Banus in the *JE*.
26. *BAFHG*, 486.

27. *BAFHG*, 514–15.

28. *BAFHG*, 205, 266, 525, and 528; *MPFC: UC*, 2.111.

29. *BAFHG*, 190, 220n11; "ascetics" in *MPFC: UC*; Magness, *Stone and Dung*, 39–40.

30. See the entries for the "Hermits" scene in *MPFC: UC*, 1.131–42; also *BAFHG*, 88.

31. "Last Exit from Leningrad," *Sunday Telegraph*, 19 March 1978: 8. The melody from this song would find its way into "You Won't Succeed on Broadway" from *Spamalot*.

32. *BAFHG*, 262.

33. See Mark 13:21 and Matthew 24:23, for example.

34. Vermes, *The Authentic Gospel of Jesus*, 182–83.

35. Magness, *Stone and Dung*, 39–40.

36. Magness, *Stone and Dung*, 40.

37. Mark 11:12–14 and 11:20–25; Matthew 21:18–22.

38. Matthew 12:39.

39. *HLTJ*, 49.

40. See the *Catholic Encyclopedia*.

41. This is the tack that Cleese, at the least, tried to take defending the film upon its release, including during the infamous interview with Palin, Muggeridge, and the Bishop of Southwark.

42. Brandon, *Jesus and the Zealots*, 7.

43. Brandon, *Jesus and the Zealots*, 7, and 110–15.

44. Horsley, "The Sicarii," 447.

45. Brandon, *Jesus and the Zealots*, 18n3.

46. Horsley, "The Sicarii," 455–56.

47. Larsen, *MPSERD*, 166–71.

48. *MPFC: UC*, 1.22, also, *MPSERD*, chapter 5.

49. *Flying Circus* Ep. 1; *Holy Grail*, "Knights Who Say Ni"; and *Flying Circus* Ep. 36, respectively.

50. Matthew 16:15–17.

51. From David Holden's "The Storming of Stormont," *Sunday Times*, 1 December 1968: 7.

52. George Gale, "A Land of Trouble," *Spectator*, 11 July 1970: 5.

53. Allessandro Casella, "Confessions of a Bourgeois," *Times*, 7 April 1971: 14.

54. "Cultural Revolution: Effects Linger On," *Times*, 21 March 1973: VIII.

55. "Angries and the Middle-Class 'Revolution'," *Spectator*, 18 July 1975: 18.

SCENE NINETEEN
"HE'S NOT THE MESSIAH" PANTO

Dawn over a large cut-out of Jerusalem. Usual dawn clichés. Cocks crowing . . . sound effects men working overtime—Drawing attention to the artifice, just as the Goons did. In the building of the *Holy Grail* Trojan Rabbit scene, all sorts of mechanical and carpentry sounds accompanied the event.[1] Here the crowing cock sounds like one produced by Jones, or rather Mandy, and it's possible she is trying to wake Brian this way.

(draft) BRIAN wakes. He sees a pretty lady asleep next to him. It is CHERYL—In the longer draft Brian has come home with "disciples" Cheryl and Karen, who will appear from under the covers in a moment, and he will hide them in a cupboard. These more amorous followers can be connected back to a number of sources, and from quite different eras. In Nikos Kazantzakis's controversial 1955 novel *The Last Temptation of Christ*, Christ dreams (while on the cross) of marrying more than one woman (Mary, then Martha and Mary) and living a long and happy life, even welcoming grandchildren. When he awakes he is still on the cross, and he then surrenders his life to God. These girls in Brian's bed had been present at a boozy (and elided) "Last Supper" scene. Brian's mother interrupts this morning-after bliss, demanding to know why these girls—who can't be disciples since "they haven't got a stitch on"—are in her home, and why there's a mob outside. The international terrorist Carlos had his own female disciples, and they were of great use to him in his work: "He had long since been taught by his instructors in subversion to 'surround yourself with pretty young girls.' It was a counsel he followed with much pleasure and assiduity. The women he seduced were mostly innocent ones, not at all involved in terrorism," write Dobson and Payne. "But he intended to use them to provide him with cover.[2] Brian's schemes aren't nearly so homely or nefarious, of course; he wants the girls (in the rough draft) and Judith (in the finished film) for more libidinal purposes. He isn't much of a terrorist (though he did try and help kidnap Pilate's wife), nor much of a revolutionary, short of painting clumsy Latin on a palace wall, but he is trying to have it all, it seems—mixing illegal work and ill-famed play with a particular maternal devotion. Dobson and Payne write again of Carlos, in about 1973:

> He flitted in and out of [England] and nobody imagined for one moment that he was a terrorist. When he was in London he lived the good life, dancing the night away, smoking cigars and eating richly until he grew even more sensitive about being El Gordo. . . . Somebody who knew him then says: "He had a ball here, always out with the birds. But his mother was always in the background. He adored her and never went against her wishes." Little did his mother know what the darker side of his life involved.[3]

When the womanizing and drinking and excessive eating in the earlier upstairs "Last Supper" scene are considered—the same scene where Brian flirted with and won both Karen and Cheryl—this revolutionary seems ready to embrace the sweet, naughty terrorist/messiah lifestyle, as long as he can keep it a secret from his mother, Mandy. Perhaps to ease the tint of debauchery on this shadow Messiah, the Pythons decided to remove the entire Last Supper they'd considered, as well as the "birds."

. . . naked sleeping form of Judith . . . apparently rude behavior has occurred during the night—In the American New Wave film *Bonnie and Clyde*, Clyde Barrow resists a physical relationship with Bonnie Parker, he says because he sees in her more than her sexuality. It also seems that he's uncomfortable with or just uncertain about his own sexuality. The moment that they do progress to a sexual union is a crucial plot pivot, the beginning of the end, dramatically; from there it's an inexorable chase to their bullet-ridden deaths. Following this formula, Brian wakes to a glorious "morning after," and after wading through the mass of adherents and the wretched, he escapes his house, is congratulated by Judith (though as a leader, not a lover), and is then arrested, leading inexorably to execution.

As mentioned earlier, the notorious Danish film project *The Sex Life of Jesus Christ* excited much talk in Britain in 1975–1976, eventually leading to the director being banned from entering the country. Newspapers published many letters to the editor condemning the proposed work and its creator, and many stories ran predicting the decline of British civilization should the film be shot or screened. *Private Eye* got in on the fun, as well, with the fictitious Rev. J. C. Flannel writing in his column "Wayside Pulpit":

> From what we have heard it does seem that there may well be real grounds for disquiet about some of the scenes that are to be shot. And yet, is there not another side to the coin? I think there probably might well be. Today more than ever surely Christians have a duty to explore every avenue of our beliefs. Mr Thoresen, it may well transpire, could discover for us some hitherto overlooked corner of the Faith. For even in the most unlikely places we may find a message of Hope. And now Hymn 95[4] in the Soho Hymns for Today, "Strip off, strip off for Jesus."[5]

It's fortunate that the amorous Brian and Judith belong to the Peoples' Front of Judea and not a group like the extremist faction of the Japanese Red Army, known as the Rengo Sekigun. In that group, disagreements about political motivations and, more pointedly, sexual activity between cadre members led to a grisly, weeks-long internal purge, a lengthy standoff and gun battle with police, and a salacious trial that fascinated and horrified the Japanese people in 1973.[6] Members of this same revolutionary group had been intent on overthrowing the Japanese government and the monarchy, and had successfully hijacked a plane for political asylum in North Korea.

Similarly, when the members of the nascent Baader-Meinhof gang went to Jordan to train with the PLO (Fatah), they quickly ran into trouble, according to one B-M member, Horst Mahler:

> There were disagreements with the PLO. These got more heated when Baader and Ensslin made a demand. They said, "We are a fighting group. We do everything together, and we should be able to sleep together." But for our hosts it was inconceivable, that men and women in a military camp would sleep together. The result was that the PLO said: "Give us back the weapons. We will make sure you get back to Berlin safely, but we don't want anything more to do with you."[7]

The co-leaders of the RAF, Baader and Ensslin, were a well-known romantic couple, and both committed suicide rather than await the results of their criminal trials.[8]

The trope of good bedfellows making for good politics could also be found in the worka-day world of twentieth-century British politics. Even as the British postwar socialist paradise that would be the New Jerusalem was being formulated in the 1950s, it wasn't all wealth redistribution, nationalization, and parliamentary heavy-lifting—the "private freedom" that Brian enjoys with Judith was one of the hallmarks of Anthony Crosland's "revisionist" version of the future, according to journalist Peter Jenkins:

> With his seminal work [*The Future of Socialism*] published in 1956 he liberated socialists not only from the encumbrances of the Marxist tradition but also from the earnest worthiness of Sidney and Beatrice Webb,[9] who had spent their honeymoon collecting information about trade unions in Dublin with no time to visit a theatre or gallery. A famous passage towards the end of *The Future of Socialism* was headed, "Liberty and Gaiety in Private Life; the Need for a Reaction against the Fabian Tradition," and it ended with the words: "Total abstinence and a good filing-system are not now the right sign-posts to the socialist Utopia; or at least if they are, some of us will fall by the wayside."[10]

Crosland preceded this paragraph with a complaint that the full weight of "society's deci-sions" had become onerous, impinging "heavily on people's private lives as well as on their social or economic welfare . . . in too restrictive and puritanical a manner."[11] Earlier, Brian had complained (in the script draft) that Judith needed to liberate herself—meaning have sex with him—when she's totally focused on larger issues like freeing Judea from the Romans and the fact that Jewish law forbids women to go to stonings. Brian manages to eventually help Judith "liberate" herself (and in the script draft he also liberates Cheryl *and* Karen), and immediately follows that act with a kind of sermon to his followers, successfully aligning his "social commitment and private freedom," like a good Crosland socialist.[12]

He throws open the shutters . . . [a] vast crowd thronging the courtyard outside his bedroom window . . ."—This is yet another moment found in the foundational *I'm All Right Jack*. After Stan has gone back to work and Mr. Kite has thrown him out of his house, Stan has to move in with his aristocratic Aunt Dolly (Margaret Rutherford). Bouquets, fruit baskets, and fan mail have piled into Dolly's sitting room as a result of Stan's assumed union-busting behavior, and outside, a chanting, singing crowd can be heard:

Aunt Dolly: Just listen to all that cheer.

STANLEY continues opening letters.

Stan: How long have they been there, Aunt Dolly?

Aunt Dolly: Hours! What a nation we British are, once we are stirred.

Dolly then pulls back the curtains to reveal a sea of singing supporters carrying placards, all in support of Stan and against the strikers and the excesses of organized labor. The gathered are singing "Land of Hope and Glory," and one enthusiastic woman, seeing the open curtain, shouts: "Three cheers for Mr. Churchill! And for Stanley Windrush! Hip-hip-hooray!" Nearby a line of girls wearing "Luv Elvis" shirts—with Elvis scratched through and "Stan" penned instead—chant "We want Stanley!" Just one scene later Stanley will be encouraged by Aunt Dolly to make an appearance outside so his supporters can have a good look at him. It contin-ues to be clear that, perhaps unconsciously, the Pythons owed a great debt to this popular film.

He is quite naked—Palin comments in his *Diaries* that director Jones wanted this scene, and was adamant—an "unshakeable commitment to full-frontals"—that both Judith and

Brian be seen fully naked. Producer John Goldstone and Cleese were reportedly much less impressed by the blatant exhibitionism—Goldstone worrying about an eventual ratings restriction (meaning a reduced audience)—and spent time on the set trying to talk Jones out of it.[13]

A period version of this elevated full frontal moment exists, of course. During Passover in about 48, Josephus reports, a certain rudeness (that would have fit nicely into either of the French soldier sequences in *Holy Grail*) caused a bloody uproar:

> But on the fourth day of the feast, a certain soldier let down his breeches, and exposed his privy members to the multitude, which put those that saw him into a furious rage, and made them cry out that this impious action was not done to reproach them, but God himself; nay, some of them reproached Cumanus,[14] and pretended that the soldier was set on by him, which, when Cumanus heard, he was also himself not a little provoked at such reproaches laid upon him; yet did he exhort them to leave off such seditious attempts, and not to raise a tumult at the festival.[15]

They raised a tumult anyway, and as the angry and frightened pilgrims ran from the garrison's approaching soldiers, as many as 20,000 were killed in the stampede. In Brian's case, his assembled followers don't even seem to notice the "last turkey in the shop" image.

MANDY: "'Popped by?'... There's a multitude out there!"—Mandy is correcting Brian, and using the more proper biblical term that appears almost eighty times in the Synoptic Gospels alone. "Multitude" is a term borrowed from the encounters Jesus had with his followers, and is a big part of the reason that those angry with him in the Jewish community were reticent to have him arrested and charged. "Swarm" is solely an OT term, and is generally associated with plagues and devastation.

CROWD: "The chosen one . . ."—*Not* an appellation used in the Gospels in reference to Jesus, the Children of Israel are the "chosen ones" (1 Chronicles 16:13), and later Ananias tells Saul that he has been chosen by "Just One," Jesus Christ, to do God's work (Acts 22:14). The phrase appears in fantasy and science fiction literature to refer to the (often unwilling) central character who must undertake his dangerous, world-saving quest. Bilbo was "chosen" by the God-like Gandalf for the adventure in *The Hobbit* (1937), while Frodo was also chosen as ring-bearer in *Fellowship of the Rings* (1954), for example. Frank Herbert's "kwisatz haderach" character Paul Muad'Dib was later born to the role in *Dune* (1965).[16]

. . . *JUDITH appears from BRIAN's bed stark naked* . . .—This image of titillation amid a politically and religiously charged event wouldn't have been unusual for the period, actually. Rupert Murdoch's newspaper *The Sun* had offered nude Page Three Girls since 1969; the West German Leftist magazine *Konkret*, for which Ulrike Meinhof wrote, also featured nude and semi-nude cover photos of both men and women (mostly women); and politically charged magazines like *Private Eye* featured nudity in cartoons and occasional photos.

The image of a revered man of faith caught *in flagrante delicto* was a bit more unusual, but might be borrowed from a very recent scandal involving the Bishop of Preveza, Stylianos. A grainy photo appearing on the covers of a number of newspapers in September 1978[17] purported to show the bishop in bed with the wife of a junior priest (Greek bishops are "eternally celibate" and may not marry[18]). Stylianos denied the accusation, calling the photo "forgery, blackmail, a communist plot to undermine my position." His Judas, according to the indignant bishop, was his former chauffeur, who harbored a grudge against the holy man, and who was seeking blackmail payment.[19] The photo and accompanying leaflets calling for the bishop's ouster were being circulated by a group calling itself, appropriately for our purposes, the "Preveza Christian Fighters." In the Pythonesque version of this scandal, of course, the followers of Brian don't seem to mind his nakedness or his association with women. Stylianos was charged by the church with "scandalizing the conscience of the Christian faithful"; Brian seems to have simply increased his stature among his faithful.[20]

MANDY: ". . . He's not the Messiah, he's a very naughty boy"—Mandy is also able to use her naming power to keep Brian's feet on the ground, though it won't save him from the cross. Idle will take this as the title of an oratorio version, *Not the Messiah (He's a Very Naughty Boy)* in 2009.

CROWD: "Behold his Mother!"—A version of Jesus's cry from the cross, "Behold thy mother!" as recorded in John 19:26. There isn't a significant Mary tradition in Jewish culture, but in Orthodox, Roman Catholic, Protestant, and even Islamic cultures, there is. In the Roman Catholic tradition, Mary took an elevated position, so it's no surprise that this crowd is perhaps renouncing whatever Jewishness it may have had in favor of what they think Brian can offer, a new version of Christianity (Brianity?). If that's the case, then Mother Mandy must be venerated, too.

CROWD: "Well . . . all right"—The crowd is doing this in one voice, of course—a hint of the pantomime to come—which Josephus mentions as a common practice of the Roman armies, as well:

> Then do the trumpets give a sound the third time, that they are to go out, in order to excite those that on any account are a little tardy, that so no one may be out of his rank when the army marches. Then does the crier stand at the general's right hand, and asks them thrice, in their own tongue, whether they be now ready to go out to war or not? To which they reply as often, with a loud and cheerful voice, saying, "We are ready." And this they do almost before the question is asked them: they do this as filled with a kind of martial fury, and at the same time that they so cry out, they lift up their right hands also.[21]

In *Flying Circus* the Pythons present beloved pantomime characters like Long John Silver, Puss, the Principal Boy, Dobbin, and even their own Pantomime Goose and Princess Margaret. In Ep. 4 the audience hisses at the evil dentist, a pantomime response. Episode 28 will devolve into a pantomime.

MANDY: "Leave that Welsh tart alone"—Like Jones, actress Sue Jones-Davies was born in Wales. A singer and performer, Jones-Davies would go on to become the mayor of Aberystwyth, Wales. In *Holy Grail*, Dennis has already complained about a "watery tart" handing out magic swords.[22]

(draft) A couple of ROMANS can be seen at the back of the crowd—In the early draft Judith[23] and Reg are actually down among the crowd, "working" to keep the emotions high, and the Romans are keeping a wary eye on the goings-on. These watching Roman soldiers are likely a nod to those that Pilate inserted into crowds around him as he addressed Jews' concerns about blasphemous images in the governor's palace, and as he answered angry cries as a result of plundering temple funds for a public works project.[24]

(draft) **WOMAN IN CROWD: "Is it right that we should pay taxes to the Romans?"**—This scene at the window, in an earlier draft, becomes more like a political news conference, with a PM answering questions from the press. Earlier drafts of the script featured tax questions, which were incredibly significant to the provincial Roman citizen, to Jew and Gentile (and to historians over the centuries), but those elements were worked out of the script prior to completion of the film.[25] The subject would have been important to Reg: "This [tax] issue . . . was the basic test of Jewish patriotism: for payment of this tribute was tantamount to denying Yahweh's absolute sovereignty over Israel—it was the issue on which the Zealots,

the nationalist action party, were prepared to die."[26] Reg had hissed that the hated Romans had "bled us white," likely a reference to the taxation demanded not for the sustenance of the Roman cult (which the Jews could have reasonably revolted against), but to keep the empire running, to pay for the garrisoning of troops in places like Caesarea and Jerusalem, who would maintain Roman law and order.[27]

Brian's answer in this draft is drawn right from the pressers of the Heath, Wilson, and Callaghan administrations of the 1970s—mealy-mouthed and obtuse: "It is one that each and every one must face . . . individually . . . at this point in time. But . . . I think we must be wary of quick and easy solutions."[28] Heath's leadership speech at the 1973 Conservative Party Conference offers these familiar lines as he discusses the problems in Northern Ireland: "We still have a long way to go. There is no easy and quick solution. There is going to be no speedy end."[29] New PM and Labour leader Callaghan's speech at the party conference at Blackpool, 1976, included the following:

> We live in too troubled a world to be able to promise that in a matter of months, or even in a couple of years, that we shall enter the promised land. The route is long and hard. But the long march has at last begun, and I hope to lead you at least some part of the way, with the Social Contract and our industrial strategy as our guide.[30]

In this earlier draft, Brian would take additional questions, becoming more politic and glib in his answers. Mandy is also a part of this sequence, letting followers in who have brought gifts, as if she's the gatekeeper to power (like a Marcia Williams) at Brian's No. 10.

BRIAN: "You've got it all wrong. You don't need to follow me. You don't need to follow anybody! You've got to think for yourselves. You're all individuals!"—This is where a thaumaturgic preacher became a foe of Rome *and* the Jews. Pilate, Herod Antipas, and the hardline Sadducees were for the most part content to allow even millennial preachers and miracle workers to operate in Judea and Galilee, so long as they never crossed the Rubicon from holy man to political man. Once Jesus was perceived, rightly or wrongly, as a potential *political* leader for tens of thousands of unhappy Jews, his fate was sealed.[31]

The other street preachers seen earlier in the film had been calling to repentance and predicting destruction—John the Baptist-like—and admonishing Jerusalemites to behave better. Such a population would be ideal Roman subjects. (Those that are listening seem disconnected from any political thought; they are pulled along by intermittent and ultimately harmless evangelistic currents.) Brian is even safe telling his multitude to not follow him, that still leaves room for obeisance to Rome or the Sanhedrin—he steps in it when he tells them to think for themselves. This puts him at odds with the Jewish elders and the Romans.[32]

This softer, almost guileless depiction is closer to the Jesus as seen in *Godspell*, the Broadway hit that reached the West End in November 1971. Critic Harold Hobson described playwright Michael Tebelak's Jesus, and his unusual look:

> Some people may, at least initially, be surprised to find Christ represented by a clown, with red paint on his nose . . . but if I had to choose a single one to show to a visitor it would be this Christ, this simple, wondering Christ played by David Essex. The shining thing about Mr Essex's performance is its manifest, stirring incapacity to perceive evil, or to recognise mockery. It inhabits a world in which there is no guile and no cruelty. But it is not a simplicity to be made a fool of: its meekness is as strong as it is true.[33]

BRIAN: "You've all got to work it out for yourselves!"—This sentiment alone might have pricked contemporary Christians like Mary Whitehouse, and groups including Festival of Light.[34] Brian is claiming that there is no need for a savior, a god, or organized religion, essentially, which may be the most visible evidence of the Pythons' credo, and their reason for making the film.

This also sounds remarkably similar to what one celebrated contributor to China's Democracy Wall posted in early December 1978,[35] a secular humanist plea for self-realization from former Red Guard Wei Jingsheng:

> We want to be masters of our own destiny. We need no gods or emperors. We do not believe in the existence of any savior. We want to be masters of the world and not instruments used by autocrats to carry out their wild ambitions. We want a modern lifestyle and democracy for the people. Freedom and happiness are our sole objectives in accomplishing modernization.[36]

The restrictive demands of political, religious, and moralist institutions across the years likely accounts for this call for freedom, a sort of collective "leave me alone" from the overwhelmed individual. Paramount leader Deng responded to Wei's call for change by having him arrested; the Democracy Wall was cleared and declared off limits in late March 1979, six months before *Life of Brian* premiered in the United States.

CROWD: "Oh no it wasn't!"—This same pantomimic exchange goes on in Ep. 28 of *Flying Circus*, when the Principal Boy breaks into a Venezuelan police station scene:

Principal Boy (Julia Breck): Hello, children!

Police Chief (Cleese): Stop! Stop this adaptation of "Puss-in-Boots"! This is the Police Department of the State of Venezuela!

Principal Boy: Oh no it isn't!

Police Chief: Oh, yes it is!

Principal Boy (*children joining in voice over*): Oh no it isn't!

All (*plus children*): Oh yes it is!

Principal Boy (*plus children*): Oh no it isn't . . .

Police Chief: Shut up! Shut up![37]

Cleese ends the scene here much the same way Reg ends many of his scenes—flustered. Mandy shuts down the panto digression very quickly, as well. In *Holy Grail*, it was an animator heart attack that stopped a fatal monster attack, and in *Meaning of Life* it will be a large building that crushes the marauding Crimson Permanent Assurance as it tries to hijack the narrative.

YOUNG MAN *(to Mandy)*: **"Are you a virgin?"**—This might be a silly, Pythonesque question, given that the mob knows this is Brian's biological mother they're addressing, meaning she's both conceived and given birth. Immaculate conception aside, Ackerman reminds us that this wouldn't be an out-of-place question (or at least consideration) given "how highly prized virgin brides were in biblical Israel."[38] Mandy is also aligned with at least some of the single, unmarried women who have had a child during this time, and seems to support herself, as Ackerman describes:

> It is not surprising, then, that only servant women, who are provided for out of the resources of their masters' and mistresses' homes; prostitutes, who assumed responsibility for their own financial well-being; and a king's daughter like Tamar, who presumably could draw on the

resources of the royal palace, are identified in the Hebrew Bible as being able to live independent of a husband.[39]

Mandy doesn't appear to be a servant working in someone's household, and she isn't a king's daughter, certainly. That only leaves the possibility of prostitute, which has been hinted at earlier in the scene with a visiting centurion in Mandy and Brian's home.

This is also a fair question for the biblical time period, especially if the questioner has read (or heard read aloud) Isaiah,[40] where a reference to a virgin with child is found, and later used by Matthew (1:23). The virgin birth is a sign given by the "Lord himself," so any potential Jesus-like messiah should come from such a conception. Mandy's indignant response confirms her *virgo intacta* status, at least to the mob. (She's already admitted to having a semi-enjoyed fling with a Roman soldier, so the bloom is clearly off the rose.) In 1975, however, the question of virginal status was put to "Jesus" himself, and money was the reason. As the multimillion dollar *Jesus of Nazareth* was in production, the "smouldering" star who had been hired to play the leading role found himself in a bit of a tricky situation, not unlike what Brian experienced moments earlier with the full frontal reveal before his mother. *Private Eye's* "Grovel" rehearses the story in mid-April 1977, when *Jesus of Nazareth* has been safely premiered:

> Lord Grade[41] has some happy news. Robert Powell, who portrays Jesus of Nazareth in the £10 million epic of that name, and his good wife Barbara are expecting their first child. A happy ending to a dangerous moment in the production of the film, two years ago, when newshounds found that Bob and Babs were cohabiting in an extramarital state. The thought of the Americans finding out that "Jesus" was living in sin made ATV apoplectic, with several hundred million dollars invested in the film. Bob obligingly got hitched.[42]

It is likely that both American and British audiences would have reacted negatively to such news, given the eventual reaction to *The Sex Life of Jesus Christ, The Love That Dares to Speak Its Name,* and even, to a lesser degree, *Life of Brian.*

In a ranging profile written by Caroline Moorhead and published in October 1977, Mary Whitehouse espoused her views on premarital sex and the importance of virginity: "'There is something very wonderful about keeping oneself a virgin, making one's virginity a gift to the man one loves.' The notion of restraint, self-denial, the antithesis of what she calls the 'I want it, and I want it now' mood of the Sixties is important to her."[43] And rather than being offended by the topic, Moorhead notes that Whitehouse freely discusses her sexual choices with interviewers, being "not averse to descending to more mundane levels."[44] Mandy isn't so free with her privacy. This same year romance novelist Barbara Cartland wrote a guest column in the *Times*, "Why Virginity Is Becoming Fashionable Once More."[45] Cartland had been selling millions of copies of her novels around the world, and was certain she could account for their increasing popularity: "Why? Because all my heroines are virgins." Her description of the ideal modern heroine sounds quite Mary-like, actually: "It is the idealized woman which every man puts in a secret shrine and worships as his wife, as the mother of his children, as his guide and inspiration." Waugh comments on Cartland's revelations, too, in both *The Spectator* and in a column in *Private Eye*.[46] In the latter he celebrates the fifty-year anniversary of the loss of Cartland's own virginity, and notes that a "small commemorative party" is in the offing.

Lastly, the tabloids were full of whispers about the country's most eligible bachelor, Prince Charles, and concerns about the potential match's vestal status floated just beneath the words in every column inch. Charles's quest for an acceptable spouse began when he was still at Trinity

College, Cambridge, in 1968, and wouldn't end until he'd decided on Diana Spencer in 1980. Not-so-coincidentally, these are the same years the Pythons could call their own, with *Flying Circus* airing in 1969 through *Life of Brian* in 1979–1980. (Historian and academic Richard Vinen also sites Margaret Thatcher's ascendancy and triumph during this precise thirteen-year epoch, 1968–1980, from a member of the Shadow Cabinet through her first year as Britain's first female prime minister.[47]) Charles was photographed with princesses and aristocrats, British debs and foreign beauties—more than twenty "serious" relationships in all, according to Wilson's count. In November 1977 *Private Eye*'s "Grovel" mentioned three he saw as potential mates, all married but all suitably unsuited to their current husbands (in his opinion), including Camilla Parker-Bowles.[48] Charles's eventual wife, Diana, would be generally accepted as virginal prior to their marriage, which became one of the biggest stories of 1980.

REVOLUTIONARIES are everywhere, carrying in a table, controlling queues . . .—This is the *Parousia* of Brian, his appearance before adamant followers, sycophants, and those seeking sundry cures and blessings. This scene became the portmanteau scene for the several that had followed it in earlier drafts. In later (elided) scenes Brian was being prodded about healing a rich man's wife, promoting food and business ventures, appearing like a combination of Robert Powell and Andy Williams at the fee-paying Sermon on the Mount, and where we are introduced to Otto and his suicide squad (Otto a Jewish Nazi seeking a Jewish homeland free from "riff-raff," gypsies, and Romans[49]). This final bit would have likely tipped the scales of at least good taste for the Jewish and Israeli communities. Including these scenes would have put off Brian's arrest for a further twenty screen minutes, at least, which is likely why they were removed.

FRANCIS: **"Now don't jostle the chosen one, please"**—There were many who believed that if they simply touched Jesus or his clothing they would be healed. In Luke 8:43–48, Jesus is surrounded by a crowd and is likely being jostled quite a bit, but when the woman who has bled for years touches his garment he knows "that power has gone out from" him. Peter even tries to tell Jesus that many were "pressing in on" him, essentially saying "pay no mind." The woman admits her touch, and Jesus blesses her and sends her on her way.

(draft) MAN: **"Will he endorse fish?"**—This was a significant theme in the later missing scenes, where Brian was being asked to endorse "Airway Fish" and buy an olive press, then lease it back to the people, as if Reginald Maudling or Marcia Williams were making Brian's deals. On the Pythons' albums, ministers sing commercial jingles on radio, while the bishops of Leicester and Bath and Wells hawk lager and frozen peas, respectively.[50]

Former PM Wilson had been famously wearing and even shilling for Gannex raincoats,[51] the maker of which, Joe Kagan, would later find his way onto the so-called "Lavender" honours list as a life peer after HW resigned.[52] Lord Kagan would be arrested for stealing from his own company, found guilty in 1980, and would spend time in prison. Tory MP Maudling had been a consistent target of the Pythons, and his shady business dealings had been in the news since the late 1960s.[53]

"REG: *(pushing mother and baby away)* **"Don't push that baby in the Savior's face"**—In Mark 10:14, Jesus is answering his disciple's questions regarding the laws of divorce when young children were brought to him "that he should touch them." His disciples rebuked the parents, likely, and were in turn rebuked by Jesus—these children were like "the kingdom of God." There is a similar scene in the 1976 film *The Passover Plot*, where scores of moaning, screaming sick run after Jesus, swamping the disciples.

GREGORY: *(from across the room)* **"Could he just see my wife? She has a headache"**—In the elided restaurant scenes this man lowers his ill wife through the roof so that Brian can cure her, a borrow from Luke 5:17–19.

REG: "The lepers are queuing"—The lepers and the "women taken in sin" are asked to queue up for Brian's ministrations, but he pushes on past all of them to be alone, outside. There had been ten lepers (mentioned earlier) who came to Jesus to be cured, and they likely queued up for Christ's ministrations.

Queuing has become something of a British institution—"a great British tradition" and "a sensible British invention"[54]—especially during and after World War II, when lines formed regularly for everything from fish to fabric to birdseed. Later, the NHS endured jibes and complaints for the dreaded patient queues, especially those needing surgeries. In August 1967, more than half a million Britons were waiting for even minor procedures, and many for major surgeries, the shorter waits being six months, and some more than two years.[55] In the Middle East region of the 1960s and 1970s, queues were a regular sight, populated by Arabs wanting to work in Israel-held lands. In *Flying Circus* Ep. 14, we are presented with a long, winding queue of brown-coated gas men waiting to help Mrs. Pinnet (Jones) with her new cooker, the line extending well into the cartoon section that follows.[56] The ever-present dole queue, finally, was a running joke in newspaper comic panels and opinion pieces, becoming especially prevalent during the 1970s.

REG: "Brian, can I introduce the gentleman who's letting us have the mount on Sunday?"—George Harrison, who financed the film (along with Denis O'Brien), makes a quick appearance here. In the missing additional Sermon on the Mount scene, it's likely this same "Mr. Papadopolis" who is allowing access, and whose man, Hosea, asks everyone to be more mindful of the donkeys' droppings. In this instance his name is spelled "Papadopoulos," for some reason. There were many open-air music festivals during this period—famously Woodstock and, infamously, Altamont, but also many in Hyde Park, for example—which the excised Brian performance very much resembles.

REG: "Those possessed by devils, try to keep them under control . . ."—Many of the physical complaints during this period were taken to be demonic possessions as opposed to medical illnesses, and were treated as such. Bringing the afflicted to a spiritual healer as opposed to a "doctor" makes sense, then. See the discussion earlier in the "Ex-leper" scene.

REG: "Incurables, I'm afraid you'll just have to wait for a few minutes"—This is one of the few rim shot jokes in the film, not unlike Reg's earlier "struggle against reality" jibe aimed at Stan/Loretta.

REG: "Women taken in sin line up against that wall, will ya?"—This might also be another crude reference to the acts of prostitution that often took place in narrow, "Gropecunt-like" alleys, where business was accomplished against the alley wall. These were mentioned earlier when Reg calls Brian a klutz.

Notes

1. Larsen, *BAFHG*, 286, 291.
2. Dobson and Payne, *Carlos Complex*, 39.
3. Dobson and Payne, *Carlos Complex*, 43.
4. Hymn 95 in the 1965 version of the Anglican Hymn Book is "Away in the Manger."
5. *Private Eye*, 17 September 1976: 9.
6. "Red Army Five Block Tokyo Trial," *Times*, 12 February 1873: 6.
7. *Baader-Meinhof: In Love with Terror*, a.t.
8. Ulrike Meinhof also hung herself in her cell in 1976.
9. The Webbs' work with the Fabian socialists led to a reworking of the Poor Law in 1909, and would become the foundation for the Welfare State after World War II.

10. Jenkins, *Mrs. Thatcher's Revolution*, 6. Crosland's *Future of Socialism* would provide a giddy, forward-looking wish list of the good things that properly revised socialism should cultivate. It reads like what the Romans brought to the ungrateful PFJ, with such improvements as

> more open-air cafes, brighter and gayer streets at night, later closing hours for public houses, more local reper-tory theatres . . . more hospitable hoteliers and restaurateurs, brighter and cleaner eating houses, more riverside cafes, more pleasure gardens . . . more murals and pictures in public places, better designs for furniture and pottery and women's clothes, statues in the centre of new housing estates, better-designed new street lamps and telephone kiosks and so on. (521–22)

This seems to be Crosland's preemptive strike at the Tories' cries over the next two decades—"What have the socialists ever done for us?"

11. Crosland, *The Future of Socialism*, 521.

12. This exchange between Brian and Judith occurs in the draft version of the script, and is found just before the stone salesman accosts them. In the finished film, Brian and his mother are walking to the stoning, Brian's just glimpsed Judith from a distance, and she won't be seen again until the Colosseum scene. Quote from Jenkins, *Mrs. Thatcher's Revolution*, 6.

13. Palin, *Diaries 1969–1979*, 493.

14. The Roman curator of Judea, c. 48–52. See also Smallwood, *JURR*, 263–64.

15. Josephus, *AJ*, 20.5.3 (Whiston, 419).

16. Herbert would say that his characters and story illustrate the dangers of surrendering to a char-ismatic leader, and that thinking for one's self was always the best option; just what Brian and Cleese would say. See Clareson's *Understanding Contemporary Science Fiction*, 169–72.

17. The news of this sensation broke the day before Palin flew off to Tunisia for shooting.

18. "Photos Found to Be Genuine: Sex Scandal Involving Bishop Shakes Church," *Sarasota Herald-Tribune* 5 September 1978: 5A.

19. "Unfrock Bishop, Say Priests," *Daily Telegraph*, 9 September 1978: 3.

20. This lurid incident played out in the press for many months—the *Daily Mail* headlines screamed "'Rasputin' of Greece Charged with Debauchery" and "The Bishop and Three Nudes"—and eventually became a popular play that would be banned, its performers and director arrested. See Nikos Kokosala-kis's "The Political Significance of Popular Religion in Greece," 43.

21. Josephus, *WJ* 3.5.4 (Whiston, 505).

22. *BAFHG*, 144–45.

23. By the final draft and shooting, "disciples" Karen and Cheryl have disappeared, and Judith has taken their place in Brian's bed.

24. See the entries for "enormous statue of Pilate" and "The Aqueduct?" above for more on these situations, one of which ended peacefully, the other in significant bloodshed and lingering animosity toward Pilate.

25. Matthew 22:15–22.

26. Brandon, *Jesus and the Zealots*, 8

27. See the entry above for "They've bled us white . . ." in "The PFJ Plan Their Raid" scene.

28. On *Monty Python's Previous Record*, Idle offers a "Teach Yourself Heath" guide for record buyers, where Heath tells the listener that "there are no quick and easy answers" (drawn from the 1971 Leader's Speech in Brighton).

29. "Leader's Speech, Blackpool 1973." http://www.britishpoliticalspeech.org/speech-archive .htm?speech=120. In fact, Heath uses the "quick and easy" phrase many times in his political speeches.

30. See http://www.britishpoliticalspeech.org/speech-archive.htm?speech=174. Labour's belief in the workability of the Social Contract would figure in Thatcher's ascension three years later.

31. See Kotker, *HLTJ*; also Maier, *Pontius Pilate*, 1968.

32. Well, it *would* have had religious consequences if the Pythons had decided to include in the world of the film the Pharisees, Sadducees, and Sanhedrin—and Jewishness in general—in anything more than a cursory way. It's possible the Pythons were simply willing to fight the "blasphemy" battle with Christians, but not Jews. It may be that, like relentlessly poking fun at Scots and giving the Irish

a miss during the run of *Flying Circus*, the troupe knew which sacred cows could be slaughtered, and which might kick. (The IRA were blowing things up, including Parliament Square at the heart of the British government.) See Larsen, *MPFC: UC* 1.123 and 2.11, 65.

33. "Rejoice, Rejoice," *Sunday Times*, 22 November 1971: 37.

34. The Nationwide Festival of Light was a grassroots Christian organization created to campaign for a return of Britain to a pre-permissive society mindset.

35. In the "real" Python world, the troupe screened the first Julian Doyle-produced cut of the film on 6 December 1978, and were pleased with the audience's response (Palin, *Diaries*, 514–15).

36. Quoted in Caryl, *Strange Rebels*, 176.

37. *ATW*, 2.28.73.

38. Ackerman, "Women in Ancient Israel," 4.

39. Ackerman, "Women in Ancient Israel," 4–5.

40. Isaiah 7:10–16.

41. Baron Grade (Louis Gradansky) was a dancer, talent manager, media mogul, and owner of ATV. Grade and his brother Leslie have been mentioned in *Flying Circus* Ep. 34 (*MPFC: UC*, 2.107). Lew was also mentioned a number of times by the Goons, and the Jewish character "Lew" (voiced by Sellers) is a likely salute to the ambitious impresario.

42. *Private Eye*, 15 April 1977: 5.

43. "A *Times* Profile," *Times*, 31 October 1977: 8.

44. "A *Times* Profile," 8.

45. *Times*, 12 January 1977: 8. The eventual Princess Diana Spencer read Cartland novels voraciously through the late 1970s. There remains a well-known image of the young Diana in a comfy chair, *c.* 1977, several Cartland novels around her.

46. *Spectator*, 12 February 1977: 6; *Private Eye*, 21 January 1977: 15.

47. Vinen, *Thatcher's Britain*, 7–8.

48. *Private Eye*, 25 November 1977: 6. Bowles eventually married Prince Charles in 2005.

49. If Otto was to have been the Pythons' take on the ironic evils of Zionism (displacing thousands of Arabs, e.g.), it's even more ironic that, as Burleigh notes, the "Zionist Establishment was either socialist or Marxist . . . evidenced by the fact that it was not until 1977 that the state of Israel elected a right-wing government" (*BRT*, 92). Idle's portrayal of this ultra-nationalist Jew, then, is as contemporary as can be.

50. Listen to "Baxter's" from *Monty Python's Previous Record* and "Treadmill Lager" from *Another Monty Python Record*.

51. For example, "Wilson, Gannex and Me," *Daily Mail*, 6 July 1976: 13; "Mr. Stonehouse Tells Court of Raincoat Meeting," *Times*, 6 July 1976: 5; also even earlier, "Politicians 'Turned into Puppets,'" *Times*, 29 April 1968: 2; and Ferdinand Mount's "The Loss of Indignation" looks closely at the lack of shame, really, in the House (Maudling, et al.), *Spectator*, 30 December 1978: 4. There are dozens of these tongue-clucking articles.

52. Also see Donoughue, *DSD*, 1.519.

53. See the entries for Maudling in *MPFC: UC*.

54. *Daily Mail*, 27 February 1973: 13, and 20 September 1969: 6.

55. "Hospital Orders Waiting List Inquiry," *Daily Mail*, 8 August 1967: 7.

56. *MPFC: UC*, 1.231.

SCENE TWENTY
BRIAN IS ARRESTED, AGAIN

JUDITH: ". . . Reg has been dominating us for too long"—Charismatic terror leaders like Carlos, Arafat, Baader, and Shigenobu could fall out of favor with followers, especially if the goals at the top don't match the foot soldiers' needs, or vice versa. When Shigenobu had to flee Japan, her minions were forced to disband or team up with sympathetic causes like Fatah; Arafat saw more violent offshoots of the PLO go their own way when talks of rapprochement began; and Baader harangued his followers to action, urging them on as he and the rest of the RAF leadership languished in prison. Brian would agree with Judith here, but when she tries to pass the PFJ's mantle to Brian's shoulders, he balks, admitting that he's not a revolutionary at all.

A familiar ROMAN CENTURION'S hand claps itself down on Brian's shoulder—There are two significant elements of this action worth mentioning. First, the authoritative "hand on the shoulder" is a "familiar" throwback to *Flying Circus*, where trench-coated inspectors appeared regularly to rein in the mayhem, often clapping a gloved hand on the shoulder of the suspect. In Ep. 29, for example, Inspector Leopard (Cleese) of the Fraud Film Squad breaks up an Elizabethan film being made by a Luchino Visconti impostor (Jones), and later Inspector Baboon (Idle) attempts to make an arrest of a blackface Michelangelo Antonioni impostor (also Jones).[1] And in the "Another Six Minutes of *Monty Python's Flying Circus*" section of that same episode (featuring "The Argument Clinic"), Inspector Flying Fox of the Yard (Chapman) breaks into the silly sketch in a very familiar way: "Right now you two me old beauties, you are nicked."[2] This characterization is a direct borrow from the very popular *Dixon of Dock Green* show the Pythons had grown up watching, and where "Evening all" was a standard greeting.[3] Inspector Flying Fox of the Yard is finally interrupted by Inspector Thompson's Gazelle of the Yard (Idle), who is interrupted by another inspector who claps him on the shoulder ("Hold it!"), followed by yet another inspector who claps him on the shoulder, and the sketch ends. *Monty Python and the Holy Grail* had ended similarly, a victim of its own reflexive, undercutting structure.[4]

Secondly, it's no surprise that the Roman authorities would continue to look for a subversive like Brian, even without an active police force. Smallwood notes that the popularity of a "terrorist" like Jesus bar Abbas kept the local Roman constabulary wary of similar irruptions of widespread anti-Roman sentiment, with Christ himself commenting on the phenomena:

> Christ's reproach to the crowd who arrested Him for treating a peaceful preacher as a terrorist by coming against Him in arms[5] suggests that the rounding up of terrorists was a commonplace in

Judaea at the time. And indeed attacks on law-abiding citizens by individual terrorists living on plunder were so much an accepted feature of the social scene then that Christ used them in His teaching without comment.[6]

This fear is demonstrated when the gathered Jews and Roman soldiers all flee as the terrifying Judean Peoples' Front race toward the crosses later in the film.

CENTURION: "You are fucking nicked me old beauty!"—Is this the "Judas" moment for Judith Iscariot? It doesn't appear so, given Judith's reaction. Brian is simply taken into custody after a brief exchange with Judith, and also after they consummated their relationship the night before.

There is no discipic Judas figure, per se, in the film, no betrayal, likely one of the early decisions about things to avoid as the troupe pondered its "Monty Python's Life of Christ" story at the earliest stages. There is a Judas moment in one of their film influences, *I'm All Right Jack*, meaning the possibility was at least on the table as they wrote what would become *Brian*. When Stanley Windrush decides to be loyal to his uncle and go back to work, crossing picket lines and disrupting the otherwise "solid" strike, he is called a "Judas" by the shop stewards and Mr. Kite.

After about the year 52, the new procurator for Judea, Antonius Felix, set about rounding up known terrorists to try and rein in the blossoming anarchy in the province. His forces were even able to ambush and capture Eleazar, the terrorist leader who had helped organize a recent attack on the Samaritans.[7] Eleazar was sent to Rome in chains and likely executed. Felix also managed the fate of the former high priest Jonathan, a different kind of threat:

> Felix also bore an ill-will to Jonathan, the high priest, because he frequently gave him admonitions about governing the Jewish affairs better than he did, lest he should himself have complaints made of him by the multitude. . . . So Felix contrived a method whereby he might get rid of him, now he was become so continuously troublesome to him; for such continual admonitions are grievous to those who are disposed to act unjustly.[8]

So Felix[9] wearies of being dressed down for his administration's and his own shortcomings. (Brian doesn't reach this level of impertinence with Pilate, though his helpful "mishearings," corrections of pronunciation, and declaration of his Roman blood seem enough to condemn him—it's the Roman guards who snigger disrespectfully.) Felix then arranged for a friend of Jonathan's to deliver the high priest into the hands of *sicarii*, Judas-like (and for the promise of money), where he was stabbed to death in a crowd by the cloaked assassins.[10] Josephus credits this as the first sicarii assassination, and bemoans the far-reaching consequences:

> And this seems to me to have been the reason why God, out of his hatred to these men's wickedness, rejected our city; and as for the temple, he no longer esteemed it sufficiently pure for him to inhabit therein, but brought the Romans upon us, and threw a fire upon the city to purge it; and brought upon us, our wives, and children, slavery,—as desirous to make us wiser by our calamities.[11]

There's no such person as Josephus in *Life of Brian*, except perhaps the manacled Ben and the doomsaying prophets, and certainly no wholesale, God-cast retribution.

JUDITH struggles briefly with a SOLDIER . . .—What she does is slap the Centurion's back armor, then his helmet, also from behind. He clearly sees her as no threat, and simply tells her to leave off.

PILATE: ". . . given us a good wun for our money"—This is an American colloquialism, but these kinds of anachronistic moments are on par for the Pythons. This rearrest is key though, for what had been happening in the world outside the film. Remember that in 1976 George Davis had escaped wrongful arrest and incarceration (he'd been sentenced to seventeen years) for a 1975 robbery, nipping away from the authorities when bumbling police couldn't prove their case against him. But his spurt of freedom was nearly as brief as Brian's. In September 1977 Davis was caught red-handed, like Brian, working as a getaway driver for yet *another* bank robbery. The entire 1975–1976 Davis case was rehashed in the news, including the "George Davis is Innocent OK" graffiti, when this new arrest came to light. The judge in the 1977 case bemoaned the fact that no death penalty meant less of a deterrent for armed recidivists such as these, and sentenced Davis to fifteen years.[12]

PILATE: "This time, I guawantee you will not escape"—There seems to be nothing *ultra vires* in relation to Pilate's statutory power, at least as he is portrayed in the film. What he is about to do was also well within his power as prefect of a Roman province. This is justice delayed, since Brian was able to escape earlier, but it is a sanctioned legal proceeding nonetheless. In a discussion of Pilate's authority to pass sentence on virtually anyone—in this case, Jesus—brought before him, Smallwood outlines that authority: "The hearing before Pilate was a regular *cognitio extra ordinem*, a trial conducted without a jury at the discretion of the governor, who could pass sentence by virtue of the powers delegated to him by the emperor; and as the prisoner put up no defence, Pilate had no option but to convict."[13] So even if the historical Pilate was more weak (Smallwood) than vicious (Philo), the Pilate in the film seems to have been ready to sentence Brian to die at either one of these two goes.

Pilate also needs to make sure Brian is punished this time, and in a public way. His crime had been one that threatened to upend the authoritarian society perpetuated by the Romans, and that potential upset had to be righted. The centurions managed to stumble into rearresting Brian (after searching for him and his poorly hidden colleagues in Matthias's house and finding only a spoon), and the promised punishment will be what rights the ship: "Pre-industrial states could rely on neither a reliable police force nor secure prisons to provide their populations with such public reassurance," Wiedemann writes. "That reassurance had instead to be provided by the punishment itself; and that explains why punishment normally had to be both cruel and public."[14] Not long after this, Pilate won't remember they even have a "Bwian" in custody, and he agrees to free him even though he's been charged with this most capital of crimes.

GUARD: "A hundred and thirty-nine, Sir, special celebration. Passover, Sir"—Pilate has embraced the democidal power he's been gifted by the emperor, though there is no historical evidence that Pilate used festivals to execute a special number of criminals. There is also significant scholarly disagreement about the celebrated release of a criminal from Roman justice at festival time.[15]

This mention of the annual festival is accurate, but the name at this point in history is anachronistic. As he looks at the dating of the Johannine Gospel, Zeitlin notes that the "use of the term Feast of the Passover . . . demonstrates that the Gospel according to John was compiled sometime after the destruction of the Temple."[16] He goes on to remind readers that in the Bible the name "Passover" is only used in "connection with the Paschal Lamb, while the festival itself is called the Festival of Unleavened Bread."[17] Zeitlin concludes: "There is no mention in the Bible of the Festival of Passover." For the Pythons (and most commercial films in general), historical accuracy can yield to convenience, since most viewers would have been stumped if the guard had answered "special celebration . . . Unleavened Bread, Sir."

PILATE: ". . . we now have 140 . . ."—The Romans weren't generally this bloodthirsty, at least outside of the arena. Mass executions were most often reserved for times of insurrection when a show of strength (proving the futility of revolt) was required. Thousands were crucified following Spartacus's slave rebellion, and in the days and weeks of Titus's siege of Jerusalem in 70, Titus's forces would round up as many as five hundred foragers a day outside the city walls and crucify them in full view of the besieged inhabitants.[18] The goal was to convince the Jews to surrender the city.

Kropotkin describes the "desperate resistance" a sitting government like tsarists (or the Romans) will put up when challenged, a resistance to change that "is savage in its repressions."[19] There's never been talk of a trial, or simply imprisonment or even exile for Brian. From the first moment he was in jail for raiding Pilate's palace the specter of crucifixion has been looming. "Rebels deserve execution," Wiedemann says of those who would refuse Rome's offer of provincial protection.[20] First the old prisoner Ben mentions the likelihood of crucifixion, given that this is Brian's first offense, and the Centurion then jokes that Pilate wants to see Brian to decide whether he is crucified head-up or head-down. It's clear that Pilate did have this kind of authority in 33, and acted on it often. Wiedemann notes that just a few decades later, in 69, the unsettled Roman Empire was targeted by groups who would take "advantage of the confusion of Rome's civil wars," for example, "Garamantine marauders."[21] These marauders were captured and publicly executed, perhaps even in a games setting with gladiators and wild animals.[22] After the fall of Jerusalem in the 70s, Titus and Vespasian would make sure thousands of Jewish captives died in bloody, well-organized games.[23]

In the 1970s, the treatment of terrorists once in custody was often less severe. Many were sentenced to long prison terms, which for a time increased the likelihood of additional attacks to ransom them out of prison. The Lod Airport survivor Kozo Okamoto *wanted* to be executed, and had even asked to be allowed to commit suicide, according to Farrell, but these requests were denied:

> Okamoto was tried under the antiterrorist law formulated during the British occupation of Palestine. The purpose of the law was to control the activities of Zionists seeking the establishment of an Israeli state through the use of force. The law was used in this case because Israeli authorities viewed the political nature of the Tel Aviv attack as a threat to the security of the state. Under ordinary criminal law, the penalty could be no greater than life in prison. However, the antiterrorism law allowed for the death penalty.[24]

Released from prison in 1985, Okamoto was granted asylum in Lebanon, where he reportedly still resides.

CENTURION: "Permission to disperse them please"—The crowds that gathered when Pilate had tweaked the Jewish population with his displays of Roman cultus images were also ordered to disperse; one refusal ended in some significant bloodshed. Our Pilate has nothing to fear from these crowds; they come armed with derision, only.

PILATE: "My address is one of the high points of the Passover"—Pilate thinks the people of Jewusalem are eagerly awaiting his address, but it wasn't likely, given his reputation. Fast forward to 1977, and the Queen's Silver Jubilee is being planned, celebrating twenty-five years on the throne. Many in Britain questioned the tact of holding such an expensive fete amid high unemployment and Callaghan's cuts across the public sector.[25] The Socialist Workers' Party (SWP) took to the streets, editorial pages, and airwaves to show their opposition to the Jubilee and the monarchy in general. SWP-created "Stuff the Jubilee" and "Abolish the Monarchy 1977" badges and posters were everywhere. The SWP also took out a small ad in *Private Eye* condemning the entire process:

Jubilee? What a load of rubbish! Arrogant, hypocritical rubbish in a year when living standards have been cut by 4 per cent, when hospitals are being closed "for lack of money," when our children are being taught in overcrowded classrooms "for lack of money," when councils have stopped building houses "for lack of money." The royal family costs as much as a new hospital every year. . . . They're costing millions more this jubilee year. Don't let them get away with it. Tell them to STUFF THE JUBILEE![26]

The Sex Pistols would have their say this same day when they played their raucous version of "God Save the Queen" while sailing down the Thames, leading to their arrest.

PILATE: ". . . Biggus Dickus has come all the way from Wome"—It was common for the nobility and wealthy to make trips across the empire for festivals, and it was very likely that Pilate, his household in Caesarea, and his friends, even from Rome, would have traveled to Jerusalem for Passover. Pilate may have first visited Jerusalem during Passover, actually, in the spring of 27.[27]

CENTURION: "You're not thinking of giving it a miss today, sir?"—"Give it a miss" is one of those more recent idioms in British English; the *OED* credits it to the early part of the twentieth century. It simply means skipping something, or passing up on an opportunity.

CENTURION: "It's just that the crowd is in a funny mood today, sir"—This was actually a concern to emperors, especially, as they attended public events like *ludi* and *munera*. The "mood" could strike different crowds to ask for releases of slaves or prisoners, to complain about price rises, and even to protest the removal of a favorite statue to an emperor's home.[28] Emperors knew that attending such public spectacles put them in the position of, for example, being asked by the demanding crowd to agree to "the manumission of a slave belonging to someone who was not the editor" of those particular games.[29] This meant the emperor had to go to the slave's actual owner and ask for such permissions, and then do what the crowd asked. These very forceful "Welease Woger"–like demands are at least part of the reason, historians believe, that Tiberius "gave up attending spectacles," while both Hadrian and Marcus Aurelius also dealt with these overwhelmingly forceful requests.[30] Wiedemann concludes that

> attendance at *munera* subjected emperors to pressure from the people, rather than diverting potential expressions of political will in other directions. Tiberius preferred to keep away altogether to avoid such pressure; but the unpopularity which this brought upon him shows that it was a mistake which later emperors knew they could not afford to repeat. . . . To appear not at all would have been a challenge to the people by denying that the power exercised at these events was shared, even if only symbolically, between emperor and people.[31]

For our purposes, the symbolic power is shared not at a games event but at a very public address from Pilate's porch, shared between the regional governor Pilate and his "wabble of wowdy webels." The people do get what they want.

This is also a comment that is an echo of the recent Passion film, *Jesus of Nazareth*. As the condemned Christ is being led out of Pilate's jails it's clear that the locals out in the streets are more agitated than usual:

A CENTURION comes through the prison gate, calls down the passageway.

Centurion: Hey Mark! Where's the prisoner? Come on.

At the far end of the passage is a JAILER.

Jailer: Here's your man.

He pulls Christ into the passageway, bent over and bleeding, tied to the heavy patibulum.

Jailer: Ahh. The King of the Jews.

Centurion: Hurry up. This crowd worries me.

The JAILER pushes CHRIST toward the bright entrance.

Jailer: Here. Take him.

The mood of the crowd has been measured by the Centurion, and the rest of the trip to the site of crucifixion is a struggle through angry, confused, or weeping citizens.

PILATE: "I'm surprised to hear you wattled by a wabble of wowdy webels"—But perhaps there shouldn't be surprise here. Judea had been one of the more restive provinces held by Rome, "having been torn by twelve major rebellions since its conquest."[32] The Jews bristled almost continuously under Roman rule, never submitting to being dominated; many of Rome's other conquests admitted to the benefits of Roman citizenship and protection.

CENTURION: "A bit thundery, sir"—A colloquialism simply meaning the threat "of an explosion of anger or passion," meaning the Centurion and Pilate are now actually speaking the same language at the same time. It won't matter, since Pilate misinterprets the Centurion's warning as reticence, and heads out to the crowd, anyway.

PILATE: ". . . and cwucify him well"—There probably weren't many failed crucifixions, though some were rescued from unattended crosses, or the nailing might be insufficient to hold the body, etc.

Notes

1. See Larsen, *MPFC: UC*, 2.40–49. The hand even comes from offscreen, just as in Ep. 29.
2. *ATW*, 2.89.
3. *MPFC: UC*, 2.43.
4. Larsen, *BAFHG*, 487.
5. Smallwood lists Matthew 26:55, Mark 14:48, and Luke 22:52 as examples.
6. Smallwood, *JURR*, 164; Smallwood further lists Luke 10:30, and John 10:1 and 8.
7. Smallwood, *JURR*, 274.
8. Josephus, *AJ*, 20.8.5 (Whiston, 421).
9. Felix is also mentioned in Acts in relation to Paul; he arrests him and interviews him, hoping for a bribe, which isn't forthcoming. Pilate never asks for nor does he seem to expect any kind of tribute from Brian—he's simply interviewing him prior to his sentencing and execution.
10. *AJ*, 20.8.5 (Whiston, 421); also *JURR*, 274–75.
11. *AJ*, 20.8.5 (Whiston, 422).
12. "George Davis Is Guilty OK," *Daily Mail*, 25 July 1978: 16–17. In September 1977 the Pythons were writing together on *Brian*. It's no surprise that the Davis case—arrest, graffiti, escape, rearrest, conviction—ended up figuring prominently into not only the film's production design, but into Brian's character arc.
13. *JURR*, 169.
14. Wiedemann, *Emperors and Gladiators*, 72.
15. See Husband, "The Pardoning of Prisoners by Pilate" (1917); Brown, *The Death of a Messiah* (1994); a contemporary, popular version can be found in Maier, *Pontius Pilate*, 130.
16. Zeitlin, "Crucifixion of Jesus Re-Examined," 351.
17. Zeitlin, "Crucifixion of Jesus Re-Examined," 351.
18. Kotker, *HLTJ*, 123.
19. Quoted in Iviansky, "Individual Terror," 45.

20. Wiedemann, *Emperors and Gladiators*, 104.

21. Wiedemann, *Emperors and Gladiators*, 15–16. The Garamantines had been a nuisance to Rome for many years. See Felipe Fernandez-Armesto's *Civilizations: Culture, Ambition, and the Transformation of Nature*, 64–65. The Romans of the time reported that these "barbarously exotic" Garamantine marauders, like the PFJ, covered their faces, though with scars and tattoos rather than veils (64).

22. Wiedemann, *Emperors and Gladiators*, 16.

23. Wiedemann, *Emperors and Gladiators*, 104.

24. Farrell, *BRJ*, 140.

25. One of the more popular placards seen on the streets read: "Cuts? Axe the monarchy!" The Queen had much earlier asked that no one go to any financial extreme in planning Jubilee events.

26. *Private Eye*, 10 June 1977: 2.

27. Meier, *Pontius Pilate*, 85.

28. Wiedemann, *Emperors and Gladiators*, 168. Tiberius eventually put the statue back, by the way.

29. Wiedemann, *Emperors and Gladiators*, 167.

30. Wiedemann, *Emperors and Gladiators*, 168.

31. Wiedemann, *Emperors and Gladiators*, 169.

32. Maier, *Pontius Pilate*, 75.

SCENE TWENTY-ONE
THE PFJ DISCUSSES

REG: "... item 4 ... attainment of world supremacy within the next four years"—One of the major influences on the Pythons, apart from the Goons, was Peter Cook. A Cambridge alum like Chapman, Cleese, and Idle, as early as 1964 Cook had formed the "World Domination League." In the group's stated goals, the date for successful domination had already passed, but they pressed on.[1] The PFJ won't seem to mind missing a deadline, either.

So the Peoples' Front of Judea are not just trying to rid themselves of the Romans, but have set their sights on ruling the world. This is quite in line with the thinking of the first-century Zealots who, according to Josephus, following an "ambiguous oracle," believed that "at that time from their country one should rule the world."[2] The Zealots believed one of their own (Judas or Eleazar?) could be this liberator, while Josephus obsequiously assured his own future by claiming the prophecy was fulfilled when Vespasian became emperor while campaigning in Judea.[3] Judas was eventually killed, Eleazar died at Masada, and Josephus became a favorite of the Flavian dynasty. One of the Qumran[4] scrolls, the *Scroll of the War of the Sons of Light against the Sons of Darkness*, actually supports the PFJ's optimism, as it "envisages a six years' struggle between the forces of Israel and the Gentiles, with varying fortunes, until God intervenes mightily to give final victory to his people."[5] This optimism is based on the "forces of Israel," meaning likely more than the dozen or so PFJ members. What's also missing here, for the PFJ, is the ask for or expectation of God's help. Reg and friends are a secular group—they are seeking miracles through militancy, not messiahs.

In 63 BC—less than one hundred years prior to the events depicted in the film—the Roman senator Catiline had planned a very similar revolt with very similar ends: the overthrow of the Roman government. Catiline was a well-born soldier and statesman who was accused of myriad crimes—including, in Sallust's history, adultery with a Vestal Virgin and beheading his brother-in-law, then parading the head around Rome.[6] The terrorist plan was discovered by Cicero, and Catiline's co-conspirators arrested, while Catiline fled. His comrades in Roman custody were executed immediately under orders from Cicero. Catiline's army fell apart in the light of scrutiny, and he died in battle with many of his followers.[7] Cicero's treatment of these terrorists is identical to Pilate's approach for Brian—summary execution.

More recently, while the PLO's charter seems to indicate a more regionally focused revolution, Dobson and Payne write of the PFLP that, having "dreams of world revolution, they had always been more internationally involved than Fatah."[8] The earliest incarnation of what would become the Japanese Red Army—in 1966 simply a more "violence-oriented" offshoot of the Japan Communist Party—"called for the complete destruction of the existing social system in Japan," this based on Japan's "complicity" with the United States in the Vietnam war effort.[9] They wanted to remake Japan in a new revolutionary image, and without the presence or influence of the United States, its military, or culture. The JRA truly "embraced the concept of a simultaneous world revolution," Farrell concludes.[10]

REG: "Francis, you've been doing some work on this?"—The PFJ is clearly all about planning, a notion the Pythons had grown up hearing, especially in the postwar years. Rather than surrender the closely held wartime control over much of the nation's production, distribution, and consumption, social engineers like Bevan, Cripps, and Beveridge saw the opportunity for a fairer Britain. In their estimations, planning at the central government level could mean every Briton works, has enough food and entertainment, and lives and retires safely and comfortably—social justice at its best. Leaving the economy to capitalist forces or the upper class would mean more of the same, with the rich remaining rich and the poor remaining poor, and an enormous, silent working class somewhere in the bulging middle. Planning was the answer to this inequality, Bogdanor mentions:

> The second element [after the Welfare State] was a belief in planning, which was a great contrast to the end of the First World War, when planning and nationalisation had rapidly been succeeded by de-control. The Labour Party, in its 1945 Manifesto, called "Let us Face the Future," said that it would plan "from the ground up." Herbert Morrison, Leader of the House of Commons, said in 1946 that, "planning, as it is now taking shape in this country under our eyes, is something new and constructively revolutionary, which will be regarded in times to come as a contribution to civilisation as vital and distinctively British as parliamentary democracy and the rule of law."[11]

The politicians and trade union representatives that the Pythons tend to present are planners, like the PFJ.

FRANCIS: ". . . I think five years is optimistic . . ."—The PFJ weren't the only terror group with overly optimistic ambitions. Lev Tikhomirov had been certain that a vigorous two- to three-year terror campaign against the sitting tsarist government in Russia would be enough to bring about collapse.[12] The Soviet Union under Stalin and the PRC under Mao laid out a series of (occasionally successful, often disastrous) five-year plans to centralize and improve the nations' vast resources and industry, using a commitment to Communist principles as guide. The revolutionary Daniel Cohn-Bendit, leader of 1968 student protests in France and then London, would many years later admit that he and his mates were also optimistic, and even "a bit naive and excessive from time to time."[13] The article continues, rehearsing names covered in these pages: "You would hear much the same from their immediate ideological descendants, Ulrike Meinhof, Donald DeFreeze, Eldridge Cleaver, Lynette 'Squeaky' Frome [sic], Leila Khaled etc., those people who made the 1970s such an entertaining place to be, with their bombs, guns and ludicrous liberationist ideologies."[14] The PFJ are meeting and talking as if they are the opposition party, actually, biding their time, waiting for the ruling party, the Romans, to run themselves out of office. Of course, the PFJ aren't actually *doing* anything, since they are currently out of power; they are the shadow party. In this they are like Thatcher and the Tories waiting for the economy to undermine Labour completely after 1975. (The economy would carry the day for the Tories, however.) As *Brian* was being produced, Britain (and people like Palin and Jones) were even smugly certain that a Tory like Thatcher could never be elected. In fact it became the Pythons' Labour Party that would remain unelected for the following eighteen years.

FRANCIS: ". . . unless we can smash the Roman Empire within the next twelve months"—First, the Roman Empire (meaning after the Republic) enjoyed a one-and-a-half millennia lifetime, give or take a few decades, meaning Francis is being optimistic, at best. In the year 33, when this film is ostensibly set, the Roman Empire was still growing; it wouldn't reach its apex, size-wise, until the third century, long after Brian, Reg, and the PFJ are gone.[15]

As has been seen, most revolutionaries overestimate their cause's popularity and influence—the masses generally don't rise up and join, and leadership often fractures after a few arrests or deaths. In the mess that was Jerusalem between 66 and 70, when groups *like* the PFJ were very active, the overly optimistic rebels had managed to seize control of the city by late 67, less than a year after the isolated hostilities—between insurgents and local Roman cohorts, then between insurgents and insurgents—burst into open fighting. This twelve-month success within the city's walls certainly led the revolutionaries to believe that licking Rome would be as easy.[16] The wealthy (those interested in "peace" and survival) would soon pack up and leave, according to Josephus: "Many of the most eminent of the Jews swam away from the city, as from a ship when it was going to sink" (or a "rat out of an aqueduct"?).[17] The bulk of the population never did join the rebels, however, and many more fled the city before the Romans arrived, or remained and died rather horribly in the privations of the prolonged siege.[18]

Second, there are six PFJ acolytes—"urban guerrillas"—in the cell meeting here. Only Judith is missing, as well as Brian, who has been arrested by the Romans. That means there are seven revolutionaries prepared to overthrow the largest and most technologically advanced empire of the ancient world. Nineteenth-century socialist Louis Blanqui had envisioned just such a possibility—a small band of committed revolutionaries overthrowing a sitting government—though he was never able to unseat the monarchy in France, and actually spent much of his life in prison as a rabid republican.[19] In nihilist Sergei Nechaev's mind, eight committed members of his "People's Justice" cell could unseat the tsarist monarchy.[20] Paucity in numbers isn't unusual, however, even for the most recent well-known terror groups, as Laqueur notes:

> Terrorist groups in contrast to guerrilla units do not grow beyond a certain limit. The basic unit usually consists of three to ten people. Some of the recent terrorist "armies" such as the Japanese Red Army, the Baader-Meinhof group . . . the Angry Brigade, the Symbionese Liberation Army, etc., numbered a few dozen members at the height of their exploits.[21]

Also recently, in 1969 Colonel Qaddafi and just "eleven other like-minded revolutionaries" were able to topple King Idris and claim Libya—but Idris was no Caesar, and Tripoli no Roman Empire.[22] Much closer to home, in the decade leading up to the creation of *Life of Brian*, the minority Provisional Army Council—or Provos—had convinced themselves "that as long as they had the support of most Catholics" in Northern Ireland, partition could be ended, and both the Irish Protestants and the British could be defeated.[23] The Provos' optimistic goal sounds familiar: "It [had] turned into a fight to force an end to the United Kingdom and to bring about the unification of Ireland."[24] Nothing short of full revolution, then, just what the Peoples' Front of Judea is calling for.

On the economic front, Ted Heath had taken as his mandate in 1970 to curb the growing powers of the unions, power that the previous Labour administrations had drip-dropped to organized labor to keep the economy running smoothly. Heath chose a frontal assault, pushing legislation that strangled income growth and hobbled strike actions, actions that he assumed would have the support of British consumers. This was "his strategic mistake," Marr writes. Heath chose to "attack union power head-on and in a single act" (like the PFJ assaulting Pilate's palace), "rather than piecemeal, as [Thatcher's] wilier government would."[25] By

1972–1973 Heath's ambitious agenda was driven onto the rocks of a miner's strike in a gale of an OPEC oil embargo—it was the perfect storm.[26] Francis's timeline is a fine example of the inapposite expectations many twentieth-century "revolutionaries" cultivated, whether they wanted to end Japan's monarchy and "occupation" by the United States, sever Northern Ireland's Westminster umbilical, upend France's higher educational system, reduce the powers of Big Labor, feed the California Bay Area's poor, or replace entirely the capitalist and imperialist governments (and influences) of Britain, Germany, or the United States. Fifty years on and more, all of these leviathans remain unslain. Even the revolutionary's spiritual leader, philosopher Herbert Marcuse, in a 1978 BBC interview cited earlier, acknowledged the blinkered shortcomings of the New Left:

> Well I would mention perhaps as a main defect the unrealistic language and in many cases the totally unrealistic strategy among the New Left, by no means general, but very definitely among the New Left, the refusal to recognize that we are not in a revolutionary situation in the advanced industrial countries, that we are not even in a prerevolutionary situation, and that the strategy has to be adopted [sic] to this situation.[27]

The always dependable Tony Benn not only helped underscore the silliness of these kinds of declarative moments, but he provided many of them over his entertaining ministerial and political career. In October 1980, just months after the much-heralded premiere of *Life of Brian*, Labour held its rather gloomy party conference in the rather gloomy Blackpool. This was also just months after Margaret Thatcher and her brand of conservatism had swept in to office, surprising most political mandarins. Party conferences are times for licking wounds, lambasting the winners, and trumpeting the "here's-what-we'll-do-next-time" plans to the faithful. The party in opposition, it had been generally agreed over time, could and did over-promise in its overly optimistic platform, with the unwritten agreement that those flights of rhetorical, political, and economic fancy could be rerouted after retaking No. 10. "You can't write a Manifesto for the Party in opposition and expect it to have any relationship to what the Party does in Government," Callaghan had said back in 1974, just *after* Labour narrowly ousted Heath and the Tories. "We're now entirely free to do what we like," he concluded.[28] "Free" doesn't mean owning up to every special interest promise in the party's manifesto; often, it actually means freedom from having to be accountable for those promises. Benn obviously liked the "entirely free" portion of this statement, and not its subtext, because at the 1980 Blackpool conference he offered his messiahship to Labour's masses, according to the *Times*:

> After the extraordinary performances of Mr. Wedgwood Benn, first at the conference where *he promised to change the face of Britain within a month* and then afterwards at fringe meetings, even some of his own followers wondered if he was the messiah[29] to lead them to the socialist promised land. A life-long member of the party said Mr. Benn was bonkers—a wonderfully expressive word suggesting a degree of unreality or willfulness far short of certification and libel. Mrs. Shirley Williams[30] wondered why he was so unambitious. "After all, it took God only six days to make the world." A senior member of the Shadow Cabinet added that it would take Mr. Benn only three days to destroy it.[31]

Mr. Benn was even more ambitious than Francis or the PFJ—he promised that in just one month after Labour took back power he would nationalize every significant British industry, abolish the House of Lords, and remove Britain from the EEC.[32] It seems to have been concluded at this off-the-rails conference that Benn—as a potential messiah bringing either redemption or destruction—would not be the face of the Labour party in the years to come . . . and he was not.[33]

FRANCIS: ". . . as Empires go, this is the big one . . ."—The Roman Empire was much smaller than many others, historically, including the actual largest, the *British* Empire, which covered a great deal of the world at its largest.[34] The Pythons are always referring to their own empire as well, of course, as through *Flying Circus* and *Holy Grail*.

What Francis might be hinting at, though, is the perhaps insurmountable revolutionary challenge presented by the Roman Empire. As was being discussed generally by terrorism experts in the 1970s, countries with "effective dictatorships" were the *only* countries escaping the scourge of terrorism.[35] Heavy-handed Communist countries like East Germany, China, the Soviet Union, and North Korea were fairly immune, thanks to effective secret police, surveillance, and limited personal freedoms, as well as harsh punishments for those who challenged the state's hegemony. The more liberal, socialist, and democratic countries—where individual liberties were protected and "rehabilitation" trumped "retribution" for lawbreakers—proved fertile nurseries for revolutionary types. Terrorists could count on lighter sentences (if they were arrested at all) in France, England, Japan, and Germany, as well as easier access to weapons, while in the United States the lack of popular enthusiasm for such underground movements (the Weathermen, the Black Panthers, the SLA) kept those cells tiny and only sporadically noticed. In Francis's Jerusalem, the sitting government has obviously arrested and is ready to execute 140 criminals of all types, the event only being "special" because it's Passover—not likely the best recruiting tool for the next batch of budding anti-imperialists. In the end, we'll see, the PFJ is back to its standard, perhaps most efficacious size—Reg, Francis, Stan/Loretta, Judith, and three unnamed others (and maybe Matthias in the background)—and while Brian is left to die on the cross as a "martyr to the cause," the Roman Empire moves on unhindered. This Pyrrhic victory cycle actually mirrors the progresses of most terror groups and organized revolutionary activity of the 1960s and beyond, Laqueur points out:

> It was easy to get publicity for almost any action or threat of action, for manifestoes and appeals. *But all this activity, however often repeated, had no political impact, nor was there any support beyond a small fringe of intellectual sympathizers.* . . . Urban terror became self-perpetuating: a major operation would be staged to seize hostages so as to assure the liberation from prison of some leading comrades. Meanwhile there would be fresh arrests and new operations would have to be planned to affect their release. Neither workers, nor peasants, nor even the intellectuals would show any sympathy, and after hundreds of bombs and thousands of lead stories in the media, the surviving terrorists, sadder and wiser men and women, would have to face *a balance sheet that was almost entirely negative*. If it was their intention to undermine the system and bring about its downfall, there were obviously more effective ways to do so.[36]

The IRA, JRA, PLO, and RAF all discovered this, to varying degrees: today there remains a British presence in Northern Ireland; Japan still has a monarchy and a military relationship with the United States; Israel exists; and Germany is now a *united* Federal Republic. The PFJ don't seem "down-hearted," though; they will live to discuss and plan another day.

STAN: "It's action that counts, not words and we need action NOW!!!"—So, *action directe*, the slogan of the nineteenth-century syndicalists.[37] Gerald Priestland stated it simply as he surveyed the economic, social, and political unrest in Britain in 1975: "Violence gives the illusion of doing something, not just talking."[38] This rather natural step was taken by most revolutionary groups, even those that *started* with (perhaps) more noble intentions, like the Tupamaros in Uruguay, or the FLQ in Quebec.[39] Brazilian revolutionary Marighella, author of the *Minimanual of the Urban Guerrilla* and spiritual father to many modern terror organizations, wrote simply that it was "the duty of every revolutionary . . . to make the revolution."[40] Laqueur explains further:

> Typical for Marighella and also for the Argentinian terrorists was the burning conviction that shooting was far more important than any other activity—especially intellectual discussion. There was contempt for ideology and "politics"—the future society (Marighella wrote) would be built not by those who made long-winded speeches or signed resolutions but by those steeled in the armed struggle.[41]

What Stan is asking for is "propaganda by deed" (*propagande par le fait*), the clarion call of the Anarchist movement, for example, across the nineteenth century in Europe, Russia, and even the United States.[42] Mikhail Bakunin had called for the spread of "our principles not by words but with deeds, *for this is the most popular, the most potent, and the most irresistible form of propaganda.*"[43] V. I. Lenin would later bemoan the preponderance of the one over the other, expressing "real anguish that his party had merely been talking about bombs but that not a single one had been made."[44]

Even those in the fray during this period saw the need—if Western imperialists were to be overthrown—for more action than discussion. Libya's Colonel Qaddafi hailed the JRA's commitment to violence following the Lod Airport massacre in May 1972:

> Fida'i[45] action must be the type of operations carried out by the Japanese. . . . Action has not yet reached the level of the true spirit of the fida'in. We demand the fida'i action is able to carry out the operations similar to the operation carried out by the Japanese. Why should a Palestinian not carry out such an operation? You will see them all writing books and magazines full of theories, but otherwise unable to carry out one daring operation like that carried out by the Japanese.[46]

Qaddafi would help the JRA conduct terrorist operations later in the 1970s.

REG: ". . . we could sit around . . . passing resolutions, making clever speeches, but it's not going to shift one Roman soldier"—This is probably the way of most nascent revolutionary groups—we have never heard of them because they never made it out the door. Bernard Donoughue would call this "left-wing claptrap," and it flowed from the Tony Benn-Michael Foot-Ian Mikardo[47] wing of the Labour Party, where Donoughue knew public appeal in 1976 didn't hang its hat, and sitting governments went to die.[48] Donoughue and his boss, Jim Callaghan, tracked a more moderate path during their administration—Thatcher would even accuse Labour of adopting Conservative policies, but half-heartedly[49]—a status quo return, essentially, just where Reg and the core of the PFJ end up as the film concludes.

In the nineteenth century, Fenian sympathizer "Professor Mezzeroff" had lectured on the virtues of explosives, teaching that "a pound of the stuff contained more force than 'a million speeches.'"[50] The Angry Brigade had graduated from fomenting revolution around the kitchen table to flinging bullets and bombs (and communiques) at government targets, as would many terror groups. Britain's own "situationist" flash-in-the-pan were the King Mob, eager but ineffective. At a Revolutionary Festival held in Essex in 1969, much was being *said*, as a description of the festival from an attendee indicates:

> The thing had fallen into the hands of the situationists, the Notting Hill King Mob lot, you know, the people who make very good slogans—one on a wall in Notting Hill that just says SCREAM, another near the Hornsey Art College which says DORIS ARCHER[51] IS A PRUDE. They're very good *provocateurs*, they've got a splendid sense of style and presentation,

but they're theoretically immature. By Monday evening the Marxist-Leninists had the festival back in control.[52]

The King Mob can't wrest the narrative from the Marxist-Leninists; the *provocateur*-ish PFJ struggle in vain with the CFG—all lose as everything sounds ridiculous.

This was an oft-heard assessment of the state of formerly volatile student movements, especially those that had made the transition to action with violence. Peter Hazelhurst characterized the feared Red Army this way in October 1975: "Japan's once powerful and cohesive radical student movements, the main fount of terrorism in the country for terrorism today, have disintegrated in recent years into feuding factions of left-wing militants arguing bitterly over ideologies."[53] Just a few years earlier, however, the embryonic JRA was the answer for a number of "radical youths," according to Farrell: "One of the most attractive features of the Red Army was its bent toward action. The appeal of doing something now, as opposed to long theoretical debates concerning the proper road to victory, attracted many of Japan's youth."[54]

REG: "This calls for immediate discussion!"—Reg has fallen back on the safest choice the PFJ could make, and the reason they are still alive and free—words, not action. They are once again shop stewards with a labor-management bone to pick. This attention to parliamentary detail also hews close to the description of the escape committee from Palin and Jones's *Ripping Yarns* episode, "Escape from Stalag 112B":

> Colonel Owen (John Phillips): We have a sort of agreement here about escapes. We have a sort of system whereby all escape plans go to Escape Committee. The Committee then recommends some of them to a full session of the Escape Board, and whichever plan has a two-thirds majority is put to a secret ballot. And the plan with the most votes then becomes the official plan and goes to the Escape Plan Review Committee, and if they like it they'll commission a feasibility study.

It turns out that the next meeting of this last committee is four months away. Major Phipps resolves to escape on his own (which he never manages).

During the exciting but dangerous days of the 1905 Russian Revolution, when secret police were active and members of an emerging soviet were increasingly targeted for arrest, "it was easier . . . to discuss tactics in the abstract than to carry them out in practice."[55] In Britain of the Pythons' day, only the Angry Brigade really crossed the line from discussion to action, setting off bombs and actually injuring one person. Their heyday lasted just nine months before they were all arrested and sent to prison; the PFJ gets about three days or so, once Brian joins, before they take their ball and go home. Andrew Marr explains why these groups found such little success:

> Though in many ways the Angry Brigade were a non-event they represent the only direct [British-born] confrontation between revolutionary protest, supposed to be one of the key ingredients of the sixties, and the evolving economy of pleasure which was the sixties' real story. Other left-wing groups, mainly Trotskyists, would argue with each other and march, protest and publish about employment and foreign affairs.[56]

The discussion-centric PFJ align themselves nicely, then, with 1960s–1970s terror groups.

Later, in a festering clash to the north, this endless discussion trope was applied by Bernard Donoughue to the Irish situation. There was a high-level meeting at No. 10 involving the Church leaders of Northern Ireland, and Donoughue characterized the confab as more of a convenient excuse for the PM to come home early from his Scillies vacation—where he was "bored"—than any pressing matter of life and death. Donoughue mentioned the "Irish crisis" as "usually a good enough excuse" for the PM, meaning the deadly struggle to the north had become nothing more than an irritant to not only Westminster, but England. Donoughue admitted: "I did not go in to the Irish meeting, since it was bound to be a lot of blather."[57] Incidentally, in 1974 bombs had detonated in Dungannon, Belfast, Dublin, Monaghan, Ballykinler, and London, killing many and causing enormous casualties and property destruction.

The newspapers (and, eventually, diary pages) of the Winter of Discontent period point up over and over again the government's inability to make decisions—what Donoughue bemoans as "dithering"—with the Parliamentary Labour Party's credibility diminishing at every new strike action and associated pay policy retreat.[58] In just a matter of weeks over the winter the polls showed Labour and Callaghan dropping from comfortable leads, and even though Thatcher was still personally disliked, the government she led in opposition grew in favorability as essential services like food delivery, sewage, and water works slowed or stopped altogether in parts of the country. Meanwhile the emerging "enemy," the powerful trade unions, dithered in their own self-destructive ways. Peter Jenkins writes of this transitional 1978–1979 period with muted alarm and certain portent. He saw a gap between the country's trade union leadership and the rank and file members, a fracture that was growing ever wider:

> If the country threatens to become ungovernable it is not because of the power of the unions, it is rather because of their powerlessness to govern their own members. Their national leaders have lost control. I have never known them to be more alarmed. They fear that this is not just another wave of industrial unrest, rather something novel, something different.[59]

Reg and the PFJ have been acting like a (trade union) leadership council for their revolutionary movement, finding safety and reassurance in the orderliness of parliamentary procedure, including the thoughtful, directed "discussion" mentioned above. Once they set Brian free, however, their "powerlessness" became apparent. Brian is acting the part of renegade shop steward or ambitious local union member—he's wildcatting. In *Holy Grail* the local syndicalist Dennis actually stood toe-to-toe with a king and argued for a devolved power structure by and for the people; he was throttled for his efforts.[60] Brian has embraced action—the graffiti, the palace assault, escaping from Pilate, falling in love, even acting the unwilling prophet— rather than the inaction of his leadership. Jenkins continues: "There was the official trade union movement, national in character and formally structured, and there was the unofficial movement, local, sectional, and informal."[61] Jenkins saw the latter group as the prosperous one, but with a high cost. The Scargills and Scanlons (and for us, Reg) were no longer calling the tune; that was happening at a more local level, and with predictably fractious results. The "something novel, something different" is what will put Brian on a cross as the film ends, while his fellow members salute him and return to their safe, symbolic struggle.

And perhaps the worst of both worlds occurred as the government took meetings with trade unions and their leaders, where everyone "dithered" quite a bit, the government giving in to irresponsible double-digit pay rises that would then encourage the next workers' group to expect the same consideration, and so on. Prices rose, the value of pay packets dropped, and manufacturing slowed. The wage-and-inflation death spiral would eventually topple both the Labour government and, ironically, turn the tide of popular support against the unions for what Donoughue called "hard-faced, grab-whatever-you-can capitalism with a union card."[62] The country was so put off that voters gave the much-disliked Margaret Thatcher the keys to No. 10.

REG: "Well obviously once the vote's been taken. We can't act on a resolution until you've voted on it"—This parliamentary, trade union "stop-go" action keeps the PFJ from reaching Brian prior to his being nailed up, and it will also keep him on the cross once they're there to affect a rescue (if they were in fact the rescue committee). In *I'm All Right Jack* the shop stewards come to the plant manager to demand that non-union-card-holder Windrush be fired. But when the manager instantly agrees with them, a "wait a tick" epiphany occurs, and, after conferring, like the PFJ, it is decided that if Windrush is fired he is being "victimised," which would constitute a strike-able action. Life provided these very moments for the Pythons to draw upon, creatively.

In October 1976 *Private Eye* reported that an ITN reporter took a camera crew to interview a group of squatters calling themselves "Mustard" (Multiracial Union of Squatters to Alleviate Racial Discrimination) in the upscale Chepstow Villas, near Notting Hill. What followed reads like a PFJ excursion:

> The chief squatter, Afro-hairstyled Michael Stewart, insisted that all the ITN men must take their shoes off before entering the house, on the premise that it was a holy place. [Reporter Geoffrey] Suchet was prepared to comply. But the cameramen refused, so they all had to go back to the office. A union meeting was then convened to discuss the issue. After much wrangling it was decided by the brothers to send a different camera team who were prepared to comply with the squatters' demands.[63]

The squatters were officially evicted that same month, with Mr. Stewart being arrested on assault and obstruction charges.[64]

JUDITH: "All you've got to do is go out of that door now, and try to stop the Romans nailing him up!"—Judith is wasting her breath, since for Reg and friends, parliamentary procedure will always, *must* always, trump "immediate action." As they hear the urgency of the situation the PFJ kicks into high gear, proposing a "completely new motion" to be discussed. The simple fact is "you can't act on a resolution until you've voted on it," Reg reminds Francis, and Judith will have to leave, frustrated and typed, as will be seen.

But Judith still qualifies as a citizen Nechaev and Bakunin would have counted on. The other half of his fifth category in *Catechism* addresses the fairer sex: "Finally, the women: some were useless and stupid and were to be treated like categories three and four [useful high-ranking people and politicians]; others were capable, passionate and devoted even though they might not yet have acquired full revolutionary consciousness."[65] Judith also likely fits into Nechaev and Bakunin's sixth category, comprising those who "had completely thrown in their lot with the revolutionaries"—these are "the most precious possession of the revolution."[66] When she finally understands what Reg is after, and she also leaves Brian to his martyrdom, then she has reached the sixth category, clearly, fully committed to the PFJ's catechism.

JUDITH: "Something's actually happening . . ."—Judith is at least energized and ready to do something, not unlike Ulrike Meinhof, a respected journalist, then activist, then terrorist. Meinhof's adopted mother, activist Renate Riemick, described admiringly her adopted daughter's commitment to change: She "put aside her Proust and her Kafka and entered the political arena."[67] The later Middle Eastern imbroglio saw the benefits of the female fellow traveler, as Burleigh writes: "Women . . . were crucial in fanning the fires of hatred across the family generations . . . reminding young males of the great deeds of their fathers, or jolting their emotions with idealised details of a way of life the family and an entire people had lost."[68]

REG: "A little ego trip from the feminists"—In *Jesus of Nazareth*, one of Christ's male disciples, upon hearing Mary's report of Jesus's resurrection, sniffs under his breath: "A woman's fantasy." Mary lashes out at him, and leaves. Margaret Thatcher was treated similarly by her political opposites, her own party, and even her Cabinet.[69] Donoughue admitted that he grudgingly respected Mrs. Thatcher, but he wasn't shy about calling her speeches "poor," that she lacked "confidence," and she was often "shrill and humourless."[70] She was known (mostly behind her back) as "that bloody woman"—by her own party and the Conservative Central Office—or "TBW" in some official communications.[71]

Notes

1. Thompson, *Peter Cook*, 175–77.
2. Quoted in Brandon, *Jesus and the Zealots*, 59; from *WJ* 6.5.4 (Whiston, 583).
3. Brandon, *Jesus and the Zealots*, 59.
4. For much more on the connections between the Qumran settlement, the Essenes, and the Zealots, see Brandon's *Jesus and the Zealots*, chapter 2, and its notes.
5. Brandon, *Jesus and the Zealots*, 60.
6. Sallust, *Catiline's War*.
7. Richard, *WWAR*, 173–77.
8. Dobson and Payne, *Carlos Complex*, 22.
9. Farrell, *BRJ*, 60.
10. *BRJ*, 87.
11. Bogdanor, "The Attempt to Construct a Socialist Commonwealth," a.t.
12. Laqueur, *Terrorism*, 49.
13. Discussed in Larsen, *MPFC: UC*, 1.355 and 2.88.
14. "Stand by for a Year of Nostalgia for 1968," *Spectator*, 5 January 2008: 18. Cleaver was a member of the American terror group The Black Panthers.
15. Mitchell, "Human Parasites," 1. And, as Mitchell points out, "while the Western Roman Empire fell in 476 AD with the conquest of Rome, the Eastern Empire with its capital of Constantinople lasted until 1453 AD as the Byzantine Empire" (1). The PFJ were tragically optimistic, as most rebel causes are.
16. See all of chapter 12 of Smallwood's *JURR* for more.
17. Josephus, *WJ*, 2.20.1 (Whiston, 497). The governor of Syria, Cestius Gallus, led forces against Jerusalem in September of 66 but retreated in November, likely due to the approaching winter weather, losing many troops along the way. This defeat acted as catalyst for the exodus from the city of Jerusalem by the wealthy—they knew that Roman recriminations were coming in the spring. See *JURR*, 297–99.
18. Kotker, *HLTJ*, 122–24.
19. Laqueur, *Terrorism*, 85.
20. Nechaev and Bakunin's *Catechism* is discussed earlier.
21. Laqueur, *Terrorism*, 108. It's also important to remember that these more modern groups possessed or had access to weapons with considerably more destructive potential—grenades, submachine guns, plastic explosives, even aircraft—outstripping the long knife a *sicarii* would have secreted beneath his robe, or the single handgun of a twentieth-century Slavic nationalist.
22. Dobson and Payne, *Carlos Complex*, 126.
23. Marr, *HMB*, 318.
24. *HMB*, 318.
25. *HMB*, 320. After the horrendous Winter of Discontent, Thatcher's government likely had an easier time justifying the "punishment" of those who had held the country hostage—public opinion was by then clearly in favor of hamstringing the unions.
26. It is Marr's opinion that "in Britain [the oil shock] arrived with special force," exacerbating the vulnerabilities of Britain's economy (340).

27. Marcuse, *Modern Philosophy: Marcuse and the Frankfurt School*, a.t.

28. Sandbrook, *Seasons in the Sun*, 276.

29. Remember that earlier drafts of the script for *Brian* contained more on-the-nose political references than the ultimate draft or finished film. On-point questions about taxes and Brian as a Christ figure, as well as near-quotations from party conference speeches, found their way *out* of the script as the film moved to completion.

30. Williams would leave Labour to help form the Social Democratic Party in 1981.

31. "Mr Healey, the Man Most Likely . . ." *Times*, 2 October 1980: 14; italics added.

32. "Appalled Reaction from Leaders over 'Demagogy,'" *Times*, 30 September 1980: 1.

33. This was the last significant government position Benn would hold; he would lose a closely contested leadership bid to Healey in 1981.

34. By 1924, the British Empire was approximately "seven times larger than the territories of Rome at their greatest extent" (Brendon, *DFBE*, 337).

35. See Laqueur, *Terrorism*, 210, for example.

36. *Terrorism*, 257–58; italics added.

37. Iviansky, "Individual Terror," 49.

38. "Gerald Priestland on Angries and Middle-Class 'Revolution,'" *Spectator*, 18 July 1975: 18.

39. The Tupamaros would give away proceeds from robberies to the poor, for example; and, from Laqueur, "the FLQ during its early years directed its attacks against establishments rather than persons" (Laqueur, *Terrorism*, 239).

40. Marighella, *Minimanual of the Urban Guerrilla*, 20.

41. Laqueur, *Terrorism*, 225.

42. Laqueur, *Terrorism*, 67–72.

43. "Letters to a Frenchman on the Present Crisis," September 1870, found at www.marxists.org.

44. Laqueur, *Terrorism*, 88.

45. Farrell notes: "*fida'i* or *fedayeen* is derived from an Arab term meaning sacrifice" (*BRJ*, 144).

46. *BRJ*, 144–45.

47. Benn was barnacle-like, willing to weather any tides as long as he kept a ministerial post, and Foot could at least be worked with, according to Donoughue and Sandbrook. Mikardo, however, was singled out by Donoughue as one of the "horrors" of the Far Left, even admitting that Callaghan hated him (*DSD*, 2.96).

48. Donoughue, *DSD*, 2.95.

49. See Sandbrook's *Seasons in the Sun*. Bernstein would later write that things in 1976 weren't as bleak as assumed, and that the IMF loan and stringent cuts might have been unnecessary as the economy had begun to improve (*Myth of Decline*, 225–26).

50. Quoted in Burleigh, *BRT*, 12.

51. A character on the long-running *The Archers* radio series, played by Gwen Berryman. *The Archers* was referenced by the Goons and the Pythons ("The Spanish Suitcase"; *MPFC: UC*, 2.25, 187, 192, 193, and 207).

52. "One Day in the Life of a Revolutionary Festival," *Times Literary Supplement*, 27 February 1969: 199.

53. "Japan's Terror Groups Raise Fears of a Police State, *Times*, 22 October 1975: 16.

54. *BRJ*, 87.

55. Laqueur, *Terrorism*, 58.

56. *HMB*, 333–34.

57. Donoughue, *DSD*, 1.270.

58. *DSD*, 2.442.

59. Jenkins, *Anatomy of Decline*, 103.

60. Dennis is both a medieval subsistence farmer and a well-versed political tannoy; the PFJ are a first-century Jerusalem terrorist group and a (slightly more) modern trade union. These kinds of bedfellows appear often in Monty Python's oeuvre. See Larsen, *BAFHG*, 117–18.

61. Jenkins, *Anatomy of Decline*, 104.

62. *DSD*, 2.439; also, see all of chapter 5 of *DSD*, vol. 2 for Donoughue's fascinating day-by-day account of the government's slow, inexorable tumble.

63. "TV News," *Private Eye*, 15 October 1976: 4.

64. "Notting Hill Squatters Evicted," *Times*, 1 October 1976: 5.

65. Laqueur, *Terrorism*, 44.

66. Laqueur, *Terrorism*, 44.

67. "Meinhof's Legacy," *Spectator*, 22 May 1976: 9.

68. *BRT*, 159.

69. Sandbrook, *Seasons in the Sun*, 666–67, and 681–82; Caryl, *Strange Rebels*, 190–94.

70. See the index entries for Thatcher in *DSD*, both volumes.

71. Bogdanor, "Thatcherism, 1979–1990," a.t.; also, Sandbrook, *Seasons in the Sun*, 666–67.

THE CRUCIFIXION QUEUE

NISUS WETTUS (Palin): "Crucifixion? Good"—His name indicates that he's both "nice" and "wet" (meaning ineffective); he doesn't fit well as a Roman soldier. Palin has faced this most of his life, and was generally known as "the nice one" as a Python. Jones had played a similarly "wet," ineffectual character, Herbert, in Holy Grail, there clearly a disappointment to his ambitious father.

MR. CHEEKY (Idle): "I can go free and live on an island somewhere"—This was actually a standard exilic pattern, but for the leading men and women of Rome, not riff-raff across the empire. Even though he has been claiming to be a Roman, Brian is here classed with the *noxii*, or criminal element selected for a degrading death. As Cook writes, "The *noxii* are a central concern of this investigation, since the individuals to be crucified were criminals whose alienation from the civic community became a matter of public spectacle." He goes on to quote Jean-Jacques Aubert's summarizing of their condition:

> Crucifixions were usually carried out outside the city limits, thus stressing the victim's rejection from the civic community. Because of the absence of blood shed out of an open and lethal wound, which evoked the glorious fate of warriors, this type of death was considered unclean, shameful, unmanly, and unworthy of a freeman. In addition, the victim was usually naked. Essential, too, was the fact that the victim lost contact with the ground, which was regarded as sacrilegious.[1]

Cook notes that in depictions such as mosaics the criminals' state of undress made them easy to spot. Brian will be stripped to a loincloth, as well, though many others on the crosses around him will remain fully clothed.

Note

1. Cook, "Crucifixion as Spectacle," 76.

SCENE TWENTY-THREE
PILATE'S PASSOVER ADDRESS

PILATE and BIGGUS . . . appear on the balcony—Inside this portico are two additional painted figures against Pompeian-red backgrounds, similar to the ones seen earlier in Pilate's room. These are also from Pompeii, based on a work known as *The Three Graces*, and origi-nally found in the House of Titus Dentatus Panthera.[1]

. . . outside in the Forum a line of GUARDS is struggling to keep back a surging crowd—This is precisely the type of setting most conducive to *sicarii* activity, though here the Pythons use the crowd as a jeering, uncontrollable audience, not a threatening mob. They aren't "surging," they are just eager to hear Pilate's speech impediment, and begin their "wagging."

PILATE and BIGGUS and the CENTURION appear on the balcony—This scene may be styled after the Antonio Ciseri painting, *Ecce Homo*, completed in 1871, or Mihály Munkác-sy's version of the same scene (1896).[2] These paintings (and many others of the same event) feature the Christ figure as well as Pilate. The Pythons decided to avoid the sticky, perhaps ultimately indefensible challenge of having a scourged Brian appear in this scene—he is with the other criminals, undifferentiated. The Pythons' version of this "Here's the man" moment is missing the man, pushing the scene further away from the life and death of Christ, and away from a possible legal entanglement with more conservative viewers and organizations who might file writs.

This is also a setting where the Roman overlords' disdain for Jewish feelings can be glimpsed. It's been mentioned that under earlier emperors—Julius Caesar and Augustus, for example—the wisdom of ruling respectfully as opposed to vindictively went a long way to keeping the peace in Judea. Jewish religious beliefs and practices were largely tolerated, yes, but principle and practice often diverged. The year 6 census, according to Brandon, struck the Jews "at the very roots of Yahweh's sovereignty over Israel—the holy land of his ancient promise was now regarded as the property of the Roman emperor."[3] Brandon continues: "The Romans not only made little attempt to placate the religious susceptibilities of their new sub-jects, they often designedly outraged them."[4] Pilate would eventually be recalled and lose his prefecture when he ran roughshod over the (particularly) religious feelings of his Jewish and Samaritan subjects. Pilate's incidents involving offending Jewish sensibilities (cataloged by Josephus) with iconic standards and shields very nearly led to earlier insurrections on a large scale. The sum total of these slights cost the prefect his job. The Pythons have *not* set out to punctiliously re-create the Holy Land settings in regard to Jewish religiosity—conspicuous by absence are the temple and its cult, the Sanhedrin, any real exemplars of Jewish religious life

(Pharisees, Sadducees), Sabbath considerations, and on. Given this more surface (or just more Christian?) approach to the Gospels, it's not a surprise to see the multiple statues of emperors and Pilate himself,[5] and Roman soldiers wearing iconic armor, in this large courtyard scene. Pilate's deployment of graven images caused outrage in the third decade, but the Pythons included them simply to re-create the "look" of a third decade Roman-occupied city. Without them, the cityscape they chose for the shoot didn't look either "Roman" or "biblical" enough.[6] They were also likely counting on the fact that audiences for this newest Monty Python film had little or no knowledge of first-century Jews and Jerusalem. Most audiences would have fallen back on their Sunday School memories or, more likely, the world proffered by the very recent *Jesus of Nazareth* miniseries, which also featured statues.

PILATE: "People of Jewusalem—Wome is your fwiend!"—Herod would address his Jerusalem subjects often, gathering residents together to hear his announcement of the rebuilt temple, to trumpet a reduction in taxes, to tell his people that he'd mended fences with his sons, and finally to announce the execution of "two of his sons several years later."[7]

Dictators and despots often use this language to convince the defeated that they are in fact in a better position "under new management" than laboring under their previous freedoms. The Soviet-installed Polish leader Edward Gierek—who, in 1970, replaced the more authoritarian Władysław Gomułka—took a friendlier tack, like Pilate:

> Gierek . . . was a natty dresser and a self-confessed technocrat who felt equally at home meeting with workers and foreign dignitaries. As soon as he assumed power, he headed off to Gdańsk to apologize to the workers there for the bloodshed and to promise a fresh beginning. Then he embarked on a series of "consultations" with various social groups to demonstrate his democratic credentials.[8]

PILATE: ". . . it is customawy at this time to welease a wong-doer fwom our pwisons"— Not likely, according to most biblical scholars. Neither Josephus nor Philo mention such a custom, nor does Tacitus. Scholarship at the time of the film's creation toed the accepted line, as it's clearly been assumed that the people of the Roman Empire could wield significant power in matters of life and death, and did so in several settings:

> In the amphitheatre, just as in the Circus and in the theatre, the people might give expression to their political opinions. . . . The people might [also] make concrete demands rather than just formal statements of approval or disapproval. . . . The most famous example is a provincial one. The sovereign power of the Roman people extended throughout the empire: as early as the reign of Tiberius, at the Jewish Passover feast, the Roman prefect of Judæa could use the right of life and death that he had received, via the emperor, from the sovereign people to allow the crowd to request the release of a condemned man.[9]

And so Barabbas may have been released, and Christ went to the cross. In true Python fashion—and true to the gloomier, more pessimistic 1970s from which the film emerges— Brian will be "released" and yet still go to the cross.

More recent scholarship disagrees. Brandon goes the next step, given the tense political situation coupled with Pilate's acknowledged disposition, asserting, "Such a custom is inherently impossible":

> Judaea was seething with revolt; its government would have been annually frustrated by having to release a notable prisoner—according to *Mark*, on this occasion a dangerous rebel, probably a Zealot, was freed. But, even if we pass over the improbability that such a custom existed, what

Mark tells of Pilate's use of it passes beyond belief. He depicts this tough Roman procurator, who was backed by a strong military force, as resorting to this custom to save a man he adjudged innocent. In so doing, he invites the Jerusalem mob to choose between Jesus and a rebel leader, Barabbas, who had killed Romans in a recent insurrection. To have given the crowd such a choice would have been the height of folly, if Pilate had sought thus to save Jesus. The mob's decision was a foregone conclusion. Led by the chief priests, they naturally chose Barabbas, to them a patriotic hero. Frustrated Pilate is represented as weakly asking the mob; "what shall I do with the man whom you call the King of the Jews?"[10]

Smallwood, writing at the time the Pythons were producing *Brian*, agrees:

Of the strange "custom" referred to here by which the Roman governor contributed to the Passover celebrations by releasing a prisoner of the Jews' choice there is no trace elsewhere; the most definite statement, in John, may be a general deduction from Pilate's action on this one occasion, or from a habit which he had adopted (as Matt. and Mark suggest) of trying to ingratiate himself with his subjects, even at the price of increasing his administrative problems by returning one of his opponents to the fray.[11]

Brandon concludes that given Pilate's well-known hardheadedness—especially in relation to his Jewish subjects—"consulting a Jewish mob about what he should do with an innocent man is ludicrous to the extreme."[12] And since Brandon also concludes that the Gospel of Mark "was written for the Christian community in Rome,"[13] it only makes sense that the Roman prefect is displayed in a favorable light if Christianity is to escape strangulation in its crib. The Pythons likely have no such concerns; they simply follow tradition, the recent *Jesus of Nazareth* example, as well as the Markan gospel version and include this oft-reproduced scene.

In the Roman Empire at large this proposal was a kind of *munus*, or act of munificence or beneficence meant to impress the crowds and even future generations—often done as editors put on games at their own expense, "intended to remind the local population of the generosity of the editor."[14] These acts were also attempts to curry favor with Roman patricians and leadership, and as political acts to impress games attendees to vote for particular candidates. The Jerusalem posited by the Pythons isn't a place wracked with uncontrollable violence or even religious schisms, and their Pilate isn't in danger of being unseated, by the emperor or the people of Judea. Therefore, Pilate's willingness to hand over a criminal as a sign of "Wome's fwiendship" is a particularly selfless sign of Roman goodwill, and therefore even more unusual, given Pilate's reputation.

BOB HOSKINS—The character leading the "wagging" assault on Pilate is named "Bob Hoskins" in the printed script. Jones plays this character, dirty and with ratty teeth, and there is no indication as to why the fellow British actor's name was chosen. Palin had been fairly certain that he could get Hoskins to play the RSM role in a *Ripping Yarns* episode in 1977, but that didn't pan out.[15] At some point they decided to just employ his name.

CENTURION: ". . . some Jewish joke, sir"—The Centurion is simply trying to protect his boss, convincing him that the Jews aren't laughing *at* him, but just among themselves. This is also one of the very few mentions of anything Jewish in the film. In Freud's *The Joke and Its Relation to the Unconscious*, most of the Jewish jokes studied by Freud were self-denigrating—Jews making fun of Jewishness—so Pilate could be mollified by this suggestion (if he's read his Freud).

PILATE: "Are they wagging me?"—"Ragging" is university slang for antiauthority pranks, boisterousness, or contentious debating.[16] By the time the Pythons were at university,

"Rag Week" was an established part of the good-natured, fundraising social scene.[17] Pilate here plays the stuffy headmaster-type being ridiculed by a churlish audience, but there's no hint of retribution from above. Chancellor Denis Healey had been booed and shouted down at the Labour Party conference in Blackpool in October 1976, as he shared with disgruntled delegates the realities of an inflationary economy, the necessity of public expenditure cuts, and the need for an IMF loan.[18] He simply ploughed through his speech anyway.

But the answer might be yes, they are "wagging" him, and with historical precedent. In the first third of the first century, the Romans assumed control of Alexandria, which had been the empire's main source of grain for many years. The city had been considered a Greek city (not an Egyptian or even African city), and the Greek population didn't accept the Roman annexation—and especially Rome's preferred treatment of the Jews in Alexandria—with grace or dignity. Generally, "the Greeks expressed their feelings by attacks on Rome's protégés, the Jews," but they also attacked Rome in a more familiar, clever way—with derision, according to Smallwood: "Once in the early 30's a gang of hooligans was organized and paid to insult the Prefect in doggerel verse (none of it, unfortunately, preserved) in the Gymnasium."[19] Our Pilate knows how this other prefect must have felt.

ANOTHER: "And a pick-pocket"—This is the third in a "comedy of threes" gag structure, a setup that falls flat when the participant clearly doesn't understand the rules (doesn't speak the language), as there are no "r" sounds in pick-pocket. In Ep. 4 of *Flying Circus*, a woman will try her hand at a joke like this, and be shamed for it.[20]

PILATE: "Sounds a notowious cwiminal"—There is no Woger or Roger to be released, even though he's attached to a laundry list of crimes, but the confusion as to who might be in Pilate's dungeons is also mirrored in the world of international terrorism in the mid-1970s. By early 1976, Carlos had fled Paris and "disappeared" into the underworld of the terror network, and his visible invisibility became almost mythical:

> He was seen in London, Paris and Bonn. In fact, the most popular expression with security police everywhere was "Carlos was here!" He became such a phantomlike figure that the idea caught on that Carlos was not a real person. The French believed he had been killed by other terrorists; the Germans said that he was no more than a code word for an international terror organization; and the Israelis, who hate for their enemies to become legends, advanced the theory that there were four different Carloses.[21]

As the city of Jerusalem moved closer to violence and anarchy (well after Pilate's rule), the incidents of street crime increased, and those anti-Romans likely longed for the order the empire had provided.

CENTURION: "Samson the Sadducee strangler . . . Silas the Syrian assassin . . . several seditious scribes from Caesarea . . ."—A list of biblical names picked likely at random, with the "ess" factor significant. Samson is a well-known OT name, while the Sadducees were the other significant political and religious body in Jerusalem. Silas was one of Paul's companions, and Josephus mentions Silas as a general appointed by Josephus himself. Jerusalem was actually ruled by the Syrian Legate during this period, and the governors of Judea depended "on the legate of Syria for help in cases of crisis," as when pilgrims caused problems and likely during any festival in Jerusalem.[22] The "seditious scribes of Caesarea" would have been hard-pressed to be too seditious, since Caesarea was Pilate's actual seat of power. Caesarea was the port city where the Romans installed their "administrative capital and military headquarters," and Herod the Great's palace became the governor's residence, according to Smallwood.[23] Pilate would have lived there most of the year, surrounded by Roman soldiers.

Recent serial-type killers included the Black Panther, the "Monster of Worcester," David McGreavy, who killed and then impaled on a fence three small children he was babysitting in 1973.[24] The Pythons had already sent up the well-known serial killer of their youth, John Christie, who had been hanged in 1953.[25] The "Monster of Florence" (Italy) had claimed a string of victims by the time this film was done, often murdering male/female couples, then mutilating the women. The killer(s) murdered at least sixteen men and women in the Tuscany area between 1968 and 1985, the grisly events covered in many newspapers of the day.[26]

Notes

1. Part of the *Pompeii 79AD* collection mentioned earlier.
2. In Ep. 24 of *Flying Circus*, Art Critic ("Gavin Millar") Cleese is rambling about the poetic gifts of Mr. Neville Shunt, saying at one point "Ecce homo, ergo elk" (*ATW*, 2.24.7).
3. Brandon, *Jesus and the Zealots*, 63.
4. Brandon, *Jesus and the Zealots*, 63.
5. True, these statues and busts wouldn't likely cause offense, since they were not part of the Roman cult of worship. But given that the Jews responded so vigorously to the aniconic shields (meaning they bore no graven images, just words celebrating Tiberius), Pilate might have been safe to assume that discretion was the better part of peaceful rule, erecting no Roman imagery where any Jew might have to see it.
6. The Pythons had discussed Israel, Jordan, Tunisia, and Morocco as possible filming locations, each with strengths and weaknesses. Jones worried "that [Tunisia] doesn't really look like the Holy Land," for example, so more props and set decorations were going to be needed. See Palin's *Diaries 1969–1979*, 394. The *Jesus of Nazareth* sets weren't overly populated with Romanesque statues and potentially sacrilegious images, meaning the Pythons didn't borrow every visual inspiration from that recent film.
7. Levine, *Jerusalem*, 172–73.
8. Caryl, *Strange Rebels*, 15.
9. Wiedemann, *Emperors and Gladiators*, 166–67.
10. Brandon, "The Trial of Jesus," 257–58.
11. Smallwood, *JURR*, 164n69; this alleged practice is discussed in Brandon, *Jesus and the Zealots*, 258–59.
12. Brandon, "The Trial of Jesus," 258.
13. Likely soon after the "Flavian triumph" in 71, when the actions of Vespasian and his son Titus triggered a new Roman dynasty (Brandon, "The Trial of Jesus," 254).
14. Wiedemann, *Emperors and Gladiators*, 16–17.
15. Palin, *Diaries 1969–1979*, 339.
16. See the *OED* entry "rag, n. 4."
17. Larsen, *MPFC: UC*, 2.174.
18. Sandbrook, *Seasons in the Sun*, 481–83.
19. Smallwood, "Jews and Romans," 237. The Caesarean Greeks seemed to have a rather clever and wicked sense of humor, too, at one point creating an elaborate parody of the Jewish sacrifice ritual that included birds and a chamber pot. The local Jews were not amused. This all spilled over, and ended with a massacre led by Florus in Jerusalem ("Jews and Romans," 318–19). Many Christians found themselves equally unhappy about the Pythons' humor in *Brian*.
20. The pun "Watteau, dear?" is her "only line," she cries (*ATW*, 1.4.43, and *MPFC: UC*, 1.76).
21. Demaris, *Brothers in Blood*, 62.
22. *JURR*, 147.
23. *JURR*, 145–47.
24. McGreavy was approved for parole in 2016.
25. *MPFC: UC*, 2.5, 9, 17, and 110.
26. "Florence Offer," *Times*, 19 September 1985: 19.

SCENE TWENTY-FOUR
THE CRUCIFIXION QUEUE, PART II

NISUS: "How many have come through?"—Miscommunication again, as the Jailer seems to hear something naughty, instead. It will become clear, though, that these characters are purposely miscommunicating. In *I'm All Right Jack*, Stanley is working his forklift on his first day, when he accidentally uncovers a group of men hiding, playing cards. They snap at him to put the crate back in place and leave them be. Stanley is told these churls are redundant, but can't actually be fired or there'll be a strike action. The Jailer and his Assistant seem to have similar attitudes toward the Romans, and similar job security.

JAILER: "You'll have to sp-sp-sp-speak up, sir"—One man hears what hasn't been said, and one man stutters—miscommunication again. And, as *I'm All Right Jack* has already been mentioned as one of the touchstones for this film for the Pythons, it should be no surprise to learn that one of the characters on the loading dock is also a stammerer: "Then what's 'e doin' on a fu-fu-fu-fu-forklift truck?" "You're right, they fu-fu-fu-fight us on every issue!" "You silly cu-cu-cu-clod!" and "Why don't you tell 'em to fu-fu-fu-photograph something worthwhile?" Unlike the stuttering of the assistant, all of these are meant to hint at a forbidden swear word before the inoffensive word emerges.

Incidentally, one of the tidbits the Pythons (and perhaps especially their de facto historian, Jones) might have culled from their historical sources is from the name of Josephus Flavius's great-grandfather, Simon the Stammerer.[1]

NISUS WETTUS: "It's such a waste of human life, isn't it?"—Perhaps meant to be one of the few voices in the film on the side of humanity, akin to the campaigners against capital punishment in Great Britain. This would have been an alien concept to most Romans, as mentioned earlier. To deny or struggle against the civilizing benefits of the empire, Wiedemann argues, was to display such antisocial tendencies as to warrant removal from civilization—imprisonment, exile, or death.[2] Perhaps Nisus is as "giving" as Augustus, though, who boasted he would often "save rather than . . . eradicate" peoples who could accept servile status.[3] In this way the "waste of human life" stops, and those like Brian and his crucifixion party could live on in grateful service to the Romans. For Nisus, this doesn't feel like clemency (he's a functionary, not a maker of rules), but an ahistorical (or maybe just atypical?) character in a period film. Perhaps he is more like the character Little Horse in *Little Big Man*, an effeminate, likely gay character who is allowed to stay in the village when the men go out to fight. The film was released in 1970, in the wake of Stonewall and the beginnings of the gay liberation movement, so it would be hard to argue there might be a significant contemporary influence. Or even Gregor in Konrad Wolf's *I Was Nineteen* (1968), a German-born Russian soldier who isn't like his Soviet comrades—or his German enemies. In other words, these kinds of characters can read more like eruptions of the time in which the film is produced. Nisus, finally, is more liberal Left than he is Roman, but he follows orders well.

BRIAN: "Could I see a lawyer or someone?"—This sounds very twentieth-century, something from the popular *The Sweeney*, or the earlier *Z Cars*. It sounds anachronistic, but it's not. This is Brian's first real attempt to exercise his rights, if granted any, as the son of a centurion, and perhaps even as a Roman citizen.[4] In Rome, and since he's not a slave, his right to a trial would have been almost certain; however, the further away he is from the seat of power, the more likely the whims of the local authority would prevail.[5] It is probably also important whether his would be considered a criminal offense (he *is* caught breaking and entering) or an act of treason or insurrection, rendering his legal rights moot. Pilate clearly sees this as a case of his own judgment being sufficient for conviction and execution, so even if Brian had the name of a lawyer on the tip of his tongue he mightn't have been allowed representation.

If he were to be granted a criminal trial, Brian might have been allowed a "defense by legal advocates," according to Richard, and Roman law, at least, was weighted in favor of the defendant, meaning Brian might have had a fighting chance:

> After 149 B.C., in most other criminal cases, the accuser and accused jointly selected jurors from special lists, each pertaining to a different type of crime.[6] Juries might contain as many as seventy-five members. Jurors listened in silence and were forbidden to speak to one another. The presiding praetor restricted himself to insuring an orderly conduct of the trial.[7]

But these magnanimous safeguards applied to a criminal accused—a slave wouldn't get this treatment, nor would a noncitizen of Rome, nor a citizen accused of treason. Brian's trial, then, has already taken place, in the court of Pilate.

When the timorous Nisus Wettus asks about a lawyer, what he's more likely asking is does Brian have any money, any resources to afford what would have been an expensive appeals process.[8] The trial procedure laid out above was generally available to the higher born. Brian of course doesn't have the funds for such an appeal,[9] nor to pay any fine that might be offered in place of corporal punishment, so—like those ahead and behind him in the crucifixion queue—he's kind of stuck. Richard does mention that those of "low or slave origin" did have legal avenues in criminal proceedings, as Augustan "urban prefects" who had "judicial knowledge [that] exceeded . . . most praetors" could hear the case: "Although low-born convicts might now be sentenced to gladiatorial schools, mines, or public works projects, there were fewer death sentences than under the republic."[10] This type of hearing would have been available for criminal and civil cases—cases of high treason generally end in death. In ancient Roman law, this high treason (a crime against the state) was known as "*perduellio*," and the guilty were banished or executed, their families forbidden to mourn them. Under Tiberius, coincidentally, the Law of Treason (*lex maiestatis*) was greatly expanded to cover either the murder of or even conspiracy to murder a high-ranking Roman official or hostages, by which Brian can easily be condemned. Punishment for a high-born so convicted would have been swift beheading and confiscation of property; for the low-born, punishment would likely have come via the more painful crucifixion, burning, or wild animal attack.

Bringing the action into the contemporary world, there are at least two interesting parallels. The first involves the case of minicab driver George Davis, mentioned earlier, who was arrested following a bank robbery, then identified by several policemen as being one of the robbers. Davis had an alibi, and he had many witnesses to support that alibi, but the testimony of policemen who were on the scene and who gave chase after the robbery carried the day. Davis's shady past was also on trial (arrests and several minor convictions)—his alibi had been supported by minor criminals like himself. The judge in the case, Mr. Justice Shaw, believed what he believed, like Pilate: "The evidence has demonstrated that you are a member of a very dangerous gang of criminals who were ruthless in what they did."[11] Davis was convicted and went to jail for more than a year before his innocence was proven. When Brian was brought before Pilate initially he was the "one survivor" of his "wowdy webels" who had dared to "waid" Pilate's palace, so Pilate knew of his links to the "very dangerous" PFJ—a summary conviction and execution is now easy. At this point, it's not likely a lawyer could have helped.

Secondly, as the 1977 trial of the Baader-Meinhof Gang got underway, the defendants refused to recognize the court's authority, refused to cooperate (even to sit down or be silent when told), and generally attacked the proceedings as a political show trial of political prisoners. According to their warden at Stammheim prison, Hans Musser: "The court could only rarely deal with the real matter of the trial. They had to deal with endless petitions, petitions for delay, petitions to see these documents, those documents, a summons for the American president to appear as a witness, and so on."[12] Brian has none of these legal options, it appears, so his trial should proceed apace.[13]

Notes

1. See the entry for Josephus in the *JE*.
2. Wiedemann, *Emperors and Gladiators*, 103.
3. Wiedemann, *Emperors and Gladiators*, 103–4.
4. There's no guarantee that the legendary "Nortius Maximus"—Brian's biological father—was actually Roman, since there were so many foreign members of the Roman military by this period. His very Roman name is assumed to be "a joke name," remember.
5. As mentioned earlier when Brian was first being interrogated, Roman emperors granted great powers of discretion and judicial authority to regional governors. The fact that Pilate was forced to return to Rome to explain his actions in relation to both the Samaritans and the Jews (compelled by Vitellius) indicates the severe, injudicial, and ruthless nature of Pilate's reign in Judea. See Brandon's "Pontius Pilate in History and Legend."
6. Again, all this is likely moot for a half-Jew accused of seditious activities, especially those that might lead to the injuring or death of a Roman governor's family, and, ultimately, the potential "smash[ing]" of the Roman Empire" in a handful of months. Rome's renowned legal largesse isn't applicable in this case, and Brian will be crucified along with 139 other poor souls.
7. Richard, *WWAR*, 50.
8. Pölönen, "Plebeians and Repression of Crime," 239n53.
9. Pölönen, "Plebeians and Repression of Crime," 238–39n53.
10. *WWAR*, 51.
11. "G. Davis, a New Name in Wisden," *Telegraph*, 20 August 1975: 1.
12. *Baader-Meinhof: In Love with Terror*, a.t.
13. Baader and Ensslin were sentenced to life imprisonment for murder and attempted murder on 28 April 1977. Meinhof had taken her life in prison the year before.

SCENE TWENTY-FIVE
PILATE'S PASSOVER ADDRESS, PART II

Pilate: "This man commands a cwack legion!"—These small scenes are playing out like extended music hall bits. Verbal humor that doesn't rely on the visual, these set pieces are reminiscent of the banter between guards and king in the Tall Tower of Swamp Castle in *Holy Grail*. By this point in *Brian*—when "crack" has become "cwack"—Pilate has lost all vestiges of authority and respect with the assembled crowd, but he can still send a man off to be crucified, as well as offer a reprieve. The "wagging" mob is in no danger, though.

   Pilate: "He wanks as highly as any in Wome!"—Mentioned earlier in relation to the "splitter" Judean Popular Peoples' Front, a "wanker" is either a disliked person (a jerk), or one who masturbates, or both. In the earlier 1970s Waugh would call Heath's Policy Review Staff the "Wank Tank."[1] PRS member Baron Rothschild was "Lord Top Wank."[2]

Notes

1. Waugh, *FCY*, 23 March 1974.
2. Rothschild was a Trinity alum and adviser to Heath and Thatcher.

SCENE TWENTY-SIX
THE CRUCIFIXION PARTY

NISUS WETTUS: "Crucifixion party?"—Here the waiting crucifixion party turns to the Roman soldier as one, like boys hearkening to their headmaster,[1] and each carries a full cross on his shoulders.[2] No one carries just the *patibulum*, as was often the case in especially public crucifixions during this period. In those cases, the rest of the cross—the post, the additional nails and ropes and any tools needed to finish the task—were to be waiting at the site of the crucifixion, according to published rules of the day. The agent in charge of the crucifixion, often a professional undertaker (contracted out by the city's leaders), had to make sure these implements were on hand, according to Cook, quoting the official contract:

> Whoever will want to exact punishment on a male slave or female slave at private expense, as he [the owner] who wants the [punishment] to be inflicted, he [the contractor] exacts the punishment in this manner: if he wants [him] to bring the *patibulum* to the cross, the contractor will have to provide wooden posts, chains, and cords for the floggers and the floggers themselves. And anyone who will want to exact punishment will have to give four sesterces for each of the workers who bring the *patibulum* and for the floggers and also for the executioner. . . . Whenever a magistrate exacts punishment at public expense, so shall he decree; and whenever it will have been ordered to be ready to carry out the punishment, the contractor will have gratis to set up stakes (*cruces*), and will have gratis to provide nails, pitch, wax, candles, and those things which are essential for such matters. Also if he will be commanded to drag [the cadaver] out with a hook, he must drag the cadaver itself out, his workers dressed in red, with a bell ringing, to a place where many cadavers will be.[3]

These would have been rules applied in the larger cities of the empire and Rome, though Jerusalem, as a holy city, might have demanded and been provided different standards. Leaving bodies out overnight, for example, would have been much more challenging anywhere near the temple.

NISUS WETTUS: "We will be on show as we go through the town, let's not let the side down . . ."—An important part of the crucifixion charge and actual execution was the spectacle, the visual proof that crime doesn't pay, especially crimes against the state. The thousands crucified following Spartacus's defeat, as well as the many crucifixions displayed outside the walls of Jerusalem as the city fell were intended as grim messages.

Most often a sport and/or school phrase, to not "let the side down" meant comporting oneself and playing well (orange sections eaten as the crucifixion party moved through the city wouldn't have been a surprise). British journalists employ the term often, but not only in sporting stories. Pakistani revolutionary Tariq Ali left the UK to return home as the first Bhutto administration began in 1969, hoping that a Pakistan socialist paradise was in the offing. But this "disappointed Trotskyite" met similar hurdles on the path to "freedom" that Reg and the PFJ encounter:

> [Ali] flew home last week on the day that President Ayub Khan's regime capitulated to 15 weeks of revolt. He appears not only to have missed the bus, but also to have found some contrast in the Pakistan left-wing camp. Mr. Z. A. Bhutto,[4] the former Foreign Minister, who led the uprising is somewhat of a revisionist, Mr. Ali has discovered. There is also a "frightening vacuum of revolutionary socialism" in Pakistan and Peking has *let the side down* and supported President Ayub Khan as the guardian against imperialism, he says.[5]

Ali was clearly hoping that China would step up and support his chosen candidate (and version of socialism).

As recently as the first days of Callaghan's administration at No. 10 in April 1976, this same sports-related phraseology was being heard as the new (and tenuously seated[6]) Labour government dealt with its first wage demand from the unions, a demand the government surrendered to completely. "Lapsing into the language of some sheepskin-jacketed football manager," Sandbrook writes, "Callaghan spoke warmly of his pride in 'Denis and all the rest of the lads,' while Michael Foot sent a warm note of congratulations for 'a Herculean feat.'"[7]

CENTURION: "Crucifixion party . . . wait for it"—There were strict, published rules governing the execution of slaves, as noted above. This isn't unlike the "regulations" mentioned by the Cart Driver in *Holy Grail*, though those rules could easily be overlooked, with the help of a cudgel and a few coins. Brian isn't a slave, nor is his mother, but whatever rights he might have had seem to have been overlooked here. As for the military "Wait for it" phrase, the Pythons have used it before, in *Flying Circus* Eps. 4 and 5, borrowing it from the Goons and many British war comedies.[8]

One man, ALFONSO, seems to be making particularly heavy weather of it—The saying "making particularly heavy weather" would indicate that the job at hand isn't all that hard, but it's being made to look harder. This is Chris Langham, who came along as part of the repertory group to fill smaller roles. He will be seen rather famously much later playing the hopelessly outmatched new minister Hugh Abbot in *The Thick of It* (2005).

SAINTLY PASSER-BY (Jones): "Let me shoulder your burden brother"—This is a "no good deed goes unpunished" moment seen often in the Python world, but it's also specifically a borrow from *Ben-Hur*. In *Ben-Hur* during the long crucifixion walk, Christ—carrying the full cross—falls. (The other two condemned are only shouldering the patibulums.) A Roman soldier grabs a man from the crowd and forces him to shoulder the cross, while Ben-Hur fetches water for the fallen Christ. There's no indication that the man forced into labor has actually taken Christ's place, but that's where the Pythons step in for the joke.

The set and prop designs around this man include a bunch of dangling candles, each either shaped like a cross, or as a man on a cross. They're not a very thoughtful design, having three wicks, so they're silly enough to be here on a Python set. Jeremias notes that the production and trade of souvenirs was an important part of Jerusalem's festival history; many pilgrims wanted to bring home trinkets to represent their devotional visit. Jewelry including signet rings, seals, and head ornaments have been documented, while votive candles (maybe not in the shape of a cross, but maybe so . . .) don't seem out of the question.[9] There is also cloth or animal skin visible with decorative cross shapes cut out of it. These people of Jerusalem are obviously observing the regular and memorable crucifixion parades as part of their Passover celebration. This is all part of the painstaking prop design Gilliam and his crew created for a believable Jerusalem, and which Gilliam was certain wasn't being appreciated.

Notes

1. There was, incidentally, a headmaster-and-class scene planned to start the film, but it found its way out of the finished product. A sex education classroom appears in *Meaning of Life*.

2. It will be seen that there are already crosses in place at the crucifixion site, none bearing victims; it's not clear where all the crosses end up once they are carried outside the city by the crucifixion party.

3. Cook, "Envisioning Crucifixion," 265–66; See also Wiedemann, *Emperors and Gladiators*, 74–75.

4. Bhutto would be executed in 1979. The Pythons mention him as a guest attending the premier of *Holy Grail* (on *The Album of the Soundtrack of the Trailer of the Film of* Monty Python and the Holy Grail). Tariq Ali attended Oxford at the same time as Jones and Palin. Ali was also a potential candidate representing the Radical Alliance in the late 1960s.

5. "Tariq Ali Assesses a Revolt," *Times*, 1 March 1969: 8; italics added.

6. Within hours of Callaghan achieving the PM's office, a Labour junior minister died in hospital, and Labour's majority was gone. As of 6 April 1976, Labour held 314 seats, and all other parties combined for 316, meaning coalition was unavoidable (Sandbrook, *Seasons in the Sun*, 465–66). This almost evenly matched House also meant that the minutiae of parliamentary democracy—Reg's voice should come to mind now—would have to be employed by its most ruthless and gifted practitioner, Michael Foot, which may at least partly account for the parliamentary fastidiousness the PFJ demonstrates (464).

7. Sandbrook, *Seasons in the Sun*, 469.

8. Larsen *MPFC: UC*, 1.77.

9. Jeremias, *JTJ*, 9, 29, 104. There is a bit of surviving footage on DVD versions of the film of Palin as a market haggler trying to hawk some of these goods.

SCENE TWENTY-SEVEN
PILATE'S PASSOVER ADDRESS, PART III

PILATE: "No Weubens. No Weginalds. No Wudolph the Wed Nosed Weindeer!"—
"Reuben" and "Reginald" are here simply because they begin with "r," but "Rudolph" and
the following "Spencer Tracy" are bare-faced irruptions of modernity like the *Star Wars* bit
earlier.[1] The Rankin and Bass version of *Rudolph the Red-Nosed Reindeer* had been a staple
on holiday television since 1964; the popular children's book made its debut in 1939, and the
song appeared a decade later. The Fleischer Brothers had produced a cinematic cartoon for
Rudolph in 1948, as well. The stop-motion animated short was running on virtually every
regional BBC station on 24 December 1976, for example.

Hollywood icon Spencer Tracy had died in 1967; he's included because his name offers
three "ess" opportunities for Biggus.

JUDITH: "Release Brian!"—Bob Hoskins and the mob are just teasing Pilate and Biggus, but Judith actually knows of a prisoner she wants released, and she also knows how to
work the Jerusalem crowd, clearly. Wiedemann writes that this is nothing new in the empire,
especially given the all-important nature of games, contests, and vocal crowds: "Suetonius
tells us that during Vespasian's reign, his son, as Praetorian Prefect, arranged for partisans
of his to be distributed among the theatre audience to demand the execution of individuals
whom Titus suspected of opposing him."[2] Judith is simply taking the crowd's good-natured
animus to poke and prod their betters and turning it to her purpose, and it works.

PILATE: "Very well. I shall welease Bwian!"—So Pilate decides to release the only man
in custody—that we know of—who is actually guilty of a capital crime. No thieves or other
brigands are offered, just Brian. This complicates the depiction of the much-battered prefect,
especially in his biblical decision to allow Jesus to meet his fate, allegedly knowing he was
innocent. The Pythons haven't simply replicated the events of the Passion here, placing Brian
in Jesus's place throughout, and calling it square. Their character is caught up in the religious
and revolutionary fervor of the period, both well documented historically, glancing across
the messianic touchstones from Gospel stories of Jesus's ministry and death. This was too
close for comfort for those who would protest the film and call it blasphemous. The problematized Pilate is an interesting Pilate, though, and was being argued in academic circles, in
Passion plays, and on editorial pages of the postwar period. This Pilate seems to be relying
on rules as opposed to laws, which will ring familiar in a moment. In an article looking at
the expectations Christians should have of themselves in relation to "world order," the *Times*

correspondent quoted Karl Barth, "perhaps the greatest theological master since Augustine, [who] spoke astringently about the behaviour of Pontius Pilate":

> He suggested that when Pilate pronounced Jesus innocent, yet handed him over, he did what all politicians do and what has belonged to the actual achievement of politics in all times: he tried to maintain order, and his own position of power, by surrendering the clear law, for the protection of which he had been installed. In him, the state abandoned its legal basis and was given over to a clique.[3]

Granted, the Pythons' version of Pilate never seems to be truly worried about losing control to the extent that his rule might be threatened; the historical Pilate was outnumbered and far from the support of Rome, or even Syria. The Pythons' version of the man is willing to give a Passover gift to the braying mob, any prisoner they want, and is also willing to put up with their "wagging" him if it means making good on his feast-time promise. This is a version of Pilate who does not sentence Jesus, nor does he give Jesus over to religious authorities knowing he will be killed. This Pilate isn't the Pilate of (most) history, the man who washed his hands to pass responsibility away from himself.

It's clear the Pythons meant to keep a distance between their Pilate and the Pilate of the Gospels (no scourging, no washing of hands, etc.), though as one of only two historical characters depicted in the film, Pilate's actions are fairly traditional—his job is to keep order in this province of the Roman Empire. In this, the Pythons are echoing to a degree the conclusions of a recent and controversial book by Haim Cohn, *The Trial and Death of Jesus* (1968). The Israeli politician, jurist, and author argued that it was Pontius Pilate and the Roman forces—and not the Sanhedrin—who tried and executed Jesus.[4] Our Pilate decides Brian's culpability and sentence on his own, which he had the authority to do, historically. One-hundred-and-thirty-nine men (and women) besides Brian will be crucified, yes, meaning Pilate has approved their sentences, but Brian is treated as indifferently as any of them, the indifference, and perhaps fairness, of law, equally applied.

Notes

1. Reuben is a name that fits, being a Hebrew name; Reginald is popular, though anachronistic, with Reg here in the film, but also other political types Reginald Maudling, Reg Birch—discussed earlier—and Reg Prentice, all in newspapers of the day. Significantly, MP Reg Prentice had left Labour for the Conservatives in 1977.

2. Wiedemann, *Emperors and Gladiators*, 167.

3. "The Christian Commitment to World Order," *Times*, 16 April 1966: 10.

4. A typical academic review of the book calls its conclusions "provocative" and its hypotheses "bold," though the book's "weaknesses" outweigh its strengths (Peter Richardson, *Journal of Biblical Literature*, 265–67). See also "Shifting the Blame from the Jews to the Romans," *Times*, 10 April 1971: 12. There existed a significant cottage industry in the post-1948 years, encouraged by the new state of Israel, for Jewish scholarship that lessened or removed total blame for the crucifixion from the Jews, while leading up to this new world, Jewish artists like Marc Chagall created more Jewish versions of the crucifixion to problematize the otherwise Christian symbolism ("Resurrecting Chagall's Jewish Jesus," *ArtNews*, 10 September 2013). To a certain extent, the Pythons are also participating in this endeavor of reexamination and rehabilitation.

SCENE TWENTY-EIGHT
LOOKING FOR BRIAN

With the crucifixion queue—

MR CHEEKY seems undeterred by this sight—The crucifixion party has nearly reached what the script is calling "Calvary" (known as "Gol'gotha" in most of the Gospels), and where *in situ* crosses can be seen. The crowd along the way is politely applauding and smiling, as if this is a cheery parade or an investiture procession. Mr. Cheeky is waving at the appreciative crowd, prompting the centurion to cuff him.

MR CHEEKY—**"I might have to give up being crucified . . ."**—As it turns out, Mr. Cheeky has escaped crucifixion before, and he will do so again today, thanks to the Romans' interest in the number of those crucified and not necessarily who they are.

In Pilate's jail—

Both the JAILER and his ASSISTANT indicate, as in charades, they're thinking of a "small word"—No becomes "n'yes," even as the Centurion storms out. More importantly, these two have obviously been toying with their Roman overseers, pretending to be mute, deaf, mad, and unable to communicate without a stutter. Cheeky taunts his abuser because he knows there's nothing worse than what already faces him—a slap is a small price to pay for some fleeting satisfaction. This is of a piece with Matthias calling crucifixion a "doddle," the crowd laughing at Pilate's and Biggus's expense, and the assembled mob not saving another authority figure, the religious official, from stoning earlier in the film.

SCENE TWENTY-NINE
THE PFJ RESOLVES

Inside MANDY'S kitchen . . .—The PFJ are likely meeting here due to Brian leading the "Fifth Legion" to their hideout earlier. There isn't any indication that this is actually Mandy and Brian's house—Matthias seems to be padding about in the background, not Mandy—excepting the scenic description.

REG: ". . . get on with it . . ."—This is connected by a sound bridge to the previous scene, where the Jailers are getting on with their story after the Centurion has left. They've passed the "get on with it" motion with "one abstention," and they can now act. In *Holy Grail*, Dingo's aside to the camera in Castle Anthrax is met with a "Get on with it!" from most of the cast, those already seen and those yet to appear.[1] In *Flying Circus*, the classic "Dead Parrot" sketch ends with the Colonel interrupting the "silly" proceedings and demanding they all "Get on with it!" to the next sketch—and they do.[2]

All this dithering means that the PFJ might be the Pythons' version of Tariq Ali, who was jibed at by other activists as "the revolutionary who has missed his first revolution."[3] *Daily Mail* columnist Vincent Mulchrone also dismisses Ali in February 1969 as a "lovable," "upper class" revolutionary who exhibits a "limpet-like devotion to our neo-Fascist land, repressive State machine and all"—which sounds very much like the PFJ and their attachment to the Roman version of Jerusalem.[4]

As for the continued time wasting on parliamentary procedure evident in everything the PFJ tries to do, British governance provided myriad examples for the Pythons to lampoon. In November 1975, Bernard Donoughue attended a meeting of his "constituency general management committee in North St Pancras," and he is attending for the first time as a General & Municipal Workers Union delegate (thanks to his position as adviser to PM Wilson). Donoughue sums up the three-hour meeting curtly, and recognizably: "As usual most of the time was spent passing resolutions denouncing the government."[5] A later meeting with this same constituency group he'd bemoan as wasted time listening to "wankers."

An interesting version of this parliamentary procedure fiddling comes from the final Wilson administration, when Benn was secretary of state for industry, and was at his most Dennisean—demanding workers' control of industry. Donoughue writes on the eve of an industrial debate:

> Before leaving I put in a green paper memo to the PM warning him that Benn's proposals on the Industry Act, to come up tomorrow at the Industry Cabinet committee (IDV), were a dangerous step to the left and a significant reinterpretation of the White Paper. Because he wants (1) powers

to direct a new NEB, (2) £1,500 million for acquisitions and (3) powers for compulsory acquisition without going through full parliamentary procedures. This must be stopped.[6]

In this case Donoughue and the PM would use procedure to curb Benn's overreach. Reg doesn't use a knobkerrie against "the feminists" or even as a face- or even lifesaving device—he's just incapable of proceeding without a vote being taken.[7]

Notes

1. Larsen, *BAFHG*, 338–39.
2. Larsen, *MPFC: UC* 1.127–42; *ATW* 1.8.106.
3. "Tariq Ali Assesses a Revolt," *Times*, 1 March 1969: 8.
4. ". . . Lickspittle Running Dog of the Neo-Fascist Society," *Daily Mail*, 6 February 1969: 6.
5. Donoughue, *DSD*, 1.578.
6. *DSD*, 1.234.
7. Francis convinces Reg to convene without "a seconder," which gets them out the door.

SCENE THIRTY
TOWARD CALVARY

To the crucifixion hill—

WORKER *removes a desiccated corpse from a cross outside the city walls*—We've already seen workers like this earlier, removing fresh body parts from the arena floor at the Colosseum. This setting is again Sousse, Tunisia,[1] one used by both *Brian* and *Jesus of Nazareth*. The looming, crenellated sandstone walls can be seen behind Brian as he carries his cross toward the others already in place. The Ribat monastery structure dates from the eighth century, but looks ancient enough to have been around much earlier, which is likely why Zeffirelli chose the location, as well, rather than shooting in Israel.[2] As they'd done for *Holy Grail*, the Pythons shot at select angles and with careful compositions so as to miss the bustling city around the monastery-fortress, capturing the stone walls and passageways instead. This Ribat structure is the backdrop for the earlier "Stoning" scene, as well.

The Pythons chose as a location this very identifiable landmark even though it was seen only months before in *Jesus of Nazareth*. An earlier sequence, when Pilate is addressing the jeering crowd, was also shot at an iconic, recognizable (even when re-dressed by Gilliam) wall of the large, inner courtyard of the Ribat monastery, the very same wall seen in *Jesus of Nazareth*, and for the very same scene—Pilate's *attempts* to speak to the Passover crowd. The Pythons used the large wall (with the staircase bisecting the wall diagonally) as their set for Pilate's porch, essentially. In Zeffirelli's film, that same wall with the diagonal staircase is in the far background; Pilate (Rod Steiger), his back to the camera, is seen in silhouette as he addresses the assembled crowd. It's worth mentioning because this is just the kind of practice the Pythons had said they wanted to avoid as they made *Holy Grail*—dressing up and then just acting silly, like a *Carry On* film. The Pythons knew they might encounter and even use some of the same vistas and buildings the much more somber Zeffirelli film employed (as well as local craftsmen and even extras), and worried about the inevitable comparisons. Once they reached the Tunisian locations for the eight-week shoot, however, they went ahead and used those same sets, and likely still hoped they weren't creating a less jiggle-and-giggle version of *Carry on Cleo*.

With the Roman soldiers—

The CENTURION *marches through the market, pushing anyone out of his way*—This scene is borrowed from the Zeffirelli version. As Christ carries his crossbar on his shoulders through the streets, the Romans clear the way of both supporters and jeering onlookers. When (in *Brian*) one Jerusalemite yells back "Bloody Romans!" at the Centurion, the Centurion pauses long enough to threaten him with crucifixion: "Watch it! There's still a few crosses left." The man has already scarpered, and the other soldiers don't leap to arrest the man, so maybe the threat isn't terribly real. In *Jesus of Nazareth*, as the phalanx of soldiers struggles through the streets with the condemned Christ, some citizens actually try and interfere. These are threatened with drawn weapons. Over the tumult can be heard the Centurion's cries: "Out of the way unless you want the same!" and "You want to die as well?"

At the crucifixion hill—

BIG NOSE: "You Roman git!"—Mr. Big Nose is right back where we first met him, as are many of the people we initially saw at the Sermon on the Mount—now threatening to punch a Roman, Parvus. A "git" is a fool, a "contemptible person," and we've seen a "Mr. and Mrs. Git" in Ep. 21 of *Flying Circus*, and it will be used by the man in the "Abuse" department in the "Argument Clinic" sketch, Ep. 29.[3] The soldier tells this "Jewish turd" to shut up.

BIG NOSE: "I'm not Jewish. I'm a Samaritan!"—He doesn't react to being called a turd, just being mistaken for a Jew. This is perhaps a spot-on indication of just where Pilate finally went wrong. After his several dustups with the Jews over sacrilegious offenses (including the bringing of Roman cultus objects into the Holy City), Pilate likely didn't have much leeway with either his subjects or his Roman employers. His slaughter of Samaritans as they attempted to reach Mt. Gerizim was the last straw. An embassy was sent to Vitellius, "who was now president of Syria," and Vitellius, obviously believing the reports of Pilate's cruelty (and, more importantly, his inability to keep order), sent Marcellus to replace Pilate.[4] Keeping the peace in Judea was at this time clearly more important than crushing the Jews' spirits. Pilate was ordered to report to Rome as quickly as possible, and his term as prefect came to a close.

GREGORY: "Under the terms of the Roman occupancy . . ."—These may not have been written down, but various procurators and prefects over Judea knew that observing Jewish religious and social customs made for a much more manageable populace. These "terms" would have included allowing Jews their particular mode of worship (to one god), access to their temple, the continued sanctity of that temple, significant religious and civic control over citizens, freedom from quartering, and no expectation of devotion to the Roman cultus or to serve in the Roman army.

GREGORY: ". . . we are entitled to be crucified in a purely Jewish area"—As the Samaritans claimed a direct ancestral relation to the ancient Israelites, and that "their temple on Mount Gerizim, and not the temple at Jerusalem, was the covenanted sanctuary of the God of Israel . . . there was a deep-rooted hostility between the Jews and the Samaritans, whose territory lay between Judaea and Galilee," writes Brandon. "Like the Jews, the Samaritans also looked for the coming of the Messiah."[5] It's no surprise, then, that Gregory and his wife would demand a crucifixion alongside Jews only.

Also, even though they'd had to take or help take the city twice, in 63 and 37 BC, both battles quite bloody, the Romans had conceded much to the Jews as part of their eventual occupation and administration. Letters or delegations from Jewish leaders to Pilate's Syrian Legate superior or even to Rome and the emperor often resulted in official and semiofficial remonstrations to the prefect.

PHARISEE: "Pharisee separate from Sadducees . . ."—At the time the Pharisees were popularly divided into seven types, including those who were falsely humble, those who worshipped with "impure motives," those who always counted their good deeds, etc.[6] The Pythons don't offer any identifiable Pharisee or Sadducee, with the noted exception of the Official at the stoning, but there are reasons they would not want to be crucified near each other:

> The Sadducees, jealously guarding the privileges and prerogatives established since the days of Solomon, when Zadok, their ancestor, officiated as priest, insisted upon the literal observance

of the Law; the Pharisees, on the other hand, claimed prophetic or Mosaic authority for their interpretation . . . at the same time asserting the principles of religious democracy and progress.[7]

The possibility that a Pharisee or Sadducee would be crucified might be remote, unless they took their religious (and democratic) beliefs to the ultimate degree of sedition. Josephus records that in the first century BC, Jannaeus crucified hundreds of Pharisee rebels, killing them in front of their families.[8] It might have been more difficult for Pilate to follow through on such an execution, given the volatile situation in Jerusalem during the time of Jesus.

VOICE: "And Swedish separate from Welsh . . ."—The silly subtitles for *Holy Grail* were made in faux-Swedish, and Jones is the troupe's only Welshman. This nationality ghettoization sounds silly, and is likely meant as such, but the Roman Empire encountered and enslaved peoples from dozens of regions, including Scandinavia and across Britain. Mannix reports that one prisoner, captured with a Germanic army, was "a Norseman, a giant with long blond hair and a beard."[9] This prisoner, armed with "an enormous two-handed sword," fought to victory in the ring against trained gladiators, and was only defeated when, succumbing to hubris, he accepted a challenge from the motivated son of a soldier who'd been killed by Germanic tribes in the north.[10]

CENTURION: "There's a hundred and forty of you lot to get up . . ."—Mass executions were part of the Roman spectacles, and became more frequent as the empire struggled to sustain itself abroad and at home:

> Wholesale crucifixions in the arena became a major attraction, and the crowd would lay bets on who would be the first to die. As with every betting sport, a lot of time and trouble was devoted to fixing the business. By bribing an attendant [like the Pythons' centurion, Parvus], you could arrange to have a certain victim die almost immediately, last an hour, or live all day. If the spikes were driven in so as to cut an artery, the man would die in a few minutes. If driven so as to break the bones only, the man would live several hours. Occasionally, though, a victim would cross you up. He might deliberately pull at the spikes to make himself bleed to death or even beat his brains out against the upright. You could never be sure.[11]

A footnote from Whiston's edition of *Wars of the Jews* affixes blame to the Jews: "Reland very properly takes notice here, how justly this judgment came upon the Jews, when they were crucified in such multitudes together, that the Romans wanted room for the crosses, and crosses for the bodies of these Jews, since they had brought this judgment on themselves by the crucifixion of their Messiah."[12] This "they only have themselves to blame" idea seems to have been prevalent among at least non-Jewish cultures across the years.

CENTURION: "Belt up!"—Another bit of Royal Air Force slang—meaning shut up—that had become part of the English-speaking lexicon after World War II. The five English Pythons grew up in the immediate postwar period. Unintelligible banter ("flipped over his Betty Harper's") heard from RAF men was the subject of a sketch in Ep. 43 of *Flying Circus*.

BRIAN: "You don't have to do this . . . you don't have to take orders"—During this period the pacifist Pat Arrowsmith was being arrested over and over again for leafletting and demonstrating against nuclear proliferation, war, and the British presence in Northern Ireland.[13] During arraignments she would lecture the judge on how "disaffected" British troops had become while deployed in Northern Ireland, essentially saying they shouldn't have to take orders and didn't want to fight.[14] The pacifist voices of the day often tried to talk past the military leaders and governments and directly to the soldiers, a sort of putting-daisies-in-gun-barrels scenario. Brian is trying to appeal to the humanity of the centurion in front of him, a man who only has one job to do—get one-hundred-and-forty people onto crosses. Unfortunately the centurion likes "taking orders," and Brian and others will be jobs that get done.

With the PFJ—

The REVOLUTIONARIES meanwhile are marching . . . rather like a trade union delegation . . .—Not "rather like," but *precisely* like. This scene is borrowed directly from *I'm All Right Jack*, though without direct attribution. The first such scene occurs early in the film, just after it's been reported to the chief steward that there is a suspected time-and-motion man infiltrating the work force. Following Mr. Kite closely, the Works Committee marches to confront this new man, rounding corners neatly and marching in lockstep. The Committee then marches, shoulder-to-shoulder, to the personnel manager (Terry-Thomas), there threatening a work stoppage if the time-and-motion study continues. In the end, just like in *Brian*, an equilibrium is reached, where the agitator, in that case Windrush, is eventually removed and both management and labor return to the peaceful status quo.

MR. CHEEKY (Idle): "Couple days up here, lots of people get rescued . . ."—The 1965 Hugh Schonfield book, *The Passover Plot*, actually posited Jesus's *faking* his own martyrdom. Schonfield writes that the revolutionary Jesus planned to be nailed to the cross, that the vinegar he was given was mixed with a sedative so that he could appear to "die," and then be rescued from the cross by his fellow insurrectionists.[15] There was a film of the same name that appeared in 1976, starring Donald Pleasance and Zalman King as Pilate and Jesus (Yeshua), respectively. In the film, Jesus decides, at Judas's urging, to accept a more militant role, like Brian, and help lead the Jewish resistance to Roman rule, plotting "a three-pronged attack on the Roman occupation."[16] Both Christian and Jewish organizations reacted negatively to the proposed film, and it received limited distribution.[17]

Mr. Frisbee isn't worried, clearly, as he's been through this before. Many Jews, having reached this point—knocking at the threshold of death—were as unafraid as Mr. Frisbee, but for very different reasons. Horsley (1979) points out that if the victim was alive during a time of "intense eschatological anticipation," meaning the general belief was that "God's final age of peace and justice was actually imminent," then torture and even death were almost welcome markers on the path to God's presence.[18] Josephus mentions that "in case of success"—where the Jews stood their religious ground and died "well"—

> "the Jews would have laid the foundations of prosperity [*eudaimon*]," [which,] translated from Hellenistic style into the language of Jewish apocalypticism, would mean that Judas and Zadok proclaimed that by carrying out the eschatological will of God they would participate in bringing about the final Kingdom of God.[19]

Josephus also records an event he witnessed involving the "rescue" of men from their respective crosses. Following the siege of Jotapata, Josephus was able to wrangle a kind of pardon from the Roman authorities,[20] including Vespasian and his son, Titus, and he set about gathering his friends and family from various states of bondage (including those held or hiding in the temple in a vanquished Jerusalem). After reconnoitering "a certain village called Thecoa" for Titus, Josephus recorded the following in *The Life of Flavius Josephus*:

> As I came back, I saw many captives crucified, and remembered three of them as my former acquaintance. I was very sorry at this in my mind, and went with tears in my eyes to Titus, and told him of them; so he immediately commanded them to be taken down, and to have the greatest care taken of them, in order to their recovery; yet two of them died under the physician's hands, while the third recovered.[21]

Even if not "rescued," corpses on crosses were guarded closely across the empire. Families of those crucified would make attempts to retrieve their loved ones' bodies for the giving of last rites followed by a proper burial, two ordinances the Romans wanted to deny their condemned. One example from the fictional writing of Petronius, provided by Cook:

> In Petronius' novel a virtuous matron of Ephesus buries her husband, who had died naturally. A soldier was guarding crosses (of crucified robbers *latrones*), lest anyone take the body for burial. . . . The soldier persuades her to take food and then seduces her. While on his errand the parents of one of the crucified men, "seeing that the watch was ill-kept, took their man down in the dark and administered the last rite to him. The soldier was eluded while he was off duty, and next day, seeing one of the crosses without its corpse, he was in terror of punishment."[22]

In this version of the oft-told tale, the matron actually suggests replacing the missing corpse on the cross with the body of her dead husband—she didn't want to lose her new lover to prison or exile or worse. Hearing the tale, others thought the woman should have been placed on the cross, instead.[23]

MR. CHEEKY: "My brother usually rescues me . . ."—This phenomenon—almost consequence-free recidivism—has historical precedent, and in this time period. The Judean procurator Festus[24] arrested *sicarii* whenever his forces could find them. Rather than follow the Roman legal procedure of a speedy trial and an even speedier execution, Festus "allowed some Sicarii to be ransomed by their relatives," according to Kotker. "In order to pay Festus, the other Sicarii attacked and robbed the rich." The next step can be guessed, and is brilliant: "They handed the money over to Festus, and the imprisoned assassins were set free to continue their crimes until they were caught again."[25] These sicarii obviously understood how the corrupt Roman legal system worked, and they (and the procurator) turned it to their advantage. Mr. Frisbee III understands how a sentence to the crosses works, and, as long as his randy brother delivers, he'll soon be free to carouse again.

MR. CHEEKY: ". . . if he can keep off the tail for more than twenty minutes . . . randy little bugger, up and down like the Assyrian Empire"—The Assyrians did manage to create an enormous empire "up and down" Egypt, the Middle East, Asia Minor, and the Caucasus. The Bridgekeeper in *Holy Grail* uses Assyria as a question, and sends Robin to his death after an incorrect answer.[26] To be "randy" is to be sexually overactive, while "little bugger" is slangy but affectionate.

MR. CHEEKY: ". . . 'Allo . . . your family arrived, then?"—Interesting use of the term, though Mr. Frisbee has just finished mentioning his own brother, so he may just assume that these are Brian's actual family members. Reg will address Brian as "sibling Brian."

Also, Brian's PFJ family doesn't include Judith, the only actual female member of the movement. For narrative purposes she must come next, of course, before Brian's mum, so that his sacrifice on the cross can be juxtaposed against *everything* he's surrendering in his nearly willing martyrdom. The treatment of Judith throughout the film—she is an "Other," always—is influenced by another powerful and ultimately polarizing political woman mentioned earlier, Marcia Williams, later Baroness Falkender. Williams had been at Harold Wilson's elbow since 1956 and right through 1976, serving as his personal and then political secretary. Her quicksilver personality and vitriolic temper combined with a grasping political acquisitiveness (and Wilson's seeming inability to separate himself from her) alienated many inside No. 10, in the Labour Party, and in the halls of British government. As the Wilson administration ended in 1976, it was widely believed that Williams had created the infamous Honours List, known as the "Lavender List," for the PM, rewarding *her* friends and business associates—some of whom later faced criminal charges and censure. Rumors that her kitchen cabinet actually ran the country during Wilson's tenures remain alive today. Clearly, she was much feared, and much disliked. Donoughue reports that Arnold Goodman, one of Wilson's political advisers, would say very little about her (she sued detractors often, vigorously, and successfully); in July 1977 Goodman told Donoughue: "But for Marcia, Harold Wilson would have been a good Prime Minister—not a great one, but a good one."[27] *Private Eye*'s Waugh was certain that "the terror of Lady Forkbender" had driven Wilson "mad."[28] Williams and Margaret Thatcher were the most visible female political figures of the Pythons' youth and then adulthood, when powerful and deadly female terrorists also occupied the headlines.

REG: "Hello, sibling Brian"—According to intimate Donoughue, PM Wilson would often distinguish between those who wanted to be closest to his ear, "draw[ing] the line between what [HW] calls the 'family' and the civil servants."[29] Wilson's family also included the mercurial Marcia Williams, who almost singlehandedly held the Labour government hostage in April 1974, when she felt her influence on Wilson slipping.[30] Donoughue recorded his feelings after one particularly vitriolic phone conversation with Williams:

> It was absolutely ridiculous that a Labour government elected to help millions of people, and its PM, should be totally absorbed in comforting and being attacked by one woman. She is suffering terribly. . . . Her insistence on attacking all who try to help her, on insisting that they put her before everything else, is intolerable. I have now been through every emotion—sympathy for her, anger at the press, irritation with her, and now, finally and totally, exhaustion and being fed up and wanting to wash my hands of it.[31]

When Judith bursts into the PFJ's meeting after Brian has been arrested for the second time, interestingly, she also was treated like "that bloody woman," the oft-ignored or put-up-with Margaret Thatcher. Judith is at least right about Brian's situation, and right about what the PFJ could do, if they chose.

On the cross, Brian is clearly part of the PFJ family, but he's about to be allowed to embrace his role as martyr to the cause, so the family can move on without him. This is reminiscent of the mind-set seen in terror groups of the 1960s, Farrell writes:

> Some very recent research on terrorist organizations (not including the Japanese Red Army) has demonstrated that group cohesiveness and identification are dominant factors in explaining behavior. Isolation from society, compartmented decision making, and dedication to a cause tend to reinforce and sustain the life of the group—even after goals and objectives have been attained. Group survival becomes the sustaining force of the movement, regardless of any political rhetoric espoused.[32]

So the PFJ unit has withdrawn and regrouped and will survive this debacle, Brian's loss certainly acting to refocus the group in their "continuing struggle."

REG: ". . . we are not in fact the rescue committee"—Marighella's *Minimanual* offers bold and quite assured support for such rescues, for "liberation of prisoners," those "ideological comrades" who have, in "the daily struggle against the enemy, [been] subject to arrest," and who likely face "unlimited" prison sentences in dungeons or on work farms.[33] Brian is on a cross in plain sight, and the Roman sentries flee at the first sign of the Judean Peoples' Front, meaning he's no longer even being guarded. His friends aren't compelled to act, though, leaving it to Brian to get the escape ball rolling, if he can. Marighella applauds this self-initiative, as well: "The imprisoned guerrilla views the prisons of the enemy as a terrain which he must dominate and understand in order to free himself by a guerrilla operation."

He concludes: "There is no jail, either on an island, in a city penitentiary, or on a farm, that is impregnable to the slyness, cleverness and the firepower of the rebels."[34] What Marighella hadn't foreseen is the terrorist group who also happens to adhere strictly to *Robert's Rules of Order*, the parliamentary system employed and rigidified by the British trade unions over the years, and the even more leader-free syndicalist movements where "the elemental mass meeting of the workers" might slow down or prevent any real action at all.[35] Fred Kite and his shop stewards are the exemplars here, and the PFJ have taken the lesson. These PFJ delegates would have to lawfully consider any such change, a new "delegation of function," which would likely take much, much longer than Brian has to live on the cross. So Brian is going to be allowed to seal his martyrdom with his death, which often happened in these desperate situations. In the more contemporary cases of the Japanese Red Army and the Baader-Meinhof Gang, the fates of the Lod Airport massacre[36] survivor Kozo Okamoto, as well as RAF leader Andreas Baader, were handled quite differently.

First, to Germany. A fan of Nechaev, Lenin, and Marighella,[37] Baader had been convicted for an arson bombing in 1968, and had fled sentencing before being captured in April 1970. In May 1970 he was serving out his sentence when, during a phony "book interview" arranged by journalist and RAF associate Ulrike Meinhof, Baader's RAF colleagues rescued him from police custody at gunpoint, seriously wounding one man.[38] This was Meinhof's initiation into the activities of the terror group. The gang would flee the country for a spate of terrorist training in Jordan, then return to bomb buildings and rob banks.

As a member of the JRA, Kozo Okamoto was likely the best-known terrorist of the period, later being eclipsed only by Carlos. Okamoto had been the sole surviving terrorist, like Brian, and he was paraded through a show "trial," like Brian, and then condemned, like Brian. In July 1976 the Entebbe hijacking participants, German and Arab nationals, had demanded that Okamoto be released from an Israeli prison in return for safe release of the mostly Israeli hostages. Writing when these wounds were still fresh (in 1977), Dobson and Payne described why Okamoto was targeted by his comrades-in-arms: "Okamoto has become something more than just a Japanese terrorist. He has become part of terrorist mythology, the only survivor of the bloodiest atrocity ever carried out by the PFLP. Like the Russians with their spies, it has become a matter of honour and credence with the PFLP to get him out of prison."[39] Brian fits the bill here, but he will not be rescued from the cross; instead, he becomes a post-probationary martyr. Likely, Brian's willingness to actually follow through on the PFJ's violent anti-imperialist agenda was more troubling, to Reg, Francis, and the lot, than the specter of the continuation of Roman rule, with its admitted perquisites. Back at Entebbe in July 1976, the terrorist's demands for Okamoto and other prisoners were duly taken into account, and then the Israeli government launched a massive rescue operation, killing all terrorists, more than thirty-three Ugandan soldiers, and rescuing more than one hundred hostages.[40] The Israelis had also expended a great deal of time and energy tracking down and eliminating those connected to Black September and the 1972 Olympics massacre.[41] The PFJ certainly fear the Roman version of that revenge, and decide to not invite the attention.

REG: ". . . however, I have been asked to read the following prepared statement on behalf of the movement"—This is the moment where Reg and the PFJ officially abandon Brian to his fate, where Reg turns aside from his oft-stated goal: the immediate overthrow of Rome. In November 1967 Harold Wilson experienced a similar *volte-face*. After months of refusing to consider, talk about, or even have a misty plan ready for the devaluation of the pound—characterizing it as "nonsense," and seeing it as potentially a personal and national disgrace[42]—the hard economic facts finally forced the government's hand. Chancellor Callaghan quickly put together a "round of cuts" that might make the embarrassing move actually efficacious, and

Wilson announced the devaluation on 18 November.[43] Like Reg, Wilson climbed down from his hobbyhorse as soon as it became politically (and for Reg, physically) dangerous. Wilson, whom Andrew Marr characterized as "curiously chirpy" after this very public humiliation—the sacrosanctity of the pound had long been "essential to his strategy"—would carry on the economic fight in a very Reg-like manner.[44] This "abandonment of principles" quirk came to characterize Wilson, Bernstein notes in his book *The Myth of Decline*. Wilson's "reluctance to try to master Labour's divisions on two key issues when they first threatened party unity"—trade union reforms in the 1960s and entry in to the EEC in the early 1970s—meant his eventual turnabouts in both areas rang false:[45]

> In both instances, he backed away from the risks of splitting the party that a showdown would have entailed. In doing so, however, he also repudiated policies that he had supported. These retreats helped to shape a view of Wilson as a man of no principles. While this judgement is not entirely fair, it is clear that preserving the unity and so the political viability of the Labour Party transcended all other issues for him. (233)

Reg has adopted the same tack, moving past overt revolutionary activity that now threatens his comrades' (and his own) safety, now happy to express revolutionary ideals in the form of proclamation, not agitation. In doing so, the core of the PFJ—including, likely, Judith—remain undivided and uncrucified: Reg has saved the Party.

It's also been clear all along that the PFJ is only effective as a revolutionary body by proxy, meaning newer, more motivated "probationary" members will carry out insurrectionary actions while the core of the cell remain free to plan revolutions, discuss procedures, and parse gender references. Most of the twentieth-century guerrilla groups structured themselves similarly, with wound-up acolytes given arms or suicide devices, then sent out to commit mayhem.[46] Attrition thus necessarily (and negatively) affected the longevity of most of these groups. Brian was set on this path by Reg's suggestion of "a little job" to make his bones—an eruption of Roman negative attention and retribution followed, sending Brian to the cross and the PFJ back into the safety of parliamentary procedure and whispered revolutionary invective. After Labour went down to defeat in the 1959 General Election, Aneurin Bevan[47] made his now-famous statement lamenting this kind of self-defeating activity: "The trade unionist votes at the polls against the consequences of his own anarchy."[48] In between elections the unions had stirred the political pot, demanding more and more, and Labour (under opposition leader Hugh Gaitskell), had promised a mutually exclusive "more spending" and "no new taxes" future. Political historian Vernon Bogdanor comments on voters' eventual at-the-polls epiphany: "I think that this is a very powerful point: people who pressed harder for wages, when it came to the election, were shocked by what happened and voted Conservative."[49] The Tories won, increasing the Conservative majority and winning a third straight election. With this official parchment Reg and the PFJ are voting at the polls "against the consequences of their own anarchy," tamping down the unwanted Roman attention and reestablishing the *status quo ante*. Conservative PM Macmillan's avuncular talk leading up to the 1959 election, reminding the British people that they'd "never had it so good," certainly resonates here with Reg and his siblings. Life was indeed quieter and safer before the firebrand Brian took up the revolutionary gauntlet, so the PFJ "vote" to return to that good life, even if it means living under the rule of the "bloody Romans" and their improved, diabolically comfortable infrastructure.

REG: "We, the People's[50] Front of Judea brackets Officials end brackets . . ."—This is an unusually positive ending for a terror group of this period. The Romans actually prided themselves on their ability to stamp out these insurrections almost as they happened, the minimum requirement being the decapitation of the movement. When the armed Samaritans followed their erstwhile prophet up Mount Gerizim, Pilate's troops were there in force to quash the action—dozens of battlefield executions took the lives of all leaders. When Judas of Galilee rebelled against the Roman census and many followed him, Roman reprisals meant "the leaders perished, and the revolt was crushed."[51] For the PFJ, however, it is the newest (and most reasonably violent) member Brian who is captured and killed; the "[Officials]" are allowed to live on, perhaps a nod to their collective lack of threat credibility to Rome's supremacy.

Brandon wonders whether the Jewish historian Josephus suffered from his own conscience in a similar manner, as he related the story of the Zealots in an unflattering way.[52] Josephus fought for the Jews and Jerusalem, yes, but he also eventually surrendered, went over to the Roman side, and became something of an apologist for Titus, Vespasian, and the Romans' right to rule their empire. Reg doesn't tear down Brian, but he clearly doesn't align himself with his acolyte—he's not willing to climb onto a cross next to him, or take his place. Reg's conscience can be assuaged by simply vowing to carry on Brian's fight. Josephus has his own conscience to deal with, according to Brandon:

> A renegade, who prospered in the service of his nation's conquerors, Josephus naturally sought to denigrate those who had led Israel into revolt. But that was not all: Josephus was uncomfortably conscious that the Zealots had sacrificed themselves and their nation, inspired by an uncompromising religious faith that he himself did not possess. In self-justification, therefore, he sought to misrepresent their motives.[53]

Again, Reg isn't tearing down, but he is misrepresenting Brian's motives—nowhere does he acknowledge that Brian started all this for the love of Judith.

REG: ". . . brackets Officials end brackets"—This official phraseology—"brackets . . . end brackets"—is yet another borrow from *I'm All Right Jack*, where the reading aloud of an official communication involved the inclusion of "brackets" where found. Stanley has been sent to almost a dozen companies for placement, and he's failed at every interview. The placement center director is writing a letter to Stan, detailing the failure: "with Mr. Bartlett, Managing Director of the British Corset Company, brackets Foundation of the Nation closed brackets Limited."

REG: ". . . on this, the occasion of your martyrdom"—The PFJ will comport themselves as any parliamentary body would, observing the agreed-upon rules even if it means Brian must be surrendered to "martyrdom." So over the course of the film the PFJ have moved from demanding the forceful overthrow of the largest empire in the world to being satisfied with a continuation of the status quo—something they sniffed at earlier, when discussing Jesus's sermon—their contradictory behavior moving them from epic to mock epic, which is a Python trope. In discussing the rise of the new powers in 1979—including Thatcher and her market agenda, a Polish pope challenging the Soviet system, the Islamic Iranian Revolution, etc.—Caryl reminds that "it was easy to underestimate just how much these leaders had actually absorbed from their opponents on the utopian Left." Already admitting that the Roman Empire has given Jerusalem and Judea much, the PFJ acknowledge this cultural and political absorption, casting their reactionary colorings into a new hue. If, as Caryl writes, "A conservative can be defined as someone who wants to defend or restore the old order," as Reg seems ready to admit now, "a counterrevolutionary, by contrast, is a conservative who has learned from the revolution."[54] The PFJ have certainly learned from their revolution, and

Brian is the exemplar of what happens to counterrevolutionaries. As often is the case, the Pythons can have it both ways. Their more modernist characters, always partly out of their time, can take advantage of both history and historical fiction—these are the kinds of characters who can lose and still claim a win, without self-contradiction (think of *Holy Grail*'s de-limbed Black Knight, e.g.). The synthesis Caryl sees in the appropriation of useful elements from the "utopian Left" by Khomeini, Deng, and even Thatcher is called by one historian "revolutionary traditionalism," a Pythonesque phrase to be sure.[55] Reg and the PFJ can continue their traditional activities and still consider themselves revolutionaries.

Bruce Anderson puts a finer point on it, writing about Margaret Thatcher and the so-called "Essex Man," the unseen, unheralded masses who elected Thatcher in 1979 and kept Labour at bay for eighteen years:

> She had a visceral hostility to the modern state and to those who tried to live off it. Her appeal was to the striving, the sharp-elbowed, the successful; they were the only people she understood. Had she been asked the question: "Chronic illness apart, if anyone fails in life, is it his own fault?" she could only have given one honest answer: yes. *But most of the population are not strivers; their fear of failure would always inhibit them from hazarding everything for success. They also have a contradictory attitude towards the state. Happy to stand on their own feet when the tax cuts came round, they also wish to be protected.*[56]

Reg and Francis and Stan are strivers who are also keen to stay alive; Brian strove and is now paying the price. At this moment, the PFJ have striven enough, they've tasted failure and don't like it, and, as it turns out, the oppressive Roman state has benefits for all the people of Jerusalem, dampening insurrectionary fervor—outrage suppressed by a "contradictory attitude." If the postwar Welfare State is the oppressive empire, then fighting against cradle-to-grave protections might eventually seem contradictory; if heartless Thatcherism is the oppressor, then the cold light of freer markets and a reduced government mean life becomes dicey again, another painful contradiction. Both play a part in *Life of Brian*.

REG: ". . . excluding those concerned with drainage, medicine, roads, housing, education, viniculture . . ."—Reg and the PFJ have already mentioned most of these, excepting "drainage" and "housing," meaning there are two *more* benefits of living as part of the Roman Empire. They've crawled through evidence of one of these Roman architectural wonders in the "Caesar Augustus Memorial Sewer," likely based on the impressive Cloaca Maxima drainage tunnels in Rome. This system channeled annual runoff, removed waste from the city, and drained the regional marshes—it was truly one of the wonders of ancient Roman engineering.

Reg also mentions housing, but the Romans don't seem to have been as keen on building homes for Jews as administrative and public service works, especially in Jerusalem. Many of the common folk lived outside the city, and many who lived in the city were attached to the city and religious governments.

REG: ". . . and hermaphrodites"—Likely just a nod to the emerging sensitivity to "Others" in this decade—meaning, for the Pythons, yet another group to make fun of—but the hermaphrodite was in the (satirical) news, and recently. In an April 1976 column for *Private Eye*, Claud Cockburn writes of "Britain's first hermaphrodite Prime Minister," known as "Snazeby." Snazeby came to power after Callaghan's four-year term ended,[57] and was generally well-received, especially after effective public relations work:

> Cynics and doubters were routed further when the Snazeby PRO squad discovered that many of the most notable people in history had been hermaphrodites in their time. A striking instance was

that of Cleopatra, who, researches showed, was also Anthony, thus explaining many ambiguities of conduct.[58]

Only Dr. Henry Kissinger "expressed disgruntlement" at having to deal with a hermaphrodite as a head of state, according to Cockburn. In the September 1977 issue of *Private Eye*, Auberon Waugh announces the emergence of a new publication, *Gay Worker*, to "cater for a ready-made market among male and female homosexualists of left wing or revolutionary leanings." He concludes, inviting Stan/Loretta types to consider applying for the post of business manager: "The successful applicant will be a Gay, left-wing, a member of NUPE, NALGO, SOGAT and SLADE,[59] possibly of lower class origins, possibly not. By first preference, the applicant should be of neither sex, *but hermaphrodites will not be excluded on those grounds alone.*"[60] The inclusion of characters like Stan/Loretta (a man who wants to be a woman and "have babies"), and then Reg's enlightened grouping of "Jews of both sexes and hermaphrodites" reminds us not only that sex and gender gags abound in middle school humor, but of the ever-present threat of the Python narrative moving sideways, distracted by the wrong infant savior, a street preacher's unfinished sentence, or the need to distinguish those in the Roman Empire whose work has actually benefited the Jews.

There are, incidentally, surviving images of Hermaphroditus at Herculaneum, as well as Pompeii, there in both the House of the Centenary and the House of the Dioscuri. The latter image is part of the celebrated *Pompeii AD79* exhibition in London.[61]

REG: "Your death will stand as a landmark . . ."—Brian is being promoted to martyr here (he was probationary before, after the failed palace raid). While in hiding beneath the city of Jotapata, Josephus was also nudged toward martyrdom by his fellows. Vespasian had sent emissaries to convince Josephus to safely emerge and talk, and Josephus, after praying, felt compelled by the Lord[62] to accept Vespasian's invitation, and to "not go over to the Romans as a deserter of the Jews, but as a minister from [God]."[63] When Josephus's fellow freedom fighters hear of his decision, they likely questioned his "revelation" and offer him a choice of suicide or murder:

> "How soon hast thou forgotten thyself! How many hast thou persuaded to lose their lives for liberty! Thou hast therefore had a false reputation for manhood, and a like false reputation for wisdom, if thou canst hope for preservation from those against whom thou hast fought so zealously, and art however willing to be preserved by them, if they be in earnest. But although the good fortune of the Romans hath made thee forget thyself, we ought to take care that the glory of our forefathers may not be tarnished. We will lend thee our right hand and a sword; and if thou wilt die willingly, thou wilt die as general of the Jews; but if unwillingly, thou wilt die as a traitor to them." As soon as they said this, they began to thrust their swords at him, and threatened they would kill him, if he thought of yielding himself to the Romans.[64]

So while Josephus's companions do applaud his impending martyrdom, it's on their own terms, and even by their own hand that they'd like it accomplished.

Reg's whole-hearted commitment to the revolutionary cause (here, of course, the PFJ's proxy is Brian) rings familiar. One of the earliest active anarchists in France, Paul Brousse echoes Reg, announcing that "propaganda by deed" was the answer to eventually winning the struggle, even if death was the only foreseeable outcome: "[Defeat] does not matter; the idea will march on, will put on flesh and sinews, and live in the eyes and on the faces of the people, who will shout for joy as it passes."[65] Brian's "supreme sacrifice" makes him a "true martyr," and so it's actually much more efficacious for the future of the movement if he stays on the cross and completes his martyrdom. Iviansky notes, importantly, that Brousse, "one of the early activists and ideologists of anarchism," would also "quickly abandon it," which sounds Reg-like.[66]

In this Reg and the PFJ sound very much like Tacitus, the republican-minded but realistic historian of Rome. Reg will continue to quietly work for "the cause," but within the system as dictated by the Romans; he's seen that full commitment means (Brian's) suffering and death, so verbal and spiritual commitment should remain the path of choice. And while Tacitus hated autocracy, he understood that it "had become a necessary evil" in the lawless present, and that "the most prudent and virtuous course of action lay in the middle ground between futile rebellion against the tyrant and complicity in his crimes ('a path . . . between abrasive obstinacy and disgusting groveling')," Richard concludes.[67] Reg and the PFJ have finally been outed as what they really are, a kind of new ideas group—a Fabian Society or IEA (Institute for Economic Affairs) or even CPS (Center for Policy Studies)—period research organizations that talked a good game of revolution but kept boots safely off the ground.[68] Caryl writes that Anthony Fisher, the founder of the IEA, understood "that what the Communists referred to as 'propaganda and agitation' stood at the center of the IEA's mission"; Reg seems to understand this careful delimitation of activities, as well, perhaps now better than ever. And this isn't a jab at Reg's dedication to the cause, either. In England, a demonstrably free society, the Fabians and the IEA didn't face arrest and imprisonment for their socialist and capitalist agendas, respectively. In a violently repressive society like the Roman Empire (or the Soviet Union or China or dozens of Third World countries in the 1960s and 1970s), great sacrifices accompany nonaligned thought and action—Reg and the PFJ are actually quite brave as they vow to "continue the fight" in Brian's memory. In *Holy Grail* Arthur retreats from the French-held castle to live and fight another day; here, Reg and the PFJ announce their "continuing struggle to liberate the parent land," and leave Brian to his own admirable destiny.

More contemporarily, the postwar, welfare state period saw the Conservatives take power from the Left in 1951, 1970, and then 1979, winning general elections in those years. Keith Joseph (and later Margaret Thatcher) would complain that rather than voicing the strongly conservative oppositions to Labour's expansion of the socialist agenda, the Tory campaigns (like in 1951) promised tradition and stability, meaning the welfare state apparatus installed after 1945 remained largely intact. The expanding socialist state was left alone or even increased after the elections of 1951, 1955, 1959, and 1970, when the Conservatives won, sometimes even increasing their margins of victory. This made no sense to Thatcher or Joseph, Thatcher calling it a "two steps forward with a half step back"[69] approach that simply ensured Labour's measures remained in place, and Tory attempts to curb these advances were quickly repealed by the following (and bolder) Labour administration. Joseph concurred, speaking in 1974:

> This is no time to be mealy-mouthed. Since the end of the Second World War, we have had altogether too much socialism. There is no point in my trying to evade what everybody knows. For half of the 30 years, Conservative Governments, for understandable reasons, did not consider it practicable to reverse the vast bulk of the accumulating detritus of socialism which on each occasion they found when they returned to office. So we tried to build on its uncertain foundations instead.[70]

It's clear here at the foot of Brian's cross that Reg and the PFJ have adopted this same safer, less turbulent approach to revolution. The oppressive Roman Empire cannot be overcome in fits and starts, and the price for failure is death, so discretion becomes the better part of valor. For the Conservative governments, the popular welfare state couldn't be undone in one go or even by regular bloodletting, the price for attempting such a thing was certain political death (or a trip to the wilderness, where prophets belong), leaving only valorous discretion for the boxed-in but resolute Tories, who at Party Conferences would read out their own proclamations about the "continuing struggle." Rather than poke the sleeping Roman Empire with a pointed stick, the better solution is to leave Brian on the cross, allowing him his martyrdom, and to build their revolution on the "uncertain foundations" of the regrettable, comfortable, but continuing Roman occupancy.

(draft) **REG: ". . . this supreme sacrifice, whereby you have supplied our cause with a true martyr, in whose proud memory we can continue the fight against the Roman Imperialist aggressors ∴ . ."**—This surrender (or tactical retreat) by Reg and the PFJ might be connected to the five-year struggle by the Labour Party to achieve Scottish devolution. Donoughue notes that both Wilson and Callaghan had undertaken the steps necessary to see devolution through, securing referenda, polling, advertising, and so on, but that when the time came for a vote (2 March 1979), the Scottish people rejected the measure—they didn't even reach the 40 percent minimum for votes cast. Wrote Donoughue on the day of devolution's failure: "The Scots might have told us during the past five years that they did not really want devolution."[71] When Reg and the PFJ finally get their chance to "do something," when Judith alerts them that "something's actually happening," they punt as well, perhaps corrupted, as the Scots would be generations later, by the "subsidies and handouts" provided by the state;[72] it's access to the dole and subsidized lifestyles for the Scots, and "sanitation and medicine and education and irrigation and public health and roads and a freshwater system and baths and public order" for the people of Jerusalem and the PFJ. Donoughue concludes:

> It is terrible that devolution has ended in this mess. We have worked at it for five years, with the Scots always, in general, saying they wanted it. Most of us in London, including the PM, did not. The polls have shown 2-1 in favour of our middle-of-the-road proposals. So we have worked to convert many sceptics in our own Party, in the Cabinet and in Parliament. We have had to mollify the English regions. We have lost one bill and fought it through the House a second time. Then suddenly the Scots change their minds. And we are left holding the baby.[73]

And Brian is left on the cross, though he's a hero to the movement.

They regroup a little way away, take their shoes off, wave them in the air, turn and sing . . .—(PSC) What they actually do here is once again copy a moment from *I'm All Right Jack*. As the Chief Shop Steward and his associates confront their boss, Major Hitchcock, for the first time (about the alleged blackleg, Windrush), they turn away for a moment, regroup ("Withdraw and consult"), and whisper about their plans. The PFJ say their goodbyes, wish Brian the best, move off, and also regroup. More like the gathering of shop stewards, though, Reg obviously calls for a vote of support for what they're about to do: sing "For He's a Jolly Good Fellow." Mr. Kite and friends consult twice, come to an agreement, and announce that the new man Windrush must *not* be fired even if he is incompetent, as that would amount to "victimisation." Also, Reg and the PFJ do not take off their shoes as their sign of agreement—they're not the mob seen earlier who followed the shoe, the gourd, etc. Perhaps the Pythons themselves were confused by this point.

ALL: "For he's a jolly good fellow"—A valediction sung by Harold Wilson's No. 10 staff to the resigning PM on his last day in office, 5 April 1976.[74] Wilson was serenaded this way a number of times, often by admiring constituents or just happy voters across Britain.[75] Wilson had also been serenaded *back* into office in 1974 the very same way. Also, the refrain is a staple it seems, being sung between 1965 and 1978 at funerals, for favorite cricketers, tennis players and retirees (including union leader Jack Jones), at football matches and for returning MPs, for Ian Smith and Enoch Powell and Ted Heath and even Margaret Thatcher.

The more political song of choice during this period would have been the "Red Flag," a sort of anthem of the Labour Party for many years, often sung to celebrate Labour legislative victories, and especially within earshot of angry Tories.[76]

When the British finally abandoned Aden in November 1967, the send-off included a bowdlerized version of Thomas Gray's *Elegy*, and a Royal Marines' band playing, appropriately, "Fings Ain't Wot They Used to Be."[77]

BRIAN *(still hurling abuse at the REVOLUTIONARIES)*: **"You bastards!"**—Brian finally realizes he's been left to his own devices by his siblings, and is understandably bitter. The other shoes waiting to drop include goodbyes from both Judith and Mandy, when Brian is truly forsaken. Again, minorities of the Welsh, Scottish, and Irish peoples had worked and hoped for "devolution" or even total separation from the United Kingdom for many years, with Callaghan's administration fielding one of the more significant devolution[78] attempts. Westminster legislation supporting Scottish devolution came to a head in February 1977, just as Jones and Palin, for example, worked together on their *Life of Brian* scenes.[79] PM Callaghan supported devolution half-heartedly, according to Donoughue, and only because he owed his administration's majority to continuing support from the SNP.[80] The bill was volatile from the beginning, and likely doomed to failure, given the Tories' (and defecting Labourites') continuing demands for a united United Kingdom. Hundreds of amendments were presented by ministers (of all factions) and many hours spent on the bill before it was (appropriately) "guillotined" in February 1977. Writes Donoughue: "The PM was quite relaxed. He said he does not mind losing the bill providing we get the credit in Scotland for 'having tried to get devolution.' I think that is his preferred outcome."[81] Reg stands at the foot of Judea's version of the guillotine, assuring Brian and siblings of the PFJ that enough has been accomplished for credit to be given, meaning Brian's glorious martyrdom and the PFJ's ability to continue the fight. Many pundits of the day seemed to have guessed Callaghan's two-fold strategy, surmising in print that Labour had to at least try and push devolution through parliament.[82] "We have not lost anything provided we handle it right," Callaghan would tell Donoughue, in a very Reg-like way, later that same night.[83] Donoughue would later describe this odd political scenario—manipulating a loss into less obvious loss—as "the reality of a minority government," and that the government was "humiliated but not defeated."[84] Reg employs this very same logic.

BIG NOSE: "I'm Brian!"—This is the Pythons' *Spartacus* moment, though their version is a self-serving one, where everyone on a cross claims to be Brian to escape the cross. The Pythonesque moment is when Brian just misses his opportunity to save himself by acknowledging his own name. This is where the idea for the film began—a man who bounces from biblical set piece to scriptural moment, always just out of step with history.

MAN (Jones): "The Judean Peoples' Front!"—Yelled as Otto's brigade is spotted approaching the crucifixion hill. The suicide squad isn't named this in the printed scripts.

Remember also that there were more and less feared revolutionary factions in the real world, as well. In Japan, home to significant political zealotry as a result of both the war and the presence of US troops and influence after the war, both the more mainstream Japanese Communists and Marxist Japanese Socialists groups had denounced the student-led (and beyond reasonably violent) Red Army and its splinters.[85] The Angry Brigade targeted symbolically, avoiding collateral damage as much as possible, while Carlos threw bombs into public places, the Red Army killed indiscriminately at the Lod Airport, and the IRA detonated bombs to kill and maim as many as possible. Some terror groups would clearly have been more feared than others.

OTTO: "Crack suicide squad"—There was an actual terrorist cadre calling themselves the Seventh Suicide Squad who attacked the Athens airport in August 1973 with machine guns and grenades, killing five and injuring fifty-five.[86] Al-Fatah would disavow this squad, initially, as being "imaginary and non-existent."[87] Idle's vocal part has been dubbed by Palin, likely due to poor sound quality from the original scene as shot. Postproduction of the Python films tended to fall to Jones, Palin, and Gilliam; it was perhaps just much easier for Palin to step into the dubbing session rather than wait for a scheduled visit by Idle.

With immaculate precision they all run themselves through, including Otto—In earlier drafts, Otto's squad had already done this, but it turned out they were all pretending.

There are actually a handful of historical moments similar to this one. When the wealthy Roman Symmachus was trying to stage an especially over-the-top version of the games in 401—"to put on some really good shows to restore national morale"—he had trouble finding wild animals, trained horses for chariot races, competent chariot drivers, and especially trained gladiators. According to Mannix: "He managed to purchase twenty-nine Saxon prisoners, supposed to be terrific fighters, but the prisoners never got out of the gladiatorial school. [Rather than fight for the Romans' amusement] they strangled each other until there was only one man left—and he beat his brains out against the wall."[88] Symmachus would admit in a letter that the "best private security" likely could not have prevented "this desperate group of men" from killing each other, and was ready to replace them with "a display of African wild animals."[89] Otto and his cadre's mass suicide are treated just as indifferently here.

Josephus reported that his companions entered into a suicide pact rather than be captured by or surrender to the Romans; Josephus was able to talk the last man out of the pact, and two survived to emerge.[90] Josephus's account is the only record we have of this miraculous escape. Also, the sicarii remnants and many women and children died by murder-suicide at Masada in 73, refusing to surrender to the Romans. Likely the suicide deaths of RAF members Baader, Ensslin, Raspe, and Meinhof, as well as the shootout death of student activist Georg von Rauch in 1971 would have raised these Germans to "martyr" status.

In the documentary *Archaeological Exploration of Masada* (1991), archaeologist Neil Silberman discusses the mixing of fact and fiction (especially useful in 1965, as the Israelis felt the need for a rousing national story):

> I think that it's fairly clear by now that Josephus, like many classical authors, was giving a melodramatic ending to a great epic. The theme of suicide as a heroic ending for classical histories was common to people throughout the Greek and Roman world. In that, Josephus was really doing nothing new, but giving an accepted end to his literary tale.

The revolutionary fervor across time has often produced groups or individuals seemingly ready to destroy themselves, though usually not before accomplishing their goal—a specific terroristic attack, for example. Russian "utopian socialist" Nikola Ishutin preached a committed, fanatical line, more Otto than Reg-like, and expected much of his followers:

> Their aim was to kill members of the government and big landowners. Lots were to be cast among the revolutionaries to establish who was to carry out the assassinations. The terrorist should live under an assumed name, break all ties with family, give up his friends, and forgo marriage. He should cut himself off from his own comrades and find his friends in the underworld. On the day appointed for the assassination, he was to disfigure his face with chemicals to avoid

being recognized. In his pocket he would carry a manifesto explaining his motives, and once he had carried out his attempt, he was to poison himself.[91]

Laqueur notes that even Ishutin, though, balked at an assassination attempt on the tsar, and most of his like-minded friends were more like the wetter PFJ—they "preferred propaganda and the establishment of schools and cooperatives" in the fight against imperialist Russia.[92]

It's also possible that given the recent grisly news from Jonestown, Guyana, it was easier to reduce these Otto/suicide scenes in the finished film. On 18 November 1978, the troubled, charismatic leader Jim Jones convinced (or compelled) hundreds of his followers to drink sedatives and poison, ending their lives in the jungles of northeastern South America. The Pythons were watching the first rough version of the completed film in mid-November, and Palin reports that the Otto sequences were feeling "dangerously like a cameo sketch."[93]

BRIAN: "You silly sods . . ."—This may be Brian's moment where he is less concerned with himself, and more with the others who have just killed themselves in front of him. This is the moment where Brian perhaps finally understands the hopelessness of the "struggle" he's been part of, if just for a few days. Discussing the "failure of revolution" as witnessed across time, Thomas Greene lists the typical explanations to account for these failures, a list that should read quite familiar: "The same is true of efforts to explain the failure of revolution: inadequate leadership, weak organization, a remote ideology, the narrowness of the movement's membership base, inappropriate economic and social conditions, the legitimacy and effectiveness of the existing political system—all may be cited to explain why defeat was inevitable."[94] The rather sad, even resigned look on Brian's face indicates he sees quite clearly why the PFJ and his own actions led them to this point, and this before both his hoped-for girlfriend and his mother appear to offer their goodbyes.

Taken in turn, Greene's sobering points can be affixed to the Peoples' Front of Judea's and Brian's actions throughout the film. Reg represents "inadequate leadership" at its nadir, given that he favors talk over action, is alarmed when meaningful acts are perpetrated, and allows his parliamentary fixation to overcome any "sibling" sentiment, leaving the movement's one true and purposeful acolyte to die on a cross. The "weak organization" that is the PFJ features a nominal leader, Reg, who hides at the first sign of danger, and this same organization invites members who merely hate the Romans "a lot." This same weak organization sends a "thank-you" committee as opposed to a "rescue committee," for example. The "remote ideology" is remote because it is at least partly removed from its time, taken from nineteen hundred years in the future. The PFJ as presented is clearly modeled on terrorist groups of the 1960s and 1970s, and their revolutionary zeal and shortcomings are sent up throughout the film. The PFJ possesses a demonstrated inability to expand membership (surviving membership, that is) beyond the handful of core members, underscoring the "narrowness of the movement's membership base." The PFJ can even claim a member who *does not* share the group's dedication to death before slavery—there is "Uh, one" who won't "gladly suffer" a glorious death for the cause. Part of the reason for this lack of total commitment and for the small size of this cadre can be attributed to the "inappropriate economic and social conditions" displayed in the film—as depicted, neither the administration of the Romans nor the daily life of the busy city seem particularly onerous or burdensome. Public order must be maintained, yes, and the Romans can be heavy-handed, but starving masses aren't part of the cityscape. A very healthy-looking, agile Ex-leper begs at one of the city gates, and he manages to get a donation, as well. What's more, on at least two occasions the PFJ completely undermine their own revolutionary foundations by acknowledging how much the Romans have done for the city, and therefore, for the Jews. From improved public health to education to public order and viticulture, life is better under the Romans. The remaining "difficulties" seem hard to get worked up over, hence, the PFJ's increasingly half-hearted cris de coeur as the narrative moves along, limping toward Brian's eventual martyrdom. Finally, as the PFJ themselves point out, the Roman Empire is the real deal. The "legitimacy and effectiveness of the existing political system" is reinforced as the various revolutionary groups are dealt with beneath Pilate's palace early in the film, then Brian is relentlessly tracked down, arrested, and finally executed for crimes against that political system. And even after these atrocities, there is no public hue and cry, no groundswell of *lumpenproletariat* support to assist in the overthrow of the empire. The Baader-Meinhof gang, the Japanese Red Army, the Weathermen, and the SLA all ran up against this same wall of public insouciance. In democratic countries boasting fairly stable economies, as has been demonstrated, these revolutionary groups failed to convince the masses that there was anything much to rebel against.

JUDITH: "Thank you, Brian. I'll never forget you"—The fact that Brian has been left on the cross by the PFJ, Otto's squad, now Judith, and soon even his mother, might not be as cruel or absurd as it seems. After the fall of Masada in 73, which culminated in the mass suicide of the last revolutionary Jews in Palestine, it was assumed by many Jews "that the Jewish religion was also destroyed," Kotker writes. "Some Jews mourned so deeply that they refused to eat meat or drink wine until the Temple was rebuilt. . . . Some refused to bring children into a world of such unhappiness and uncertainty."[96] Surviving rabbis would admonish the faithful to grieve, but within reason, saying "it was wrong, even sinful, to mourn too deeply," or to purposely not have children.[97] They were to remember the Lord's commandment of happiness, to be fruitful and multiply, which is very forward-looking. Perhaps the PFJ and the others, even Mandy, are moderating their grief similarly, which does prepare the audience and everyone on the crosses for the upbeat closing musical number. Essentially, the defeated Jews were being asked to look on the bright side of life.

MANDY: ". . . go ahead . . . be crucified . . . see if I care"—Well, if the Mandy-Brian relationship is meant to be metaphoric for Israel—"As a mother comforts her child, so I [God] will comfort you; you shall be comforted in Jerusalem" (Isa. 66:13)—then no one's being watched after, and no one is getting comforted. This turnabout is standard for the Pythons' version of God's love to His people.[95] (Remember, He was an obstreperous, shirty God in *Holy Grail*, prone to shortness, anger, and punishments.) This is hardly the crucifixion scene in *Spartacus*—though it's meant to remind us of it—where Spartacus's wife, Varinia, and his "free" son look up at him longingly, cinematically. Varinia begs Spartacus to "Please die," a bit more poignant than Mandy's sorrowful "Go ahead, be crucified, see if I care."

Notes

1. Palin, *Diaries 1969–1979*, 496.

2. Palin reports that the Pythons had actually been invited to shoot in Israel, and had also considered Jordan and Morocco (*Diaries 1969–1979*, 494).

3. Larsen, *MPFC: UC*, 1.331; see entries for "Argument Clinic" in Ep. 29 (2.40–49).

4. Josephus, *AJ*, 18.4.1–3 (Whiston, 380); Josephus goes on to say that Vitellius went immediately to Jerusalem, released the citizens from certain taxes, and gave them back the priestly vestments.

5. Brandon, "Pontius Pilate in History and Legend," 528.

6. Jeremias, *JTJ*, 114 and 114n22.

7. *JE*, "Pharisees."

8. *AJ*, 13.14.2 (Whiston, 285).

9. Mannix, *TAD*, 27–28.

10. *TAD*, 28.

11. *TAD*, 132.

12. 5.11.1n19 (Whiston, 563).

13. Arrowsmith—CND cofounder and Radical Alliance candidate—was fined £2, for example, in 1962 for "obstruction" as she campaigned to "ban the bomb" ("Pat Arrowsmith Fined £2," *Daily Mail*, 8 May 1962: 9).

14. From *Wildcat Inside Story, Disaffection, 1797 to 1974*, available at theanarchistlibrary.org.

15. "Jesus 'Planned His Crucifixion': New Theory in Book," *Sunday Times*, 17 October 1965: 3.

16. "Gospel of the Guerrilla," *Sunday Times*, 14 March 1976: 14.

17. A little more than a month after this controversy erupted, the Pythons officially decided to do a "Life of Christ" film (Palin, *Diaries 1969–1979*, 310–11). *The Passover Plot* was actually nominated for a costume design Academy Award; it's a beautiful, flawed, compelling film.

18. Horsley, "The Sicarii," 443.

19. Quoted in Horsley, "The Sicarii," 443.

20. This "pardon" has led many to assume Josephus had gone over to the Roman side, betraying the Jewish people, a charge Josephus denies vehemently.

21. *Josephus*, 20–21.

22. Cook, "Envisioning Crucifixion," 278.

23. Cook, "Envisioning Crucifixion," 278.

24. Porcius Festus was procurator from 59 to 62.

25. Kotker, *HLTJ*, 111.

26. Larsen, *BAFHG*, 471.

27. Donoughue, *DSD*, 2.222; see also Sandbrook's *White Heat* and *Seasons in the Sun*, as well as Joe Haines's 2001 reprint of his 1976 book *Politics of Power*.

28. Waugh, *FCY*, 3 November 1975.

29. *DSD*, 1.122.

30. The press had been hounding her (and her family) for alleged land speculation (known as "the Slagheap Affair") and influence-peddling exploits, and Wilson was doing his best to keep his government clear of the mess. See Sandbrook and Donoughue. Just over a month later Wilson offered Williams a life peerage, likely hoping to quiet her and free himself from her clutches (*DSD*, 1.125). The press explosion echoed for years after she became Lady Falkender.

31. *DSD*, 1.97.

32. Farrell, *BRJ*, 41–42.

33. Marighella, *Minimanual*, 60.

34. Marighella, *Minimanual*, 60–61.

35. See the discussion of Tom Brown and syndicalism in *BAFHG*, 129.

36. Discussed earlier in "The PFJ Plan Their Raid," "In the Court of Pontius Pilate," and "Hiding with the PFJ."

37. Burleigh, *BRT*, 233.

38. Aust, *The Baader-Meinhof Complex*, 58–61.

39. Dobson and Payne, *Carlos Complex*, 185.

40. "Israel Rejoices at the Success of Raid to Free Entebbe Hostages," *Times*, 5 July 1976: 1.

41. Operation "Wrath of God" (or "Bayonet") had begun in fall 1972, and was still in force in 1979. Many of the targets were only distantly connected to the original attack, if at all, but were killed on principle (see *BRT*).

42. *BAFHG*, 60–61, 67n107–8, 133, 408.

43. The devaluation amounted to a 14 percent drop in the value of the pound. This embarrassment would cost Callaghan his position; Callaghan would still become the King's First Minister in 1976, leading the country until 1979.

44. Marr, *HMB*, 299.

45. Bernstein, *Myth of Decline*, 233.

46. Ilich Ramírez Sánchez is an example of a figure who both planned and then carried out such acts of terror, rendering him infamously as "Carlos," and putting him on "most wanted" lists around the

·world. Carlos would eventually be hunted to ground and incarcerated. Reg and the PFJ want to avoid this kind of denouement.

47. Bevan had established the NHS when serving as minister of health in the postwar Attlee government. In 1959 he was serving as shadow foreign secretary.

48. Bogdanor, "Collapse of the Postwar Settlement," a.t.

49. Bogdanor, "Collapse of the Postwar Settlement," a.t.

50. Here the printed script (in book form) has spelled "People's" differently than most other places in the script. Likely a typo. As seen in the *Holy Grail* script, the spelling of "Launcelot" (or "Lancelot") depended on who was typing that scene.

51. Brandon, "The Zealots," 634.

52. The mentions of Zealots in the Gospels are also clearly more pro-Roman, written at a time when cultivating that stance was more beneficial than antagonizing the Romans by praising the Zealots as freedom fighters (Brandon, "The Zealots," 637).

53. Brandon, "The Zealots," 637.

54. Caryl, *Strange Rebels*, xiv.

55. Caryl, *Strange Rebels*, xiv.

56. "The One Thing Wrong with the Essex Man," *Spectator*, 29 March 1997: 10; italics added.

57. Callaghan's term had just begun when Cockburn wrote the satirical article and would end just over three years later, in May 1979.

58. *Private Eye*, 16 April 1976: 14.

59. These are, in order: National Union of Public Employees, National and Local Government Officers Association, Society of Graphical and Allied Trades, and Society of Lithographic Artists, Designers and Engravers. These all unions Waugh and *PE* have tilted with (and been sued by).

60. 30 September 1977: 17; italics added.

61. *Pompeii AD79*, 70.

62. Critics wonder whether he was listening to the voice of the Spirit, or a voice of self-preservation; Brian will wonder about the PFJ's motivations as they leave him on the cross.

63. Josephus, *WJ*, 3.8.3 (Whiston, 515).

64. *WJ*, 3.8.4 (Whiston, 515).

65. Quoted in Iviansky, "Individual Terror," 45.

66. Iviansky, "Individual Terror," 45.

67. Richard, *WWAR*, 187–88.

68. Caryl, *Strange Rebels*, 162–64. Caryl mentions that both the IEA and CPS, though more conservative and certainly formed in opposition to the sitting Labour governments and the welfare state in general, kept themselves unallied to any party, to be ideologically pure *and* protect their charitable status in the eyes of Inland Revenue (164). Reg is equally pragmatic.

69. From a *Daily Telegraph* article penned by Thatcher (30 January 1975), and quoted by Bogdanor in "Thatcherism, 1979–1990."

70. Quoted in Bogdanor's "Thatcherism, 1979–1990," a.t.

71. Donoughue, *DSD*, 2.453.

72. This is one of Donoughue's lamentation sections, which crop up more often as the days of his government in power wane.

73. *DSD*, 2.453.

74. Sandbrook, *Seasons in the Sun*, 428.

75. See for example: "More Enthusiasm Than in 1964," *Times*, 31 March 1966: 12; "Labour Women in Militant Mood," *Times*, 18 May 1967: 2.

76. "Same Old Song," *Daily Telegraph*, 30 January 1971: 10.

77. Brendon, *DFBE*, 513.

78. The "devolving" of administrative power from Westminster to, for example, Ulster, Cardiff, or Edinburgh, where (sub)national parliamentary bodies could undertake "domestic" issues while remaining legally "British."

79. They were chatting about the comedic potentials of an affected Pontius Pilate character, for example (Palin, *Diaries 1969–1979*, 367).

80. Deaths of sympathetic ministers and unhelpful by-elections had erased Labour's majority on Callaghan's very first day as prime minister. A fragile coalition kept Labour in power, but to a certain extent lashed the major party to the whims of the fringe. See Sandbrook and Donoughue for more on this fascinating period.

81. *DSD*, 2.152.

82. The *quid pro quo* nature of Callaghan's support is made clear in, for example, "Callaghan Stands Firm" *Sunday Times*, 8 August 1976: 2, as well as John Grigg's "For Whom the Tumbrils," *Spectator*, 12 February 1977: 4.

83. *DSD*, 2.152.

84. *DSD*, 2.165. In 1979 a referendum offering a Welsh Assembly was rejected by almost 80 percent of Welsh voters; Irish independence continues to be a matter of bloodshed to this day.

85. See Richard Harris, "A Kamikaze Touch Returns to Japanese Extremism," *Times*, 1 June 1972: 14. This article also connects the rootless violence of the Japanese leftists to the PLO; rootless because, unlike the Middle Eastern guerrilla organizations, the Red Army had no manifesto for the overthrow of an occupying power or call for radical change at home ("no cause worthy of their dramatic dying" in Japan), so were striking piecemeal and abroad, instead.

86. Dobson and Payne, *Carlos Complex*, 134.

87. "Israel Court Jails for Seven Years," *Times*, 9 August 1973: 5.

88. *TAD*, 139.

89. From Shaw's *Spartacus and the Slave Wars*, 50; see also Wiedemann, *Emperors and Gladiators*, 91.

90. *WJ*, 3.8.5–9 (Whiston, 515–16).

91. Laqueur, *Terrorism*, 46.

92. Laqueur, *Terrorism*, 45–46.

93. Palin, *Diaries 1969–1979*, 510. Palin does not mention the Jonestown massacre in his diaries.

94. Greene, *Comparative Revolutionary Movements*, 2–3.

95. King and Stager, *LBI*, 49.

96. *HLTJ*, 135.

97. *HLTJ*, 135.

SCENE THIRTY-ONE
"ALWAYS LOOK ON THE BRIGHT SIDE OF LIFE"

MR. FRISBEE III: "Cheer up, Brian. You know what they say"—In the intervening years this song has taken on a life of its own, finding its way onto football terraces, including Aston Villa, Manchester United, and Sheffield Wednesday, and as the closing number in the successful musical play *Spamalot* and the *He's Not the Messiah* oratorio. Anecdotally, it's also sung at many, many funerals.

MR. FRISBEE III: "Don't grumble, give a whistle"—In the 1940 home front documentary *London Can Take It*, five long weeks of the Blitz haven't dampened the spirits of Londoners, says the narrator:

> Doctor Joseph Goebbels said recently that the nightly air raids have had a terrific effect on the morale of the people of London. The good doctor is absolutely right. Today the morale of the people is higher than ever before. They are fused together not by fear, but by a surging spirit of courage the like of which the world has never known. . . . They would rather stand up and face death, then kneel down and face the kind of existence the conqueror would impose upon them.[1]

Frisbee's is a particularly British song, calling for smiling stoicism in the face of ultimate adversity, here a sort of "Jerusalem Can Take It" declaration. During the worst of the Blitz, songs were often sung in air raid shelters and down on Tube platforms—ostensibly to calm the children and drown out the horrors above—particularly English songs like "White Cliffs of Dover," "There'll Always Be an England," and even "Knees Up Mother Brown."[2] "If you're up to your neck in hot water," the wartime Vera Lynn song went, "be like the kettle and sing."[3] Idle was likely inspired by this popular song, "Be Like the Kettle and Sing," from the wartime film *We'll Meet Again* (1943), as some of the lyrics attest:

> Tell that umbrella man he's just an also ran
> Think of a kid on a swing
> When you're up to your neck in hot water,
> Be like the kettle and sing.
> You'll find that life's always got a funny side
> So come over on the sunny side
> And wear a great big smile
> It makes your life worthwhile
> You'll have the world on a string
> When you're up to your neck in hot water,
> Be like the kettle and sing.

In the film, a performance is underway as German bombs are falling outside, and the audience is frightened. The emcee isn't "getting over," the girls backstage fear, as he tells the conductor to strike up a song so that the audience can sing. "Pretend you're in the bathtub!" he coaxes as the music vamps. No one sings. "Don't be bashful, just let yourself go!" Young Vera begins to sing offstage, then is pulled front stage, and by the time she reaches the lines: "When your troubles are boiling over consult this recipe / Everybody can be in clover, happy as can be," the audience is singing along merrily, drowning out the falling bombs outside. Everyone then sings together, on stage and in the audience:

> When all the skies are grey, and it's a rainy day
> Think of the birdies in spring
> When you're up to your neck in hot water
> Be like the kettle and sing.

When the song finishes the raid is over, and the "all clear" sounds. Idle as Frisbee is simply singing through the Blitz, showing the pluck that the English have exhibited since those dark days.

    MR. FRISBEE III: "Just purse your lips and whistle . . ."—Whistling was a fairy common portion of many music hall songs, but this idea that whistling can lift spirits and make tasks bearable is more particular. One likely source is the well-known Frank Churchill and Larry Morley song "Whistle While You Work," from Walt Disney's *Snow White* (1937). We also can't forget the "Colonel Bogey March" sections from *The Bridge on the River Kwai* (1957), where British troops marched into a prisoner of war camp blowing their patriotism through pursed lips.

    MR. FRISBEE III: ". . . you come from nothing. You're going back to nothing. What have you lost? Nothing!"—This sounds like a *creatio ex nihilo* argument, and it's a concept we've not heard in the film. A supernatural being, Jesus, is presented at the beginning of the film ("He is the son of God"), suggesting something beyond and before this life, and Brian's "followers" are keen to find out the secret to eternal life, which they believe truly exists. Brian even preaches about a God who watches over his birds, flowers, and children on Earth, and it sounds as if he might even believe it. Brian later preaches self-reliance, asserting that no earthly master should be followed. He does this without denying the existence of God or an afterlife, so Mr. Frisbee is the voice of, perhaps, the new faith in the 1960s and beyond, when the concept of a caring, watchful, "up there somewhere" kind of god took a real hit. This isn't the 1 Timothy citation, either, where "we brought nothing into this world, and it is certain we can carry nothing out" (6:7), though it might be the human, stoical version of this concept coming from a man nailed to a cross and facing the end of his earthly existence. As the victims dance on crosses at the end of the film, then, crucifixion is truly a doddle, and the Centurion would have shaken his head at this disturbing, "oddball" behavior.

    MR. FRISBEE III: "See? The end of the film"—The man on the cross can see the beginning of the titles. Cf. Plautus's fourth-wall breaking (context smashing) in his plays, where characters know they are in plays, and where actors speak about the producer's role, and so on. For example: "When Chrysalis triumphs, he tells the audience, which is expecting the clever slave to deliver the standard, grandiose, satirical speech employing the language of a conquering general, that he refuses to do so because this comic bit has been overdone and abruptly leaves the stage."[4]

    MR. FRISBEE III: "Incidentally, this record is available in the foyer"—Like a concert, where tour memorabilia and records could be had on the way out of the show. The Pythons had recently finished a wildly popular series of shows in New York, which is likely where the elided popstar Sermon on the Mount came from.

MR. FRISBEE III: "Who do you think pays for all this rubbish?"—EMI was on board to fund the film, but got cold feet when the Christian backlash began to be predicted. George Harrison and HandMade Films stepped in to put together funding.

MR. FRISBEE III: "I told them: 'Bernie, I said to him, they'll never make their money back'"—The film actually made about five times its production budget, which would be considered a box office success. Sales of the album for the film could also be factored in, as well as sales of the book, and later videotape and DVD sales.

"If you have enjoyed seeing this film, why not go and see La Notte?"—This is a bit of captioning at the end of the credits. Mentioned in Ep. 29, the film was directed by Michelangelo Antonioni, and premiered in 1961.[5]

Notes

1. Narrated by Quentin Reynolds.
2. "Britain at War: Singing through Air Raids," *Telegraph*, 30 October 2008; "Life in an Air-Raid Shelter," *WW2 People's War*, BBC; Freedman, *Whistling in the Dark*. The Goons used bits of these songs, as well.
3. Freedman, *Whistling in the Dark*, 132.
4. Richard, *WWAR*, 200.
5. Larsen, *MPFC: UC*, 2.46.

BIBLIOGRAPHY

"1978–1979: Winter of Discontent." Libcom.org. https://libcom.org/history/1978-1979-winter-of -discontent.

Abel, Lionel. "Seven Heroes of the New Left." *New York Times*, 5 May 1968.

Ackerman, Susan. "Women in Ancient Israel and the Hebrew Bible." *Oxford Research Encyclopedia of Religion*. April 2016. http://religion.oxfordre.com/view/10.1093/acrefore/9780199340378.001.0001/ acrefore-9780199340378-e-45?rskey=qlpgfF&result=1.

Aldrete, Gregory S. *Floods of the Tiber in Ancient Rome*. Baltimore, MD: Johns Hopkins University Press, 2007.

Ames, Cody Scott. "Herodian Judea: Games, Politics, Kingship in the First Century BCE." *Journal of Ancient History and Archeology* 2, no. 2 (2015): 5–15.

"Ancient Roman Toilets Did Not Improve Sanitation." *Popular Archaeology* 11 (June 2013).

"The Anger of the Middle Class." *London Times*, 11 January 1975: 13.

The Angry Brigade. "Communique 5." theanarchistlibrary.org.

Annan, Thomas. *The Photographs of Old Closes and Streets of Glasgow 1876/77*. New York: Dover, 1977.

Aust, Stefan, *The Baader-Meinhof Complex*. London: The Bodley Head, 2008.

Avigad, Nahman. *Archaeological Discoveries in the Jewish Quarter of Jerusalem: Second Temple Period*. Jerusalem: Israel Exploration Society, 1976.

Baader-Meinhof: In Love with Terror. Dir. Ben Lewis. BBC, 2002.

Barnes, Clive. "Stage: Screaming and Intact, 'Monty Python Live!'" *New York Times*, 16 April 1976: 11.

Bauckham, Richard. "For What Offence Was James Put to Death? In *James the Just and Christian Origins*. Leiden, The Netherlands: Koninklijke Brill NV, 1999.

Bauman, Richard A. *Human Rights in Ancient Rome*. London: Routledge, 2000.

Beckett, Andy. *When the Lights Went Out: Britain in the Seventies*. London: Faber and Faber, 2009.

Behind the Fridge. Peter Cook and Dudley Moore. Dir. Peter Faiman. 1971.

Bell, J. Bowyer. *The Secret Army: The IRA*. Cambridge, MA: MIT Press, 1983.

———. *Terror Out of Zion*. New York: St. Martin's Press, 1977.

Benn, Tony. *Conflicts of Interest: Diaries 1977–80*. London: Hutchinson, 1990.

Ben-Sasson, Haim Hillel. *A History of the Jewish People*. Cambridge: Harvard University Press, 1976.

Bentwich, Norman. *Josephus*. Philadelphia: Jewish Publication Society of America, 1914.

Bergson, Henri. *Laughter: An Essay on the Comic*. Ed. Wylie Sypher. New York: Doubleday, 1956.

Bernstein, George L. *The Myth of Decline: The Rise of Britain since 1945*. London: Pimlico, 2004.

Beveridge, William. *The Beveridge Report: Social Insurance and Allied Services*. London: HMSO, 1942.

Black, Lawrence, and Hugh Pemberton, eds. "The Winter of Discontent in British Politics." *Political Quarterly* 80, no. 4 (2009): 553–61.

Black, Lawrence, Hugh Pemberton, and Pat Thane, eds. *Reassessing 1970s Britain.* Manchester: Manchester University Press, 2013.

Bogdanor, Vernon. "The Attempt to Construct a Socialist Commonwealth." *Britain in the 20th Century.* Gresham College Lectures, 2011–2012.

———"The Character of the Postwar Period." *Britain in the 20th Century.* Gresham College Lectures, 2011–2012.

———. "The Collapse of the Postwar Settlement, 1964–1979." *Britain in the 20th Century.* Gresham College Lectures, 2011–2012.

———. "Thatcherism, 1979–1990." *Britain in the 20th Century.* Gresham College Lectures, 2011–2012.

Booker, Christopher. *The Seventies: The Decade That Changed the Future.* New York: Stein & Day, 1980.

Borg, Marcus, and John Dominic Crossan. *The Last Week: A Day-by-Day Account of Jesus's Final Week in Jerusalem.* San Francisco: Harper, 2006.

Borowski, Oded. *Daily Life in Biblical Times.* Atlanta, GA: Society of Biblical Literature, 2003.

———. *Every Living Thing: Daily Use of Animals in Ancient Israel.* Walnut Creek, CA: AltaMira Press, 1998.

Bough, Jill. *Donkey.* London: Reaktion Books, 2011.

Brandon, S. G. F. *Jesus and the Zealots: A Study of the Political Factor in Primitive Christianity.* Manchester: Manchester University Press, 1967.

———. "Josephus: Renegade or Patriot?" *History Today* 8:12 (1958): 830–36.

———. "Pontius Pilate in History and Legend." *History Today* 18, no. 8 (1968): 523–30.

———. *The Trial of Jesus of Nazareth.* New York: Stein and Day, 1968.

———. "The Trial of Jesus: The Enigma of the First Good Friday." *History Today* 16, no. 4 (1966): 251–59.

———. "The Zealots: The Jewish Resistance against Rome." *History Today* 15, no. 9 (1965): 632–41.

Brendon, Piers. *The Decline and Fall of the British Empire, 1781–1997.* New York: Vintage, 2010.

Brown, Raymond E. *The Death of the Messiah: From Gethsemane to the Grave.* New York: Yale University Press, 1998.

Burke, Edmund. "Frantz Fanon's *The Wretched of the Earth.*" *Daedalus* 105, no. 1 (Winter 1976): 127–35.

Burleigh, Michael. *Blood and Rage: A Cultural History of Terrorism.* New York: HarperCollins, 2009.

Caillois, Roger. *Pontius Pilate.* New York: Macmillan, 1963.

Calabro, David. "Gestures of Praise: Lifting and Spreading the Hands in Biblical Prayer." In *Ascending in the Mountain of the Lord: Temple, Praise and Worship in the Old Testament,* ed. Jeffrey R. Chadwick, 105–21. Salt Lake City, UT: Deseret Book, 2013.

Carlton, David. *Britain and the Suez Crisis.* Oxford: Basil Blackwell, 1988.

Carr, Gordon. *The Angry Brigade.* Dir. Gordon Carr. BBC and PM Press, 1973.

———. *The Angry Brigade: The Cause and the Case.* London: Victor Gollancz, Ltd., 1975.

———, dir. *The Angry Brigade: The Spectacular Rise and Fall of Britain's First Urban Guerilla Group.* Hole in the Wall Productions, 1973.

Caryl, Christian. *Strange Rebels: 1979 and the Birth of the 21st Century.* Philadelphia: Perseus, 2013.

Castle, Barbara. *The Castle Diaries 1974–1976.* London: Weidenfeld and Nicholson, 1980.

Catanzaro, Raimondo. *The Red Brigades and Left-Wing Terrorism in Italy.* London: Pinter, 1991.

Chapman, Graham. *A Liar's Autobiography: Volume VI.* London: Methuen, 1980.

———, John Cleese, Terry Gilliam, Eric Idle, and Michael Palin. *Monty Python's "The Life of Brian" (of Nazareth).* New York: F. Jordan Books, 1979.

———. *Monty Python and the Holy Grail (Book).* New York: Methuen, 1977.

———. Monty Python's Flying Circus*: All the Words, Vols. 1 and 2.* London: Methuen, 1989.

Chilton, Bruce D., and Craig Allen, eds. *James the Just and Christian Origins.* Leiden, The Netherlands: Koninklijke Brill NV, 1999.

Christian Believing. Church of England Doctrine Commission. London: S.P.C.K., 1976.

Churchill, Winston. "The End of the Beginning." Churchill Society. http://www.churchill-society -london.org.uk/EndoBegn.html.

Clareson, Thomas. *Understanding Contemporary Science Fiction*. Columbia: University of South Carolina Press, 1990.

Cleese, John. *So, Anyway*. New York: Three Rivers Press, 2014.

Cockerell, Michael. *The Lost World of the Seventies*. BBC 2, 2012.

———. *Roy Jenkins: A Very Social Democrat*. BBC, 1996.

Cohen, Jennie. "A Wise Man's Cure: Frankincense and Myrrh." *History* 27 June 2011. http://www.history.com/news/a-wise-mans-cure-frankincense-and-myrrh.

Cohn, Haim. *The Trial and Death of Jesus*. New York: Kvat, 1968.

Cook, John Granger. "Crucifixion as Spectacle in Roman Campania." *Novum Testamentum* 54 (2012): 68–100.

———. "Envisioning Crucifixion: Light from Several Inscriptions and the Palatine Graffito." *Novum Testamentum* 50 (2008): 262–85.

Cook, Wendy. *So Farewell Then: The Untold Life of Peter Cook*. New York: HarperCollins, 2006.

Coopey, Richard, and Nicholas Woodward, eds. *Britain in the 1970s: The Troubled Decade*. New York: St. Martin's, 1996.

Cowley, Philip, and Matthew Bailey. "Peasants' Uprising or Religious War? Re-examining the 1975 Conservative Leadership Contest." *British Journal of Political Science* 30, no. 4 (Oct. 2000): 599–629.

Crosland, C. A. R. *The Future of Socialism*. New York: Macmillan, 1957.

Cullman, Oscar. *Jesus and the Revolutionaries*. New York: Harper and Row, 1970.

Cumming, George, and Stephen Sayles. "The Symbionese Liberation Army: Coming Together, 1973." *History Compass* 9, no. 6 (2011): 485–97.

Cupitt, Don, and Peter Armstrong. *Who Was Jesus?* London: BBC, 1977.

Dal Masio, Cinzia. *Pompeii: The Art of Loving*. Milan: 24 ORE Cultural, 2012.

David, Ariel. "Ancient Romans, Jews Invented Trash Collection, Archaeology of Jerusalem Hints." *Haaretz*, 29 June 2016.

Davies, R. W. "Police Work in Roman Times." *History Today* 18, no. 10 (1968): 700–707.

Demaris, Ovid. *Brothers in Blood: The International Terrorist Network*. New York: Scribner's, 1977.

Denham, Andrew, and Mark Garnett. *Keith Joseph*. Oxford: Routledge, 2014.

Dennan, James, and Paul McDonald. *Unemployment Statistics from 1881 to the Present Day, Labour Market Trends*. London: The Government Statistical Service, January 1996.

Dimont, Max I. *Jews, God and History*. New York: Signet, 2004.

Dobson, Christopher, and Ronald Payne. *The Carlos Complex*. London: Coronet Books, 1978.

———. *The Terrorists: Their Weapons, Leaders and Tactics*. New York: Facts On File, 1979.

Donoughue, Bernard. *Downing Street Diary: With Harold Wilson in No. 10*. London: Pimlico, 2006.

———. *Downing Street Diary: With James Callaghan in No. 10*. London: Jonathan Cape, 2008.

Doré, Gustave. *The Divine Comedy: The Inferno, Purgatorio, and Paradiso*. Trans. L. G. White. New York: Pantheon Books, 1948.

———. *The Doré Bible Illustrations*. Introd. by Millicent Rose. New York: Dover, 1974.

———. *Masterpieces from the Works of Gustave Doré*. Ed. Edmund Ollier. New York: Cassell Publishing, 1887.

Dowty, Alan. *Israel/Palestine*. Cambridge: Polity, 2012.

Doyle, Julian. *The Life of ~~Brian~~ Jesus*. Leicester: Matador, 2011.

Eckstein, Harry. "Terror as a Weapon of Political Agitation." *Internal War, Problems and Approaches* (1964): 71–99.

Edersheim, Alfred. *Sketches of Jewish Social Life*. New York: James Pott & Co., 1881.

Ehrman, Bart D., and Zlatko Pleše, eds. *The Apocryphal Gospels*. Oxford: Oxford University Press, 2011.

———. *Misquoting Jesus: The Story Behind Who Changed the Bible and Why*. San Francisco, CA: Harper, 2005.

Eisler, Robert. *The Messiah Jesus and John the Baptist*. London: Methuen, 1931.

Emmerich, Anne Catherine. *The Dolorous Passion of Our Lord Jesus Christ*. London, New York: Burns & Oates, 1890.

Engen, Darel Tai. "The Economy of Ancient Greece." In *Economic History Net Encyclopedia*, ed. Robert Whaples. 31 July 2004. http://eh.net/encyclopedia/the-economy-of-ancient-greece/.

Erickson, Lynda. "Youth and Political Deference in England." *Canadian Journal of Political Science* 10, no. 3 (September 1977): 573–95.

Evans, Craig A. *Jesus and His World: The Archaeological Evidence*. Louisville, KY: WJK, 2012.

Fanon, Frantz. *Black Skin, White Masks*. New York: Grove Press, 1967.

———. *The Fanon Reader*. Ed. Haddour Azzedine. London: Pluto Press, 2006.

———. *The Wretched of the Earth*. New York: Grove Press, 1966.

Farrell, William R. *Blood and Rage: The Story of the Japanese Red Army*. Lexington, MA: Lexington Books, 1990.

Fernandez-Armesto, Felipe. *Civilizations: Culture, Ambition, and the Transformation of Nature*. New York: The Free Press, 2001.

Ficacci, Luigi. *Piranesi: The Complete Etchings*. Köln, Germany: Taschen, 2000.

"First UK Hijacking: Questions Raised." *Flight International*, 16 January 1975.

Flanders, Judith. "Slums." British Library. https://www.bl.uk/voices-of-science/sitecore/content/home/romantics-and-victorians/articles/slums.

Follain, John. *Jackal: The Complete Story of the Legendary Terrorist, Carlos the Jackal*. New York: Arcade, 2011.

Freedman, Jean R. *Whistling in the Dark: Memory and Culture in Wartime London*. Lexington: University Press of Kentucky, 1999.

Freese, Brett Leslie. "Medicinal Myrrh." *Archaeology* 49, no. 3 (May/June 1996). http://archive.archaeology.org/9605/newsbriefs/myrrh.html.

Freud, Sigmund. *The Joke and Its Relation to the Unconscious*. Tr. Joyce Crick. New York: Penguin, 2002.

Fromm, Erich. *The Fear of Freedom*. London: Routledge & Kegan Paul, 1952.

Fuchs, Jacob. *Horace's Satires and Epistles*. New York: W. W. Norton, 1977.

Garfield, Simon. *Private Battles: Our Intimate Diaries*. London: Ebury Press, 2007.

———. *Our Hidden Lives: The Remarkable Diaries of Postwar Britain*. London: Ebury Press, 2004.

Garnett, Mark. *From Anger to Apathy: The Story of Politics, Society and Popular Culture in Britain since 1975*. London: Vintage, 2008.

Gaskill, Alonzo. "The 'Ceremony of the Shoe': A Ritual of God's Ancient Covenant People." In *Our Rites of Worship*, ed. Daniel L. Belnap. Provo, UT: Religious Studies Center, 2013.

Gershuny, Theodore. *Soon to Be a Major Motion Picture*. New York: Henry Holt, 1982.

Geva, Hillel, ed. *Ancient Jerusalem Revealed*. Jerusalem: Israel Exploration Society, 1994.

Gilliam, Terry. *Animations of Mortality*. London: Eyre Methuen, 1978.

———. *Gilliam on Gilliam*. Ed. Ian Christie. London, New York: Faber and Faber, 1999.

———. *Gilliamesque*. New York: Harper Design, 2015.

Gillmeister, Heiner. *Tennis: A Cultural History*. London: Leicester University Press, 1997.

Goldberg, G. J. "The Popularity of John the Baptist." http://www.josephus.org/JohnTBaptist.htm#Popularity.

Grant, Michael. *Gladiators*. New York: B&N, 1967.

———. *The History of Ancient Israel*. New York: Charles Scribner's Sons, 1984.

Grant, Ted. "Labour's Programme—1964–70: Disaster Was a Warning." *The Militant*. https://www.marxists.org/archive/grant/1972/09/programme.htm.

Greene, Elizabeth. "Women Present, No 'Second Fiddle' in Roman Military." *Western News*, 5 February 2015. http://news.westernu.ca/2015/02/women-present-no-second-fiddle-in-roman-military/.

Greene, Thomas H. *Comparative Revolutionary Movements*. Upper Saddle River, NJ: Prentice-Hall, 1974.

Greer, Germaine. *The Female Eunuch*. London: MacGibbon & Kee, 1970.

Guelich, Robert A. "The Matthean Beatitudes: 'Entrance-Requirements' or Eschatological Blessings?" *Journal of Biblical Literature* 95, no. 3 (Sep. 1976): 415–34.

Haas, N. "Anthropological Observations on the Skeletal Remains from Giv'at ha-Mivtar." *Israel Exploration Journal* 20, nos. 1–2 (1970): 38–59.

Haines, Joe. *The Politics of Power*. London: Jonathan Cape, 1977.

Hammerton, J. A. *Wonders of the Past*, 2 vols. New York: Wise and Company, 1952.

Hankoff, L. D. "Religious Healing in First-Century Christianity." *Journal of Psychohistory* 19, no. 4 (Spring 1992): 387–407.

Hansen, Søren, and Jesper Jensen. *The Little Red Schoolbook*. London: Stage 1, 1971.

Harrison, Tony. *Tony Harrison: The Mysteries*. London: Faber and Faber, 1985.

Hay, Colin. "Narrating Discourse: The Discursive Construction of the 'Winter of Discontent.'" *Sociology* 30, no. 2 (May 1996): 253–77.

"The History of Plumbing in Jerusalem." *Plumbing and Mechanical*, July 1989.

Hendrix, Holland L. *Jews and the Roman Empire*. PBS *Frontline*, 1998.

Hewison, Robert. *Monty Python: The Case Against*. New York: Grove Press, 1981.

Hitchens, Peter. *The Abolition of Britain*. London: Continuum, 2008.

Hobsbawm, Eric. "The Forward March of Labour Halted?" *Marxism Today* (Sep. 1978): 279–86.

Hofstader, Richard. *The Paranoid Style in American Politics*. London: Jonathan Cape, 1966.

Holland, Tom. *Rubicon: The Triumph and Tragedy of the Roman Republic*. London: Little, Brown, 2003.

Hope, Valerie M. "Contempt and Respect: The Treatment of the Corpse in Ancient Rome." In *Death and Disease in the Ancient City*, edited by Valerie M. Hope and Eireann Marshall, 104–27. Florence, KY: Routledge, 2000.

Horace. *Horace's Satire and Epistles*. Tr. and ed. Jacob Fuchs. New York: Norton, 1977.

Horsley, Richard A. "Josephus and the Bandits." *Journal for the Study of Judaism* 10, no.1: 37–63.

———. "The Sicarii: Ancient Jewish 'Terrorists'." *Journal of Religion* 59, no. 4 (Oct. 1979): 435–58.

———. "The Zealots: Their Origin, Relationships and Importance in the Jewish Revolt." *Novum Testamentum* 28, no. 2 (1986): 159–92.

Horvath, Tibor. "Why Was Jesus Brought to Pilate?" *Novum Testamentum* 11, no. 3 (July 1969): 174–84.

Hubbard, David. *The Skyjacker—His Flights of Fantasy*. New York: Macmillan, 1971.

Hughes, Geoffrey. *An Encyclopedia of Swearing*. London: Routledge, 2015.

Humphry, Derek, and David Tindall. *False Messiah: The Story of Michael X*. London: Hart Davis, 1977.

Husband, R. W. "The Pardoning of Prisoners by Pilate." *American Journal of Theology* 21, no. 1 (January 1917): 110–16.

I'm All Right Jack. Dir. John Boulting. Charter Film Productions, 1959.

Iviansky, Ze'ev. "Individual Terror: Concept and Typology." *Journal of Contemporary History* 12, no. 1 (January 1977): 43–63.

Jay, Douglas. *The Socialist Case*. London: Faber and Faber, 1937.

Jenkins, Peter. *Anatomy of Decline: The Political Journalism of Peter Jenkins*. Eds. Brian Brivati and Richard Crockett. London: Indigo, 1995.

———. *Mrs. Thatcher's Revolution: The Ending of the Socialist Era*. Cambridge, MA: Harvard University Press, 1988.

Jeremias, Joachim. *Jerusalem in the Time of Jesus*. Philadelphia: Fortress Press, 1969.

Jessop, Bob, and Russell Wheatley, eds. *Karl Marx's Social and Political Thought, Vol. V*. London: Routledge, 1999.

"Jews and the Roman Empire." In *From Jesus to Christ*. PBS Frontline. April 1998. http://www.pbs.org/wgbh/pages/frontline/shows/religion/portrait/jews.html.

Jewish Encyclopedia. http://www.jewishencyclopedia.com/.

Johnson, Kim Howard. *Monty Python's Tunisian Holiday: My Life with Brian*. New York: St. Martin's Press, 2008.

Joseph, Keith. "The Stockton Lecture: Monetarism Is Not Enough." The Centre for Policy Studies. London: Chichester & London, 1976.

Josephus: Complete Works. Trans. William Whiston. Grand Rapids, MI: Kregel, 1960.

Joyce, James. *Ulysses*. New York: Vintage International, 1990.

Judt, Tony. *Postwar: A History of Europe Since 1945*. New York: Penguin, 2005.

Kemna, Friedhelm. "Death of a Nightingale." *Encounter*, September 1974: 60–62.

Kemp, Arnold. *Confusion to Our Enemies*. London: Neil Wilson, 2012.

BIBLIOGRAPHY

King, Philip J., and Lawrence E. Stager. *Life in Biblical Israel*. Louisville, KY: Westminster John Knox Press, 2001.

Kokosalakis, Nikos. "The Political Significance of Popular Religion in Greece." *Archives de sciences sociales des religions* 64, no. 1 (1987): 37–52.

Koloski-Ostrow, Ann. *The Archaeology of Sanitation in Roman Italy: Toilets, Sewers, and Water Systems*. Chapel Hill: University of North Carolina Press, 2015.

Korb, Scott. *Life in Year One: What the World Was Like in First-Century Palestine*. New York: Riverhead, 2010.

Kotker, Norman. *The Holy Land in the Time of Jesus*. New York: American Heritage, 1967.

Krassner, Paul. "The Parts Left Out of the Patty Hearst Trial, Parts 1 and 2." disinfo.com.

———. *Patty Hearst and the Twinkie Murders*. Oakland, CA: PM Press, 2014.

Lalvani, Kartar. *The Making of India: The Untold Story of British Enterprise*. London: Bloomsbury, 2016.

Lansford, Tyler. *The Latin Inscriptions of Rome: A Walking Guide*. Baltimore: Johns Hopkins University Press, 2009.

Laqueur, Walter. *Terrorism: A Study of National and International Political Violence*. London: ABACUS, Sphere Books, 1978.

Larsen, Darl. *A Book about the Film* Monty Python and the Holy Grail. Lanham, MD: Rowman & Littlefield, 2015.

———. *Monty Python, Shakespeare and English Renaissance Drama*. Jefferson, NC: McFarland, 2003.

———. Monty Python's Flying Circus: *An Utterly Complete, Thoroughly Unillustrated, Absolutely Unauthorized Guide to Possibly All the References from Arthur "Two Sheds" Jackson to Zambesi*. Lanham, MD: Taylor Trade, 2013.

Lasky, Melvin J. "Ulrike Meinhof and the Baader-Meinhof Gang." *Encounter*, July 1975: 9–23.

Lawrence, Benjamin. "Servi Poenae." In *The Historical Encyclopedia of World Slavery*, edited by Junius P. Rodriguez, 577–78. Santa Barbara, CA: ABC-CLIO, 1997.

Lee, Stephen J. *Aspects of British Political History 1914–1995*. London: Routledge, 1996.

Levine, Lee I. *Jerusalem: Portrait of the City in the Second Temple Period*. Philadelphia: Jewish Historical Society, 2002.

Levy, Leonard Williams. *Blasphemy: Verbal Offense against the Sacred, from Moses to Salman Rushdie*. New York: Knopf, 1993.

Lifshitz, B. "Inscriptions latines de Césarée (Caesarea Palaestinae)." *Latomus* 22, no. 4 (October–December 1963): 783–84.

Ligasor, Tim. "The Art of Attrition: The Erosion of Peoples Temple and Jim Jones." http://jonestown.sdsu.edu/?page_id=29409.

Lindvall, Terry. *God Mocks: A History of Religious Satire from the Hebrew Prophets to Stephen Colbert*. New York: New York University Press, 2015.

Little, Alan M. G. *A Roman Bridal Drama at the Villa of the Mysteries*. Kennebunk, ME: Star Press, 1972.

London Can Take It. Dir. Humphrey Jennings and Harry Watt. 1940.

Look Back at Grunwick. Concord Media, 1980.

MacDonald, William. *The Architecture of the Roman Empire*. New Haven, CT: Yale University Press, 1965.

Madan, Rev. M. *Juvenal and Persius*. Dublin: Brett Smith, 1820.

Magness, Jodi. *Stone and Dung, Oil and Spit: Jewish Daily Life in the Time of Jesus*. Grand Rapids, MI: Eerdmans Publishing, 2011.

———. "What's the Poop on Ancient Toilets and Toilet Habits?" *Near Eastern Archaeology* 75, no. 2 (June 2012): 80–87.

Maier, Paul L. "The Fate of Pontius Pilate." *Hermes* 99, no. 3 (1971): 362–71.

———. *Pontius Pilate*. New York: Doubleday, 1968.

Malik, Sarita. *Representing Black Britain: Black and Asian Images on Television*. London: Sage, 2002.

Mannix, Daniel P. *Those about to Die*. New York: Ballantine, 1958.

Marcuse, Herbert. "Interview with Herbert Marcuse." *Modern Philosophy: Marcuse and the Frankfurt School.* Interviewer Bryan Magee. London: BBC, 1978.

Marighella, Carlos. *Minimanual of the Urban Guerrilla.* St. Petersburgh, FL: Red and Black, 2008.

Marin, Pater. "Meditations on the Jesus Movement: Children of Yearning." *Saturday Review* 58, no. 2 (6 May 1972): 58–62.

Marr, Andrew. *A History of Modern Britain.* London: Macmillan, 2007.

Martin, Ernest L. *New Evidence of the Site of the Temple in Jerusalem.* Review response. Associate for Scriptural Knowledge. http://askelm.com/temple/t001211.htm.

Marwick, Arthur. *British Society since 1945.* London: Penguin, 2003.

McDonald, Fiona. *The Popular History of Graffiti: From the Ancient World to the Present.* New York: Skyhorse, 2013.

McKeown, J.C. *A Cabinet of Roman Curiosities.* Oxford: Oxford University Press, 2010.

Miller, Casey, and Kate Swift. *Words and Women.* Garden City, NY: Anchor Press, 1976.

Milligan, Spike. *The Goon Show Scripts.* New York: St. Martin's, 1972.

Mitchell, Piers D. "Human Parasites in the Roman World: Health Consequences of Conquering an Empire." *Parasitology* 144, no. 1 (2017): 48–58.

Montefiore, Simon Sebag. *Jerusalem: The Biography.* London: Weidenfeld & Nicolson, 2011.

Monty Python and the Holy Grail. Dirs. Terry Gilliam and Terry Jones. 1974.

Monty Python's Life of Brian. Dir. Terry Jones. 1979.

Monty Python's the Meaning of Life. Dir. Terry Jones. 1983.

Monty Python's And Now For Something Completely Different. Dir. Ian MacNaughton. 1971.

Moorehead, Caroline. "The Captive Mind." *London Times,* 12 January 1980: 6.

Morgan, Kenneth O. *Britain Since 1945: The People's Peace.* Oxford: Oxford University Press, 2001.

———. *Callaghan: A Life.* Oxford: Oxford University Press, 1997.

———. *The Oxford History of Britain.* Oxford: Oxford University Press, 2001.

———. "Symbiosis: Trade and the British Empire." *BBC History* 17 February 2011. http://www.bbc .co.uk/history/british/empire_seapower/trade_empire_01.shtml.

Morris, James. *Pax Britannica: The Climax of Empire.* London: Penguin, 1968.

Muddiman, John, and John Barton. *The Oxford Bible Commentary: The Gospels.* Oxford: Oxford University Press, 2001.

Murray, Peter. *Piranesi and the Grandeur of Ancient Rome.* London: Thames and Hudson, 1971.

Nash, David. *Blasphemy in the Christian World.* Oxford: Oxford University Press, 2007.

Neufeld, Edward. "Hygiene Conditions in Ancient Israel." *Biblical Archaeologist* 34, no. 2 (May 1971): 41–66.

The New Partridge Dictionary of Slang. New York: Routledge, 2006.

Newton, Michael. *The Encyclopedia of Kidnappings.* New York: Facts On File, 2002.

O'Hehir, Andrew. "Insane Time and Place." *Salon,* 18 August 2016. http://www.salon.com/2016/08/18/ patty-hearsts-america-what-american-heiress-gets-wrong-and-right-about-an-insane-time-and -place/.

Orsini, Alessandro, and Sarah J. Nodes. *Anatomy of the Red Brigades.* Ithaca, NY: Cornell University Press, 2011.

Palin, Michael. *Michael Palin Diaries 1969–1979: The Python Years.* London: Thomas Dunne Books, 2007.

Pasolini, Pier Paolo. *The Gospel According to St. Matthew.* 1964.

Pathrapankal, Joseph M. "Jesus: Freedom-Fighter or Prince of Peace?" *Indian Journal of Theology* 24, nos. 3–4 (July–December 1975): 79–86.

Paul VI. *Marialis Cultis.* 1974. papalencyclicals.net.

Pearce, Edward. *Denis Healey: A Life in Our Times.* London: Little, Brown, 2002.

Pellison, Maurice. *Roman Life in Pliny's Time.* Philadelphia: George Jacobs, 1897.

Penny, Nicholas. *Piranesi.* London: Bloomsbury, 1978.

Petronius. *Satyricon.* Tr. Alfred R. Allinson. New York: Panurge, 1930.

BIBLIOGRAPHY

"Pharisees: Their Dress." *Bible History Online.* http://www.bible-history.com/pharisees/PHARISEES Dress.htm.

Philo. *The Embassy to Gaius.* Trans. F. H. Colson. Cambridge, MA: Harvard University Press, 1962.

Piranesi, G. B. *Etchings by G.B. Giovanni Batista Piranesi, 1720–1778.* London: P. & D. Colnaghi and Co., 1973–1974.

———. *Piranesi: Etchings and Drawings.* Ed. Roseline Bacou. Boston: New York Graphic Society, 1975.

Pitchford, Mark. *The Conservative Party and the Extreme Right, 1945–1975.* Manchester: Manchester University Press, 2011.

Pölönen, Janne. "Plebeians and Repression of Crime in the Roman Empire: From Torture of Convicts to Torture of Suspects." *Revue Internationale des droits de l'Antiquité* 51 (2004): 217–57.

Pompeii AD79. Bristol: Imperial Tobacco Ltd., 1977.

Porter, Bernard. *The Lion's Share: A Short History of British Imperialism 1850–1983.* Essex: Longman, 1984.

Prawer, Joshua. *The History of Jerusalem.* New York: New York University Press, 1996.

Radin, Max. *The Jews among the Greeks and Romans.* Philadelphia: The Jewish Publication Society of America, 1915.

The Red Army/PFLP: Declaration of World War. Dir. Masao Adachi and Kôji Wakamatsu. Lebanon, 1971.

Rawson, Hugh. *Wicked Words.* New York: Crown, 1989.

Reich, Ronny. "The Question of the Biblical 'Zinnor' and Warren's Shaft." https://www.youtube.com/watch?v=YFmCfbnOh_g.

Reich, Ronny, and Eli Shukron. "Light at the End of the Tunnel: Warren's Shaft Theory of David's Conquest Shattered." *BAR,* January/February 1999: 22–33, 72.

Reisner, Robert. *Graffiti.* New York: Parallax, 1967.

Ricciardi, Alessia. *After La Dolce Vita: A Cultural Prehistory of Berlusconi's Italy.* Stanford, CA: Stanford University Press, 2012.

Richard, Carl J. *Why We're All Romans.* Lanham, MD: Rowman & Littlefield, 2010.

Roberts, Andrew. *A History of the English-Speaking Peoples since 1900.* New York: HarperCollins, 2009.

Roberts, J. M., and Odd Arne Westad. *The Penguin History of the World.* New York: Penguin, 1976, 2013.

Rodriguez, Junius P. *The Historical Encyclopedia of World Slavery.* 2 volumes. Santa Barbara, CA: ABC-CLIO, 1997.

Roller, Duane W. *The Building Program of Herod the Great.* Berkeley: University of California Press, 1998.

The Roman Empire in the First Century. Hugo Godwin, researcher; Bruce Robinson, writer. PBS. Devillier Donegan, 2001.

Rosenblatt, Samuel. "The Crucifixion of Jesus from the Standpoint of Pharisaic Law." *Journal of Biblical Literature* 75, no. 4 (December 1956): 315–21.

Rothwell, Kenneth S. "Roman Polanski's *Macbeth*: Golgotha Triumphant." *Literature/Film Quarterly* 1, no. 1 (Winter 1973): 71–75.

Sabbagh, Karl. *Britain in Palestine: The Story of British Rule in Palestine 1917–1948.* Stroud, UK: Skyscraper, 2012.

Safrai, Ze'ev. *The Economy of Roman Palestine.* London: Routledge, 1994.

Sallust. *Catiline's War.* London: Penguin, 2007.

Sandbrook, Dominic. *Never Had It So Good: A History of Britain from Suez to the Beatles.* London: Little Brown, 2005.

———. *Seasons in the Sun: The Battle for Britain 1974–1979.* London: Allen Lane, 2012.

———. *State of Emergency: The Way We Were: Britain 1970–74.* London: Allen Lane, 2010.

———. *White Heat: A History of Britain in the Swinging Sixties.* London: Abacus, 2007.

Sanders, James A. "The Dead Sea Scrolls—A Quarter-Century of Study." *Biblical Archaeologist* 36, no. 4 (December 1973): 109–48.

Sandnes, Karl Olav. *Belly and Body in the Pauline Epistles*. Cambridge: Cambridge University Press, 2002.

Sapir, Boris, ed. *"Vpered!" 1873–1877: From the Archives of Valerian Nikolaevich Smernov*. Dordrecht, Holland: D. Reidel, 1970.

Schain, Martin. *The Marshall Plan: Fifty Years After*. New York: Palgrave, 2001.

Schiffman, Lawrence H. "Inverting Reality: The Dead Sea Scrolls in the Popular Media." *Dead Sea Discoveries* 12, no. 1 (2005): 24–37.

Schlaeger, Hilke. "Vernunft gegen Gewalt Studenten, Professoren, Polizei: in Berlin, Heidelberg und Frankfurt zum Beispiel." *Die Zeit*, 17 January 1969.

Schneer, Jonathan. *The Balfour Declaration: The Origins of the Arab-Israeli Conflict*. Toronto: Anchor Canada, 2012.

Schreiber, Mark. *Shocking Crimes of Postwar Japan*. Tokyo: Yenbooks, 1996.

Schürer, Emil, et al. *The History of the Jewish People in the Age of Jesus Christ*. London: Bloomsbury, 1973.

Scott, Jonathan. *Piranesi*. New York: Wiley-Academy, 1975.

Seaford, R. A. S. "The Mysteries of Dionysos at Pompeii." In *Pegasus: Classical Essays from the University of Exeter*, edited by H. W. Stubbs. Exeter: University of Exeter, 1981.

Seldon, Anthony, and Kevin Hickson, eds. *New Labour, Old Labour: The Wilson and Callaghan Governments, 1974–79*. London: Routledge, 2004.

The Seventh Seal. Dir. Ingmar Bergman. 1958.

Shanks, Michael. *The Stagnant Society*. London: Penguin, 1972.

Shaw, Brent D. *Spartacus and the Slave Wars*. New York: Palgrave Macmillan, 2001.

Shepherd, John. *Crisis? What Crisis? The Callaghan Government and the British 'Winter of Discontent'*. Manchester: Manchester University Press, 2013.

———. "Labour Wasn't Working." *History Today*, January 2009: 43–49.

Sherman, A. J. *Mandate Days: British Lives in Palestine, 1918–1948*. New York: Thames and Hudson, 1997.

Silberman, Neil Asher, and Eric M. Meyers. "The Politics of First-Century Judea." *Archaeology* 47, no. 6 (November/December 1994): 30–41.

"Simeon bar Giora." Jewish Virtual Library, http://www.jewishvirtuallibrary.org/simeon-bar-giora.

Simon of the Desert. Dir. Luis Bunuel. 1965.

Smallwood, E. Mary. "Jews and Romans in the Early Empire: Part I." *History Today* 15, no. 4 (1965): 232–39.

———. "Jews and Romans in the Early Empire: Part II." *History Today* 15, no. 5 (1965): 313–19.

———. *The Jews under Roman Rule: From Pompey to Diocletian*. Leiden, Netherlands: E. J. Brill, 1976.

Smith, Jason E., and Andre Moncourt, eds. *The Red Army Faction: A Documentary History*, Vol. 1, *Projectiles for the People*. Montreal: Kersplebedeb, 2009.

———. *The Red Army Faction: A Documentary History*, Vol. 2, *Dancing with Imperialism*. Montreal: Kersplebedeb, 2009.

Smith, Morton. "Zealots and the Sicarii, Their Origins and Relation." *Harvard Theological Review* 64 no. 1 (January 1971): 1–19.

Smith, William. *A Dictionary of Greek and Roman Antiquities*. London: John Murray, 1875.

Sounes, Howard. *The Seventies: The Sights, Sounds and Ideas of a Brilliant Decade*. London: Simon and Schuster, 2007.

Stanton, Graham. *The Gospels and Jesus*. Oxford: Oxford University Press, 2002.

Stevenson, Walter. "The Rise of the Eunuchs in Greco-Roman Antiquity." *Journal of the History of Sexuality* 5, no. 4 (April 1995): 494–511.

Stillman, Edmund, ed. *The United Kingdom in 1980: The Hudson Report*. New York: Halsted Press, 1974.

"Stoke Newington 8 Defence Group: A Political Statement." https://hackneyhistory.wordpress.com/2012/01/10/stoke-newington-8-defence-group-a-political-statement/.

Sugarman, David. "Melville in Jerusalem." *Tablet*, 16 August 2012. http://www.tabletmag.com/jewish-arts-and-culture/books/109333/melville-in-jerusalem.

BIBLIOGRAPHY

Taylor, Joan E., ed. *Jesus and Brian: Exploring the Historical Jesus and His Times via "Monty Python's Life of Brian."* London: Bloomsbury, 2015.

Thatcher, Margaret. Margaret Thatcher Foundation. http://www.margaretthatcher.org.

Thiessen, Gerd, and Annette Merz. *The Historical Jesus.* Minneapolis: Fortress Press, 1996.

Thomas, Donald. *Villain's Paradise: A History of Britain's Underworld.* New York: Pegasus Books, 2006.

Thompson, Harry. *Peter Cook.* London: Hodder and Stoughton, 1997.

Thompson, John O. *Monty Python: Complete and Utter Theory of the Grotesque.* London: BFI, 1982.

Timmers, J. J. M., and A. Van Der Heyden. *The Glory of Rome.* New York: Funk & Wagnalls, 1975.

Tiratsoo, Nick, ed. *From Blitz to Blair: A New History of Britain since 1939.* London: Weidenfeld & Nicholson, 1997.

"A Tomb in Jerusalem Reveals the History of Crucifixion and Roman Crucifixion Methods." *Bible History Daily,* 22 July 2011.

Tomlinson, Jim. "The Politics of Decline." In *Reassessing 1970s Britain,* ed. Lawrence Black, Hugh Pemberton, and Pat Thane. Manchester: Manchester University Press, 2013.

Toner, Jerry. *The Day Commodus Killed a Rhino.* Baltimore: Johns Hopkins University Press, 2014.

Toye, Richard. "'The Gentleman in Whitehall' Reconsidered: The Evolution of Douglas Jay's Views on Economic Planning and Consumer Choice, 1937–1947." *Labour History Review* 67, no. 2 (August 2002): 185–202.

"TUC: History Online." http://www.unionhistory.info/timeline.

Tuchman, Barbara. *Bible and Sword: England and Palestine from the Bronze Age to Balfour.* New York: Ballantine Books, 1984.

Turner, Alwyn W. *Crisis? What Crisis? Britain in the 1970s.* London: Aurum, 2008.

Tzaferis, Vassilios. "Crucifixion—the Archaeological Evidence." *Biblical Archaeology Review* 11, no. 1 (1985): 44–53.

Varon, Jamie. *Bringing the War Home: The Weather Underground, the Red Army Faction, and Revolutionary Violence in the Sixties and Seventies.* Berkeley: University of California Press, 2004.

Vermes, Geza. *The Authentic Gospel of Jesus.* London: Penguin, 2004.

Vikman, Elisabeth. "Ancient Origins: Sexual Violence in Warfare, Parts I and II." *Anthropology & Medicine* 12, no. 1 (April 2005): 21–31, 33–46.

Vinen, Richard. *Thatcher's Britain.* London: Simon & Schuster, 2009.

Von Ehrenkrook, Jason. "Effeminacy in the Shadow of Empire: The Politics of Transgressive Gender in Josephus's Bellum Judaicum." *Jewish Quarterly Review* 101, no. 2 (Spring 2011): 145–63.

Wasson, Donald. "Roman Citizenship." *Ancient History Encyclopedia.* http://www.ancient.eu/article/859/.

Watson, Bruce. "For a While, the Luddites Had a Smashing Success." *Smithsonian* 24, no. 1 (April 1993): 140–54.

Waugh, Auberon. *A Turbulent Decade: The Diaries of Auberon Waugh 1976–1985.* Ed. Anna Galli-Pahlavi. London: Private Eye, 1985.

———. *Four Crowded Years: The Diaries of Auberon Waugh 1972–1976.* Ed. N. R. Galli. London: Private Eye, 1976.

Weekend. Dir. Jean-Luc Godard. 1967.

We'll Meet Again. Dir. Philip Brandon. Columbia British Pictures, 1943.

Wharton, Ken. *Wasted Years, Wasted Lives: The British Army in Northern Ireland,* vol. 2. Solihull, UK: Helion, 2014.

Wheen, Francis. *Strange Days Indeed—The 1970s: The Golden Age of Paranoia.* New York: Public Affairs, 2010.

White, Lawrence G. *The Divine Comedy.* New York: Pantheon, 1948.

Whitehead, Phillip. *The Writing on the Wall: Britain in the Seventies.* London: Michael Joseph, 1985.

Wiedemann, Thomas. *Emperors and Gladiators.* Oxford: Routledge, 1992.

Williamson, Adrian. "The Case for Brexit: Lessons from the 1960s and 1970s." *History & Policy.* 5 May 2015.

Williamson, G. W., ed. *Josephus: The Jewish War.* London: Penguin, 1970.

Wilmut, Roger. *From Fringe to Flying Circus*. London: Methuen, 1980.

Wise, Michael, et al. *The Dead Sea Scrolls*. San Francisco, CA: HarperCollins, 2005.

WW2 People's War. "Dunstable Town Centre" and "Life in an Air-Raid Shelter." BBC. http://www.bbc.co.uk/.

Yadin, Yigael. *Excavation of Masada*. Jerusalem: Israel Exploration Society, 1965.

———, ed. *Jerusalem Revealed*. Jerusalem: Israel Exploration Society, 1975.

Zeitlin, Solomon. "The Crucifixion of Jesus Re-Examined." *The Jewish Quarterly Review* 31, no. 4 (April 1941): 327–69.

———. "The Crucifixion of Jesus Re-Examined (Continued)." *The Jewish Quarterly Review* 32, no. 2 (October 1941): 175–89.

———. "The Idolatry of the Dead Sea Scrolls" *The Jewish Quarterly Review*, 48, no. 3 (January 1958): 243–78.

———. "History, Historians and the Dead Sea Scrolls" *Jewish Quarterly Review*, 55, no. 2 (October 1964): 97–116.

Zias, Joseph, and Eliezer Sekeles. "The Crucified Man from Giv'at ha-Mivtar: A Reappraisal." *Israel Exploration Journal* 35, no. 1 (1985): 22–27.

INDEX

ABOUT THE AUTHOR

Darl Larsen was born and raised in central California and has been part of the film faculty at Brigham Young University since 1998. He took degrees at UC Santa Barbara, Brigham Young University, and Northern Illinois University. He is professor in the Media Arts department and the Center for Animation at BYU, teaching film, animation, screenwriting, and popular culture studies. He has written extensively in the area of Monty Python studies and his books include *Monty Python, Shakespeare, and English Renaissance Drama* (2003) as well as Monty Python's Flying Circus: *An Utterly Complete, Thoroughly Unillustrated, Absolutely Unauthorized Guide to Possibly All the References* (Scarecrow Press, 2008; Revised, Taylor Trade, 2013) and *A Book about the Film* Monty Python and the Holy Grail: *All the References from African Swallows to Zoot* (Rowman & Littlefield, 2015). Larsen lives in Provo, Utah, with his family.

Albert Schweitzer

Albert Schweitzer

A BIOGRAPHY

Second Edition

James Brabazon

*In Celebration of the 125th Anniversary
of Albert Schweitzer's Birth*

SYRACUSE UNIVERSITY PRESS

Library of Congress Cataloging-in-Publication Data
Brabazon, James.
Albert Schweitzer : a biography / James Brabazon.—2nd ed.
p. cm. — (The Albert Schweitzer library)
Includes bibliographical references (p.) and index.
ISBN 0-8156-2875-7 (alk. paper) — ISBN 0-8156-0675-3 (pbk. : alk. paper)
1. Schweitzer, Albert, 1875–1965. 2. Missionaries, Medical—Gabon—Biography. 3.
Theologians—Europe—Biography. 4. Musicians—Europe—Biography. I. Title. II. Albert
Schweitzer library (Syracuse, N.Y.)
CT1018.S45 B72 2000
610'.92—dc21
[B]   00-044668

Manufactured in the United States of America

Contents

Illustrations

Preface

IT IS WITH MIXED FEELINGS that a biographer learns of important new material that may dramatically change the perception that the world has of his subject. Will it integrate with what he has already written or conflict with it? Support it or undermine it?

In this case the letters that have been found between Schweitzer and Hélène Bresslau, written during the ten years before their marriage, expose not only a long, secret, and very unusual relationship, of which even their closest friends knew almost nothing, but also facets of Schweitzer's personality and the development of his thinking that he took immense trouble to hide from the world. The letters, then, fill a huge gap in our understanding.

His secretiveness toward all others meant that he desperately needed a confidante: someone totally trustworthy, totally understanding, yet able to counsel and guide him. Hélène filled the bill, and to her he poured out his heart without constraint. The letters are so rich in interest and insight that it is very difficult to make a selection; the temptation is to include many whole exchanges. Because this is not possible here, I recommend that those interested in Schweitzer beg, buy, or borrow the recently published letters for themselves.

The bulk of this new material is to be found in chapters 9 and 12 although it also affects several other chapters. The other main change in the book is to be found in chapters 26 and 27. I deal in greater detail with the antagonism that developed between Schweitzer and the governments of the West, particularly the United States, as they tried to keep secret the fall-out hazards of the hydrogen bomb tests and show how successful he was in exposing them.

Born in Africa, **James Brabazon** returned as a child to England, where he attended public school and won a scholarship to read Classics at Cambridge. World War II interrupted this plan, and he obtained an external degree while also working in a statistics department of the Admiralty.

After the war he pursued a career as actor and writer in the theater before moving to television, where he worked as story-editor for a major BBC drama slot, moving on to direct and produce for Granada Television and London Weekend.

Now an independent writer/producer, one of his major projects is a feature film about Schweitzer, focusing on the profound influence Schweitzer and his ideals had on the banning of hydrogen bomb tests.

Preface to the First Edition

ALBERT SCHWEITZER DIED on September 4, 1965. A presence that had made itself felt throughout the world was now an absence. He was mourned by Japanese schoolchildren as by European intellectuals, by peasants as by politicians, by blacks and whites, communists and capitalists, employers and wage slaves. Magazine articles had already appeared with headlines that described him as a twentieth-century saint and the greatest man of our generation. At his death, the superlatives poured again from the presses of the world.

Many of those who actually met him felt that the force of his personality came at least within measurable distance of living up to the myth. The impact of his physical presence was certainly tremendous. He existed in the confident, indisputable way that animals and children exist, his concentration at every moment focused completely on whomever or whatever then occupied his mind.

When he was part of the company, whether the company consisted of colleagues, friends, or strangers, jungle Africans or Nobel Prize winners, he was the center of interest. He commanded attention by his knowledge, by his training as a preacher, which had taught him how to make people listen to him, but mostly by sheer personal magnetism—a combination of physical power, charm, dominating will, and a quick responsiveness to everything around him.

A formidable man. A man difficult to say no to. A man of whom a friend said that his enjoyment of his own dominance was as naïve and endearing as that of a little girl with a new frock. Others found it less charming. But for good or ill, the power was there. Schweitzer was a force to be reckoned with.

Response to life was the mark of his personality. Reverence for Life was the key phrase of his philosophy. The things he stood for were the things for which the new generation stands: a return to the earth and a respect for nature, peace, simplicity, spontaneity, the stripping away of the false values of a materialistic civilization to rediscover the true values of human relationship—relationship with other people and with the whole of creation.

The thing that made him unique was that in proving his point he was not prepared to rely on statements or pronouncements or arguments. He was a great scholar, but for him scholarship was not enough. He lived his belief. He claimed to "make his life his argument."

When he died, the things he was doing were left unfinished. The hospital he designed, built, and presided over for so many years was still growing. The books in which he had hoped to explore the wider implications of his philosophy remain a series of disconnected notes, which others are still trying to put together. But his life was ended. There was no continuation. In that sense it is complete; the argument has been stated.

The statement he made by his life was intended to be about all life. To investigate his life, therefore—to see whether it has the universal relevance he claimed—is not only a matter of doing justice to him; it may be of crucial importance to us.

My own quest for the truth about Schweitzer was spurred on by a sense that much could be learned from a philosopher who was not content with philosophy, a theologian who went beyond theology. It also seemed important to look for the hidden flaws, the human failings in the man who has been beatified by the popular press; and to discover which were right, those who were "for" him or those who were "against" him, or whether, perhaps, those words had no meaning.

He has often been hailed as an exceptionally good man. But a close friend of his said, "He was not so much righteous, as right." The world has utmost need of people who are right. Was Schweitzer? If so, his life must have been right because he made his life his argument.

With this in mind, I set about trying to understand Schweitzer's life.

Acknowledgments

I WAS WELL INTO THE WRITING of this book before I fully appreciated what I should have realized from the start—how rash it is to try to get to know second hand a man of Schweitzer's magnitude, and how hard it is to hold in balance and to convey in proper perspective what one hopes one has discovered. To those who unstintingly helped me to understand, I owe a tremendous debt of gratitude—and an apology where I have failed to pass on to the reader what they tried to tell me.

First among these must be Mrs. Clara Urquhart, who provided me with the initial impetus to embark on the project, as in the past she provided the impetus to many others to get to know Schweitzer.

Next I must thank Schweitzer's daughter, Mrs. Rhena Schweitzer Miller, for the confidence she placed in the book, for the help and encouragement she has given me, and for the labor of reading and checking the manuscript for accuracy. To her, too, I owe the authorization for the many quotations from Schweitzer's books, speeches, sermons, and letters. Most of all, perhaps, I am grateful for her objectivity about her father, a man about whom objectivity was not always easy.

I also thank Ali Silver, for twenty years Schweitzer's right hand at Lambaréné and later the devoted and delightful keeper of the Central Archives in Günsbach, Alsace, and Mrs. Erica Anderson, whose Albert Schweitzer Friendship House in Great Barrington, Massachusetts, was for me a treasury both of written material and of recollection.

My first impression of the quality of Schweitzer as a man came from the quality of the many relatives and friends of his that I met—a most attractive combination of friendly directness and warm vitality. From his sister-in-law, Mme. Emma Schweitzer, who knew him in his teens, to his granddaughter, Christiane, following in his footsteps as a doctor and musician; from M. Leon Morel, who was already a missionary on the Ogowe River when Schweitzer first decided to go there, to Dr. Weissberg, who ran the government hospital near Schweitzer's during the last years of his life; from Schweitzer's nephews, Gustav Woytt and Albert Ehretsmann, who knew him at home in Alsace, to Dr. Mark Lauterburg, who worked in Africa with him in the 1920s, and Dr. James Witchalls, who did so forty years later; from all these and many others I gained not only the information I needed but also something else—an idea of the kind of man Schweitzer must have been if he could impress, and sometimes overwhelm, people as varied and yet as vigorous as these. To all of them my warmest thanks both for what they told me and for what they gave me of themselves.

Sources of quotations, where they are not fully identified in the text, are indicated in the notes and in the bibliography. Readers who do not care for notes are reassured that these contain no additional information but are confined to source references only.

More formally I acknowledge my gratitude for permission to use quotations from the following:

Erica Anderson. *Albert Schweitzer's Gift of Friendship* and *The Schweitzer Album*. Reprinted by permission of the author.

James Cameron. *Point of Departure*. Reprinted by permission of Weidenfeld and Nicholson/Arthur Barker/World University Library. Articles from the *News Chronicle* by permission of Associated Newspapers Group. Broadcast talk by permission of the BBC and Nicholas Thompson.

Pablo Casals and Albert E. Kahn. *Joys and Sorrows*. Copyright © 1970 by Simon and Schuster. Reprinted by permission of Simon and Schuster and Hughes Massie.

The *Christian Register* and the *Register Leader*. Articles by Charles R. Joy and Melvin Arnold reprinted by permission of the Unitarian Universalist Association.

Winston Churchill. *My African Journey*. Reprinted by permission of Neville Spearman.

The *Convocation Record of the* Albert Schweitzer International Convocation 1966. Reprinted by permission of the Aspen Institute of Humanistic Studies and Elizabeth Paepcke.

Norman Cousins. *Doctor Schweitzer of Lambarene*. Copyright © 1960 by Harper and Row. Reprinted by permission of Harper and Row.

The *Daily Herald*. Letter from Albert Schweitzer reprinted by permission of I.P.C. Newspapers.

Albert Einstein. Letter to Albert Schweitzer and statement about him by permission of the estate of Albert Einstein.

Frederick Franck. *Days with Albert Schweitzer.* Copyright © 1959 by Holt, Rinehart and Winston. Reprinted by permission of Holt, Rinehart and Winston and Peter Davies.

John Gunther. *Inside Africa.* Reprinted by permission of Harper and Row and Hamish Hamilton.

Hermann Hagedorn. Correspondence with Albert Schweitzer by permission of Mrs. Hermann Hagedorn and Mary H. du Vail, the George Arents Research Library for Special Collections at Syracuse University, and the Collection of American Literature, Beinecke Rare Book and Manuscript Library, Yale University.

Dag Hammarskjöld. Letter to Albert Schweitzer by permission of the trustees of Dag Hammarskjöld's papers.

Charles R. Joy. *Music in the Life of Albert Schweitzer.* Copyright © 1951 by Harper and Row. Reprinted by permission of Harper and Row and A. and C. Black.

Charles R. Joy and Melvin Arnold. Articles in the *Christian Register* and the *Register Leader.* Reprinted by permission of the Unitarian Universalist Association.

Nikos Kazantzakis. Letter to Albert Schweitzer by permission of Helen Kazantzakis.

Oskar Kraus. *Albert Schweitzer—His Work and His Philosophy.* Reprinted by permission of A. and C. Black.

D. H. Lawrence. "Thought." From *The Complete Poems of D. H. Lawrence,* edited by Vivian de Sola Pinto and F. Warren Roberts. Reprinted by permission of Lawrence Pollinger and the estate of Frieda Lawrence. In addition, copyright © 1964, 1971 by Angelo Ravagli and C. M. Weekley, executors of the estate of Frieda Lawrence Ravagli. All rights reserved. Reprinted by permission of the Viking Press.

Gerald McKnight. *Verdict on Schweitzer.* Reprinted by permission of Frederick Muller and John Day.

Charles Michel and Fritz Dinner. Report of the funeral of Albert Schweitzer. Reprinted by permission of the authors.

Dr. David Miller. Report of the death of Albert Schweitzer. Reprinted by permission of the author.

John Middleton Murry. *Love, Freedom and Society.* Reprinted by permission of the Society of Authors as representative of the estate of John Middleton Murry.

Conor Cruise O'Brien. Article in the *New York Review of Books,* August 1964. Reprinted by permission of the author.

Suzanne Oswald. *Mein Onkel Bery.* Reprinted by permission of the author.

D. Packiarajan. Letter to Albert Schweitzer. Reprinted by permission of the author.

"Panorama." Television program for Albert Schweitzer's ninetieth birthday. Quoted by permission of the BBC.

The Paris Mission Society. Correspondence with and about Albert Schweitzer by permission of Service Protestant de Mission et de Relations Internationales.

Werner Picht. *The Life and Thought of Albert Schweitzer.* Reprinted by permission of George Allen and Unwin.

Jean Pierhal. *Albert Schweitzer—The Story of His Life.* Reprinted by permission of the Philosophical Library.

Emory Ross, a "Portrait of Albert Schweitzer." Reprinted from the *American Scholar,* volume 19, no. 1 (Winter, 1949–50). Copyright © 1949 by the United Chapter of Phi Beta Kappa. By permission of the publishers.

Jean-Paul Sartre. *Les Mots.* Copyright © 1964 Editions Gallimard, reprinted by permission. By permission also of Hamish Hamilton. By permission also of George Braziller. From *The Words* by Jean-Paul Sartre, reprinted with the permission of the publisher. English translation copyright © 1964 by George Braziller.

Albert Schweitzer and Hélène Schweitzer. All by permission of Rhena Schweitzer-Miller.

Religion in Modern Civilization. Copyright © 1934 by the Christian Century Foundation. Reprinted by permission from the November 21 and 28, 1934, issues of the *Christian Century.*

George Seaver. *Albert Schweitzer—The Man and His Mind.* Reprinted by permission of the author.

Ali Silver. Extract from the British Bulletin of the Albert Schweitzer Hospital Fund, by permission of the author.

Adlai E. Stevenson. Correspondence with Albert Schweitzer and statement by permission of Adlai Stevenson III and the Princeton University Library.

Lawrence S. Wittner. *Blacklisting Schweitzer,* article in the *Bulletin of the Atomic Scientists, May–June 1995,* by permission of the author.

Marie Woytt-Secretan. Extract from the British Bulletin of the Albert Schweitzer Hospital Fund by permission of the author.

Permissions for translations are as follows:

Albert Schweitzer—Hélène Bresslau, The Years Prior to Lambarene, Correspondence 1902–1912, translated by Antje Bultmann Lemke. By permission of the translator.

"Childhood Recollections of Old Colmar," translated by Jon Russel. Reprinted from *Albert Schweitzer—An Introduction,* by Jacques Feschotte. By permission of A. and C. Black.

"Le Choeur de St. Guillaume de Strasbourg—Un chapitre de l'histoire de la musique en Alsace," "Deutsche und Französische Orgelbaukunst

Albert Schweitzer

1

Childhood
1875–1885

SCHWEITZER SIMPLY MEANS SWISS. The family seems to have lived in Switzerland until the end of the seventeenth century. What they were called there nobody knows, but when they moved north to Alsace after the Thirty Years' War, they were called Swiss as a means of identification, and for a while the name came to signify the occupations they had at that time—carers for cows and makers of cheese.

The Thirty Years' War had been a dreadful and consuming struggle. Luther's great challenge to the Roman Church a hundred years before had been followed by mounting religious bitterness, culminating in a vicious conflict that tore Europe apart. In some towns, it was said at the time, there were only wolves for the wolves to feed on, and now in many places, dead men's land was to be had for little more than the asking. In Alsace, softer and more fertile than the country they had come from, the Schweitzers settled, spread, and flourished.

Alsace is a lovely homeland. The people are cheerful and energetic, and the soil is beneficent. On the mountainsides the timber grows straight and dense, and in the valleys the vineyards produce some of the most delicious white wines in the world. There is a saying that the Alsatians, who have no unnecessary scruples about taking the best of both worlds, eat as much as the Germans and as well as the French.

In this pleasant place the family took root. During the next two hundred years, they contributed to the community a variety of sound citizens, among them a rich sprinkling of schoolmasters and pastors—leaders of their communities, cultivated people, often with a bent for music—the kind of solid bourgeoisie that Alsace values. There was little to suggest, though, that suddenly at the end of the nineteenth century, they were to

1

produce two of the most influential Europeans of their age, Albert
Schweitzer and Jean-Paul Sartre.

Despite all of its virtues—partly, indeed, because of them—Alsace
has one great drawback. It is very vulnerable and, from the point of
view of the large powers on either side, very desirable. Its borders, the
crest of the Vosges Mountains on the west side and the Rhine on the
east, are both natural barriers whose control is militarily important.
Alsace was a battleground in Roman times when the legions set up
their outposts along the Rhine to protect their empire against the Vandals. Ever since then it has played the role of buffer between France and
Germany, much more so than Lorraine, its neighbor on the west, which
has only been linked historically with Alsace because they share control
of the important passes over the mountains that divide them. Whenever
France and Germany have resumed their perennial conflict, Alsace has
become first a battlefield and then, when the struggle was over, part of
the spoils of war.

So it is that an Alsatian might be born a Frenchman and die a German,
or vice versa, according to the outcome of the latest bout. Had Albert
been born five years earlier, he would have started life as a Frenchman.
But the Franco-Prussian War had ended with victory for Prussia and the
founding of the German Empire, and so he was born a German citizen.
For this crime he was to be imprisoned by the French during the First
World War before being transformed into a Frenchman in 1918.

The Alsatians have had enough of this kind of thing to make them
humorously resigned to the follies of international politics—although it
also makes them understandably alert to any shift in the political wind.
But although their natural feeling about their two large and aggressive
neighbors is to wish a plague on both their houses, they have also contrived to win what they can from the situation by adopting as their own
whatever suits them best from each side. Their eating habits have already been mentioned. In the same way they have developed their dialect, an unwritten language that is largely formed by taking from French
or German whichever offers the shorter and simpler way of saying things.
Alsatian speech tends to he pungent, practical, and economical, like the
people themselves.

All this is very relevant to Schweitzer, for he was completely a man of
Alsace. One can begin to understand him better if one begins by understanding this obstinate, friendly, self-reliant little region; a region that can
never afford to ignore the march of history but refuses to be impressed
by it, that lives close to the soil because the soil is good and profitable
and is all that people have.

Especially relevant is the way Alsatians and their neighbors have handled
religious differences. After the Thirty Years' War, they were faced with all

the usual problems of communities where Catholics and Protestants coexist, but there was also a special complication introduced by Louis XIV.

Soon after the war, Louis quietly annexed Alsace for France. In many of the towns, Catholic minorities had no place of worship, and Louis undertook to remedy this lack by a simple and ruthless method. Lutheran pastors were forced to hand over the chancels of their churches for the permanent use of their Catholic neighbors, and to allocate certain times each Sunday when the Catholics could have the whole church for the celebration of mass.

Part of Louis's intention was to humiliate a defeated enemy, and the natural reaction would have been one of extreme bitterness. The war that had just ended had been over precisely this issue, and numbers of Alsatians had died in it. Louis was giving Alsace every opportunity to develop a festering unease that could sooner or later break out into a painful sickness like that of present-day Ulster. But the mischief-making failed. The Alsatians, making the uncommon decision to put common sense and loyalty before dogma, used the occasion to develop a degree of friendly and cooperative understanding between priest and pastor. Inevitably, there were hard feelings among individuals—there still are— and the Catholics took the opportunity to cling to the rich plain-land while the defeated Protestants tended to retreat into the hills. But in village after village, God was worshiped in different ways at different times in the same church, and the congregations did not suffer. The two men of God cared together for their joint flock.

The Schweitzers set a good example of this kind of tolerance. Most families leaned to one side or the other, and there were not many houses where one would find, as one would in Pastor Louis's study, French and German classics side by side on the bookshelves, Rousseau and Luther both having a say.

Kaysersberg, where Albert was born, is a typical enough little Alsatian town. Half-destroyed in the Second World War, it has been so lovingly rebuilt that only by looking very carefully can one see which houses are new. Beautiful, compact, damaged by wars, but nearly untouched by the cruder forms of progress, it reflects history from every corner of its timbered courtyards and every cobble of its winding roads. The very name means "Caesar's Mountain," and here, on the hill that dominates the town, the Romans built a fort that commanded the mouth of one of the main valley routes over the Vosges into Gaul.

The ruins of a castle still crown that hill, but this was built much later against a threat from the opposite direction. Emperor Frederick II had trouble in the thirteenth century controlling the depredations of the Dukes of Lorraine, who came raiding over the pass and down the valley, and the castle was there to send them back before they broke out into the open plain.

So the past hovers above the town. And beneath it, behind a wire grille in the crypt of the church, one may still see a great pile of bones removed from a medieval plague pit. Here is the very imminence of mortality, the very presence of history in the jumble of dead burghers.

Even today's livelihood is owed in some degree to the soldiers who set out in the sixteenth century to campaign in Hungary and brought back vines from Tokay. Wine is a very serious matter in Alsace—a means of combining business with pleasure, with pride added into the bargain. And Albert Schweitzer as a boy was glad to boast that the year of his birth, 1875, was an excellent vintage year.

He was born on January 14, a Capricornian subject. People born under Capricorn are supposed to combine the spiritual and the practical to an unusual degree, and although he would have laughed at the idea, Schweitzer might have been born to endorse that particular theory. It is tempting also to find symbolism in the place of his birth, standing as it does midway between France and Germany, between Catholicism and Protestantism, between mountain and plain. But the fact that Schweitzer turned out to combine in himself many opposing elements—the dreamer and the man of action, the traditionalist and the innovator, the servant of mankind and the hardy egotist—has nothing to do with symbolic connections. It is a simple matter of cause and effect. He was what he was because he was faithful to the place of his origins and its trick of absorbing multiple influences.

His father, Louis, was pastor to the Lutherans of Kaysersberg—a gentle, kindly man in his late twenties, with an inclination to ill health that was far from typical of the Schweitzers. There was already a daughter, Louise, a year or so older than Albert. But the pastor must have been eager for a son, for at Albert's birth this placid, bookish man jumped right over the crib in his excitement.

The vicarage where the family lived is a beautiful, sturdy old house with a spacious courtyard. It is at the upper end of the town where the street begins to widen as it leads out toward the hills. The room where his mother gave birth to Albert looks out over the street, muffled then with the January snow, past the big clock on the adjoining wall toward the inn, the tree-lined square, and the castle on the hill.

Schweitzer's mother was herself a pastor's daughter from one of the villages in the next valley southward. Here Louis had wooed and won her when he was assistant pastor to her father. The family moved back to this valley a few months after Schweitzer's birth, when his father was transferred to the smaller parish of Günsbach, only a few miles from his mother's childhood home in Mühlbach. Her father was dead now, but he was far from forgotten. His name was still a byword in the neighborhood for eccentricity, wide learning, a passion for organs, and a fierce temper. For her, at least, the move was a homecoming.

Kaysersberg was predominately Catholic. Günsbach, farther from the plain, had a majority of Protestants. And in Pastor Schweitzer's new parish the ancient edict of Louis XIV was still effective, entitling the Catholic minority to a share of the time and space of his church. Dominating the little chancel was a gilded altar, with tall candlesticks, and above that two gilt statues stood and gazed down the aisle at Catholic and Protestant worshipers alike.

The house at Günsbach was an unhappy change from the one they had left at Kaysersberg. It was hemmed in by other houses, dark, and, what was more serious, damp. About the time of the move, Albert had developed a severe fever, and the new house did him no good. In August, when his father was inducted to the parish and the visiting pastors' wives peered into the crib at the infant Albert, he lay so yellow and wizened amid the splendor of his frills and ribbons that the good ladies could find nothing pretty to say about him, even to the daughter of the notable Pastor Schillinger of Mühlbach; and Mrs. Schweitzer, unable to stand the embarrassment, carried off her puny offspring and cried over him in the privacy of her bedroom. The story was told to Schweitzer frequently by his mother, but in the account as we have it in his *Memoirs of Childhood and Youth*, the exact illness is not specified: jaundice, perhaps—the yellow skin suggests it—and so severe that the child's life was despaired of and ninety years of remarkable living were nearly canceled before they began.

Another boy, Paul, and two girls, Adèle and Margrete, were added to the family, and the pastor's stipend began to feel the strain a little. Although they were better off than the peasants who were their neighbors, they had a position to maintain and their hospitality was unstinting. Nevertheless, they managed well enough. And Europe remained at peace while the children grew.

We know very little about this childhood except what Schweitzer himself has told us in his books. His was not a family of diarists or letter writers; nor were they communicative about their feelings and experiences. True, Pastor Louis had some literary skill. He used to collect stories from the valley villages and published a little book of them, the names of participants tactfully altered. The stories are simple, but shrewdly and vigorously told, and quite without ecclesiastical taint. He seems to have written little else, however, until the First World War, when he began to keep a diary, largely for the benefit of Albert, cut off in Africa, about the progress of parish affairs and the impact of a war that brought terror and death to the family's very doorstep.

But even had there been an ardent diarist in the family, he would have found only the most ordinary events to record. The peace that prevailed between nations was matched by the harmony within the family. The cycle of seasons and the normal incidents of growing up provided all the excitement that came Albert's way. The hard-packed snow in winter, the sunny vineyard in summer; picnics; the harvest; lessons at the village school; visits to friends and relatives in Colmar, the nearest big town, out on the plain beyond the mouth of the valley; and the occasional expedition as far as Strasbourg, Alsace's capital city, fifty miles to the north; these were the framework of Schweitzer's first ten years. But for a chance meeting that resulted in his writing his *Memoirs of Childhood and Youth* when he was in his forties, almost nothing would remain to tell us of his intense interior response to these gentle events.

The book is one of the small classics about childhood—truthful, observant, and wise; quietly mocking (of himself besides others) and full of amused understanding. But it leaves huge gaps in our knowledge. It was intended as a group of tales for use in a young people's magazine, and a great many things that we would like to know are not recorded in it. And so we see the boy Schweitzer in a series of disconnected images, as though caught by the intermittent flashes of a great strobe light. The images are vivid and important. But between them lies darkness.

Maddeningly lacking is any clear picture of Albert's relationship with the rest of the family. We hear, for example, almost nothing of his brother and sisters. We are told only that the family was happy, loving, yet reticent about personal feelings. And if this seems improbable to a generation taught to believe that all genius stems from the repression of early family trauma, it seems, nevertheless, to be perfectly true. Although no one still living remembers those early years, there are several who visited the Günsbach vicarage regularly at the beginning of the new century and knew the Schweitzers well. And an account of the teenage Albert by his sister Adèle, brief as it is, brings the family to life in all its unspectacular normality.

The family reticence, of which Schweitzer had his full share, is quite enough to explain the gaps in his narrative—together with the fact that the family was not the subject of the book. Schweitzer was writing about his own early experiences, and these were mostly solitary. Struggles and agonies there certainly were; indeed, they were the mainspring of his life. But they were never repressed. They were fully conscious from the beginning and jealously guarded for their importance. And they had nothing to do with the family.

Instead, the family was the stable basis for his inner security, the strength that enabled him to make his struggles fertile. Out of those first placid ten years in Günsbach flow all the different streams of Schweitzer's life. In his memoirs we can see, clearly marked because they spring from unforgettable experiences, the sources of each stream as it arose. And if his mature achievements are remarkable in scope and scale, they are the more astonishing for having sprung not from the compression of energies that had been thwarted in some way but simply from a natural, free development of what was born and bred in a normal small Alsatian boy.

The *Memoirs of Childhood and Youth* are thrown together, as Schweitzer admits, just as they occurred to him; their chronology is not always obvious, and here and there remarks occur whose significance is concealed by their apparent casualness. Only when one begins to fit the fragments together in their context and in the context of the rest of his life does the importance of some of the small pieces become clear.

We first see Schweitzer, through the eyes of his forty-year-old self, when he is very small—still in petticoats. He is sitting in a corner of the manse courtyard watching his father collect honey from their beehives. A bee settles on his hand and begins to crawl over the skin. He watches it with interest and approval—until it stings him and he howls.

Great excitement. The servant girl is trying to kiss it better while his mother is scolding his father for not putting the child in a safer place. The hubbub is highly enjoyable—so much so that when Albert suddenly realizes that the pain has gone, he goes on crying in order to prolong the satisfaction of being the center of all this fuss. But later, when everyone has calmed down, he grows so ashamed of having exploited the situation that he remains miserable for the rest of the day. So he records.

For the rest of the day? That argues impressive emotional stamina at a very early age. But something made that day stick in the memory— something more than the hurt and the crying, for those must have been frequent. The unforgettable thing was the little boy's vivid awareness of himself, the enjoyment with which he dominated the situation, commanding the limelight with tears, and then the uncomfortable realization that he was cheating—getting a larger share of sympathy than he deserved and outraging that just and proper balance between behavior and consequence that children instinctively recognize and value.

About the same time that he was learning this lesson in honesty, his churchgoing began. When he was three or four, he was, he says, "allowed" to go to church. Unlike many clerical parents, Albert's father managed to give him the feeling that coming to church was a privilege, not an imposition. Louis probably achieved this by the simple means of believing it himself, for children are dangerously sensitive to hypocrisy in such matters.

Church had its excitements for the small boy, and its terrors. He had the satisfaction of seeing his father presiding over the congregation, the respected focus of the village's attention; years later he still remembered the feel of the servant girl's cotton glove on his mouth when she tried to stop him from yawning or singing too loudly. He remembered, too, the lady who sometimes came and told tales of strange heathen folk overseas and who collected sous for the conversion of these poor creatures. Nearer home and more alarming was the vision of the devil, who frequently peered down the aisle at the congregation but vanished whenever the pastor was actually praying—a clear proof of the power of prayer, which, wrote Schweitzer, "gave quite a distinctive tone to my childish piety."[1]

The vision turned out to be nothing more diabolical than the reflection of Daddy Iltis, the organist, looking in his mirror for his cue to play. Much worse than the devil, who, after all, was safely caged in the House of God and controllable by prayer, was the village gravedigger, sacristan, and humorist, a veteran of the Crimean War, Jägle by name. Jägle's sense of humor led him to divert himself by persuading the pastor's son that he had horns growing. Albert's forehead had distinctive bumps, which lent credibility to the story. So Jägle would trap the terrified boy and feel the bumps for signs of growth while Albert stood hypnotized, longing to run away but powerless to move. Months passed before he could bring himself to speak to his father, even indirectly, about horns on human foreheads and so exorcise his fear. Then Jägle had other jokes up his sleeve. He told Albert that the Prussians were going to put all boys into armor, and that the blacksmith would need him for a fitting. Schweitzer calls this humor dry, but sour would be a better word. There are Jägles in most communities, and although their cruelty may be unintentional, it can be harmful. In the long run, however, they sometimes provide their victims with an early inoculation against alarmist fantasies and teach them a useful skepticism about the statements of their elders. Later on, Jägle tried to teach Albert to follow in his footsteps as a humorist, but Schweitzer comments, "I found his school a little too hard for me."[2]

On the whole, though, these were years of contentment before school placed its dreaded restrictions between Albert and his liberty. He used to go out tending the pigs and cows of the local farmers, and it became his one ambition be a swineherd forever, roaming the countryside all day long for the rest of his life. Günsbach is surrounded by an almost endless variety of hill and field, forest and vineyard. Behind the village rise the slopes of the Rebberg, the little mountain among whose folds lie secret valleys quite cut off from the world. Follow the stream up, past the clustering houses, and one can soon be high above the villages, or one can lose oneself in thick woodland, or stay in the valley and go fishing in the little river Fecht or walking by the lake in the little park, or keep an eye on the progress of the vines, some of them planted by Pastor Louis himself.

Albert knew when he was well off. He had no wish to grow up, no envy of the big boys who went to school. When the time for school finally came, he had to be led there, and he cried all the way.

His fears were well founded; the academic life did not improve on acquaintance. School and Schweitzer simply did not agree. He was dreamy and vague, and found even reading and writing too much for him. Soon his father was reduced to begging him at least to learn enough to become the local postman; the Schweitzers were not the sort of people to produce swineherds. Albert's maternal grandfather, that famous Pastor Schillinger of Mülbach, had been a great student of current events in the political and scientific world and would wait in the street after the Sunday service to pass on to his parishioners news of the latest invention or discovery. When the skies showed something of interest, he would set up a telescope in front of his home for public use. Could his daughter have produced this dunce?

Schweitzer, looking back, remembered his mother's eyes as frequently red with weeping over her son's school reports. But nobody seemed able to do anything about him. He continued to sit at his desk, staring out of the window and chewing his pencil, considering the immense advantages of a swineherd's life over any other and quite unprepared to accept the opinion of parent or teacher that he might be wrong. Book learning he regarded as a waste of time, and he found it "terribly unnatural" that his father should be forever reading and writing in the musty study where he could barely breathe for the smell of books.

But the country and its creatures were not the sum total of his interests. Both sides of the family had produced musicians—particularly organists—with grandfather Schillinger eminent among them. He had been a great improviser, both on the organ and on his square piano, and on his death the piano had come to his daughter and son-in-law at Günsbach. Louis, too, had a talent for improvisation, and Albert would spend hours listening when his father played and then learning how to do the same himself. Before he went to school, he was already able to devise his own harmonies to the tunes of the songs and hymns he knew.

The singing teacher could only pick out tunes with one finger, and she and the backward Albert discovered with mutual astonishment that he could do at least one thing better than she could. But as with the story of the bee sting, the satisfaction of mastery was more than outweighed by his sense of shame and embarrassment. He was afraid he might seem to be showing off and trying to set himself up against the teacher—a complex, introspective child. One would have expected, because he had so little success at school, that where he did find himself doing well he would have made the most of it. But things were not as simple as that.

The few early photographs we have of him, aged five onward, all show a dark, intense little face, watchful, almost wary, the deep eyes considering us from beneath lowered brows. No doubt some of his hostility is owing to the circumstances. The unfortunate child has obviously been dressed up in the most uncomfortable garment for the occasion—stiff collar, huge bow, and what appears to be a velvet suit—and his hair has been plastered down, which he hated. After all that, after the posing and waiting and the standing still for the exposure, an angelic smile is not to be expected. But in pictures taken in groups, with the family or with his class, the same observant look singles him out, as though the blinds of his own spirit were down and from behind them he was gravely absorbing the evidence of his senses, reserving judgment.

Although he refused to read or write, there were always stories. Despite philosophies and techniques of psychology the story is still as good a device as any that man has hit upon for understanding himself. A good story sticks in the subconscious and breeds all kinds of reflections and responses. And Günsbach was full of stories.

Albert's father was collecting tales of the valley people for his book, and his mother would tell him stories about her family, particularly grandfather Schillinger and her much-loved half-brother Albert, after whom Schweitzer was named. In a settled pastoral community the past remains very close, and these dead were almost as present, as potent an influence as the living.

The spirit of Pastor Schillinger was unavoidable. He lived in the stories about him; he lived in the square piano on which the family played; but he also made himself felt through his daughter, who had inherited, along with some of his sternness and lack of humor, his alert, inquiring mind. While Albert's father concerned himself with the local interest of the valley, Mrs. Schweitzer was the one who followed world events and hated it when a public holiday deprived her of her morning paper.

Schweitzer's recollections of his mother as being frequently in tears—about his school reports, about his father's chronic ill health, about the family finances—might suggest weakness in her character. Wrongly, if so. She was the elder of the two parents by four years and had the more powerful personality. Her tears were the result not of inadequacy but of depressions as deep as her temper was violent. Both temper and depressions were inherited from her father. Both were passed on to her son. Their daughter-in-law, Paul's wife, speaks of her as "very hard, very severe." And one may guess from her photographs that she was a formidable woman in a rage. The features are strong, masculine, and far from beautiful. But the eyes are warm, and the lines bespeak firmness and justice rather than harshness. She seems to have avoided, perhaps because of her husband's softening influence, the extreme rigidity of old

Schillinger, who insisted on parishioners dressing in frock coats when visiting him and who draped all mirrors in black when young women stayed in his house. The virtue Mrs. Schweitzer seems to have prized above all was kindness. And she had a deep romantic love of nature, especially of the countryside of her valley, a love bordering on sentimentality. Schweitzer quotes her as saying of a lake where they often walked, "Here, children, I am completely at home. Here among the rocks, among the woods. I came here as a child. Let me breathe the fragrance of the fir trees and enjoy the quiet of this refuge from the world. Do not speak. After I am no longer on earth, come here and think of me."[3]

When Schweitzer recalled those days, he himself was an old man, and the sentiment may have been affected by his own knowledge of approaching death. But the sensual richness of the Schweitzers' identification with nature is unmistakable—a depth of emotion that in some of the family may have substituted for sexual warmth and freedom of expression in personal relationships, but which in Albert himself was to prove the ground bass to the whole theme of his life.

Writing in 1944 to the American poet and biographer Hermann Hagedorn, who had asked him for details of his early years, he recalled:

> Even when I was a child I was like a person in an ecstasy in the presence of Nature, without anyone suspecting it. I consider Nature as the great consoler. In her I always found calm and serenity again when I was disturbed. And this has only become accentuated during the course of my life. . . . Unforgettable pictures of the country are engraved on my memory. I roam among these memories as in a gallery in which are hung the most beautiful landscapes painted by the greatest masters It is said I am a man of action. But at bottom I am a dreamer, and it is in reveries, reviving the living contact with Nature, that I gather the powers that make me an active being.[4]

Like his mother, Albert had difficulty in talking about deep feelings for people but none in expressing his love for nature. This shared delight seems to have been one of the strongest links, unspoken but acknowledged, between them. As a young man he spent some very hard-earned pocket money on sending her and his sister Adèle for a walking holiday in Switzerland, for whose mountains she had a passion. And she always hoped that one day, when he was rich and successful, he would take her to Scotland. The hope was never fulfilled. He had the wrong kind of success.

The relationship between these parents and their children was not an unusual one in Europe at that period: the dominant mother and gentle retiring father, the lack of any show of sexual feeling between parents, extending to an emotional reticence between parent and child. The only

account of this family, apart from Schweitzer's own, is from Jean-Paul
Sartre. It was written almost a century later and was dependent on impressions gathered much later during visits to the vicarage as a child—
Sartre was nearly thirty years younger than Schweitzer—and on his
recollection of the recollections of his grandmother.

Sartre was brought up in unhappy circumstances in Paris, in the house
of his grandfather, Charles Schweitzer, Albert's uncle. His mother, who
had been widowed soon after his birth, had been forced to return with
her child, penniless, to the parental home she had only just left. Here, so
Sartre suggests, she had been resented and humiliated although she struck
up a lifelong friendship with Albert, who used to walk Jean-Paul out in
the pram when staying in Paris as a young man. At all events, Sartre
grew up feeling unwanted and out of place—a sensitive Parisian among
robust Alsatians. His view of the Schweitzer family is accordingly jaundiced. His grandmother, so he believed, had not enjoyed her marriage to
Charles Schweitzer; his mother was even more embittered, and his own
sympathies lay with the female side of the family. But his acid little
sketch of the family is worth quoting, nevertheless. His evidence, although that of a hostile witness, is revealing in a way that he may not
have intended.

Here, then, is his version of a visit to Alsace by his grandmother and
grandfather, Charles and Louise, in the early years of their marriage.
(The brothers mentioned are, of course, Albert's father, Louis, and his
uncles, Charles and Auguste, both of whom had settled in Paris.)

> They spent a fortnight in Alsace without leaving the table; the brothers
> told each other scatological stories in dialect; now and then the pastor
> would turn to Louise and translate them out of Christian charity. It was not
> long before she produced good enough reason to exempt her from all
> conjugal intercourse and to give her a right to a bedroom of her own; she
> would speak of her migraine, take to her bed, and began to hate noise,
> passion and enthusiasm, all the shabby vulgarity and theatricality of life
> with the Schweitzers.[5]

So the Schweitzer household was noisy, passionate, and enthusiastic.
Nobody would guess it from Schweitzer's own temperate account. But
they are not bad qualities among which to grow up. There may be some
literary license in the portrait of the genteel Louise, unaccustomed to
country language and the presence of a vigorous man in her bed, marching off to have her lonely migraine. Other children were there during
those holidays—Schweitzer's nephew and niece among them—who remember the little, sharp-eyed Jean-Paul sitting with his ironic smile,
absorbing but taking no part, and who remember the ladies tut-tutting at

some of the language being used in front of the women and children, as ladies tut-tut the world over. It was no more serious, they say, than that. Jean-Paul's own grandfather, Charles, with whom he had an intense love-hate relationship, was the most ebullient of the family and used to annoy Albert's humorless mother with his jokes. The Schweitzers, for example, took their hospitality seriously enough to keep a visitors' book, whose flyleaf carried the inscription from Hebrews: "Be not forgetful to entertain strangers; for thereby some have entertained angels unawares." Charles added, "Others have found the devil slipping in," which Mrs. Schweitzer did her utmost to erase. Sartre adds this about their language: "Creatures of nature and puritans—a combination of virtues less rare than people think—the Schweitzers loved coarse words which, while they minimized the body in true Christian fashion, manifested their willing acceptance of the natural functions."[6]

Did they minimize the body? Charles used to jog Jean-Paul on his knee and sing, "I ride upon my bidet, and when it trots it leaves a fart."[7] Jean-Paul giggled and blushed, knowing that this was rude. The subject matter for the family's vulgarity was excretion rather than sex. But as an adult Albert exhibited a perfectly normal countryman's interest in the processes of procreation, animal and human, and although he had a strong dislike of immodesty, appears to have been quite without prudishness. "He had no quarrel with the way God made men and women," said a friend. It is possible that he achieved this attitude in the teeth of his upbringing, but there is no evidence of any struggle of this kind in his youth. And looking at the lifestyles of the two men, one can scarcely feel that it is Sartre to whom one would go for a free and balanced attitude to human physiology.

The Schweitzers lived life with gusto and good humor, and there was none of the pious hypocrisy suffered by the families of many Protestant clerics. But from Sartre we can safely accept that this bustling, energetic household lacked that physical intimacy, that easy tender relationship between husbands and wives that leads to easy tender relationships between parents and children. In families of this kind the mother often places more emphasis on action and achievement than on contentment and fulfillment—or, perhaps, such mothers equate the two. Certainly, that period produced large numbers of men of achievement, explorers and adventurers, men who welcomed hardship. And many of them had mothers who, like the Spartan women, expressed their love by spurring their sons to endeavor and by discouraging weakness.

But despite Mrs. Schweitzer's vehement temperament, her varied interests, and her passion for information, the man she taught her son to admire most was not her learned and imperious father but her gentle half-brother Albert.

The older Albert had been pastor at St. Nicholas Church in Strasbourg. When Strasbourg was threatened with siege during the Franco-Prussian War, he went in a hurry to Paris to fetch drugs and supplies for his parishioners. Getting what he needed was not easy, and by the time he finally returned, Strasbourg was already surrounded. The Germans allowed the supplies to be sent through, but Albert Schillinger was held, suffering agonies of guilt for fear his parish would think he had deliberately chosen to avoid their hardships. So when the war was over and there were food shortages, his guilt reinforced his natural benevolence, and he suffered considerable deprivations to help others who were in need. Because he had a weak heart, this was not simply kind but dangerously sacrificial; two years later he was rewarded for his selflessness by a sudden heart attack that killed him as he stood talking with friends. The young Albert became haunted by the idea that he ought to provide some sort of continuation of the man whose name he had been given.

Such were the ever-present dead. From the living there were other lessons to be learned, and, unlike school lessons, once learned they were never forgotten. Coming home from school one day he had a friendly wrestling match with a bigger boy, George Nitschelm. Albert won the fight and pinned the boy down. A triumph. But what happened next turned the tables on Albert forever. Lying there defeated, George said, "Yes, if I got broth to eat twice a week, as you do, I'd be as strong as you are."[8] And Albert, so he says, staggered home, overcome by this end of the game.

The excuse is not a particularly good one. It is scarcely likely that George starved in that rich countryside. Albert might reasonably have dismissed the remark and forgotten the incident, or he might have been secretly pleased to have his superiority recognized. So what overcame him? The real accusation behind George Nitschelm's words was that Albert belonged to a different class, one of the alien bourgeoisie.

Albert certainly knew something about socialism. A relation of the family was Eugene Debs, whose father had emigrated from Colmar to the United States, and who was himself to become a leading trades union organizer there, even running for the presidency. The Schweitzers of Günsbach had maintained contact with Debs—Mrs. Schweitzer had a family photograph taken specially for him. So she would certainly have talked to the children about the poverty in the United States at the time and the appalling conditions that Debs and other Socialists were fighting to improve.

Albert, his instincts always siding with the weak and disregarded, could not endure to be thought of as one of "them," the better off, the exploiters. More than anything he wanted to be exactly the same as the other boys so that they would forget that he was a sprig of the gentry, bred from a line of pastors and, worse, schoolmasters. But he was caught in a cleft stick: nothing he could do could alter the facts, and in a way his very determination set him farther apart. The harder he struggled to escape his bourgeois background, the more he was proving himself an exceptional child.

He refused to wear an overcoat that had been made for him out of an old coat of his father's, not a particularly high-class garment, but the other boys had none at all. He refused to let his mother buy him a sailor cap and made such a commotion in a Strasbourg shop that the customers came running to see what the trouble was. Before he could be pacified, the shop assistant had to delve into the unsalable stock for a brown cap that could be pulled down over the ears, "like what the village boys wear,"[9] said this uncouth boy in the big Strasbourg store. To the added embarrassment of his mother, he dragged it on there and then, such was his need to establish his difference from the middle-class shoppers who were staring and whispering.

A school photograph adds point and poignancy to the story. There sits Albert among his classmates, the only one with a wide collar and a fancy suit, the young master to the life. The respectability of the Schweitzers shouts from the picture.

It became a running battle, poisoning, he says, their lives. Coat and cap were not the only issues. Gloves entered into it—he insisted on fingerless mittens; and boots—he would wear only clogs, except on Sundays. He endured beatings as well as entreaties, and against both he stood firm.

Oddly enough, his father was more perturbed about his deviation from propriety than his mother. Perhaps the dignity of the ministry was at issue. The gentle pastor was not too gentle to administer beatings to his "sacré imbécile" of a son. But Mrs. Schweitzer seemed to understand that there was more involved than willfulness. Albert was unable to explain to either of them. Against all beatings, reasoning, and entreaty he stood firm and won by sheer obstinacy.

It was to no avail. The boys were not to be fooled by his disguise. In brown cap and clogs, fingerless gloves and no coat, he was still not one of them. They went on calling him a sprig of the gentry, and he went on suffering.

The difference must have been fairly evident and concerned more than parentage or clothes. At its simplest, a boy who can teach the teacher how to harmonize is unlikely to find it easy to merge with the herd. But there were other, deeper differences.

In a neighboring village lived a Jew, a dealer in land and cattle, and reputedly a usurer, named Mausche. Jew-baiting was an accepted way of enjoying oneself in Günsbach as elsewhere, and the village had no Jew of its own; so when Mausche appeared with his donkey cart and drove through the village and out over the bridge across the Fecht, he was pursued by a horde of jeering boys. Albert, when he reached an age to join in this sport, ran jeering with them, thus announcing, as he says, that he was beginning to feel grown-up. But he was also announcing his identity with the rest of the boys. He did it for no reason but because the others did. And he admired the daring boys who folded a corner of a shirt into the shape of a pig's ear and waved it in Mausche's face.

Mausche drove on, apparently unmoved. But once or twice he turned and smiled. That smile, like George Nitschelm's excuse about the broth, was never forgotten. "Embarrassed but good-natured"[10] Schweitzer called it—the smile of the perennial outcast. It taught him, he says, what it means to keep silent under persecution.

One need not be persecuted to know what persecution is. Children's imaginations leap ahead of their experience. But when this happened, the boy was already beginning himself to know what it meant to be singled out for scorn. His sympathy went out to Mausche. He never again ran with the pack when the Jew and his donkey drove through; instead, he greeted him politely. Coat or no coat, clogs or no clogs, this was not the way to win acceptance and approval from his classmates. He would have done better to join the boys who turned their shirttails into pigs' ears if he had really wanted more than anything else to be one of them.

Out in the fields and on the hillsides he had already become deeply affected by the sufferings of animals, both in the course of nature and at the hands of human beings. Not that the Alsatians are particularly cruel to animals. Jägle, the gravedigger, had a pet calf that he wept over when it ceased to recognize him after a season's hill pasturing. And when researching this book I met a clog-maker living opposite the house that Schweitzer built in Günsbach whose dream it was to stand still on a hillside until the birds came and settled on his outstretched arms. But country people are unsentimental about animals, sometimes indifferent. In Colmar Albert once saw an ancient bony horse being dragged and beaten to the knacker's yard. And there are the marks of nature's harshness in every dried-out shell of a bird caught by a cat, in every pile of rabbit's bones in the fields, every small scream in the night, every maggot that infests the dead or living flesh. For Albert these were enough to make him add privately to the prayers that his mother said with him each night a special prayer for "all things that have breath," for he saw no reason why human beings should have the exclusive right to compassion.

In a much-quoted passage he writes, "Youth's unqualified joie de vivre I never really knew,"[11] adding that he doubts that he was alone in this.

It is highly unlikely that youth's unqualified joie de vivre exists at all outside the sentimental memories of adults. But the statement is worth setting against his claim to have had a very happy childhood, for these small clouds of distress were the beginning of a darkness that had immense results.

The thing that differentiates Schweitzer is not that he suffered, both in himself and on behalf of other people and creatures, but that the feeling remained fresh and active in him, whereas in others it becomes overlaid or dismissed. And experience with him was remembered and its lesson learned. This was the result partly of the violence of his experiences, partly of the obstinacy with which he clung to them as something that he knew to be fundamental and true. Although he learned gradually to be more patient and tactful than he had been over the issue of the overcoat and the sailor cap, the pattern of events was constantly the same as when George Nitschelm gasped out the fatal words and set Albert on a collision course with his parents. Experiences came to him with a vividness that forced him to a decision from which subsequent events and the argument of the others had no power to deflect him.

It was not that he was an unnaturally good child, in the sense of being squeamish or inhibited. His understanding of pain included the inflicting of it besides the suffering of it. People who hate cruelty only because they have been at the receiving end are in danger of becoming tyrants themselves if their chance comes to turn the tables. A safer basis for compassion is to have found the roots of aggression in oneself at an early age.

The Schweitzers had a dog, somewhat learnedly named Phylax, Greek for "Guard." Phylax's technique for guarding the family was to bite anybody who came to the door in uniform. He had once been rash enough to bite a policeman, but it was the postman who was regularly in danger and needed protection. Albert, the eldest son, was given the responsibility of holding off Phylax, and he liked to pretend to be a wild-beast tamer and pen him into a corner of the courtyard with a switch, striking him whenever he tried to break out. "When later in the day, we sat side by side as friends, I blamed myself for having struck him; I knew that I could keep him back from the postman if I held him by his collar and stroked him. But when the fatal hour came round again I yielded once more to the pleasurable intoxication of being a wild-beast tamer!"[12]

A neighbor's asthmatic old horse also learned to be wary of the young Albert Schweitzer, who was inclined to whip him into a trot although he was too old for trotting. Afterward Albert would "look into his tired eyes and silently ask forgiveness," but next time he was allowed to drive, the same thing happened. The excitement of mastery over other creatures was too much to resist.

There were other experiences, less painful, that went as deep and had as lasting an effect. They are mostly to be found in the memoirs, but they are worth mentioning here not for curiosity value but because they show us the child who is, if any child ever was, the father of the man.

Standing outside the classroom, waiting for a lesson, he heard inside the older boys at their singing lesson. They were singing Alsatian folk songs in two-part harmony. For some reason Albert had never heard this particular style of singing before or, more probably, he had simply never heard it done properly. He was, once again, "overwhelmed"; he had to clutch the wall to prevent himself from falling, such was the ecstasy. And when in Colmar he first heard a brass band in procession, he nearly fainted away again.

One thing is evident from all these experiences. Albert's dreaminess was not the result of any vagueness or lack of interest in life. His mind may have been absent from where the teacher wanted it, but it was vividly present somewhere else. Herding swine lost its appeal, and his imagination reached after other, more distant occupations. For a long while he wanted to be a sailor, and he covered his schoolbook with pictures of ships. The world was full of romantic possibilities, and some obstinacy refused to let him pretend to be fascinated in the schoolroom when the schoolroom threatened to distract him from what he was really learning. "No one," he wrote, "can do anything in defiance of his inner nature."[13] The remark is worth bearing in mind, coming from one who is commonly supposed to have been a model of self-sacrifice.

The early backwardness of brilliant men is not uncommon. Perhaps it is simply this, that most of us allow our natural turn of mind, to which we might apply all the energy of a growing creature, to be diverted into the common course of primary schooling out of respect for our elders and fear of getting into trouble. We are slowed by preformed ideas, our wheels stuck in the ruts. But the interior direction of some men is so demanding that it will not be deflected; and so in the long run they travel faster.

Still hankering after his freedom to enjoy the open air, Albert used to take his homework to a rock seat halfway up the hill above the village commanding a view of the length and breadth of the valley. There he thrust his pencils into a crack in the rock and let his mind wander. A large pink statue now stands, or rather sits, on this rock—a piece of sculpture of which one of the few noteworthy features is the accuracy with which the sculptor has observed the odd way in which Schweitzer held his pen or pencil, not between his finger and thumb but between first and second fingers. There is nobody left to tell us whether he already had this trait when he sat there as a boy. He is sometimes said to have developed it later as a result of writer's cramp. But his daughter has it and says it was not learned from him. Could such a characteristic be instinctive and hereditary?

Still his work did not improve. His mother's tears at his bad school reports distressed him but were unable to reform him. In the years of his fame he never forgot how much cleverer the boys of the village had been than he was—boys who remained farm workers and shopkeepers. The village school had made it impossible for him to be an intellectual snob, and he was grateful.

Not even the annual agony of writing, or failing to write, Christmas thank-you letters could spur him to work harder. These dreaded sessions took place in the pastor's study between Christmas and New Year's Day, and the anticipation was sometimes enough to reduce Albert to tears on Christmas Day itself. As he sat despairing in front of his piece of paper while his clever sister Louise rattled off letter after letter, each one different and yet each obeying the specified formula, and his friends "whizzed down the road behind the church on their sledges," the iron ate into his soul. Instead of emerging from the ordeal with a strengthened ambition to do better next year, he merely found himself confirmed in his "horror of studies and letter writing," a horror that took years to shake off.

Others, however, benefited in due course, for he determined that when he grew up, the recipients of his presents should never salt their soup with their tears as he had done. And as he determined, so he did. Gifts to nephews, nieces, and godchildren were accompanied by notes forbidding them to write their thanks.

Colmar, for Albert, was "the big world." Bicycles had not yet reached Günsbach. The first penny-farthing arrived there while he was still at the village school, and half the village turned out, adults and children, to see this strange object leaning against the wall of the inn and to watch its rider emerge from the inn and pedal away—a sight even stranger than the bicycle, for who had ever seen an adult in knickerbockers?

So there was no getting away from Günsbach, except for the regular holiday visits to his godmother's house in Colmar. But Colmar was sufficient. Here were parks, processions, brass bands, a museum, and real boats on a real river—of which more later. In addition, Colmar presented Albert with moral issues more complex than any he had yet had to face.

One afternoon his godmother sent him out for a walk escorted by the two maids—at that time even the petite bourgeoisie boasted two maids. The maids took him instead to the local fair where they spent the time dancing. They danced, all three of them, hand in hand, Albert between the girls in the long row of dancers, and on the other side of each girl "a cavalier who interested her much more than I did!" So he learned the contredanse, a dance, which he reports regretfully, "you don't see any more."

On the way home the girls made it clear that there was no need to mention to his godmother that they had been to the fair. "I came face to face," he says, "with the problem of Guilt. On the one hand I was on fire with chivalry. On the other, I should have to tell a lie if I was to keep faith with these sterling girls." We learn a lot about Schweitzer from the capital G that he gives to Guilt, the mock pomposity saving the story from any hint of pretentiousness. And there is no moral. "Luckily, as it happens at times to all of us, I was spared the ordeal."[14] His godmother asked only whether they had had a nice time. Yes, they said. Nobody mentioned where they had been.

Another brush with Evil in Colmar left its mark. Albert's godmother sent him out with a friend to play. The friend was a Colmar boy, a little older than Albert and a good deal more sophisticated, and Albert was put in his care with the strict injunction not to go near the river and, above all, not to go boating. The boy led Albert through narrow unfamiliar streets till eventually they reached the edge of the town—and the river. Albert was thrilled, for he had never before seen a real river with real boats on it "that floated on the water, with great loads of vegetables on board and a man in the stern to steer them." Besides, he had recently abandoned plans to become a coachman or a pastry cook in favor of going to sea as a sailor.

"Let's find one that's not properly tied up," said the boy, and promptly did so, jumping aboard and telling Albert to follow. Albert was shocked. He begged the boy to remember what they had been told. "We mustn't do it," he said. Then came the revelation. "He didn't deign to reply, but looked at me as if I had fallen out of the moon and was speaking some unknown language. He didn't even try to find excuses for not obeying. He merely implied by his attitude that obedience, in his eyes, was a prejudice to be abandoned: a notion so far beneath him that there was no point in acknowledging it. It was an attitude of mind that I had not imagined possible. When later, towards 1893, as an undergraduate, I read what Nietzsche had written a few years before—it was beginning to make something of a stir—I found nothing surprising in his intention to go 'beyond good and evil.' There was nothing in Nietzsche that had not been revealed to me, without a word spoken, in that scene on the banks of the Lauch. And for an instant, as I boarded the boat under the imperious gaze of my companion, I had been one with Nietzsche."[15]

Here, in the quiet deflation of the overblown elements in Nietzsche's philosophy, is the essential Schweitzer—the man who was not to be frightened by big words and pretentious notions but would always check them against simple human experience. Europe would have been saved a great deal if the German nation had had a greater share of his Alsatian common sense and humor.

His Nietzschean escapade, like Germany's, ended badly. The boys were seen, reported, and punished. "Still," concludes Schweitzer, "guilty or not, I'd been out in a boat!"

The museum at Colmar was the object of regular expeditions, and here Albert found a great deal to interest him. This museum is remarkable for so small a town, and the attendance there is said to be second only to the Louvre in all France. The most notable exhibits are the paintings of two fifteenth-century Alsatian masters, Grünewald and Schöngauer. Both painted religious subjects with a great deal of realism, placing the life of Christ in Alsatian surroundings with much naturalistic detail. The Grünewalds, which today are proudly and centrally displayed, were then badly placed and badly lit, but Albert singled them out for special attention. Life in Alsace had changed so little since the fifteenth century that the wooden bathtub that Grünewald had given to Jesus was just like the ones in Günsbach. And as at Günsbach a chamber pot lay handy. The color, too, pleased Albert—"brilliant and unexpected"—but the naturalism impressed him most. Jesus was no mystery, for here he was surrounded by people and things that Albert knew. Most gratifying of all, it seemed that St. John had a mop of unruly hair like his own.

Albert's hair was totally uncontrollable, and the maid whose hopeless job it was to try to flatten it with fearsome brushings and a stick of brilliantine used to make disquieting remarks about the way in which hair could indicate character. "Unruly without, unruly within," she would pronounce, and Albert was beginning to wonder if his hair really did presage something like a criminal career. Grünewald's St. John reassured him.

Schweitzer's disposition to let this kind of thing prey on his mind was characteristic. Jägle had poisoned his life with the threat of horns. The maid was able to "darken the skies" with her old wives' tales of character reading by hair. These things fed a deep anxiety about existence, about nature, and about his own character that he was unable to shake off and that was growing toward a climax.

Another of Colmar's sights, too, pointed to that climax—the big statue in the Champ de Mars of a reclining black man. The statue was made by Bartholdi, a native of Colmar, who also designed New York's Statue of Liberty. It was destroyed during the Second World War, but the head is preserved—dignified, leonine, pensive, a highly idealized conception of the noble savage. It touched the strong romantic chords in the boy's nature. He visited the statue again and again.

Why did this particular image appeal to Albert? It was only one of four that surrounded the main statue, which celebrated an admiral of local fame. The other three statues all represented races from other distant countries. We can only guess what was special about this one; but something in the pose of the head, lowered and brooding, is not unlike those early photographs of Schweitzer himself. St. John had hair like Albert's. Perhaps the Bartholdi black man seemed to the boy to share his sense of sadness.

So the long quiet years of childhood stretched out, undramatic but full of incident. One exciting day Mrs. Schweitzer returned from Strasbourg looking years younger because of her new set of teeth. Friends and relations constantly visited for the country walks and the mountain air. In summer there were frequent family picnics led by father—bread and cheese and homegrown wine—and when young Paul was likely to be left behind, because they were going farther than he could walk, Albert knocked together a cart and towed him rather than see him deserted. In the winter evenings the pastor would settle down with his piano or his books, the girls with their embroidery, Mrs. Schweitzer with her cooking or her mending, and Albert, unless some demand roused him to unwilling effort, with his dreams.

Spring would come, and the storks would fly in from the south to build their nests and to bring good luck to the houses where they settled. When the time came for spring cleaning, Mrs. Schweitzer would shut the dog out of the house so that his muddy paw-marks would not undo her labors. Ordinary events, but in every ordinary event Albert found significance. From images as simple as that of the exiled dog he would build the foundations of his philosophy.

His father was still far from robust in health. His digestion was unreliable, and Mrs. Schweitzer wondered guiltily if the cause was the cheaper food that the growing family made it necessary to buy. He suffered occasionally from rheumatism as well, to which the dampness of the house contributed.

In such circumstances as these an elder son takes on any tasks and responsibilities that his size and strength allow. The boy was certainly not driven hard, for he was to look back longingly to this period when he came up against a stricter disciplinarian in his great aunt a few years later. "My parents," he says, "trained us for freedom."[16] But during these growing years, when the father was often either ill or in his musty study, the mother and the strong son, working together, learned to understand and respect each other, and although their mutual reserve meant that they almost never spoke freely of their deeper feelings, she passed on to him a full share of her interest in world affairs, her love of kindness and her passion for nature. He understood only too well her shyness, her flaring temper, and those acute depressions. The constant troubled references in his memoirs to her reddened eyes show how aware he was of her mental state; aware and probably more than a little guilty.

In his ninth year important things happened. The first was simply that his legs finally grew long enough to reach the organ pedals. This was a great event, for the organ was in his blood, and as we have seen, he was never inclined to fight his heritage. Daddy Iltis encouraged him to practice whenever he could; perhaps from sheer good-heartedness, perhaps partly because he had an eye to the moment when he could take some time off and leave the accompaniment of the occasional service to an enthusiastic deputy. If he had anything of this sort in mind, he was not disappointed. Within a year Albert's face began occasionally to appear framed in the organ mirror as Satan's stand-in.

Besides being the organist, Daddy Iltis was also teacher to the senior section of the school, to which Albert had now graduated. And at last, under his friendly guidance, Albert began to show a little interest in learning. The ability to read and write, laboriously acquired and unwillingly exercised, were suddenly seen to have some purpose, and once that happened, there was no stopping him. One of the first books he asked for was a Bible; when his father gave him one, he plunged into it with enthusiasm.

This was not simply a pious exercise. He had never yet had a satisfactory answer to his question: if Jesus' parents were given frankincense, myrrh, and especially gold by the Three Wise Men from the East, how was it that they remained poor? Other things puzzled him too. Forty days and nights of rain were said to have drowned even the mountaintops when Noah was afloat in his ark. In Alsace it rained nearly as long as that one summer, and the water never even reached the houses. Albert's father had explained this by the theory that in those days it had rained bucketsful, not mere drops, but, unfortunately, this was not confirmed by the Scripture teacher. Clearly, the Bible held clues to these and other mysteries; and Albert had an urgent need to know more about those important days when Jesus lived—about the springs of the religion to which his father and so many relatives had given their lives.

His ninth year, then, saw the beginning of Schweitzer the organist and Schweitzer the biblical scholar. But more important still—more central— was a third development, an event, a moment, which hardened his childish tendencies and inclinations into a crucial conviction.

It happened a little before Easter. The soft snow had melted from the surrounding fields and now lay only on the high slopes distantly visible at the head of the valley. Where it had lain hard packed in the streets, it had been chipped up to bare the buried cobbles. The naked branches were beginning to mist a little with leaf buds. What better time, thought Albert's friend Henry Bräsch, to take one's new catapult up the warm hillside and kill a few birds? Henry proposed the expedition to Albert, who found himself in his familiar dilemma. He prayed for the safety of birds—why should he shoot them? On the other hand, refusal might mean further mockery from his fellows.

The story has often been told and justly. A vital thread of his life runs unbroken through this experience, the greatest of his childhood, through the greatest experience of his manhood thirty-two years later, and straight on to the end of his life. For a moment as important as this there are no better words than his own.

> We got close to a tree which was still without any leaves, and on which the birds were singing beautifully to greet the morning, without showing the least fear of us. Then stooping like a Red Indian hunter, my companion put a bullet in the leather of his catapult and took aim. In obedience to his nod of command, I did the same, though with terrible twinges of conscience, vowing to myself that I would shoot directly he did. At that very moment the church bells began to ring, mingling their music with the songs of the birds and the sunshine. It was the Warning-bell which began half an hour before the regular peal-ringing, and for me it was a voice from heaven. I shooed the birds away, so that they flew where they were safe from my companion's catapult, and then I fled home. And ever since then, when the Passion-tide bells ring out to the leafless trees and the sunshine, I reflect with a rush of grateful emotion, how on that day their music drove deep into my heart the commandment: Thou shall not kill.
>
> From that day onward I took courage to emancipate myself from the fear of men, and whenever my inner convictions were at stake I let other people's opinions weigh less with me than they had done previously. I tried also to unlearn my former dread of being laughed at by my schoolfellows.[17]

The dilemma was resolved. The life of "things that have breath" was more important than the fear of being laughed at. The terror of being different from the others was at last overcome; not in a moment, naturally, for the conflict continued, never entirely to be resolved, between the need to stand out alone and the need to be one of the company. But the priorities were now clear and were never again to be in doubt. When at the age of nine and a half he went on to the Realschule in Münster, roughly two miles away, he would walk by himself over the hills, which is not the direct route, rather than go with the other boys along the road.

One other incident is undated but should be reported. It must have happened about this period. One of the guests at a wedding that his father conducted was a crippled girl. Albert in his innocence asked whether this was the bride. They laughed at him; who would want to marry a girl with deformities? Albert privately determined that if that was the way the world went, he would he different. He would marry a cripple. It was one of those silly quixotic resolutions that children do make and then, when they learn better, forget about. But in Albert's case such resolutions often stayed with him, and he lived to make them seem normal and reasonable. About this decision it is less easy to decide how important it was, and what, if anything, it meant to him later in life.

In the year in which he tramped across hills to the Realschule, he saw the Münster valley in every seasonal mood and fell more and more deeply in love with it. He tried to express his feelings in poetry and in sketches; both were complete failures. Only in musical improvisation did he ever feel he had creative ability. In fact, though, there are the marks of a major artist in the use he makes of imagery in his books and sermons. It is nearly always nature imagery. The countryside through which he tramped became the natural landscape of his thought.

Imagery of this kind can bring an argument down to earth and at the same time bring it to life. He would have said that bringing to life and bringing down to earth were one and the same thing. Everything that happened to him was teaching him the same lesson: truth lies in the concrete. Dogma and theory must check with common human experience. Eternity starts from here and now, or nowhere. Grünewald reinforced it with the chamber pot near Jesus' crib, and at the Realschule Pastor Schaffler, the teacher of religion, had the gift of dramatizing Bible stories to such effect that when he wept over the story of Joseph making himself known to his brothers, rows of boys would sit sobbing on their benches in sympathy.

At this period Albert was nicknamed Isaac, "the Laugher," because he could so easily be made to giggle in class, and his schoolfellows made the most of this weakness. But this laughter was not the sign of cheerfulness. "I was by no means," he says, "a merry character."[18] Introspection still pursued him, and he had not yet learned to neutralize it by putting it to work. His giggles were of that uncomfortable kind that come from tension and self-consciousness.

The tension is made clear by one tiny incident, casually mentioned in the memoirs but full of consequence. He was playing a game with Adèle, one of his younger sisters. Even in games he found it impossible to relax and enjoy himself. He played "with terrible earnestness, and got angry if anyone else did not play with all his might."[19] Not an entirely attractive boy, it must be admitted; it is little wonder the other boys enjoyed making him laugh in class.

Adèle took this particular game less seriously than Albert thought she should, which infuriated him so much that he hit her. His mother had told him that he must never hit a girl, but most mothers say something of the sort to most sons at some time or other. More than a mother's reprimand is needed to account for the consequence, which was simply that Albert stopped playing games.

All he writes is this: "From that time onwards I began to feel anxious about my passion for play, and gradually gave up all games. I have never ventured to touch a playing card."[20]

The key word is *passion*. Sartre wrote of the noise, passion, and enthusiasm of the Schweitzers. *Noise* and *enthusiasm* fit Albert badly at this age. He was the dreamy one. But *passion* is absolutely right. The passion for play, and that passion for dominance he felt in taming the snarling dog, came head-on into conflict with the passion for kindness and justice. The struggle was cruel because the feeling was so intense. That same intensity that peers out at us from the early photographs, that "overcame" him after his fight with George Nitschelm, that almost stunned him when he heard two-part harmony sung well, that drove him to those long and bitter fights with his parents over what he was to wear, now turned inward. He recognized a force in himself over which he was in danger of losing control. He had to tame it for his own peace of mind. His own violence now had to be penned into a corner and stopped from biting. His desire for mastery had to be turned on to himself.

Jesus said, "If your eye offends you, pluck it out." Here was a child who set about plucking out his love for games because it offended him. He might easily at this point have swung fiercely toward puritanical self-repression, but some instinct saved him from this. The search for a right way of living continued, forced on him by the ease with which he felt he might go wrong. From now on he was to seek for a course by which his vehement nature could express itself positively, not destructively.

Instead of the subconscious wound the psychoanalysts seek, the thing that troubled him was his awareness of the division and conflict in existence itself. In nature there was creation and there was cruelty. In himself there was love and violence. Something was fundamentally at odds and out of balance in the very stuff of which life and the universe were made. Once again, the exceptional thing about this particular boy was not that he felt this, for multitudes of people feel it, at all ages; what singles him out was the depth of feeling, the insistence with which it pursued him, and his refusal to evade it. The wound was not a personal one of his own. It was in everything, and it had to be faced.

In all these developing tensions of his mind, there was one sure place of peace and reconciliation, and ironically the thing that gave it its special quality was the ill-intentioned edict of Louis XIV. The Catholic chancel of the Günsbach church, with its gilded altar and the two golden statues flanking the east window, was a vision of mystical wonder to the Lutheran boy. Beyond the vision, through the window, he could see the real world of roofs and mountains, trees and sky. This world, he recollects, "continued the chancel of the church into an infinity of distance, and was, in turn, flooded with a kind of transfiguring glory imparted to it by the chancel. Thus my gaze wandered from the finite to the infinite, and my soul was wrapped in peace and quiet."[21]

Günsbach had given him everything he could need—quiet and disquiet, deep roots in the country and the community, and yet enough freedom to question and break away into his own world. As long as he lived it was part of him.

But now the time had come for him to leave it. His elderly great-uncle in Mulhouse, who was also his godfather, made it possible for him to go to the Gymnasium there for his secondary education by offering to board him free of charge. In addition, he would have a small scholarship as a pastor's son. For such an opportunity one should be truly grateful.

He was not grateful. Secretly, he wept for hours at the prospect. "I felt as if I were being torn away from Nature."[22] The ten years to which he was saying goodbye were his whole lifetime to date, years in which the most startling events in the physical world had been the arrival of the first bicycle in the village and the first appearance of that alien and suspicious vegetable, the tomato; but in which he had laid down irrevocably the pattern of his life.

2

The Dark Years
1885–1893

MULHOUSE IS AN INDUSTRIAL TOWN, as dreary as Colmar is enchanting. In this uninspiring spot Albert's uncle Louis occupied a gloomy residence that was actually part of the Central School; for after a lifetime of schoolteaching Louis had now become a school inspector. So Albert lived in a permanent atmosphere of education. The boy who hated school was now at school for twenty-four hours a day.

As though this were not enough, the discipline, too, was strict and pedagogical. Louis and his wife, Sophie, were of the old school. Childless themselves, they did not believe, as Albert's parents did, in bringing up children for freedom. The day was carefully regulated, to each task its proper time, to each hour its task. Aunt Sophie would encourage the lethargic boy with worthy considerations: "Think how lucky you are to be strong enough to make your bed!"

Looking back later in life, he was to discover that he had learned something from Aunt Sophie, but at the time he was not impressed. Even piano practice (between lunchtime and afternoon school, and again if he finished his homework early) became a chore to which he had to be dragged. He was not allowed out walking alone, and visiting was confined to one or two carefully selected and approved friends. When he was finally old enough to be permitted to go for walks by himself, the lanky boy would make a pilgrimage to the top of a nearby hill, from which on a clear day he could see the distant outline of the mountains, a shadowy reminder of home.

What sort of correspondence passed between the two Louis Schweitzers, father and uncle, about the ill-disciplined boy and the need for a firm hand? It has all vanished. Sophie did her best to instill in him a proper respect for literature. Reading was a good and proper activity, but only within a prescribed period—in her case for one hour before supper and two after. Albert's homework restricted his time far more severely, and his method of leaping on a book when he had the chance and devouring it at one sitting, skipping the dull bits, was entirely deplorable and needed correction. How could one appreciate the style if one read like that?

Albert privately disagreed. He believed that if there were bits one wanted to skip, the book was badly written. If it were good enough, the style commanded attention automatically. But he kept his opinion to himself because argument might endanger what little reading time the schedule allowed.

Things came to a head over newspapers, which he read as avidly as he did anything else. The only time he had for this was during the quarter of an hour while supper was being laid, but his aunt was convinced that he only looked at the murder cases and the fiction in the Literary Supplement, and she tried to persuade her husband not to allow him the paper. Albert claimed an interest in politics. His uncle, wise to the deceits of eleven-year-olds, instantly tested him on his knowledge of recent political events. When Albert had reeled off the names of princes and premiers in the Balkans, the three previous French cabinets, and the substance of a recent speech in the Reichstag, the grownups submitted. From then on Albert would solemnly discuss politics with his great-uncle over meals; but much more important, he was allowed additional time for reading the papers.

"Naturally," he wrote, "I used this time to refresh my soul with stories from the Literary Supplement."[1] For stories remained his passion. And even in his fifties, when he was traveling about Europe, he would get someone to keep any installments of a serial that he might have missed so that he could finish it when he got back home.

The battle of the newspapers was one triumph in a period that otherwise was largely disaster. Aunt Sophie's stern regime failed to work. The donkey in Albert's character, the beast that would never be driven in any but the direction that suited him, dug his heels in. One teacher after another found him totally unresponsive, and the day came when the headmaster had to speak to his father about the waste of time and money involved in keeping him on at the Gymnasium. He was the dunce again. Of all the lessons he gratefully remembered having learned from Aunt Sophie, one of the most vivid and valuable was how not to educate the young.

The ax did not fall. He was allowed to stay at Mulhouse, working at lessons he did not understand or want to understand, living in the house of rules, regulations, etiquette, and discipline, musty with the odor of those who, however kind and well-intentioned, were old not only physically but at heart. His feelings when he heard he was not to be expelled back into the Eden of Günsbach must have been mixed indeed.

Nor did Mulhouse do anything to help Albert with his shyness. Rather he sank deeper into himself. His struggles had always been solitary, even in the heart of his family. Here he was more isolated than ever. The never-ending schedule of activities at school and at his uncle's house kept his body occupied but gave him no escape from his loneliness or his private thoughts. So deeply did his problems enwrap him that he barely noticed the distress his lethargy was causing. When his father came to see the headmaster about his possible removal from the school, the only reaction Albert could summon up was amazement that he was not scolded. It never occurred to him that his parents' worry had gone too deep for anger.

In practical ways, though, he was a dutiful and considerate son, prepared, when the family finances were at a low ebb, to freeze all winter in a summer suit rather than admit to his mother that his winter one was too small and he needed a new one. His aunt characteristically encouraged this Spartan gesture. His schoolmates laughed at him for his impoverishment, which was unpleasant, but at least the reason was no longer his superiority. Perhaps he found some satisfaction in reflecting that he was now among the underprivileged.

In Günsbach he had determined that he would never allow himself to become insensitive to the pain of the world. He would fight his way through the problem rather than take Peer Gynt's way, round about. "Even while I was a boy at school," he wrote in his autobiography, "it was clear to me that no explanation of the evil in the world could ever satisfy me; all explanations, I felt, ended in sophistries, and at bottom had no other object than to make it possible for men to share in the misery around them with less keen feelings."

He would not evade the issue or forget the experiences that had forced it on him. "It seemed to me a matter of course that we should all take our share of the burden of pain which lies upon the world."[2] Somewhere beneath the lethargic exterior the determination smoldered on, but it was now so damped by the rigidity of his godparents, by homesickness, and the longing for the lost world of the countryside that he himself was barely aware of it.

Aunt Sophie, however, had another lesson to teach him by reverse example. Withdrawn by nature, he found in her someone who was withdrawn on principle. Etiquette and decorum were her watchwords. Going to see friends was known as "knocking about outside."[3] Spontaneity was discouraged and humanity in general kept at arm's length.

This was a change from the vigorous, hospitable life of Günsbach, and Albert, seeking a way out of his distress, had to decide which was better. Aunt Sophie lost. Formal rules of society, Albert concluded, were not the key to relationships with the outer world. In Sophie he saw his own reserve writ large and sealed with adult approval, and he saw that it ran counter to his convictions about the unity of all life. Spontaneous warmth, the thing he was no good at, was the proper approach to fellow creatures. So he set out to achieve it.

A deliberate decision to be spontaneous sounds like a contradiction in terms, but the contradiction is more apparent than real. He was not really aiming to change himself—simply to release his true nature. Some native insight told him that the search for love and warmth is not a journey to a far country but the uncovering of a hidden spring. The difficulty of finding it is not that it is remote or alien but that it has been half obliterated by the superstructures of social taboo and the rubble of one's own attempts at self-preservation. It takes an act of faith to start excavating, for if the pessimists are right and the heart of man is desperately wicked, the well, once disclosed, will turn out to be foul-smelling and poisonous, not fresh and life-giving. Albert, fortunately, had not been brought up in that negative stream of Christian thought, and he believed that man, once liberated, was inherently good. So he made his act of faith. But such a decision is only a beginning. Hard work follows. Habit and social sanction set like concrete over the spring water, and the man swinging the pick has his work cut out to get through.

Not that Albert was completely friendless. He had at least two good school-friends (awarded his godparents' seal of respectability), one of whom came regularly to Günsbach for the Whitsun holidays. But an odd feature is that in both cases he seems to have valued one of the parents as much as the son. One was a pastor—yet another pastor!—"an extraordinarily learned man." In the other case it was the mother whom Albert singled out. He describes her as "a woman much above average" and makes the rather curious comment that because of her "it was a great advantage to me to go so often to the house of Ostier." Not pleasure; advantage. Similarly, he says of Anna Schäffer, a schoolteacher—yet another schoolteacher!—who also stayed with Louis and Sophie, that "with her wise and kindly personality she contributed much more to my education than she ever suspected."[4] All the time the search is for understanding rather than delight. Surrounded by pedagogues and ecclesiastics, Albert stood a good chance of maturing into a sanctimonious prig.

Anna Schäffer, however, appears to have provided some relief from the strictness of the household, and what she taught him had more to do with how to treat people than how to analyze a sentence or a specimen.

She and Mrs. Ostier were the first of a long line of women whose help and approval he was to enjoy and rely upon throughout his life—a humanizing, counterdogmatic influence that mattered a great deal to him. Not that he was sexually precocious—far from it. At puberty he began to worship an occasional schoolgirl from afar, like most middle-class boys. But it was older women whose company he sought. He could learn from them, and he found them easy to get on with.

And there were still occasional moments when something happened vivid enough to penetrate the miasma and stir the impressionable mind to its old, excited response. Such a moment was his first view of the astonishing Marie-Joseph Erb, a virtuoso pianist from Paris, who came to give a concert at Mulhouse. Sixty years later Schweitzer still remembered the gowned women eating candy while they awaited the maestro and the inadequacy of his own outgrown suit; he remembered the whirling fingers and his own thunderstruck attempts to work out how those incredible runs and "cascades of arpeggios" had been achieved. Afterward he could not understand how the audience could go back to exchanging sweetmeats as though nothing special had happened. The concert was a revelation of the possibilities of the piano, and at practice that evening he even worked hard at the studies that were "starred with sharps and double sharps, which I had so detested before."[5]

He devised a system for mitigating the tedium of these scale exercises, at least when at home during the holidays, by propping a novel or a magazine serial on the music stand and reading while his fingers ran up and down the keyboard. The rest of the family, going about their business, had no such alleviation of the interminable din and felt more than a little sore. He alone sat happily insulated from boredom, refreshing his soul with fiction. It is unlikely though that he tried this trick at Mulhouse. One can imagine the comments of Aunt Sophie had she caught him at it.

His music teacher at Mulhouse was Eugène Münch, an organist of considerable distinction, whose nephew Charles was to become the conductor of the Boston Symphony Orchestra. Eugène was an enthusiastic teacher and a tireless seeker after perfection, but he could do no more with this tedious boy than anyone else and called him "the thorn in my flesh." The problem was that Aunt Sophie could lead Albert to the piano, but she could not make him practice properly. Münch gave him various pieces to learn, but Albert preferred to sight-read something that caught his fancy or to improvise as he had learned to do on the old square piano at Günsbach. Perhaps from time to time he became in fantasy Mr. Erb of the flying fingers. So he came to his lessons ill prepared and got into trouble. His surprise at not being scolded by his father about his bad report is only one indication that at that time trouble was more or less his native element.

The determination to break out of his shell was at work within him, but these decisions take time to become effective. With Albert it was a new teacher who made the first crack—not, needless to say, by any new form of stick or carrot for the donkey Albert. Those had all been tried and abandoned as hopeless. What forced itself through the fog of Albert's inattention was the single fact that Dr. Wehmann did his job properly. Exercise books were handed out, collected, and corrected at the proper time. The boys were not expected to be the only ones who were in the right place at the right time with all their work done. Dr. Wehmann, too, had his obligations and met them. The implication, unstated in Schweitzer's account but clearly enough implied, is that the rest of the staff were not like Dr. Wehmann. The same sense of justice that told Albert that animals had as much right to compassion as human beings also said that boys and masters had an equal obligation to work at lessons. Dr. Wehmann became his hero.

In one of his letters to Hermann Hagedorn about his early life, he wrote: "I could never tell you how indebted I am to him. I and many of my schoolmates feel that we owe our sense of duty to the mere example of his life. . . . He had a rare gift for encouraging his students."[6] And in his autobiography he writes, "Thanks to Dr. Wehmann I became firmly convinced that a deep sense of duty . . . is the great educative influence, and that it accomplishes what no exhortations and no punishments can."[7]

But the word *duty* here must not be confused with that thin-lipped attitude that often serves as a substitute for love. Schweitzer never preached or practiced that rigid, external type of duty, which is, in fact, the enemy of the spontaneity he was seeking. What Schweitzer is writing of is example, the willingness to be the first to do what you are asking others to do and an orderliness that enables good intentions to become effective.

The response to Wehmann's example was immediate, and the result startling. Between Christmas and Easter Albert moved from the bottom of the form to somewhere near the top. Any teacher who had written on Albert's school report "could do better" would have been absolutely accurate. It was not that he had been unable to work—simply unwilling. He had not seen the point of it. Now he did. The spirit of enlightenment, as he put it, awoke in him in his fourteenth year.

In music, too, the time for the opening of the floodgates had arrived. Münch one day gave his unrewarding pupil a "Song Without Words" by Mendelssohn saying, "I suppose you'll spoil this like everything else. If a boy has no feeling, I certainly can't give him any."

Albert was hurt. His problem was that he had, if anything, too much feeling but did not care to exhibit it. Münch's remark meant that now he could put his whole heart into playing the Mendelssohn and yet not feel he was endangering his carefully guarded emotional underbelly. He was simply answering a challenge. He practiced for once with great care, and at the next lesson gave Münch a considerable surprise. Münch's response was to sit at the piano himself and play another of the "Songs Without Words." Albert was accepted. They were musicians together.

The breakthrough was happening on all fronts. In music as in lessons the pent-up talent, once released, soared immediately to undreamed-of heights. At fifteen, after his confirmation, he began to have lessons on the big organ at St. Stephen's. At sixteen he was deputizing there for Münch at church services. And not long after that he was playing the organ accompaniment at a concert performance of Brahms' Requiem. A puff of wind from the right direction and the smoldering fire burst out and leaped heavenward with a ferocity redoubled by its long suppression.

There came a new broadening of his musical horizon—a new experience to stun him and send him walking about the streets in a dream for days afterward—Wagner's *Tannhäuser*. It was his first visit to a theater— often exciting enough in itself to a susceptible boy. Wagner overwhelmed him. Where Bach fed the religious instinct in him and the need for reason and order, Wagner nourished the wild romantic, the ecstatic side of his nature.

The release was longest delayed in religion—perhaps because in religion it mattered most. His teacher was Pastor Wennagel, an old man who, if he had ever had it, had by now lost the fire to which Albert's fire could answer. What he taught, he taught well. But in Albert there raged questions that Wennagel's kind of instruction never even knew existed, let alone how to answer. And, in particular, there was one fundamental difference between the ideas of the teacher and the pupil. Albert, fighting his way through to a command of his impulses and an understanding of life, had adopted Grandfather Schillinger's devotion to reason as his guiding light. Christianity was not exempt from its rule. Dogma, revelation, the tradition of the Church—all were subject to questioning, all had to be seen to stand up to rational examination. For Pastor Wennagel faith was a matter of submission to authority; Albert's probing into the mysteries of received truth seemed to him not only meaningless but bordering on blasphemy. The boy, approaching his confirmation with reverence and exaltation, knew instinctively that to bring his questions to Wennagel would be to expose both of them to fruitless hurt; so he hugged to himself both his questions and his joyous conviction of the universal power of reason to embrace the highest religious experience. To Wennagel's gentle questions about his feelings he could only give evasive answers, and the old man concluded with disappointment that Albert did not care. Had he persevered with sympathy he might well have discovered the passionate emotion that seethed beneath the demand for reason. Albert was, in fact, "so moved by the holiness of the time that I felt almost ill."[8] Wennagel's disappointment awaits all adults who have the "correct" answer in mind when they question children, and it is their own fault, for the question is not sincere. They seek their own image in another person and are hurt when they find that the other is truly other. Clergy and schoolmasters, upholders of tradition, are peculiarly prone to this mistake, and it is remarkable that Albert, with the blood of both professions thick in his veins, surrounded by both for most of his early life, managed to resist their pressures and retain his independence of mind. Even more astonishing perhaps is that he was able to do this without any violent or rebellious reaction, without ever kicking over the traces like the traditional daughter of the parsonage who flees from the restriction of her upbringing to the arms of a multiplicity of lovers. Albert managed the difficult feat of remaining a lone sheep without ever leaving the fold. The worst that happened was that when he finally broke through the crust of his reserve, he began to exhibit one or two alarmingly wolfish characteristics.

In the perspective of history, that period of his life simply looks like an abnormally late spring. Delayed by the frosts of shyness, of the struggle with his own passion, of uncomprehending adults, he finally blossomed into a sudden simultaneous flowering. For him, the release was almost a second birth. But for the bystanders it was an explosion, and it was wise to stand clear of the blast. The tall, quiet lad was suddenly a prickly streak of aggressive argument. No unexamined statement was allowed to pass unchallenged. Casual remarks were subjected to scrutiny they were never intended to stand up to. The passion for reason reached an unreasonable pitch as the search for truth switched from the inward landscape to the world outside. He became an intolerable nuisance, not to be taken anywhere with any degree of comfort. His aunt said he was insolent, and his father had to implore him, when they were visiting friends, to keep his mouth shut and not spoil yet another day.

Insolence was not the intention. All he wanted was to find out the truth. Other people seemed not to care about it, and it had to be pointed out to them that this would not do. How could one go through life cheerfully making inaccurate statements based on false assumptions? No wonder the world was in a mess! Like Socrates, Albert demanded only that people should use the brains they were given to ask questions, to pull apart accepted notions, to think for themselves.

History began to fascinate him. Here was one vital key to human life and behavior. And the natural sciences were important, for they dealt with objective fact. The only trouble with science lessons was that there were not enough of them. Something also was wrong with the textbooks, for they pretended to know too much.

Today the thought that science has its limitations is a familiar one. We have seen too much of the consequences of trusting our lives to purely technical criteria. But in the closing years of the nineteenth century science appeared to those who believed in it at all as a shining light, the probable guarantee of a bright and constantly improving future. The mysteries of nature were capable of being dissected, analyzed, described, and eventually controlled. It was to conventionally religious minds that it mostly appeared a threat, likely to replace hallowed belief with some mechanical explanation of the world's development such as evolution and natural selection. Worthy archdeacons contemplated suicide at the very thought.

This was not what worried Albert. He had no quarrel with the truth, from whatever direction it came. If his grandfather could set up his telescope for the village to peer through at the night sky, Albert was not going to be an obscurantist about the universe. His problem was simply that science was not scientific enough. If one stated that a thunderstorm was caused by electrical discharges, this did nothing to explain it: it merely provided a rather more accurate way of describing it. But the new description then needed further explanation. What was electricity? Where did it come from? The confidence of the textbooks (which in any case were out of date almost as soon as they appeared) was laughable and pitiful. "It hurt me to think that we never acknowledge the absolutely mysterious character of nature, but always speak so confidently of explaining her."[9] Behind each new contribution of science is always further mystery. However deeply our knowledge penetrates, the only proper attitude to the basis of nature is mysticism—wonder. And this conclusion is reached not through a rejection of science but through the use of reason to assess the proper place and function of science. "Thus I fell gradually into a new habit of dreaming about the thousand and one miracles that surround us, though fortunately the new habit did not, like my earlier thoughtless day-dreams, prevent me from working properly. The habit, however, is with me still, and gets stronger. If during a meal I catch sight of the light broken up in a glass jug of water into the colours of the spectrum, I can at once become oblivious of everything around me, and unable to withdraw my gaze from the spectacle."

History, too, came under the same judgment. "I gradually recognised that the historical process, too, is full of riddles, and that we must abandon forever the hope of really understanding the past. In this department also, all that our faculties allow us to do is to produce more or less thorough descriptions."[10]

In religion, truth began with personal experience. Because history was so suspect, so capable of distortion, the historical side of religion must always be treated with suspicion: finally one could only trust

one's own heart and mind. This was one reason why he so much respected his father, whose sermons were as often as not a way of sharing
his own thoughts and problems with his congregation. This was not
particularly clever, but it was true. And who needed cleverness, if not
to discover truth?

Albert was a strong boy now, tall and thin, with a physical strength
capable of matching the mental energy that had been released by the
explosion of his spirit. The world was his oyster now, and he set about
opening it. And if there were subjects that he found particularly difficult,
he began to look on them as challenges, not as tiresome irrelevances.
Languages, for example, never came easily. Nor did mathematics.

Such was his determination that when he wanted to earn some pocket
money by giving private tuition, it was mathematics that he taught—
because mathematics was in demand. The reason he needed money was
a compelling one. He wanted a bicycle. Bicycles had come a long way, in
every sense, during the previous ten years, and were no longer the oddi-
ties they had been. To Albert his bicycle was the magic steed that opened
to him the gates of the countryside. Mulhouse at last was no longer a
prison, mentally or physically.

He saved up more money and gave a bicycle to his young brother,
Paul. He sent his mother and sister on holiday to Switzerland. He found
himself able to talk to anyone about anything. Everything was delight
and exhilaration, whether exploring the countryside with his brother
during the holidays, conversing with pig farmers or professors, making
a nuisance of himself in the cause of truth, or flooding a church with the
sound of a big organ. And yet his very delight carried with it a penalty.
The greater his happiness, the stronger grew his feeling that he owed
something to somebody in return for it. Where this sense of debt came
from is difficult to say, but it was strong in him. It may be that those first
few stifling years at Mulhouse taught him the value of his parents, his
home valley, and his childhood freedom as nothing else could have done,
and this, too, was a backhanded lesson from Aunt Sophie. Whether this
was the cause or not, a little cloud now hovered intermittently in the
bright sky of his newfound happiness. It was not yet a very large cloud,
but it was there, and it would not go away.

Finals were passed, if not in a blaze of glory, at least respectably. They
were marred by only two things, his obstinacy and his trousers. The
latter, which he had borrowed for the occasion (examinees were required
to attend in black frock coat and trousers), were far too short. With singular lack of foresight he had failed to try them on until the day they
were needed. He could eliminate the gap at his ankles by adding bits of
string to his braces, but then the gap reappeared at his waist. Apart from
the embarrassment, they must have been very uncomfortable. But Albert,

who had once so hated being laughed at, was now prepared to turn like a mannequin to let his fellow candidates appreciate the full effect, which was best of all from behind. When the students entered the examination hall, the school staff enjoyed the vision, but the visiting commissioner was not amused and leaned heavily on the buffoon in the funny trousers.

The obstinacy lay in the fact that, as usual, Albert had not troubled to learn things that he considered irrelevant, and he could see no reason whatever to suppose that it mattered how Homer described the beaching of the Greek ships at Troy. The commissioner took the view that as part of the examination syllabus it did matter, and Albert was only saved at the last moment by his interest in history, which turned out to be the commissioner's subject. Albert finished with a special mention, and his days at Mulhouse were over.

Liberated from his shyness and looking back at the days of his enslavement, what he regretted most was failure to express his gratitude. He was genuinely grateful to many people—Uncle Louis and Aunt Sophie not excluded. Sometimes he was grateful for what they had given unwittingly, the chance remark finding the exact spot at the right moment; sometimes for what they intended, for the goodwill offered even if not accepted. He could scarcely be said to have been easily influenced. The Rock of Gibraltar was more yielding than Albert Schweitzer when his mind was made up. But when he was searching, as he so often was, for a clue, a direction, then his response to the right stimulus was instant and uncompromising. These deep, barely acknowledged moments of communication he felt were the most important and precious gifts that human beings could give each other. They could happen by a word, an action, perhaps simply a smile, and their effect was unforeseen and secret.

So education for him consisted as much as anything in being constantly ready and available with the healing and necessary presence. He assumed, generously, perhaps, but probably rightly, that other people were as anxious as he was to find their proper path and needed, as he did, moments of guidance. Their search was their own affair, not to be dictated from outside; but they could be helped at any and every moment by the responsiveness of people they met. One must be ready, therefore, to give oneself freely wherever one was needed; but one must never demand results, for these might be long delayed or very different from what was anticipated. All that was necessary was the readiness to give and the humility to know that the choice of gift was not for the giver. Only the receiver knew what he needed, and even he might not be able to find words for it.

Albert was conscious of debts of gratitude that it was now much too late to repay. He had been too shy at the time or had taken things too much for granted or had not recognized what it was he had been given.

But if the debts could not be paid where they were owed, they could go back into the common pool of humanity. Benefit could be acknowledged by being passed on to others. And this became the plan of his life.

The cloud then was a cloud of obligation. The debts were piling up, and something in him was saying that sooner or later they would have to be reckoned with. But not yet. For the moment there were new avenues opening up in all directions. Life had become full of possibilities.

3

—

Strasbourg
1893–1896

AT HOME THINGS HAD GREATLY CHANGED for the better. The son of a former pastor of Günsbach had died and left his house to the parish as a vicarage in place of the old one. The house was well built and dry, with a substantial cellar and a good garden, and the move had a rapid effect on Louis's health. Shortly after this, a small legacy solved the worst of the family's financial problems.

The children had grown up with their mother's keen interest in all manner of things, and there was never a dull moment at the vicarage. With the easing of the financial stringency the Schillinger passion to be up to date showed itself in Mrs. Schweitzer as a love for trying out new foods, new gadgets, whatever was the latest thing.

The family's pleasure at having Albert home was not entirely unalloyed, although by this time the worst of his argumentative phase was over and they could at least look forward to having a meal in peace. But he was still inclined to moodiness, and as always after he returned from Mulhouse it was some time before he was able to relax. He went about the house withdrawn and stiff, still dogged by the starchy image of Aunt Sophie, and from time to time, when he was not thinking, would call his mother "Aunt."

Even after the family atmosphere had reasserted itself and he had begun to thaw out, the visible manifestations of his inward struggles continued to plague those around him. One never knew when he would turn up late for meals (a considerable crime) or fly into a sudden rage. He would hurt his father by refusing to take part in the traditional stroll after church on Sundays or by making it very evident that he only did so under protest. He preferred to loiter and dream. He would do his best

40

to avoid any task requiring practical effort. He would practice his scales and arpeggios incessantly, despite all protest, or make abrupt and imperious demands of his poor sisters that they leave everything and pump the bellows of the organ while he practiced and keep them there till they nearly dropped.

But these things were endured not only because he was a beloved son, not only because he was a big brother, but because it was becoming increasingly apparent that the *sacré imbécile*, the dunce of the village school and the near-despair of the Gymnasium, was developing into someone to reckon with.

Not that the family, even at the height of his fame, ever allowed themselves to show more than a surprised amusement that Bery, as they called him, should have attracted so much attention. And they did their best, as he did, to avoid meretricious publicity. But forty years later Adèle was prevailed upon to write about her memories of those adolescent years, and she makes it clear that even as early as this, and even to those who suffered most from his uncertain temper, something marked him out. They all felt the increasing dominance of his personality and realized that what drove him was a passion for truth and a hungry quest for perfection. They understood what he called "the conviction that human progress is only possible if reasoned thought replaces mere opinion,"[1] and they realized that anyone who held such a conviction was unlikely to live a very contented life.

Young Paul was different—all charm, thoughtfulness, and good humor, never any trouble, and without any of his brother's prickliness, but also without the inner fire that gave meaning to his brother's flaws. They were different enough, both in age and temperament, these two, to be without jealousy or rivalry. Each admired, but had no wish to emulate, the other.

Schweitzer's pursuit of truth, it must be reported, did not preclude the odd social evasion. He was searching, he said, for what was "true and serviceable," and sometimes a lie appeared a good deal more serviceable than the strict truth. One day he and a cousin, feeling the need of beer, explained to their grandfather (on a visit to Pfaffenhofen) that they were going to see an uncle. No sooner were they settled at the inn than grandfather appeared and sat down at their table. "An old man isn't as blind as you might think," he said. "And he's often just as thirsty as the young ones. Now pour me a drink." It was the sort of lesson that Schweitzer regarded as eminently serviceable, and he continued to tell the story till he was an old man himself.

With a month or two to spare between finals and the start of the university term, the student traditionally travels. No longer a schoolboy, no longer a slave of the timetable, he stretches toward manhood, he comes into his own as a free member of the human race and wishes to survey his inheritance.

Arrangements had been made for Schweitzer to visit his uncles in Paris. Here, one might think, was truly the big world, outclassing Colmar, Mulhouse, even Strasbourg. Fin-de-siècle Paris was at that time widely regarded as the center and height of Western Civilization. But this Paris, the Mecca of sensitive Americans, where Left Bank artists experimented with new forms, where poets sought significance through every degree of perverse experience, the Paris of Baudelaire and Rimbaud, Cézanne and Gauguin, where death came early from alcoholism, drug addiction, or syphilis—this was not the Paris Schweitzer came to know. His Paris was largely a kind of colony of Alsace, populated by those who had fled there when their country came under German rule at the end of the Franco-Prussian War.

These Alsatians were mostly professional people. The very fact that they had been able to make the move to Paris meant that they had a certain amount of enterprise and at least moderate means, sufficient to provide themselves with a fresh start and somewhere to live. They had none of the language problems that most expatriates suffer from, so they had no need to herd together physically. But they naturally kept in touch with one another and helped each other through the first difficult years. As expatriates often do, they throve, needing to work harder than the natives to achieve security in a strange land. Alsatian shrewdness and energy gave them a great advantage; but there was another reason for their success. Unlike the Bohemian colony of artists on the Left Bank, Parisian bourgeois society at that time was restricted by the most rigid conventions. "Paradoxical as it is," Schweitzer wrote, "no other citizenry in the world is for good or bad as conservative as that of the modern French Republic."[2] The more flexible Alsatians could maneuver with much greater freedom than the formal Parisians; when they wanted things done, they did not allow convention to impede them.

Uncle Auguste and Uncle Charles had both in their different ways achieved distinction and prosperity, and both were able to introduce Albert to a prosperous circle of friends and acquaintances. He was less of a country cousin in the big town than he might have been, being much among his own countrymen, who to some degree at least retained their native outlook and native accent. But when he ventured among the true Parisians he discovered, for example, that a visit to a friend necessitated a formal call rather than a casual arrival and that certain afternoons were set aside each week for receiving. Besides, the trams never seemed to go where one wanted them to go. Any spontaneous impulse to strike up friendships was nipped in the bud.

Inevitably, therefore, such friends as he did make tended to come from within the Alsatian community. Auguste, with whom he stayed, was able to put him in touch with the business world. Charles had put his bilingual upbringing to good use by becoming a teacher of German at the Collège Janson de Saylly where he used a new and advanced method about which he had also written a textbook. His circle was, accordingly, more academic and, because he was something of an amateur both in poetry and music, artistic. A poem of his that has survived shows more enthusiasm and sentiment than talent and suggests that there may have been something in Sartre's portrait of him as a histrionic figure, a striker of attitudes. But looked at another way, he was an impressive and memorable man, larger than life, flamboyant and highly entertaining.

Among the Alsatians the social life to which Schweitzer was introduced was not unrewarding, to judge by the one event we know of. This was the wedding of a M. Herrenschmidt, whom Schweitzer must have known passably well, for he was chosen as best man. One of the children of that marriage, Marcelle Herrenschmidt, grew up a friend of Schweitzer's, and it was remembered in the family that he danced all through that night, the first record we have of Schweitzer as the enthusiastic dancer, the man who in his eighties, when invited to condemn jive, said, "Any young person who does not dance is an idiot."

At the wedding also was a Mlle. Adèle Herrenschmidt, the bridegroom's sister—a woman of forty, a teacher, who later became principal of a girl's finishing school. Between these two, says Marcelle, a great mutual attraction grew up.

Paris is renowned for its tales of the sexual initiation of young men by older and more experienced women, and it might be tempting to make conjectures along these lines. The only reference to Adèle Herrenschmidt in Schweitzer's autobiography is one passing mention: "While in Paris I also saw a good deal of Mademoiselle Adèle Herrenschmidt, an Alsatian lady occupied in teaching."[3] This is as brief and unemotional as the sentence with which he relates his mother's death. Schweitzer was discreet to the point of total obfuscation about his emotional life, and by the standards of reticence in his public statements, this sentence might well be a declaration of passionate involvement.

Recently, however, a great deal more has been discovered about the inner Schweitzer, and what we have learned makes it unbelievable that the relationship was sexual. We do know that although younger women were much attracted to him, and he was certainly not unaware of their attractions, with older ones he had a different, and to him more important, relationship: they guided, encouraged and inspired him. With his Aunt Mathilde, in particular, he had an intense mutual devotion and spiritual understanding, and he never ceased to mourn and remember her. His friendship with Adèle Herrenschmidt was of a similar nature. In the years before the First World War, when he took his annual holiday, he would join Adèle and some of the family (young Marcelle included) and they would all journey to Grimmialp, a remote village in the depths of a little-known Swiss valley near Interlaken, where they spent ten days with the world shut out by the surrounding mountains. This friendship lasted until Adèle's death in the early 1920s, and it is clear that this intelligent and sophisticated lady was one of the two or three women to whom he looked for guidance and inspiration.

Hugely important in a different way was the fact that among Uncle Charles's circle of acquaintances was the organist of St. Sulpice and organ teacher at the Conservatoire, Charles-Marie Widor.

Twenty years earlier Widor, then only twenty-five, had succeeded César Franck at the Conservatoire. Now he was the most famous organist in France; and as a composer he was respected even in Germany where French music on the whole was regarded with some disdain. For Widor, as for Schweitzer, the organ was more than a mere musical instrument. It was a means of reaching out to the infinite and the eternal. "Organ playing," he told Schweitzer, "is the manifestation of a will filled with a vision of eternity."[4]

Such an attitude inevitably led him toward Bach; and through a variety of historical accidents Bach's original style of organ playing had been passed down with much less distortion through the French school than through his native German tradition. Widor, therefore, was an acknowledged king among the interpreters of Bach, and the pupils whom he handpicked exclusively from the students at the Conservatoire were the elite of their calling. Besides this, the organ at St. Sulpice, recently rebuilt and enlarged by the great organ builder, Cavaillé-Coll, was recognized as one of the most magnificent in the world.

So an introduction to Widor was something of an awe-inspiring occasion for any budding organist. Schweitzer confessed to a continuing shyness in company, which must have added to his nervousness, however confident he may have been in his abilities when he presented himself at St. Sulpice one October day with his aunt's letter of introduction in his pocket.

Thus they came face to face, the small elegant Parisian with his punctilious courtesy and his secure international reputation and the tall, abrupt country lad with the thick accent and the big hands, whom he was obliged, for politeness sake, to hear play the organ. He enquired what Schweitzer would like to play. "Bach, of course," said Schweitzer.[5]

The answer was not as obvious as it might now appear. In the first place, one of Widor's own compositions might have seemed the more diplomatic choice. But apart from considerations of tact, Bach was not the acknowledged emperor of the organ that he is today. His rediscovery, after years of neglect, was comparatively recent and not yet by any means complete. Schweitzer's "of course" might not everywhere have won agreement. But here, as it turned out, it was the right answer.

The playing was even better. So far had he come since, five years before, he had hated the sharps and double sharps and had made himself the thorn in Münch's flesh, so well had he made use of the panting efforts of his sisters at the bellows of the Günsbach organ, that Widor instantly broke his rule of only taking on pupils from the academy although, "I still don't understand why he did it,"[6] wrote Schweitzer at the age of seventy.

For both men the meeting was important—for Schweitzer vital. No encouragement could have given him greater confidence. Although there was little time during this stay to take advantage of Widor's offer, those few first lessons meant that he could embark on a fundamental improvement in his technique. *Plasticity* was the key word—a word that denotes the careful molding of a phrase so that each note contributes its proper value to the entire musical structure. Smoothness is essential, but it must be achieved without loss of definition. Every note must be distinct, yet integrally linked with its neighbors. Structure was an aspect of music of which Schweitzer had hitherto been too little aware.

So he was able to return to college with a great deal to think about, a great deal to work on. Behind him he had the approval of the great man and the knowledge that he could return to Paris at any time to take up instruction where he had left off.

No longer the reluctant scholar, Schweitzer seems to have settled instantly into college life. It was an exciting time to be an undergraduate, and Strasbourg was as good a place as any to appreciate it. In every way the university was young. Founded only twenty years before, after the Franco-Prussian War had left Strasbourg in German hands, it had been provided by an astute government with some of the brightest young professors in Germany. The rising intellectuals of Alsace were to be wooed into the liveliest streams of German thought. As a result, the university offered ideas that were largely free from the trammeling influences of tradition and the prejudices of aging professors. "A fresh breeze of youthfulness," wrote Schweitzer, "penetrated everywhere."[7] The prevailing mood among thinking people was set by the cheerful view of Hegel that, however the pendulum of events might swing to and fro, the hour hand of history was advancing steadily toward the perfecting of civilization. It followed that nothing but good could come of the rather startling thoughts being put forward by Nietzsche and by those who were opening up a new approach to the study of man, known as psychology. One might happily and without qualms explore any new road, however dark or devious, for the truth was great and would prevail, regardless of individual error. Indeed, it was only through individual error that it could prevail, for it was precisely the clash and conflict of views that would lead to further light.

The insights of psychology were being pounced on with glee and with varying degrees of appropriateness. All was grist to the mill of this new investigative technique. Some scholars, not content with demonstrating that the belief in Christianity, along with other religious faiths, was neurotic in origin, went on to claim that Jesus himself could be shown to have suffered from paranoia, schizophrenia, or at the very least hallucinations.

The excitement about Nietzsche went less deep, for the students found it hard to take his excitable mental antics seriously. But as his major books became known, they began to read him for the brilliance of his style and the entertainment value of his epigrams. (Schweitzer thought his *Beyond Good and Evil* one of the two most perfectly written books in the German language. The other was Luther's translation of the Bible.) The young people enjoyed Nietzsche's shrill attacks on every shibboleth, his witty, catty disrespect for every moral and intellectual cliché, his demolition of the idea that pomposity was the same as profundity, his mistrust of any philosophy that tried to cram all of life into a system, his intoxicating combination of common sense and hysteria. It never occurred to them that his demand for nobility would become an excuse for self-aggrandizement or that his accusation that the Christian Church encourages weakness could be used to justify the abandonment of pity. He appeared to them a stimulating court jester, little more.

He was, of course, much more. His books opened the door to the abuses that the Nazis committed in his name, but he himself really cannot be held responsible for them. His own ideas were truly noble—but unbalanced. He proclaimed the need for self-transcendence, and he was right. He demanded that life should be affirmed, not denied, and he was right. He was even right when he pointed out that meekness and humility are encouragements to political and religious oppression. But he was wrong in saying that humanity should, therefore, discard meekness and humility. A virtue that can be abused is not, therefore, a vice. The vice is the abuse. Nietzsche, reacting against one abuse, opened the door to another.

Schweitzer understood this. Like many great men, he valued what was great in others, and he responded powerfully to Nietzsche's demand for heroism and the vision of the superman, who could rise above his own weakness to his own full potential stature. It was of a piece with his own belief that reason was a better guide to behavior than convention, and it had echoes in the noble spiritual aim behind the grandiose romanticism of Wagner's operas, which moved Schweitzer so deeply.

But he was not at all happy with the implication that ordinary simple qualities were to be despised in the process of self-improvement. He was only puzzled that none of the theologians and religious philosophers seemed able to answer Nietzsche, to take his ideas apart and show where they were inadequate.

This conflict in his feelings about Nietzsche he later expressed strikingly in a letter to Hélène Bresslau: "I read Nietzsche: *Beyond Good and Evil*—this great and beautiful call to life, to acceptance of life; I hear miraculous strange harmonies that would be mine too if my duty would leave me time. . . . In Nietzsche was something of the spirit of Christ. . . . But he lacked action; for this reason his 'pride' paced inside a cage like a captured lion, instead of coming out of his cave to attack his prey, he tore himself to pieces in the end. But he was noble, this man. Had he lived twenty centuries earlier, he could have become St. Paul."[8]

At this time, however, these thoughts were no more than whiffs of apprehension. For the most part he went along with the general feeling among the young that any of the old beliefs that failed to survive the shovel of the psychologists and the gadfly attacks of Nietzsche were not worth keeping anyway. They embarked cheerfully on their voyages of discovery, and nobody at that time could be expected to foresee how many of those expeditions of the mind would end in wasteland or swamp, or whether some of the things being jettisoned to make the journey possible would later turn out to have been valuable and perhaps irreplaceable. One difference between Schweitzer and Sartre was simply that Schweitzer's intellectual life was given its direction at a time of hope, Sartre's at a time of disillusion.

Schweitzer's lodgings were at St. Thomas College, overlooking the river on the edge of the old town. Old Strasbourg, laced with little waterways, threaded with narrow streets, and revealing a rich variety of timbered houses at every turn, was exactly calculated to feed the romantic heart of the young student, particularly because it resembled the town of his holidays, Colmar.

Not far from St. Thomas College is St. William's Church, where Ernest Münch, brother of Eugène, who had taught Schweitzer at Mulhouse, was energetically building up an audience for concerts of Bach's music. A great revival of interest in Bach had been going on for the past forty years, some of which had taken the misguided form of trying to "modernize" the music by performing it as though it had been composed in that century. But Ernest Münch was of the other party—those who were beginning to seek out the composer's original manuscripts in search of clues to his precise intentions.

Schweitzer lost no time in introducing himself, and before long he and Münch were up half the night discussing points of interpretation, pacing to and fro, banging chairs on the floor to emphasize an argument, and falling asleep over the pages. Münch's three children woke sometimes in the night to hear the commotion: Fritz, who himself was studying the organ; Charles, who was to become the conductor of the Boston Symphony Orchestra—and Emma, to whom Albert's arrival was most fateful of all. She was to marry Albert's young brother, Paul. She lived to a ripe old age in Günsbach, and it is to her that we owe much of what we know of Schweitzer's student life in Strasbourg.

The academic subjects he had elected to study were theology and philosophy. He was still eagerly interested in biblical history although his approach was now somewhat more sophisticated than in the days when he puzzled over the poverty of the Holy Family. Again he was lucky; for anyone with such interests, to be in Strasbourg in the last decade of the nineteenth century was to be in exactly the right place at exactly the right time.

About a hundred years earlier a professor of Oriental languages named Hermann Samuel Reimarus had first dared to suggest that it was possible, even desirable, to apply historical judgments to the life of Jesus. Before that all had been a fog of piety, and nobody had thought fit to peer through the haze of omissions and contradictions in the gospels and try to distinguish a recognizable story of a recognizable man. The fact that the creeds, devised fifteen centuries before, had stated that Jesus was "true god and true man" had not encouraged the priests to take his manhood seriously and ask, "What really happened to him?" The life of a man who was also a god could evidently be a confusing series of jumbled incidents instead of a consecutive history. Besides, it gave so much more scope for that enjoyable form of self-expression known as interpretation.

Luther's attack on the mystifications of the Roman Catholic Church, and his insistence that the New Testament be published and read in a language that ordinary people could understand, had gradually borne fruit. It was in his country and his language, although not until two hundred and fifty years after his death, that Reimarus made the breakthrough with a series of witty, scathing, and impassioned attacks on the priestly nonsense that surrounded the stories in the Bible. It was a bold venture, so bold that his work was not published at all during his lifetime, and after his death only in fragments, and anonymously. But once published by a courageous admirer, it could be seen for what it was—the first approach of rationalism to the New Testament—and then there was no stopping the avalanche of violently polemical works that it set in motion. Theory followed theory, each demolishing the last, each fatally weak at some point or other, which became the target for the next attack. The orthodox continued to abide, as they always had done, by the principle laid down by Osiander in the sixteenth century, that if an event is recorded more than once in the Gospels, in different connections, it happened more than once and in different connections. So Jesus twice cleansed the temple and raised the daughter of Jairus from the dead several times over. But in the German theological schools the battle for the definitive historical life of Jesus raged on, sometimes going around in circles, sometimes making a little progress, but forever revealing fresh abysses of incomprehensibility in those four odd little books that the Christian Church regards as containing the ultimate revelation of God to man.

The battle was still in full swing when Schweitzer arrived at Strasbourg. In fact, his own lecturer, Heinrich Julius Holtzmann, had recently published a scholarly salvo on the origin of the Synoptic Gospels; the book had been very well received, and the views he put forward naturally formed the basis of his lectures on the subject.

On one or two points there was general agreement—that none of the Gospels had been written until at least forty years after Jesus' death and that the Gospel of St. John was the least historically reliable, having more of the character of a personal commentary on the significance of Jesus' sayings than of an accurate account of events. But the precise relationships connecting the other three Gospels, the so-called Synoptics, which at least presented a recognizable similarity of outline, was still heatedly discussed.

Holtzmann had made a powerful case for what was known as the Marcan hypothesis. He believed that Mark's Gospel, being the simplest and least elaborated, was therefore likely to be the earliest and most reliable. He was far from being alone in this belief, but the narrative in Mark has so many gaps that even when the decision has been taken to follow Mark in preference to the other Gospels, the scope for interpretation is still nearly limitless.

The method chosen for filling in the gaps naturally affected the kind of Jesus that emerged: his personality and his purposes could be read a dozen different ways according to the way in which the interpreter laid together the elements left by Mark. The temptation was to read the story according to one's own predispositions and to impose one's own outlook on that conveniently shadowy Jesus.

Holtzmann was a kindly and right-thinking European liberal. The Jesus he saw in Mark was an idealist, like himself, who set out to found an ideal Kingdom of God, succeeded for a while in carrying his hearers with him, but, encountering increasing opposition, began to see himself as a suffering Messiah and finally put his fate to the test when he went up to Jerusalem to his death. The skillful way he told the story, the effective use he made of detail from Mark's Gospel, was so much to the taste of the time that it carried enormous conviction. When Schweitzer sat to hear his lectures he was the acknowledged and loved master of his subject, the man who had cracked the riddle of the Gospels and had given to that eager, optimistic generation a Jesus they could understand and identify with. In its general lines, of course, the picture is still recognizable as the Jesus of innumerable European and North American pulpits today.

Schweitzer, eager to please such a distinguished tutor, studied hard. His first term, disrupted by the usual problems of settling down, was also bedeviled by the difficulty of learning Hebrew, not an easy language at the best of times and particularly difficult going for him, with his problem about languages. But once he had mastered its elements and passed the initial examination at the beginning of his second term, he was able to concentrate better on the Gospel problems.

In April he began his year's national service, but this did not seriously interfere with his studies. It was administered with a sane flexibility very unlike the strictness we have since learned to think of as the mark of German militarism. His captain arranged matters so that he could get away to attend the most important lectures, and he continued to grapple with both the Synoptic Gospels and the history of philosophy.

He enjoyed his military service. Physical activity was a pleasure to him, and he had grown into an exceedingly robust young man. His frame was filling out, and he was able to make do with very little sleep. So the extra work was no hardship; indeed, he now took delight in pitting himself against a challenge.

The discipline, too, was something he appreciated. Dr. Wehmann had taught him its value, but self-discipline still did not come easily and he relied more on enthusiasm and impulse. External discipline was a help. So for a while the military and the academic existences continued side by side.

In the autumn, however, the national servicemen had to go on maneuvers, and there was no more college life. Meanwhile, Schweitzer had applied for a scholarship, and to qualify for this he was due to take an examination at the beginning of the winter term. Although students doing their national service were required to take only one subject in this examination instead of three, Schweitzer was anxious to shine in that one, which was the Synoptic Gospels. So in his haversack, when he set off on maneuvers, was a copy of the Greek New Testament from which he wanted to study the text at first hand to see how much he could remember of Holtzmann's commentaries. While his fellow recruits dozed around him, he was deep in the Greek original of the Gospels.

And so it was that in St. Matthew he came upon a problem. At first it merely puzzled him, then startled him when he discovered that nobody else had taken much note of it, and finally proved the key to his whole interpretation, which, so far as I can ascertain, has never been successfully challenged. Nor has it been openly acknowledged because acknowledgment would be most uncomfortable for orthodox Christianity. It has simply been quietly absorbed as the unspoken basis for a great deal of modern thinking about Jesus.

What he noticed was as simple as his observation that forty days of rain is not enough to cover a mountain. His achievement in each case was simply to take quite practically something that hitherto had always been regarded as having only a "spiritual" meaning, and "spiritual" in this sense was all too often used to describe something that should not be brought into focus or looked at too closely, for it contradicted reason. In such circumstances it was thought best to allow the spiritual and the rational to pursue their separate courses. The invaluable word *mystery* was invoked a great deal more than it should have been, for although it may legitimately be used to describe a phenomenon that can be observed but not fully understood or expressed, it has all too often been used to mean "something that *you* cannot understand, but is an open book to me, thanks to my superior connections with the Godhead."

Schweitzer, as we have seen, expected reason to be able to embrace every side of human experience, the spiritual included. There might be occasions on which it was not enough; there might even be times when reason itself said that reason here could go no farther. But it must never be abandoned while it had anything to contribute. And—one more important point—reason to him was not a dry logic. The German word *denken* has a much wider, deeper meaning than the English *think*. It covers all the faculties of the concentrating, absorbed mind, which include intuition and experience besides logic.

By now, of course, Schweitzer had long known that much of the Bible had been written by storytellers whose purposes were more complex than the mere description of facts and historical events and who embellished their tales accordingly. Such embellishments were clearly at work in the stories of the Ark and the Flood. And passages in the Gospels themselves appeared to have received similar treatment. But he could see no reason why this should be true of the first half of chapter 10 of St. Matthew.

The chapter begins thus:

> And he called to him his twelve disciples and gave them authority over unclean spirits, to cast them out, and to heal every disease and every infirmity.
> [After naming the twelve it continues]:
> These twelve Jesus sent out, charging them, "Go nowhere among the Gentiles, and enter no town of the Samaritans, but go rather to the lost

sheep of the house of Israel. And preach as you go, saying, 'The kingdom of heaven is at hand.' Heal the sick, raise the dead, cleanse lepers, cast out demons. You received without paying, give without pay. Take no gold, nor silver, nor copper in your belts, no bag for your journey, nor two tunics, nor sandals, nor a staff; for the labourer deserves his food. And whatever town or village you enter, find out who is worthy in it, and stay with him until you depart. As you enter the house, salute it. And if the house is worthy, let your peace come upon it; but if it is not worthy, let your peace return to you. And if anyone will not receive you or listen to your words, shake off the dust from your feet as you leave that house or town. Truly I say to you, it shall be more tolerable on the day of judgment for the land of Sodom and Gomorrah than for that town.

Behold, I send you out as sheep in the midst of wolves; so be wise as serpents and innocent as doves. Beware of men, for they will deliver you up to councils, and flog you in their synagogues, and you will be dragged before governors and kings for my sake . . . and you will be hated by all for my name's sake. But he who endures to the end will be saved. When they persecute you in one town, flee to the next; for truly I say to you, you will not have gone through all the towns of Israel, before the Son of Man comes.[9]

According to the Marcan theory, so stoutly defended by Holtzmann, there was nothing in Matthew of any significance that was not to be found, at least in simple form, in Mark. But the counterpart in Mark: 6,[10] although it mentions a mission, says nothing at all about the nearness of the Kingdom of God. Was it, therefore, unimportant? A later fabrication? Certainly there was one very good reason for preferring to dismiss Matthew's addition, and that was that it seems to lead nowhere at all. The incident is incomplete. The twelve are sent off on an urgent missionary journey to warn the faithful of the imminence of the Kingdom of God and are themselves warned of all the dire experiences that they are to expect—hatred, persecution, beating—before the kingdom arrives. Most solemn of all, they are promised that even before their task is finished, the kingdom will be upon them.

The episode is never mentioned again. There is no record of the disciples actually setting out on their journey nor of any persecutions or disasters. Nor is there any explanation as to why these predictions were not fulfilled. Admittedly, the chronology is so sketchy that the order of events is far from obvious, but within a few verses the disciples are around Jesus as before, and there is no mention of the great mission and the nonappearance of the kingdom. The incident comes from nowhere and goes nowhere. It is untidy and pointless. Clearly, it would be easier to ignore it or explain it away. But this fails to answer the real question: if it is so inconclusive, if it shows Jesus making plans that get nowhere and prophecies that are never fulfilled, why on earth would anyone want to invent it? Why should the faithful, two generations later, preserve this evidence of the fallibility of their master if it were false? Its very improbability proved, to Schweitzer at least, that it was not a valueless addition to Mark but a genuine record from some other source.

One thing the passage does, then, is to cast doubt on the sufficiency of the Marcan hypothesis. But this is not its only or even its main importance. The really fundamental question concerned this Kingdom of God that Jesus foresaw, for which he was forever urging preparedness.

We are accustomed to think of the Kingdom of God in a spiritual sense as a condition of peace that the individual can by grace or by endeavor achieve in this life and that may one day, if enough people achieve it, come to reign over the whole world. Schweitzer's knowledge of and instinct for history told him that this was not the Jewish view. For the Jews the Kingdom of God had a very specific, very material meaning, handed down by the prophets. It meant deliverance from their oppressors and the appearance of the Messiah, the Son of Man—a chosen human being to whom God would give command over the nations. He would bring the old order of violence and evil to an end and inaugurate a totally new age, without tears or sickness or death, a world remade. But it would not be a separate world, in the sense of an afterlife or a spiritual realm distant from earth. It would be the same world, renewed and perfected. And all that was necessary for its coming was that enough of the Chosen People should believe in it and prepare themselves for it by a change of heart.

This, said Schweitzer, was what every Jew of that period understood by the Kingdom of God. And where, in all the Gospels, was there any indication that Jesus meant anything different? Where was there any suggestion that he wanted to "spiritualize" the phrase? If he had told the disciples that they were expecting the wrong kind of kingdom, that all Jewry had been misled by the prophets, and that they were going to have to find their own kingdom within the same old suffering world—in that case would there not have been great emphasis in the Gospels on this startling new interpretation?

If, then, Jesus believed in the same physical kingdom as his contemporaries and urgently predicted its arrival at a time when quite evidently it failed to arrive, what did this imply about the ministry of Jesus? Clearly, it meant for one thing that he was fallible, as other men are fallible. This would be no great shock to Schweitzer, brought up on the down-to-earth paintings of Grünewald and the whole Lutheran tradition of a human and comprehensible Christ. But, asked Schweitzer, what must it have meant to Jesus himself to expect the cataclysmic coming of the kingdom and to find himself wrong? What did that do to his own beliefs, and how did it affect his subsequent behavior? In short, Schweitzer saw that this passage, if authentic, must be a vital key to the progress of Jesus' thought and career and one that nobody before had noticed.

This is a bald, brief, and unsubtle outline of the argument, which, indeed, was not yet an argument when he first began to wonder about Matthew chapter 10 in the Alsatian hills. It was simply an uneasiness, a subject for private study. And it was complicated by a further problem in chapter 11.

This was a more abstruse and scholarly question, concerning the meaning of the Greek phrase "'ο ἐρχομενος." It is translated into English as "he who is to come." John the Baptist sent a message to Jesus asking if he was "he who is to come." Jesus in reply said neither yes or no. His messengers are simply to tell John that Jesus is performing miracles of healing and preaching the good news to the poor.[11]

We are so accustomed, said Schweitzer, to the notion that John the Baptist was the forerunner of the Messiah that we take it for granted that he himself was aware of it. But in those confused days, with fanatical religious and religio-political sects abounding, united only by their hatred of the occupying Romans, who was sure of what? John anointed Jesus in the Jordan but never named him the Messiah. Jesus, on the other hand, describes John to his disciples in the same chapter as "'ο ἐρχομενος."

Moreover, in the Jewish tradition it was not the Messiah but his forerunner who was expected to come performing miracles, signs, and wonders. The Messiah himself was expected to come in glory, not before but with the new kingdom. Could it be, wondered Schweitzer, that John, thinking of himself as simply a prophet, was not, in fact, asking Jesus "Are you the Messiah?" but "Are you the Messiah's forerunner?" For Jesus had given no word or sign at this stage that he regarded himself as the Messiah. Indeed, had he done so, the people would have been uncontrollable, and the authorities would quite certainly have been forced to act.

Further, Jesus' reply suggests, by its emphasis on the miracles, that he is sending a cryptic indication that he is, indeed, that forerunner although later he is speaking of John as "'ο ἐρχομενος." The puzzles multiply.

The point about these puzzles, whose pursuit took Schweitzer years of work and which are far too complex to be gone into in detail here, is that they both centered on the same question: the question of the Messiahship of Jesus. The Christian Church has worshiped him for two millennia as the Messiah, adapting the meanings of that word and the phrase "Son of God" to suit its own beliefs and requirements. But Jesus was not a Christian; he was a Jew. Did he know he was the Messiah? And when did the disciples know? And what did they expect? And what did he expect when he went to the Cross? Had he really, without a word, renounced the ancient Jewish hope of the age of peace—he who said he had come to fulfill the prophets?

Many of these questions had been the subject of attention from the writers who since Reimarus had been looking into the history of Jesus. Schweitzer was not exploring uncharted territory. Only he had a new starting point from which to set out and make his own map—the unfulfilled mission on which Jesus sent the twelve disciples as recorded in Matthew: 10.

It was evident that if his investigations were to lead in the direction he suspected, he would come into head-on collision with his respected tutor, Holtzmann, on Holtzmann's pet subject. He was not ready for this, nor did he want to hurt the kindly professor who examined him so gently on his summer's work when the scholarship time came. So in his replies he said nothing of his doubts about Holtzmann's theories.

Schweitzer was to get so enwrapped in his project that he did less work than he should have done on his set subjects. "No one can do anything in defiance of his inner nature," and his inner nature had not changed since the days when he rejected his schoolbooks for dreams of being a swineherd or a sailor. He still dreamed his own dreams, he still chose his own path, although now his deviations were less noticeable, because at least the path now led through the same countryside that he was officially supposed to be treading. And besides, he had grown craftier, or more tactful, at concealing what he was about. The impetuous quest for truth bequeathed him by Grandfather Schillinger was no less headlong. But he had learned that it was sometimes better pursued in quietness and solitude if it was to reach its goal.

He lived very simply. He could afford nothing else. Beer was cheaper than wine, so beer he drank, and very little of that. His room was without comforts—a workshop, not a place for relaxing or entertaining. He found relaxation in music, entertainment in the conversation of friends and the occasional visit to the theater, generally to hear Wagner. Wagner had "overwhelmed" him. Like everything else that overwhelmed him, Wagner was to receive passionate and lifelong attention. Schweitzer not only listened to the music; he studied the scores, analyzed the productions, and generally made himself acquainted with every aspect of Wagner's work. His first emotional reaction was confirmed. "His music is so great, so elemental," he wrote to Hermann Hagedorn in later years, "that it makes of Wagner the equal of Beethoven or Bach. Such assurance in composition, such grandiose musical architecture, such richness in his themes, such consummate knowledge of the natural resources of each instrument, such poetry, dramatic life, power of suggestion: it is unique, unfathomable in its greatness, a miracle of creative power! Forgive me, my enthusiasm is running away with me."[12]

The same thoroughness that he gave to Wagner meant that in his study of the organ he was not content with learning to play it; he discovered how organs were built, compared their virtues, and studied how effects were achieved. His work with Ernest Münch on Bach's manuscripts led to further research on organ construction; understanding the music was helped by knowing the kind of instrument it was written for.

He had plenty of opportunity for playing, sometimes in concert conditions. When Münch conducted his Bach concerts, his brother Eugène would come from Mulhouse to play the organ for him. Schweitzer would stand in for Eugène at rehearsals and in due course took over at the actual performance if for any reason Eugène was unable to come. Because the concerts at St. William's were acknowledged as among the leading expositions of the new, authentic style of playing Bach, Schweitzer found himself in the forefront of musical advance. The Strasbourg orchestra with which he played was noted for its excellence, and there are few spurs to achievement like the challenge of playing in the company of first-class players.

St. William's had not, of course, been designed for this kind of enterprise. The organ, a magnificent creation by the eighteenth-century organ builder Silbermann, was so positioned that it was impossible to accommodate anything but a small choir and orchestra near it. When a full choir and orchestra were needed, they had to be positioned behind the congregation, under the bell tower, where they could only be accompanied by a small organ with a single manual. When Münch gave a performance of the St. Matthew Passion with its two orchestras and two choirs, the audience had a very early and rather surprising experience of stereophonic sound, having one choir, one orchestra, and one organ behind them and another small choir and orchestra in front, under the great organ. Schweitzer played the latter although he had only been at Strasbourg a year. "In spite of the distance," he wrote, "we obtained a perfect ensemble. But the audience was still a bit disconcerted by listening to music coming from two opposite sides. For us the experience was very interesting."[13]

The only solution to the problem was to move the organ farther back, to make room for the choir and orchestra in front of it. This distressed Schweitzer, for the organ's tone was matchless and even visitors who knew the Cavaillé-Coll organs at St. Sulpice and Notre Dame were astonished at it. But the move had to be made. The problem was how to pay for it.

The finances at St. William's were already under some strain because of the concerts. Münch wanted his music to be available to all comers, and he made no charge for entry. A collection taken as the audiences left was never enough to cover expenses. This led to fierce disagreements with the church treasurer, Herr Frick, who shared the view of the church council that the upkeep of a choir for church services was all very well but that concerts were quite a different matter. Both Münch and Frick had violent tempers and disagreements grew heated. The choir's continued existence was threatened.

Surprisingly enough, it was to young Schweitzer that Münch turned as his mediator. Schweitzer's own temper was none too even; he never did master it entirely. But he was already learning to keep it in check when it was clear that a polite approach would pay dividends. He handled Frick with kid gloves; allowed him to let off a little steam, and then played on his pride in the fact that St. William's choir was regularly mentioned in the newspapers. The obdurate Frick softened under the Schweitzer treatment.

After a while it was decided that certain seats would have to be reserved at a mark each to ease the strain. But even after that, and even with donations from wealthy supporters, the cost of moving and renovating the organ was much too great, and long-drawn-out negotiations for assistance from the city authorities themselves were necessary before the plan could finally be put into effect.

The reviews for the first concert after the moving of the organ were unexpectedly poor, and Schweitzer now learned something about publicity. "As we thought it over we came to the conclusion that this might have been because the musical critics were all seated together, so that if one shook his head or puckered his eyebrows at some passage, none of his colleagues would risk giving a completely favourable report for fear of compromising himself. From that time on we saw to it that the critics did not sit together, and thus had their impartiality safeguarded; and this had a good result in their articles. The principle was once more proved that nothing must be left to chance."[14]

The significance of all this is that Schweitzer did not only concern himself with music at St. William's. He immediately plunged into the center of the whole enterprise, involving himself in all its aspects. He was part of an idealistic pioneering venture that constantly faced the quicksands of financial disaster and the thorns of other people's uncomprehending opposition. He learned that the idealist must be more practical than the realist because he stands alone—that successful idealism cannot live on pure enthusiasm but demands a willingness to muddy one's boots in incessant tedious detail and a certain cynical cunning in dealing with those who are in a position to be helpful or otherwise. It was a valuable foretaste of the difficulties of his own great adventure to come. It impressed on him unforgettably "that nothing must be left to chance."

The Münch family and their circle seem to have been his closest friends. If there were others, their names have been lost. If there were girlfriends, he kept them quiet, in accordance with his principle that a person is entitled to the privacy of his private life. We know from photographs that he was developing into a very attractive young man, and Emma Schweitzer, née Münch, remembered that there were plenty of girls who were fully aware of the fact. Who they were at this time she was not prepared to say, even if she remembered. But it is clear that she herself was not immune to his charm; she remembered that he was very fond of dancing and flirting and said that he was not merely romantic but sentimental. As we shall see, he had a partiality for "rendezvous," and when we add the comment that he himself made to a friend toward the end of his life, that he regretted the introduction of lipstick for one reason only— that it added unnecessary hazards to a stolen kiss—we have some clues as to Schweitzer's love life as a student.

Certainly, it seems that there was one fairly serious attachment, and for Schweitzer serious would mean serious: in nothing that he did was he superficial. But whether there was just one or several, much of his leisure time was spent in groups. Cycling parties jaunted into the country on weekends along the flat empty roads that led out of the city, through a couple of villages, and up into the hills. It is pleasant to think of early romances budding within these groups of energetic students pedaling forth with the young ladies of Strasbourg. In the evenings they would dance deep into the night in the country inns among the folds of the mountains; and Schweitzer achieved such a reputation as a dancer that he was regularly invited to private dances although his dancing was energetic rather than elegant, for he was not a physically graceful man; and he himself swore he was only invited when they needed someone who was prepared to play the piano all night long.

The occasional visit to a Wagner opera would provide a welcome romantic evening, ardent souls carried away on a flood of melody. But we are fairly safe in assuming that whatever encounters there were went little further than walks in the country, kisses, and romantic handholding. Schweitzer's upbringing, although not strict, had been entirely conventional in sexual matters, and he showed no signs of rebelling against it. Besides, his many other interests would scarcely have given him the time for the prolonged assault necessary to overcome the scruples of the average young lady from the respectable middle classes of the day.

He joined a student association attached to St. Thomas, which ran a kind of Robin Hood service, begging twice a year from the rich and distributing weekly to the poor. The conditions of the poor were nothing new to him. But he really dreaded the begging expeditions, which aggravated his natural shyness and sometimes made him extremely clumsy. He learned that "begging with tact and restraint is better appreciated than any sort of stand-and-deliver approach."[15] One can imagine the sort of reactions he must have aroused before this lesson sank in when he stood, large and embarrassed, on the doorstep of the big house, aggressively explaining the moral obligation of some wealthy merchant to hand over a part of his ill-gotten gains.

The battle with shyness continued, and he was making progress. But it required constant effort. He would take trouble to speak to any and everybody, in the street in Günsbach, on the train, in cafés and shops, wherever life took him. There were four classes on the trains, and he would always travel fourth class. It was an economy, true, but it was also where he met people he wanted to meet—"the real people," he called them—swineherds and sailors, for example, no longer to argue with them or persuade them to pursue the truth, simply to get to know and understand them. He made it his business to make everybody's business his own—to share their interests and concerns, their work, their jokes and stories. From bakers he learned the secret of making dough, from carpenters the tricks of cabinet making. He grew in his understanding of life, this theologian, this academic, from the point of view of those who lived it; from the underside, where things look very different from the perspective of the theorist; more varied, more interesting and funnier, as well as truer.

He still enjoyed stories above all, including those rude and ribald stories that delighted the heart of Uncle Charles. The semiliterate passengers of the fourth class were full of them. Schweitzer would sit quietly in his corner, scribbling notes and ideas on his cuff and listening to the conversation, until the opportunity came to join in. Quickly building up a repertoire of stories of his own, he was not an unwelcome companion. The faultless memory that was to win the respect of biblical scholars was at work storing up excellent little *blagues*—partly for sheer entertainment, partly for what they said about human nature.

These things made Schweitzer much loved by those who came to know him, the villagers of Günsbach, the shopkeepers near St. Thomas in Strasbourg. The few who still remember him speak of his cheerfulness and the way he would stop for a chat and a joke with everyone. Nor was it only talk. One day in the street he met an old lady who turned out to have no mattress. Schweitzer went to his room, fetched the mattress off his own bed, and carried it on his back to her house.

He was nineteen and a half when he first stumbled upon the mystery of Matthew 10 and decided to treat it as a mystery in the detective rather than the supernatural sense. In the eighteen months that followed he was busier than he had ever been as he pursued all the different interests that absorbed him. He would work late into the night, his head wreathed in clouds of smoke—he was deeply devoted to his pipe—scribbling illegibly in his haste. His room was strewn with books, musical scores, and sheaves of notes, more or less neatly arranged from a practical point of view, so that he could lay his hand quickly on what he wanted, but the despair of anybody who tried to sweep or dust. Both here and at home, Adèle complained, he was untidy, impractical in day-to-day affairs, and impatient of anyone who tried to alter him. Work was all-important, all-absorbing, both in term-time and vacations. He hated to be dragged away. Adèle and the youngest sister, Margrete, were at school at the Lutheran convent of the Good Shepherd in old Strasbourg, not far from St. Thomas, and Adèle recalled how reluctantly her brother came to take them out on Sundays—how ill at ease he sat in the parlor waiting for them, shy at the presence of so many girls and impatient to get his duty over with.

Chronically behind schedule, he would pelt from appointment to appointment on his bicycle, his energy responding to the unending pressure, his interest kept at high pitch by the constant change of subject. At the same time he was learning that to do all these different things he had to concentrate totally and exclusively on each in its turn.

He was happy. This was the life that his ancestry and his childhood had prepared him for, now raised to a level his forebears had never approached. All things came together for his good, and he knew it and reveled in it. But that was not the whole story. In this complex young man were many strands of character, each counterpointing the other. As an embryo exhibits at different times the different characteristics of its species' history, so the boy Albert Schweitzer had been through phases in which first one side of his nature took control, then another: the dreamer, the romantic introvert, with flashes of passion and insight, was followed by the determined rationalist forced by his own temperament to learn control; the shy boy nervous of others' laughter became the bold conversationalist and raconteur; the inattentive scholar developed immense powers of concentration. But the earlier Schweitzer was never replaced by the later. The two existed side by side, thread behind thread. And now in his twentieth and twenty-first year, the threads were weaving themselves into a complex but complete personality in which each aspect settled into a harmonious whole. The whole was not without tension; that would not have been possible with so many extremes balanced at the center point. But the tension was always controlled and guided toward creation; never released to destruction.

So in the most active and happy eighteen months of his life so far other forces were at work below the busy surface. The energy and pace of his daily life is easy to envisage. But there was another side. A night's study is a long, lonely affair. Two o'clock in the morning is an awesome time, especially for a romantic youth. And a long organ practice alone in a darkened church with an instrument that speaks of sublimity and power is another experience fraught with profound feeling. These two kinds of vigil were a regular element of this outwardly hectic life; and both were centered on one image—the figure of Jesus.

Bach's sonatas address Jesus intimately, confidently, as friend and master. They speak of a whole life interwoven with Jesus. Studying Bach, Schweitzer could not avoid being aware of the deep personal religion that gave meaning to the music. Alongside that, his own intense search through the Gospels was a search for the same man, the man with whom Bach shared his happiness and his agony, his hopes and fears. Schweitzer was saturating himself with Jesus—not as a scholar analyzing a remote historical personage but as a man searching for the mind and motives of a man. All his capacity for emotional intuition, his ability to feel with other creatures besides his intellectual and historical skill were bent on understanding Jesus.

The two quests—the quest for a knowledge of his fellow man and the quest for a knowledge of Jesus—were not wholly separate, although they occurred at different levels. The love of God and the love of one's neighbor—the two great commandments—are not so alien to one another. In humanity Schweitzer found the raw material of Jesus, in Jesus the completion of humanity. And along with these studies—linked with them—there grew that sense of debt that had begun to make itself felt earlier; the happier he grew, the more the feeling oppressed him that he owed something to somebody in return. Other children's homes were so much less happy than his had been. Other students lacked his health and energy or simply a godfather who would board them free of charge.

The German word for debt is the same as the word for guilt. Protestantism talks all too much about guilt and has been responsible for unjustifiable guilt complexes and puritanical self-abasement of a most unhealthy kind. But translated into "debt" the word loses a lot of its venom because debt is repayable. What in some men might have become a load of intolerable, irrational guilt became in Schweitzer simply a need to repay.

In a peasant society, never very far from hardship, debt is important. What is borrowed is not easily afforded; simple justice demands its return at the first moment possible. And Schweitzer's family had to count the pennies. At his paternal grandfather's house in Pfaffenhofen he had been taught, when he ate an apple, to keep the core for the pigs and the stalk for the fire. Schweitzer understood debt. These first years at the university, the years when he was learning to master all the elements of his nature and harness them to his purpose; when he first began to feel the full potential of his mind and spirit; when through the Gospels and through Bach he spent so many hours face to face with the figure of Jesus—these were the years when that little cloud, the size of a man's hand, grew to cover the whole sky. The greater his satisfaction, the greater his debt. The cloud was becoming more than he could bear.

One stiflingly hot summer month, a certain Professor Lucius held a course of lectures on the history of missions. The heat and the unpopularity of the subject reduced his audience to half a dozen or so. One of these was Schweitzer, who as a boy had enjoyed his father's afternoon mission services and the letters that missionaries of the Paris Mission Society had sent from distant lands.

Lucius's theme was to do with debt. He spoke of the damage that white colonists had done in black countries and the way in which missionaries could do a little to make up for these depredations.

Ten years later Schweitzer recalled:

> It was there that I was struck for the first time by this idea of expiation. It had an extraordinary effect on me. Till then, in Dogmatics and New Testament commentaries, this word "expiation" had seemed heavy to handle—it had to struggle to explain why Jesus died for the world's sins. Everything we had hitherto been told was lifeless and petrified, and we noticed in the way the lecturers spoke of it that they seemed ill at ease and were none too clear about it themselves. But now, launched as an appeal to work under the banner of Jesus, this word took on life, it was a cry, a shock, something which sank into you and took hold of you—and as that day ended I understood Christianity better, and I knew why missionary work was needed.[16]

The word worked within him, reinforcing all that he already felt. And in the Whitsun holidays of 1896, a few months after his twenty-first birthday, he woke one morning of brilliant sunshine with the conviction that the debt must be repaid, the cloud must be lifted—or persuaded to fall in fertile rain. What was to be done?

In his childhood we have seen how experience was followed by decision, decision by action. He had not changed. "Proceeding to think the matter out at once with calm deliberation, while the birds were singing outside, I settled with myself before I got up, that I would consider myself justified in living till I was thirty for science and art, in order to devote myself from that time forward to the direct service of humanity. Many a time already had I tried to settle what meaning lay hidden for me in the saying of Jesus 'Whosoever would save his life shall lose it, and whosoever shall lose his life for My sake and the Gospel's shall save it!' Now the answer was found. In addition to the outward, I now had inward happiness."[17]

What the direct service was to be he had yet no idea. He had nine years to look into that. But the decision had been taken—a decision that was in no way startling, for it had been prepared for by everything he was and had been. When he finally put it into effect, it was to appear to observers as though a whole lifetime had been wrenched violently off-course in unnecessary self-denial. From within it seemed no more than a natural development—one that was so much part of the man that the real self-denial would have been to refuse it, because that would have deprived him of inward happiness.

4

—

Paris

1896–1899

OUTWARDLY, EVERYTHING WENT ON AS BEFORE. The time bomb that Schweitzer had set for 1905 ticked imperceptibly. Not one of his family or his friends was consulted. Not one was even informed. Nothing could better illustrate how the separate layers of this complex character lay one beneath another than the way he kept this vital secret all the time that he was studying to be easy and outgoing in company. This was no longer compulsive shyness but a matter of controlled reason and the will.

Not that he ceased to be regularly "overwhelmed" by one experience or another—the molten lava of emotion still seethed beneath the hardening crags of character. Knowing of his passion for Wagner, kind Parisian friends gave him tickets for a production of Wagner's entire *Ring of the Nibelungs* at Bayreuth—the first time the whole cycle had been performed since Wagner had first presented it there himself twenty years before at the opening of his dream opera house. Now, after his death, that enormous operatic event was being faithfully repeated under the direction of his widow Cosima; not with a new production, for who could ever improve on the master himself? So far as was possible everything was identical with the original performance.

The occasion was not to be missed. The tetralogy was the biggest theatrical event of the century. The opera-house-cum-temple in which it was performed was equally unique, born of an unlikely union between an opinionated genius of a composer and an enthusiastic young emperor, Ludwig II. Wagner, turning upside down every accepted canon of operatic presentation, aimed at a total experience—musical, theatrical, practical, religious—to which nothing less than a complete new building would do justice. In fact, Wagner went some way toward personifying for young

Europeans the superman that Nietzsche had demanded. Rising above bourgeois considerations of financial solvency and marital morality—Cosima was another man's wife when she became his mistress—he inhabited a higher sphere, he achieved things that others barely dreamed of. To see his masterpiece at Bayreuth was to share in the consummation of the century.

Schweitzer, as we have seen, had his share of admiration for the Nietzschean ideal, and he responded to the event. "The very simplicity of it made it so marvellously effective," he wrote, and contrasted this production with others that he saw later, which had "all sorts of stage effects claiming attention alongside the music, as though it were a film show."[1]

Wagner had only himself to blame if recent producers have over elaborated the settings, for his stage directions are far from simple, demanding, for example, an underwater scene with a mermaid swimming gently in the middle distance. But it would appear that for such a scene he himself was content with a huge dominating painted backdrop and a few papier-mâché boulders—a setting that casts an awe-inspiring mood over the whole action—and eschewed the mechanical tricks, which, as Schweitzer noted, are admired for themselves rather than for their contribution to the performance.

To pay for his train ticket Schweitzer had to make do with only one meal a day but turned this to advantage by taking lunch each day with members of the orchestra and listening to their views on the imposing Cosima, views that were respectful but by no means unanimous about the advantage of having "a woman of such an imperious will as Madame Cosima directing the performances."[2]

In fact, the disadvantage, as he came to see himself later, lay not in the will but in the fact that it was directed toward a sterile repetition rather than a recreation, an act of personal homage rather than of artistic understanding. At the time, however, he was vastly impressed by the dominating spirit of Wagner that brooded over the production. Schweitzer's character showed a marked degree of hero worship; but the heroes he chose were of the highest caliber.

On his way back to Strasbourg he broke his journey to sample the quality of a new organ in the Liederhalle at Stuttgart. It had been much publicized for the technical innovations that had been built into it, as into many new organs in Germany about that time—devices in the main made possible by the application of electricity to the bellows and to the linkages between key and pipe and between different sections of the organ. This sudden access to new power opened up possibilities of swift fingering that before had been limited by the relatively cumbersome series of wooden push-rods and pivots that connected the finger to the pipe valve—the principal one of which was known as a "tracker." In these new German organs the tracker was on the way out. At the same time the output of the organ could be increased and the control of volume could be much simplified by bringing into action a revolving drum that, at one touch of hand or foot, activated an overall crescendo or diminuendo. Previously, a complicated series of movements had been necessary to build up the volume by bringing in the different voices one by one. Finally, having liberated the organist from these chores, the designer felt able to add a multiplicity of new hand stops for the variation of tone. Each new organ had a different layout, according to the designer's perception of how to exploit these innovations.

Schweitzer was already suspicious, so he claimed, that in seeking new technical efficiency the designer had lost sight of more important factors. But his suspicions had not prepared him for the revelation that Stuttgart afforded him. He was to call it his "Damascus," after the Damascus road on which St. Paul in a blinding flash saw the error of his ways.

The parallel is not very good, for it was the error of others' ways, not his own, that was revealed to Schweitzer at Stuttgart. His work with Widor at St. Sulpice had given him an excellent point of comparison. And when a good local organist played him a Bach fugue on the Stuttgart organ, he found it quite impossible to follow the separate lines of the music, on which the whole effect of contrapuntal music depends. It was "a chaos of sounds."[3] Not only this, but the tone, too, was harsh and dry.

His suspicions more than confirmed, he made it his business during the following years to seek out and play all kinds of organs wherever he went, in substantiation of his case. The quest did nothing for his popularity in the German musical world, for organists there were intoxicated with the novelty of their toys and were not at all pleased to be told that the despised and old-fashioned French were still doing these things better. But steadily, over the next nine years, Schweitzer went on building up his evidence.

In Strasbourg his life continued as the sort of peaceful rush that many students know: too many things to do, not enough time, but never any real pressure, never any anxiety. The vacations at Günsbach were an unfailing refreshment. Nothing much changed there, except that Louise had married a Mr. Ehretsmann and gone to live in Colmar. She and her husband, however, and the children as they arrived, came regularly to the vicarage at weekends and holidays. And in the new, dry vicarage with its big flower-filled garden, and its cellar filled with chalk-marked casks of home-grown wine, the old pastor's health held up and constantly improved. The few small blemishes there had been on the family's happiness, poverty and ill health, seemed to have been permanently removed.

When the academic year began in the autumn of 1897, a fresh impetus was given to Schweitzer's New Testament studies when the subject was set for the government test, a preliminary examination to be held the following May. Students were to write a thesis, *"The Last Supper— Schleiermacher's View Compared with the New Testament Conception and the Confessions of Faith of the Reformers."* Schweitzer studied Schleiermacher on the Last Supper and in due course passed the examination. But a thought that Schleiermacher dealt with in passing and then never pursued to a conclusion led Schweitzer down a new track in his investigations into Jesus' sayings about the Kingdom of God.

Certain words reported as spoken by Jesus over the broken bread and the wine at that Last Supper form the very heart of the eucharist, mass or communion service, which is, in turn, the heart of Christian worship. But not all the words that the priest says in that solemn consecration are recorded in Mark and Matthew, the early Gospels. According to those Gospels, Jesus did say, of the bread, "Take, eat; this is my body." He did not say, . . . "which is given for you. Do this in remembrance of me." Of the wine he said, "Drink of it, all of you. For this is my blood of the covenant, which is poured out for many for the forgiveness of sins." He did not say, "Do this, as often as you shall drink it, in remembrance of me."[4]

According to the most authentic documents, then, Jesus never gave his disciples any instruction to repeat the supper. Yet had he done so, how could any account have omitted anything so awesomely memorable—especially when the early Christians did, in fact, repeat the meal? No—if Mark and Matthew (and even some versions of Luke) say nothing of such instructions, it is more than reasonable to assume that Jesus never gave them. They were inserted by the early Christians to account for and justify their continuance of the sacred meal.

There are other words, however, which are recorded in all three Gospels, but which the Christian ritual omits. They are similar in all the Synoptic Gospels. In Mark they read: "Truly, I say to you, I shall not drink again of the fruit of the vine until that day when I drink it new in the Kingdom of God."[5] Here again, at this moment of ultimate solemnity, is the insistence on the coming kingdom, which, Schweitzer believed, had one meaning for Jesus' Jewish hearers and one only.

What then was the true significance of the meal? If Schweitzer was right in thinking that Jesus genuinely believed in a kingdom whose arrival was only days away, would this not account for Jesus' words as the Gospels report them? No repetition would be necessary because this would be not merely Jesus' last supper but the last supper of any of them in the old order, a preparation, in Jesus' eyes, for the First Supper of the new kingdom. Was it as such that the early Christians celebrated it freshly each week, as they still waited for their master's reappearance and arrival of the Apocalypse? And was it because the kingdom never came that they were forced to change the meal's significance to one of remembrance and to insert the words that explained this?

Schweitzer was not ready to make his conclusions public. As with the scholarship examination three and a half years earlier, he confined himself at the government test to what he was asked and kept his own investigations to himself. He still needed to do a great deal of work, for example, on the Old Testament prophecies and the influence and meaning they had for the Jews of Jesus' time, the people who heard him speak.

Schweitzer did well enough in the test for Holtzmann to propose him for another scholarship worth twelve hundred marks a year for six years; not a princely sum—barely enough to live on—but it obliged the holder to take the degree of licentiate in theology within those six years. Applying for this, Schweitzer was committing himself to academic life.

He won the scholarship. Already he was evidently a prize student, the protégé and pet of poor Holtzmann, who still knew nothing of the theological rebellion hatching in the young man's bosom. Ironically enough, that very licentiate in theology for which Holtzmann was grooming him was to be the occasion for Schweitzer's declaration of independence.

Meantime, however, Schweitzer switched for the moment to philosophy. He had two excellent tutors in the subject, one of whom specialized in ancient Greek philosophy, the other, Theobald Ziegler, an ex-theologian and an expert in ethics and the philosophy of religion. The philosophers who interested Schweitzer most at that time were the speculative school of the seventeenth and eighteenth centuries, on the one hand, and, on the other, the "modern" school, who had finally declared the speculatives bankrupt and had begun to look for the secret of life in their own responses to it, in emotion and will rather than abstract thought. Of these Schopenhauer and Nietzsche were the outstanding examples. But the eighteenth century was where Schweitzer really felt intellectually at home. He liked the eagerness for truth and justice that he found in the philosophers of that period, and he wanted to know why it had now dwindled into disillusion and skepticism.

One great man of the eighteenth century, however, he found difficult to understand. His tutors seemed enthusiastic about Goethe, but their enthusiasm puzzled Schweitzer. At a time when thinker after thinker was striving to grasp the secrets of the whole of Creation and weld them into a gigantic pattern of thought, Goethe was humbly studying natural science. Instead of speculating, he was observing. Instead of trying to master nature, he made himself its servant. He appeared totally unmoved by the whole exhilarating impulse of his age, and Schweitzer, deeply admiring that age, dismissed Goethe as a man out of step. One of the remarkable things about Schweitzer was how swiftly his intuition normally seized upon what was important to him and how very rarely he changed his mind. Further experience nearly always confirmed rather than contradicted his first impressions. Goethe was to be the exception that proved this rule.

In the brilliant young man who was combining theology and philosophy Ziegler saw a student after his own heart and before long suggested a subject for study that suited them both well. Huddled together against the rain one day under Ziegler's umbrella they decided that Schweitzer should work at a dissertation on the religious philosophy of Kant for his philosophy degree.

Of all the great logic-chopping philosophers of the German speculative school, Kant was the one most calculated to appeal to Schweitzer—precisely because he had views on ethics that transcended logic.

This kind of philosophy means little to anyone but an expert in the field. It needs a special vocabulary for its own purposes; and it deals in abstractions, using them as counters for an elaborate game whose rules and results are obscure and, to the uninitiated, quite lacking in practical outcome.

For our purpose it is enough to note how Schweitzer fared in this field, so artificial compared with his other interests; and what effect it had on him. For out of every new mental encounter he took something that he needed, leaving the rest behind. He picked out the kernel and threw away the husk—never making the mistake of assuming that there was no kernel just because the husk was dry.

In the autumn of his twenty-third year, 1898, he went to Paris to work at the Sorbonne. The library there was more comprehensive, and the instruction should have been better than at Strasbourg. Besides, it was an opportunity to see more of Widor.

For this period of intensive study he decided not to stay with Uncle Auguste. The select and spacious northern suburb where Auguste lived in the Boulevard Malesherbes was three or four miles from the university and St. Sulpice, which lie within half a mile of each other in the center of the city, near the Luxembourg Gardens. The tram service was of little use, and for Schweitzer, accustomed to working any or all hours of the twenty-four, the restrictions imposed by the obligations of hospitality and the consideration owed to a family home would have made his kind of concentration impossible. So he took a small room in the rue de Sorbonne and set to work.

It quickly became apparent that however superior Paris might be in the matter of organs, the planning of its university left much to be desired.

The lectures at the Sorbonne were excellent, but the organization of the syllabus made it impossible for students to get full value from them. At Strasbourg, Schweitzer had been used to courses of several lectures that comprehensively explored their subject from many angles. Here the lectures were confined to special subjects, unrelated to their background. Schweitzer did not attend many lectures.

The National Library was equally disappointing. The system of obtaining books for the Reading Room was so cumbersome that the impatient Schweitzer decided that he had no time for it; he would ignore all that had been written about Kant and concentrate instead on what had been written *by* Kant. The instinct was typical—disregard the rubble, go for the foundations.

One thing that must be said about his *Sketch of a Philosophy of Religion in Kant's "Critique of Pure Reason"* is that he seems when it suited him to have been able to adopt the abstract philosophical style and to match the subject of his study in obscurity. It never happened in any of his other writings, which are limpidly clear and unpretentious. But here he was capable of whole pages of this kind of thing: "Thus, in the inter-relationship of transcendental hypotheses with the assumptions of reason for practical purposes, there lies, at the same time, the relation of critical idealism to the philosophy of religion which is based on it."[6] To be fair we have to remember, apart from the difficulty of translation, that this, unlike his other writings, was intended for the eyes of professional philosophers only. When he wanted his philosophy to reach a wider public, his style was very different.

There are several good reasons why Schweitzer was interested in Kant and why we should be interested in his interest. Kant was the most outstanding thinker of the eighteenth century, a child of the Enlightenment—that period when reason began to dispel superstition, at least among thinking men; when philosophers began to attack the intolerance of the Christian Church and question its dogmas; when a whole series of thinkers set about reexamining the most basic presuppositions about human nature, the purpose of society, and man's place in the universe. They refused to accept the priests' assertion that God was this or that, even that God existed; they wanted proofs of their own, logical and unanswerable. They wanted to know what morality meant, whether good behavior was desirable as an end in itself or as a means to happiness or simply as a social necessity to keep the community stable. They even questioned the nature of knowledge itself—whether it came entirely from experience, or whether there were things that the mind could know or could discover by a process of pure logic quite independent of experience. In France, Germany, and England philosophers rang the changes on these themes, and their ideas began to have an effect outside their academic circles. Whole nations felt the impact, for these philosophers concerned themselves with the happiness of mankind in general, not merely of the chosen few; and happiness here and now, not only in the afterlife. They concerned themselves with the meaning of freedom, the search for justice, and the proper conduct of authority. Kings and ministers listened to them. Voltaire, who chastised the French government mercilessly at any sign of persecution or injustice, was for a few months the honored intimate of Frederick the Great; had he lived two years longer he would have seen torture abolished in France as a result of the new humanitarian wave of thought. The effects were not enormous, perhaps, and in the perspective of the whole century it could be argued that harm resulted besides good. Both the violence and the splendors of the French Revolution can be laid at the door of a belief in the rights of the common man. But for Schweitzer, as for grandfather Schillinger, the eighteenth century was a time when philosophers had both hearts and heads in the right place, when reason was both humane and effective, and when Europe at least took a few hopeful steps toward universal justice.

Among the philosophers of the Enlightenment, Kant had a special place. As a young man he followed his teachers in believing that the existence of God and the basic principles of ethical behavior could be known and proved without either divine revelation or the experience of the senses. He himself was not a man of much experience of the world: his whole life was dominated by academic study; and at the age of thirty-eight he was still engaged in the rarefied pastime of proving the existence of God by purely intellectual propositions.

But he was coming under the influence of English and Scottish philosophers who, as Britons are apt to do, had a more practical, empirical approach; that is, they insisted that knowledge and understanding can come only from experience, and that metaphysics, which claims that it is possible to know through intellectual reasoning alone, is (in Hume's phrase) "nothing but sophistry and illusion."

Hume's attack on metaphysics woke Kant, so he said, from his "dogmatic slumbers," and he embarked on his first great work, A Critique of Pure Reason. "Our age," he wrote, "is essentially an age of criticism, to which everything has to submit." Now he decided to turn reason onto reason itself to discover its scope and limitations.

It would be irrelevant to this book to attempt a full account of Kant's "critical idealism"—to delve into the definitions and redefinitions, the qualifications and distinctions that go to make up the argument. Suffice it to say that, once convinced of the inadequacy of pure reason but concluding that sense experience was also insufficient to account for all human knowledge and behavior, he introduced a new idea that fell between the two and shared, so he felt, the advantages of both. This was practical reason. *The Critique of Pure Reason* was supplemented by the *Critique of Practical Reason* in which Kant concluded that certain propositions, which could never be proved by pure reason, must, nevertheless, be assumed for practical purposes by ordinary men if they were to give their lives any meaning at all. These he reduced to three ultimate "postulates": God, freedom, and immortality, belief in which he showed to be necessary to human beings as guarantees of the value of ethical conduct. There was no point in people trying to behave well unless they could depend on these three postulates to support their efforts: God, as the ultimate giver of the moral law; freedom, without which one could not choose whether or not to obey it; and immortality, as the end toward which the individual, obviously unable to achieve complete goodness in this life, could look for an opportunity to complete his self-perfection.

So one point at which Kant's thought suited Schweitzer was in his desire, without losing the guidance of reason, to find value in the ordinary man's experience and way of thinking. An even stronger link lay in the conviction that for Kant was more fundamental than anything else— the conviction that an understanding of the moral law, a respect for right conduct, was the basic, unalterable fact of human consciousness. This moral sense, he believed, was not the product of teaching or experience. It was inborn. Nor was it conditional on circumstances. It was categorical. He sought by long analysis to define this law, rejecting all definitions that were partial or provisional or questionable.

In the end he defined this universal obligation thus: "Act only on a basis which you can will to become universal law." This was his "categorical imperative": the one unquestionable starting point for all ethics, and all religion. Even God was only to be understood as the founder and guarantor of this law.

This emphasis on a basic principle of ethics impressed Schweitzer more than anything else about Kant. In fact, the main part of Schweitzer's thesis is devoted to showing that Kant's concept of the moral law grew deeper and deeper and in the end destroyed the arguments put forward in the *Critique of Practical Reason*; that his search for a rational design in the universe came into conflict with the search for ultimate morality; and it was reason that, almost unnoticed, got left behind as he was driven back, against his own logic, to a conviction that somewhere in man is a need for righteousness and right action that has nothing to do with the hope of immortality or any other reward or guarantee. This, said Schweitzer, was the real greatness of Kant, that despite his dry academic approach, his moral intuition was so powerful that it shattered his elaborate intellectual structure.

And, as ever with Schweitzer, his tough reasoning was reinforced by a deep emotional response. To Hélène Bresslau he wrote, "Whenever I take this book [*The Critique of Practical Reason*] into my hands, it opens by itself to this section; here I find my innermost thoughts." He quotes two paragraphs, beginning "Duty! Thou sublime and great name that dost embrace nothing insinuating but requirest submission." "Sometimes," he writes, "I feel as if I were the first who really, deeply, understands him— 'the disciple who loved his master.' No, he is not a pedant; only on the surface. I love him as my Christmas friend, as my great educator, as my comforter."[7]

This devotion does not save poor Kant from Schweitzer's ruthless analysis of his destructive contradictions and inconsistencies, which he claims to be the first to have noticed. In the summary that concludes his thesis he boldly states, "every type of reflection has been investigated by itself, and only after it was thoroughly understood compared with the reflections in other writings and brought into relationship with them." As a result, he claims to have demonstrated that "a philosophy of religion tailored and oriented to the pre-suppositions of critical idealism is a product which is disintegrating."[8]

Kant, like other speculative philosophers, attempted to erect a huge and indestructible edifice of thought on basic presuppositions that simply could not stand the weight of the structure. It is the classic blindness of academics; they become so involved in their mental gymnastics as the scaffolding grows higher and higher that they never notice how the whole thing is tilting where the joints are weak, so a few taps from a critical hammer at the right point can bring it all crashing to the ground. The ruin can be interesting and instructive but is not for living in. As Winston Churchill is reported to have said, "The only trouble with great thinkers is that they generally think wrong." It would take a professional philosopher to say whether Schweitzer's long and detailed thesis really justified his claim to have found the flaws in Kant. But his tutor Ziegler said afterward, "A new philosophical genius is arising in our midst."

One other point about the Kant thesis is of great importance in showing the development of Schweitzer's mind at this time. One of Kant's works with which he deals is *The Critique of Aesthetic Judgment* in which Kant considers the relationship between nature and art "although," as Schweitzer dryly observes, "he was without native artistic ability or any close contact with the performing arts."[9] Schweitzer's analysis of the argument is of no general interest until the moment when he unexpectedly takes off at a tangent, more or less deserting Kant, and develops his own account of artistic theory. This then extends into a statement about genius—first about artistic genius and, then, by further development, about religious and moral genius. There are those who claim that Schweitzer himself was certainly a moral genius, probably a religious one, and perhaps a musical one, so his own views on the subject at the age of twenty-four are worth some attention.

He begins by stating that any object is dependent on certain ideas in the viewer before it can become art. "Thus a heap of rubble on a mountain becomes art because around it hovers the romantic spell of the Middle Ages. If we were to discover that it was contemporary, we would fail to find in it any aesthetic unity; it would remain . . . a picture of loathsome disorder. A couple of broken columns and a bit of blue sky, and the landscape becomes art if the viewer's memory, and his insight into the splendour of ancient Greece, should awaken; failing this, the infertile imagination cannot complete the vision."[10]

Genius, he goes on to say, is the ability to extend the range of appearances that can be seen as art, "to accomplish an aesthetic unity at a point where it had not been accomplished before."[11] And for this reason genius is often misunderstood. Genius has perceived a unity that is not perceived by others: to them it is still loathsome disorder. "Thus when Bach breathed into counterpoint, which in itself is an empty pattern, the idea of a unified development, by virtue of which all his works possess such a surprising perfection and unity, his music was felt, particularly by capable contemporary musicians, to be noise."[12]

Then he turns to religious genius:

> If it is the religious or ethical nature of the person which seizes the world of appearances and its events in a corresponding unique unity, one calls it moral or religious genius. Therefore, the nature of every religious genius is shown in that he constructs a unity by working over the wreckage of a religion destroyed either deliberately or unconsciously as the exigencies of his religious personality dictate, without concern as to whether, for the average person, the broken pieces do fit together into a structure or not. The genius seizes only what he needs for his new, unified image, lit by his own light—and the rest becomes blurred in the shade. Thus, for Jesus of Nazareth, only that exists in the Old Testament which proves to be in harmony with his religious talent. It is from here that light is shed: "On these two hang all the law and the prophets." Thus Luther, being the religious genius that he was, fits together the most contradictory portions of medieval dogma because he brings a unified principle to bear on it; he voices contradictions, but he never felt them.[13]

Thus Schweitzer also? We shall see. It is even possible that, more or less consciously, he was defining his own process.

There are many echoes of Kant's ideas in Schweitzer despite the arrogant young man's confident dismissal of his philosophical system as "self-disintegrating." Both of them hold the conviction that the moral principle in man is a starting point, and both search for the fundamental moral law. Both maintain that reason can be practical, can take account of common experience, without ceasing to be reason. And both believe that in thinking of God, we have to start with what we know of man. Less important, but noted by Schweitzer as significant, is Kant's abandonment of the idea of immortality as prerequisite for morality. Schweitzer, too, was to express strong doubts about immortality.

Which came first? Was Schweitzer interested in Kant because he already held similar views? Or did he develop these views through his study of Kant? Evidently, some of each. Schweitzer was initially attracted because Kant tried to hold together religion, philosophy, and ethics—Schweitzer's preoccupations—in one grand design. But Kant, in turn, reinforced Schweitzer's convictions that all things could and should come under the sway of reason and that a fundamental principle of life should be sought and could be found. Although Kant had failed, Schweitzer felt, he had failed nobly. Those who had followed him had done worse and had gradually abandoned reason altogether as a guiding principle in favor of instinct, or nature, or the State. Kant pointed in the right direction and gave his pupil courage.

This was the last time that Schweitzer ever concerned himself with purely speculative philosophy, except to dismiss it as too abstract. But it would be a mistake to suppose that even this encounter was purely cerebral. Nothing was ever purely cerebral for Schweitzer. Other philosophers could, and often did, lead lives that appeared to be totally unaffected by their theories and speculations. Not so with Schweitzer. We are watching a young man who was to make his life his argument. At this stage in his career he was still developing the argument. After that he made his argument his life. Only in the final process did he make his life his argument. But at every stage there was the closest possible connection between the two. This is the significance of Kant for our present purpose: that every mind that Schweitzer encountered added something vital to the pattern of his living and that this kind of critical analysis provided him with much more rigorous intellectual exercise than many theologians are called upon to face.

The tussle with Kant was not the only reason, nor in the long run the most important, for this trip to Paris. Kant he could have studied anywhere. But Paris meant Widor; it meant music.

Since he first met Widor five years before, the promising lad fresh from school had become a confident young man with the beginnings of a reputation of his own. His studies on Bach in Strasbourg had taught him things that he could teach his teacher, and, according to Widor himself, it was during this period that a conversation took place that was to lead to two heavy volumes and the founding of Schweitzer's reputation as one of the world's foremost authorities on Bach.

Widor was puzzled. He understood the musical logic of the fugues, indeed of all the instrumental works, except some of the choral preludes. These troubled him because they "passed abruptly from one order of ideas to another, from the chromatic to the diatonic scale, from slow movements to rapid ones, without any apparent reason."[14] Schweitzer, as a German-speaking Lutheran, might know what literary idea Bach was trying to express by these odd and unexpected progressions.

Schweitzer knew exactly. The words of the chorales on which the music was based were quite familiar to him—he had them by heart. As he recited them, the meaning of the music's changing moods became clear to Widor: "Music and poetry were tightly clasped together, every musical design corresponding to a literary idea. In this way the works which I had admired up to that time as models of pure counterpoint became for me a series of poems with a matchless eloquence and emotional intensity."[15]

This was a revolutionary insight. The current school of Bach interpretation emphasized that he was above all a mathematical composer, in contrast to the romantics, the Berliozes, the Wagners, who expressed rich personal emotion in their music. There was war in the musical world between the adherents of the romantic and the classical, and the latter required that the music of their hero, Bach, should be austerely remote from the changes and chances of life, obeying only the laws of its own changelessly beautiful world.

So it needed the many-sided Schweitzer to open Widor's eyes to a whole new dimension of Bach's art. And although still instructor and pupil, the relationship was approaching that of colleagues and friends. Widor now taught Schweitzer free of charge and proudly introduced his young lion of a protégé to a much wider circle of artists and intellectuals in Paris than Uncle Charles could command. This did not, of course, include the socially questionable avant-garde of art on the Left Bank, for that was not the world of the fastidious little professor from the Conservatoire; it was mainly the musical establishment, sharing the rigid social code of middle-class Paris, that opened its doors to Schweitzer. He enjoyed the social life, but found it far from irresistible, and dragged himself away without difficulty to the little room with the oil lamp where he and Kant were trying conclusions.

Widor taught only the organ. For the piano Schweitzer needed somebody else and, in fact, went to two teachers, widely differing in approach. The more interesting of these, Marie Jaëll-Trautmann, was very advanced indeed. As we have seen, Schweitzer found the native Parisians a pretty conventional lot, and it is not surprising to find that Marie Jaëll was Alsatian by birth. This formidable lady, a friend of Liszt, married to a piano virtuoso and herself a notable concert pianist, had abandoned performance to develop her theories about touch and fingering in piano playing. Like all the best teachers, whether of art or of life, she aimed to liberate the natural talent, to release the performer from the tensions that inhibit his own instinctive control. In piano playing this meant that the student had to discover and isolate all the muscles from the shoulder down, so that none of them should be affected by involuntary tensing, conscious or unconscious.

Other teachers might recommend exercises that aimed at strength or flexibility of the fingers, a purely mechanical virtuosity. Marie Jaëll believed that that would all follow once the finger was put into uninterrupted touch with the mind. Once the muscles have been brought out of the bondage of unwanted tension, they can convey the player's intuition to the fingertips without obstruction so that it seems as though each finger is thinking for itself. The finger must be aware not only of the movement required but of the actual sound it wants to produce. And it must be aware that the sound is affected not only by the way the key goes down but also by the way it comes up. Phrasing depends on the right sequence of movements, either joining the notes in an organic unity or separating them by the subtlest rolling of the fingers in different directions as the notes are pressed. So the fingers grow increasingly sensitive to the relationship between touch and tone, and the player becomes acutely conscious of tone color.

To make sure that her theories were physically sound Marie Jaëll called in a physiologist, a M. Féré, to advise her. And the voluntary guinea pig at their experiment (as though he had not already enough to do) was Albert Schweitzer. It was all worth it. He learned an immense amount in a comparatively short time, proving once again that the "liberating" technique of teaching is not only surer but swifter than the "hammer-it-into-them" technique. It sharpened his musical ear and "completely altered" his hand. "I became more and more completely master of my finger, with great benefit to my organ playing."[16]

But he went only so far with Marie Jaëll. She was afflicted by that terrible need of pioneers to find in their discoveries some kind of universal key to the whole of nature, and this led her into strange extravagancies in the books she wrote, which for many people concealed the practical value of her teaching. Schweitzer, maintaining his almost infuriating common sense even in the midst of the most progressive experiments, hedged his bets by going at the same time, and unknown to Marie Jaëll, to another piano teacher, a conventional, traditional pedagogue, J. Philipp. "This protected me from what was one-sided in the Jaëll method."[17] He got the best out of both by never telling either that he was studying with the other, for they each mistrusted the other's teaching and would have regarded him as a disloyal and less-than-serious student had they known.

Even his fingers had to learn to conceal from each teacher that they had been practicing with the other. They had to play "with Marie Jaëll in the morning à la Jaëll and with Philipp in the afternoon à la Philipp"— in itself something of a feat of concentration and technique. But Schweitzer's ethics never dealt in any commandment as simple as "thou shalt not lie." As we have seen, he agreed with Kant that morality had its origin not in the needs of society but in those of the individual. Nietzsche was emphasizing this at the time with his appeal for moral heroism and the dismissal of bourgeois scruples in the interest of a higher standard. Like others in the intellectual swim, Schweitzer believed in making his own moral rules, not in having them made for him. If telling a little less than the whole truth was necessary to maintain good relations with two people both of whom he valued, the trouble the dissembling caused him was a fair price to pay.

So the winter wore on. There were nights without sleep and days with too little to eat although Widor often decided that the large young man needed nourishment and took him to the Restaurant Foyot, his regular eating place near the Luxembourg; and sometimes he would dine with one of his increasing circle of friends in the university and musical worlds before going back to the midnight oil.

To keep himself awake as he worked he sat with his feet in a bowl of cold water and he smoked—ceaselessly. He worked with his head wreathed in clouds of smoke, and even reached that grim condition in which a cigarette is necessary before it is possible to get up in the morning.

But on December 31 he made a New Year's resolution. On January 1, 1899, he gave up the habit, and never smoked again for the remaining sixty-six years of his life. He thought he had detected a weakening of his memory—that extraordinary memory over which people marveled until the end of his life and which nourished him not only with the facts he needed for his intellectual work but also with the recollections of people, places, and events that fed his spirit.

Nine days before this resolution, on the Friday before Christmas, he stopped work for a while to write a letter to a little girl, his niece and goddaughter Suzanne, Louise's eldest child, not yet two years old. It is an odd letter, full of a homesickness that perhaps he could not quite express directly to adults; and it is worth quoting at length, for it is the first personal utterance we have from these ill-documented years.

My Suzi cherie !!!—Now stay still and don't make faces,—you are in front of me, leaning against a book by Kant. Ordinarily you are on the mantelpiece, because on the table you distract me too much. I have kissed you and placed you in front of me on the table. You are the only photograph in my room.

I have just been dreaming a little and thinking about you. Do you remember when you didn't want to be alone when you went to bed, and I had to hold your hand? You cried—I opened the door; "Pa'ain, pa'ain" [her word for *parrain*—godfather]. I couldn't resist such tender trust—I came to your side, you took my hand; and you were calm and peaceful. It was dark in the room and I talked in a low voice—I told you things you didn't understand. Sometimes I passed my hand over your forehead as my mother does over mine, loving me. I said "Suzi" very softly—I thought you were asleep—but no—I started to get up—"Pa'ain, pa'ain"—I tried to creep out on all fours—"Pa'ain, Pa'ain!"—oh, I believe I can hear you say the word now.

He goes on to talk of Christmas:

Papa has written that he has chosen a pine from the forest for the Christmas tree and it was snowing. . . . O Suzi, Suzi! Last year I carried you in my arms! You had a lovely long dress, you couldn't yet say "Pa'ain" and I loved you all the same. Do you know, will you ever know what you are to me? What place you hold in my heart? And on Sunday I shan't be with you! . . .

Grandmama from Günsbach and your mama will cry a little—you know, they love me a great deal.

A little later, a didactic note creeps in:

You are right, you know, to be gay at Christmas as long as you can; plenty of sad Christmasses will come later—my first sad Christmas was when I brought back a bad report, grandmama cried, and I couldn't bear to see her cry, I took her head in my hands and kissed her and promised to work. It was then that I realised I loved her more than I could tell her. I've kept my promise.

When you're big, you'll re-read this letter . . . what shall I be then? Perhaps they'll tell you that I'm hard and cruel, that I'm heartless. And you will know that I'm not heartless—I have almost too much heart; when one loves deeply, one is not happy.

And now as I look at your photograph, I have to smile. Do you know what they'll say? Pa'ain is writing to his Suzi, but Suzi doesn't know how to read! . . . But it isn't true. You will understand better than all the rest; they will say: it is a sad letter—and you will smile. Pa'ain has written me a letter, he has told me a lot of things and the others think it's sad, because they don't understand. . . . It's funny, people imagine one must know how to read before one can understand a letter—no, it's only necessary to love pa'ain to decipher it.[18]

Here for the first time we have clearly on display that sentimentality of which he was accused and that vulnerable heart, which was so frequently overwhelmed by this experience or that. Schweitzer used to say of himself, in his later years, "I have the heart of a dove inside the hide of a hippopotamus."

Apparent also is the distance Schweitzer has progressed in that quest for spontaneity that began sixteen years earlier, that day in Lent when he spoiled Henry Bräsch's bird-shooting expedition. About that incident he wrote: "From that day onward I took courage to free myself from the fear of men. . . . I tried also to unlearn my former dread of being laughed at by my school-fellows. . . . "[19] And in the *Memoirs of Childhood and Youth*, about the struggle he had with his shyness and reserve, he says: "The law of reserve must be broken down by the claims of the heart, and thus we all reach a moment when we should step outside our aloofness, and to some fellow man become ourselves a man. . . . I gained courage to try to make my actions as natural and hearty as my feelings were."[20]

Certainly, in this letter there is a perfect clarity of expression, the feeling flowing as freely as intention flowed from brain to fingertip under Marie Jaëll's, piano instruction. But this was something Schweitzer found easy in letters, at least letters to those with whom he had a warm and loving relationship. How far he had achieved the same ease in personal contact is more difficult to say, but everything suggests a great loosening up of his character, as in the impulse that made him unhesitatingly take the mattress from his bed and carry it cheerfully through the streets to a needy old woman.

Plato has an image of the life of man as a chariot drawn by two horses, the emotional impulses, which if not controlled constantly by the charioteer, reason, will pull in different directions and overturn the chariot. Schweitzer's horses were magnificent, powerful creatures, and his reason fought to keep them both at full stretch and yet in complete harmony. Such a fight never ends. Some who knew him said he was a man of will, a hard man. Others were conscious only of a glowing warmth. Once, when somebody's insecurity was mentioned in conversation, he asked, "Who is secure?" And in this letter the most revealing and moving thing of all is the sudden outburst of doubt: "What shall I be then? Perhaps they'll tell you that I'm hard and cruel, that I'm heartless." What made him think that? Had anything been said to him? And if so, why? We do not know. Later he was called hard because he ignored all advice and pleas when he went to Africa; could he already have been anticipating such a development and the reaction to it? Or was it simply that his family had begged him to be home for Christmas and he had refused, feeling that his work was more important, his concentration must not be broken? Certainly, he must have known that this letter would be passed around the family at their Christmas festivities, and they would all read his plea for understanding, the admission of a chink in his armor, and, perhaps, the hint of the change to come.

To understand Schweitzer we have not only to be aware of the balance he achieved between the different sides of his nature; we have also to know how precariously it was maintained, the effort it continually cost. I have found a tendency, not only in others but in myself, to feel about Schweitzer that he had it too easy to be a good guide. We feel somehow that because he mastered himself, he lived too high above the struggle to be able to help those who are embroiled in it. Those thinkers and writers like Sartre who not only suffered the full sickness of the century but explored its fever-chart with gusto seem more sympathetic. "They understand," we say; "therefore, they can heal."

But, unfortunately, the blind cannot lead the blind. All they can do is commiserate more easily with each other's infirmities as they totter together into the ditch. They can also condemn as patronizing any seeing person who suggests that they might be better off on the path and offers to lead them there. And, certainly, the sick can get little comfort from the hearty encouragement of a healthy optimist who has never known what sickness is. The nervousness of the twentieth century was a valid reaction against the false optimism of the nineteenth; and it is very easy to see in Schweitzer a figure of robust, uncomplicated health, and to feel that he has nothing to offer us.

It is not true. He stood exactly between the two centuries. Although he used the phraseology of the nineteenth, he spoke of the despair of the twentieth. He felt, sooner than most, the abyss that lay under the crust of progress, and before existentialism was a word, he was an existentialist—with this one difference from the others, that where they often seemed interested in sickness for its own sake, his only interest in disease was how to cure it. In a sick time, Schweitzer was for health.

He himself experienced its sickness—less dangerously than others, because of the solidity of his upbringing, but acutely enough to make him devote his life first to doctoring himself and then to finding medicines for civilization. Until his stay in Paris the points where he had been conscious of something wrong were in his own personal life and in the common agonies of the world at large—pain, poverty, sickness, and cruelty. But now he began to be increasingly aware of a special sickness— the stink of a decaying civilization, which in Paris was more noticeable than elsewhere. With that political sensitivity which he had shown at his uncle's dinner table at the age of eleven, he found himself contrasting the high concerns and noble intentions of Kant and the Enlightenment with the general attitude of society to the events of his own time. "My impression was," he wrote, "that the fire of man's ideals was burning low without anyone noticing it or troubling about it. On a number of occasions I had to acknowledge that public opinion did not reject with indignation inhumane ideas which were publicly disseminated, but accepted them, and that it approved of, as opportune, inhumane courses of action taken by governments and nations."[21]

In fact, although Schweitzer barely mentions it, Paris in 1898 was buzzing with a political scandal so poisonous that it is still an international household word—the Dreyfus case.

In 1894 Alfred Dreyfus, a young Jewish army officer, had been found guilty of selling military secrets to the Germans and sentenced to life imprisonment. His brother Mathieu, convinced of his innocence, had spent the intervening years gathering evidence of a miscarriage of justice and collecting allies—one of whom, incidentally, was an Alsatian, M. Scheurer-Kestner, who had risen to be vice-president of the Senate.

On November 15, 1898, a month before Schweitzer wrote to Suzi, Mathieu Dreyfus had shocked Paris by claiming that the documents in question bore the handwriting not of Alfred Dreyfus but of a dissolute and aristocratic officer, Major Count Esterhazy. Esterhazy demanded an opportunity to clear his name and on January 9 was acquitted by court-martial. Clemenceau, at this time forwarding his career by a deep involvement in journalism, took an interest and four days after the court-martial published Emile Zola's famous letter, "J'accuse," alleging miscarriage of justice and corruption in high places.

France was split in two. The Royalist/Catholic faction felt that the honor of France, her army, and her nobility was at stake; it was expedient that one unimportant officer (Jewish at that) should be sacrificed for its preservation. The other party, tending to be Lutheran and Republican in its sympathies, supported Dreyfus and Zola in their attempt to get justice done. The pro-Dreyfusards formed themselves into an organization with a title calculated to please Schweitzer—the League of the Rights of Man. The anti-Dreyfusards countered with The League of the French Motherland.

The case rolled on for eight months, its ripples widening. In the distant Alsatian hills, Schweitzer's mother was moved to write a passionate letter to the papers about it. Little by little the lies and forgeries that had convicted Dreyfus were uncovered, and in September he was finally pardoned and released. As the anti-Dreyfusards had feared, the honor and self-confidence of France was shaken for years to come, and by their own conduct.

For Schweitzer the case was no more than the boil where a deep-seated poison had come to a head. Indifference to justice, he felt, was far too widespread. Too many people were abandoning true patriotism for "a short-sighted nationalism." The banner that they carried bore the word

Realpolitik, and all the nations of Europe were infected. "From a number of signs," he wrote, "I had to infer the growth of a peculiar intellectual and spiritual fatigue in this generation which is so proud of what it has accomplished. It seemed as if I heard its members arguing to each other that their previous hopes for the future of mankind had been pitched too high, and that it was becoming necessary to limit oneself to striving for what was attainable."[22]

With the ending of the century, people were looking around them and summing up the achievements of the past hundred years. Material progress had been enormous and was clearly only beginning. This gave a sense of confidence that to many spelled advance, unalterable and unending. To these people, man had now reached his highest point so far, and was poised to go higher. But Schweitzer's own impression was that "in our mental and spiritual life we were not only below the level of past generations, but were in many respects only living on their achievements . . . and that not a little of this heritage was beginning to melt away in our hands."[23] Reason was giving way to superstition, and astrology was growing popular, with its implication that human effort could not affect events predestined by the stars. It made Schweitzer very uneasy that people suffering from this sort of moral exhaustion should imagine that they had really advanced since the eighteenth century. The little pool of light where he and Kant met night after night seemed a haven of sanity and security, surrounded by advancing shadows.

5

Berlin

1899

IN MARCH HE TOOK his completed thesis back to Strasbourg and read it to Ziegler, and Ziegler made his pronouncement about the advent of a philosophical genius.

If there was genius in the thesis, it was the result of a combination of three qualities: first, that characteristic instinct to bypass the commentators and get to grips with the original writings of the man himself; second, the intuition that searched beneath the words and the arguments for the character of the thinker and valued him for his aspirations more than for his logic; and third, that infinite capacity for taking pains that led Schweitzer to track various key words through the different writings, to count their frequency, and to analyze the way their meaning varied as the thought of Kant developed. Genius or no, the sum of these qualities is impressive. Ziegler looked hopefully forward to the second part of the examination, the viva voce interview, which was set for July. Schweitzer had four months to prepare.

He decided that this time he would try Berlin, which boasted excellent lecturers in philosophy. Theology, too, was well represented, and although that was not the subject on the agenda at the moment, Schweitzer would not have been the man he was if he had resisted the temptation to drink at all the springs at once.

Three years had already passed since his decision to abandon the academic life at the age of thirty. Only six of his nine years were left; into them he needed to cram as much as possible of the life he loved and excelled in. Meanwhile, he was searching for the path that his service was to take when the time was up. He had no idea yet what it was to be.

He took a room on the third floor of a courtyard house in the Kochstrasse. In his reading in Berlin he intended to get a good working knowledge of all the major philosophers, ancient and modern, besides rounding out his study of Kant. But Berlin proved much more seductive than Paris in distracting him from his syllabus. In the first place there was none of that rigid social etiquette that made it so hard to penetrate French family life. Here the hospitality was easy and swift, and social life so much the more enjoyable. Similarly the intellectual life was informal and vigorous: one did not encounter professors only at lectures but might find oneself invited to their homes, there to meet others and carry on the debate among friends.

Intellectual leaders thronged to the house of Frau Curtius, widow of a great scholar of ancient Greece, whose stepson, Frederick, was district superintendent of Colmar and an excellent administrator in the Lutheran Church. Schweitzer knew Frederick a little and through him was made welcome in the Curtius household. Every fortnight Frau Curtius would hold open house, and everyone who was anyone in the academic world would drop in for beer, sandwiches, fruit, and conversation about the day's work. Schweitzer would retire shyly into a corner, and for the most part was content to listen as the discussions of his elders and betters raged furiously, but without rancor, around him. Looking back from fifty years later he remembered particularly Wilhelm Dilthey, H. Diels, and above all Hermann Grimm, a theologian who backed the highly unfashionable view that St. John's Gospel was historically consistent with the other three and who was forever trying unsuccessfully to enlist Schweitzer's support for this view.

All around were lectures to be sampled, interesting theories to be followed up, organs to be tried out. He found the organs, on the whole, displeasing, also the style of the organists. The same openness to new ideas that made Berliners more attractive to him than Parisians also made them more vulnerable to the blandishments of technical progress, and many of the organs had been renovated on the same lines as the new instrument at Stuttgart. He found their sound "dull and dry," and their organists more concerned with speed and virtuosity than with Widor's "plasticity of style" or Marie Jaëll's sensitivity to tone. He played regularly, however deputizing for the organist at Kaiser Wilhelm Memorial Church; and at the organist's house he met musicians, painters, and sculptors and so was able to keep one foot in the academic camp, one in the artistic.

Among the lectures that meant a great deal to him, although they were no part of his present studies, were those of the great Adolf Harnack, a highly fashionable preacher and theologian, a man of immense charm and erudition. His learning was so overwhelming that it actually reduced Schweitzer to a total inability even to answer his questions; so Schweitzer records.

There might, however, have been another reason for his paralysis. Harnack's view of Jesus was diametrically opposite to the one burgeoning in Schweitzer's mind. Schweitzer was convinced that the clue to Jesus' thought lay in taking seriously the fact that he was a Jew. Harnack on the other hand believed that the Jewish background was quite irrelevant: Jesus had come to preach the brotherhood of man under the fatherhood of God, and the fact that he happened to have been born in Roman-occupied Palestine was quite without significance. The proper way to study the Gospels, then, was to eliminate all the historical circumstances and to lift out the essential, universal Jesus, freed from his "Jewish old clothes." Harnack's famous series of lectures on this theme, "The Nature of Christianity," was delivered the following winter to enormous acclaim. Before such a compelling opponent, the speechless Schweitzer had plenty of opportunity to check the validity of his theories.

Among the philosophers was Georg Simmel, to whose lectures Schweitzer, sipping here and there, was drawn back time and again. Simmel was concerned with the work of Nietzsche and the philosophy of self-transcendence, which, as we have seen, intrigued and troubled Schweitzer. Nietzsche, gradually going mad from syphilis, had in a lucid moment pumped out a final burst of frantic works, including *The Twilight of the Idols*, *Antichrist*, and *Ecce Homo*. In these, with increasing hysteria but enough uncomfortable insight to make them impressive, he flayed the hypocrisy of Europe's Christian bourgeois standards and appealed to everyone to do what he himself in his weakness impotently yearned to do—to stand alone, to think alone, to act alone, heroically, without reference to others and responsible to no one. As we have seen, the doctrine of standing alone easily became a doctrine of stamping on anyone whose mediocrity impeded one's self-perfecting. Already in Nietzsche's own books there were signs of this ruthless arrogance.

Simmel's lectures were an attempt to disentangle the good from the bad in Nietzsche, placing the emphasis on self-transcendence that involved no conflict with others. The actual self had to be overcome in order to release the higher self, which was potentially already in existence. The notion is far from unfamiliar, being a philosophical restatement of a basic religious idea, the idea of self-denial, of losing one's life in order to save it.

At one level Simmel's lectures were important for Schweitzer because, with his dual interest in philosophy and religion, he needed to find ways of expressing religious thought in nonreligious terms. Not only Nietzsche but the whole current of feeling was swaying against established Christianity, and the old religious language was suspect. But if religious ideas could be proved in philosophic terms, it was a guarantee that they were still valid outside the context of the Church. For Schweitzer, philosophy and theology were not so much separate subjects as different approaches to the same truth. And because every instinct told him that the greatest truths were the simplest, it followed that anything that mattered could be said without using ecclesiastical jargon.

There was a deeper and more personal reason for Schweitzer's interest in self-transcendence. As we have seen, the notion of losing one's life in order to save it had haunted his thoughts for a long while. Self-denial and self-transcendence summed up in one way what his whole life had been about, since the time when he conquered his desire to lash the dog Phylax like a lion-tamer, since he abandoned games when games led to uncontrollable anger, since he learned to stop worrying about other children's laughter, since he quit smoking when he thought smoking threatened his memory. It had become rooted in his mind that if he wanted to achieve his potential—the greatness that Nietzsche and Jesus asked for—it could only be at the cost of some sacrifice.

And still, in the list of things that occupied him in these astonishingly crowded four months, we have not reached the principal distraction from his work on Kant—the intriguing investigations of Carl Stumpf.

Stumpf was an experimental psychologist who was also something of a philosopher, and his view of the eighteenth century was quite different from Schweitzer's. He regarded it as the Dark Ages, when foolhardy thinkers speculated on matters about which they had no real knowledge at all. Stumpf had no interest in conclusions or systems. All he wished to do was observe facts. Until sufficient facts had been observed with sufficient thoroughness, he believed it was impossible even to start to construct a philosophy. He was a man, in his way, far ahead of his time and probably a considerable influence in the weaning of Schweitzer from the speculative philosophers to that great observer of nature, Goethe.

Stumpf concentrated particularly on the psychology of sensation. Too many philosophers had discoursed freely about sense experience without knowing what it really was. So he investigated the actual effects on human beings of heat, light, and especially sound.

Once again Schweitzer stepped forward as the willing guinea pig. His ear, trained by Marie Jaëll, was cocked to analyze the effects of simple tones, of variations of pitch and intensity. What happened when one added echo? Or tried to eliminate it? And how did one isolate a note from its overtones? And what did that do to its psychological coloring?

Stumpf and Schweitzer spent hours at this fascinating game, in churches, halls, and rooms of different sizes. Kant took a back seat. At the very end of the nineteenth century Schweitzer was plunging into the experimental techniques of the twentieth. Although he may have mistrusted the aberrations of technical progress, he never believed that the remedy was to retreat into a prescientific past. His argument was not with physical discovery but with the unthinking use that people made of it. The way forward was through more knowledge, not less, but knowledge itself must be exercised in the service of a true ideal, such as the ideals of the eighteenth century. Nor was any of this inconsistent with Christianity because Schweitzer was convinced that "truthfulness in all things belongs to the spirit of Jesus."

In this conviction he stretched his mind in all directions. He worked hard and long, but without rush and without strain. His sister Adèle says that however hard he worked he never appeared to lose his inward serenity. And this is borne out by a second letter we have to his god-daughter Suzi, dated simply "Berlin, June '99, one Thursday evening." Like the first, it reads like a love letter, long and warm and leisurely. And it makes it quite clear that a close correspondence of letters and gifts flowed between him and the rest of the family. "Grandma tells me in her letter that the strawberries sent from Colmar did something unpleasant to your digestion; this is the kind of thing that often happens in this world." He describes the house where he lives: "As you come in you have to take care not to step on the porter's feet as he sits smoking his pipe; remembering the days when these delights weren't forbidden me, I slow up to catch a noseful of it." He describes his young friend, Hänschen Müller, who "is very well brought up, better than you (but that need go no further)," and who tends to get beaten for other children's crimes. "The latest thing was that the others shouted 'old Schachtel' after a lady who was climbing the stairs; his father was listening at the window and Hänschen caught it; it was only later that the lady came along and said that he was innocent. I couldn't help thinking of the number of times my father beat my bottom when I wasn't guilty; it didn't happen often, but the memory is comforting. . . . Kiss Grandmama for me and tell her that her letter delighted me all evening. Help Grandpapa when he bottles the wine to send me. . . . Give my regards to Turk [the family's latest dog] when you take him for a walk and tell him a bit about what I'm doing, he'll find it interesting."[1]

Before Schweitzer returned to Strasbourg, yet another seed was sown, almost by chance, in the highly fertile pasture of his mind. A group who had attended a session at the Prussian Academy of Sciences had gathered for afternoon coffee at Frau Curtius's house to discuss it further. Through the hubbub of conversation a phrase reached Schweitzer in his corner: "Why, we are all of us nothing but *epigoni*." He never knew who said it, but "it struck home with me," he wrote, "like a flash of lightning."[2]

Epigoni is a Greek word without an exact English meaning. It is something like "followers on," "successors," "latecomers," "heirs of something past." The idea was not particularly novel or striking. But it summed up all that he had been feeling about European civilization. A chance incident as slight as this often sets the seal on a whole semiconscious complex of ideas in the mind of a writer. It is the spermatozoon that fertilizes the egg. And now Schweitzer was pregnant with a book.

It was to be called *We Epigoni*. Fired by the thought, he discussed its theme with his friends, but they were not particularly impressed. They thought the idea was a good example of paradox and fin-de-siècle pessimism, but none of them found it actually true or significant. How could they, when Germany, so recently unified, was growing steadily more powerful and influential, and an infectious national euphoria bathed each new day in a hopeful halo? Schweitzer, the alien Alsatian who knew too much about history, gave up talking about his book.

So he returned to Strasbourg, full of his experiences, full of his book, but somewhat empty of research on his proper subjects. In his written thesis he had been able to conceal the fact that he had skipped the commentaries and read only Kant himself. But it became painfully apparent under questioning. His examiners, full of expectation, had to admit to being disappointed and somewhat let down. The bud of genius appeared a little blighted. Harnack, Simmel, and the experiments with Stumpf had eaten away more time than they should have.

But a favored student has to be allowed to stray a little. There was no question of his failing. And in August 1899 Schweitzer had his first degree.

6

Two Examinations

1899–1900

FOR THE NEW ACADEMIC YEAR Ziegler, undeterred by his disappointment, urged Schweitzer to go on to the next step in philosophy by qualifying as Privat-Dozent, or lecturer/tutor. Meantime, a warm recommendation from the generous Holtzmann ensured publication of the thesis despite its length and the obscurity of the author.

Unfortunately for his plans, Ziegler happened to mention that if Schweitzer were to continue on the philosophy side he would have to give up any thoughts of preaching. It was time now to decide between the two fields of study, and sermons from a professor of philosophy might be regarded as out of place. That settled it for Schweitzer. He had already had experience in preaching, both in his father's church at minor services and in village churches to which he was sent as part of his theological training. Generations of pastors and schoolmasters had left their mark on his character, and "preaching," he wrote, "was a necessity of my being. I felt it was a wonderful thing to be allowed to address a congregation every Sunday about the deepest questions of life."[1]

So he decided instead to study for his licentiate in theology, which in any case he was bound to take by the terms of his Goll scholarship. He had plenty of time; nearly five years remained before the scholarship expired, and its twelve hundred marks a year would keep him in the modest style to which he was accustomed until he was within a few months of his thirtieth birthday and the end of his academic career. The moment seemed ripe to travel farther afield.

He had sampled university life in Paris and Berlin, the two capitals whose languages he spoke already. Now he looked forward to seeing new countries, learning new languages, taking at least a small step toward those far-off lands that had fascinated his childish imagination and that, once he had embarked on his life of service, were likely to be lost to him forever. At least part of his study for the licentiate he hoped to do in England.

While he was planning this, he learned of the plight of another student, Jäger by name, whose brilliant career in Oriental languages was threatened by lack of funds to continue his studies. Jäger needed scholarship money. He needed, specifically, the Goll scholarship. But the Goll money was Schweitzer's until the end of his six-year term—unless he released it by taking the licentiate. For Jäger's sake Schweitzer gave up all plans to go abroad and decided to attempt the licentiate as soon as possible. The earliest opportunity to take the examination was the following July—a very tight schedule, for a licentiate was more than an ordinary degree and qualified its holder for a full professorship.

Because he was staying in Strasbourg, he had to find somewhere to live, for having graduated, he was no longer entitled to his beloved rooms in St. Thomas. But by a special dispensation he was allowed to stay there as a paying guest at a rate that, if he were careful, he could just afford. "It seemed to me the fittest place for the work which now lay before me."[2]

What lay before him was no less than the upheaval of all established views of the life and mind of the founder of Christianity, for the subject of his thesis was a foregone conclusion. Now was the time to put together all his thoughts and studies on the meaning of the Gospels, focusing them on the Last Supper—the moment when, Schweitzer believed, Jesus felt the old order passing over into the new. The twenty-five-year-old son of the village pastor, the ex-dunce of Mulhouse Gymnasium, was setting himself, apparently without a qualm, a task that had baffled theologians and historians alike and that was bound to bring him into conflict not only with the academics but with the whole bulk of the Christian Church, of every persuasion. All this he knew. But the ideas had been maturing in the dark of his mind long enough. Now it was time to set them in order and put them on display. It was not the mind of Kant that he sought now in the pool of light on his desk but the mysterious figure of Jesus, on whom half the world laid its hopes, calling him Savior, Lord, and Son of God. Schweitzer was proposing to tell them in the name of Jesus that through the centuries they had never known who Jesus was but that he, Schweitzer, could set them right.

This was the task of the quiet hours. Meanwhile, organ playing still took up as much time as ever. Eugène Münch had died unexpectedly of typhoid fever the previous September when he was only forty-one years old; and Schweitzer, in the midst of his other activities, had written a touching tribute to him for his family and friends. Now Schweitzer was

St. William's official and permanent organist. He also had to think of providing himself with an income of sorts. The scholarship was barely enough to cover his expenses and that would cease as soon as he received the licentiate. He applied for the post of deacon, a sort of noncommissioned officer of the church, licensed to preach but not to hold services, at the church of St. Nicholas, across the river from St. Thomas College.

St. Nicholas is an unpretentious church, but an obvious choice for Schweitzer, for he was already bound to it by many links. His uncle, Albert Schillinger, had been incumbent here thirty years before, and Herr Gerold, one of the two elderly ministers who now staffed it, had been Uncle Albert's closest friend. The other minister, Herr Knittel, had been pastor at Günsbach before Schweitzer's father.

He was accepted as deacon on the first of December. The same month, the last month of the century, saw the publication of his thesis on Kant—his first published work apart from his memoir of Eugène Münch.

Life now was more restricted than ever before. It revolved around a few fixed points: the growing book in his room at St. Thomas, music at St. William's, the preaching and work of a junior assistant at St. Nicholas. A time of steady and serene concentration set in. His inaugural sermon took as its text St. Paul's advice: "Be joyful always."

The originals of most of Schweitzer's sermons were destroyed by fire in the Second World War. We shall never know what else went up in smoke during one or other of the wars, but we know that he was a tireless correspondent and that later in life he liked to preserve the letters he received, so the loss was probably considerable. The recent discovery of letters between Schweitzer and his wife-to-be is not likely to be repeated.

Fortunately, typed copies of about a hundred and fifty of the sermons were made by a friend during World War II, and these survive. Fortunately, because, like his father, Schweitzer used sermons not to huff and puff with inflated rhetoric, not to expound subtle points of doctrine, not to distribute condemnation or praise, but simply to share with a congregation his feelings "about the deepest questions of life." He himself was reluctant to allow publication of his sermons, particularly those he preached in Africa. But the very grounds he gave for refusal—that they were designed as explorations of a subject with friends rather than a full and final statement—is the reason why they are so valuable to us. The sermons are more personal than anything else that has come down to us except the letters. In them we hear his own true voice speaking about his deepest convictions.

In May he preached a series of sermons on the Beatitudes, that great series of statements of blessedness that many, Schweitzer among them, would say are the heart of Jesus' teaching. On the twenty-fourth he was struggling with "Blessed are those who weep, for they shall be comforted," the eternal problem of unhappiness, the great mystery that had overwhelmed him as a boy and driven him to set his life from the age of thirty in the balance against it. Now the apprentice preacher was trying to find the words to reconcile his congregation to the harshness of the world. The sermon, it must be said, is comparatively conventional. The young deacon (not yet even a curate) has not yet achieved the experience and the ruthless honesty that mark his later sermons. But already we find notable features.

First the simplicity. The scholar who could not only unravel the knots of Kant's verbiage but also create a few entanglements on his own account now studies to be understood by every member of the congregation. "I do not preach as a theologian," he said, "but as a layman." Clear, vigorous, and confident, this style is unmistakably the man.

Then the warmth. One gets the sense of a strong and practical hand stretched out to help and reassure—above all to reassure. And behind the reassurance is a secure confidence in Jesus as the source of reassurance and compassion. "This is exactly what is marvelous about Jesus: he does not address himself only to our spiritual being, but he puts himself also on our level, he understands us man to man. . . . Christianity has been accused of consoling believers for the evils of the world by making them gaze at the mirage of the promise of heavenly bliss. This is wrong, Jesus was never touched by such thoughts, for he did not say 'Happy *shall be* those who weep today,' but 'Happy *today* are those who *today* weep.' " And against those who through the ages have seen suffering as a punishment from God, he quotes the story of the man blind from birth, of whom Jesus was asked, "Who has sinned, he or his parents, to bring this evil on him?" And Jesus said, "No one."

"Now we have reached the heart of the meaning. It is this: 'Do not despair. Do not believe that God wants to chastise you, to punish or reprove you, but know that in suffering also you are in his kingdom, you are still his children and he sustains you in his fatherly arms.' " But Schweitzer had not yet eliminated all traces of pious cliché. The sermon ends by asking, "What teacher was the first to show you that we do not live for ourselves alone? Suffering. . . . What bred in you the desire for a more noble life? Suffering."[3] And so on, and so on. Schweitzer has still not really suffered himself. Mental battles, yes, powerful emotions, depressions—but not real suffering. The reconciliation is too easy.

But it is hard not to warm to the humanity of the preacher and what Georges Marchal calls his smiling and virile confidence. There is confidence in the way in which he invokes the friendly Jesus who "understands us as man to man"—the human Jesus whose portrait, as we know though his hearers did not, was nearing completion on his desk.

Along with the licentiate thesis, however, he was also required to prepare for another examination, which would qualify him for ordination as a curate. The situation was somewhat absurd, as though a racing driver, in training for a Grand Prix, should find himself compelled to pass an elementary driving test. And, in fact, Schweitzer nearly failed his driving test.

The two examinations were held within six days of each other, that for the curacy first. A curate's qualifications do not include controversial views on higher theology, and the examiners were mostly elderly clerics of a fairly orthodox and prosaic turn of mind. It is not surprising that Schweitzer, with the licentiate giving him more than enough to think about and with an unconquered disposition to neglect what did not interest him, failed to observe his own precept of leaving nothing to chance. He left a great deal to chance here and trusted to spur-of-the-moment improvisation to see him through. It was a close thing. One question, about the authorship of a certain hymn, he tried nonchalantly to turn aside by saying that the hymn was too insignificant for him to trouble himself over. Regrettably, the hymn had been written by the father of one of the examiners. Aging clerics do not love to feel belittled by clever young fellows with a superior air, especially if the young fellow is suspected of advanced ideas.

But as in his final examination for the Gymnasium, a common interest with an influential examiner tipped the scales at the last moment. Old Pfarrer Will was an expert on the history of dogma, and Schweitzer's knowledge of the subject saved him from humiliating failure. With anything but unanimous acclaim, he became a curate, a minister of the Lutheran Church.

The examiners for the licentiate were of a different breed. Scholars themselves, they could recognize the scholarship and enthusiasm that had gone into the thesis on the Last Supper. Whether or not they were convinced, they were definitely impressed. Within a week of his curate's examination Schweitzer had won his second degree and lost the Goll scholarship. It so happened that his curate's stipend exactly equaled the scholarship money, so he was no worse off; but had he not scraped through to the curacy he would have gone very hungry. No doubt this fact added to the annoyance to which he confessed when Jäger, after all that, failed to make use of the scholarship.

Four and a half years ahead loomed the watershed of Schweitzer's thirtieth birthday. Four of those years he might have spent, without financial worries, traveling and meeting new minds. Instead, he was a pastor, committed to a job, and so far as he knew, he would never again have the chance to see the world. "I never ceased to regret," he wrote, "this misplaced consideration for others." Those who suspect Schweitzer of being too "good" may be reassured by this evidence that his goodness had nothing to do with masochistic self-denial but was concerned with very practical ends.

What was done, however, could not be undone. And the Last Supper thesis had not exhausted what he had to say about the life of Jesus. There was plenty of work ahead.

7

The Scholar-Curate

1900–1901

THERE WAS SIMPLY TOO MUCH TO DO. Schweitzer had to earn a living, and at the same time he was interested in too many different things. Moreover, whatever caught his interest involved him to the limit. That ever-questing, never-satisfied, all-or-nothing spirit led him into challenge after challenge, each of which had to be defended, often against all received opinion. Everyone who knew him in Strasbourg at this time says the same thing. Social life? Where would he find the time? Girlfriends? Where would he find the time? Dancing? Where would he find the time? Yet, as it turned out, he did find the time for the most momentous encounter of his life.

In any case, he scarcely needed social life because a good pastor's life is constantly social—Schweitzer's more than most, urged on by his determination to become what his convictions had told him he should be—the man for all men, the universal neighbor. Whether in his everyday affairs or in his great intellectual interests Schweitzer could only understand life by understanding people. Reading his books, we find that his thirst for understanding always emerges as a need to enter into the mind of a human being. His theological books were quests for the minds of Jesus and St. Paul; his book about Bach sought for the man behind the music; and even the great books about civilization were in the last analysis a search for himself. In them he mined for what in himself was absolutely fundamental and universally human. He sought, therefore, for humanity.

To this understanding everything was relevant. To know a man one needed to know his interests. Schweitzer wanted to hear about a man's trade or his craft, his problems and victories, the way business was going

96

and what he thought of the political situation. When it came to a person's private life, for Schweitzer it was indeed private and no more to be discussed in public than the secrets of the confessional, although he knew well enough what went on, and he was not a man to be shocked. When family problems were brought to him, as they are to any pastor, he was gentle and understanding, never censorious.

It is true, however, that he could never, all his life, accustom himself to the new freedom of discussion of sex in public, and in old age was upset by a photograph of the birth of a baby—an event that he had witnessed times without number and always rejoiced in. He even tore from a magazine an article on prostitution. Such matters were only to be spoken of between friends, not to be paraded in print.

Outside sex, though, family life was as interesting as public life, and he saw no conflict between the two. In his book on Bach he confesses to a frustrated curiosity about "Bach's intimate life," and as to Jesus' rejection of his family, Schweitzer always found that sad. He could only suppose that it happened "because his relatives wished to take him home and obstruct his public ministry." But he could never quite fathom why universal love should come into conflict with family ties although it was a conflict from which he was himself to suffer before the end.

Every moment then was filled with the need to know more about people and the things people did and suffered. In conversation, in his study, in the pulpit, this was what exercised him. The philosophies he studied he judged not by their interior logic but by their truth to life. What was the value of a magnificently coherent system of thought that never touched ground? To interest Schweitzer, truth must be serviceable, and its service must be to all men.

He came back constantly to the ideas behind his *epigoni* book. What was happening to civilization? Somehow or other, his intuition told him, civilized man had lost sight of civilization's purpose. He searched the philosophers to find out if any of them dealt with anything as fundamental, basic, or "elemental" as this. No. They all took civilization for granted, along with the ethics that make civilization possible. The tree had grown so large, and the branches so complicated, that the roots had been forgotten. Worse, the stem had been attacked and the sap was ceasing to flow. Among thinkers, only Tolstoy seemed to be writing about the elemental factors, love and compassion, and he was an artist, a man of imagination rather than logic.

What was it that civilization had lost? Nobody seemed to have a compelling ideal to set against Nietzsche's vision of proud and dominating individualism, which was everywhere gaining ground.

One quality that soldiers and politicians are said to need is the instinct for the jugular—the knowledge when and how to go for the kill. In philosophers, Schweitzer looked for something else and rarely found it—the instinct for the tap root, the root that draws nourishment from the soil. He himself had it. He believed that civilization, like everything else, needs constant nourishment if it is not to wither and die. What is that forgotten nourishment? It must be some quality deep in the nature of man; indeed of life itself.

Schweitzer found himself dissatisfied with any philosophy that confined its attention to human life. Kant had tried to capture the whole universe in a web of thought. That had proved a failure; the universe was too vast for that kind of thinking. But at least Kant had known that man does not live in isolation from the rest of Creation. Schweitzer scanned the philosophers for any sign that they acknowledged other life than human. In childhood he had included in his prayers "everything that had breath." Now, seeking for the root principle of the way we live together on earth, he again felt an emptiness if animal life were not included. None of the philosophers included it. Even in the Bible, the only words he could find of compassion toward animals were in Proverbs 12: "A righteous man regards the life of his beast." The taproot instinct told Schweitzer that in this respect philosophy and the Bible were less rich and less real than everyday life, where animals were man's constant, valued companions and assistants, with as much right as any human creature to the world they were born into. Philosophy and religion should be man's servants, not his masters. They existed for man, not man for them. Schweitzer measured the great thinkers against the man in the street, and the thinkers were found wanting.

Had Schweitzer been Anglo-Saxon he might well have stopped worrying about the thinkers and got on with living. But being what he was, deeply imbued with the German need for a pattern in life, he found it impossible to let go. Instinct and thought must be brought into harness. His own passionate nature still needed the guidance of a ruling principle, an ideal. His misfortune was that the principles that satisfied others left him cold; wherever he looked he found ideas that had lost touch with life. "I have often thought," he said in later life, "how lucky I was not to be brilliant. It forced me to be profound."

Such a man could never dwindle into the average kind of curate. Nor was it so. Within a month of the examinations we find him preparing a lecture, the first of a series, for the Foreign Language Society of Paris. The subject was his old bugbear, Nietzsche. While he was working on it, he heard that Nietzsche had finally, after his years of madness, died. The lecture became a kind of obituary, a valediction. Schweitzer saluted Nietzsche's courage, originality, and honesty but was sad about his limitations, warned against his conclusions, and wished that superhumanity could have been achieved without sacrificing humanity.

A few weeks later he had managed to get to Bayreuth for more of his beloved Wagner. And meeting there with his much-loved Aunt Mathilde, he accompanied her to Oberammergau for the Passion Play. "She wanted someone to look after the baggage," he said.

He liked the scenery—the mountains behind the open-air stage—better than the play. He admired the devotion of the performers and the way in which they struggled to preserve the simplicity of the original design in face of the flood of foreign visitors. But the structure of the play he found wanting, the display excessively theatrical, the text imperfect, and the music banal. It has to be admitted that a biblical scholar with a specialist interest in Bach might be as difficult to please as anyone in the Oberammergau audience that year, but his criticisms are not unjust.

Back in Strasbourg life settled to a steady rhythm that was to last without serious disruption for the next six years. The restrictions were less severe than he might have feared because Gerold and Knittel, proud of the attainments of their new curate, were thoughtful and helpful about arranging free time. He was generally required to take the afternoon service and the children's service on Sundays and an hour's confirmation class for boys three times a week. Occasionally, he would deputize for one of the old gentlemen at the morning service as well, but he enjoyed the more intimate afternoon services better. Person to person he was at ease. In front of a crowd less so.

His comments on his confirmation class are worth quoting, not least because of the contrast between his teaching methods and those of Aunt Sophie of Mulhouse:

> I tried hard to give them as little homework to do as possible, that the lessons might be a time of pure refreshment for heart and spirit. I therefore used the last ten minutes for making them repeat after me, and so get to know by heart, Bible sayings and verses of hymns which they might take away with them from these classes to guide them throughout their lives. The aim of my teaching was to bring home to their hearts and thoughts the great truths of later life so they might be able to resist the temptations to irreligion which would assail them. I tried also to awake in them a love for the Church, and a feeling of need for a solemn hour for their souls in the Sunday services. I taught them to respect traditional doctrines, but at the same time to hold fast to the saying of St. Paul that where the spirit of Christ is, there is liberty.... In these lessons I first became conscious of how much schoolmaster blood I have in me from my ancestors.[1]

Mrs. Clara Urquhart, his long-standing friend in later years, has said that if one element in him predominated over others, it was the teacher.

For the younger children, who went to L'Ecole de Dragon, St. Nicholas' Sunday School, Schweitzer adopted the bribery technique. Each week he came to class primed with a story, which he saved up to tell in the final few minutes if the children had been good. Fritz Schnepp, who went to Sunday School at L'Ecole de Dragon all those years ago, remembered the joy of the stories until his old age, stories mainly of animals, of adventure, and hunting in distant lands. The big, energetic, friendly young man was more than capable of inspiring hero worship in the boys with his ready laugh, his swift understanding, and his spurts of amiable fury. "His temper was quick," says M. Schnepp, "but never frightening." And Dr. André Wetzel, who also knew him from the early days, says, "There was so little humbug about him that people were often amazed to hear he was a pastor."

As to his afternoon sermons, Schweitzer regarded these, he says, "as simple devotional exercises rather than sermons," so much so that they often lasted less than a quarter of an hour, and a complaint was lodged with Pastor Knittel about their inadequacy. "He was as much embarrassed as I was. When he asked what he was to reply to the aggrieved member of the congregation, I replied that he might say that I was only a poor Curate who stopped speaking when he found he had nothing more to say about the text. Thereupon he dismissed me with a mild reprimand, and an admonition not to preach for less than twenty minutes."[2]

Confirmation classes were Schweitzer's only obligatory task, and because they only occurred during the school terms, he was free during the holidays to find a replacement preacher and to go where he would. This gave him one month at Easter, which he generally spent in Paris, and two in the late summer, which he took at home in Günsbach. But besides these he frequently had to make hurried journeys to Paris to play the organ at some concert with the Jean Sebastian Bach Society, whose official organist he now became. Sermons were written on the train or while waiting at stations. Cuffs were covered with thoughts that occurred en route. The trouble about these dates was that they sometimes clashed with his organ duties at St. William's, and now the wheel was coming full circle there: just as he had deputized eight years before for Eugène Münch, so now some of the young organ pupils whom he and Ernest Münch had trained were called upon to stand in for him.

When he made these forty-eight-hour dashes to Paris for a quick rehearsal, a concert, and back the next day, there was no time to reach his uncle's house in the suburbs, no money for a hotel. At any hour of the day or night he would hammer unceremoniously on the door of any handy friend who was used to his informal ways. Pfarrer Christian Brandt remembered being awakened at five in the morning by an apparently tireless young man who wanted a bed for a few hours and, in the manner of the perennial student, was prepared to cadge one without shame or apology.

During the longer spells in Paris Schweitzer stayed with his uncle. Happy hours were spent with Widor at the organ of St. Sulpice, hours that, he wrote in 1962, "count among the most beautiful of my life."[3]

This was also his opportunity to extend his knowledge of French-built organs, which he was still busy comparing and contrasting with the new German organs. The two kinds of organ demanded different methods of playing, and Schweitzer studied the French style not only with Widor but also with Fr. Alexandre Guilmant, organist of the Church of the Trinity, and Eugène Gigout of Saint Augustine, both of whom were composers as well as performers. Guilmant, like Widor, had studied under the great Belgian organist Nicholas Jacques Lemmens, who himself had been a pupil of Adolf Hesse, the brilliant and faithful interpreter of Bach who had made his church in Breslau a place of pilgrimage for Bach lovers at the beginning of the nineteenth century when Bach's name was almost forgotten. With the aid of these two French organists, heirs of the true Bach style, Schweitzer was building up a crushing case against German organ building.

The attack was on three main fronts: ease of manipulation, touch control, and tone. On manipulation the issue was one of hands versus feet. Schweitzer states it graphically:

> The basic principle of the French system is the arrangement of all the resources of the instrument in the pedals. The French organs have no pistons under the keyboards. What system shall we decide upon?
>
> I do not sit for five minutes beside Father Guilmant on the bench of his beautiful house organ at Meudon without his asking me, as if he had just remembered where we left off last time: "And in Germany do they still build pistons? That I can't understand. See how simple it is when one has everything under one's feet." And the short agile feet press couplers and combination pedals silently then in a trice let them up again.
>
> On another day Widor, for the twenty-fifth time, begins on the same subject. "Tell my friend Professor Münch at Strasbourg that he must point out for me a single place in a Bach prelude or fugue when he has a hand free for a moment to reach for a piston. Let him name anyone who can play on the manual and at the same time press the piston on the key strip with his thumb."
>
> I keep my silence, for the first German organist into whose hands I fall a few weeks later, and to whom I put this controversial question, answers me invariably, "The French are very backward. Formerly we too had all this in the feet; now, however, we have our beautiful pistons."[4]

Schweitzer summed up in favor of the French system. An organist often has a free foot, seldom a free hand; he had heard the jarring hesitations and dislocations of rhythm on German organs when the hand had to leave the keyboard to reach for the piston. And if helpers were introduced to pull the stops, something always went wrong.

The question of touch control was the issue between pneumatic action and tracker action. When the electric bellows made unlimited power available to organ builders, they made use of it to eliminate the pushrod system connecting the key to the valve that opened the pipe.

Now the lightest possible touch instantly produced the note; no pressure was required, the finger had no "knowledge" of the moment the valve opened and closed, no sensitivity was needed. The difference was something like that between a manual and an electric typewriter, except that a dead precision is a desirable quality in a typewriter, not necessarily so in a musical instrument.

> The player must exert himself to overcome this dead precision. It lacks the vital and elastic quality of the lever. . . . With the tracker the finger feels a certain tension exactly when the tone comes; it feels the contact point. And the depressed key pushes up under the finger, in order that, when the finger shows the slightest impulse to leave it, it may immediately rise with its own strength and lift the finger up with it. The strength of the keys co-operates with the will! With the tracker even the mediocre organist cannot smear. With pneumatics there is no such co-operation on the part of the keys. It makes the playing worse instead of better, and brings to light the slightest fault.
>
> Only with the tracker does one come into really intimate relationship with one's organ. In pneumatics one communicates with one's instrument by telegraph.[5]

The effect of Marie Jaëll's lessons on touch is apparent here. He went so far as to say that the average pneumatic organ was an instrument "which one leaves in a high state of nervous despair."[6]

For judging tonal quality Schweitzer devised a technique of his own:

> In order to judge the tone of an organ, one first pulls out all the eight-foot stops and plays a polyphonic movement. In the midst of the web of tone the alto and the tenor must come through well; and the tone, even when the stops are played in the upper register, should never be unpleasant. Thereupon one lets the four-foot and two-foot stops enter, and repeats the test. Finally, one plays Bach fugues for a half-hour without interruption on the full organ. If the hearer is able to follow the voices clearly, and if he finds the sustained fullness of tone is not exhausting, then the organ is good.[7]

German organs often failed this test because of their makers' tendency to build in too much power. The high pressure of an electric bellows could increase the volume, but at the expense of tone. "A fat person," commented Schweitzer disparagingly, "is neither beautiful nor strong. To be artistically beautiful and strong is only to have a figure with a perfect play of muscles."[8]

Schweitzer himself was both beautiful and strong. A glance at the photographs taken about this time shows that he had grown strikingly handsome. But almost more impressive than the good looks is the powerful masculinity of the face—the piercing eyes, dark springy hair, and strong square jaw and cheekbones would turn heads in any company. It is not a face to suggest deep devotional piety or profound scholarship and long, late hours of study. A scholarly reputation combined with vigorous physical authority is a very attractive combination.

He also possessed a quality that his friend Werner Picht described as "total presence." To illustrate this quality Picht described an occasion that he witnessed some years after the time we are now concerned with, when Schweitzer's work on organ building had borne fruit in the form of commissions to design new organs. But because we are talking of the impression that Schweitzer could make, I quote it here. At twenty-five he may have had it to a lesser degree than at thirty-five, but it was assuredly already well developed.

> Total presence in every situation is the infallible sign of the significant human being. Schweitzer has this sign in the highest degree. Napoleon needed an actor's training. But with Schweitzer the effect is unconscious and obtained without any gesture. During his years in Strasbourg a new organ was built in the Sangerhaus according to his instructions. The organists of Strasbourg came together at the inaugural celebration, and each sought to demonstrate the capacities of the new instrument and his own mastery of it. When everyone else had played his piece, the man who had created the organ walked slowly up to it in his usual fashion, his arms hanging loosely by his side, sat down at the organ, and played the Chorale—it was Advent—"*Wie soll ich dich empfangen*"—and then walked away again. And yet the one figure that moved with the least fuss is the one which remains in the memory after the passage of half a century.[9]

This "presence" arose from a total and unselfconscious concentration on the business at hand. Because he was unaware of it, it did not detract from his gaiety and good humor, and in addition he possessed that swift apprehension and sympathy that appeals to women. Besides all this, he was becoming something of a dandy—so he himself related in old age to Mrs. Erica Anderson, the documentary filmmaker whose film about him won an Oscar in 1958 and who became a close friend. Fortunately, we have a photograph that shows what he meant. There he sits in all his glory—straw hat, cane, and all—the very model of a maiden's prayer, posed with conscious elegance on a rock in the middle of a field. His brother took the photograph, so it may have been intended for the family album. But the impression it makes is less that of the pious and devoted son of the vicarage, more that of the debonair young man about town.

An odd little story he told to Mrs. Anderson adds to the picture of the dandy. He was out for a walk with relations one day when a fashionable hat came flying over a clump of bushes and landed at his feet. "It was a nice hat, so I tried it on. It fitted well enough and I was very much tempted to accept this unexpected gift. But in the end I tossed it back where it came from."[10]

Those, of course, were the days when the appearance of a camera was the cue to strike a pose—a habit he never entirely grew out of. The informal Schweitzer cannot be found in early photographs or in his published works, in both of which he appears, as it were, in his Sunday best.

In life, however, he had by now achieved a naturalness, a way of making himself instantly at home, which was one of his greatest attractions. He was the kind of man who would follow a housewife into her kitchen to steal a bun fresh from the oven (for his was a very sweet tooth) and do so with such charm and appreciation that it was a compliment, not an impertinence. The self-transcendence he demanded of himself never descended to the petty self-sacrifices of giving up sugar in his coffee or seeking physical discomfort for its own sake and for the sake of appearing superior.

At dances, both in Paris and at Strasbourg, he would go out of his way to dance with the wallflowers. True to the spirit that as a boy had made him vow to marry a cripple, his sympathy went out to the girls who, for whatever reason, sat around the dance floor partnerless. With the boldness of conquered shyness he put his sympathy into practice, and enjoyed the happiness he gave. Not for him the priggish self-satisfaction of an unpleasant duty done. He gave pleasure and he took pleasure, physical and mental. "He was," say his friends, "a man for touching"—the light touch on the elbow or shoulder. Gaiety, activity, and contact with other human beings were the gifts of God. Delight itself was a duty; unhappiness was the enemy. The unhappiness of others diminished one's own happiness, so kindness was the practical thing for one's own good as well as that of others.

Fifty years later, when he was visiting Europe in the intervals of his spells at Lambarene, Erica Anderson used to act as his chauffeur to save him the trouble of long and tiring train journeys. Modern life offers few better opportunities for intimate conversation than a long car journey.

Enclosed, uninterrupted, unable to do anything but talk, on these occasions Schweitzer could relax with a trusted friend more completely than anywhere else. On one long drive from Günsbach to Paris, she remembered, he talked nearly all the way about the women in his life. She did not say who they were nor what exactly is meant by "the women in his life," nor, perhaps, should she because Schweitzer himself took such care to protect not only his own private life but that of everybody he knew. But she said that several appear to have lived in Paris and that he seemed to have had a partiality for Jewish women.

In view of the lack of firm information as to the identity and number of Schweitzer's lady friends—quite apart from the precise role they played in his life—it might seem wiser not to go into the subject any farther. By passing it over, however, I run the risk of giving an impression that may well, I believe, be false, namely, that Schweitzer never knew the physical love of a woman until his marriage at the age of thirty-seven.

It is impossible, of course, to prove that he did not have love affairs. And if anyone was ever in a position to prove that he did, they have never come forward. Schweitzer was not the sort of man whose confidence one would breach any more than he breached that of others.

But the newly discovered letters between him and Hélène Bresslau, his long-time confidante, later to be his wife, throw some light on this, as on other aspects of his life. These will emerge in due course, but for the moment let us note a couple of revealing remarks, one serious, one teasing.

The first comes from an early period of this correspondence: "You know from the most intimate of my letters . . . that I had an affection about which I did not speak, and which I have not completely overcome—I know that I will conquer it, but it is very hard."[11] The second comes when it has finally been agreed, after a long period when it seemed that was not to be their path, that they will marry: "A little letter from the other Hélène which suggests a rendezvous in Switzerland. . . . I do not know whether I will stretch out my hands for this delicious meal [a reference to a meal in Homer's *Odyssey*]. I would like to, all right, because I feel that soon I will only know what the word 'rendezvous' means by looking it up in the dictionary."[12] To which Hélène replies: "When and where will the rendezvous with Hélène Barrère be? I can't quite believe in this lack of familiarity with rendezvous, after all those recent meetings with sweet and pretty ladies!"[13]

It seems clear from this that, despite contrary reports, Schweitzer did find the time for a little light romance. It is difficult to say what the word *rendezvous* means here; it could range from almost nothing to something fairly serious although the openness with Hélène shows that there was not a trace of secrecy or guilt about it in this connection.

His mother, it seems, complained that his friends were almost only women, which he indignantly denied in a letter to Hélène: "She does not think of Curtius, Ziegler, Widor.—But, you know women have more strength and are more naturally in tune with life than men. I am sure that no friendship with a man would have helped me, would have taught me as much as you have, not to forget my aunt and Miss H. (Adèle Herrenschmidt). There is an elemental superiority and naturalness in a woman—or did only I meet those?"[14]

He took an interest in fashion, and along with his new social poise he was developing a great and gallant charm. Something of this charm is captured in letters he wrote to women friends and continued to write almost till the day he died.

Some of the letters to Hélène have this style. I have seen others, too, mostly from his later years, but the style is so like that of those early letters to his goddaughter Suzi that we are safe in assuming that this was a lifelong style—tender, playful, intimate, and quite free from the formality that dogged most of his other correspondence. Although they carry no implication of physical liaison, these can really only be described as love letters and could only have been written by a masculine man to a woman whose femininity he valued.

Add to this a passing remark in one of his lyrical letters about nature to Hélène:

> Now nature gives in. Two days it fought and wrestled against its ageing. . . . An overnight peace has come. Nature now smiles in bright sunshine. . . . Shiny rose-hips and dark sloes decorate nature as if it were blossoming again. It puts brilliant jewelery on its dark and serious robe.—How beautiful and moving this is. This is how women fight until they surrender, and then comes Fall, smiling, when all charms and richness, which they hide inside, unfold.[15]

It is a comment very much of its period, but it does suggest some experience. His dandyism, too, suggests an awareness of sex, a courting instinct, and a self-confidence that must have come from a knowledge that he was found attractive. Mrs. Clara Urquhart, his translator, confidante, and close friend in later years, is certain that as a young man he fell deeply in love, as the passage above suggests. Erica Anderson, whose excellent and characteristic remark, "He had no quarrel with the way God made men and women," has already been quoted, also says, "Schweitzer believed in experience. He wished to experience everything, for he believed it was the only way to learn. There was no rigidity about him. The only rule was that one must never treat experience lightly or irresponsibly; and one must try never to hurt other people." "Schweitzer," she says, "was a complete man."[16] And Schweitzer's daughter, Mrs. Rhena Schweitzer-Miller, says, "There is only one phrase to describe what he had, and that is sex appeal."[17]

That such a man should reach his thirty-seventh year without experiencing sexual love I find incredible. To others it may not seem so. If love affairs did occur, I am certain that he would have felt them deeply and taken them seriously although he would certainly have been wary of any involvement that threatened to overmaster him and his work. And if, in fact, he never did make love with a woman, it was surely because he knew he could never give the relationship the time and consideration it demanded and deserved.

But if, as I think probable, his eagerness for life embraced this experience as it embraced others, then Paris in the early years of the century seems the most likely place and time for it to have happened. His life in the college at Strasbourg was too much of an open book for romances to have passed unnoticed, and it is those who knew him in Strasbourg who all swore that he had no time for such things. In Paris he was free from the constraints of his position as professor and pastor and with a little leisure. Here, as in Strasbourg, he was in touch with people from many different walks of life—business people, teachers, artists, musicians, students—besides the shopkeepers and artisans with whom he was everywhere on good terms. There was no shortage of possible partners. As to his partiality for Jewish women, Mrs. Anderson has suggested that an association with someone from a different religion would be less likely to burden him with any sense of spiritual responsibility.

Should it be asked whether even this amount of discussion of Schweitzer's private life is legitimate, I can only answer yes and for two reasons. The first is the same that he himself gave for publishing what he believed about Jesus, even though it would be unpalatable for many and to some destructive of their faith: "Truth is in all circumstances more valuable than untruth, and this must apply to truth in the realm of history as to other kinds of truth." And, quoting St. Paul, "We can do nothing against the truth, but for the truth."[18]

The second is that Schweitzer has far too long been a plaster idol removed from the sphere of ordinary feeling. His name is a byword for inhuman perfection, which is grossly unfair to a most human man. The care with which he protected his relations with women has led the world to believe that he was spotlessly chaste and made it possible for the puritans to quote him as their hero. But although the myth elevates him as a shining example for aseptic preachers to point at, it also removes him from the common run of humanity, who were his true friends. The ordinary sensual, life-loving human being finds the Schweitzer figure too pure for understanding or sympathy.

As the twentieth century wore on people grew steadily less inclined
to believe that physical abstinence is necessarily good and that holiness
involves a denial of the body. They were more likely to feel that if a man
knows nothing of the love of a woman until he is thirty-seven, it is a
defect rather than a mark of perfection. They were beginning to understand holiness in its proper sense, as wholeness.

If it could truly be shown that Schweitzer had no relations with women
before his marriage, then, of course, that should be clearly said. But I
believe that the evidence points the other way. I believe he was a whole
man.

During the summer breaks at Günsbach, he was capable of relapsing
into the moody lad whom elsewhere he had outgrown. Here he could for
a while relax from the effort of will that went into the rest of his life and
forget the self-imposed struggle for ever-increasing self-mastery. The
family routine was unchanged. Meals were on the table at the stroke of
the clock, and woe betide anyone who was not in his place. Traditional
food was taken to traditional picnic places. Year after year fruit was
bottled, jam was made, and sometimes, after a family expedition, the
whole house would smell of the wild strawberries that they had picked.

But Schweitzer never forgot his work for long. The very peacefulness
of the vicarage and its ordered ways would aggravate his restlessness
and make him irritable and abstracted. When the bell sounded for lunch
all the family would appear except Albert. Albert would be sent for.
Albert would explain that he would be down when he had finished this
paragraph. But the paragraph would spread into a page, or two or three,
before Albert appeared and took his place with a somewhat querulous
expression on his face. He would gaze out of the window through the
rest of the meal, saying nothing; and make it clear, if any remark was
made about his lateness, that he had better things to worry about than
punctuality.

On the whole the family bore it well. They were increasingly proud of
him and convinced of his rightness. Perhaps the old pastor was the least
impressed, being something of a disciplinarian, and seeing no reason
why Albert should spend so much time over theological notions that he
was convinced nobody would take seriously. But he recognized—he could
scarcely help recognizing—that his son now dominated the house when
he was home. And mother was as proud as could be, only a little grieved
that Albert rested so little and could spare so little time for the family.

Louise would often be there with her husband, Jules, and the family,
little Suzi and her baby brother. Jules shared Albert's apprehensions about
the increasing size and power of the great industrial empires with their
insistence on a slavish loyalty to predigested schemes rather than initiative and free thought. And this insistence on conformity and crushing of

individuality was infecting churches as much as nations, political parties, and industrial concerns. Realpolitik, the worship of expediency and self-interest, was rife everywhere. The forebodings Schweitzer had felt in Paris and in Berlin about the way Western civilization was going grew steadily more gloomy. Increasingly, he felt himself "out of step with his age," and the more Europe seemed to be dispensing with individual thought and succumbing to the cozy dogmas of nationalism and material progress, the more convinced he became that civilization began with the individual. Individual reason alone could find the way through the fashionable parrot-cries to the "elemental" in man; individual will could carry out the decisions of reason. Enslavement to causes, however worthy, was the end of truth and liberty.

All this was very like Nietzsche. The difference lay in what Nietzsche and Schweitzer regarded as elemental. For Nietzsche it was man's power to dominate. The individual he had in mind would rise above humanity to a splendid pagan nobility, freed from normal human concerns. For Schweitzer, the free man was Jesus, the figure he traced in his study and his prayer and his preaching. Jesus was no idealistic vision, but a man who actually had delved into himself for the essence of humanity, and in pursuit of his conviction had forced the authorities to kill him. What Nietzsche had said about the need for heroism, which was becoming increasingly relevant in an unheroic world, added fuel to the fire of Schweitzer's admiration of Jesus—an irony that might not have pleased the author of *Anti-Christ*.

In Schweitzer's room the new Jesus was almost ready to make his appearance.

8

—

The Historical Jesus

1901

IN MAY 1901 an extraordinary thing happened. The principal of Strasbourg's Theological College had died, and a certain Gustav Anrich was appointed to the post. Anrich needed some time to wind up his affairs in his parish, and an interim deputy was required. Schweitzer was only twenty-six, had earned his degree a mere nine months before, and was not even a fully fledged pastor. Yet by general agreement of the theological faculty he was the only serious contender for the position; such was the esteem in which he was held. And, evidently, he made a success of it, for two years later, when Anrich went on to another post, Schweitzer was an automatic choice as his successor.

He held the deputy principalship from the beginning of May to the end of September when the new term began. And now, during this term of office, the book at last came out: *Das Abendmahl. Das Messianitäts und Leidensgeheimnis. Ein Skizze des Lebens Jesu* (The secret of the Messiahship and Passion. A Sketch of the life of Jesus). Only the latter part was translated into English (and that not until 1914) under the title *The Mystery of the Kingdom of God*.

If you ask English-speaking scholars the name of the book about Christ for which Schweitzer is famous, the chances are that they will say *The Quest of the Historical Jesus*. They may well add that it was a highly important work for its time, impressively researched, unconvincing, overemphatic, and, unfortunately, they have never read it.

Still less have they read *The Mystery of the Kingdom of God*. The reason is partly that although it is the earlier book, it was translated later, and the furor that was caused in England by *The Quest* had blown over by the time *The Mystery* arrived on the scene. It, therefore, seemed somewhat déjà vu because the arguments it puts forward are summarized in *The Quest*.

But the arguments are far more closely knit and compelling in the earlier book. *The Quest* had quite another purpose: it was designed as a survey of all the previous attempts to make historical sense of the Gospels; and Schweitzer, having already put forward his own solution in *The Mystery of the Kingdom of God*, saw no reason to repeat his ideas in full. He sketches them in as a conclusion to the Quest, and inevitably they are not wholly watertight or convincing in this form.

The Mystery of the Kingdom of God, then, is the important book. Schweitzer never found cause to alter the views there expounded, and although one will find scholars who claim that he was only able to hold to his theories by totally ignoring subsequent developments in theology, his introduction to the third edition of *The Quest*, written when he was seventy-five, shows that, in fact, he had remained closely in touch with these developments but found nothing in them to make him change his mind.

Indeed, his views had not changed in any material respect since he first hit upon the problem while on maneuvers at the age of nineteen. The intuition that then struck him had now broadened and deepened into considered conviction, and he had confirmed it by wide-ranging studies of other possible theories, of the historical background of Jesus' life, and of the texts themselves in Hebrew and in Greek. The theory no longer depended on the passage in Matthew about the sending out of the disciples and the prophecy that the kingdom would be on them before they returned. This was now only one of many passages, all of which combined to prove in Schweitzer's mind that Jesus lived in constant expectation that the world was about to be remade and that he would reappear as its Lord, the chosen one of God.

In comparing Schweitzer's books with those of other theologians one is struck by one great difference that permeates all his writing. He does not *read* like a theologian. There is a sort of transparency about his presentation; the thoughts come clear and unmuddied. No preconception comes between Schweitzer and the subject under discussion; no dogmatic discoloration tinges his observation. With every other writer one is aware that some undeclared bias is tilting the argument to port or starboard. Centuries of Church teaching about Jesus have so impregnated the imagination of Christians that fact and dogma have become indistinguishable. For example, a scholar may know very well that the phrase "Son of God" could be applied by a Jew to every male Jew—to be human was to be a child of God. Yet when the phrase is applied to Jesus he finds it nearly impossible to forget that for seventeen hundred years the

Christian Church has used the phrase to mean something quite different—the divine second person of the Holy Trinity, a unique creature, part of the Deity Himself. The two images become confused. And because our scholar is writing as a Christian for Christians, he may also be afraid of seeming to betray his own faith if he really manages to drive all Christian reactions from his imagination. It takes great courage to divest the mind of the doctrines that support and comfort it—great courage and a rare imaginative power, the power to enter an alien thought-world without feeling challenged, frightened, and defensive. Many of the reactions to Schweitzer's books show symptoms of this anxiety.

Schweitzer shows no such fear. There is a fine defiance, almost a ruthlessness about the way in which he claims the right to make up his own mind: "the judgment of the early Church," he writes, "is not binding upon us."[1] Such a claim is, of course, easier for a Lutheran than for a Catholic, for the latter is committed to the view that the Church is itself divine, that it possesses Christ's spirit and is, indeed, in some mystical way the continuation of Christ's own body. But Protestants, too, have a sense of the holiness of the Church, and to set oneself up against its judgments, although absolutely necessary for Schweitzer's purpose, can feel something like blasphemy.

Schweitzer's unique quality, then, was his ability to look at the subject afresh, undeterred by the claims of loyalty or the fear of what disastrous consequences his discoveries might provoke. On the crucial question of Jesus' Messiahship, for example, he writes, "One should not forget that if Jesus did not take himself to be the Messiah, this means the death blow of the Christian faith."[2] No mystical doctrine, he believed, could possibly justify a Church that posthumously promoted its founder to a status he never claimed in his lifetime.

In the twentieth century we saw how the Che Guevaras of this world can be transformed after their deaths into demigods to satisfy the need of their followers for someone to worship. Schweitzer was right. If this is how the Church was founded, it is proof only that man can set up a dead hero higher than he stood when he lived and that Jesus was less than the image they made of him. This was the danger Schweitzer faced, and he knew it. And, perhaps, he exulted in it a little. His book glows with a sense of enjoyable challenge. And he did, after all, believe in heroes—the one man pitted against the many.

As we have seen, Schweitzer's instinct, whether dealing with philosophy, music, or religion, was to drive straight through to the mind that gave it birth. Instead of treating the texts as a series of abstract propositions, he paid Jesus the unusual compliment of acknowledging that he was both a comprehensible human being and a Jew of his time. The most pious Christian is committed to believing that Jesus was Man as well as

God. Schweitzer took this seriously, knowing that the side that was God is not approachable by the historical method, but the side that is Man can be understood in the way we understand other men—by sympathy and imagination combined with an understanding of the surrounding circumstances.

Most professional theologians are less noted for their imaginative insight into human behavior than for their skill in literary analysis or dogmatic manipulation. Schweitzer, entering the battle as a human being trying imaginatively as well as intellectually to understand the story of another human being, gave himself an excellent chance of discovering things that others had failed to notice. But at the same time he put himself outside the club. He was not working entirely within the rules. And this may be one reason why the theological fraternity, while respectfully acknowledging his industry, his versatility, and his admirable humanitarian work in the jungle, has failed to take his arguments as seriously as they deserve.

To understand these arguments at all we must plunge briefly into the history of the period. The little Jewish nation in Jesus' day was already well acquainted with suppression and the resentful acceptance of domination by a foreign power that did not understand or care about their God. Since the great captivity in Egypt and their long flight to the Promised Land, their history had been a succession of enslavements by aggressive neighbors. Their holy books were almost all concerned not with the mysteries of internal prayer or personal salvation but with the promises made by God that he would deliver the nation from this captivity or that. They dealt also with the behavior required by God as a condition of deliverance. But the hope to which they looked was not that of individual bliss or a vision of God in another life but of the Jewish society living in peace and perfection, harmoniously obeying its own laws and worshiping its God. Different prophets offered different pictures of the coming society and different prescriptions as to what kind of offering would be acceptable to the Lord before he ushered in the kingdom to come; some spoke of sacrifices of beasts, some of repentance of heart, and one, the second writer of Isaiah, foretold the sacrifice of one just man for many.

But in all of them the future glory would be found in a specific human community, altered certainly almost beyond recognition, but on earth and in time. In this sense the religious instincts of the Jews were social and political rather than spiritual in the common modern sense of "otherworldly."

For some of the prophets, the kingdom would be ruled over by God in person. But for Daniel, God was too great, too transcendent for such a restricted task; he would send instead his chosen one, the Son of Man, to rule on his behalf. The Son of Man would be human, but his origin would be heavenly. Other prophets had spoken of the Messiah, a king descended from David, who would rule in heaven on God's behalf. By the time of Jesus' birth, these various concepts had become an amalgam of ideas and hopes. But at all events it was widely agreed that the kingdom was coming—that the prophet Elijah would reappear as the forerunner of the kingdom, announcing himself by doing signs and miracles—and that the Messiah, now identified with the Son of Man, would then appear in glory to usher in the kingdom. When this happened, he would select the faithful and rule over them in peace and justice forever—the faithless having been consumed in the disasters that attended the inauguration of the new order. These beliefs and hopes are now summed up in the word *eschatology*, the study of the ultimate things.

When Jesus was born, a great many Jews had cause to believe that the kingdom might be due. Apart from sayings in the prophecies that upon calculation put the date at about this time, many contemporary events suggested that deliverance was necessary. Half a century before, the Romans had occupied Israel, and a Roman general had walked boldly into the Temple's Holy of Holies, into which nobody but the high priest was allowed. Since then the occupation had become increasingly harsh and repressive, in answer partly to the resistance movements that had sprung up among the Jews. Herod the Great had imposed what was almost a police state, impious and detested. On top of this there had been earthquakes, droughts, and pestilence, quite enough to convince the pious that the end, and the beginning, were near.

Many groups had left the cities and awaited the cataclysm in the desert, and communities of believers flourished. Others, although they might pursue their normal lives, could not fail to be aware either of the all-pervading presence of the occupying forces or of the hope of divine intervention and deliverance. On or below the surface, Palestine at that time was emotionally turbulent, sometimes hysterical, electric with apprehension and revolutionary fervor. And the fervor was both religious and political because the two things for the Jews were the same.

Into this society, desperately alert to every possible hint of the arrival of salvation, came Jesus, born of the family of David, with a personality and style of preaching that drew crowds to him in his lifetime and that have echoed unceasingly down the whole of subsequent history.

The only records of Jesus' life that have come down to us, the four Gospels, are absurdly confusing and incomplete. Why? To this question all scholars of any note are in agreement in answering that, whatever Jesus himself may have thought, his followers after his death were convinced that his return as the Messiah was to be expected at any moment. This is why nobody troubled to write his history; his life story was not needed. And in any case his life so far was of little significance; it was merely the overture to the perfected life to come. It was only when the kingdom failed, day after day, month after month, year after year, to break upon the world—when some of the disciples had died and new recruits had to be instructed in the expectations of the group—that people began to collect the stories told of Jesus and to write them down.

But they were still not interested in Jesus' life history, only in what he had said and done that was of significance and value in fostering and refreshing the disciples' faith in the return of the Messiah and the birth of the kingdom.

As time passed and the kingdom was still delayed, it became obvious that someone had made a mistake. That it should be Jesus was unthinkable. By definition the Messiah does not make mistakes. So it must have been the disciples. They must have misunderstood him. And so the great game of reinterpretation began, open to anyone with a theory that could remotely be made to fit those ambiguous brief records in the Gospels. The game has gone on ever since, with efforts being made from time to time by the various churches, notably the Roman Catholics, to check the confusion by laying down a party line and reinforcing it by the claim that it had been dictated by the Spirit of Jesus, which had entered the disciples at Pentecost and dwelt in the Church ever since.

After a time it began to be seen, in retrospect, that since the Spirit of Jesus dwelt still in the Church, the kingdom had, in fact, come after all. It had been in the world all the time, ushered in by Jesus and held in trust by the Church. Thus, it could be shown to everyone's satisfaction that nobody had made a mistake after all. God had moved in a mysterious way, the kingdom had arrived, and *this* was what Jesus had been talking about all the time.

But was it? The Church's claim to the exclusive representation of Jesus in the world has had good results and bad. Often it has imposed order, the order of conformity, on conflicting sects. Great and holy men have sprung from its soil (although also from other soils). It has also been responsible for some of the most disgusting horrors in human history. Who can say whether the scales tip toward good or ill in the long run? The parable of the Grand Inquisitor, in Dostoyevski's *The Brothers Karamazov*, is probably the world's greatest statement of the pros and cons. But one thing the Church has not done. It has not been able to make its image look even remotely like the image that rises from the pages of the Gospels. But because the Church cannot do without Jesus, we are back to the question—who was he? What was he? What *did* he mean?

We have seen that Schweitzer's tutor, Holtzmann, believed that all the really essential historical material about Jesus could be found in Mark's

Gospel and that the additions in Matthew, having been inserted by the writer for some purpose of his own, could, therefore, be disregarded as historical information. The story that Holtzmann picked out from Mark was essentially the one still told today in a great many pulpits.

Jesus came to tell the Jews—indeed, to tell the world—that God's Kingdom was not, after all, to be the crudely materialistic world in which the rivers were eternally full of fish, the trees of fruit, and the fields of corn, where love and peace reigned and there were no more tears. (The fact that churchmen dismissed this vision as being "too sensual" shows what extraordinary people churchmen can be, but many of them did.) Instead, Jesus offered them a new concept, a new way of living in the world as it is today. Love and peace not through a change in the world but through a change of heart. He came as an example, to show how it could be done besides proclaiming that it should.

At first his mission met with great success and popularity. But later he encountered opposition and increasing misunderstanding. And concluding that he must now make the ultimate gesture of love and self-giving by incurring a humiliating and agonizing death, in which he would take on himself the pain and guilt of all the world and by his own suffering reconcile God to the wickedness of humanity, he went to Jerusalem and allowed the authorities to crucify him.

The fourfold arguments by which Schweitzer demolishes this picture involve a close knowledge of the text and need not concern us here. Suffice it to say that he found no evidence (1) that Jesus ever spoke of a new concept of the kingdom. The few passages that are regularly brought forward to prove that he did so, such as "the Kingdom of God is within you,"[3] have other possible meanings: this particular sentence can also be translated "the Kingdom of God is within your grasp" or "suddenly the Kingdom of God will be among you." The new Revised Standard Version of the Bible, accepted by all major denominations, translates it as "the Kingdom of God is in the midst of you." (2) He found no evidence that there was any "unsuccessful" period in his mission, crowds continued to surround him from beginning to end, or (3) that Jesus ever gave the disciples the idea that he was offering himself for the world's sins. This idea was put forward by St. Paul as an explanation of the crucifixion *after* it had happened.

What was Schweitzer's alternative? What *did* Jesus mean when he spoke of the Kingdom of God, and how much did he speak of it? This crucial problem gave Schweitzer's book its title. The Mystery of the Kingdom of God does not mean, as it would in the hands of many theologians, "the Mysterious, Mystical Fact of the Kingdom of God." It means "The Puzzle of the Kingdom of God." Schweitzer was not writing a metaphysical tract but a detective story.

Although in Mark we find a number of instances where Jesus speaks of the Kingdom of God, they are much more frequent in Matthew. Holtzmann and the Marcan school put this down to the fact that Matthew himself was a convinced eschatologist, an "end-of-the-world" man, and has, therefore, put his own views into Jesus' mouth. But Matthew's Gospel, like the other three, was approved by followers of Jesus as a true and proper record. Were they all blind to the fact that Matthew had overdone it to the extent of making Jesus, the beloved Lord, utter false prophecies—he who had in other passages been so scathing about false prophets?

The standard procedure for theologians, when faced with awkward questions of this kind, is to reject the passage as "unauthentic." They decide what they want Jesus to say, select the passages that support it, and reject the rest. Christians thus let themselves off the hook of disagreeing with their Lord.

Schweitzer's clinching point was that if we accept that Jesus was a man of his time and did, in fact, believe what Jews of his time believed, nothing has to be rejected. Everything fits. Everything makes sense. To the question, for example, whether or not Jesus regarded himself as the Messiah, Schweitzer's account points out that the Messiah was not expected until the kingdom came. By definition he was the ruler of the new kingdom. So Jesus knew that he was called to Messiahship, but not yet. Not until the kingdom came. For the present he was only the man whom God had chosen for future glorification. The secret was imparted to him when John the Baptist baptized him in the river Jordan. There was no need to tell anyone because all would be revealed when the world ended. Meantime it was a secret between Jesus and God, shared later in strict confidence with the disciples. The first and only time he openly claims to be the Messiah, he is on trial before the high priest, and the claim means certain death. He brought his death upon himself because he believed the moment of the kingdom had come. By the manner of his death he hoped to save his followers—all the believers who had gathered to hear him in the previous months—from the woes and calamities that were supposed to precede the kingdom and thereby purge Israel of its sins; because it was also said in Isaiah, "Surely he has borne our griefs and carried our sorrows . . . he was wounded for our transgressions, he was bruised for our iniquities . . . and with his stripes we are healed."[4] Jesus, steeped in the prophets, took the salvation of the Jews on himself, fulfilled the prophecies deliberately, and deliberately died, having warned the disciples in parables what to expect. The fact that they did not fully understand was of no importance. All would be made clear at the day of rejoicing.

Throughout his preaching period Jesus allows the crowds to think that he may be, at best, the expected forerunner of the Messiah—or else simply one of the prophets. But when he realizes that the kingdom is not coming as soon as he expects and concludes that the Chosen People are not yet faithful enough, he decides to sacrifice himself before God to atone for their shortcomings. From then on he plans his own death. He reveals to the disciples the secret of his Messiahship, knowing that if this is discovered by the authorities, it will mean his arrest—something he has hitherto carefully avoided. And he knows there is a traitor in the group—Judas. When Judas excuses himself and leaves the Last Supper, Jesus knows where he is going—and encourages him. The message that Judas takes to the authorities is not, as commonly supposed, where Jesus is. Jesus' whereabouts are no secret; he has been constantly in and around the temple. The message is that Jesus claims to be the Messiah. At last the authorities have evidence against him.

Even so, false witnesses have to be bribed, because Jesus is too popular with the people. But in the event they are not necessary. Here, where it is most fatal to make the direct statement, he makes it. "Are you the Christ, the Son of the Blessed One?" "I am." And then comes the great defiance: "And you will see the Son of Man seated at the right hand of Power and coming with the clouds of heaven."[5] He has condemned himself to death.

The story here summarized is, of course, supported in Schweitzer's book by chapter and verse. And it is interesting that the only other "life of Jesus" that I have been able to find that proposes a similar outline is one written by a Jew, Dr. Hugh J. Schonfield. Dr. Schonfield's book, *The Passover Plot*, shows, with great scholarship and a deep admiration of Jesus, how that extraordinary career can look to someone not brought up in the Christian tradition. It was published in 1965, and there is no reason to suppose that the author had ever read Schweitzer's book, from which it differs in some respects, bearing more heavily on the political circumstances. But the similarity is a remarkable tribute to Schweitzer's insight and his ability to enter into the Jewish thought-world of the period.

There is no question that at this level Schweitzer is extremely convincing. It is true, as he claims, that to read the Gospels afresh after studying his arguments is to bring a great deal that was obscure and "mysterious" into clear light and sharp focus. But what remains then of the Christian Jesus? What does Schweitzer think of the Resurrection? Of the miracles? Of the transfiguration of Jesus on the mountain? And how can he go on claiming to be a Christian if his Christ is so fallible, so limited by his own time and place?

This last is, of course, the most crucial question of all and is the challenge that has been thrown at Schweitzer's theology from that day to this. He did answer it, in his own way, although it was a way that his critics consistently failed to understand. We look at that in a moment.

First, the Resurrection and the other supernatural events in the Gospels. What place have they in Schweitzer's story?

Schweitzer was a skeptic—a doubting Thomas. He would certainly have wanted to thrust his hand into the wounded side of the risen Jesus, to test if it was really he. To this extent he was a true child of the Age of Reason that he admired and of the Age of Doubt that bred him. He was a scientific-thinking man in the sense that he only trusted what he could personally observe and test. This does not mean he was a materialist, for he found it perfectly possible to observe and test consciousness, emotional reaction, and thought itself. But the metaphysical, the supernatural, were no part of his world. A visitor to Lambarene in 1954, Richard Kik, quoted him as saying, "I never could understand anything over-spiritualized . . . and as for the transcendental, I've never been able to understand it at all."[6] The theologian in him was always under the strict eye of the rationalist philosopher.

Immortality and the afterlife, therefore, he regarded as not proven. And he knew enough about psychology to be very wary of claims to visions and so forth. His reading of the miracles was that some of them were cases of faith healing—the effect of Jesus' personality on sufferers from psychosomatic complaints. Others he regarded as the experiences of highly excited minds, which had become amplified in the process of word-of-mouth retelling down the years before they were put on paper.

Into this category he put such reports as the turning of the water into wine, walking on the lake, and so on. The feeding of the five thousand, he suspects, was actually a symbolic meal of the same kind as the Last Supper—a ritual sharing of bread among those who had gathered to Jesus, who were, simply by being there, believers in the kingdom. The transfiguration of Jesus, observed by three disciples only on top of a high mountain, occurred very shortly after an event of the most intensely emotional nature. Jesus had declared himself to be the Messiah; had enjoined strict secrecy; had demanded their total dedication to his cause; and, finally, had promised "there are some standing here who will not taste death before they see that the Kingdom of God has come with power."[7] The emotional effect on a group of Galilean fishermen, says Schweitzer, would put them into the ideal condition for experiencing hallucinations.

And similarly, he suspects, the distraught disciples after Jesus' death found themselves "seeing" him; as widows and widowers "see" the loved one whom they cannot believe dead. Such was the Resurrection. Armed with these visions and the memory of Jesus' promises, the disciples set about preaching the doctrine of Christ, the risen Messiah. But Christ was not risen in the flesh. He was dead. He had been wrong.

"You are probably right about it," Schweitzer's father said, "but no one will believe you." And so it proved. None of the theologians was convinced. Indeed, little attention appears to have been paid to the book at all, except by Holtzmann (to whom, incidentally, Schweitzer had dedicated it, "with sincere respect and devotion," calling himself "his grateful pupil").

Holtzmann's reaction was inevitably motivated by a degree of personal pain. "You have ruined everything I taught," he told Schweitzer. And in his own next book, *Das Messianische Bewusstsein Jesu*, he referred to Schweitzer as "this crushing critic" with his "merciless edifice of theory."[8] The book did nothing to refute Schweitzer's arguments, simply granting him a few points in his eschatological claims, but asserting, without evidence, that he had taken it much too far and reiterating that there was a spiritual side to Jesus' teaching that Schweitzer had not allowed for. Christian Brandt, who was a young student at the time, and used to read Schweitzer's proofs for him, remembered meeting Holtzmann at Baden and asking him what he really thought of Schweitzer's ideas. Holtzmann seemed very agitated. "He is right," he said, "but only partly right."

Unfortunately, Schweitzer had not left room for the "partly right" verdict. His own phrase for his contribution to the study of Jesus was "*Konsequente Eschatologie*." It is generally translated "thoroughgoing Eschatology," but this scarcely does justice to the phrase. *Konsequente* means coherent, logical, consistent. And Schweitzer made it clear that in his view the attempt to have it both ways was a lost cause.

A theologian called Weiss had written a book shortly before Schweitzer's, asserting the importance of Jesus' sayings about the Kingdom of God. Where Schweitzer had pushed matters farther was by saying, in effect, "If a man is forever saying that the Kingdom of God is around the corner, he will inevitably behave accordingly." And finding that word and action matched and that on this simple basis the whole Gospel made sense, he declared a position of no compromise. A man who speaks and acts in the belief that the world is coming to an end in a couple of weeks does not hedge his bets. Either he believes it or he does not. The suggestion that he believes it part of the time, but part of the time is thinking in terms of normal history stretching out ahead, is simply psychological nonsense. "If *any* of Jesus' sayings about the kingdom are true," says Schweitzer, in effect, "then the whole of my theory inevitably follows. If on the other hand you believe that Jesus was spiritualizing the message for generations to come, you must reject *all* the eschatological sayings as later interpolations. *Tertium Non Datur*—there is no third alternative. Jesus was not a man to blow hot and cold, nor to say one thing and mean another."

With his uncompromising *Tertium Non Datur*, Schweitzer left no room for equivocation. It was impossible to slide out of the alternatives he posed with a "but" or an "if" or an "on the other hand." And being still, as he said himself, the same "intolerable young man" who had made everybody's life hell as a schoolboy with his demands for truth, he had not written too tactfully about the theories he was now attacking. Here, for example, is what he says at one point about the way in which "the modern-historical school" (that is to say, Holtzmann and all the leading "liberal" theologians) account for the crucifixion of Jesus: "It is after all a lifeless thought! The feeble modernity of it is visible in the fact that it does not get beyond a sort of representative significance of Jesus death."[9] Feeble! Lifeless! One begins to see perhaps why scholars found it preferable to ignore a book that attacked so vigorously but to which they appeared to have no convincing answer.

One can see, too, why people found it difficult to assess Schweitzer's situation in the university. A much-respected young acting principal of a theological college, a working curate, comes out with a book that appears to demolish large parts of the faith he is working for. Is he right? Then where is Christianity? Is he wrong? Then should he go on holding office?

Although he did not know it till later, two members of the faculty protested against his acceptance as a lecturer, fearing that he would "confuse" the students with his unorthodox approach. It was Holtzmann, whom he had hurt most, who with characteristic generosity and integrity threw his authority into the balance and swung the vote in Schweitzer's favor.

It hurt Schweitzer that Holtzmann was hurt. He found it painful that his conclusions must inevitably wound a lot of Christians. "The satisfaction which I could not help feeling at having solved so many riddles about the existence of Jesus was accompanied by a painful consciousness that this new knowledge in the realm of history would mean unrest and difficulty for Christian piety. . . .[10] I find it no light task to follow my vocation, to put pressure on the Christian Faith to reconcile itself in all sincerity with historical truth. But I have devoted myself to it with joy, because I am certain that truthfulness in all things belongs to the Spirit of Jesus."[11]

We must postpone for a moment looking at the paradoxical claim that the spirit of Jesus led Schweitzer to announce that Jesus was fallible and dead. It lies at the heart of that difficult question—what kind of Christian could he call himself now? But for the moment we are considering only the reactions to his historical theories.

It was Schweitzer's ruthless logic, the dominating clarity of his argument, and his refusal of compromise that most perplexed the readers of

The Mystery of the Kingdom of God. The silence that greeted its publication was almost audible. The two professors who opposed Schweitzer's lectureship did so in secret. Dr. Walter Lowrie, in the excellent introduction he wrote to the English translation in 1914, says:

> Obviously it was not the weakness of the book, but rather its strong originality and in particular the trenchant way in which it demolished the "liberal life of Jesus" which accounts for the passive hostility with which it was greeted. In fact it contained more than could be readily digested at once either by a liberal or a conservative mind. Most of the New Testament students in Germany had collaborated in the fabrication of the "liberal life of Jesus" and they could not patiently endure to see their work destroyed. Those among us who fancy that German professors are bloodless beings who live in an atmosphere purified of passion and prejudice, need to be informed that on the contrary they are human, all too human. The animosities of party and school and the jealousies of the cathedral have been proverbial for generations. The reception accorded to Schweitzer's work does not seem creditable. It was met by something like a conspiracy of silence.[12]

Christian Brandt confirmed that the silence by no means indicated assent. "They all thought he was wrong," Brandt told me. "But he only tapped the side of his nose with his finger and said, 'I can wait.'"

Schweitzer is still waiting. Through all his theological writings he never changed his mind about Jesus although he kept in touch with all the subsequent developments in theology. We can only assess his achievement, therefore, if we look to see how later theologians reacted to his viewpoint, after the first stunned silence, and whether any of them, from that day to this, has found any convincing proof that he was wrong. For this purpose we must consider the reactions to *The Quest of the Historical Jesus*, which appeared in 1906, and to *The Mystery of the Kingdom of God.*

The German attitude can, perhaps, be summed up at its most charitable by Holtzmann with his "he is only partly right" and at its most uncompromising by the Olympian Harnack, who wrote, "If anyone finds it impossible to accept the antinomy 'the Kingdom is future and yet present,' argument with him is useless."[13]

In England Schweitzer fared better, at least for a time. Canon William Sanday, a professor at Oxford, read *The Quest of the Historical Jesus* in German and welcomed it in a series of lectures in 1907, endorsing almost everything that Schweitzer had to say. Before long the students at both Oxford and Cambridge were in a furor about the new ideas, and Schweitzer looked set for the leadership of the new theology at least in England. Two years later, however, Professor Ernst von Dobschutz came to Oxford to give a series of lectures and brought with him the official line: Schweitzer had gone too far, had pressed his alternatives too hard, had not allowed for the ambiguity that clearly lay in Jesus' words and that Jesus had evidently intended.

At this point it became clear that Canon Sanday, in his championship of Schweitzer, was not wholly disinterested. He disapproved of the whole tendency of the Protestants in Germany to "modernize" Jesus, and what he liked most about *The Quest* was Schweitzer's exposure of the weaknesses in the modernizers' case. He had not, however, read the earlier book, *The Mystery of the Kingdom of God*, where Schweitzer's own case is most closely argued.

Von Dobschutz's lectures shook the shallow roots of Sanday's enthusiasm, and in 1910 Sanday published a recantation in the Hibbert Journal, Britain's foremost philosophical and theological magazine. In it he apologized for having been "attracted unduly by Dr. Schweitzer's freshness and force" and overimpressed by his "audacity and exaggeration." Sanday now found that he could not agree with Schweitzer's "tendency to push things to extremes at the dictates of logical consistency." "Such drastic logic" he claims, "was not to be looked for on the soil of Palestine."[14]

This last remark is a good example of the befogging of issues that was the order of the day. In the first place he seems to be saying that Jesus, along with all the other Jews, was unable to coordinate thought with action—a suggestion that is unsupported with reference to the race in general, but in the case of Jesus is an attack more damaging to the founder of the Church than any mounted by Schweitzer.

More basic, however, is Sanday's failure to understand where the logic lay. Schweitzer does not claim that Jesus was logical in the intellectual sense (although there is no reason why he should not have been). Schweitzer claims that he himself is logical in saying that if a man is obsessed by the end of the world, that obsession will underlie all his words and actions; a part-time obsession is not possible. It is not logic that makes such a man connect his sayings with his belief. It is the necessity of his being. Either Jesus was obsessed or he was not. There is no third alternative.

Once again we see that other theologians trade in words, without understanding the reality behind the words, where Schweitzer trades in understanding of human beings. Once again we see how his very strength, his honesty and common sense, make him an odd man out in the theologians' club.

So Sanday (who had still not read *The Mystery of the Kingdom of God*) retreated from Schweitzer's logic into ecclesiastical double-think, and the waves of the establishment closed over him. In 1910 *The Quest of the Historical Jesus* was published in English with a preface by Professor F. C. Burkitt of Cambridge. In recommending the book Burkitt suggests that the most important element is not Schweitzer's own solution, but his survey of all the other solutions. "It is not to be expected," he writes, "that English students will endorse the whole of his view of the Gospel History, any more than his German fellow-workers have done."[15] It is a typical scholar's approach. The game is the study of problems, not the discovery of answers. But Burkitt's coolness, which has been echoed down the years, is also partly the result of the accident that *The Quest* appeared in the English language before *The Mystery*. Having read it, people assumed they had Schweitzer's arguments in their entirety and could the more easily dismiss them.

The British reviews clung fairly closely to Burkitt's line. The *Glasgow Herald*, for example, praised *The Quest* as "the only book in which any attempt has been made to give a full and connected history of the whole course of that wonderful movement of the German mind . . . which has had for its single aim to reach the exact truth about the Christ of history. In this aspect the book is invaluable." But the reviewer is not much impressed by what he calls "Dr. Schweitzer's 'stand-and-deliver' style of calling upon the Christian world to declare itself either eschatological or non-eschatological."[16] The same phrase that Schweitzer himself used of his less successful attempts at begging for charity, "stand and deliver," suggests one reason why his book failed to endear itself to its readers.

The *Manchester Guardian,* too, spoke admiringly of "fullness of detail and brilliant perception" in Schweitzer's summary of previous books, but "some readers will feel that his own solution has become an obsession, and they will possibly resent the extreme dogmatism of his tone."[17]

The *Nation* rated the book "by far the ablest work which has hitherto appeared in this difficult and tantalising field,"[18] and summarized its conclusions with fairness but was quite convinced that eschatology was foisted on Jesus posthumously by ecstatic disciples.

Several reviewers were so confused by the fact that Schweitzer's Jesus does not believe in a "spiritual" kingdom that they told their readers that the teaching, too, of this Jesus was without spiritual or even ethical content—the exact opposite of the truth. Others, more perceptive, were glad to be able to agree with Schweitzer's final conclusion that the Jesus of the heart is independent of historical discoveries, so their historical disagreements scarcely matter.

What is quite evident, through the various degrees of nonacceptance and dismissal, is that the book had caused a considerable flutter in British theological dovecotes. And we are not surprised to find the *Times* reporting that the shadow of Schweitzer had fallen across the Church Congress held that year.

It had also made enough impression to be accorded considerable space in an *Encyclopaedia of Religion and Ethics* published in 1912. Professor I. A.

MacCulloch, contributing the section on eschatology, has this to say: "The Eschatological theory, that Christ thought that the Kingdom would be inaugurated immediately after a short period of messianic woes . . . cannot be proved . . . nor can it be certain that Christ looked forward to an immediate coming of the [future] Kingdom."[19]

Having dismissed the whole theory on this bare assertion, he goes on to counter it with a series of unsupported guesses ("if he is correctly reported his purpose may have been to show that") and upholds the view that St. John is more accurate than the other Gospels simply because its interpretation is more spiritual.

In his anxiety to give no quarter to the dreaded eschatologists, MacCulloch translates and interprets biblical phrases in a manner that gives no indication that there are other possible meanings, proving the opposite to what he desires; he starts an argument with an "if" or a "perhaps" and then proceeds to a conclusion as though his "perhaps" were an established certainty; and he never genuinely queries the assumption that Christ thought what the later Church required him to think or seeks truthfully to start from the beginning. He exhibits all the characteristics of what we have learned in a different context to call brainwashing. Schweitzer, hopeful that "truth belongs to the spirit of Jesus," had reckoned without the conditioning that affected the outlook of so many members of Jesus' Church.

Such were the initial reactions of the theological world. *The Mystery of the Kingdom of God* was not translated into English until 1914, a bad year in Britain and the United States for books with German-sounding authors. It seems to have passed almost without notice in Britain where it was not reviewed seriously until the second impression in 1925. In the United States the publishers grew so alarmed at having a "German" author on their hands when war broke out in Europe that they sold the whole edition to jobbers at ten cents per volume, and the jobbers got rid of them at twenty-five cents apiece at the drugstores. By the time the war was over the whole eschatological issue was old hat. Theologians had moved on to other problems, and Schweitzer was accorded a respectful wave of the hand as someone who once made "a useful contribution" but could now be ignored. It was convenient that he had meanwhile disappeared into the jungle, and everybody could then change the subject by talking about his saintly self-sacrifice.

The fact is, of course, that when Schweitzer posed his stark alternatives, he committed the grievous error of leaving no room for discussion. This was not playing the game. Theologians in their disputes are far from gentle creatures, as Dr. Lowrie points out. Their works are liberally scattered with warlike images: the opposition routed in hopeless disorder, and so forth. Schweitzer played this game as well as any of them. But in most cases the routed opposition could, and did, rally and reform and fight a return battle. That was part of the fun.

Schweitzer's challenge was different: that third choice which he denied his readers was vitally necessary to their comfort. They could not deny the force of the eschatological argument, but if they accepted it with the unshrinking honesty of Schweitzer, they found that the beliefs on which they had pinned their faith and hope vanished like sand through their fingers. So the third choice *had* to be true. The spiritual Jesus, operating through the ages, had to coexist with the eschatological Jesus who lived for his own time. How? A mystery! Schweitzer's book, rejecting that mystery as impossible, was like one of those remarks dropped by a stranger into the middle of a pleasant party discussion, which all of a sudden demolishes the basis of the whole conversation and leaves an embarrassed hush behind.

As on those occasions, the first thing that everybody did was to change the subject and pretend the remark had never been made. Suddenly, it became the mode to dismiss the whole search for the historical Jesus as useless. The Gospels are so difficult to interpret, it was decided, that we must abandon any attempt to read them for information about Jesus; we must now read them for what they can tell us about the people who wrote them and for whom they were written, that is to say, the early Church. Behind the early Church we know there lies a misty figure, almost certainly an actual person but possibly not even that, called Jesus. We are not concerned with what that figure really said and did—only with what the Church said he said and did and why they said it.

This new approach is called "form criticism," and it studies the Gospels as a series of totally unconnected episodes that have been thrown together in a manner so arbitrary that we now have no hope of disentangling them. In studying these episodes we first decide in each case what purpose the writer hoped to serve by telling this particular story, for the stories fall into several groups, each with its particular form (hence the name of the method), and the form suggests how the story was used; for example, miracle stories would be needed to convince doubters of the Messiahship of Jesus, pronouncement stories might be required to give the young Church guidance on conduct or doctrine, and so forth. So only those parts of Jesus' life and teaching that were useful for the daily survival of the early Church would have been preserved, and these would have been so adulterated and altered in the process of being used as propaganda that their historical value is nil. Schweitzer's whole labor, and that of all his predecessors was, therefore, a waste of time.

Schweitzer was not unaware of these developments. Introducing the third edition (1950) of *The Quest* he says, "My book deals with practically all conceivable arguments against the historicity of Jesus. Here the old is always appearing in a new form."[20] And it is true that something very like form criticism had appeared in the middle of the nineteenth century in the work of Bruno Bauer; Schweitzer spends twenty-three close-packed pages on it in *The Quest* and concludes that the figure behind the Gospel stories must be more solid and comprehensible than this theory allows.

Farther on in the introduction he writes, "Later works on the life of Jesus cannot be included here. The introduction of new chapters, owing to the size of the book, would necessitate considerable abbreviation of what I have already written. But I cannot bring myself to spoil the thoroughness with which I have treated the earlier period. I therefore bequeath to another the task of introducing order into the chaos of modern lives of Jesus, which I performed for the earlier period."[21] Nobody has yet come forward to take on this task, but Schweitzer evidently had no qualms about his ability to demolish twentieth-century theories of the life of Jesus as effectively as he did those of the nineteenth.

For the moment let me say simply that form criticism itself unwittingly provides the most convincing proof possible of Schweitzer's eschatological theories.

Let us assume that none of the Gospels incidents can be proved to have originated with Jesus; they are derived from his sayings and acts, yes; but their selection and their final form are dictated by the needs of the young Church.

This Church is waiting for the second coming of the Messiah; all the records agree at least about that. They expect it daily. They feel some embarrassment that it delays so long. The very fact that the Gospels have to be written means that some fairly desperate measures have become necessary to preserve the faith—measures undreamed of in the first twenty or thirty years after Jesus' death.

At this juncture, any remark that Jesus might have made about a new, spiritual meaning of the kingdom, would have been, literally, a Godsend. It would have explained the whole delay if someone—anyone—had remembered Jesus telling them that the kingdom was not of the kind they expected, that history was to go on, and that they must find the kingdom in themselves. According to the rules of form criticism, such a hint would have been exploited to the full, both to comfort the Church and to turn aside the jeers of outsiders.

The fact that the Gospels contain no accounts of this kind is conclusive proof that Jesus never spoke to his disciples in these terms. If he was concerned to spiritualize the kingdom, he died with his secret unspoken. It was not the early Church, but a much later one, forced by history to spiritualize the idea of the kingdom, that put that thought by hindsight into his mind.

Form criticism has been the more sophisticated branch of recent New Testament study. Along with it has gone a new version of the old way of thinking, adorned with a new label, "realized eschatology." Schweitzer's influence is acknowledged by the word *eschatology*, but his meaning is obliterated by the whole phrase, which refers to the notion that Jesus did, in fact, usher in the kingdom simply by appearing on earth. The end of an era did arrive, although for some reason nobody noticed the fact for some while afterward. The disciples, awaiting the arrival of the kingdom, had already begun to live in it by virtue of the new vision of life bequeathed them by Jesus. Similarly, for all Christians thereafter, the kingdom is here and now, in love and faith.

Professor C. H. Dodd, doyen of British theologians in the 1970s, was a leading exponent of this theory, which was widely accepted as a satisfactory solution of the eschatological question. It is, of course, nothing of the kind. It may adequately represent what has perforce happened to the Church over the years, but it evades all the historical difficulties about Jesus' own expectations that were thrown up in those hundred years of searching German criticism as though they had never been.

So we are left hanging between those who, for all practical purposes, accept most of the Gospels as "Gospel" and continue with the game of "interpreting" them to their own convenience and those who reject them totally. Schweitzer is not merely forgotten but was actually suppressed by the religious establishment. The BBC's attitude, for example, when challenged in the early 1940s by a keen Schweitzerian, Colonel E. M. Mozley, was that Schweitzer's theories must not be discussed on the radio on the grounds that they were "not in the stream of the Christian tradition."[22] This ban was lifted only in 1947.

Apart from the way in which theological schools have avoided the issue of eschatology, what did more recent individual theologians have to say about Schweitzer himself?

In Switzerland a small group headed by Martin Werner continued to work on his lines, applying his insights to the later history of the Church. In Britain, however, you may look in vain for any serious consideration of his work.

Such attention as there is still concentrates on *The Quest of the Historical Jesus*, rather than on *The Mystery of the Kingdom of God*. The latter appears to be totally unknown, or ignored. The former is treated with the sort of distant respect accorded to the great statues of Easter Island. "A seminal work," said Professor Evans of Kings College, London, when I spoke to him, "since which nothing can be the same again; but flawed unfortunately by faulty methodology." He quotes that passage in Matthew that gave Schweitzer his starting point as being of doubtful authenticity anyway. He seems not to have realized that the full structure of Schweitzer's theory has no longer any need of this passage; the full-grown tree dispenses with the seed it sprang from.

Professors Davidson and Leaney, joint authors of *The Pelican Guide to Modern Theology*, call it "one of the most brilliant and interesting books of the century" and then proceed to misunderstand it so radically that they can write, "Such a reconstruction rendered a view of Jesus which saw him at his end a deeply disillusioned man, uttering a cry of despair from the cross as he died."[23] On the contrary, Schweitzer's Jesus died in the full hope of immediate reawakening into a world made new.

Professor A. M. Hunter, of Aberdeen University in Scotland, said that Schweitzer, "having destroyed the liberal portrait of Jesus, set about painting a new one in terms of his own eschatology—a portrait which satisfied no one but himself and reminds us, as Streeter says, 'of the Superman of Nietzsche wearing Galilean robes.' "[24]

The only way in which Schweitzer's Jesus resembles the Superman is in his heroic stature. In every other way, as we have seen, he is totally unlike. Apart from that enormous error, the striking thing is Hunter's happy assumption that Jesus existed to satisfy modern Christians. This comforting belief finds echoes in many writers. W. J. Wolf says that *The Quest* "brought an end to the 'Liberal lives,' but presented a Jesus totally foreign to our day."[25] The fact that the figure is foreign apparently makes it unnecessary to decide whether it is true. Jesus is not allowed to be foreign (which he obviously was) because thereby he becomes less useful to the modern Church. It is a curious criterion of truth.

Several New Testament authorities whom I approached simply admitted that they know too little about Schweitzer to be able to make any useful comment. Their knowledge is secondhand. We have seen enough of the travesties committed by firsthand commentators to realize that those present-day theologians who have relied on them have gained a quite inaccurate impression of Schweitzer's work.

This might account, for example, for an extraordinary paragraph about Schweitzer in D. M. Baillie's book, *God Was in Christ*. Elsewhere Professor Baillie admits that since the "Jesus of History" movement there is an almost universal recognition that Jesus' knowledge was limited by human conditions and that likewise his healing activities and his moral and religious life were fully human. But of Schweitzer's Jesus he writes: "The effect of Schweitzer's own interpretation, as he saw plainly, was to produce a portrait of the historic Jesus so grotesquely 'eschatological' in outlook as to make Him a complete stranger to our time, so remote, mysterious, and even unintelligible to us that it seemed to bring to an impasse the whole attempt to make the historic Jesus real as a basis for the Christianity of the modern world."[26] The picture Baillie draws of Schweitzer's Jesus is so entirely different from Schweitzer's own that he must surely be supposed to be making it up from hearsay. On top of this he claims that Schweitzer "saw plainly" what Baillie sees. In fact, what Schweitzer says of this "grotesquely eschatological stranger, remote, mysterious, and unintelligible," is this: "Even if the historical Jesus had something strange about him, yet his personality, as it really is, influences us much more strongly and immediately than when he approached us in dogma ánd in the results attained hitherto by research."[27]

In fact, even Schweitzer overstated the strangeness involved. Among theologians it may not be customary to exercise the imagination; but among writers it is well known that a figure placed firmly in its true historical context will always have a more universal significance than one set in some sort of limbo. We can identify much more easily with a genuine person whose circumstances, climate, and mental background are different from our own than we can with some kind of faceless creature with no definable place or time. We do not find it difficult, for example, to understand the predicament of King Oedipus although his thought-world was not remotely like ours. We can detach his problem with ease from its circumstances and apply it to our own. Only the Church's self-imposed blinkers make it difficult to do the same with Jesus.

All too often the spokesmen of the Church impose on Jesus the humiliating discourtesy of employing him as a helpless prop for their own preconceptions. He is required to be like themselves and judged according to that likeness. C. H. Dodd writes, "We no longer accept a saying as authoritative because it lies before us as a word of Jesus, but because we are rationally convinced that it is a word of His, and that will mostly mean in the last resort, because we are convinced that it is worthy of Him, that is, true and important."[28]

We are, it seems, to be the judges of truth and importance. It leaves Jesus at our mercy, the all-purpose symbol of any nation that goes to war, of authority and of rebellion, of Black Power and white racism, of Protestant and Catholic at each other's throats. Small wonder that Schweitzer wrote, "How strong would Christian truth now stand in the world of today, if its relation to the truth of history were in every respect what it should be! But instead of allowing this truth its rights, Christianity has mistreated it in various ways, conscious or unconscious, whenever it became embarrassing, but always by either evading, or twisting, or suppressing it."[29] Things have not changed.

Schweitzer spoke of his own work on the Gospels as "scientific" and "historical." By adopting these standards, he put himself out of the game. In a race where most runners have their feet tied in a sack of dogmatic preconceptions or emotional dependency, he cut loose and ran on two good legs. He reached the post first but found himself disqualified. As he mildly remarks in the introduction to the third edition of *The Quest*, "The fact remains, however, that the eschatological solution has not succeeded in dominating the latest writing on the life of Jesus, and is not within sight of doing so. . . . It is an axiom for tradition that Jesus preached truth utterly beyond and above the time-process. But this is contradicted by the eschatological picture of Jesus, which shows him sharing the expectations of his contemporaries. Faith is asked to give up something which it has always held and cannot contemplate abandoning."[30]

My own feelings are better summed up in a passage he wrote about the earliest of biblical critics, Reimarus, which could be applied word for word to himself and the fate of his books:

> The fact is there are some who are historians by the grace of God, who from their mother's womb have an instinctive feeling for the real. They follow through all the intricacy and confusion of reported fact the pathway of reality, like a stream which, despite the rocks that encumber its course and the windings of its valley, finds its way inevitably to the sea. No erudition can supply the place of this historical instinct, but erudition sometimes serves a useful purpose, inasmuch as it produces in its possessors the pleasing belief that they are historians, and thus secures their services for the cause of history. In truth, they are at best merely doing the preliminary spade-work of history, collecting for a future historian the dry bones of fact, from which, with the aid of his natural gift, he can recall the past to life. More often, however, the way in which erudition seeks to serve history is by suppressing historical discoveries as long as possible, and leading an army of possibilities out into the field to oppose the one true view. By arraying these in support of one another it finally imagines that it has created out of possibilities a living reality.
>
> This obstructive erudition is the special prerogative of theology, in which, even at the present day, a truly marvellous scholarship often serves only to blind the eyes to elementary truths, and to cause the artificial to be preferred to the natural.[31]

Schweitzer's historical instinct, like a water diviner's rod, led him unerringly past the dry places of fruitless academic bickering to the spot where the important truths lay hidden. There he began to dig. He himself was scarcely aware what a large part instinct played in his research. He attributed all his results to reason. But in every field of discovery it is instinct, a kind of esthetic sixth sense, that tells the great investigators what questions to ask. To answer needs only application and skill. Many people have those qualities. The real secret is in the asking.

Truth belongs to the spirit of Jesus. Yet truth declares that Jesus died a terrible death in pursuit of a mirage. This is the apparent contradiction in Schweitzer's argument. There is no connection, say the critics, between Schweitzer's historical theories and his Christian devotion. What kind of Christian can he be if the Christ he follows is no more than a deluded rabbi? The question has rankled down the years with Schweitzer's admirers and detractors. Books and articles have been written showing that he was, or was not, a Christian, and in what sense.

In many cases these assessments have started from a definition of Christianity that Schweitzer would not have accepted. And their authors frequently appear not to have read what he himself said on the subject, or to have read it with very little attempt at imaginative understanding.

Schweitzer made a first step toward clarifying his attitude at the end of *The Mystery of the Kingdom of God,* and although later he refined and amplified the statement he then made, his answer always remained essentially the same.

Jesus' death, says Schweitzer, changed everything, but not in the way Jesus intended. Jesus and the disciples expected the Kingdom of God in the eschatological sense. The spiritual understanding of the kingdom was forced on the Church by the failure of the eschatological Kingdom to arrive. The Church had to interpret—and misinterpret—the belated records of Jesus' sayings so as to make them fit in with a future that Jesus never envisaged. But such was the immense ethical and religious power of Jesus' personality that it did now become possible for those who followed him to live in a totally new way—to live, in fact, in a "kingdom within-the-world" that Jesus himself never envisaged. "The Christian view of the world which he founded by his death carries mankind forever beyond eschatology."[32]

But we must not, says Schweitzer, impose these later ideas onto the historical Jesus. That is where untruth starts because we all begin to saddle Jesus with the outlook and ideas of our own place and time. If we allow Jesus to remain in every way a man of his time, conditioned by the beliefs prevalent in his place in history, we can then see how superhuman his personality really was. His spirit was such that he attempted to bring history to an end—the most heroic act that anyone of his time could conceive of. Schweitzer uses a marvelous image in *The Quest of the Historical Jesus*: "In the knowledge that he is the coming Son of Man [Jesus] lays hold of the wheel of the world to set it moving on that last revolution which is to bring all ordinary history to a close. It refuses to turn, and he throws himself upon it. Then it does turn. And crushes him. Instead of bringing in the eschatological conditions, he has destroyed them. The wheel rolls onward, and the mangled body of the one immeasurably great man, who was strong enough to think of himself as the spiritual ruler of mankind and to bend history to his purpose, is hanging upon it still. That is his victory and his reign."[33]

We can see the influence of Nietzsche in Schweitzer's vision of Jesus as the hero. Nietzsche had looked in the wrong direction for his superman, sickened as he was by the hypocrisy of the very people who profess to follow the hero of Galilee. Jesus, dying in the greatest cause the world could offer, a cause foredoomed to failure, shattered the eschatological dream. But the spiritual power that led him to that adventure is untouched by the fact that he was mistaken about results. With his limitations as a man he had no choice but to follow the highest that he saw. It was a mirage. With its disappearance his spirit is freed to be applied anew to all other situations and civilizations. The liberated spirit can pervade all history as it once "quickened and transfigured Jewish eschatology. . . . Theology is not bound to graze in a paddock. It is free, for its task is to found our Christian view of the world solely upon the personality of Jesus Christ, irrespective of the form in which it expressed itself in his time."[34]

Schweitzer intended in due course to trace the process whereby the Church was forced to adapt its thinking little by little until it finally formulated the Creeds several hundred years after Jesus' death. The outlines of the process were already clear in his mind—particularly the first great steps taken by St. Paul, whose brilliant and deeply religious mind was confronted by the agonizing problems caused by the nonappearance of Jesus and the kingdom.

The book on St. Paul was not to be completed for many years yet, and the later one, about the subsequent development of the Church's beliefs and the formulation of the Creeds was so whittled away by the lack of time that it finally appeared only as a short essay. But following the trail through the years, one finds that Schweitzer accounts as convincingly for the errors of the Church as he did for the errors of Jesus. Not only is he convincing—he is deeply sympathetic. He sees the necessity of what the Church did, and he believes, moreover, that in one sense those early churchmen were right. They did the only thing possible. A spiritual understanding of the kingdom was the only course left open to them. They had to learn to see the existing world afresh, in the spirit of Jesus. This is precisely how Schweitzer himself lived.

But however right they were spiritually, they were absolutely wrong historically. The error of Jesus echoed down the ages, forcing fresh errors on generation after generation as they attempted to reconcile the first great mistake with the facts. The complicated dogmatic formulae of the Creeds were efforts to fit all the conflicting and paradoxical pieces together. Thus, Jesus became more and more strange because Greek ideas of what a God should be became mixed with the original Jewish expectations, and the resulting God-man of the Christian Church was born, flanked by the other two persons of the Trinity. Christians now find the Jesus of Schweitzer strange only because they have been accustomed from childhood to believe in the far stranger Jesus of the catechism.

So Schweitzer's Christianity was nothing more nor less than a total devotion to the spirit of the original Jesus—a man who was limited by the knowledge of his time, but whose spirit was so great that he attempted to crack open time and reveal the kernel—the hidden realm of God. Success or failure was not the issue. The grandeur of the attempt made Jesus superhuman, even divine, supremely worthy of devotion.

But what kind of devotion can this be, to the spirit of a mortal man? And in what sense can it be called religious?

Although he did not understand the transcendental or the supernatural, Schweitzer understood mysticism—because he experienced it. Indeed, he found it a universal human characteristic, in one form or another. The highest form of mysticism, he believed, "takes place through an act of thinking. Whenever thought makes the ultimate effort to conceive the relation of the personality to the universal, this mysticism comes into existence. . . . It attains the power to distinguish between appearance and reality, and is able to conceive the material as a mode of manifestation of the spiritual. It has sight of the eternal in the transient."[35]

We have already noted that the German *denken* has a much wider and deeper meaning than the English *think,* and embraces overtones of awareness and contemplation as well as cogitation. "Thinking" mysticism, in this sense, was Schweitzer's manner of understanding Jesus—not because Jesus was a resurrected God, but because his spirit had manifested the eternal truth of heroic humanity as nobody before or since. Schweitzer found communion with Jesus deep in himself, in the depths of contemplation.

In a sense, therefore, it might seem that the whole quest of the historical Jesus was a scholarly irrelevance. Schweitzer's allegiance was to the Jesus within, not to the Jesus of history. But things are not so simple as that. In Jesus the eternal was manifested in a real man—not a figment. His reality was essential—a guarantee that the greatness of his spirit was not an invention. The Kingdom might have been a mirage, but Jesus was not. The connection between the inner Jesus and the historical Jesus is a close one, after all. "Whoever preaches the Gospel of Jesus must settle for himself what the original meaning of his sayings was, and work his way through the historical truth to the eternal. During this process he will again and again have opportunity to notice that it is with this new beginning that he first truly realizes all that Jesus has to say to us."[36]

At the end of *The Mystery of the Kingdom of God,* Schweitzer wrote [author's italics]: "The judgments passed upon this realistic account of the life of Jesus may be very diverse, according to the dogmatic, historical, or literary point of view of the critics. Only with the *aim* of the book may they not find fault: *to depict the figure of Jesus in its overwhelming heroic greatness and to impress it upon the modern age and upon the modern theology.*"[37] At the end of *The Quest of the Historical Jesus* he wrote a passage that has been quoted again and again, often for the wrong reasons: "He comes to us as One unknown, without a name, as of old, by the lakeside, He came to those men who knew Him not. He speaks to us the same word: 'Follow thou me!' and sets us to the tasks which He has to fulfil for our time. He commands. And to those who obey Him, whether they be wise or simple, He will reveal Himself in the toils, the conflicts, the sufferings which they shall pass through in His fellowship, and as an ineffable mystery, they shall learn in their own experience who He is."[38] It sounds magnificent. "Unknown"—"Without a name"—no wonder it pleased those readers who were dismayed by the clarity of the rest of the book. It seemed that Schweitzer had at last relented and would allow his reader a Jesus who is vague, unfocused, faceless, drifting like a wraith by the water.

But it means nothing of the kind. Schweitzer has simply pulled out the stops of his pulpit oratory for the last few chords of the book. What he is really saying is clear if you add the sentence preceding the quotation: "The names in which men expressed their recognition of Him as such, Messiah, Son of Man, Son of God, have become for us historical parables. We can find no designation which expresses what He is for us."[39] All Schweitzer is saying is that "Messiah" and "Son of God" are now meaningless phrases; our Jesus must do without these titles. The compelling power of his spirit is what remains, dominating the lives of his followers.

What then is this power? What exactly was it about the spirit of Jesus that made him so unique, yet so universal? Simply this, that without altering his vision of what the kingdom would be, Jesus totally altered men's vision of what was required to enter it—"the mighty thought underlying the Beatitudes of the Sermon on the Mount, that we come to know God and belong to him through Love."[40] He did not speak of the kingdom because he took that for granted. "The subject of all his preaching is love, and, more generally, the preparation of the heart for the Kingdom."[41]

The unique ethical insight with which Jesus spoke of the preparations needful to bring in God's Kingdom—*that* was universal, *that* was divine—Jesus' total understanding of the human heart, of what man must become before the world can be renewed. That, for Schweitzer, was what mattered about Jesus; because regardless of the changing views of the

universe or the meaning of God, the deepest needs of man and his society remain unaltered. We still yearn for the kingdom of love and peace
that has not yet dawned. If it is ever to come, it will always require the
same change in men's hearts that Jesus demanded. Therefore, we must
follow Jesus. So still for us today, "The one important thing is that we be
as thoroughly dominated by the idea of the Kingdom as Jesus required
his followers to be."[42] "The true understanding of Jesus is the understanding of will acting on will. The true relation to him is to be taken
possession of by him. Christian piety of any and every sort is valuable
only so far as it means the surrender of our will to his."[43] So Schweitzer
wrote in *Out of My Life and Thought* at the age of fifty-six.

His critics want to know how he could write this about a fallible,
dead human being. Is it logical to submit one's will to the will of a
man two thousand years dead? Perhaps not. One can only say that for
Schweitzer truth was a matter of experience and observation, not of
logic. It was clear from the evidence that the historical Jesus was
dead. It was clear from the evidence that the spirit of Jesus was alive.
Does that seem unreasonable? Schweitzer claimed always that his
thought was based on reason (which is not the same as logic). And
reason told him that to believe the facts of one's experience, even if
they seemed contradictory, was more reasonable than to deny experience because it seemed at first sight unreasonable. Must history and
the spirit obey the same laws? If they clearly did not do so, reason
must accept it.

Werner Picht, who knew Schweitzer from the Strasbourg days, and
who married into the Curtius family, wrote in his fine book about him,
"He is present *in person* in his scholarly writings to an extent which is
regarded as quite improper in the scholarly world."[44] In something of the
same sense, Nietzsche wrote of his love for what was written with the
author's blood; those who wrote with blood, he said, would learn that
blood was spirit.

There were overtones to Nietzsche's remark that Schweitzer would
have totally rejected, yet he, too, wrote with his blood. He wrote what his
blood told him. He entered by intuition into his subject and then applied
reason to what he found. Thus, he was saved from both extremes, mind-
less emotional indulgence and sterile logic. Between the two he held a
precarious balance, trusting, Picht says, to a sleepwalker's instinct that
skirts precipices. I would prefer to say that he trusted something much
more wide awake—a sort of inspired normality. Professors find it difficult
to understand what Schweitzer means. It is easier for peasants. He was
a peasant—born where many opposites meet. However long he took to
prove it, what he had to say was always in the end very simple. He

returned to the center, where things are real. He was the scholar of the obvious. He is to be trusted because he kept his eyes fixed on the facts, both internal and external, and refused the seductive satisfactions of intellectual consistency.

In a letter to Oskar Kraus, dated February 5, 1926, he wrote,

In spite of external differences in form, I feel that Jesus' outlook on the world (Weltanschauung] is identical with mine in what I would call the simplicity, the infinity, the heroism of his ethics. Through the outlook on the world and view of life which gradually developed in my mind, I was able to understand the eschatological views of Jesus and was thus enabled to do justice to the historical Jesus. What attracts me so tremendously in him is the simplicity of the rationalism inherent in his fantastic outlook on the world.

Jesus, in short, reasoned out the implications of his beliefs, however strange they may be to us, and followed them to the uttermost in simple faithfulness. And—here the final piece of Schweitzer's theory clicks into place—it was precisely because the end of the world was so near, because God was so near, that his ethics were the purest ever preached. There was no need to compromise anymore. In those last few months, love and goodness could be absolute, with no glance over the shoulder at the consequences. What though you went hungry or cold, or were beaten or imprisoned? The reward was in sight, a hundred-fold. At the end of the race you may push the car to its limit. It was precisely because Jesus believed in a mirage that he could be the greatest hero and teacher in history, totally without reservation, therefore totally right. No subsequent doctrine, alloyed by the continuation of history, could match that blazing purity. Thus, Jesus was the Lord.

When he was older, Schweitzer would generally evade the question, "Do you call yourself a Christian?" But once he said, "There are two sorts of Christians—the dogmatic and the undogmatic. The latter follows Jesus and accepts none of the doctrines laid down by the early Church or any other church. That's the sort of Christian I am."

The Churches naturally find it difficult to acknowledge such a person as a Christian at all. But outside the Church's ranks are millions of people, disillusioned with organized religion, who feel much the same way about Jesus as Schweitzer did, yet have little intellectual foundation for their feeling. They may look to Schweitzer for their authority.

Schweitzer's view of Jesus offers us as it were a filter with which we may separate the temporary from the eternal in Jesus' thought. We are not obliged to accept or reject the package as a whole or to swallow obvious untruths along with deep spiritual understanding. Schweitzer makes it possible to be a skeptical rationalist and at the same time a disciple of Jesus, without dishonesty.

To found a church would have been the last thing Schweitzer wished to do. But to reassure millions of individuals that they had as good a right to their respect and love for Jesus as anyone else—indeed, that to meet Jesus face to face, as individuals, was the only true way—that would have been his wish.

9

—

Hélène

IN THE PREVIOUS CHAPTER we have surveyed most of what Schweitzer wrote and said about Jesus at various periods of his life. It seemed right to do so because even the ideas that for lack of time were not written down for nearly half a century were already clear in his mind by 1902. And so consistent was he that once we have grasped what he said at twenty-seven, we know fairly accurately what he would have said at any moment in the following sixty-three years.

But a certain change of emphasis occurred as time went on. In the early books, *The Mystery of the Kingdom of God* and *The Quest of the Historical Jesus*, comparatively little stress is laid on Jesus' doctrine of love. What seems to impress Schweitzer the most is his heroic stature, the will that measured itself against the end of history. Schweitzer's need for hero worship is expressed in romantic statements, such as "Before that mysterious person . . . we must be forced to lay our faces in the dust, without daring to wish to understand his nature."[1] This is pulpit rhetoric, deeply felt, no doubt, but carrying still a slightly hollow ring, a touch of Germanic self-abasement; it has little in common with the confident investigations of the rest of the books and the easy assurance of that sermon in which Schweitzer speaks of Jesus understanding us "as man to man."

The emphasis on love comes later, in letters, in Schweitzer's autobiography, in the essay on the history of the Church, all written after he had abandoned the academic life and learned in his own person something about the suffering that he recommended as so beneficial.

For now, when *The Mystery of the Kingdom of God* was published, he was still a good and obedient Lutheran pastor, and in his sermons we find a much more conventional approach than in the book. Orthodox doctrine is still struggling to work in harness with unorthodox research,

139

and when in February he preached "On the meaning of the death of Jesus," although he says nothing that contradicts his theological findings, the tone is quite different: "He [Jesus] declared that his blood would be shed for many, for the remission of sins. But why and how? He kept silence on this point, that it might remain a mystery, the source of adoration. . . . He indicated what kind of death he was to die, not only to allude to the cross on which his blood was to be shed, but to make us understand the deep and hidden meaning which this holds for us as well."[2]

And, coming back to suffering: "To suffer and to endure, this is to feel the clasp of the Lord's hand, the hand who seizes us and encourages us: 'Higher! Always higher!' "[3]

He spoke rather differently of pain when he knew more about it.

In March he was finally inaugurated as privat-dozent in spite of those two dissenting professors. His inaugural lecture was on St. John and the new Greek doctrines that John and others were grafting onto the ideas of the young Church in an effort to account for the phenomenon of the Messiah who had never returned. "In the beginning was the Word," declares St. John. No Jew knew of a Messiah who was the Word of God. The very word *logos* is Greek. Jesus was well on his way to becoming a mystical, more-than-human figure.

A sermon Schweitzer preached that May shows vividly how his ideas were moving away from the academic and toward the active. The sermon was about the seventy men whom Jesus sent out to preach the kingdom and about whom, when they returned exulting in their success, Jesus thanked God who had "hidden these things from the wise and understanding, and revealed them to babes."[4] Schweitzer comments: "Thought and analysis are powerless to pierce the great mystery that hovers over the world and over our existence, but knowledge of the great truths only appears in action and labour."[5] He had always known this. Speculative philosophy had seduced him for a while. Now he was shaking himself free. As he did so his style began to expand from the cramped diction of academic argument into the great natural images that became a hallmark of his mature thought. "Knowledge of life is like a man, sitting at his window, who looks at the flight of the billowing black clouds, chased by the March wind, and says: 'How sad and desolate it is!' And that's as far as he goes. At the same time the farmer, working in the fields, also watches the columns of cloud chased by the wind. But he goes further. He feels the passing of the breath of life, everywhere at work in the universe, the triumphant force of renewal which nothing can hold back. He alone understands the purpose of the March wind."[6]

And then, the deathblow of the intellectuals:

You all know the name of the philosopher Schopenhauer who tried to convince men in his writings that the greatest wisdom was to see in life nothing but suffering and struggle and distress. I can never open one of his books without asking myself this question: What would have become of him if, instead of retreating with distinction into his ivory tower, far from professional and human contact, he had been forced to take the post of schoolmaster in a poor mountain village, where he would have had the task of turning a haphazard mob of children, with slack habits, into self-respecting men? He would never have written the books that made him famous, never have been surrounded by clouds of incense, nor had the crown of laurels placed on his white locks; but he would have had more understanding; he would have acquired the deep conviction that life is not only a battlefield, but that it is at one and the same time a struggle and a victory.[7]

Here, too, was a text for Schweitzer the fighter. "These undying words [of Jesus], 'Rejoice, for your names are enrolled in heaven,' are not spoken to the fortunate nor to those who rest from their labours, but to the combatants, to those whom Jesus Christ has chosen to announce the victory."[8]

Schweitzer was turning now to his new hero, Goethe, the odd man out in eighteenth-century philosophy, the man who let speculative thought pass him by and involved himself in every kind of activity, town planning, bridge building, economics, playwriting, poetry, and natural science. Goethe was to have a greater influence on Schweitzer than anyone except Jesus and, perhaps, St. Paul.

This interest in action was inevitably connected with the abiding problem: What was to be the manner of Schweitzer's service when he reached the age of thirty? He had decided initially to leave it to circumstances to guide him. Circumstance now pointed toward some kind of social service for the poor, an area of need that he constantly encountered.

As in intellectual life, so in social awareness, Strasbourg was very advanced. The central government at Berlin had recently confirmed the appointment of a young and enterprising mayor named Schwander, who had risen from the ranks of local government. He had devised a half-professional, half-amateur organization for the relief of poverty and distress. Simple tasks such as the distribution of food and fuel and the delousing of uncared-for children were entrusted to a corps of volunteers. Where problems were more complicated, the paid social workers took over.

Among the volunteers was a group of young people attached to the university. Members of this group also formed the nucleus of the cycle club with which Schweitzer rode out on free days into the country—to explore a castle, to picnic by the river, to gather flowers—although

Schweitzer himself preferred to leave the flowers growing where they were. The group included Paul and Adèle, who were living in Strasbourg at the time and with whom Schweitzer lived for a while after his deputy principalship was over. Others were the Münch children, among them Charles, Fritz, and Emma; the Curtius girls, and their literary brother, Ernst Robert; Elly Knapp, daughter of the rector of the university, whose husband, Theodor Heuss, was to became chancellor of Germany immediately after World War II; and an energetic gray-eyed German-Jewish girl, daughter of a distinguished professor of history—Hélène Bresslau.

Though Hélène's parents were Jewish by blood, her father had severed all connections with the Jewish community and had had his children baptized as Christians. He might even have become a Christian himself, his granddaughter believes, but that his pride and integrity would never let him take a step that might seem to have been motivated by expediency. Like many of the older generation at that time, like Schweitzer's godfather and to some extent like his father, Professor Bresslau could be strict and disapproved of laxity, and to some of the young of Strasbourg he appeared uncomfortably stern. But his granddaughter remembers him as a gentle and kind man.

Hélène's social conscience was almost as highly developed as Schweitzer's and in addition she had enthusiasm, efficiency, and a fine disregard of social convention. She worked among verminous children at a state orphanage. She helped to found and run a home for unmarried mothers, which was not at all a proper thing for nice young ladies to do. She was one of the first women skiers. She played the organ. At a time when young women were taking eagerly to emancipation all over northern Europe, she was as liberated a woman as Strasbourg could offer. And she had decided, like Schweitzer, that she must one day devote herself entirely to social service—only her deadline was the age of twenty-five, not thirty. She was four years younger than Schweitzer, almost exactly; so her moment of decision was due one year ahead of his.

All the girls adored Schweitzer, we are told. But Hélène Bresslau, with her practicality and zeal, had more to offer him than most. She offered him criticism instead of flattery, and at the dinner party at which it seems they met she asked, "What gives you the courage to go into the pulpit every Sunday and preach in that awful Alsatian dialect? The accent's ugly and the grammar's dreadful."

So began a relationship which for sheer intensity and passion would be difficult to match—but which involved almost no physical contact until their marriage more than ten years later.

It has always been assumed—not least by the present writer—that this was a purely practical attachment, an agreement about desirable action that in due course it seemed sensible to translate into a full partnership.

The letters between the two that have recently been discovered by their daughter are a revelation. How could we have guessed so wrong?

The answer is because the couple made it their business to see that nobody should guess right. And if they successfully deceived all their friends for all those years, it is scarcely surprising that we, too, should have been misled. "We met," Hélène wrote in 1945 to one of Schweitzer's biographers, George Seaver, "with a mutual feeling of responsibility for all the good that we had received in our lives, and a sense of duty to pay for it by helping others. It has been the joy and pride of my life to follow and assist him in all his activities."[9] And in Schweitzer's autobiography the sole reference to Hélène reads, "I left my residence on the St. Thomas Embankment, in order that with my wife—Hélène Bresslau, the daughter of the Strasbourg historian, whom I had married on June 18, 1912— I might spend the last months [before going to Africa] in my father's parsonage at Günsbach."[10] So bare, so bald, so totally misleading.

Rhena, their daughter, was not looking for the letters when she stumbled on them as she went through old possessions early in the 1980s. She had no idea they existed, having been given the impression they had all been destroyed. To her, the discovery "verged on the miraculous." For here were not merely facts about the relationship but everything that her father had taken such pains to keep hidden about his own inner being, the turbulent feelings of a passionate, sensitive, contradictory man, searching for his path in life. And, in addition, here was the revelation of the quite extraordinary influence her mother had had on this strange, compelling man and his destiny.

It will be necessary to dwell for some time on these letters because here we see Albert Schweitzer as only one person has ever seen him before, in all his innocence and his toughness, his pride and his humility, his confusion and vulnerability, his ambition, his tenderness and his anger as he searches for his meaning and the thoughts and emotions tumble over one another in their haste to reach the page. And as we read, we begin to understand what it was that they uniquely found in each other.

It is nearly impossible to summarize the letters. They are too dense; the phrasing of them is almost as important as the meaning. So I hope the reader will forgive me if I quote extensively from them and will, perhaps, go along with me and share my absorption in them.

For the next ten years, then, we look at two separate, parallel lives: the active, confident, open Schweitzer, whom his friends and parishioners knew and who has come down to us from previous sources, and the new man, the writer of midnight letters, the enclosed dreamer, increasingly frustrated with the restrictions of his bourgeois, academic life, the romantic communer with his heart, with nature—and with his new guardian angel, Hélène. For that, at this point, was what he needed and what she was to him.

Few romantic couples can have taken more care to mark the significant dates of their developing closeness. It would seem that that first important dinner party happened on August 6, 1898. Ten years to the day later he wrote: "I see the table very clearly before me, and how we and 'they' sat there. But I can no longer remember what your face looked like in those days. The face that impressed itself so deeply on my spirit later erased that first impression. Only I believe that you are much more beautiful now than you were then . . . or was I not yet so receptive in those days?

"In the evening we took you home. What would have turned out differently in our lives without that meeting? When I say 'ten years' a shudder passes over me. . . . Ten years which I took from your life; you could be married and the mother of growing children if I had not stood in the way."[11]

But it was not until two years or more later that the really important meeting took place. The first note we have is polite and playful, thanking Hélène for keeping a two-year-old promise to send him a book, ("I find in it deep and natural, practical feeling combined with a plastic view and ideal sense of history. This greatness of thought is lacking in most moderns") and confirms that Schweitzer had not forgotten her strictures on his style: "For this card I wrote three drafts late at night so the sentence structure might meet with your approval. Awake or asleep, I worry about my untidy style—with time I hope that it will improve."[12]

That was in March 1901. And he remembered, from presumably about the same time, "the professor's little girl who asked the poor little privatdozent while they were cycling at the polygon: 'What is your language then, Doctor?', and that so bluntly and saucily."[13]

A year or so later she evidently invited him to some event that he had to refuse because it clashed with a Confirmation class, but "An afternoon excursion, however, would be most welcome if you can arrange one."[14]

The day they always celebrated as the real beginning of the "friendship" was March 22. Time and again he comes back to that magical day. On March 25, 1904: "Do you still remember how we walked back from our excursion to the flood dam with our bicycles while I spoke with you?

"Now the weather is the same as it was then: the long waiting for Spring. Yet, all the same it is beautiful, this holding back, this timidity of our northern nature—Italian Spring is not for me, it is too beautiful, it does not know these small, chilly flowers under bushes, which alternately weep and laugh, depending upon wind or sun."[15]

On March 22, 1910: "It was a forest in spring. . . . It seemed to me that a prophetic spirit had spoken through me when I dismounted from my bicycle and offered you friendship . . . asked the question—'Do you believe in friendship between . . . ' from which our life grew."[16]

On March 21, 1912: "this wonderful enchantment of things which brought us together and is leading us to a far land . . . and over everything a breath of spring, of newly-budding branches, of little blue and yellow flowers. . . . If you had dreamed where this question, 'whether a friendship existed' would lead you . . . that those minutes when we walked along together beside our bicycles contained the deciding moment of your life."[17]

And Hélène, on March 18, 1912: "The 18th! Blue flowers—sunshine—a tree-trunk in the Neuhofer Forest—is my dear friend thinking of that?"[18]

So what exactly did happen between them that spring day? The first letter we have from Hélène, in May of that year, suggests that the progress of the relationship was not entirely smooth, that Hélène started out with different expectations from his:

> My Friend,
> You made me feel good, but you have also hurt me; therefore, I would like to continue our discussion. Actually, I would like to thank you because I have advanced through our exchange—I have gained new insights.
> You are probably correct in your views about development, as far as we think of it as a slow, gradual becoming. I believe that everything that lies in us is dark and we are not conscious of it until a word or an event coming from the outside suddenly brings it to our consciousness, or puts it into a new light. In this way, rather by spurts, we advance a step and recognize this only afterwards. This is what happened to me.
> I often asked myself in the past: . . . Why does God put this boundless desire for happiness into our hearts if he denies us fulfilment? . . . One wants to rebel against the exclusion from this fulfilment! That was my struggle and the end of my philosophy. . . .
> You too must know the struggle of that part in us that is so filled with longing. How else could you have understood the silent cry of the cherry trees in Günsbach? Or did you always know that your path to life would pass by the closed gate of happiness? You see, my friend, this is the very view that you gave me yesterday; here is not the end, here the road only divides and your path leads ahead, it goes further, wherever it may lead; what matters is the "moving ahead," the way beyond which I was not able to find. And now this seems so simple and clear to me, so reassuring. And yet, I never would have found this on my own; I wanted to convert you to my theory which seemed so much kinder and brighter, yet it only led me to desperation.
> Well, I do not yet know my way—it is so much easier for a man whose profession gives him direction—will you help me to find mine? "Why would we need friends if we did not need them?" I always despised that phrase,

but there is some truth in it. A young woman is dependent upon her talents, and if she does not have any special ones, she is in a predicament. Perhaps in this case, too, I might receive sudden help, as happened yesterday.

My friend, don't be mad at me that I tell you all of this. I feel as if these renunciations contain a hidden trait of sympathy between us. . . . If you want to tell me anything before we meet again, just write—if you send it with the morning mail it will reach me directly—my parents know about our friendship. They know as much as they have to so they don't draw wrong conclusions. This is not a breach of trust, what our friendship is, and what it means to us is between us alone. A young woman has to account for her ways differently than a man who is independent. You will understand, my friend, won't you? Our friendship will remain a well-kept secret with my parents.

So again: I thank you! Always in good Friendship.

Hélène Bresslau.[19]

How are we to read this? It is necessary to bear in mind that just three weeks before that first March meeting, Schweitzer's beloved Aunt Mathilde had died. Aunt Mathilde had been the best, wisest, and most understanding of his "guardian angels." His letters refer again and again to "the one that lies at Père Lachaise cemetery," the one to whom he had been able to open his soul. The man who could open his soul to almost nobody had lost the best of his confidantes. This was what he needed as he spoke to an attractive young woman who turned out to share a great many of his idealisms and yearnings for nobility.

It is difficult to avoid the conclusion that there had been some passionate mutual avowal from which she had gained one sort of expectation and he another. Finally, in May, he had made it clear that his way was not the way of marriage and domesticity, but of renunciation: that he was in the grip of some "higher destiny." So their paths must divide. To her this meant the end of the relationship, but he had persuaded her that it only meant a fork in the road: they would go on together, but separately, as friends of a special kind, united by something greater than the normal satisfaction she (perhaps both of them) longed for. It had been hurtful, but in the end she had accepted that this could be a greater happiness than the other, which had only led her to desperation.

The struggle went on. Schweitzer was only too aware that his need for a guardian and guide was likely to conflict with Hélène's other interests, that his dominant personality put an unfair pressure on her. Constantly, his letters contained ecstatic rhetoric about the greatness that he was offering her and in the same paragraph pleas that she would not let herself be sacrificed unless she was quite sure, the thoughts tumbling over each other in their uncontrolled urgency:

I do not have the courage to tell you what you mean in my life, and all that you have become for me; you are my friend if ever a woman was the friend of a man. Why do I tell you this? You see it in the openness with which I speak to you in my letters. Why do I tell you this? I am always afraid to tie you too closely to me and to block your road to happiness. But tell me—have you become richer with me, have you become somebody—you also have found happiness, the horizon of your life has changed, it has become brighter,—please tell me; I know it, but I want to hear it from you. Is it true that I have given you the true concept of life? Do you feel that I awakened a cadence that slumbered in you, but that nobody had been able to bring to life? And is the happiness I brought you most precious to you? Tell me and look deep into my eyes.

You too have given me much: you forced me to open up, you have torn my thoughts out of me, you told me with pride: I have a right to know—when I was lonely and sad you came to me and you gave me everything a woman can give that is noble and beautiful, not without a struggle, but without egoism, you were woman, we drowned the little daughter of the professor in the Rhine—You have given me great support: the esteem and the affection of a noble person that watches over you everywhere, to the depth of your thoughts, and that does not permit you to falter because one always thinks: what would she say? Would I still be worthy of speaking to her as I do, of looking into her eyes, of accepting her respect and friendship?—this noble woman is something of a guardian angel. You came to me when I was alone, when the first guardian angel had left me. I fought against you, I did not want you to take her place, out of respect for you, and not to awaken the jealousy of the dead because you were a German, you were only a marriageable young lady—you conquered me, you overwhelmed me and I was forced to make space for you in my thinking and in my life. And only now do I wholly perceive the woman in you—and because I know you differently from the others, who only see the young lady, I cannot act naturally in company, I want to keep it a secret at all cost that I know you, for fear that somebody could interfere with our friendship. . . .

And now you search for your path: I do not have the right to hold you back: "we bring each other bad luck"; that is true, not in its petit-bourgeois meaning, but in the great sense that we draw each other into our own fate. I do not know whether, without you, I had the strength to continue my fight, whether I would have become unfaithful to my calling. But you were there, you held on to the best in me, and if I had become weak I would have lost your respect and more than that: I would have humiliated you, I would have deceived you.—And I am the one who caused you to turn from the right path: I plead with you once more: wait, hold on to the thought to pursue your happiness as woman, believe me, it is your fate to found a family, give yourself two more years—I plead with you with all my heart—but I plead without the right to hold you back. Is it I who brought you into the hustle and bustle of the intellectual world in which one progresses because one must, because one cannot stand still—Go straight ahead—towards the sun—if only our life has significance for us, what does it matter, whether it has been "happy" or "unhappy" measured by the events, the only true value is the one we give it; that is real and eternal value.

May God bless and protect you.[20]

"Gave me everything a woman can give that is noble and beautiful"? Surely in most situations this would imply something sexual. But here it seems to link with the thought that Hélène was the new guardian angel, in the place of the wise Aunt Mathilde, and what she gave him was that warm womanly guidance and support that he normally sought from older women. Thus was the little girl drowned and the mature woman rose from the waves to meet his needs.

One remarkable thing about the whole situation is how infrequently these two actually met. When they met socially it was impossible to talk intimately, and any public acknowledgement of serious involvement was out of the question because it would have been seen as a prelude to engagement, and this, of course, was not any part of Schweitzer's plan.

For all his intense thoughts of her, he loved to be alone. In a letter dated November 2, 1902, we have a remarkable glimpse of what his aloneness meant to him and also of his rather disconcerting trick, when thinking intently of someone, of suddenly switching from writing *about* that person to addressing him or her, for he frequently did it about Hélène.

I finished everything and now I am *all alone. All alone*—that is glorious. I turned off the lamp and I followed the flickering of the fire in the stove and the sound of the church bells penetrated the November dusk. It is Saturday evening.

Then I went over to the piano and played Beethoven's sonata for the fortepiano. To perform for others is nothing, no—one has to be alone because one can rejoice, laugh, cry and weep—. Oh, this heavenly exuberance—and then this dreamy, blissful world which wafts through these transparent chords—and I was by myself—and it was glorious, glorious.

Is that selfish? Well—I don't care, it may be so—no, we were two, Beethoven and I.—How I thank you that you let me have a glimpse into your world [now addressing Beethoven]—in your beautiful, paintorn, sun drenched, peacefully dying world. How many have thanked you? How many will thank you? You great prophet of overcoming and of struggle for joyful serenity![21]

Such a man was not to be diverted into domesticity. His was a solo destiny. So meetings with Hélène had to be few and covert, and letters were necessarily the chief means of keeping the relationship alive. Failing her real presence Schweitzer would often visualise her in his room:

> Come, take the armchair, move it toward the table, and we will talk to each other—how good it would be if you could chat with me a little. You don't mind that I am wearing an old jacket? It is a little worn at the sleeves and one button is missing. . . .
>
> Give me both your hands—we are at the Rhine, I imagine—the smell of the hay—, just as at that time when I revealed the secret of my life to you. You were so happy to be the sister of my thought, and I felt miserable because I had opened myself so completely. But then I did not regret it— now I feel relieved in the knowledge that you, such an honest and noble soul know my inner thoughts.[22]

One might suspect in these circumstances that the real person would be lost behind an idealized image, a projection, and to some extent I think this happened. The raison d'être of the relationship was Schweitzer's need for a guide and guardian angel. So often does he refer to her pure and noble soul that one gets the impression that he is reminding her— and himself—of her function rather than addressing a normal human being. Indeed the whole point of the relationship was that it was not normal. It had to be superb, heroic, almost beyond credulity. It inspired Schweitzer to go to the limit in discovering the full potential for greatness that he felt within himself but had little idea how to direct.

So we find that many of the letters are outpourings of disconnected ideas, confessions, streams of consciousness, as he used Hélène as a sounding board for the thoughts that flooded through him.

> Why am I that way, that I have an inner fear of all humans, even those who are close to me, afraid that they take my solitude away from me. There are only a few people to whom I have given the right to share in my thoughts, with whom to have dialogue. But with those few I feel so rich.[23]
>
> The room was dark, but a glimmer came from the street, and in the soft light I could recognize everything—vaguely. This is how life lies ahead of me, the life I will spend in these rooms—dark yet brightened by a gentle, distant light—so be it—may God guide and bless me.—I would like to know what it is—this God whom I implore—does he exist?—What is the spirit that forces me to follow my path—I who am not naive, but critical, not 'humble" but "proud"—what do I know? Let us go on—the spirit that speaks to me is a *reality*, the only supernatural reality that really exists for me—the rest is only a symbol, based on the only reality: *I believe because I act*—that action is, for me, the essential reality—and while I act I will be both humble and proud—truthful as cutting steel.

> *To be humble*—not only to have the *right and the strength* to be truthful—
> that is what I want—to proclaim the whole truth and to confirm it with my
> life, to gain strength from it—for this alone I sacrifice the happiness of life.
> You may tell me that this is a *self-delusion*—whatever: *I live from it* I suffer
> with it, I cry, I laugh about it I am *happy* about it. And as long as a few
> women of noble spirit support me with their fair sympathy, I can go my
> way alone.
>   Be content and be quiet—
>   Higher and higher—
>   The peace of God, *which surpasses all understanding.*
>   Shall keep your hearts and minds through Jesus Christ.[24]

An unkind reader might wonder whether he had taken a little too
much wine with his dinner. But for this impassioned dreamer that was
probably not necessary.

> I feel as if this whole life is an immense dream: people around me do not
> understand me anymore; they suspect something which they do not know;
> they cannot understand that I feel removed, and especially why I don't
> care about my "career" as professor! As if that would be my goal, the
> career of a professor!—No, I want to "live," live my life—you understand
> me! Listen to the wind in the big tree, our friend.[25]
>   I know that my activity as I want to develop it with the renunciation of
> conventional happiness is necessary, not for myself, but for our time, and
> it will prove its merit only through renunciation. I feel that I do not deceive
> myself, that it is not some will o' the wisp idea that leads me astray; it is
> that quietest calm, the peace of a torn soul—you know that I hate St.
> Augustine, it is not the peace of a pious man: I am not pious. If I should
> come to the conclusion tomorrow that there is no god, and no immortality,
> and that morality is only an invention of society—that would not touch me
> at all. The equilibrium of my inner life and the knowledge of my duty
> would not be shaken in the least.[26]

As he keeps returning to the theme of renunciation, on which the
whole relationship was based, the lectures of Georg Simmel seem to
have relevance. Simmel was the philosopher who tried to separate the
notion of self-transcendence in Nietzsche from its concomitant arrogance toward others. This would be entirely to Schweitzer's taste as he
strove to rise above himself, aiming for greatness, the one who stands
alone, yet still a man among men. Renunciation is very much a part of
self-transcendence, of losing one's life to find it. This was what
Schweitzer expected of himself—and of anyone who wished to be near
him.

To be alone, to stand alone—these held no terrors for him.

Sometimes it seems, as if I had arrived beyond clouds and stars, and could see the world in the most wonderful clarity. And therefore the right to be a heretic! To know only Jesus of Nazareth; to continue his work as the only religion, not to bear what Christianity has absorbed over the years in vulgarity. Not to be afraid of Hell, not to strive for the joys of Heaven, not to live in false fear, not the fake devotion that has become an essential part of our religion—and yet that one understands the one Great One, and that one knows that one is his disciple.

Last night before I went to sleep, I read the 25th chapter of the Gospel of St. Matthew because I especially love the verse: "Truly I tell you, just as you did it to one of the least of these who are my brothers, you did it to me." But when it came to the last judgment and the separation of the "sheep from the goats" I smiled: I do not want to belong to the sheep, and in heaven I would certainly meet quite a lot whom I do not like: St. Loyola, St. Hieronymus and a few Prussian church leaders—and to be friendly with them, to exchange a brotherly kiss? No, I decline. Rather to Hell. There the crowd will be more congenial. With Julian Apostate, Caesar, Socrates, Plato and Heraclitus one can have a fruitful conversation. Yes, I serve him, because of him, only because of him—because he is the only truth, the only happiness.[27]

We preach about texts—prescribed texts—so we do not have to tell our own thoughts, and in the end we have run away from our own thoughts that we don't know any more. And one can only preach what is based on one's own thoughts. That this is not taught us in our pastoral training, I will hold against the professors forever. They shaped us into skilful practitioners, but did not want us to strive for something higher.[28]

Gripped by his own need to communicate, it does not seem to have occurred to Schweitzer what chaos would ensue if every lesser pastor were encouraged to tell his own thoughts: those pastors, for example, with whom he himself most ardently disagreed.

Interspersed with these struggles was the specific struggle about Hélène. The tension culminated in a desperate series of letters on November 1 and 2, 1903.

Last night I went home sad, because I always fear that people take the liberty to talk about you and me, to suspect a little affair—but then, when I am alone with you, alone in my room when I call you in my thoughts, then I can talk with you without inhibition. Don't we have this, this being by ourselves, when we imagine each other close together? Yes, you are here, on my wastepaper basket with the cover, between my armchair and the window, in that comfortable corner, that, from now on, is your place here. But do not talk, watch how the leaves, one after another, fall from the big tree. . . .

Listen carefully. I blame myself for not trying hard enough to disengage you from me. How often I tell myself: if you were to succeed in playing a less important part in her life and thought, yet maintain some relationship with her, she would look for affection somewhere else and find somebody who could make her completely happy. But no, you write her letters, you open your innermost self to her, you share your thoughts with her . . . who will deliver you from the accusation that you have taken possession of her, and that you have taken everything she can give, without having the courage and the right to accept her totally, to make her your own? . . .

One day she will tell you; without bitterness she will say: you led me the wrong way. I was a woman. I had the right to enjoy the happiness of a woman. Because of you I looked for another kind of happiness, a sublime one, that is true, and I engaged all my energy, I have experienced indescribable moments of bliss, but in spite of this, I went the wrong way . . . if you speak to me like this some day, not reproachfully, gently and without bitterness, what will I answer? You cannot deliver me from my self-accusations. . . .

Saturday morning

. . . I will be totally frank: I do know that when you are married I will not have the right to take this place in your thoughts, to write you letters like this one. I know that this will be a loss for me, but that is nothing compared to the happiness for which you must search. We have both arrived at a point of intimacy which makes any explanation unnecessary. You will remain for me what you are: I will come to find the warmth at your hearth and as a "complete" woman you will be more for me than you are now, when the thought that you are "a marriageable young woman" (don't laugh, I am serious), always covers the ideal which you personify for me, I mean an independent woman and a friend, and it often spoils everything for me, my naturalness, my spontaneity. . . .

I worry so much about you. Forgive me—; I only ask: Think about it.

Saturday evening

My dear friend—I don't dare to read my pages from this morning again— what will you say when you read them?

I wanted to be totally honest—you will find in them the admiration I feel for you—and my fears—my great fears. These are thoughts that demand an answer—please let me have one.[29]

Last evening when I saw you at the stairs with Elly, both looking into emptiness—both so sad—I had to tell myself: I would only have to say one word and everything would be different, but I do not have the right to say it—I don't have this right and you know it. But to let you depart, to let you go into this world shrouded in mist—and when will I see you again? Promise me one thing: if you meet somebody with whom you could share your life and who asks you to accompany him: do not refuse; do not refuse![30]

Can these ragged, contradictory, painful thoughts come from the man who is so confidently tearing Kant apart, preaching with such serenity, controlling the mighty and complex power of a great organ in a Bach fugue? Here nothing is solid beneath his feet, his thoughts and feelings slide uncontrollably to and fro as he tries to catch and express them.

Her reply was not the answer he was looking for; it didn't even give him the comfort of knowing where he stood:

> Thank you for everything [she wrote] thank you for being so completely open. But don't ask for an answer from me—I cannot write; let us leave it as you wish: you speak to me and I am there, I listen to you. Burn this card and do not worry about me—you see many things very differently from what they really are. I do not want to hurt you, you know that—you must be *refreshed, enjoy your work, and be happy.* The first condition for this is: Stop your struggles, I want it. You must be at one with yourself. I trust that you do not misunderstand me.[31]

What did she mean by his seeing things very differently? A letter she wrote nearly eighteen months later tells us that she did, in fact, write other letters at this time, but "I could not send them to you at the time because I did not want to let you know how much I suffered . . . don't forget to read them in the knowledge that they were written by someone whose soul was, at that time, really ill."[32]

Her daughter believes that she destroyed some of her letters. If so, these may well have been among them. We can only guess at what this illness of soul really was, but it cannot have been helped by the emotional pressure put on her by Schweitzer.

Her letter reads like the sort of thing that many a woman has said to a besotted and deluded lover, and the truth is that Schweitzer was besotted. But as with many cases of besottedness, it was the image that besotted him, not the real person. This is not to say that the image is valueless: in this case it is the image of a greatness he aspired to, as Dante found in Beatrice the image of heavenly glory. But a young woman is not a guardian angel, although the notion may flatter her; she is a young woman. In one of his letters, Schweitzer says that she idealizes him. This may well be true, but it is truer still that he idealized her. He read into her simple, honest, practical advice something unique and magical. This kind of idealization often occurs when an adolescent is in the grip of unrequited or unconsummated sexual love, and this may have something to do with this case. To be honest, Schweitzer's letters do often read like the outpourings of an adolescent fighting for his identity. But in this case surely it also comes from the identification of Hélène with Aunt Mathilde. This confusion of identity would account for the shock he felt when he saw her dressed up at a party and for his curious confession that he didn't particularly want to meet her. As a student of Freud, he must have been aware of the concept of sublimation, and it is difficult to believe that he knew himself so little that he did not recognize something akin to this in himself. He may have done so and yet welcomed it.

Sublimation is often regarded today as nothing but a perversion; but as its name suggests, it can be seen as a way of turning something ordinary into something sublime—in a word, self-transcendence. However that may be, one of the developments that we can trace through these letters is the emergence of a true and practical tenderness and concern out of a self-regarding and basically insensitive exaltation of emotion.

At all events, it is clear that at this moment Hélène was unable to share all his ecstasies, his feelings of mystical union, and at the same time unable to reject him.

He did not burn the card. Nor, oddly enough, did she, when she collected the correspondence for preservation. This may have been because, after this, the agonies seem to have died down, perhaps simply from emotional exhaustion, and some sort of mutual understanding prevailed that led them forward together. That the relationship survived at all is quite extraordinary. But sometimes one gets the impression that it was so vital to Schweitzer that, once he had put all his strength into trying to free her, he was thereafter simply not going to allow it to fail, and exerted all his emotional and literary skills to ensure that it didn't.

And there really was something in Hélène that responded to his high-flown passion and the demand for renunciation. From her point of view, this was a powerful experience, far different from the conventional pairings going on around her—deeply romantic, almost mystical—added to which Albert was a very desirable, very unusual young man, and he was hers in a very special way: to control, to criticize, to adore.

Because it was Hélène who preserved the letters, it is natural that the majority are from him to her rather than from her to him. So we have little idea how much she actually did to steer him, or whether what he needed was simply trust and encouragement. But a passage in one of her letters, about the middle of this ten-year correspondence, gives some idea: "Last night, when at five o'clock I lay down again, I thought of those nights when I got up, secretly, desperately, to write to you to help you out of your sadness and to save you from a dark day, and to pull myself out of my own desperation, and I was filled with gratitude. How everything has changed and turned out well!"[33]

And in one she even dared to complain, very delicately but none the less poignantly, about the trials of working on his drafts.

> I congratulate you on the good news. You see, your friend did not give you bad advice in all these years when she said that there must be a German edition of the *Bach*. This nation has a right to have one! But your friend is resigned, she foresees that your promise will not be kept in this case, as in all other promises about co-operation. If it does not already exist, one will invent a very special orthography and punctuation which an

uninitiated cannot comprehend, is it not true? And in the end everything will be done under great pressure and whole nights will be spent working? How well one knows this and one gives up even being surprised or disappointed. Oh, how disobedient our friends are! Once in a while one has to scold a little, don't you agree? I am afraid he has been spoiled recently. And in the end he does not want to have anything to do with the one who speaks her opinion freely. And then?—well, you understand—perhaps one has to change one's tune in order to overcome a great disappointment.— Why hide things from oneself? And why hide something from you that I cannot hide from myself?[34]

One thing the German *Bach* did for them was to provide a respectable excuse for them to meet. And her letter suggests that Schweitzer's German writing owed her a very great deal; although he learned so well from her that a few years later she was worried that she could not be reading his drafts very carefully because she could find so few errors.

One possible reason why things became more relaxed was that Schweitzer now started to channel his discontentment with academic life into a new and practical outlet for his energies. He decided to adopt and raise a number of abandoned boys or orphans and approached Mayor Schwander about it. For a while this seemed to him to be the path that his life was to take, and his letters were full of cheerful anticipation of doing something useful.

At about the same time, January 1904, Hélène started to train as a nurse at Stettin City Hospital. He felt that she, too, had found her path and was happy for both of them. (It is worth noting that she began medical training before he did, contrary to earlier opinions that she only did so to help him.)

She wrote from the hospital, mentioning that there she was known as Sister Hélène. Schweitzer promptly wrote back:

> Can you imagine that I would miss the opportunity to call you "Sister Hélène"? Oh no. Good evening, Sister Hélène. Take the armchair; wait a moment—I will move it closer to the table, now sit down, Sister Hélène. Are you comfortable, Sister Hélène? And now I am there for you, let us have a long conversation. Excuse me for one moment, I have to stoke the fire, so we will not get cold. And now give me your good hand, Sister Hélène.[35]

As the year passed without any boys being offered to him, despite applications elsewhere and advertisements in the papers, he became increasingly depressed. He had started out on a new course with a sort of self-satisfaction at his boldness, an assurance that this was what Jesus had in mind for him, and it was not working. But he persisted in trust and hope.

In October Hélène's father threw a grand party. He was now chancellor of the University, and she was hostess and star. Schweitzer was invited. Here was a situation fit for any romantic drama. It elicited a long letter, in several parts.

What I felt when I saw you was a shock—. At last I saw your sincere eyes again—And how handsome you looked in your suit. Nobody dares to tell you this. You looked so charming, more attractive than ever. Forgive me my clumsiness. It will be difficult to court you—let us joke a little—

Things are a little better. The affairs of the Seminary are improving. I had an awful fight with Nowack, who again pokes his nose into things that are none of his business. I am deadly tired from my work. When will I be able to give you the completed *Bach*? . . .

IV

I come from the Knapps, where you were too, to celebrate the birthday of Else Gütschow. I don't like your blouse! It is not beautiful. Please, do not wear it again when you go anywhere where I am. What a tyrant I am. Please forgive me! When my fingers went over the keys of the piano, we were at the Rhine. You wore the lace collar with your old blouse, and we did not speak. . . . I was exhausted when I got up from the piano—not one note for the others, all, all for you.

V

After the return from the soirée of his Magnificence . . . [her father]

Was I formal enough? You have to tell me.

While I ate the delicacies that were served, I was only dreaming. What a happy idea to at least seat me where I could see you. While you conversed with your neighbors, I told myself: it is thrilling to tell myself that I know her better than anybody else who is here, and she too knows me so well,—with my struggles, my goals, with the idea that keeps me alive— and that I know that she is more than the daughter of the Magnificence, she is a noble, a great woman, a unique soul—who searches and fights—I heard you talking with me on the road to the Fischbodle—I saw you sitting on the rock. . . .

But I want you to marry! An honest man—are you listening! It is your fate to be a wife and mother. You know that otherwise my happiness is not complete. Frequently, when I see a man whom I respect, I ask myself: If he would marry her!![36]

But in the same letter: "If only you knew how despondent I am at times. Waiting and waiting in order to realise my plans. The boy I hoped to take in, one of my candidates for confirmation, was adopted by his aunt."[37]

It has always seemed odd to students of Schweitzer that this respectable curate and university shining light should have been frustrated in this plan of his, but now that we know more about him it is less remarkable. The authorities may well have sensed the decidedly unstable character that lurked under that academic exterior. They may have felt as Hélène did when she wrote to him after hearing one of his sermons: "In it you are yourself: arrogant and humble—and slightly paradoxical."[38]

A month or two later, February 1905, there was another party. Here the paradoxical relationship has become even more pronounced. Whatever the words may say, this is the letter of a lover:

> I come from a party—I must speak with you. If I did not restrain myself with all my willpower, I would sit here all night with the sheet of paper before me and converse with you. . . . In the check room when I saw the seating order, I knew before I read it that I would lead you to the table. And when I felt your arm in mine, I felt happy. How one learns to be satisfied with little. But it is good this way.
>
> I could not speak with you—only very little—but I spoke with you in my thoughts and looked at you from a distance. Since we met on the street I wish nothing but that you accept the position with Schwander [a position at the Social Services Department of the City, where she worked with homeless children, but which she was unable to take up because of her mother's illness]. Please do it, I beseech you, I can see that you will be very happy!! . . . Imagine, I sometimes think that one day we will meet facing a great task and our paths will unite, I am sure of that! . . .
>
> Did I play my role well with the gentleman with whom we are "vaguely" acquainted? Was I indifferent enough in the presence of the people? In spite of the great ideas I have for your future, I always try to look among the unmarried gentlemen for the one whom I would like to see as your husband. Mrs. von Dobschütz! (Ernest von Dobschütz was professor of New Testament Theology 1904–10.) That would be the right thing. While my colleague tried to engage you in a conversation as only a gentleman of the world approaches a lady, I kept saying to myself: "Mrs. von Dobschütz. I forbid you to accept this one. He is another edition of your friend Kuck, and he would never understand you. . . . "
>
> I stole your place card, of course. Yours and mine are together in an envelope.[39]

Alas, we do not have Hélène's response to these intimate, indeed impertinent messages. But very soon came a turning point in Schweitzer's life to which she did respond. On February 25 he wrote in despair:

> Everything is lost! I searched in vain.
> Either the children I try to find do not exist, or people don't want to let me have them and take my plans as fantasies. I had to swallow a

lot. . . . Have I told you that I changed my plan? I would like to take in young men who leave School, so they may learn something solid, or to see that they can become teachers. You see, I have so much love to give, I will be so happy. When I meet a homeless person—and they come around every day—and when I hear that he grew up as an orphan, I tell myself that he would not be in this condition if I had met him. . . .

I am in the grip of a terrible despondency. But I never tell myself that my ideas are fantasies. I am too logical, too rational to indulge in fantasies. But I want to free myself from this bourgeois life that would kill everything in me, I want to *live,* I want to do something as a disciple of Jesus. That is the only thing in which I believe—and in your friendship. Because I believe in it! But people don't allow us to step outside the ordinary, to detach the conventional ties. Yes, I would perish in those. I must free myself. . . .

Look, I do good deeds. I gave all my money to the poor. On New Year's I had nothing in my pockets. But what I want to give, my love, my life, my time—that I am not permitted to give. And that is for me a true need, more than my life. See, Lene, I don't deceive myself.

This thought not just to contribute through scholarship, but through my life, came to me in an unexpected way. Like a small cloud from the distance, on the horizon, so it seemed to me.

While I wrote my book on Kant, I felt the cloud coming closer: its shadow enveloped me. In my Kant I have said more than I realized at the time: I destroyed everything that is essential in religion; I left the *categorical imperative* as the only reality. And now the cloud has become larger. I see nothing of what I once saw. Scholarship has become pale—I feel only one thing: I must act. Everything else feels like a comedy. I feel like I am play-acting; as long as I have not accepted this reality, my whole life is a comedy. . . . I have given up the ambition to become a great scholar, I want to be more—*simply a human.* That will become the theme of your *Wir Epigonen.* We are not true humans, but beings who live by a civilization inherited from the past, that keeps us hostage, that confines us. No freedom of movement, nothing. Man, everything in us is killed by our calculations for our future, by our social position and cast. You see, I am not happy—yet I am happy. I suffer, but that is part of life. I live, I don't care about my existence, and that is the beginning of wisdom, i.e. to search for a value for this existence which the others don't know at all, and which they don't accept. Not a professorship, a comfortable life—but something different. I have found it, I believe that I possess this value: *to serve Jesus.* I am less at peace than if my only goal were to attain a professorship and a good wife, but *I live.* And that gives me the tremendous feeling of happiness, as if one would see a ray of light in a deep pit, as if one would hear music. One feels uprooted, because one asks—what lies ahead, what decisions I should I make—but *more alive,* happier than those who are anchored in life. To drift with released anchor.

I know one thing: If I cannot realize my plan to educate, to take care of young boys, I cannot remain here: I would despair. I would envy all those who serve Jesus, even the lowliest woman at the Salvation Army. I would conclude that I have to search for another kind of realization and would offer my services to the French Mission in the Congo or at the Sambesi River, because people are needed there. If I were to listen to myself, I would leave here tomorrow instead of playing this comedy as I waste away. . . .

I am at this point. It is difficult to write you this instead of telling it as "in the beginning," on the bank of the Rhine surrounded by flowers and sun. But look, difficult issues begin with an idyll, then the idyllic parable perishes, and what remains is the burden. This burden, however, unites those who know each other so well. But the idyll was beautiful—wasn't it?—I would never want to lose a second of it. All is well, whatever happens. . . .

Do you remember that I have a promise from you, from the bank of the Rhine. "If you need somebody some day, promise that you will call me." I promised you—and I often think of that. If I ever need you, I will call you, you can be sure. I guard your promise as something precious, like a jewel to call upon.[40]

We often hear that it is only when one hits bottom that things get better. In this letter, when he feels he has hit bottom, when the flowery idyll has faded, when the confident plans are shattered in humiliation, we can see the seeds of so much that grew into the full tree of his life: the decision to make his life his argument; the purpose of renunciation; the first stirrings of the thought of working in Africa; the vague sense that in some way this may involve Hélène. None of these are yet clear; they are, as he felt, a ray of light in a deep pit. Looking back at the time when these letters were at their wildest and most incoherent, we can see that two separate struggles were going on at the same time, the struggle to distinguish between Hélène the woman and Hélène the guardian angel, and the struggle within himself between the academic and conventional side of his nature and the urgent need to release the romantic in him, to break free into something completely new, completely his own.

He seems also to have made some demand on Hélène that we do not know about. For the moment, her response, like the one eighteen months earlier, was veiled and half-hearted. She was nursing her mother and had little time for a long discussion. It is clear, however, that she shared his growing discomfort with conventional bourgeois life.

In that circle [the Knapps's] I suffocate from the attention that is given to the merest trifles, and to the manner, the thought that is engaged to deal with trivia in order to cultivate the art of conversation. . . . yet I love my friends, and Elly Knapp was so close to me. I too have love to share. . . .

In reply to his question, however, she says:

I have always been very proud of my friend, that he never asked me anything—although he knew that I would do anything he might ask from me—that I would not do gladly and with joy. But this time—although he understood that I could not write—he demands an answer from me!—You see, my friend, there is much that I would like to tell you, exactly concerning the reasons why you suffer so much right now, but that cannot be put into written words. Any moment my mother may call, the household needs me, I could never finish such a letter. And to begin while realizing that one cannot communicate completely, makes no sense. . . . I can do only one thing: be an example that there are ways to come out of the deepest abyss of desperation to be at the top again. Will that give you some courage?[41]

Here it is very clear how she now saw her role in this relationship—to guide, to comfort, to direct this powerful, headstrong creature, inwardly battered by so many tides of emotion and ambition. But such a responsibility demanded time, consideration, and care if she was to give him what he needed.

And in his way he did the same for her. Between that and her next triumphant letter, a couple of months later, there must have come the chance she wanted for them to communicate completely. And for Hélène it resolved everything.

My friend, my great, beloved friend, I must thank you—as three years ago. Thank you that you are so much for me, and that I can be so much for you. This is all so wonderful, so much more beautiful than we could have hoped, or even dared to believe. I thank you for your faith with which you guided me, all the good forces you released in me and sustained, how you assisted me in my struggles, even when I fought against you and against myself. I am grateful that you trusted me, that you held on faithfully to our friendship, even when you felt it to be your duty to warn me, to doubt myself, my strength, and the strength of our friendship. I thank you for all the warm and good feelings which you have for me and cherish, and that I always could feel although you never spoke about them. You made me feel calm, at peace and protected, and assured me of the continuation of this trust that fills me with affirmation of life and with confidence. . . .

Is it because we have paid our tribute in advance, through our struggles and suffering? Now we do not have to fear anybody, not the gods, not humans, not ourselves, you agree my great friend? We have the right to everything we have, even the secrecy which weighed so heavily and frequently on my mind, because those close to me, those to whom I owed the truth, and in whom I wanted to confide did not comprehend the faith I put in them, perhaps they were not able to comprehend it—so they misused my confidence to pull me away from my own, strongest convictions. That I allowed them to do this, that I granted them that much influence over me has brought both of us much sorrow and this will always remain my great guilt toward you.

I tell you this today, so you know that I am aware of it. At the same time I ask you to bear this guilt, together with me, so it will not cast any shadow on our future happiness.[42]

What had caused this sense of guilt? Perhaps her half-heartedness, her fear of commitment, her anxiety about secrecy. Yet she seems also to blame him that in trying to persuade her to think of another man, of marriage and children, he had not sufficiently trusted her devotion to him.

In any event, she too has finally broken free from the bonds of convention. Something had now swept away all the doubts and fears between them. Now he writes like a confident, successful lover to the woman he has won:

I want you to be a little proud of me—just a little. Others give their women jewellery, pearls, diamonds; I give you only my thoughts, my thoughts, thoughts not repeated, not borrowed from somebody else,—my thoughts borne out of my own spirit. My thoughts which, laughing or crying, I have brought forth with an arrogant pride; to have created thoughts, to be a thinker. No, fundamentally, I am not modest because to create thoughts that live is given only to a few people, and if they have some, they offer them to the world, let themselves be admired, and everybody refers to them. Mine belong to me and to those with whom I want to share them, and the most beautiful belong only to you and me. These are my precious stones. You cannot adorn yourself with them. But you have something that only few people in this world could give you.[43]

As a friend once said of him, years later, he knew who he was!

All the same, the demands he made on her were heavy. Committing herself to such an all-or-nothing man, such a driven visionary, whose energy and stamina were "superhuman" (her word) was never going to make life easy, and at this time at least he had little sympathy for weakness in his partner. Nor did she ask for it:

It made me so happy to feel your strength, that you do not feel sorry for me, that it does not affect you when I am weak and downcast. . . . What strangers think, I can ignore, a wasted hour or at most a lost afternoon are bearable,—but the quiet grief of my mother is hard to bear; she feels that there is more, something secretive that she cannot grasp, and about which I cannot tell her more. I would like to help her to understand, to soothe her worries, but she only shows disbelief, hostility, and lack of understanding.

Forgive me for writing all this—I would not have done so if I were still afraid that this would upset you. This was the fear I had the other day when I said—"leave me lying by the roadside"—because I was afraid to see the fear and worry in your face that my complaints had caused. Now I can speak freely so some of your strength flows over to me and sustains me. This was indeed strength, your joyful "I have no pity for you, none!"—strength, and not only self-discipline or concealment of real worries—that made me happy, that gives me courage to speak freely—I could not continue to hide anything from you and to pretend. I need your strength, which returns to me when I can tell you everything, and I feel how you are not touched by it, that you can pass over it—you must go ahead.[44]

Courage indeed, and before the end it was to take its toll on her.

A few weeks later comes almost the only moment in all these two hundred letters that actually uses the word love:

> . . . to share my thoughts with . . . the one who does have all rights—is this not more than a "declaration of love" which I never stated formally? And I will never do it. Because I do not want the shadow of external customs on our friendship. We found each other, and nothing on this earth could be more beautiful than that. To do, each in his sphere, or together if destiny wills it, to comprehend life and, together, walk the high peaks, to be indebted to each other and to give to each other. We are rich through each other! . . . Us, and our relationship I only understand correctly when I think of Him, our Lord. It is he who brought us together, not in any wrong or mystical way, but as two laborers whom he met in the morning on the street and whom he sent into his vineyards. We are on that road.[45]

Nearly two years earlier, reading what he called "Our Book" [*Letters which Never Reached Their Destination*, by Elisabeth von Heyking], the book of which he told Hélène, "You could have written all those letters," he had trembled when he read "the sentence in which she says that a man owes what he has seen, felt and thought to another being who has awakened what had been slumbering in him. Lucky, those who meet those who are destined to awaken that which slumbers in them."[46] Undoubtedly he felt that Hélène had done exactly this for him—awakened what had been slumbering in him or, at least, directed what had been lying unformed and undirected. And it may well be that it was through her practicality that he started to feel the hollowness in the academic world and that her nursing activities encouraged his own inclinations toward medical work.

As to what had now so dramatically demolished Hélène's doubts and hesitations, Schweitzer's autobiography probably gives us the key.

> One morning in the autumn of 1904 I found on my writing-table in the College one of the green-covered magazines in which the Paris Missionary Society reported every month on its activities. A certain Miss Scherdlin

used to put them there knowing that I was specially interested in this Society on account of the impression made on me by the letters of one of its earliest missionaries, Casalis by name, when my father read them aloud at his missionary services during my childhood. That evening in the very act of putting it aside that I might go on with my work, I mechanically opened this magazine, which had been laid on my table during my absence. As I did so, my eye caught the title of an article: "The needs of the Congo Mission."

It was by Alfred Boegner, the President of the Paris Missionary Society, an Alsatian, and contained a complaint that the Mission had not enough workers to carry on its work in the Gabon, the northern province of the Congo Colony. The writer expressed his hope that his appeal would bring some of those "on whom the Master's eyes already rested" to a decision to offer themselves for this urgent work. The conclusion ran: "Men and women who can reply simply to the Master's call, 'Lord, I am coming,' those are the people whom the Church needs." The article finished, I quietly began my work. My search was over.[47]

The autobiography simplifies what the letters tell us was a more reluctant and gradual decision. Even after the decision was made, he was very, very cautious. But by May 1905 he must have been ready at least to hint that the search was over, that he had found the path, and that he wanted her to be his ally in this great enterprise. His midnight letter of June 1–2 speaks of "your promise (or mine, because I suggested it to you)—, to call you where and when I need you. I think that one day I may have to fulfil a major task for which I will need you—and then I will just simply ask you to work with me—and that, perhaps, providence will lead us towards working for the same cause. . . . But this is on the far horizon.—One should under no circumstances think about it before one has a close look at the work—."[48]

She had already said that she would do anything he asked of her. Although Schweitzer was still, even with her, reluctant to let his deepest thoughts out of his sole possession, still only moving step by cautious step toward the fulfilment of his plans, the understanding was there, and it made them happy. Both knew that at last they were true partners. Now there was no longer any doubt about what she meant to him, or he to her.

10

Bach

1902–1904

FROM NOW ON the letters deal far more with events, practical matters, than with interior agonies and ecstasies although often the exaltation bursts through again.

But we have to go back a little in time and look at what was happening in Schweitzer's other world, the daylight world.

By the end of 1902 another book was on the way. The germ of this one was that conversation between Widor and Schweitzer four years earlier when Schweitzer explained that the curious progressions and key changes in Bach's cantatas were reflections of the words. Since that time Widor had been troubled that the French had no book about Bach's music, only about his life, and had asked Schweitzer to fill the gap by writing an essay for his pupils at the Conservatoire.

Schweitzer had set about this in the autumn holiday. But in his usual thorough way he had found himself writing much more than he had intended. It became clear that the essay "would expand into a book about Bach. With good courage I resigned myself to my fate."[1]

He was lucky enough to pick up, very cheaply, a set of the complete edition of Bach's music that the Bach Society had been publishing, bit by bit, for the past fifty years—a landmark in the new appreciation of the composer. Armed with this, he set to work.

For once he felt slightly alarmed at his own temerity. He felt himself to be an amateur in musical history and theory. His sole ambition, he explained, was that "as a musician I wanted to talk to other musicians about Bach's music."[2]

But he had something new to say, and knowing what a fighter he was, we are not surprised to find that the book took shape as a challenge.

164

Even the title throws down the gauntlet: *J. S. Bach. The Musician-Poet*—this about a man who was regarded as the most mathematical, least poetical composer ever to dot a crochet.

The musical world was fiercely divided at this time into two main schools, classic and romantic. The romantics loved the sweeping emotionalism of Wagner, Mahler, and Tchaikowsky. The classicists defended the formality of Bach, which was supposed to be emotionless, rarefied, and cerebral. Wagner, in particular, had stirred up violent enthusiasm and equally violent reactions among the writers of the time. Men as different as Baudelaire, Thomas Mann, and Tolstoy found music both fascinating and frightening. Like the sea, it could carry you into deep waters and drown you.

Schweitzer understood and loved the emotional flood. The sound of a great organ at full volume is as overwhelming as any in the world, comparable to the superamplified din of modern pop, which young people use to reach states of cataleptic ecstasy. But he had no fear of it. Nor was he afraid to step between the two warring factions with his assertion that Bach, the idol of the antiromantics, was himself a painter of emotional colors.

Schweitzer, we are beginning to see, was never happier than when taking a lone stand against the consensus of the world. Once he had picked his cause, he always did it the fullest justice. To his own consternation, the book grew and grew and was not to be ready for nearly two years.

An incidental effect of this book, the first he had to write in French, was to clarify his style. Although the family normally corresponded in French, it was not their native tongue. Alsatian is closer to German, and under German rule the main language taught in the schools was German. Schweitzer found French difficult, its rhythms more exacting.

He came to the conclusion that nobody is truly bilingual. "My own experience makes me think it only self-deception if any believes that he has two mother-tongues. He may think that he is equally master of each, yet it is invariably the case that he actually thinks in only one, and is only in that one really free and creative. If anyone assures me that he has two languages, each as thoroughly familiar to him as the other, I immediately ask him in which of them he counts and reckons, in which he can best give me the names of kitchen utensils and tools used by carpenter or smith, and in which of them he dreams. I have not yet come across anyone who, when thus tested, had not to admit that one of the languages occupied only a second place."

As to the difference between the two languages, he writes, "I can best describe it by saying that in French I seem to be strolling along the well-kept paths in a fine park, but in German to be wandering at will in a magnificent forest.

"Always accustomed in French to be careful about the rhythmical arrangement of the sentence, and to strive for simplicity of expression, these things have become equally a necessity to me in German. And now through my work on the French *Bach* it became clear to me what literary style corresponded to my nature."[3] His criterion once again is a personal one but now influenced by the "higher criticism"[4] of Hélène.

Hélène's name appears for the first time in the Günsbach visitors' book in the Easter holiday of 1903. The new generation of children there christened her Tante Anstand, "Aunt Prim and Proper." With her it was always "Sit up straight," "Wash your hands." They were not entirely at ease, these country Alsatians, with the well-born German-Jewish lady, however much they admired her classical features and respected her courage in involving herself with Strasbourg's flea-ridden orphans. But they were accustomed by now to entertaining all kinds of notable people, professors and musicians and politicians, besides students and local folk. No ceremony was observed. Visitors had to take the Schweitzers as they found them. Hélène, at all events, became a fairly regular visitor.

Gustav Anrich, the principal of St. Thomas College, for whom Schweitzer had briefly deputized in 1901, now moved, only two years later, to a different post. Without opposition, it seems, Schweitzer was elected to take his place. The students, once having had a taste of Schweitzer, were only too delighted to have him back so soon.

Principal is, perhaps, a slightly misleading word. A *Stiftsdirektor* has no administrative functions; he is charged with the direction of students' studies and generally with oversight of their spiritual and mental welfare—a high responsibility for a man of twenty-eight, and one which, had he wished, he could have held for the rest of his life.

On October 1, the start of the new academic year, he moved his belongings into the "roomy and sunny official quarters on the second floor [in Britain, it would be called the first] of the College of St. Thomas"[5] although even now he still kept his book-littered study for his literary work.

The beautiful new quarters were no match for Schweitzer. Despite a stipend of two thousand marks a year to add to his curate's pay he had no inclination to change his way of life. The new rooms soon acquired a topsoil of books. All his belongings were kept in a quantity of linen baskets, which served in place of cupboards and chests. There was a grand piano, littered with scores of his favorite composers—Bach, Wagner, Mendelssohn, Widor, César Franck—on which at a moment's notice he would expound, with illustrations, the inner significance of anything from a Bach cantata to the whole of Wagner's *Tristan.*

As principal he seemed almost like one of the students. He ate in the students' dining hall, and he was at their disposal at any time. A standard nickname for principals—slightly disrespectful—was *"Popel."* Nobody ever called Schweitzer *Popel. Popel* was for "them"—the superiors—and Schweitzer was not like that.

He taught Greek and Hebrew and twice a week directed a course on the Old and New Testaments. With these, and his curate's duties, and the book on Bach, he was again working late into the night. His letters to Hélène were often written at midnight, and sometimes he worked until 7:30 in the morning. Then he would tell the maid to keep the students quiet, and he would sleep for two or three hours while she kept watch.

He never needed to be roused. He could wake himself at any time. Like many of those who work exceptionally hard, he knew how to take catnaps. Sometimes in the middle of a discussion he would say, "I'm tired. Come back in twenty minutes." He would sleep for twenty minutes and wake of his own accord, fresh for hours more.

This was enough to earn the students' respect. What earned their love was that in the midst of it all, if any of them was sick or in trouble, he would come to his room at any hour of the day or night and ask what he could do.

As we have seen from the letters, he was working on a plan to adopt a number of orphaned or abandoned children and educate them himself. Thus, he would have virgin soil in which to implant his ideas about life, and along with them he would implant his own sense of indebtedness so that the children would grow up to care for other derelict children in their turn, a self-perpetuating form of kindness.

Whether, in fact, he would have succeeded in imbuing them with the gratitude that came naturally to him is a matter for doubt. Human beings do not seem notably grateful for charity. But if anything could have done it, it would have been his faith and optimism, his trust in the hidden goodness of human beings.

His feelings about gratitude come out clearly in a sermon he preached some fifteen years later when he spoke of the biblical story of the ten lepers whom Jesus healed, only one of whom returned to thank him. For Schweitzer this did not prove that the other nine were ungrateful—he was sure that they never forgot what they owed to Jesus. But they were too taken up with their delight and the excitement of their families to express their thankfulness. The trouble with neglecting to express one's gratitude was that it made men believe that kindness was pointless. It "paralyses moral action in the world."[6]

Even those of us who feel, with Schweitzer, that people are basically good are often afraid to say so openly or to put the belief into action. It leaves us vulnerable, we feel, exposed to exploitation. So we, in turn, cover up the good that we feel, and the vicious circle continues. One of

Schweitzer's great gifts was his readiness to stand unprotected by cynicism. And in the end he gained from it far more than he lost.

From the letters we know of the despair he felt as stuffy bureaucracy frustrated his first sorties into the world of charitable action. "For example, when the Strasbourg orphanage was burnt down I offered to take in a few boys, for the time being, but the Superintendent did not even allow me to finish what I had to say."[7] Knowing something of his temper, we can guess at the feelings that made him remember that incident so clearly when, twenty-seven years later, he wrote of it in his autobiography.

He made efforts to find other channels for his service, such as the welfare of tramps and ex-convicts, but all the time, as we have seen from the letters to Hélène, that need for a task that was his alone was struggling to the surface. The welfare work he had in mind needed the resources of an organization, and he was a loner, a soloist, anything but an organization man, however worthy the organization. He needed the space to stretch his wings, freedom to work at his own pace and in his own way. Perhaps it was arrogance, which he knew was in him, or romanticism, hungering for something grander than the benevolent societies of Strasbourg could offer; or heroism, which some have called it—he said destiny: "Thank you, destiny. Others will call you God, providence, accident. I call you destiny."[8] In the end it was largely an instinct that guided him past the blind alleys where his talents would have been smothered and kept him waiting until the right road opened ahead.

Still he said nothing about his imminent change of course. He went about his work as though nothing had happened or was going to happen. There must have been times, when plans for the future were being discussed in the college or the church, that caused him some embarrassment. But he was not going to make his decision public until the details were clear in his mind. His instinctive fear of the opposition of his friends (justified, as it turned out) was reinforced by the example of St. Paul, who after his conversion to Jesus "did not confer with flesh and blood" and waited three years before getting in touch with the disciples. But his main reason was simply that "I am by nature very uncommunicative as to everything that concerns my personal life. I have to make an effort to be articulate to others."[9]

In his autobiography he says that only one person—"one trustworthy friend"[10]—knew what he was planning. He kept the identity of this friend secret till the end of his life, and, indeed, when in 1944 Hermann Hagedorn included in his inquiries the specific question, "Who was the trustworthy friend?" Schweitzer replied, "This is unimportant. Permit me not to answer it"[11]—so faithful was he to that ancient vow of secrecy.

We now know, of course, that the friend was Hélène and that it was far from unimportant. At one time I thought that the friend might be Werner Picht, who in the introduction to his book, *The Life and Thought of Albert Schweitzer,* describes himself as "The man who, as a youth, sat at the feet of the preacher of St. Nicholas Church at Strasbourg, who sat at his side at the desk in Günsbach when *Bach* was written, who drew the stops for him at the ancient Silbermann organ of St. Thomas's in Strasbourg, who was with him when his decision to go into the wilderness was first conceived, and who accepted it at once as a matter of course."[12]

Picht was undoubtedly very close to Schweitzer, and it may well be that he was trusted with the decision and unique among Schweitzer's friends in accepting it. As to the others: "Almost more than with my contemplated new start itself [my friends] reproached me with not having shown them so much confidence as to discuss it with them first. With this side issue they tormented me beyond measure during those difficult weeks."[13] So he felt justified in having protected Hélène against the jealousy of others.

Two Sundays before his thirtieth birthday was the Feast of Epiphany, the day devoted to the celebration of missionary work. None of those who heard Schweitzer's sermon on this occasion—except perhaps one—knew that what they were listening to was an announcement of his intentions and a discussion of his reasons. From the pulpit he could speak openly of his secret plan, and even those who knew him well had no means of knowing what he was telling them. Afterward, looking back, we can understand.

The sermon is a long one. I have picked out, as it were, the themes. For at this crucial moment all the major themes of his life come together, as at the climax of a great fugue: the theme of human compassion; the theme of devotion to Jesus; the theme of the degeneracy of civilization; the theme of fascination with faraway lands; the theme of action; the theme of simplicity.

He was to make his life his argument. But now the argument is still in words. And here it is, the *apologia pro vita sua*. In this magnificent sermon he gives an account of his life not after he has lived it, but before. And nobody knew what he was doing.

"Jesus said to them, 'I will make you fishers of men' "; this was the text. Other festivals, says Schweitzer, look backward to past events. But this festival is one "when we look straight ahead of us, when it is not the past that we summon, but the present hour and the future, and when we prepare ourselves to face the tasks of tomorrow." He goes on to look at missions as they are, with an undeceived eye.

Missions are not popular; you have no more illusions on that subject than I have. . . . Recently in Paris a generous donor said in my presence to a lady who was collecting: "You can always call on me. My door and my purse are always wide open. But never in any circumstances ask me for anything for Missions—not a farthing. It's money thrown out of the window." As for me, I have argued so much, I have broken so many lances on behalf of Missions, by sea and by land, in coach and train, mountain and plain, with friends and strangers, that I know pretty well all the objections that people bring against them.

The first objection, endlessly repeated, is this: we must leave those races their religions, we must not go to them and take away the beliefs which have kept them happy hitherto, for that does nothing but disturb their spirit. To that I reply: "For me, a mission does not concern itself primarily or exclusively with religion. Far from it! It is above all a task of humanity, which neither our governments nor our peoples have understood. . . . "

What is it our governments and our peoples think of when they look beyond the seas? They think of the lands which they will take, as they say, under their sovereign protection, which they can attach to themselves in one way or another; they think of what they can seize from them for their own greater profit . . . Our States, these States so confident of their high civilisation, come to grief there. They are nothing more than predators. Where in these highly civilised nations are the workmen, the craftsmen, the teachers, the wise men, the doctors, who will go to those distant lands and do the work of civilisation? Where can one see our society undertake some effort in this direction? Nowhere, absolutely nowhere!

The only true civilisation consists in living as a disciple of Jesus, for whom every human being is a person who has a right to our help and our sacrifice. . . .

Ah, fine civilisation, which can talk in such edifying terms of human dignity and the rights of man, and which at the same time mocks and tramples on human dignity and the rights of man among the millions of beings whose only crime is living overseas, having skin of another colour, and being unable to manage their affairs single-handed.

If anyone were to ask me why I think Christianity is the unique religion, dominating all the others, I will happily throw in the dustbin everything we have been taught about the relationship between religions, about the hierarchical structure, about the criterion of excellence, and I will only hold onto one thing: that in the first command the Lord gave on earth, a single word stands out: the word "man." He does not speak of religion, faith, the soul or anything else, only about "men." "Come. I will make you fishers of men."

In short, Missions are nothing but an expiation for the violence committed far away by nations that call themselves Christian.[14]

By today's standards what he says could be called paternalistic. He sees the black races as poor, distressed, needing help and the true

Christian as the benefactor who from his abundance can offer health, education, an improvement of life. But the word *paternalistic* begs too many questions to be useful. The question to ask is whether Schweitzer's words were true. They were. Were his motives sincere? They were. Did he place the responsibility and the blame where they belonged? He did. There is nothing patronizing about his attitude. To say what he said about white imperialism, when he said it, from a pulpit, was as enlightened, courageous, and farsighted as it was possible to be at that time. Nearly a century later the powerful predators among the white races are still about their dirty business.

In these same days, leading up to his birthday, he was sitting for a portrait. He had handed over a room in his official residence on St. Thomas' quay to a painter friend who needed a studio—Ada von Erlach, sister-in-law of that Frederick Curtius whose mother kept open house for the academics of Berlin. Ada had recently had a serious operation, halting although not curing a fatal disease, presumably a cancer. Her aged mother, the Countess von Erlach, lived with Frederick in Strasbourg—a wise old lady who had been the governess of a grand duchess. Schweitzer was treated as a member of the family, and to solace the old lady for not being able to get out any longer to concerts, played the piano to her for an hour every evening. In return she took him in hand and helped him, so he says, "to round off many a hard angle in my personality."[15]

It was the old countess who persuaded Schweitzer to sit for his portrait by Ada, hoping that by getting back to her painting Ada would gain a fresh interest in life that would help her back to health.

The last of these sittings happened to fall on his thirtieth birthday, January 14, 1905. This was the day he had long settled on as the day for a final decision on his future. "I always, always have to think of how serious you were on your thirtieth birthday,"[16] wrote Hélène five years later.

He must have gone over the pros and cons many times before in those long solitary night hours, but on this significant day, sitting there motionless—not his favorite occupation—he had plenty of time to sum them up and face the implications of his plan. He was "like the man in the parable who 'desiring to build a tower first counts the cost whether he have wherewith to complete it.' "[17]

What was the cost? First and most obviously the loss of his job, his respected place in the university. We now know that this was the least of his worries. Indeed, he could scarcely wait to escape: "A few weeks ago," he wrote to Hélène, "Reverend Knittel told me: you will receive a unanimous vote to become my successor, and after a few years you will be the Canon of St. Thomas and member of the Church commission.—I suffocate."[18] And: "Today we had our Faculty meeting. . . . [W]hen the program of courses was determined, I thought with a shudder that perhaps I might have spent my whole life preparing course schedules."[19]

Then there were his friends, and, perhaps, more important than the loss of them was the loss of their sympathy and understanding. Above all, there was the loss of his music: the concerts in Strasbourg, the happy spells in Paris, the daily practice, the Sunday services, the freedom of the organs of Europe. What he was going to do could be seen as a continuation, in a way, of his pastoral and even his theological work. But music must be lost. And music, to a man who rested so little, *was* his rest—his balm, his solace, his relaxation. That would really be hard to leave.

There were more practical considerations. For several reasons it seemed better not to think of going to Africa as an ordinary missionary. The steady veering of his thoughts toward practical action, his disenchantment with theory, with words, urged him toward something different. Besides, he had enough experience of what the average Christian divine thought of his theology to doubt whether missionaries would find him particularly suitable as a preacher to the heathen. The Paris Mission Society had always been his father's favorite because it was less inclined than most to talk in "the sugary language of Canaan":[20] there was an exceptional liberality about their attitude. But even so, Schweitzer thought them likely to balk at his ideas.

The society, however, desperately needed medical help. The missionaries on the spot were constantly reporting their distress at the physical condition of the Africans who came to them. As a medical missionary surely he would be acceptable. Active, practical, merciful—everything pointed to this as Schweitzer's field of work, except that he knew no medicine.

He was thirty years old. How long would it take to learn? Could he learn it, starting so late in life? Could he face the effort of starting from the beginning in a totally new field? Such were the costs he had to count.

By the end of his birthday the decision was confirmed. He would step down from professor to student at the start of the next university year, when the medical course began, and in due course offer his services as a doctor to the Paris Mission Society. The prospect was daunting. But the will that he had already trained to ignore the laughter of schoolfellows, exhaustion, and the disapproval of theological colleagues was equal to the new challenge.

Still, however, he would tell no one what he intended—or only one or possibly two: Hélène and Werner Picht. First, he must cross the river and set the boats on fire. Then there would be no going back. Even Hélène, it would seem, had to wait till after March before he was ready to discuss the full details of his thought, the details including her. From the rest of the world his plans remained secret for another nine months as he went about his many occupations as before.

The Bach book was finished. He had been sending the chapters one by one to Widor as he wrote them and in October the previous year, with the end in sight, he had asked Widor to supply the introduction he had promised. Widor, holidaying in Venice, promptly obliged. Schweitzer could scarcely have asked for a more enthusiastic recommendation:

> Better than all the speeches in the world, the pages you are about to read will show the power of Bach's extraordinary brain, for they will give you examples and proofs. . . .
> As we read Monsieur Schweitzer's book, it seems to us that we are present at the inauguration of a monument; the last scaffolds, the last veils have fallen; we walk around the statue to study its details, then we withdraw a little to a point from which our eyes can survey the whole; and then we pass our judgement upon it.[21]

Although the book disagreed with most current opinion about Bach and trod on a few toes in so doing, the musicians were more generous than the theologians had been. Schweitzer had only intended to fill a gap in the musical education of French students; he had not felt qualified to do more. But the combination of scholarship and insight in the book attracted attention in Germany as well, and he was soon asked for a translation—Hélène also urging it and promising her help. What with one thing and another it was a year or more before he found time to attend to this commission, but when he did, he found that the difference between the two languages made a simple translation impossible. He would have to begin afresh.

Let us break the chronology of the story and consider the German edition now. For although it turned out to be nearly twice as long, everything in it was already in his head when he wrote the French version. The scale of the project was all that had changed. And perhaps one can detect a slightly less reverent note in the later book (on which the English translation is based) as though the company of medical students had rubbed away a faint trace of pastoral respectability in Schweitzer's outlook and left him freer to look without alarm at his hero's foibles and failings.

When the time came to begin the new edition, he found it difficult to get down to it. This was cold meat reheated, and he still had trouble concentrating on what did not catch his interest. The impulse to start finally came at Bayreuth in the summer of 1906. He returned exhilarated to his hotel room after a particularly exciting performance of *Tristan* and found that at last the words were beginning to come. Once started, that evening in the Black Horse Inn at Bayreuth, "while the babel of voices surged up from the Bierhalle below into my stuffy room,"[22] he wrote all night and on past sunrise.

The English translation (beautifully done by Ernest Newman in 1911) runs to two volumes, a total of 926 pages; and Bach is not even born until page 99. In his usual thorough way Schweitzer has led up to his subject by going into the history of German music that produced his hero and an account of the extraordinary musical family into which he was born. In the French edition this is much more sketchily dealt with, but in the long run the long-winded German method pays great dividends in understanding, partly because Schweitzer by now was writing so well that length is not matched by tedium.

The next 125 pages are devoted to Bach's life—another 40 to the cause of his reputation since his death—and the rest of volume one to a detailed survey of the instrumental works and the proper manner of playing them.

The first part of volume two goes into Bach's approach to writing for the voice. Here we come to the controversial part of the book, the argument that Bach is essentially a painter of pictures in his music, different motifs in the music representing specific images: dragging footsteps, placid water, storms, steep ascent or headlong downfall; that he deliberately and brilliantly illustrates the main theme of the words he is setting to music; and that he was happiest and most successful with words whose image was strong and clear. The argument is chiefly directed at Philipp Spitta, who had recently published the first full biography of Bach. Spitta's historical work was admirable, particularly in view of the scarcity of information about Bach, and Schweitzer made good use of it. But Spitta was a leader of the fashionable view that Bach's work was at the opposite pole to the descriptive composers, Berlioz, Schubert, Wagner, and obeyed only the pure laws of music; in short, that Bach was, as the phrase has it, "the celestial sewing machine." Spitta believed that the occasions when the music of a cantata seemed pictorial were subconscious accidents, to be ignored by the listener. Although how anyone could ignore, for example, the desperate, heartbroken wail in the *St. Matthew Passion* that tells of Peter's remorse at betraying Jesus, when he "wept bitterly," is difficult to understand.

Schweitzer believed that these descriptive elements were of the essence of the music and, moreover, that proper performance was impossible until the performer had understood the pictorial purpose of the writing. With enormous care Schweitzer goes into the precise function of tied phrases, staccato notes, and so forth, showing how these build up the detailed rhythmical pattern that sets the scene. The whole vitality of this sort of music depends on this wealth of delicate and precise detail, rather than on the emotive masses of sound, swelling crescendos, dramatic climaxes, and tapering diminuendos of composers from Beethoven onward.

In one fascinating chapter on art in general, Schweitzer suggests that whatever medium they may work in, all artists experience the same artistic impulse. Their particular talent dictates how this impulse is expressed, whether in music, poetry, or the pictorial arts. This being so, he says, we often find a painter whose vision is poetic, even perhaps narrative, another whose painting is closer to music. A poet may be half musician or half painter. And a musician may paint pictures in his music or may evoke the emotional overtones of poetry. For Schweitzer, Bach was the painter, dealing in tableaux; Wagner was the poet, creating in the mind not visual images but flooding sensations.

Perhaps these classifications of the different types of artist and musician are too precise. Perhaps we can accept here the charge that was brought against Schweitzer's views on Jesus—that he pushes the argument too far. For, as he says himself, all writing about art is imprecise and subjective, incapable of either proof or disproof. Statements about art are oblique: they have the nature of parables. But even if we find it impossible to go along with Schweitzer all the way, this section of the book is full of stimulating ideas and insights and well worth reading on its own. (I find myself using here almost exactly the same terms as critics who wrote about *The Quest of the Historical Jesus*. This suggests that they thought of the Gospels as some sort of art form about which one could be stimulating, imprecise, and above all subjective, whereas Schweitzer, as a historian, was trying to be objective and asking others to make the same effort.)

The four hundred pages that conclude the second volume, in which Schweitzer deals exhaustively with all Bach's vocal works, are not for general readers although they form a marvelous work of reference and the writers of the blurbs on record jackets still regularly quote what he had to say about this cantata or that motet. It is not difficult to see why. No one before or since has combined such extensive technical knowledge with such esthetic insight, enthusiasm, and power to express himself.

One typical example must suffice:

The other alto cantata, Widerstehe doch der Sünde (No. 54) begins with an alarming chord of the seventh—

The trembling of the basses and violas, and the sighs of the violins, between them give the movement a somewhat disturbing effect. It is meant to depict the horror of the curse upon sin that is threatened in the text. Of a similar character is the aria "Wer Sünde tut, der ist vom Teufel" (The sinner is of the devil). It is strict trio between the voice, the violas and the violins. The theme runs thus—

Harmonically the movement is of unparalleled harshness.

The opening aria of the solo cantata for tenor, "Ich armer Mensch, ich Sündenknecht" (No. 55) is, as a rule, phrased so inanimately that the whole sense of the despairing wail is lost. The characteristic accent should fall on the second beat. The orchestra must phrase thus—

This passage—

should be played with a strong crescendo, the last quaver being always heavily accented in contradiction to the beat, thus obstructing the rhythm, as it were. This motive belongs to the words "Ich geh' vor Gottes Angesicht mit Furcht und Zittern zum Gerichte" (I go in fear and trembling into the presence of God). It suggests painful striving, as in the theme of the introduction to the cantata "Herr, gehe nicht ins Gericht" (No. 105), of which it strongly reminds us.[23]

Perhaps what is most impressive in this book is the extraordinary memory and the concentration that seems able to seize on so many facets of a subject—historical, esthetic, technical, and human—all at once. Bach is

seen simultaneously as a man, gentle and friendly, but capable of mean-
ness and bad temper and chronically unable to control his pupils; as a
historical climax to a whole musical movement; as a virtuoso keyboard
player (his chief, almost his only fame in his own day); as a supreme
artist, who paid so little heed to his own talent that his manuscripts were
never properly preserved and their classification is still in a state of chaos;
and as a mystic, whose passionate, almost morbid attachment to Jesus
and to the death that would unite him to his Lord was in a totally separate compartment from the contented family life of a man who liked the
good things of the world and knew the value of money.

The historical element is vital, for it was not only Schweitzer's musical
insight that led him to the pictorial function in Bach. Reaching back into
the eighteenth century, he was simply disinterring a musical language,
commonplace then, which the nineteenth century had buried. Bach was
one of a school of composers that "took for itself by preference the title
of 'expressive' (affektvoll) in distinction from all others, meaning to indicate thereby that its purpose was graphic characterisation and realism.
Although our musical aestheticians must have known this—for the histories of music testify sufficiently to it—they made no attempt to examine the music of that epoch thoroughly and to enquire what light it might
throw on the nature of the art, but took the line of sweeping aside these
phenomena as merely transitory pathological perversion of pure music."[24]

At the very beginning of the nineteenth century one man, Johann
Nicolaus Forkel, a musical historian, wrote of Bach as "the greatest musical
poet and greatest musical rhetorician that has ever existed, and probably
that ever will exist."[25] But his voice was barely heard in the surrounding
silence, the mood of reaction that found Bach simply old-fashioned.
Another twenty years were to pass before the great rediscovery began
and thirty more before it was really under way. But even then the words
of Forkel were not taken seriously. Schweitzer's steady perseverance, his
relentless amassing of detailed evidence, were necessary before people
could again see Bach as he saw himself—an "expressive" man.

As we have noted, although Schweitzer was so unforthcoming about
his own private affairs, he had no qualms about investigating Bach's
daily life. In the French edition he laments, "Unfortunately we possess
very few details about Bach's intimate life, about the husband and the
father of a family."[26] And in the German edition he writes of "the shame-
less curiosity that characterises our boasted historical sense."[27] That he
condoned this curiosity in himself may make us easier about our curiosity toward him.

Amusing to note are other parallels between Bach and himself: "The
other deliverances upon him [Bach] run on general lines of admiration
and amazement and rhetorical analogies from ancient mythology. . . . We

would gladly exchange all these for a single sentence of someone who, at the first performance of the St. Matthew Passion, had an intuition of the real spirit of Bach's music."[28] We suffer in the same way from the unthinking adulation of Schweitzer. How closely, too, Schweitzer describes himself in these words about Bach: "He is one of those rare personalities that do not become, but always are"[29] although in Schweitzer's case it took Hélène to bring out the hidden man. We see the practical Schweitzer emerging from the academic when he writes:

> Bach was self-taught, and as such had an aversion to all learned theories. Clavier-playing, organ-playing, harmony, composition—he had learnt them all by himself; his sole teachers had been untiring work and incessant experiment.
>
> To a man who had made the fundamental rules of art his own in this manner, many theories that were interesting or new for others were a matter of indifference, for he had been to the roots of things. Now Bach lived in the epoch when it was thought that the perfect art could be discovered by aesthetic reasoning, while others, again, thought that salvation for music lay in mathematical speculations upon the numbers that underlie intervals. To all these endeavours Bach opposed a robust indifference.[30]

And we see the sort of humor that pleased Schweitzer in his obvious enjoyment of the anecdotes he relates. Bach's tightfistedness amused him so much that he mentions three times the letter in which Bach wrote: "My position here is worth about 700 thalers, and when there are rather more funerals than usual the perquisites increase proportionately; but if the air is healthy the fees decrease, last year, for example, being more than 100 thalers below the average from funerals."[31]"He cannot help showing," says Schweitzer, "his indignation over the healthy year 1729, when the Leipzigers took so little pleasure in dying that the burial fees brought the cantor a hundred thalers less than usual."[32]

A close link between author and subject was Bach's dislike of working under the imposition of a governing body. At St. Thomas, Leipzig, Bach was answerable to both the church council and the consistory. But arguments broke out between the two bodies about his responsibilities. "We cannot say," says Schweitzer, "that Bach suffered from this tension. It ministered admirably to his own need for independence, for he played the consistory off against the council and the council against the consistory, and meanwhile did what he liked."[33]

These personal notes enliven the long learnedness of the book. Schweitzer never forgot the man behind the masterpieces. But above everything else what attracted Schweitzer about Bach was his religion. All Bach's technical skill, like all Schweitzer's, went to serve an overriding mystical purpose. Things must be done beautifully because that was the clearest, most unencumbered path to the vision of eternity. It is worth noting in this connection that however much Schweitzer loved and admired Mozart and Beethoven (and we know that he did), the Protestant composers delighted him most: Bach, Mendelssohn, Wagner—as unlikely a trio as you could assemble, in style and talent. They are united only by a specifically religious mystical fervor that was not in the nature of Mozart or Beethoven, greater though they were than Wagner and immeasurably superior to Mendelssohn. Indeed, if it were not for Bach, we would have to say that Schweitzer's musical taste was almost deplorably romantic. The truth is that whatever his aesthetic insight he ultimately valued the intention, the mystical frame of mind, almost as much as the achievement.

Although most of the technical sections of the Bach book are to be skipped by any but practicing musicians, one of the side issues is of great general interest—both in itself and because it shows that Schweitzer had already reached conclusions that he only published in full a good deal later. It concerns the type of bow that Bach had in mind for the soloists in his violin works.

It was not until 1932 that he returned to this subject, in an article entitled "The Round Bow" in the *Schweitzerische Musikzeitung*. But here in the Bach book we find him already hot on the trail.

Compositions for stringed instruments often include chords besides single notes. The only way to play a chord of more than two notes on a modern violin with a modern bow is by playing the notes in quick succession, altering the angle of the bow to touch one string after another. The chord thus becomes a sort of swift arpeggio. But the word *bow* really means exactly that—a bow, a curved piece of wood with a string stretched between the ends held taut by the spring in the wood. This was the early musical bow, as can be seen in paintings of the time. By Bach's day the straighter bow, with a screw for tightening the strings, was coming into use. But the old bow was still in evidence, and Schweitzer was convinced that Bach had the old bow in mind when he wrote chords. For the strings of a bow of this kind, pressed firmly down across the strings of a violin; will give a little so that they are touching all the strings of the instrument at once and can play a simultaneous chord.

The straight bow, its strings screwed tighter than the old bow could ever be, has a brighter, more piercing tone, and can fill a larger hall. By comparison the old bow produced a softer, mellower sound. You can reproduce the tone of an old bow, said Schweitzer, by unstringing a modern one, turning it upside down, and restringing it with the strings above the violin strings and the wood under the neck of the violin. Draw this across the strings and you get an idea of Bach's violin tone.

A Norwegian named Ole Bull, who had died as recently as 1880, had played with a round bow, but Schweitzer never heard a bow of this kind being used properly until 1929. Nobody was prepared to sacrifice the strength of tone produced by a modern bow or to learn the complicated technique of using the thumb to tighten and relax the tension of the bowstrings.

Schweitzer's constant insistence on old organs and old bows was accompanied by a dislike of modern pianos, at any rate for Bach's music. To his ears all the later developments had added power at the expense of beauty. The accusation often leveled at him that he lived in the past and was not interested in the present or future is only true to this extent, that his historical sense enabled him to feel the pulse of a bygone culture, to live imaginatively within it, more completely than most of us, who observe it only from outside.

The pulse of the eighteenth century was very different from our own. But it is reasonable to suppose that a mind tuned to that pulse would be in a better position than most of us to compare old sounds and new. Schweitzer's experiments with Marie Jaëll and Carl Stumpf showed that he was far from reactionary. He had listened more widely and carefully than most men of his day. He never advocated a return to the imperfect techniques and instruments of a past age. All he asked was that modern ingenuity should seek ways of preserving and increasing beauty, not destroying it.

What would he have thought of the way in which Bach became the darling of pop groups and was synthezised on an electronic organ? Bach's vitality, fortunately, lifts him clear of the clutch of his less-discriminating admirers, but it must be said that some of them leave him temporarily a little bruised.

The campaign that Schweitzer launched a little later for his kind of organ has very largely been won. The harpsichord and other keyboard instruments that pluck rather than strike the strings have found a new popularity since Schweitzer's time. But the round bow is still as dead as the dodo and shows no signs of resurrection.

The accusation against all three of them was of softness, gentleness, a lack of volume that made them unable to be heard properly in a large concert hall. Perhaps another technical innovation can solve this problem. Electronic amplification need not always be crude and unmusical. Sensitively amplified, the sound of a clavichord can fill any hall or can be heard on records in the intimacy of one's own home. Perhaps with this help the round bow, too, will come back into its own.

While he was working on the book, Cosima Wagner came to stay in Strasbourg with her daughter, Eva. She had heard about Schweitzer's new views on Bach and wanted to learn more of them; so Schweitzer accompanied her as she walked about Strasbourg and played for her on the organ of the Temple Neuf.

Hitherto he had only met the great lady at Heidelberg when she was imperiously receiving visitors after a concert. Now they got to know each other better, and Schweitzer was bowled over by her as by none of the young women of Strasbourg. Christian Brandt remembered the casual pride with which Schweitzer introduced her when they met accidentally on the college stairs. And she, in her turn, must have been impressed by the intense and knowledgeable young man, for when he went to visit her in her declining years after the war, the news of his arrival put her into such a flutter that she was unable to see him.

Schweitzer's theories about music were born of practical experience. And, in turn, the theories bore practical results. A new organ was required for his church, St. Nicholas, and, as we may imagine, the design incorporated many of his ideas. The stops and the couplings were planned as a compromise between the French and the German systems, aiming at the fullest flexibility combined with simplicity of operation. The result seems to have been most successful, and it must have delighted him enormously to see his notions taking physical shape. The new design cost only marginally more than a conventional one would have done, a point he stresses in writing about it, for many churches were being seduced by the cheapness of the "factory" organs that were beginning to dominate the organ-building world, in which smart complicated consoles were featured at the cost of inferior metal in the pipes and corner-cutting in quality all around. The treasurer of St. Nicholas was, no doubt, breathing down Schweitzer's neck, and it must have been a relief to both of them that the custom-built instrument performed as anticipated and still only added two hundred marks to the bill.

Meantime, in Paris Schweitzer had banded together with several of his musical friends and associates to found a new society—the Paris Bach Society. The leading light was the conductor Gustave Bret, but he was supported by Widor, Guilmant, Gabriel Fauré, Vincent d'Indy, Paul Dukas, and Schweitzer himself, a cross section of French music that excluded only the three greatest names of all—Debussy, Ravel, and Saint-Saëns.

They met in Widor's rooms at the Conservatoire and Schweitzer's function, apart from contributing to the interpretation of the music, was to play the organ accompaniment at the society's concerts and to write their program notes, a few of which survive.

It is interesting sometimes to note the things Schweitzer did *not* write about, the people he apparently did not find important. Debussy, although a very different composer from Wagner, feminine and sensitive in his music where Wagner is aggressively masculine, followed closely in Wagner's footsteps as a composer of the music of "sensations," and his friendships with Mallarmé and Gide and the direct influence he had on Impressionist painters helped him to fulfill in his own way Wagner's demand for a linking and unity of all the arts. Yet Schweitzer never mentions him. The reason, I feel sure, is temperamental. The "softness" of Debussy (and of the Impressionists) was not for him.

The planning of the Paris Bach Society's concerts naturally involved a good deal of correspondence. Schweitzer was already a good and reliable letter-writer, but his previous activities had never stimulated such a volume of correspondence as began now. The society was one cause, the book another. Congratulations, questions, and challenges began to pour in. It was as well he had no idea how this correspondence would increase, how nearly it would overwhelm him as his name became known in other, wider spheres.

The next stage in the great adventure took place in July: "My hand shakes a little: I just put the letter in the mailbox in which I tell the Director of the Paris Mission that I am ready and willing to leave in February, 1910. The letter has been written: clear, precise, without any sentiments, almost like a business letter. I carried it to the mailbox; when I returned I stood still for a moment and looked at the two towers of the Thomas church which stood above the courtyard enveloped in a soft light. . . . I am happy. It is done. I am not afraid that I might regret anything."[34]

The confidence did not last long. The following day he writes: "My head aches. I had a restless night, and this morning I feel as if my soul does not live in my body. It follows my letter, wants to bring it back; wants to be free again to decide, to make the decision."[35] Then followed the experience of many a job seeker. After ten days: "I am desolate, it is almost an attack of despair. I wait in vain for an answer from Paris . . . every morning I wake up and wait for the mail—nothing; at eleven o'clock again—nothing. Today on my way to the confirmation class . . . the eleven o'clock mailman shook his head again. . . . I felt like breaking my cane on the railing of the bridge and throwing it into the water."[36]

We have seen that the Paris Mission Society—La Société des Missions Evangéliques chez les Peuples non Chrétiens—was one of which his father approved as having a more liberal outlook than most. There were, unfortunately, no missions specifically belonging to the liberal sections of Protestantism. The dogmatic elements in the churches had been the quickest to send representatives to preach to the heathen at the beginning of the nineteenth century, their purpose being simply "to save souls"—meaning thereby to baptize as many black people as possible. By contrast, the liberal Christians wanted, as Schweitzer put it, "to set the Gospel working primarily as a force for the restoration of mankind and the conditions of human society in the heathen world."[37] But this kind of Christianity had no spokesman in the mission world, which is why missions gained the bad name that still clings to them. Liberal Christians, therefore, tended to support the dogmatic missions for lack of anything better, and naturally they gave the most support where they discerned the most liberal spirit.

While the wait continued, life went on. Hélène, working in England, heard a lecture about mission work in the Congo (which at that time included the present Gabon) and wrote:

> [He] spoke, not as much about the work of the missionaries . . . as about the awful conditions under which the poor natives have to live in the Belgian Congo. He wanted to appeal to public opinion to shake people up so they would contribute to the development of this area into a genuine state with a government instead of being at the mercy of one single person who, although a King, has almost only commercial interests. . . . [I]t was horrifying, even if only half of the cruelties he reported are actually committed there. I told my parents about this evening and, for the first time, mentioned the Congo to them. I wrote that, if the description of the atrocities are based on fact, no responsible person could remain a calm observer.[38]

In the summer of this year Schweitzer discovered that his students, studying the life of Jesus, had been given no idea what previous work had been done on the subject. It so happened that the university library was uniquely well equipped with relevant books and other material, and Schweitzer, after consulting his old mentor Holtzmann, decided to lecture on the subject. "I attacked the work with zeal, but the material took such a hold of me that when I had finished the course of lectures I became absolutely absorbed in it."[39] So began *The Quest of the Historical Jesus*.

At the same time something else needed winding up; his conclusions about organ building must be made public before he vanished into his new life. With so little time left, he went at the two things like a whirlwind: the booklet, which, in the long run, was to change the face of organ construction; and the huge tome, with its wealth of learning, which was to land rather like a dud shell in the battlefields of theology.

Meantime, he had finally had a reply from the Paris Mission. On October 12 he wrote to Hélène:

> I spoke with the Director of the Missions in the Parc Montsouris, and after five minutes we were friends! . . . I explained to him how I arrived at the idea. He was moved by the simplicity and the logic of my thought. He himself is quite liberal, but there are people on the Committee who are afraid of an assistant professor from Strassburg; but he is sure that I can win them over through the simplicity of my words.

I will, however, see to it that the question of dogma does not come up.

Well then: two years from now the Mission Society will call me to the place where I am needed. If they have a vacancy before that time, I will go. I leave the Seminary and will begin my medical studies already this winter. If the Society considers it useful to let me complete my medical studies, they will let me do so. This is the solution I like best, because then we both feel more at ease. My religious views will then be a private matter. But if they need a missionary sooner, I will not finish my studies. Officially, the Society knows that one week from today I will be available.

These men are simple and of great depth. No veneer. One of them asked with a sad voice, whether there was anybody in this assembly who would come and help him in the Congo. . . . If there is an invisible communication between souls, he must have heard my Yes.[40]

But Schweitzer rapidly discovered that the director, an Alsatian named Boegner, had been a little too sanguine about the committee, and the simple, humane attitude of the missionaries themselves was no reflection of the policies of the society's head office. Boegner, who had himself written the article that had made up Schweitzer's mind for him, had to confess that he was somewhat oversimplifying when he wrote, at the conclusion of his article, "Men and women who can reply simply to the Master's call 'Lord, I am coming,' those are the people whom the Church needs." Schweitzer had indeed said, "Lord, I am coming." But he had not also said, "I believe in X and Y and Z," and, therefore, members of the committee were likely to raise objections, evidently feeling that the souls of their converts might be infected by the healing touch of a less-than-true believer. The two Alsatians, Boegner and Schweitzer, decided to wait and see whether the intervening years would bring these frightened people to what Schweitzer called "a truly Christian reasonableness."[41]

In fact, as it turned out, a more liberal mission organization did exist, the General Union of Evangelical Missions, based in Switzerland, under whose auspices Schweitzer could have gone, he reckoned, as either doctor or missionary and on his own terms. But he made no attempt to do things this easy way for two odd and very Schweitzerian reasons. First, that "my call to Equatorial Africa had come to me through the article in the Paris Mission Magazine"[42] and, therefore, a sort of emotional loyalty tied him to that society. And second, sheer obstinacy, "I was tempted to persist in getting a decision on the question whether, face to face with the Gospel of Jesus, a missionary society could justifiably arrogate to itself the right to refuse to the suffering natives in their district the services of a doctor, because in their opinion he was not sufficiently orthodox."[43] Behind that persistence one senses the same anger that crept up on him when pious souls told him he must believe in the Resurrection before he could believe in the living Jesus. His notorious temper must have had a trying time in these months when he felt himself surrounded by people who not only did not understand him but did not understand the Christianity they all professed. One cannot help suspecting that he learned the hard way the lesson he speaks of in his autobiography:

> These favoured persons [that is, those like himself who are lucky enough to be able to strike out on an independent line] must also be modest, so as not to fly into a passion at the opposition they encounter; they have to meet it in the temper which says: "Ah well, it had to be!" Anyone who proposes to do good must not expect people to roll stones out of his way, but must accept his lot calmly even if they roll a few more upon it. A strength which becomes clearer and stronger through its experience of such obstacles is the only strength that can conquer them. Resistance is only a waste of strength.[44]

Under these stresses, Schweitzer's already powerful will was being tempered into a flexible but truly formidable weapon.

The following day he slipped an explosive fistful of letters into a Paris letterbox, announcing to his unsuspecting family and friends that "at the beginning of the winter term I should enter myself as a medical student, in order to go later on to Equatorial Africa as a doctor."[45] Another letter resigned his post as principal of St. Thomas College. There could no longer be time for those responsibilities.

He makes a point of the date in his autobiography. Knowing how he disliked superstition, it is tempting to wonder if this was some kind of defiant gesture—except that even this could seem to give superstition more than its due. But, for the record it was Friday the thirteenth.

11

Medical Studies

1905–1908

HIS MOTHER SEEMS to have been the hardest hit. She had defended him in his dreamy days and encouraged his ambitions. She had watched the seeds she planted in him burst into an unheard-of flowering. Her passion for knowledge and novelty had become in him an unremitting search for truth, saluted by great men. How she must have basked in the praise and admiration he constantly provoked! There seemed to be nothing to prevent him going higher and higher, conquering one territory after another. And now this! All of it wasted on a quixotic, self-destructive impulse! She made efforts to understand and to hide her disappointment and disapproval, but she was never reconciled.

Whatever support he may have hoped for or expected from friends and relatives was not forthcoming. As is the manner of friends, they resented not having been taken into his confidence. No doubt they felt betrayed that this frank and cheerful companion could have chatted and joked with them and yet kept so great a project, the best of himself perhaps, hidden from them. It was bad enough that he was going, throwing away God's gifts, but could he not at least have consulted them first? Most of us have found to our cost that our friends think they know better than we do what is good for us. Schweitzer was no exception, and it was a very shrewd instinct indeed that told him to leave his great plan gestating, nine years and nine months, before he revealed it, fully formed, to his startled friends.

He was dismayed to find that the theological friends were the least understanding of all. He quoted the precedent of St. Paul, and the three silent years he had spent before declaring his conversion. But they seemed

186

not to be able to see things as simply as Schweitzer himself. St. Paul had not had to throw away such gifts, such achievements.

Widor told Schweitzer he was "like a general who wanted to go into the firing line with a rifle."[1] A lady, of whom Schweitzer says only that she was "filled with the modern spirit," demonstrated that he could do more for the Africans by lecturing than by action. She told him that "that saying from Goethe's Faust 'In the beginning was the deed' was now out of date—today propaganda was the mother of happenings."[2] The modern spirit has evidently altered very little in the last ninety-odd years.

And Elly Knapp, the enterprising young lady who with Hélène startled respectable citizens by running a home for unmarried mothers, was surprised, looking back, that they all had been so little aware of Schweitzer's qualities. "We students," she wrote, "were unmercifully critical of one another."[3]

So this was a traumatic time for Schweitzer. The simple confidence that friends who knew the Gospels must understand what he was doing was constantly shaken. He was reluctant to expose his feelings and speak of "the act of obedience which Jesus' command of love may under special circumstances call for,"[4] and when in desperation he did so, he found himself accused of conceit. Or if in defiance of his habitual reserve he allowed people "to have a glimpse of the thoughts which had given birth to my resolution,"[5] they did not believe him. They were convinced that something else lay behind it: disheartenment about his career or an unhappy love affair. So for the most part he did not trouble to explain. Werner Picht remembered his saying, "My friends have no more patience with my paradoxes. It's time for me to go."[6] "He said, 'J'irai!' (I'm going!), and that was that."

Many people can still be found who will explain with a shrewd and knowing air some theory that they have either read or invented for themselves about Schweitzer's decision to go to Africa. I have met clergymen who believe that he went to atone for the dreadful things he had done to Jesus in his books. Others, of course, bring his mother into it somewhere, believing that Freud has the answer to all things. It may encourage such people to know that they are in the good company of Schweitzer's own friends, who could not possibly believe it was as simple as he said it was.

In a way he had himself to blame, having kept his thoughts hidden so long. But he certainly found himself confirmed in the wisdom of his silence. "How much I suffered through so many people assuming a right to tear open all the doors and shutters of my inner self! . . . I felt as a real kindness the action of persons who made no attempt to dig their fists into my heart, but regarded me as a precocious young man, not quite right in the head, and treated me correspondingly with affectionate mockery."[7] Schweitzer had always known, and now had engraved on his heart, that simple truth, so rarely observed, that the greatest kindness we can do to anyone is to let him be himself.

In Schweitzer's case, his long self-searchings meant that he knew himself pretty well—far better than his well-wishers did. His own estimate of himself is worth quoting: "I held the venture to be justified, because I had considered it for a long time and from every point of view, and credited myself with the possession of health, sound nerves, energy, practical common-sense, toughness, prudence, very few wants, and everything else that might be found necessary by anyone wandering along the path of the idea. I believed myself, further, to wear the protective armour of a temperament quite capable of enduring an eventual failure of my plan."[8] We have seen his doubts and hesitations revealed in the letters to Hélène, but this is not the estimate of a neurotic seeking escape from some childhood trauma or theological guilt.

To his congregation he would say what he could not say to his friends. On November 19 he preached a sermon. He took as his text the story of the disciples on the dark lake, beating against the wind to the far shore, who saw Jesus coming across the water toward them in the night and thought he was a ghost; when Peter, always requiring practical proofs, said, "Lord if it is you, bid me come to you on the water"; and Jesus said "Come"; and Peter stepped out of the boat, but then grew frightened and began to sink, and Jesus stretched out his hand and saved him.

For Schweitzer this was not a miracle but a parable that had been transformed into a miracle in retrospect, and the parable spoke directly to him. To an age battered by winds of doubt Jesus appeared like a phantom, and nobody knew whether he was real. There was only one way to find out—to go toward him and see. If one became frightened and seemed to be sinking, then his hand would be there to protect and save.

This sermon, like others, could appear unremarkable enough (apart from Schweitzer's usual sturdy style) if we did not know what was going on in his life at the time. But this was no pious exhortation from a book of published orations—it was like his father's sermons, a sharing of his own struggles. Listen then to Schweitzer, beleaguered by his friends, misunderstood, and attacked on all sides, stating his case.

> It is hardly an uplifting task to be a pastor in these days of doubt and indifference. One wishes to give the people of our time some spiritual encouragement, to bring them the message of Jesus, and that is not possible. The age wants its doubts dissolved without trouble or effort. But if the proclamation of the gospel were simply the dissolution of doubts and

the defence of a doctrine, the preacher's would be the most taxing and thankless of tasks; that would be as though one were trying to enrich people's lives by straightening out their sums on a piece of paper. Fortunately it is not that at all—it is much, much finer. It is saying to people: "Do not stay where you are, but move ahead, move towards Jesus!" . . . Do not ask yourself whether the road is firm or practicable, fit for the man who follows his inclinations, but look only to see that it is really the road that leads straight to Jesus. Peter is able to walk towards him, the moment he dismisses all human considerations. . . .

How is Jesus alive for us? Do not attempt to prove his presence by formulations, even if they are sanctified by the ages. Of late I have very nearly lost my temper when some pious soul has come to me saying that no one can believe in the living presence of Jesus if they do not believe in his physical resurrection and the eternal existence of his glorified body. Jesus lives for everyone whom he directs, in matters great and small, as if he were here among us. He tells them "Do this or that." And they answer, quite simply, "Yes!" and go about their job, humble and busy. . . . The fact that the Lord still, in our days, gives his orders, proves to me—and for me it is the only proof—that he is neither a ghost nor dead, but that he lives.

If you will let me explain in my way this living presence, I will say to you: "The eternal body of Jesus is simply his words; for it was about them that he said 'Heaven and earth shall pass away, but my words shall not pass away!' "[9]

To the music critic Gustav von Lüpke he wrote more simply, but the message was the same.

I hope you will give me the pleasure of showing a deeper insight than most people . . . and that you will find the course I am taking as natural and right as I do myself. For me the whole essence of religion is at stake. For me religion means to be human, plainly human in the sense in which Jesus was. In the colonies things are pretty hopeless and comfortless. We—the Christian nations—send out there the mere dregs of our people; we think only of what we can get out of the natives . . . in short what is happening there is a mockery of humanity and Christianity. If this wrong is in some measure to be atoned for, we must send out there men who will do good in the name of Jesus, not simply proselytising missionaries, but men who will help the distressed as they must be helped if the Sermon on the Mount and the words of Jesus are valid and right.

Now we sit here and study theology, and then compete for the best ecclesiastical posts, write thick learned books in order to become professors of theology . . . and what is going on out there where the honour and the name of Jesus are at stake, does not concern us at all. And I am supposed to devote my life to making ever fresh critical discoveries, that I might become famous as a theologian and go on training pastors who will also sit at home, and will not have the right to send them out to this vital work.

I cannot do so. For years I have turned these matters over in my mind, this way and that. At last it became clear to me that this isn't my life. I want to be a simple human being, doing something small in the spirit of Jesus. . . . . "What you have done to the least of these my brethren you have done to me." Just as the wind is driven to spend its force in the big empty spaces so must the men who know the laws of the spirit go where men are most needed.[10]

The sermon echoes the letters. There is no conflict between the private and the public man, and there can be no mistaking why Schweitzer went to Africa, nor what kind of Christian he was—at least at that time, and probably for the rest of his life. He himself used the word *heretic*, by which he meant someone who is not particularly interested in the formulations of a quarrelsome group of anti-Semitic elders of the church, as they struggled sixteen hundred years earlier to define the indefinable and to make some sense of the confusion left by the evangelists who themselves were trying make sense of a Messiah who had promised to return but failed to do so; elders who, to give their deliberations an unchallengeable stamp of approval, had claimed that they were informed by the Holy Spirit, and that on this basis they were entitled to expel from the knowledge of God anyone who dared to question their formulae. If this was heresy, Schweitzer was happy to be a heretic.

Writing in his autobiography twenty-five years later about his decision to abandon a good career and go to Africa, he acknowledged that he had been lucky in his time. In those days "anyone who gave up remunerative work could still hope to get through life somehow or other, while anyone who thought of doing the same in the difficult economic conditions of today would run the risk of coming to grief not only materially but spiritually as well. I am compelled therefore, not only by what I have observed, but by experience also, to admit that worthy and capable persons have had to renounce a course of independent action which would have been of great value to the world, because circumstances rendered such a course impossible."[11]

The claim to be a hero, which others often make for Schweitzer, was one he never made for himself: indeed, he specifically renounced it. "There are no heroes of action," he wrote, "only heroes of renunciation and suffering. Of such there are plenty. But few of them are known, and even these not to the crowd, but to the few."[12] In his letters to Hermann Hagedorn, too, he steadily reiterated that there was nothing exceptional or unique about him.

When, later on, others came to him for advice about their wish to make the same sort of break that he had made, he would discourage any who seemed to be suffering from restlessness or frustration in their own jobs. "Only a person who can find a value in every sort of activity, and can devote himself to each one with full consciousness of duty, has the inward right to undertake some out-of-the-ordinary activity instead of that which falls naturally to his lot."[13] Extremely practical and clear-sighted. But despite this plenty of people have accused Schweitzer of the very thing he warned against, running away from something that he could not face to lose himself in the anonymity of the jungle. It is difficult to see what he could have been running away from. As he points out himself, "I had received, as a young man, such recognition as others usually get only after a whole life of toil and struggle."[14]

No, there is no doubt that for years he had been loved, admired, successful, and happy. He was simply running true to form, to that obstinate necessity of his being that since his childhood days had linked action inevitably with experience and thought. He felt—he considered—he acted. In the Gospels he had found the guidance he needed, not in a set of rules to obey but in a man to follow. He was complete—his course was set. In a sense everything that happened afterward, exciting though it was, although it brought him worldwide fame and esteem, was now programed. He had set the countdown in motion. It was only a matter of awaiting the liftoff and the actual adventure.

The situation was quite irregular as far as the university was concerned. Professors in one subject could not enroll as students in another. And, unfortunately, only duly enrolled students were allowed to take examinations at the end of courses. Schweitzer seemed to have no alternative but to resign as a professor, but this he was not inclined to do. He enjoyed both teaching and preaching far too much to give up either until he was compelled to. Apart from all else there was a financial problem. He had sent in his resignation as principal, and when this took effect in the following spring, he would lose both his official residence and his comfortable salary.

The university, once over its astonishment, proved admirably cooperative and flexible. The professors agreed to let him attend lectures free, not as a student but as a colleague, so his resignation was not required. And he was to be allowed to sit for the examinations on the strength of certificates from the professors stating that he had attended.

So he gave in his name to the dean of the medical faculty (whose first reaction was to hand him over to the psychiatric department), and one day of thick fog toward the end of October he set out for his first lecture on anatomy.

Although it was difficult to begin again at thirty, learning a totally new subject, he rejoiced in the practicality of it. He had had enough of words. He had always loved natural science but had largely deserted it for subjects where speculation and argument were interminable and proof was impossible. Now he was dealing with solid facts, capable of demonstration and conclusion, and it was a great relief.

The closeness with Hélène was not diminished. In the outer world they met occasionally, and she listened to and gave her judgment on his sermons; but at the deeper level she was always with him:

> Yesterday my birthday was celebrated at the Seminary in the evening because earlier it would have distracted me too much from my lecture. The students said, "Stosst an, Frauenlieb lebe . . . " [lift your glasses to the love of women] and everybody probably thought about one girl, or several whom he courts. Their eyes were happy. Mine too, but in a different way . . . because I know the true meaning of a "woman's love." . . . what struggles, what strength, what renunciation, what richness . . . and one shakes and trembles when one accepts another's existence so totally, the other's thoughts, the other's fate, and at last one no longer resists accepting the responsibility . . . because one feels that here is something stronger than anything else in this world.[15]

When the time came to leave the principal's quarters, his friend Frederick Curtius came to the rescue. Curtius's official residence as president of the Lutheran Church of Alsace was inside the same big building that housed the principal's rooms, and he offered Schweitzer four small attics in his residence, one of them equipped as a kitchen. Schweitzer wrote wonderingly to Hélène: "This is the last letter I will write you from the Seminary. . . . What has become of the person who had planned to end his days here, dreaming under the tree? This artist-monk . . . Dead and buried! I feel as if I had never known him, so far removed is he now. I feel and now understand what it means: 'If someone is in Christ, he has become a new creature.' . . . How our values do change!"[16]

So, "on the rainy Shrove Tuesday of 1906 the students carried my belongings out through one door of the house on the St. Thomas' Embankment and in through another."[17]

Here Schweitzer installed himself and his books, now augmented by fat medical tomes. *The Quest of the Historical Jesus* and the long essay on organ building had been finished in the winter, before he moved. Now, for the moment, there was no literary work going on—only his pastoral work, his theological lectures, his organ playing, and his medical studies. The German edition of the Bach book had been commissioned, but he was—understandably—finding it difficult to settle to it.

In April he took a holiday in Italy, accompanied by Tata (Adèle Herrenschmidt). Hélène had toured there in 1898 and had told him what to look out for, but Schweitzer was not impressed with Italy.

My general impressions? I had not been wrong: Italy is not for me! I felt like a stranger from beginning to end! I was homesick for the North, for the sparse spring in our land. . . . I had not realized that I am such a barbarian. I truly suffered.

On the other hand, your friend is too demanding! He cannot enjoy anything surrounded by all those curious people who walk around with their Baedekers; those people to whom the essence of this country has been sold. Fiesole seemed like a beauty with make up, to whom one pays homage. . . .

I could have cried. Impossible to dream in the countryside, to love it. Everything was noisy, presented to be admired. No concentration!

Oh, San Marco! This peace! But to be there by myself, to dream, to weep, to hope . . . and not always those curious people, with their books in hand, who come for five minutes and behave as if they were at home, and who spoil the silence with their endless cackling. Why is all this sold to foreign visitors? I am so selfish, so selfish for the countryside and the art! I could commit murder to get rid of them, they don't leave me alone when I need it.

How I did laugh when I saw the Duomo of Milan! It is a masterpiece fresh from the confectioner. . . .

Only Michelangelo . . . You must tell me about Michelangelo, lady friend.

A monk played the sophisticated guide, to entertain my friend. He was blessed with heavenly bliss, a fat paunch, and he smelled from his feet to his mouth! And he was stupid too. Another one who will keep me from entering paradise. Would you be kind enough to share hell with me?[18]

Entertaining enough, but it does seem part of Schweitzer's grand self-centeredness that he never noticed that he, too, was one of those same tourists, or wondered what might give him the right to have San Marco all to himself.

He was increasingly in demand for his organ playing. There were the Bach Society's concerts in Paris, which he could not afford to turn down, for he needed the fees to help out his diminished income. And he had caught the eye of Luis Millet, conductor of the Orfeo Catala of Barcelona, who invited him to play in the Bach concerts there.

One of these concerts was to be held before the king and queen of Spain, and Schweitzer felt that the occasion demanded something better than the clothes he normally wore. Many, many years later he told the story of the frock coat to Frederick Franck, a dentist working in his hospital in central Africa.

I had my frock coat when I had to play the organ for the King of Spain in Barcelona. It was in 1905, yes, 1905. Or was it 1906? No, no, it was 1905. I remember it very well, for I said to my friend the tailor in Günsbach, "You have to make me a frock coat for I have to play for the King of Spain." He got very embarrassed. "You mean to say, Albert, I have to make the frock coat you are going to play in for a king?" With a worried expression on his face he then said "All I can do is my best." It really became a beautiful frock coat, very strongly built, and I have always worn it on all great occasions. Of course I haven't got it here, so I can't show it to you, for in Africa it's no use. I keep it in Günsbach. But I wore it when I performed the marriage of Theodor Heuss, the present President of Western Germany, in the church of St. Nicholas in Strasbourg in 1907, when I was minister there. Of course I wore it, too, when I gave the lectures in Edinburgh, when I got the Goethe Prize, when I received the Nobel Prize, and when the Queen of England decorated me. And the last time Theodor Heuss saw it he said, "My, my, Albert, don't you look elegant. You must have a very good tailor in Günsbach."[19]

After the concert the king asked Schweitzer, "Is it difficult to play the organ?" "Almost as difficult as to rule Spain," replied Schweitzer. "Then," said the king, "you must be a brave man."[20]

That summer, at Bayreuth, his literary inactivity came to an end when, inspired by *Tristan*, he began the German edition of the Bach book. He was busy also with thoughts about St. Paul. If eschatology provided such dramatic clues to the puzzles in the Gospels, might it not be fruitfully applied also to the parts of Paul's Epistles that still baffled scholars?

While preparing a series of lectures on the subject, he became convinced that he was onto something. It was generally thought at that time that the difference between Paul's notions and those of other early Christians was owing to the fact that he had been brought up in Asia Minor, where the Greek Mystery religions were dominant; and that this accounted for his opposition to the Jewish law and his mystical image of dying and being reborn "in Christ." The Greek Mysteries centered around a God who died and was reborn. Mithraism, too, had a similar central myth. What more natural than that Paul should introduce these ideas into the Christ story?

Schweitzer, however, claimed that these religions did not reach a state that would make sense of this theory until a hundred years after Paul. So either the Epistles of Paul were written much later and foisted onto Paul to give them authority, or there must be another explanation of Paul's novel ideas. Working on this, Schweitzer was once again seized by the old need to begin his research with a survey of all that had hitherto been

written on the subject. So he started collecting material for a brief historical introduction to his own discoveries; but like the Bach book, the thing
stretched and grew under his hand, and he realized that he was going to
have to write a whole separate book, leading up to the book he really
wanted to write.

And so the overcrowded months passed in what he described as "a
continuous struggle with fatigue."[21] Günsbach provided a relaxation, and
when really overtired, he recharged his energies by getting out into the
country and drawing strength from nature. Sometimes his goddaughter,
Suzanne, would climb with him up the hill behind the village and sit
happily while he made notes in his notebook or, if the notebook ran out,
on his cuffs.

She remembered how even then, long before his philosophy of Reverence for Life was formulated, he would take the greatest care of every
living creature and teach her to do the same. Above all, he would teach
her to be grateful. Nobody could know, he would say, where we came
from or where we are going. The only sure thing was existence, and the
only way to affirm life was to take responsibility for our existence. Thankfulness strengthened the good in the world. For him it was a matter of
the greatest thankfulness that he could call this beautiful valley home.

His young cousin, Jean-Paul Sartre, who had been born in Paris a year
or so earlier, was to pick up the theme that all we could be sure of was
existence itself, never its purpose. But for Sartre this meant futility and
distress, not thankfulness. The word "Existentialist" could be applied to
both; but it was Sartre's version, not Schweitzer's, that gained currency
in the philosophical world. And Schweitzer, the champion of existence,
never laid claim to the title of Existentialist; indeed, he rejected it outright, for the associations it came to have were entirely alien to him.

When he was late for lunch at the manse, it was often Suzanne who
was sent to fetch him. She knocked first, and if there was no reply put
her head around the door—cautiously, because as often as not it would
be greeted by a flying book. Schweitzer was still unpunctual and disin-
clined for domestic chores. It was his job to draw the wine for the meal
from the cask in the cellar; one day he dropped the jug on the stairs, and
his father said, "That's the last time the *sacré imbécile* draws my wine!"
The job thereafter was Suzanne's, and she had the impression that godfather Albert had achieved what he intended.

Hélène, too, was by now a welcome visitor at the vicarage. Pretending
that that was all she was, he wrote:

Dear Miss Bresslau: Your cake arrived in excellent condition. My mother
admired how perfectly I delivered it here. Everybody thought that it was

charming of you and Mrs. Schweitzer proved to be the genuine mother of her son when she began immediately to eat the orange slices! That is called Atavism. My father was a little disappointed: he had hoped that it would be a yeast cake that you can dunk in your coffee. I promised him that at your next visit, Saturday night, you would bake such a cake. He cannot believe that you actually made yourself what I brought with me.[22]

And a month or two later: "When we took a walk, my father said: 'If the day should come on which you tell me, "Hélène Bresslau will be my wife," this would be one of the most wonderful days for me!' . . . My father is already looking forward to having somebody to whom he can pay court. You also have to bake something for him while you are here."[23]

That year, 1907, Widor, too, came to stay at Günsbach en route for Germany, and Schweitzer met him off the express at Colmar. Widor had been traveling first class, as befitted his age and distinction. But for the last eight miles up the valley on the local train he traveled fourth class with Schweitzer.

Widor was quite a surprise to the family at the manse. They had met a variety of people, but never had they entertained anyone who kissed his hostess' hand at breakfast every day, and they were astonished at the courtly way he would reply to a hospitable offer, "I am quite overwhelmed, madame." It gives us some idea of the force of Schweitzer's character that he could prevail on such an elegant old gentleman to travel fourth class among the peasants.

That force could still erupt in anger. Suzanne's younger brother, Albert, remembered a day when Schweitzer was helping him with his Latin translation. He made no mistakes at all, and Schweitzer sent Albert to his grandfather to tell him how well he had done. When Albert returned, Widor was with Schweitzer, and Schweitzer made him do it again for Widor. This time he made a mistake, and Schweitzer slapped him so hard it made his nose bleed. Thereafter, Schweitzer swore he would never help him again. Not till years later did he apologize and asked if Albert had minded very much.

Schweitzer's energy was volcanic. As when a child he had struck his sister over a game and then determined to give up games, so still he had to fight to fetter and guide that impatient energy. The wisdom that we find in his books is not the wisdom of a man to whom it was easy to be right, but that of a man who knew that if wisdom failed, the abyss was waiting.

In September, as he was nearing the end of the massive German Bach book, exhaustion finally caught up with him. His beloved Adèle Herrenschmidt took him to Pontresina, in Switzerland, for a rest. From here he wrote to Hélène:

I can think very clearly, but I am exhausted and have spells of nausea. This afternoon I was very pale, but now I can breathe normally again. . . . The hotel is awfully elegant; I don't fit here with my worn suits. If it were not for Tata, I would not stay here. . . . . Good bye, I want to take a little walk to get my blood going, to look for a piece of bark to carve a little boat! Yes, a real boy.[24]

And two days later:

Tomorrow I will begin to work on a very special piece of bark, for whom? You must guess. My hand hurts from so much writing.

. . . Yesterday we were invited for brunch by friends of hers at the Grand Hotel at St. Moritz. Luxurious hotel, elegant dresses, music, champagne, beautiful ladies: in short, in my shabby gray suit I felt like a flea under the shirt of a beautiful woman. I tried to make conversation with a pleasant young girl, and at the same time tried to keep my thoughts with the plans for my chapter. Suddenly Tata, who had read the music program, called laughing from the other table: "Albert, they play the waltz of the beautiful Hélène by Offenbach." General amazement. I blush. Lottie bursts with laughter. Tata is very amused and they ask: "Who is the beautiful Hélène?" At that moment Tata, who had just gotten her champagne, lifts her glass: "I ask all of you to drink to the beautiful Hélène," and the glasses clinked with a beautiful ring. Where were your ears yesterday at 1.25?[25]

The hand worried Hélène more than the exhaustion. Rest can cure exhaustion, but his hand must be looked after. She wrote him a little lecture about it, and she was right: writer's cramp troubled him all his life. And when he returned, she seems to have nursed him through the end of the Bach book: "You were so self-sacrificing and kind to the exhausted man, you helped him, encouraged him, and the shared work on Bach has brought us even closer. I relive every moment of our vacation again."[26] Her care for him was much appreciated by his parents, and when at the end of the month he had finished the Bach book: "We drank to Bach and to my recuperation; then my father lifted his glass and asked us to drink to the health of 'intelligent women in general, and to that of Miss Bresslau in particular.' What do you say to that?"[27]

On the thirtieth Schweitzer wrote to Gustave Bret, conductor of the Paris Bach Society: "I take the first morning of the first week of liberty— the ms of the Bach book was finished on Wednesday 25th September 1907 at 6.45 P.M.—to study the question of cuts." The cuts refer to a projected performance of the *St. John Passion,* and Schweitzer lists a number of points: "The general principle is to keep the action intact, and as many chorales as possible." . . . "Fifty years of Purgatory if you suppress the first Kreuzige." Of the *Air avec Choeur* he comments: "To tell the truth nobody knows how it should be sung. One is only aware of the contest between the bass and the orchestra." He suggests replacing the *oboe di caccia* by the *cor anglais*—"identical instruments"—but, "on the other hand we have a marvellous *oboe d'amore* if you want one." And he proposes adding a piccolo, to bring out the flute parts. "Above all, use plenty of oboes, and put them right in the forefront, *in front of the violins.* The effect is superb!"[28]

From this letter, and from an article that Schweitzer wrote for the Berlin magazine *Die Musik* about the difficulty of organizing a choir in Paris, we get an idea of the considerable part he was playing in the running of the Paris Bach Society. This article has so much in it of social besides musical interest that it demands some attention. It gives us some idea of the meticulous thoroughness with which he approached every one of his enterprises.

> When my friend and I a few years ago started to organise a Bach Society in Paris to produce the Passions and cantatas, people everywhere expressed the opinion that sooner or later our enterprise would certainly go on the rocks, since it was impossible to keep a good choir together very long in Paris. When we said that what succeeded elsewhere should certainly be possible there as well, we received only sympathetic shrugs of the shoulders.
>
> The fact is that none of the choirs composed of society volunteers has enjoyed a very long existence in Paris. Usually they died with their founders, if not before. For the most part they were not purely Parisian organisations, but were undertaken by the Alsatian community resident in the capital city. This is the reason that Paris had the best mixed choirs in the middle of the eighties, when the Alsatian community and its adherents from the departments of the east, by virtue of the exodus from Germany after the year 1870, had achieved the greatest importance and had taken a leading place in politics and intellectual culture.

He goes on to complain of the high cost of running a choir with professional singers; the result being too few rehearsals, and "under these circumstances a profound analysis of the works is impossible."

> The discipline is not very rigorous. It has always impressed me how little the conductor is heeded even in the choirs of the Conservatory concerts. More than three-quarters of the singers watch their notes from beginning to end for lack of discipline and skill. The director must make all possible concessions to them. The rehearsals are usually conducted with the singers seated. Men and women often keep their hats on. Intermittent pauses are numerous. And under no circumstances may the time agreed on be lengthened.[29]

The lack of enthusiasm and morale Schweitzer attributes to a complex of social causes. The inadequacy of the tram service was a contributory factor, making it necessary for a woman going out at night always to take a carriage unless she lived close to a main street. But the main difficulty lay in the Parisian attitude to family life. The fact that young unmarried women were never allowed out unchaperoned made for a permanent shortage of sopranos. And the Parisians' devotion to their families to the exclusion of any larger social unit meant that the conductor of a choir was forever fighting the prior claims of family visiting days. Once at rehearsal, French individualism came into conflict with choir discipline. The French singer "does not become a member of the choir, a stop that the director pulls, but remains Mr. So-and-So or Mrs. So-and-So, who wants to be recognised as such. The modern Frenchman has an instinctive anxiety about anything that is called discipline; he sees in it nothing but a submission that is unworthy of a free being."[30]

Schweitzer contrasts this approach with the musical tradition in Germany and Switzerland, which had originated with the choirs and orchestras maintained by the small separate states and their courts in the eighteenth century. In France the monarchy had sucked the life out of the provincial cities.

> Most of all, however, the general musical education suffers from the lack of choirs. Only by rehearsing together and singing together can we arouse an interest in polyphony. Anyone who has never experienced a work of art which he has helped to create, in the midst of which he stands as it passes by, which he hears from within out, never emerges from the position of mere musical feeling to that of genuine artistic perception. The educational value of choral singing, which we may assume as a matter of course in the German people—at least for much the greater part of them— is lacking in the French. The feelings of the French are probably just as elemental and vital as those of the Germans, but the power of judgement that can be gained only through artistic activity is wanting.[31]

As to Schweitzer's musical contribution, a rare glimpse is given us by a Dr. A. T. Davison, who sang in the choir at that time, when he was studying the organ with Widor, and who went on to become a professor of music at Harvard University. In an article in the *Albert Schweitzer Jubilee Book of 1945,* he describes how Schweitzer's playing stood out against what he calls "the mechanical and heartless perfection of the choir and the orchestra." Bret's conducting he thought "more competent than inspired," and the somewhat underrehearsed choir lacked fire. "Schweitzer's contribution," he felt, was "easily the most distinguished of all."

I was struck first of all by Schweitzer's indifference to any "effective-ness" in registration or manner of playing, the entire process being concentrated in the presentation of the music in its proper setting without the slightest effort to make it "telling" of itself. And it must be remembered that the question was not of the great organ compositions; it was solely of the organ background to, let us say, one of the cantatas. My early studies had centred about the instrument as a vehicle of display, and from Widor I was discovering that the organ and the organist were the servants; the music—specially that of Bach—the master. The unpretentious accompani-mental parts must always be a pretty routine affair to the organist who loves his playing better than the music he plays. Schweitzer however, never once obtruding himself, lavished upon them all the scrupulous attention they deserve but all too seldom receive. I realise now that my feeling about his skilful and appropriate support was primarily a technical one, albeit an as yet undiscovered clue to the impulse that converted these stylistic mar-vels into an almost biographical record of Bach himself.[32] [Widor himself had described Schweitzer as "One of the most skilful and experienced players that any conductor could desire to have at the organ during the performance of a Bach cantata or Passion."][33]

As far as I can remember [Davison continues] Schweitzer, in spite of his authoritative knowledge, was never consulted—publicly, at least—regard-ing any of the questions involved in the performance of Bach's music. In fact the only occasion upon which I remember his forsaking the near-ano-nymity of the organ bench was at a rehearsal when the conductor, wishing to judge an effect from the rear of the hall, put his baton in Schweitzer's hand and asked him to direct the choir and orchestra. At that time, at least, Albert Schweitzer was in no sense a conductor, and it is significant that he made no pretense of being one. Turning his back squarely upon both or-chestra and choir, one hand thrust in his trousers pocket, his head back, staring up into the dark of the Salle Gaveau, his arm moving in awkward sweeps and unorthodox directions, it was quite obvious that if he gave himself a thought—which I doubt—it was only to consider himself the agent who should bring the music to life. Beyond that he had no respon-sibility. It was for the conductor to judge whether the balance of tone or the seating of the participants was satisfactory. Above all, there was complete detachment; entire absorption in the sound of the music. To this day I can remember the intense admiration I felt for Schweitzer's indifference to externals. How I swelled with indignation at the pitying smirks of the orchestral players as they condescendingly shrugged their shoulders and ostentatiously disregarded the vague gestures of the conductor pro tem. It was then, I feel sure, that I first sensed the stature of the man.[34]

Schweitzer was not yet a solo concert organist. It was circumstance, the need to collect money, that resulted in that development. At present he was still only—and happily—an accompanist, a member of the ensemble.

In March 1908 there was cause for concern about Hélène. She wrote: "I don't want to talk about myself, that's so boring. And now I have had so much light shone through me that there is nothing secret left. . . . I couldn't go to the Cahns' this afternoon, because I needed to have a third X-ray; the first two showed that there is something there, but not in enough detail; in any case it is nothing serious, perhaps a harmless bone splinter. So there is not the slightest cause for alarm; I will go to my professor on Wednesday and on Friday I will tell you what he said."[35]

Evidently it was not regarded as serious, for nothing more was heard about it for the moment; but throughout the following years she was afflicted by spells of unexplained exhaustion besides more dramatic complaints.

With a short while to go before the first medical examination, it became clear that Schweitzer had indulged once too often in his passion for trying to learn everything about a subject, rather than confining himself to the issues in hand. He enjoyed working on the physical sciences so much that he tried to cover the whole field and neglected the syllabus. He was not helped by the fact that he could not, at thirty, rely on a memory as perfect as he had enjoyed when he was twenty. In the last few weeks his young fellow students finally persuaded him to join a cramming club, which studied previous examination papers and the sort of answers required.

When, four weeks before the examination, he officiated at the wedding of his friend Elly Knapp with Theodor Heuss, a delayed birth at the gynecological unit barely gave him time to exchange his white gown for his frock coat, and some of the guests were surprised to note that the handsome young pastor smelled so strongly of iodoform.

The examination began on May 13, 1908. The subjects were anatomy, physiology, and the natural sciences. When he entered, his fatigue was greater than at any other time of his life; so at any rate he wrote in 1931— when of course he did not know what was to come. But he passed, and passed well, better than he had ever expected. Now, the worst over, the back of the new subject broken at last, he could drive on with fresh confidence to clinical study and his finals.

12

The Departure

1908–1913

SO THE ODD STUDENT toiled on, ten years older than the rest of the class, a professor one minute, a pupil the next, and the next again an organist of rising international reputation. His greatest difficulty was staying awake hour after hour at medical lectures.

Traveling to Paris or to Barcelona on the train, he dug deep into the resources of his extraordinary stamina, all the time strengthening it still further, making of himself what he wanted to be, the man without needs who was always at the disposal of the needs of others. He did not always, however, travel fourth class, or even third. On the way to Paris one day, he reported: "All alone in my compartment. And next to me is a nice first-class compartment, completely empty; I will get into it in Avricourt, since it will fill up after Nancy."[1] Food he did like—that was an essential fuel—but he was able to go for long periods even without food when occasion demanded.

When he did take a holiday, the routine was still the same: first, to travel to Switzerland and there to join Adèle Herrenschmidt, now a woman of fifty-three and head of a finishing school at Neuilly, and her niece, Marcelle. Once among the Alps at Oey they took a horse-drawn carriage up the small side valley for two hours or more till the mountains were all around them and they reached the lonely Kurhaus Grimmialp where year after year they had the same table and year after year Schweitzer would say: *"Hier ist wo die Welt zu ist"* (This is where we leave the world outside.)[2]

English has no equivalent for the word *Kurhaus*, which is somewhere between a sanatorium and a hotel, a place where the air is good and treatment is available. The only treatment Schweitzer needed was the

202

remoteness and the quiet; the only person it seems that he trusted to share it, Adèle Herrenschmidt. They stayed ten days or so at Grimmialp, and even here he spent most of the day working. Then they drove back down the valley, back to trains and hustle and civilization; Schweitzer refreshed for his breakneck life by his perennial nurse and consoler, nature.

To have taken a holiday with the other guardian angel would, of course, have contravened the whole basis of the relationship. So while Schweitzer was at Grimmialp in August 1908, Hélène was lying on a beach far away—she loved the sea rather than the mountains—trying in her own way to recover her energy.

Hélène's recuperation was less successful than his. When she got back to Strasbourg, she wrote despairingly:

> You see, Bery—I don't know if you can understand this—I have such an unquenchable need for rest. . . . The fact that my beloved sea was too strong for me showed me how much I need to recover . . . all I want to do is lie on the sofa all day, I have not the smallest wish to see or do anything— quite the contrary, I shrink from it. I am going to Günsbach, to a house where people are as good and kind to me as if I belonged there—and where all their goodness and kindness cannot give me the feeling of belonging—quite the contrary, from time to time they make me conscious of the fact that I have no right to it. You may call it oversensitive, but that doesn't mean that I can prevent it happening again. . . . I am not ill, but I am at the same point, perhaps even a little further back than when I went to the seaside. This journey which was began with so much hope was a failed experiment which no one can do anything about because no one— least of all myself—knows what is the problem with my foolish nerves.[3]

He wrote back encouragingly:

> I have a kind of deep premonition that you are moving towards recovery. I understand all your considerations, absolutely. . . . Now I want to tell you what my mother thinks. She tells herself that you are the woman who means infinitely much in my life, something deep and holy, and then that you shared the work with her son when he could not have gone on without you! And that makes her proud, thankful that someone is dedicating herself in such a way to her son . . . . and proud to have this woman with her . . . I implore you: do not come for your sake or for my sake, but for my mother's sake . . . and partly for us, too. When will we have such holidays again? The happiness of your friend who is resting will heal you. . . .
>
> Tata says that the sea was certainly too strong, but that you won't begin to feel how much good it has done you for 10 days! She is determined to comfort me. . . . And then the "population shortage" in the country! Surely your strength will suffice for culling beans.[4]

A month later he wrote, "So there it is, the news. It is what I had expected, and now it is a question of possessing one's soul in patience and doing one's duty. But I am already relieved at the thought that you are doing something for yourself."[5] This appears to confirm their daughter's belief that Hélène had a slight attack of tuberculosis as a result of overwork, and it must have thrown a serious shadow over the hope of her being able to partner Schweitzer in Africa. Lightening the tone a little, he wrote again the next day: "My mother thinks that it would be wise for you to wear a very well-fitting corset for a time. I pass the advice on to you without insisting on it: in questions of the wardrobes of my lady friends, I only get involved if it is a matter of outer garments."[6]

His booklet on organ building had begun to show results. The eighteenth century Silbermann organ in St. Thomas needed attention, and Schweitzer managed to persuade the church council not to scrap it and replace it, as all the other churches were doing, but to restore and renovate it. The man they commissioned to supervise the restoration, on Schweitzer's recommendation, was none other than that virtuoso pianist Marie-Joseph Erb, whose dazzling fingerwork had stunned the young Albert in his schooldays at Mulhouse and driven him back, reinspired, to his sharps and flats.

Erb now lived in Strasbourg, and Schweitzer had got to know him a little. He was not only a pianist but also an organist and a composer, not only a virtuoso but also a mature musician. Schweitzer, Erb, and the organ builder, Härpfer, spent a great deal of time planning how best to replace the worn-out parts and to introduce new diapason pipes into the old organ without sacrificing any of its quality.

When it was done, Schweitzer was well satisfied. Thirteen years later, the same Archibald Davison who had admired Schweitzer's playing in Paris had the chance to hear him play the renovated St. Thomas organ, and for the first time was able to see and hear for himself the kind of organ for which Bach wrote. "There it was, very much as it was in Bach's day, devoid of all the labor-saving devices of the modern instrument, cumbersome, and, from the point of view of one who had been used to the mechanically effortless instruments of America, calculated to set up for the player almost every conceivable impediment to easy and comfortable manipulation."

When Schweitzer began to play, Davison noted that "The 'machinery' of the old organ was plainly audible" and that when the assistants had to pull out a number of stops in the middle of the G-Minor Fantasia and Fugue, it caused a "terrific clatter." But Schweitzer appeared not to be aware of the noise; and he himself barely noticed it "so overpowering was the effect of the music and its registration."[7]

This picture gives us a good idea of what Schweitzer did and did not think important about organ building. He would have been totally un-interested in the technical fussiness that goes into today's recordings, the obsession with exploiting electronic effects, and so forth. If the spirit was right, it obliterated other imperfections. If not, what possible profit could there be in polishing something that was hollow at heart?

Hélène had been recovering well. But now something happened that was to have a fateful and permanent consequence. One day of thaw, she went out to ski with Schweitzer's brother, Paul. She was, we know, a skillful and intrepid skier. Schweitzer, feeling the thaw, was worried that the snow might be treacherous and warned them not to go. They went, nevertheless, and Hélène fell badly. When Schweitzer saw her after the fall, he knew that the injury would affect her for the rest of her life. The damage was to her back. Accounts speak of a slipped disk and a broken spine. It can hardly have been as serious as this, however, for by March 1909 she was on her way to Russia, bad back and all.

She had always been a passionate traveler, and her romantic side might well have found Russia very appealing. In addition, it was a long way away, and she seems to have needed at this point to put a distance between herself and Schweitzer. But the distance did not put an end to the correspondence. Sitting on his favorite rock he wrote to her:

Hyelyena! [The Russian pronunciation of her name and the ease with which she got on there suggest that she spoke the language]
    It has just struck 8:30 from the Günsbach church. Sülti [his dog, Sultan] and I have settled down on the rock and are celebrating the first Thursday evening with you. You can imagine the picture. I told him what is going on, and he has a suitable expression on his face. It is lovely, very lovely weather. . . . Dog-roses are blossoming on the rock, and the scent of elder comes from the distance . . . there are caterpillars there too, but I pretended I didn't see them, because tonight is a feast day. Is it really true that you have arrived? I can't believe it, for since Tuesday evening I keep seeing you in the compartment . . . what are you doing? The waiting is so long! But I am not worried (although I know that your back is hurting you now). But now rest . . . The time will come when you must work . . . how the river roars!
    Now it is striking nine. By your time it is already later, and perhaps you have already lain down and are waiting for "10 o'clock." ["Ten o'clock" was a time that they had agreed they would be sure to think of each other every day and recurs in a number of their letters.]

Not long after the restoration of the St. Thomas organ, Schweitzer was invited to prepare an address on organ construction for the Third Con-gress of the International Music Society, which was to be held in Vienna from May 25 to 29, 1909. The organizer, Guido Adler, had decided that organ building was a question of sufficient importance to warrant the creation of a special study group in the congress and presumably expected some sort of recapitulation of Schweitzer's booklet. But having cause to suspect that support for his views was thin on the ground, Schweitzer, despite all his other preoccupations, decided first to conduct an opinion survey. He sent a questionnaire, financed by the society, to organists and organ builders all over Europe. The questions were grouped under twelve headings and covered everything from the desirability of different sorts of wind-chest to the prices of the organ installations. Paragraph 5, for example, runs: "5. What dimensions do you consider the best for manuals and pedals? Are you for little or big keys, for keyboards near one another or rather far apart? Do you prefer the straight or the curved pedals? How should the pedal lie under the console? What range of notes should it have?"[9]

Schweitzer wrote later:

> This effort revealed how little sympathy there was for raising the question of organ construction at all. Instead of answering to the point, many of those addressed came out with threats against those who would encroach upon the freedom of the organ builder, and, as one man wrote, "would like to make all organs on one last." Worst of all were the answers of many organ builders and many organ inspectors. There were organ builders who did not understand what it would mean to them to have minimum prices set which would permit them to do artistic work. They saw only that a movement was on foot that would make it impossible for them to drive their new rivals from the field by underbidding or by means of the newest inventions.[10]

These responses were counterbalanced, however, by a great many positive replies, which Schweitzer analyzed and incorporated into his lecture. When the congress began, the members of the organ-building study group immediately put their heads together and decided that this opportunity should not be missed, and ignoring the social side of the congress, they set about drawing up a list of regulations for the guidance of future organ builders. The Alsatian, Härpfer, who had rebuilt the St. Thomas organ, was there. And Schweitzer's own initiative is clear from the fact that he was cochairman of the group's sessions; the other chairman also coming from Strasbourg, Dr. Xavier Matthias of the Catholic theological faculty. Barely taking time to eat or sleep, the group completed the fifty pages of regulations in the four days of the congress, laying down a detailed set of standards that were subsequently accepted by the society and circulated to the same list who had originally received the questionnaire.

The results took time to emerge, but even within the next year or two it was evident that the tide was turning, that people were everywhere beginning to rethink their assumptions about organ building and to experiment with ways of using technology to maintain quality, not simply to cut down price or to devise complicated and unnecessary additions. By 1927 Schweitzer was able to write, "Today the fight is won";[11] not that the destruction of fine old organs had been halted (it still goes on even now), but when it happens now, it is generally through the ignorance of parish councils rather than the recommendation of the profession itself.

The letters to Russia continued. Unhappily some of them failed to reach Hélène because "Copying the filthy Russian letters makes me wild! Please send me 1 or 2 addressed envelopes in every letter."[12] To which she gently replied:

It is a little bit your fault, because you are not capable of copying the Russian properly—but the fact that you are not capable of doing what everyone else can do is a serious sign of the nervous condition in which my poor G. finds himself. And his friend is so far away and cannot even help him in correcting and mailing off the proofs—that is really sad. . . . You want to know how my back is doing. It has had a good rest—like all of me—and almost always remembers its duty to my G. to keep nice and straight, and what is more important, it is strong enough for it and capable of doing it. It only arouses a faint memory of former pains when I have been forced to keep it bent for a very long time, but since I am not doing much work there is seldom occasion for that.[13]

(This abbreviation, "my G," was a kind of nickname that they had become accustomed to using for each other. It stood for "My Great One," which is much more usual in French and less pretentious than it would be in English, but which did, in a half-serious, half-playful way, describe what each was to the other.)

Whatever difficulties there may have been with Hélène's parents, Schweitzer was evidently making a calculated effort to overcome them.

On Sunday evening I dined with the Bresslau parents . . . just the three of us! It was very nice. During the meal I told the story of the journey to Vienna; I said that I had accompanied you to the station: then your father bewailed the fact that you certainly had not had enough money, and asked me if I hadn't given you any. To this I replied . . . since I could not bring a "No" to my lips . . . that I gave you 15 crowns in Austrian currency, but you would pay it back to me on your return. It was also enjoyable to show the Bresslau parents that one is taking care of Mademoiselle Hélène and that it is even permitted to become involved in her financial affairs.

Later we went over to the sofa, and I began to pay discreet court to Mother Bresslau . . . just as one runs one's hands over the keys of the instrument . . . it produced a good tone.[14]

Hélène continued to send long and detailed accounts of Russia, of the weather that ruined the harvest, of a magnificent Christ painting, of her train journeys, of the people who entertained her, and generally she added an injunction to get to bed earlier.

By the end of August she was back and in Günsbach while Schweitzer was in Grimmialp, starting work on a new subject: now it was the turn of St. Paul for the Schweitzer treatment.

He was determined if possible to finish the work that had begun with *The Mystery of the Kingdom of God* and show through the book on St. Paul how the process that started with Jesus' expectation of the new order had shifted gradually but inevitably toward the Church's quite different interpretation.

By the end of September Hélène was again working at the hospital. Things settled back to normal. But now yet another distraction had entered Schweitzer's life. Schirmer's, the New York music publishers, had asked Widor to edit Bach's organ works with advice about the best way to play them. Widor agreed only on condition that Schweitzer collaborated with him, and Schirmer's accepted the stipulation. In fact, Schweitzer did all the donkey work: he prepared the first draft, which he then worked over with Widor. Anyone who has done work of this kind will know how much easier it is to amend and refine something that has already been put on paper than it is to arrange those first thoughts and find those first words. All this, of course, necessitated numerous extra visits to Paris although twice Widor came to Günsbach for a few days to get on with the work without disturbance.

Schirmer's commission was a recognition that Widor's style of playing Bach was the nearest possible to an authentic reproduction of Bach's own. And this edition still holds an honored place on organists' bookshelves.

Widor and Schweitzer had firm ideas about everything to do with the performance of Bach's organ music—proper phrasing, proper fingering, (bearing in mind that Bach crossed one finger over another rather than turning the thumb under), proper registration, which corresponded to what was possible on Bach's own organs, and moderation of volume so that the individual lines of melody remained clear and were never swamped by an indiscriminate fortissimo such as Bach could not have achieved even had he wished to. But these suggestions were never incorporated in the actual score. That was left as Bach left it, or as nearly so as could be discovered. The comments were separate, to be used or ignored as the player wished. Schweitzer had had enough of those editions that offer the player, even while he is playing, "the fingering, the phrasing, the fortes and pianos, the crescendos and decrescendos, and not infrequently even the pedantic analyses of some editor or other, even when I entirely disagree with them."[15]

The recommendations in this edition, incidentally, do not hark back to Bach's ways with total rigidity. After explaining what the limitations of Bach's days imposed on the composer himself, they go on to suggest "experiments to discover how far beyond that use could be made, without spoiling the style, of the variations in the volume of sound and its tone—colours which are desirable and possible on the modern organ."[16]

There were other distractions:

> Yesterday I was in Karlsruhe at the premiere of the new opera by Siegfried Wagner. I left after the afternoon sermon. Afterwards I dined with the family (Siegfried, Chamberlain and his wife, Thode) and Thomas. It is beautiful music, really admirable. But the text ruins everything! Ficker, who was also there, said: "Thode and Chamberlain ought to keep an eye on him in these matters,'" and I thought, "You are missing one thing, Siegfried! You don't have a Hélène, a cruel, severe, self-willed Hélène, as I do! (only displaying these characteristics in matters of authorship, of course!) . . . Then you could create magnificent operas."[17]

When their anniversary date came up in March 1910, neither was able to make the meeting for the occasion. But Schweitzer wrote:

> I dreamed, while my head, still weary from the warm sun, did its duty and produced its sermon. . . . We were both in the forest in spring. . . . I saw the yellow branch from which you broke off a blossoming twig on the second 22nd . . . the avenue down below, where the path leads to the wooden bridge. . . . Then it gradually became darker and colder. I went to church. And when I went back home, happy to have done my duty well . . . read and be amazed . . . I telephoned Mama B. and invited myself to the birthday dinner to replace her daughter. That is something new which was not always on the program for the 22nd. And I thought of how you always took care to get home on time. . . . Your parents did not know what thoughts I had as I sat with them at table. . . . And Mother Bresslau serves me a tart and says that it is her dear daughter's favorite tart, and I must do it justice.[18]

It was not long, though, before Hélène's health was again a cause for anxiety:

> Your little letter was so alarming. . . . It is just striking 10 o'clock. . . . This afternoon I met the entire Bresslau family. They told me about your letter,

and Bery sat in on the family council while your affairs were discussed, on the sofa next to your mother. How times have changed! Well: I am of the opinion that you should give notice immediately if your health is suffering—oh, why did I have to hear again about your back! But if it is exhaustion and depression, then you should take that into account and not reach a decision until after your vacation. If I know you, you will be depressed if you have wasted these eight months for nothing; the business with the external exam will not work out.

In your place, I would drop surgery, I would try to get into the Internal Division and to get leave soon; what comes next will follow in due course. But above all you must do what you think is right . . . your health is everything. . . .

If only I could speak with you for one single hour. Do you want me to have some business in organ matters down there and to visit my dear aunt in Frankfurt for a few hours if you cannot get leave? I could arrange it! And what are a few hours in the train compared to the homesickness and loneliness which you cast off after a peaceful hour with your Bery and how much hope and sunshine I would like to give you. Say the word and it will be done . . . in spite of the semester.

My dear, I am putting into these lines everything which I bear within me for you, pleas, admiration, pride, comfort. On this piece of paper it sounds so cold, but you know what it is in reality . . . everything that the word "my great one" contains. . . . I wish that it would come and carry you over the hesitations of these days and make you "buoyant" again. . . . But be sure that everything that you decide is right.[19]

Despite his buoyant confidence that his strength could support her, something of the strain he himself suffered at this time is shown by the number of letters to him that mention that he had been ill. Ernest Newman, who was busy translating the German edition of the Bach book into English, writes on November 5, 1910, thanking him for the French edition and the correction of a mistake in it; "I am grieved to hear of your ill health," he writes, "you work too hard, I am afraid." When one considers all the other activities, preaching, taking part in concerts, and writing books, that were going on while he was in the thick of his medical studies, one can only marvel that he did not collapse altogether. His extraordinary ability to relax totally and dream, allowing the subconscious mind to work in peace, his capacity for drawing refreshment from nature—these would seem to be the clues to what kept him going. And perhaps, too, his tender concern and sense of responsibility for Hélène may have had something to do with it—a far cry from the "no pity" of five years earlier.

Hélène's health improved: "Now I . . . may rejoice from the depths of my soul in the progress of your back. You can imagine what reading those lines meant to me! . . . Now this is the doctor talking: no, don't go to the opera! Be careful, let *weeks* go by before you put any strain on your back at all! (by sewing, dinner invitations, etc.). I implore you! Don't give up halfway. Do you understand my pleas? We will go to the theater when you are quite strong, when I don't have to worry at all about how you are sitting. When that day comes, these terrible, terrible memories of coming to visit you and seeing you in pain will be extinguished."[20]

Negotiations with the Paris Mission were proceeding gently, and on May 5, 1911, he was able to write to Hélène:

> The conference lasted from 4:30 to 6:30. In attendance: Boegner, Couve, Bianquis and I. It was simple and beautiful.
>
> So: (1) I am offering myself as an independent medical helper at the mission, which will provide me with accommodations. I will try to collect what I need every year. What I cannot raise will be provided by the mission.
>
> (2) On the problem of nationality: I will remain German. They understand that. As regards the right to practice as a doctor without a French licence, Monsieur Reinach (because of his wife) will smooth the way.
>
> (3) Inventories of supplies (for ladies too) will arrive one of these days (As main question, I threw the leather sofa into the conversation. It can't come.)
>
> (4) The mission would welcome it if I were to find a nurse, and would welcome it all the more if it could be arranged that a person with these skills was willing to bind herself to me in such a way as to bear my name. I said that at the moment I could only express myself theoretically on this point.
>
> (5) Departure is set for the 25th of June or the 25th of July? This will mean arriving at the best season and having two months to acclimatize oneself before the rainy season . . . which would be especially important for a woman, I am told.[21]

This is the first time in the correspondence that marriage is mentioned although the off-hand way it is introduced shows that he did not expect it to be a shock to her. Indeed, one would guess that by now it was well understood between them that it was a practical part of a practical partnership. It does appear that Hélène had long left out of her calculations any hopes of a more normal kind of romance. One thing, however, that this mention does make clear: since at this time the Bresslau parents had not been told of the plan to go together to Africa, the theory that it was they who insisted on the marriage for respectability's sake no longer holds up.

But by the end of the month Hélène was still not really well: "Bery, things are really on the way up! I can tell that by the fact that I overcome things more quickly. It was only on the first night that I slept badly, I hardly feel the lumbago back now, I can stand up nice and straight and enjoyed walking for 1¹/₂ hours yesterday. It is true that I am dreadfully cautious, I am careful to avoid catching cold and wrong movements; I will begin exercising as soon as I have felt nothing *at all* from my back for a couple of days."[22]

As things improved further: "[A]ll honor," he wrote, "to whatever is worthy of honor in my friend's state of health." And, making good use of his training: "During the time when you are taking the waters, please take only a thyroid pill every third day, because your metabolism is raised anyway."[23]

In August came an argument. It was about politics. As we have seen, Schweitzer's political antennae were always acute, and now there was an issue that threatened to affect their plans. As it was to turn out, it affected the rest of their lives: the prospect of war.

"Politics—thanks for the article—I find very sad. Probably 'our Congo' [French at that time] will go to Germany. . . . [T]he present missionaries must give way to others . . . or tensions will increase, and then my plan of founding a humanitarian effort with both nations will be impossible. Alas for the wretched nationalistic age!"[24] And a week or two later: "It has just struck 10 . . . I held my head in my hands and all the worries about politics and all the bitterness against country-devouring patriotism were carried out by the bells into the distant valleys, and you came and laid your hands in mine."[25]

Hélène, a German, was sensitive to the charge that the Germans had devoured Alsace in the Franco-Prussian war forty years earlier. She hastened to their defense:

[Y]our bitter observation in yesterday's letter has kept running through my head. Don't you see, the "devourers of countries" are the French this time; they are not satisfied with what the Algeciras agreements granted them and think they can get what they want because they feel England's jealousy behind them. But Morocco means such a colossal increase in power for France that Germany may indeed feel uneasy at such a shift in the balance, and since it has genuine interests of German subjects to protect— which were already threatened in the previous situation—, it is probably justified in demanding reparations. France definitely wants Morocco, but both nations wish to avoid war (only England wants that!), and so the idea of compensation for the Congo does not seem so improbable to me. And I—first without thinking of the two of us!—would be happy to see it (although as a colony it cannot make up even remotely for Morocco), because it is just through a really significant increase in France's power that England's ever-watchful suspicion of us, which is constantly stirring up intrigues, could be diverted.

But for us, what would it mean if the Congo were to become German? If I call to mind your reasons for choosing to go there, there are three of them: (1) to snatch the intelligent and educable natives there from the burgeoning influence of Islam; (2) to help the French Protestant mission, *which needs people*; (3) to prove that human labor can and should rise above all the national differences which separate us. *As long as the Fr. mission remains in the country* all these reasons are independent of the nationality of the region itself. Now if the Congo were really to become German, it seems to me that it is a worthy task for anyone who desires peace and the labors of peace to work (and then to work with the mission itself) to bring it about that it stays in the country. In the interests of the country, but in its own interest too, for I think that it cannot lightly give up a field of labor into which it has put so much... Farewell—and if you must consider me a complete baby politically, keep on loving me a little bit anyway! From my heart, your G.[26]

He replied immediately:

I am far from thinking you a baby politically. On the contrary. But this one time you do not see what lies behind it all. The treaties of Algeciras were not a solution, but only a source of further disputes... the reason being that Germany wanted to put the thing off so that 1. France would get very annoyed, 2. the Mannesmann brothers [important German industrialists] would buy lots of mines and lots of land, 3. it could arm its own fleet to be able to fight England if need arises. Here under heading number 3 is the fly in the ointment! What Germany wants above all is an Atlantic harbor so that it can make an enormous military harbor out of it, maintain an Atlantic fleet and thus threaten England from east and west, since England now only has to defend itself against the North Sea. An Atlantic German fleet is impossible because it would have no ports for coal, etc. But in England's case it is not envy but the purest self-preservation that it can never permit Germany to have a military port on the northern coast of Africa near the ocean. The fact that the only object of Germany's world policies is to get the upper hand over England and threaten it with invasion by a German army is as clear as daylight.... And that is the nasty part. Germany has to acknowledge the current state of ownership... but it still wants to triumph over England; then it can take as many colonies as it wants. Hence the coalition against Germany, (thank God!) Hence the danger of war, whether now or in a year makes no difference. In the long run Germany cannot survive this insane mobilization, and is bound to collapse. That is why it must risk everything before that happens, a life-or-death risk... only because of insane plans for greatness.... That is the truth.... By the way, I developed the theory of the war harbor for you two years ago.... You see how right I was.

And with regard to our Congo, if it becomes German the German God, who made iron grow [German patriotic poem by E. M. Arndt], will have to come in at the same time. The French missionaries will have to move out of the area at once and leave it to a German society. Then the children will have to learn 'Hail the victor's crown' [German national anthem until 1914], etc., in German right away. By the way, France would do just the same if it took over a German colony. It is the insane nationalism which always comes first. Then there is no place for me, I do not wish to torment myself to pieces in such senseless periods of transition! But we will find something somewhere else. Perhaps the missionary society will settle somewhere else . . . or, as is more probable, Germany will strike a milder chord and will not get the Congo. As the documents stand it would have to fight against France and England; Italy can't say a word, or the fleet just concentrated in the Mediterranean by the excellent Delcasse will set sail (France has assembled all its squadrons in the Mediterranean and is leaving the fight in the North Sea to England). . . . You know that I do not hate Germany; I honor it. But this delusion of grandeur, to which decency, honesty, morality, etc., are no more than empty concepts, is unworthy of this people. . . . Is this a political letter, my little baby? My ink even ran out along the way.[27]

It seemed worth quoting these at some length, not only for their inherent interest as documents concerning the perceptions of two intelligent and well-informed people at the build-up to World War One but to show how aware they both were of the hazards of their situation—that they went into it with eyes wide open. Schweitzer's analysis, of course, was by far the more accurate. And the little joke at the end, designed to take the sting from the letter, is a foretaste of his ability, when running his hospital, to use humor to defuse a tense situation.

Two days later he had a new thought:

At 10 o'clock I hung your portrait on its nail in the window niche and I looked at you from time to time. . . . Then I suddenly had the oddest feeling, that one day a day will come when it is not the picture but the person who is near to me, and can approach me in the middle of the night and ask about the end of laboring . . . and will express wishes and commands about it. . . . And I did not know, it came over me so strangely, whether I should rejoice (I trembled inwardly!) or be afraid of this new situation which will necessarily limit my freedom (and thus also to some degree my work and my night work).

Here I sit with a weary head, at the end of this heavy task, it is 2 o'clock, and I think of all these things, the serious part and a couple of silly things (e.g., whether someone appearing to admonish me will be wearing a beautiful kimono?).[28]

She replied in another letter heavy with prophecy:

Tell me, Bery, do you really believe in a limitation of your freedom, and are you afraid of it? Don't you know that you are always, always free and would be completely free, yes, m. G., utterly and completely free the moment you might wish for it? You *do* know it, and I understand what you meant. But consider that this image of someone coming up to you during the night and interrupting you has never risen before me—I don't think I would ever have dared to interrupt you, and I would never do anything but what I am already doing now: beg you in advance to consider your health and not to let it get too late.

In the same letter she wound up the political argument, writing of

the realization—which does not trouble me any more, but is like a scar which one must not touch—that there is something on which our thinking is fundamentally different. We will speak no more about politics. And may Heaven grant that it has no role to play in our lives.[29]

In September, a month before his finals began, Schweitzer went for a week to Munich for the Festival of French Music where Widor was to conduct a new work of his, the *Symphonia Sacra* for organ and orchestra. Schweitzer was to play the difficult organ part; he needed the fee to pay for his examination charges. At the beginning of the week's rehearsals he was eating in small restaurants for economy's sake, but a wealthy count who bottled champagne, and had to eat at the hotels to which he sold, came to Widor and asked if he knew of any students who would care to keep him company at lunch and dinner. Widor suggested Schweitzer, who, thus, suddenly found himself living off the fat of the land, champagne being naturally a regular feature of the menu. At the count's table, incidentally, Schweitzer met Saint-Saëns for the first time, but what they thought of each other remains a fascinating mystery.

The evening of the concert Schweitzer and Widor were both invited to dinner. Schweitzer thought it prudent to decline, but Widor went. The rest of the story is best told in the words of C. R. Joy in his excellent collection of stories and writings, *Music in the Life of Albert Schweitzer:*

At eight o'clock, when they were to begin, Widor was not there. At five minutes past be had not arrived. At ten minutes past he appeared, rushed to the rostrum, and began at once to conduct the orchestra with one hand while he searched for his glasses with the other. He was unable to conduct the symphony without the score, and neither he nor the orchestra was thoroughly familiar with it. With his baton first in his right hand and then in his left he searched in his pockets, one after the other. They were a quarter of the way through before he found them. Had not Schweitzer been so sure of himself and supported so well with the organ, the whole thing would have been disastrous. Said Schweitzer afterwards, "You see, I was right in not accepting the invitation."[30]

The state medical examination, the climax to six years' work, began in October and ended on December 17, 1911. When it was finished, "I could not," he wrote, "grasp the fact that the terrible strain of the medical course was now behind me. Again and again I had to assure myself that I was really awake and not dreaming."[31] The surgeon who conducted his last examination was telling him that but for his excellent health he would never have got through those last months and years, but he scarcely heard him, the voice seemed to be coming from far away.

What the surgeon said of that time was true of Schweitzer's whole life. His achievements were only possible for a man of great physical strength. "Energy," said Blake, "is eternal delight." Lack of energy can bring to nothing all kinds of brilliance, insight, and good intention. Even love can fall a victim to weariness; to express it can become too much effort. This is not to decry the passion and determination that made Schweitzer what he was, and it may well be that by remaining true to himself and to his vision of excellence he saved himself from those interior complications and conflicts that can lead to neurotic illness. His goodness, in short, may well have contributed to his health; but his health certainly helped him to make the most of his goodness.

When Schweitzer walked unbelievingly out into the night, he still had a thesis to write for his medical degree, and he still had to take a specialist course in tropical medicine before he could go to Africa. Moreover, although he did not then know it, there was trouble ahead from the Paris Mission.

Now that he had his qualifications it was time to let the world in on his secrets although he still found it difficult to do so. On December 22 he wrote to Hélène from Paris:

> I am still in bed, obeying you and getting a good rest. . . . It is nine o'clock. . . . My stay here is sad: it is raining the whole time, no carriages, no automobiles (because of the strike), almost no streetcars because of construction on the streets. . . . Yesterday I had to run all my errands on foot and got dreadfully wet. . . . No Christmas mood to make Christmas music.
>
> Your letter has just arrived . . . such a letter as only you could write . . . Yes, there is something like an undertone of melancholy when I think of binding you to my uncertain life, but with you everything is possible, and blessing will come from all this.
>
> I am constantly thinking about announcing our decision, but I have not yet become clear about it.[32]

Yet the same day he did make up his mind:

Paris. 80 Boulevard Malesherbes, 22.Dec., 1911
Dear Professor Bresslau, dear Mrs. Bresslau,

I come to ask your permission to call on you next Sunday between 10 and 11 o'clock—because I have services at other times, to discuss with you a matter that is of great concern to you and me. You will not be inordinately surprised when I tell you that it concerns your daughter, and that I venture to ask you to permit your daughter to accept my name and to accompany me to the Congo. I am aware of the severity of this request. Ever since this plan became a reality in me, I have felt a pain when I look at you and know about the sacrifice I have to ask from you. It is a heavy burden for me. I come to you and ask you to let your daughter go with me, without being able to promise her a secure existence for her future, and with the intention of moving to a place where the sun may cause many dangers to our health.

But I have a large circle of faithful and well-to-do friends who will support my overseas work, whom I can trust and who will not abandon me. And if I should be forced, for reasons of health, to give up my activities, there are always opportunities for church positions in Alsace. This is a reassuring thought. As far as the health issue is concerned, all those who work in the Congo have assured me that one can avoid the dangers if one observes the correct precautions, and especially if one returns every two to three years for several months to the northern climate, which is my firm intention.

I know that all these considerations cannot ease my heavy responsibility or your worries about your daughter when she becomes my companion . . . and yet, I dare to come to you with my request and hope that you will not reject it. The thought of joining our lives in common work grew steadily in your daughter and in me, and in the course of time and events became a firm resolution. We have thought about this, considered everything carefully, and finally found that we both have the right to make this decision, and that through everything we have thought, worked and experienced together we belong together.

I beg you, esteemed professor, to have confidence in me. Even if I cannot offer your daughter a brilliant existence, or even a steadily secure one, I will strive with all I have to make her happy and—for the great sacrifice she brings me—to be hers in deep gratitude to my last breath.

I have told my parents and my sister and brothers about my plans. They love your daughter very much and would be happy to receive her into our family.

I am barely able to express myself adequately and clearly, since I am writing these lines with deep emotion. Please do understand what I could not express quite as I would like. In case you want to receive me on Sunday between 10:00 and 11:00, it is not necessary to leave a message at Thomasstaden. I return home on Saturday.

With feelings of deep respect,
Your Albert Schweitzer[33]

Within a few days the families got together: "It was so beautiful yesterday to see the complete accord between our families. And what my mother said to you was so beautiful! . . . Such times. . . . How strange your friend is. . . . He feels a pang that our secret does not belong to us any more, and that now all the world will talk about it. . . . But he soon regains his composure at the thought that this will be the path to our new seclusion, far away from the world."[34]

The engagement took at least the younger members of the family by surprise. They knew that the two families did not entirely get on. His was too Alsatian, hers too German—and Jewish into the bargain. Hélène's mother was a sweet woman, but her father was not much liked by some of the Schweitzers. Besides—the old cry—they really didn't think Bery had time for that kind of thing.

But it had happened. The engagement party was held at Strasbourg. Champagne was drunk, Mrs. Schweitzer wiped her eyes, the men smiled indulgently, and Suzi had a loving pinch on the arm from her Uncle Bery.

As the new year, 1912, began, he wrote to Hélène: "Day has just begun. . . . I was standing at the window when the twelve strokes sounded from the cathedral. . . . Oh how different this is from last year, when I was full of fear, full of fear. . . . Will you ever know what I suffered for you?"[35]

For his degree thesis he decided to combine two of his fields of study and put into practice something he was increasingly preaching—the harnessing of religion with science. He would write a psychiatric study of Jesus. At least the subject was unlikely to encounter much competition from other medical finalists!

In fact, he had something of a personal reason for choosing the subject. With the recent upsurge of interest in psychopathology, a vogue had arisen for applying psychological tests to Jesus. Three writers had published theories that Jesus suffered from one kind of mental abnormality or another: he had a tendency to delusions and hallucinations that amounted, they claimed, to paranoia, the definition of which was a good deal more chaotic than it is now.

Among those who were supposed to have contributed to the notion of a mentally disordered Jesus was Schweitzer. Holtzmann and others, so he tells us in the preface to his thesis, were constantly reminding him that he "had portrayed a Jesus whose object-world looked like a structure of fantasies."[36] A Jesus, they felt, who believed in the coming of a practical Kingdom of God was obviously out of his mind; and Schweitzer had done as much as any man to establish how central this was to Jesus' thought.

Schweitzer's existing knowledge was already more than enough to make mincemeat of the books that made Jesus out a madman, on two main scores. First, the three authors had been entirely uncritical about their historical sources; the bulk of the passages they used to make their points came from St. John, whom no reputable scholar regarded as historically reliable. And second, they had ignored a very basic and very obvious principle in the analysis of ideas that look like delusions, namely, that these ideas should be investigated in relation to the ideas current in the society of the time. As Dr. Winifred Overholser pointed out in her introduction to a new translation of Schweitzer's booklet in 1948: "To the Haitian native a belief that necromancy may be employed against him is a part of the folkways, is 'normal'—for the educated resident of Park Avenue such a belief would properly be classified as delusion."[37] It was as normal for Jesus to believe what he did as for the men before Copernicus to believe that the sun moved around the earth.

Equipped though he was with these potent arguments, Schweitzer, in accordance with his principle of getting to the bottom of any subject he touched, read deeply about paranoia and other forms of psychosis, so far as they had then been studied, and took a year over writing his thesis. So his mistrust of psychoanalysis cannot be blamed, as it often is, on ignorance. Indeed, the opening paragraph of his thesis is actually a defense of the method and puts the blame where it belongs, on imperfect practitioners:

> The psycho-pathological method, which conceives its task to be the investigation of the mental aberrations of significant personalities in relation to their works, has recently fallen into disrepute. This is not because of the method, which with proper limitations and in the hands of professional investigators can produce and has produced valuable results, but because it has been faultily pursued by amateurs. The prerequisites which are essential for successful work in this field—exact source knowledge, adequate medical, and particularly psychiatric, experience, both under the discipline of critical talents—are very seldom found together.[38]

So deeply did he believe in truth, including psychiatric truth, that he embarked on his analysis of his beloved Jesus with his eyes open to the possibility that he might, in fact, find genuine signs of mental disorder there.

> Should it really turn out that Jesus' object world must be considered by the doctor as in some degree the world of a sick man, still this conclusion, regardless of the consequences that follow from it and the shock to many that would result from it must not remain unuttered, since reverence for truth must be exalted above everything else. With this conviction I began the work, suppressing the unpleasant feeling of having to subject a great personality to psychiatric examination, and pondering the truth that what is great and profound in the ethical teachings of Jesus would retain its

significance even if the conceptions in his world outlook and some of his actions had to be called more or less diseased.[39]

As it turned out, however, he found no cause to alter his belief that Jesus was perfectly sane, no reason to suppose that the ethical genius sprang from an unbalanced vision; always assuming that he was, as Schweitzer insisted, a man sharing the life and thought of his fellow men.

While this booklet was in the making, a great many other things were happening. To study tropical medicine he had to go to Paris; Strasbourg could not teach him all he needed to know. So now, at last, he was forced to give up his teaching at the university, his preaching at St. Nicholas. The last series of lectures he gave, in the winter of 1911–12 insisted on the belief behind his thesis and went deeply into the reconciliation between religion and science, a subject that concerned him more and more. With his combination of mystical apprehension and vigorously disciplined research he was qualified to speak for both as few others have been. What was science? What was religion? Both were life, both were truth. The names were unimportant.

On the religious side there is one subject on which we have not yet heard his views—sin. Sin would seem to be an important part of a preacher's concerns, but Schweitzer was not particularly interested in it. He touched on the subject in a sermon he preached in January 1912.

> I cannot speak to you about sin like those terrifying preachers of peni-tence who have arisen through the ages. And I would not wish to. They always remind me of those fearful storms which beat on the earth but give it none of the refreshment that a fine rain gives when the water, instead of falling in torrents and carrying all before it, gently penetrates the soil. John the Baptist was a powerful orator. But Jesus, speaking to the people gently, certainly touched them much more deeply and convinced them more deeply of their sin. Whoever speaks to others of guilt and sin should preach as a sinner; everything he says that is true is an episode from his own experience.[40]

The thought is echoed in his autobiography when he writes: "It is not where sinfulness is most talked about that its seriousness is most forcibly taught. There is not much about it in the Sermon on the Mount. But thanks to the longing for freedom from sin and for purity of heart which Jesus has enshrined in the Beatitudes, these form the great call to repen-tance which is increasingly working on man."[41]

On February 25 Schweitzer preached his last afternoon sermon to the congregation that had shared so many of his thoughts. His text this time was "Be faithful unto death and I will give you the crown of life." "No doubt," he told them, "you have often noticed that during these last years I have been tired out, and have only been able to do my work by drawing on the last of my strength; and I have had the impression, as I came down from the pulpit, that you have had to be very indulgent with me . . .

"And now that our ways are going to part, we must find a vantage point from which we can encompass a huge horizon. . . . You will understand that this saying—'be faithful' offers us just the wide view that will rule our meditation."[42]

Faithfulness, he said, is the interior force of life through which we direct our lives into strong-flowing channels and save ourselves from spreading into shallow streams like a river with weak banks. There is faithfulness to oneself, without which our soul is wounded and slowly loses its blood. There is faithfulness toward men, which means nothing less than responsibility for everything we do to every man and woman alive. There is faithfulness to the spirit of Jesus, which lies in placing ourselves at his service.

And the crown of life is not some prize to be awarded after it is all over. "The crown of life is simply the joy and peace which fill the heart of the man who is faithful, which never desert him, but which grow more and more brilliant like the sinking sun, that at the very moment of its setting floods the whole world with light."[43]

So he said good-bye to St. Nicholas and the university, and going around Strasbourg afterward, he could scarcely bear to look at the places where he had taught and preached throughout those ten crowded years.

In Paris, he got in touch with M. Boegner's successor at the Mission Society, M. Jean Bianquis. The basis of the agreement with the committee that had gradually been reached over the years was that Schweitzer would come without involving the society in any expense whatever: "I know what heavy expenses the overseas missions represent for you. . . . I am counting on devoted friends who have given me to understand that they will help me within the limits of their capacities."[44]

Schweitzer, in fact, had been going around Paris and Strasbourg ringing the doorbells of the wealthy and influential Protestant families he had come to know. And although he found that the tone of welcome changed noticeably when he mentioned the subject of his visit—particularly when it became clear that he was asking for money for a project that did not even exist yet—his personal involvement finally got him the help he needed. His experience of begging for the poor as a student in Strasbourg stood him in good stead. One family would suggest another, and so he begged his way around the cities.

Part of Schweitzer's preparations consisted of an assiduous picking of useful brains. He had always gone out of his way to understand and share the problems of butcher, baker, and candlestick maker. Now his interest was more personal, for in Africa he would have to combine all those functions and many more in himself. He had to discipline himself to the chore of making orderly and accurate lists, of estimating budgets and keeping accounts. He learned a good deal about handling money from a Mrs. Fischer, whose husband had been a professor of surgery at Strasbourg but had died young. Having undertaken to go to Africa independently, Schweitzer could not count on any support from anywhere once he was out there. There could be no cables to headquarters for more funds or a couple of extra nurses. There could be no replacements for himself unless he himself found them. If a house needed repair, he would have to repair it. And all this in an environment totally strange to him, full of problems he had never encountered.

Everything must be foreseen now, or it would be too late. One particular apprehension was nagging at him. The Russian representatives in Paris were now openly saying that war was not far away. And in both France and Germany civil servants were increasingly being paid in paper money, not in gold. Gold was being held back. It seemed ominous. For Schweitzer in the Gabon would be an alien—a German citizen on French territory. His political antennae twitched, and he made provision for taking two thousand marks in gold, which would keep its value regardless of developments.

On the literary and artistic side three projects were still unfinished: the thesis on the psychology of Jesus, the Bach organ works, and a new edition of *The Quest of the Historical Jesus.* The last was made necessary by a number of British writers who had been attracting attention with the theory that Jesus never existed at all; he was a mythological figure, they said, invented like the Greek gods as a symbol of a new faith.

In answer to this entertaining theory, which still enjoys periodic resurrections, Schweitzer demonstrated at some length that although it may be difficult to prove that Jesus existed, it is quite impossible to prove that he did not. Like those writers who had tried to prove Jesus mad, these Britishers—notably Robertson, Smith, Frazer, and Drews—seemed to have no knowledge of the critical work that had been done on the differences between the Gospels and used all four indiscriminately to make their points. But more important, they never tackled the real issue, which was that if the early Christians had wanted to invent a mythological founder, it was inconceivable that they would have invented the Jesus who appears in the New Testament—a Jesus full of inconsistencies and hard sayings, quite unfitted to be the mythical hero of a folk cult. This section of the book, unfortunately, never found its way into English translation.

In March he had welcome news from Hélène:

[A]fter 14 more days the last great separation will be over—can it be true? . . . Berylein, my dear, you are getting a healthy wife who will be able to endure things once more. And even if I had learned nothing at all in the clinic—but you learn heaps of things there every day—I would have been happy to have gone there simply because I see how well I am taking it. I am there in the morning at 8, 8:15 at the latest, and on my feet until 1 or 1:30 and am getting on famously. They let you get at something right away, giving injections, catheterizing, today I applied bandages and was in charge of the instruments in a minor case. And the sister shows me everything very charmingly and gives me good advice on the care and maintenance of the instruments and of everything else. And today she also told me that I was the most envied girl in Strasbourg. Can you guess why? Don't rack your brains over it, my dear, I will tell you: because I—am getting such a famous husband! I really have to laugh. If I were only to be envied because of his fame![45]

From him, on Easter Eve:

6 April 1912 at night . . . The Faustian night which will vanish on Easter morning when the Easter bells will ring it to its grave. . . . Now, however, I go to bed—not a poetic act, admittedly but I comfort myself with the realization that I do not have to be like Faust in all aspects, and I don't want to be. I would rather take my Gretchen with me to Africa than leave her behind. This is (1) more pleasant, (2) more honorable, (3) more profitable. And there must not be a poodle either, but a wire-haired dog, as large as possible . . . . I do not have to confess how late it is.[46]

In April he found a new way of raising money. He had never, it seems, given a solo organ recital in public before, but now he did, as part of a concert given by the Paris Bach Society "for the benefit of the Ogowe Mission." Gustave Bret said later that this was the first time that Schweitzer was recognized as a virtuoso soloist. The concert was a great success.

Meanwhile collections were being made in parishes in Alsace, whose pastors had been at college with him. Strasbourg professors contributed, even though they were German and the enterprise was for a French colony. There was another concert at Le Havre and a lecture to go with it. And, of course, there had been substantial advances from the Bach book, and royalties were still coming in.

And so, when he had enough money for all the necessary equipment, for the voyage, and for the first year's running expenses, he told the Mission Society, in a letter dated May 11, 1912, that he was fully equipped and ready to go, asking only for a piece of ground and, if possible, some sort of building. On May 13 M. Bianquis, with an almost audible sigh of relief, agreed.

But in the meantime a new pastor had joined the committee, a M. Edouard Sautter, and, naturally, the situation now had to be explained to him. M. Bianquis spoke to him, and found him somewhat disapproving. He then wrote to him, a long, closely reasoned and fervent letter, pointing out how much the mission would benefit from the presence of a doctor, particularly one who came full of love for Jesus, having trained for just this task. He summarized the history of the case, mentioning how the other committee members had had their doubts but now had been persuaded of Schweitzer's fitness to be associated with their work. He was confident that M. Sautter would also come to see it in this light.

M. Sautter quite failed to see it in this light. M. Sautter knew clearly what a Christian was, and Schweitzer was not one of them. He was obdurate. And he swung one or two other members of the committee to his way of thinking. M. Bianquis sent Schweitzer copies of his correspondence with Sautter, and his letters grew increasingly desperate. Schweitzer, already at the end of his tether, already beginning to make lists of equipment, already in communication with a M. Ottman in Africa about what to bring (tough crockery—the Africans break it—and envelopes *without glue*), suddenly found himself requested to appear before the committee and satisfy them as to his religious orthodoxy. Schweitzer was very wary. He knew of a minister whom the society had refused to accept simply because he was not prepared categorically to say that the fourth Gospel was written by the apostle John. The minister was right; the evidence is not conclusive. But his historical integrity branded him as undesirable.

Schweitzer accordingly sent a message to the committee that the more rigid among them must have seen as the confirmation of their worst fears. He refused to be examined by the committee and "based my refusal on the fact that Jesus, when He called his disciples, required from them nothing beyond the will to follow Him. I also sent a message to the Committee that, if we are to follow the saying of Jesus: 'He that is not against us is on our part,' a missionary society would be in the wrong if it rejected even a Mahommedan who offered his services for the treatment of their suffering natives."[47]

Instead, he offered to meet all the twenty or so committee members individually, to give them a chance to make a personal assessment, and this was agreed. As he went the rounds, it became clear that some at least of the committee were afraid that with his great learning he might "confuse" the missionaries and also that the temptation to preach might become too much for him even though he went as a doctor. Only when he solemnly promised that if he went he would be "as dumb as a carp" on the subject of religion did they relax and give him their blessing, as well they might, because they were sending out a fully qualified doctor, dedicated, humane, and hardworking, tamed, muzzled, and obedient, at no cost whatever to themselves.

Even so, at some moment during this struggle it seems that the Swiss-based Union of Evangelical Missions actually wrote to Schweitzer, offering him a post on his own terms—the easy way out of his difficulties. When exactly this happened is difficult to determine because we only have a reference to this offer in another letter written in 1921. But Schweitzer's obstinacy, his desire to prove his point in his own way, had clearly not softened with the years, and he turned the offer down.

This crisis, on top of all his other worries and his physical exhaustion, was finally too much for him and led, in his daughter's words, "to a physical and psychic breakdown which lasted several months. He suffered from queasiness, nausea, fevers and heart problems."[48]

The wedding was arranged for June 18. Earlier that month a stranger arrived at the Günsbach manse to pay his respects to Schweitzer, but Schweitzer was upstairs in bed, worn out, and the stranger had to be content with talking to his mother. "You have an important son," said the man. "If he was less important I might see more of him," she replied, and then the unhappiness came out: "When he has something new in his mind he gets it all ready secretly, and when it's too late for anyone to do anything about it he lets people know. Now he's off with his wife to Africa as a mission doctor."

"What?" asked the man. "He's got a wife?"

"He will have, if he finds the time to marry her."[49]

He did find the time, although he was still not fully recovered on the day, and "Aunt-Prim-and-Proper" became a real aunt. So the letters came to an end, and a relationship that was strangely founded on renunciation reached an equally strange consummation. In addition to the spiritual and intellectual comfort that each had from the other, there was now the simple physical comfort that most people seek and find in marriage. How much this meant to these two, after so many years of great spiritual closeness, whether it was a passionate fulfilment or merely another step along the path of a remarkable partnership, is something that readers will have to guess at for themselves.

But this may be the moment to try to answer one or two of the key questions about this man: What was it that made him so frightened of other human beings? What was it in him that he so desperately needed to hide? And how did this relate to his other qualities? To pretend to be conclusive would be arrogant besides being impertinent. But tentatively, I suggest that the secret of Albert Schweitzer was that tremulous passion with which he encountered every aspect of life. The ecstasy with which he first heard harmony as a child, the awareness of the pain of other creatures, the aching sensibility with which he empathized with the small, chilly spring flowers and with the friendly tree outside his window that shared his midnight thoughts—all these were of a piece with the sense of passionate identity that he felt toward Kant—and toward Hélène—and toward Jesus. His letters are full of moments when "I trembled," "I shook." Inwardly, he was one aching wound, vulnerable to people, to nature, to ideas, to all of existence. He did not forget things, because the vividness of every experience imprinted itself so indelibly on his mind and heart. And this, in turn, forced him to control these reactions with the strictest mental discipline, to save his sanity. It was this two-edged sword, passionate instinct and tight reasoning, that enabled him to cut through to the heart of every subject he encountered. This was his weakness, his strength, the source of his sense of greatness, and the thing that had to be kept close to his heart; partly because he did not wish to be laughed at by worldly wise friends, but also, perhaps, because of a feeling that if he allowed others to pluck out the heart of his mystery, the power and the greatness would somehow leak away. What he required from older women, his guardian angels, was that they should be the trusted recipients of the chaotic profusion of his responses to life, that they should not laugh at him as younger women might but respect his vulnerable heart and nurse it toward wholeness and understanding. Young people saw nothing special in him because he would not let them. What he saw in Hélène was a union of the two, youth and maturity. He saw it, but for a long time it was too astonishing for him fully to trust it. And indeed it was a two-way process: as he came to trust her, so she came to see what he needed and grew able to deserve that trust.

For many obvious reasons, there was no honeymoon worth the name. And it was clearly out of the question for them to set off that summer, as they had hoped. The great adventure had to be postponed. It was not until January 1913 that Schweitzer felt strong enough to undertake the journey in March.

Meantime, he went on working. The Bach organ edition would never be finished in time; that was obvious. Despite all he could do, three volumes, dealing with the Choral Preludes, still remained to be dealt with when he left for Africa. But while he was in Europe work went on ceaselessly on the first five.

A Psychiatric Study of Jesus, the thesis for his medical degree, was finally completed early in 1913. Now Schweitzer was three times a doctor—of philosophy, of theology, and of medicine. Whether the triple doctorate is indeed unique, as some claim, I do not know. But certain it is that there have not been many of them. And we may be fairly sure that no one else has ever taken a third doctorate with the precise intention of escaping the academic world of the first two.

One further administrative problem faced Schweitzer. His doctor's diploma was a German one, and he wanted to practice in a French colony. Here the "old-boy network" came into action. Influential friends in Paris went to work, and special permission was granted. All the formalities were over. All that remained was the packing and the going.

The Paris Bach Society, which Schweitzer had helped to found seven years before and for which he had played so faithfully, presented him with a magnificent parting gift—a piano specially equipped with a pedal attachment, on which he could simulate playing an organ. From Samkita on the upper reaches of the Ogowe, where the missionaries waited with eager excitement for the doctor they needed so badly, he received instructions from M. Ottman how to preserve the precious piano, lining it with zinc against the ravages of the ubiquitous insects.

In deciding on the best site to commence operations, Schweitzer had consulted a M. Morel, another missionary from the Ogowe River, who was also an Alsatian. The Ogowe was navigable for several hundred miles inland from Cape Lopez, and in the days when the jungle had not yet been pierced by road or rail such a river was the main, almost the only, highway. A hospital at a strategic point on the river would be accessible to villagers for many miles up and down stream.

The Ogowe had already been opened up by traders in the nineteenth century, and settlements of both Catholics and Protestants were scattered along its shores. (The book that appeared in the 1920s purporting to be the memoirs of Trader Horn was based, whether fictionally or not, on the experiences of one of the Ogowe traders. After the traders came the missionaries.) About 150 miles from the coast lies the village of Lambarene and a few miles beyond that the mission station of Andende. Here Schweitzer, on M. Morel's advice, had requested and been granted a house for himself and his wife and a site for some sort of hospital building. Thirty or forty miles farther upriver lay Samkita, where M. Morel and M. Ottman worked.

So the last of the equipment and provisions were bought, the crates were packed and labeled (one of the cellars of St. Thomas Church having been pressed into service as a storeroom and packing place, somewhat to the verger's displeasure), and, finally, in February the packing cases— seventy of them—were sent off in advance to Bordeaux. It only remained to conclude the arrangements by which fresh supplies could be ordered and sent on to Africa and then to say good-bye.

Apart from the personal leave-takings there was a last good-bye to be said from the pulpit, and Schweitzer returned to St. Nicholas for a sort of farewell guest appearance on March 9. The text he chose for this occasion was that passage from St. Paul's letter to the Philippians that is so often used as a blessing at the end of a service: "And the peace of God which surpasses all understanding keep your hearts and your minds in Jesus Christ." Schweitzer had always used this parting benediction and now used it for a greater parting. But what he wanted to say about it was slightly different from what the congregation might have expected. He wanted to emphasize that St. Paul was talking about minds as well as hearts. He wanted to strike another blow against an age that was increasingly separating thought (i.e., science and technology) from faith (i.e., religion). His last lecture series was about the reconciliation of the two, but those lectures are lost to us. In this sermon we have a glimpse of the way he was thinking, and it is important for what was to come later.

Schweitzer had now spent more than six years working among medical men, studying the hard facts of natural science and biology. He had a right to speak for science. And he believed, more and more deeply, that thought led to religion. If it did not, that was because it did not go deep enough but gave up too soon. If the mind did not lead toward God, of what use was the mind? Was God irrational? If so the very heart of things must be irrational, and reason was of no use at all. But reason was one of men's noblest functions. Therefore, God must be at the heart of reason as well as at the heart of love. All the true and excellent capacities of man must meet at the same point; and that point must be in some way divine.

> The more I felt I grasped the personality of Jesus, the stronger grew my conviction that in him there was an inter-penetration of faith and simple natural thought. The further I went in my study of the history of Christianity, the clearer it seemed to me that so many errors and conflicts amount to this—that from the first generations to our own day people have constantly renewed the opposition of faith and piety against reason, and so dug a ditch in the hearts of men where God placed a harmony.

Then he defines what he means by reason—or what it is not.

> You realise that reason is quite frankly not just the ability to think about superficial everyday affairs; it is the light which illuminates the spirit from within, which helps us to unravel the meaning of things, of the world, of the enigma of existence, the value and the purpose of our own being, and which allows us to discover the guiding thread of our own life. And this can only be what leads to the peace of God, the harmonisation between ourselves and the outside world. . . .

And how does this peace surpass all understanding?

> Just as the distant snow-covered peaks, shining in the sun, seem to rise in a solitary jet above a horizon of mist—but in reality stand behind the mountainous fortifications over which they tower, and which noone can reach without first crossing all the intervening country—so does the peace of God seem to tower in the distance beyond reason, but in truth stands upon it.

So for Schweitzer reason was always driving farther because "true happiness only breathes from the depths of inward peace." Reason "increases our thirst for peace. It drives us to climb the steep flanks of the mountains, and when we reach the shining barriers of the glaciers it encourages us—Higher! Higher! Always higher! On to the shining light of the peaks, to the peace and the silent grandeur of the summits."[50]

So Schweitzer spoke, like one of those doomed heroes of Ibsen who are drunk with the romantic intoxication of the far-off peaks of the spirit. But Schweitzer, as we have seen, was the man who contrived to balance the extremes at the center point, and while he kept one eye on the distant snow, the other scanned every step of the way. As he spoke, his seventy cases were on the way to Bordeaux and his two thousand marks in gold were ready for packing in his hand baggage.

One final gesture: he took a ninety-nine-year lease on the Rocks of Kanzenrain—those rocks on the hill above Günsbach where he had sat and looked out over the valley since he was a child, finding peace and inspiration. A piece of the land that had bred him now waited for his return, and nobody could touch it without his knowledge. And so the last few days passed and the morning of March 23 dawned, Good Friday, 1913—almost to the day the anniversary that he and Hélène kept.

His mother was still not reconciled to what she regarded as a waste of a career. Suzanne was in Günsbach and remembered how it was. How Mrs. Schweitzer got up early and went about the house with her face set; how Schweitzer came down and asked for his favorite breakfast, and Mrs. Schweitzer left the room tight-lipped. The uneasy morning passed, and lunchtime, and it was time to leave the village and cross the stream by the bridge where the children used to chase and mock Mausche the Jew on his donkey cart and wait in the station for the single-track train that would come down the valley and take them to Colmar for the Strasbourg connection and the Paris express. The church bells rang for afternoon service—the same bells, at much the same time of year, as had rung thirty years before and cued the boy Albert to drive away the birds from the threatening catapults. If it seems sentimental to mention this, we must remember that he *was* sentimental—particularly about his homeland, his village, and his father's church. Throughout his life this had been home; there had been no break, no reaction to interrupt the flow of his feelings toward it.

The train arrived as the bell ceased, and Schweitzer and Hélène climbed onto the platform of the last coach, from which they could wave good-bye and look for the last time at the valley. The train started and they all waved—except Mrs. Schweitzer. The hard Schillinger spirit would not melt. The will that drove the son to Africa held back the blessing of the mother. He was not to see her again.

Schweitzer and Hélène spent the night in Strasbourg. On Saturday they took the Paris train and on Sunday went to the Easter celebrations at St. Sulpice and heard Widor at his organ. At two o'clock they were off again, to Bordeaux.

That Easter day was brilliant with sunshine, warm with spring, and the people were out in their holiday clothes. Finally to be on the move after seven grinding years of preparation, and on such a glorious day, seemed like a dream.

It would be fair to suggest that the level-headed calculation that Schweitzer had put into his plans had been somewhat jeopardized by his insistence on doing so many other things at the same time and that it was asking for trouble for two people to set out on so great a task having half killed themselves merely in getting to the starting post. But here they were. The dream had taken flesh.

What was ahead was totally unknown. Everything that foresight and imagination could do had been done, but the break with past experience was complete. Schweitzer was going to Africa to work, to serve, to heal, to try to pay back something of what the white races owed the black. But behind that dedication was also the romantic child, unable to attend to his lessons for dreaming of foreign lands and drawn constantly back to the great sad figure of the noble black man on Colmar's Champ de Mars. His whole life had been a preparation for this moment. Poised between one life and the next, he looked out at the sunshine and knew that whatever sacrifices he might have made, whatever happiness he might have left behind, he had made the right choice. It would have been more difficult to stay.

13

Africa

1913

WHEN ONE THINKS one has thought of everything, there is always something one has not thought of, for example, that the customs offices at Bordeaux will be closed on Easter Monday. The ship waited at Pauillac, thirty miles farther downriver. The boat train from Bordeaux was due to leave for the docks before long, and the big packing case that had been sent in advance sat inaccessible in the customs. The situation was fraught with disaster, for customs officials are not noted for their willingness to bend the rules in the interests of distracted travelers. Somehow or other, however, Schweitzer found an official who was prepared to do just that, and with minutes to spare the baggage was hurried by motorcar from customs to train, by train from Bordeaux to Pauillac, and was soon on board the steamship *Europe.*

After the jostling and shoving and finding the cabin, (comfortably forward, away from the engines), and cleaning up and settling in, lunch was served. The Schweitzers felt "poor untraveled home birds" among the old Africa hands at their table: a couple of doctors, some officers, two wives returning to their husbands in the colonial service. Schweitzer "could not help thinking of the fowls my mother used to buy every summer from Italian poultry dealers to add to her stock, which for several days used to walk about among the old ones very shyly and humbly."[1] And he noticed "a certain expression of energy and determination"[2] in his fellow passengers.

The Bay of Biscay provided further unforeseen hazards. The traditional foul weather set in, and the storm lasted three days. The Congo steamers were particularly shallow of draught, to enable them to go far

231

up the Congo, and they rolled accordingly. Schweitzer, unprepared, had not made the baggage fast, and in the night the cabin trunks "began to chase each other about. The two hat cases also, which contained our sun-helmets, took part in the game without reflecting how badly off they might come in it, and when I tried to catch the trunks, I nearly got one leg crushed between them and the wall of the cabin. So I left them to their fate and contented myself with lying quietly in my berth and counting how many seconds elapsed between each plunge made by the ship and the corresponding rush of our boxes. Soon there could be heard similar noises from other cabins and added to them the sound of crockery, etc., moving wildly about in the galley and the dining saloon."[3]

That passage comes from Schweitzer's first book about Africa, *On the Edge of the Primeval Forest*. The style is new. Neither the formal style of the scholarly books nor the near-rhetorical style of the early sermons, here is the style that is the man himself. Disasters and dangers are treated with humor, and even rampaging baggage elicits a sort of affectionate sympathy, as though it had a right to its "game."

This, I feel sure, was the Schweitzer his friends loved, the Schweitzer by whom every living creature, and by a comic extension every inanimate object as well, was appreciated and enjoyed simply for existing, for doing what was its nature to do.

And what did the man of God do as the ship was flung to and fro? Did he pray? No. With a more scientific spirit he counted the seconds between the lurch of the ship and the suicidal rush of the baggage. Perhaps he prayed as well, but that is not what he remembered and reported.

Eventually, the storm ended and the ship plowed on to calmer, sunnier waters. Schweitzer occupied himself in picking up tips from more experienced passengers. A lieutenant expounded his views on the evil ways Mohammedanism brought in its wake—not because the religion was false but because, so he said, it made the Africans anti-European, opposed to material improvements, and, therefore, idle. A military doctor gave Schweitzer two hours' discourse every day about his experiences of tropical medicine.

Once past the Canary Islands the troops on board were ordered to wear sun helmets when on deck. Schweitzer was surprised because the weather was not particularly hot. But he was warned by an old Africa hand that in tropical latitudes the sun was man's worst enemy, to be dreaded even more in the cool of sunrise and sunset than at midday. He took the hint to heart, for he was to become notorious for his insistence that all staff and visitors at his hospital should wear something on their heads, often clashing with travelers who had gone bareheaded in tropical climates for years before meeting him. But before he became so rigid, he was to have some practical experience of sunstroke himself, not personally, but in colleagues.

More curious—indeed extraordinary—is the fact that he also wore a hat after sunset. This seems to have had no practical reason at all, nothing but the fulfilment of an apparently pointless promise. The promise was made to the old Countess of Erlach, Frederick Curtius's mother-in-law, in the days when Schweitzer used to play the piano for her in the evenings in the chapter house of St. Thomas. An uncle of the countess who had worked for years in the tropics had told her that the reason he never contracted malaria was because he never went bareheaded out of doors after sunset. The old lady, who had greatly taken to Schweitzer and had decided to exercise a civilizing influence on him, made him promise to do the same. Schweitzer kept his promise. And never, as a matter of fact, caught malaria, although, as he says himself, "of course the disease does not result from going with uncovered head in the tropics after sundown."[4]

What can we make of this blind obedience to an irrational promise? Schweitzer did not normally feel himself tied by bonds of sentiment when they turned out to be contrary to sense or to his own convictions. Truth normally reigned over all other considerations, and the truth was that the opinions of the countess' uncle carried no medical weight at all. So this obligation to which Schweitzer bound himself was no more than a gesture. I can only think it was a combination of two threads in Schweitzer's character, both of which were so deeply part of him that he had no alternative but to do as the countess said.

The first was his sense of debt. He owed the countess a great deal, and he could repay it only by doing as she wished. The other was his almost romantic sense of fidelity. When in old age he said, "*Je suis fidèle*," he was speaking of fidelity to the influences that made him what he was. All his life he was faithful to the deep experiences of his early years because in them dwelt a richness of feeling that he never wished to lose. Without them "the soul lost its blood." I think that this habit of wearing a hat after sundown was a ritual of remembrance by which he not only acknowledged gratitude but remained in touch with one of the sources of his strength. For despite his Protestantism, despite his scientific turn of mind and his hatred of humbug and his incomprehension of the transcendental, he had a strong sense of the value of ritual. As a boy he had loved the Catholic chancel of the Günsbach church. He remembered and honored anniversaries and birthdays. His wife said of him, "He really does know how to give presents."

His rituals were the rituals of his own life and experience, not the imposed rituals of an organization. But they were no less important to him for that.

At Dakar came the first symbolic landing on African soil, and the first taste of African cruelty to animals. When he saw two Africans sitting on a loaded cart that was stuck in the mud and beating their horse to make it pull harder, Schweitzer rapidly had the two astonished blacks off their cart and pushing. "If you can't bear to see animals ill treated," said the lieutenant, "don't go to Africa."[5]

Schweitzer was well prepared for the horrors that the white man had brought to Africa. Whether he was ready for the Africans' own defects is more difficult to say. The statue in Colmar was romanticized. Was he, at least subconsciously, expecting to find the noble savage sadly but with dignity enduring the rule of the white man? Mrs. Urquhart thinks he was. She thinks that the real Africa was a deep shock to him. Even on the Ivory Coast, where he saw finely built blacks who might have been models for the Colmar statue, he noted in the seaport Africans' eyes a "haunting vision of sullen and unwilling subjection, mixed with insolence."[6]

As the ship sailed, close inshore, past the Pepper Coast, the Ivory Coast, the Gold Coast, and the Slave Coast, Schweitzer's imagination was dwelling on the suffering those lands had seen. The sympathetic insight that had taken him into the minds of Bach, Paul, and Jesus was focused now upon the slaves who had been dragged in their thousands from these shores to the plantations of the New World. The schoolboy dreamer, the lover of travelers' tales, the follower of Jesus—all the layers of his personality were touched. And as he sat at table he tried similarly to guess at the thoughts, the responsibilities, the experiences, and the ideals of his fellow passengers. "If everything could be written down that is done during these years by all of us who are now here on this ship, what a book it would be! Would there be no pages that we should be glad to turn over as quickly as possible?"[7]

The heat grew more intense. It was worse when the sky was overcast than on the clear days, and the intermittent storms did nothing to cool the air. After nearly three weeks they finally reached the equator and the capital city of the Gabon, Libreville—so called because freed slaves were landed here in the days when France and Britain had finally abandoned slavery and with the enthusiasm of reformed sinners had suddenly turned from capturing slaves to capturing their captors.

In Libreville the Schweitzers were welcomed by an American missionary. Mr. Ford, and because it was a Sunday were introduced to some of his black congregation. Schweitzer noticed that they showed none of the sullen looks of the seaport blacks, but looked "free and yet modest."[8] Mr. Ford was to prove a useful friend when war came. The last few miles, from Libreville to Cape Lopez, at the mouth of the Ogowe, were spent in worrying how much duty they would be charged on their equipment. The other passengers had told frightening tales of the ferocity of customs charges. But again they were lucky and in due course transferred to the paddle steamer *Alémbé*, which was to take them upriver. The equipment, however, had to be left behind. There was no room in this boat; and the next was not for another fortnight.

And up the river, into Africa, they went. Any first visit to the tropics is not merely a new experience, it is a new kind of experience. The feelings it arouses are unlike anything one has felt before. One does not recognize them. One does not recognize oneself. One is a new creature, with new perceptions. And so Schweitzer found, for all the care with which he had prepared his imagination.

River and forest ... ! Who can really describe the first impression they make? We seemed to be dreaming! Pictures of antediluvian scenery which elsewhere had seemed to be merely the creation of fancy, are now seen in real life. It is impossible to say where the river ends and the land begins, for a mighty network of roots, clothed with bright-flowering creepers, projects right into the water. Clumps of palms and palm trees, ordinary trees spreading out widely with green boughs and huge leaves, single trees of the pine family shooting up to a towering height in between them, wide fields of papyrus clumps as tall as a man, with big fan-like leaves, and amid all this luxuriant greenery the rotting stems of dead giants shooting up to heaven. ... In every gap in the forest a water mirror meets the eye; at every bend in the river a new tributary shows itself. A heron flies heavily up and then settles on a dead tree trunk; white birds and blue birds skim over the water, and high in the air a pair of ospreys circle. Then—yes; there can be no mistake about it—from the branch of a palm there hang and swing—two monkey tails! Now the owners of the tails are visible. We are really in Africa!

The scale, too, overwhelms the mind.

Each new corner, each new bend, is like the last. Always the same forest and the same yellow water. The impression which nature makes on us is immeasurably deepened by the constant monotonous repetition. You shut your eyes for an hour, and when you open them you see exactly what you saw before. The Ogowe is not a river but a river system, three or four branches, each as big as the Rhine, twisting themselves together, and in between are lakes big and little. How the black pilot finds his way through this maze of watercourses is a riddle to me.[9]

Let me quote the impression of two other writers about these African jungles, for it was among these jungles, and partly because of them, that

Schweitzer found the key to all his thinking. Here, then, is Mary Kingsley, a magnificently humorous and intrepid English spinster who journeyed in the 1890s up this same river and wrote a book of unparalleled adventure, comedy, and scientific interest, *Travels in West Africa*.

> Not only does this forest depend on flowers for its illumination, for there are many kinds of trees having their young shoots, crimson, brown-pink, and creamy yellow: added to this there is also the relieving aspect of the prevailing fashion among West African trees, of wearing the trunk white with here and there upon it splashes of pale pink lichen, and vermil-ion-red fungus, which alone is sufficient to prevent the great mass of vegetation from being a monotony in green.
>
> All day long we steam past ever-varying scenes of loveliness whose component parts are ever the same, yet the effect ever different. Doubtless it is wrong to call it a symphony, yet I know no other word to describe the scenery of the Ogowe. It is as full of life and beauty and passion as any symphony Beethoven ever wrote: the parts changing, interweaving, and returning. There are "leitmotifs" here in it, too. See the papyrus ahead; and you know when you get abreast of it you will find the great forest sweeping away in a bay-like curve behind it against the dull gray sky, the splendid columns of its cotton and red woods looking like a facade of some limitless inchoate temple. Then again there is that stretch of sword-grass, looking as if it grew firmly on to the bottom, so steady does it stand; but as the "Mové" goes by, her wash sets it undulating in waves across its broad acres of extent, showing it is only riding at anchor; and you know after a grass patch you will soon see a red dwarf clay cliff, with a village perched on its top, and the inhabitants thereof in their blue and red cloths standing by to shout and wave to the "Mové," or legging it like lamplighters from the back streets to do so, and through all these changing phases, there is always the strain of the vast wild forest, and the swift, deep, silent river.[10]

But it was Winston Churchill, writing in *My African Journey* of the Uganda forests, who expressed something else about them that entered Schweitzer's soul—a sense of awe at the unimaginable energy with which in these jungles life destroys life and then arises again from death.

> One becomes, not without a secret sense of aversion, the spectator of an intense convulsion of life and death. Reproduction and decay are locked struggling in infinite embraces. In this glittering Equatorial slum huge trees jostle one another for room to live: slender growths stretch upwards—as it seems in agony—towards sunlight and life. The soil bursts with irrepressible vegetations. Every victor, trampling on the rotting mould of exterminated antagonists, soars aloft only to encounter another host of aerial rivals, to be burdened with masses of parasitic foliage, smothered in the glorious blos-

soms of creepers laced and bound and interwoven with interminable tangles of vines and trailers. Birds are as bright as butterflies; butterflies are as big as birds.[11]

Scattered throughout this immensity are the people Schweitzer has come here to care for.

> After a long run we stop at a small negro village, where, stacked on the river bank, are several hundred logs of wood, such as bakers often use, and we lie to in order to ship them, as wood is the fuel used for the engines. A plank is put out to the bank; the negroes form line and carry the logs on board. On the deck stands another negro with a paper, and as ten logs have passed, another on the plank calls to him in musical tones, "Put a one." When the hundredth log comes, the call, in the same pleasant tone, is, "Put a cross." The price is from four to five francs a hundred, which is rather high when one considers that the logs are all windfalls and only have to be collected.
>
> The captain abuses the village elder for not having had logs enough ready. The latter excuses himself with pathetic words and gestures. At last they come to an agreement that he shall be paid in spirits instead of cash, because he thinks that the whites get their liquor cheaper than the blacks do, so that he will make a better bargain.
>
> Now the voyage continues. On the banks are the ruins of abandoned huts. "When I came here fifteen years ago," said a trader who stood near me, "these places were all flourishing villages." "And why are they so no longer?" I asked. He shrugged his shoulders and said in a low voice, "L'alcohol [sic]."...
>
> I feel more convinced than ever that this land needs to help it men who will never let themselves be discouraged.[12]

So long as the moon is high they can continue by night while "a heat that is almost unendurable"[13] streams out from the forest wall. They move on till past midnight. This also is strange in the tropics, that because of the heat, night has a different nature. In cooler climates one is glad to be indoors at night; the air grows chilly. But near the equator it is a good time to move, to go out, to be active—so long as one can see and so long as one is not in danger. One can sleep by day when it grows too hot to stir.

So at first light, five o'clock, they are on the way again. And finally, well over a hundred miles from the coast, they see at last the village whose name the world has learned to link with Dr. Schweitzer's—Lambarene, which in the local dialect means "Let us try."

The mission station itself is not in the village but farther upriver still, an hour's journey by canoe. Mr. Christol and Mr. Ellenberger have come to meet the Schweitzers in two canoes rowed by boys from the mission school, singing and racing.

The dugout tree trunks seem very unstable—and are. The river is wide and full of dangerous beasts. The boys decide to race the paddle steamer. The Schweitzers grow very nervous. But after half an hour they manage to relax. The canoes swing into a side stream. In the distance a group of buildings gleams white on the side of a hill—the end of the journey—the terminus of a decision made seventeen years before between waking and getting out of bed—the beginning of a life's work.

1. Kaysersberg, Schweitzer's birthplace.

2. Pastor Louis Schweitzer's
   vicarage in Kaysersberg.

3. Schweitzer's maternal grandfather, the eccentric Pastor Schillinger.

4. Schweitzer's parents.

5. Schweitzer's collar singles him out among his classmates.

6. Schweitzer, age seven.

7. The Schweitzer family. Albert stands in the middle.

8. The Schweitzer family at the Günsbach vicarage. Albert stands at far left.

9. The statue of a black man that
fascinated young Schweitzer.

10. Schweitzer as a student in 1900.

11. Schweitzer as a dandy, age thirty-one.

12. Young Schweitzer and friends on a night out.

13. Hélène Bresslau.

14. Schweitzer in prison
in France, 1918.

15. Friends help pack for the second expedition in 1924.

16. The first house in Africa, at the Andende mission.

17. Building the first hospital at Andende. Schweitzer's first African assistant, Joseph, stands at the foot of the ladder.

18. The chicken-house surgery.

20. View upriver from Andende.

19. The Andende settlement. The mission building and the Schweitzers' house on the top of the hill, the hospital at the foot.

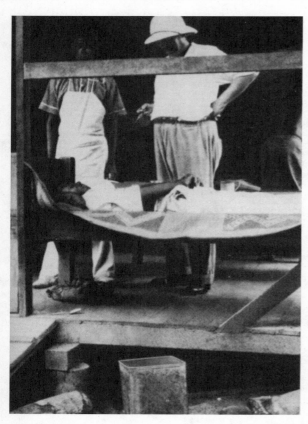

21. A ward in the new hospital.
Marie Woytt-Secretan, Strasbourg

22. Schweitzer treats an ulcer.
Marie Woytt-Secretan, Strasbourg

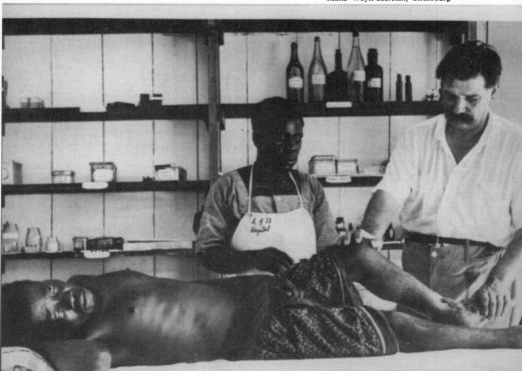

23. Schweitzer the foreman.

Marie Woytt-Secretan, Strasbourg

24. Patients live as they do in their own villages.

Clara Urquhart

25. Left: Schweitzer in his fifties.

Marie Woytt-Secretan, Strasbourg

27. Right: Ground plan of the hospital in 1954.

Marie Woytt-Secretan, Strasbourg

26. Below: In the operating room.

Clara Urquhart

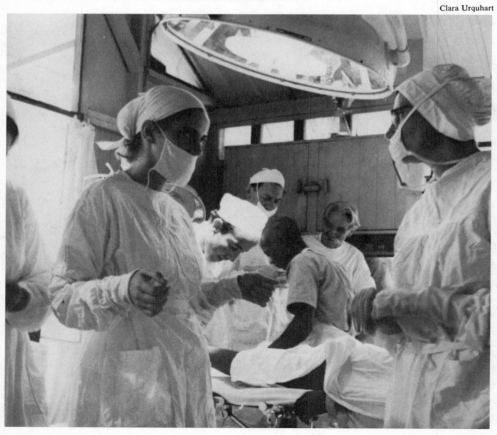

PLAN OF THE HOSPITAL
OF DR. ALBERT SCHWEITZER AT LAMBARÉNÉ

French Equatorial Africa

GABON

**THE HOSPITAL, THE PLANTATION
AND THE LEPER VILLAGE**

The Hospital has beds for 350 patients. The leper village has accomodations for 250 lepers. Two lepers occupy a room and a kitchen. The leper village was completed in June 1955.

The large trees are Kapocks which serve as lightning conductors.

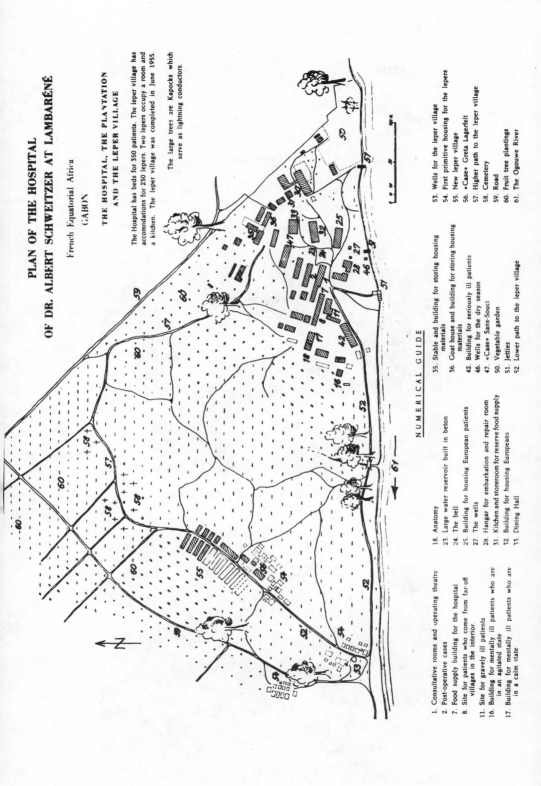

NUMERICAL GUIDE

1. Consultative rooms and operating theatre
2. Post-operative cases
7. Food supply building for the hospital
8. Site for patients who come from far-off villages in the interior.
11. Site for gravely ill patients
16. Building for mentally ill patients who are in an agitated state
17. Building for mentally ill patients who are in a calm state
18. Anatomy
23. Large water reservoir built in beton
24. The bell
25. Building for housing European patients
27. The wells
28. Hangar for embarkation and repair room
31. Kitchen and storeroom for reserve food supply
32. Building for housing Europeans
33. Dining Hall
35. Stable and building for storing housing materials
36. Goat house and building for storing housing materials
42. Building for seriously ill patients
46. Wells for the dry season
47. «Case» Sans-Souci
50. Vegetable garden
51. Jetties
52. Lower path to the leper village
53. Wells for the leper village
54. First primitive housing for the lepers
55. New leper village
56. «Case» Greta Lagerfelt
57. Higher path to the leper village
58. Cemetery
59. Road
60. Fruit tree plantings
61. The Ogowue River

28. The working end of Schweitzer's room.

29. The sleeping end of Schweitzer's room.

30. Schweitzer's piano in the tiny
room adjoining his living room.

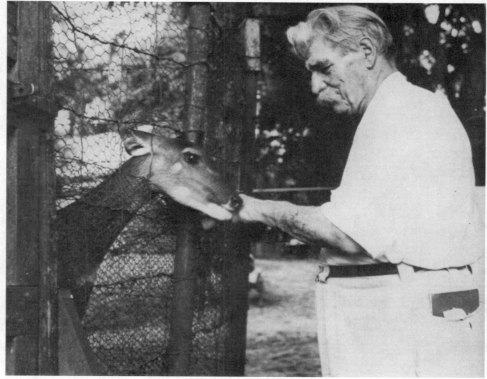

Clara Urquhart

31. One of his pet antelopes uses Schweitzer's arm as a saltlick.

32. A family walk with his daughter Rhena, her husband, and their four children.

Marie Woytt-Secretan, Strasbourg

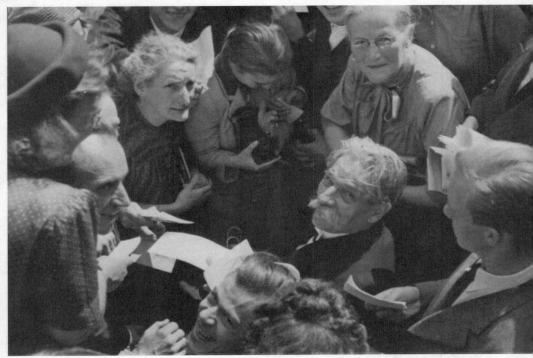

33. Schweitzer besieged by autograph hunters.

34. The graves of Schweitzer and Hélène, Lambarene.

14

Andende

THE FIRST HOSPITAL

1913

THE WOODEN BUNGALOW that the Schweitzers had been allotted stood on rows of iron piles, which lifted it above the threat of the torrents that regularly flowed down the hill after the storms. A veranda ran all around, shaded by the wide roof. In every direction the view was of forest, although the river broke the middle distance on one side, and a range of hills stood blue on the horizon.

A little after six, before they were properly settled in, darkness fell suddenly and the hot, moist night began. Twelve hours of darkness, twelve hours of light—the rhythm of days scarcely varies so near the equator. Schweitzer sat on a packing case and listened, entranced, as the children's evening hymn floated through the night air, competing with the din of the crickets.

An enormous spider crept down the wall. "An exciting hunt," he wrote, "and the creature is done for."[1] More slaughter followed. The house, left empty for a while, had become infested with spiders and flying cockroaches, and Schweitzer, lover of life in all its forms, began his sojourn in Africa with an evening of mass destruction before he and Hélène could get to bed. An unreasoning sentimentality was never part of his philosophy, and the first priority here was to make their new home habitable.

At 6:00 A.M. the sun rose, the bell rang, the children sang their dawn hymn, the day began.

So did the stream of patients. Strict instructions had been issued that the doctor was to be given time to settle in, but they were ignored. There had been white men in Lambarene before with medical skill, and the

239

villagers had learned to trust them. The news of the new doctor's coming had spread wide, and the sick were not going to wait.

Unfortunately, there was nowhere to treat them except in the open air. The local timber traders had been enjoying a good season and had attracted all the available labor at rates the missionaries could not hope to compete with; so the corrugated iron "hospital" Schweitzer had been promised had not materialized. Moreover, the bulk of the equipment and drugs was still a hundred and fifty miles away on the coast, and the black teacher whose services Schweitzer had counted on as interpreter and assistant (he had been in correspondence with and about him for a year) had failed to turn up because he was engaged in a legal dispute in his village. Legal disputes, Schweitzer was to discover, were very popular with the Africans and took automatic precedence over any other project or promise. This, said the missionaries, was the beginning of his education: you could never rely on an African.

So the job started, without accommodation, equipment, or assistance. All Schweitzer had was a small quantity of medicines in his trunk and, of course, the patients.

From east and west they came—the cannibal Fangs from the interior (the French called them Pahouins), from downstream the Galoas and others, survivors of the coastal tribes decimated by the slave trade and by intertribal warfare. Now Schweitzer could begin to study on the spot the results of the white man's interference and greed, the debt he had come to lighten.

There was little here of the noble savage of Colmar. For centuries the slavers had taken the strongest and best of the stock. The tribes nearest the coast had themselves turned slave traders and had raided up the river, draining the villages. Even when the English and French slavers saw the evil of their ways, other nations found it comparatively easy to evade their gunboats, and the trade went on. When, finally, the United States abolished slavery, and the demand fell off to the point where the risks were no longer worth running, the tribes' troubles were not ended. White traders found their way at last through the devious channels of the estuary and up the river—a route that the coastal Africans had so far kept secret—and the porters they brought with them from the Congo carried smallpox and sleeping sickness to districts that had never known them before. Half the population around Lambarene died in the first smallpox epidemic.

Into the lands of these weakened tribes came the warlike Fangs from the highlands farther up the river, and there was almost no resistance to their slaughtering.

At last the white man did something toward undoing the harm he had caused. The killing was stopped, the Fangs held in check. The point where their dominance came to a halt was roughly at Lambarene. Peace of a sort prevailed, but there was no love lost between the tribes.

Then the missionaries came; and the Ogowe, unlucky in climate and in history, was at least lucky in its missionaries. The first who ventured up the river was an American, Dr. Nassau, who came with a group of American Presbyterians to the west coast of Africa and from there explored deep into the interior. Mary Kingsley believed he might have ranked with Livingstone and Burton as an explorer had he troubled to take notes of his expeditions.

Nassau established a mission station at Andende, and for a while the Americans ran it. Then the French authorities decided that all instructions to Africans in their colonies must be given in French, and the Americans had to withdraw, handing the station over to the Paris Mission Society. Schweitzer's judgment in picking on this particular station is confirmed by Mary Kingsley, who had very little use indeed for missionaries in general but who wrote of the Andende group that their "influence upon the natives has been, and is, all for good; and the amount of work they have done, considering the small financial resources behind them, is to a person who has seen other missions most remarkable, and is not open to the criticism lavished upon missions in general. . . . I regard the Mission Evangelique, judging from the results I have seen, as the perfection of what one may call a purely spiritual mission."[2]

Such, briefly, was the history of the hill on which Schweitzer, hemmed in by the immeasurable forest, under the beating sun of what experienced travelers have called the worst climate in the world, set up his open-air clinic for the sad dregs of half a dozen lowland tribes and their cannibal foes.

He knew, of course, what diseases he might expect to encounter, but he had never imagined the sick would be so numerous nor that so many patients would be suffering from so many diseases at the same time. A curious myth has arisen that Schweitzer's hospital dealt solely, or mainly, with leprosy. In fact, practically every disease under the sun was represented, not only the specifically tropical diseases but European ones as well. Cancer and appendicitis seemed not to have reached Africa, but everything else cropped up sooner or later, from pleurisy and whooping-cough to nicotine poisoning. Schweitzer listed the commonest as "skin diseases of various sorts, malaria, sleeping sickness, leprosy, elephantiasis, heart complaints, suppurating injuries to the bones (osteomyelitis) and tropical dysentery."[3] Hernias were also very frequent, often becoming strangulated and causing intense pain followed by death, and, unprintable in those days but widespread, nonetheless, venereal diseases brought by Europeans. "Here among us," said one man, "everybody is ill." "Our country," said one old chief, "devours its own children."[4] Almost worse than the multiplicity of the diseases was their sheer extent. Africa does nothing by halves. An ulcerated leg would be simply one running, stinking open sore. All kinds of creatures burrowing beneath the skin set up irritations all over the body that were scratched until they, too, developed into open wounds. The swellings of elephantiasis can be so huge one can barely believe that people could still carry on something like normal existence with these burdens.

So of the walking wounded who came to Schweitzer's clinic many were in a state that, had they been Europeans, would have had them in hospital long since or, perhaps, on a mortuary slab. The hardihood that kept them alive, active, and even cheerful was Schweitzer's only ally against the ubiquitous onslaught of death.

Among other things that contributed to the general ill health of the area was the poverty of diet. Staple foods that other countries can rely on—corn, rice, and potatoes—produced no usable crops in the intense damp heat of the Ogowe climate. The people lived mainly on manioc (the ground-up root of the cassava tree), on yams, and on bananas. Even these were not indigenous but had been introduced from the West Indies by the Portuguese. In the districts where they had not been established the people lived permanently near famine level, and a great many would eat earth in their starvation. In defiance of the comforting belief that a man who knows the forest need never starve, these jungles produced no nourishment whatever: a man lost there would certainly and swiftly die.

Apart from the physical diseases there were mental and psychological complications to deal with. Taboos, curses, and the dread of witch doctors dominated the patients' minds; no amount of medicine would cure a man who was convinced he had broken a taboo and would die. Poisoning was common; the fear of it commoner still. Terror and superstition were as deadly as bacilli.

These things Schweitzer learned little by little. For this first fortnight he could do little more than ease pain and begin to build up trust. When work was over in the evenings, he and Hélène would walk with the missionaries the length and breadth of the station—650 yards one way, less than 120 the other—cramped quarters for a man who for years had regarded half of Europe as his workshop. Little wonder that he wrote, "One seems to be living in a prison." But tiny and airless though the station was, it was better than the suffocating tracks that led through the tall dense forest to near-by villages. At least on the station there were fruit trees planted by earlier missionaries: mango and paw-paw, citrus fruits, coffee, cocoa, and oil nut palms.

After a fortnight the steamer came upriver again, and Schweitzer's cases arrived in Lambarene village. A fleet of canoes fetched them up to

Andende, a monster dugout taking the crated piano. Dozens of African helpers hauled the equipment up the hill to Schweitzer's bungalow, but where was it to go?

There was one empty building on the station; one of the missionaries, M. Morel, had used it to house his hens. The roof leaked, the main room had no window, and, naturally, it was filthy, but Schweitzer decided to promote it to the rank of hospital. "I got some shelves fixed on the walls, installed an old camp bed and covered the worst of the dirt with whitewash, feeling myself more than fortunate."[5] Here the work went on and, at least, did not have to be interrupted by a rush to the veranda when the rainy season's regular evening storm began. Even so, most of the medicines still had to be kept in the bungalow, for lack of space, and Schweitzer had to cross the yard to prepare each prescription, wasting time and energy when both were in short supply.

Hélène, suffering like her husband from the first impact of the stifling heat, put all her vitality into the work to which she had given her heart and for which she, like him, had prepared so long. The housekeeping alone in these circumstances took a great deal of thought and effort, more particularly because a demarcation of function worthy of the toughest trade union operated among the black servants: each when his job was finished went and lay down, and any task that none of them catered for was left to Hélène. On top of this she sterilized the instruments, prepared patients for surgery, assisted at operations, and kept the bandages and linen washed.

One day an unusual patient arrived. He spoke French well and seemed particularly intelligent. His name was Joseph Azowani, and had the Schweitzer story been fiction, he would have figured among the notable lieutenants of literature. He had trained as a cook, and when Schweitzer, impressed with his ability, asked him to act as interpreter and general medical assistant, he was inclined to refer to the various sections of the patients' anatomy as though they were joints of meat on a butcher's slab. "This woman has a pain in her upper left cutlet, and her loin."[6] A human leg would be a *gigot*, French for a leg of lamb. Or a man would have a wounded fillet.

He was no fool, however. Schweitzer came to rely on him more and more, and as Joseph learned from Schweitzer, so he also taught him, steering him through the tricky thickets of African prejudice and superstition. Unusually for an African of that place and time he had no fear of blood and pus, which normally they would never touch. With a few lapses he was to remain faithful to the hospital, an unmistakable figure with his strutting walk, until the distant end, more than fifty years ahead.

With Hélène and Joseph, Schweitzer now had something of a team, and the work routine was laid down. At 8:30 the patients were waiting in the shade by the fowl house, and the doctor's standing orders were read out in both dialects.

1. Spitting near the doctor's house is strictly forbidden.

2. Those who are waiting must not talk to each other loudly.

3. Patients and their friends must bring with them food enough for one day, as they cannot all be treated early in the day.

4. Any one who spends the night on the station without the doctor's permission will be sent away without any medicine. [It happened not infrequently that patients from a distance crowded into the schoolboys' dormitory, turned them out, and took their places.]

5. All bottles and tin boxes which medicines are given in must be returned.

6. In the middle of the month, when the steamer has gone up the river, none but urgent cases can be seen till the steamer has gone down again, as the doctor is then writing to Europe to get more of his valuable medicines.[7]

The arrangement Schweitzer had made with the Paris Mission was evidently conditional on a trial period, for on June 18, about six weeks after his arrival, we find him writing to Paris to say that he now wants to make the agreement permanent and to stay "as long as God gives me strength and as long as the Mission can accommodate me."[8] He had by this time decided that the place originally suggested by the missionaries for the hospital building was not the most suitable—too small, and too far from his bungalow—and he now asked for permission to start building on the lower part of the hill between the bungalow and the river. This request had to be considered by the conference of missionaries, which was to be held at the end of July, thirty odd miles upriver at Samkita. At four o'clock one morning Schweitzer and two of the missionaries embarked with twelve rowers in their canoe for the long day's paddling against the swift current.

The conference confirmed Schweitzer's guess that the missionaries themselves, unlike the Parisian head office, had better things to worry about than doctrinal niceties. "Necessity," he wrote, "compelled them to put forward Christianity as before all else an ethical religion"[9] (necessity being the simple need to be understood by the Africans). The sermons of the missionaries centered around the great but simple statements of the Sermon on the Mount, which Schweitzer regarded as the heart of the Gospels.

M. Morel, the only survivor of those distant days when I was writing this book, could scarcely remember what all the fuss was about and obviously regarded the head office ban as absurd. "He was a pastor, wasn't he? So he should preach." But Schweitzer adhered strictly to his vows to remain "as dumb as a carp" on theological matters and simply enjoyed "the refreshing atmosphere of love and goodwill."[10]

The missionaries in their turn warmed to Schweitzer, and before long came to trust him so far that they released him from his vow of dumbness and invited him to share in the preaching. So one of the happinesses that he had sacrificed to come to Africa was restored to him—and in good measure, for he found a special delight in speaking of his own simple devotion to Jesus among people whose reactions were not straitjacketed by centuries of dogma.

The conference fully approved Schweitzer's building plans and voted four thousand francs toward the cost. But if the thought even crossed his mind that his troubles were now over, he was rapidly disabused. It was almost impossible, with the timber trade in full swing, to find laborers even to level the site of the first building. And once they were found, it proved quite impossible to make them work. This put the fiery Schillinger temper under heavy strain; and Schweitzer, knowing he would never be able to contain himself at the sight of such frustrating idleness, took precautions against his own wrath. He selected from the jungle sticks of a wood that snapped on the slightest impact so that when his own breaking point was reached he could lash out with one of these and relieve his feelings without doing any harm. In the end the laborers had to be dismissed, eight porters were borrowed from a nearby timber merchant, and Schweitzer himself took a spade and led the work "while the black foreman lay in the shade of a tree and occasionally threw us an encouraging word."[11]

The building itself was to Schweitzer's own specification based on suggestions from missionaries. Already, as early as this, he had worked out the basic elements of the design he was to use for all his hospital buildings, from now until the day he died, a design that owed little to tradition, something to experience, but most of all to applied common sense, but which was still more comfortable than the air-conditioned concrete of a luxury hotel and which was to draw groups of architects to Lambarene from all over the world.

The main principles were two: first, the buildings should run east and west, along the line of the equator, so that the unvarying route of the sun traveled along the length of the roof and never penetrated under the wide overhanging eaves, and second, the long sides of the buildings, instead of having walls and windows, were made entirely of tough mosquito netting, The ends were corrugated iron or, later, hardwood, and ran right to the tops of the rooms. Thus, the sun never entered, but every breath of air circulated in the house almost as freely as outside. And the warm rising air was never trapped in the ceiling but flowed out and added to the circulation. The ceiling itself was made of stretched calico, against mosquitoes. The floor was of beaten earth, wood, or concrete, and the roof was of stitched palm leaves, which were cool but not very durable and constantly needed to be renewed. In later buildings Schweitzer made the roof of corrugated iron, which normally makes for great heat, but which was the only available material of sufficient strength and durability. He also added a wooden ceiling, forming an insulating cavity under the iron roof to absorb the heat. Wooden shutters were provided for the open sides as a protection against storms. Apart from its coolness, this design had an additional advantage—that the whole building was mosquito-free—unlike the average European house in the tropics in which mosquito netting only covers the bed, involving complicated struggles on retiring and a permanent hazard if one has to get up in the night.

Thus, from the start Schweitzer's hospital was in a special sense his own, paid for by money he earned or begged and built to his own requirements—requirements that not only reflected his personality, homespun yet original, but fitted exactly both the needs and the facilities of the upper Ogowe.

The largest rooms in this first "hospital" building were only thirteen feet square: the casualty room and the surgery. The dispensary and the sterilizing room were smaller still. With the aid of the mission's two practical workers, Schweitzer himself lending a hand, it was finished in November, early in Lambarene's "summer," which is the rainy season. After that, work began on a hut for Joseph and a dormitory for the patients, the first of whom constructed their own beds—dried grass hammocks lashed to upright poles driven into the earth floor. About forty patients a day soon needed housing and along with them the friends and relatives who had brought them.

When the dormitory was finished, another hut was started, on the opposite bank, for sleeping-sickness patients. Isolation was a perennial problem, as was sanitation. Increasingly, Schweitzer found his time divided between medical work and building. Without his presence as supervisor and exemplar, no progress was made. The tension of deciding how to divide his time between the two was worse than the actual work. In Strasbourg he had credited himself with sound nerves and a tough temperament. Now he was to find that

I belong unfortunately to the number of those medical men who have not the robust temperament which is desirable in that calling, and so are consumed with unceasing anxiety about the condition of their severe cases and of those on whom they have operated. In vain I have tried to train myself to the equanimity which makes it possible for a doctor, in spite of all his sympathy with the sufferings of his patients to husband, as is desirable, his spiritual and nervous energy.[12] With this continual drive, and the impatience of the waiting sick, I often get so worried and nervous that I hardly know where I am or what I am doing.[13]

As an indication of what this "continual drive" amounted to, Schweitzer and Hélène treated nearly two thousand patients in the first nine months—this in addition to the building work.

Perhaps Schweitzer's anxiety was connected with another discovery, about suffering. In his sermons in Strasbourg he had proclaimed the value of suffering as a searcher of souls, a strengthener of faith. Now he was less sure. "Pain," he wrote "is a more terrible lord of mankind than even death himself." The remark comes in a passage that he wrote in June 1914, a passage that has often been quoted, but generally without the medical detail. Without that detail the passage is all sweetness and light—the guts are gone—which is less than fair to Schweitzer. The full passage reads thus:

[The blacks] also suffer much oftener than white people from strangulated hernia, in which the intestine becomes constricted and blocked, so that it can no longer empty itself. It then becomes enormously inflated by the gases which form, and this causes terrible pain. Then after several days of torture, death takes place, unless the intestine can be got back through the rupture into the abdomen. Our ancestors were well acquainted with this terrible method of dying, but we no longer see it in Europe because every case is operated upon as soon as ever it is recognised. "Let not the sun go down upon your—strangulated hernia," is the maxim continually impressed upon medical students. But in Africa this terrible death is quite common. There are few negroes who have not as boys seen some man rolling in the sand of his hut and howling with agony till death came to release him. So now, the moment a man feels that his rupture is a strangulated one—rupture is far rarer among women—he begs his friends to put him in a canoe and bring him to me.

How can I describe my feelings when a poor fellow is brought to me in this condition? I am the only person within hundreds of miles who can help him. Because I am here and am supplied by my friends with the necessary means, he can be saved, like those who came before him in the same condition and those who will come after him in the same condition, while otherwise he would have fallen a victim to the torture. This does not mean merely that I can save his life. We must all die. But that I can save him from days of torture, that is what I feel as my great and ever new privilege. Pain is a more terrible lord of mankind than even death himself.

So, when the poor, moaning creature comes, I lay my hand on his forehead and say to him: "Don't be afraid! In an hour's time you shall be put to sleep, and when you wake you won't feel any more pain." Very soon he is given an injection of omnipon; the doctor's wife is called to the hospital, and with Joseph's help, makes everything ready for the operation. When that is to begin she administers the anaesthetic and Joseph, in a long pair of rubber gloves, acts as assistant.

The operation is finished, and in the hardly lighted dormitory, I watch for the sick man's awakening. Scarcely has he recovered consciousness when he stares about him and ejaculates again and again: "I've no more pain! I've no more pain!" His hand feels for mine and will not let it go. Then I begin to tell him and the others who are in the room that it is the Lord Jesus who has told the doctor and his wife to come to the Ogowe, and that white people in Europe give them the money to live here and cure the sick negroes. Then I have to answer questions as to who these white people are, where they live, and how they know that the natives suffer so much from sickness. The African sun is shining through the coffee bushes into the dark shed, but we, black and white, sit side by side and feel that we know by experience the meaning of the words: "And all ye are brethren" (Matt.: xxiii.8). Would that my generous friends in Europe could come out here and live through one such hour![14]

Emotion apart, how good a doctor was he? Good intentions are one thing, results another. In fact eight months after arriving he was able to record with some pride, but even greater relief, a success rate for his operations of 100 percent. For a man with no previous experience, limited equipment, minimal assistance, and nobody to turn to for advice or a second opinion this speaks for itself, particularly because Schweitzer never adopted the practice, common in all medical communities and strongly urged by the practical Joseph, of refusing to operate on the more difficult cases for fear the patient should die under the knife and injure the surgeon's reputation.

As trying as anything else was his isolation. He notes briefly how he envies doctors in Europe, who can always ask a colleague for a second opinion. Dr. Weissberg, who thirty years later was to go through much the same experience in the Government hospital on the island of Lambarene (one borrowed lantern between him and his wife, so that if he needed it for an emergency operation, she had to sit in the dark), puts in more strongly: "I always think," he says, "of Charlie Chaplin. The bomb lands, the General hands it to the Colonel, the Colonel to the Adjutant, the Adjutant to the Corporal, the Corporal to Charlie Chaplin. Charlie looks round for somebody else but there's nobody. Out there, you are always Charlie Chaplin. With one hand you hold the patient, with one hand you hold the lantern, with one hand you hold the knife, and you trust to luck." Weissberg became a friend and ally of Schweitzer in the later years and had no doubt that he was a good doctor.

From the first Schweitzer established the principle that those who could do so should offer some token payment for their treatment. The payment might be an egg, a bunch of bananas, or money. It helped the hospital to survive, but also it served as a reminder that there were benefactors in Europe who by some effort and sacrifice had made the treatment possible. Schweitzer's sense of debt, of mutual help and mutual obligation, never let him take any benefits for granted, and he would not let others do so either. This constant awareness of the value of what he was given, particularly the small gifts that cost the giver a good deal, is the clue to some decisions in later years that have puzzled a number of observers.

All the while Schweitzer was learning more about the life around him. Slavery, he discovered, still existed, although not in any organized way. Sometimes it survived because it still suited the slaves themselves, who preferred the total dependence and the lack of responsibility that went with it. Cannibalism was much feared and probably did go on, but so secretly it could never be confirmed. The domination of witch doctors and taboos was all-prevailing, and much of Schweitzer's trouble came from fighting the psychological influence of superstition, particularly when the witch doctors began to resent his influence and to put pressure on his patients. His own name among the Africans was Oganga—Fetishman— the only name they had for a man with the power of curing (and also causing) disease. The fact that Schweitzer, with his anesthetics, could kill a man and then bring him to life again cured, made him a very great fetishman indeed.

The Africa that Schweitzer came to know was, of course, one of the most primitive, undevelopable areas in the whole continent, indeed in the world. To find an equivalent today one would have to search among the tribes of the upper Amazon. The people were wretched—undernourished and without hope of improvement. Much of the slavery was owing to the starvation of the tribes of the interior; they would rather sell a child into servitude downriver, where it had a chance of survival, than watch it starve among the earth eaters.

Schweitzer was especially interested in the relationship between black and white, the effects of the confrontation of the two ways of life. He discovered rapidly that for all their subservience to superstition the Africans had a keen interest in the meaning of life and questions of right and wrong and that for all their indifference to his building program, they were far from completely idle.

Faced, for example, with the need to build a new village (which frequently happened, either because the banana plantation had exhausted the soil and they had to clear a fresh part of the forest or because a feud within a village led to a split), they would work almost without stopping for days on end. Or they would row tirelessly for hours and days to bring a sick friend, black or white, to the hospital. But for anyone with whom they had neither personal nor tribal connections they would not lift a finger. Humanity at large was no concern of theirs, and the notion of universal love was so novel to them as to be more or less meaningless.

For any white man trying to get work done on the Ogowe this presented problems. Schweitzer's own difficulties were echoed by all the traders up and down the river, particularly the timber merchants. Coming from the timber country of Alsace to the timber country of the Gabon, Schweitzer took a great and knowledgeable interest in the problems of the Ogowe's main export—the huge trees of mahogany, okoume, rosewood, coralwood, and ironwood. Profitable though this trade was, it was attended by every kind of complication and hazard. Trees had to be found close to the river, for it was impossible to shift the gigantic trunks more than a few yards from their felling point. Once safely in the water and floated down to the estuary they might be caught by an offshore wind and driven irretrievably out to sea. And the problems created by nature were compounded by the attitude of the Africans, who would work just so long as they needed money for a specific purpose, such as buying a wife or a pair of shoes, and no longer, and if a fiesta called, they would let pass the few precious days in the year when the river was high enough to float trunks lying some distance from the river bank and leave timber worth hundreds and thousands of pounds to rot into uselessness before the next year's floods.

In July 1914 Schweitzer himself fell ill with an abscess that needed attention. He went with Hélène to Cape Lopez to see the military doctor there, and while convalescing, he wrote an essay on the timber trade and also began to set out his thoughts on what he called "Social Problems in the Forest." The seventeen pages in which he wrote these thoughts down, while a slow trading steamer took the couple back to Lambarene, still stand up as a concise and acute analysis of the colonial situation. Schweitzer saw the problem, he foresaw the future, he faced the tragedy. The roots of all the subsequent conflicts between black and white are here laid bare.

First, he inquired why it was that the African would not work when he was required by the white men to work and answered that it was not because he was lazy but because he was a free man. Within his village he could find all that he actually required for existence. He did not need money. He only went out to earn it when he or his wife wanted some luxury such as sugar, tobacco, rum, dress material, or a pair of boots. Once he had what he wanted, why go on working? He was still the master, not the servant, of his economy.

Such casual, unpredictable labor was useless to the white man, enslaved by the demands of productivity. Trade and state, therefore, combined to create need in the African, so as to force him into permanent work. The state imposed taxes (for the building of schools, hospitals, and roads, which, indeed, were often very needful), and trade seduced him with desirable objects such as sewing machines, safety razors, collars and ties, corsets, open-work stockings, concertinas, and music boxes.

Still, however, the African would not work steadily. His freedom was too deeply ingrained. And here the real tragedy began. "The child of nature becomes a steady worker only so far as he ceases to be free and becomes unfree,"[15] so the white man learns never to let him work near his village, for there he is his own man, and never to pay him the whole of his wages, for then he would be content and stop working. Half his money is put by till the end of the year.

What happens?

> Many get homesick. Others cannot put up with the strange diet, for as no fresh provisions are to be had, they must as a rule live chiefly on rice. Most of them fall victims to the taste for rum, and ulcers and diseases spread rapidly among them, living, as they do, a kind of barrack life in overcrowded huts. In spite of all precautions they mostly get through their pay as soon as the contract time is up, and return home as poor as they went away.
>
> The negro is worth something only so long as he is in his village and under the moral control of intercourse with his family and other relatives; away from these surroundings he easily goes to the bad, both morally and physically. Colonies of negro labourers away from their families are, in fact, centres of demoralisation, and yet such colonies are required for trade and for the cultivation of the soil, both of which would be impossible without them.
>
> The tragic element in this question is that the interests of civilisation and of colonisation do not coincide, but are largely antagonistic to each other. The former would he promoted best by the natives being left in their villages and there trained to various industries, to lay out plantations, to grow a little coffee or cocoa for themselves or even for sale, to build themselves houses of timber or brick instead of huts of bamboo, and so to live a steady and worthy life. Colonisation, however, demands that as much of the population as possible shall be made available in every possible way for utilising to the utmost the natural wealth of the country. Its watchword is "production," so that the capital invested in the colonies may pay its interest, and that the motherland may get her needs supplied through her connection with them. For the unsuspected incompatibilities which show themselves here, no individual is responsible; they arise out of the circumstances themselves.[16]

Some colonial states enforced compulsory labor. This, too, tended to drag men away from their village roots. In some districts large commercial companies with concessions wielded more power than the state itself, making all the local Africans dependent on them. The power might be used with wisdom and discretion, but there was no guarantee of this, and in any case the principle was wrong.

Because the white man's influence falls heaviest on villages near the white man's towns, those villages vanish, only to reappear far away in the jungle. A no-man's-land grows up between white and black. Enforcement becomes more difficult and more severe. The breaking up of villages goes on in an increasing spiral.

Schweitzer goes on to look at the problem of "the educated native":

> Both Government and trade require natives with extensive knowledge whom they can employ in administration and in the stores. The schools, therefore, must set their aims higher than is natural, and produce people who understand complicated figures and can write the white man's language perfectly. Many a native has such ability that the results of this attempt are, so far as intellectual knowledge goes, astounding.
>
> But what becomes of these people? They have been uprooted from their villages, just like those who go off to work for strangers. They live at the store, continually exposed to the dangers which haunt every native so closely, the temptations to defraud and to drink. They earn good wages, indeed, but as they have to buy all their necessities at high prices, and are a prey to the black man's innate love of spending, they often find themselves in financial difficulties and even in want. They do not now belong to the ordinary negroes, nor do they belong to the whites either; they are a tertium quid between the two.[17]

Civilization for the African, says Schweitzer, should not start with book learning, but with industry and agriculture, "through which alone can be secured the economic conditions of higher civilization."[18] This is a prophetic comment, belatedly being put into practice in a number of African countries today. The timber trade, sporadically attracting every able-bodied male, made any sort of regular employment impossible. And Schweitzer complains of the way in which cheap European goods are destroying the African's craft of making household utensils out of wood and bark fiber. He speaks of the dilemma of governments who, even if they wish to abolish the import of cheap liquor, never do so because they have no other equally profitable revenues to replace the tax on them.

On the issue of polygamy Schweitzer sees clearly that it suits the local conditions far better than monogamy. (He used to say that the emphasis on monogamy arose when a society became settled and the men began to value the permanence of their possessions—their land, their houses, their wives. A nomadic culture had different values.) Polygamy safeguards the children in a society where the only milk available is mother's milk and the mother must suckle her child for a long time. While she does so, other wives can solace the father, leaving her to give her time to the child. Polygamy ensures that every woman can be married in a society that has no place for the unmarried woman. Polygamy protects the widows and orphans, who can simply join another family. In short, to abolish it on doctrinaire grounds could only cause the greatest confusion and hardship. (My own aunt once met Schweitzer on a lecture tour in Switzerland. When asked what he would speak about, he said that to such a respectable bourgeois community he would like to commend the benefits of polygamy.)

Wife purchase, too, seemed to work well enough, and Schweitzer concluded that "we should accept, but try to improve and refine, the rights and customs which we find in existence, and make no alterations which are not absolutely necessary."[19] He believed that changes would come of their own accord, if and when they were needed.

One should not pretend that Schweitzer's opinions on African marriage customs were particularly advanced or daring. Most observers who went there from Europe with an open mind came to the same conclusions, and Schweitzer himself wrote that his views have been reached "after conversation with all the best and most experienced of the white men in this district." The cry to change the ways of the villagers came only from the more rigid type of missionary and the more obtuse and unimaginative sort of visitor—the same sort who was later to be horrified at the way Schweitzer ran his hospital.

Most liberals of today would probably agree with Schweitzer's analysis of the situation so far. The white man, committed to productivity, encounters the unconcern of the black man, free from such commitment. Slavery is no longer permissible, so the free black man must be bound by other means. New needs must be created in him, which he can only satisfy by offering the white man his labor. And the white man ensures the fulfilment of the contract by separating him from the source of his freedom, his village. The dreadful labor camps that recently disfigured South Africa were the logical conclusion of the process, the new slavery incarnate, as evil as the old with a touch of hypocrisy added.

The only point at which Schweitzer and the modern liberal might part company is that Schweitzer also understands and sympathizes with the white man, whose job depends on the willingness of black laborers to do what they have promised and who finds that, for his purposes, they are totally unreliable.

Which brings us to the vexed question of paternalism—the word that has been thrown at Schweitzer a great many times—as at many other whites of his generation. Like all such emotive and generalizing words it is best abandoned as soon as mentioned, but it must be mentioned before it can be abandoned. What matters is not the word, with all the taking up of attitudes and judgments that it presupposes, but the truth. Was Schweitzer in some way patronizing and "superior"? The key passage is to be found in the essay on social problems in the forest, and it runs thus:

A word in conclusion about the relations between the whites and the blacks. What must be the general character of the intercourse between them? Am I to treat the black man as my equal or as my inferior? I must show him that I can respect the dignity of human personality in every one, and this attitude in me he must be able to see for himself; but the essential thing is that there shall be a real feeling of brotherliness. How far this is to find complete expression in the sayings and doings of daily life must be settled by circumstances. The negro is a child, and with children nothing can be done without the use of authority. We must, therefore, so arrange the circumstances of daily life that my natural authority can find expression. With regard to the negroes, then, I have coined the formula: "I am your brother, it is true, but your elder brother."[20]

So Schweitzer takes for granted what the modern African and the modern liberal white man would at least question if he did not hotly dispute: that the African—that is, the primitive Ogowe African whom he knew eighty-five years ago—is a child, and that the white man must exercise his natural authority over him.

He quotes two stories to illustrate what happens when this natural authority breaks down. One concerns a missionary who some years before had left the mission staff "to live among the negroes as their brother absolutely. From that day," says Schweitzer, "his life became a misery. With his abandonment of the social interval between white and black he lost all his influence; his word was no longer taken as the 'white man's word,' but he had to argue every point with them as if he were merely their equal."[21]

From this and from the other story, about a black cook who took advantage of his employer's easy ways to grow overfamiliar, it is evident that at this time Schweitzer, however enlightened about the causes of the situation, could not envisage anything so revolutionary as a white man genuinely abandoning his superior position and putting himself on a level with the blacks as a partner.

The missionary was certainly unwise to want to live as the brother of the blacks if he was unprepared for the implications. He wished to be their brother yet not their equal, and Schweitzer seems not to have noticed the inconsistency. The cook, too, was expected to understand that white men draw the line on social freedom at a certain point and to know where the line is and not overstep it. The moral that Schweitzer seems to have drawn from such tales, as did almost everyone else of his generation, was that social freedom must not be allowed to go too far, for it opens the floodgates to total equality, which is unthinkable.

In Schweitzer's particular situation, of course, total equality was indeed unthinkable. He was not a missionary with a spiritual task only: he was the controller of a jungle clinic with lives at stake, and anywhere in the world a man in such a position must have authority or his work is destroyed. He was undoubtedly right in thinking that on the Ogowe the only way to maintain such authority was by preserving a distance between himself and the tribesmen, for the Africans were simply not accustomed to thinking on the lines necessary for self-discipline and voluntary cooperation. Authority had to be imposed. And we shall see in a moment how for all that authority, their lack of discipline regularly endangered the hospital. But there was another reason why Schweitzer needed authority in Africa, and that was because he needed it everywhere. It was in his schoolmasterish nature. His paternalism, if we must use the word, was not toward the blacks only but toward everyone. He had come to Africa to avoid theorizing argument and to put his feelings into action, and he was not likely, once there, to suffer interminable palavers with his staff and his patients, whether black or white. Without authority he could neither have been what he was nor done what he came to do.

But he did not believe that authority was something automatically conferred by black upon white.

A white man can only have real authority if the native respects him. No one must imagine that the child of nature looks up to us merely because we know more, or can do more than he can. This superiority is so obvious to him that it ceases to be taken into account. It is by no means the case that the white man is to the negro an imposing person because he possesses railways and steamers, can fly in the air, or travel under water. "White people are clever and can do anything they want to," says Joseph. The negro is not in a position to estimate what these technical conquests of nature mean as proofs of mental and spiritual superiority, but on one point he has an unerring intuition, and that is on the question whether any particular white man is a real, moral personality or not. If the native feels that he is, moral authority is possible; if not, it is simply impossible to create it. The child of nature, not having been artificialized and spoilt as we have been, has only elementary standards of judgment, and he measures us by the most elementary of them all, the moral standard. Where he finds goodness, justice and genuineness of character, real worth and dignity, that is, behind the external dignity given by social circumstances, he bows and acknowledges his master; where he does not find them he remains really defiant in spite of all appearance of submission, and says to himself: "This white is no more of a man than I am, for he is not a better one than I am."[22]

Schweitzer, too, measured men by the moral standard, the most elementary of them all. For all the differences in their social backgrounds Schweitzer found more spiritual affinity with the Ogowe African than with the industrial European. Authority then, for Schweitzer, must be fairly won. It is not a guaranteed attribute of Europeans, a side-effect of whiteness. And he himself was not in Africa looking for a respect he had failed to win in his own country. He had held authority—intellectual, spiritual, and physical—over students, musicians, theologians, philosophers, and women in the capitals of Europe. He was not born with it— he had achieved it. Schweitzer had the right to speak of authority in Lambarene as elsewhere.

Having put the case as fairly as he can for the Africans, Schweitzer now has something to add about the white colonists.

I am not thinking merely of the fact that many unsuitable and not a few quite unworthy men go out into the colonies of all nations. I wish to emphasise a further fact that even the morally best and the idealists find it difficult out here to be what they wish to be. We all get exhausted in the terrible contest between the European worker who bears the responsibility and is always in a hurry, and the child of nature who does not know what responsibility is and is never in a hurry. The Government official has to record at the end of the year so much work done by the natives in building and road maintenance, in service as carrier or boatman, and so much money paid in taxes; the trader and the planter are expected by their companies to provide so much profit for the capital invested in the enterprise. But in all this they are forever dependent on men who cannot share the responsibility that weighs on them, who only give just so much return of labour as the others can force out of them, and who, if there is the slightest failure in superintendence, do exactly as they like without any regard for the loss that may be caused to their employers. In this daily and hourly contest with the child of nature every white man is continually in danger of gradual moral ruin.

The greater the responsibility that rests on a white man, the greater the danger of his becoming hard towards the natives. We on a mission staff are too easily inclined to become self-righteous with regard to the other whites. We have not got to obtain such and such results from the natives by the end of the year, as officials and traders have, and therefore this exhausting contest is not so hard a one for us as for them. I no longer venture to judge my fellows after learning something of the soul of the white man who is in business from those who lay as patients under my roof, and whose talk has led me to suspect that those who now speak savagely about the natives may have come out to Africa full of idealism, but in the daily contest have become weary and hopeless, losing little by little what they once possessed of spirituality.

That it is so hard to keep oneself really humane, and so to be a standard bearer of civilisation, that is the tragic element in the problem of the relations between white and coloured men in Equatorial Africa.[23]

So the blame he laid on the whites from his pulpit in Strasbourg was not so easy to apportion on the spot. Two ways of life come face to face, and there is a good chance that they will destroy one other. Again South Africa shows the consequences writ large. The struggle there crushed the blacks physically. Morally, it rotted the whites. The blame is theirs, for they were in control. But beyond the blame is the tragedy.

Remembering that Schweitzer had deliberately chosen to work among some of the most primitive, remote, and socially ruined tribes in the world, it is important to hold a clear picture in our minds of what exactly the difficulties were that the traders faced, that made Schweitzer call the Ogowe Africans "children," and that drove him to an unceasing use of his rational authoritarianism. For he was, indeed, driven to it. He had not expected or wished to have to waste time imposing his will. "When, before coming to Africa, I heard missionaries and traders say again and again that one must be very careful out here to maintain this authoritative position of the white man, it seemed to me to be a hard and unnatural position to take up, as it does to every one in Europe who reads or hears the same."[24]

But, in fact, he found he had to tell the Africans the same things over and over again—not because he was white and they were black, not for the pleasure of dominating them, but simply, for example, to make sure that they came at the right time for their injections and remembered to take their medicine. He found he had to lock everything up, to become a "walking bunch of keys,"[25] not for the preservation of private property, for he never locked up his own belongings, and certainly not to save time and effort, simply because everything left unlocked was liable to "take a walk," and once gone could not be replaced for months, if at all. Medicines, instruments, equipment were not his to take risks with. They had been bought from the gifts of dozens of benefactors, many of them far from wealthy, and he owed it to them (and to the patients) not to lose them.

He found that nothing could safely be left to Africans to do by themselves; all had to be supervised and checked.

Not long ago the termites, or white ants, got into a box which stood on our veranda. I emptied the box and broke it up, and gave the pieces to the negro who had been helping me. "Look," I said to him, "the ants have got into it; you mustn't put the wood with the rest of the firewood or the ants will get into the framework of the hospital building. Go down to the river and throw it into the water. Do you understand?"

"Yes, yes, you need not worry." It was late in the day and, being too tired to go down the hill again, I was inclined to break my general rule and trust a black—one who was in fact on the whole intelligent and handy. But about ten o'clock I felt so uneasy that I took the lantern and went down to the hospital. There was the wood with the ants in it lying with the rest of the firewood. To save himself the trouble of going the twenty yards down to the river, the negro had endangered all my buildings![26]

It is fair to ask the critic, "What would *you* have done—what would you have thought—given the remoteness, the responsibility, the lack of assistance, the climate, the weariness, the many better things one might wish to do?" In a European the action would have amounted to criminal negligence or sheer idiocy. By a kind of perversity it is now often suggested that it would have been kinder always to judge Africans by European standards, that not to do so was deplorably patronizing, was "paternalistic." In Schweitzer's context simply to state that view is to show how nonsensical it would have been, how fatal would have been the results.

Finally, we must remember that "child" in Schweitzer's vocabulary was by no means a derogatory word. Schweitzer's hero had told his listeners: "Except ye become as little children ye shall in no wise enter the Kingdom of Heaven." It was not simply a question of being fond of children. Most people are fond of children. For Schweitzer, as for Jesus, the child had understandings that the adult had lost. Likewise the African.

They both had the gift of simple, direct response to life, an appreciation of what really matters. Martha, in the Gospels, was irritated with her sister Mary for much the same reason as the whites were irritated with the blacks. Mary sat about talking and listening instead of helping with the housework. Jesus sided with Mary. Schweitzer in his childhood had been a Mary, dreaming when they wanted him to do something useful. Now perforce he was a Martha and was to remain one for the rest of his life. But at least part of him remained the dreamer, and he had every sympathy, even while he tongue-lashed them into activity, with those who would rather have sat and let life flow around and into them.

For his own relaxation and refreshment he had always in the past relied upon nature and music. Here nature was all around him, to an oppressive degree. As for music, although he had gone to great trouble to bring his organ-pedaled piano all the way to the equator, he made little use of it at first. It reminded him too vividly of the delights he had given up and would never, he believed, taste again. "The renunciation," he thought, "would be easier if I allowed fingers and feet to get rusty with disuse."[27]

But there were three volumes left uncompleted of the Bach edition he had undertaken with Widor. In his spare time he put in some work on these; and one evening, playing a fugue "in melancholy mood" he was struck by the thought that here in Africa, with no concerts to perform for, he could work gradually, at his own speed, on deepening his understanding of the music. He could perfect his technique and study individual works in the greatest detail, eventually learning them by heart. So once again, as when he was a student, he began to use music as a retreat from stress and found new depths in Bach as he played into the hush of the jungle night.

15

War

1914–1915

TWO YEARS WAS GENERALLY REGARDED as the longest a white man should stay in that climate before coming back to Europe to regain energy. According to Dr. Weissberg, the white mortality in the Gabon in 1913 was 20 percent per year. According to Mary Kingsley, the strong, robust, full-blooded type was the most likely to succumb. After a year and a quarter Schweitzer was exceedingly tired.

We have to remember that he was already suffering from periods of total exhaustion before he went out to Africa, and in one of his long and very conscientious reports to the committee he writes of the extra fatigue of a night journey upriver on the steamer to treat a patient at another station.

By this time he was already adding to the plantation of fruit trees and had started a garden. During the dry season every growing thing had to be watered daily. He used the families of the patients for this chore, giving to each one a cup of rice if they would carry a jar of water to the garden. Tomatoes, radishes, and beans were on the way, and trees were already bearing oranges and mandarins. At least in that climate nature helps those who help themselves, and crops, once planted and watered, are swift and heavy. Pineapples were a weed.

The Schweitzers began to plan their first trip home. After one more rainy season they would take a break in the spring of 1915.

It was not to be. Europe went to war. On August 5, 1914, in the evening, the Schweitzers were informed that, as German citizens, they were to regard themselves prisoners of war.

He had seen it coming, of course. And its consequences. He had the gold, which he had brought instead of paper money. But it was of little use because he was now placed under house arrest and forbidden to practice as a doctor. A black officer and four men were posted outside the bungalow to see that he and Hélène spoke to nobody, white or black.

The guards' task was a thankless one. The local Africans, who had no idea what the war was about, were only aware that suddenly they could get no treatment and that some of their fellow blacks were ordering the doctor about. The guards became very unpopular.

For Schweitzer life had suddenly come to an abrupt halt. For the first time for perhaps thirty years, instead of too much he had nothing whatever to do, except think. And the thoughts were not happy. His own family and friends, and Hélène's, were in the direct line of fire between the two main combatants, as Alsatians always were. They themselves were unlikely to hear from their families because communications now ceased between German-occupied Alsace and French-occupied Gabon.

Had Schweitzer's temperament been other than it was, he might well have sunk into a despairing lethargy. Instead he instantly made the best of the situation and almost with relief went back to his writing. The book on St. Paul was so nearly finished that it was the obvious first task.

When he started to think about it, however, Schweitzer found something else in the forefront of his mind. Long ago in Berlin he had sat in the corner of the room, a shy student, while the great brains of the university exchanged ideas, and had heard someone say: "We are nothing but *epigoni*." He had planned a book then, but no one had been interested in his thoughts on the decay of civilization, and the whole idea had been overwhelmed by all that had happened since. Now it was clear that he had been right in his pessimism about the way Europe was going, and the teacher in him was eager to analyze the reasons why. By the second morning of his internment he was at work on his philosophy of civilization.

At first the writing was only for his own satisfaction. It was his way of combating the stress of the news. Whether it would ever reach publication he doubted, for the authorities might not allow him to keep the manuscript. He was not even sure that he would ever see Europe again. He worked with a sense of detachment born of complete isolation, cut off, as he was, not only from his home, his work, and his friends but also from his future.

Little by little the isolation eased. The idiocy of having a doctor idle while sick people went untended aroused such protests that the local district commandant began, before long, to send sufferers to Schweitzer with special notes to the guards to let them pass—isolated cases at first, then in increasing numbers. Meanwhile, his friends in Paris—Widor in particular, but also the influential friends of Uncle Auguste—had been active on his behalf, and at the end of November the internment order was lifted and he was free to go on practicing medicine as before. What he could not do, however, was return home. So the two-year stretch in the tropics was extended indefinitely.

Now he made time in his schedule to go on with the philosophy of civilization. In his imagination he was with the soldiers in the trenches and with his family at home. This imagination was the stimulus for the book. Such a horror must be traced to its root causes.

Schweitzer knew as much as or more than most people about the immediate political events leading up to the war. He had always been politically aware, as his godfather had discovered when he was only eleven. We have seen the argument he had with Hélène about the rights and wrongs of prewar developments, and he is reported to have said sharply to her, when she complained one day about the postal services in Alsace, "What do you expect? You [the Germans] are so busy building warships you have no time to organize the mail."

But the book was not about this kind of cause of war at all. The specific incidents were irrelevant for him. The search was not a survey or conglomeration of facts. (Spengler, who was also trying to account for the breakdown of European civilization, approached it that way, and his two massive, incredibly knowledgeable, totally unreadable volumes were for a while very popular among the intelligentsia after the war.)

Schweitzer was interested in the attitudes behind the incidents, the spirit that allowed the incidents to happen and that, if these incidents had not happened, would have allowed others, with the same result. The precise tracing of events was not "elemental" enough for him. He believed, after all, that he had, at the start of the century, discerned the trend long before the events occurred.

So the book was to be about what people expected of civilization and what they were prepared to give to it. When it finally achieved publication, the opening chapter was entitled "How Philosophy Is Responsible for the Collapse of Civilisation," and the opening words announced the theme: "We are living today under the sign of the collapse of civilisation. The situation has not been produced by the war: the latter is only a manifestation of it. The spiritual atmosphere has solidified into actual facts, which again react on it with disastrous results in every respect."[1]

After several months of isolation, an occasional letter began to arrive via neutral Switzerland. Hélène's father, wealthier and with better contacts than Schweitzer's parents, was more successful in getting messages and letters through and wrote asking if the couple would like pressure exerted to get their internment transferred to somewhere in Europe. It would seem that they replied in the negative; at least where they were they could go on working.

Schweitzer was a less dutiful correspondent than his wife. Hélène wrote conscientiously to her parents, and the Bresslaus passed on messages to the Schweitzers and transmitted their replies.

Pastor Schweitzer, meanwhile, had begun keeping a diary of these wartime days to show his son when he should return. It is one of the most valuable and revealing documents we have of this relationship and of the whole gentle, unremarkable atmosphere of the Schweitzers' family life.

By the summer of 1915 Günsbach was really in the front line. The Germans had dug themselves defensive positions on the hills on either side, dominating the valley. The French were challenging the heights. The villages were all taken over by the military, and not only the vicarage but even the church was occupied; Louis Schweitzer could no longer hold services, and his house was no longer his own. All he could do was minister to his parishioners and, when it was necessary, bury the dead— of both sides—and write to the next of kin. In his diary he wrote of parish news and of the war almost in the same sentence. He had one consolation: the local commandant was billeted in his house, which meant he could usually arrange some sort of military transport for his visitors. This was just as well, for the passenger trains no longer ran up the valley from Colmar, and even army trains stopped at Hammerschmeide (now La Forge), three or four miles down the valley. After that it was horse-drawn transport or a long walk.

Stray bullets and shells made it dangerous to move about in the valley by day, and the villagers grew accustomed to doing much of their work by night. The cellars of the vicarage proved invaluable as protection. Mrs. Schweitzer tended to be very nervous, understandably, because one day in August a mortar shell came through the roof and landed on the dining-room table. After this she went to Colmar for a while to stay with Louise and her family, but after a month or two she rejoined her husband in Günsbach.

In Lambarene Schweitzer was suffering from nothing worse than tiredness and a heavy cold caught after a sudden drop in temperature. All day he treated the physical ailments of his patients; by night he went on with the diagnosis of Europe's disease.

Europe, he believed, had gone to war because Europeans had lost touch with their own ideals. He blamed Nietzsche as much as anyone. Philosophy might seem remote from international politics, but he had himself experienced the way in which Nietzsche's influence had seeped down from the academic heights and had permeated politics, business, and everyday life, not in its pure form but distorted and oversimplified. Europe had taken happily to the idea that the victory of the strong man over the weak led toward the perfection of the species.

From Hegel people had acquired a general feeling that progress inevitably developed out of conflict and that mankind automatically advanced by the sheer processes of history. Scientific and material improvements seemed to confirm this. So if history itself provided the world with a sort of automatic pilot, who needed compasses? The search of the eighteenth-century philosophers for some kind of rational pattern in nature by which men should set their sights had been abandoned as both hopeless and unnecessary.

So the war into which Europe had stumbled was marked by two new and hideous features: the absence of ideals and the presence of machine guns. Schweitzer was going to tell the world why it had happened.

The book as we have it, *The Decay and Restoration of Civilisation,* is the result of two separate drafts, one written after the war. But the lines on which he was thinking out there in the jungle are clear enough; and they are startlingly modern. Today we are still complaining that we are drilled and dominated by large impersonal organizations. We are aware that great cities cut us off from the natural life of the country. We know that long hours of meaningless factory work cannot be dignified by the name of honest labor, and that after a day in the office or on a production line the mind is in need of vacuous entertainment rather than meaningful recreation. We know that we are stunted by specialization, that few people have the satisfaction of mastering a complete job, that the word "creative" has become so debauched that it is now applied without a smile to advertising copywriters. And we know that we suffer from having too many acquaintances and associates and too few friends. All these are concomitants of the highly organized industrial society devoted mainly to production and the growth of the gross national product.

But we feel that the period before 1914 was part of the golden age before any of this had begun to happen. The postwar generation is generally held responsible for the beginning of the end of the old values. Not so, according to Schweitzer. He had felt it in the air years before and had seen or foreseen all these developments.

In the book he pinned them down with his usual accuracy and economy. At this stage of the writing of the book Schweitzer was still only concerned with the causes and the symptoms of Europe's disease. He had reached the conclusion that a specific mental conflict had crippled the image that Europeans had traditionally held of the world they lived in. Briefly, the argument runs thus: Europeans in general believe that life is worth living. They have, that is to say, a positive approach to life on this earth (unlike, for example, Buddhists, who believe that the way to perfect oneself is to detach oneself as far as possible from life because all worldly satisfaction is illusory). The endeavor of European philosophers has been to prove that this positive approach to life is justified by the fact that the universe itself is beneficent—that goodness, or love, is part of the nature of things. Many splendid theories have been evolved to demonstrate the excellence of the universe, and they all had two things in common: that their ideals were admirable and that they had the practical advantage of confirming people in general in their trust in divine providence (or whatever it might be called).

Unfortunately, each theory in turn (Kant's included) proved vulnerable to criticism. And when finally in the nineteenth century the study of natural science began to be taken seriously and people began to look for truth not in academic theories but in physical observation and experiments, it soon became clear that there is really nothing at all in nature that one can truly call loving. Nature is an indifferent force, creating and destroying impartially. For every sign of kindliness there is an opposing cruelty. The idealistic pictures drawn by philosophers, clerics, and moralists were simply wish-fulfilling figments of the imagination.

Because European morality had always depended on this supposed universal pattern (man's mind being seen in some way as the mirror of the universal mind), the shattering of the pattern left morality without any basis. It was now felt that because nature moved blindly ("evolution" was the new watchword), man could afford to do the same and evolution would take care of the results. Civilization abandoned all the ideals that had hitherto sustained it and believed it could do without them. Philosophy ceased to be the study of ethics and human improvement and became a matter of observation and description, without moral content. "Value judgment" became a dirty phrase. In short, because man could find nothing in nature on which to peg his ideals, he was free (this was never quite stated but was implied) to become as amoral as nature.

Such, put crudely, was Schweitzer's "apparently abstract, yet absolutely practical thinking about the connection between civilisation and world-view." But for him to leave anything at a negative stage was quite against his nature. "Everything," Erica Anderson remembers him saying, "should end in a major key." Suddenly, one day in the summer of 1915, it came to him that criticism was not enough. "I awoke," he wrote, "from a sort of stupor."[2]

And the search began for the antidote to Europe's sickness. Somewhere, Schweitzer felt, some basic principle of civilization had been missed, or mislaid—a principle that would underwrite the validity of human ideals, proving that love was not simply a sentimental invention or a convenient way of holding society together. He could never return to the old-fashioned view that the universe itself was kindly—more particularly since he had been exposed to nature's blind and destructive force on the Ogowe. But what other connection could there be between ethics and the universe at large? This now became the great question, hammering at him day in, day out, while he worked. It was now not only a matter of rescuing civilization; in his own person he now faced the ultimate question: Have we any sort of guarantee that it matters in the least whether we behave well or badly? Was his devotion to other human beings no more than a romantic whim? If so, not only was civilization doomed but so in a way was he.

Being Schweitzer, he was never in any danger of being content with any political or economic formula. The suggestion that a redistribution of wealth, however desirable, would guarantee civilized behavior was a nonsequitur of absurd proportions. The question went much, much farther back. What did a human being really need? What indeed *was* a human being? What was the indestructible, rock-bottom fact about humanity, from which everything began?

What we want badly enough we generally find. It could be claimed that what happened next to Schweitzer was simply the result of his great need. It could also be said that intuition strikes truest where the need is greatest. This is for the reader to decide.

The actual event I shall leave to Schweitzer's own words. I hope the reader will not blame Schweitzer for the fact that some sentences sound so clumsy in English. Translation of this kind of passage, where some words have no English equivalent, is an impossible task. I only ask the reader to try to penetrate to the sense, noting merely that the phrase "world-and-life-affirmation" *(Welt- und Lebensbejahung)*, so impossibly cumbersome in English, is Schweitzer's phrase for the European attitude we have noted—that life is valuable and the universe is beneficent and that the two things are connected.

So it was necessary [he wrote] to undertake to grasp as a necessity of thought by fresh, simple and sincere thinking the truth which had hitherto been only suspected and believed in, although so often proclaimed as proved.

In undertaking this I seemed to myself to be like a man who has to build a new and better boat to replace a rotten one in which he can no longer venture to trust himself to the sea, and yet does not know how to begin.

For months on end I lived in a continual state of mental excitement. Without the least success I let my thoughts be concentrated, even all through my daily work at the hospital, on the real nature of the world-and-life-affirmation and of ethics, and on the question of what they have in common. I was wandering about in a thicket in which no path was to be found. I was leaning with all my might against an iron door which would not yield.

All that I had learnt from philosophy about ethics left me in the lurch. The conceptions of the Good which it had offered were all so lifeless, so unelemental, so narrow, and so destitute of content that it was quite impossible to bring them into union with the world-and-life-affirmation. Moreover philosophy could be said never to have concerned itself with the problem of the connection between civilisation and world-view. The modern world-and-life-affirmation had become to it such a matter of course that it had felt no need for coming to clear ideas about it.

To my surprise I had also to establish the fact that the central province of philosophy, into which meditation about civilisation and world-view had led me, was practically unexplored land. Now from this point, now from that, I tried to penetrate to its interior, but again and again I had to give up the attempt. I was already exhausted and disheartened. I saw, indeed, the conception needed before me, but could not grasp it and give it expression.

While in this mental condition I had to undertake a longish journey on the river. I was staying with my wife on the coast at Cape Lopez for the sake of her health—it was in September 1915—when I was summoned to visit Madame Pelot, the ailing wife of a missionary, at N'Gomo, about 160 miles upstream. The only means of conveyance I could find was a small steamer, towing an over-laden barge, which was on the point of starting. Except myself, there were only natives on board, but among them was Emil Ogouma, my friend from Lambarene. Since I had been in too much of a hurry to provide myself with enough food for the journey, they let me share the contents of their cooking pot. Slowly we crept upstream, laboriously feeling—it was the dry season—for the channels between the sandbanks. Lost in thought I sat on the deck of the barge, struggling to find the elementary and universal conception of the ethical which I had not discovered in any philosophy. Sheet after sheet I covered with disconnected sentences, merely to keep myself concentrated on the problem. Late on the third day, at the very moment when, at sunset, we were making our way through a herd of hippopotamuses, there flashed upon my mind, unforeseen and unsought, the phrase, "Reverence for Life." The iron door had yielded: the path in the thicket had become visible. Now I had found my way to the idea in which world-and-life-affirmation and ethics are contained side by side! Now I knew that the world-view of ethical world-and-life-affirmation, together with its ideals of civilisation, is founded in thought.[3]

When the phrase came to him, it was not of Christianity that he thought, not of Goethe, not even of Jesus. His mind went eastward, to Buddha. The antecedents of his great idea were worldwide.

That same month, September 1915, half-trained French troops crept up the mountain slopes of the Lingen, above Münster, and tried to storm the entrenched German positions on the crest. By the end of the battle thirty thousand men had died and the military situation remained unchanged.

16

"Reverence for Life"

1915

FROM THIS MOMENT ON, almost everything that Schweitzer did, almost everything that Schweitzer wrote, led back in some way or other to Reverence for Life. In a sense it had always been so since the first apocalyptic moment when the church bells rang and he frightened the birds away rather than catapult them. The discovery of the phrase Reverence for Life was a turning point only in the sense that it was the recognition and naming of something that had always been there.

What first of all, does it actually mean? And what does Schweitzer mean when he says it is "founded in thought," or more positively, that it is a "necessity of thought"?

Reverence for Life is a translation of the German *Ehrfurcht vor dem Leben*, and the word *reverence* is really not quite adequate although it comes closer in some ways than the French translation, *respect de la vie*. *Reverence* can, perhaps, carry some of the sense of mystical awe that is present in *Ehrfurcht* (although lacking in the rather matter-of-fact *respect*), but it is more specifically religious in tone than *Ehrfurcht*, and it lacks the German word's overtones of "fear before an overwhelming force." *Ehrfurcht* is respect carried to ultimate lengths. It holds reverberations of the feelings we experience on the tops of high mountains, in a storm at sea, or in a tropical tornado. This was the element that the African jungle gave to Schweitzer's thinking—the acknowledgment of immensity and of overwhelming power. Like the farmer in his sermon, listening to the fierce winds, Schweitzer felt the force of continuing life in the vastness of nature.

This is a Wagnerian concept. Or, perhaps, in English we should look rather to Wordsworth, Blake, or Walt Whitman, the great mystic nature poets, for a parallel. At all events, it is a poetic concept. It came to him after much diligent thought, true, but it came out of the blue, an intuition, not a logical answer to an intellectual problem. So how can he call it a product of thought, or worse still, a necessity of thought?

Numbers of readers of Schweitzer have been troubled by this problem. John Middleton Murry, who was so impressed by Schweitzer that he wrote half a book about him in 1948, spent chapters berating him for failing to notice that Reverence for Life is *not* a necessity of thought, that no logical sequence of propositions compels any man to arrive at Reverence for Life. It is instead, said Murry (and many others), simply Schweitzer's own personal view of life summed up in a phrase, and thought has nothing to do with it.

This is a tempting conclusion to draw. Many thinkers tend to start with the presuppositions that their own natures require and then try to rationalize them. Schweitzer seems a blatant example.

"Schweitzer," says Murry, "does not see that he has, throughout his recorded career, been bent on imposing himself upon experience. He began with various elements in his character: a very pronounced will, a desire to relieve human misery, a determination not to subordinate himself to any organization, and a conviction that whatever was true in the Christian religion could be established by rational thinking. These were the main distinguishable elements. The will was the driving force behind the other three."[1]

There is certainly some truth in this. If it were the whole truth, we might take off our hats to a man whose nature is so generous, so universal, that it leads him to find Reverence for Life as his guiding star; but we would have no obligation to follow him, for he would have failed to establish it as a principle for all human beings.

It is, of course, so patently obvious that Reverence for Life is *not* a necessity or a product of *logical*, step-by-step thinking that one is only amazed that anyone troubled to pursue that line of argument. Murry failed to ask the simple initial question: Is "thought" an adequate translation of what Schweitzer wrote? We have already seen that *denken* does, in fact, carry other connotations, of meditation, of brooding absorption in a subject, which the word "thought" does not encompass. Murry would have saved himself a great deal of irritation and effort if he had realized this. Curiously enough, in the other half of his book, which is a study of D. H. Lawrence, he quotes a poem of Lawrence's that is the precise answer to his problem:

> Thought, I love thought.
> But not the juggling and twisting of already existent ideas,
> I despise that self-important game.
> Thought is the welling up of unknown life into consciousness,

Thought is the testing of statements on the touchstone of the conscience.
Thought is gazing onto the face of life, and reading what can be read,
Thought is pondering over experience, and coming to conclusion.
Thought is not a trick, or an exercise, or a set of dodges.
Thought is a man in his wholeness wholly attending.

That precisely, is *denken.*

Murry himself was, in fact, trying hard to find in Schweitzer a confirmation of his own idealistic socialist ideas and was not truly attending to what Schweitzer wrote. Otherwise, he would have noticed the similarity between Lawrence's poem and Schweitzer's own definitions of thought at various points in his writings. For example, in *The Decay and Restoration of Civilisation,* he writes, "[T]hought is no dry intellectualism, which would suppress all the manifold movements of our inner life, but the totality of all the functions of our spirit in their living action and interaction."[2] And in his Hibbert lectures in 1934 he says, "Thinking is a harmony within us."[3]

Perhaps the clearest statement of his attitude and the way he reached it comes from a statement he made in an interview on Radio Brazzaville in 1953:

> I was always, even as a boy, engrossed in the philosophical problem of the relation between emotion and reason. Certain truths originate in feeling, others in the mind. Those truths that we derive from our emotions are of a moral kind—compassion, kindness, forgiveness, love for our neighbour. Reason, on the other hand, teaches us the truths that come from reflection.
>
> But with the great spirits of our world—the Hebrew prophets, Christ, Zoroaster, the Buddha, and others—feeling is always paramount. In them emotion holds its ground against reason, and all of us have an inner assurance that the truth of emotion that these great spiritual figures reveal to us is the most profound and the most important truth.
>
> The problem presented itself to me in these terms: must we really be condemned to live in this dualism of emotional and rational truths? Since my particular preoccupation was with problems of morality, I have always been struck by finding myself forced to recognize that the morality elaborated by philosophy, both ancient and modern, has been meager indeed when compared to the morality of the great religious and ethical geniuses who have taught us that the supreme and only truth capable of satisfying man's spirit is love.
>
> I reached a point where I asked myself this question: does the mind, in its striving for a morality that can guide us in life, lag so far behind the morality that emotion reveals because it is not sufficiently profound to be able to conceive what the great teachers, in obedience to feeling, have made known to us?

This led me to devote myself entirely to the search for a fundamental principle of morality. Others before me have done the same. Throughout history there have been philosophers who believed intuitively that reason must eventually succeed in discovering the true and profound nature of the good. I have tried to carry their work further. In so doing, I was brought to the point where I had to consider the question of what the fundamental idea of existence is. What is the mind's point of departure when it sets itself the task of reflecting on humanity and on the world in which we live? This point of departure, I said to myself, is not any knowledge of the world that we have acquired. We do not have—and we will never have—true knowledge of the world; such knowledge will always remain a mystery to us.

The point of departure naturally offered for meditation between ourselves and the world is the simple evidence that we are life that wishes to live and are animated by a will in the midst of other lives animated by the same will. Simply by considering the act of thinking, our consciousness tells us this. True knowledge of the world consists in our being penetrated by a sense of the mystery of existence and of life.

If we proceed on the basis of this knowledge, it is no longer isolated reason that devotes itself to thought, but our whole being, that unity of emotion and reflection that constitutes the individual.[4]

In his preface to *Civilisation and Ethics*, the book in which he first unveiled the notion of Reverence for Life in all its glory, Schweitzer writes time and again of the way in which rational thought must give way in the end to the nonrational. Only "inexorably truth-loving and recklessly courageous thought is mature enough to learn by experience how the rational, when it thinks itself out to a conclusion, passes necessarily over into the nonrational."[5] In this passage the key phrase is "by experience." There is no *logic* by which the rational must arrive at the nonrational. We simply discover the fact, says Schweitzer, by experience:

If rational thought thinks itself out to a conclusion, it arrives at something non-rational which, nevertheless, is a necessity of thought. This is the paradox which dominates our spiritual life. If we try to get on without this non-rational element, there result views of the world and of life which have neither vitality nor value.

All valuable conviction is non-rational and has an emotional character, because it cannot be derived from knowledge of the world but arises out of the thinking experience of our will-to-live, in which we stride out beyond all knowledge of the world. This fact it is which the rational thought that thinks itself out to a conclusion comprehends as the truth by which we must live. The way to true mysticism leads up through rational thought to deep experience of the world and of our will-to-live. We must all venture once more to be "thinkers," so as to reach mysticism, which is the only direct and the only profound world-view. We must all wander in the field of knowledge to the point where knowledge passes over into experience of the world. We must all, through thought, become religious.[6]

Schweitzer's experience was that rational thinking led inevitably to "thinking experience" and so to mystical apprehension, and this whole process he called "thought." As a result, he could speak of the "thinking man" when he meant not the academic but the man who is aware of the depths in himself and of his deep links with the rest of nature—the man who has not blocked off, in the interests of "growing up," the warm instincts of childhood.

This point is so important and so alien to our technological way of thinking that I make no apology for quoting two other passages. The first is from *Civilisation and Ethics*, chapter 19. Schweitzer is describing the role which thought plays in the origin of ethics. "It seizes on something of which a preliminary form is seen in an instinct, in order to extend it and bring it to perfection. It apprehends the content of an instinct, and tries to give it practical application in new and consistent action."[7]

The other passage comes from the beginning of *The Mysticism of Paul the Apostle*, the book that he had had to leave unfinished when he went to Africa. Here he is distinguishing between different kinds of mysticism: the superstitious mysticism of primitive races, the magical mysticism that involves sacramental initiations, and the mature mysticism that is a personal comprehension of the universal.

> When the conception of the universal is reached and a man reflects upon his relation to the totality of being and to Being in itself, the resultant mysticism becomes widened, deepened, and purified. The entrance into the super-earthly and eternal then takes place through an act of thinking.
>
> In this act the conscious personality raises itself above that illusion of the senses which makes him regard himself as in bondage in the present life to the earthly and temporal. It attains the power to distinguish between appearance and reality and is able to conceive the material as a mode of manifestation of the Spiritual. It has sight of the Eternal in the Transient. Recognising the unity of all things in God, in Being as such, it passes beyond the unquiet flux of becoming and disintegration into the peace of timeless being, and is conscious of itself as being in God, and in every moment eternal.
>
> This intellectual mysticism is a common possession of humanity. Whenever thought makes the ultimate effort to conceive the relation of the personality to the universal, this mysticism comes into existence.[8]

In this process then of instinct, reason, and mystical intuition, what are the steps by which Schweitzer reaches his goal, the foundation of civilization, Reverence for Life?

First comes the clearing away of the rubble. "If a man wishes to reach clear notions about himself and his relation to the world, he must ever again and again be looking away from the manifold, which is the product of his thought and knowledge, and reflect upon the first, the most immediate, and the continually given fact of his own consciousness.[9] With a single sweep Schweitzer dismisses the doctrines and traditions of the churches, the theories of philosophers, the folklore of nations, all that man had thought or written or handed down. These are merely "the product of his thought and knowledge." They are partial and fallible. The only thing man really is certain of is his own existence and his awareness of it. From there he can start. Descartes began, "I think; therefore I am." *Cogito, ergo sum.* "With this beginning," says Schweitzer, "he finds himself irretrievably on the road to the abstract.[10] For *cogito* is the word for intellectual reflection, which is certainly not the first step. Existence and its awareness come long before we reach the point of cogitation. "The most immediate fact of man's consciousness is the assertion: 'I am life which wills to live, in the midst of life which wills to live.' "[11] So Schweitzer lays down the basis of his thinking—the simplest, most fundamental or, as he would say, "elemental" starting point of consciousness. It is universal and elemental as well. I live. I want to go on living. So, too, do others live and want to go on living.

(As to those individuals and philosophies that claim that life is not worth living, Schweitzer observes that if they were consistent, they would simply expire; so long as they go on living, there must be *some* will-to-live stronger than the will not to live. The true despair of the suicide is, of course, something totally different.)

From this simple beginning Schweitzer proceeds: "As in my will-to-live there is ardent desire for further life and for the mysterious exaltation of the will-to-live which we call pleasure, while there is fear of destruction and of that mysterious depreciation of the will-to-live which we call pain: so too are these in the will-to-live around me, whether it can express itself to me, or remains dumb."[12]

With the next step we begin, perhaps, to enter the nonrational: "The man who has become a thinking being feels a compulsion to give to every will-to-live the same reverence for life that he gives to his own. He experiences that other life in his own. He accepts as being good: to preserve life, to promote life, to raise to its highest value life which is capable of development; and as being evil: to destroy life, to injure life, to repress life which is capable of development. This is the absolute, fundamental principle of the moral, and it is a necessity of thought."[13]

It could well be argued that the contrary is true. The world being what it is, my will-to-live is likely to find itself in conflict with other wills-to-live. It does so every time I eat a lamb chop. As Schweitzer himself writes, a few lines later: "The world, however, offers us the horrible drama of will-to-live divided against itself. One existence holds its own at the cost of another; one destroys another."[14] So finding my will-to-live in conflict with others my reaction is surely to strengthen myself against them, to prepare to destroy them before they can destroy me. This, the law of the jungle, could certainly be described as logical, therefore rational. But this is not the thought of Schweitzer's "thinking man." "In him," says Schweitzer, "the will-to-live has become conscious of other will-to-live, and desirous of solidarity with it."[15] Schweitzer's type of thinking process leads to a precisely opposite conclusion to the logic of the law of the jungle.

At this point it becomes important to decide whether or not we accept Schweitzer's mode of thinking as a proper approach to philosophy. This semirational, semimystical technique may be all right for poets; it may even yield important insights that we apprehend more with our pulses than with our brains. But can it be made the basis of a complete view of life? Can it convey something that is sufficiently accurate to be generally acceptable?

In the mystical stage of his thinking, is Schweitzer not really being subconsciously swayed by the Christian teaching of his childhood? Is he not generalizing from his own particular good fortune and subconsciously seeking for a philosophical justification for his own uncommon impulse to goodwill? Is he not alloying true thought with other mental functions to reach the goal he desires? Is thought not really much more calculating than he makes out, leading us to the behaviorists' belief that we are conditioned creatures who operate according to learned reflexes that enable us to survive and that love itself is only another such reflex, a useful cement for securing the fabric of society?

These are questions that we must all answer for ourselves. Do we agree with Schweitzer in experiencing thought as something more than a logical thread of reason? Are we conscious of an impulse toward solidarity with other creatures? And if so, do we believe that impulse to be something rooted in our nature and in all nature? Or is it the result of some sort of social brainwashing?

Schweitzer's own childhood history seems to make the brainwashing theory less than convincing. His reactions at that time were often violently emotional, even uncontrollable, and very much his own. They certainly do not seem to have been designed to please his parents. Yet these reactions were the start of his mystical identification with nature.

Indeed, he himself claimed that the brainwashing was the other way— that life and adult society took pains to eliminate the spontaneous loving response of the child, so that growing up was a process of mental impoverishment. If he was right about this, then the kind of thought that is merely rational is artificially attenuated. The rich contents of the mind have been diminished to a colorless adding machine; and for some reason this adding machine has been regarded as much more scientific than the more complex mechanism it has replaced—as though science were concerned only with semihuman creatures.

This notion that science is only concerned with the physical, the practical, the technical has arisen because the physical and the practical are so much easier to approach scientifically than the mental and spiritual; they are easier to measure and assess. We have even been assured that because mental and spiritual factors cannot be measured accurately, they do not exist—or at any rate have no significance.

The true difference, however, between the scientific way of looking at life and any other way is simply this—that the scientist is prepared to make the most careful observations possible before forming a theory and then to check his theory by experiment. This is certainly difficult in studying mental processes, but not impossible. What is extremely unscientific is to ignore complicated mental phenomena simply because they are difficult. A truly scientific approach takes account of all phenomena, emotional impulses included.

In any case, Schweitzer is far from being alone in finding that "thought" is much more than emotionless intellectualization. Einstein said that there was no logical path to a great scientific discovery; the mind had to make a leap, like that of a great painter or poet. And Arthur Koestler, in his monumental book, *The Act of Creation*, sets out to show how all discovery, scientific or artistic, occurs as a flash of vision, unexpected although not unsought, which instantly perceives a connection between things never before connected, making a new pattern never perceived before— a concept close to Schweitzer's own definition of genius.

After the vision comes the difficult work. The scientist begins his experimental checks. The artist begins the laborious business of transferring the vision to paper or canvas. Neither of them can trust the vision unless it works in physical terms. If it does, the vision was a true one. If not, not.

So with Schweitzer, Reverence for Life came upon him as *Peer Gynt* came upon Ibsen or the theory of relativity came upon Einstein. Ibsen had to write the play and make it work. Einstein had to find the mathematical proofs. And Schweitzer had first to check his vision against the theories of other philosophers and then, because he was talking about life, had to make his life his argument.

The word *thought* really is a red herring. Schweitzer, trained in the academic schools of philosophy, remained under their influence even when he had rejected their results. Goethe, with the same kind of vision, expressed it in poetry. Schweitzer could not. He wrote books of reasoned argument. He went back through all the types of philosophy he knew of—Chinese, Indian, and ancient Greek as well as European—checking the new vision against them and them against the vision. If there is something uneasy about the endeavor, it is because it often brings together two different kinds of thought, academic and visionary. But the purpose is clear: to check whether it can be shown that previous philosophies have all failed for lack of this one life-giving foundation.

The only way for the reader to satisfy himself about this is to read *Civilisation and Ethics.* The final chapters should be read in any case, for they are the fullest and most exhilarating exposition of Reverence for Life that he ever wrote, a paean of delight in the new possibilities of living. But the earlier chapters are optional, for the real experimental checks on the theory are to be found not in the writings but in the rest of his life.

Let us recapitulate a little. Schweitzer, concentrating his whole mind upon his whole mind, observed that deep within it was an ethical impulse. The impulse to solidarity with other creatures is so profound that it is almost a part of that first element of consciousness. "I am life, that wills to live, in the midst of life that wills to live." He believed that the impulse had been there since infancy. It was not implanted; it was inborn. It was not invented; it was discovered. It was undeniable. The fact that it was discovered at the heart of all consciousness by the brooding mind, and once discovered could not be denied, led Schweitzer to call it a necessity of thought.

Moreover, he had discovered it and believed that everybody else could discover it without any appeal to supernatural causes. To discover it one did not need any belief in God or in Divine Providence or Eternal Essence or any transcendental pattern beyond earth. One simply sought in the depths of one's own being. The fact that this human impulse found no reflection in Nature or the Universe or History or any other of those great abstractions was puzzling, because human beings in general had always felt that there must be a Divine Pattern to which our nature corresponds, and philosophers had always obliged by attempting to discern it.

The attempt had finally collapsed, as we have seen, demolished by the study of natural history—the last blow, perhaps, delivered by Darwin when his *Origin of Species* showed that the only "pattern" needed to account for man's superiority to other animals was the pattern of natural selection and the survival of the fittest, a doctrine that gave plausibility to Nietzsche's plea that man should become dominant rather than good. The belief in goodness and gentleness had so long and so completely depended on a belief in the Divine Pattern that it was unthinkable that the two could be separated.

Schweitzer separated them. In his own eyes he seemed extremely daring. Long chapters are devoted to the novelty of the claim that one *could* be agnostic about the design of the universe and still find significance and the foundation of ethics in mankind—that world-view could be dissociated from life-view. "To understand the meaning of the whole—and that is what a world-view demands—is for us an impossibility. . . . I believe I am the first among Western thinkers who has ventured to recognise this crushing result of knowledge.[16] So he writes in the Preface to *Civilisation and Ethics*, and many passages echo the same idea. A world-view is inaccessible to knowledge. It remains a mystery. The only valid attitude to it is resignation; we can never know. We can only know ourselves. And from *that* knowledge we can build an affirmation of life and in a sort of way an affirmation of the world as well, not because we *know* it but because we experience it.

Schweitzer never fully explores the possibility that man affirms the universe precisely because he affirms himself—that he projects his own secret knowledge of the solidarity of all life onto the universe and then seeks to find an intellectual justification for what he has subconsciously done by inventing Divine Patterns, reversing cause and effect. On this view there could be a connection, but a psychological one, not the philosophical one Schweitzer's training led him to argue against.

Be that as it may, he is much to be honored for what he did. It was a brave and truthful thing for any man at that time, particularly a pastor, to dispense with Divine Patterns without, at some time, succumbing to disillusionment and cynicism. The philosopher-scientist John Wren-Lewis makes this point strongly and goes on to point out how subsequent scientific developments have confirmed Schweitzer's conclusions.

For ever since then our understanding of the physical universe has been changing. What we know now about the formation of matter, the origin of the stellar system, the operation of the brain, and so on, are far from complete, but they are totally different from what Schweitzer knew at the time of the First World War. Any belief about man based on man's relationship with the physical universe has been irreparably shattered time and again in the intervening years as Darwin and others shattered the beliefs of the nineteenth century. We have reached the point of being able to control and alter nature to an ever-increasing degree—even to alter man himself, his very brain structure. No settled relationship is possible any longer. All we have is ourselves, in whom we may or may not find something we call divine. Where other prophets and philosophers have repeatedly become out of fashion, Schweitzer's elemental discoveries are still valid. The man whom many regard as old-fashioned is still up-to-date.

It would not be true to say that Schweitzer saw these implications when he divorced life-view from world-view. But events have shown that the human heart *could* come first. It *could* mold the world to its will rather than be molded by the whim of the elements. To interfere with nature seems sacrilegious to those who feel that nature contains some divine order. To those who feel that this view is superstitious, an aftermath of the centuries when man was at nature's mercy, it may seem a responsibility to be seized with thankfulness, courage, and good hope. And whether it works out well or ill lies certainly not in the stars but in the human heart.

Schweitzer's bold stroke, then, which still discredits him in the eyes of conventional philosophers, seems to point accurately to the future. He himself was not troubled about that. Enough for him that his intuition, which had led him to his own personal, profound understanding of Jesus, of Bach, and of St. Paul, now like an opening shutter printed indelibly on his mind a vision of life itself. The haunting passion for nature that he had felt since childhood fused with his desperate quest for the foundation of human ethics, and the vision was born. Everything led to life itself, everything stemmed from it. Good is what promotes and preserves life. Evil is what destroys and injures life. That is enough.

One of the difficulties about Reverence for Life is that it seems so extraordinarily naive. Schweitzer believed in and trusted naïveté, but at first sight this is so oversimple as to be meaningless. Not until one begins to consider the consequences of living by such a simple belief does one realize its potency.

In the first place, Reverence for Life is so basic an idea that it is difficult for anyone to refuse to acknowledge it. Unlike pacifism, vegetarianism, or any political or religious creed, it is an attitude of mind, not a code of rules or a set of propositions. It commands nothing. It forbids nothing. All it requires is that whatever is done should be done in full and deep awareness. Unlike creeds and codes, which provide human beings with preconstructed decisions and take away the need for choice, Reverence for Life lays on everyone the responsibility for every action. Imagine what the result would be if no human being could appeal any longer to country or party or creed to justify his actions but had to give a personal account for all he did.

Reverence for Life involves awareness—it begins with sinking deep into oneself, as in meditation—but it does not stop there. It proceeds to action. It must, because life is everywhere under attack and needs protection and enhancement. Its wounds cannot be ignored. In this way Reverence for Life bridges the chasm between the contemplative and the active. It avoids the kind of busy and unconsidered helpfulness that often stems from guilt feelings and sometimes does as much harm as good, and it avoids the self-centeredness of dedicated navel-gazing. Its very simplicity makes it a kind of zero point on a scale: the point where measurement begins. Because if one does not know where to begin, one has no idea what one's measurements represent. Reverence for Life is not in itself an activity. It is a means of checking all activity.

Often, when writing of Reverence for Life, Schweitzer made the point that every previous attempt to find the basis for morality had confined itself to the human species. Ethics were always seen either as a technique for perfecting the individual human soul or for improving human society. Very rarely did anyone include other forms of life.

In fact, although Schweitzer never mentions it, Jeremy Bentham, writing in the eighteenth century of the need to treat all individuals with equal humanity, had this footnote to add about animals [author's italics]:

> The day *may* come when the rest of the animal creation may acquire those rights which never could have been withholden from them but by the hand of tyranny. The French have already discovered that the blackness of the skin is no reason why a human being should be abandoned without redress to the caprice of a tormentor. It may one day come to be recognized that the number of the legs, the villosity of the skin, or the termination of the os sacrum, are reasons equally insufficient for abandoning a sensitive being to the same fate. What else is it that should trace the insuperable line? Is it the faculty of reason, or perhaps the faculty of discourse? But a full-grown horse or dog is beyond comparison a more rational, as well as a more conversable animal, than an infant of a day, or a week, or even a month, old. But suppose they were otherwise, what would it avail? The question is not, "Can they *reason?*" nor "Can they *talk?*" but "Can they *suffer?*"[17]

The idea then had been mooted, but only as a footnote, not as an essential part of the argument. And even so, Bentham referred only to animal life, not to life as a whole, which included vegetable life. For Schweitzer even the cutting of a flower or the lopping of a tree were matters for responsible consideration. What Bentham tacked on in a footnote Schweitzer made a central point of his thought. The sense of solidarity with life to which his brooding had brought him made this inevitable. One could only, Schweitzer believed, understand civilization by understanding life. One could only understand life by sharing life. Unless one went as deep as this, one was always faced with conflicts and difficulties that arose from the principle being insufficiently inclusive. Even humanity was not embracing enough, for the one absolute value shared by all humanity was life itself, and that was shared also by all other creatures.

Journalistic distortion has presented Reverence for Life as a sort of perverted love for mosquitoes. And it is true that Schweitzer, with a thorough-going consistency that would almost seem absurd were it not the very reason for his achievements, would put a mosquito out of a room rather than kill it. "What?" cry the critics. "A doctor saving the life of a disease carrier?" The action is indeed a *reductio ad absurdum* of the argument and for that reason valuable, for the responsibility of Reverence for Life meant in Schweitzer's instance that he was never prepared to kill if there were any other means of self-defense. In the hospital there were other means. As we have seen, his mosquito netting side-walls were a better protection for people indoors than any amount of swatting and slaughtering. And out-of-doors there were drugs for protection, on which Schweitzer was very insistent; besides which, what good would the death of one mosquito do among so many millions?

Few people would be so meticulous about the details of their belief. Schweitzer was in a special case, feeling that he had to be a living embodiment of his argument. But he was right in a sense. Half-heartedness would have been the death of the argument. The validity of a law is best seen in extreme cases. Blake, with the same kind of vision as Schweitzer's, wrote: "A robin redbreast in a cage, Puts all Heaven in a rage." Many would accept that proposition, from love of robin redbreasts. The real issue arises when one asks whether a poisonous spider in a cage would put all heaven in a rage. I suspect Blake would have answered yes. Schweitzer certainly would have unless, of course, it was caged for its own good or the safety of others. Schweitzer was quite prepared to restrain or, if necessary, kill creatures that were genuinely harmful—witness the spider hunt on his first night in Andende. Not to do so would itself be an offense against Reverence for Life, for where life is harmful to other life a choice must be made.

The choice, for Schweitzer, always involved qualms. The exercise of responsibility for death, even the death of harmful bacilli, visible only under a microscope, he found painful. He cultivated this sensitivity; for he concluded that the loss of sensitivity was what had led the world astray. And the tough hide he had grown since childhood to protect his sensitivity against the jeers of his fellows was now quite capable of dealing with accusations of sentimentality. The formula he used to recommend, the soul of a dove in the hide of a hippopotamus, was accurate enough of himself; he cultivated it and carefully maintained it, using determination to reinforce conviction, conviction to stiffen instinct.

That his sensitivity did not make him sentimental is evident from a number of stories. James Cameron, who visited the hospital in 1953, tells one in his book *Point of Departure*.

One day luncheon began with a reprimand, the Doctor was concerned at my having walked alone up the forest track past the settlement: Did I not realize the danger from gorillas? This was a bad place for gorillas, I said, with rather fatuous lightness (since I did feel guilty), that it might be possible that by now the neighbouring gorillas had themselves developed the rudiments of Respect for Life.

He replied with acerbity: "Doubtless if you communicated to the gorilla that you were a member of the British Press, he would stand aside; if by chance you had no time to do so he would first break your arms, then your legs, one by one: following that he would tear off your scalp. Gorillas I know."[18]

Clearer still is the story told by Dr. Frank Catchpool, who worked with Schweitzer for a number of years in the fifties, speaking at a convocation at Aspen, Colorado, after Schweitzer's death:

As I was going down to the pharmacy one day, I saw Dr. Schweitzer's pelican struggling in for a landing. He made three attempts to land and I saw something was wrong with the undercarriage, because one hand was hanging down. I watched it carefully and it tried again, again and again . . . these birds with a five foot wing span, they fly so beautifully. Finally it made a clumsy crash-landing and came to a halt and I sent a message with Ali and said: "Tell Dr. Schweitzer that his pelican has a broken leg." An hour or so later Dr. Schweitzer came to the pharmacy and he said, "Do you have a moment? I would like you to come and consult with me about my pelican." I said, "*Sofort*, Doctor, I come. He said, "No . . . your patients first!"

This was important to me and I was glad he said that. He had very clearly established the priorities of medical treatment: humans first, the worst cases first, and his own pelican, which he loved very much, was not to be put ahead of even the most minor human case. After lunch we went and looked at the pelican. Its leg did not seem to be broken but it was paralyzed in some peculiar manner, but we couldn't see anything else wrong with it. Then I noticed a couple of specks of blood on its feathers and I said, "Well, could it possibly have been shot at? As it flies around it is such an easy target for someone with a shotgun." So, I said, "May I take an X-ray?" He said, "Well, X-rays are precious and hard to come by . . . if you like to. I'd like to know what's wrong with my pelican, too."

This is another point I'd like to bring out. We had all things we needed in X-ray for making accurate diagnosis. On this picture you can see some of the pellets are flattened out against the bone, indicating the shot had considerable velocity. Also, from the nature of the spots it was pretty certain that the intestines of the pelican had been perforated in numerous places. I said: "Dr. Schweitzer, this pelican is going to die. I can't do anything for it, unless you like me to open it up and we can sew up all these multiple lesions that he's got." He said, "Are you crazy?" He said, "No, leave this pelican alone. I don't want you to waste your time. I don't want you to waste the materials of the hospital on this. I'll look after my pelican." So, he put his pelican outside his window. After four or five days went past and the pelican wasn't eating . . . he tried forcing it to eat himself, he went to me one day at lunchtime and said, "Do you have another minute . . . will you come and look at my pelican?" I said, "Yes, it's dehydrating, it's not taking any fluids, it will surely die." Dr. Schweitzer said, "If he's not better tomorrow I'll chop his head off." This, again, to me is important to show that this man would not let his sentiment overrule his reason. He knew that this animal was doomed, he couldn't save it. He knew he was troubled by this animal's suffering. So, he brutally said, "I will knock its head off."[19]

The Alsatian countryman, bred of those Schweitzers whom Sartre found so crude of speech, is still there.

Attempts were made from time to time to persuade Schweitzer to tabulate Reverence for Life, laying down an order of priority among creatures. From Dr. Catchpool's story it is clear that human life came before animal life in Schweitzer's own personal tabulation although several people noted that he was more able to demonstrate his tenderness to animals than to humans. But he refused to lay down a scale of values for others. To ask for a scale of values, in fact, implies a considerable misunderstanding of the whole idea of Reverence for Life. Reverence is an attitude of mind, not a set of rules. Schweitzer was asking that people should follow him in sinking into their own minds and hearts and finding there, as he was convinced they would, a place where separateness from other life ceased and solidarity began. Once there, they would not need rules. Each person would have to make decisions from time to time about the relative importance to him or to her of different creatures. To keep alive a fallen nestling one must find worms. To keep a falcon one must sacrifice mice. Each decision must be personal but must be taken under the overall guidance of Reverence for Life. Nothing must be arbitrary or irresponsible. The moment one publishes a list of priorities one takes away that personal responsibility, that fresh openness of heart and spontaneity of reaction that is of the essence of Schweitzer's thinking.

Responsibility is a difficult thing. Most people prefer to accept some common code of behavior that takes from them the need to make choices and leaves them simply with the obligation to obey. No doubt Schweitzer's teaching would have been much more enthusiastically received had he issued clear instructions about the relative value of cats and birds, birds and caterpillars, caterpillars and leaves. It was not his way. Schweitzer was the ultimate revolutionary, who will not take orders even from revolutionaries but only from his own conscience and asks only that others do the same. "It is not by receiving instruction about agreement between ethical and necessary, that a man makes progress in ethics, but only by coming to hear more and more plainly the voice of the ethical, by becoming ruled more and more by the longing to preserve and promote life, and by becoming more and more obstinate in resistance to the necessity for destroying or injuring life.

"In ethical conflicts man can arrive only at subjective decisions. No one can decide for him at what point, on each occasion, lies the extreme limit of possibility for his persistence in the preservation and furtherance of life. He alone has to judge this issue, by letting himself be guided by a feeling of the highest possible responsibility towards other life."[20]

Responsibility being a hard thing, so is Reverence for Life. In his hospital Schweitzer lived face to face with decision all the time. When young pelicans were brought in by African boys who had shot the parent birds, fish had to be caught to feed them. Life demanded death. So, said Schweitzer, the responsibility for Reverence for Life demands constant guilt. There is no way of avoiding the awareness that in preserving we destroy, and we are responsible. If we are not aware of this, something is wrong with us. "We must never let ourselves become blunted. We are living in truth, when we experience these conflicts more profoundly. The good conscience is an invention of the devil."[21]

This aspect of Schweitzer's thinking needs to be clarified. We are accustomed to the post-Freudian notion of guilt as purely destructive. For Schweitzer it simply meant an awareness of our involvement in the harsh necessities of life; it meant a refusal to pretend to be outside or above them. It meant too (the German word *Schuld*, meaning debt as well as guilt) that something or someone is constantly having to pay for our decisions, however honestly and wisely we try to make them. To the creatures that have to pay—the fish for the pelicans, for example—we owe a debt that we are not entitled to ignore.

Such awareness, in fact, should have a precisely opposite result to the deadening effect of a destructive guilt complex. To be conscious of the price paid should sharpen the value of the life for which it was given. Schweitzer's own legendary alertness is the outward and visible sign of the state of mind he was talking about.

This alertness, this responsiveness, is perhaps the most obvious effect of Reverence for Life. Once reverence is established, everything that exists is important. Boredom is not possible. There can be no superiority, no isolation, no detachment. Everything is a subject for concern; nothing is beneath notice. The world is there to be appreciated and enjoyed. As Schweitzer once wrote of a girls' school that had adopted his principles:

"The awareness of the meaning of my philosophy of kindness towards all creatures had made them at once serious and gay."[22]

The gaiety he spoke of arises from the freedom offered by Reverence for Life. To make up for the burden it imposes of responsibility for choice, Reverence for Life lifts many other burdens and demolishes many other problems. It overrides questions of nation and of party and every kind of limited loyalty to race or creed. For although at first Reverence for Life may seem a vague ideal, the consequences if it is taken seriously are very practical. Cruelty, any kind of cruelty, for any purpose, becomes impossible. Racism and all prejudice become impossible. Censoriousness and self-righteousness become impossible (because one's regard for other beings depends only on their existence, not on any virtues they may possess). So also does that prevalent modern disease, self-hatred, become impossible. For oneself is also part of life, demanding reverence. As the second great commandment of Jesus was to love your neighbor *as yourself*, implying that you must love yourself before you can love your neighbor, so Reverence for Life can operate from a secure foundation only if the life of others is valued as a result of valuing one's own.

In *Civilisation and Ethics* Schweitzer makes this point clearly and with power.

> Why do I forgive anyone? Ordinary ethics say, because I feel sympathy with him. They allow men, when they pardon others, to seem to themselves wonderfully good, and allow them to practise a style of pardoning which is not free from humiliation of the other. They thus make forgiveness a sweetened triumph of self-devotion.
>
> The ethics of reverence for life do away with this crude point of view. All acts of forbearance and of pardon are for them acts forced from one by sincerity towards oneself. I must practise unlimited forgiveness because, if I did not, I should be wanting in sincerity to myself, for I would be acting as if I myself were not guilty in the same way as the other has been guilty towards me. Because my life is so liberally spotted with falsehood, I must forgive falsehood which has been practised upon me; because I myself have been in so many cases wanting in love, and guilty of hatred, slander, deceit, or arrogance, I must pardon any want of love and all hatred, slander, deceit or arrogance that have been directed against myself. I must forgive quietly and unostentatiously; in fact I do not really pardon at all, for I do not let things develop to any such act of judgement. Nor is this any eccentric proceeding; it is only a necessary widening and refining of ordinary ethics. . . . It is not from kindness to others that I am gentle, peaceable, forbearing, and friendly, but because by such behaviour I prove my own profoundest self-realisation to be true. Reverence for life which I apply to my own existence, and reverence for life which keeps me in a temper of devotion to other existence than my own, interpenetrate each other.[23]

In this philosophy there is nothing negative, nothing repressive or divisive, there is no conflict either between man and beast, man and man, or man and himself.

The liberating effect of Reverence for Life makes it the enemy of every form of establishment, every authoritarian code of ethics. One reason why the appeal of Schweitzer's philosophy fell for the most part on deaf ears was that the period just after he wrote his book saw the emergence into history of the theories of another thinker, whose books had been written sixty years before—Karl Marx. Intelligent Europeans between the wars found themselves faced with very practical issues as communism began to emerge as the hope of the exploited classes, and capitalism and fascism fought back. In this situation people of conscience had no serious choice. Whatever the defects of communism (and they only gradually appeared), it was for most thinking people the only viable opposition to social injustice, and he who was not with the Marxists was against them. A generation of generous souls dedicated themselves to the Marxist future, and found itself destitute when that ideal turned to ashes in Stalin's Russia.

The great socialist ideal lived on, and large numbers of honest men and women felt it a virtue to sacrifice their identity to the party good, even though commitment meant signing away their power of individual judgment and their conscience to a cause that could and often did override humanity.

At such a time the voice of Schweitzer proclaiming that the individual is supreme had as much chance of being heard as a solo flute in an artillery barrage. "With the spirit of the age I am in complete disagreement," he wrote in his autobiography, "because it is filled with disdain for thinking. . . . The organised political, social and religious associations of our time are at work to induce the individual man not to arrive at his convictions by his own thinking, but to make his own the convictions that they keep readymade for him. Any man who thinks for himself and at the same time is spiritually free is to them something inconvenient and even uncanny."[24]

Plenty of people are still convinced that ethics consists of dedicating oneself unreservedly to a party or a cause, so it is worthwhile quoting Schweitzer at some length on the subject not only to make it clear how unlikely he was to get a hearing but to show how early he saw the flaws that took years to become apparent to others.

> It is impossible to succeed in developing the ethic of ethical personality into a serviceable ethics of society. It seems so obvious, that from right individual ethics right social ethics should result, the one system continuing itself into the other like a town into suburbs. In reality however, they cannot

be so built that the streets of the one continue into those of the other. The plans of each are drawn on principles which take no account of that.

The ethics of ethical personality is personal, incapable of regulation, and absolute; the system established by society for its prosperous existence is supra-personal, regulated, and relative. Hence the ethical personality cannot surrender to it, but lives always in continuous conflict with it, obliged again and again to oppose it because it finds its focus too short.

In the last analysis, the antagonism between the two arises from their differing valuations of humaneness. Humaneness consists in never sacrificing a human being to a purpose. The ethic of ethical personality aims at preserving humaneness. The system established by society is impotent in that respect.

When the individual is faced with the alternative of having to sacrifice in some way or other the happiness or the existence of another, or else to bear the loss himself, he is in a position to obey the demands of ethics and to choose the latter. But society, thinking impersonally and pursuing its aims impersonally, does not allow the same weight to consideration for the happiness or existence of an individual. In principle humaneness is not an item in its ethics. But individuals come continually into the position of being in one way or another executive organs of society, and then the conflict between the two points of view become active. That this may always be decided in its own favour, society exerts itself as much as possible to limit the authority of the ethic of personality, although inwardly it has to acknowledge its superiority. It wants to have servants who will never oppose it.

Even a society whose ethical standard is relatively high is dangerous to the ethics of its members. If those things which form precisely the defects of a social code of ethics develop strongly, and if society exercises, further, an excessively strong spiritual influence on individuals, then the ethic of ethical personality is ruined. This happens in present-day society, whose ethical conscience is becoming fatally stunted by a biologico-sociological ethic, and this, moreover, finally corrupted by nationalism.

The great mistake of ethical thought down to the present time is that it fails to admit the essential difference between the morality of ethical personality and that which is established from the standpoint of society, and always thinks that it ought to and is able to cast them in one piece. The result is that the ethic of personality is sacrificed to the ethic of society. And an end must be put to this. What matters is to recognise that the two are engaged in a conflict which cannot be made less intense. Either the moral standard of personality raises the moral standard of society, so far as is possible, to its own level, or it is dragged down by it.[25]

We have seen, and still do see, plenty of examples of personal moral standards being dragged down by the moral standards of society—to such an extent that people in public life have come to be regarded with a sort of despairing disgust. Whatever their party allegiance, none is seen to be any better than the others. Corruption and dishonesty corrode every organization and every party.

But, in the ironical way in which history often works, Schweitzer's ideas, largely neglected in his own time despite all the personal admiration he received, are now being followed by a new generation that knows little or nothing about him. The course of history has forced them to acknowledge what he saw years before.

The young of today, or at least a large and articulate body of them all over the world, have like Schweitzer come out wholeheartedly for life as a whole. They have seen, as he did, the lunacy of pretending that we can survive separately. The disastrous results of unfettered nationalism, unfettered capitalism, unfettered industrialization and technological progress have been felt in this generation's bloodstream. They need no telling that polluted air, earth, and sea are bound up with the very existence of themselves and their children and that unless we reverence life we all die. Just as Schweitzer did, they have, therefore, rejected the traditional ethics that were limited to loyalties to one small community or another, one self-important creed or another. Life itself is precious, and the old divisions that made people kill each other for living in the wrong place or thinking different thoughts are seen as so ridiculous as to be almost incomprehensible.

To determine the extent to which this can be traced directly back to Schweitzer's influence is impossible. What is sure is that the new generation badly needs a prophet who combines mystical insight with common sense and practical knowledge, as Schweitzer does. If they can find a secure foundation from which to go on challenging the nations and institutions that bred them, we have some hope of consolidating the radical change of outlook that alone can master the social and technological turmoil of our age.

Schweitzer's banner, which looked so irrelevant and old-fashioned in the 1920s and 1930s, could well now lead the field.

17

Internment

1915–1917

NOW SCHWEITZER HAD A PHILOSOPHY that satisfied both his instinct and his intellect, that provided a place where religion and philosophy met. Once he had hit upon Reverence for Life as the starting point (although all its implications were not yet worked out), it more or less took the place of Christianity in his mind. Jesus, of course, remained what he always had been—the supreme man. But Schweitzer was convinced that he had thought his way to a level deeper than the churches dealt with; their language and ideas were no longer adequate for his purposes. So, for example, although he continued to use the word God when that would best convey his meaning to his hearers, or when not to use it would only upset or startle people, he used it less and less in general conversation and not at all in his writings. For he had declared himself agnostic about one of the manifestations of God, as creator and ruler of the universe, and the spirit he discovered within himself he preferred to define a good deal more closely as "Will to Live, seeking communion with other Wills to Live." He felt that here he was in touch with some sort of universal Will, but the word God was so blurred by a hundred other connotations that it was useless as shorthand for what he was talking about, and he was only prepared to talk about what he himself had experienced.

Medical work continued as before, and now, to maintain supplies, Schweitzer began to run in debt. He could no longer get into touch with his sources of financial assistance in Strasbourg, and he had not budgeted for so long a stay. Joseph fell victim to the inevitable economy drive; Schweitzer had to ask him to accept a cut in pay, and Joseph felt that it was beneath his dignity to work for so little. So he went. And Schweitzer's work increased.

By December he and Hélène were both beginning to feel the effects of tropical anemia. The four-minute walk up the steep hill to the bungalow grew quite exhausting. "In the tropics a man can do at most half of what he can manage in a temperate climate. If he is dragged about from one task to another he gets used up so quickly that, though he is still on the spot, the working capacity he represents is nil."[1] Adding to all the other labor was the savage rate of depreciation in the tropics. Floods, termites, weevils, traveler ants—life was a perpetual battle against the depredations of any or all of these. While one foe was being thwarted, the others were creeping in. "Oh, the fight that has to be carried on in Africa with creeping insects! What time one loses over the thorough precautions that have to be taken! And with what helpless rage one has to confess again and again that one has been outwitted!"[2] Meantime, reserves of European food were running short, and the Schweitzers trained themselves reluctantly to eat monkey flesh. At Christmas they burned the stubs of the candles they had saved from the previous year.

Letters to and from Europe were getting through fairly regularly now, and news arrived also by telegraph from Libreville or Cape Lopez. Newspapers that reached them seemed unbearable, not only because of the news they brought but because they appeared so grotesquely shrill and feverish. "All of us here live under the daily repeated experience that nature is everything and man is nothing. . . . It seems something almost abnormal that over a portion of the earth's surface nature should be nothing and man everything!"[3] At sermon time on Sundays Schweitzer was faced with the complicated task of explaining how it was that the whites, professed followers of Jesus, had turned on each other in a destructive fury quite incomprehensible to the Gabonese blacks. "About this time it became known that of the whites who had gone home to fulfill their military duties ten had already been killed, and it made a great impression on the natives. 'Ten men killed already in this war!' said an old Pahouin. 'Why, then, don't the tribes meet for a palaver? How can they pay for all these dead men?' For, with the natives it is a rule that all who fall in a war, whether on the victorious or on the defeated side, must be paid for by the other side."[4]

Time passed and weariness became a part of living. But Schweitzer went on working on his book, for he reckoned that the work he did on that was recreation rather than an additional burden. "Mental work one must have, if one is to keep one's self in moral health in Africa; hence the man of culture, though it may seem a strange thing to say, can stand life in the forest better than the uneducated man, because he has a means of recreation of which the other knows nothing. When one reads a good book on a serious subject one is no longer the creature that has been exhausting itself the whole day in the contest with the unreliability of the natives and the tiresome worry of the insects; one becomes once more a man!"[5]

In the dry season, from May to October, the temperature dropped and the river shrank, leaving broad sandbanks exposed. One could walk there and enjoy the breeze blowing up the river. The work eased, too, in these cooler, drier, healthier months. In July 1916 Schweitzer was writing about this relief in one of the occasional essays that he still wrote in the hope that sooner or later they would reach his supporters. He did not know that early in the month his mother had died, her premonition fulfilled that she would never see him again.

In his autobiography Schweitzer says only this: "My mother was knocked down and killed in 1916 by cavalry horses on the road between Günsbach and Weier-im-Tal,"[6] a statement so bald that some writers have assumed from it that Schweitzer cared little for his mother. Others, their imaginations working in different directions, have dramatized the scene by describing her as having been "trampled to death."

The truth about the whole sad, pointless accident is told in Louis Schweitzer's diary. On Monday, July 3, a sultry, wet day, he and Mrs. Schweitzer went to lunch with a friend, Frau Kiener, in Walbach, only a mile or two down the valley. After lunch the two women contentedly fed the ducks and hens, they all strolled for a while in the park, and the Schweitzers left about 6:00 P.M. Their friends came with them as far as the bridge where they all stopped and looked at the scenery. Then the Schweitzers strolled on.

They took the footpath through the fields as far as Weier where they sat and rested awhile on a bench. When they moved on it began to rain, so they put up their umbrellas and kept to the left of the road, under the trees. At a bend in the road two soldiers came galloping up behind them, one whipping his horse all the way, and rode past. When these were a hundred yards or so ahead, a third soldier, also riding hard, swung around the bend behind the Schweitzers. With the rain splashing on their umbrellas they only heard him when he was almost on them and then, "Mama turned to see what was coming—I couldn't pull her back." The horse struck her and she fell with a cry on the back of her head, her arms outstretched. There she lay, her eyes closed, foam on her mouth, her breathing deep and heavy.

The soldier came back, explaining that his horse had been out of control; and then went for help. Meanwhile, a friend passed with a cart loaded with grass. They lifted Mrs. Schweitzer onto the bed of grass and set off for the village. A doctor from Strasbourg who came by diagnosed a fractured skull and returned with them to the manse. There the doctor bandaged Mrs. Schweitzer's head and tried to ease her breathing by massage and arm movements, meanwhile sending to Sulzbach for camphor. At 8:30 a doctor came from Sulzbach with the camphor, which was injected, and Mrs. Schweitzer's breathing improved briefly.

Before long, both doctors had to leave. Mrs. Schweitzer's condition remained unchanged till 2:00 A.M. Then her pulse weakened. Then stopped.

Louis wrote to Louise, then slept uneasily for an hour or two. From 8:00 A.M. onward the villagers came to offer their sympathy, and at 11:00 Louise and Jules arrived, Louise badly shaken.

At 8:00 that evening shooting began in the valley, and they had to go frequently to the cellar. The following day at 8:00 in the morning Mrs. Schweitzer's face began to swell because of the bandage.

It so happened that the village she came from, Mühlbach, where her father had been pastor and where Louis had first met her, was largely destroyed about the same time. The destruction included the church and the organ on which her father had lavished such enthusiasm and which Albert had helped to restore before he went to Africa. In Lambarene Schweitzer had already read of the damage to Mühlbach in a Swiss newspaper by the time the letters come through with the news of his mother's death.

It was August 15. On that day he wrote to Louis: "I write to tell you that I know that mother lies in the graveyard. The omens were remarkable. When the boat's siren sounded in the distance, I knew what news it brought. Through the room her picture greets me. Today we decorate it with palms and orange blossom. I am still too shattered to make sense of it, and I see in my mind's eye the corner of the graveyard in all its summer beauty; and I think how it will be when Hélène and I greet her on our return home.[7]

None of this found its way into Schweitzer's public writings. "At the end of the summer," he wrote, "we were able to join our missionary neighbours, Mr. and Mrs. Morel, of Samkita, in a visit of some weeks to Cape Lopez, where a trading company, several of whose employees had benefited by our treatment and hospitality during illness, placed three rooms in one of their stores at our disposal. The sea air worked wonders for our health."[8] That is all he says about that summer.

They had occasionally spent recuperative weeks at Cape Lopez before. They were there in December 1915, and Schweitzer wrote that he felt so refreshed his philosophical work must be good. Now, with the rainy season approaching again and Hélène's health getting worse, they planned to stay there throughout the winter months. A timber merchant had offered them a house now lying vacant because of the war, and by the middle of October the baggage was packed and ready for the journey to the coast. It comes as something of a shock to discover that the baggage included not only chickens, but parrots and antelopes—fifty crates all told. The Schweitzers were traveling with a menagerie; as, indeed, they presumably had to, for who was to look after their animals if they left them behind?

Perhaps Hélène was not entirely delighted about it all. Aunt Hélène, so Schweitzer wrote to his niece, still had problems about respectability; her beloved pet dwarf antelope was inclined to wet all over the place and make little balls wherever it fancied.

A doctor is never entirely on holiday. Someone is always needing attention, everywhere. But the medical work at Cape Lopez was only occasional, and most of Schweitzer's time was divided between his book—at low tide—and at high tide helping to roll huge logs up the beach. This was to preserve the logs until they could again be shipped back to Europe; it was Schweitzer's way of paying the timber merchant for his lodging. They swam, too, and lived, Schweitzer wrote, the life of Robinson—presumably a reference to *The* Swiss *Family Robinson,* that classic adventure story about a family on a desert island. As to food, the bay was alive with fish. One day Schweitzer caught four hundred herring. They grew tired of eating fish.

In January 1917 Schweitzer formally rented the cottage, together with some land, for his use or the use of any of the society's members who were passing through. The contract stipulated that he might build accommodation for Africans visiting the coast and also chicken houses. But one clause shows that Schweitzer was far from certain about the future. It provided that should the authorities compel him to return to France, the contract was nullified by *force majeure.*

They stayed a long while at Cape Lopez while the war rolled on in Europe, and Louis Schweitzer recorded in his diary: "5th April, 1917. America declared war on Germany. I heard the first cuckoo in Altenbach."

Schweitzer and Hélène finally gathered their cases together and went back up the river to work some time in the early summer. There was much to do. In addition to the normal ailments of the local Africans, dysentery was rife among military carriers from the Cameroons who were passing through. They had not long settled to the task when the half-expected blow fell. The suspended sentence of internment that had hung over their heads for so long suddenly became a reality.

Clemenceau had decided that security in the French colonies was far too lax (and judging by Schweitzer's case he would seem to have had some justification for the view). He wanted the laxity stopped, and the Schweitzers found themselves ordered immediately to Europe. Mercifully, the ship that was to take them was a few days late, so they had time at least to make some dispositions of their effects.

The contract for the cottage at Cape Lopez had to be torn up, invoking the *force majeur* clause. And on October 9 Schweitzer wrote a letter to M. Félix Fauré, head of the mission station, that reads like a will. The whole pharmacy as it stands, surgical instruments and all, is left to the mission station; he estimates the value at about six thousand francs. The microscope is a personal gift to M. Fauré. The piano is to be left where it is, if possible in its zinc-lined case; and the harmonium is to go to the American missionary, Mr. Ford, who happened to be in Lambarene on a visit from Cape Lopez at the time. To Mr. Ford, also, Schweitzer entrusted his precious drafts of *The Philosophy of Civilisation* for safekeeping until the end of the war. It was written in German and was scarcely likely to survive French internment, besides which it would make a weighty item out of the 110 pounds that was all they were allowed to take with them. Mr. Ford undertook the task with some reservation, for he himself believed philosophy to be a dangerous waste of time. If he ever brought himself to read the manuscript entrusted to him, he must have felt better about his responsibility, for he would have discovered how closely Schweitzer agreed with him. For his own purposes Schweitzer made a brief summary of the book's ideas, in French, disguised as a harmless study of the Renaissance, wholly irrelevant to contemporary life.

In the previous year or two Schweitzer had occasionally met people on their way to prison camps and had always given them a supply of medicines from his own dwindling store with careful instructions how to use them. Few things would be more useful in the conditions to which they were going. Now he crammed as much as he could in the way of medicines and equipment into his own limited baggage.

Even while they packed, an African was brought in with a strangulated hernia. Among the packing cases, Schweitzer performed the last operation of these four and a half years.

Two days later, an hour before they boarded the river steamer, he went to see an English timber-merchant friend and exchanged his carefully hoarded gold for French notes. Then they went aboard. Before they could push off, the father superior of the Catholic Mission thrust his way through the guard to shake hands with Schweitzer and thank him for all he had done for the country. Then they set off—all that they had built, all their friends, all the patients, all the animals, left behind.

On the way down the river they sewed the French money into their clothing, and thus clad they boarded the liner at Cape Lopez. Once again, as when they were first treated as dangerous prisoners of war three years earlier, they were isolated under guard. Last time Schweitzer had begun writing. That was not possible this time, so instead he set about memorizing some Bach fugues and Widor's *Sixth Organ Symphony*. He had them by heart before they reached Bordeaux. And he practiced the organ with a table as keyboard and the floor as pedals as he had done when a child.

It was November when they disembarked in Europe. After four and a half years of tropical heat they found themselves in a chilly army barracks, without winter clothing, facing the sharp nip of late autumn weather. Even the normal barrack comforts were missing, because the place was designed for troops on the move through the port. On the seventeenth Hélène and Schweitzer wrote to their respective homes, both in much the same terms. Hélène's letter arrived first—so much so that Louis Schweitzer heard the news of his son's arrival in Europe on December 17 via the Bresslau family, two days before his own letter arrived from Albert. Louis's diary for the nineteenth records:

> At last a letter from Albert in Bordeaux, dated 17th November like Hélène's. He writes, "Dear Father: This note to say we have arrived in Bordeaux. You have doubtless heard the news—(where from?)—that an order came for us to leave Africa by the next passage, for internment in France. For the moment we are temporarily interned at Bordeaux, at 136 rue Belleville, where there are also some refugees. It is normally a barracks. At the moment it only houses civilians. Luckily the weather is dry, which allows us to get re-acclimatised. Don't worry too much about us. If you can make any representations about us, such as you spoke about earlier, that would be good, for the mountains would be what's most beneficial for our health—Hélène and I send our love. Greetings and news to our friends. Yours, Albert Schweitzer."
>
> To start with [Louis continues] I was delighted at the news that they had come to Europe. But since Albert's letter, the more I think about it the more puzzling the affair becomes. Why have they got to leave Africa and be interned? Why just at the time of year when the passage from the tropics to Europe must be so injurious to the health? Have Albert and Hélène deserved no better consideration? Have written to Albert and the Bresslaus.

In Louis's suggestion that Clemenceau should have postponed his plans until the weather suited Albert and Hélène better, there sounds the authentic note of parental indignation. But he was right to worry. Hélène in her letter had been more explicit about the temperature: "Our only discomfort is the cold, which is natural after so sharp a change of temperature following a long spell on the equator. But we have been able to procure some warm clothes, which we were short of." Despite the warm clothes, Clemenceau and the Bordeaux barracks achieved what all the bacilli of the Ogowe had failed to do. Albert and Hélène were only there three weeks, but during that time they caught dysentery, which the medicines they carried with them failed to arrest, presumably because they were so run down.

In addition, so Schweitzer later told his nephew, Gustav Woytt, Hélène also contracted tuberculosis in those barracks from infection left behind by previous occupants. Whether or not her lungs still bore the scars from her previous infection, this one was not to be thrown off lightly. From the aftereffects of this brief incarceration Schweitzer was to suffer for at least two years, Hélène for the rest of her life. Those three weeks were a tragic turning point for both of them, for never again was Hélène fully fit to work beside her husband in Africa.

They had their wish for mountain air, however, for Garaison, where they were sent, lies close to the Pyrenees, and the peaks shine in the near distance. The internment camp had, in fact, once been a monastery devoted to healing; the very name means healing, for "Garaison" is Provencal for *guérison*. Despite the cold, the couple began to feel better here.

During the previous year the inmates of the camp had done a great deal to put the abandoned monastery into good repair. The governor was a fair and tolerant man, and matters could in many ways have been worse. Heating was minimal, but the food was tolerable, the couple had a room to themselves, and provided one did not give in to apathy, there was more to be learned from this haphazard collection of prisoners, gathered from every race, every class, and every profession, than one could normally gather in a lifetime.

Some of the bread that Schweitzer had earlier cast upon the waters returned deviously in the form of a table. In Lambarene one day he had given medicines to a man destined for a prisoner of war camp in Dahomey. This man, sent subsequently to a camp in France, had cured the wife of a mill engineer by means of Schweitzer's medicines. Now the mill engineer was at Garaison and wanted to repay the debt. The table he made for Schweitzer out of wood rifled from the loft meant that now Schweitzer could write again and "practice the organ."

Further alleviation came when a group of gypsy musicians decided to enroll him as one of themselves because he figured in Romain Rolland's book, *Musicians of Today*. After a while the initial prohibition against his practicing medicine was sensibly lifted, as it had been in Africa, and he was busy as a doctor again.

Friends were active in Paris on the Schweitzers' behalf all this while, for it was indeed ridiculous that Schweitzer should be imprisoned by a country that was half his own, many of whose distinguished citizens were his relatives and friends, and in whose capital he had made his name as a musician.

Meantime, the Bresslaus sent them fifteen hundred francs, and a local lady, Madame Dessacs, used to send in food. In later life Schweitzer never failed, when in that area, to visit her grave.

They wrote home that they were getting over their chills and holding their heads high, so far as it was possible with the tropical tiredness that still pursued them. Schweitzer was studying prison mentality and the killing effect of despair. The ones who had given up interest in life, he found, were most difficult to treat. Medicines could not reach their disease.

After a while the activities of the Paris friends resulted in their being offered a choice of prison; they replied that they would stay where they were. The climate was not bad, they had made friends here, and there was work to be done among the sick. When Hélène was sent some warm material, tailors competed for the job of making it up, to have something to do.

Further revelations about human nature came early in 1918 when the French authorities decided to use some of the internees as pawns in an international blackmail game. The Germans had taken certain unpleasant measures against civilians in Belgium, and in return the French threatened to send the more distinguished inmates at Garaison to a special reprisal camp in North Africa. Schweitzer was obviously one of those in danger. Some of the notables, however, turned out in this crisis to be less notable than they had let it be supposed. "Head waiters, when delivered here, had given their profession as hotel directors so as to count for something in the camp; shop assistants had elevated themselves to the rank of merchants. Now they bewailed to everyone they met the danger which threatened them on account of the rank they had assumed."[9]

The Germans, fortunately, yielded, and the distinguished persons remained at Garaison, some of them less distinguished than before. The effect a reprisal camp might have had on Schweitzer, sick and exhausted as he was, is not difficult to imagine. It might well have been the end of the Schweitzer story.

The winter was severe, but spring came at last and with it the order to move again to a camp at St. Remy, set aside for Alsatians only. The Schweitzers appealed against the move, but it seems their freedom to choose their place of incarceration had been withdrawn, and nobody took any notice. Even the camp governor put in an appeal. He wanted to keep them. But on March 27 they were moved, regardless. Louis Schweitzer did not receive the news till June 1, the day he picked his first strawberries.

The camp at St. Remy had also been a monastery, but it had also been something else.

> The first time I entered the big room on the ground floor which was our day-room, it struck me as being, in its unadorned and bare ugliness, strangely familiar. Where, then, had I seen that iron stove, and the flue-pipe crossing the room from end to end? The mystery was solved at last; I knew them from a drawing of Van Gogh's. The building in which we were housed,

once a monastery in a walled-up garden, had till recently been occupied by sufferers from nervous or mental diseases. Among them at one time was Van Gogh, who immortalised with his pencil the desolate room in which today we in our turn were sitting about. Like us, he had suffered from the cold stone floor when the mistral blew! Like us, he had walked round and round between the high garden walls.[10]

Here, too, the governor was a reasonable, jovial man, and here the Schweitzers met many people they already knew. True to the pattern, Schweitzer was barred from practicing medicine at first, but once he had gained the governor's trust, and when the camp doctor was sent home in an exchange of prisoners, he graduated to camp doctor and, indeed, was let out occasionally to attend the local sick. But the climate was very different from Garaison and did not suit Hélène at all. The bleak winds and the cold stone floors troubled her greatly. And Schweitzer himself was suffering from the aftereffects of the dysentery attack at Bordeaux, a languor that he could not shake off and that made him unable to join the vigorous walks that were organized for the inmates' exercise. Hélène, too, was too weak for these walks, and "we were thankful that on those days the Governor used to take us and other weaklings out himself."[11]

It was here, chilly and tired and unwell, that Schweitzer begot his first and only child. Why now? That child herself, Rhena, thinks that her parents must have been practicing some form of contraception hitherto, which now, through mischance or carelessness, failed. Certainly, it scarcely seems the time or place to begin planning a family. Hélène was approaching forty and in no state to bear the extra physical trials of pregnancy. And it must immediately have been clear to the Schweitzers that this pregnancy threw great doubt over future plans for Lambarene—for Hélène at least, probably for both of them.

Among the relics that Schweitzer kept from this time is a poem written by a fellow prisoner, Harry Wollman, about the eternal beauties of sky and earth outlasting pain and grief and about the mothers of the world, with their soft hands, standing waiting at their doors for the return of their children. A poem of yearning, of homesickness.

And home was at last in sight. The efforts of friends had placed the Schweitzers' names on a list of prisoners to be exchanged (although by accident only Hélène was listed at first, and Schweitzer himself was added at the last moment), and on July 12 they were roused in the middle of the night with orders to get ready to go home.

As the sun rose we dragged our baggage into the courtyard for the examination. The sketches for the "Philosophy of Civilisation" which I had put on paper here and at Garaison, and had already laid before the Camp

Censor, I was allowed to take with me when he had put his stamp upon a certain number of pages. As the convoy passed through the gate I ran back to see the Governor once more, and found him sitting, sorrowful, in his office. He felt the departure of his prisoners very much. We still write to each other, and he addresses me as "mon cher pensionnaire" ("my dear boarder").[12]

They were taken to the railway station at Tarascon to await their train. Neither Schweitzer nor Hélène was in any fit state by now to carry their baggage, and as they dragged themselves through the shingle between the tracks toward the freight shed where they were to embark, a cripple, whom Schweitzer had treated in the camp and who had no possessions of his own to carry, offered to help them. Much moved, Schweitzer accepted. "While we walked along side by side in the scorching sun, I vowed to myself that in memory of him I would in future always keep a look-out at stations for heavily laden people, and help them. And this vow I have kept."[13] Years later, companions were sometimes embarrassed by Schweitzer's irrepressible eagerness to carry the baggage of puzzled strangers.

At one stop on the way the party was entertained to an excellent meal by a welcoming committee who, it turned out, actually intended the feast for a group of French being repatriated from Germany rather than Alsatians returning from France. By the time the mistake was realized the food was gone, and the Alsatians journeyed on to Lyons full and contented without ever discovering what happened when the correct group steamed in from the other direction.

More and more coaches joined the train filled with internees from other camps until they reached the Swiss frontier. Here they had to wait a long while for cabled confirmation that the trainload for which they were being exchanged had also reached the frontier. When they at last reached Zürich, early on July 15, Schweitzer found himself greeted, to his great amazement, by a group of friends who had known for weeks— longer than he had—that he was coming home.

Louis Schweitzer, too, had known for some time that the couple were soon to be released. This particular day, July 15, he chanced to meet a man who had had a telegram from a friend reporting that Schweitzer and Hélène had passed through Zürich that morning and were now in Constance, safe and well. He went to Strasbourg to wait for them, staying with his daughter Adèle at nearby Oberhausbergen.

Constance, lying on the border, separated prosperous, war-free Switzerland from a Germany nearing defeat. "Dreadful was the impression we received in Constance. Here we had before our eyes for the first time the starvation of which till then we had only known by hearsay. None but pale, emaciated people in the streets! How wearily they went about! It was surprising that they could still stand!"[14]

Here Schweitzer stayed till the formalities were completed while Hélène was allowed to go straight on to her parents in Strasbourg. According to his father, Schweitzer stayed on an extra day to help fellow internees with their papers. He did not reach Strasbourg till late on the seventeenth, long after dark. "Not a light was burning in the streets. Not a glimmer of light showed from any dwelling-house! On account of attacks from the air the city had to be completely dark. I could not hope to reach the distant garden suburb where my wife's parents lived, and I had much trouble in finding the way to Frau Fischer's house near St. Thomas's."[15]

His sister Louise was waiting for him at Mrs. Fischer's. So was his niece-godchild, Suzanne, now in her early twenties and too old to be called Suzi anymore, with whom he had kept up a steady correspondence. This was the first reunion. At eleven the next morning the three of them went to meet Louis off the train from Oberhausbergen. "We meet again," Louis wrote, "after five years and four months."[16]

In the afternoon Louise went back home to her family in Colmar. Albert went with his father to stay with Adèle, and soon Louis was worrying about the unaccustomed unreliability of Albert's stomach.

There was no question of Schweitzer's going to Günsbach yet to greet his mother's grave. A pass was needed to go up the valley into the battle zone, and these passes were not easily come by. Louis had to go back to his parish alone, and two weeks passed before he received a letter from Louise to say that Albert and Hélène were coming to Colmar. Two days later, on August 7, a telegram arrived asking him to pick up Albert and Hélène in Colmar at 9:00 A.M. The passes had finally, "after many visits and many entreaties,"[17] been granted.

Presumably the picking up in Colmar was arranged by courtesy of Louis's military friend, Captain Frick, the area commander, who lodged at the vicarage. Hélène and Schweitzer arrived at 11:30 after a night of gunfire.

> So this was the peaceful valley to which I had bidden farewell on Good Friday 1913! There were dull roars from guns on the mountains. On the roads one walked between lines of wire-netting packed with straw, as between high walls. These were intended to hide the traffic in the valley from the enemy batteries on the crest of the Vosges. Everywhere there were brick emplacements for machine-guns! Houses ruined by gun-fire! Hills which I remembered covered with woods now stood bare. The shellfire had left only a few stumps here and there. In the villages one saw posted up the order that everyone must always carry a gas-mask with him.[18]

The inhabitants of Günsbach had grown so accustomed to having the fighting on their doorstep that bringing home the hay crop by night had become a matter of course, as had the periodic rush to the cellars and the constant possibility that a threatened attack might mean immediate evacuation of the village. Louis Schweitzer no longer even retreated to the vicarage's capacious cellars during a bombardment but sat it out in his study.

Much more than by the war the villagers were worried by drought. The harvest was in serious danger that year. "The corn was drying up; the potatoes were being ruined; on many meadows the grass-crop was so thin that it was not worth while to mow it; from the byres resounded the bellowing of hungry cattle. Even if a storm-cloud rose above the horizon it brought not rain but wind, which robbed the soil of its remaining moisture, and clouds of dust in which there flew the spectre of starvation."[19]

They visited the grave after lunch. The same day, records Louis, the poppy harvest began.

Albert stayed for the next ten days, till the eighteenth, when the people of Günsbach held a festival, arranged without the pastor's knowing, to celebrate the forty-third anniversary of his installation in that parish— that installation when the yellow baby Albert had caused such embarrassment to the visiting pastors' wives and such distress to his mother. Now Albert, who was in on the secret, played the organ and preached for his father's festival, and the church was packed.

The following day he went to Strasbourg for a few days, but was soon back, seeking the long-awaited rest and recuperation of his native climate and his native hills, trying to throw off his languor and the intermittent fever that had troubled him since the last weeks at St. Remy. He got worse instead of better. The fever became more acute, and he was in increasing pain. The dysentery at Bordeaux had left a legacy in the form of an abscess of the rectum. By the end of the month he could not conceal the extent of his illness from his father, and on the thirty-first Louis records that when fetching Louise and "Bebby" (Suzanne's younger brother, Albert, the one who suffered Schweitzer's fury over the Latin lesson) from a military train at Türkheim, he also collected medicine for his son from the chemist.

When he returned, two crises faced him. Albert's fever was acute, and Captain Frick had had disturbing news. An attack seemed imminent and two fresh battalions were coming to Günsbach. Everyone who did not absolutely have to stay must, unfortunately, leave. Nor, he was sorry, could he offer them transport. Had he known it earlier, he would not have let Louise and Bebby come.

An empty munitions train was leaving Walbach for Colmar an hour before midnight. Louise and Bebby set off immediately to catch it. At 9:30 Schweitzer and the pregnant Hélène also set off down the road for the walk of three and a half miles to Walbach; with them went Suzanne, who had been staying at the vicarage. To distract himself from the pain Schweitzer sang chorales, interspersed with tirades against the idiocy of all the politicians who had failed to prevent the war and now were incapable of bringing it to an end, but he laughed when he asked Suzanne what she had in her basket, and she replied, "Love letters, a prayer of yours and my washing things."[20]

He managed to reach Walbach, but could go no farther. While the others went on to Colmar in the munitions train, Schweitzer and Hélène stayed at the house of their friend, Frau Kiener. The next day Hélène went back to Günsbach for some belongings that had been left behind and then returned to Schweitzer. Frau Kiener found a carriage and on this Schweitzer was taken to Louise's house in Colmar. Suzanne was immediately sent to fetch a doctor, but it was 7:00 P.M. before she found one. The doctor diagnosed the abscess and prescribed immediate surgery. At 8:30 Schweitzer, on a stretcher, was on a train to Strasbourg, accompanied by Hélène and Louise. The pain was now almost unbearable. They reached Strasbourg at 11:30 and had to wait half an hour in the waiting room while an ambulance was fetched from the hospital. With the ambulance came an assistant, who gave Schweitzer opium.

At 9:30 the next morning Schweitzer was operated on—a fairly straightforward operation, lasting only a quarter of an hour. It appeared completely successful.

Hélène reported that while she stayed with him that day, he talked a great deal. About what we are not told. But that experience of pain gave him a new understanding of suffering. It added to his sense of debt that he had been delivered from the agony and danger of his illness by medical knowledge and skill. He conceived a new notion—"the Fellowship of those who bear the Mark of Pain."

Who are the members of this Fellowship? Those who have learnt by experience what physical pain and bodily anguish mean, belong together all the world over; they are united by a secret bond. One and all, they know the horrors of suffering to which man can be exposed, and one and all they know the longing to be free from pain. He who has been delivered from pain must not think he is now free again, and at liberty to take up life just as it was before, entirely forgetful of the past. He is now a "man whose eyes are open" with regard to pain and anguish, and he must help to overcome those two enemies (so far as human power can control them) and to bring to others the deliverance which he has himself enjoyed.[21]

18

The Lost Coin

1918–1924

WHILE SCHWEITZER RECOVERED, the war ground at last to an end. On October 6 the Germans made peace overtures to President Wilson. Wilson replied on the tenth. And on the thirteenth, Schweitzer preached a sermon at St. Nicholas Church, his first for five and a half years—years of shattering experience for his congregation, and for him years of remoteness, of an existence whose perspectives were quite unlike theirs. "I have looked forward Sunday by Sunday to this day when I should be permitted to speak to you again. . . . And now this dream so long awaited becomes fact, at a moment especially crucial and agonising, when our destiny is about to be decided and our future is darker than ever."

He spoke of the sufferings they had seen, every one of them, and recalled the words of benediction he had left with them in 1913: "the peace of God which passes all understanding." How to reconcile these things? How to arrive at resignation to the will of God? (For here he still spoke of God although he also used the phrase "universal will.")

The passage that follows is truly magnificent in its resolute refusal to pretend that things are other than they are or that horror is anything but horror.

> How to arrive at resignation to the will of God? Are we to confront this idea face to face, and gaze fixedly at it till we are enveloped and hypnotised by it? I would not dare to set you on that path, for I very much doubt whether it leads to the true peace of God. Forcing oneself to yield to the idea that everything comes from God seems to me the despairing act of those who have given up thinking: they shatter their own intelligence, they renounce the making of natural and reasonable judgements on things, they

302

empty themselves of energy. They have peace, but only because their spring
is broken.

Not a trace is left now of the pious cliché, of the comforting phrases
about the nobility of suffering.

It often happens, certainly, that looking back we discover some sense in
what at the time seemed obscure; so we decide that good has come out of
evil, and reason has emerged from the absurd. . . . The tumultuous threat of
the mountains that loomed round us as we travelled through the valleys is
transformed to tranquil ranges when we see them from the distant plain.
But there also exists . . . a multitude of occasions in which the absurd does
not change into the reasonable, nor the evil into the good.

Anyone who tries to explain why a mother has to lose her only son,
why friend betrays friend, why empty phrases carry greater weight than
the truth, will only entangle himself in the undergrowth.

All we can know, says Schweitzer, is that the will of God tends toward

the blossoming of the spirit. . . . You who have passed through so many
grievous experiences, you have certainly found the consolation of feeling
inwardly free in face of the blows of fortune. You have amazed yourselves,
at those moments when to human thinking you should be crushed by
misfortune, by finding yourselves, on the contrary, uplifted by the triumph
of spiritual forces over material catastrophe. . . . If we can lay hold of this
passing experience as a permanent conviction, this is where the peace of
God begins.

The peace of God is not rest—it is an active force. . . . It is finding a
progress within oneself that marches through life's events. Men and women
of all nations can and must find this together—not through politics, not
through "grand conferences about this League of Nations which they wish
to found." What we must seek is the Kingdom of God, which arises naturally where men's thoughts are noble. . . .

[F]rom the depths to which we have fallen let us proclaim our faith in
the future of humanity and our desire to rescue it from destruction as the
most precious ideals to bequeath to the coming time and the rising generation. The sun of hope does not shine on our path. Thick night still covers
us, and the dawn of better days will not brighten for our generation. But
if we have succeeded in preserving our faith in the sunrise which must
come, the quivering light of the stars will be enough to illuminate our way.

May the peace of God fill our hearts and uphold our courage.[1]

Schweitzer had some need of courage at this time. His abscess did not
properly clear up, and although his friend, Mayor Schwander, offered
him work in the Municipal Hospital and St. Nicholas took him back as

curate, he had the debts of the war years at the hospital hanging over him and no means of repaying them.

Strasbourg had changed greatly. The war had bred antagonisms between pro-French and pro-German factions, and the less scrupulous had used these to enhance themselves at the expense of their rivals. A new generation had sprung up who knew and cared nothing for Schweitzer's reputation. He felt, he said, like a coin that has rolled under a wardrobe and been forgotten. Nothing went right at this time. One day early in November he was driving back from Günsbach in a borrowed two-wheeler when one of the wheels caught in some tramlines, the horse slipped on the cobbles and fell, and Schweitzer and the driver were thrown out. The frightened horse, struggling to regain its footing, kicked Schweitzer's arm and caused a slight fracture. Not a serious accident, simply an additional nuisance, with Hélène now seven months pregnant.

Then came the revolution in Germany, the Kaiser's abdication, and the armistice; the end of the shooting and the sleepless nights. Günsbach was suddenly full of French troops instead of German, and French officers were quartered in the manse. And with the ceding of Alsace to France, Schweitzer was now a French citizen. For a while he found himself in sole charge at St. Nicholas. M. Gerold had been openly anti-German and had been dismissed by the German authorities. When the armistice came and Strasbourg came under French rule, his colleague, M. Ernst, was removed because he was anti-French. It took a little while before the new authorities reappointed M. Gerold, and meanwhile Schweitzer, who had offended nobody, had to do all the work.

For once in his life Schweitzer had no objective—and no spirit to seek one. In these bad times he still remembered those worse off still and regularly sent what food he could to friends in Germany. He would cross the border at the Rhine bridge with a rucksack full of provisions and dispatch the parcels from Kehl. One of the friends he made a point of helping was the aging Cosima Wagner, now desolate among the neglected splendors of Bayreuth.

On January 14, 1919, his own forty-fourth birthday, Hélène bore him a daughter. Rhena Fanny Suzanne arrived at 11:00 P.M. in the clinic at Strasbourg hospital. Amid all the rejoicing it must have seemed as though Albert Schweitzer was a man with a great future behind him, settling down now to a belated domesticity.

The drafts of *The Philosophy of Civilisation* had not arrived from Africa, so Schweitzer, his mind still full of the importance of Reverence for Life, began the book all over again. As yet he had never spoken in public of his idea, apart from a brief use of the phrase in a sermon in December in memory of the dead. Here he had asked, as everyone at that time was

asking, that the dead should not have died in vain; if life were rever-
enced, such deaths would never again be required of human kind.

The sermon is notable for its graphic insistence on the ghastly details
of death when so many sermons were inclined to surround such details
in a comforting cocoon of rhetoric:

> Piercing bullets have drained them of their blood; lying in the barbed
> wire, they have groaned and suffered all day long and no help has been
> able to reach them; stretched out on the frozen earth, they have died of cold
> in the night; exploding mines have entombed them, or flung them into the
> air, sliced to pieces; or else on the deep sea, the water has come boiling into
> their ship; they have fought the waves till exhaustion came; or imprisoned
> in the hull of the ship they have clung to the bulkheads, seized with help-
> less terror. And those who have not perished on the battlefields or at sea
> have succumbed after weeks and months in military hospitals, fighting to
> hold onto a life of mutilation.[2]

All this, he said, had happened because the world had not taken seriously "human life, that mysterious and irreplaceable value"—a world
"which plays the fool with Reverence for Life."

A month after Rhena's birth, however, he could contain himself no
longer. He needed, as of old, to share with his congregation the thoughts
that mattered to him. This first public announcement of his great discovery, taking place as it did in a religious context, is stated in religious
terms. And what terms! For if in his philosophical books he had to show
the inadequacy of every previous philosophy of ethics, so now he had to
prove the shortcomings of every previous religious statement—including
those of Jesus!

On February 16 he preached the first of two successive sermons on
Reverence for Life. He took his text from Mark 12; the passage in which
Jesus, questioned as to which is the greatest of the commandments, answers that there are two: first, to love the Lord your God with all your
heart, with all your soul, with all your mind, and with all your strength,
and second, to love your neighbor as yourself. The sermon begins by
asking, as Schweitzer had asked himself in Africa, what is the fundamental basis of all ethics. For Christian morality "has become bankrupt in the
world. It has not penetrated men's souls in depth, it has been accepted
only superficially, and always more readily in words than in deeds.

"This is why it is a waste of time ceaselessly to repeat and to comment
upon the commandments of Jesus, as if thus they must in the end wear
a path into men's consciousness." And moreover, "It is not easy to present
them in a form that makes them applicable in practice. Let us take, for
example, the verses of the first and great commandment. What can it

really mean—to love God with all one's heart, and for the love of God never to do anything but good? Pressing the idea to its depths, a host of questions arise: have you ever done something good solely for the love of God, and can you say that without this love you would have chosen to do ill?

"As to the second commandment. 'You shall love your neighbour as yourself,' it is truly magnificent. I could expound it to you with the most edifying examples. But is it truly applicable? Suppose that from tomorrow you were to decide to abide by it to the letter, where would you find yourself at the end of a few days?"

Because these commandments are so impossible to act upon, he goes on to say, there is a great danger that people will content themselves with exalted lip-service. Another danger—it is an open door to pride. "While we pardon our enemies, we glorify ourselves for our nobility of soul; when we render some service to someone who needs us, we admire our generosity. . . . [O]ur sin of vanity brings us lower morally than those who act without pretending, as we do, to conform to the commandments of Jesus."

Now he summons reason to help solve the problem—reason and the heart together—and defines reason thus: "I understand by reason a force of comprehension which penetrates to the heart of things, which grasps the entirety of the world and which seizes the control-handle of the will." Reason is "at one and the same time a thirst for knowledge and a thirst for happiness, mysteriously amalgamated within us." This thirst for knowledge tries to penetrate into the numberless forms with which life clothes itself; it seeks to comprehend the miracle of an ice crystal, it realizes that "the beetle stretched out dead by the side of the road was a creature which lived, struggled for existence, like you; it experienced fear and suffering, like you; and now is no more than matter in decomposition, as you will be, sooner or later. . . . ."

"To respect the endless immensity of nature—no longer to be a stranger among men—to participate and share in the life of all. . . . Thus the final result of knowledge connects with the commandment of the love for one's neighbour. Heart and reason are at one. . . ."

"To found a new world everyone must "decipher, letter by letter, this single commandment, as great as it is simple; Reverence for Life—a commandment more charged with meaning than the Law and the Prophets."[3]

One could scarcely make a greater claim. Those who believe that Schweitzer suffered from megalomania could find their text here, for the claim seems so much more startling in religious terms than it does in philosophical. Christian doctrine, unlike philosophy, claims to be revealed truth, once and for all absolute. Schweitzer is treating it like any other human attempt at understanding—magnificent but incomplete. There is no sign here of the doctrine of the Trinity. God is simply, "the unfathomable principle of eternity and of life that we call God." So the claim to be able to criticize the great commandments of Jesus, and to improve on them, is not quite so extraordinary. Schweitzer is not, as some of his critics have claimed, setting himself up as God, or pretending to be a second Jesus. He is asserting his right as a man to his own discoveries about life— discoveries he could never have made without a lifetime's absorption in the insights of Jesus.

It would be unfair to assess this sermon without reading it all, and to set it all down here is out of the question. In any case, a sermon is not a theological treatise: it is inevitably a simplified exposition, designed to convince by inspiration as much as by reason. There is no time for more. In this summary I have tried simply to show the way Schweitzer's mind was working in relation to the religion of his upbringing.

In the second sermon he amplified a number of points and dealt with some difficulties. "The great enemy of ethics is insensitivity." Several times he uses a word about the processes of nature that now seems strikingly modern; he talks of their "absurdity." In recent years the notion that life has an element of absurdity has become fashionable, in contrast to the old conception that a hidden providence guided all things. Schweitzer was saying it in 1919. "Nature knows nothing of reverence for life. She creates life in a thousand ways with a prodigious ingenuity, and destroys it in a thousand ways with an equally prodigious absurdity. . . .

"Her cruelty is so absurd! The most precious life is sacrificed to the benefit of the most ignoble." And he goes on to speak of a child's life destroyed by a tubercle bacillus, an African ravaged with pain and moaning all night because of a few minute organisms ten to fourteen thousandths of a millimeter long, the carriers of sleeping sickness.

But why the notions of the Good and of Reverence for Life arise in man but not in nature, that is a question he asks but leaves unresolved. The puzzlement and confusion that this arouses he regards as the first great hazard to be faced in devoting oneself to Reverence for Life, and we have no choice but to accept this puzzlement as one of "the contradictions which flow from the nature of the world like a devastating tide."

Two other hazards, or "temptations," threaten the follower of Reverence for Life. The first is the thought that "it will do no good! All that you, do all that you *can* do, to prevent or mitigate suffering and to maintain life, is insignificant in relation to what goes on in the world around you, of which you cannot change one iota."

Schweitzer's answer is interesting, for it shows how clearly he realized that his work in Africa fulfilled his own needs besides benefiting others and how strongly he believed that by yielding to their impulses toward good others could fulfill themselves in the same way. It is true, he says, that "compared with the size of the task the little you can do is no more than a drop of water in the midst of a torrent; but it gives your life its only true meaning and its value. Wherever you may be, and to whatever extent things depend on you, your presence should bring deliverance." For "compassion and mutual help are an inner necessity to you."

The final temptation is the thought that "to feel compassion for others means suffering. Anyone who is one day seized with the grief of the world can never again rediscover happiness, as mankind thinks of it. . . . In the middle of a group where gaiety reigns, suddenly his spirit is elsewhere." And the tempter comes, saying, " 'Come on, not so much sensitivity! Do as others do and stop thinking, if you want to live a reasonable life.' " To this temptation Schweitzer replies that "compassion also brings with it the ability to rejoice with others. If your compassion is blunted, you lose at the same time the possibility of responding to others' happiness."[4]

The "temptations" Schweitzer spoke of are so frequently brought forward in any discussion about the psychology of a life devoted to others that Schweitzer's own facing of them and answers to them are a necessary part of our understanding of the man. As to the effectiveness with which he applied them, there are plenty of people who will tell you that he did often, simply by his presence, bring deliverance, and that he did enjoy the rejoicing of others as much as he grieved over their unhappiness. He himself was an illustration that his method of enriching life could actually work.

This year, 1919, held less interest and excitement than any in Schweitzer's life before or after. Neither he nor Hélène was fully recovered in health. Tropical exhaustion had eaten deep, and their resilience was a long while returning. Schweitzer himself had to have a second operation in the summer, about which we know very little, except that it was a follow-up to the first. Either just before or just after the operation, in a sermon on his perennial theme, gratitude, he spoke of hospitals: "A sick man is in hospital at Strasbourg's surgical clinic, and he is due for an operation; to whom will he owe his recovery? Not only to the doctor who performs the operation, to the assistants who renew the dressings and the nurses who have cleaned him up; but also to many others, shadowy figures from the past."[5]—the founders of the hospital, for example, and the discoverers of anesthetics and disinfectants.

Here is Schweitzer's morality at work. He is deliberately cultivating his sense of debt, as Baudelaire cultivated his hysteria. He is feeding his imagination with thoughts designed to nourish gratitude and solidarity. Thus he continually refreshed the springs of his personality.

In October, briefly and unexpectedly, the world opened out again for Schweitzer. His friends of the Orfeo Catala in Barcelona invited him to give a concert there. Permission to travel was difficult to get—so was money—but the invitation meant a great deal and he went. He had been playing regularly, of course, in church, but whether because the disruptions of war had put a stop to all concert-going or because those who were now arranging concerts did not know him, this was the first time since the war that he had played in front of an audience rather than a congregation.

He was hurt by the neglect of Strasbourg where once he had ridden so high. "This first emergence in the world let me see that as an artist I was still of some value."[6] Equally painful, if not more, was the indifference of the academic world. "In learned circles I could have believed myself entirely forgotten, but for the affection and kindness shown me by the theological faculties at Zürich and Berne."[6]

The neglect was not personal. Seven years is a long time in the life of any institution, and groupings change. For ten years and more he had been one of the darlings of his group of professors, and his circle of friends was like a family. All this was broken up; the more so because Strasbourg University, as we have seen, had enjoyed the special favor of the German government that now was no more. Political divisions existed in the university as elsewhere, and the new European situation was reflected in the staffing.

Failing other musical activities, Schweitzer tried to get on with the remaining volumes of the Bach edition for America. But the notes he had made for these were with the manuscript of *Civilisation*, which he had left in Africa; and the publisher was less enthusiastic than he had been, not surprisingly, for the arts suffer first when war comes and recover slowly. Bach was as important as he had ever been to Schweitzer, but not to the rest of the world.

In this disheartenment Schweitzer turned to Eastern religions and philosophies. In his studies for *The Philosophy of Civilisation* and in the revelation of Reverence for Life he had already discovered in his thought strong affinities with Buddhism. Now he began to explore the differences and the similarities between the two, using as a criterion his distinction between philosophies that were "world-and-life-affirming" and those that were "world-and-life-denying." The latter contained no impulse to ethical activity and to the betterment of human conditions but were content to concentrate on personal spirituality in detachment from the world; despite his emphasis on mysticism Schweitzer had no use for these. But he did admire the emphasis in Buddhist mysticism on the thought that all life was one, a thought that he found nowhere in the West.

Hinduism and Christianity he saw as having in common an attempt to combine affirmation and denial of the world and of life. In Hinduism denial was the stronger element. In Christianity, as he saw it, denial had predominated throughout the Dark Ages, the centuries during which the Catholic Church reigned supreme in Europe and when the world was seen as a vale of tears to be endured in the expectation of bliss after death; affirmation of this life had only broken through with the Renaissance, which is why Schweitzer loved the seventeenth and eighteenth centuries when the Renaissance came to flower. No similar movement had occurred in India where personal mysticism was still the be-all and end-all of religion. And in Europe, he felt, the negation that had been rejected in the eighteenth century had begun to creep back in the nineteenth; to that extent "Christianity ceases to be a force making for civilisation and begins to attract attention as a hindrance to it, as is amply shown by the history of our own time."[7]

Schweitzer was still suffering from the aftereffects of his abscess. The second operation had been no more successful than the first, and the wound would not heal. So discomfort, embarrassment, and world-weariness combined with the loss of his aim in life, the restrictions of movement, the poor food and the all-pervading postwar shock to pull him down.

George Marshall in his recent study of Schweitzer goes so far as to say that at this time Schweitzer was suffering from a nervous breakdown. He brings to bear, I believe, some extremely dubious evidence, including a chance visit to a psychiatrist who happened to be a friend of his and the fact that Schweitzer on several occasions set about repairing and cleaning out old organs. This, says Marshall, was a special work-therapy for his condition.

In fact, of course, Schweitzer was forever plunging into work of this kind. He had come to enjoy and value manual labor, particularly when it was in the interest of one of his beloved old organs. It certainly proves nothing about his mental health.

All the same it was a period of profound depression. "Nervous breakdown" is misleading only in that it suggests a specific period of collapse, followed by treatment; there is no evidence of this whatever. As Marshall points out, however, there is a photograph of Schweitzer as an internee which, even allowing for the well-known lying characteristics of the camera, tells a story. Schweitzer sits hunched up like a morose Charlie Chaplin, almost unrecognizable as the vigorous character of most of his photographs.

Such was the outlook as Christmas approached—a Christmas that the Schweitzers "expected to celebrate in sorrow and distress as we had all the other holidays since the beginning of the war,"[8] he wrote thirteen years later in a grateful memorial article to Archbishop Nathan Söderblom, the man who brought him back to life.

Before the war, Schweitzer had known of Söderblom as a scholar of historical religions with a particular interest in the relation of religion to science. In the meantime, unknown to Schweitzer, the scholar had become Archbishop of Sweden. Also unknown to him, Söderblom knew about Schweitzer—knew his work and knew that he had been interned. In fact, the archbishop was actually under the impression that Schweitzer was still detained.

Söderblom was involved in the organizing of an annual series of lectures sponsored by the Olaus-Petri Foundation at the University of Uppsala and had a number of distinguished names on his list. He had somehow heard that Schweitzer was formulating a new theory of ethics, and so Schweitzer figured on the list, although not at the head of it. But it occurred to Söderblom that an invitation to give the coming year's lecture might help release Schweitzer from the imprisonment in which he believed him to be languishing. Accordingly, he asked the Archbishop of Canterbury (presumably as representing the war's victors) to find out where Schweitzer was and pass on the invitation. And so it came about that a letter arrived belatedly at Schweitzer's lodgings two days before Christmas and sat on the mantelpiece waiting when he came home from work. "I was not after all so completely forgotten as I had thought."[9]

So run-down was he that he seriously thought of refusing the archbishop's invitation. But Söderblom dismissed these doubts. The change of air would do Schweitzer good, and the food in Sweden was better than in the defeated German dependency. Another difficulty, the travel restrictions imposed on Alsatians, was overcome by admirers of Schweitzer's who had authority to secure him a visa.

How long Schweitzer might have continued in his trough of depression had he not been able to get out of the cramping circumstances of postwar Strasbourg into the freedom and cheer of Sweden no one can say. But it is important to realize that at this time he was a defeated man. Without money, energy, or position, he would have had to drag himself back by his own bootstraps, and that might have been too much even for him.

Söderblom was right. The air and the cheerful and vigorous company gave him a new lease on life. And, perhaps, even more important was the opportunity to spread out his ideas in a place where they would be noticed and the promise of publication after delivery of the lectures.

Schweitzer and Hélène reached Uppsala in April 1920. The archbishop, they found, was a remarkable man. When part of his rod of office was mislaid, he cut a syringa twig and happily marched with that in procession. Even more impressive, Schweitzer found, was the way he conducted local church business. Schweitzer went into his room one evening to find him sitting on a trunk settling the problems of the local priests, who were strewn over the sofa and the archbishop's bed. He had a genius for combining authority with informality. This kind of episcopal relationship with the priests struck Schweitzer as something the Alsatian church sadly lacked.

A day or two after the last lecture, as Schweitzer was preparing to go home, Söderblom took him out for a walk one rainy evening, the two of them under one umbrella. Schweitzer spoke of his anxieties about the debts he still owed to the Paris Mission Society and to friends in Paris—debts he saw no means of repaying. Söderblom, practical and vigorous, said that the obvious solution was to tap some of the money that had come Sweden's way during the war. Collecting money was out of the question in either France or Germany now, but the war had brought prosperity to the nearby neutral countries. Söderblom was convinced that a tour of organ recitals and lectures about his African experiences would pay Schweitzer handsomely. And he set about arranging it, planning the itinerary, writing letters of introduction, and arranging accommodation. He also got in touch with a publisher, Lindblad, about the subsequent publication of a book based on the lectures. Schweitzer, the dynamic organizer, was for once being organized. And to good effect.

Sweden responded to Schweitzer unforgettably, the country districts even more than the cities. He toured for six weeks, from mid-May to the end of June, and by the end of that time was well on the way to paying off the seventeen thousand francs he owed. His spirit, too, was so refreshed that now there was no doubt in his mind that he would go back to Africa. "If Archbishop Söderblom had not called me to Sweden and stimulated interest in my life work as a doctor in the primeval forest among his countrymen, I am not at all sure that it would have been possible for me to return to Lambarene."[10]

What did the decision cost Hélène? "For the fact that she so far sacrificed herself as to acquiesce under these circumstances, in my resumption of work at Lambarene, I have never ceased to be grateful."[11]

She must, of course, have known that she had no real choice. Suffering from tuberculosis and with Rhena to look after, she could not possibly go back with Schweitzer, and every principle she believed in, every passionate ideal they had exchanged when planning their adventure, made it impossible to deny him the work that was so important to both of them and that he had now proved he could do. But the sacrifice was very real. Whatever misgivings she may and must have felt, they were fully justified. She and Schweitzer were never again to be so close as they had been, and she was to see other women working at his side as she had dreamed of doing and then so notably succeeded. Mercifully, though, she could not have known at this time the extent of the sacrifice, for she fully intended to rejoin her husband when she was stronger and Rhena was a little older. She could not have foreseen how long the years of illness stretched ahead nor how totally Schweitzer would become attached to Lambarene.

But Schweitzer, as he wrote to Suzanne, felt like a fir tree that shakes off the snow and straightens up after the winter. Back in Strasbourg he went full tilt at the book for Lindblad and had it finished by August. Because it was for the general public, it had to be a good deal shorter than anything he had hitherto written: a salutary discipline, he felt—he was learning to condense his thought.

It appears that in the previous year Schweitzer had begun to make moves toward rebuilding an academic career, this time in Switzerland, and in the summer of this year he was made an Honorary Doctor of Divinity at Zürich University. But all that became irrelevant now. Africa's call was insistent.

The manuscript that he had left with Mr. Ford in Lambarene at last reached Strasbourg, and he set to work with a fresh eagerness to collate his two drafts and get this book finished as well. Now once again life offered him the variety he throve on. After the deadening sameness of the past years he was again doing everything at once: writing, planning, lecturing, and playing the organ, often traveling miles to do so.

Apart from the book, there were the letters to write—letters, for example, on philosophical matters to Oskar Kraus, an admirer who wrote anxiously from Prague beseeching him to have the first chapters of his uncompleted book translated into English. In England, said Kraus, everyone is talking about Spengler and *The Decline of the West*; Schweitzer's book was needed as a corrective.

There were letters to his old friend, Morel, on leave in Rothau from Lambarene, who reported how the antelopes and monkeys were faring out there and how much everyone was looking forward to having Schweitzer back.

And then there were letters to the Paris Mission Society with whom negotiations had to begin all over again. Schweitzer's first spell on the Ogowe had evidently failed to convince the society's central committee that he was a totally acceptable type, however well he had got on with the missionaries on the spot. In spite of these complications he clung obstinately, as before, to his intention to begin again at Lambarene and nowhere else although he received renewed offers from Zürich of posts wherever he wanted and on his own terms.

He went again to Barcelona to play at the first performance ever given there of the *St. Matthew Passion*. In Strasbourg he saw a lot of his friend Mr. Erb, the organist and composer, and Widor called upon him as he passed across Europe. The old rhythm of life was reasserting itself.

In June 1921 the book about Africa was published: first in Sweden, translated by one of Schweitzer's hostesses on his Sweden tour, Baroness Greta Lagerfeld; soon after that in Switzerland, Germany, and England; and finally in Holland, France, Denmark, and Finland. *Zwischen Wasser und Urwald* was the German title (Between water and jungle.) In English we know it as *On the Edge of the Primeval Forest*.

With its combination of adventure, humor, and practical morality, all attractively served up in Schweitzer's sturdy style, the book was immediately successful, and with its success Schweitzer's fame spread out from the confines of the specialists into the broad reaches of the general public.

Success meant money, too, and before long Schweitzer was able to resign his curacy and his medical post in Strasbourg and move with the family to the Günsbach vicarage, where his father still lived, a hale old gentleman. Here he was able to concentrate on his plans for the future, and from here he made frequent money-raising forages to parishes all around. A chance meeting with an Englishwoman and her son in Colmar was to prove fruitful. He kept in touch with young Noel Gillespie and was to take him out to Africa with him when he went two and a half years later.

This was the first of many such meetings with enthusiasts for his work who were to provide the steady flow of volunteer help on which his hospital lived. From now on, wherever in the world he went, Schweitzer was never short of offers of hospitality and help.

It was in this busy summer of 1921 that one evening in Strasbourg Professor Davison heard Schweitzer play on the organ of St. Thomas Church; that evening when, despite the clatter of the aging mechanism, Davison felt "the realisation of that so oft-dreamed ideal, the artist at one with the composer," and sat, he and his students, talking to Schweitzer long after the concert at an open air café in the warm summer night.

Meantime, Schweitzer was arranging an ambitious tour, and by autumn it was organized. It was to last well into the following year, and, indeed, he was seriously thinking of extending it as far as the United States where he was in touch with Emmanuel Church, Boston. A Mr. Elwood Worcester was trying through friends at Harvard and Columbia Universities to arrange for a series of lectures there, but the chief drawback, outwardly at least, was that "Americans as a rule are not very good linguists and the number of persons who would be able to follow your thought in either the French or German language would be limited."[12] This disadvantage, however, had not proved insuperable in other countries, given a good interpreter. Perhaps the additional cost and even a persisting mistrust of German-sounding names might have been the real reasons. It is interesting, however, in view of the number of occasions in later years when Schweitzer was implored to visit America and had to refuse for lack of time, to find him at this stage the proposer of the trip. The connection with Boston, too, is noteworthy. The Unitarians there were to prove an immense source of assistance during and after the Second World War, but this early correspondence has hitherto lain undiscovered in the files.

The tour, on which it seems Hélène accompanied him at least for some of the time, began in the wealthy countries, neutral in the war, which had already given him a welcome—Switzerland and Sweden. From there Schweitzer went in January to England, less war-torn than any other combatant country, where he had been invited to lecture at Oxford, at Cambridge, in London, and at the new Selly Oak College in Birmingham.

Anyone who followed him around England would have gained a good panoramic view of his intellectual preoccupations: Oxford had a preview of the coming book *The Decay and Restoration of Civilisation*; Cambridge was treated to "The Significance of Eschatology"; in London the Society for the Study of the Science of Religion heard about "The Pauline Problem"; and at Selly Oak he gave a series of lectures on his most recent study, "Christianity and the Religions of the World."

These last lectures were later published in book form—somewhat to Schweitzer's embarrassment. He felt he had failed, in so brief a compass, to do justice to a subject that he regarded as of great importance, and he was taken to task from time to time by people of other faiths for misrepresenting them. The book is of great interest, however, if only as a defense of Christianity against the fashion then beginning in Europe (and still with us) for upholding the religions of the East as far richer and more profitable.

Schweitzer had the greatest respect for Eastern religions and considered that Christianity could learn something from all of them, a view that brought him into frequent conflict with more orthodox Christians. But he still believed that Christianity possessed some insights deeper than any of theirs.

Brahmanism and Buddhism, says Schweitzer, are logical, consistent religions, whose spirituality consists of a withdrawal from the world. They can have no ethical content; to do good is for them pointless, for it happens in a world in which good does not exist, in which the only good is to get out of it. Christianity, too, rejects worldly values but for quite a different purpose. "The Brahmans and Buddha say to men: 'As one who has died, and to whom nothing in the natural world is of interest any longer, you should live in the world of pure spirituality.' The gospel of Jesus tells him, 'You must become free from the world and from yourself, in order to work in the world as an instrument of God.' "[13] Hinduism, he believes, is tarred with the same brush as Buddhism. Although it has adopted an ethical element (perhaps from Christianity) and tries to be more closely in touch with the real world, the lure of world abandonment and pure spirituality is really still there at the bottom. "Hinduism tries in vain to hide the chain fastened to its foot."[14]

The Chinese philosophers, however, have mostly tried to find morality in learning to imitate the virtues of nature, to reflect in man's behavior the quiet but irresistible forces of the natural world. Where the Indians find salvation in totally rejecting nature, the Chinese totally accept it and try to conform with it.

But for Schweitzer, as we know, nature was far from benign. He could not accept that the cruelties of nature were a necessary part of some higher process. So the Chinese thinkers, too, although noble in their pleas to mankind to stop fighting and struggling and to "live in accordance with the meaning of existence,"[15] lacked the positive compassionate will that informed Christianity.

Again and again he comes back to his central point: logical consistency is not enough. The strength of Christianity is that within a world whose values it rejects, it yet finds another value that is as real if not more so—compassionate love. Inconsistent it may be, illogical perhaps, but true. Schweitzer proclaims the need for a special kind of naïveté, the kind that has examined all the clever and consistent philosophies and is prepared to say that they are irrelevant, because the facts tell a different story.

With his usual thoroughness he had prepared for his lectures by studying how best to make himself understood through an interpreter. He had first practiced the technique to some extent in his services at Lambarene where his addresses had been translated into the Fang and Galoa languages as he went along. But George Seaver in his excellent biography records that the seed was sown earlier still.

In 1934 Schweitzer prefaced his Hibbert Lectures at Oxford by saying, "I first learned that it was possible to talk to others whose language I could not speak when, many years ago, I heard your Gerard Booth speak through an interpreter at Strasbourg—the gift I had from him I now return to the country that gave it."[16] And this is how, in his autobiography, he describes the technique:

What is most important is to speak in short, simple and clearly constructed sentences, to go through the address with the interpreter with the greatest possible care beforehand, and to deliver it in the shape which he expects. With this preparation the interpreter has to make no effort to understand the meaning of the sentence to be translated; he catches it like a ball which he throws on at once to the listeners. By following this plan one makes it possible to deliver through an interpreter even scientific addresses, and it is a much better way than for the speaker to inflict torture on himself and his hearers by speaking in a language of which he is not fully master.[17]

Reports from his audiences indicate that the method was highly successful; hearers often found that soon they quite forgot that they were listening to an interpreter. But all the same Schweitzer did want to learn English. When Noel Gillespie went to Lambarene with him in 1924, one of his functions was as English tutor.

From this tour we get for the first time an account of the impact of the fully formed Schweitzer personality, that personality which was the outward sign of the character he had been molding for himself since, as a boy, he had decided to break out of his reserve and seek warmth and spontaneity. When he was a young man, people remembered him for his energy and intensity, his masculinity, his acts of kindness, but no one spoke or wrote of him quite as Dr. Micklem of Selly Oak College wrote in his introduction to the published lectures. "It is not easy to explain in words that will not appear extravagant how greatly we were drawn to the man himself. We knew he was strong, but we found him gentle; we have not often seen such intellectual freedom coupled with so evangelical a zeal."[18]

Again and again, from now on, we have the same kind of reaction: "his personality was indescribable." People who met him speak of his complete concentration, a total, delighted, childlike interest in what was happening. He had learned to be permanently in touch with his own depths, his response coming always from the heart, unshadowed by self-consciousness or guile. Like Blake, he was a man without a mask. Whether chatting with a child about earwigs, rehearsing alone in Westminster Abbey for a recital, or talking to a church group about Lambarene, he withheld nothing. The art he had learned from Marie Jaëll of freeing the muscles of the arm so that the musical will went directly to the fingertips had also been used to free the personality from inhibition, and the result was overwhelming.

A good conversationalist is often less effective as a public speaker, and vice versa. Schweitzer had no such limitations. In private he would always give his companions his fullest attention. On a platform he knew how to hold huge audiences breathless with a power that came from a marrying of deep emotional conviction with hard-won technique.

This new flowering of his personality, after the winter of sickness and depression, owed something to a special happiness—that all that he had sacrificed when he went to Africa had been restored to him—indeed, had now become an essential part of the enterprise. He had renounced his joy in teaching; it was replaced by the joy of lecturing on his own favorite subjects. He had renounced playing the organ at concerts; now he played all over Europe in the cause of his hospital. He had renounced financial independence when he resigned his salaried posts; now his own efforts were bringing in more than ever before, and he was no longer dependent on charity.

How was Hélène able to keep up with the surging energy of this new elation? A young journalist, Hubert le Peet, who later became editor of *The Friend* and also of the British edition of Schweitzer's hospital bulletins, went to Oxford to interview Schweitzer and found himself appropriated as his guide in London. He wrote of those days as "a strenuous time, conveying the burly black-cloaked figure from theologian to theologian, from organ to organ. . . . He sometimes forgets that other people are not quite so tireless as himself, and I've sometimes been quite sorry for dear Madame Schweitzer!"[19]

He returned home from England the way he had come, giving fresh lectures in Sweden and Switzerland en route, and only reached Günsbach in March. The correspondence with the Paris Mission Society was dragging on all this while, and at the end of April he received a letter from Mr. Bianquis to which, by some chance, a copy of his answer has been preserved. At this distance we can see the archetypal comedy of the conflict between the committee mind and the creative mind, but at the time the raw edges of frustration must have been very sore. The letters deserve lengthy quotation:

MY DEAR FRIEND,

I do not know where you are at the moment but I am sending this letter to Mr. Dieterlen who will certainly know how to get it to you. Our committee at its April meeting, has taken note of the discussion we had with you on March 10th. I was asked to produce a resumé, which I did from memory four weeks after our meeting, but I think it is sufficiently accurate. I enclose a copy.

After hearing this . . . the Committee has instructed me to write to you again to clarify certain parts which were the subject of long discussion at this meeting.

We are delighted to see you return to Lambarene to give your services, both to Africans and to the Europeans of the Ogowe, and in particular to our missionary personnel, and we are grateful for the great efforts you are making to collect the necessary funds. We are sorry, on the other hand, that you have not been able to accede more completely to the views of the Committee and take steps to hasten the building of your hospital and your dwelling at a certain distance from the mission station. However, we understand the reasons you give, and we are quite prepared to welcome you fraternally for a second spell on the following conditions:

1. The committee requests you to choose, as soon as possible after your arrival at Lambarene, the plot of land on which you wish to establish yourself, and to communicate this to us within a maximum of three months.

2. This plot should be at least 1 kilometre from the buildings of the mission station, either outside our concession, or on the concession's territory.

3. In this latter case our society will not agree to sell you the land upon which you build, but it is willing to lend it to you free of charge for so long as you yourself remain in the Gabon. On your departure the buildings which you have raised on this land will remain our property, like the land itself.

4. For the construction of these buildings we will put at your disposal one of our workmen, and even two if necessary, but all the expenses which arise will have to be your responsibility. Some of us even feel that we should require of you a certain indemnity for the time which our workmen spend in your service. In any case, the whole work will have to be effected during the dry season of 1923, and must therefore be finished towards the end of September 1923.

5. As to the hut which hitherto has served you at Lambarene as a consultation room and store for instruments and medicines, our society is prepared to grant you the title free of charge but asks you to see to its removal to the hospital area as soon as possible, at your cost.

6. Finally, certain members have expressed the desire that our workmen should be asked as from now to prepare on the station itself a small hut, divided into two compartments, which can serve as your lodging from the time of your arrival and during the period of the building of your final domicile. This hut will subsequently be used by our missionaries for the benefit of their work.

We are afraid, in point of fact, that there is no room we can offer you in the actual Mission buildings if we add, as we wish, a second school-mistress in addition to Mlle Arnoux, and if the Hermann family is required by the Conference to settle at this station at the same time as the Lortsch family, M. Pelot and M. Tanner.

I should have sent you this letter a fortnight ago, for the committee would have wished to have your reply for its meeting of 1 May. I'm afraid now that it may be too late, particularly if you are in Sweden. But would you please reply as soon as possible, and forgive the delay which results from my excessive work in these last weeks.

I hope that you have no objection to agreeing to the committee's wishes. I know that you do not much like written contracts, and that you would prefer to have carte blanche to reach verbal agreement with our missionaries. But it is very natural that our committee wishes to formulate clearly the conditions of a collaboration which, despite everything, is of a slightly delicate nature. We continue, you and we, to maintain the independence of our two kinds of work, vis à vis each other; but on the other hand there is between us an obvious solidarity.

I hope, my dear friend, that you are not tiring yourself too much before leaving! And I send, as you know, the most affectionate good wishes for your next trip.

Your devoted,
Jean Bianquis[20]

The letter found Schweitzer at Günsbach, and on April 30 he wrote back. Here and there the letter—hand-written like all his letters—is illegible with age, but the bulk of it is clear enough.

DEAR DIRECTOR AND DEAR FRIEND,

I have just received your communication through the good offices of M. Dieterlen and I am replying straight away. I am forced to be brief, since I have a touch of writer's cramp which troubles and impedes me.

First of all I must correct one mistake in the résumé of our discussion. I have never thought of asking that M. Pelot or any other missionary-workman should be put at my disposition for my building. That would be tactless on my part. Perhaps M. Pelot and his colleague will be busy on other work, or tired. I have only ever spoken of *consulting* M. Pelot, for whose experience and knowledge I have great respect. . . .

2. *The question of the kilometre.* First of all I must point out that it is not so easy to measure a kilometre through the bush. Besides, the question of the distance has not the same importance if my hospital is separated from the mission station by a stretch of water. That would be the case, if I were to establish myself either up-stream or down-stream of the station.

Furthermore, you may find that there are missionaries at Lambarene who will express their views against the kilometre and who will ask me to do them a favour and settle closer to the station! My hospital should oblige them by giving its services to the workers and to the children in the mission school! This is very important for them, seeing that there are a good number of rainstorms every day. If the hospital is at any distance from the station, it can no longer fulfill these functions.

Furthermore, the station benefits from my hospital as regards its provisions. In return for my medicines I receive fresh fish, hens and sweet bananas, which I am accustomed to sharing straightaway with the missionary households. This is important. If I moved too far away, the missionary tables will no longer be provided from the overflow from the hospital, because the "boys" of the missionary's wife could not be summoned quickly enough. . . .

If M. Hermann is still in your service, it is because during his fever in February 1914 I was able to stay with him for four weeks at Talagouga, since my hospital was under the supervision of the Lambarene mission. With the distance which you wish to impose on me, I can never do anything of the kind. I could give a consultation to a missionary when summoned, and that would be all, for I would not be able to abandon my hospital to robbery. It might well be that if it were decided that I am to place my hospital outside the station, I would put it two or three kilometres away, with all the disadvantages which would then result as regards the services rendered to the Lambarene mission station in general! In demanding this kilometre you are acting against the interests of the missionaries themselves. Please consult them.

3. *Construction of the buildings*—You ask me to agree that if you permit me to build on your land—which you refuse to sell me—the buildings are to belong to you. It will be difficult for me to agree to this clause. My death might occur at a time when my work was in deficit. In that case my heirs, who are responsible for the debts of my hospital, must be able to sell the materials of my buildings to cover the deficit. The great advantage of building on land lent by the Mission consists in this—that I can begin to establish myself without wasting months in asking the Government for my own concession. (You know the African bureaucracy!) For you the stretch of ground which you would lend me has no value. So why not let me have it, particularly if it is at a distance from the station?

I am sure that we shall still have time to discuss this question when we know whether I am interested in asking you for a stretch of land, when we know its situation, and when the missionaries of the Gabon have considered the question as it appears to them out there.

4. As to the length of time which you would like to fix for relieving the station of my presence, it is useless for me to agree today to dates which neither you nor I can accurately assess. Your situation in this is extremely simple. If you judge that the thing is going on too long for your convenience, you send a message to Lambarene, giving me my notice. So far as I am concerned, you will be obeyed within twenty-four hours. I will go and fix myself up somewhere in a bamboo hut. I can only repeat what I told you in our discussion—it is I who have the greater interest, once the question of principle is agreed, in establishing myself as quickly as possible outside the station. Why go on whipping a galloping horse?

5. Thank you for continuing to offer a corrugated iron hut. All the same, I only accept it, as I have already told you, if the missionaries there have no objection. The cost of moving I accept as my charge.

6. To conclude, let me once more say to you that only questions of principle, (as I said to you in our discussion) can be decided in Europe. Agreement on practical questions must be reached out there. Have no fear

that my poor dialectic will carry away your missionaries. For the rest, believe me, they will make no decisions without consulting you.

My feeling is that we should not treat these matters like diplomats working out a treaty, but like Christians working for Christ and trusting in one another. I do not think I have abused your confidence nor that of the missionaries of the Ogowe. So I see no reason why we should impose on each other the torment of elaborating clauses as the diplomats do, instead of being towards each other what we wish to be; Christians who act in the spirit and who have confidence in the spirit.

Please accept my best wishes and pass on what I have written to the members of the committee. Please say a thousand good things from me to M. ———.

Your devoted,
Albert Schweitzer

P.S. In the heat of the argument I almost forgot to say how touched I was by your thoughtfulness in lending me M. Tanner and M. Pelot for my building. As to the hut which you propose constructing for my temporary lodging, do nothing about it! If M. Hermann is at Lambarene he'll find a little place for the doctor to stay, believe me! You do not take into account the difficulties of the smallest construction at Lambarene. Since the whole land is on a slope, it is necessary first to level an area and that is only done with great difficulty because of the rock which one encounters everywhere-Unfortunately I cannot get this reply to you by the 1st May. Forgive me. I did not receive your letter in time.[21]

This uncompromising blast was thrown together so hastily, clumsily, and sometimes ungrammatically that Schweitzer almost certainly decided to make a fair copy when he had cooled down a little, and kept the first draft as a reference, which is why we are lucky enough to have it.

Soon after the letter reached Paris, the missionaries themselves, aware of Schweitzer's difficulties, tried to lend a hand. On May 6 they passed a resolution at Talagouga that ran:

The Medical Problem and Dr. Schweitzer

Our Conference has been called upon to re-affirm the absolute necessity for our Mission of possessing an organised and continuing medical organisation. The conclusions of the report which M. Lortsch sent you on this subject in September 1921 grow more and more apparent to those who want a proper foundation for our work.

In response to our needs, the arrival of Dr. Schweitzer might appear providential. He tells us we may expect his return in the month of September. We shall greet him with great joy, asking God to smooth over the difficulties which might prevent his establishment in our midst, and to grant us a fruitful collaboration with him for the good of the Africans and also of the missionaries. May He also permit him to give our medical installation the development and the stability which we would like. On his arrival, the most urgent questions concerning his position here will be examined by the board of the Conference in the spirit which you have indicated, and the others will be submitted to you.

We allow ourselves finally to point out that if a doctor seems indispensable to us for our work below, so much the more will he be for our work above.[22]

But before this could reach Paris, Schweitzer's broadside had achieved its purpose, for on May 11, M. Bianquis was able to write again to say that, without waiting for the committee's next meeting, he had contacted the executive members, who had taken counsel and agreed that since his return was "desired by all our missionaries out there," they were "confident that you and they can arrange the practical questions of your installation on the spot, each granting the other the maximum independence, but allowing for the mutual service each is called upon to render the other."

"I should like to believe," continues M. Bianquis, "that the Committee itself will recognise the force of your observations and will no longer insist on the somewhat trifling conditions that it felt it should impose."[23]

Together with this more or less official reply, M. Bianquis sent a very friendly personal note. He was evidently delighted at the outcome. The battle was won.

The following he was gaining through his tours now added a great deal to Schweitzer's correspondence. Small quantities of money came in a steady stream to the Günsbach house, and when he was not there himself, his father would acknowledge these contributions and make a list for Albert. But for Schweitzer the important thing was to keep the cash flowing, and wherever his travels had taken him, he began organizing the translation and distribution of newsletters and bulletins, which he intended writing from the hospital to maintain the interest of his supporters. In addition to these tedious but vital activities he was writing to various experts about new drugs for gonorrhoea, about the best sort of motorboat to order, about a hundred and one matters that needed dealing with before he went back to Africa. Small wonder his mother's writer's cramp was catching up with him.

Hélène's health had not kept pace with her husband's, and that summer they decided to build a house at Königsfeld, a village in the German part of the Black Forest. Hélène knew Königsfeld from earlier visits, and it had much to recommend it. In the first place the economic collapse of postwar Germany had made house building in that country very cheap; elsewhere Schweitzer might not have been able to afford it. On the one hand, the air was excellent. In those days clear mountain air was believed to be essential for sufferers from tuberculosis, but on the other hand, Hélène's heart would not permit her to live at too great an altitude. Königsfeld offered the perfect compromise. Although quiet and secluded, it was easy to reach from the main road and railway line to Strasbourg. And, finally, it was the home of a branch of the Moravian Brethren, a strict sect of the Lutheran Church for whom Schweitzer had great respect, their hallmarks being simplicity of life, devotion to the Bible, and freedom from dogma. This was the sort of atmosphere in which Schweitzer would be happy to have his child grow up while he was away. So here they lived, mother and daughter, and Schweitzer was with them when he could be.

But in the autumn he was off again, in his worn suit and homespun overcoat, with his two big linen bags for correspondence (one for answered letters, the other for those still to be dealt with) and his selection of small linen bags carrying currency of the different countries he was to visit. After Switzerland he went this time to Denmark. And in November, Oskar Kraus wrote inviting him to come to Prague and lecture on the Philosophy of Civilization.

He went in January, and a great friendship with Kraus began, which three years later was to result in Kraus writing a book about his friend. There is something touchingly comical about Kraus's attitude to Schweitzer, whom he regarded as totally wrongheaded, but at the same time unequaled "in originality, in many-sidedness, and in the intensity of his intellectual, his artistic and above all his ethical qualities."[24] He himself was an unshakable disciple of a nineteenth-century speculative philosopher named Franz Brentano, and his book on Schweitzer is full of an infuriated perplexity that anybody could be as brilliant as Schweitzer and still not see that Brentano was right. Kraus is a glorious example of the kind of thinker, trained in the German schools of philosophy, who the half-German Roman Catholic philosopher and theologian Baron von Hügel says in The German Soul is much too inclined to think ideas important and meaningful just because they are efficiently and elaborately ordered. Such thinkers cannot rest content unless they can reduce the world to a verbal formula, to which end they are forever pulling apart phrases, comparing terminologies, referring every idea to another idea, and pouncing on paradoxes as though they were a proof of invalid thought.

With enormous triumph Kraus manages in his book to prove (what is partly true but quite irrelevant) that "Schweitzer's mysticism is nothing more nor less than a logically unjustifiable short cut to a desired aim which he is unable to attain in a logically justifiable way or which he prematurely despairs of ever attaining."[25] It never seems to occur to him that ideas need to be referred to life, and that inconsistencies can correspond to something inconsistent in reality. The fact that Schweitzer refused this kind of artificial consistency is just what marks him out from the German school and makes nonsense of the claim that he had a typically German outlook.

Back in Königsfeld, while he was struggling to finish the two volumes of *The Philosophy of Civilisation*, preparations for Lambarene continued. One day samples arrived from the Rockefeller Foundation of a new sleeping sickness drug, Tryparsamide, with the request that he would test it under tropical conditions, an indication of how widely he was becoming known. In fact, this proved to be one of the first of the great advances in tropical medicine that revolutionized Schweitzer's work during his lifetime.

Finally the books were finished, The *Decay and Restoration of Civilisation*, which is a fairly general statement of the problem and of Schweitzer's approach, and *Civilisation and Ethics*, in which he plunges, characteristically, into a historical survey of the course of civilization and the influence upon it of varying world-views before concluding with his own solution, the adoption of Reverence for Life as a basis for all future ethical and political systems. I have already summarized the theme of the books, but they should be read in full, so rich are they in insight and a sort of revolutionary common sense. Every page of my copies is marked, often in a half-dozen places. It is impossible to begin to quote. I hope that readers will seek out the books for themselves.

Schweitzer sent the books to Harper's in London, who before the war had expressed interest in a book on his philosophical ideas. But Harper's had changed their minds. When he told the story many years later to Norman Cousins, editor of the *Saturday Review*, Schweitzer attributed the trouble once again to that German-sounding name of his. But his Berlin publisher was equally discouraging, and in desperation he gave the manuscript to Mme. Emmy Martin, a pastor's widow who since 1919 had been helping him with secretarial work, to take with her to München and dispose of as best she might.

Knowing nothing about publishers, Mme. Martin offered it to a firm named Beck, which specialized in legal books. Herr Beck was not available, but one of his associates, Herr Albers, after looking through a few pages took the manuscript home with him, and before long the *Philosophy of Civilisation* had a publisher.

It was some time, however, before the books appeared, for this was the period of galloping inflation in the German economy and the government needed the printing press on which the books were to be printed to make paper money.

It so happened that thanks to Albers, Beck was already the publisher of Oswald Spengler's *Decline of the West,* which was enjoying great popularity at the time. One of Schweitzer's favorite stories was of the occasion when Albers, Spengler, and Schweitzer were all going to lunch together, Albers walking between his two authors. Schweitzer burst out laughing. "It reminds me," he said, "of a farmer with his two milk cows."

In May, Schweitzer was again in Switzerland. Some idea of the schedules he kept can be gained from the following list of engagements for this month, bearing in mind that excellent though the public transportation system was in Switzerland, the mountainous nature of the country added to the complications of traveling and that Schweitzer liked to go third class, unless there was a fourth:

3 Mai	Frau Moser Kreuz Herzogenbuchsee	Cant. Bern
4	Prfr. Ziegler Burgdorf	" "
7	Weiss Olten	" "
abends	Schmid Baisthal	" Solothurn
8 Mai	Gaun Liestal Baselland	
9	Blumenstein Biberist	b/Solothurn
10	Ludwig Biel	Cant. Bern
11	Meier Baden	Cant. Aargau
12	Nissen Schwarzenburg	Cant. Bern
14	Friedli Ober—Diesbach	b/Thun
abends	Dürrenmatt Kariolfingen—Stalden	Cant. Bern
15 Mai	Buchmuller Huttwil	Cant. Bern
16	W.Hopf Lutzelfluh	b/Burgdorf
17	Matthys Worb	Cant. Bern
18	Rohr Thun	" "
19	Waber Munsinger	" "
20	Roochuz Spiez	a/Thunersee
21	P. Hopf Steffisburg	b/Thun
abends	Ammann Trubschachen—Emmental	
22 Mai	D. Müller Langnau	Cant. Bern
23	Von Schulthess Männedorf	a/Zurichsee
25-	Weber Menziken	i/Seethal
abends	Lehrer Merz Rheinfelden Baselland	
27 Mai	Jac. Keller Winterthur	
28–29 Mai	Herrn Robert Kaufmann Belsitostrasse 17	Zürich
30 Mai		Günsbach Elsass

As he crossed and recrossed Switzerland he found himself one afternoon with an hour or two to spare in Zürich and called upon his friend Oscar Pfister, which is where, so to speak, we came in. Schweitzer lay and rested, Pfister persuaded him to speak of his early memories, and the result was *Memoirs of My Childhood and Youth*. This was the meeting that George Marshall, in his recent biography, quotes as additional evidence that Schweitzer after the war suffered "a nervous breakdown." In fact, by this time Schweitzer had been back on the top of his form for nearly three years, and there is a small epilogue to the story that clinches the matter. When, years later, Schweitzer damaged his hand and was taken by Erica Anderson to a Zürich doctor to have it attended to, the doctor's nurse turned out to be Oscar Pfister's daughter. She remembered the occasion well as a cheerful social visit and nothing more. The truth is that the worst thing Schweitzer suffered from at this period was an attack of otitis media, or inflammation of the middle ear.

Dr. Micklem, writing the preface to *Christianity and the Religions of the World* about this time, says that Hélène's illness postponed Schweitzer's return to Africa; but for that, he would already have been back in Lambarene. This certainly seems probable, but the delay was not to last much longer. By the autumn, when the proofs of the *Civilisation* books arrived for checking, he was busy in Strasbourg packing, as he had packed with Hélène eleven years before. He was due to sail in February.

The friendship with Oskar Kraus led to further expeditions to Prague before he left, and on one of these occasions he decided to break his return journey to visit Bayreuth again. This was not so simple, for a special visa was needed at that time to stop in Bavaria, and Schweitzer had no such visa. At the frontier all passengers without visas were directed by the police to the express that went straight through Bavaria without stopping. Schweitzer, never an inconspicuous figure, was made the more noticeable by the large bunch of white roses that he had been given after a concert in Prague, and which he now wished to present to Cosima Wagner. But somehow, taking advantage of the inattention of the police, he crept onto the forbidden train.

As the reader already knows, it was all in vain. Sad enough that the great theater where Schweitzer had spent so many enraptured evenings was now unworkable, that there was no money to restore it to working order, and that no one knew whether or not there was still an audience for Wagner. But the final blow was to discover that the great lady herself had grown very nervous and was often unable to see visitors. When she heard of Schweitzer's arrival, she became so overexcited that her daughter grew anxious about her, and Schweitzer, leaving the roses for her, went on with his mission unaccomplished. How he explained himself at the frontier is not recorded.

Kraus meantime had been badgering Schweitzer with questions designed to make him clarify his ideas. It was intolerable, felt Kraus, that a thinker should "vacillate" so. And on January 2, 1924, Schweitzer wrote him a letter, selections from which Kraus quoted in his book. One passage he quoted has become famous: Kraus' persistence had forced Schweitzer to set down, clearly and foursquare, the meaning he attached to the word "God" and the relationship he saw between philosophy, religion, and ethics. Looked at from Kraus's point of view, Schweitzer could see that what he had to say was not at all satisfactory. Yet he had to say it because it seemed to him true.

Here is the passage.

Hitherto I have followed one principle; in philosophy I never express more than I have experienced as a result of absolutely logical thinking.

Because I express no more than I have experienced, I never speak in philosophy of "God" but only of "the universal will-to-live," which comes to consciousness in me in a two-fold way: first, as creative will perceived as manifestations in observable phenomena external to me; and secondly, as ethical will experienced within me.

Certainly there is a probability inference of which you speak that does suggest the existence of an external God, but it seems to me doubtful whether it is the province of philosophy to draw this inference.

Also it is doubtful that in making such a probability inference there is a gain thereby for the *Weltanschauung* or for the energy of such a total world-view.

I prefer therefore to stop with a description of the experience of thinking, leaving pantheism and theism as an indecisive mystery within me. I am always thrown back to the reality of my experience.

When I must use the language of traditional religious idioms, however, then I employ the word "God" in its historical definiteness and indefiniteness.

Similarly I speak in ethics of "love" in place of "reverence for life."

When I use the language of religion, it is a matter of fidelity for me to convey the experience of elemental thinking in all of its affirmative vitality and in its relationship to our inherited religiosity.

In using the term "God" in this way, I distort neither my philosophy of nature nor the realities of traditional religion.

In the language of experience and the language of religion the content remains absolutely the same. In both idioms I renounce final knowledge of the world and I affirm the primacy of the universal will-to-live experienced in myself.

My lectures on religion contain much criticism of religious thought. But the views expressed in the lectures are put forth as universal experiences so natural that they do not hurt anyone. For ultimately the center of elemental religious concern is, in the traditional idiom, "the being grasped by the ethical will of God."

I am not able to get around the renunciation of all metaphysical knowledge of the world nor beyond the conflict: pantheism-theism. I say this in the philosophical as well as the traditional religious sense.

Ah, dear friend, how much would I rather follow together with you the unbroken lines which lead all the way to Brentano. But ever since my fifteenth year I have had to be content with discontinuity in my philosophy.

It is my fate and my destiny to think out while living how much ethical content and religiosity can be realized by reason in a *Weltanschauung* which dares to be incomplete.

But the point on which we are precisely and absolutely in agreement concerns the quality of active love as the ethical ordinance of the world-view, which I call "the commanding power of the world-view."

Our agreement on love and service makes clear our high task.[26]

On February 21, in pursuit of his high task, Schweitzer embarked at Bordeaux, accompanied by the young Englishman, Noel Gillespie. Hélène and Rhena stayed behind in the Black Forest.

19

Adolinanongo

THE SECOND HOSPITAL

1924–1927

SCHWEITZER LOVED THE VOYAGE. He always did love that voyage—the only holiday, he said, he ever had. This time he traveled on a cargo boat, to avoid interruptions by passengers, for this was a holiday rather in the sense of a change than a rest; the large sack of unanswered letters went with him, to be eroded en route. The customs men were incredulous and deeply suspicious and spent some time searching for smuggled currency.

The steamer made more frequent calls at the ports of West Africa than did the passenger liners. Schweitzer was anxious to learn as much as possible about these other regions. He was even exploring the possibility of extending his activities by starting a second hospital at Nyasoso, in the British part of the Cameroons. Noel Gillespie and he left the ship at Douala to spend a fortnight looking at the country and discussing possibilities with the British Resident. The plan came to nothing—probably because in the event Lambarene itself was more than enough to handle. But Schweitzer suffered, as we all do, from the persistent illusion that next year all will be different, everything will be under control, and we can relax, look around, and make fresh plans.

The journey continued in the mail liner *Europa*, and two days later they reached Cape Lopez where Schweitzer and Hélène had spent the rainy season of 1916–17, seven years before, living on fish, and where the beaches are lined with the lost logs from the timber rafts of the Ogowe. Cape Lopez had been renamed since he was last there and was now called Port-Gentil.

They went up the river on the *Alémbé*, the boat that had first carried Schweitzer that way in 1913 but which was a good deal older now and much the worse for wear. Schweitzer was comparing the country with the richer Cameroons and Gold Coast—richer because the very wealth of the Ogowe, its timber, took the labor off the land and left it quite uncultivated. The riverside tribes one and all followed the timber trade, and whenever the demand was high, they moved to where the uncut trees stood and lived off imported food. Their lives had no continuity, no security against the whims of international trade. When trade was good, they suffered from dysentery brought on by rice and canned meat. When it was bad, they starved. At present, with postwar reconstruction still going on and two international exhibitions needing timber, trade was excellent, and nobody was left to prepare manioc or even to roof the village huts.

This nomadic, impermanent life of the Ogowe tribes was an important cause of their backwardness. In other areas clinics could be set up and local people trained to staff them. In a village forever on the move because its menfolk were periodically tempted by irresistibly high wages, this was a hopeless task.

Schweitzer and Noel reached Lambarene on April 19, 1924, Easter Eve. The war had torn six and a half years out of Schweitzer's life since he last saw the scattered town on the long, narrow island. The hot, rainy season was drawing to an end, and the river was full. The mission station dugouts toiled the half-mile up the river, hugging the bank to avoid the current, rounded the sharp nose of the island, and dropped more swiftly down the river's other branch, which sweeps the island's north side. From the moment they rounded the point they could see the Andende settlement, a mile and a half ahead, the river disappearing around a bend below it. This was unchanged.

But the hospital was changed. It barely existed. When men drop their guard, the jungle moves in very fast. The buildings Schweitzer had worked on so hard were roofless and overgrown; the path up the steep little hill from hospital to house was invisible.

The work began again from the beginning.

This meant, first, putting a roof on the buildings that still stood. But even the makers of leaf-tiles (raffia leaves stitched over bamboo) had made none lately, so easy was it to earn more money from the timber merchants. Only by a hut-to-hut search, village by village, followed by bribery, cajolement, and the threat of refusing treatment to the sick (unenforceable and disbelieved), did Schweitzer and Noel manage even to get a roof over their heads.

Schweitzer missed Hélène sorely, everything reminded him of her absence. Joseph, like every able-bodied African, was busy on the timber trade. Noel Gillespie, young and enthusiastic but quite untrained, turned his hand to whatever needed doing—building, typing letters, and all kinds of unskilled medical assistance.

The patients came, nevertheless—and many died, either because they came too late, their conditions were too extreme, or because to treat them properly in those circumstances was more than one man could do; or sometimes because lying in the roofless huts they caught fatal chills.

The hospital's mortality rate was boosted by another factor. "The praise-worthy habit of dumping sick persons at my hospital and then making themselves scarce has not been lost by the Ogowe people. . . . A woman from a village not far from Lambarene has been deposited here. She has no one at all belonging to her, so no one in the village troubles about her. A neighbour's wife, so I am told, asked another woman to lend her an axe that she might get a little firewood for the old woman to keep her warm during the damp nights. 'What?' was the answer. 'An axe for that old woman? Take her to the doctor, and leave here there till she dies.' And that was what happened."[1]

Sleeping sickness had increased. So had leprosy. For the latter the treatment was still at that time pitifully inadequate; the discovery of the sulfone drugs was years ahead yet. One sleeping sickness patient had fits of mental disturbance that made him violent, and a crude wooden cage had to be built for him. The enclosure was impossibly primitive but better than the treatment his own people often gave to the mentally sick—to tie them up and pitch them in the river.

In June and July this desperate state of affairs began to ease. A Swiss missionary, M. Abrezol, arrived, bringing with him a powerful motor-boat for the mission station. On the same day, all Schweitzer's packing cases finally reached Lambarene. Then the husband of a sleeping sickness patient turned out to have some carpentry experience. ("The dread of being left without a carpenter at all made my lips so eloquent that under the mango tree at sunset I wrung from him the promise to stay. He cost me 300 francs a month besides his food [80 francs], and he cannot read measurements.")[2] Joseph returned to the hospital. And a nurse, Mathilde Kottmann, arrived from Strasbourg.

Here in a nutshell is the unpredictability of the struggle that was Schweitzer's lot from now on. For who could guess that within eight weeks M. Abrezol would be inexplicably drowned while bathing, al-though a strong swimmer; that the motorboat, which only he could master, would have gone aground; that Monenzali, the African carpenter whom Schweitzer had persuaded to stay, would work faithfully on till his death years later; and that Mathilde Kottmann would live and work at Schweitzer's side till Schweitzer himself died in 1965?

Such were the swings and the roundabouts of Lambarene life. Noel Gillespie had to go home in August. In October a trained doctor arrived, an Alsatian named Victor Nessmann, who had been a fellow medical student of Schweitzer's. For the first time the immense burden of being the only doctor, besides administrator, caterer, and builder, was lifted from Schweitzer's shoulders.

Now Schweitzer could, when necessary, leave the medical side of things to others to concentrate on the expansion or consolidation of the hospital, on the correspondence with Europe that had to be kept alive, and on all the administrative details. From this time, too, stems the title the Africans gave him, *Le grand Docteur*, a title that has been taken to imply some sort of self-aggrandizement but which, in fact, only means "the old doctor," in contrast with the various younger assistants who joined him from time to time, who were *les petits Docteurs*.

The migrant timber laborers from the even more primitive tribes in the interior were a special problem. Unfamiliar even with the use of an ax, they were prone to every sort of accident and arrived in considerable numbers at the hospital where they set new standards of blatancy in thieving and breaking things.

The rainy season was exhausting and depressing. Painful foot ulcers, brought on by constant injuries while building new wards, sometimes meant that Schweitzer had to be carried down to the hospital to work there at all. But after a wretched Christmas and a miserable fiftieth birthday, when all the white staff were feeling ill and despondent, the new year looked brighter. Another motorboat arrived, a present from Sweden. And when in March a third doctor, Mark Lauterburg, joined them from Switzerland, the team began to look really workable. Nessmann took the motorboat up- and downriver to deal with the cases that could not be brought in and to initiate some preventive measures while Lauterburg dealt with major surgery, and Schweitzer, apart from his supervisory work, concentrated on experiments with the new treatments for leprosy and sleeping sickness.

At this stage the hopes of a second hospital at Nyasoso were still very much alive, and the British government had offered full support. A long fund-raising letter to the *Times* that August from Schweitzer's British Committee (including four bishops!) describes it as "a feasible project."[3] But the very success of the hospital began soon to pose problems. The ever-increasing number of patients constantly threatened to overwhelm the facilities. New buildings were needed to house them, and the arrival of each new doctor or nurse meant additional building, all of which took away from time that could be spent on medicine.

Then, in the early summer, just after Schweitzer had received the long-expected but grievous news of his father's death, the number of dysentery cases began to increase alarmingly. The disease was reaching epidemic proportions.

This was a new type of dysentery, that did not respond to Schweitzer's medicines, and nothing would persuade the Africans of the vital importance of avoiding infection. Men would sooner catch the disease and die than be separated from their friends.

It was in the middle of this desperate time that Joseph made a remark that has gone into the Schweitzer legend. Some of the up-country tribesmen had once again been drawing infected water to drink, and Schweitzer, in despair, fell into a chair saying, "What a blockhead I was to come to Africa to doctor savages like these!" "Yes, doctor," said Joseph, "here on earth you are a great blockhead, but not in heaven."

The story is, of course, tailor-made for the more inspirational accounts of Schweitzer's life. But these all too often omit the comment with which Schweitzer ends the story, which is rather less edifying: "He likes giving utterance to sententious remarks like that. I wish he could support us better in our efforts to hinder the spread of dysentery!"[4]

In case readers find Schweitzer's word *savages* less edifying still, let me point out that the French *sauvages* from which it is translated is not quite so derogatory. As a description of wild, undisciplined, violent, and primitive people it is accurate, if not particularly polite, and Schweitzer was always more interested in accuracy than tact.

The new rainy season approached, and the leaf-tile roofs were full of holes. Dreading what damp huts might do to his patients, Schweitzer ordered corrugated iron from Europe although he had no idea how or whether he could pay for it.

And on top of everything came famine. The traders had miscalculated how much food would be needed for all the migrant labor, the weather had been worse than usual, and a supply ship had been wrecked. It added up to starvation. Schweitzer, having as usual scented trouble early, had laid in large quantities of rice, so his patients were better off than most. But an exclusive rice diet was conducive to dysentery. Among the hospital inmates were "dozens of walking skeletons."[5]

The realization was forced upon Schweitzer that in one major respect his foresight and his courage had failed. In bargaining with the Mission Society he had rejected the idea of starting afresh outside the station, largely because of the bureaucratic complications involved in getting a concession from the government for his own piece of land. But in staying within the mission grounds he had limited himself to an area that, as he wrote to his supporters in 1928, "was hemmed in on every side. On one side was the river, on another a steep hill, on another the graveyard of the Mission Station, on another a swamp."[6] He could never satisfactorily isolate infectious cases, never house noisy mental patients in any tolerable way or at a distance from the others, and never accommodate all the helpers he needed in any sort of comfort.

The only alternative to an ever more hopeless overcrowding was to write off all the work of the past eighteen months and begin absolutely afresh somewhere else. So much for the dream of getting all the building finally done and being able to concentrate on doctoring.

A possible site existed, very nearby. From the veranda of Schweitzer's house, one could see it, less than two miles upriver, on a slight headland. Today one can walk there in half an hour, along the riverside forest track, but in those days swamps made this impossible.

The site had once been the headquarters of the Sun-King of the Galoas, N'Kombe, and so the trees there were younger than elsewhere, the bush less dense, the soil at least a little less hard. Many of the trees were oil palms: the oil crushed from their nuts was a valuable addition to the local diet. On a wide front the ground sloped gently up from the river. In addition to the hospital there was room for a garden and a big fruit tree plantation, and Schweitzer was desperately aware of the need for the hospital to grow its own food and not to be dependent on supplies that could be interrupted by accident, by war, or by the varying fortunes of the outside world. The name of the place, which the world came to know as Lambarene, is actually Adolinanongo, which means "it looks out over the nations."

Schweitzer had long been tempted by Adolinanongo: even during his prewar spell here he had had an eye on it. Famine and epidemic now forced his hand. True to form he kept his thoughts to himself until, his mind made up, he had been to see the district commissioner.

The commissioner was cordial. The formalities would be long-drawn-out, but in view of the urgency and the improbability of any opposition Schweitzer was given a provisional go-ahead. The concession he asked for was about 170 acres, which he would, of course, have to measure out for himself in the thick bush. The land remained the government's, but any building or development would be Schweitzer's property. A condition of granting the concession was that a quarter of the area must first be cultivated, but that was not hard to promise. The first thing Schweitzer intended to do was to provide the hospital with food.

When he announced the move to the assembled white staff, they were first stunned, then overwhelmed with delight. In Schweitzer's own case the delight was tempered not only by the thought of the immense task ahead but by the fact that now he would not be able to go back to Europe and his family, as planned, the following year. As before, his two-year spell was going to have to be stretched. No one else had the building experience or the ability to supervise the workers. Whatever the demands of his wife and his growing daughter, now six years old and much in need of a father, the hospital, for him, came first.

The work began. Workmen as such were nonexistent, so each morning all the more-or-less able-bodied men who could be mustered were herded into canoes and sent off upstream. The able-bodied were not many, for the dysentery epidemic raged on. In the hospital the medical work was as heavy as ever. Instead of the original forty or so, the patients now numbered well over a hundred although additional nursing help had just arrived in the sturdy form of Emma Haussknecht, a former teacher from Alsace who was to be one of the hospital's greatest pillars of strength, sweetness, and good humor until her death in 1956.

The one ace in Schweitzer's hand, as he gathered his squad of hungry reluctant hobbledehoys, was that he had food, and in those famine-stricken days the offer of a little extra food for a day's work was a bribe few could resist. In the second of the bulletins, which he now began to send, more or less regularly, to his supporters in Europe, he described his method of recruiting his laborers:

> I choose them from the fifteen to twenty persons among the 120 patients, women accompanying their husbands, children, slight cases, convalescents or ex-patients who are willing to give a few days' work out of gratitude. . . . They are told that friends in Europe are helping to support the hospital and have a right to expect each inmate to help the work in return. This truth does not easily make its way home to the hearts of my savages. They seem to believe in a "perfection of bounty" and that I should feed them, heal them, and leave them all day in the sociable circle telling stories, and even furnish them with tobacco to smoke! It is no easy task to embark them in the canoes for the plantation each morning. They prove, with every gesture of conviction, that their health requires that on this particular day they should rest at the hospital. . . . Naturally our convalescents work only to the degree their strength allows. Some on account of wounds cannot walk. They pull out weeds seated on the ground.[7]

It was autumn 1925. When the first tree fell at Adolinanongo, the site that was to become identified with Schweitzer, he was already nearly fifty-one.

So far as I can ascertain, the project for a second hospital in the Cameroons was never again seriously considered. As Schweitzer was known to say in his later years, when criticized for failing to do this or that, "One man can only do so much."

The measuring, pegging, clearing, felling, chopping up, snake killing, stone breaking, leveling, pile driving, lifting, carrying, sawing, hammering, and tree planting went on for more than a year. Schweitzer supervised it all, dovetailing it with the continuing needs of the old hospital and himself laboring harder than anyone. In *More from the Primeval Forest*, a fresh selection from the reports he sent to his supporters, he sets a typical day to music:

> A day with these people moves on like a symphony. Lento: They take very grumpily the axes and bush-knives that I distribute to them on landing. In snail-tempo the procession goes to the spot where bush and tree are to be cut down. At last everyone is in his place. With great caution the first blows are struck.
>
> Moderato: Axes and bush-knives move in extremely moderate time, which the conductor tries in vain to quicken. The midday break puts an end to the tedious movement.
>
> Adagio: With much trouble I have brought the people back to the work place in the stifling forest. Not a breath of wind is stirring. One hears from time to time the stroke of an axe.
>
> Scherzo: A few jokes, to which in my despair I tune myself up, are successful. The mental atmosphere gets livelier, merry words fly here and there, and a few begin to sing. It is now getting a little cooler too. A tiny gust of wind steals up from the river into the thick undergrowth.
>
> Finale: All are jolly now. The wicked forest, on account of which they have to stand here instead of sitting comfortably in the hospital shall have a bad time of it. Wild imprecations are hurled at it. Howling and yelling they attack it, axes and bush-knives vie with each other in battering it. But—no bird must fly up, no squirrel show itself, no question must be asked, no command given. With the very slightest distraction the spell would be broken. Then the axes and knives would come to rest, everybody would begin talking about what had happened or what they had heard, and there would be no getting them again into train for work.
>
> Happily, no distraction comes. The music gets louder and faster. If this finale lasts even a good half-hour the day has not been wasted. And it continues till I shout "Amani! Amani!" (Enough! Enough!), and put an end to the work for the day.[8]

The framework of the buildings was to be hardwood, the Ogowe's most plentiful product. This one commodity at least was much cheaper here than in Europe. True, it was extremely hard to work, blunting saws and bending nails; but softwoods would have swiftly been eaten by termites. "Any termite that tries to eat my hospital," Schweitzer told Erica Anderson, "will have to see a dentist."

For roofing, the corrugated iron he had already ordered would be invaluable. Leaf tiles were far too much trouble. This hospital, however simple, must be weatherproof. Heat would be reduced by the insulating cavity between roof and ceiling.

All the buildings were raised on piles to let the storm waters pass beneath. The piles had to be brought from sixteen miles upriver where there was a plantation of especially hard wood and then charred for extra preservation. Schweitzer had to supervise the charring, to make sure it was done enough and not too much; and had himself to move the heavy piles into their final position, for the Africans could not grasp the need for such precision. (Nor could they understand why, if a nest of ants were found where a pile was to sink, the doctor should carefully remove the ants rather than crush them. But so he did.)

The head carpenter, Monenzali, although industrious and reliable, could not read even a tape measure, so Schweitzer cut a series of sticks for him to the required lengths. In these circumstances the odds are high that a building will arise somewhat out of true. The price of a square and upright house was constant vigilance.

To create a garden, Schweitzer leveled a series of terraces near the water, each level protected by planks from being washed away by the rains. Stones broken into gravel formed the base, through which excess water could drain off, and leafmold was laid down to create soil. The goats and hens contributed their droppings, and the swift processes of decay in that hot, steamy atmosphere soon rotted it all down to a fertile compost. Early in 1926 beans and cabbages were sown and were eaten a few months later. In that dry season Schweitzer carried water every day for hundreds of fruit tree saplings. To stop the Africans from stealing fruit was impossible. The only solution was to have so much fruit that stealing would no longer be a crime.

In response to an appeal to Europe for a carpenter, a young Swiss, Hans Muggensturm, arrived in April and took over supervision of the building work. The first building completed was a store hut for the tools, to save carrying them to and fro each day; then a hut for the workmen, Monenzali and his assistants. After that there was no need to waste time each day in rounding the men up, transporting them by canoe, and getting them back home before the light failed. Things moved faster.

At Andende, Dr. Nessmann was replaced by Dr. Trensz, another Alsatian, who argued with Schweitzer about the design of the main hospital building and won the argument. "I often think that if I had not followed his advice," Schweitzer said later, "I might not have such a well-organized main building."[9] Frédéric Trensz also distinguished himself by improvising a simple laboratory and identifying in the river water a bacillus similar to that of cholera. It became clear that this was the bacillus responsible for many of the cases that had previously been diagnosed as bacillus dysentery. Schweitzer had, in fact, already had some success in experimentally treating dysentery patients as for cholera, but this had been a matter of lucky instinct, not scientific research.

Trensz was now able to prepare a vaccine, and as a further precaution Schweitzer lost no time in having a well dug for drinking water. The discovery, in fact, revolutionized Trensz's career. He published a learned paper on the subject; having gone out to Africa a surgeon, he returned well on the way to becoming a distinguished research bacteriologist and later ran a highly successful laboratory in Strasbourg.

This was only one of many medical improvements. The new sleeping sickness drugs proved notably effective, and new methods were discovered for treating the agonizing phagedenic ulcers of the feet, from which Schweitzer himself had suffered along with about a third of the hospital's patients.

Sometime in the dry season Joseph married a wife and being unable on his hospital pay to support her in the manner to which she (and her relatives) felt she was entitled, left for a second time for the fleshpots of the timber trade.

And so the work went on until, on January 21, 1927, a fleet of canoes moved the patients to the new hospital.

> Night was falling as I made the last journey and, with Dr. Lauterburg, brought up the last of the patients, among them the mental cases. These, however, sat quite quiet, filled with great expectations. They had been told that in the new hospital they would have rooms with wooden floors; this was, to them, as if they were going to live in a palace. In the old hospital the floors of their rooms had been merely the damp earth.
>
> I shall never forget that first evening in the new hospital. From all the mosquito-curtains there looked out contented faces. "What a fine house you've built us, Doctor!" was the universal exclamation. The fact was that for the first time my sick were housed as elementary humanity requires the sick to be housed, and you may think how I thanked God for that. And how thankfully also I thought of the friends in Europe whose kindness has permitted me to face the cost of the removal![10]

The quarters for the staff were not yet built, so two doctors and a nurse moved into the house for European patients at the new hospital, and the rest stayed at Andende. Schweitzer set about demolishing all the buildings at Andende that belonged to him, to use every beam, plank, and nail for the fittings of the new hospital—the bed frames, cupboards, and shelves.

In March someone arrived from England who must be mentioned although in the early bulletins she asked to remain anonymous. Mrs. C. E. B. Russell proved as much at home supervising the workers on the plantation as later she showed herself translating Schweitzer's lectures: a lady of great talent and character.

> Early in July the chief buildings are finished, though there is still much to do in the matter of internal arrangements.
>
> The big pile-built village has quite a dignified look! And how much easier the work is now, for at last we have space enough, air enough, and light enough! How delightful we feel it, doctors and nurses all, to have our new rooms distinctly cooler than our old quarters were!
>
> For the isolation of the dysentery cases wise precautions have been taken. Their rooms have no opening towards the hospital, and are approached on the side next to the river. But from the river they are separated by a fence, so that they cannot pollute the water.
>
> For the mental patients eight cells and a general sitting-room are in prospect.[11]

Here, in fact, is the nucleus of the hospital as it existed till Schweitzer's death and for many years after—more than half a century—and which despite the inroads of the termites still survives as a museum today.

20

Fame

1927–1929

AT LAST HE WENT HOME. Apart from anything else funds were running very low, and a new money-raising tour was imperative. The hospital was probably the cheapest ever built, with crippled labor and materials that either grew on the spot or were bought secondhand, but still the enterprise was more than had been budgeted for. Only Schweitzer could raise the necessary cash; so a real rest was out of the question.

Three nights only he spent at Königsfeld with the wife and child he had not seen for three and a half years before he was off on his comfortless, third-or-fourth-class travels across Europe, fulfilling engagements he had arranged before he left Lambarene.

In such circumstances little intimacy can have survived between husband and wife, but there remained a total and unquestioning loyalty and respect, which in itself is remarkable. Between father and daughter there appears to have been no particular tension such as one might have expected. About her feelings then Rhena writes, "I really don't know if I loved my father as a child or not. I certainly was happy when he was with us but I also adjusted when he left. I accepted his absences as a normal thing in my life."[1]

Children can and do accept almost anything as normal, but only if they are allowed to do so. Rhena's ability to adjust tells us a great deal about the atmosphere of equanimity that her mother must have created in the home and her acceptance that the demands of the hospital were supreme.

She still cannot have realized, however, that they would remain so for the rest of Schweitzer's life. Neither in Africa nor in Europe was there to be any escape. From now on his life was to be an alternation between physical work at Lambarene and fund-raising in Europe, with only one departure from the routine when he went briefly with Hélène to the United States after the World War Two.

Just beginning, and henceforward increasing to an almost monotonous flow, was the stream of honors that the world heaped upon him.

In the previous year he had been awarded the Universal Order of Human Merit at Geneva "for the eminent services rendered by you to civilisation and humanity in the midst of the black peoples of Africa." This was his first award that had nothing to do with his academic achievements, but simply recognized his increasing fame as a humanitarian.

Another honor that had been offered him, but which he had had to refuse, was that of being the first recipient of an annual Goethe prize, also for Service to Humanity, which had just been inaugurated by Goethe's city, Frankfurt. The first presentation was made this year, 1927, on August 28, Goethe's birthday. Schweitzer had no hope of getting there, but he accepted the offer of the following year's prize.

Schweitzer was now fully in the world's eye. Wherever he went he was excitedly reported, not only for his hospital work but also, inevitably, for what he had been before and what he had given up to go to Africa. Whether or not he wished it, this was the story that brought money to the hospital; he had to make use of it or lose the income he so desperately needed to pay an increasing staff, to buy increasingly expensive medicines, and to feed and house an ever-increasing number of patients and their families.

Being in the world's eye brought another obligation—to be in himself the visible embodiment of Reverence for Life. He had set out to make his life his argument. He had mocked the Schopenhauers of this world for not living in accordance with their philosophy; now he was committed to making his argument unanswerable. The passion for what was true and serviceable, which had given him the strength for his merciless attacks on the flaws in philosophical and theological traditions, could scarcely let him get away with any inconsistency in his own behavior.

Not that this was particularly difficult for him. Had there been any hypocrisy in him the strain would have been enormous, and, doubtless, the cracks would have shown. But he had been working on his own character since childhood, eliminating the bogus, finding his ideal in the depths of the natural man, and putting his truest impulses into action. "I am simply a man who does what is natural. The natural thing, however, is lovingkindness."[2] This was his true and tested belief.

The natural, however, is also other things: weariness, irritation, and in his case a continuing shyness, a fiery temper, and the need to be right. However vigorously he had molded himself, body and mind, to eliminate these accidental personal qualities and to let the basic loving-kindness through, he was, as he wrote in *Memoirs of Childhood and Youth,* "essentially as intolerable as ever."[3]

Before we go on then, let us look more closely at the self-portrait he gives us in that book, for it adds depth to the pictures we have from the letters to Hélène and from those who met him, on tour and at the hospital, in this last long stretch of his life. He is writing in his forty-ninth year about his teens.

> Between my fourteenth and sixteenth years I passed through an unpleasant phase of development, becoming an intolerable nuisance to everybody, especially to my father, through a passion for discussion. On everyone who met me in the street I wanted to inflict thoroughgoing and closely reasoned considerations on all the questions that were then being generally discussed, in order to expose the errors of the conventional views and get the correct view recognised and appreciated. The joy of seeking for what was true and serviceable had come upon me like a kind of intoxication, and every conversation in which I took part had to go back to fundamentals. . . .
>
> The conviction that human progress is possible only if reasoned thought replaces mere opinion and absence of thought had seized hold of me, and its first manifestations made themselves felt in this stormy and disagreeable fashion.
>
> However, this unpleasant fermentation worked itself off and left the wine clear, though I have remained essentially what I then became. I have always felt clearly that if I were to surrender my enthusiasm for the true and the serviceable, as recognized by means of thought, I should be surrendering my very self. I am, therefore, essentially as intolerable as ever, only I try as well as I can to reconcile that disposition with the claims of conventional manners, so as not to annoy other people.
>
> But how often do I inwardly rebel! How much I suffer from the way we spend so much of our time uselessly instead of talking in serious fashion about serious things, and getting to know each other well as hoping and believing, striving and suffering mortals! I often feel it to be absolutely wrong to sit like that with a mask on, so to say. Many a time I ask myself how far we can carry this good breeding without harm to our integrity.[4]

That was the picture from within. How did he appear to others? The accounts of people who met him in Europe show a quite extraordinary consistency. Even more unvarying are the letters he wrote, thousands of them: to friends, to the famous, to unknown contributors, to those who wrote for his advice. The biographer searching through this mass of material for the odd illuminating inconsistency, the flash of idiosyncrasy, is in for disappointment. The only striking thing is the contrast between the Schweitzer people met in the flesh, full of sparkling personality and resilient energy, and the Schweitzer of the letters, unrelaxed, a little formal, and generally complaining of weariness and a sense of mild desperation at the prospect of unending toil.

To record in detail the comings and goings of the next few years would be tedious in the extreme. Let us instead try to build up a picture of the man, his appearance, the sound of his voice, and the impression he made upon those who heard him, who escorted him, who went to visit him, who offered him hospitality. The exact dates are unimportant. He did not change from year to year, not at least until at last he began, much later than most, to grow old.

Even his clothes were always the same and, apparently, everlasting. In Africa his outfit consisted of baggy trousers, white shirt, and a single clip-on bow tie, which he took in his pocket on his way to formal occasions such as calling on government officials, to be donned at the last possible moment and removed directly the interview was over. In Europe he fetched out the black suit that the Günsbach tailor had made for him when he played in Barcelona before the king of Spain in 1905. His one and only hat went with him everywhere. At best, if someone suggested it was time he had a new one, he would examine it carefully and might concede that it needed a new band. On one occasion Emmy Martin actually bought him a new hat, identical in style with the old, and left it on the hat stand in place of the old one. Schweitzer was going out to visit someone who had suffered a bereavement, and as he went to the door he had his mind fixed on understanding and sharing the loss so that what he said might have some meaning. Absent-mindedly he picked up the new hat, put it on, and went out. Mme. Martin was triumphant. But when he came back, he said, "This is not my hat. What have you done with my hat? I want it back." And he had it back.

All this, with his canvas bags and haversacks, seemed often to be a pose. People could not believe that there was not something perverse, an inverted flamboyance, about this ostentatious simplicity that was unaffected by time or circumstance. And certainly Schweitzer was not unaware of its effect. But the reasoning behind it was all of a piece. The money had been contributed for the hospital, not for him, and it was not his to spend. "Anything I spend on myself I can't spend on my Africans." His Lambarene trousers grew shorter and shorter as the bottoms frayed and he stitched them to a new level. And his shirts reached a condition in which observers could scarcely tell which was darning and which was original material. He remained the canny peasant, whose grandmother had taught him to put the stalk of the apple in the fuel box and give the core to the pigs, who wrote his lists and letters on the backs of old envelopes, undid and preserved every piece of string, flattened every piece of used wrapping paper, straightened every used nail, and only for birthdays and similar celebrations allowed such luxuries as wine and butter on the menu at the hospital.

In a sense it was a demonstration. In Africa he was setting an example that was vital to the hospital, where waste was madness. In Europe he was flying a flag against the technological world of overconsumption and when pressed could defend himself to some effect. He told a lady in America that his tie had been worn on ceremonial occasions by his father. She was astonished. "I know men," she said, "who have a hundred ties!" "Really?" asked Schweitzer, "For one neck?" The flag he flew was a true symbol of himself; to behave otherwise just because he was becoming notable would have been to be false to himself, to acknowledge that simplicity was not really important, that he was prepared to abandon it when it was no longer forced upon him. "*Je suis fidèle*," he said.

And, perhaps, he needed his fidelity as a bulwark against the extraordinary tide of flattery that suddenly swept about him. He knew his strength came from his roots in the hills of Alsace, and his mind constantly returned there, even if his body could not, to draw fresh sap. His clothes and his habits were a statement that the traditions of his home were still strong within him. And although he often said he was a citizen of the world, he made it clear that he was also "a pine-tree of the Vosges,"[5] which would not change its characteristics, transplant it where one would.

As to the world's reactions to the way he looked, although he understood it, he was certainly not concerned about it. He was interested in his function, not in himself. Some part of the power of his personality and the effect he had on others must certainly be accounted for by the fact that he had put himself at the disposal of something beyond himself. Such people present a paradoxical spectacle in that their very self-abandonment enables them to be more themselves. They are not troubled, as others are, about their "images," so they inhibit themselves less and present themselves with greater force. In religious terms the experience of self-abandonment is expressed in a sermon that Schweitzer preached in 1905, the year of his decision to take up medicine, but which is appropriate to quote now, when we are trying to find clues to the mature personality that burst on the world at this time of 1927–28.

> To content oneself with becoming small, that is the only salvation and liberation. To work in the world as such, asking nothing of it, or of men, not even recognition, that is true happiness. . . . There are things which one cannot do without Jesus. Without Him one cannot attain to that higher innocence—unless we look to Him in the disappointments of life, and seek in Him the strength to be childlike and small in that higher sense.

> Whoever has gone through the world of smallness has left the empire
> of this world to enter into the Kingdom of God. He has gone over the
> border as one goes over the border in a dark forest—without taking note
> of it. The way remains the same, the surrounding things the same, and only
> gradually does he realise that whilst everything is familiar it is different,
> that life is the same and yet not the same because of the clarity which lights
> up in him, and because of the peace and the strength which have taken
> possession of him because he is small and has finished with himself.[6]

This is not the false humility of the man who pretends he is unimportant. It is the ability to see oneself in perspective, judging oneself by the importance of the work one has to do and to be thrown neither to one side nor the other by the waves of popular hysteria. It amused him very much to find himself "as famous as a prize-fighter," or, perhaps, not quite as famous, for he also loved to tell the story of the autograph hunter who said to him, "Now I've got three Albert Schweitzers I can swap them for one Max Schmeling." Wherever he went he might have been entertained, had he so wished, by the rich and the famous, by distinguished citizens and celebrity hunters who would have made much of him. In fact, he often left his arrangements to the last moment and trusted to luck to find a bed.

After he had spent two hard days in London, with rehearsals and recitals at St. Margaret's, Westminster, and St. Paul's, not to mention an impromptu talk to the Choir School, the wife of his organ assistant, Mr. Ashby, discovered that he had no plans for food or lodging that night. The Ashbys gave him supper and a bed, and their Putney home became his *pied à terre* in London for years thereafter.

In Amsterdam a widow, Mrs. Obermann, heard about Schweitzer in 1927, and with the help of friends made a great effort, collected a thousand guilders in a week, and sent them to Basel to a Mr. Baur, who acted as Schweitzer's collecting agent. Schweitzer wrote his thanks, and in his letter said that he would seek out Mrs. Obermann next time he was in Rotterdam and shake her hand personally. He came in 1928, to lecture in a church, and Mrs. Obermann managed to get a seat, although the church was packed to overflowing and mounted police were on hand to control the hundreds who were turned away. But she heard nothing from Schweitzer. She had not really expected to do so.

Throughout the introductions, while he waited to speak, she watched him sitting quietly "like a heap of tiredness." His turn came and he rose. His burly form had filled out now, and he was positively portly, although his face was extraordinarily young for a man of fifty-three, and his hair sprang dark and uncontrollable as ever. His arms hung loosely by his side, totally relaxed, in his characteristic pose, heavy and without grace, a peasant stance. He began quietly, in a voice which was unexpectedly high-pitched for such a big man, a pitch that he may have learned so as to overcome the abominable acoustics of churches and church halls.

"People often ask me, why did you go to Africa?" There was a long pause. He seemed to be brooding. The silence held through the packed church. Into the silence, slowly: *"Weil mein Meister es mir gesagt hat"*— "Because my master told me to." With its timing, its simplicity, its sincerity, the statement was one of those that makes an audience's skin prickle. Then, as he often did, he spoke of Africa as Lazarus, the beggar at the table of the rich man that was Europe. Whatever else the speech was, this was great oratory, a control of the audience coming from the personality but also learned in the schoolroom and the pulpit. American journalists in Lambarene in later years reported that Schweitzer's simple Bible readings after the evening meal outdid Billy Graham in their ability to grip an audience. A professional in all things, he had mastered his technique until it could be forgotten and the man himself was revealed.

The evening ended, and Mrs. Obermann went home. There was a telephone call: "Did you receive my letter?" No, she hadn't. "I would like to take a meal with you tomorrow." So began a long friendship of a kind that was repeated in numberless cities and towns of Europe.

On one occasion when he arrived, Mrs. Obermann's house was already full of relatives and friends, and she suggested a nearby hotel. "Haven't you a seamen's home here?" he asked. She happened to be on the committee of the seamen's home, and he picked up the haversack in which he carried his belongings and walked there to find a bed. Next morning he reported that he had enjoyed it very much because of the view.

Another time he had traveled all night and had rehearsed in the morning for an organ concert in the evening. These rehearsals were exhaustive and exhausting. Schweitzer would find an organ-playing friend to play the piece in question while he stumped about the church checking the effect of the different stops in different parts of the church. Having decided upon the ideal registration to use for the concert, he then began his own rehearsal. After he had rehearsed he went back to Mrs. Obermann's house and lay down to rest. His hostess told her children to be particularly quiet when they came back from school for their lunch. When he got up, Schweitzer asked where the children were—had they stayed at school? When he heard that they had been in the house but had kept quiet on his behalf, "If you ever again tell your children to be quiet just for me, I'll buy each one of them a trumpet."

His consideration had its limitations. When he really needed something, he had no hesitation in asking for it, and one thing he always needed was a companion. A part of his shyness that he never lost was a real reluctance to go into a room alone. Whenever he visited Paris, for example, he would ring the Herrenschmidt household and demand that Adèle's younger sister (for Adèle had died in 1923) should drop everything and steer him around the city for two or three days. Did she ever refuse? "He was not a man one said no to," says her daughter. But did she not resent it? "No, she loved it." He had a way of dominating women that many of them adored. It was done with charm and warmth; he had not lost the art of the rendezvous, and his manner of giving all his attention to his companion of the moment made it seem a compliment and a privilege. Even when he was ordering people about it was with a sort of attractive gruffness, like a terrier.

For the occasions when his displeasure was provoked (and such occasions were not infrequent in a man so sure of his own rightness and with so much of the teacher in him), he had learned a way of expressing it that took away much of the sting. His threat to Mrs. Obermann to buy all the children trumpets was typical. Another instance: he hated to see men wear short trousers; he thought them undignified. So he would say to someone who failed or refused to do what he thought best, "If you don't do what I say I'll come out wearing shorts tomorrow."[7]

His biographer, George Seaver, whose book was published in 1948, gives many descriptions of encounters with Schweitzer, often from firsthand sources. After writing of the effect of the lectures he gave in England in 1928, Seaver goes on:

> Even more striking was the "terrific impact" of his presence within doors—a veritable tornado—with a riot of people surging round him; secretaries with their typewriters relegated to the bathroom and stairs; important and importunate callers, with whom he had light-heartedly made appointments and had forgotten all about, demanding interviews, their indignation melting, when admitted eventually, "like wax in the sun." And when before his departure, itself an uproarious occasion, Miss Royden[8] tried to express in halting French their gratitude for his visit and the "honour" that she and her household felt in entertaining him as their guest, the Doctor, gravely shocked, drew her aside and besought her never to use such a word as that, *"parce que ce n'est pas convenable parmi les chrétiens."*[9]

In another encounter:

> So moved was Mr. Hudson Shaw by an address on Lambarene given by the doctor to a meeting of which he was chairman that, without a thought, he cast his gold watch into the collection. Remembering later that the watch, precious though it was to him, was of old-fashioned make and probably worth not more than the value of its gold, he offered to "ransom" it for a much larger sum. Somewhat to his surprise, Dr. Schweitzer asked if he

might keep the watch for a few days longer. It was soon returned, but this time with an inscription: "Rev. Hudson Shaw et Dr Albert Schweitzer—fratres. 21/5/28." The considerate thoughtfulness of this gesture was noted by Miss Royden as characteristic of the "quality of perfection—and I should add, of exquisite care—that gives a grace and fitness to all he says and does—trifles in themselves perhaps—but not trifles to those to whom beauty is as precious as strength."[10]

A singer, Clara Faisst, who had asked Schweitzer to hear her sing, wrote, "I have never been listened to as by you. . . . I felt your reviving force."[11]

Yet during these outpourings of energy, physical and psychic (for to listen as he evidently listened to Clara Faisst demands the energy of great concentration), it seems that scarcely anybody actually saw him tired; generally he easily outlasted his companions. "He was the easiest of visitors to entertain," wrote Mrs. Ashby, "but a tyrant to work with; indefatigable himself, he would work others to exhaustion; and I remember his good-tempered but dismayed surprise when I told him so!" He would snatch his rest as and when he could, curled up in a wooden-seated third-class compartment or stretched across a couple of hard chairs. The ability to relax, instantly and completely, in any circumstances is probably the secret of his stamina. We have seen how, under great pressure in his twenties, he knew how to take time off to do absolutely nothing. And even when Mrs. Obermann saw him as a "heap of tiredness," he was more probably in a state of deeply concentrated relaxation.

Only the letters, with their constant and increasing complaint of weariness, provide the curious counterpoint. One wonders whether this became a more or less automatic ploy to excuse himself for the fact that he was so often late in replying; for the mountain of mail was now swelled by dozens of letters a week, from all over the world, asking him to solve the writers' personal problems. He had become, as well as everything else, a guru.

It was a sad fate for one to whom, as he admitted in *Memoirs of Childhood and Youth*, letter writing never came easy. He never forgot those dreadful post-Christmas sessions in his father's study as a boy when he sat and envied his big sister's facile flow. Like thank-you letters, all his correspondence tended to fall into an unvarying mold: first the apology for lateness in writing and the statement that he must be brief because his writer's cramp was troubling him; then a somewhat formal message, which, if on a philosophical or theological subject (and this would include life in general), would summarize the views set out in his books, sticking always to principles rather than individual cases; often a short rundown on the latest tasks awaiting him at the hospital, with a complaint about his weariness and the difficulty of getting things done; and a warm but formal conclusion. Even the signature was unrelaxed, amazing in a man who so studied to be natural in his relationships. Face to face he would ask people to address him by the intimate *tu*. But in letters, even to close friends, even to his daughter, he signed himself, not Bery, not Albert, not Papa, but the full and formal "Albert Schweitzer."

Why was this? Was it that the written word was too permanent and he too aware of the position he had taken up to be able to unbend on paper? He did once say of Goethe, "If the poor man had known they would write down everything he said, he'd never have opened his mouth." Was he aware that he was moving into the same danger?

Or did he find it impossible to relate in a personal fashion unless the person were physically present? He certainly hated the telephone on the grounds that it was impossible to talk properly to someone whom one could not see.

Or were those Christmas letters so traumatic that the very thought of "letter writing" subconsciously and uncontrollably stiffened his mind as it stiffened his fingers around the pen? Did the father image hang over him saying, "You haven't written enough. Your aunt won't be satisfied with that." For he certainly often wrote much more than was strictly necessary. But it was wasted effort, for it said nothing new. Perhaps he was aware of this, for he did himself say that the colorful Gabonese stamps on the envelopes were the most interesting parts of his letters.

Königsfeld and Günsbach provided brief interludes from this Flying Dutchman existence. Here for short spells he could be with his daughter and she with him. Hélène saw more of him, for she sometimes traveled with him and even did a little lecturing of her own.

During these breaks, Schweitzer worked on *The Mysticism of Paul the Apostle,* the book that had been so nearly ready when he first went to Africa fifteen years earlier. His retirement from the academic world had evidently not blunted his theological skill, for this is regarded by theologians as his finest achievement although the subject is much less pertinent to the ordinary reader and never likely to attract the same attention as the books about Jesus.

But even Günsbach, even Königsfeld no longer provided complete sanctuary, for friends, acquaintances, correspondents, and now sightseers as well pursued him to every resting place, and a combination of his inherited hospitality and his own deliberate openness to all comers meant that nobody was ever turned away.

So when, in August 1928, he went to Frankfurt to receive his Goethe prize, he had already decided what he would do with the money. He would build a house in Günsbach that could be his European headquarters and also serve as a guesthouse for his visitors. During the following year or two it was under construction to his design. By his wish it was not set back, but opened directly onto the road, without even a pavement between, so that working at the window of the front room he could be close to the comings and goings of the villagers and chat with them as they passed by. It is this kind of touch (and there are many like it) that makes one ask oneself to what extent he, shy as he was, *really* wanted things this way and to what extent it was a demonstration of a conviction. The only way I find I can answer this is by saying that the conviction was as much a part of him as his shyness; by his own reckoning a more important part because it was the product, as he always insisted, of thought, whereas shyness was an accident of inheritance. This is what he meant when he wrote to Professor John Regester in 1931, "I only understand myself from the philosophical point of view." He had dug his philosophy out of the depths of himself; now he molded everything about him to his philosophy.

The speech he made at the presentation of the Goethe prize is inevitably concerned with this interlocking of thought and life, for it was with Goethe's help that he first weaned himself away from the elaborate fairy tales of speculative philosophy and onto the "simple, homely nature philosophy," which "leaves the world and nature as they are and compels man to find his place in them."[12] The speech, with its characteristic title "My Debt to Goethe," is Schweitzer's first public acknowledgment of the man whom he used to call "my father in thought." It describes how his admiration had developed into something like a personal relationship; how Goethe's example had strengthened him whenever practical tasks had seemed likely to overwhelm intellectual ones, as a curate, as a medical student, and recently as a building laborer. For Goethe, too, had lived by "the union of practical work with intellectual activity."[13] And when in Africa Schweitzer had been compelled to leave his medical work to others while he superintended the clearing of the jungle for the new hospital, "I thought, whenever I got reduced to despair, how Goethe had devised for the final activities of his Faust the task of winning from the sea land on which men could live and feed themselves. And thus Goethe stood by my side in the swampy forest as my smiling comforter, and the man who really understood."[14]

On the surface there were enormous differences between Goethe, the temperamental, many-sided creative genius, and Schweitzer, the single-minded ethical teacher. Werner Picht, who knew Schweitzer well, makes the most of these differences in his book *The Life and Thought of Albert Schweitzer:*

The expansiveness of Goethe's nature stands against the homogeneity of Schweitzer's. Into a ripe old age Goethe still remained open to all possibilities of human activity, whereas from his earliest youth Schweitzer's way of life was already determined. Goethe added ring after ring to his personality like a growing tree, Schweitzer's nature is more that of the solid monolith. . . . For Goethe the all-important thing was to give permanency to the moment. . . . for Schweitzer the meaning of life lies in ceaseless ethical activity. . . . The sensuality which combines Goethe rhapsodically with nature "in all her glory" is not for him. For Schweitzer thought is the legitimate path to knowledge. Goethe attaches great importance to intuition. Schweitzer abstracts where Goethe keeps to the concrete.[15]

Rash though it may be to disagree with so fine a thinker as Picht, and one who actually knew Schweitzer, I feel certain that he undervalues the intuitive in Schweitzer. Schweitzer did, I am convinced, experience that rhapsodical sensuality, combining him with nature: only he did not find it enough. He had seen also nature's absurd cruelty in Africa, and that made a great deal of difference. "Nobody really knows me," he said, "who has not seen me in Africa." He was speaking of himself as a man of action rather than intellect, but also as a man in the midst of nature rather than in the midst of civilization. Africa's harsh indifference and man's insanity in the war had convinced him that the rhapsody needed directing. Indeed, I believe it was precisely this tension, between the rhapsody and the despair, that forced him to think his way to his conclusions and that provided the motive force for his life.

So there was a genuine community of souls between Goethe and Schweitzer although Schweitzer's style is the more formal and controlled. And the crucial link lies in what Schweitzer said, in 1932, speaking at Manchester University on "The Philosophical Development of Goethe": "With him thought and conduct were one, and that is the best thing one can say of any thinker."

Although he spent the Goethe prize on his Günsbach house, he felt badly about taking money out of Germany at a time when Germany needed every mark she could get for reconstruction and for the help of the crippled and widowed. So all the money he earned at this time from his concerts and lectures in Germany went not into the Lambarene fund but instead to German charities, until the full value of the prize had been equaled. And, indeed, from this time on, now that money came so comparatively easily, Schweitzer would often divert his takings to some other cause that he felt was especially needy, rather than to his hospital. His sense of justice was troubled by the feeling that the hospital enjoyed an unfair advantage in his ability to fill churches and halls and with them the hospital coffers. This was one of the reasons, not often understood, why the hospital remained simple when one might have expected it to be able to grow wealthy and elaborate. Schweitzer wished it so, certainly, on principle. But there was no vast fund lying idle, as has been alleged. The surplus was quietly distributed elsewhere.

In 1929, Schweitzer was fifty-four. A Leipzig publisher by the name of Felix Meiner decided that this was an appropriate age for him to embark on his autobiography. Schweitzer did not agree. A letter from Schweitzer to Meiner, on the latter's seventieth birthday in 1953, lets us into the genesis of the book.

> If you had not forced me to write *Aus meinem Leben und Denken* [Out of My Life and Thought] I never would have thought of it.
>
> If you dear friend, had not enjoyed Oskar Kraus's co-operation, I doubt whether you would have succeeded. I did not like the whole thing, because at the age of 54 years I believed I was still too young to write a report of my life. An old clergyman in Strasbourg had stopped me in the street: "What have I been told, Albert, that you are writing your life already? That is a symptom of vanity. A man should do that only after his 70th birthday. I want you to hear this from me. Don't be offended." He spoke these words and left me. I did not think he was wrong, but it so happened that Mr. Felix Meiner thought differently.[16]

The book was commissioned, and Schweitzer wrote it the following year at Lambarene. But although he thought fifty-four was too young for an autobiography, he evidently felt it was time to think about who was to succeed him when he retired. Knowing as we do that he went on for another thirty-six years and that the succession was unclear to the very end, it seems odd to discover that he appointed a successor as far back as this, but, in fact, he did.

He was a young Swiss doctor, the son of a pastor, and his name was Erich Dölken. "Years before," wrote Schweitzer in one of his bulletins, "he had resolved to devote himself to my Hospital, not for a time only, but permanently."[17] But Dölken died before even reaching Lambarene. On the trip going to Africa, he was found dead in his cabin one morning—presumably from a heart attack—and was buried at Grand Bassam. It was the first of several abortive attempts to find the right successor.

One wonders what would have happened had Dölken lived. Would Schweitzer, in fact, have retired? Or would Dölken have been content to work as his assistant all those thirty-six years till his death before taking over? Or would the long haul finally have proved too much for Dölken? Would he have lasted just so long (as many others did), and then, through sickness or clash of temperament, the need to be his own master or the need to further his career, have moved on—back to Europe or away to found a hospital of his own in some other unhealthy part of the world?

Dölken had been due in Lambarene in the autumn. Schweitzer was booked to return there on the next sailing of the same ship, arriving at Christmas, and for months ahead was superintending the fresh supplies he would take with him. We have a photograph that shows the room in the Rue des Greniers in Strasbourg where the preparations went on. Here volunteers packed the cases, made by other volunteers, with drugs, rubber gloves, operating gowns, mosquito netting, sheets, blankets, etcetera, which had been bought, transported, stitched, hemmed, or otherwise contributed by hosts of yet other volunteers. It reminds us of something easily forgotten about this particular hospital—that the whole backup organization, which in other cases would be provided by some mission society or some government department, had to be created and supported by Schweitzer alone. A multitude of friends and friends of friends gave up time to help; and among these a few key figures, honorary secretaries, honorary treasurers, honorary odd-job men of all sorts, unsung but beyond value for their industry and reliability, worked for years on end to keep the supplies flowing. It is highly probable that Hélène played a major part in all this, but finally it was Schweitzer's responsibility and no one else's that everything needed on the Ogowe was thought of, obtained, and dispatched. Doctors, nurses, and patients must all have what they needed . . . and even the patients' families must be housed and fed, which is not a usual hospital facility.

This time when Schweitzer sailed, Hélène came with him, leaving Rhena behind with friends. The decision had not been easily reached, for Hélène's health was still far from perfect, and they both knew all too well how merciless that climate could be to the weak. But simply to see the new hospital, to have that share at least in the work she had partnered, that was her desire and her right.

With them went a Dr. Ann Schmitz and a trained nurse cum bacteriologist, Marie Secretan, the latter charged particularly with the care of Hélène on the voyage and at Lambarene. Marie Secretan's account of that journey makes intriguing reading.

> I had been told that this journey was dreadfully tedious, but we very soon discovered that no one who travels with Dr. Schweitzer can be bored. A bundle of proofs of his book, *The Mysticism of St. Paul,* which were awaiting correction, made the 22 hours seem quite short. . . . Then came the voyage—my first! . . . People had talked about the tedium of a three-weeks' voyage, but here too Dr. Schweitzer provided a way to make the time pass. He wrote while on board the final chapter of *The Mysticism of St. Paul,* and

Fr. Schmitz and I provided him with two copies of it, in case the one sent to the printer should get lost. That also made the time pass very quickly.[18]

What kind of man is it who can prevail upon two healthy young women to check proofs and make copies of chapters of deep theology amid the booming racket of an express train and the heaving and lurching of a coastal steamer, and make them feel he has done them a good turn?

Hélène, too, wrote about the return to Africa and her joy at seeing Lambarene again and the new hospital. What she does not mention is that on the voyage her tubercular condition flared up again with a high fever. After many years of waiting to come back and work at her husband's side this was a devastating blow—a sad indication that her full health was never likely to return. Long discussions took place on the ship as to whether she should continue the journey or whether she and Marie Secretan should transfer to a liner returning to Europe. Such a capitulation to weakness, however, was not in Hélène's nature, and she went on. They reached Port-Gentil on Christmas Eve 1929. Quite unexpectedly, Mathilde Kottmann appeared with the motorboat in which she had come downriver from the hospital to smooth over the customs formalities and organize the transfer of the 128 packing cases to the special tug she had hired. So Schweitzer was able to come upriver with the rest of them, instead of having to stay on the coast to deal with the paperwork and wait for the riverboat's next sailing. He spent Christmas Day chugging up the Ogowe and writing the preface to the St. Paul book. His last major book was finished.

At Lambarene there was further evidence of smooth and efficient planning. A timber merchant had lent a motor lighter to take the cases to the hospital. Another had offered the services of twenty of his African employees for the loadings. The barely completed cluster of huts that Schweitzer left behind had in the past two and a half years been completed to his specifications and had become a well-oiled medical machine, housing and treating between 250 and 300 patients. The staff now, including the African orderlies, the cooks, the washing and mending women, and the people who crushed the palm nuts for their oil, numbered about thirty-five. Among them, once more, was Joseph; the timber trade had let him down again. When Hélène had worked there, thirteen years earlier, she, Joseph, and Schweitzer were more or less the entire personnel.

21

Life at the Hospital

1929–1932

FROM HIS COMMENT soon after arrival that the management and discipline were better than when he left,[1] it is evident that so far as the medical side was concerned his staff was perfectly capable of running the hospital without him and that they could also organize the building and the garden maintenance that he had left in their care.

What they could not do was give the place the particular stamp that he gave it. Nor did they have to raise money for it, nor organize supplies, nor take responsibility for additional building. And this, it was instantly apparent, was already necessary.

The particular need was for a new mental ward, for the original one had had to be used for dysentery patients. Such a ward must be strong enough to restrain the mental patients during their violent disturbances, yet not too uncomfortably restrictive at other times. Pencil and hammer in hand, blue notebook with its string-threaded leaves in one hip pocket and folding rule sticking out of the other, Schweitzer set about it—and about any repairs and renovations that were required.

Although he still did a certain amount of doctoring, the hospital was now so complex that general supervision and administration, added to his building work and the writing of his autobiography, amounted to a full-time task. As time went on there were always improvements to be made: a big new building with partitions so that each family could have privacy from the others; a cement reservoir to collect rainwater from the roofs, all of them built with the same kind of laborious effort that had raised the main part of the hospital.

But the more he built, the more the patients came. Demand for treatment always exceeded supply. The spirit of mercy became indistinguishable from the struggle to keep abreast of the situation. Any romance that might be left was liable to disappear beneath the weight of what he called "the prose of Africa." It was vital that he preserve those moments when, in philosophical work, in music, and in memory, his mind returned to the rich soil of the country and culture that had bred him and drew from it the fresh sap he needed.

At the same time the peasant in him also needed the manual labor, the challenge of physical mastery without which he found the intellectual world meaningless. Although he constantly sought sympathy—and received it—for the way in which practical details kept him from his desk until deep into the night, he once confessed, in a quiet moment many years later, that he was unable to settle down to writing unless he had first done a hard day's work, that whether or not the work was needed, he needed the work. Since his university days, work had always been a necessity—almost a drug. To wake each morning with the knowledge that the day held too much was the only way he knew how to live. Grumble though he might, his complaints were like those of a dedicated mother about her children: the tasks that were his burden were also his fulfilment.

At this time the fulfilment was great. The hospital was in that happy stage when a young, expanding project is full of life and growth. When Dr. Nessmann left in 1926, he had said it was like leaving paradise, not because the humidity was 90 percent and the place full of crippled, half-starved, desperately sick people, but because of the spirit of hope, cooperation, and achievement in face of odds. However great the contributions of others, this kind of atmosphere is always the creation of the leader of the enterprise, and, perhaps, it is the most satisfying creation of all.

For Hélène, however, it was too much, and at Easter she had to go home. She had been able to do no work, and for much of the time her weakness had forced her to remain sitting on the balcony of her room, watching the activity go on around her. Finally, to her bitter regret, she had to acknowledge defeat. She said good-bye to the hospital, her husband, and the brisk women who could work with him in that climate and set off on the long voyage to Europe, health, and loneliness.

But, at least, she had seen and lived in the new hospital, and now when news came, she could visualize and understand it. She knew the effort each task represented; she knew the feel of the dawn and the dusk, the routine of the day.

From that time till Schweitzer's death the routine scarcely varied. With days always the same length there was no change even from season to season. Doctors and nurses came and went, the hospital grew, medicines improved, but the long and detailed description Schweitzer sent to his supporters in 1936 of "A Day at the Hospital" can stand as a pattern for all the days from 1931 onward. This historic document is reproduced as appendix A and is the most complete and authentic account of the hospital's activities that we possess, one that, incidentally, answers a great many questions, misapprehensions, and criticisms about the way it was run.

Schweitzer's own day began with a little Bach on the battered piano in the smaller room next to his own small room and a shave in cold water on the veranda, with a small mirror hung on a nail in one of the beams. After the day's work and the evening meal, when the oil lamps had gone their separate ways from the dining room through the rustling darkness to the various rooms, Schweitzer's own lamp sat in his window while he played again and then wrote late into the night: letters, lists, and fresh pages of the projected third volume of *The Philosophy of Civilisation*. To prevent nibbling by ants or goats they were threaded on a piece of string and hung on nails above the windows, "like pheasants."

The work of healing was often complicated by the witchcraft, taboos, and superstition that still ruled the lives of the Gabonese. A patient's relatives, encouraged by a witch doctor, would attribute his sickness to poisoning by some enemy, and if the patient died, it could trigger a retaliatory murder. So the cause of every death had to be explained very carefully and convincingly to the relatives although even then it was impossible to tell what random retribution might be exacted when the party got back to its village.

Within the confines of the hospital Schweitzer also had to act as headman and administrator of justice when one of the Africans' interminable legal arguments arose. Here is his account of one such occasion.

In the night a patient had taken another man's canoe and gone out fishing by moonlight. The owner of the boat surprised him as he returned at dawn and demanded for the use of the canoe a large monetary compensation as well as all the fish he had caught. By the laws current among the natives, this was his actual right.

The case was brought before me and, as often before, I had to act as judge. First I made known that on my land not native law, but the law of reason of the white man is in force and is proclaimed by my lips. Then I proceeded to examine the legal position. I established the fact that both men were at the same time right and wrong. "You are right," I said to the owner of the canoe, "because the other man ought to have asked for permission to use your boat. But you are wrong because you are careless and lazy. You were careless because you merely twisted the chain of your canoe round a palm-tree instead of fastening it with a padlock as you ought to do here. By your carelessness you led this man into temptation to make use of your canoe. Of laziness you are guilty because you were asleep in your hut on this moonlit night instead of making use of the good opportunity for fishing."

"But you," I said, turning to the other, "were in the wrong when you took the boat without asking the owner's permission. You were in the right because you were not so lazy as he was and you did not want to let the moonlight night go by without making some use of it."

In view of the established legal usage, I then gave sentence that the man who went fishing must give a third of the fish to the owner as compensation, and might keep one-third for himself because he had taken the trouble to catch the fish. The remaining third I claimed for the Hospital, because the affair took place here and I had to waste my time adjudicating the palaver.[2]

On Sunday only essential work was done. In the morning Schweitzer held a service, for the business of transporting everybody by canoe to the Andende mission would have been much too complicated; and besides, it satisfied a need in him.

At nine o'clock an orderly went around the hospital with a bell, summoning people to prayers. For the next half-hour Schweitzer sat playing on "the little harmonium" in the lane between the two main wards, under the shade of the wide roofs, while the people slowly came together, or else someone would play something appropriately religious on the gramophone. When, eventually, everyone had arrived, Schweitzer began, not with a hymn, because nobody knew the hymns, and not with a prayer, because newcomers would not understand, but with a sermon. An interpreter on his left translated it sentence by sentence into Bendjabi, for the benefit of the tribes of the interior; another on his right translated into the Fang dialect. Most patients knew one or the other, more or less.

I cannot [he wrote) pretend that my hearers are as quiet as the faithful of a church in Europe. If anyone is in the habit of cooking their dinner on the spot where we are gathered, I let them get on with it. Mothers wash their children and comb their hair; men mend their nets, slung beneath the roofs; a native shamelessly lays his head in a companion's lap for a delousing. It is much better to let them go on than to interrupt the proceedings with remarks about discipline, which would have to be repeated each week, with this ever-changing audience. Sheep and goats run bleating about the gathering. The weaverbirds that nest in the nearby trees make a deafening din. Even Mrs. Russell's two monkeys, let loose on Sundays, go through their tricks in the palm-trees and on the corrugated iron roofs, and finally snuggle up on their mistress's shoulders.[3]

In later years the Bendjabi language was replaced by Galoa when fewer of the patients came from the wild interior tribes. And as literacy grew among the Africans Schweitzer provided hymn books, and hymns were sung beautifully and with great enjoyment.

The sermons were rather different from those he had preached at St. Nicholas, Strasbourg, simple though even those were.

I restrict myself to the simplest experiences, whatever my point of departure, I always come back to the central idea; letting oneself be seized by Christ. So even if someone only hears me once he has at least a hint of what it means to be a Christian.

I try to be as concrete as possible. No vague generalisations to explain, for example, Peter's question to Jesus: "How many times should I forgive my brother? Should it be seven times?" (Matthew 18.21). I talk to my people with complete realism, and I use everyday incidents to illustrate the meaning of forgiving seven times in a single day. This is how I recently tackled it:

"One morning, you have just got up, and you leave your hut. Coming towards you you see a man whom everybody thinks is a scoundrel. He does you an injury. You remember that Jesus has said that one should forgive; you keep quiet instead of starting an argument.

"Next your neighbour's goat eats the bananas you were keeping for your dinner. Instead of seeking a quarrel with him, you merely tell him what his goat has done and that it would be fair if he replaced your bananas. But if he contests this and pretends that it wasn't his goat, you go on your way peacefully and you reflect that the Almighty has provided so many bananas on your plantation that it's not worth the trouble of starting a fight over the odd bunch. . . . "

After another four misadventures evening comes and—

"You want to go fishing but you discover that your canoe has disappeared. Someone has gone off in it to do his own fishing. Angrily you hide yourself behind a tree to await him, and you promise yourself that when he gets back you'll seize his fish, you'll make a complaint against him and make him pay a fair compensation. But while you lie in wait, your heart starts to speak. It keeps repeating to you the words of Jesus: 'God cannot forgive us our sins if we do not forgive each others.' You have to wait so long that the Lord Jesus once more wins the victory. When the other fellow comes back at the crack of dawn, and stands all confused when he sees you step out from behind your tree, you don't start punching him, but tell him that the Lord Jesus forces you to forgive him; and you let him go. You do not even claim the fish which he has caught, unless he offers them of his own accord. But I think that he will give them to you, from sheer amazement that you haven't made a fuss.

"Then you go home, happy and proud that you have succeeded in forgiving seven times. But suppose that very day the Lord Jesus comes into your village; you introduce yourself to him, imagining that he will praise you before all the world for your good deeds. Not at all. He will tell you, as he told Peter, that seven times is still not enough—that one must forgive yet another seven times, and yet again, and a fourth time's seven times and plenty more times, if you also want God always to forgive you."[4]

Schweitzer, again and again confronted with the same indifference, the same negligence, the same thievish predilections, had ample opportunity to practice the limitless forgiveness he preached.

To complete the picture, the laughter must not be forgotten. Ali Silver, after nearly twenty years at the hospital, missed the fun more than anything else. Schweitzer's warm humor infected the whole place, and there was often plenty to laugh about in the absurdities of human or animal behavior. Almost anything could happen on the Ogowe, and Schweitzer treasured the comedies of life. From a collection of such incidents in the Günsbach Archives:

> My Uncle Charles was a great man, you know. He was a teacher at the Janson-de-Saylly College and much feared by his pupils. One day an African ran in to fetch me, because a white man had travelled up the river to visit me. That means a journey of three days! Flattered, I put on my Sunday jacket and went down to the landing stage, where the white man was waiting for me, surrounded by a crowd of gaping blacks. When he saw me in the distance he shouted, "Are you Albert Schweitzer?" I bowed. "Listen; your uncle is a rotten dung-heap. He failed me in my exam. So . . . ! I have only come here to tell you that." He turned round, clambered back on the motor-boat and left me standing there in my Sunday glory—and I laughed and laughed.[5]

Such a visit was a rare event. Mostly the comedy came from the hospital's own inhabitants, human and animal: the parrot that shouted "Get out of here!" to departing visitors; the lady who said, when Schweitzer mentioned a passage in one of St. Paul's Epistles, "In our village we don't read other people's mail"; and the local post office clerk who regularly ordered goods from Paris for people in his village and when they arrived sent an official letter saying "Purchaser Deceased" so that nobody had to pay the bill. "That man," said Joseph, "is not stupid at all."

Such was a week at the Schweitzer hospital. Fifty-two such weeks in every year were what Schweitzer created on the banks of the Ogowe. The routine is something between that of a village, a hospital, and a farm, for it was really all three of these things although for the sake of convenience we must continue to call it a hospital.

One of the things that gave it its paradisical quality (although not everyone would have agreed) was the population of goats, antelopes, cats, pelicans, monkeys, sheep, chickens, and dogs that shared Adolinanongo with the human beings. They added a touch of the Garden of Eden, for in that atmosphere of security the most diverse creatures played together.

The reason for the animals' presence were often practical enough. Some had been found wounded, nursed to health, and kept as pets. The chickens were there for eggs and for meat; the goats for their manure, for their meat, and also because Schweitzer, anxious as much as anything to teach the local tribes how to feed themselves better, hoped to get milk from them. Milk was unknown on the Ogowe because the tsetse fly killed the cows. Schweitzer, unfortunately, found that without a great deal of attention the goats suffered, often fatally, from mange. But he kept trying.

Alongside the practical reasons for keeping the animals, however, was, of course, the spirit of Reverence for Life. Even before he had hit upon the phrase, he had felt that life without animals was only half life; in Alsace he had always had a dog, in Africa a selection of antelopes, and so forth. Now his natural feeling of the community of all life had become the central tenet of his philosophy, and the whole hospital was permeated by it. The animals were not merely used as a farmer uses his stock, although they were used. They were not merely loved as a lapdog is loved although they were loved. They were respected. They had their inalienable place in the scheme of life. That was what made the difference. Attempts to pen them in always collapsed because patients, on their way to steal fruit or to steal the animals themselves, made short work of wire-netting enclosures. Besides, the patients' own animals, which came with the families, were quite uncontrollable, so the effort was scarcely worth it. When, later on, European visitors came to Lambarene and found the creatures roaming more or less unchecked through the hospital, their reservations were understandable. A goat in the wards of a European or American hospital might well seem out of place. We will look at the criticisms that then arose when we reach that part of the story. For the moment we are only concerned to see how the hospital developed and why it developed as it did.

Schweitzer's, in fact, was not the only hospital that looked more like a village. Dr. Clement Chesterman, for example, who was setting up a hospital in the Congo at about the same time, had also to face the fact that Africans could only be persuaded to come in for treatment if they were able to live there as they lived at home. They would not be separated from their families. They would not eat food cooked by anyone outside the family for fear of poisoning. And the cooking had to be done outside the hut, in the traditional way. As late as 1970, when African staff at the Schweitzer hospital were given new concrete homes with built-in kitchens, they refused to cook in them.

Late in life Schweitzer recalled that when he was planning his hospital two men from the Catholic Mission had said to him, "You must build a hospital here—but not up into the heavens, keep it close to the earth." He should not be credited with any exceptional foresight or insight. He built his hospital in the only way that supplies allowed or patients would accept. It cannot be emphasized too much that he never envisaged the size it would grow to, tiny though it still is compared with a big hospital in America or Europe. "I only meant to build a *small* hospital," he would say. And once—"It often seems to me as though I did it all half in a dream."[6] He simply wanted to be a doctor in the bush. He was forced to build a village because the Africans came in such numbers, families and all, and because their own villages were too impermanent for the setting up of clinics.

He was forced to grow vegetables, plant fruit trees, and keep livestock because otherwise his patients and their families starved. He was forced to organize a supply of doctors and nurses from Europe because the backwardness of the Gabonese made it impossible to find black staff who could even read. The town of Lambarene, which even when Schweitzer died was no larger than a sizable English village, is the Gabon's third largest town.

From the start—from the day when Joseph began to help in 1913—Schweitzer used all the local staff he could. He did not, it is true, set up a training course for Africans—"One man can only do so much," and Schweitzer was primarily interested in teaching the Africans the elements of agriculture, handicrafts, and mutual help so they might become independent of the pressures of Western trade. Many thinking Africans have come around to a belief in the same priorities.

The only qualifications he could hope for in a population that had almost no book learning were honesty and reliability. Africans who wanted to stay and help were given undemanding tasks at first, until it was clear whether they really had some firmness of intention. If this sounds patronizing, one can only point out that people's lives were at stake, and Schweitzer did not feel like putting them in the hands of people who might decide to go fishing when an operation was due.

A number of black orderlies were already at work when Schweitzer returned in 1929, and through the following years they increased in number and responsibility. But he never had a black doctor there. Why? Because Schweitzer depended on volunteers, and no black doctor ever volunteered. The few who qualified in the Gabon stayed—understandably enough—in Libreville or headed for Paris. They felt no debt toward the ravaged tribes in the interior. Let the whites see to that.

Think then of Schweitzer as a headman in his village, a peasant on his farm, a superintendent in his hospital—all at the same time. He dispensed justice like a headman. He mended fences, dug drains, improvised outhouses, and tended the livestock like a farmer. He administered the hospital, saw to the welfare of the staff, planned for the future, authorized expenditure, took responsibility for treatment, like a superintendent. At important operations he was always present, day or night.

Indeed, he insisted that the whole staff should be ready for work at any hour, if work was needed. Suffering did not keep strict hours, nor could its alleviation. His own ear was the sharpest to hear the approach of a canoe in the night. His experience and instinct were often the quickest to diagnose trouble. Dr. Frank Catchpool, who worked with him in the 1950s, said:

> He had a real understanding of when a man was sick, these critical moments in a doctor's career when he must decide to hold off treatment sometimes. When he was just causing the man more misery he would instinctively feel it. He could tell when a man was near death and he could tell—I can remember him ordering me to incise a big abscess sometimes when I thought I'd just wait another day. He'd say: "No, now, today, this minute, you must incise it today, no more delay." And he was right, every time. There would be a pint or two of pus in this man's leg—these big tropical abscesses.[7]

Whatever went on in the hospital, Schweitzer knew. As the number of doctors and nurses increased, the chances of emotional entanglement grew. The doctors were mostly young and vigorous, the nurses often young and pretty. The sun set at 6:00 P.M., and then little work could be done, there was nowhere to go, nothing to do to while away the time after dinner but to visit other people's rooms, talk, maybe play a gramophone. The place was as enclosed as a monastery, but for both sexes. The moon rose mistily above the palms, and love affairs, jealousies, gossip, and enmities were inevitable. The rooms might be mosquito-proof but they were far from soundproof, and although the sound of a gramophone can do a good deal to cover a whispered conversation, having to wind it up every few minutes makes for a somewhat piecemeal romance, and the love affairs (and hatreds) were mostly common knowledge.

Surprisingly, though, for a man so emotionally disciplined as Schweitzer, he was never censorious of other people's sexual indiscretions. Their lives were allowed privacy such as he wished for his own—so much so that when the irate father of one of the doctors demanded from Schweitzer confirmation and details of his son's liaison with a visitor to the hospital, he simply said, "You may tear me in pieces but I will tell you nothing."[8]

He did, however, dislike immodesty: he found it indecorous and possibly prejudicial to hospital discipline. Nurses were required to wear long dresses with high necks, and when a white woman patient received

Schweitzer in a nightgown of dramatic décolletage, he instructed the nurses to find her something more Christian to wear.

This was a matter of taste, however, not of moral condemnation. He never set himself up as any man's or woman's judge in matters of behavior. Only when passion interfered with the running of the hospital did he take action. And if the situation became so serious that those involved had to leave the hospital, he would make all possible arrangements for them to start afresh elsewhere.

Otherwise, no judgments were made. Anyone who came for sanctuary was welcome, and no questions were asked. A man who had been expelled from a mission for sexual misconduct stayed for years at the hospital, working in the garden. The only thing Schweitzer did require of anyone who stayed was that they undertook a share of the work, whatever their capacity, which was often not very great. But all could stay as long as they wished and would be housed and fed.

As a result of this acceptance of all comers, Schweitzer was sometimes accused of being a hopeless judge of character. He was too naïve, it was said, to know whether people who came to him for sanctuary were genuinely desperate cases or confidence men looking for free board and lodging. The truth is that he did not care which they were. If that was naïve, he had always said, he was not ashamed to be naïve.

In fact, he knew something that the knowledgeable folk of this world do not know—that nobody can really tell the genuine from the bogus. The very need to abuse someone's confidence can often hide real desperation. A beggar whose only comfort is alcohol will never dare ask money for a drink; he will say he wants it to visit his sick mother. If one gives him money and he spends it on liquor, one has only oneself to blame for assuming the right to judge what he needs and whether that need is reprehensible or laudable. Nothing is more paternalistic than the view that is only slightly satirized in the cartoon of the well-dressed lady who says, "I never give food to tramps; they only eat it." Schweitzer would have nothing to do with such an attitude. He knew that the main reason for not judging others is that one can never be sure of being right. And he believed that people became trustworthy by being trusted. (Only persistent bitter experience and his responsibility for the hospital's survival forced him to become mistrustful toward the Africans; even so he was constantly on the lookout for those whom he could trust, and to them he gave responsibility.) Combined with his lifelong refusal to pry into private lives, these considerations led him to make what many regarded as mistakes about the people he helped.

But he was careful enough about those accepted as his helpers. Applications came thick and fast from doctors and nurses, and their motives were by no means unmixed. Some wanted the cachet of Schweitzer's name to help them, after a few months at Lambarene, in their careers. Some were running away from failure or unhappiness at home—the thing Schweitzer had been accused of. Some simply wanted a romantic interlude in a humdrum life. Knowing the stresses not only of the work but of the confined life and the irritating climate, he could not give responsibility to anyone of an unstable temperament. "Idealists," as he said, "must be sober."[9] This, as much as considerations of language, accounts for the high proportion of Alsatian, Swiss, and Dutch names on the hospital records. These are races of low volatility. An equable temperament was as important as medical qualifications for his work, and his investigations before accepting new medical staff were suitably thorough.

Once accepted, such a person would receive the most meticulous instructions as to his requirements and his journey; his ticket would be arranged, and Schweitzer would write personally (and by hand: he never used a typewriter because the sound disturbed him and the mechanism came between him and his correspondent) to all the authorities whose approval was needed, to ease his passage. One of the recommendations to young doctors on the voyage out was that at ship's dances they should dance with the wallflowers, as Schweitzer had in his younger days.

Apart from the one or two faithful nurses—Mathilde Kottmann; Emma Haussknecht; Maria Lagendijk, who first went in 1938 and worked there till after Schweitzer's death; and later Ali Silver—the staff turnover was fairly rapid. Few people wanted to devote a lifetime to Lambarene. Few, for that matter, had the stamina to do so. Schweitzer, by nature a teacher, with autocracy bred into him from the Schillinger side, had autocracy thrust upon him in Africa because nobody could match his experience of local conditions. He had, after all, gone there because he wanted to do things his own way. He had trained, studied, and observed, with all the formidable application of which he was capable, to become the complete bush doctor. He had designed the hospital himself and was personally responsible for its financial upkeep. So he had some excuse for claiming that he knew what he was doing and little time for any arguing or explaining. The charge that he was an autocrat is true. The question is whether he was a good autocrat.

Dr. Mark Lauterburg, one of the few who worked with him in the early days and was still living when I first researched this book, said (as do most people who worked there) that it took him a long time, a matter of months, before he fully realized why Schweitzer did things the way he did. One had to learn by experience that certain obvious "improvements" were, in fact, impractical because of the climate, the behavior of the patients, or the distance from the source of supplies. To take the simplest thing: to maintain a supply of running water would have required a mechanical pump, and a pump meant fuel, spare parts, and a certain elementary understanding of and respect for machinery. Fuel was expensive: it had to be transported from Europe. And supplies were not guaranteed: a ship stranded, a world shortage, a war somewhere, and the flow would dry up, leaving the whole system useless. Spare parts were even less easily available. And every section of the system would be vulnerable to the ignorance and curiosity of tribesmen, who had never seen such a thing before and had no conception of its frailties. Better therefore, an old-fashioned well and a hand pump one could rely on (although even that went wrong) than a complicated system that only worked some of the time.

Because running water was impractical, toilets had to be primitive: a hut for women, a hut for men; a hole in a piece of wood and a smell that pervaded the hospital when the wind was easterly. That was for the Europeans. The Africans simply used the bush as they did in their villages. Visitors sometimes found this alarming, if not appalling, but the place was not designed for visitors, and what was the alternative? Such a system had served peasant communities throughout the centuries and was entirely appropriate to this village. The huts were set on the outskirts of the clearing and were known as *Hinter Indien*—"Beyond India," a traditional German phrase for the end of the world. *Hinter Indien* became part of the legend of Lambarene. It was noted with some envy that Schweitzer, acute though all his other senses were, seemed quite oblivious to smell, but, in fact, this was not the case. He could smell flowers well enough and perfume (which he disliked). He was simply able to ignore what he could not alter.

Such conditions obviously necessitated careful attention to hygiene. But plenty of visitors to coastal resorts on the Mediterranean will confirm that few things are less hygienic than a flush toilet that has ceased to flush. The open hole is greatly to be preferred. And this was the principle on which many of Schweitzer's decisions were made. An electrocardiograph machine would be very nice but quite useless unless fully tropicalized against dust, humidity, and creeping things and accompanied by a technician who could service it. Better to perfect one's skills in diagnosing with the aid of a stethoscope, which would never go wrong.

Dr. Lauterburg remembers questioning Schweitzer's judgment on one point only—should he not have had an X-ray machine? Because Lauterburg was in Lambarene in the twenties, during the move from the old hospital to the new, the chances are that so complex a machine would have been beyond Schweitzer's pocket at the time, even if it had been technically feasible. When, in fact, Schweitzer was offered an X-ray machine in 1938, it was reluctantly and with very good reason that he refused it. As will be seen, he had a much more urgent use for the money. Apart from the X-ray machine, however, Dr. Lauterburg in the twenties, like Dr. Catchpool in the fifties, finally concluded that Schweitzer knew what he was doing. Here is Dr. Catchpool again:

> I asked to introduce a new drug into the hospital for treatment of hookworm disease. I wasn't familiar with the drugs that he was using. I had been taught that these drugs were sort of out of date. Dr. Schweitzer asked me very sharply, he said: "What is this drug you want to use? Why do you want to use it? What advantages does it have over what I have been using with good effect over all these years? I know my drugs are toxic, but I have laid down exactly how they should be given, and we don't have toxic effects, because I have covered all of this with my patients, we don't allow this to happen." He said: "You know, I had a doctor who wanted to use a new drug for treatment of hookworm disease. I foolishly allowed him to do it, and we had three deaths. I have never forgiven myself for this." He said: "What proof do you have that this drug you want to use is efficient?" So I brought in the evidence. He said "Good, we shall do it." Then, later on, as he had a little bit more confidence in me, he made it quite clear that the medicine in the hospital should be practised in his hospital according to the way the doctors who were practicing medicine in the hospital at that time deemed they were able to best practice medicine. In other words, he said: "Whatever you want, tell me what you need, I'll get it for you. Whatever drugs you want, tell me what you want, we'll get them. You shall not want for any drug or any materials, or any instruments. You shall have everything you need." This he made quite plain to me. In this hospital we had all the facilities that we needed for doing even the most extraordinary work.[10]

The crucial thing was winning his confidence. The same point is made by Dr. Anna Wildikann, who worked at Lambarene before and during World War Two:

> Anyone who won his confidence had a free hand and could work independently. When new medicines were ordered, Dr. Schweitzer asked each of us if we had any special requirement. In the first week after my arrival in 1935, Dr. Schweitzer asked me if I needed any special medication. "Yes," I said, "I would very much like to have a new remedy for malformed bones which I have already used in Europe, but it is very expensive." His answer was: "I did not ask you about the cost, but about your wish. If the remedy is good, you shall have it."[11]

Schweitzer needed convincing that the new treatment, whatever it was, was not only new but better than the old and would work not only in Europe but in Lambarene. Once convinced of that, he would move heaven and earth to get it. There is a story that he refused to use antibiotics. It is totally untrue. So familiar did antibiotics become at Lambarene that animals were named after them. But Schweitzer did refuse to allow young doctors, intoxicated with the success of the new wonder drugs, to use them indiscriminately when there was not due cause. Sensational though they were, he saw no reason why they should be exempt from the law that, if overused, a drug will in the end produce an immunity to its action. "The old idiot is still living in the nineteenth century," some said. But the old idiot saw a good deal farther than they did.

An illustration of the way in which Schweitzer gained a reputation for rejecting medical advance was the story of a visitor to the hospital (this was in the later years when visitors grew common) that he was seen pitching a crate of medicines unopened into the river. The story gained wide circulation, and Schweitzer, as was his custom, did not trouble to explain. The truth was, however, that on this occasion, as on several others, a consignment of medicines had been sent inadequately packed for the tropics and the contents had become useless. It is unlikely that these were medicines ordered by Schweitzer, for he would have ensured that these were properly packed. But pharmaceutical companies would sometimes send quantities of surplus drugs to Schweitzer for tax deduction purposes and no special care was taken over their dispatch.

How keen he really was to find new solutions to medical problems emerges from an anecdote told by Dr. Ernest Bueding, who was working at the Pasteur Institute in Paris in 1934.[12] A new yellow fever vaccine had been discovered there but not fully tested for side effects when "a doctor from Colmar" telephoned for information about the new drug. On hearing of the possibility of side effects he came to Paris the next day and insisted on being injected with the vaccine himself despite strong warnings that this was unwise at the age of fifty-nine. Schweitzer, who, of course, had been recognized by this time, was very impatient when the institute hospitalized him for two days as a precaution. But he suffered no serious reactions and immediately put in an order for the vaccine.

Schweitzer, it is true, never liked technology for its own sake, and in this he was consistent from his youth onward. Claims that science could explain nature, when, in fact, all it did was to break it up into smaller pieces and give it new names, never impressed him. In this, too, he was ahead of the field. Physicists today recognize that every time they draw aside one veil they are faced by new mysteries; education is often, in Arthur Koestler's phrase, "a package of information wrapped around a vacuum."[13]

As he grew older, Schweitzer liked the twentieth century less and less. He used his motorboats as little as possible, preferring a canoe paddled by lepers. It was good for the lepers to feel useful, and it was much more peaceful. He welcomed DDT at its first appearance, and it was regularly employed in the operating theater although he discouraged too widespread a use of it throughout the hospital, even when it might have simplified the nurses' work. It killed indiscriminately and did not, like antibiotics, specifically attack the carriers of disease. He would not have been at all happy, for example, about the wholesale destruction of ants. He was fond of ants, which he regarded as useful scavengers about the hospital, and he used to leave small pieces of food on his desk while he worked so that he could watch them crawl up the leg in a column and return beneath the floorboards with their booty; when the cat began to join in by sitting in wait for them and killing them with its paw, he protected them with a basket. He truly did love creatures simply for being alive and refused to endanger anything, ants, mosquitoes, rats included, which did him and his hospital no obvious harm.

Inevitably such behavior seemed to some of his colleagues to be eccentric to the point of idiocy, so alien was it to everything they had been taught at medical school. There were battles that could only be ended by Schweitzer finally saying, "This is my hospital. While you are here you do as I say." Some doctors did not stay long enough to be convinced that Schweitzer's way worked. Others in the end decided that, against all their preconceptions, it did work, and they were prepared to let a few idiosyncracies go for the sake of the atmosphere of dedication and the obvious high success rate of the hospital.

One such idiosyncrasy was on the question of sun-helmets. The warnings about sunstroke that Schweitzer had been given by old-timers on his first voyage out had been reinforced by cases within his own experience, and he was absolutely rigid about the need for his staff to wear something on their heads at all times. When people disputed this on the grounds that they had survived in other parts of the tropics without hats and the pressure of a hat simply added to their discomfort in the humid heat, Schweitzer was adamant. He had known of cases, he said, where a few moments in the sun or a stray shaft through a hole in the roof had made people very ill. He was not going to let that happen in his hospital where he was responsible.

There seems little doubt that in this instance he was less open to reasoned argument than usual, and there may be some connection with that curious promise he made to the old Countess of Erlach that he would never go bareheaded in the tropics, even after sundown. Rational or not, however, his orders were nearly always obeyed.

After his death the sun-helmet became almost obsolete in the hospital because it was found that sunstroke did not automatically follow exposure. Except when in the open for long periods without shade, a covered head became the exception rather than the rule on the Ogowe, and no harm followed. Perhaps, as some believe, the climate had altered in those fifty years. More probably it is a question of diet, for sunstroke affects the undernourished and we are better fed today. Or it is possible that Schweitzer was simply wrong, misled by incorrectly diagnosing the cases he came across, but this is unlikely for he was rarely mistaken in his diagnosis.

When journalists began to visit him after 1950, men well experienced in the tropics, the sun-helmet issue became an immediate cause of misunderstanding, for the first thing he did was to try to force headwear on them as well, thus branding himself a relic from nineteenth-century colonialism. This snap judgment was confirmed by his dislike of technology and his peasant ways, and so the report grew that here was somebody who had retreated from progress into the jungle and had no understanding of the twentieth century, a well-meaning but irrelevant anachronism.

What, finally, was his real relationship with the Africans in his hospital? He had gone to Africa full of idealism. He had found himself in a region of greater poverty, disease, and backwardness than he had ever envisaged. He had suffered from the ingratitude and unreliability of those he came to help. He had seen other men lose patience with the blacks and take to cursing at them, and despite his own clear and compassionate analysis of the reasons why a tribesman could not and would not understand the Europeans' attitude to work, he, too, had often been driven to despair.

Now he had reached a kind of tolerant hopelessness toward them. Writing of them he used phrases that could be taken as very patronizing, "Mes sauvages," "Mes primitifs." Day after day the struggle was renewed to persuade them to take their treatment at the right time, in the right dosage; to discourage them from taking off their dressings to show their friends where the pain came out; to dissuade them from cooling their open sores in the infected river; to find help for the building work and the garden, and to keep them from drifting quietly away behind the bushes and disappearing. And day after day, at least some of the Africans defeated him. They failed to turn up for their medicine, they went for a swim, they consulted the witch doctor, they cut down a fruit tree for firewood; a lady being treated for gonorrhea spent a night entertaining a canoe full of gentlemen callers, themselves infected; and so on and so forth. In the end he was constantly shouting at them, he was calling them monkeys, and very occasionally, he was hitting them.

A nurse who worked in Lambarene for two spells of more than a year each, Trudi Bochsler, says that no one can judge Schweitzer who did not work at Lambarene for at least six months. The confinement, the climate, the endless frustrations and setbacks, the depredations of man and beast sooner or later take their toll and one is a different person from who one thought one was. "If anyone who worked there for any length of time tells you that they never struck a native, they're lying," she says. She herself, a twenty-year-old idealist, finally struck a large African who was telling Schweitzer lies about her work. Schweitzer was horrified. "I never thought *you* would do that," he said.

Schweitzer himself horrified the great British journalist James Cameron, who visited Lambarene in 1953, by his violence of word and deed toward the African although Cameron admits that a group of Africans he saw, who were supposed to be working, "moved with a deliberation I should scarcely have thought possible. It was like watching a slow-motion film! Sometimes work slowed down to a point where movement, if it existed, was imperceptible; it was like studying the hour-hand of a watch."[14]

Cameron was not the only visitor to be dismayed at finding this hero of so many uplifting articles and books shouting like a slave driver at his black crew and even sometimes laying a hand on them. The question is not, however, what James Cameron or any other brief visitor thought about it, but how the Africans themselves reacted. Few of the observers whose indignation was aroused on behalf of the humiliated blacks seem to have asked the victims for their views. Had they done so, the answers might not have been very reliable, for underprivileged people are not noted for confiding in rich, inquisitive strangers. But if they had reached the truth, it might have been very different from what they expected.

Schweitzer was a man for touching: he was not afraid of physical contact. And he could be impatient. He hit his young nephew for a mistake in Latin. He hit one of his nurses a considerable whack with a pick handle when she would not do things the way he told her to do them. The passion that in childhood made him strike his sister for not paying sufficient attention to their game was still there, however carefully held in check. His temper and his hand would flash out. A moment later, all would be over, and the swift reconciliation followed.

The Africans, too, were physical creatures, accustomed to physical expression of feelings. They understood the reasons for Schweitzer's impatience, and they understood his way of expressing it. They knew that the shouting and the playful slap on the backside meant no ill will, and they knew something that educated Westerners, as prim about violence as their grandparents were about sex, have forgotten—that the ability to give or take blows without rancor is a mark of comradeship. A blow can only confidently be struck if no harm is intended. It is only when tension is high that it must be withheld, for then it would really matter.

The Africans knew, too, that the way he treated them had nothing to do with their blackness. His impatience, like his authoritarianism, was the same for everyone, and it was only the visitors' own color consciousness that made them so uncomfortable. Clara Urquhart has an excellent story that when she was watching him supervise some Africans, he grew so impatient with one that he said to her, "I should like to slap that fellow. I don't suppose I will, but if I should, just close your eyes and pretend I'm slapping a white man, and then you'll feel all right."[15]

The understanding between Schweitzer and the Africans lay much too deep for penetration by those who came briefly to Lambarene. It was to help the Africans that he came to their country, and kept coming—and the Africans knew it. They knew that they were secure in his heart, and he in theirs. Between such people, as between a long-married couple, small rows can flare and blow over and the underlying relationship is untouched. It is only with those we know less well that we must always be polite.

Schweitzer had no time for politeness. "I hate good manners," he said to Frederick Franck—although Franck qualified this by saying, "He has the most exquisite manners one could expect of a gentleman of the Old World. . . . What he really hates are the ape-like automatic tricks we indulge in."[16] At table everybody was told to reach for the food they wanted; there were better things to concentrate on than passing one another the potatoes. Nor did he care for any "After you" hesitations in a doorway; it was first come, first through. Hélène would have liked to refine him a little, but never succeeded.

Nor was he polite to Africans. If they were idle, he shouted at them. If they still would not move, he abused them. For the most part they would shout back. But they would, even if briefly, move. And grin as they did so. "We do not become angry," a leper said to Norman Cousins. "How could we? Could a man become angry at his own father for telling him what to do?"[17]

But when Schweitzer shouted and nagged, he knew what he was asking of them, undernourished as they were. Norman Cousins tells how, one day when he was at the hospital, Schweitzer suggested that he and three other whites should try taking over the jungle-clearing work the blacks had been doing. "After about ten minutes we looked as though we had been working ten hours. Our white shirts and khaki pants were drenched. All the while the Africans stood by, looking on us with boundless compassion and appearing desperately eager to spare us further effort." Schweitzer had "just wanted us to have some respect for the requirements of physical labour in Lambarene."[18]

When he first came back to Africa in 1924, Schweitzer evidently hoped for and looked forward to a less-dominant relationship. He has been criticized for never having learned an African dialect, for having always played the part of an overlord, never that of a collaborator with the Gabonese of the Ogowe. A passage from *More from the Primeval Forest* shows that he was aware of this and knew it to be a shortcoming:

I daresay we should have fewer difficulties with our savages if we could occasionally sit round the fire with them and show ourselves to them as men, and not merely as medicine-men and custodians of law and order in the hospital. But there is no time for that. All three of us, we two doctors and Nurse Kottmann, are really so overwhelmed with work that the humanity within us cannot come out properly. But we cannot help it. For the present we are condemned to the trying task of carrying on the struggle with sickness and pain, and to that everything else has to give way.[19]

If he had truly wanted to know the Africans as man to man, though, would he not have found time, or made time? Perhaps. And perhaps he would, as he suspected, have got more from them if he had. But although he respected their views on life and understood the origins of their superstitions, he never joined in their celebrations or tried in any way to share their lives. The fashionable modern fascination with primitive cultures that takes film cameras into the intimate lives of lost tribes wherever they may be found he would have regarded as voyeuristic curiosity and an unpardonable invasion of privacy. He did not go to Africa to make clever discoveries about cultures that led people to eat one another, poison one another, and behave with total indifference to the suffering of anyone from the next tribe. He was there to improve their lot, and he did it the way he found he could do it best. Possibly if he had learned a couple of Gabonese languages and lived closer to them, he might have accomplished more. On the other hand, he could already talk with most of them in French. And, perhaps, by working side by side with them, ten times as hard as they, and bawling at them when things grew too much for him, he really grew as close to them as anybody could.

What news of these brusque encounters reached the supporters in Europe? None at all, before 1950. Schweitzer's lectures and the bulletins that from time to time emerged from Lambarene were purged of such detail. They were sober, factual accounts, designed to give a brief picture of achievements and difficulties and to stimulate interest and the flow of cash. They were not dishonest, but they were far removed from the warts-and-all, now-it-can-be-told candid journalism that became fashionable later.

As a result, legions of good Christian people in Europe grew acquainted with an imaginary Lambarene, where the warts were somehow idealized and where sweat, pus, bad temper, and bad smells had no place. It was not surprising that when these people began to arrive to see for themselves the sanctified jungle clearing, they often experienced fierce symptoms of reaction or that hardened journalists, whose experiences had given them a deep mistrust of heroes and dislike of halos, should begin to scent another clay-footed idol and to itch to bring him down.

"No one knows me who has not seen me in Africa." It was true. And almost no one ever had seen him in Africa. He was as remote, as mysterious, as legendary as the gorilla or the pygmy, and romance built up around him in Europe while in Africa the sweat fell off him in rivers as he wrestled with disease and mud, concrete and evil spirits, storms, snakes, other people's stupidity, and his own unquenchable temper.

And yet to Michael Scott, the priest who worked in South Africa from 1943 on, who truly tried to identify with the Africans and truly made their cause his own, Schweitzer said, in a moment of heartbreaking humility, "I helped Africa the easy way. You did it the hard way."[20]

22

Another War

1932–1945

SO SCHWEITZER SHUTTLED between his two lives, the myth thickening around him.

The year 1932 was spent in Europe, where the new guest house in Günsbach was finished and Mme. Martin, a pastor's widow, was installed as secretary. This is the house where the main Schweitzer archives are now held. Here Schweitzer spent much of his time when he was not actually traveling, and here all sorts of visitors came to see him, invited and uninvited. Here all were welcomed and fed, and the cry often went upstairs to the first-floor kitchen: "Four more for lunch. Put some more water in the soup."

Plenty of these visitors have left a record of their impressions and of the homely everyday life into which they were absorbed. However distinguished, they were never allowed to disrupt the routine, for Schweitzer the theological rebel had never seriously questioned the simple traditions of Alsatian life, and now they were an essential part of his stability.

Time after time in these accounts we find the same elements—a sense of simple delight, a touch of hero worship—and the same incidents noted and treasured: Schweitzer's insistence on carrying the bags from the station; the family meals at which not only the family sits down but visitors, old friends, and staff from Lambarene; the strolls in the village and into the neighboring hills; the recruitment of visitors to do a little helping in the office or the kitchen; the constant interruptions of telephone calls or fresh arrivals; the evening sessions at the organ. Schweitzer preaches in his father's cassock and Geneva bands. Schweitzer chats with the villagers about their school days together. Schweitzer sits at his window, writing, writing, while neighbors leave little gifts on his windowsill: eggs, fresh vegetables, fruit from their gardens or picked wild on the hill.

Sometimes Schweitzer would decide to sit at the piano and launch into selections from *Der Rosenkavalier* or even an interlude of *"Yotz,"* which is the Alsatian way of pronouncing "jazz." For his own private moments he preferred the place on the hill above the house where he had always sat since boyhood, the Rocks of Kantzenrain.

Hélène was often with him at Günsbach, but not always. Even here she felt out of things as the activity buzzed about her. When Schweitzer was at Strasbourg, organizing matters in the Rue des Greniers and often sleeping there, she would stay in the Rue St. Aurelie with their mutual friends Christian Brandt and his wife.

As Schweitzer's star rose, hers declined, and it is easy to feel the pathos of the picture: Schweitzer the center of attention, vital, brilliant, and admired, while Hélène sits half-noticed in an unlit corner, talking of the old days. So easy indeed is the pathos that it is essential to remember that this was *not* a case of a beautiful marriage wrecked on the harsh shores of ambition. It was a case of a partnership of idealists that for practical reasons became a marriage and then through nobody's fault became unworkable. Tragic—and the tragedy spared neither of them—Schweitzer and Hélène had always understood and accepted the conditions of the partnership. Hélène's ill-health and the arrival of Rhena had meant that only one of the partners could go on with the work that both believed in, but neither would seriously have considered that the work be abandoned altogether to preserve the form of a conventional marriage.

Schweitzer himself, with his uncomfortable logic, saw the family tie as resembling the tribal tie of his Africans, which limited goodwill to the tribe alone at the expense of the rest of the human race. He criticized the same restricted vision in French family life. And steeped as he was in the Gospels he must have considered the relevance of the last verses of Matthew 12: "While he was still speaking to the people, behold, his mother and his brothers stood outside, asking to speak to him. But he replied to the man who told him, 'Who is my mother, and who are my brothers?' And stretching out his hand towards his disciples, he said 'Here are my mother and my brothers! For whoever does the will of my father in heaven is my brother, and sister, and mother.' "

Hélène's tubercular condition, which had recurred on the way to Lambarene in 1928, had since been checked by a Dr. Gerson, an advocate of natural foods and a salt-free diet. According to Erica Anderson, Gerson actually saved Hélène's life at that time although, of course, he could not restore the affected lung tissue to its original elasticity. But Schweitzer was so impressed by Gerson's methods that he adhered to many of his principles, including avoidance of salt, to the end of his life.

Rhena saw almost nothing of her father. She could leave Königsfeld very little because of her schooling, and when Hélène was in Alsace, she stayed with friends. Hers was not an easy life although she made the best of it and enjoyed her father's brief visits while they lasted. He made great efforts, she remembers, to compensate for his absences, and she, was grateful. Nor did she pine when the visits came to an end, for she says: "I always was objective with my father. I recognised his greatness and the importance of his work, even as a child, and I accepted my life as it was."[1] But she did find the Moravian Brothers uncomfortably strict. And when she was twelve, something happened that caused her great distress: she caught her mother's tuberculosis.

Schweitzer had warned Hélène to take great care against infecting the child, but throughout the critical years of puberty, till she was eighteen, Rhena suffered from tuberculosis of the skin. Her face was affected, the skin pocked with holes full of matter, so that other children would not sit next to her. Although Schweitzer found it impossible not to blame Hélène, there must also have been some feeling the other way—that had father been at home this might never have happened.

Before Schweitzer set off on the usual circuit of fund-raising engagements, a special occasion had to be fitted in. On March 22, the centenary of Goethe's death, he was to deliver a memorial oration in the Opera House in Frankfurt.

The gathering was notable, the audience distinguished, the Opera House packed. One hundred years after Goethe's death, to the exact hour, Schweitzer began to speak.

What he had to say was full of foreboding. With Germany still in a state of economic and political chaos after the war, thinking Germans were finding themselves forced into one extreme camp or another— Nazism or communism. Schweitzer saw in Goethe the man who had stood supremely for the individual and for spiritual independence from any sort of mass will. He himself had been watching the approach of the mass will and warning against it ever since he had first seen the dangers in Nietzsche's philosophy in the 1890s. Now it was everywhere, overwhelming. Everyone sought, or had found

the magic formulas of some economic or social system. . . . [A]nd the terrible significance of these magic formulas, to whatever school of economic and social witchcraft they may belong, is always that the individual has to surrender his material and spiritual personal existence, and may continue to live only as belonging body and soul to a plurality which controls him absolutely.

The material and spiritual independence of the individual, insofar as they are not already crushed, are on all sides threatened most seriously. We are commemorating the death of Goethe in the most stupendous hour of fate that has ever sounded for humanity. And in this hour of fate it is his mission, beyond that of every other writer or thinker, to speak to us. As the most untimely of all men, he gazes into our era, because he has absolutely nothing in common with the spirit in which it lives. But as the most timely he tenders his advice, because what it needs to hear he has to say.

What is it he says to our era?

He tells it that the frightful drama which is now being played through can only come to an end, if it removes from its path the economic and social magic to which it has surrendered itself, unlearns the incantations with which it has been befooled, and is determined, whatever the cost, to get back to a natural relationship with reality.

To individuals he says: "Do not abandon the ideal of personal, individual manhood, even if it run contrary to circumstances such as have developed. Do not believe this ideal is lost, even when it no longer seems tenable beside the opportunistic theories which endeavour simply to adjust the spiritual to the material. Remain human with your own souls! Do not become mere human things which allow to have stuffed into them souls which are adjusted to the mass-will and pulse in measure with it!"[2]

So Goethe spoke through Schweitzer and Schweitzer through Goethe, for this speech is deeply revealing of Schweitzer himself and not only on the political level. Hundreds of people listened in dead silence that day to prophetic words whose truth they were to prove in their own minds and bodies in the next twelve years. They were breaking away from nature, he told them, and surrendering themselves to "a monstrous unnaturalness." Looking back from the end of the century, we can see how exactly Nazism fulfilled his prediction. But it would be wrong to suppose that he was speaking only of Nazism or that the end of Hitler left the world with a clean bill of health. All the time and everywhere the individual will is still threatened and submerged by the mass will. If Schweitzer was right, the evil of Nazism was not simply that the dogma it forced on individuals was false and cruel; the imposition of any dogma by force or coercion must in itself be evil.

The argument against him is that nothing can be achieved by individuals, that only united masses can be effective, and that if necessary, unity must be created by coercion. In this speech in 1932 he did not evade that issue.

There arises a question which even half a lifetime ago we should have regarded as impossible: Is there any longer any sense in holding on to the ideal of personal human individuality, when circumstances are developing in just the opposite direction, or is it not on the contrary our duty to adjust ourselves to a new ideal of human existence, in accordance with which man is destined to attain a differently constituted perfection of being in unreserved absorption into organised society?[3]

Schweitzer had no doubt about the answer: this was precisely that "monstrous unnaturalness" he spoke of.

After that he went on with his tour, visiting Holland, Britain, Sweden, and Switzerland as well as Germany, the pace as furious as ever. "You can't burn the candle at both ends," someone said. "You can if it's long enough," said Schweitzer. "What do you think of the architecture of the city?" someone said. "I'll begin sightseeing when I'm seventy-five," said Schweitzer. (Although even that proved a pious hope.)

In the summer Oxford gave him an honorary degree in divinity. He went to Scotland, the country to which he had wanted to take his mother, for the first time in his life. Edinburgh University gave him degrees in divinity and music; St. Andrews in laws. He loved the long light mid-summer evenings in Scotland, especially after the six o'clock sunsets of Lambarene. The students of St. Andrews were evidently impressed, for two years later they nominated him for rectorship of the university. A cable from the Students' Union dated November 1, 1934, says, "Nomination already well supported only difficulty speech in English essential." Despite desultory attempts to learn English, and ever-increasing ability to understand it when spoken, he was unable to oblige.

He stayed in Europe for the winter of 1933 and set off again for Lambarene in March. Hélène stayed behind, but not in Königsfeld. Hélène was Jewish by birth and Hitler was in power. She and Rhena moved to Switzerland and settled in Lausanne, much to Rhena's delight, for the move freed her from the rigidities of the Moravian Brothers.

The hospital was doing well. No special crises or disasters arose, the new building that was necessary was manageable, the surgeons completed more than 500 operations in the year; and a special fund raised in Alsace purchased the hospital's first refrigerator. Leftover food could now be kept fresh, and for the first time the parched workers had cool water to drink.

To ensure the continuity of the hospital a legal arrangement came into effect on October 13 whereby on Schweitzer's death the ownership passed automatically to the association that looked after his interests in Strasbourg.

So 1933 passed, and in 1934 Schweitzer was in Europe again. The notable events of this year were two major lecture series: the Hibbert Lectures on Religion in Modern Civilisation, first given at Manchester College, Oxford, and repeated at London University, and in Edinburgh the Gifford Lectures, a series of ten lectures on "The Problem of Natural Philosophy and Natural Ethics."

The two sets of lectures covered much the same ground although the latter had a much greater range. Both were elaborations and variations on the themes of the first two books of *The Philosophy of Civilisation*, and both led up, inevitably, to Reverence for Life. "Everything that happens in world history rests on something spiritual. If the spiritual is strong, it creates world history. If it is weak, it suffers history."[4] Schweitzer was troubled that contemporary theologians were denying this powerful bond between the spiritual and the social, between religion and history. Karl Barth especially, he felt, was quite disastrously in tune with the spirit of the age when he taught that man's relationship with God was something quite apart from his everyday life.

> The terrible thing is that he dares to preach that religion is turned aside from the world, and in so doing expresses what the spirit of the age is feeling. The spirit of the age dislikes what is simple. It no longer believes the simple can be profound. It loves the complicated, and regards it as profound. It loves the violent. That is why the spirit of the age can love Karl Barth and Nietszche at the same time. The spirit of the age loves dissonance, in tones, in lines, and in thought. That shows how far from thinking it is, for thinking is a harmony with us.[5]

True and harmonious thinking, Schweitzer claimed, saw the progress of civilization as the expansion of Jesus' ethic of love into ever wider spheres: from tribe to nation, from nation to all mankind, and finally, with Reverence for Life, from mankind to all living creatures. The Gifford Lectures, leading to the same conclusions, began with a long section on Eastern philosophy. The subject had increasingly attracted Schweitzer, and his book *Indian Thought and Its Development* was nearing publication.

Two memorable meetings occurred in Edinburgh: the first with Sir Wilfred Grenfell, who was, as it were, a Schweitzer of the snow. What Schweitzer was doing in the hot swamps of Africa, Grenfell was doing in the frozen waters of Labrador where he had founded a hospital for fishermen. A mutual friend invited them both, and they met on the doorstep. George Seaver tells the story: "We began at once," says Schweitzer, "to question each other about the problems connected with the management of our hospitals. His chief trouble was the disappearance of reindeer for their periodic migrations; mine the loss of goats, from theft and snake-bites. Then we burst out laughing: we were talking not as doctors concerned with patients, but as farmers concerned with livestock!"[6]

When they signed the visitors' book—the dark, burly doctor from the African river and the white-haired doctor from the snows—Schweitzer was impelled to add under his signature, "The Hippopotamus is delighted to meet the Polar Bear."

And the great cellist, Pablo Casals, who was there for the first performance of a new cello concerto by Sir Donald Francis Tovey, wrote in his autobiography, *Joys and Sorrows:*

> I had looked forward eagerly to meeting Schweitzer. Not only was I familiar with his writings on Bach, but I had of course an intense admiration for him as a man. On that occasion in Edinburgh there were a number of public and private concerts, and Schweitzer became very excited over my playing of Bach. He urged me to stay on—he wanted to hear more Bach—but I couldn't stay, because of other engagements. I had to catch a train after my last performance, and I had gotten my things together and was hurrying down a corridor when I heard the sound of running footsteps behind me. I looked around. It was Schweitzer. He was all out of breath. He looked at me with that wonderful expression of his which mirrored the great compassion of the man. "If you must leave," he said, "then let us at least say goodbye with intimacy." He was speaking in French. "Let us tutoyer one another before we separate." We embraced and parted.[7]

The rest of the tour took Schweitzer the length and breadth of England: Harrogate, Leeds, Peterborough, Sheffield, Manchester, Birmingham, London, and so back to the Continent. For his sixtieth birthday, in January 1935, Strasbourg named a park after him. All over the world, in fact, people took an interest in his birthday—even, surprisingly, in Nazi Germany.

Schweitzer had vowed never to set foot on German soil so long as Hitler was in power. The distaste was mutual. The Nazi Party had been going out of its way to find fault with Schweitzer's notions, which were clearly not complimentary to them. But on his sixtieth birthday it seems to have occurred to their propaganda ministry that he might be useful to their image, and, accordingly, they tried to get in touch with him through an old friend of his, Emil Lind, and to offer him various tempting musical posts in Germany. Lind realized that they were using him to set up Schweitzer as an example of "National Socialist Bach worship" and warned Schweitzer what to expect. When Goebbels, the minister of propaganda, wrote shortly afterward to Schweitzer, he concluded his letter, *"Mit Deutschem Gruss"* (with German greetings). Schweitzer, declining to have anything to do with the plan, signed off "With Central African Greetings, Albert Schweitzer."[8] And three weeks after his birthday, back to central Africa he went.

This time he was in Lambarene for only seven months. Expansion was again necessary, for the hospital was full to overflowing with thirty patients awaiting operations.

I could no longer close my ears to the frequent complaints of doctors and nurses that our consulting room had become too small. On the days when three or four doctors are all questioning patients, medicines are being dealt out and many injections of Salvarsan, Tryparsamide and Antileprol are being given, it is thronged as if there were a fair going on. And often through all the din are heard the groans of a native maternity case lying behind a curtain. For the consulting room has also to serve for accouchements![9]

Slowly the spread of technology was making itself felt, for better or worse. The hospital was given a petrol lamp, which made it possible in an emergency to operate at night. And airplanes began to fly over Lambarene on an air route that had opened between Europe and the Congo. One witch doctor explained that this portended a month's darkness, and his village cut all their plantains in readiness for the long night that never came.

In October Schweitzer was back in Europe again, a Europe perturbed by Mussolini's invasion of Abyssinia, which threatened the stability of the whole of Africa. The chickens of dictatorship were beginning to fly wide before coming home to roost. Schweitzer's ear was cocked. He knew the sound of the wings of war.

Honors were falling thick around him now. All over the world, from Seville to New South Wales, organizations and cities were competing in offering him honorary citizenships, honorary memberships, honorary whatever they could think of. The previous spring a number of organizations in Austria, Switzerland, Sweden, Czechoslovakia, and England had made a determined effort to get him the Nobel Peace Prize, but without success.

In London he was asked if he would go to China with the Dean of Canterbury and Dr. Wilfred Grenfell to help with reconstruction work after the flood disaster of the previous year. He would gladly have gone, he told them, but he was an old carthorse who could still do some useful work in the old shafts but might not do so well in new ones.

The months passed much as usual, but one meeting is particularly interesting. Jawaharlal Nehru was due to be released after one of his regular spells in a British jail, and Mahatma Gandhi wrote to ask if Schweitzer would look after him for a few days while he accustomed himself to freedom. So Nehru was briefly the guest of the Schweitzers in Lausanne. The book on Indian thought had been published a short while before. In it Schweitzer had written at some length and with enormous sympathy and respect about Gandhi although he had one or two minor criticisms to make as well. Had Gandhi read this? And did Schweitzer discuss it with Nehru? How far did either of the great Indians agree with Schweitzer's interpretation of Indian philosophy? And what did they think of Reverence for Life? It would be fascinating to know. But at least it is pleasant to think that Gandhi and Schweitzer, who from such totally different backgrounds had reached such similar conclusions, had at least this one very human and practical contact.

One mystery remained to be solved in the Schweitzer story: the mystery of the third and fourth volumes of *The Philosophy of Civilisation*. He was constantly reported to be working hard on these, and, indeed, he himself said so. Sheaves of notes were hanging on a nail in Lambarene out of reach of the goats. This summer of 1936, for example, is one of the periods when he apparently put in a great deal of work on volume three. Yet volume three never appeared. For a man who could produce long and complicated books in six months or less, this seems extremely odd.

There have been reports for years that work is being done on an edited version of his notes, and now, thirty-five years after his death, I am told that a selection, at least, is shortly to be published.

It is clear that Schweitzer simply had too much to do to be able to organize the floods of ideas that came to him, and as he said, he found it difficult to hold onto the thoughts till he could get them onto paper. But was it more? Was he grappling with something that even he was unable to master? It is important to know. For his subject was the application of Reverence for Life to society and to politics, and this is precisely where for many people the philosophy fails to convince. As a personal creed, yes. But how, for example, can politicians apply it to international affairs? The theme of the value of the individual in the face of vast impersonal forces is as crucial as ever as the world is swamped by the depredations of unfettered global finance. Was Schweitzer's answer among those notes he worked on for so many years?

In the autumn another project loomed, which meant forgetting everything else for a few weeks. The Columbia Gramophone Company had already recorded Schweitzer's playing of a number of Bach works in London for the Bach Organ Music Society. The organ he had played on was that of All Hallows in the Tower. These first six works, advertised as "played by Dr. Albert Schweitzer, the greatest interpreter of Bach," had proved so successful that the company now wished to make fifty-two more records.

Although he liked the organ at All Hallows, Schweitzer had not been entirely happy about the arrangements there. The rector had not been very enthusiastic about the enterprise, and Schweitzer had been able to work there only at nights. Moreover, much of the time he had spent on stepladders stuffing the windows with cotton wool to prevent vibration. He proposed instead the organ of St. Aurelia in Strasbourg—an organ built by his favorite organ builder, Silbermann, and restored by his friend Frederic Härpfer. The secretary of the Bach Organ Music Society went especially to Strasbourg to hear it and was so impressed by the organ's tone that Columbia agreed to spend a great deal of money sending their recording equipment from London to Strasbourg for what was at that time the "largest plan of consecutive gramophone record making ever undertaken by an artist."[10] The recordings were made in October, and took two weeks. They are now of course virtually unobtainable. But they sold extremely well, and Schweitzer must have earned a very large fee.

He stayed in Europe for his birthday, and on January 29, 1937, embarked again from Bordeaux. He arrived to find the hospital overcrowded as usual, with the additional complication that the rainy season had been less rainy than usual and many patients and their families could not go home because the river was too low. His determination not to get involved in any more building lasted a month or two, but in the end he had once more to give in to the pleas of the staff for more space, so the situation was back to normal. In addition, it was found that some of the charred posts that formed the foundations of the huts had rotted more quickly than had been expected and were now dangerous. They had to be renewed.

Another task was the digging of a new well. The concrete cistern and the single well both dried up in a long dry season, leaving the patients with no choice but to drink the river water, which carried the risk of infection. In this predicament "I had the great good luck," Schweitzer wrote, "to come upon a spring of water which never runs dry."[11] And here he dug a well, lined it with concrete, and provided it with a good pump.

Now came the moment when Schweitzer had to turn down the offer of an X-ray machine. The grateful Europeans of the Ogowe had decided to show Schweitzer their appreciation. Many of them owed their lives, or those of wives or husbands, to the hospital, for often they would delay coming in until the last moment because of the difficulty of travel and the amount of money they stood to lose by abandoning their work at a crucial moment, and it required all the resources of the hospital to save them. Ninety thousand francs they collected, and an X-ray machine was the present they had in mind.

But Schweitzer had scented war, and much though he desired an X-ray machine, he had a feeling that his first need was going to be a large and varied stock of drugs. Ninety thousand francs' worth would go a long way to ensure the hospital against a breakdown of supplies, and he persuaded the donors of the money to let him spend it his way.

The year 1938 rolled onward. Schweitzer was still building and, in addition, was extending the garden. As ever, each extension was undertaken with great reluctance, and each was to be the very last. Meanwhile, Lambarene town achieved the hallmark of civilization—a radio station.

In November and December of this year Hélène and Rhena went on a lecture tour of their own to the United States. Schweitzer himself had never been able to find time to go, and although *My Life and Thought* had sold out there in 1932 (the name was slightly changed to *Out of My Life and Thought* and the first impression of three thousand copies sold out in three weeks), he was, inevitably, less well known in America than in the European countries. This tour of Hélène's sowed seeds that were to bear fruit at a critical moment for the hospital when it might well have collapsed without American help.

On January 12, 1939, almost two full years after his last sight of Europe, Schweitzer set sail for a change of climate. But he was already too late. At every port they put into, warships lay at anchor. On the ship's radio he heard the saber-rattling speeches of politicians. Hitler had already occupied Czechoslovakia, calling the bluff of the rest of Europe, and now, as the ship crossed the Bay of Biscay, was busy announcing that he had no further territorial ambitions. Schweitzer, who was supposed to be naïve, was not so gullible as some politicians at that time: he did not believe a word of it. Before they reached Bordeaux, he had booked his berth on the return voyage; he wanted to prepare his hospital for the war, and to be with the Africans who needed and trusted him when it came.

This gave him just ten days in Alsace before he had to head back for Bordeaux and the Gabon. He spent them ordering all the drugs and equipment he could afford—and seeing his family from whom he had been separated for two years. Rhena was now just twenty and engaged to be married to Jean Eckert, an organ builder working for Cavaillé-Coll in Paris. Although she had toured the United States with her mother on behalf of the hospital, she had never actually been to Lambarene, and during Schweitzer's brief visit it was decided that she must now see the place that had kept her father away from her for most of her childhood. He left them making preparations, and on May 16 Rhena and Hélène sailed from Bordeaux in his wake.

They stayed only a few weeks. Rhena was anxious to return to her fiancé, and the last thing anyone wanted was to have these two trapped in Lambarene throughout a long war. Schweitzer expected hostilities to break out at any moment although few people showed his pessimism. The general belief was that either there would be no war, or it would be very short, or anyway it would not seriously interrupt shipping and supplies. As a result, Schweitzer, on the lookout for food to hoard, found that several traders were anxious to sell him quantities of rice at bargain prices because it was of inferior quality; it had weevils in it, and they were sure they could replace it. Schweitzer warned them that they might regret the sale but was ignored. The hospital lived on this rice for three years.

In September the war broke out. Two nurses and two doctors had gone back to Europe in the spring and the summer. That left four nurses, including the perennial Emma Haussknecht, and one other doctor besides Schweitzer, Dr. Ladislas Goldschmid, who had been attached to the hospital since 1933 and had recently returned from leave in Europe.

One other doctor, Dr. Anna Wildikann, reached Lambarene in January 1940 before the war really began to blaze. But the optimists had to reconsider their outlook when the liner *Brazza*, which had several times carried Schweitzer between Bordeaux and Port-Gentil, was torpedoed near Cape Finistère and sank with almost all aboard. Nobody from the hospital was among the passengers, but the last consignment of drugs and equipment was lost.

Schweitzer was not at all sure that the war would be short, and as soon as it began, he started to send home all but the most serious cases. He had not the food, the medicines, or the staff to keep the hospital running for any length of time at its current rate:

> What sad days we spent sending these people home! Again and again we had to refuse the urgent entreaties of those who, in spite of all, wished to stay with us, again and again we had to try to explain what to them was inexplicable—the fact that they must leave the hospital. Many of the homeward bound were able to travel on steamers and motor-boats whose owners were kind enough to take them. Others were obliged to make their way to distant villages by long and difficult jungle trails. At last they had all gone and the heart-rending scenes were at an end. How dead the Hospital seemed with such a diminished number of inmates![12]

A few of those inmates were replaced by white women, wives of Europeans who had settled in lonely houses in the bush and were now called up. Unlike the Africans, these had no means of reaching their homes and rather than face the jungle alone they sought sanctuary at the hospital.

When France fell to Hitler in June 1940, all her colonies followed suit in surrendering, except one—the bleak plateau country of Chad in central Africa. Félix Eboué, the remarkable and universally respected African governor of Chad, hated the Nazis and instantly responded to the call of Charles de Gaulle, exiled in England and rallying the forces of French resistance. A touch of persuasion and a little intrigue, and three other French colonies—the French Congo, the Cameroons, and Ubangi-Shari—followed Chad in declaring for Free France. Only the Gabon was left, and although for a while it looked as though the Gabon, too, would declare for de Gaulle, a pro-German submarine and various troopships that appeared off Libreville made the governor think again. This did not

suit de Gaulle at all, for the Gabon was of enormous strategic importance. If he controlled the Ogowe, he had a direct route to Chad and the
heart of Africa, and from Chad the allies could harass the Italians in
Abyssinia from the south and prevent them from moving any farther
into Africa.

Moreover, he could offer the British a route to the Middle East and
India—invaluable now that the Mediterranean was controlled by the
dictatorships. With the Gabon, de Gaulle would have something of real
importance to contribute to the Allied cause. Without it his position was
intolerably weak for so proud a man. In September the Gaullist troops
advanced from three sides into the jungle of the Gabon, making for the
coast and Libreville, the capital.

It was at Lambarene that the defending troops made their one and
only stand. Tiny as it is, Lambarene stands at the junction of river and
jungle track and commands both. From October 13 to November 5 the
battle for Lambarene continued. The hospital, a mile or two from the
town, was declared neutral territory, and both sides forbade their aircraft
to bomb it. All the same Schweitzer and the inmates hastily barricaded
the windows against stray shots, and, in fact, a few accidental bullets did
whistle across the water from the island.

On November 5 the occupying forces surrendered, the Free French
moved on downriver to the coast, and before long, the Gabon had fallen
to de Gaulle and the whole of French Equatorial Africa was his. Félix
Eboué was installed at Brazzaville in the Congo as governor-general of
the whole vast area.

Every channel of communication with Germany or occupied France
was now closed. Schweitzer's lifeline was definitely cut. But as one door
closed another opened, and his friends in Britain and the United States
could now contact him. Before the year was out, he had received two
offers of help from America. Dr. Edward Hume, secretary of the Christian Medical Council for Overseas Work, who had visited Schweitzer at
Günsbach, offered to send medicines. And Professor Everett Skillings of
Middlebury College, Vermont, wrote that he was collecting money.
Schweitzer put the two in touch with each other. To Dr. Hume he sent a
list of the most urgently needed medicines and equipment, the quantity
to be determined by the size of Professor Skillings' collection.

Another year, however, was to pass before the consignment arrived.
Sending across the Atlantic anything that was not connected with war
was not the simplest of tasks. Meanwhile, the gaps on shelves where the
drugs were stored grew wider each week.

Those yawning shelves pointed up, as nothing else could have done,
the vulnerability of Schweitzer's position and his responsibility. It had
been his decision to run his hospital without support of an organization;

his decision, too, to hand over considerable quantities of his collections to other charities. Now he was reaping the results pinned as he was in Africa and unable to go around with the collecting bowl.

Those who criticize him for being publicity-hungry doubtless forget that it was his name, and that alone, that stood between the hospital and bankruptcy; often, indeed, it stood between several hundred people and starvation. Publicity for Schweitzer was survival for the hospital. Such critics also forget—or perhaps do not realize—that until he was more than seventy the publicity he received was not of the inflated kind, blown up by journalists in search of a good story. He had won it honestly, the hard way, and had done everything he could to ensure that the people who contributed to the hospital funds had the chance of actually seeing the man they supported. He had lectured to them, had played the organ for them, and multitudes of them knew him personally. For person to person was the only sort of communication he thought valuable. Without that communication he was crippled.

While the hospital was waiting for the medicines from across the Atlantic, help arrived in a totally unexpected form. On August 2, 1941, Hélène stepped onto the landing place, having managed to find her way from occupied France. She must have known what she faced, and that there was little hope of her going back till the war ended. She was sixty-two and not strong. Yet she had made that hard and dangerous journey alone and on her own initiative, a feat that in itself shows that, despite all the difficulties of the marriage, here was a woman who was still a match for Schweitzer in determination.

Early in the war she had joined Rhena and her husband in Paris, but when the Germans came they made for Bordeaux, a nightmare journey that took about a month. They slept mostly in the car and ate when they could find something to eat.

To George Seaver, who wanted to know how she had contrived to get from there to Lambarene, she later wrote:

I am glad to answer your enquiry, especially since it gives me the opportunity of paying a tribute of gratitude to your country, from which such efficient help came to my undertaking; and next to it, the most kind and active assistance from the Red Cross Society in Geneva. Knowing that a British visa was necessary, I asked the Red Cross to supply me with the address of the office in London to which to apply, stating as my reason the fact that I was the oldest of the nurses at Lambarene, and might be of some use since no young nurses were available. They replied that their delegate was on the point of leaving for London and would present my application, but that the reply might take a long time. It took a very long time. But then I had a wonderful surprise: a telegram, followed by a letter, informed me— not of the address I had asked for, but—that I was at liberty to proceed at

once! Moreover, the competent authorities in London had given instructions that my journey should be facilitated as much as possible!

The next step was to ask for permission to leave France. When this
question had been discussed before, I had been told that if only I could
obtain the authority to prove admission to the colony, there would be little
or no difficulty in procuring a permit. But when—contrary to all expectation—I had received this authority, it took seven weeks to collect the necessary papers and permits to proceed from Bordeaux; and later on, four
weeks longer, to continue my journey from Lisbon; in fact, I received my
last permit just half an hour before the ship was due to leave that port!

My journey on the neutral [Portuguese] steamer was without accident,
in broad daylight and brilliantly lit by night, and my reception in Angola
quite in accord with the kind suggestions made by the competent authorities in London. I was relieved also of another trouble. I had prepared myself,
with some apprehension, for a long and lonely journey of 3 months through
the bush in unfamiliar territory, but found to my great relief that this was
reduced to a week's drive by car on new roads, and finally to a cruise along
the well-known river to the Hospital which I reached on August 2, 1941.

On my arrival I found that I was the first person—and so far as I know
the only one hitherto—who has succeeded legally in coming here from
France since 1940. Once again and with deep gratitude I would acknowledge my debt to that miraculous help which I have so often received in my
life, and to so much undeserved kindness, to a large extent from strangers,
which has made it easier to stand what would otherwise have been sad
and difficult.[13]

Hélène stayed until the end of the war, deputizing in turn for each of
the nurses, so as to give each one a break, and helping Schweitzer with
his correspondence and administration.

Her health stood up unexpectedly well although she did at one point
have to have an operation on her foot. For fifty-six months she did not
even go to the coast for the rainy season.

Schweitzer was, of course, having to do more doctoring than he had
done for some time. Several times a week he was assisting Goldschmid
at operations. Besides this he was taking advantage of the collapse of the
timber trade and the consequent cheap labor to extend the fruit tree
plantation and to renew deteriorating garden walls, drains, paths, and
buildings. "I run from right to left, what with pumps to repair, missing
keys to find, tools to mend, the refrigerators to set going, wood to fetch
for the kitchen and laundry: bananas, cassava, and maize to buy from the
natives who bring it in—*et que sais-je encore.*"[14]

Funds kept trickling in—not enormous, but enough to keep the hospital working at reduced speed—from Britain, the United States, and the
Swedish Red Cross. And in May 1942, only just in time, the first consignment arrived from America—twenty-eight cases of medicines,

instruments, extra-large rubber gloves for Schweitzer, who had been operating in a size too small, kitchen utensils, and every kind of useful article. In 1943 further shipments came from both America and Britain, and money with them, so that it again became possible to start taking in more patients. Numbers of these patients were whites, who were succumbing to the strain of their long enforced stay in the tropics and the inadequate diet. At the same time Dr. Goldschmid took a holiday in the Belgian Congo, and Schweitzer was himself operating three mornings a week. "Not to fall ill—to keep fit for work—is our constant care,"[15] he wrote.

Although things remained much the same at the hospital, the world outside was altering rapidly and constantly coming closer. Roads were driven through the jungle from west to east, from north to south, for military transport. The main highway, such as it was, that ran the full length of Africa from Algiers to Capetown passed through Lambarene, crossing the two branches of the Ogowe on motor ferries. They were only red dirt tracks, these roads, but they brought the mail from the coast by truck in hours, instead of by boat in days. And the seeds for the garden now came from Capetown.

Politically, too, an immense change was brewing. Early in 1944 de Gaulle attended a conference at Félix Eboué's headquarters at Brazzaville and took the first step toward granting full French citizenship, with voting rights, to the black populations of the French colonies. The move was, of course, political, an act of acknowledgment for the help they had given him and an encouragement to further cooperation rather than a farsighted piece of statesmanship. But by such gestures of expediency history is often pushed along, and two years later, when the war was won, the agreement was to be ratified—to the fury of most of the white colonists. The tragedy was that Eboué was not there to see the new era in, having died soon after the Brazzaville conference.

As one might expect, Schweitzer viewed the whole thing with the darkest suspicion. He understood very well the political motives behind it and was not impressed, nor did he think it particularly sane to give the vote to people who could not read or write and who knew nothing of the issues they were voting about. For years he had been trying to teach them the basic principles of agriculture and carpentry so that they could feed and house themselves properly and cease to be the slaves of the seasons. He had hammered them about theft, foresight, honesty, and application, believing these to be the first essentials for the creation of any kind of stable community free from fear. His efforts had rolled off them like water off a duck's back.

He was convinced that in offering them any sort of self-government at this stage Europe was simply adding to its crimes by refusing responsibility for the mess it had got them into. European officials must remain, he believed, to protect them against exploitation by European trade.

He was thinking, of course, only of the Gabon, the only part of Africa he knew. And the Gabon was less able to become a political entity than almost any other area because of the lack of education and communications and because of the large number of different tribes who did not like each other, did not understand each other's language, and did not wish to do so. After hundreds of years during which these tribes had been torn from their traditional ways of living, physically decimated and morally confused by the slave trade, the timber trade, and the liquor trade, to leave them now to their own devices was something like criminal negligence. So Schweitzer believed. When he said, as he often did, that an authoritarian system was the only one that would work in Africa, these were his reasons.

Other developments pleased him more. Those who claim that he ignored and mistrusted advances in medical techniques should read the notes he made during these years: "If only we had penicillin!" Of sulphonamides—"How much the existence of this valuable drug means to us!"[16] For heart disease—"Now we have from Switzerland a preparation of squills (Scilla maritima) which is far less dangerous than digitalis. . . . Recently there has been hope of important progress in the treatment of leprosy. French doctors in Madagascar have since 1937 been making promising experiments with a drug obtained from a plant found on the island (Hydrocotylus asiatica). With this treatment they are achieving rapid cures of leprous ulcers. In America a drug called promin, related to the sulphonamides, is also being tried with success."[17] As to DDT, here he is writing in 1944 of termites, "these wicked insects," which crawl into everywhere and eat everything, "nothing so far had been of any use against them, but lately we have been trying DDT."[18]

For the first time, too, the government was lending a hand with medical problems.

We have been less troubled with sleeping sickness than in earlier years because a Government doctor has been concerned with fighting it in our district. There is a large camp for sleeping sickness patients a little down the river from Lambarene. To carry on the fight against the disease in the right way it is necessary that at regular intervals the doctor or a white assistant should visit every village in a given district and examine all the inhabitants to discover by microscopic tests whether the germ of the disease is to be found in their blood or spinal fluid. Our concern is now limited to passing on to the Government doctor any patients in whom we suspect sleeping sickness.[19]

Unfortunately, though, even this relief boomeranged: the government doctor was called up, and Dr. Goldschmid had to take his place so that he was able to work only part-time at the hospital. And everyone grew more and more tired. Schweitzer's letters kept coming back to it.

> I dare hope that the greatest part of the work in regard to the maintenance of the buildings is about to be completed. I am glad about it, as I could never tell how much I suffered in these years when I had to sacrifice so much of my time to such work, besides my other activities. . . .[20] My wife is again well enough to help in the household, which is precious. I am always on my feet, though I need rest. . . .[21] If I started going on holiday I would soon find out how tired I am. I prefer to work from day to day. . . .[22] I surprise myself by the way I am able to carry on with my work, week in, week out. . . .[23] My capacity for sound sleep enables me to carry on like this and keep going without a day's rest. But oh! for one free day when I could at last sleep enough to get rid of the fatigue which more and more invades me; to concentrate entirely on finishing my book, to study my music and play the organ at leisure; to walk, to dream, to read for pure refreshment's sake. When will that day come? Will it ever come?[24]

In October 1944 he wrote:

> We continue to go on well, although tired. I have more work than ever. I begin in the morning at 6:45 and go on until 12:45. At 2 o'clock I start again and continue until 7 P.M. All this time I am on my feet in the hospital and doing secondary things. I belong to myself only after supper, but at 11 o'clock at night I am going on my last round in the hospital.
>
> My wife is also at work all day long. Mlle Emma looks after the garden, besides her other occupations. Mlle Koch does the household and has charge of the kitchen. What luck that she returned safely!
>
> How intensely I have been thinking of my friends in London when I learned that you have been bombed again! But I do hope that is going to be finished now, once and for all.[25]

It was, at last, nearly finished. One more wartime Christmas, one more wartime birthday. He was seventy years old. For eight continuous years he had been laboring in the sweaty confines of the hospital, and the hope of finding a successor was farther away than when he had first given the matter thought fifteen years before.

When in the evenings he sat down to write his thank-you letters, as his debt to his benefactors compelled him to do, he was so weary that he could find little but his weariness to write about although often one can see, reading these letters, how the enjoyment of communicating with his friends lifted his spirits and restored his strength as he wrote, and a letter that begins with apologies for lateness and brevity, using the standard excuses of overwork and writer's cramp, ends by enlarging on the problems of the hospital for three or four pages. But his harping on his tiredness, however justified, sometimes came dangerously close to self-pity, a sentiment that was far from his true feelings, for, in fact, he regarded himself as lucky to have escaped involvement in the war.

The seventieth birthday did not go unnoticed by the world. France and Germany were deep in the last few desperate months of fighting, and Alsace, after a war that had left it comparatively undisturbed by military action, was now the scene of rearguard battles as the Germans were driven back over their borders by the Allies. But in Britain, stretched to its utmost but now sighing with relief as the bombing eased and Hitler was clearly on the run, Schweitzer was richly remembered. London newspapers offered congratulations, if not canonization. One paper wrote: "If sainthood consists in making the good life attractive, Albert Schweitzer is a saint of our century. Yet his example does not belittle our own lives. He ennobles us, who are made of the same human clay. His story is a living sermon on the brotherhood of man. It gives perspective to the sufferings of our time." And the BBC broadcast a talk by Schweitzer's old friend, Nathaniel Micklem (somewhat patronizing about Schweitzer's theology, it must he said, although complimentary about everything else), and one of Schweitzer's organ recordings. Schweitzer actually heard it himself on the radio of a white patient, for this was another manifestation of the Brave New World that occasionally the hospital could hear news of Europe direct by radio. Otherwise they relied on summaries fetched every few days from the radio station in Lambarene town.

While in Europe the war moved toward a cease-fire, Schweitzer was preoccupied by a new threat—one that mercifully had not loomed during the earlier war years, when it would have been totally disastrous—famine. The dry season of 1944 had not been dry enough, and the villagers had been unable to burn the bush and make their plantations of plantain and manioc. When this happened, as it occasionally did, the Africans, sooner than make the effort of digging up the trees and shrubs that would not burn, simply starved. Foreseeing the shortage, Schweitzer sent his empty rice sacks by truck to a region farther in the interior called Tschibanga, where a farsighted district commissioner had been growing rice since 1942, and bought as much as possible for the hospital.

And then,

The news of the end of the war in Europe we received on Monday, May 7th, 1945, at midday. While I was sitting at my writing table after dinner finishing urgent letters which had to reach the river steamer by 2 o'clock there appeared at my window a white patient who had brought his radio set with him to the Hospital. He shouted to me that, according to a German report relayed from the radio station at Leopoldville in the Belgian Congo, an Armistice had been concluded in Europe on land and sea. But I had to go on sitting at my table in order to finish the letters which must be sent off immediately. Then I had to go down to the Hospital where the heart cases and other patients have appointments for treatment at 2 o'clock. In the course of the afternoon the big bell was rung and when the people at the Hospital had gathered, they were told that the war in Europe was over. After that, in spite of my great fatigue, I had to drag myself into the plantation to see how the work was getting on there.

Only when evening came, could I begin to think and try to imagine the meaning of the end of the hostilities and what the innumerable people must be feeling who were experiencing the first night for years without the threat of bombardment. Whilst outside in the darkness the palms were gently rustling, I fetched from its shelf the little book with the sayings of Laotse, the great Chinese thinker of the 6th century B.C., and read his impressive words on war and victory: "Weapons are disastrous implements, no tools for a noble being. Only when he can do no otherwise, does he make use of them. . . . Quiet and peace are for him the highest. He conquers, but he knows no joy in this. He who would rejoice in victory, would be rejoicing in murder. . . . At the victory celebration, the general should take his place as is the custom at funeral ceremonies. The slaughter of human beings in great numbers should be lamented with tears of compassion. Therefore should he who has conquered in battle bear himself as if he were at a festival of mourning."[26]

While Schweitzer quietly rejoiced that the disastrous weapons of war had been laid aside at last in Europe, the most disastrous of all was being primed for its first public performance. On August 6 the first atom bomb was dropped on Hiroshima, three days later, the second, on Nagasaki.

Mankind had discovered the opposite of Reverence for Life.

23

America

"THE GREATEST MAN IN THE WORLD"

1945-1950

THE FIRST TO ARRIVE from Europe was the resourceful Mathilde Kottmann, who had been pining to get back to Lambarene and who managed by dint of some string-pulling to get a much-sought-after seat on a flight from Paris to Libreville. From there she traveled by car to Lambarene, the first to reach the hospital from Europe in days rather than weeks. Soon after she arrived, Hélène, who had endured those four and a half years in Africa remarkably well, went home, along with numbers of whites who had been living, more or less bedridden, at the hospital.

But if Schweitzer himself had hoped to be relieved as soon as the war was over, he was disappointed. Permissions and papers were almost as difficult to get as ever, and although two doctors were ready to come, they were unlikely to reach Lambarene before the new year.

And in the new year they came. So did fresh nurses. So, also, did the New Gabonese Constitution. "Now we are all Frenchmen," said the Africans, "we don't have to work anymore." To Schweitzer one said, "You can stay. The rest, we'll slit their throats." Allowing that these stories may come from biased observers, there can be no doubt that the niceties of democratic government were far from clear to the tribesmen of the Ogowe. A good many, when they were first required to vote, wanted to know where they should put their cross for Dr. Schweitzer.

For the hospital itself the change meant a steady increase in paperwork. Nobody had hitherto troubled Schweitzer with that kind of thing; once through customs he was his own man, and the hospital records, although meticulous, were written on pieces of brown wrapping paper, luggage labels, and the like. They were for the use of the staff alone.

Now Schweitzer was answerable to a new government; what was more, to a black government, which inevitably had a strong antiwhite element and a vested interest in rejecting the works of all Europeans.

Schweitzer was forced to take his paperwork seriously, to justify his hospital not only to his patients on the spot but to the officials in Libreville. In fact, the officials were mostly on his side; to anyone but a totally fanatical antiwhite his record spoke for itself. But still he was an alien, even if a friendly one, and to some extent on sufferance in the Gabon.

Despite the efforts of supporters in Britain and the United States, the hospital was beginning to run into debt. But for the bounty that had been flowing in from America it would have foundered long before; and when Schweitzer wrote of the work of the Albert Schweitzer Fellowship of America, "it seems to me in the nature of a miracle,"[1] he was scarcely overstating the case. The Fellowship had spread from the East Coast to the West, collecting thousands of dollars in California, and had even stirred inquiries in New Zealand. The Congregational and Episcopalian Churches had added their blessings and their collections. The organist of the New York Philharmonic Orchestra, an Alsatian named Edouard Nies-Berger, had organized benefit concerts among the American Guild of Organists, and other musicians, too, had contributed. All this in a land where Schweitzer was as yet barely known to the general public and where even the moving spirit of the Fellowship, a one-time missionary named Emory Ross, had never met him personally.

Ross made up for this as soon as the war was over. He and his wife, flying the Atlantic to visit Lambarene in 1946, were probably the first two people in the history of the hospital to come from a far land simply to have a look at what was going on. They were certainly not the last. They were, in fact, the first swallows of an Indian summer that, along with great benefits and new friendships, brought all kinds of fresh complications.

But despite all the efforts of all the committees money was still an urgent problem. Prices were soaring. Food, wages, drugs, fares—the cost of running the hospital had quadrupled since before the war and at the same time benefactors in Europe had grown poorer. Schweitzer was not sure that it would be possible to go on at all. "Something has to happen in someone's heart before anything happens in Lambarene," he said,[2] but when the pockets of well-wishers were empty, the heart was less effective.

"My great and continued concern is how to feed them all," Schweitzer wrote in 1946. And as fresh doctors and nurses arrived from Europe, as the success of the new American sulfone drugs against leprosy brought greatly increased numbers of lepers into the hospital in search of treatment, the food problem grew more and more acute; by the summer of 1947 the hospital account was thousands of francs overdrawn. Schweitzer, struggling to get things back into peacetime running order before returning to Europe to raise fresh funds, was in an acute dilemma.

At this juncture—according to one version at the very moment when he was on his way to the bank to discuss the possibility of closing the hospital—two Americans, Dr. Charles R. Joy and Mr. Melvin Arnold, arrived at Lambarene. With them they brought a check for more than four thousand dollars, more than enough to cover the debts and put the account into good shape for the future.

Joy and Arnold had been sent by the *Christian Register,* a Unitarian magazine published in Boston, Massachusetts. Dr. Joy was an administrator of relief programs, Arnold, editor in chief of the Beacon Press, a Unitarian publishing house.

The Unitarians had a special interest in Schweitzer, for they found his theology very much to their liking with its refusal to worry too much about the doctrines of the Trinity or definitions of the divinity of Jesus. The Unitarian Service Committee, with the *Christian Register* as its mouthpiece, had already been active in collecting money for the hospital during the war. And now Melvin Arnold, on taking up his post with the Beacon Press, had decided on "a long term publishing program seeking to make America as familiar with the work of Albert Schweitzer as is Europe."[3]

Charles Joy, in fact, had already collected an anthology of Schweitzer's writings, which the Beacon Press was in the process of publishing, and this had occasioned considerable correspondence with Schweitzer, so perhaps the doctor was not totally taken by surprise when Arnold and Joy and the check arrived at Lambarene. But they were, nonetheless, welcome, and the visit was the beginning of a long friendship that was of value not only to the hospital (and presumably to the Unitarians) but also to the present-day biographer of Schweitzer, for Joy's enthusiastic researches brought to light and preserved a great deal of material that but for him would have vanished completely. With Joy and Arnold the Indian summer began in good earnest.

They returned to Boston, and their contribution to a special Albert Schweitzer number of the *Christian Register* in September 1947 put the Schweitzer bandwagon firmly on the road in the United States.

Not that their articles were the first to salute him with superlatives. *Reader's Digest* had already, a year before, published an article about him by a Fr. John O'Brien entitled "God's Eager Fool—The Story of a Great Protestant, Told by a Catholic Priest." An eminent divine had described him as "the greatest soul in Christendom"; and a poll taken in Europe and quoted in the *Christian Register* had classed him alongside Goethe and Leonardo da Vinci as one of the three all-round geniuses of Western Europe.

These plaudits, however, had not yet become part of a full-scale campaign. *Reader's Digest*, it is true, had a tremendous circulation; but this periodical discovers a new genius or saint every other month. A new one from central Africa was nothing to stir the pulse especially. America had been softened up a little, that was all, for the barrage of publicity which now began. *Life* magazine, one of the biggest guns of all, ran a major article on October 6, 1947 (almost simultaneously with the *Christian Register's* special number), headed "The Greatest Man in the World— That Is What Some People Call Albert Schweitzer, Jungle Philosopher." After that nothing could stop the runaway myth.

Arnold had described how on leaving Lambarene he had written in Schweitzer's visitors' book "a few lines, telling what it meant to have the privilege of knowing 'the greatest soul in Christendom.' "[4] Schweitzer instantly crossed it out; thereby, of course, confirming his greatness. The tale itself became part of the myth.

For the America of that time, a label such as "the greatest man in the world" was irresistible. Schweitzer grew furious when he heard of it, but what could he do? His story had moved uncontrollably beyond the level of personal encounter at which be had tried to keep it in Europe and into the realm of the mass soul, which he dreaded and disliked. And what was more, those unrelieved, overstrained war years at Lambarene had turned the big, bull-like figure into something highly suitable for canonization by popular demand. The springy hair, although just as vigorous and unruly, was going gray. The face was growing lined, the eyes were a little gentler, the frame a little stooped. Schweitzer was ideal for the sort of presentation America loved, as the craggy old he-man saint, the peasant philosopher who had seen it all, the frontiersman with the homespun wit and unquenchable kindliness.

So much popularity was, of course, very good for the hospital's finances: the money that now flowed in made its reestablishment merely a matter of time. But before Schweitzer left for Europe, two things happened that were to have a long-term effect on the hospital. Ali Silver arrived, the bright, energetic, and totally devoted young nurse from Holland who, with Mathilde Kottmann, was to support and serve Schweitzer to the end, still nearly twenty years ahead. And over in Lambarene town a new hospital came into existence, founded by the Gabonese government. It began almost as modestly as Schweitzer's had, with a few mud huts, very little equipment, and a young doctor and his wife as the entire staff.

Dr. Weissberg's first encounter with Schweitzer was not auspicious. When, stammering and nervous, he came face to face with the great man, he began by explaining that he had read some of his books, then failed to remember which, then asked if Schweitzer enjoyed hunting. The story is a fair illustration of the sort of awe-inspiring figure that Schweitzer, the prophet of simplicity, had by now become in the world's eyes.

But after this unpromising start the friendship eventually ripened—Weissberg stayed only a few months on this occasion but returned a few years later—into a mutually valued collaboration, a very different relationship from the one described or implied by many of the reporters from postwar Lambarene, who wanted to use the government hospital as a stick with which to beat Schweitzer's.

Enough for the moment to say that what Schweitzer had gone through in 1913 and 1923, Weissberg in some degree repeated in 1947 and the 1950s. It was Weissberg who said that out there one was always Charlie Chaplin when the bomb dropped; one looked around for somebody to hand it to, and there was no one. Schweitzer's hospital at that time seemed to Weissberg a place of dazzling equipment and gleaming efficiency.

In 1948 approaches began to reach Schweitzer from the American universities. First, Dubuque offered rectorship. Then Yale proposed an honorary degree in divinity, which had to be refused because acceptance involved appearing in person to receive it. (Some universities were prepared in Schweitzer's case to waive this rule and grant an honorary degree "in absentia," but not Yale.) And Princeton invited Schweitzer to come and finish his philosophical work in peace and quiet at the Institute of Advanced Studies, run by Robert Oppenheimer, the physicist who had been so closely involved in the development of the atom bomb. The reasons for Schweitzer's refusal to go to the States are obvious enough, but they are spelled out in a letter he wrote in April 1948, to Albert Einstein, who lived and worked at Princeton.

DEAR FRIEND,

Many a time have I written you in thought, because from afar I follow your life and your work and your attitude towards the happenings of our time. But my writer's cramp, an inheritance from my mother, hinders me, so that many letters planned in thought remain unwritten. But now that circumstances make it impossible for me to meet you in Princeton I really must tell you in writing how sorry I am about it. And now in an issue of *Life* magazine which came into my hands I see pictures of the Institute which further increase my regrets about the renunciation. The picture of Dr. Oppenheimer with you is touching. When I see a picture of you there always comes back the memory of the beautiful hours I spent with you in Berlin.

Through Dr. Oppenheimer you will have heard about the reasons for my renunciation. I am no longer a free man; in everything I have to consider my hospital and have always to be alert and ready for any action required for its running. Every enterprise is nowadays so burdened by all possible regulations, records and the like that it needs firm guidance all the time. So my absences from Lambarene are limited by this need for constant alertness. At present I have no doctors who are thoroughly acquainted with the hospital's management. The two who are with me now will this week have finished their two years and will be replaced by two new ones whom I will have to introduce to the work. And for the management as a whole I have nobody who could take over the necessary decisions and responsibilities.

For instance—at one time it began to "smell" like inflation of the franc (in spite of official reassurances that this would not happen), and in order to convert the shrinking paper currency into merchandise before it was too late I had to risk putting all available money into rice, petroleum and other materials which could be had in the factories and stores. In this way I risked having insufficient funds later on to pay outstanding bills and the wages of the numerous black personnel of the hospital. Nobody else could have taken the risk of getting the hospital into great financial difficulties by emptying the money chest, which was already in a precarious situation. I took the risk and saved thousands through hurried buying which was above our means. It saved the hospital from the financial crisis in which it would have been involved if we had had to pay the prices which soared high on the day of inflation. This is just one of many examples. How could I, a good theologian, ever have thought that I would become a speculator and a gambler to keep the hospital above water? However, though I have become a slave to the hospital, it is worth it.

Nonetheless, I am not giving up the hope of being able to continue with my other work. One thing to which I still rigidly adhere is practising the piano with the organ pedal, even if it is only for three-quarters of an hour, to keep in form and also to improve.

The Philosophy I carry with me constantly. Many chapters of the third volume of the Philosophy of Civilisation are finished and others are so far completed in thought that they can be put on paper right away. Only I must first get much extra work behind me (some of it masonry work), in order to be able to keep at it with some degree of quietness and regularity.

At the moment I am trying to eat my way through a mountain of thick gruel to reach the "Lubberland," the land of the lazy. It will be a very modest "Lubberland" but it will suffice my desires. These consist in having the morning and night hours to myself and to use the afternoon for work at the hospital. And if I can achieve that, even in a modest way, I could still give "The Philosophy of Reverence for Life" its definitive form. The whole question is: will I have around me efficient people who are capable of relieving me of as much work as possible, especially the stupid secondary work? The third volume is conceived as a symphony of thoughts—a symphonic performance of themes. Never before in my life have I thought and felt so musically as in these last years. In the third volume I have worked in chapters about mysticism and religion, as revolving around ethics.

We are at present three doctors and seven white nurses, among them an American. Without the material help of the U.S.A. the hospital could not be kept above water despite the economies we practise. My special field is Urology. At the same time I am the Top Apothecary, working out all the orders and keeping the large Pharmacy in order. At the moment I am especially occupied with the treatment of leprosy. We are using the new American remedies Promin and Diasone, which actually achieve what the former remedies could not. At present we have about fifty lepers under treatment. Leprosy is widespread here.

I am enclosing a map of the hospital. A Swiss engineer who passed through here made it and gave me several copies. Most of these buildings I erected with our black carpenter; in particular I did the masonry work. Among the new generation of natives there are none of the good workmen we used to find among the old ones. The old ones went through the regular apprenticeship and fellowship at the Catholic and Protestant labour missions. Those of the new generation get their knowledge at the so-called Industrial Schools. They consider themselves too good to become workmen. On the whole, what will become of the native population in all the colonial territories now that the tendency of the present generation is directed towards emancipating itself from the tilling of the soil and from trade! Nearby and seen from within, rather than from outside and from a distance, colonial problems look quite different.

Now I have let myself go and imposed upon you many pages of my scribble. But it was a pleasure for me to be with you in thought at my desk in these night hours. When will it be granted to us really to be together? Will it even happen?

I read in the "Aufbau,"[5] which I receive regularly, that you received a prize which imposes on you a flight around the world. I hope you will be able to play hooky, to use a good old college expression. . . .

Please remember me to Dr. Oppenheimer. I would have liked to make his acquaintance. How is your violin?

> With best thoughts, your devoted
> Albert Schweitzer

The writer's cramp hand has stood up well this evening. My wife is at present in Europe, staying in the Black Forest in Switzerland. She is relatively well. My daughter lives in Switzerland with her husband and four children.[6]

Einstein's reply was brief but warm:

I regret of course that you cannot visit the Institute, as you had intended. I am convinced, however, that the work you have pursued for so long is much more important. You are one of the few who combine extraordinary energy and many-sidedness with the desire to serve man and to lighten his lot. If there were more persons such as you are, we would never have slid into so dangerous an international situation as now prevails.

Against the blindness of human beings there unfortunately does not yet exist any remedy.

With warmest regards and wishes,

Yours

Albert Einstein[7]

Schweitzer's long letter is interesting for several reasons. It is a good example of the stiffness of his letter-writing style, even when writing to old friends, and of the repeated themes of all his correspondence. (Ten years later he wrote another letter to Princeton, to the president of the university, most of which might have been written on the same day.) But the fact that he was already in correspondence with Oppenheimer is also interesting, in view of Oppenheimer's subsequent stand against the development of the hydrogen bomb and Schweitzer's deep involvement, along with Einstein, in banning atomic testing.

The brief mention of Hélène in the postscript concealed the fact that she was, in fact, not at all well and very unhappy. No sooner had she returned to Europe than she was hankering to get back. "I was pretty miserable in Europe, more than I could tell you," she wrote on June 25 to Hermann Hagedorn.[8] And that dry season she did fly out for a brief and happy interlude. Then she had to return to extract their Königsfeld house from the military authorities who had requisitioned it and to put it straight again, all of which proved very tiring.

A tantalizing feature of Schweitzer's letter is the reference to the "symphony of thought" in the long-awaited third volume of *The Philosophy of Civilisation*. The previous year either Joy or Arnold had actually touched the famous third volume. Their account in the *Christian Register* relates with awe:

> The last night that one of the American visitors was to be at the hospital, the doctor called him in and told him to hold out his arms. Then the doctor reached up to a shelf and began piling into the visitor's arms stacks of sheets of paper, yellowed and brown with age. He continued until the paper stood a foot high, and then he exclaimed: "Third Volume!"
>
> So this was it: the distilled wisdom of this scholar, for which the learned world had long been waiting.
>
> "How soon?" the visitor asked. The doctor chuckled, and spread his hands. There are more chapters to write, and rewrite. Some of the chapters already have been done six times.
>
> Looking at the oil lamp on the desk and thinking of the inflammability of this single copy of the precious manuscript, the visitor suggested microfilming. The doctor laughed: Microfilming? Too modern! His manuscript was durable. "Look—see how these chapters have survived the teeth of the antelopes!"[9]

In September 1948, at long last, Schweitzer set sail from Port Gentil. Air travel had arrived since he was last there, but nothing would induce him to fly. He enjoyed the sea voyage too much.

Apart from the one hurried round trip to Günsbach and straight back in 1939, he had scarcely moved outside that tiny, hemmed-in cluster of huts on the riverbank for eleven years and seven months.

The homecoming was triumphant. Jacques Feschotte, an old friend of Schweitzer's and a regular visitor at the Günsbach house, wrote:

> I cannot describe with what joy he was welcomed by those who had waited so long. The road to Günsbach was soon crowded with pilgrims. They found the Doctor at seventy-three as strong and as upright as ever. His hair had silvered over and his face was thinner, but his eyes—if such a thing were possible—seemed even keener than before. The whole of Alsace was bent on fêting him. His native town, Kaysersberg, Colmar, Strasbourg, his University, and representative bodies of every kind vied with one another in their touching expressions of regard for this great son of Alsace.[10]

There were, of course, those four grandchildren to visit in Switzerland, none of whom he had ever seen. But for the most part the next few months were extremely peaceful and static by Schweitzer's standards as he fell back into the rhythm of Günsbach life, writing, talking, strolling in the evenings, playing the organ, and entertaining visitors by the score. Thanks to the stir going on in America, there was no pressing need to go on tour for the moment. Wealthy, enthusiastic, generous, and very, very large, the United States represented a newly discovered fairy godmother to the hospital.

Nor had Americans given up hope of inducing Schweitzer to cross the Atlantic. Yale and Princeton had failed. Harvard had invited him to deliver the Lowell lectures, but he had not risen to that bait either. But a more seductive attempt came in the form of an invitation to speak at Aspen, Colorado, on the occasion of the bicentenary of Goethe's birth.

Aspen was originally a silver-mining town. A wealthy enthusiast named Walter Paepcke had founded an organization known as the Aspen Institute for Humanistic Studies, which held its meetings in a huge specially designed tent in Aspen although much of the planning was done in Chicago.

About the beginning of January 1949, Paepcke sent a cable to Schweitzer asking him to come and speak at Aspen the following July and offering a fee of five thousand dollars. Before long came the reply: Dr. Schweitzer regrets. After a little consideration a new cable went to Günsbach, offering the same sum, only this time in francs, and payable to the hospital. It arrived soon after Schweitzer's seventy-fourth birthday and was accepted. Goethe, the money, the chance of visiting the pharmaceutical companies that produced the sulfone drugs, and, most important, the chance of saying thank-you in person to the people who had kept the hospital alive all added up to an irresistible proposal.

In accepting, Schweitzer was apparently unaware that Aspen was half a continent away from Chicago, the origin of the cable. He was under the impression that it might be a suburb of the city or a nearby town. "Schweitzer would never have come to America in the first place," said Mrs. Paepcke later, "had the great doctor not laboured under an illusion."[11] A confirmatory letter arrived toward the end of February, clarifying matters, but by now Schweitzer was committed, and during the following months he worked on his speech, as well as on the legendary third volume and on an important epilogue to a projected book on his theology by the Englishman, Colonel E. N. Mozley.

In England, meanwhile, the first serious criticism of Reverence for Life had appeared in the form of Middleton Murry's book, already mentioned, *The Challenge of Schweitzer*. Although Murry's whole exasperated argument is destroyed by his failure to understand what Schweitzer meant by "thought," the book is important as giving the intellectuals in England their first respectable lead in questioning the perfection of Schweitzer's ideas.

America was troubled by no such doubts and prepared excitedly for the arrival of the World's Greatest Man. The University of Chicago had seized the occasion to offer him an honorary degree in laws, which he accepted. The date for its presentation was three days after the Aspen speech, which was to be given twice, once in French, once in German, early in July.

Schweitzer had never aimed to be great, only to be human. And when the liner SS *Nieuw Amsterdam* docked at New York on June 28 and sixty-eight reporters and photographers thronged around him and Hélène, he appeared to enjoy himself greatly, posing for the photographers in his Günsbach suit, his high wing collar, and his father's bow tie, and back-chatting the reporters. "What do you think of the New World?" they asked him. "You live here," he replied, "you tell me." ... "I was afraid I'd find you all so materialistic," he said, "but here you are treating a philosopher like the King of England or a prize-fighter."

Dr. Emory Ross went with him to Colorado, marveling at his child-like enthusiasm, his swift absorption of what he saw and heard, the extraordinary range and accuracy of his knowledge, the "quality of understanding, solidarity, oneness with others quite different from himself," and in particular that special vision that gave him the constant flow of images of everyday life with which he made his points. For example, here is Ross's account of an interview with Fulton Oursler for

Reader's Digest. They are talking about the practical application of Reverence for Life.

> Man should forgive wrongs against himself, yes. Before the wrongdoer has asked forgiveness? Certainly, replied Schweitzer, and cheerfully, freely without grudging or reservations—just sweep it out clean, and again and again if required. That's the only way a man can live at peace within himself, and have a room free within for enjoyment and growth. He remembered a fortnight before, in New York's Pennsylvania Station. He was waiting with Mrs. Schweitzer and their small party of friends to board the train for Aspen, Colorado. The usual crowds were milling before the gates. It was the first American railway station he had ever encountered. There must have been a thousand things to see. But Schweitzer saw a sweeper with broom and pan. He was steadily sweeping up paper, cigarette-stubs, refuse, moving among the people. He swept a space clean and moved on. When he looked back, there was more paper and refuse already thrown by people. Did he fume and fuss and hate? Not at all. He went on steadily, serenely sweeping. That was his part. He did it. In the business of forgiveness, we must always be using our broom and pan.[12]

During the two thousand–mile journey an incident occurred that no book about Schweitzer can omit. The story has many versions; the most authentic is probably that from the 1951 bulletin to British supporters, vouched for by Mr. and Mrs. T. D. Williams, the treasurer of the Schweitzer Hospital Fund in Britain and his wife. Both had traveled with Schweitzer from Europe:

> As they were travelling over the plains of the Midwest two ladies stopped diffidently at the door of Schweitzer's compartment and asked, "Have we the honour of speaking to Professor Einstein?" "No, unfortunately not," he replied, "though I can quite understand your mistake, for he has the same kind of hair as I have (rumpling his up), but inside my head is altogether different. However, he is a very old friend of mine—would you like me to give you his autograph?" And he wrote, "Albert Einstein, by way of his friend Albert Schweitzer."[13]

Schweitzer and Einstein, incidentally, were to figure as first and second, respectively, in a nationwide poll conducted in December 1950, by the *Saturday Review of Literature* to select the world's greatest living nonpolitical persons.

Aspen turned out to be eight thousand feet high—a great deal higher than anything in the Vosges—and the altitude did not suit Schweitzer. "Aspen," he said, "is built too close to heaven." All the same, despite a late arrival caused by a rock-fall on the rail track, he was up bright and early on his first morning there, to the embarrassment of his hostess, Mrs. Elizabeth Paepcke.

The Schweitzers had been told that breakfast was at 8:00 sharp. But at 7:45 the bathroom flooded while Walter Paepcke was showering, and Mrs. Paepcke related how she was still endeavoring with mop, bucket, and sponge to control the situation when "our Victoria clock chimed 8:00. The front door opened. There stood the great man himself, amused brown eyes, immense drooping mustache, thin black folded tie, old-fashioned long coat . . . and on his arm an elderly lady in gray and garnets who looked like a pale moth. 'Dénouement.' I stared at the doctor.

" 'Oh.' I cried, 'our plumbing has backed up, there is water all over the floor, and I have to rescue my husband from the bathroom.'

" 'I see,' said Dr. Schweitzer slowly, as he looked me over from tousled hair to bare feet and mop. 'I see,' he repeated, 'Mrs. Schweitzer and I are just in time to witness the second flood.' "[14]

The first lecture, in French, was translated by Emory Ross. When Schweitzer repeated it in German, two days later, the translator was the novelist and playwright Thornton Wilder. "Schweitzer stood," Mrs. Paepcke remembered, "with folded hands, hardly moving, speaking in a surprisingly high and childlike voice. He wore his usual long, black coat, and high, stiff winged collar, but instead of looking pontifical in these he gave the illusion of frailty and extreme vulnerability. It was hard to believe that this man was he who had hewn a hospital with his bare hands out of a disease-infested jungle."[15]

The audience included all kinds of distinguished people. José Ortega y Gasset was there, Artur Rubinstein, Gregor Piatigorsky, Martin Buber; and Ernst-Robert Curtius, son of the Frederick Curtius who had helped Schweitzer in his student days, had come all the way from Strasbourg for the occasion. *Life* magazine managed to take a photograph in which Schweitzer was surrounded by philosophers, theologians, and historians from Spain, France, Holland, and Norway, as well as Harvard and Washington.

The content of the lecture would not have been unfamiliar to anyone who already knew Schweitzer's other lectures on Goethe. He went into the different sides of Goethe's personality in greater detail than on previous occasions, and there was none of the lowering sense of coming disaster that had marked the last one in Frankfurt in 1932. But the main theme was the same: Goethe's attachment to nature, to simplicity, to resignation in the face of mystery, to common sense and observation and action, as opposed to speculative and sterile intellectual exercises. Schweitzer is, as usual, singling out the elements in Goethe that he himself valued and is puzzled here and there by elements that he cannot sympathize with.

We do not understand for instance, his behaviour toward Christiane Vulpius. They live as man and wife for eighteen months before he legally marries her and gives her, in the eyes of the world, the status to which she is actually entitled. How is it possible for him to prolong a situation which must bring him, and especially her, so many difficulties and so much humiliation? How shall we understand, in general, the spirit of indecision which he displays on more than one occasion?

And this lack of naturalness which he also exhibits! When his prince and friend, Karl August, dies, he does not render to him the last honors, which he should have done in any case as the prince's prime minister. Instead he asks Karl August's son and successor to excuse him from taking part in the funeral ceremonies, so that he may retire to the country to master his grief. He does not even take part in writing the necrology.[16]

Schweitzer the traditionalist breaks through here, the man who, for all his other revolutionary notions, valued the stabilizing force of the rules and rituals of society. A later generation than his came to feel that these rules and rituals were themselves often the forces that destroyed individuality. Rejecting these rules, they could, perhaps, understand that side of Goethe better than Schweitzer did. But the society that bred Schweitzer had given him his individuality, not taken it from him, and he was faithful to it.

For the most part, however, the lecture is one of gentle and understanding admiration. "This is Goethe—the poet, the sage, the thinker and the man. There are persons who think of him with gratitude for the ethical and religious wisdom he has given them, so simple and yet so profound.

"Joyfully I acknowledge myself to be one of them."[17]

Schweitzer did not stay long on the heights of Aspen, but while he did the reporters were around him in droves, wanting a good quote or two. One, who had been keeping him from his dinner, said to him, "You're a great man, but what is this business of Reverence for Life?"

"Do you want to practice it," asked Schweitzer, "or do you want me to explain it to you?"

"You explain it first," said the reporter, "and I'll decide if I want to practice it."

Schweitzer liked that.

"If you let me go and eat my soup while it's warm," he said, "you've already practiced Reverence for Life."

It proved a successful and lasting quote.

After leaving Aspen, he rested for a day at Denver then went on to Chicago where he received his honorary degree, which was followed by a luncheon reception in the Grand Ballroom of the Stevens Hotel. Among those who paid him tribute at that luncheon was Governor Adlai Stevenson, and the Grand Ballroom (as Schweitzer noted on his copy of the program) held more than seventeen hundred people. The invitation with which the lady who organized it drew them all there deserves reprinting in full, for surely it must be one of the high points of the legend, the ecstatic call of a Maenad to the worship of her deity:

CONFERENCE OF CLUB PRESIDENTS AND PROGRAM CHAIRMEN
A WONDERFUL DREAM COME TRUE!
You are to have the high honor of presenting the award
FOR DISTINGUISHED SERVICE TO HUMANITY
TO
DR. ALBERT SCHWEITZER
Philosopher—Musician—Doctor—Theologian—Writer—"Man of God"
"The Thought of him was always a Beatitude, a Great Light,
a Wind of Courage"
JULY 11—12:15 NOON, STEVENS HOTEL GRAND BALL ROOM—CHICAGO

Schweitzer would not have been human had this kind of adulation left him completely untouched. For one thing it must have affected those around him, making it less and less possible for anyone to treat him as an ordinary human being. And now *Time* magazine gave him a front cover, as well as an article, and another article appeared in *Life*. *Reader's Digest* added their piece. He was on every bookstall and in every cinema, blown higher than any human creature could survive. If not the greatest, he was certainly the world's most admired man, with several popularity polls to prove it. From now on there was nowhere he could go in the world's estimation but down, and who could wonder that among journalists there was a feeling that the bubble should be pricked sooner or later and speculation as to who would be the first to prick it.

But whatever dismay, amusement, satisfaction, embarrassment, or sheer amazement Schweitzer may have felt at finding himself the world's favorite, shrewd amusement and a childlike delight in all that was happening were his most apparent reactions, and his lifelong sense of proportion ensured that in essentials he was unchanged. He continued to play any organ he could lay his hands on until he was dragged away (organ playing, he used to say, is the best exercise in the world). He went to see friends in Cleveland, Ohio, he visited pharmaceutical works in New York, and on July 22 set sail again for Europe.

It was at this high point of his fortunes that many of the books about Schweitzer appeared, publishers naturally being keen to ride the wave. George Seaver's book had come out in 1947, and others by Hermann

Hagedorn, Colonel P. N. Mozley, Joseph Gollomb, and Jacques Feschotte followed in 1948, 1950, 1951, and 1954, respectively.

Most of these books, as one might expect, were to a greater or lesser extent hagiographies. They made little attempt to comprehend Schweitzer, but simply accepted that he was some kind of force of nature to be wondered at and, if possible, emulated rather than understood.

The correspondence between Schweitzer and Hermann Hagedorn in 1944 and 1945 shows how little Schweitzer did to encourage this adulation. Hagedorn, whose *Prophet in the Wilderness* is one of the most imaginative and appealing of the books about him, was anxious to fill in some of the gaps, factual and emotional, in the autobiography *Out of My Life and Thought*, and many of the questions he asked were very pertinent. They dealt mainly with the early years, the Strasbourg years; and the striking thing about Schweitzer's answers is his refusal to claim any special quality for himself. In question after question he cuts away the ground from beneath the biographer's feet. Hagedorn, for example, writes about the temptations Schweitzer must have felt to abandon the resolution he made at twenty-one and to go after the honors that were beckoning at thirty; about "the spiritual struggles that you must have known. The inward story remains untold." What does Schweitzer reply? "I did not know the temptations of which you speak. . . . I was so absorbed in work during those years that I didn't have time to think of myself. I am no superman. Far from it. There is no 'inward story' of those years. I was very happy, very busy, very tired, and I lived in the shadow of St. Thomas' Church; when I wanted to relax I often went there at ten o'clock at night to play the organ—it was a fine instrument—in the dusky church." And again and again: "Don't forget one thing: people thought very little about me. . . . I don't believe that Catholic Scholars attached any particular importance to my book. I was a quite unknown young man. . . . I was no prodigy, one way or another. I got somewhere thanks to good teachers, and thanks to my industry. . . . There is nothing 'unique' about me whatsoever."[18]

Schweitzer's own valuation of himself was borne out by Elly Knapp (that friend of Hélène's whom Schweitzer married to Theodor Heuss in 1908) in her book *Ausblick vom Münsterturm*. At that time, she remembered, nobody paid any special attention to him. But now the glory of the present shed a transforming light on the past. All the same, Schweitzer was less than totally open when he claimed that there was no "inward story" of that period, that he had no time to think of himself. The inward story was not the one that Hagedorn suspected, the temptation to abandon his chosen path, but we have seen, through the letters between Schweitzer and Hélène, that there were struggles indeed and that even if he did not think of himself as a superman, he certainly was for a while obsessed with Greatness.

Only Colonel Mozley's book ignored the saintly figure with the shaggy head and twinkling eyes, brooding with patient wisdom over the world, and went with enthusiasm for the theology, which had long been neglected or at best regarded as just another alpha plus for the prize boy.

With indignation Mozley discovered that the Church had failed either to answer Schweitzer or to take him seriously, and his book summarized, in seventy-five good clear pages, all Schweitzer's conclusions. This was important and timely. More so still was the epilogue that it drew from Schweitzer himself, in which he followed up his theories about the early Church and traced the course of Christianity thereafter. We have already glanced at this in chapter 8 but it is worth reminding ourselves, that now, fifty years later, Schweitzer still retained these thoughts not only as an intellectual conviction but as the very foundation of his daily activity.

As Schweitzer saw it, the vivid expectation that Jesus originally had of the coming of God's kingdom had inevitably been whittled away over the centuries after his death. Gradually, as the kingdom receded into the future, the hope of a new age for all mankind had become transmuted into something quite different—the self-centered attempt of isolated individuals to ensure their ticket into bliss after death. The Church's function had changed from that of fostering communal life in the spirit of Jesus to that of forgiving sinners so that they could die "in the sure hope of glorious resurrection."

In Schweitzer's view this aberration must now be reversed:

> We are no longer content like the generations before us, to believe in the Kingdom that comes of itself at the end of time. Mankind today must either realise the Kingdom of God or perish. The very tragedy of our present situation compels us to devote ourselves in faith to its realisation.
>
> We are at the beginning of the end of the human race. The question before it is whether it will use for beneficial purposes or for purposes of destruction the power which modern science has placed in its hands. So long as its capacity for destruction was limited, it was possible to hope that reason would set a limit to disaster. Such an illusion is impossible today, when its power is illimitable. Our only hope is that the Spirit of God will strive with the spirit of the world and will prevail.
>
> The last petition of the Lord's Prayer has again its original meaning for us as a prayer for deliverance from the dominion of the evil powers of the world. These are no less real to us as working in men's minds, instead of being embodied in angelic beings opposed to God. The first believers set their hope solely upon the Kingdom of God in expectation of the end of the world; we do it in expectation of the end of the human race.
>
> But there can be no Kingdom of God in the world without the Kingdom of God in our hearts. The starting-point is our determined effort to bring every thought and action under the sway of the Kingdom of God. Nothing

can be achieved without inwardness. The Spirit of God will only strive against the spirit of the world when it has won its victory over that spirit in our hearts.[19]

The apocalyptic end of the world that Jesus saw coming had made a new appearance in the world in the shape of the threat of atomic destruction. But if the end came, there was no promise this time that God would send a new ruler and a new world order after it. Only man could do that through the spirit of Jesus that now had a new name, Reverence for Life; and it must be done before the disaster, not after it. The confrontation between Life and limitless Death was imminent.

This epilogue was a brief sketch for a longer book that Schweitzer contemplated and on whose manuscript he did, in fact, work in 1950 and 1951, but which was never published in his lifetime. It was found among his effects after his death and published under the title *The Kingdom of God and Primitive Christianity*—his last statement about God, about the Church, and about life.

A couple of months in Europe for packing and preparation, and Schweitzer was en route once more for Africa, Hélène still with him.

From there, soon after he had completed three-quarters of a century's living, he wrote: "I am still standing. That is really something. . . . I am in the process of giving to the hospital the impulsion so that it may go on one day when I am no longer in this world, in my tradition and in my spirit."[20] He had not only made his life his argument, he had made his hospital his argument, for his hospital was now his life.

How long had Schweitzer been aware of the hospital as something embodying his spirit and his tradition? For most of its life it had simply "grown half in a dream," reflecting his personality to some extent, certainly, but mostly reflecting the sheer forces of necessity.

But now, with the world's eyes on him, with all the Albert Schweitzer councils and committees all over Europe and the United States thriving and multiplying, he could take the hospital's survival for granted and think more about preserving its style.

For with the publicity came also the pressures. It would have suited many of the big international companies well to sponsor the hospital to the tune of thousands of dollars and garner the glory. Schweitzer received several such offers. He might have raised, had he so wished, air-conditioned palaces with spotless antiseptic wards and long, echoing concrete corridors full of all kinds of equipment that humidity made useless in his wooden village. In return, he would only have had to allow the use of his name—and lose control of his hospital. For whatever promises he might have been given, he must have known that the image-makers of any respectable American concern would never have allowed life to go on at Lambarene as it now did. He had enough experience already of the shock registered by hygiene-conscious Europeans when they saw his open drains and found chicken dung in the wards to know that his Africans' needs would have to take second place to the demands of the benefactor's publicity men. An army of white technicians would have arrived to install and maintain the new-style hospital. The Africans would have been separated from their families, forced to eat unfamiliar food cooked by strangers, and imprisoned in impersonal wards functionally designed not for living in but only for being ill in.

No amount of superior equipment, Schweitzer felt, could make up for the psychological harm that would follow. In his hospital the whole cycle of life and death was integrated. Health and enjoyment were there, as well as pain and disease. The place asserted life in a way no American or European hospital could do. And probably most important of all, it was a teaching hospital.

The constant criticisms that Schweitzer did not teach the Africans medicine and did not contribute to medical knowledge miss the point that all the time he was trying to teach them something else, something much more basic and essential: how not to get ill in the first place; how to grow food; how to plan for the future; how to avoid infection; how to defeat suicidal superstitions and hatreds—in short, how to live.

Schweitzer had originally come to Africa to be independent, in his service of mankind, of a civilization he thought was on the wrong road. He was not going to sell out to that civilization now, however great the inducements it offered him. His creation was not just a hospital, which could be improved by spending money, but a way of life. That was what he meant by his spirit and his tradition, and that was not for sale. It could be passed on only by personal example and personal influence. All the millions of the drug companies and the film companies (for Hollywood was vainly offering huge sums to make a film about him) were powerless to do that simple thing.

More and more, as the outside world increased the pressure in the ensuing years, Schweitzer was forced into autocracy. It seemed self-evident to a great many people that his hospital was as it was only because he could not afford to make it any better. Now that money was available for the asking, why did he pig-headedly cling to its primitive inadequacies? His reasons, although they were quite capable of rational explanation, lay deep in his instincts—as had his reasons for going to Africa in the first place. And just as then he had grown tired of the hopeless task of convincing his friends by argument and had simply said, "I'm going," so now he laid down the law and let everybody think what they pleased. *"Fais ton devoir sans discuter,"* he used to shout at the Africans, "Get on with your job and don't argue about it." And so he did himself.

He had always been a difficult man to say no to. As with age and pressure he grew more dogmatic and less inclined to discuss his decisions, the chances of his sometimes being wrong increased. The marvel is how rarely it happened. The only person with the courage to tell him when it did happen was Hélène. She had always been irritated by some of his characteristics, and now the unquestioning deference he received really exasperated her. So, of course, did her impotence as the young and vigorous nurses took over and she found herself again without a function at Lambarene. The tension between husband and wife was inevitable and not always well concealed. For example, Hélène had much less love for animal life than he had, and would keep a stick handy against any creature that presumed too much on her reverence for its life.

All the same, Schweitzer may have needed that touch of acid in his life and may have known it. For although he very humanly liked to be admired, he hated to be separated from other people by too much respect, and one thing he missed very much at Lambarene was the company of his intellectual equals and the chance of exercising his wits with them. At least Hélène's skepticism offered him something to push against, even though it was complicated by personal emotion.

But in July 1950 Hélène had to go back to Europe. The hurly-burly of the American tour and the hurried preparation in Alsace had told heavily on her remaining energies. Schweitzer accompanied her to Port-Gentil and put her on the ship. "The farewells at Lambarene," he wrote to America, "were moving for it is scarcely probable that my wife will return. . . . [T]ogether we looked at the hospital until at the bend of the river it disappeared from our horizon. I still cannot get myself away from the emotion of that farewell."

In the hospital, though, all was well. "The doctors and nurses are doing their work well . . . the spirit is excellent . . . my dream is accomplished."[21]

It seems to have been during this happy period, when the hospital was running smoothly, there were no financial worries, and the Schweitzer spirit ruled unquestioned in Lambarene, that he wrote a tiny, odd little book of immense charm, which, like *Memoirs of Childhood and Youth*, tells us more about the man himself than all his philosophies do.

Three young pelicans had been brought in by Africans and were named Parsifal, Lohengrin, and Tristan. Parsifal became Schweitzer's own favorite and lived in the hospital until his death from the pellets of a hunter's shotgun, already described in Dr. Catchpool's story.

For Schweitzer's birthday Dr. Anna Wildikann presented him with a collection of photographs of Parsifal, with which he was delighted. Dr. Wildikann was shortly leaving the hospital to work in Israel, and Schweitzer knew that she needed a car for her new work. So he sat down and in one night wrote the biography of Parsifal to go with the photographs, so that she could buy her car with the royalties.

The book is called *The Story of My Pelican,* and it is told in the first person by the pelican himself: "I am the pelican, the hero of this book." The story begins with the pelican's "confused recollections" of his infancy, with his brothers, in a high nest above the river and the forest.

My exact memories start from the moment when some black men, shouting and waving branches, drove my parents off and carried us away, all three of us, with our feet bound together. In the village we were placed in a basket in which we could not move. . . . [They are then taken by canoe on a three-day journey till they reach a place where] among the palms and the mangoes are many red roofs. . . . Dogs flung themselves yelping in our way and I promise you we were very frightened. Then a powerful voice broke in, restoring silence, and there appeared a man of burly stature accompanied by a person in white. It was, I discovered from what followed, Dr. Schweitzer and the nurse Emma Haussknecht.

For a moment or two the doctor looked at our kidnappers and our basket. Then he said, "Three pelicans to feed, that's all we needed!"

After that there was another silence, at the end of which the doctor spoke to the two blacks: "Didn't you know it's a sin to take little ones away from their parents? How could you do that? Just wait and see; the good Lord will surely find a way of punishing you! Didn't the missionary tell you that at school?"

The doctor's expression was fearsome, and the blacks were uneasy. But they quickly pulled themselves together and said: "We thought that you liked pelicans and that's why we've brought them. If you pay us for them you can have them. If not, we'll take them to another white man.

The doctor went all red: "Out of the question! Do you think I'm going to let you drag these poor creatures around half dead with hunger? They'll stay here. Here you are, here's a couple of coins for the cost of the journey and the fish you had to buy for them. And now, clear off!"

So the pelicans stayed, and were fed, and "the doctoresse" [Anna Wildikann] came and looked at them, and said: "They have a remarkably stupid look about them! But aren't they nice, with their little round behinds all covered with down." They would have liked to pick us up and stroke us, but we dealt out a few sharp nips all round.

[After that the doctor set about building a hutch to keep them warm at night.]

He busied himself all afternoon under the house, crawling about and making no attempt to hide the bad temper these extraordinary activities put him in. I never had any experience of man and I found it very strange that such a good man could grumble such a lot. . . .

[The story continues, the pelican grows up, and the doctor teaches him to fly.]

At the end of the dry season, when the other pelicans returned to the region of the lakes and swamps, my brothers went with them. "Good riddance" said the doctor to Miss Emma; "let's hope the little one will follow suit."

But the little one—me—I'd no intention of doing them such a favour. At the hospital I was at home. . . . I swore that the doctor wouldn't get rid of me so easily. I know better than he does what's good for me.

From time to time lady pelicans have made suggestions to me about leaving the hospital and making a home with them, somewhere a long way away, in a tree. But I've always stuck to the hospital grounds and I intend to go on sticking to them.[22]

It is impossible to convey at second hand the warmth and the humor and the loving enjoyment of people and creatures that glow from this book. Sentimentality and whimsy are somehow effortlessly avoided, and in their place, in a frivolous vein, is that same entering into another's world that marked Schweitzer's understanding of Jesus and of Bach. Perhaps his word *solidarity* is as good as any to describe the process.

Almost as attractive is the gentle self-mockery. Here is a man who finds himself as amusing as the rest of creation, and who is so self-confident that he can display his weaknesses without apology. One can scarcely imagine those other philosophers, his bugbears Schopenhauer and Nietzsche, writing thus of themselves.

Everyone who knew Schweitzer speaks of his eyes. They were alert, they were direct, they fixed you, they were amused, they twinkled. Reading *The Story of My Pelican*, I find I can see those eyes as clearly as in any photograph.

24

Schweitzer on Film

1950–1954

THE HOSPITAL NOW HOUSED four hundred patients, of whom half were lepers attracted by the efficacy of the new sulfone drugs. The staff numbered twenty-four, of whom about two-thirds were white.

Apart from one or two who had made Lambarene their life's work (Emma Haussknecht, Mathilde Kottmann, Ali Silver), these white doctors and nurses came for spells of two years at the most, frequently less. Some returned for a second period, but most moved on elsewhere.

In a sense, therefore, the larger the hospital grew the less continuity it had, for the proportion of people who were untried and new to the work was always increasing. These doctors and nurses comprise a roll of honor that is and always will be unsung in Schweitzer's story, but we must not forget the sum of adventure, enterprise, and often self-sacrifice represented by this ceaseless flow of trained medical personnel to the Ogowe, nor the constant efforts of Schweitzer's allies in Europe and now in America to find and persuade the right people to go out there, nor from Schweitzer's point of view the ever-increasing paperwork—negotiations, instructions, tickets, permits, passports—which he insisted on seeing to personally.

For the biographer, who has been troubled by the underdocumentation of the early years, the problem now is rather that of an excess of information. For although the outlines of the story are clear enough, different accounts often contradict each other in detail, and, meanwhile, the inward Schweitzer, whom we have been trying to follow and comprehend, is in danger of becoming swamped under a torrent of facts.

Because Schweitzer's autobiography came to an end twenty years earlier, we no longer have his own vision of his life to go by. He published no more books. And the bulletins he wrote and the vast bulk of his letters concerned only the practical needs and problems of the hospital.

More and more people could claim to have met Schweitzer, but very few of those could claim to know him, and even of those few none could know his every side; human communication does not allow such total identification. So one of his closest friends could say to me, "Schweitzer could never have written such a thing," when, in fact, he did write precisely that. Another could claim that he occasionally struck Africans in momentary anger while a third will hotly deny that he could ever have administered more than a friendly slap on the backside. One nurse will say that he was remote and authoritative, another that he was warmly human toward everyone. And on a simple point of fact, someone who was a long while at the hospital will say that Schweitzer was never concerned about fire because everything there was always so damp while his own remarks in his bulletins show that possibility did worry him and that for that reason he replaced wooden walls with corrugated iron and also abandoned wooden floors in wards and went back to earthen ones.

But what is clear from every account is that for all the increasing complexity of the hospital Schweitzer never did lose the "inwardness" he valued so much nor his sense of wonder and delight. "The prose of Africa" might overwhelm his days so that there was rarely time to give himself, as man to man, to those who worked with him or those for whom he worked, but the impulse never died nor did the need to withdraw and commune with nature. Clara Urquhart remembered how he would say to her, "Come and sit with me," and they would go to a bench overlooking the hospital and sit together hand in hand for half or three quarters of an hour without speaking, as once he used to go, alone or with his god-daughter, Suzi, to the Rocks of Kantzenrain above his village in Alsace. Times like these were his only holidays.

The great influx of leprosy patients into the hospital posed very special problems, the most obvious of which was that there as simply not enough accommodation for them, especially in view of the long period during which they needed to be kept under observation before the disease could be considered checked. They were inclined to vanish back to their villages as soon as the pain ceased, only to return, much worse, when it recurred.

Into this situation came an enthusiastic young nurse, Trudi Bochsler, who immediately made these patients her special concern. Soon, indeed, she began to argue with Schweitzer and fight hospital regulations in her determination to see that "her" lepers got their fair share or, if possible, more than their fair share of the available facilities. She noted that the effectiveness of the new drugs was often reduced because the patients were suffering from other diseases or from malnutrition, and their systems were unable to benefit as they should. The other complaints, therefore, had to be diagnosed and treated before the leprosy treatment could begin, and this made fresh demands on the hospital in general.

It is probably from this time that the popular imagination began to identify the Schweitzer hospital exclusively with leprosy, and it is worth reiterating that until the end of World War Two leprosy treatments were so laborious and ineffective that lepers made a very small proportion of the patients. Ten or fifteen years later the hospital's usefulness in the leprosy campaign was ending as the government took it over, and once again lepers were in a minority there. But at this particular juncture Schweitzer's hospital was the only place for hundreds of miles offering the newest treatment.

The place where the leprosy patients were treated was not even a building, simply a leaf canopy to keep off sun and rain, and their accommodation was the isolation building at the top of the hill, a few minutes' walk from the main hospital. Here, before long, Trudi Bochsler was taking upon herself the building of a number of huts for her patients. Here she coaxed and bullied and cajoled the lepers, who now loved and trusted her like a mother, to do for themselves, so far as their maimed limbs allowed them, what no one else had time to do—build themselves a village. Defying Schweitzer when she disagreed with him, oblivious to the problems she caused in the rest of the hospital, she yet wrung from him such respect that he granted her an autonomy within the organization that no one else had achieved.

Another arrival at the hospital at this time was the filmmaker Mrs. Erica Anderson, who has already been quoted but now met Schweitzer for the first time. With her she brought her camera equipment and an assistant—in defiance of Schweitzer's wishes, for when she had first broached the idea of making a film about him, he had refused permission as he had done to numbers of other applicants before her. To Clara Urquhart, through whose good offices Erica had first managed to contact Schweitzer, he had written, "I would rather burn in hell than have a film made of my life."[1]

He had, however, invited Erica to come, if she wished, to the hospital, but *not* to film. She had only brought her equipment because a collector of African art had asked her to shoot some film for him in the Congo although she also had a secret hope that once at Lambarene she might overcome Schweitzer's objections.

And so it proved. After a while she had regretfully reached the conclusion that Schweitzer was right—anyone making a film would only interrupt hospital routine and be an extra and unproductive mouth to feed—when Schweitzer sent for her. Having come to know her, he had changed his mind—with two stipulations. There must be no publicity for the film, and it must not be released until after his death.

So began a friendship that Erica was to record in her book *Albert Schweitzer's Gift of Friendship*—by far the most vivid and, I suspect, the most accurate portrait of Schweitzer ever put into print, lovingly written and full of the kind of significant day-to-day detail that so many books about him lack.

With her independence from hospital routine and her different background from the nurses Erica was able to see Schweitzer in a different light than did the medical staff. She saw him as someone whose gaiety and spontaneity was inhibited by his responsibilities at the hospital, and she felt that to some extent, at least, his authoritarian pose was forced on him by the need of some of the medical staff for a father figure. He told her, for example, that he much disliked being called *"le grand Docteur,"* the title that some of the staff insisted on using. To Erica he would refer to himself humorously as "Grandfather," or "the old idiot."

The staff, in turn, tended to mistrust Erica as an alien force in the atmosphere of Lambarene. But nobody could fail to admit that her film, when it was finally shown several years later, was a loving and unique record of the hospital and of Schweitzer himself and his home in Alsace.

He returned to Alsace in May 1951, this time only for six months. He was growing older, and Europe was growing more exhausting. Although he undertook no further tours and went only briefly to Holland, Scandinavia, and England on more or less private visits, he was inundated by visitors of all sorts, among them the queen of the Belgians, who came quietly and privately to see him.

Erica Anderson had already returned to America to develop the film she had shot and to report progress to her producer, the railroad millionaire James Jerome Hill. He sent an album of her photographs to Günsbach and shortly received an ecstatic letter from Emmy Martin, thanking her for such "an abundance of beauty" and inviting her to Alsace. "On the 28th July, the anniversary of Bach's death, Dr. Schweitzer will play a concert in St. Thomas's Church in Strasbourg. You should be present! It would also be good if you could be here in Günsbach between the 7th and 14th of August, because there will be much music in our house."[2]

Such an invitation was exactly what Erica had hoped for, and Jerome Hill decided to come with her. They arranged to be in Strasbourg in time for the concert but not to disturb Schweitzer by calling on him before it. Erica's account of what followed provides a good example of Schweitzer's captivating charm.

The night of the concert we arrive at St. Thomas Church at six o'clock. Hundreds of people are already gathered there, standing outside the church, though the concert does not start until seven-thirty. We've inched our way forward to about the fourth row of standees, when Schweitzer arrives. His European clothes strike me as very strange: a black Loden coat, a large black hat, an old-fashioned collar and black tie. He looks very much the proverbial German professor, quite different from the worker of Lambarene with his sun helmet, sand-colored trousers, and the white, open-collared shirt.

He walks briskly, waves at the crowd, but does not stop to talk with anyone before entering the church. A few minutes later the church door opens and Mme. Martin beckons to someone in the crowd. I turn instinctively to look for that someone behind, not believing she could mean me. But I feel myself pushed forward.

"Yes, I mean you," Mme. Martin says. "The Docteur told me that he made you a promise. Follow me."

Schweitzer is already in the organ loft when we reach him. "An elephant does not forget," he says, taking my hand. "Didn't I promise you that someday you would be with me when I played on a beautiful church organ, instead of an out-of-tune piano with pedal attachments?"[3]

After the concert Schweitzer spent hours signing autographs (having refused to let the police "protect" him from the crowd) and at last went to the restaurant where he had arranged to meet with, among a number of others, Jerome Hill.

Hill remembered how that evening Schweitzer went methodically from table to table, concentrating unhurriedly on each group of people who wanted to meet him, and how when he came to Hill's table and spoke to him, Hill immediately felt entirely at ease, as though he had known him all his life. "Schweitzer's power was to bring out the person you really were," writes Erica. "'So you are the generous soul who let this creature come to Lambarene despite all my objections' are the words with which Schweitzer takes Jerome's hand. 'The girl's stubborn as a dog,' he continues. 'Like a flea which digs in where the dog can't scratch. That's the way she is. I just could not refuse her.' "[4]

Before long, as filming progressed at Günsbach, Jerome Hill began planning to bring tape recording equipment there to record a concert for the film on Schweitzer's own village organ. The two Americans entered closely into Günsbach life, and both grew close to Schweitzer's heart. They saw how "he is asked to aid all kinds of human suffering. A father comes to him, in deep despair about placing his Mongoloid child in a mental home; a young bride terribly disillusioned by her marriage; a lonely widow. Schweitzer offers far more than general advice. There is something deeply and distinctly personal in his dealings with people.

When the widow is leaving him, for instance, Schweitzer follows her a few steps away from the house. 'This is the spot where your husband said good-bye to me for the last time,' Schweitzer tells her gently. For some astonishing, inexplicable reason, he remembers the day, the month, and the year of the event, though it happened thirteen years ago!"[5]

Hélène was there most of the time, her bowed figure contrasting with the uprightness of her husband. Although the flesh was shrinking on his broad figure and the face falling into the lines of old age, he was still a formidable physical presence. The secret of life was, he believed, to live "as a man who never gets used up."[6] But Hélène was used up. Her body gave her no choice.

Rhena, too, was a frequent visitor, bringing one or more of her children as her aunts had brought their families up the valley before her to visit the old manse. She was all too aware of the tensions between her parents and of her mother's jealousy of Mme. Martin, on whom Schweitzer relied completely.

The old jangling doorbell rang unceasingly with visitors or with mail arriving. Honors were still pouring in—offers of honorary degrees, invitations to become a freeman of a city, or president or vice-president of charity committees and musical organizations. Schweitzer can never have known that so many organizations even existed. He would generally accept, so long as all they wanted was his name on the letterhead and no work or responsibility was required.

The happiest occasion was when a prize of ten thousand marks was awarded him by the West German Association of Book Publishers and Book Sellers for his contribution to world peace. It happened at Frankfurt. His last visit there for a public occasion had been for the centenary of Goethe's death in 1932 with the Nazi threat looming. Things were different now. The president of West Germany, who presented him with his prize, was one of his oldest friends, Theodor Heuss, whom Schweitzer, reeking of anesthetic, had married to Elly Knapp in 1908. We have already heard the story of the famous frock coat, which Schweitzer wore to that wedding and wore again today. And Heuss congratulated him on the excellence of his Günsbach tailor.

The prize money Schweitzer gave to German refugees and destitute writers. He could afford to do so now so long as he kept his hospital simple and made the Africans work for what they got. The council that organized collections for him in Britain had a balance of ten thousand pounds or so, of which he only asked them to send about a tenth to Africa. The rest he wanted to set aside as a pension fund for his workers; for this purpose he trusted sterling more than the other European currencies.

A visit to Stockholm to receive the Grand Medal of the Red Cross of Sweden and membership in the Swedish Royal Academy of Music gave him a good story to add to his repertoire. At a dinner at which the king of Sweden was present a fish was placed before him that he was not familiar with—a complete fish, head, tail, bones, and all. Not knowing what to do with this fish or whether he liked it, he waited till nobody was looking and slipped it into his pocket. A newspaper report the next day noted that the famous doctor had learned some interesting habits in central Africa, for he could swallow an entire fish and leave no trace behind. Unfortunately, Schweitzer forgot about the fish, and a day or two later Hélène grew seriously worried about the drains before the decomposing corpse was traced.

On October 6 Jerome Hill's recording van arrived in Günsbach, and work began on that section of the film. Schweitzer was naturally delighted with the fidelity of the recording and the instant playback, making it possible to check and rerecord unsatisfactory passages. He began to ask about the possibility of recording a whole series of works the following autumn—Bach, Widor, César Franck, and Mendelssohn. Jerome Hill immediately put the wheels in motion.

Although Schweitzer's days were filled with vigorous enthusiasm, his letters, as usual, told a different story. He wrote at this time to friends in America:

"Since I have been in Europe I have not had one day, one afternoon to rest. There are visitors, journalists, friends.

"I cross one crisis of fatigue after another. On shipboard I have given definite form to two important chapters of *The Kingdom of God*, but in Europe not a single hour on it. I am in despair because of this! I am trying to work on the chorales of Bach which I promised to Schirmer before the First World War. Nies-Berger is helping me with this."[7] Edouard Nies-Berger's own recollections of the time are somewhat different—a humbling amazement at finding himself quite unable to keep pace with a man, almost twice his age, who worked with unflagging delight and passion and seemed to need neither rest nor sleep.

Schweitzer, it may be remembered, had been working with Widor on this edition of the complete Bach organ works for Schirmer's of New York before the First World War but had not been able to finish it before going to Lambarene in 1913. After the war, Schweitzer's German-sounding name and the general chaos of the economy had discouraged the publishers from going ahead with the project. But now that that same name represented such glowing publicity value, the scheme was resurrected and urged to a conclusion.

Although Schweitzer did not in the end manage to complete the edition himself, Nies-Berger went on to finish it alone, and this monumental work, the fruit of all the detailed research Schweitzer had put into fingering, registration, and ornamentation, besides the original score, finally saw print in its entirety.

While this was going on, Erica Anderson had been happily making herself useful by acting as chauffeur. When the filming and recording were finished, she went on to Germany to visit friends, leaving word that she was at Schweitzer's disposal if he needed her, and it was not long before she was summoned back into service.

The summons was courteous but peremptory:

DEAR ERICA,

Now I have to call on you, if it is possible for you to be at my disposal. I arrive in Heidelberg from Hamburg on Thursday, November 1 at 5:05 P.M. I have to visit friends in Württemberg. The train connections are very bad, and I would lose a day that way. Now my request: Wait for me on the Heidelberg train station on November 1 at 5:05 P.M. Drive me to the place where I have to be, and the next day on to Strasbourg. Should I not arrive at 5:05 P.M. wait in the station restaurant until ten in the evening. Then take a room in a hotel as near to the station as possible. Then wait for me on November 2 from eight in the morning on, again in the station restaurant, until I show up. You help me out greatly. I thank you from my heart and I am happy to see you again. In haste with kind greetings,

Yours,

Albert Schweitzer[8]

When Schweitzer took such journeys by train he went alone, so we have no way of knowing what happened. Thanks to the fact that he never learned to drive a car and relied on a chauffeur we have Erica's account of this trip, and it adds valuably to our knowledge of him. A few extracts will have to suffice here:

On the way to Heilbronn, Schweitzer tells me about his recent trips through Sweden, England, and Germany, about the enthusiastic response of new friends and old to his philosophical ideas. His talk is so animated, his voice so youthful, that in the dark of the autumn evening I feel as though I have a very young man next to me who has just returned from his first trip into the world.

I am not sure of the road, and in the darkness it is difficult to read the signs. But it is always Schweitzer who jumps out of the car to seek directions, grabbing the hand of whomever we encounter, and always displaying such a rare combination of politeness, directness and warmth.

When in the dark they lost their way and the car became stuck in a muddy ditch, Schweitzer, although he had been two days and two nights in a third-class train compartment, insisted on walking off across muddy plowed fields in search of help.

Fortunately, Erica managed to extricate the car by herself, and when he was back in it again, "The adventures we experience!" he says. "One must allow life to come up with such accidental situations. It is always they which turn out to have been the most memorable."

Erica left Schweitzer with his friends for the night and herself went to the local inn, picking him up again in the morning.

In daylight the road is much easier to follow. . . . Dr. Schweitzer talks in a constant flow about the poet Mörike, who grew up in this part of the world, about art, politics, philosophy, and he grows more exuberant as the sun rises higher and the day brightens. Every well-cared-for field we pass gives him joy, every little cart, every dung-heap. Especially dung-heaps! He explains to me their importance: "Once when a journalist asked me about civilisation, I answered, 'It all begins with the dung-heap. If a dung-heap is looked after well and built as it should be, you can be sure that the people who built it are civilised.' I'm afraid that journalist did not understand what I meant, but ever since then I say, 'Civilisation starts with the dung-heap, the *Misthaufen*.'" While he talks on, the sun shines in his eyes, and like a boy who has taken a day off from school, he says: "Think of it. No one in the world knows exactly where we are!"

A little girl, braids flying in the wind, is running down the road ahead of us.

"Pull over," he says. "Maybe we can give her a lift." Then to the child: "Hey, you, little frog, where are you off to in such a hurry?"

"To the pharmacy," the little one pipes up. "My mother is sick, and I have to get her some medicine."

"To the pharmacy then," replies Schweitzer. "Get in, and we'll take you there. Tell me, does the druggist give you some licorice when you buy something?"

"No. Never," replies the little girl.

"Then tell him that the old fellow who gave you a lift is a doctor," says Schweitzer. "And that when he was a child, he always got some free candy in a pharmacy. It's a good old custom and should not be abandoned. What do you want to be when you grow up?"

After a slight pause, the small high voice rings out: "A fashion designer!"

"Fashion designer," Schweitzer says, imitating her high voice. "Tell me," he continues in his own, "do you know how to sew?"

"No. But I can draw beautifully," the child replies.

"That is good," says Schweitzer. "But you must also learn how to sew. That way you will be a better fashion designer later on. And don't make skirts that are too short, do you hear? And the same applies to your hair— leave it long, whatever fashion dictates."

Later they gave a lift to a young man who, despairing of the purpose of life, was on his way to enter a monastery.

> For seven miles Dr. Schweitzer tries to touch something in the young man which still has a glimmer of faith, a spark of hope. I can feel that the young man, although by no means easily convinced, is listening intently. At last he speaks too, slowly, but with less bitterness and self-pity than before.
>
> "Maybe you have something," he says. "Maybe it is not a coincidence that you picked me up. I did not even bother to raise my hand for a lift any more. I was sure that people didn't care, that people are no good. I have no friend—"
>
> Here the Doctor interrupts him.
>
> "You must not expect anything from others," Dr. Schweitzer says. "It's you yourself of whom you must ask a lot. Only from oneself has one the right to ask for everything or anything. This way it's up to yourself—your own choice. What you get from others remains a present, a gift!"
>
> "Thank you," says the young man when he steps out of the car. "I'll think about what you said. I will take time before I make a decision."[9]

Finally, after visiting another friend of Schweitzer's in the mountains of the Black Forest, a professor of geology who had been exiled by the Nazis and never reinstated by the French and whom Schweitzer had not seen for twenty years, they drove home.

Although Schweitzer grew accustomed to cars and appreciated the time they saved, he never quite accustomed himself to the guilt involved in traveling in the softly sprung American limousine. "It's like a pram," he said, and he tried to assuage it by insisting on offering lifts to all and sundry. As with his passion for helping people with their baggage, the impulse occasionally got a little out of hand and led to situations that were humorous rather than helpful. But that was a small price to pay for adherence to his principle of giving himself to all humanity and for the constant contacts he made with all kinds of people on his travels.

25

A Crack in the Myth

1951–1954

WHEN HE RETURNED to Lambarene in December, 1951, Schweitzer found everything in very good running order, except the leprosy situation. The number of lepers was still increasing, and the huts they had built under the driving encouragement of Trudi Bochsler were of the very vulnerable bamboo and leaf-tile construction that needed constant repair. There was nothing for it but to build a complete new section of the hospital, a permanent village, for the leprosy patients alone—somewhere for them to live out their lives even after the disease was arrested, for their villages often refused to have them back.

Monenzali, the carpenter who had helped Schweitzer build the beginnings of the hospital, had retired to his village. He was too old, he said, to work any more. Schweitzer sent a message that if he came back and built again he would grow younger every day; and Monenzali came.

His relationship with Trudi, fighting for her patients with a single-mindedness that took no account whatever of the interests of the hospital as a whole, remained unsettled, and his famous Schillinger temper was often on display—as was his technique of swift reconciliation. At the end of one row he shouted: "Don't you know you're talking to Albert Schweitzer? Get out of the room and don't come back!" Before she had reached the door, which could not have been more than three paces, he said "Do you like books?" She stopped and said she did. "Take any book you like from my shelves," he said. She took her time and chose a book by Kierkegaard, a philosopher she thought she should know more about. She thought Schweitzer showed signs of regretting his offer, but he said nothing, and she carried the book off to her room. The moment was typical. Schweitzer never actually apologized; he simply did something to show that the incident was canceled.

The Kierkegaard book turned out to be underlined and annotated so heavily that there was barely any white space left on the pages. Schweitzer's Bible, too, was black with annotations, but that one might have expected. It is more interesting in the book of a philosopher whom he mentioned little, and then often dismissively, but who shared with him the conviction that religion is a matter of the individual soul's deep response to God, beyond reason and beyond dogma.

Kierkegaard is often quoted as the father of Christian Existentialism, the apostle of the personal, immediate encounter with God in the circumstances of daily life. Allowing for tremendous differences of temperament, one could easily make the same claim for Schweitzer. When I first started researching this book, I was struck by this similarity and asked Dr. Hermann Baur, who has made a deep study of Schweitzer's thoughts, whether Schweitzer had ever mentioned Kierkegaard. Dr. Baur had never read nor heard of any serious comment by Schweitzer on the subject, and I was surprised and disappointed by the implication that Schweitzer had failed to take note of so important and relevant a philosopher. But the incident with Trudi shows once more the comprehensiveness of Schweitzer's interests and the concentration he gave them. One can never assume that he has ignored or dismissed anything of importance simply because there is no recorded utterance on the subject.

Erica Anderson was in Lambarene again in March, continuing to shoot her film. Six more years were to pass before it was finished. And the correspondence with Jerome Hill about the new recordings at Günsbach was touched with an intimacy very rare in Schweitzer's letters. He is overwhelmed, he says, by the money that Hill is spending on him in putting that marvelous recording apparatus at his disposal again. "I'm afraid one day an article will appear in 'The New York Times': 'Doctor Schweitzer has ruined Jerome Hill.'" And, meanwhile, he hears from Erica that Hill is sending him an incomparable new record player as a belated birthday present. "Don't trouble to send an electrician—we have plenty of people who can install it, given clear instructions. But send the most essential spare parts."[1] He leaned, too, on Hill's advice about the contracts for the sale of the recordings. Hill planned to do this through the American Columbia Company, and the contract excluded the British section of Columbia to whom Schweitzer felt he owed gratitude for recording him when he was less well known. "Gratitude has been one of my guiding stars. Now I look like having to renounce it."[2]

As to the film, he reiterated that it must not be shown before his death. "How can I allow such personal scenes to be shown while I am still alive? How could I possibly bear it? This is impossible. I could not do it because I have given myself to you both with all my heart. I have unlimited confidence in you both that you will not only make a good film but also do it with great tact. To no-one else but you would I show such trust."[3] It ran quite counter to his reserve, and particularly to his dislike of personal adulation, to think of himself as the subject of a film. His work, yes. Himself, no.

In fact he had grown so involved in the film that he decided to write the commentary himself, but not in a hurry. "I can't hurry. It must be a good and beautiful job." There was plenty of time because the film was not to be shown in his lifetime, and "I have more imagination than is usually believed of me."[4]

On the leprosy village front things were less smooth. In the end Trudi Bochsler crossed him once too often, and in May she went home after a final confrontation. She went to various centers in Switzerland to study the latest treatments of leprosy, and Schweitzer continued the village without her.

July saw him on the boat for Bordeaux again for a brief five months in Europe during which the new recordings were made. Nies-Berger came from New York for further work on the Bach edition, and Schweitzer was installed as a member of the French Academy of Moral and Political Sciences. In his address to the academy on October 20, entitled "The Problem of Ethics in the Evolution of Human Thought," he covered much familiar ground; but one thought is, perhaps, given clearer articulation than before.

> The term "Reverence for Life" is broader and, for that reason, less vital than that of love, but it bears within it the same energies. This essentially philosophical notion of good has also the advantage of being more complete than that of love. Love only includes our obligations towards other beings. It does not include our obligations towards ourselves. One cannot, for instance, deduce from it the necessity of telling the truth; yet this, together with compassion, is the prime characteristic of the ethical personality. Reverence for one's own life should compel one, whatever the circumstances may be, to avoid all dissimulation and, in general, to become ONESELF in the deepest and noblest sense.[5]

In November he completed the recordings in Günsbach church. Rhena's husband, the organ builder Jean Eckert, who himself took a keen and informed interest in the problems of recording music, had always tried to dissuade Schweitzer from using the Günsbach organ for recording purposes, not because the organ was unsatisfactory, but because the acoustics of the small church muffled the effect. But Schweitzer, it seems, was not interested in making perfect recordings, only in preserving the sound of his beloved instrument. He was well satisfied with the result, but the recordings certainly appear to lack the clarity and definition of which this beautiful little organ is capable and on which he himself laid such emphasis.

The recordings over, he went back to Lambarene, this time for eighteen months. More and more now Lambarene, not Günsbach, was home. In Lambarene he was his own man, he could organize his life, he could give himself time to think.

For extraordinary though it may seem, no major journalist had yet actually penetrated to the hospital or seen what actually went on there. And although visitors were becoming more frequent, they were still for the most part people who already had some personal interest in Schweitzer and his work. The tourist trade had not yet discovered Lambarene.

For a year things went more or less smoothly in the hospital. The building of the leprosy village took up the greater part of Schweitzer's time, for the clearing and the leveling of the site meant moving quantities of hard rocky soil by hand.

> Why did we not hand the work over to a building contractor instead of doing it ourselves? If we had engaged a white contractor, who would have had to employ native workers and earn something for himself, the cost would have been prohibitive. Nor could I, to reduce his wage bill, let him use the able-bodied lepers, because I would have had no guarantee that he would look after them properly, while they on their part would not have wanted to work under him or obey him. Now, as before in the Hospital, the village has had to be built with the labour of the inmates who are able to work, and those lepers whose general state of health is more or less satisfactory. And since I am the only one with the authority to keep them at the job I have to be my own contractor again.
>
> Moreover, I regard it as a matter of principle that those who find shelter and care in this Hospital maintained by gifts should serve it with the labour of which they are capable, and so acknowledge what they are receiving. They owe it to those who make donations to the Hospital to do their part in keeping the costs of its maintenance and operation as low as possible.
>
> At the end of the week, of course, those working on the building site get some money, and two or three times during the week they are given some good confectionery; they also like gifts of sugar. They have a right to all their clothes, and on Sunday the women who during the week have been carrying earth can be recognized by their pretty dresses and headscarves.[6]

A timber merchant helped by lending Schweitzer a length of light rail and some trucks in which the earth could be carried more easily, but it was still a formidable task.

From the outside world, pressures were now being exerted on Schweitzer from various sources to involve himself in politics, especially in the efforts to get international agreement on the control of atomic bombs, for many people thought his moral influence would be invaluable. But he always refused. His method had always been the slow, personal one, not the high-level political approach, and besides, he was not sure that he knew enough about the subject.

In November 1953, however, something happened that had been on the cards for a long time. He was awarded the Nobel Peace Prize. And this had several results, the first being that he could afford to buy and import corrugated iron for the roofs of the village, for the prize was worth thirty-six thousand dollars. Without that money the huts, although built on concrete and of hardwood, would, apparently, have had raffia roofs.

The question immediately arises why Schweitzer did not plan to use his reserves in Britain for this purpose, and there is no way of knowing the answer, for he kept these decisions very much to himself. At a guess, however, he was determined not to find himself without a sizable contingency fund if war came again, which in those uneasy years, when the threat of atomic war was always at the back of everyone's mind, seemed not at all unlikely.

The prize had to be awarded in absentia and was accepted on Schweitzer's behalf by the French ambassador to Norway, for Schweitzer was much too involved in the building of the leprosy village to get away. But it was, of course, widely publicized. And this was the moment when at last a British journalist decided to make the great expedition and confront the doctor in his mythical habitat. James Cameron took some pride in having been the first actually to penetrate to the lair of the legend, but his achievement was not so tremendous when one considers that inexperienced young nurses now made the trip regularly and it was possible to fly all the way to Lambarene's own airstrip. Schweitzer had been doing it the hard way for forty years.

Cameron wrote a series of three articles for the *News Chronicle* about Schweitzer and the hospital, which he adapted fourteen years later into a chapter for his semi-autobiographical book *Point of Departure*. He also broadcast a talk on BBC radio. Some of what he wrote has already been quoted. But now it is time to go into it more thoroughly, for Cameron was, in fact, the first man to open a few cracks in the surface of the myth—the reaction the world was ready for.

The effect of Cameron's articles was the result of a combination of factors. He was the first man to have visited Lambarene and reported it with an eye unprejudiced in Schweitzer's favor: he had no ax to grind; he wrote much more vividly and entertainingly than most of Schweitzer's adulatory biographers had done; and he was known as a paragon among journalists for sensitivity and integrity. He was a man to be trusted.

Much of his report ran along fairly familiar lines. He found that he liked Schweitzer ("the only man in this century," as he described him in his radio talk, "who has become famous by being good")[7] more than he had expected. He had come prepared to find him smug, expecting to be preached at. This did not happen. "It may be hard to communicate that a man may be good, and testy; of legendary resolution, but frail; capable of universal tolerance and sudden superb impatiences; full of Christ and fun. . . . I often forgot in the mornings that Albert Schweitzer was The World's Finest Man: I felt him merely to be one of the friendliest." (In the heat of the afternoon nobody was quite so good-tempered.) He liked his "famous and intensely expressive moustache—a massive affair of no especial shape; or rather of a multitude of shapes, since it appears to pay great attention to the doctor's mood; now a battery of questioning antennae, now an unpromising curtain." He enjoyed the way "he roared at the dog chasing hens: 'Stop that! Don't you know this is a Peace Prize house? Be a Nobel dog, and quick.'" And he admired Schweitzer's "prodigious wink."[8]

Cameron's broadcast used mostly the same material as the articles, and we can hear from his tone of voice how much he liked the fact that in Schweitzer's ethic there was no fanaticism, only reasonableness, and that the sole rule was kindness. He liked the way Schweitzer's conversation ranged between the state of the world, the best way to eat a mango, and the will of God. He respected the fact that most thefts were merely irritating, but that it was a desperately sad day when somebody stole some penicillin. And in a voice of great warmth he told how Schweitzer, asked when he would go for his Peace Prize, said, "I can't go yet. If I do these lazy brutes will never get their houses built. And they need them so badly!"[9]

Although he found himself somewhat disconcerted when Schweitzer talked "like a Kenya settler" about the idleness of the Africans, he conceded in the articles that "in this context he could of course say what he liked. . . . You do not negate 40 years of selfless devotion to the African by reacting to his more maddening aspects. I liked it. He made people work, and did most of it himself."[10]

But however much he liked Schweitzer personally, evidently bearing no ill-will over the inevitable tussle about wearing a hat in the sun ("If you are determined to become ill, become ill elsewhere, near some other doctor," said Schweitzer),[11] the things that disconcerted him were bound to disconcert his readers over the breakfast tables in December 1953 even more. Fair though he tried to be, Cameron's understanding of Schweitzer was far from complete, and the majority of his readers were much less well informed than he was about the reasons why things at Lambarene were done as they were.

Early in the first article, for example, comes the description of "the primitive dugout canoe that fulfils the doctor's insistence on remoteness, self-containment, his resistance to progress." For those who skimmed over the page and did not even read the text there was a picture of the hospital with the caption LIFE IN THE GIMCRACK COLONY OF HOPE. And of the hospital itself ("a place of surpassing ugliness"), Cameron writes, "I would say that the hospital today exists for him rather than he for it. Here it is: deliberately archaic and primitive, deliberately part of the jungle around it, a background of his own creation which probably means a good deal more philosophically than it does medically."[12]

That was very damaging, and irresponsible in its inaccuracy. And what must the good Liberal readers of the *News Chronicle* have thought when they read that Schweitzer shouted at his native workmen, "'Run, you! Work like a white man, can't you?' "[13] Nor can they have liked Schweitzer's reported views on the subject of African self-government: " 'They have citizens' rights now, but no citizens' responsibilities. They destroy most things they touch. . . . You ask whether the *indigène* can ever develop to responsibility without us, and the answer is No, they cannot. Others disagree. The United Nations Trusteeship Commissions and so on—they think in terms of *politics*. Do they ask who plants the trees that the African can eat, who bores the wells that he can drink? No, they say, How are they progressing to self-government? Self-government without resource, without thrift? Democracy is meaningless to children!'"[14]

Out of the context of the upper Ogowe these, too, were damaging, however accurate, and it is clear that Cameron did not ask the right questions of Schweitzer to get a complete picture—or else that Schweitzer did not take Cameron seriously enough to give him the full answers.

In a rather perfunctory attempt to explain the hospital Cameron wrote, "There was the theory, or heresy, that somewhere in this monument to sacrifice rests a trace of spiritual pride—the mystique that maintains the hospital as a slum, because it is thus that Schweitzer has always seen it; that denies to his patients and staff the minimum of amenity, and indeed human contact with le grand Docteur himself, because his mind is elsewhere.

"The doctor's answer is very nearly clear: this is a mission before it is a hospital: it is maintained in African squalor because it is indeed part of Africa: in any case were it otherwise no African would come. One asks why, with tuberculosis patients the hospital should refuse offers of essential radio-therapy, and the answer again is simple: Dr. Schweitzer does not like it. That answers everything: it may be right."[15]

The consistent philosophy that lay behind everything that Schweitzer did had evidently escaped him, leaving him with the belief (headlined by the subeditors of the *News Chronicle*) that "here was not one man but two,"[16] the moral impulse and symbolism of being good, its practical expression worthless.

Reading the later version in *Point of Departure,* one finds that time has hardened Cameron's negative feelings about Schweitzer. Perhaps as the warmth of Schweitzer's personality faded from the memory he was left with only his indignation at the doctor's views. He was probably affected, too, by the growth of the antimyth that he himself fostered and that had become firmly entrenched by the time of Schweitzer's death, for reasons that we shall come to.

But although these feelings may have grown through the years, they were certainly there in embryo from the start. And Cameron was sensitive enough to remember and record a small stab that Schweitzer made at his profession. Cameron had raised the question of "the many shadows of despair that haunt this continent and seemed somehow this week to obsess me," but Schweitzer would not be drawn. " 'I am a man of limited experience,' " he said. " 'A man must occupy himself with what he knows and lives among. I would suggest there are too many people hurrying around having everybody's troubles at once. Yours must be a distressing occupation: rather useless.' " "It was," says Cameron, "the only acid remark he allowed himself."[17]

What also emerges from *Point of Departure* is that even in 1954 a heavy undertow of reaction already existed against the Schweitzer image. Cameron ends his section on Schweitzer thus:

> When I returned to England there was much pressure to write a book on the visit, which had, it seemed, been the first. I did not; I am uncertain why. Among the wistful fancies that had haunted the reveries of biographers and journalists for years with a guilty and unreasonable itch was the definitive exposure of Dr. Schweitzer. There, it had been felt, would be the really outstanding essay in tastelessness, the truly resounding iconoclasm. The endurance of the Schweitzer legend was a permanent challenge to explode it, or at least to question it: to examine with some sort of objectivity the man who through half a century conned the world into an adoration in which the mere investigation of his pretensions was a sort of heresy.
>
> It was not hard to know what had for years been argued only by a few; that while the original achievements of Schweitzer were considerable and his sacrifices notable, yet his accomplishments were negligible: his mission an illusion; his hospital in the Equatorial forest medically valueless, or even dangerous, existing solely as a frame for his immeasurable ego; his own philosophical contribution to the advancement of Africa rather worse than negative.
>
> Everything lay in the decision of timing, and this I mistrusted. When I stayed with the patriarch in Lambarene it was long ago, before the Doctor began to discover and enjoy the reverent pilgrimages of journalists and TV

teams. Then did the theme become popular; that the Schweitzer hospital was no place of light and healing but a squalid slum, from which the Doctor excluded all the advantages he was forever being offered simply because he did not personally understand them; that his immense personal vanity insulated him from anything less than sanctimonious worship; that his celebrated "Reverence for Life" contrasted bitterly with the cruel loneliness imposed on his own wife and daughter, just as his arrogant contempt for those around him contrasted with his cultivation of the rich dilettante women who affected to nurse at his shrine. To that could be added that it was the Doctor who proposed to me his opinion that the most salutary influence on the African race question had been the late Dr. Malan; that he had never in forty years taken an African to table, and that indeed in no circumstances could he contemplate even the possibility of an *indigène* being seated in his presence. There was at the time the baffling suspicion that he was pulling my leg; only later I knew he was not.

I reflected much on these things, and came to the decision that while the life of Dr. Schweitzer was indeed a paradox with very unwholesome undertones, to argue so would almost certainly be defined as unreasonable sensationalism, and probably rightly. Numbers of people were presumably deriving some sort of value from the inspiration of the Schweitzer mystique, and if the price of that were to let this strange old man perpetuate his peculiarities, then it might be dishonest, but was not particularly harmful.

It was possible that in redressing the balance of unreasonable devotion one could be ungenerous to those aspects of Schweitzer's life that must command admiration—the almost inhuman industry of the young Alsatian who *did* become a distinguished scholar, theologian, musicologist and all the rest; to surrender such a rare virtuosity for the sake of a dream was not a small thing, albeit the end was so little.[18]

When I spoke to Cameron about this, he reiterated his belief that in some way and to some people the myth was of value, so must not be destroyed, in its way a less ruthless attitude than Schweitzer's own about Jesus. But, in fact, his articles had damaged the myth considerably. And although in the *News Chronicle* he had written nothing as damning as the reference to Dr. Malan or those phrases about Schweitzer's accomplishments being negligible, his mission an illusion, and his hospital valueless or even dangerous, he must have let these views be known to his colleagues in Fleet Street and elsewhere, all of them eager to hear about Schweitzer at firsthand. Dr. Malan, in particular, was political dynamite, for as leader of the South African Nationalist Party and Prime Minister of South Africa at that time he was setting in motion the policy of separate development of black and white known as apartheid—although in a less vicious form than it later assumed.

Perhaps as regards Schweitzer's accomplishments and his mission readers of this book should be left to make up their own minds. They have the information with which to do so. The statement that the hospital was medically valueless (which was echoed by various doctors then and later and almost certainly came from medical sources) begs the question—to whom?

It was, indeed, valueless to medical research. It was not equipped for that nor designed for it. But to the patients? The question answers itself and in doing so reveals the horrifying self-centeredness of some of the medical profession to whom sickness is a matter of professional interest rather than compassion and a place that merely makes people suffer less is valueless.

With regard to the criticism about Schweitzer's behavior toward his family, Cameron admitted that he knew neither Hélène nor Rhena. "It would seem," he said, "from what one hears, that he behaved very badly towards them," a piece of hearsay reporting that scarcely commands much respect.

The Malan issue, however, must be faced, and here Cameron's comments were interesting. After admitting that the Ogowe Africans were much the most primitive of the continent, he went on: "Schweitzer argued, and I think with some reason, that Malan was a patriarchal tyrant, rather than a fascist tyrant, the way his successors became. And I think there's something to be said for that." And he said, "Although Schweitzer was totally undemocratic, and refused to discuss anything, that may have been exactly what these chaps [the Gabonese] liked about him."

This, however, would by no means fully explain Schweitzer's apparent defense of Dr. Malan. Malan, for example, was a nationalist of the most extreme kind; Schweitzer detested nationalism. Malan admired Nazi Germany; Schweitzer had abominated it. Malan's policy was that South Africa should become an all-white territory and that the blacks should be moved from their homes to new areas of separate development; Schweitzer was on record that such enforced movement was a crime by the white man against the black. If Cameron assumed that Schweitzer approved of everything about Malan, he misunderstood him completely.

The key to the misunderstanding lies in Schweitzer's "no discussion" attitude. He had grown tired of theoretical arguments before he was thirty. More recently he had grown accustomed to doing without the company of his intellectual equals. Nor was there time for going over and over the same ground with new people. We know already that he had spent immense care studying Kierkegaard, whom he once in a letter dismissed as "that psychopath." And he much distressed Cameron by apparently speaking contemptuously of Gandhi as someone with a great gift for education who had been misled into politics. This was conversational shorthand tinged with a certain amount of sheer naughtiness, as

Cameron would have realized had he read the thirteen pages on Gandhi in chapter 15 of Schweitzer's *Indian Thought and Its Development*.

"The philosophy of Mahatma Gandhi," Schweitzer there begins, "is a world in itself." And after exploring that world with the greatest sympathy and admiration he ends: "By a magnificent paradox Gandhi brings the idea of activity and the idea of world-and-life-negation into relationship in such a way that he can regard activity in the world as the highest form of renunciation of the world. In a letter to the Brahmin ascetic, he says, 'My service to my people is part of the discipline to which I subject myself in order to free my soul from the bonds of the flesh. . . . For me the path to salvation leads through unceasing tribulation in the service of my fellow-countrymen and humanity.' So in Gandhi's spirit modern Indian ethical world-and-life-affirmation and a world-and-life-negation which goes back to the Buddha dwell side by side."[19]

Such was Schweitzer's true assessment of Gandhi, as opposed to his curt remark to Cameron. And what increasingly emerges from the whole of Cameron's article is that Schweitzer was not taking Cameron very seriously: the exchange about the gorilla, Schweitzer's comments on Cameron's profession, the remark about Gandhi—all suggest that Schweitzer was teasing Cameron a little and deliberately trying to shock what he regarded as Cameron's somewhat overdelicate and theoretical sensibilities.

There are many other accounts of Schweitzer's liking to tease overearnest visitors. Frederick Franck, the dentist who worked at Lambarene in 1958, relates the reply he made to a visitor who at lunch embarked on a solemn speech asking the Lord to preserve Schweitzer in health for many years to come. All Schweitzer said in reply was, "Let us hope the Lord is listening."

"On such occasions," writes Franck, "he has a twinkle in his eye which no professional snake charmer could improve on, and usually the twinkle is followed by a special wink which will disappear from this earth with Schweitzer."[20] I suspect that the twinkle and the wink were in evidence when he talked with Cameron, whether Cameron realized it or not, for nothing could have been more calculated to arouse the reactions of someone whom Schweitzer suspected of sentimentality toward the blacks than praise of Dr. Malan.

Similarly, the remark about never taking an African to his table and never contemplating the possibility of an African being seated in his presence gives an impression so totally at variance with the facts that some grave misunderstanding must have occurred, whether deliberately induced or otherwise. Africans sat, lay, and sprawled in Schweitzer's presence all the time, even while he was taking the Sunday morning service. It is true that no African took a meal in the staff dining room, for two reasons, reasons which might well have led Schweitzer to say that he could not imagine it ever happening. The first, as we have seen, was a matter of discipline. As head of the hospital he believed, from sufficient experience, that his authority would be diminished to the detriment of the patients if he allowed the Africans to feel that he and they were socially identical. Some separation was necessary for the efficiency of the hospital. The second was the Africans' own refusal to eat from any pot but their own, a refusal that had its origin in fear of poisoning but had become an unbreakable social custom. But, naturally, when in the course of time Africans—mostly officials—came to the hospital as visitors, they ate in the staff dining room like any other guests. Schweitzer was the man who in Alsace had insisted on traveling fourth class in order to be among the real people. Whatever he may have said to Cameron, the implications of the way Cameron reported it are totally foreign to Schweitzer's nature.

Although Schweitzer may not have taken Cameron too seriously, Cameron unfortunately took Schweitzer very seriously indeed. Schweitzer knew what he was talking about when he said of Goethe, "If he had known they would write down everything he said he would never have opened his mouth." And perhaps he was unlucky that the first writer to take a critical line about him was the well-respected and widely read James Cameron.

Not long after Cameron came the equally popular and distinguished American writer, John Gunther, who was working on his book *Inside Africa.* Unlike Cameron, Gunther came by personal invitation. Friends had recommended him to visit Schweitzer after a family tragedy, and Schweitzer had no idea that he intended to write a chapter in his book about the hospital.

Gunther's piece was much better informed than Cameron's and showed more understanding of the local conditions. His description of Schweitzer as "august and good . . . but cranky on occasion, dictatorial, prejudiced, pedantic in a peculiarly teutonic manner, irascible, and somewhat vain"[21] was as reasonable a thumbnail sketch as one could expect. And although he got a few facts wrong, his research was remarkably thorough and accurate. The things that upset Cameron about the hospital Gunther took in his stride: "The hospital startles some visitors because almost everybody thinks beforehand that it will be like an Indian ashram, an aseptic harbor of tranquillity, spirituality and out-of-worldness." What distressed Gunther was being told never to leave anything unlocked. "It was sharply disillusioning, in this community dedicated to good works, to find that there should be so much overt distrust."[22] Perhaps when Gunther was there nobody stole any penicillin.

He did appreciate the reasons for many things however—that the smoke from the Africans' outdoor fires, blowing through the buildings, kept down the mosquitoes; that the animals were not only loved but made use of: "as we walked into lunch one day Schweitzer encountered Thekla, the red pig, and calmly wiped his shoes on her. Obviously the pig enjoyed this process, and her stiff bristles gave the Doctor's shoes a formidable shine."[23]

Medical standards were high, said Gunther, nor did he see any harm in shouting at workmen who "were not too ill to work, but just plain lazy."[24]

Gunther's piece, though written second, actually appeared before Cameron's, and despite its well-informed and moderate approach aroused Schweitzer's indignation. Schweitzer very rarely protested about what people wrote about him; he made it a principle not to do so. So his letter to Gunther on this occasion is surprising and is probably to be explained by the fact that he felt he had been caught unfairly off guard. "I spoke with you naturally and openly," he wrote.[25] Cameron had come unashamedly as a journalist and as such had suffered Schweitzer's irony and watchfulness. Gunther had outraged Schweitzer's feeling that personal and public statements must be kept separate and that nothing of his must be published that had not been carefully drafted and redrafted into a formal statement.

Paradoxically, though, his very guardedness with Cameron had produced much worse results than his openness with Gunther. As for his protest to Gunther and his request that certain passages be omitted when the article appeared in Gunther's book, that produced no result at all. He never attempted such a thing again.

After these two articles, Cameron's especially, the antimyth began to gather momentum on both sides of the Atlantic. To most people Schweitzer remained a selfless saint, a dedicated healer. But to a small but growing group, a modish minority, he was suddenly a self-centered bully, a publicity-seeking tyrant who knew nothing of medicine and sought only to grope his way to a questionable heaven. Both views were absurdly wide of the mark. And, perhaps, at that time it was really not possible for any writer to see things properly in perspective, especially if at the same time he was trying to hold the interest of a public to whom illusion and disillusion seem equally desirable, but who often find the truth more than a little tedious.

A note from the hospital bulletin about this time discusses the Africans' wearing, or not wearing, of sandals. Some time later a distinguished visiting South African physician, Dr. Jack Penn, seeing a number of Africans walking barefoot, noted that more good might be done by providing all the patients with sandals than by the equivalent value in medicines. The suggestion was sensible and well-meant, but like many such suggestions was made in ignorance of the practical problems and, of course, implied that Schweitzer had not thought of such a simple piece of preventive medicine. Here, however, is Schweitzer:

> Our native inmates have decided to wear sandals. From the very beginning I tried to persuade them to make themselves sandals of thin wood or hide as a protection against thorns and stones and the splinters of glass that lie around their dwellings. But I was preaching to the deaf. Not even when I told them that Homer makes the god Hermes tie sandals on his feet before every journey, even a journey through the air, could I arouse any interest in this kind of footwear. The pictures which they saw in the illustrated newspapers and magazines that fell into their hands showed that whites, men and women alike, wore shoes and not sandals. And for them that settled the matter. Since the cost of shoes was prohibitive, they preferred to go around barefoot, and took no notice of me. When I tried to persuade them to wear sandals it was also because the patients who wore foot bandages would no longer get them dirty, wet and muddy.
>
> Just as I had about resigned myself to failure, the illustrated papers began publishing photographs of elegant ladies wearing sandals, and so now for about ten years our natives have been wearing them too. All the hospital inmates wear them, not only those with bandaged feet. We can't afford to get them in Europe, but a native who sits on a cobbler's stool on the veranda by my room puts together sandals out of old tyre tubes which we are given locally. The soles are made of cloth and the rubber is used for the straps. We have to thank the ladies of fashion that the bandages on the feet of our lepers remain clean.[26]

The Africans whom Penn saw were backsliders, immune for some reason to the influence of fashion.

Another great medical advance was the installation, at long last, of X-ray equipment. It was specially designed for tropical use, and Dr. Emeric Percy, who for a long while had been one of Schweitzer's chief assistants, went to the Philips factory in Holland where it was built to study its operation and maintenance before bringing it back.

Schweitzer himself was doing less and less actual medical work. The leper village occupied most of his active hours although he still made sure he was present at all major operations so that he could take responsibility. Correspondence took up more time than ever although he delegated much of it to various assistants and nurses. One extraordinary fact is that the handwriting of all the three chief nurses who helped him, Mathilde Kottmann, Emma Haussknecht, and Ali Silver, came to look almost identical with his own. Mathilde Kottman's, in particular, was said to have been seen by handwriting experts and pronounced indistinguishable from Schweitzer's. (Friends of Schweitzer's once sent a sample of his handwriting to an expert for analysis—without, of course, saying whose it was—and then reported the result to Schweitzer. The expert, so Schweitzer related later, "said some very nice things about it, but added that there was a tendency to despotism.")

One letter that he wrote about this time links the old days, when the hospital was cut off from the world, with the new period of Schweitzer's emergence into international affairs. The subject was Dr. Goldschmid, who had stood by Schweitzer through the war years. The addressee was Dag Hammarskjöld, secretary-general of the United Nations.

DEAR MR. HAMMARSKJÖLD,

When you were elected Secretary-General of the United Nations I learned through an English review that you had sympathy for my ideas and that your device was To Serve. I intended to write you at that time, not to congratulate you on your election—for you should not be congratulated on having to fill one of the most difficult of posts—but to send you my good wishes. But as I am overwhelmed by work and fatigue, this letter to you was never written—as has been the fate of a good many others. But I did send you my best wishes through my thoughts.

Now I am writing to ask you for information and perhaps a favor.

The doctor who had served my hospital from 1932 to 1944, and who was subsequently, from 1945 to 1953, in the service of the Government of French Equatorial Africa, has now reached the age limit of 54. It would still be possible for him, with his vast medical knowledge and great experience as a physician and surgeon; to make a place for himself in France, but he would much prefer to have a position where he would continue to serve in colonial lands and use his experience relating to these regions.

Dr. Goldschmid's qualifications followed, and Schweitzer concluded:

Perhaps I shall some day have an opportunity to see you in Sweden. I go there during each of my European sojourns, especially to see my friends the Lagerfelds at Gammalhil. Baronne Lagerfeld, my Swedish translator, has been seriously ill for many months and has become nearly blind. I am also to go to America, but do not know when my work and my fatigue will allow it. In any case I should be very happy to make your acquaintance,

With my good wishes,
Your devoted
Albert Schweitzer

I apologize for making you decipher my handwriting. I do not use a typewriter because of the noise it makes.[27]

Hammarskjöld's reply was swift:

13 January 1954

DEAR DR. SCHWEITZER,

I have received your kind letter of December 19, 1953, and wish to tell you how touched I am by your good wishes and what encouragement I found in it. . . . I know no better way to reply to what you have so kindly said about me than to send you herewith the text of a brief talk I am to give on television in the near future, and which will show what a source of inspiration your own life and thought has been to me.

From the information you have given me, it would indeed seem that Dr. Goldschmid is fitted to render great services in an international organization concerned with the welfare of the peoples of Africa. I naturally think first of all of the World Health Organization. This Organization, as you are no doubt aware, has a regional office at Brazzaville which serves the territories to the south of the Sahara and which concerns itself with public health and the fight against certain tropical diseases.

Hammarskjöld promised to consult not only the director general of WHO, but also the director of UNICEF and the director general of UNESCO, and the letter continued:

I am delighted at the prospect of meeting you. Please do not fail to keep me informed of your plans for travel to Sweden and the United States. There are so many things I would like to talk with you about, in the realm of pure thought, as well as about the services which the United Nations can render those indigent peoples who have so long been the object of your preoccupations.

I must not end this letter without mentioning the Nobel Peace Prize which has recently been awarded to you. The Nobel Institute has acted with great discernment; no man of the present day has contributed more than you have to the development of the spiritual conditions required for world brotherhood and a lasting peace.

Please accept, dear Doctor Schweitzer, my cordial and devoted good wishes

Dag Hammarskjöld
Secretary-General[28]

So there were compensations for the overburdened, ill-paid, and ill-equipped workers at the Lambarene hospital: a note of recommendation from *le grand Docteur* was a passport to work and recognition anywhere in the world.

26

The Nobel Peace Prize and the Bomb

1954–1957

IF EVER A PROPHET earned the right to say "I told you so," it was Schweitzer. Before 1914 he was already warning the world against rampant nationalism, the dehumanizing effects of technology, and the growth of vast, soul-demanding organizations, whether commercial or political.

In the Second World War irreverence for life had reached new levels in the torture and slaughter of the Jews and in the mass killings of the atom bomb. Things that human beings would never, except under extreme pressure, dream of doing on their own behalf, they did cold-bloodedly in the name of some national or political mystique. And as their humanity dwindled, their power grew.

Schweitzer's moral stature was enhanced by his very rejection of size and power. And after the announcement of his Nobel Peace Prize people who knew about the diabolical effects of atomic radiation began increasingly to see him as a valuable champion of their cause against the ambition of politicians and the apathy of the public.

Schweitzer had for long been in touch with people close to atomic development as we know from his letters to Einstein and Oppenheimer at Princeton. And he had concerned himself with finding out the results of research on the survivors of Hiroshima and Nagasaki. But he had resolutely refused to be drawn into any public discussion and had asked that anything he wrote in letters remain confidential and not be passed on to journalists. He wanted to be able to say freely what he thought.

Early in 1954, however, things reached a pitch he could not ignore. Russia and Britain had already tested their atom bombs, and the United

States, terrified that Russia was catching up in the nuclear race, had been secretly going ahead with the development of the hydrogen bomb. On March 1, 1954, they exploded their first hydrogen bomb on Bikini Atoll in the Pacific. It was not long before the world became aware of the effects of the fallout on Japanese fishermen who happened to be eighty-five miles away. Professor Alexander Haddow proposed that the United Nations should set up a conference of scientists on the subject, and the London *Daily Herald* approached Schweitzer for his comments. On April 14 the *Herald* gave half a page to his reply, complete with photographs of himself and his signature and a potted biography ("the scholar-genius who renounced the world to become a medical missionary").

Schweitzer's contribution was characteristic. The first three paragraphs explain how tired he is and that, therefore, an article of eight hundred words is out of the question, and one wonders anew at the obstinacy that makes him write these laborious longhand letters, writer's cramp and all, sooner than risk becoming glib by learning to dictate to a secretary or to use a typewriter. The letter continues:

> I am, however, most anxious to give my views to you personally. The problem of the effects of H-bomb explosions is terribly disturbing, but I do not think that a conference of scientists is what is needed to deal with it. There are too many conferences in the world today and too many decisions taken by them. What the world should do is to listen to the warnings of individual scientists who understand this terrible problem. That is what would impress people and give them understanding and make them realise the danger in which we find ourselves. Just look at the influence Einstein has, because of the anguish he shows in face of the atomic bomb. It must be the scientists, who comprehend thoroughly all the issues and the dangers involved, who speak to the world, as many as possible of them all telling humanity the truth in speeches and articles. If they all raised their voices, each one feeling himself impelled to tell the terrible truth, they would be listened to, for then humanity would understand that the issues were grave. If you and Alexander Haddow can manage to persuade them to put before mankind the thoughts by which they themselves are obsessed, then there will be some hope of stopping these horrible explosions, and of bringing pressure to bear on the men who govern. But the scientists must speak up. Only they have the authority to state that we can no longer take on ourselves the responsibility for these experiments, only they can say it. There you have my opinion. I give it to you with anguish in my heart, anguish which holds me from day to day. With my best wishes and in the hope that those who must advise us will make themselves heard.

Schweitzer wanted to bring into the open the personal, individual fears and obsessed thoughts that scientists had expressed in letters to him. These personal nightmares of the scientists never found their way into the prepared statements and public attitudes that they brought to conferences, so conferences were useless. Conferences had agendas and nightmares were out of order. In the hope of publicizing their anguish, Schweitzer revealed his own. And the *Herald* made the most of it with its huge headline THE H-BOMB: THERE IS ANGUISH IN MY HEART, SAYS DR. ALBERT SCHWEITZER.

The most important effect of this letter was to make known to the public, anguished itself but kept totally in the dark, that their anguish was shared by those who knew the facts. But Schweitzer's hope that the scientists might now speak out for themselves was for the most part doomed to disappointment, for the scientists were in trouble. Governments were touchy about the bomb, being involved in the desperate race to build bigger and better ones in order not to be at a disadvantage when the next one fell. Scientists, therefore, who condemned the bomb were as good as committing treason. Robert Oppenheimer himself, after rising to dizzy heights in the American scientific and political world, fell under suspicion of communist leanings that year because he voiced his doubts about the ethics of proceeding with the atomic arms race and suddenly found himself stripped of office and barred from any access to the work of the U.S. atomic energy program.

Schweitzer went back to Europe in May. In the autumn he was due to collect his Peace Prize in Oslo and to make an acceptance speech. The hopes of those who thought he might take the opportunity to preach a really passionate sermon on the evils of atomic testing were unfulfilled, for he was still waiting for others to speak, more qualified than he. The speech he worked on throughout that summer was in his other style— a historical survey of war, its causes, its results, its justification or other- wise—very coolly argued and to tell the truth, considering the potential of the subject, rather dry and dull. It was to sober reason, not to emotion, that Schweitzer was appealing.

The occasion itself was anything but dull, however. To begin with, the domestic tension at Günsbach suddenly flared high when Hélène flatly refused to go to Oslo with Schweitzer if Mme. Martin went. Schweitzer was not used to being blackmailed in that way and, besides, he needed Mme. Martin, he said, to guide him through the throng of notables he was to meet. And he set off for Oslo without his wife.

The progress was triumphal, the stations the train stopped at jammed with people. Everybody wanted to shake his hand, and he had to exer- cise a long-learned discipline to drink very little because it was so difficult to get away to the toilet. An article appeared in a Norwegian newspaper suggesting that everyone who wanted a handshake should instead give a krone to the hospital; and that one article gave Schweitzer as much again as the prize.

The style of it all troubled Schweitzer. He had to travel first class at the Prize Committee's insistence. He found running water in his hotel at Oslo and wanted to know, "What do I need running water for? Am I a trout?" Bouquets of flowers were banished from his room, because he hated to see flowers wither. He tried to see everyone who came but refused to speak into an impersonal microphone.

Erica Anderson was there, as well as Emmy Martin. So was Clara Urquhart. Charles Joy, who with Melvin Arnold had brought succor to Lambarene from the Unitarians after the war, had arrived from Boston to report on the presentation. And then came a message from Rhena that her mother was now on the way, in a very bad humor and quite prepared to destroy the whole thing by publicly threatening divorce. On his side Schweitzer was equally at the end of his emotional tether. "Let her," he said.

It never came to that. Hélène arrived and sat by her husband's side through the ceremony, but they did not speak to each other. Whether anybody outside the Schweitzers' immediate circle knew of the private stress of the speaker is difficult to say. But Charles Joy noted that "Dr. Schweitzer was not an effective speaker with his manuscript. He seldom looked up from it; his voice was not strong and had little resonance; his inflections were regular and monotonous. The occasion was too important for extemporaneous utterance, but Dr. Schweitzer would have made a much more dynamic impression if he had spoken directly from his heart."[1]

It was not like Schweitzer, however important the occasion, to read from his written speech. Normally he would write and rewrite, thereby making sure he knew what he had to say and how to say it, and then he would speak without reference to the written word at all. In this case, however, he was suffering from the fact that on arrival at Oslo he had had to cut the talk from eighty minutes or so to thirty-five, a butchery he was not at all happy about, feeling that he could not properly develop his points in the time. "For a moment," he told Norman Cousins later, "just before I got up to speak, I was tempted to reach for the full message even at the risk of being stopped halfway through my speech. But I downed the temptation out of courtesy to my hosts."[2]

So everything combined to make it difficult at this moment to speak directly from the heart: the importance of the occasion, the truncation of his speech, and the tensions of his private life.

His theme was simply that organizations could never, by themselves, bring about peace.

I am well aware that there is nothing essentially new in what I have been saying about the problem of peace. I am profoundly convinced that the solution is this: we should reject war for ethical reasons—because, that is to say, it makes us guilty of the crime of inhumanity. Erasmus of Rotterdam, and several others since his day, have proclaimed this as the truth to which all should rally. The only originality which I claim for myself is that not only do I affirm this as true, but I am convinced, intellectually convinced, that the human spirit in our time is capable of creating a new attitude of mind: an attitude based upon ethics. This conviction persuades me to affirm that truth anew, in the hope that my testimony may perhaps prevent its being set aside as a well-meaning form of words. People may say that it is "inapplicable to reality"; but more than one truth has long remained dormant and ineffective for no other reason than that nobody had imagined that it could ever have any application to reality.[3]

The speech was simply an affirmation of faith. Now, Schweitzer believed, it was for the specialists, the scientists, to say their say, and for the politicians then to do their job of peacemaking.

As soon as might be he returned to Africa and to work, reaching Lambarene in December although for a while he found himself among the patients there, having slipped and hurt his leg at Port-Gentil. The role did not suit him. His impotence exasperated him, and he vowed to be rid of his crutches by January, which he was.

The Peace Prize address, although it gave heart and strength to individuals and organizations all over the world who were fighting to get a hearing for the voice of humanity, produced little immediate result. The letter to the *Daily Herald*, however, had the effect of stimulating a young French atomic physicist, Noel Martin, to publish some of his conclusions about the effects of radiation in a communication to the Paris Academy of Sciences. His calculations had shown that, quite apart from the fact that hydrogen bombs were "terrible and inadmissible death-dealing machines," their explosions also resulted in "numerous irreversible and cumulative phenomena, which will irremediably affect the existence of life."[4]

In December he wrote to Schweitzer to say that as a result of this communication to the academy the press of the whole world had publicized his conclusions, and he was now sought after by radio, newspapers, and television. He was the man of the moment. And he would like Schweitzer, whose letter had been the starting point of the whole chain of events, to contribute a preface to the book he was writing on the subject.

Schweitzer wrote very warmly in reply but declined to provide the preface, on the usual grounds of not wishing to become involved in specific issues on which he was not qualified to speak. And he had good reason to be cautious at this particular moment because a small cloud of hornets was buzzing around his head as a result of his having agreed to become honorary patron of a German Communist Youth organization.

Such honorary appointments he often accepted, whatever their political background, if their aims seemed humane, and this organization claimed to be interested in peace and cooperation and humanity. Schweitzer was somewhat dismayed, therefore, when letters from friends suddenly began pouring in warning him gravely of the way in which this communist group was certain to exploit his name for ends very different from the ones he approved of. Schweitzer took alarm and swiftly withdrew his patronage. It was the first of several occasions in his last ten years when he found himself in political trouble as often as not simply through an undiscriminating politeness and goodwill. But his goodwill was now, quite against his wishes, valid political currency, and he had to learn painfully that in the world of 1955 it could not with impunity be distributed to all and sundry. Age, seclusion, and the rapidly changing world were at last robbing him of some of the sureness of his political instinct. For he had reached eighty.

Among the plaudits that came thick and fast to the little red-roofed settlement was a statement by Einstein:

> I have hardly ever met a person in whom kindliness and the desire for beauty are so completely fused as in Albert Schweitzer. This is a particularly fortunate blessing in someone who enjoys robust health; he is fond of using his arms and hands in order to create what his nature urges him to achieve. This robust health, which makes him very active, as well as his moral sensitivity, have kept him from being a pessimist. In this way he has been able to preserve his joyfully affirmative nature, in spite of all the disappointments which our time inflicts upon every sensitive person.
>
> He loves beauty, not only in the arts proper but also in purely intellectual efforts, without being impressed by sophistry. An unerring instinct helps him to preserve his closeness to life and his spontaneity in everything.
>
> In all his activities be has avoided rigid tradition, and he fights against it whenever the outcome is promising. This can be clearly felt in his classical work on Bach where he exposes the dross and the mannerisms through which the creations of the beloved master have been obscured and were impaired in their simple effectiveness.
>
> It seems to me that the work in Lambarene has been to a considerable extent an escape from the morally petrified and soulless tradition of our own culture—an evil against which the individual is virtually powerless.
>
> He has not preached and he has not warned, and he never expected that his dream would become a comfort and a solace to innumerable others. He simply acted out of inner necessity.

There must be apparently an indestructible good core in many people, or else they would never have recognized his simple greatness.[5]

The statement reached Schweitzer in a special Birthday Volume from his admirers, and he replied swiftly and delightedly: "Even without writing we are united in thought, because we experience our terrible times together and in the same way, and we worry together about the future of mankind. When we met in Berlin we could never have imagined that we should be united by such a bond. It is strange how often our names are linked in public. It delights me that we have the same first name."

The progress of events had evidently caused him to change his mind about conferences, for he went on:

About the new tests with the latest atomic bomb, it amazes me that the United Nations Organisation cannot make up its mind to set up a conference about it. I get letters asking that you and I should speak up and demand that UNO should do something of the kind. But we have spoken up enough. We cannot dictate to UNO. It is an autonomous body and must discover for itself the incentive and the responsibility for trying to halt the disaster that threatens. From this distance I cannot make out what it is that prevents them from rising to the occasion. If they failed at least the attempt would have been made, and the opposition would have been forced to show its hand.[6]

He was, indeed, a long way from the involved personal, national, and international politics that were plaguing the United Nations. The individual protesters were in a weak position. The dynamic Oppenheimer was discredited and powerless. The gentle Einstein was old and sick and in despair. And Noel Martin, the man whom Schweitzer had encouraged to speak out, was learning the cost of his honesty: in a letter to Schweitzer he described how as a result of publicizing his findings he had been discreetly but swiftly dismissed from the National Centre of Scientific Research, where he had been on the point of getting his doctorate; and how even his colleagues now looked askance at him.

In April came the news of Einstein's death. "Why won't they listen? Why won't they listen?" he had repeated hopelessly before he died. Schweitzer was haunted by his despair.

He was in Europe in May, his friends and family gathering around as ever. His younger brother Paul, now a retired businessman, lived opposite the Günsbach guest house, with his wife Emma, née Münch.

Britain, the first country to recognize Schweitzer's theology and one of the first to offer him honorary degrees, had one last great honor to bestow. Only one other non-Briton had ever received the Order of Merit, and he was a general who as Allied Supreme Commander had led the British Armed Forces to victory over Hitler's Germany—Dwight Eisenhower.

Schweitzer went to England in October to receive his Order of Merit from the queen. His private audience with Her Majesty delighted him, and he decided that other European countries had made a great mistake in abolishing royalty. He wrote a thank-you letter to the Privy Secretary: "Please convey to Her Majesty my great and respectful gratitude for the friendly way she deigned to receive me on October 19th. It touched me deeply. Would you please also ask if she would be kind enough to accept these two copies of my "Memoirs of Childhood and Youth" which I have signed for Prince Charles and Princess Anne. I wrote them for children, and to be read to children. I would be very happy if Her Majesty would kindly pass them on to her children one day when they are old enough to read."

Three days after his visit to Buckingham Palace he went to Cambridge where he was presented with an honorary doctorate of laws. ("Laws is for general excellence," wrote the master of Magdalene College. "A degree in Medicine, Letters or Music would be too specific.") And while at Cambridge he insisted on visiting Grantchester to see the grave of Professor F. C. Burkitt, who had been responsible for getting his youthful theological work translated into English. Schweitzer always had a liking for visiting graves of friends when the friends were no longer to be visited alive. It was a part of his "inwardness" to be able to summon up the past in an awareness of how it had nourished the present, in much the same way that he summoned up the mountains and woods of Alsace to nourish him in Lambarene.

During the few days he spent in London Schweitzer himself was treated somewhat like royalty, holding court in a back room of his friend Emil Mettler's restaurant in Petty France, by St. James's Park. A "closed" notice was hung on the door, and the famous lined up to meet him. A nurse from Alsace who worked then in a London hospital was invited by Mettler to attend the reception and she watched, awed, as the great men arrived. The composer Vaughan Williams, also an Order of Merit (O.M.) and three years older than Schweitzer, was led to the head of the line. Bertrand Russell followed and Dr. Leslie Weatherhead; and George Seaver, Schweitzer's biographer, met him for the first time, to be overwhelmed by his personality. Augustus John, yet another O.M., had persuaded a friend to stay all night with him to make sure he remained sober and woke up in time for the interview, and he sat sketching Schweitzer for nearly an hour. Between the celebrities came the dozens of ordinary people who simply wanted an autograph or a word with the great man. An Indian wanted to kiss his feet, but Schweitzer gently forbade him. "We should love each other," he said, "but one should never stand in awe of another human being."

So he left England for the last time. In November his old friend Theodor Heuss presented him with the German Order of Merit, to the accompaniment of the usual throngs, and in December he went back to Africa. A little while later Hélène joined him. She found the long pointless months without him even worse than the humid climate and the prickly relationships at Lambarene. She was truly a sick woman now, walking with difficulty, drawing breath with difficulty. Some of those who knew her had little sympathy for her, finding her snobbish and catty. Others admired her courage, her proud intelligence, and her refinement. But she was certainly a tragic figure. However weary he became, it is doubtful whether Schweitzer ever experienced the exhaustion of body and spirit that a chronic weakness imposes, except, perhaps, in those few far-off months before he and Hélène first sailed for Africa and again after the World War One, just after Rhena was born and before he "straightened himself like a pine-tree shaking off the snow" and obtained Hélène's agreement that he should go his own way alone.

In Lambarene town Dr. Weissberg had arrived back at the government hospital, and a friendly partnership began. On the whole it was the government hospital that benefited the more because Schweitzer had a trained and dedicated staff whom Weissberg could borrow, besides equipment and drugs. Weissberg himself had no white staff, and he swore that so far as his experience went the difference between white and black was that the blacks had no concept of dedication. The midwife would turn up for duty when it pleased her, not when she was needed; nurses would have no interest in healing patients from a rival tribe. He envied Schweitzer a great deal.

On his side he could, as time went on, offer to keep drugs for Schweitzer in his large refrigerators, and he would help Schweitzer with his paperwork, "his weak point," says Weissberg. "He would send a message to me saying, 'Come as quick as possible. I need you.' When I got there he would show me all these papers. 'What am I supposed to do with these forms?' he'd say; 'You'll have to help me. Do you think Beethoven could ever have composed his symphonies if he'd had to fill up so many forms?' He was never really organized," says Dr. Weissberg.

The hospital was now well and truly on the tourist circuit, and the day of the rubberneck had come. Travel agents arranged visits for parties without knowing anything of the conditions there. One day Weissberg was summoned by Schweitzer (there was no telephone) who waved a letter in his face and said, "Seventy Norwegians are arriving tomorrow and they all want a room with a bath. What are we going to do?" When the laughter had died down, beds of a sort were found for twelve at Schweitzer's hospital, for twenty at Weissberg's. After their first night Dr. Weissberg saw his twenty marching off with their luggage and an indignant expression on their faces, looking for something better. Some hours later they crawled back, very tired, very apologetic, and very glad to have somewhere to lie down. What happened to the remaining thirty-eight is not recorded.

Naturally, all visitors, after they had been shown around the hospital, felt entitled to see and speak to the real object of their pilgrimage, Dr. Schweitzer. "Why, it's a zoo!" cried one disenchanted tripper. "Yes," he said, "and I'm the chief gorilla."[7] A tourist association invited him to become their honorary president, an honor he felt was not really suitable: "As the new type of elephant which the tourists come here to shoot—not with guns but with cameras—I feel it would hardly be fitting for me to be president of your association."[8]

To deal with the hordes Schweitzer had inevitably to develop something of an act, a performance that could be switched on and would keep an awe-struck group entertained for half an hour or so. He gave good value; he could amuse, instruct, and charm, and the visitors went away happy. But what they went away with was not the real Schweitzer. "Anyone who only met Schweitzer once," said Clara Urquhart, "met only the myth."

Erica Anderson was finishing off her film, and Schweitzer wrote to Jerome Hill: "As I write to you it seems to me very strange that there was ever a time when I did not know you and say 'tu' to you. For a long while you were simply the mysterious boss of Mrs. Erica; I thought of you as an elderly stiff gentleman who had succeeded in doing a very strange thing—persuading this strange creature, me, to have a film made about me; without even being sure whether it would ever come to anything."

Trudi Bochsler, the nurse who had left after disagreements with Schweitzer about the lepers, had returned. After extensive study of new leprosy treatments, she had been to other leper colonies elsewhere and found them too much influenced by politics for her taste. Schweitzer or no, Lambarene had much to be said for it. Schweitzer, for his part, knew how the leprosy village missed her, and the hatchet was buried. When she came, Schweitzer gave her responsibility over the new village, which had been laboriously growing while she was away. There she became, in Norman Cousins's phrase, "general manager, nurse, interne, teacher, confidante, minister and family head."[9] Medically and psychologically her effect on the patients was excellent. Even so, some of the nurses found it difficult to forgive Schweitzer for forgiving Trudi. She had committed high treason, and even Schweitzer was not allowed to condone that.

Truth to tell, Schweitzer was not finding it easy to imbue all the staff all the time with the authentic Schweitzer spirit. There was no difficulty now in recruiting staff; the problem was to select the right ones from the huge numbers of young doctors and nurses who were anxious to begin their careers here, many of whom wanted mainly to borrow a little glory to help them on their way. So the very success of the hospital began to militate against the maintenance of its unique qualities. And although Schweitzer himself was able to withstand the demands for change, he knew they existed not only in the world outside but within the hospital itself. "They can turn it upside down when I'm gone," he said once or twice, "but while I'm here it stays the way it is."

All, of course, hung upon finding the right successor, and Schweitzer was not satisfied that he had done so. A regular theme in his letters now and for many years is that "I have a permanent staff of very good and devoted doctors, but no-one is really capable of taking over the entire management of the hospital. In the backwoods everything is more complicated than in Europe or the U.S.A."[10]

In fact the search for a successor was complicated by another problem—that nobody knew what the government would do with the hospital once Schweitzer was gone, and in any case, it would be a bold man who would take over from a myth with the eyes of the world's press on him.

In April 1956 Emma Haussknecht died. If anyone could be described as having been Schweitzer's right hand in the later years, it was she. Thirty years earlier, when Schweitzer decided to move out of the old, small hospital and build a new one, she was there and but for her spells of leave had stayed ever since. Of the three women who, like Schweitzer, gave their whole lives to Lambarene, she was the most like him in temperament, sturdy and cheerful and compassionate. The penalty of living too long is that one's friends die around one, but Emma's end was quite unexpected. A sudden illness, a return to Europe, a quick operation, and death.

Her ashes were returned to Lambarene, and over them, in a service attended by the whole hospital, Schweitzer made a short speech of recollection and thanks: "She did not live to herself. She lived for her duties, and to be kind to others. She had indeed a good heart. All those who had anything to do with her knew this."[11] And then came a little ceremony: "He asked that each one present should throw a little earth into the grave, himself the first, followed by his staff, and then all who were there. It took half an hour for all the men, women, and children to file past. The old people were helped, the blind were led, there were lepers with bandaged feet, and last of all came Joseph, Dr. Schweitzer's old orderly at the hospital.

"Dr. Schweitzer himself stood with bowed head by the open grave, watching how it gradually filled, now and then himself drawing a little Alsatian soil [brought specially from Alsace with the urn] from the small bag in his hand until it was empty. Then he received from Mlle. Kottmann two small wreaths from Emma Haussknecht's homeland, and tied them on to the wooden cross underneath the date palm."[12]

Erica Anderson had at last finished her film. More than that, she and Jerome Hill had succeeded in making Schweitzer change his mind about not showing it until after his death. One reason was, no doubt, that he had come to trust them as he had never expected to do and had got closely involved in the making of the film, himself writing the commentary. But the immediate reason for its release was the fact that screens the world over were changing shape. The panoramic screen was taking over from the old "academy" shape in which every film had hitherto been shown, and Hill was afraid that his film might seem too old-fashioned in a few years' time to get a showing.

Hill's idea was that the proceeds should go to the hospital, but Schweitzer was anxious that he should first recover the costs of making it, and if money were left over that other charities should benefit. "It's a question of tact. My hospital gains a great deal of sympathy in the world because I myself am well known. This gives it a tremendous advantage over other works of benevolence; so I am vulnerable to the world's criticism simply for accepting this privilege. . . . and also one has to take into account the possibility that one day my hospital may cease to exist. . . . Finally I would like to ask you if one can't allow my four grandchildren to benefit in Switzerland to some small degree. With the difficulties of transferring money from France to Switzerland I haven't been able to help these children as I would have liked to." In fact, for whatever reason, the children never did benefit from the film.

In January 1957 Erica wrote an article for *American Weekly*, which told the story of her making of the film, and announced that it was shortly to be shown in New York with Fredric March speaking Schweitzer's words and Burgess Meredith doing the narration. The film was a great success, and rightly. The fact that it was about Schweitzer would in itself have ensured its popularity, but this was a very good film. It attracted huge audiences, earned a lot of money, and the following year won an Academy Award. Schweitzer was delighted although he himself did not see it till 1959.

For the last three years Schweitzer's determination to avoid being involved in the politics of atomic radiation had been coming under increasing pressure. Dag Hammarskjöld himself, secretary-general of the United Nations, had written to him in 1955 in terms that must have been difficult to refuse.

> You know, as I do, that the whole world absolutely needs an ideology which can confer a valid meaning to the efforts of all nations and give fresh and solid bases to the principle of 'coexistence.' Thus, I am persuaded that it behoves you, even within the strictly political field that concerns the United Nations, to send forth an essential message to the world. I have already had an opportunity to tell you that in my opinion it would be possible to animate international life with a new spirit by making better known the very attitude that you have tried to explain to the men of our generation. It is precisely for this reason that we at the United Nations have contracted a debt of gratitude to you for what you have done and what you symbolize; but this is also why we make bold to hope that you will perhaps choose to add your powerful voice to the appeals made in favor of mutual respect among nations, in the very sense that we understand this term at the United Nations.[13]

Schweitzer had held firm at that time. But as the months passed it became evident that the politicians would never of their own accord adopt the humanitarian line. Indeed, they were continuing to hush up the scientists' fears. At the same time his sense of debt was coming into play again: "They gave me the Peace Prize—I don't know why. Now I feel I should do something to earn it." And at the same time a plot was being hatched among friends of his, which was to swing the balance.

Emory Ross, still head of the Schweitzer Fellowship of the United States, first approached the editor of *Saturday Review,* Norman Cousins. Cousins, who had made a name for himself as a champion of cultural freedom and public morality and had written and lectured a great deal on the problems of the atomic age, had already published an editorial entitled "The Point about Schweitzer," taking issue with the critics of Lambarene's "primitiveness"; he was also involved in discussions with J. D. Newth of A. and C. Black, Schweitzer's London publishers, about how to persuade Schweitzer to finish and deliver the famous Third Volume of *The Philosophy of Civilisation.*

Thirty-three years had passed since the first two volumes appeared, and all that existed of the third was those yellowing, curled, goat-chewed pages now lying haphazard in a trunk in Schweitzer's room at Lambarene. No carbons, no photocopies, no security at all.

The two projects—to rescue the Third Volume and to persuade Schweitzer to speak out about the atomic horror—came together. Clara

Urquhart lent her influence, and early in 1957 she and Cousins arrived in Lambarene. With them they brought a letter from President Eisenhower and the good wishes of Pandit Nehru, now India's prime minister.

In the few days he stayed there Cousins achieved a great deal. First he persuaded Schweitzer to look in the trunk where he kept his manuscripts, to extract *The Kingdom of God and Primitive Christianity*, and to spend several hours sorting it out before handing it over to be photocopied.

> I opened the bundle [Cousins wrote]. Here, for all I knew, was one of the most important books of our time. The sheets had been perforated at the top and were tied together by a string. But I gasped when I saw the kind of paper that had been used for the manuscript. There were sheets of every size and description. Dr. Schweitzer had written his book in longhand on the reverse side of miscellaneous papers. Some of them were outdated tax forms that had been donated to Lambarene by the French colonial administration. Some were lumber requisition forms used by a lumber mill not far away on the Ogowe River. Some came from old calendars. I couldn't even begin to count the number of manuscript pages which were written on the reverse sides of letters sent to him many years earlier.[14]

Cousins had less luck with the bigger manuscript, the Third Volume. It already amounted, it seemed, to something like four hundred thousand words, and to put it into order would take days of uninterrupted work. Schweitzer admitted he had done very little work on it for several years although his mind had been ticking away "like an old clock a long time after the key has been lost."[15]

What had certainly happened was that the life had gone out of the book. Any writer knows that an idea must be given birth within its proper time or it dies in the womb; and Schweitzer once told Erica Anderson that the most difficult thing in his life was to keep his thoughts warm and vital until he had time to get them on to paper. He may well have found his ideas going cold and had worked and reworked them, trying to breathe fresh life into them, until he himself scarcely knew where they began or ended.

On the atomic question, however, his response was swift and positive. Cousins spoke to him of the hazards of the arms race, of the immorality of the tests that were spreading radioactive dust across the world, of the rapid increase in radioactivity in certain foods as a result of the fallout from test explosions, of the genetic hazards for future generations. But Schweitzer needed no telling. The questions in his mind were practical ones: first, should he make a statement at all, and what good would it do? Second, if he did make a statement, should it be about peace and disarmament in general or about the more limited subject of nuclear testing? And third, what form should it take?

After a night or two of consideration Schweitzer had answered his three questions. To the first the answer was:

"This crisis intimately concerns the individual. The individual must therefore establish a connection with it. . . . The leaders will act only as they become aware of a higher responsibility that has behind it a wall of insistence from the people themselves. I have no way of knowing whether I can help in this. Perhaps I may be justified in trying."

In answer to the second question he felt it was better to aim first for the limited objective, the banning of nuclear tests. The issues here were clearer, the involvement of peoples worldwide, the chances of success greater. "If a ban on nuclear testing can be put into effect, then perhaps the stage can be set for other and broader measures related to peace."

As to the form of the pronouncement, Cousins felt that "a direct statement, released to all the news agencies, might be effective." Schweitzer disagreed. He had serious doubts about the news-release type of story. What it gains in immediate attention it tends to lose in long-term impact. "Besides one runs the risk of competing with all the other news that may be breaking on a certain day."

"I am worried about present-day journalism," he told Cousins. "The emphasis on negative happenings is much too strong. Not infrequently, news about events marking great progress is overlooked or minimized. It tends to make for a negative and discouraging atmosphere. There is a danger that people may lose faith in the forward direction of humanity if they feel that very little happens to support that faith. And real progress is related to the belief by people that it is possible."[16]

When Cousins departed, he took with him the photocopied manuscript and a letter to President Eisenhower:

DEAR MR. PRESIDENT

I send you my heartfelt thanks for your friendly letter in which you send me your good wishes and those of Mrs. Eisenhower on the occasion of my eighty-second birthday. This expression of your good wishes was the first birthday greeting I received. Your generous and kind thoughts touch me deeply. In my heart I carry the hope I may somehow be able to contribute to the peace of the world. This I know has always been your own deepest wish. We both share the conviction that humanity must find a way to control the weapons which now menace the very existence of life on earth. May it be given to us both to see the day when the world's peoples will realize that the fate of all humanity is now at stake, and that it is urgently necessary to make the bold decisions that can deal adequately with the agonizing situation in which the world now finds itself. I was very happy

to have Mr. Cousins, who will take this letter to you, here with me in
Lambarene. It was rewarding to spend time together and to see how many
ideas and opinions we shared.

With assurance of my highest esteem, I am,

Yours devotedly,
Albert Schweitzer[17]

Schweitzer was left to work out the details of his statement. And
within a week or two we find him writing to Gunnar Jahn, president of
the Nobel Peace Prize Committee in Oslo. He has been pressed, he
says, because of his views on Reverence for Life, to express publicly his
concern about the increase in radioactivity from nuclear tests. And he
has decided he would like to do so by radio from the Peace Prize city,
Oslo. Would Gunnar Jahn please talk to the director of Radio Oslo
about this?

The arrangements were quickly made. After his experience at the Peace
Prize presentation, Schweitzer wanted unlimited time "to develop the
facts very fully. I don't want to be criticised for leaving large gaps in the
argument." He would, however, compress it as tightly as possible, making it simple and universally comprehensible. But "don't ask me to come
to the microphone myself," he wrote. He did not like speaking to large
faceless audiences, and the difficulties of recording the statement at
Lambarene were too great; there were no glass windows to keep out the
noises of the hospital and the jungle. Someone else had better do it.[18] If
other national radios wished to broadcast the statement, they might do
so simultaneously with Radio Oslo or later, but in no case before, and
then only with Radio Oslo's permission.

On April 24, 1957, Schweitzer's "Declaration of Conscience" was issued by Radio Oslo and simultaneously by several other national radio
stations. As he had intended, it was carefully documented as to the history of atomic tests, the quantities of fallout, and the effects of radiation,
short- and long-term.

All these things were known to the statesmen of the atomic powers,
he said,

and we must also assume that they are alive to their responsibility.

At any rate, America and Soviet Russia and Britain are telling one another again and again that they want nothing more than to reach an agreement to end the testing of atomic weapons. At the same time, however,
they declare that they cannot stop the tests so long as there is no such
agreement.

Why do they not come to an agreement? The real reason is that in
their own countries there is no public opinion asking for it. Nor is there
any such public opinion in other countries, with the exception of Japan.

This opinion has been forced upon the Japanese people because, little by little, they will be hit in a most terrible way by the evil consequences of all the tests.

An agreement of this kind presupposes reliability and trust. There must be guarantees preventing the agreement from being signed by anyone intending to win important tactical advantages foreseen only by him. Public opinion in all nations concerned must inspire and accept the agreement.

When public opinion has been created in the countries concerned and among all nations, an opinion informed of the dangers involved in going on with the tests and led by the reason which this information imposes, then the statesmen may reach an agreement to stop the experiments.

A public opinion of this kind stands in no need of plebiscites or committees to express itself. It works through just being there.[19]

That was the message. It was broadcast in English, French, German, and Russian. "The broadcast," wrote Dr. Kaare Fostervoll of Radio Oslo, "was incredibly successful." And so it was, with the general public and with those who had no vested interest in the tests. Where it was less appreciated was among the Western governments that were concerned with developing atomic weapons, notably the United States and Britain. In fact, they were considerably alarmed. So far from wanting their citizens to know what they were up to, they were doing their utmost to prevent it.

It must be remembered that this was not, at least to the authorities concerned, a clear-cut issue of right and wrong. Western governments were genuinely fearful of Russia (as was Russia of them) and saw it as their duty to their citizens to be ahead in any arms race, lest Russia think it worth starting a war. This immediate responsibility outweighed the longer-term and to them less-proven risks of genetic and other damage from fallout. This was the reason for their efforts to silence or subvert their own scientists and to keep the public in ignorance of the facts about fallout, and they had been reasonably successful. But Schweitzer was a different matter. How was he to be silenced?

After the broadcast, things moved fast. The day after the broadcast an American physicist attached to the U.S. Atomic Energy Commission (AEC), Dr. Willard Frank Libby, published a reply to Schweitzer, claiming that the radiation involved was insignificant compared with normal quantities from other sources.

At the same time, Schweitzer, keeping an eye on the world's reactions, was writing to Norman Cousins complaining that the American media, unlike the rest of the world, had not covered his speech adequately. Cousins passed this on to the CBS television network, who contacted the AEC to find out whether they would cooperate if a special program were set up to deal with the Schweitzer statement and whether Libby would appear on air with a reply. The public relations director of the AEC, Everett Holles, said he needed a better idea of what the program might contain, but he felt that after the respectful, scientific reply Libby had already made it was probably unnecessary for him to appear on air. Holles sent a memo to Libby relating all this. He noted that a communist newspaper, the New York *Daily Worker*, had also claimed that the media had "suppressed" the story, which, he said, had helped to minimize the attention paid by CBS to Cousins's "agitation."[20]

Anyone talking the same language as the Soviets was at that time suspect as ipso facto anti-American and more than likely in the pay of Moscow, so for Cousins to be seen saying the same thing as a communist newspaper was, of course, an automatic bar to be taken seriously and a useful weapon in the hands of the U.S. authorities.

The truth was, however, that the American media really had been very casual about Schweitzer's "Declaration of Conscience." No American radio station broadcast it, and few publications had paid it much attention. The *New York Saturday Review*, edited by Cousins, covered it fully, as one would expect, but his support was predictable and discounted. The *New York Times* was not impressed, and the New York *Daily News* impolitely suggested that Schweitzer should "pull in his horns," claiming that he was repeating stale communist propaganda and recommending its readers to listen to the scientists who said there was almost no danger from fallout.

Such a lukewarm response in the United States is not to be regarded as anything sinister in itself, rather as an indication of the success with which the administration had already brainwashed the public and so of the difficulty of getting through to them. A public that believes itself to have a free press and an open government is far more vulnerable to insidious propaganda than one that has learned to regard its rulers as barefaced liars. America had yet to learn that the price of freedom is eternal cynicism, at least about the government.

A few days later Kaare Fostervoll wrote to Schweitzer, asking if he wished to reply to Libby's statement.[21] Schweitzer had already dealt with Libby's argument by pointing out how even insignificant amounts of radioactive material in river water became stored in ever-increasing quantities in the river plankton and in the creatures that lived on the plankton and particularly in their reproductive systems, so that the radioactivity in the egg yolks of river birds on such a river was a million times higher than that in the water itself. Libby was a physicist; the people who should be consulted were the chemists and biologists who understood the effects of fallout on internal organs. Libby's letter was precisely the kind of "reassurance propaganda" from the Establishment that he was fighting. But he had no intention of involving himself in disputes. He preferred to make his statement and leave it to make its effect. "Do not reply to the Libby letter," he cabled.

In May, Norman Cousins offered Libby the chance to write an open letter to Schweitzer in the *Saturday Review*. Libby merely repeated his previous claims, leaving matters where they were.

If Schweitzer had hoped for a grass-roots movement to make itself felt at a political level, he was disappointed: at this point the effect of all this on the policies of the West was negligible. At a more sinister level, however, the authorities were working away on Schweitzer. In August, a memorandum reached Admiral Paul Foster of the AEC from Gerard C. Smith, special assistant to the secretary of state, John Foster Dulles, attaching a memo from the Central Intelligence Agency (CIA). The CIA's memo, for the attention of Lewis Strauss, chairman of the AEC, in turn attached copies of four letters from Dr. Schweitzer. It drew attention to passages in the letters that gave Schweitzer's reasons for making himself the spokesman on this subject, including a disparaging reference to "the esteem in which he believes he is held as a result of his philosophies."[22]

This memo was classified secret at the time but was declassified in the 1990s along with a number of other documents on this subject. The interesting thing, however, is that the letters from Schweitzer that the memo refers to were not declassified at the same time; they remain unavailable. Equally interesting is the question of how the CIA came by this personal correspondence in the first place.

Some light may be thrown on this by Schweitzer's request to Fostervoll about this time: "Address letters and cables to Mlle. Mathilde Kottmann. Journalists are getting at my letters, I don't know how."[23]

In fact, journalists were frequently to be found ensconced, rather uncomfortably, in Lambarene town, making interesting offers to postal officials for a sight of Schweitzer's correspondence. Several things drew them there: the hope of an interview, the possibility of Schweitzer's death, and, according to several people I have spoken to, the desire to discredit him and his campaign against nuclear testing. This last allegation looks a good deal better founded as a result of the new material from the U.S. State Department. Professor Lawrence S. Wittner, of the State University of New York, Albany, who wrote an exhaustive study of the world nuclear disarmament history, has made no bones about his belief that the secret campaign against Schweitzer was known and approved from the very top—President Eisenhower and Secretary of State Dulles, no less—and involved instructions to the Federal Bureau of Investigation (FBI) and CIA to "investigate" him.[24]

The only reason we know about the four letters in the possession of the CIA is because of the declassification of the covering memo, which mentions them. This was presumably an oversight by the declassifiers: the whole lot should have been left secret, then we should never have known of the existence of the letters. But it raises the question: How much else is still on the files and still unrevealed?

I contacted the CIA in April 1997, requesting sight of their Schweitzer files under the Freedom of Information Act. At first they were very forthcoming, promising a swift reply. It was some weeks, however, before the reply finally came. After a paragraph explaining the responsibilities and authority of the director of the CIA in accordance with section this and subsection that: "Accordingly, your request is denied on the basis of FOIA exemptions (b) (1) and (b) (3). By this action we are neither confirming nor denying the existence or non-existence of such records." Over the page is the explanation of these exemptions: (b) (1) "applies to material which is properly classified pursuant to an executive order in the interest of national defense or foreign policy." And (b) (3) "applies to the Director's statutory obligations to protect from disclosure intelligence sources and methods, as well as the organization, functions, names, official titles, salaries or numbers of personnel employed by the Agency, in accordance with the National Security Act of 1947 and the CIA Act of 1949, respectively."[25]

So either Albert Schweitzer is still a grave threat to U.S. national security, thirty-five years after his death, or the administration has, even now, something to be very ashamed of in its dealings with him.

The one major political figure who did react to Schweitzer's statement was Adlai Stevenson, with whom Schweitzer had been in touch for some time. Stevenson, a runner for the presidency and the one significant American politician to call for a halt to nuclear testing, was highly thought of by a large number of intelligent Americans and was, accordingly, a target for the wrath of Eisenhower and Dulles, who had gone to a great deal of trouble to demonize him.

His correspondence with Schweitzer was another result of Clara Urquhart's benevolent diplomacy. The previous year, when Stevenson was for a second time running for the presidency against Eisenhower, Schweitzer had written to him:

> I take advantage of the letter Madame Clara is writing to you, to say Hello. I read with great interest everything that concerns you, and I admire your courage in throwing yourself again into the electoral struggle. What emotions and fatigues you have in prospect!
>
> I too have a difficult life, but less difficult than yours. I do my work far from this world, in the forest, at the end of a river. I enjoy a certain solitude which gives me the strength to do my work. I have no vacation, no free day, no Sunday. But nevertheless I have the privilege of belonging in a way

to myself. This year I cannot go to Europe. I am enjoying Madame Clara's visit, and having news of you through her.[26]

In his reply Stevenson had written with deep envy, "I think your felicitous phrase 'belonging in a way to myself' comes close to identifying what I long for most in this exposed and relentless life."[27]

In June 1957, while the to-do about the "Declaration of Conscience" was still simmering, Stevenson finally came to Lambarene, combining the trip with an inspection of the mines and dams of the Gabon. Afterward he issued a statement:

> Dr. Schweitzer is gratified by the world's reception of his declaration in April on the dangers of testing atomic devices. Heretofore man has had to obey nature. But now he has learned how to subjugate nature and Dr. Schweitzer considers this the most dangerous period in history. He commented that his views were not as widely reported in the United States, Britain and France as elsewhere. But he feels that his declaration may have encouraged scientists to express their views more freely, and he was much pleased by the recent petition signed by two thousand American scientists calling for an end of nuclear bomb tests.
>
> His information agrees with the reports I brought him, and he feels that public opinion, led by scientists who know the facts, is now moving rapidly in the right direction and will soon influence governments.[28]

It was surely no coincidence that this petition was signed by two thousand American scientists so soon after the "Declaration of Conscience" and that the following February the Campaign for Nuclear Disarmament was launched in Britain by Bertrand Russell and Canon Collins. Both events represented precisely what Schweitzer had urged: the raising of the voices of the people against the apparent blindness of their rulers. Schweitzer had opened a door. Information was starting to leak out, and with it a demand for more information. In the end the flood was to prove unstoppable.

27

The Last of Europe

1957–1959

FOR EIGHTEEN PAINFUL MONTHS Hélène had not left Lambarene. She had stayed through the rainy season, health failing more and more. In January Norman Cousins had noted that "the blue veins stood out against her forehead and seemed stark against the pure whiteness of her skin. She had lovely grey-brown eyes, but they seemed to look at you through a mist. When she spoke, it was with considerable effort. Her breathing was labored. Despite her difficulties she would not allow anyone to treat her as an invalid. She insisted on coming to the dining room for lunch and frequently for dinner. It was easy to see how much of a struggle it was for her, even with the aid of a cane, to negotiate the two dozen or so steps across the compound and climb the short stairs to the dining room."[1] In fact, as the autopsy was to show, she must have had several slight heart attacks during these years, and the lung tissue, although completely cured by Dr. Gerson's treatment in the twenties and thirties, was so extensively scarred that much of it was useless. In an atmosphere that took away the breath of the healthiest, she was breathing on severely limited capacity. But in her case there was the worse burden, the weariness of spirit when there seems no longer to be any purpose in life. Her spring was broken.

But the decision to stay was hers. When her husband urged her to go back to Europe, she would complain to friends that he was trying to get rid of her. She must have known all too well that her presence was a worry to him, and he must have resented the fact that she knew it: a sore relationship now, perhaps mitigated, perhaps aggravated, by those early years. What was left of that extraordinary closeness, of the mutual quest for greatness? It cannot have been forgotten, but they must both have been aware that she had never been fitted for that climate and that work. Did they now blame each other, as couples do? One thing, however, had certainly endured—her courage.

In May 1957, a few weeks before Adlai Stevenson's visit, she could hold out no longer. A Dutch nurse, Toni van Leer, was flying back to Europe to her sick father, and Hélène, who certainly could not have made the journey alone, said a final good-bye to Lambarene and set off with Toni to Paris. There Rhena met her and took her to a clinic in Zürich. Ten days after she left Lambarene she was dead. Had she left sooner she might have lived longer, but probably not much, for the doctor who performed the autopsy told Rhena that the organism was completely used up. From the start of her relationship with Schweitzer she had spent herself heedless of cost. She had paid and reckoned it was worth it.

Some staff members were surprised how silent and sad the Africans were, not for their own loss, but for him. "But the doctor and Mrs. Schweitzer weren't happy together," one nurse said. "Perhaps," said the Africans, "but she was his wife." As for Schweitzer, his feelings had never in his life been on display, least of all about her. Nor were they now. Nobody knew what he felt; but perhaps, knowing more now about the way the partnership began, knowing more about that secret, vulnerable heart, we have a better idea than we did before.

In August, as soon as he could get away, he went to Europe to clear up Hélène's affairs. The house at Königsfeld was handed over to the Moravian Brothers, and all Schweitzer's belongings were moved from there to Günsbach. Meticulous as ever, he made out an inventory, like the ones he and Hélène had made out together the first time they went to Africa.

Objects which Dr. Albert Schweitzer is moving from his house on the Rue de Schramberg in Königsfeld, where he will not be living any more, to his house in Günsbach, Upper Rhine, on the road to Münster:-

Used Books (1300)	value: 30,000 francs
Used Music notebooks (400)	value: 25,000 francs
Packets of notebooks with choir notes (12)	no value
Manuscripts of Dr. Schweitzer (12 packets)	no value
Notebooks with notes (15 packets)	no value
Old white paper (2 packets)	no value
Concert programmes (1 packet)	no value
Little boxes of old writing materials (2)	no value
Old letters (2 sacks)	no value
1 70 year old piano, out of tune	no value
A plain wooden bed, used	6,000 francs[2]

Erica Anderson was in attendance with her car, and we find Schweitzer writing to Jerome Hill:

> I was very happy to see Madame Erica at my return here, for I have had to make a journey of four days from Günsbach to Switzerland, from Switzerland to Frankfurt and then to Stuttgart—partly to assist at the anniversary of Goethe's birth, and afterwards for other reasons. During this period I shall have to travel a good deal from Alsace to Switzerland and Königsfeld to put my wife's affairs in order. I don't know about Madame Erica's plans but if she still finds a little time to help me in my journeys I shall be extremely grateful. I hope that the film will be as great a success in Switzerland as it has been in the States, France and Germany. I hope also to see you in Alsace.[3]

Jerome Hill had had a new electric heating system put into the Günsbach church, and "this afternoon I went with Madame Erica, Mlle. Mathilde and my brother to the church. What a joy it was for me to see it in this state!—despite the fact that I was so attached to those horrible furnaces. The electric heating which has replaced them is very well installed."[4]

Among the friends Schweitzer visited was Nikos Kazantzakis, one of the great Greek novelists and poets of this century, best known as the author of *Zorba the Greek* and *The Greek Passion* (in Britain entitled *Christ Recrucified*). Two years earlier he had visited Schweitzer and had afterward written him a lyrical note. "I am still under the charm of your presence. That blessed day of 11th August was an astonishment to me. It seemed for the first time that our ideal can be realised on our hard earth without being compromised. You have renewed my confidence in man and in his high possibilities."[5]

Now, on a sudden impulse as they drove through Freiburg, Schweitzer went to see Kazantzakis, only to find that he had just had a relapse after recovering from an infection that he had contracted when vaccinated in China against his will. Now he was mortally sick, and three days later he died.

Equally important to Schweitzer was the old woman in a remote Swiss village who for years had sent him the money from selling the eggs from her small farmyard. It was because of her, and such as her, that the hospital had existed at all and because of her and such as her that Schweitzer refused to allow any unnecessary expenditure, even when he might have done so.

By November Jerome Hill was beginning to inquire what kept Erica in Europe, and Schweitzer was writing:

> I'm afraid I've kept her here in Europe against her will, because I fractured my little right finger. I have lost a lot of time and I needed her very badly;

particularly for following the news about the danger of radio-activity in the newspapers, and the journals in German, French and in particular English and American. I have to stay up to date on this question. My time and my eyes don't let me do this work, and so I asked her to do it and she's done a tremendous service in cutting out interesting articles and making me a packet every day; the result is that I'm now up to date with the results or non-results of all the congresses and the discussions exchanged between the east and the west bloc and I can judge what point the situation has reached.[6]

This broken finger was the result of an accident climbing up to his favorite old sitting place, the Rocks of Kantzenrain. Admirers had installed a bench on the spot, and Schweitzer insisted on going up the steep path in the rain to look at it properly before thanking the donors. The eighty-two-year-old gentleman was not as sure of foot as the boy who had first found the place, and slipped on the wet soil.

Immediately after the accident his travels took him through Zürich, and Erica took him to a doctor there for treatment. The nurse turned out to be the daughter of that same Oscar Pfister, the psychiatrist, who had persuaded him to recollect his childhood and youth in 1923. A happy couple of hours were spent in reminiscence.

On Christmas Day Schweitzer arrived back in Lambarene, bringing with him Hélène's ashes. They were interred near those of Emma Haussknecht, close below Schweitzer's window, and Schweitzer carved the cross.

For his birthday that January there was a guest at the table who was also celebrating a birthday—his daughter, Rhena. It was years, she had written to him, since they had celebrated their joint birthday together. All right, he had replied, come to Lambarene for this one. And she had come.

Despite the difficulties of her childhood, Rhena had loved her mother dearly and still wanted the love of the father she scarcely knew. Once, in Lausanne, when she was about sixteen, he had waltzed with her at a party and waltzed very well. Once he had borrowed a book of hers about American Indian trappers and retired with it to his room. "You'd better come and fetch it back in half an hour," he said, "because once I'm into it I shan't be able to put it down." Such domestic memories were few. She had married young, and friends thought it might have been because she needed love and a home of her own. She had borne and raised three daughters and a son, and when Clara Urquhart first visited her, the impression she had left with Clara was of a highly domesticated woman smothered in children and chows.

Now the children were in their teens, and her marriage was beginning to go wrong. She had a feeling that the course her life had taken had been without her full understanding and consent, and she wanted to do something of her own before it was too late. As a child she had wanted to be a doctor, and her father had discouraged her. The life was too hard, he said. Now it was too late for that, but the Lambarene that she had only once in her life visited still exerted a great fascination. She might yet do something there, she thought, or failing that, she might try publishing.

On this trip to the hospital, for her thirty-ninth birthday and her father's eighty-third, it struck her that what the hospital really lacked was a good pathology laboratory. Perhaps she should train as a pathologist. On her return home she wrote to her father with this proposal. His reply was crushing: "You won't even let me die in peace," he wrote; explaining later that he did not like the idea of his daughter working under him alongside the doctors, the relationship might be uneasy.

But she was not his daughter for nothing, and she was stronger now than in her teens. She went ahead with the training. It was a two-year course, and before it was even finished, while she was in Lambarene again during her vacation, Schweitzer gave her sole charge of the laboratory.

Apart from his daughter, Schweitzer's concerns at the hospital were all too familiar—more patients than ever, more nurses, and more doctors: five doctors by now, fourteen nurses, and room for 360 African patients, besides the 200 lepers. The problem of feeding them all was complicated by the shortage of rice, so a switch had to be made to bananas and manioc for a staple diet. How were they to collect enough? In a talk in Switzerland the following year Schweitzer told a group of helpers on their way to Lambarene about the coming of "modern times" to the hospital. This talk, so eloquent of Schweitzer's charm, his humor, and his whole approach to life, is printed as appendix B. It tells of the great moment when the automobile came at last to the hospital in the form of a Mercedes-Benz truck that Schweitzer had to buy to collect the bananas. It tells of the road that had to be built by hand for the truck to run on. And it defines once and for all Schweitzer's attitude toward machinery.

But although he gave in with good grace when the internal combustion engine proved itself really necessary, there is no denying the glee with which, some time earlier, he had announced one lunchtime at the hospital: "The twentieth century has finally arrived here. There are only two motor vehicles in the district, and today the inevitable happened. They collided. We have patched up the drivers. Anyone who feels reverence for machinery is welcome to look after the vehicles." Nor did he ever use a motorboat when a canoe could serve the purpose. But could anyone, reading that talk, suppose this was a man blinded by a Canute-like prejudice against progress?

The progress of the world toward nuclear self-destruction can have given him little cause to reconsider his mistrust of technology. Negotiations in London had collapsed in the summer, and Russia had walked out of a United Nations conference in the autumn.

In December a request came from Linus Pauling, organizer of the petition signed by nine thousand American scientists earlier in the year. Now he was collecting signatures from scientists around the world for a new appeal against the proliferation of nuclear weapons and wanted Schweitzer's signature to add to it. Schweitzer signed, and again Pauling collected more than nine thousand signatures, thirty-six of them from Nobel Prize winners.

But Schweitzer felt that still more was needed. By chance he had met Kaare Fostervoll of Oslo Radio in Basel while shopping for medicines in the autumn, and he was wondering about another broadcast. In February 1958 he wrote to Fostervoll and to Gunnar Jahn about it: "Since October I have spent the greater part of my time in keeping myself informed about the progress of atomic weapons; and I am in touch with experts on the subject." He had in mind two talks on the radio, one of about thirty minutes, "Peace or Atomic War," another of forty or forty-five minutes on the renunciation of atomic weapons.[7]

In the end there were three, of twenty minutes each, entitled *The Renunciation of Nuclear Tests*, *The Danger of an Atomic War*, and *Negotiations at the Highest Level*. The broadcasts were scheduled for April 28, 29, and 30, 1958. The American ambassador to Norway, Frances E. Willis, had a preview of the texts and on the twenty-fourth cabled Dulles in considerable alarm. The talks "generally supports [sic] Soviet propaganda line," wrote the ambassador, adding that the previous year's broadcast had produced a striking reaction, including a large-scale signature campaign in its support, and warning that these talks were likely to generate a demand that the Norwegian government should take an initiative along the lines of the talks. By pouch she was sending the texts of the talks. The following day, on second thoughts, she cabled again, cancelling the phrase "generally supports Soviet propaganda line," and replacing it with "in many instances coincide with the Soviet line."[8]

It was an especially difficult moment for the United States and Britain. They and Russia had been playing dangerous diplomatic games of brinkmanship. Russia, having walked out of the United Nations conference nine months earlier and now having completed a series of tests, had just proposed disarmament, almost certainly knowing full well that they were not trusted and that the West would feel obliged to reject the proposal, thus putting themselves in the wrong. A summit meeting between the political heads of the three powers was impending. It was in this situation and atmosphere that Schweitzer spoke out much more directly than before. Now he was really entering into the political world. Avoiding generalization, he quoted facts and figures in impressive detail, and he named the villains.

> The Soviet Union has recently made a disarmament proposal. . . . [T]he proposal is difficult for the United States and Britain to accept. They spoke against it when the matter was discussed in the spring of 1957. Since then ceaseless propaganda had been directed against the view that the radiation following nuclear tests is so dangerous that it is necessary to stop them. The American and European Press is constantly receiving abundant propaganda material supplied by government atomic commissions and scientists, who feel called upon to support this view.[9]

Going in some detail into this "reassurance propaganda," with quotations from various American physicists including Dr. Libby, he was scathing about the way in which the physicist "Edward Teller, the father of the dirty hydrogen bomb, sang a hymn of praise to the idyllic nuclear war to be waged with completely clean hydrogen bombs." He continued:

> Neither the United States nor the Soviet Union is thinking of producing this less effective bomb for use in a possible war. The American War Department has quite recently declared that the irradiation of whole areas has become a new offensive weapon . . .
>
> It is not for the physicist, choosing to take into account only the radiation from the air, to say the decisive word on the dangers of nuclear tests. That right belongs to the biologists and physicians who have studied internal as well as external radiation, and those physicists who pay attention to the facts established by the biologists and physicians.
>
> The declaration signed by 9,235 scientists of all nations, handed to the Secretary General of the United Nations by the well-known American scientist, Dr. Linus Pauling, on 13th January 1958, gave the reassurance propaganda its death-blow. The scientists declared that the radioactivity gradually created by nuclear tests represents a greater danger for all parts of the world, particularly serious because its consequence will be an increasing number of deformed children in the future.[10]

He spoke of the new intercontinental ballistic missiles, with a range of five thousand miles, and quoted the statement of an American general to some congressmen: "If at intervals of ten minutes 110 H-bombs are dropped over the U.S.A. there would be a casualty list of about 70 million people, besides some thousands of square miles made useless for a whole generation. Countries like England, West Germany, and France would be finished off with 15 to 20 H-bombs."[11]

He warned against "the extreme danger of an error in interpreting what appears on a radar screen, when immediate action is imperative, resulting in the outbreak of an atomic war."[12]

As a practical suggestion, he begged that the nuclear powers separate the disarmament issue, on which there was little chance of agreement, from the banning of further tests, which concerned the whole world and was a feasible first step.

The day after the first broadcast, Ambassador Willis suggested letting Teller and Libby have copies of the text, in case they wished to comment on the "sarcastic attacks" of Schweitzer. The same day, the Atomic Energy Commission held a meeting at which Strauss and Libby were present, along with about thirty others, at which the first item on the agenda was a reply to Schweitzer. Bernard Baruch had suggested that such a reply would be most effective if made by a distinguished public figure with a large popular following and offered to find such a figure if Libby would prepare the material. This plan seems to have been dropped, however, and Dulles shortly cabled Willis to say that any official response might be counterproductive, and rebuttals by individual scientists in, for example, the *Bulletin of Atomic Scientists*, would be a better idea. One might almost get the impression that distinguished public figures and serious atomic scientists who would challenge Schweitzer were becoming increasingly difficult to find. As a final desperate throw, Ambassador Willis thought it might be worth finding out who had actually written down Schweitzer's message—presumably with the notion that it would be a scoop to discover that it had been ghost-written by a communist. Alas, she had to report back that the whole thing had been received in Oslo in manuscript form in old-fashioned German.

Now the U.S. administration tried a new tack: much of the funding of the hospital from America came via the Albert Schweitzer Fellowship in New York. Lewis Strauss asked the notorious J. Edgar Hoover, head of the FBI, to investigate this potentially anti-American organization. Still no luck: Hoover had to report that the Fellowship was clean as a whistle— just a charitable foundation supporting good works.

In June, the American consul in the Congo, James Green, reported to Washington his intention to visit Schweitzer. Far away from the hothouse politics of the Cold War and clearly a simple and honest man, he had no idea what he was stepping into when he asked whether the State Department would like him to deliver greetings from Eisenhower or Dulles or to pass on any message as to current thinking on the suspension of nuclear testing. "Under no, repeat no, circumstances discuss nuclear policy or disarmament," came back the reply, and "no, repeat no, message of greeting from a high United States official contemplated."[13]

Green went, nevertheless, and because Schweitzer immediately started to talk about the tests, Green had no option but to join in. He reported back in a five-page dispatch, from which it is clear that Schweitzer simply repeated all that he had already said, but here, in face-to-face conversation, more vividly and angrily than elsewhere. Green's ill-informed attempts to put the American case were brushed aside with ridicule. Schweitzer claimed that Linus Pauling and other scientists had never been given a chance to present their views, and Einstein had not been listened to. As to Libby and Teller, they were experts on the bomb but not on its effects. They had created the bomb—and may God have mercy on their souls—but they did not realize what they had created. They were merely Dulles's chained dogs, whom the secretary of state used to support his propaganda.

Another point Schweitzer made (which he had also raised in his Oslo broadcasts) was that the testing of thermonuclear bombs was a violation of international law, the law (Grotius had written) that underlay all law and defended the rights of all peoples. This is one of Schweitzer's thoughts that has never yet been followed up but, perhaps, in the fullness of time will be.

Green's conclusions from the interview were that although Schweitzer's convictions happened, unfortunately, to coincide with current Soviet policy, it should not be concluded that he had any sympathy with communism. On the contrary, he was acting from deep humanitarian convictions. In his innocence, Green suggested that the department should send him concrete evidence that Linus Pauling and other opponents, American and foreign, of further testings, had been free to air their views in the press and on radio and television.[14]

Now, however, with Linus Pauling's 9,000 dissenting scientists in the United States and 9,235 in the rest of the world, with the Campaign for Nuclear Disarmament growing increasingly noisy in Britain, with Gallup polls around the world reporting an abrupt change in the attitude of ordinary people—those in favor of the tests dropping from 64 percent to 27 percent—the voices of the people were becoming difficult to ignore. As early as April 8, before Schweitzer's second set of broadcasts, Eisenhower had secretly suggested that "continued rigidness on nuclear testing may well lead to [the] moral isolation of the United States." In July, Dulles told a British official that "in face of public pressure" the United States "would have to suspend tests."[15] In August Eisenhower told his hardliners that world opinion could be even more powerful than nuclear weapons.[16] And at the end of August, Eisenhower announced the suspension of nuclear testing by the United States as of October 31.

So the head of the world's mightiest power had capitulated to an over-worked middle-European doctor from the back of beyond. For this was precisely what Schweitzer had foreseen: that the voice of ordinary people was the only weapon that could defeat the bomb. And if any one man was responsible for making that voice heard, it was he. He had cracked the citadel of misinformation created by the champions of democracy and done it by truly democratic means. He had won a straight fight with the hawks of the U.S. military, the president included, over what can justifiably be called the most crucial issue of the twentieth century. If for nothing else, this could entitle him to a claim to be one of the most significant figures of our times. For it was not only his fame and his independence that made him the only man who could have achieved what he did; it was also that life-long insistence on going to the bottom of things, of making his case unanswerable, of leaving nothing to chance.

The American public showed that they, at least, did not resent what Schweitzer had done, for his status in late 1958 had risen from fourth to third most admired man in the world, according to a Gallup poll. The politicians, however, showed themselves poor losers. Birthday greetings from Eisenhower were vetoed by White House officials in January 1959, and any suggestions that Schweitzer should be invited to the United States were firmly rejected by the State Department on the same old grounds of his dubious political attitudes and adherence to the communist line.

Even when the Kennedy administration came in, with high ideals, there were further tensions. The Western governments had ceased to describe airborne radioactive fallout as harmless and claimed that they wanted to put a stop to it. But the talking went on, and Schweitzer wrote worried letters to Adlai Stevenson about the way the heads of state were flying to and fro uttering banalities without making any practical moves toward peace. He received warm and anxious replies from a man who thought very much as he did but had to deal with the sluggishness of popular reaction: "I am afraid that most Americans think of peace as peace on our terms and unconditional surrender by the Soviet. Nor do our politicians or press do much to erase this naïveté."[17] But the talking survived the hesitancies and the bad faith and, however slowly it came to fruition, it did end with the Test Ban Treaty five years later. Now, at last, Schweitzer and the president of the United States were on the same side—Schweitzer's side.

All this increased Schweitzer's incoming correspondence even more. He continued to keep in touch with the international situation, so far as he could from Africa, by corresponding with people in high places and low. But the mass of the letters was still from the common people, terrified of nuclear war for themselves and their children. For all the help he had from Mathilde, Ali, and anyone else who could be pressed into service (even typewriters were welcome so long as they were kept out of ear-shot), there was no hope of keeping up with it all, especially when the hospital paperwork was increasing all the time. A plebiscite was held in the Gabon in 1958, as a result of which the country became fully self-governing, and the documentation required of Schweitzer changed again and still increased.

Among the incoming mail were invitations from Princeton and Yale. Yale offered the Howland Memorial Prize, worth three thousand dollars, but with the qualification that it must be received in person. Princeton offered an honorary degree, with appeals both from Robert Oppenheimer and Adlai Stevenson that Schweitzer should come. But nothing could tempt him across the Atlantic again.

One more trip to Europe was arranged, however, during which he received the Sonning Prize (the bequest of a Danish journalist) in Copenhagen and the Joseph Lemaire Prize in Brussels; he received the freedom of the City of Frankfurt and visited Switzerland, Holland, Sweden, and France. In Paris he spoke at a meeting of the French Association, of which his old friend Jacques Feschotte was vice president.

His speeches here and at the Lemaire Prize presentation have been preserved, probably transcribed from tape recordings. They are condensations of all he believed, pithily expressed, the opposite of verbose German philosophy:

> No philosophy can have the assurance or the simplicity of those which existed before Einstein gave the world his insights.
> The mystery of being, the mystery of life, dominate our age.
> The distinctions between the learned man and the man without learning is leveled down by this mystery of being.
> All beings are together in the foundations of the essence of life.
> If you have the same feelings as I have, try to speak to others about spiritual things. I guarantee you one thing. You will find that without your realising it the spirit in these other men will understand you.[18]

In Günsbach this last time Schweitzer was helping to organize the restoration of the organ. It had been rebuilt in 1932, but the parish then had not been able to afford new material throughout, and many of the parts used had been salvaged from the original seventeenth-century instrument. These had now deteriorated seriously.

Moreover, the rebuilding had been done at a time when organ builders had abandoned tracker action for pneumatic linkage. Since then Schweitzer's disquisition on organ building had brought tracker action back into favor, and organ builders had relearned how to install it. With financial help from the American Guild of Organists, from Jerome Hill and elsewhere, a complete new restoration was embarked upon.

And in Münster Schweitzer finally saw the film he had helped to make about his life and work. A cinema had recently opened in the town, seating about five hundred people. By word of mouth alone the cinema was packed to overflowing that Saturday night, and the film had to be run twice. No lights showed in the houses as Schweitzer's party drove in Erica Anderson's car the two miles from Günsbach. "You've started something, Erica," Schweitzer said. "Movies now on Saturday night! Where will it end?"[19]

He refused a special seat and pushed his way among the people, perching with two children on his knees. Erica watched his reactions and noted that "he seems particularly moved when he sees photographs of his father and mother and hears his own confession: 'They educated us for freedom. My father was my dearest friend.' "[20]

Let the commentary that he wrote for this film, full of the unashamed emotions he had always felt for the place of his upbringing, round off his life in Europe.

> I long once more to have the freedom to live in memories, to be allowed to wander among them. I recognise how wonderful it is that in my old age I can be at home where I was in my youth, that the themes of the beginning of the symphony of my life resound again in the finale.
>
> This privilege is to be twice valued in a time when so many men, as a result of the terrible events of two wars, are denied the right to enjoy the home of their youth. This loss has brought homesickness to their hearts.
>
> Yet to me it has been given in my old age to be at home in the village in which I grew up, in the surroundings where I received my first impressions. Because of the demands of the work of my student days I had to deny myself much that I longed for. But I do not want to give up now the heartfelt wish which I have cherished so long of enjoying the splendor of being at home once more and searching out those places that remind me of my youth. So let me, after these long years of work, be light-hearted again in the most beautiful sense of that word. The autumn sun calls to me; there is no autumn sun in Africa, only here.
>
> I remember four or five periods of my life when nature spoke to me here when I was small, before I went to school. In the vineyards which my father had newly planted and which bore their first harvest, my father called me to hunt for grapes. When I found none, he showed me finally where some were hidden in the leaves. And here along the line of the brook, in the small valley behind the hills, we walked to the interior of the Günsbach valleys. Here at these rocks I used to sit so often during my later student days, reflecting on my plan to go to Africa to help. Here in the meadow covered with flowers we rested. And then we went further up on a winding mountain trail. And suddenly the valley stopped, shut off from

the world outside. Here the mountains drew together and I could no longer see the way to the valley leading to the plain.

I came here many times before leaving for Africa, to experience the mystery of remoteness from the world. Here on the path along the woods one can look beyond the valley on to the plain and the world. My mother loved this path and this view. Always in the first days of vacation we came here with her and rested in the grass. I would suggest that the ruins at the end of the valley lifting high above the plain be the boundary for our excursion. Lying on the wall, I looked down on the castle and considered what would rule my life. How I have loved the castles of Alsace! In the shadow of the proud castle of Kaysersberg I was born. Often I have returned to it, to the wonderful church at the foot of the hilltop castle. I always imagine that men such as I who are rooted in the past have a special relationship to it for their entire lives.

Now I come down into the valley to a small mountain lake. How often we walked here with my mother after the four-hour journey from Günsbach, to sit here with her. When she came down from the high mountains around the end of the valley she would say "Here children, I am completely at home. Here among the rocks, among the woods. I came here as a child. Let me breathe the fragrance of the fir trees and enjoy the quiet of this refuge from the world. Do not speak. After I am no longer on the earth, come here and think of me." I do think of you, Mother. I love as you did this refuge from the world, this niche.

Now I have left the mountains and the castles and the woods. I stand before the church and see the swallows once more. The swallows are gathering for the journey south. We will set out together. But a time will come when I will not see you when you gather for this journey, and you will set out for the south without me, for I will have gone on a longer journey from one world to another. Hurry with your going, so that cold and death from starvation do not surprise you here! Farewell, until we meet in Africa under the southern sky.[21]

28

The Final Years

1959–1965

IN NOVEMBER 1959 Schweitzer was offered an honor that could well be regarded as the most extraordinary of all. The new government of the Gabon, under Leon M'Ba, asked him to represent the African states on the French delegation to the United Nations Commission on the Rights of Man. So much for the contention that all the Africans mistrusted him and his paternalism. If any Africans might have had cause to resent him, it was the government of the Gabon. They might well have felt that his hospital was some sort of reproach to their own medical services, staffed as it was by whites and run by a man who was known not to believe in African independence. The invitation does credit to them as well as to Schweitzer. But the reply was predictable; scribbled across the invitation is "Impossible. My hospital needs me."

On the ship going back to Africa, Clara Urquhart received a message that a very old friend of Schweitzer's was dead—Emil Mettler, the Swiss at whose restaurant Schweitzer had set up headquarters when in London. When Clara told Schweitzer, he showed no sign of emotion at all. His grief was certainly deep; he later wrote a memoir of Mettler that shows how deeply attached the two had been. But he had seen much death. And whatever other spontaneities he had learned, personal grief was still something for himself alone. The story is a warning not to suppose, as many did, that they could divine Schweitzer's feelings, or lack of them, by what he did or did not do. Feelings as powerful as these he took deep into himself to the place where death and life were all part of life's significance.

He reached Lambarene on December 31, a fortnight before his eighty-fifth birthday, never to leave again. And still the hospital grew.

Still Schweitzer built, still he did not rest, still there was more to do than he could ever find the time for. In the midst of all the normal activities, a stream changed course, cutting across the road taken by the banana truck, and they had to build a new concrete bridge. And there were the everlasting letters. "Long after I'm dead I feel I'll still be answering letters."[1]

The pathology laboratory was finished and in operation, and Rhena was working there full time. Among those who had helped her to set it up was Joseph Bissengai, "young Joseph," who had been at the hospital only twenty-five years, in contrast to "old Joseph," Joseph Azowani, who was Schweitzer's first assistant at Andende forty-six years before. Old Joseph did little work now, preferring to yarn with visitors about his early days with the doctor and maybe pick up a tip or two. But he was still there.

Like everyone else, Rhena had her fights with Schweitzer. She was disobedient about sun-helmets and would hide when she was hatless and saw him coming. And there was a battle over the use of electricity for the laboratory. But, like everyone else, she found she had only to prove that her proposals were necessary, practical, and economical, and she would get her way.

The world outside was seething. In the United States the hawks were after the blood of Linus Pauling; he was summoned before the Internal Security Subcommittee of the Senate Judiciary and questioned about the petition he had organized against nuclear testing. His action, it seemed, had been somewhat un-American. He appealed to Schweitzer for help. Although the McCarthy era was over, Pauling was for a while in some danger, and the committee seems to have allowed the case to drop only because they did not wish to be in the position of prosecuting a Nobel Prize winner.

Trouble was also brewing in the Belgian Congo, which gained full independence in August 1960, about the same time as the Gabon. But where the Gabon had been reasonably well prepared, the Congo was hurled into independence hastily and without forethought. Chaos ensued, and soon civil war. Dag Hammarskjöld flew over the hospital on his way to Brazzaville to seek a solution and cabled his good wishes to Schweitzer.

And Adlai Stevenson was appointed ambassador to the United Nations at the end of the year by newly elected president John F. Kennedy.

Tucked away in his wooden hut on the Ogowe Schweitzer maintained his contact with the protagonists of these great events; but all his correspondence constantly reiterated that his letters were personal, not for publication. And before long he had good cause to regret it when someone did not honor his request.

Walter Ulbricht, head of East Germany, had written to Schweitzer earlier to congratulate him on an honorary degree conferred on him by the East Berlin Humboldt University where he had studied in 1900.

Schweitzer had, in fact, as much sympathy with Russia and East Germany as he had with America and the West. He was constantly pointing out to Adlai Stevenson that America's insistence on encircling East Germany with nuclear missiles was bound to make Russia nervous and invite reactions. And despite the fact that he had no more sympathy with communism than with any other dogmatic political creed and in letters referred to Ulbricht as a tyrant, he replied as politely as he would have done to anyone else, adding a few lines about the importance of peace and Reverence for Life and concluding with his good wishes.

Unfortunately for him he was late, as so often, in replying, and in the meantime the situation between East and West Germany had reached a point of high tension, for this was the time of the Berlin crisis and the building of the Berlin Wall. When Ulbricht received Schweitzer's letter he published it, and the reaction in Europe, especially in West Germany, was violent. It was alleged that at this critical moment he had declared himself in favor of the East German Democratic Republic. Schweitzer was hurt and indignant. They were calling it, he said, the end of the Schweitzer myth of political impartiality. Why? All he had done was to offer Ulbricht the same courtesy as he did to anyone else.

The result was that when Bertrand Russell wrote in September of that year, 1961, to ask for his support in making protests about Berlin and about the nuclear threat, Schweitzer replied that, although he fully agreed with Russell and would sign whatever Russell wished, he felt too out of touch, as well as too busy and too tired, to write the text.

Indeed, he was so busy and so tired that he did something he had never considered at any previous time—he gave up playing Bach. It was a real sign of capitulation when he crated up the famous piano with organ pedal attachment, which the Paris Bach Society had given him in 1913 and which had been his daily solace for almost fifty years, and sent it back to Günsbach.

For all his caution the year was not to end without another misunderstanding, another indiscretion, and another row. George Marshall, minister of the Church of the Larger Fellowship, Unitarian Universalist, in Boston, and an associate of Charles Joy and Melvin Arnold, had written to Schweitzer in April, suggesting he might like to become an honorary member of the Unitarian Church. In reply Schweitzer, seeing no harm, wrote back (in November!):

I thank you cordially for your offer to make me an honoured member of the Unitarian Church. I accept with pleasure. Even as a student I worked on the problem and history of the Unitarian Church and developed sympathy for your affirmation of Christian freedom at a time when it resulted in persecution. Gradually I established closer contact with Unitarian communities and became familiar with their faith-in-action. Therefore I thank you that through you I have been made an honoured member of this church.[2]

George Marshall published Schweitzer's letter in its entirety on the front cover of his church's News Bulletin for Religious Liberals; and very naturally a great many people, Unitarians and others alike, took it to mean that Schweitzer, whose orthodoxy in the Lutheran Church had long been highly dubious, had now finally thrown in his lot with the Unitarians.

The religious rumpus was as noisy as the political one had been over the Ulbricht letter, and for once Schweitzer was persuaded to break his habit of not replying to criticism. In an interview in *Time* magazine, which had followed up the story, he stated: "For a long time now I have had connections with the Unitarian Church. But there is no question of my breaking with the Lutheran Church. I am a Protestant, but above all I am a scientist, and as such I can be on good terms with all Protestant Churches."[3]

The Belgian Congo situation was growing worse. Within weeks of the declaration of independence, the wealthy Katanga area had seceded from the rest of the Congo and set up its own government. The Belgians had prepared the country so badly for independence and granted it in such haste that the central government in Leopoldville (now Kinshasa) had no chance of imposing order on the situation.

Katanga, with its huge deposits of copper, possessed all the wealth of the country, and the great international mining companies that operated there had brought with them organizing ability and technical skills that the rest of the country totally lacked. Katanga, in fact, was the industrial center of the whole of the Belgian Congo without which the rest of the country was bankrupt. The secession, headed by Moise Tshombe, was backed by Belgian money and Belgian mercenary soldiers, for part of the stated policy of the new Leopoldville government was to rid the country of whites, and in Katanga, at least, the whites intended to stay.

Dag Hammarskjöld had persuaded the Security Council of the United Nations to send troops to the area, in the hope of forcing Tshombe to allow the large earnings of Katanga to be spread over the rest of the Congo and thus make it possible for the new government to control and develop the whole country. And in August 1961, after a series of atrocities, murders, plots, counterplots, alliances, and betrayals, UN forces were ordered into action against Katanga.

World opinion was bitterly divided. A month later Hammarskjöld was on his way to negotiate with Katanga when his plane crashed and he was killed—the victim, many believed, of another murder.

Sporadic fighting went on for another year more. And in December 1962 Schweitzer broke his rule of political silence and made a statement.

His thesis was simple: Before the Belgians colonized that part of the world, Katanga and the rest of the Congo had nothing to do with each other. Colonization welded the two together quite arbitrarily, simply because Belgium happened to occupy both. Therefore, when independence was granted and colonization was reversed, the two territories reverted to their old separation. There was no legal or historical reason whatever why Katanga should feel any responsibility toward the new Congolese Republic or vice-versa.

Moreover, because Katanga was well organized, wealthy, and well disposed to cooperation with the whites, it deserved its prosperity. To hand over large amounts of that prosperity to the totally disorganized, feckless, and malevolent Congolese would simply be to throw away good money, which itself was a feckless and irresponsible act.

There is, of course, a certain cold logic about this argument. What it ignores, astonishingly, is precisely the thing that sent Schweitzer to Africa in the first place—the debt owed by the white man to the black. For the bulk of the money from the mines was not going to Katanga at all; it was going back to Belgium. Tshombe's support came from Belgian interests of an entirely selfish nature. Belgium had exploited the whole of the Congo, and the only reason Katanga had done better was because that was where the mines were and that was, therefore, where the money had been invested. The rest of the country was impoverished and inefficient for precisely the same reasons as the Ogowe was impoverished and inefficient: the capitalist countries had put money in only where they hoped to get more money out. Hammarskjöld and thousands with him agreed with the new government that it was now time to restore the balance and to use the Congo's assets to feed the whole country.

Schweitzer was quite sincere. It clearly hurt him to find himself opposing the views of a man he admired as much as Dag Hammarskjöld. And when Bertrand Russell wrote to say that European interests were bribing Tshombe and milking Katanga and that they should be forced to help the Congo to industrialize, he replied that the only trouble with the Congo was that its government was corrupt and inefficient, whereas Katanga's was efficient, hardworking, and peaceful. "Please forgive me for not being able to agree with you," he wrote, "because I know the facts."[4]

The facts that Schweitzer referred to were local, not international. The white traders and engineers he personally met were none of them rascally exploiters; they were mostly humane men struggling to earn a living in very difficult conditions. These were not the men who bribed governments and organized private armies of ruthless mercenaries to protect their investments. They were themselves cannon fodder for the financial field marshals who sat in the capitals of Europe and disposed of millions of francs. Things, as Schweitzer often said, looked very different from out there.

But it does appear that for once his respect for thrift, order, and legality, combined with his oft-stated mistrust of black self-government, had overwhelmed his sense of natural justice and the rights of man as man.

Across the Atlantic the nuclear threat reached a climax with the Cuba crisis of October 1962. Both Kennedy and Defense Secretary McNamara said that they were prepared to use nuclear weapons if necessary to keep Russian missiles out of Cuba. Full-scale nuclear war seemed very possible, and Schweitzer wrote in great perturbation to Bertrand Russell: "We must act!!"[5]

No action Schweitzer took could, in fact, have had any significant effect at that critical moment. His great strength lay in his ability to speak to the ordinary people of the world and to remind them that their futures were at stake. This he had already done, and that worldwide call and the tide of popular feeling to which it had given impetus certainly had their effect on the peaceful outcome of the Cuba crisis. More he could not do.

In the long-term issue, too, that of nuclear testing, the humanity to which he had appealed was gradually winning. The talks that began in 1958 resulted in a formal Test Ban Treaty in August 1963, and Schweitzer began to see President Kennedy in a new light. When Kennedy was assassinated in November of that year, Schweitzer wrote to his mother, Mrs. Joseph P. Kennedy: "I do not know who else has his clear-sightedness, his tenacity and his authority and could continue his great humanitarian and political work.

"At present we walk in the dark again. Where are we going? Your son was one of the great personalities of the world's history. Millions of us mourn with you."[6]

But at least the treaty was signed. And not the least of Schweitzer's rewards must have been the many letters he received from the ordinary defenseless folk who stood in most danger from atomic radiation—and from some who already knew what it was. Here is one, from Sueo Muta, Hospital for Atom Victims, Nagasaki, Japan.

DEAR DOCTOR SCHAITZER [*sic*] AND MRS. ECKERT!
I wish you a Merry Christmas and a happy new year.
　　Looking at the photograph taken on the occasion of your visit to our hospital, I am thinking of you at far distant land in Africa. I wish that doctor Schwaitzer is in good spirits. My health comes to a state of lull. It is difficult to me to get good health. Thanks to endeavour of doctor Schwaitzer and other peace-makers a partial atom-bomb test ban was realized in the last sommer. It is big joy for us. From now we need not fear

rain and air contaminated by radioactivity which causes atomdiseases to many persons.

But production, storage and use of nuclear arms are not yet prohibited and minace [sic] humanity. I hope that the coming year 1964 will be the year of annihilation of nuclear arms and of establishment of eternal peace.[7]

Einstein had died in despair at what science had let loose on the world. Schweitzer was luckier: he saw at least a milestone on the road he had pointed out back to sanity.

Earlier in 1963 he had passed another landmark, one he could never have expected: the fiftieth anniversary of his arrival at Lambarene. He had come in April 1913, his achievements all put aside for the sake of one ambition—to give something back to the Africans whom the West had used and abandoned; fifty years later that gift to the Africans had itself become his greatest achievement. He had come with his wife to a single bungalow; fifty years later his daughter was able to write:

Lambarene hospital is in great degree an African village, which now comprises 72 buildings grouped around the central core: operating theatre, X-ray room, laboratory, dental clinic, delivery room, doctor's offices, and a dispensary where drugs are issued and injections given, and where, in cases of accidents, first aid is administered. About a thousand operations a year are performed, mostly hernias, but including urological, gynecological, abdominal, orthopedic and some eye surgery.

About 350 babies are born each year at the hospital. Besides the 450 to 500 hospitalized patients, we also treat a large number in our outpatient clinics.[8]

All he had wanted was a small hospital, but it had grown and grown. Since 1927 he had been trying to get it finished, to get the building over and done with and to concentrate on his medical work, his writing, his philosophy. But the hospital had defeated him. Rhena writes, "His most important task now, however, is the construction work, especially during the dry season. The roofs of the new houses must be on before the rains start at the beginning of October."[9]

In fact, the hospital was growing faster than ever. Between 1961 and 1964 the number of patients rose from 450 to 600. It was so big that Schweitzer no longer knew everybody by name. He was in his late eighties, still working a longer, harder day than his daughter could, but here and there the hospital was beginning to slip out of his control. He had not had a single day off for many years. And when suddenly he felt very tired and for two days was not seen around the hospital, it was as though the sun had failed to rise. After those two days he was back at work, but for a while he himself had thought that he might die.

In a letter to Wernher von Braun, the rocket physicist, who wrote to him that year about immortality, he had said, "At eighty-eight a man is rather like an over-ripe plum hanging on a tree—it only needs a little gust of wind to shake it off." But he was not tempted, as the old so often are, to console himself with thoughts of everlasting life. "I do not believe that life after death is a field for deep religion. Deep religion is a matter of a spiritual way of life, in which man enters into the life of the spirit with which Jesus came into the world. Deep religion does not make demands as to the continuation of life after death. Religion leaves all this to God. In religion the point is to follow the saying of Jesus: 'Go up into the heights.' "[10]

It was the same answer that he would have given at thirty. Nothing had changed. His fidelity still held.

In the administration of the hospital he was helped by his two "archangels," Mathilde Kottmann and Ali Silver. As it grew bigger and he grew more tired, more and more responsibility devolved upon them. They had been there so long—Ali for sixteen years, Mathilde for nearly forty, that they had reason to feel they knew his mind. They worshiped him, and he relied on them. To look after him and the hospital was their joy and privilege, and to Ali, writing in the British bulletin for 1963, all was for the best in the best of all possible hospitals.

> There is something of a small paradise about Lambarene. We live and work in mutual trust and confidence, each trying in the best way he can to alleviate suffering. Whenever necessary doctors and nurses work without regard for hours or time, day and night. The patients have freedom throughout the hospital: they fish in the river, they take their firewood from the forest, they eat all they wish of the fruits of the plantation, and they have no cares concerning payment, for everything is free for them. Children are playing everywhere, the little ones often completely naked, enjoying the sun or the waters of the Ogowe river. The animals know that they can live in security here, they are not killed for food and when they die they die a natural death.[11]

Ali was not the only one to feel this. It was the raison d'être of the hospital, and the feeling to a greater or lesser degree affected everyone who worked there for any length of time. In Erica Anderson's film something of the enchantment comes across, and the viewer is captivated by the atmosphere of a life that is busy and purposeful yet unhurried, serious but light-hearted, and in which the companionship of all creatures is taken for granted. Schweitzer's own personality had become, as he had wished, the spirit of Lambarene, and those who allowed themselves to respond to it were warmed and enriched, men as well as women, although men were the more inclined to resist the spell.

But the sunshine of that paradise was not always unclouded. Ali herself had grown so furious on one occasion that she almost left, and Schweitzer had implored her to stay "at least until I die." Mathilde had grown stiff-lipped with disapproval when Schweitzer forgave a man who stole drugs and allowed him back into the hospital for treatment; also when he took back the heretic Trudi Bochsler and gave her charge of the leprosy village.

Some of the other doctors and nurses resented the power of the archangels—particularly when, in those last few years, Schweitzer grew too tired to dominate them. Almost by definition anyone who came to work at Lambarene was a person of exceptional personality, someone who had made a break from the accepted pattern. Such people held strong and far from identical views. To hold these people together, in those cramped and wearying conditions, needed a personality as large as Schweitzer's. For him they would do what they would do for no one else. As his dominance began to wane, clashes of interest and temperament became more apparent.

Part of Schweitzer's great strength as a leader was that the fierce authoritarianism that he wielded in hospital matters gave place to a total generosity in everything else. People's religious beliefs, their sexual inclinations, their taste in music and the way they spent their spare time—these were their own affair. Schweitzer might tease them—and some sensitive souls might find the teasing a little heavy-handed—but he would never judge and never interfere. Indeed, he would greatly enjoy the kaleidoscope of character. And when he wanted something, he knew how to handle people with kid gloves. "Please don't make me sad," he would say when deviations occurred from the Schweitzerian way.

Nor did it escape him, as was commonly supposed, that some of his helpers were less dedicated than others. "Some come to help," he said once, "and others come to help themselves."[12] To both kinds he indiscriminately offered a place in the hospital. And here we must mention the well-publicized tale that Schweitzer encouraged wealthy socialites to cluster around him, feeding on their money and their flattery.

The two who were specifically cited were Marion Preminger (subsequently Mrs. Marion Mayer) and Olga Deterding, daughter of an oil millionaire. They must be mentioned only because they have figured so largely in other books and articles (one book contrived to devote almost a whole chapter to the two of them) that they are now, willy-nilly, part of the story.

The idea of poor little rich girls working among the tumors and the leprosy was much too good to escape the journalists, and they made the most of it. In England, if one were to ask almost anybody what name they associate with Albert Schweitzer, they would say Olga Deterding—

a fine example of both the power and the perspective of the press. In Lambarene she was no more important than any other guest although it was tiresome that from time to time she had to be hidden from reporters and photographers who had come a long way to get at her.

Marion Preminger's function in the hospital was to collect money for it and to arrive every year for Schweitzer's birthday to hand out expensive and incongruous gifts to all and sundry. On the strength of this she called it "my hospital."

To both Schweitzer offered precisely what he offered hundreds of others—if they wanted to come they were welcome. If they wanted to stay, a place would be found for them. If they wanted to help, with work or with money, so much the better. "I'm a past master at putting people to work," he said, and money was always welcome. But no one was going to force them. And if a rich woman wished to spend some of her money on exotic gifts, although the staff might feel the money could have been better spent, Schweitzer would not judge. He would, as Erica Anderson said, like you for what you were—whatever you were—even if you were rich; and he would try to give you what you needed, even if what you needed was a sense of your own bounty or an escape from your own uselessness.

The archangels could not be expected to have the same breadth of vision. For years they had tried to protect Schweitzer from his own generous refusal to discriminate, his giving of himself to activities and people they thought unworthy of his time. He had had to fight for the right to make his own decisions as to what was important. At last he began to give in and to allow himself to be organized. He allowed the archangels to take decisions he would once have taken and to come between him and the people of the hospital.

Minor inefficiencies increased. We have Dr. Weissberg's word for it that Schweitzer was never really organized, and his sisters were always astonished that their dreaming brother had gained such a reputation for efficiency; it never seemed evident at home. He had run the hospital on the basis of intimate personal knowledge of its every aspect. As the details slipped out of his grasp, gaps appeared in the smooth running of things that, although they had little effect if any on the actual medical excellence of the hospital, loomed large in the minds and the gossip of the workers there. One nurse, for example, badly needing fresh linen, was denied the key to the store and broke in, only to find it infested with rats. It had always been next to impossible to keep rats and termites out of the stores (much of the trouble with the famous out-of-tune piano in the dining room was diagnosed as caused by rat urine), but the nurse felt that this piece of neglect would not have happened had Schweitzer been fully in charge.

The small beginnings of the hospital became an ever more obvious liability. Schweitzer might build houses and import staff and buy trucks and jeeps, but the drainage, such as it was, was never designed for such numbers. An outside toilet that is adequate for half a dozen people is a very different matter for a staff of twenty plus a dozen or more visitors. The open drain down the middle of the village, which was intended to serve at most forty or fifty patients with their families, now carried the litter of ten times that number, and some of that litter consisted of pus-and-blood-soaked dressings torn off by patients or by animals and dropped by the wayside. To keep this Augean stable in order was a Herculean task, and its Hercules was growing old.

Rhena, too, had her difficulties. Suspecting the well water, of which her father was so proud, she analyzed it and found it to be more infected than the river water. When she told Schweitzer, he was furious and ignored her suggestion that a pipe should be run out into midstream where pollution was minimal, and water pumped into the hospital from there. But when, next dry season, all the wells, fortunately, ran dry, Schweitzer did exactly that, and she noticed that he did not go back to the wells. Before long he was showing off his water supply to visitors as if it were his own idea.

But still the patients came—and were cured. The opinions of doctors about the hospital's efficiency varied tremendously, and one has only to consider the wrangles that divide and subdivide the medical profession on every possible subject to know that no such thing as an objective medical opinion exists.

Dr. Stanley Browne, an expert on leprosy and later in charge of the British Leprosy Research Association, visited the hospital after Schweitzer's death and pronounced it a disgrace, chiefly on the grounds that it was not occupied in preventive medicine but concentrated on what he regarded as the more showy side of doctoring—surgery.

At least one television program has been based on this view, which ignores the fact that at this time the Schweitzer hospital was handing over the early treatment of leprosy to a government campaign in the villages. The leprosy village itself remained for one reason only—the cured patients refused to go home. "This is now our village," they said, "and if you turn us out we will build ourselves a new village nearby." And indeed several who did return to their original villages found themselves rejected and driven back to the leprosy village. Schweitzer promised that they might stay there as long as they lived.

Stanley Browne's life was dedicated to the fight against leprosy. The fact that the Schweitzer hospital was not concentrated on that one thing was enough to damn it in his eyes.

Dr. Jack Penn, however, a South African plastic surgeon who began by calling the hospital "a magnificent failure," later revised his opinion after working and operating there. He told Clara Urquhart, "This show is a Rolls-Royce; maybe a fairly ancient model, but still a Rolls-Royce. To my mind nothing could be gained by changing anything so as to make a streamlined Ford—even the very latest model—out of this tried and tested Rolls-Royce."[13]

But even he, as has already been quoted, is said to have remarked that a consignment of sandals would do more good than a lot of surgery— as though Schweitzer had not been trying to get the Africans to wear sandals since he first came.

Finding fault with Schweitzer, in fact, had become something of a fashion. And the more one studies the evidence the more one is forced to the conclusion that the opinions of anyone who did not actually stay and work with him are almost worthless. Time and again a criticism that looks intelligent and valid proves to be so ill-informed as to be quite irrelevant. So, although figures, too, can lie, let me refer to some that were collected by a Swiss doctor, Rolf Müller, who did work for some while at Lambarene and who published these figures in leading medical journals in Geneva and Munich.

These show that the number of patients treated rose from 3,800 in 1958 to about 6,500 in 1963. The number of operations performed in 1962 was 802, in 1963, 950, an average of more than three in every working day. The operation mortality rate was lower than 1.17 percent, less than the European average.

The equipment in the operating theater, which now had two operating tables, each with powerful modern electric lamps, was better according to one visitor than that in the average large Swiss hospital, and the same was true of the supplies in the dispensary.

Schweitzer himself had, of course, long ceased to do any surgery personally although he sat daily in the dispensary, keeping himself informed of all that went on and ready to give any advice required. And he still insisted on authorizing serious surgery, for he was responsible to the families of the patients.

The only relief he found from the pressure of his overgrown creation was in his visitors. Although he complained regularly about yet another day wasted on tourists, in fact he welcomed them gladly and sometimes appeared restless if several days passed without any arrivals. He would show them proudly around and talk to them about his philosophy. Perhaps the performance that, as we have seen, he was compelled to put on for their entertainment (and from appendix B we have some idea of the quality of that performance) also gave some satisfaction to him. In age the bones of character, like the bones of the body, begin to show through, and Schweitzer, by his own account a schoolmaster, was by now the headmaster of a school for living. A few inmates had access to the real man. For the rest it was "No discussion." The myth spoke and was not to be questioned.

Among the visitors came a writer called Gerald McKnight. After a few days' stay and a couple of conversations with the doctor, he felt equipped to write his *Verdict on Schweitzer,* a book that deserves to be passed by in silence but for one thing—that in many libraries, in Britain, at least, it was for a long while the only work to be had on the subject and was, therefore, the source book and compendium of nearly the whole range of misinformation about Schweitzer. The book needs some attention so that people with a vague feeling that Schweitzer was a fraud should be quite clear about the origin of that feeling.

To itemize the inaccuracies, false insinuations, and out-of-context quotations in McKnight's book would take a chapter in itself. A few samples will have to suffice although they cannot hope to indicate the range and frequency of his distortions. The difficulty is to select from such a rich crop.

The preface immediately establishes McKnight's view that Schweitzer's hospital appears to some people to be "in reality, a jungle sore suppurating into the fresh body of emergent Africa, hampering the advance of clean, clear-minded and progressive Africans who are now building modern and fully equipped hospitals in the vicinity . . . in a word Schweitzer's hospital is redundant . . . an old man's private dream-world overtaken by realities he refuses to accept."[14] What it appears to be to others McKnight does not trouble to state.

In fact, the only "modern and fully equipped hospital in the vicinity" (Dr. Weissberg's) was described by one of the few reporters who actually went there, a Swiss named Roman Brodmann, who went to Lambarene in 1962 armed with all the standard prejudices against Schweitzer. Here are his words:

> I found at the hospital a young French doctor who was responsible for the running of the place. He showed me round the building. which was of stone and disgustingly dirty (*Time* Magazine: "A modern anti-septic hospital") and shrugged his shoulders in resignation. "I'm a doctor, not a charwoman." The beds are of iron. The mattresses have a doss-house look about them—a real paradise for germs. The operating theatre is inadequately equipped, which is relatively unimportant since there is a complete lack of a second doctor to assist at any operation that presents any difficulty. So the doctor sends cases that are at all complicated across the river to Schweitzer's hospital. I found nearly half the beds unoccupied at the government hospital; Schweitzer's hospital is full to overflowing, and being expanded all the time.[15]

And Frederick Franck, in his delightful and perceptive *Days with Albert Schweitzer*, writes:

> I saw many much better equipped hospitals in Equatorial Africa [than Schweitzer's]. I was shown modern government hospitals after having been told that they put the Schweitzer Hospital to shame. And, indeed, they had better buildings, cleaner wards, mosaic floors, and sometimes better equipment. The quality of the medicine practised, however, was often incomparably poorer. In some of these hospitals the staff consisted of a single overworked doctor who, having to waste most of his time on useless paper work and statistics, was forced to leave treatment to incompetent orderlies. Often there was no doctor at all and a lonely, overburdened nurse had to try to diagnose and treat everything from toothache to leprosy. Intricate instruments, no longer in working order, were standing around; gleaming electro-cardiographs or anesthesia machines had become corroded and irreparable after a short time in the equatorial humidity.[16]

Having discussed the hospital, McKnight goes on, in a chapter entitled "How Good a Doctor?" to assess Schweitzer himself. He makes the point that Schweitzer was not a brilliant surgeon and that for many years he had practised very little medicine or surgery himself, and continues, "We must accept the fact that Schweitzer did not have any great stomach for healing men's bodies, while his time could better be used in trying to patch up their doomed souls,"[17] a statement diametrically opposite to the truth that Schweitzer went to Africa precisely to get away from word spinning and to devote himself to physical healing.

It was McKnight, too, who if he did not invent them, gave a great boost to the titillating tales of desperate women with an unhealthy longing for self-sacrifice, offering their lives to Schweitzer in a sick and hopeless devotion and loving him for the ruthlessness with which he sucked them dry. It was McKnight who devoted a chapter to Olga Deterding and Marion Preminger. The chapter is called "Beauty in the Jungle." Out of twenty chapters, four others are devoted to this exciting theme: "Women and the Lure," "Eccentrics' Goal," "The Novice," and "Unsung Heroines."

The chapters on "The Bach Book," "Is Schweitzer a Christian?" and "Philosopher of Doom" also have their special highlights. Conor Cruise O'Brien remarked in the *New York Review of Books* that "Mr. McKnight's writing has the worst features of the kind of British journalism which formed it; cockiness, ignorance, carelessness, prurience, innuendo, and lip-service to the highest moral standards."[18]

Finally, we come to the "Verdict." Here McKnight poses the wholly fatuous question, "Is Schweitzer a saint or a fraud?"[19] and then brings evidence that he is not a saint. So he had to be the other thing. Schweitzer was unlucky to live just long enough to see the fashionable tide swing against him, and now in magazine after magazine the new cry was taken up, "Schweitzer is a fraud." Schweitzer refused to reply or to let anyone do so for him. He never believed in justifying himself. "The philosophy of stoicism has its advantages," he said.

Frederick Franck has some pleasantly scathing things to say about the myths perpetrated and then perpetuated by journalists who spent an hour or two at the hospital. The British, he says, are most likely to have invented the doctor's morning swim in the Ogowe (actually full of bilharzia); the French are responsible for the rumor that he was living with a rich young petroleum heiress; the hymns after lunch came from a devout Scandinavian pastor; and the soulful Bismarck with fluorescent eyes roaming the nocturnal Ogowe sounds like a German creation. (While we are on the subject, Franck's *Days with Albert Schweitzer* is highly recommended as the clearest, sanest, most vivid picture we have of the hospital and its inhabitants. It teaches us one invaluable lesson—that it was not difficult to love the African patients. It is all too easy to picture a sort of undifferentiated mass of black bodies and faces, toward whom the whites felt a generalized goodwill. Schweitzer's own rather stiff, sometimes didactic prose fails to convey the warmth of the relationship. Franck, working there as a dentist for a year, paints individual pictures of Africans that come glowing from the page, sometimes with love, sometimes with the heat of fury. It is clear that doctors, nurses, and Schweitzer himself found a huge reward in doing what they did for these richly human patients, with all their varied and vivid personalities. Franck makes it clear why Ali Silver missed the "fun" of the hospital, and that one of the things Schweitzer found there was the open contact "as man to man" that he valued so highly.)

McKnight's book came out in the middle of 1964. That summer Schweitzer had his coffin made. And to look after the medical side of the hospital after his death he sent for Dr. Walter Munz, who had worked with him already for some years, to return as physician-in-charge. But still he had apparently not nominated an administrator to succeed him. To inquiries—and there were many—as to what would happen when he died, he was evasive.

For his ninetieth birthday BBC television sent out a team to do a program for the Panorama series, and the interviewer, Michael Barratt, asked him, "What arrangements have you made for the future of Lambarene after you're no longer able to run it?" Schweitzer replied: "The one who will take over as leader of the Hospital when I am dead— but (laughingly) I am not going to die too soon—he's already been nominated and is already on the staff. That's all been taken care of."[20]

But still nobody knew who the successor was. Schweitzer had not told even the two archangels. The mystery thickened. He could not have been referring to Munz, for the interview took place before January 11, and Walter Munz had not yet come back to Lambarene to take up his position. In any case, the post of physician-in-charge was not the same as Schweitzer's successor.

The conflicts that were bound to break out at his death were already casting a shadow before them. Should the hospital survive? And if so, in what form? As an indication of how far it had changed already, it now boasted six refrigerators, two deep-freezes, two jeeps, an American convertible donated by Erica Anderson, traffic signs requesting a speed limit of ten kilometres per hour, and a parking area. ("If they park anywhere else I'll put down tin tacks," said Schweitzer.)[21]

There was air conditioning in the windowless X-ray room. One nurse had made a start on preventive medicine by taking a traveling inoculation clinic to nearby villages. The number of patients had risen to six hundred, with six doctors and thirty-five nurses to look after them. Sometimes they had to rent beds in nearby villages to accommodate the walking patients.

But the aged motorboat was never used. Schweitzer felt no need of it. The toilet facilities were unchanged, and when a nurse, Joan Klent, was discovered building a lavatory for her patients, Schweitzer was furious although in the end, as usual, if anyone stood up to him, he growled, "You'll never change," and gave in.

Rhena found that she could never predict exactly how her father would react. Although she was his daughter, she was only now beginning to know him properly, and her feelings toward him were a curious mixture of love, irritation, admiration, and detachment. For all his unshakable consistency at the elemental level—perhaps because of it—he could be whimsical, he could change his mind, he could give in to impulse. And if she began: "But yesterday you said," he had a standard answer: "I'm not a book with a well-constructed plot. I'm a man, with all a man's contradictions."

A man who lays down rules may be allowed to break them and knows when they should be broken. It was more difficult for Mathilde and Ali, indoctrinated with his belief that what was good enough for the Africans was good enough for those who tended them and in love with a way of life they felt was threatened. They resented the force of the change they could feel coming, and their rigidity was resented in turn.

Among those who wanted change was Rhena, not a great deal of change, but some. She wanted, for example, running water, and electric light throughout the hospital. Schweitzer would not budge. It was not necessary, so it need not be. He had doctors, nurses, patients, and a good medical record. Why change? His view was entirely reasonable. Rhena, however, thought that the people who came to work there deserved better than a bucket to sluice over themselves for a shower and oil lamps to read and write by.

During those last years Rhena not only worked in the laboratory, she also traveled all over the world on her father's behalf, speaking, showing slides, and collecting money. She went to Scandinavia, to South America, and most successfully of all, to Japan. Japan took to Schweitzer's thought more enthusiastically than any other country, and in many Japanese schools his books became required reading. (From these visits comes the reference in Sueo Muta's letter to "your visit to our hospital." Schweitzer himself never went—only Rhena).

Schweitzer's writer's cramp was now getting serious. But he still wrote letters, as many as ever. Bertrand Russell was trying to persuade him to join the campaign to look into the assassination of President Kennedy, but he declined, on the grounds that he knew too little about it. "People have too often criticised me for concerning myself with the world's affairs, though I live in the virgin forest. You would not wish to expose me to this criticism again."[22]

The atomic issue was different. Schweitzer felt that they should campaign against Barry Goldwater's election to the presidency, on the grounds of his strongly conservative and isolationist views and his vociferous support for the nuclear program, and Russell agreed. Schweitzer signed a manifesto.

Thousands of letters still went unanswered. A sad Indian who had written once and had no reply writes desperately: "I expected your kind word of comfort and appreciation from your own hand would arrive to console and encourage the heart of this poor despairing boy. But God did not will it so far. But, truly, my dear Grandfather, I am left by Him as a miserable ship with its destination of a high goal but struggling in the midst of great agitating waters of impediments both of body and of circumstances. Really my position is thus. I find no other go but to run to you crying for help and a lift by your own strengthening arm."[23] What a burden of responsibility, the knowledge that so many hung so on his words! No wonder he confessed to Trudi Bochsler that he was sometimes afraid of not being able to live up to his professions.

As he grew weaker and had to be driven in the jeep on his visits to the leprosy village, everyone around him was constantly concerned for his health. They worried about the effect on him of the sudden spate of malice directed toward him in the world press. He was often said to be untouched by criticism, but it was not true. "He strides through his self-created world," said the commentary of the Panorama film, "impervious to criticism from outside and deaf to it from the people around him." But to Dr. Weissberg he said, "Always ask yourself how much of the criticism is justified." And on his ninetieth birthday he said to the assembled Africans, "Do you want me to leave you? If you say so, I will." They howled him down because they loved him deeply. But he had never needed to ask such a question before.

Another blow awaited him. *Les Mots*, the autobiography of Jean-Paul Sartre, came out with its dismissive references to the family in general and especially Sartre's grandfather, Schweitzer's Uncle Charles. Schweitzer had always visited Sartre's mother when he was in Paris and they got on well together. He visited Sartre too, when he could, and had read all his books and plays. He admired them even if he did not like them. But Sartre seems to have neither liked nor admired Schweitzer in return. "I am sad," wrote Schweitzer in a letter to a friend, "that he writes so derogatorily about his grandfather, who had a good knowledge of German literature and had a great love for his only grandchild."

And he went on, with one of the few personal asides in his correspondence:

> I met Sartre very early, when he was still in his baby clothes. I lived near my uncle, close to the Bois de Boulogne, and so my cousin often asked me to push the pram to the park for her. I was supposed to lift him out of the pram to do a wee-wee; but he never did it when he was lifted out, only in the pram. One could see that he was already himself in that pram.
>
> Sometimes he spent his holidays with his mother at the vicarage in Günsbach. He is supposed to have written his first pieces in the vicarage garden, when he was still a pupil. We are correct and friendly with one another, but we have no deep relationship. His philosophy is witty and clever but not profound. He is a follower of Husserl and Heidegger. His plays are better than his philosophy. In them he deals with ethics, which have no place in his philosophy.[24]

That year Ali Silver began to sleep in a hammock in Schweitzer's room to be near him at all times. But he kept going. If any whisper of illness escaped, the deluge of inquiries about his health doubled the normal flow of letters. So he still took care always to be seen around the hospital. And, indeed, he seemed to be as fit as ever—only a little less active.

But in June there was concern about his blood sugar, which was 265. Sweet things were cut from his diet, but he was not a good patient. He resented even being asked how he felt and was as difficult as a spoiled child about his food. He would try to snatch a piece of cake if it was within reach, and nobody seemed willing or able to stop him. His color was not so good as usual, especially the color of his hands, and his memory was growing erratic.

Rhena's situation as laboratory nurse was made more difficult by the fact that the patient was not only a crusty authoritarian but also her father. Nevertheless, she sent particulars to her husband's doctor in Zürich, a specialist in diabetes, who prescribed Orinase. This brought the blood sugar down to 165, and Schweitzer seemed better.

For a number of years now he had not eaten meat (he could no longer bear, he explained, to eat anything that had been alive), and now he lived largely on soup—often lentil soup—of which he never tired.

Erica Anderson had been at the hospital during the spring and early summer, and when she left in the middle of July, there was no immediate cause for concern.

On August 10 Schweitzer wrote to Jerome Hill, and his handwriting, usually so consistent and firm, was spidery and wandering, the final sentence almost illegible. The letter is of no great interest in itself—he wants Jerome Hill to help a friend while he is in Europe. And, "If you are able in one of your journeys to pass by Lambarene, which has an airport now, I would be very glad to see you again."

It was one of the last letters he penned himself. Two days later a small group of friends arrived, including Charles Michel, who for so many years had supervised the purchases and deliveries of supplies to the hospital from Strasbourg, and Fritz Dinner, the vigorous leader of the Swiss Committee. "He looked very well for his age," they wrote, "though he was a little more stooped and his movements were slower than in previous years. His voice was softer but extremely clear."[25]

He worked every day, as usual, in the pharmacy, in his room, or on the building site, and still took most of his meals with the staff and read the Bible after the evening meal.

On Monday, August 23, instead of the Bible reading, he announced in a clear, firm voice, his instructions in case of his death. That same day he dictated and signed a letter to the Strasbourg Association of the Hospital, who would become responsible for the hospital on his death:

> To the Association of the hospital of Dr. Albert Schweitzer, Lambarene, Gabon, Strasbourg.
> To the Members of the Association,
> GENTLEMEN, I the undersigned, Albert Schweitzer, doctor of medicine in Lambarene, Gabon, declare that my daughter, Mme. Rhena Eckert Schweitzer, Uetikon a See, shall take over the direction of my hospital at Lambarene after my death. Given at Lambarene, the 23rd August, 1965.

It was the first Rhena had known of it.

From that moment he began to fail. He was not always present at meals; he was not always out at work. On Thursday and Friday he had himself driven through the hospital grounds, and on the Friday he walked through his orchard. Walter Munz said, "His last walk was wonderful. Once more he passed through the orchard supported by his cane. He identified every tree he had planted, praised them for their sturdy growth and for their beauty. From the top of the hill he looked over the hospital and was very happy about it."[26]

Once when the criticism had been high, he had sat and looked at his hospital and said quietly, "All the same, it is a charming hospital." Walking through the orchard, he said good-bye to his charming hospital.

On Saturday the twenty-eighth he had breakfast in the dining room, and the staff could see that a change had taken place. Then he went back to his room and talked to Rhena. He said he was very, very tired.

He tried to walk a little way but got no farther than the porch outside his room. He returned to his bed.

Dr. David Miller wrote the medical report:

The terminal illness of Albert Schweitzer was caused primarily by cerebral vascular insufficiency which manifested itself quite abruptly on August 28, 1965, with impairment of consciousness and of cerebral regulation of cardiac and respiratory function. During the preceding week he had seemed more fatigued than usual, with some unsteadiness on his feet.

On the evening of August 29, because in his semi-comatose condition he was unable to take sufficient fluid by mouth, he was given an intravenous infusion of physiologically-balanced electrolyte solution, slowly through the night.

For the most part thereafter he remained semi-comatose and bed-ridden, with transient periods of increased reactivity. Until September 3, he was able to take clear fluids, including beer (which he had asked for) in small amounts by mouth. His blood pressure was well maintained until nearly the end, and an electrocardiogram on September 2 revealed no evidence of myocardial infarction.

On 3 September, his fluid intake and urinary output diminished, his temperature rose gradually, his respirations became more rapid with evidence of diminished aeration of the right lung, and his coma deepened.

Because of the evident irreversibility of his condition—deepening cerebral coma, increasing uremia and developing pneumonitis—no further diagnostic measures or specific therapeutic measures were carried out. He continued to receive constant and excellent nursing care but he did not require any analgesic medications, for at no time was there any evidence of suffering. Over the last few hours of his life his pulse grew weaker and his coma deepened further. At 11:30 P.M. September 4, 1965, he passed away quietly in peace and dignity in his bed at the hospital he had built and loved.[27]

Fritz Dinner and Charles Michel's account of the funeral was published in the hospital bulletin, the American Schweitzer Fellowship's *Courier,* and elsewhere:

His mortal body was laid in the coffin which had been made during the summer of 1964 according to his instructions, and with him the little sack filled with rice which he used to carry with him constantly, and leaves of the wild vine climbing his Günsbach house; his old felt hat from which he never parted was placed there too and his loden coat was spread over him.

On the eve of his impending death the natives of the hospital had gathered and all of them, irrespective of creed, had held a moving service for their "Papa pour nous" with singing and Bible reading, expressing their love and devotion.

On Sunday 5th September at 5:30 in the morning the big hospital bell tolled and was joined by the bell from the leper village to signal the death of the "Grand Docteur." The tom-toms of the natives began to mingle with the bells to spread the sad news.

From six o'clock in the morning onwards, without interruption until the funeral in the early afternoon, the inmates of the hospital, the people of the leper village and those who had come from the surrounding countryside filed past the coffin in the room in which he had lived and died, to take leave in reverent dignity of their beloved dead.

The grief of these African men and women as they expressed it in their songs was deeply touching—an audible witness of their gratitude, their devotion, and most of all their love for their "Grand Docteur" who had helped them and had understood their actions, their joys and their sorrows.

The funeral took place on 5th September at three in the afternoon. The coffin was placed on a small platform under the palm trees in front of Doctor Schweitzer's room. The only tributes on the red shining coffin, made from native wood, were a small wooden cross and a sprig of red blossoms from the African jungle, placed there by one of the doctor's workmen who has served him for many years, Obiange.

In spite of the short time between the announcement of Doctor Schweitzer's death and burial, a great grieving multitude had gathered. There were members of the Government, the Minister of the Interior, the Minister of Defence, and the Minister of Public Health; the Director of the Cabinet of the President of the Republic of Gabon, the Prefect of the Moyen Ogowe, the Under-Secretary of Lambarene, representatives of the Gabonese and French Administrations. Deputies of citizens of Libreville and Lambarene, as well as many from surrounding villages. Representatives of Catholic and Protestant Missions and presidents of many different organisations had come, and Ambassadors or those representing them from France, Germany, England, America and Israel. A guard of honour of the State Police appeared and paid their respects to the bearer of the highest decorations of the French and Gabonese Governments. Uncountable people from near and far filled the big compound of the hospital.

Dr. Walter Munz officiated at the service, during which hymns were sung by the European nurses of the staff, by the Protestant evangelists, and by the people of the leper village. The choirs of the natives, singing with emotion, expressed their immeasurable sorrow at the loss of their "Grand Docteur" in a deeply touching way.

Following the religious service the official representatives of the Gabonese Republic honoured the great personality of Dr. Schweitzer in speeches in the warmest terms. Finally, Monsieur Michel, as representative of the Strasbourg Association of the Hospital, and speaking for the diverse other supporting organisations in different countries, as well as in the name of the entire staff of the hospital and of those from Dr. Schweitzer's distant homeland, Alsace, addressed the last words of gratitude and the last farewell to the beloved dead, in these simple words:

"I thank you, dear Docteur, in the name of all—for all you did."

In the name of Mrs. Rhena Eckert-Schweitzer he thanked all those who had come that day for the sympathy they showed and the grief they shared.

After this, the mourning visitors gathered round the grave. Four African and four European helpers carried the coffin and lowered it into the African earth under the palm trees beside the Ogowe river. After the blessing of the grave, the final prayer, and the Lord's Prayer spoken in unison there followed a chorale sung by the hospital community. Then innumerable hands let African earth fall on the coffin as their last greeting and thanks to their "Grand Docteur" so deeply beloved.[28]

Epilogue

THE MAN WAS DEAD. The myth lived on—and the antimyth. So, against many expectations, did the hospital. This book is not about the hospital but about Albert Schweitzer, but perhaps it should be reported here how it fared after he died.

Disagreements arose, as was inevitable, about whether and how far it should be changed. When I went there eight years after his death, it was still there and still working. Running water had been added; there were shower and toilet blocks. Electric light was available throughout the hospital until the generator was switched off at ten each night. But the room the visitor slept in was identical with the room James Cameron and hundreds of others had slept in; the wards, the surgery, and the operating theater were still the simple, tough, hardwood buildings Schweitzer put up for his patients in the years before the hospital grew famous and the money easier. Survivors still lived in the leprosy village. The staff still gathered for meals in the dining room although the old long table had gone and had been replaced by several small ones. There had been reports of a morbid Schweitzer mystique—of meals set in his empty place—but these were certainly not true then and I was assured never were. On Sunday a service was still held by one of the staff, a Fang interpreter on one side, a Galoa on the other although now it was held in the new recreation hut, not in the open space between the wards. The rest of the hospital continued to work efficiently and was valued by the government, specializing in difficult cases, and particularly in surgery.

Schweitzer's room remained as he left it—a memorial and a museum for the many visitors who wished to see where he lived and worked.

Since that time the whole of the old hospital has become a museum, visited by great numbers of people, but the termites are now sadly winning their long battle with its timbers. A new hospital has arisen on the neighboring site, partly funded by the Gabonese government but still largely supported by the donations of Schweitzer Committees all over the world, and still provides specialist care.

Has the Schweitzer spirit survived? Well, even when I was there, the goats were gone. The hospital no longer grew all its own vegetables, for labor was no longer obtainable on the old barter system. There were minimum wage rates to be considered, and it was now sometimes cheaper to buy the vegetables. Pets were still common, but anywhere in the world people keep pets. The Garden of Eden touch had vanished. People there surely believed in and to some extent practiced Reverence for Life, but nobody any longer passionately embodied it. Things had become more ordinary. The myth was evaporating.

This would not have troubled Schweitzer too much. It was his Lambarene, but as he said to his granddaughter Christiane, when she wanted to go there to help, "You can have your Lambarene anywhere." The true heirs to Schweitzer's hospital are other hospitals, many of them directly inspired by his—Dr. Mellon's in Haiti, Dr. Binder's in Mexico, Dr. Rhee's in Korea, Dr. Humberto's in Brazil—and not only hospitals but many other ventures undertaken with the same concern and dedication. The criterion is not that others should try to preserve what Schweitzer made nor even to imitate it but that they should try to find a true and valid expression, in action, of their own most humane and human impulses.

For the hospital, as Schweitzer said himself, was really only "an improvisation." He made it up as he went along. The theme on which he was improvising was a certain attitude that, once the name had come to him, was called Reverence for Life. Other people's improvisations on the theme could be, and should be, quite different. What mattered was the theme.

Unlike the hospital, the theme was anything but improvised. From his early childhood he had been aware of it, and all his life he had worked at its perfecting. Rabbi Leo Beck said that Schweitzer's greatest achievement was his own personality. Jung said that he seemed to have no neurosis. However much or little this book can convey, it can never present the personality, which, whether admired, loved, or resented, was always overwhelming.

In the autobiography we find the events and the thoughts that built up the man. In the books of philosophy the thoughts are expanded and enriched. In the sermons the soul's deeper feelings are revealed. But it is in the slighter, more casual works, that came from him almost by accident, *Memoirs of Childhood and Youth* and *The Story of My Pelican*, that we come nearest to the flavor of that personality: childlike without being in the least childish, undeceived without being critical, loving without being indulgent, and in every way appreciative. He drank life and savored it.

With the poet Terence he could say, "I am a man. No human thing is foreign to me." Further he could say, "I am life. No living thing is foreign to me." Because he entered so simply into the realm of living creatures, he seemed its king.

By another paradox, the thing that made him rich was his overwhelming sense of indebtedness. In fact, although he appears not to have noticed it, his sense of debt was very selective. He felt no urge to pay anyone back for harm done to him, only for good. He was aware of being privileged and of owing that privilege to various people in particular and also to life in general.

Guessing wildly, we might wonder whether his near-fatal illness in infancy left him with a profound subconscious gratitude for being alive at all. It is the only clue as to what might have made him different from his brother or from many other children born in similar circumstances.

His theology will probably never satisfy the theologians; it ignores all the fascinating blind alleys they love to explore. His philosophy will never satisfy the philosophers; it fails to put the universe in its place, and it fails to pursue verbal distinctions down long dark burrows leading nowhere. It speaks to the whole man, not to the intellect alone.

Even his ethics will never satisfy the students of ethics. They fail to lay down clear and definitive regulations as to what to do in all circumstances. (Two years before his death, a Roman Catholic journal in Iowa, in a gesture toward the new goodwill between churches, published a very friendly article about Schweitzer by Fr. Ernest Ranly, CPPS; but Fr. Ranly found it a great failing in Schweitzer's ethics that he could not tell us "how or to what degree we are to help others, pay our taxes, work for social justice and obey civil laws.")[1]

On the other hand, the ethics of ethicists, the philosophy of philosophers, and the theology of theologians will never satisfy ordinary people. Schweitzer's might.

The things that Schweitzer believed and fought for are believed by millions and millions of people already. Is there anything startlingly new in the proposition that life is to be preserved and encouraged, and death, disease, and human destructiveness to be fought against?

Did Schweitzer carry this to excess with his plea that no life, animal or vegetable, large or small, shall be taken without due and careful thought for the consequences? It seemed so to a great many people. But within a few years of his death that thought of his received grand new names— conservation, and ecology. The casual use of pesticides which he was mocked for banning, has been found to have effects that reach out and threaten the whole world's balance of existence.

For some years now the economists of the world have been executing a hasty, ragged, and rather humiliating about-turn to fall into line with the ecologists—and with Schweitzer. We all know now that simplicity, thoughtfulness, and the cherishing of our world is the precondition for survival. We have not yet understood (and perhaps an even deeper crisis yet is necessary for this) that to cherish each other is also something more than morality. It is, as Schweitzer said, a necessity of thought. It is common sense, practical politics, and the health of the human soul.

We may be thankful for Schweitzer's schoolmasterishness and passion for teaching, whatever authoritarian quirks they may have led him into. For they forced him to demonstrate with a grand QED something that the world badly needs to know: that goodness works; that to be effective it is not necessary to belong to a huge consortium or to indulge in political intrigue or the power game.

The vast majority of people, as he knew, are at heart peaceable and neighborly; and for that very reason they never reach the places of power where the world's fate is decided. The dilemma has always been that power and influence go to the ambitious and the aggressive so that gentleness and humanity are less to be found in the corridors of power than anywhere else, and it comes to be accepted that the simple neighborly values in some way unfit a person for responsibility. Schweitzer put into the service of kindness a personality that could have dominated governments, thereby proving that goodness was not after all a disability.

I began this book by quoting Erica Anderson: "He was not so much righteous, as right." That does not mean that everything he said or did was correct, but that he was normal, he was human, he was balanced, he was sane, he was free. He was normal, in fact, to an abnormal degree. He was superhumanly human. He was excessively balanced. He took simple, everyday qualities, gave them intellectual respectability, and then pushed them to their limits and proved that they worked in practice.

Great men usually achieve greatness at the cost of some distortion of personality. They pay for their exceptional strength in one sphere by exceptional weakness in others. In Schweitzer two things only were truly exceptional: his conviction that his simple instincts were not to be despised but were desperately important and his sheer physical stamina.

The passionate boy who would not wear an overcoat; the passionate youth who was forever arguing the truth; the passionate young man who had learned the uselessness of argument and instead kept his thoughts and intentions to himself till they were ready to be acted upon; the passionate explorer of music, the hero-worshiper of Jesus, of Wagner, of Goethe; the never-satisfied searcher for the root of all human impulse; the unwavering, uncompromising exemplar of his beliefs; at every stage of this consistent progression he was dependent on the ability of his body to stand up to the demands his passion imposed on it. In one of his last letters, with the pain of the writer's cramp very visible in the writing, he says: "The hand has stood up to it after all. My body generally sees reason in the end."

Once the passion and the strength are understood, many of the seeming paradoxes of Schweitzer's life fall into place. That a man so consistent and so basically simple could have so many divergent interests is not really surprising. Everything mattered to him; the only limitation on the things he could do was the number of waking hours in a day, and his waking hours were more than most. That he should be both musician and philosopher, pastor and physician, is only surprising to those who believe that specialization is in the nature of things. Most people are interested in all kinds of things, but few have the energy and determination to do more than dabble outside their own professions.

Schweitzer never allowed the false distinctions of convention to trouble him. Conventional thinking opposes reason to instinct, art to science, theory to practice, tradition to revolution. Schweitzer was not interested in such labels. Both reason and instinct are aspects of mental concentration; art and science are forms of creative discovery; practice is useless without theory and theory without practice; revolution loses itself without knowledge of tradition, and tradition stiffens without revolution. Most people are temperamentally disposed to one or the other of each pair, and the balance of society depends on the interaction of opposing and complementary types. With Schweitzer all the elements came together in a single man. His imagination and intelligence took him into the deep places of the mind where all these things begin. His ecstasy before the manifestations of nature led him into the origins of thought and will and impulse where nothing human—indeed nothing conscious—could be denied, where the mind is aware of its solidarity with all consciousness.

Reverence for Life is the acknowledgment that deeper than all division is the mystery of solidarity. Solidarity is not unity, nor is it identity, nor is it love. It respects the separateness of individual lives as the very condition of their mutual concern and interdependence. In finding that mystery and deliberately giving himself to it, Schweitzer released a force in himself that encompassed the whole range of existence. "With consciousness and with volition I devote myself to Being. I become imaginative force, like that which works mysteriously in nature, and thus I gave my existence a meaning from within outwards."[2]

So Schweitzer described what he was trying to do. The result was described by his close friend Werner Picht:

> During the years the goodness inherent in his nature . . . has permeated his being into its uttermost recesses like yeast. It manifests itself in the least

significant word and in the most casual action. His self-renunciation is complete. His life is spent absolutely and exclusively in the service of love, caritas. But this, as the ethic of reverence for life clearly shows, is exclusively based on the consciousness of solidarity with everything living and the responsibility which flows from it. It is humanitarian. It is compelling not by its theoretical justification, but by its perfection.[3]

Schweitzer was a practical mystic, whose mysticism led him into the ordinary lives of men and women and of all creatures—into a normality filled with significance.

He was a genius, one might say, in the art of living, using the word *genius* in his own sense of one who constructs a new unity out of what appeared before to be divided. He was certainly a religious genius, breaking down old structures and taking from them the pieces he needed to build a new unity. But the religious genius was inseparable from his genius in living in which he welded an unprecedented new unity out of elements that normally divide men within themselves: intuition, reason, and will.

To do this he had to learn to use himself to the limit. Once he had discovered where the center of his life lay, and learned not to be ashamed of it but to express it, the joy of that liberation lasted a lifetime. In his teens it made him insufferable. In old age people would say of him, "He is the most self-centered man I have ever met." That self-centeredness was the visible sign of the concentration he gave to being true to himself. It was the price he paid, and made others pay, for his fidelity to his vision.

And the vision? He himself would have said that everything that mattered was in his books, that he understood himself philosophically, that as a fallible individual he was unimportant.

The books, it is true, are vital. They explain and complement the life. But all the same, the image of a living man is more potent and more effective than any sermon or symbol or set of exhortations. Schweitzer was not the ultimate or only illustration of his vision; he was formed by Alsace, by liberal Protestantism, and by the nineteenth-century German academic tradition, and he carried the marks of that place, that time, and that mental discipline. But through that particular individual the vision shone with a power that is the greater because it is more personal. The theory, in short, worked.

The life was the argument, and a very strenuous argument it was. After ninety years, eight months, and some days the body that had carried it grew very tired and lay down for the last time.

With it, his case rests.

Postscript to the
Second Edition

WHILE PREPARING this second edition, a quarter of a century after first writing this book, I have been surprised to find that I am now less pessimistic about the future of the world than I was then.

This can, perhaps, be put down to the end of the Cold War and the consequent lifting of the threat of world annihilation that seemed real enough then. But I am sure that there is more to it than that. I sense that around the world more and more of the things that Schweitzer begged for are coming to pass.

In his Nobel Peace Prize address of 1954, *The Problem of Peace in the World of Today,* he said, "I am profoundly convinced that the solution [to the problem of peace] is: we should reject war for ethical reasons—because, that is to say, it makes us guilty of the crime of inhumanity."

He realized that people might set this aside "as a well-meaning form of words; that people might say that it was 'inapplicable to reality.' " "But more than one truth," he said, "has long remained dormant and ineffective for no other reason than that nobody had imagined it could ever have any application to reality."

In this past twenty-five years, a generation has been growing up in many parts of the world to whom it hardly needs saying that the world is our responsibility; to them it is simply obvious that we are all members one of another, all forms of life included, and that inhumanity is quite simply wrong. The arguments about controlling the conflicts in the former Yugoslavia have not centered on whether or how each nation's legal situation is affected but on whether it is *right* for nations to unite to try to stop grievous inhumanity wherever it may occur. It is the ethics of the situation, not the realpolitik, that concern us. And the notion that the

505

United Nations could even suggest to a nation like Russia that they place individual human rights above the need for winning a war, and that Russia would be compelled by world opinion at least to listen if not to accede, would have been unthinkable half a century ago.

There are, of course, complications, and always will be. Power must be exercised in preventing abuse of power, and this power can itself be abused. There are plenty of people who still think of fighting old wars for old reasons in old ways. But they are becoming isolated. In large and important parts of the world soldiers today are being trained as peace-keepers, not war-makers. Reporters try to make us aware of the evils, not just of our enemies, but of war itself.

If I am right, a gentle but irresistible tide is turning, an undertow of human consciousness, not imposed from above and not determined by self-interest, but growing in human hearts and minds where, as Schweitzer believed, goodness lies. If so, whether we realize it or not, we have a lot to thank him for.

In the spirit of Schweitzer's remark that "you can have your Lambarene anywhere," there are numerous organizations and initiatives around the world that are specifically Schweitzer based. There are also many that acknowledge his inspiration although they do not use his name. There are certainly many, many more that may never have heard his name but that passionately espouse his principles and ideals without realizing their debt to him.

It would be impossible to list all the organizations with specific links to Schweitzer, and in any case such a list would rapidly become out of date. For any reader who may wish to contact such an organization, the following are the principal centers, that will be likely to have up-to-date information about the worldwide movement:

The Schweitzer Hospital, Lambarene, Gabon, West Africa. It is now owned by the Fondation Internationale pour l'Hopital du Dr. Albert Schweitzer à Lambaréné, which has its headquarters in Lambarene.

International Albert Schweitzer Center, Maison Albert Schweitzer, Günsbach, 68140 Münster, France. Based in the house that Schweitzer built and that served as his base when he was in Europe, it houses archives and a small museum and is visited by Schweitzer enthusiasts from all over the world.

The Albert Schweitzer Fellowship, 330 Brookline Avenue, Boston, Mass. 02215, (Tel: (617)667-5111). The Fellowship was founded to support Schweitzer and his hospital and was largely responsible for its preservation after World War Two. Extensive archives are also to be found here, and it continues to fund activities based on Schweitzer's work and his philosophy, including sponsoring medical students working in local communities in many of the United States. In common with Johns Hopkins University and the Albert Schweitzer Institute for the Humanities, it gives regular Schweitzer awards to students and others whose work best embodies the ethic of Reverence for Life and follows Schweitzer's example, "his life was his argument."

Appendixes
Notes
Bibliography
Index

A Day at the Hospital

by Albert Schweitzer

Reprinted from British Bulletin no. 12 (Spring 1936)
of Dr. Schweitzers Hospital Fund
(the British Committee for the support of the hospital)

WHEN THE FIRST GONG SOUNDS at 6:45 a.m. the doctor who for a week is taking the duty of making the first round of the wards, the nurse whose turn it is for early service and the nurse who has charge of the workmen descend to the Hospital. The latter calls the roll of the paid labourers, the companions male and female of the patients who are eligible for work and the convalescents who are in like case, deals out to them axes, saws, spades, rakes and bush-knives and sends or leads them to where they are to work, whether it be in the forest, in the plantation, in the garden, on a building-site or in the laundry. At the same time the nurse in the consulting room is calling over the names of the native orderlies and visiting the people who are seriously ill.

At 7:30 the gong summons us to breakfast. It is only after breakfast, at 8 a.m., that the real Hospital work is supposed to begin. But in spite of all exhortations I cannot prevent nurses and doctors, even when it is not their turn for early work, from being down in the Hospital at 7. The nurse who has to do the bandaging in the operated patients' ward generally begins soon after 6. But nevertheless I hold fast to the principle that the main work in the Hospital shall only begin at 8, for in this equatorial climate one must economise one's strength. One can only get through three-fifths of the work of which one is capable in Europe. The newcomers and the overzealous often pay dearly for their contempt of this truth.

It must also be remembered that doctors and nurses do not always enjoy undisturbed rest, but are often fetched down to the Hospital two or three times in the course of one night. It is often the greatest savages who have the least consideration for their need of sleep and have them called without any urgent reason.

When we come down at 8 a.m. the six Hospital washerwomen have the boilers on four big fires under a roof which protects them from sun and rain. They get the water from a pump nearby. These women who work down by the Hospital have to wash the bandages and operation linen. Their place is just in front of the consultation room, so that the nurses can overlook them from its windows and stop their gossiping and idleness by calling to them. Up near our dwelling houses six other women are busy with our household washing. We need far more clean linen in the Tropics than in more temperate zones. In the hot season we may each of us need a change three times a day.

At least six men are occupied every day with the felling, cutting-up and transport of the necessary firewood. In the course of the years the plantation has pushed in between the Hospital and the forest, so that the forest is now a good half hour's walk from the Hospital. Carts are no use in such hilly country so all the wood must be carried by hand. It is not only the washerwomen and the women who are making palm oil who use up the firewood, but there are fires burning nearly all day long for disinfecting the surgical instruments, and for cooking the food prepared for the very sick and the mental patients under the supervision of the nurses, and there are fires in the dysentery ward (to which relations are not allowed access) kept burning day and night. And in addition there is the firewood required for our own kitchen, for the bread oven and for our laundry.

Often we get whole rafts of splendid okoume wood as presents from timber merchants who for one reason or another cannot sell their logs. A nurse takes a crew and goes to fetch them, but the sawing of these huge logs is a laborious business.

As the washerwomen and the palm oil women are recruited from those who have come with patients and are constantly changing, it is impossible to think of training them to economy in the use of fuel, or to reasonable methods of work. This causes the nurses much trouble.

The patients and their friends fetch their own firewood from the forest for the fires over which they cook their meals, fires which they keep burning from early morning till far into the night. As unfortunately we have not enough sheds which can be locked up they often manage to help themselves from our stores, and even the beams and planks ready for use in building are not always secure from their depredations.

At 8 o'clock the patients and out-patients begin to congregate on the landward side of the consulting room. Plank beds are arranged under the big ward for the operated patients which lies opposite and stands on piles, and on these they sit or lie protected from sun and rain.

Three times a week, on the days when injections are given, the Hospital orderly Dominique goes through the wards at 8 a.m. with a big cow-bell, and summons the sleeping-sickness and elephantiasis patients, the lepers, the tuberculous and the patients who need injections of Neo-Salvarsan. An hour passes before he has collected at all events the majority. So that they may not promptly melt away again, they are shut up in a big wire-enclosed room alongside the consulting room and fetched out one by one when their turn arrives. But when a doctor calls the roll of those on his list for injections, at least a third are missing. Then Dominique, who is the shrewdest of the orderlies and has most authority over the patients, starts out again. He looks for the dawdlers among the patients who sit gossiping on the steps by the landing stage, among those who are bathing, those who are fishing, those who are fetching firewood, those who are gathering palm nuts, and drives them in front of him to the Hospital like a flock of sheep. He does not attempt to get the "Incorrigibles." These go off into the forest or the plantation for the whole morning and then appear in the consulting room in the course of the afternoon or towards evening reproachfully to establish the fact that they have not yet been "pricked." It is nothing to them that the necessary solution must be prepared afresh, and it is in vain that we try to make clear to them how they render our work difficult by their heedlessness about days and hours. They cannot even be trained to punctuality by the loss of their rations for a day or two if they repeatedly fail to attend at the right time for their injections. They always find helpful friends who let them share the contents of their cooking-pots, and thus they need not be unfaithful to the principle that freedom is the highest good.

The injections are given by Hospital Orderly N'Yama. He has held this office for years and is a master of the art of finding veins which defy both eyes and fingers when sought. He prepares the solutions under the supervision of a doctor who tells him the exact quantity required for each patient. When it is a question of Tryparsamide, which is used for sleeping sickness, or of various other drugs, the doses are calculated by the weight of the patients. At the request of Mr. Holm, the Swedish doctor, who had the care of the sleeping sickness cases, a Swedish lady gave us a weighing machine, and this enables us to weigh these patients every week.

The work is generally distributed among the three doctors as follows: one has the white patients, the mental patients and the urological cases, undertakes the main part of the work in the operating room and looks after the dispensary. The second is mainly concerned with leprosy, sleeping-sickness, tuberculosis, tropical ulcers and native confinement cases, and supervises all patients who regularly receive injections. The third undertakes some of the operations, is responsible for the bandaging of all who have undergone operations and all accident cases and has the care of the dysentery patients.

Of the eight nurses three are occupied with the housekeeping, garden, kitchen and live-stock. One of the three looks after the little motherless babies who are brought up on bottles. These infants—of whom there are usually ten or twelve—pass the day in an airy room protected from mosquitoes, in charge of a native woman. They spend the night with the relatives who have brought them. We make these relatives stay with us to wash the babies' clothes and, if they are capable, to work for the Hospital in return for the milk given to the children. Usually it is the father, or an old aunt or a grandmother who is with the baby. I have built a house with eight rooms near the crèche for these people so that the infants can always be under the nurse's supervision.

A fourth nurse has charge of the workpeople. Her chief responsibility is the upkeep of the plantation, the supervision of the harvesting of the bananas and palm nuts, and the care of the young fruit trees, which are greatly endangered by fungi and grasshoppers. She also directs the clearing of the forest and has to provide the Hospital with the necessary amount of firewood.

The four nurses who serve in the Hospital divide their work as follows: The first serves in the operating room, sterilizes the linen and bandages and supervises the washerwomen who wash these things. The second bandages the operated patients and those wounded by accidents, has charge of the white patients and assists the operation sister. The third serves in the consulting room, dispenses the medicines as the doctor directs, looks after the native confinement cases and the newborn infants and supervises the people who are seriously ill in the various wards. The fourth bandages the tropical ulcers (this work claims many hours of the day), looks after the mental cases, supervises the women who make palm oil, buys the plantains and manioc (cassava) needed to feed the patients, gives the rations, and sees to it that the wards and surroundings of the Hospital are kept clean.

At 11:30 this nurse has a horn blown to announce that the distribution of the rations is about to begin. This is done from a room on a level with the ground with a large window with a counter inside it. The patients file past the window and each takes his ration from the counter. But before receiving it he has to hand in his card with his name and number so that the nurse can mark his name on her list as having received his day's ration. Otherwise the same person might fetch a ration four times over.

The ordinary patients and those who accompany them are not given cooked food, but materials to form two meals, which they prepare as they please over their own little fires.

When we have enough plantains and manioc the ration consists entirely of these, with the addition of a little salt and a large spoonful of palm oil. Two or three times a week we also give a piece of dried fish.

If there are no plantains and manioc to be had, we give rice. Plantains are far more nourishing than bananas, hut when we are obliged to give rations of rice we add bananas. In our plantation we only grow bananas, not plantains, as the former require far less labour. If we were to cultivate plantains they would cost us more than those we buy from the villagers.

All the inmates of the Hospital have permission to fetch from the plantation all the palm nuts, bananas, paw-paws, lemons and mangoes they need. In this way we know that if we are compelled to feed them on rice they will nevertheless get enough vitamins.

The nurse who distributes the rations has a difficulty in the fact that those who file before her also fetch the food for the lying-down cases. She knows the ration is given but cannot be sure that it reaches its destination. A thorough savage will think nothing of gobbling up the share of a lying-down patient who has been committed to his care.

Both the nurses who have to look after the patients lying in the wards have great difficulties with those who are unaccompanied by relatives. There are plenty of people who are only suffering from slight illness and can he detailed to act as attendants. But it is quite another matter to get these to fulfil their duties properly, namely cook the patients' food and give it to them, fetch their drinking water, and be constantly about ready to render any necessary service instead of passing their time as best they please.

We hesitate to ask anybody to be a patient's attendant unless he belongs to the same tribe, for we know in advance that he will regard the request as outrageous. In many cases it is impossible to get a man to render neighbourly service to a "stranger" either by kindly exhortation, presents, threats or punishment. But even people of the same tribe do not readily consent to undertake such duties and, when they do, need very strict supervision. The nurses are often quite in despair about the difficulty of the problems concerned with the patients who cannot leave their beds.

Our eight native orderlies are so busy that they cannot devote as much time as is necessary to individual patients in the wards. We cannot think of facing the expense of having more paid attendants when the people with slight illnesses can perfectly well perform these duties. So we still take the trouble to try and teach savages that the patients assigned to their care are their neighbours. When we succeed in making them understand, we are happy indeed.

Three mornings a week are devoted to consultations for out-patients and the reception of new patients, and three to operations. But we cannot observe this routine very strictly. Sometimes for weeks at a time it is necessary to perform operations every morning as otherwise we could not get through the surgical work. On the other hand we cannot prevent out-patients and new patients from arriving on the operation days. For we cannot restrict those who come long distances by canoe to landing on certain days, nor even if it is an operation day can we refuse to receive sick people brought by some canoe which is going to Lambarene on business when its occupants have given them a passage out of compassion. Many patients, especially the old and the lonely, can only reach the Hospital if they can find such an opportunity.

A card like a luggage label is filled up for each patient. On it is inscribed the date of the consultation or reception as an in-patient, his name, his Hospital number, his age, where he comes from and the diagnosis. If it is an in-patient, a note is also made to show whether he is to receive the ration or not. People who come from a short distance—up to about twenty-five miles around—are not provided with food, as their relatives ought to bring them plantains and manioc. And similarly patients who are not altogether poor are expected to provide their own meals. It is not always easy to decide who ought to have the ration. The new doctors generally refer the question to one of riper experience. I have laid down as a principle that it is better to give food to a patient who might perhaps provide it for himself than to let him go hungry when he ought to be having the ration.

It also happens that people who are able to provide their own food for a time have to be supplied by us later on when they have spent all their money or their relatives are weary of spending whole days bringing them plantains or manioc. A few weeks ago I had to give orders that a well-to-do chief from the interior who had come to us for an operation should along with his two wives receive the ration. On a journey far from his own village he had been forced suddenly to resolve to get freed from the hernia which was troubling him badly. So the rich chief was with us like any poor stranger and his wives had to condescend to laundry work in order to earn their food. He promised to give the Hospital a fine present in return for his operation and board, but it has not yet arrived.

Those who accompany a patient are also given cards. On each of these is the name and number of the patient, the name of the companion and a note as to whether he is entirely occupied with his duties as attendant or whether he can also work for the Hospital. So by a glance at the card each of us can quickly know all about every native he meets at the Hospital.

For every patient a second, larger card is filled up on which is entered the history of his illness, the diagnosis and the treatment. This card is kept in the consulting room and the results of later examinations and an account of the course of the disease are added from time to time.

When a patient is discharged, he keeps his little card to show if he ever returns for treatment. But one corner, the corner in which it is marked that he is to receive the ration, is snipped off, otherwise he would leave it to a friend who would thus be enabled with two names to fetch a double ration, if the nurse were not very observant. It has actually happened that patients about to leave have pretended their cards were lost so as to be able to give them to others with the instruction to give the ration still intact.

As a rule we have not finished with the consultations when the gong summons us to dinner at 12:30.

From 1 to 2 p.m. the doctors and nurses are supposed to rest in order to be fresh for their afternoon work. On the Equator a siesta is almost a necessity.

After 2 p.m. the doctors are busy with the out-patients who have come for consultations or with the reception of new patients for whom there was no time left in the morning. But our principal work in the afternoon is with the serious cases lying in the wards. It is at this time that we undertake the often lengthy examinations necessary to pronounce or confirm a diagnosis. How glad we are to be several doctors and able to consult each other! It is a principle among us that any doctor who has a serious case under his treatment shall introduce it to his colleagues. And each of us is entitled to talk to his colleagues about all his cases, to communicate his opinion about the diagnosis and get advice about the treatment. In very difficult cases the doctor who has been longest at the Hospital decides on the treatment to be employed and assumes the responsibility.

In so far as their work permits all the doctors make the evening round of visits together.

As I have mentioned in previous reports, we have great difficulty in repatriating the patients who have come from far distant districts. We have to rely on passing steamers or motor boats taking them with them. So that no opportunity may be missed, the two nurses who are busy in the consulting room with a view thence of the landing stage have the duty of inquiring of the owner or native skipper of each boat that calls whether there is any possibility of taking some of the patients who have been restored to health. The owners and skippers are naturally not very enthusiastic about giving our natives a free passage and thus adding to the weight of their generally overloaded boats. So if we do not take the initiative by inquiring as to the goal of their voyage and begging them to take some patients, they simply go on. There are but few so far advanced in virtue that they come and offer to take some people with them.

When it becomes clear that a boat is available, Dominique is hastily sent through all the wards with a bell such as railway porters use, and as he goes he shouts, "An opportunity of sailing in the direction of ———! Anyone who wants to go is to come to the consulting room at once!" And in the consulting room all other work comes to a standstill while a doctor decides whether the aspirants can really be discharged. Whilst he writes for the successful a recommendation to the officials through whose districts they must pass on their journey, and the nurse puts up a stock of provisions for several days and finds presents for those who have been workers, the patients who may leave fetch their belongings from the wards. But they cannot be left to do this by themselves. A native orderly must go with each to make him hasten and prevent him from going all round the Hospital to take a long farewell from all his acquaintances. The captains of the boats are in a hurry to go on, but for our savages time is nothing. Often the people who ought to be going have to be fetched out of the plantation. So in spite of all the trouble we take, frequently more than an hour goes by before all are on board the boat. Doctors and nurses are left quite exhausted by the running up and down and the shouting of directions. And then we are always afraid that the affair did not go well enough, so that that owner or skipper will not touch at the Hospital again for a long time lest he run the risk of having to take people with him and so losing time.

It is but seldom we know in advance when a boat will be passing so that we can quietly assemble the travellers and equip them for their journey.

On the afternoon of the last day of the month the monthly roll-call is held. As our natives often depart without announcing the fact, we have to make sure from time to time who is still on the list as a Hospital inmate and who is missing. And in addition the roll-call gives us an opportunity of questioning the patients and their companions when we can all discuss them together. At 2 p.m. the doctors and Hospital nurses with the orderlies around them sit down at a table in the consulting room. To begin with, the nurses display the cards of the bed-patients for which each is responsible, whilst Dominique assembles the people outside. First come the labourers sent to us from the big timber camps or from other employers or missions, and then come the rest. It takes about four hours before the three hundred patients and their companions have filed past the doctors and nurses, for all haste while calling the roll is prohibited, and all the questions which arise in connection with any inmate are quietly discussed. The diagnosis and treatment of the patient's malady, his right to receive a ration, the length of his residence and other details are all passed in review. Every inmate can make complaints or express his wishes; but he must also be prepared for nurses and orderlies bringing up against him any acts of insubordination of which he has been guilty.

The roll-call is also the hour of judgment, especially feared as such by the companions and wives of the patients and by the convalescents. For doctors, nurses and orderlies now discuss whether this woman or that attendant is still needed entirely for nursing the patient, or whether they cannot also work for the Hospital, and which of the convalescents is far enough advanced towards health to be able to render some service until such time as he can he sent home.

The nurse who supervises the workpeople sits, notebook in hand, watching for her victims. Now a washerwoman or a palm-oil woman is assigned to her, now a man for cracking palm nuts, now a woman for weeding the garden, now a woman for carrying water, or a man to fetch water for the garden, now people who are fit for any kind of work, even for felling trees. Each of these has a note entered on his or her card to the effect that he shall now no longer fetch his rations from the nurse who distributes food to the patients, but from her who supervises the workpeople so that he becomes dependent upon her.

It avails nothing to be an absentee from the roll-call, for fate is decided even in absence. When such people come to fetch their rations next day they are refereed to the nurse in charge of the workmen. They cannot even escape work by always remaining invisible when the doctors make their morning and evening rounds and by renouncing their claims to a ration by begging a miserable living from other people's cooking-pots or finding what they can in the plantation. Attention has been directed to them by the study of their cards at the roll-call, and they may be sure that on one of the following days an orderly, a nurse or a doctor will stop them and hand them over to the nurse in charge of the workers. And if they have once been seen by her, she will not let them disappear from view again.

It is one of our principles that all people capable of work who are not needed in attendance on the sick, whether they receive the ration or provide their own food, shall in some way or other work for the common good in payment for the treatment and drugs provided for themselves or their relatives. There is always any amount of work to be done.

Of course those who take trouble to remain un-noticed sometimes succeeded in escaping work for a time, especially if we are very busy with the sick people or there are new nurses at the Hospital who are not sufficiently familiar with their dodges. "The savages are cleverer than I am," said one of the new nurses at a recent roll-call when it came out that a Hospital inmate owed several days of delightful idleness to her inexperience.

We keep such strict watch over the inmates and are so careful that each carries a card-label, because without these precautions our wards would become lodging houses and places of refuge for all the riff-raff of the neighbourhood.

When there is room, we gladly receive as lodgers genuine unemployed until they can find work. They draw the ration and a little payment according to what they do.

When they leave we also give convalescents and companions of patients money or a present in return for the services they have rendered. Good washerwomen or palm-oil women can go home wearing fine head-cloths or loin-cloths.

We see that evening is approaching when the poultry and duck-herd and the sheep and goat-herd come down to the Hospital and drive the livestock up the hill to their quarters near our dwelling houses. When the birds and animals are fetched it is a sign to doctors and nurses that it is time to begin the evening round of the wards.

A little before 6 p.m. the gong is sounded to announce that work is at an end. The workers are already back from the forest and from the plantation, having known the time by an alarm clock carried by one of them on a cord. Now there is a great throng round the room where the tools are kept. Axes, saws, bush-knives, spades, pickaxes and rakes are given back, and the nurse in charge has to be careful that this does not happen too quickly so that she has time to see that all she gave out has been brought back. If the tools were not counted, many men would put the best axes and saws aside for their own use or leave them in the forest to save the trouble of carrying them home. The last of the tools may be put away by lantern-light. For we are close to the Equator. At six o'clock—the difference between winter and summer is only about a quarter of an hour—night suddenly descends.

We all find it unpleasant that darkness comes so quickly. One has to break off work instead of finishing it at leisure. For with the darkness there immediately come the mosquitoes which spread malaria. We are specially in danger from them because the Hospital contains so many malaria patients. As the consulting room, like the rooms in our dwelling houses, is protected by wire mosquito netting, people who are urgently requiring attention can be brought to it on stretchers or on their light wooden beds. The two operation rooms, the room for confinements, the bandage room and the large and small dispensaries are similarly protected.

At 6:30 p.m. a second gong reminds the over-zealous to cease work so as to change and rest before supper, which is announced at 7 o'clock by a third gong. The meal is followed by prayers. Then we often remain together for another half-hour. At 8:30 the evening bell—which except at this time is only rung for the Sunday Service—sounds, and after that there must be no more noise. Even the white patients' gramophone must be silent. The nurses visit each other's rooms with their needlework. The doctors read medical journals with an ear on the river in case a motor boat is approaching with fresh patients.

By 10 p.m. most of the lights are out, but this does not mean that all are sleeping. To begin with there are the cicadas and toads which make a tremendous noise from 9 p.m. till 2 a.m. And often the white patients' house contains mothers with new-born infants which sleep by day and cry by night. Or the two hippopotami that live in front of the Hospital engage in a bellowing competition. Or one, if not several, of the lunatics drums for hours at a time on the wooden walls of his cell. Or in one of the villages across the river there is dancing all night to the sound of the *tam-tam*. When Dr. Goldschmid complained to the chief of a village in which the *tam-tam* did not cease during the whole of a night illuminated by the full moon, he replied, "But Doctor, what will become of a people that does not get any amusement?"

But we are compensated for all these disturbing noises by the mild, fragrant night air and the mysterious rustling of the palms.

I am very glad that during my last stay I was able to enlarge the rooms for the examination and treatment of the patients. It makes the work quite different. Each of us now has enough room for his work, whereas up to now we kept getting in each other's way.

The airy new ward for the T.B. patients has places for about twenty and will soon be in use.

I should like friends all over Europe to know how grateful we are to them that their kindness enabled us to make these building improvements in such hard times and so allow us to fight the misery of disease more efficiently than before.

Albert Schweitzer

From *Albert Schweitzer's Gift of Friendship*

Part of a talk given by Albert Schweitzer to Swiss and Alsatian helpers of his hospital before they went to Lambarene—summer, 1959. Reprinted from Albert Schweitzer's Gift of Friendship *by Erica Anderson, pp. 144–48.*

IN HISTORY, every schoolboy can tell when modern times started; in regard to the hospital I, too, can determine this pretty accurately. Modern times at the hospital started in the year 1958. I will tell you how. The year before I had made a vow that no one would ever persuade me to build again. We had enough space and did not need any new buildings. I really thought that I was old enough to say sincerely: "I will not build any more. I have no one to help me with such things anyway. Therefore, all that's finished." This was a nice thought for me, but it worked out differently, because very strange things happened.

I first had to face the fact that we needed some space to store petroleum for our generators, and it had to be stored a good distance from living quarters in case it should be struck by lightning and start a fire. So I decided to build near the garden, away from our houses, a room where we would store oil and petrol.

But I said to myself: "This is only a little diversion. My vow of not building still holds." So I was getting set to start that when something else happened. An engineer from Zürich offered to build me a house, a prefabricated house made of aluminium.

First I thought, what would we do with aluminium? But the fellow finally convinced me that the house would be good for us and that it would be good for everybody to find out what experience one can have with aluminium in the tropics. So I told him: "Yes, and thanks."

Then they said: "You know, of course, you only have to make the foundation, but that is a trifle." Then they gave me the blue-prints. Just to read them was a nightmare for me. I am so used to building without plans. But then they told me that the foundation did not have to fit to the exact millimeter. Some story that was! If I'd not had a doctor who was knowledgeable about construction, I would have had to give up the thing at the start. But I had to work at that foundation for weeks and weeks. I who swore never to build again!

So this became building project number two, and I have to admit that the building was important because I did not really have enough space for all my patients. We have about three hundred and fifty couchettes, or mats covered with straw and a blanket. On these they sleep well enough, but there aren't enough of them. Because we have so many patients, I decided to agree to that aluminium building. This is the one that has worried me most and completing it has taken months. But when I left Africa, all was going well, and a fortnight ago I got the message that it is finished. How well an aluminium building fares in the tropics we shall soon see.

Now to building number three. I could ask you to guess what I might be referring to, and no one would. Could you imagine what else we would need in Lambarene? No one knows? Well, I did not know it either. A building for an automobile, a Mercedes-Benz truck weighing five and a half tons, imagine that! How did such a thing come about, and why? You might think that we got high-hatted, that the hospital became big and that we got proud and modern, but those who know me know that the danger of my becoming too modern is not great. But necessity stepped in, namely, the problem of feeding the hospital patients and of being sure that we always had enough to eat; we have to have twenty-seven tons of rice on hand in advance, because there may be months when no shipment comes from Saigon. At least that was always my working principle, to have that much rice on hand.

But suddenly in the year 1958, no rice is forthcoming. I asked in Lambarene: "What is this? No rice has come. Are there no ships bringing rice from Saigon?" They answered me: "Oh. be calm, Monsieur. It will come. This is Africa. Don't worry. It will come. You must have patience. It does not come just when you wish, but it will come." So I kept my patience, as they had advised. Oh, yes. But one sack of rice was eaten up and then another and another and another. Finally I said, "What is this? We have only enough left for another week. What will happen?" So I went again to the officials in Lambarene, and again they answered: "Don't worry. It will come. It will come."

But I'd heard enough of that. No, I thought, this is a time when more exact information is needed, and I found out that through political circumstances the rice traffic had been interrupted. Saigon had left the business pact with France, and did not accept payments in French money any more. It wanted dollars. You can imagine that we did not have too many dollars around. Anyway, we could not count any more on a regular supply from Saigon. The day had come when I had to admit that I had not enough food for my people. What could I do?

I went to the local administrator and said: "Listen. I have no more food for my people. I want to give up my hospital. Half of my patients I will send away and the other half I will bring to you, and you must feed them and care for them." This did it. The man finally understood what it all meant and he answered: "What can we do, cher Docteur?" Then I replied that the only alternative was for him to put a car at my disposal so that I could get to villages and buy bananas for my people. He said: "But certainly, of course, absolutely, Docteur." And he finally sent a car. So we had to change our staple from rice to bananas, a very serious thing.

How does the banana market operate in the tropics? In the old times, while the hospital was small, we had almost enough bananas. They were delivered to us by river-way. But not from down the river, only from up the river. This is because one cannot expect the men to paddle upstream with a heavy load of bananas. They can paddle back upstream after unloading the bananas. But with this system we were not getting enough bananas.

Then the Government built a road linking Libreville and Lambarene because they also need bananas from the villages, where there are lots of plantations. One cannot expect the *indigènes* to carry bananas on the paths through the jungle to the Lambarene hospital, because bananas are very heavy. Another disadvantage is that they spoil quickly and so cannot be stored for long. In fact, after four days in the tropics they start to rot. So I stood facing the problem, "How can I get hold of enough bananas quickly and steadily?"

After a week my great friend, the administrator, decided that I had used his car long enough. He said that he needed it for other projects. My luck had run out. But there was an *indigène* who did have a car and I told him I would make an agreement with him. I said: "On Thursday you drive from the hospital about twenty miles to those villages which sell bananas. I will send a nurse along with you. She will take along a scale to weigh the bananas, and help you load and unload!" That was fine, he told me, and so we made a contract. But one thing I forgot—to examine the car.

European people from Lambarene came to me and said, "Docteur—How can you send your nurses off in a car which may burst into flames at any moment? It is a dangerous thing, and how its brakes ever work not even the Good Lord knows." I also realized that no such car would ever solve the problem permanently since we now required eight tons of bananas a week. What we obviously needed was a truck. But the road was not strong enough for a truck, so we also needed a new road. And a road that would even hold after heavy rains. At that point the connecting link to the government road was only a narrow path: moreover, it mounted to a steep hill.

So I had to build a road, and that turned out to be one of my biggest adventures. I even confessed to myself: "This you can't do." And in truth it was most unlikely that I could ever finish it because the road had to be widened about two and a half meters, and the foundation had to be filled in to about one meter, and the earth had to he carried by my good workmen.

But they are not favorably inclined to shovel tons of earth. Not very enthusiastic, at first they had to carry heavy earth for about half a kilometer, and the soil was wet besides. So you can see the beginning was one of the most difficult performances I started in Lambarene. At first the *indigènes* really did not want to co-operate. We also had to hew the stones out of the ground, carry them to the road, and stones that were too big we had to crush with a hammer. I told myself: "Now, I, myself, will have to stand for at least four months to supervise this job."

I who promised myself never to build again! I who had vowed to do only the hospital work from now on!

But at this point a miracle happened, a genuine miracle. A Volkswagen appeared on the horizon. Now a Volkswagen has a good reputation. Half of the cars that travel through the Sahara are Volkswagens. It's one of the few cars that can travel through sand. Anyway, from this Volkswagen four youths from Hamburg emerged, one of them slightly injured from an accident in a ditch. We took good care of him, and his companions walked through the hospital, looking very interested. They watched us work, and it was not long before they said to me: "Docteur, we have seen how hard you work, and we've decided to stay a while and help you build that road."

They took the tools and started to hew the big stones from morning till night, and the ambition of these German fellows had a most infectious effect on the *indigènes*. They became different people and started to work, as though it were fun. The spark took, and in three months we finished that road. It is a great road, sweeping behind the hospital in a big turn, and it rises to a hill of about thirty meters, and it serves well. Now the big question was, what kind of automobile would be must useful? I held a meeting of mechanics and asked them. Unanimously, they replied: "A Mercedes-Benz, five-and-a-half-ton diesel."

"Perhaps that is right," I thought. I had just read a report that the President of the French Republic and the German Chancellor had embraced each other at a political meeting, so I figured the time was ripe to buy a German car even if living in a French territory.

You see how wonderful it is when two people suddenly start up a friendship which no one would have expected! Anyway, I was lucky again. I contacted the Mercedes firm, and they delivered me the truck for a truly Christian price, I must say.

And so all is in order. The truck travels well on the new road; once a week it brings us about eight tons of bananas. Thus we've become independent of the arrival of rice. I need rice only for the summer months when bananas are more scarce. So fifteen tons of rice suffice. And that is how my hospital has entered into the modern age. But one thing I will guarantee you—modern times will not alter the old spirit of modesty and economy, the spirit of small beginnings. In this spirit the hospital developed, and in this spirit it shall live on.

Notes

UNLESS OTHERWISE INDICATED, all works are by Schweitzer. Shortened titles and last names of authors are used after the first reference.

1. Childhood, 1875–1885

1. *Memoirs of Childhood and Youth,* p. 10.
2. Ibid., p. 13.
3. Commentary written for Erica Anderson's film, but not used.
4. Letter dated Dec. 16, 1944, now in the Hermann Hagedorn Collection, George Arents Research Library, Syracuse University, N.Y.
5. Jean-Paul Sartre, *Les Mots,* p. 60.
6. Ibid., p. 7.
7. Ibid., p. 36.
8. *Memoirs,* p. 17.
9. Ibid., p. 19.
10. Ibid., p. 16.
11. Ibid., p. 39.
12. Ibid., p. 42.
13. Ibid., p. 49.
14. "Childhood Recollections of Old Colmar," in Jacques Feschotte, *Albert Schweitzer— An Introduction,* p. 110.
15. Ibid., pp. 111–113.
16. *Memoirs,* p. 81.
17. Ibid., pp. 40–41.
18. Ibid., p. 34.
19. Ibid.
20. Ibid.
21. Ibid., p. 65.
22. Ibid., p. 33.

2. The Dark Years, 1885–1893

1. *Memoirs,* p. 51.
2. *My Life and Thought* (1966), p. 195.

3. *Memoirs*, p. 52.
4. Ibid.
5. From "Un Grand Musicien Français: Marie-Joseph Erb," translated by Charles R. Joy as "My First Concert," in Joy, *Music in the Life of Albert Schweitzer* (1959), p. 6.
6. Letter dated Feb. 12, 1945, Hagedorn Collection.
7. *Memoirs*, p. 55.
8. Ibid., p. 60.
9. Ibid., p. 72.
10. Ibid.

3. Strasbourg, 1893–1896

1. *Memoirs*, p. 75.
2. "Warum es so schwer ist einen guten Chor in Paris zusammenzubringen," translated as "The Chorus in Paris," in Joy, *Music* (1959), p. 56.
3. *My Life and Thought* (1966), p. 86.
4. "Deutsche und Französiche Orgelbaukuost und Orgelkuost," 190, translated as "The Chorus in Paris," in Joy, *Music* (1959), p. 168.
5. Preface by Charles Widor in *J S. Bach* (German ed).
6. Letter dated Dec. 16, 1944.
7. *My Life and Thought* (1966), p. 10.
8. Letter to Hélène Bresslau dated Sept. 6, 1903.
9. Matt. 10:1, 5–18, 22–23.
10. Mark 6:7–13.
11. Matt. 11:2–6.
12. Letter to Hagedorn dated Feb. 12, 1945.
13. "Le Choeur de St. Guillaume de Strasbourg—un chapitre de l'histoire de la musique en Alsace," in Joy, *Music* (1959), p. 37.
14. Ibid.
15. *My Life and Thought* (1966), p. 76.
16. Sermon preached at St. Nicholas, Strasbourg, Jan. 6, 1905. From *Reverence for Life*.
17. *My Life and Thought* (1966), pp. 74–75.

4. Paris, 1896–1899

1. *My Life and Thought* (1966), p. 15.
2. "Mes souvenirs sur Cosima Wagner," in Joy, *Music* (1959), p. 58.
3. *My Life and Thought* (1966), p. 63.
4. Matt 26:26–28; Mark 14:22–24.
5. Mark 14:25.
6. "Philosophy of Religion," in Thomas Kiernan, ed. *A Treasury of Albert Schweitzer*, p. 235.
7. Letter to Hélène Bresslau dated Dec. 21, 1902.
8. "Philosophy of Religion," p. 336.
9. Ibid., p. 312.
10. Ibid., pp. 325–26.
11. Ibid., p. 329.
12. Ibid.
13. Ibid., p. 330.
14. Preface by Widor in *J. S. Bach* (French ed).
15. Ibid.

16. *My Life and Thought* (1966), p. 20.
17. Ibid.
18. Suzanne Oswald, *Mein Onkel Bery*, pp. 77–80.
19. *Memoirs*, p. 41.
20. Ibid., pp. 95–96.
21. *My Life and Thought* (1966), p. 122.
22. Ibid.
23. Ibid., p. 123.

5. Berlin, 1899

1. Oswald, *Mein Onkel Bery*, pp. 80–83.
2. *My Life and Thought* (1966), p. 122.

6. Two Examinations, 1899–1900

1. *My Life and Thought* (1966), p. 25.
2. Ibid.
3. Sermon preached at the afternoon service at St. Nicholas, Strasbourg, May 14, 1900. Strasbourg in *Reverence for Life*.

7. The Scholar-Curate, 1900–1901

1. *My Life and Thought* (1966), p. 27.
2. Ibid.
3. Letter to Felix Raugel.
4. Joy, *Music* (1959), p. 144.
5. Ibid., p. 152–53.
6. Ibid., p. 152.
7. "Zur Reform des Orgelbaues," in Joy, *Music* (1959), p. 224.
8. "Orgelbaukunst," in Joy, *Music* (1959), p. 156.
9. Werner Picht, *The Life and Thought of Albert Schweitzer*, p. 198.
10. Narrated by Erica Anderson.
11. Letter to Hélène Bresslau dated Sept. 6, 1903.
12. Letter dated Aug. 30, 1911.
13. Letter from Hélène Bresslau dated Sept. 2, 1911.
14. Letter dated Mar. 13, 1906.
15. Letter dated Sept. 18, 1902.
16. Author's conversation with Anderson.
17. Author's conversation with Rhena Schweitzer-Miller.
18. *My Life and Thought* (1966), p. 48.

8. The Historical Jesus, 1901

1. *The Mystery of the Kingdom of God*, p. 6.
2. Ibid., pp. 5–6.
3. Luke 17:20.
4. Isa. 53:4–5.
5. Mark 14:61–62.
6. Picht, *Life and Thought*, p. 46.
7. Mark 9:1.

8. H. J. Holtzmann, *Das messianische Bewusstsein Jesu*, pp. 8–9.
9. *Mystery*, pp. 18–19.
10. *My Life and Thought* (1966), p. 48.
11. Ibid., p. 54.
12. *Mystery*, pp. 18–19.
13. Adolf Harnack, *The Sayings of Jesus*, p. 232.
14. *Hibbert Journal*, no. 32 (July 1910).
15. *The Quest of the Historical Jesus*, (3d ed.), p. xviii.
16. Glasgow *Herald* (May 20, 1910).
17. Manchester *Guardian* (May 20, 1910).
18. *The Nation* (June 11, 1910).
19. *Encyclopaedia of Religion and Ethics*, vol. 5, p. 382.
20. *Quest*, (3d ed.), p. xii.
21. Ibid., p. xiii.
22. E. N. Mozley, *The Theology of Albert Schweitzer for Christian Enquirers*, p. 77.
23. *The Pelican Guide to Modern Theology*, vol. 3., "Biblical Criticism," p. 256.
24. A. M. Hunter, *The Work and Words of Jesus*, p. 13.
25. W. J. Wolf, *A Handbook of Christian Theology*, p. 57.
26. D. M. Baillie, *God Was in Christ*, p. 24.
27. *My Life and Thought* (1966), p. 51.
28. C. H. Dodd, *The Authority of the Bible*, p. 233.
29. *My Life and Thought* (1966), p. 48.
30. *Quest* (3d ed.), p. xiv.
31. Ibid., p. 25.
32. *Mystery*, p. 248.
33. *Quest* (3d ed.), pp. 368–69.
34. *Mystery*, pp. 251–52.
35. *The Mysticism of Paul the Apostle*, p. 2.
36. *My Life and Thought* (1966), p. 51.
37. *Mystery*, p. 274.
38. *Quest* (3d ed.), p. 401.
39. Ibid.
40. *My Life and Thought* (1966), p. 50.
41. Ibid.
42. Ibid.
43. Ibid., p. 51.
44. Picht, *Life and Thought*, p. 88.

9. Hélène

1. *Mystery*, pp. 274–75.
2. Sermon preached at the afternoon service at St. Nicholas, Strasbourg, Feb. 23, 1902. In *Reverence for Life*.
3. Ibid.
4. Luke 10:21.
5. Sermon preached at the afternoon service at St. Nicholas, Strasbourg, May 11, 1902.
6. Ibid.
7. Ibid.
8. Ibid.
9. George Seaver—*Albert Schweitzer: The Man and His Mind*, p. 160.
10. *My Life and Thought* (1966), p. 95.

11. Letter dated Aug. 8, 1908. Unless otherwise indicated, all letters quoted from here to the end of chapter 12 are between Schweitzer (AS) and Hélène Bresslau (HB) and are to be found in *The Albert Schweitzer-Hélène Bresslau Letters, 1902–1912,* trans. Antje Lemke (Syracuse: Syracuse Univ. Press, 2001).

12. Letter dated Mar. 2, 1901.

13. Letter dated Aug. 15, 1908.

14. Letter dated Mar. 9, 1902.

15. Letter dated Mar. 25, 1904.

16. Letter dated Mar. 22, 1910.

17. Letter dated Mar. 21, 1912.

18. Letter dated Mar. 18, 1912.

19. Letter from HB to AS dated May 5–6, 1902.

20. Letter dated Nov. 1, 1903.

21. Letter dated Nov. 15, 1902.

22. Letter dated July 4, 1903.

23. Letter dated Dec. 21, 1902.

24. Letter dated Sept. 25, 1903.

25. Letter dated Nov. 26, 1903.

26. Letter dated Sept. 6, 1903.

27. Letter dated May 1, 1904.

28. Letter dated Feb. 6, 1905.

29. Letter dated Nov. 1, 1903.

30. Letter dated Nov. 2, 1903.

31. Letter HB to AS dated Nov. 8, 1903.

32. Letter HB to AS dated Mar. 1905.

33. Letter HB to AS dated Aug. 27, 1906.

34. Letter dated Sept. 5, 1905.

35. Letter dated Jan. 19, 1904.

36. Letter dated Oct–Nov, 1904.

37. Ibid.

38. Letter HB to AS dated Feb. 2, 1904.

39. Letter dated Feb. 2, 1905.

40. Letter dated Feb. 25, 1905.

41. Letter HB to AS dated Mar. 1905.

42. Letter HB to AS dated May 5/6, 1905.

43. Letter dated May 20, 1905.

44. Letter HB to AS dated June 25, 1905.

45. Letter dated July 1, 1905.

46 Letter dated Sept 6, 1903.

47. *My Life and Thought* (1966), pp. 76–77.

48. Letter dated June 1–2, 1905.

10. Bach, 1904–1905

1. *My Life and Thought* (1966), p. 55.

2. Ibid., p. 56.

3. Ibid., p. 56–57.

4. Letter dated Aug. 21, 1905.

5. *My Life and Thought* (1966), p. 75.

6. Sermon preached at St. Nicholas, Strasbourg, July 27, 1919.

7. *My Life and Thought* (1966), p. 75.

8. Letter dated May 20, 1905.
9. Letter dated Dec. 16, 1944.
10. *My Life and Thought* (1966), p. 77.
11. Letter dated Dec. 16, 1944.
12. Picht, *Life and Thought*, p. 16.
13. *My Life and Thought* (1966), p. 77.
14. Sermon preached at the afternoon service at St. Nicholas, Strasbourg, Jan. 6, 1905.
15. *My Life and Thought* (1966), p. 88.
16. Letter HB to AS dated Jan. 12, 1910.
17. *My Life and Thought* (1966), p. 77.
18. Letter dated May 20, 1905.
19. Letter dated Dec. 18, 1905.
20. *My Life and Thought* (1966), p. 83.
21. Widor in Preface to *J. S. Bach* (French ed.), trans. Charles R. Joy, in Joy, *Music* (1959), pp. 65–66.
22. *My Life and Thought* (1966), p. 58.
23. *J. S. Bach*, vol. 2, pp. 253–54 (English ed.).
24. Ibid., p. 2.
25. Johann Nicolaus Forkel, *Uber Johann Sebastian Bachs Leben, Kunst und Kunstwerke*, p. 69.
26. *J. S. Bach* (French ed.), in Joy, *Music* (1959), p. 74.
27. *J. S. Bach* (German ed.), vol. 1, p. 20.
28. Ibid., vol. 1, p. 183.
29. Ibid., vol. 2, p. 131.
30. Ibid., vol. 1, pp. 188–89.
31. Ibid., vol. 1, p. 137.
32. Ibid., vol. 1, p. 158.
33. Ibid., vol. 1, p. 114.
34. Letter dated July 9, 1905.
35. Letter dated July 10, 1905.
36. Letter dated July 20, 1905.
37. *My Life and Thought* (1966), pp. 82–83.
38. Letter from HB to AS dated Aug. 28, 1905.
39. *My Life and Thought* (1966), p. 40.
40. Letter dated Oct. 12, 1905.
41. *My Life and Thought* (1966), p. 84.
42. Ibid.
43. Ibid.
44. Ibid., p. 80.
45. *My Life and Thought* (1966), p. 74.

11. Medical Studies, 1905–1908

1. *My Life and Thought* (1966), p. 78.
2. Ibid.
3. Elly Heuss-Knapp, *Ausblick vom Münsterturm*, p. 64.
4. *My Life and Thought* (1966), p. 78.
5. Ibid.
6. Picht, *Life and Thought*, p. 162.
7. *My Life and Thought* (1966), p. 78.
8. Ibid., p. 79.

9. Sermon preached at the afternoon service at St. Nicholas, Strasbourg, Nov. 19, 1905.

10. Letter to music critic Gustav von Lüpke, quoted in Jean Pierhal, *Albert Schweitzer: The Story of His Life*, p. 59.

11. *My Life and Thought* (1966), p. 80.

12. Ibid.

13. Ibid.

14. Ibid., p. 78.

15. Letter dated Jan. 25, 1906.

16. Letter dated Feb. 27, 1906.

17. *My Life and Thought* (1966), p. 88.

18. Letter dated Apr. 29, 1906.

19. Frederick Frank, *Days with Albert Schweitzer*, p. 166.

20. Joy, *Music* (1959), p. 180.

21. *My Life and Thought* (1966), p. 81.

22. Letter dated Mar. 1907.

23. Letter dated May 24, 1907.

24. Letter dated Sept. 2, 1907.

25. Letter dated Sept. 4, 1907.

26. Letter dated Oct. 25, 1907.

27. Letter dated Sept. 29, 1907.

28. Letter to Gustave Bret, Princeton University Library collection, date unknown.

29. From an article in *Die Musik*, "Warum es so schwerist einen guten Chor in Paris Zusammenzubringen?" (Why is it so difficult to organize a good choir in Paris?), trans. as "The Chorus in Paris" and reprinted in Joy, *Music* (1959), pp. 48–49.

30. Ibid., p. 53.

31. Ibid., p. 55.

32. Archibald T. Davison, "The Transcendentalism of Albert Schweitzer," in *The Albert Schweitzer Jubilee Book of 1954*, pp. 200–201.

33. Preface by Widor to J. S. Bach (German ed.).

34. Davison, "Transcendentalism," p. 201.

35. Letter from HB to AS dated Mar. 9, 1908.

12. The Departure, 1908–1913

1. Letter dated Nov. 22, 1908.

2. Interview with Marcelle Herrenschmidt, Lyon, June 1972.

3. Letter HB to AS dated Aug. 22, 1908.

4. Letter dated Aug. 24, 1908.

5. Letter dated Sept. 23, 1908.

6. Letter dated Sept. 24, 1908.

7. Davison, "Transcendentalism," pp. 202–3.

8. Letter dated Mar. 20, 1909.

9. Joy, *Music* (1959), p. 254.

10. Ibid., p. 202.

11. Ibid., p. 206.

12. Letter dated June 28, 1909.

13. Letter dated Aug. 5, 1909.

14. Letter dated June 10, 1909.

15. *My Life and Thought* (1966), p. 113.

16. Ibid., p. 112.
17. Letter dated Jan. 24, 1910.
18. Letter dated Mar. 22, 1910.
19. Letter dated May 1, 1910.
20. Letter dated Jan. 5, 1911.
21. Letter dated May 5, 1911.
22. Letter HB to AS dated May 30, 1911.
23. Letter dated July 20, 1911.
24. Letter dated Aug. 5, 1911.
25. Letter dated Aug. 23, 1911.
26. Letter HB to AS dated Aug. 26, 1911.
27. Letter dated Aug. 28, 1911.
28. Letter dated Aug. 30, 1911.
29. Letter HB to AS dated Sept. 2, 1911.
30. Joy, *Music* (1959), p. 181.
31. *My Life and Thought* (1966), p. 92.
32. Letter dated Dec. 22, 1911.
33. Letter to Prof. and Mrs. Bresslau dated Dec. 22, 1911.
34. Letter dated Dec. 27, 1911.
35. Letter dated Jan. 1, 1912.
36. *A Psychiatric Study of Jesus*, p. 27.
37. Ibid., p. 14.
38. Ibid., p. 33.
39. Ibid., p. 28.
40. Sermon preached at St, Nicholas, Strasbourg, Jan. 21, 1912.
41. *My Life and Thought* (1966), p. 194.
42. Sermon preached at St, Nicholas, Strasbourg, Feb. 25, 1912.
43. Ibid.
44. Letter dated Mar. 4, 1912.
45. Letter HB to AS dated Mar. 18, 1912.
46. Letter dated Apr. 6, 1912.
47. *My Life and Thought* (1966), pp. 97–98.
48. Letter from Rhena Schweitzer Miller to the author dated Oct. 12, 1999.
49. From the Günsbach archives. The stranger is not identified.
50. Sermon preached at St. Nicholas, Strasbourg, Mar. 9, 1913.

13. Africa, 1913

1. *On the Edge of the Primeval Forest*, p. 14.
2. Ibid.
3. Ibid., pp. 14–15.
4. *My Life and Thought* (1966), p. 89.
5. *On the Edge of the Primeval Forest*, p. 14.
6. Ibid., p. 21.
7. Ibid., p. 19.
8. Ibid., p. 21.
9. Ibid., pp 21–22.
10. Mary Kingsley, *Travels in West Africa*, pp. 129–30.
11. Winston S. Churchill, *My African Journey*, pp. 101–2.
12. *On the Edge of the Primeval Forest*, pp. 22–23.
13. Ibid., p. 23.

14. Andende: The First Hospital, 1913

1. *On the Edge of the Primeval Forest*, p 25.
2. Kingsley, *Travels*, pp. 214–5,.
3. *On the Edge of the Primeval Forest*, pp. 30–31.
4. Ibid., p. 32.
5. Ibid., p 28.
6. Ibid.
7. Ibid., pp. 28–29.
8. Letter dated June 18, 1913, in the Günsbach archives.
9. *My Life and Thought* (1966), p. 119.
10. *On the Edge of the Primeval Forest*, p. 36.
11. Ibid., p. 37.
12. *My Life and Thought* (1966), p. 118.
13. *On the Edge of the Primeval Forest*, p. 65.
14. Ibid., pp. 69–70.
15. Ibid., p. 85.
16. Ibid., pp. 85–86.
17. Ibid., p. 90.
18. Ibid.
19. Ibid., p. 95.
20. Ibid.
21. Ibid., pp. 95–96.
22. Ibid., pp. 96–97.
23. Ibid., pp. 97–98.
24. Ibid., p. 96.
25. Ibid., p. 51.
26. Ibid., p. 98.
27. *My Life and Thought* (1966), p. 120.

15. War, 1914–1915

1. *The Decay and Restoration of Civilization*, p. 1.
2. *My Life and Thought* (1966), p. 124.
3. Ibid., pp. 129–30.

16. "Reverence For Life," 1915

1. John Middleton Murry, *Love, Freedom and Society*, p. 187.
2. *Decay and Restoration*, p. 88.
3. "Religion in Modern Civilisation," summary of Hibbert Lectures in the *Christian Century*, Nov. 28, 1934. p. 1520.
4. Interview on Radio Brazzaville, 1953, quoted in Erica Anderson, *The Schweitzer Album*, p. 153.
5. *Civilisation and Ethics*, pp. 12–13.
6. Ibid., p. 13.
7. Ibid., p. 197.
8. *Mysticism of Paul the Apostle*, p. 12.
9. *My Life and Thought* (1966), p. 130.
10. Ibid.
11. Ibid.

12. Ibid., pp. 130–31.
13. Ibid., p. 131.
14. Ibid., p. 132.
15. Ibid.
16. *Civilisation and Ethics*, p. 9.
17. Jeremy Bentham, *The Principles of Morals and Legislation*, chap. 17, sec. 1.
18, James Cameron. *Point of Departure*, pp. 169–70.
19. Talk by Dr. Frank Catchpool, printed in the *Convocation Record* of the Albert Schweitzer International Convocation at Aspen, Colo. (May 1966), sec. 6, pp. 27–28.
20. *Civilisation and Ethics*, p. 221.
21. Ibid.
22. "Albert Schweitzer Speaks Out." Article in the *World Book Year Book of 1964*, p. 148.
23. *Civilisation and Ethics*, p. 218–19.
24. *My Life and Thought* (1966), p. 179.
25. *Civilisation and Ethics*, pp. 198–99.

17. Internment, 1915–1917

1. *On the Edge of the Primeval Forest*, p. 115.
2. Ibid., p. 103.
3. Ibid., p. 108.
4. Ibid., p. 109.
5. Ibid., p. 108.
6. *My Life and Thought* (1966), p. 7.
7. Letter dated Aug. 15, 1916.
8. *On the Edge of the Primeval Forest*, p. 109.
9. *My Life and Thought* (1966), p. 141.
10. Ibid., p. 142.
11. Ibid., p. 143.
12. Ibid., p. 144.
13. Ibid.
14. Ibid., pp. 145–46.
15. Ibid., p. 146.
16. Louis Schweitzer's diaries in the Günsbach archives.
17. *My Life and Thought* (1966), p. 146.
18. Ibid.
19. Ibid., p. 147.
20. Oswald, *Mein Onkel Bery*, p. 97.
21. *Primeval Forest*. pp. 124–25.

18. The Lost Coin, 1918–1924

1. Sermon preached at St. Nicholas, Strasbourg, Oct. 18, 1918.
2. Ibid., Dec. 1, 1918.
3. Ibid., Feb. 16, 1919.
4. Ibid., Feb. 23, 1919.
5. Ibid., Aug. 17, 1919.
6. *My Life and Thought* (1966), p. 151.
7. Ibid.
8. Memorial article for Archbishop Nathan Söderblom, May 1933, Hagedorn Collection.
9. Ibid.

10. Ibid.
11. *My Life and Thought* (1966), p. 158.
12. Letter from Elwood Worcester dated Sept. 27, 1921.
13. *Christianity and the Religions of the World,* p. 46.
14. Ibid., p. 68.
15. Ibid., p. 54.
16. Introduction to the Hibbert Lectures, quoted in Seaver, *Albert Schweitzer,* p. 80n.
17. *My Life and Thought* (1966), p. 153.
18. Foreword by Nathaniel Micklem to *Christianity,* p. 8.
19. Seaver, *Albert Schweitzer.* p. 86.
20. Letter dated Apr. 25, 1922, quoted by permission of Le Service Protestant de Mission et de Relations Internationales, Paris.
21. Letter dated Apr. 30, 1922.
22. Resolution passed by the missionaries of Talagouga, May 6, 1922. Permission of Le Service Protestant de Mission et de Relations Internationales, Paris.
23. Letter dated May 11, 1922. Permission of Le Service Protestant de Mission et de Relations Internationales, Paris.
24. Oskar Kraus, *Albert Schweitzer: His Work and His Philosophy,* p. 1.
25. Ibid., p. 50.
26. Letter dated Jan. 2, 1924.

19. Adolinanongo: The Second Hospital, 1924–1927

1. *More from the Primeval Forest,* p. 24.
2. "Dr. Schweitzer's Hospital Fund," Bulletin no. 2 (Summer 1926). pp. 3–4.
3. Letter to the *London Times* (Aug. 22, 1925).
4. *More from the Primeval Forest,* pp. 80–81.
5. Ibid., p. 84.
6. Bulletin no. 3 (Spring 1928), pp. 3–4.
7. Bulletin no. 2 (Summer 1926), pp. 2–3.
8. *More from the Primeval Forest,* pp. 91–92.
9. Anderson, *Albert Schweitzer's Gift of Friendship,* p. 143.
10. Bulletin no. 3 (Spring 1928), p. 6.
11. *More from the Primeval Forest,* p. 126.

20. Fame, 1927–1929

1. Letter from Rhena Schweitzer Miller to the author dated May 24, 1974.
2. Picht, *Life and Thought,* p. 199.
3. *Memoirs,* p. 75.
4. Ibid., pp. 75–76.
5. Letter dated Dec. 16, 1944.
6. Sermon preached at the afternoon service at St. Nicholas, Strasbourg, June 6, 1905.
7. Related to the author by Anderson, June 1973.
8. Maude Royden, DD, CH, pioneer of the women's movement,.
9. Seaver, *Albert Schweitzer,* p. 109.
10. Ibid., p. 108.
11. Letter from Clara Faisst in Günsbach archives.
12. Goethe Prize Address, Aug. 28, 1928.
13. Ibid.
14. Ibid.

15. Picht, *Life and Thought*, p. 169.

16. Letter to Meiner, quoted in Anderson, *Schweitzer Album*, p. 138.

17. Bulletin no. 4 (Spring 1930), p. 4.

18. Ibid., pp. 14–15.

21. Life at the Hospital, 1929–1932

1. Bulletin no. 4 (Spring 1930), p 10.

2. *From My African Notebook*, pp. 101–2.

3. "Un Culte du Dimanche en Forêt Vierge," *Cahiers Protestants*.

4. Ibid.

5. From the Günsbach archives.

6. Picht, *Life and Thought*, p. 166.

7. *Convocation Record* (May 1966), sec. 6, p. 26.

8. Related to the author by Anderson, June 1973.

9. *My Life and Thought* (1966), p. 78.

10. *Convocation Record*, sec. 6, pp. 26–27.

11. Ibid., p. 38.

12. Postscript by Skillings to *My Life and Thought* (1966), p. 204.

13. Interview with Arthur Koestler by Norman Moss in *the Sunday Times Magazine*, Oct. 14, 1973.

14. James Cameron, *Point of Departure*, p. 166.

15. Related to the author by Clara Urquhart.

16. Franck, *Days with Albert Schweitzer*, p. 32.

17. Norman Cousins, *Doctor Schweitzer of Lambarene*, p. 94.

18. Ibid., p. 95.

19. *More from the Primeval Forest*, p. 53.

20. Related to the author by Anderson, June 1973.

22. Another War, 1932–1945

1. Letter from Rhena Schweitzer-Miller to the author dated May 24, 1974.

2. "Goethe's Message for Our Time." address on the centenary of Goethe's death, Mar. 22, 1932, in *Goethe: Three Studies.*

3. Ibid., pp. 49–50.

4. From a summary of the Hibbert Lectures printed in *the Christian Century,* Nov. 28, 1934, p. 1484.

5. Ibid.

6. Seaver, *Albert Schweitzer*, p. 148.

7. Pablo Casals and Albert E. Kahn, *Joys and Sorrows*, p. 215.

8. Roland Schütz, *Anecdoten um Albert Schweitzer*, p. 56.

9. Bulletin no. 11 (Autumn 1935), p. 8.

10. Bulletin no. 13 (Autumn 1936), p. 6.

11. Letter to Dr. Maude Royden, quoted in Seaver, *Albert Schweitzer*, p. 155.

12. Bulletin no. 18 (Spring 1946), p. 3.

13. Seaver, *Albert Schweitzer*, pp. 159–60.

14. Ibid., p. 161.

15. Bulletin no. 18 (Spring. 1946), p. 11.

16. Ibid., p. 12.

17. Ibid., p. I5.

18. Ibid., p. 16.

19. Ibid., pp. 14–15.
20. Bulletin no. 17 (Jan. 1945), p. 4. Letter dated May 24, 1944.
21. Ibid. Letter dated Apr. 30, 1944.
22. Ibid. Letter dated May 24, 1944.
23. Ibid. Letter dated Sept. 21, 1944.
24. Seaver, *Albert Schweitzer*, p. 162.
25. Bulletin no. 17 (Jan. 1945), p. 5. Letter dated Oct. 25, 1944.
26. Bulletin no. 18 (Spring 1946), pp. 17–18.

23. America: "The Greatest Man in the World," 1945–1950

1. Postscript by Skillings to Schweitzer, *My Life and Thought* (1966), p. 217.
2. Anderson, *Schweitzer Album*, p. 60.
3. *Christian Register*, vol. 126, no. 8 (Sept. 1947), p. 324.
4. Ibid.
5. The German-language paper published in New York.
6. Letter dated Apr. 30, 1948.
7. Letter from Albert Einstein dated Sept. 25, 1938.
8. Letter dated June 25, 1948, in the Collection of American Literature, Beinecke Rare Book and Manuscript Library, Yale University.
9. *Christian Register*, vol. 126, no. 8 (Sept. 1947), p. 327.
10. Feschotte, *Albert Schweitzer*, pp. 62–63.
11. *Convocation Record*, sec. 1, p. 12.
12. Reprinted from "Portrait: Albert Schweitzer," by Emory Ross, in *American Scholar*, vol. 19, no. 1 (Winter 1945–50), p. 85.
13. Bulletin no. 19 (June 1951), p. 6.
14. *Convocation Record*, sec. 1, pp. 13–14.
15. Ibid., p. 14.
16. "Goethe—His Personality and His Work," address at the Goethe Bicentennial Convocation, Aspen, Colo., July 6 and 8, 1949. In *Goethe: Five Studies*, pp. 58–59.
17. Ibid., p. 65.
18. Letter dated Dec. 16, 1944.
19. "The Conception of the Kingdom of God in the Transformation of Eschatology," epilogue by Schweitzer in E. N. Mozley, *The Theology of Albert Schweitzer for Christian Enquirers*, pp. 107–8.
20. Letter dated Feb. 7, 1950, quoted in the *Courier*, (Autumn 1968), p. 11.
21. Letter dated July 7, 1950, quoted in the *Courier* (Autumn 1968), p. 11.
22. *Histoire de mon pélican*, pp. 10–40.

24. Schweitzer on Film, 1950–1954

1. Erica Anderson, *Albert Schweitzer's Gift of Friendship*, p. 89.
2. Ibid., pp. 89–90.
3. Ibid., p. 90.
4. Ibid., pp. 91–92.
5. Ibid., pp. 91–92.
6. *Memoirs*, p. 101.
7. Letter dated Oct. 23, 1951, quoted in the *Courier* (Autumn 1968), p. 12.
8. Anderson, *Schweitzer's Gift*, p. 95.
9. Ibid., selections, pp. 96–103.

25. A Crack in the Myth, 1951–1954

1. Letter dated Feb. 3, 1952.
2. Letter dated Mar. 31, 1952.
3. Letter dated May 9, 1952.
4. Letter dated Apr. 14, 1953.
5. "The Problem of Ethics in the Evolution of Human Thought," printed as an appendix in Feschotte, *Albert Schweitzer,* pp. 129–30.
6. Bulletin no. 22 (Jan. 1955), p. 10.
7. Radio broadcast by James Cameron, BBC, London, Jan. 14, 1955.
8. Articles in the *News Chronicle* (Dec. 7, 8, 9, 1953).
9. Radio broadcast, by James Cameron, BBC, London, Jan. 14, 1955.
10. Articles in the *News Chronicle* (Dec. 7, 8, 9, 1953).
11. Ibid.
12. Ibid.
13. Ibid.
14. Ibid.
15. Ibid.
16. Ibid.
17. Ibid.
18. Cameron, *Point of Departure,* pp. 173–74.
19. *Indian Thought and Its Development,* pp. 237–38.
20. Franck, *Days with Albert Schweitzer,* pp, 158–59.
21. John Gunther, *Inside Africa,* p. 698.
22. Ibid., pp. 706–7.
23. Ibid., p. 710.
24. Ibid., p. 709.
25. Letter dated July 28, 1954.
26. Bulletin no. 22 (Jan. 1955), p. 16.
27. Letter dated Dec. 19, 1953.
28. Letter from Dag Hammarskjöld dated Jan. 13, 1954, in the Günsbach archives.

26. The Nobel Peace Prize and the Bomb, 1954–1957

1. *Christian Register* (Dec. 1954), p. 17.
2. Cousins, *Doctor Schweitzer of Lambaréné,* p. 186.
3. "The Problem of Peace in the World Today," Nobel Peace Prize Address delivered Nov. 4, 1954, pp. 18–19.
4. Letter dated Dec. 5, 1954.
5. Statement by Albert Einstein, from *To Albert Schweitzer. A Festschrift Commemorating His Eightieth Birthday,* privately printed by Homer A. Jack.
6. Letter dated Feb. 20, 1955.
7. From Anderson's film, *Albert Schweitzer.*
8. Clara Urquhart, *With Dr. Schweitzer in Lambaréné,* p. 39.
9. Cousins, *Doctor Schweitzer,* p. 147.
10. Letter to Robert F. Goheen, president of Princeton University, dated Mar. 27, 1959.
11. Bulletin no. 23 (July 1957), p 7.
12. Ibid.
13. Letter dated July 21, 1955.
14. Cousins, *Doctor Schweitzer,* p. 171.
15. Ibid., p. 122.

16. Ibid., pp. 173–76.

17. Ibid., pp. 189–90.

18. Letter dated Feb. 20, 1957.

19. "A Declaration of Conscience," radio address broadcast on Apr. 24, 1957, printed as an appendix to Cousins, *Doctor Schweitzer*, pp. 235–36.

20. Everett Holles to Willard Libby, Apr. 26, 1957, Box 60, AEC Series, Lewis Strauss Papers, Herbert Hoover Library, West Branch, Iowa.

21. Letter dated May 3, 1957.

22. Gerard Smith to Paul Foster, Aug. 7, 1957, John L. McGruder to Strauss, Aug. 13, 1957, Box 100, AEC Series, Lewis Strauss Papers.

23. Letter, Schweitzer to Fostervoll dated Feb. 25, 1958.

24. Lawrence S. Wittner, "Blacklisting Schweitzer," *The Bulletin of the Atomic Scientists*, May–June 1995, p 55.

25. Letter from the CIA to the author dated June 27, 1997.

26. Letter dated Aug. 14, 1956.

27. Letter from Adlai Stevenson dated Sept. 18, 1956.

28. Statement by Adlai Stevenson dated June 24, 1957.

27. The Last of Europe, 1957–1959

1. Cousins, *Doctor Schweitzer*, pp. 108–9.

2. Anderson, *Schweitzer Album*, p. 112.

3. Letter dated Aug. 30, 1957.

4. Ibid.

5. Letter dated Aug. 1955.

6. Letter dated Nov. 24, 1957.

7. Letter dated Feb. 25, 1958.

8. Frances E. Willis to Secretary of State, Apr. 24, 1958, 957.40/4–2458, Deptartment of State (DOS) Records.

9. *Peace or Atomic War*, pp. 5–7.

10. Ibid., p. 9.

11. Ibid., p. 15.

12. Ibid., p. 17.

13. Herter, DOS, to James F. Green, May 28, 1958, DOS Records.

14. James F. Green to Secretary of State, June 19, 1958, DOS Records.

15. Wittner, "Blacklisting Schweitzer" quoting Pfau, *No Sacrifice Too Great: The Life of Lewis Strauss*, and British Foreign Office Records, Public Record Office.

16. Ibid., quoting A. J. Goodpaster *Memorandum of Conference with the President*, Aug. 12, 1958, Box 3, Alpha Subseries, Subject Series, White House Office of the Staff Secretary Records, Eisenhower Library.

17. Letter from Adlai Stevenson dated Feb. 8, 1960.

18. Address by Schweitzer to the French Albert Schweitzer Association, Nov. 6, 1959.

19. Anderson, *Schweitzer's Gift*, p. 150.

20. Ibid., p. 152.

21. Anderson, *Schweitzer Album*, pp. 19–20.

28. The Final Years, 1959–1965

1. Anderson, *Schweitzer's Gift*, p. 69.

2. News Bulletin of the Church of the Larger Fellowship, Unitarian Universalist, Boston (Nov. 24, 1961).

3. *Time Magazine*, Dec. 8, 1961.

4. Letter dated Feb. 7, 1963.

5. Letter dated Oct. 24, 1962.

6. Letter dated Dec. 19, 1963.

7. Letter dated Nov. 29, 1963.

8. *Courier* (May 1964), p. 150.

9. Ibid.

10. Letter dated Feb. 10, 1963.

11. Article by Ali Silver, Bulletin no. 26, (Apr. 1963), p. 4.

12. Anderson, *Schweitzer's Gift*, p. 53.

13. Urquhart, *With Dr. Schweitzer in Lambarene*, p. 24.

14. Gerald McKnight, *Verdict on Schweitzer*, pp. 13–14.

15. Roman Brodmann, "La Vérité sur Lambarene," reprinted in "Albert Schweitzer dans la vérité: Hommage pour ses quatre-vingt-dix ans," From *Saisons d'Alsace*, no. 14, p. 136.

16. Franck, *Days with Albert Schweitzer*, pp. 80–81.

17. McKnight, *Verdict*, p. 217.

18. *New York Review of Books*, Aug. 20, 1964.

19. McKnight. *Verdict*, p. 16.

20. BBC "Panorama" television program, Jan. 19, 1965.

21. Related to the author by Anderson, June 1973.

22. Letter dated Oct. 9, 1964.

23. Letter from D. Packiarajan in the Günsbach archives dated Aug. 25, 1963.

24. Letter to Herbert Spiegelberg dated Apr. 4, 1965.

25. Bulletin no. 28 (Nov., 1965), p. 3.

26. Quoted by Charles R. Joy in the *Register Leader* (Dec. 1966), p. 3.

27. From the Günsbach archives.

28. Bulletin no. 38 (Nov. 1965), pp. 4–6.

Epilogue

1. *Catholic Messenger*, Aug. 29, 1963.

2. *Civilisation and Ethics*, p. 190.

3. Picht, *Life and Thought*, p. 198.

Bibliography

MY PRINCIPAL ARCHIVE SOURCE was the central archive at Günsbach, Alsace. I also consulted the collection of Erica Anderson at the Albert Schweitzer Friendship House at Great Barrington, Mass., now housed at the Schweitzer archives at Syracuse University and with the Albert Schweitzer Fellowship, Boston, Mass. The Bulletins cited are the British Bulletins of the Albert Schweitzer Hospital Fund at Kenwood Cottage, Croydon, near Royston, Herts. Many items there were taken from the regular bulletins circulated by Lambarene to all Schweitzer support committees.

American Scholar (Winter 1949–50).
Anderson, Erica. *Albert Schweitzer's Gift of Friendship.* New York: Harper and Row, 1964.
———. *The Schweitzer Album.* New York: Harper and Row, 1965; London: A. and C. Black, 1965.
———. *Albert Schweitzer Album.* Documentary. Albert Schweitzer Fellowship, Boston, Mass.
Anekdoten um Albert Schweitzer. Edited by Roland Schütz. Munich: Bechtel Verlag, n.d.
Baillie, D. M., *God Was in Christ.* London: Faber and Faber, 1948.
Begegnung mit Schweitzer. Festschrift. Edited by Hans Walter Bahr and Robert Minder.
Bentham, Jeremy. *The Principles of Morals and Legislation.* London: Basil Blackman, 1948.
Bremi, Willi. *Der Weg des Protestantischen Menschens.* Zürich: Artemis Verlag, 1953.
Brodmann, Roman. "La Vérité sur Lambaréné." Reprinted in "Albert Schweitzer dans sa vérité: Hommage pour ses quatre-vengt-dix ans, *Saisons D'Alsace*, no. 14. Strasbourg: Istra, 1965.
Cameron, James. *Point of Departure.* London: Arthur Barker, 1967.
Casals, Pablo, and Albert E. Kahn. *Joys and Sorrows.* London: Macdonald, 1970.
Christian Register and *Register Leader.* Publications of the Unitarian Universalist Association, Boston, Mass.

Churchill, Winston. *My African Journey,* London: Holland Press and Neville Spearman, 1962. Reprinted from the original edition of 1908.

Clark, Henry. *The Ethical Mysticism of Albert Schweitzer.* Boston: Beacon Press, 1962.

Convocation Record. The Albert Schweitzer International Convocation at Aspen, Colo., May 1966. Sponsored by the Aspen Institution for Humanistic Studies, the Schweitzer Fellowship, and the Johnson Foundation.

The Courier. Publication of the American Albert Schweitzer Fellowship.

Cousins, Norman. *Doctor Schweitzer of Lambaréné.* New York: Harper and Brothers, 1960. London: A. and C. Black.

Davison, Archibald T. "The Transcendentalism of Albert Schweitzer." In *The Albert Schweitzer Jubilee Book of 1954,* edited by A. A. Roback. Cambridge, Mass.: Sci-Art Publishers, 1954.

Dodd, C. H. *The Authority of the Bible.* London: Collins, 1960.

Encyclopaedia of Religion and Ethics. Edited by James Hastings. Edinburgh: T. and T. Clark; New York: Charles Scribner's Sons, 1908–26.

Feschotte, Jacques. *Albert Schweitzer, an Introduction.* Translated by John Russell. London: A. and C. Black, 1954. Boston: Beacon Press, 1955.

Forkel, Johann Nicolaus. *Uber Johann Sebastian Bachs Leben, Kunst und Kunstwerke.* Leipzig: Hoffmeister und Kuhnel, Bureau de Musique, 1802.

Franck, Frederick. *Days with Albert Schweitzer.* London: Peter Davies, 1959, New York: Holt, Rinehart and Winston, 1959.

Gollomb, Joseph. *Albert Schweitzer: Genius in the Jungle.* London and New York: Peter Nevill Ltd., 1951.

Goodpaster, A. J. Memorandum of Conference with the President, Aug. 12, 1958. Box 3, Alpha Subseries, Subject Series, White House Office of the Staff Secretary Records, Eisenhower Library.

Gunther, John. *Inside Africa.* London: Hamish Hamilton, 1954; New York: Harper and Brothers, 1955.

A Handbook of Christian Theology. Cleveland: World Publishing, 1958.

Harnack, Adolf. *Das Wesen des Christentums* (What is Christianity?). Leipzig: Hinrichs, 1901.

Heuss-Knapp, Elly. *Ausblick von Münsterturm.* Tübingen: Rainer Wunderlich Verlag Hermann Liens, 1952.

Hibbert Journal, no. 32 (July 1910).

Holtzmann, Heinrich Julius, *Das messianische Bewusstsein Jesu.* Tübingen: Verlag von J. C. B. Mohr (Paul Siebeck), 1907.

Hunter, A. M. *The Work and Words of Jesus.* London: S. C. M. Press, 1950.

Jack, Homer A., ed., *To Dr. Albert Schweitzer: A Festschrift Commemorating His Eightieth Birthday.* New York: Profile Press, 1955.

Joy, Charles R., tr. and ed. *Music in the Life of Albert Schweitzer.* New York: Harper, 1951; London: A, and C. Black, 1953; Beacon Paperback, 1959.

Kant, Immanuel. *A Critique of Aesthetic Judgement.* Oxford: Clarendon Press, 1911.

———. *A Critique of Practical Reason.* Chicago: Univ. of Chicago Press, 1949.

———. *A Critique of Pure Reason.* London and Toronto: J. M. Dent, 1934; New York: Macmillan, 1963.

Kiernan, Thomas. *A Treasury of Albert Schweitzer.* New York: Citadel Press, 1965.

Kingsley, Mary, *Travels in West Africa.* London: Charles Knight, 1972.

Koestler, Arthur. *The Act of Creation.* New York: Macmillan, 1964.

Kraus, Oskar. *Albert Schweitzer—His Work and His Philosophy.* Translated by E. G. McCalman. London: A. and C. Black, 1944.

Langfield, Gabriel. *Albert Schweitzer: A Study of His Philosophy of Life.* Translated by Maurice Michael. London: George Allen and Unwin, 1960.

Lawrence, D. H. "Thought." From *The Complete Poems of D. H. Lawrence.* London: Viking Press, 1964.

Lemke, Antje Bultmann. *The Albert Schweitzer–Hélène Bresslau Letters, 1902–1912.* Syracuse: Syracuse Univ. Press, 2001.

Marshall, George. *An Understanding of Albert Schweitzer.* New York: Philosophical Library, 1966.

Marshall, George, and David Poling. *Schweitzer.* New York: Doubleday, 1971; London: Geoffrey Bles, 1971.

McKnight, Gerald, *Verdict on Schweitzer.* London: Frederick Muller, 1964; New York: John Day, 1966.

Michel, Charles, and Fritz Dinner. Report on Schweitzer's funeral in the *Courier* and British Bulletin no. 28, Nov. 1965.

Moss, Norman, "Koestler in Wonderland," From the *Sunday Times Magazine,* (Oct. 14, 1973).

Mozley, E. N,, *The Theology of Albert Schweitzer for Christian Enquirers.* London: A. and C. Black, 1950. New York: Macmillan, 1951.

Murry, John Middleton, *Love, Freedom and Society.* London: Jonathan Cape, 1957.

New York Review of Books. Aug. 20, 1964.

Oswald, Suzanne, *Mein Onkel Bery.* Zürich: Rotapfel Verlag, 1971.

Pfau, Richard. *No Sacrifice Too Great: The Life of Louis Strauss.* Charlottesville: Univ. Press of Virginia, 1984.

Picht, Werner. *The Life and Thought of Albert Schweitzer.* Translated by Edward Fitzgerald. London, George Allen and Unwin, 1964.

Pierhal, Jean. *Albert Schweitzer: The Story of His Life.* New York: Philosophical Library, 1957

Ross, Emory. "Portrait: Albert Schweitzer," *American Scholar* 19, no. 1 (Winter 1949–50).

Sartre, Jean-Paul, *Les Mots.* Translated by Irene Clephane. London: Hamish Hamilton, 1964; Paris: Gallimard and Cie, 1964: New York: George Braziller, 1964.

Schütz, Roland. *Anekdoten um Albert Schweitzer.* Munich and Essingen: Bechtle Verlag, 1966.

Schweitzer, Albert. "Albert Schweitzer Speaks Out." *World Book Year Book of 1964.* Reprinted in *The Courier,* May, 1964.

———. "Archbishop Nathan Söderblom." May 1933. Hagedorn Collection.

———. "Childhood Recollections of Old Colmar." Part of a speech given at a reception in Colmar, Feb. 23, 1949. Printed as an appendix to Feschotte, *Albert Schweitzer.*

————. *Le Choeur de St. Guillaume de Strasbourg—Un Chapitre de L'Histoire de la Musique en Alsace.* Compiled by Erik Jung. Strasbourg: P. H. Heitz, 1947. Reprinted in Joy, *Music in the Life of Albert Schweitzer.*

————. *Christianity and the Religions of the World.* Translated by Johann Powers. London: George Allen and Unwin; 1923, New York: Henry Holt, 1939.

————. *Civilisation and Ethics.* Translated by C. T. Campion and Mrs. C. E. B. Russell. London: A. and C. Black, 1923; New York: Macmillan, 1929, 1950.

————. "The Conception of the Kingdom of God in the Transformation of Eschatology." Appendix to E. N. Mozley, *The Theology of Albert Schweitzer for Christian Enquirers.*

————. "A Declaration of Conscience." Radio broadcast, Apr. 24, 1957. Printed as an appendix to Norman Cousins, *Doctor Schweitzer of Lambaréné.*

————. *Deutsche und Französische Orgelbaukunst und Orgelkunst.* Leipzig: Breitkopf und Härtel, 1906. Reprinted in Joy, *Music in the Life of Albert Schweitzer.*

————. *Goethe: Five Studies.* Translated by Charles R. Joy. Boston: Beacon Press, 1961.

————. *Goethe: Three Studies.* Translated by C. T. Campion and Mrs. C. E. B.. Russell. London: A. and C. Black, 1949.

————. *Un Grand Musicien Français; Marie Joseph Erb.* Strasbourg-Paris: Editions Le Roux et Cie. Translated as "Marie-Joseph Erb," in Joy, *Music in the Life of Albert Schweitzer.*

————. "The H-Bomb." *London Daily Herald,* Apr. 14, 1954.

————. *Histoire de mon pélican.* Paris: Albin Michel, 1963.

————. *Indian Thought and its Development.* Translated by Mrs. C. E. B. Russell. London: Hodder and Stoughton, 1936. Reissued by A. and C. Black, 1951. Boston: Beacon Press, 1936.

————. *J. S. Bach.* 2 vols. Translated by Ernest Newman, with alterations and additions at Schweitzer's request, from the German version of 1908. Leipzig: Breitkopf und Härtel, 1911; reprint, A. and C. Black, 1923; New York: Macmillan, 1950.

————. *J. S. Bach, Le Musicien-Poète.* French ed. Paris: Costallat, 1905; Leipzig: Breitkopf und Härtel, 1908. Translated in part by Charles R. Joy and reprinted in Joy, *Music in the Life of Albert Schweitzer.*

————. "The Kingdom of God and Primitive Christianity" ("Reich Gottes und Christentum"). Translated by L. A. Garrard. London: A. and C. Black, 1968.

————. *Memoirs of Childhood and Youth.* Translated by C. T. Campion. London: George Allen and Unwin, 1924; New York: Macmillan, 1931.

————. "Mes Souvenirs sur Cosima Wagner." *L'Alsace Francoise* 25, no. 7 (Feb. 12, 1933). Reprinted in Joy, *Music in the Life of Albert Schweitzer.*

————. *More from the Primeval Forest.* Translated by C. T. Campion. London: A. and C. Black, 1931; New York: Macmillan, 1948.

————. *My African Notebook.* Translated by Mrs. C. E. B. Russell. London: George Allen and Unwin, 1938; New York: Henry Holt, 1939.

————. *My Life and Thought.* Translated by C. T. Campion, London: George Allen and Unwin, 1933; Unwin Books, 1966 (paperback ed.); New York: Henry Holt, 1948.

———. *The Mystery of the Kingdom of God*. Translated by Walter Lowrie. London: A. and C. Black, 1914; New York: Dodd, Mead and Co., 1914; New York: Dodd, Mead and Co., 1914; New York: Macmillan, 1950.

———. *The Mysticism of Paul the Apostle*. Translated by William Montgomery. London: A. and C. Black, 1931; New York: Henry Holt, 1931; New York: Macmillan, 1955.

———. *On the Edge of the Primeval Forest (Zwischen Wasser und Urwald)*. Translated by C. T. Campion. London: A. and C. Black, 1922; New York: Macmillan, 1948.

———. *Paul and His Interpreters*. Translated by William Montgomery. London: A. and C. Black, 1912; New York: Macmillan, 1912.

———. "Peace or Atomic War." Three broadcast talks transmitted on April 28, 29, and 30, 1958. London: A. and C. Black, 1958; New York: Holt Rinehart and Winston, 1958.

———. "The Problem of Ethics in the Evolution of Human Thought." Address given before L'Academie des Sciences Morales et Politiques, Institut de France, Oct. 20, 1952. Printed as an appendix to Feschotte, *Albert Schweitzer*.

———. "The Problem of Peace in the World of Today." Nobel Peace Prize Address. London: A. and C. Black, 1954; New York: Harper and Brothers, 1954

———. *A Psychiatric Study of Jesus*. Translated by Charles R. Joy. Boston: Beacon Press, 1948.

———. *The Quest of the Historical Jesus*. Translated by W. Montgomery. London: A. and C. Black. 1910, 1954 (3d ed.); New York: Macmillan, 1945.

———. "Religion in Modern Civilization." *The Christian Century*, Nov. 21 and 28, 1934.

———. *Reverence for Life*. London: S.P.C.K. Press, 1966.

———. *Die Religionsphilosophie Kants von der Kritik der Reinen Vernunft bis zur Religion innerhalb der Grenzen der blossen Vernunft*. Freiburg, 1899. Translated by Thomas Kiernan and reprinted as *Sketch of a Philosophy of Religion in Kant's Critique of Pure Reason*, in Kiernan, *A Treasury of Albert Schweitzer*.

———. *Strassburger Predigten* (Strasbourg sermons). Edited by Ulrich Neuenschwander. Munich: Verlag C. H. Beck, 1966.

———. "Warum es so schwer ist einen guten Chor in Paris Zusammenzubringen." *Die Musik* 9, no. 19. Berlin: Bernard Schuster. Reprinted in Joy, *Music in the Life of Albert Schweitzer*.

Seaver, George. *Albert Schweitzer, A Vindication*. London: James Clarke and Co., 1950; Boston: Beacon Press, 1951.

———. *Albert Schweitzer: Christian Revolutionary*. London: James Clarke and Co., 1944.

———. *Albert Schweitzer: The Man and His Mind*. London: A. and C. Black, 1948; New York: Harper and Brothers, 1947.

Stevenson, Adlai E. Statement, June 24, 1957. Papers of Adlai E. Stevenson, Princeton University Library.

Urquhart, Clara. *With Dr. Schweitzer in Lambaréné*. London: George C. Harrap, 1957.

West, Richard. *Brazza of the Congo*. London: Jonathan Cape. 1972; New York: Holt, Rinehart, and Winston.

Wittner, Lawrence S. "Blacklisting Schweitzer." *Bulletin of the Atomic Scientists*, May–June 1995.

Wolf, W. J. *A Handbook of Christian Theology.* Cleveland, Ohio: World Publishing, 1958.

Woytt-Secretan, Marie. Extract from the British Bulletin of the Albert Schweitzer Hospital Fund.

Index